FIRST
PRINCIPLES
—— OF ——
ECONOMICS

FIRST
PRINCIPLES
—OF—
ECONOMICS

RICHARD G. LIPSEY

Sir Edward Peacock Professor of Economics, Queen's University,
Kingston, Ontario

COLIN HARBURY

Professor of Economics, City University,
London

WEIDENFELD AND NICOLSON · LONDON

to Claudia

George Weidenfeld and Nicolson Ltd
91 Clapham High Street, London SW4 7TA

ISBN 0 297 78845 0 cased
ISBN 0 297 78846 9 paperback

Phototypeset by Keyspools Ltd,
Golborne, Lancs.

Printed and bound in Great Britain by
The Bath Press, Avon

Contents

Preface

This new book is an introduction to economic principles for complete beginners. It is pitched at the level of the average A-level candidate, which should make it suitable also for students taking the economics examinations set by the major professional bodies, such as the Institutes of Chartered Accountants, of Bankers, of Actuaries, of Chartered Surveyors etc. Many first-year undergraduates who do not have A-level economics under their belts will, we believe, also benefit from this book, although it may not go quite far enough to cover fully some parts of their university or polytechnic syllabuses. In any case the book stops well short of the coverage and degree of rigour to be found in Richard Lipsey's *Introduction to Positive Economics* (Weidenfeld, 6th edn 1983, 7th edn 1989).

There is, of course, no shortage of alternative texts on offer at this level. Hence we should make clear the distinctive features of ours. The most important are, in our view, clarity and readability. We have given top priority to writing thoroughly understandable explanations of basic economic principles. This can be seen from the fact that this book is longer than many others, because we took as much space as we needed to expound each topic fully, rather than making a ritualistic bow to it.

While we have avoided embracing novelties to differentiate our product, and hope it will find favour as a reliable, up-to-date and clear treatment of mainstream fundamentals of economics, readers will notice a number of distinguishing characteristics (which we obviously think are valuable). The prime example is the development of a totally new framework for the use of elementary supply and demand analysis (Chapter 10)[1], which replaces the conventional 'problems' chapters of many other standard texts. Secondly, we would mention the pains taken to weave the new wave of aggregate-supply/aggregate-demand analysis comprehensibly into elementary macroeconomics.

A third distinctive feature is the structure of the book, which is designed to allow flexibility in the order of reading. There are five parts: (1) Introduction, (2) Elementary Microeconomics, (3) Intermediate Microeconomics, (4) Elementary Macroeconomics, and (5) Intermediate Microeconomics. After reading Part 1, students may choose to move on to either elementary micro or elementary macroeconomics. The full set of choices for covering the material in this book is discussed in the Preface to Parts 2–5 on page 42. We leave individual teachers to follow their own preferences as to ordering, but cannot resist telling you that our own preferred order is either 1,2,3,4,5 or 1,2,4,3,5 (because we feel that nowadays it is difficult to make sense of even elementary macro without a firm understanding of basic microeconomics).

The coverage of economic theory in this book is full, as may perhaps be most readily seen by glancing at the comprehensive summaries which end every chapter. Moreover, while the textual treatment calls for only minimal mathematical background, we have provided an ultra-elementary guide to the use of graphical and mathematical methods in three Appendices. There

---

1 A shortened version of this chapter appeared in *Economics*, vol. XXII, Part 3, No. 95, Autumn 1986.

are, however, two omissions. The first is material on the UK economy which, in order to prevent the book becoming excessively long and too early outdated, is only sparsely covered here. There are other books which concentrate on applied economics. The reader will not be surprised to learn that we recommend our own *Introduction to the UK Economy* (Harbury and Lipsey, 2nd edn 1986, Pitman), which we update regularly (so use the latest edition) and to which we cross-reference repeatedly in this book.

The second omission is that, again to prevent excessive length, there are no questions or problems in the book itself. We do however believe, and strongly too, that the best way of learning economics is to apply the principles you learn to problems, and we therefore encourage you to acquire an appropriate student workbook to use alongside this book. We think that you will find that Colin Harbury's *Workbook in Introductory Economics* (Pergamon, 4th edn 1987) is such an appropriate companion, although there are of course others (and you will also find that Stilwell, Lipsey and Clarke's *Workbook to accompany An Introduction to Positive Economics* (Weidenfeld, 1983) contains some questions and problems which are equally within the scope of a reader of this book).

Many people have helped to make this book possible. We owe a particular debt to Claudia Lipsey, whose careful reading of the book in its various drafts has greatly improved the readability of the entire text. Diana Lipsey, David Tash and David Whitehead have also contributed important suggestions on various parts of the manuscript. Dana Miltchen and Elaine Fitzpatrick have coped with mountains of messy manuscript. We end with the disclaimer that we have no one to blame other than ourselves for the content of this book.

We truly hope that the reader who masters the principles of economics presented here will do more than pass his or her exams successfully. Economic principles, even at this level, are extraordinarily powerful tools that allow the significance of many current events to be appreciated. They also aid you in reasoning sensibly, and arguing persuasively, about the merits and demerits of policies put forward to deal with the economic problems of the day.

January 1988   RICHARD LIPSEY
                                                       COLIN HARBURY

Part 1

INTRODUCTION

The Nature of Economics

Work, leisure and unemployment; gross national product and living standards; income taxes, and VAT; scarce rented flats, and plentiful but expensive houses; uneconomic coal mines, expensive atomic energy, and North Sea oil a dwindling resource; shortages of skilled labour and education cuts; pollution, depletion of natural resources, and discoveries of new supplies; exports, imports, and the European Community: emigration and immigration; poverty in Central Africa, and affluence in Western Europe and North America.

These are items of everyday press headlines, of TV news commentaries, of articles in the weeklies, and of the research of learned scholars.

Many of these items are also important concerns of ordinary people. Will I find a job when I leave school? Will my father be made redundant? Is my own city fated to decline as industries close or move away? If I marry, will we be able to find a house that we can afford? Are immigrants threatening my job prospects? Should I emigrate to find a better job? If I set up a small business, what kind of records must I keep, and will I be able to sell in Europe? Will Japanese imports outsell me in my own market?

These items also provide important topics for economists to study by asking such questions as: How can we explain the existence of unemployment or of regional inequalities in the UK? How can we get higher living standards, more housing, more of all the goods and services that we enjoy? How can we avoid unemployment, inflation, pollution and the other things we dislike?

When you study economics, you will be studying issues such as those listed in the first paragraph. Of course, you must not expect to find all the answers to the questions raised by these issues in one introductory book. Many of the questions remain unsettled after two centuries of study by some of the world's greatest thinkers. But even a single introductory study should give you some real insight, both into the issues involved and into tentative answers to many of these questions.

The Boundaries of Economics

Economics is one of a group of subjects collectively known as the *social sciences*. (The other main social sciences are sociology and political science.) These subjects all deal with how people behave in society. As with any closely related group of subjects, the topics covered by each tend to overlap. Let us consider a simple example.

Most people know that economics deals with supply and demand. An example is of the demand for ice-cream. What determines the number of ice-creams that the public will buy in one particular week in July? Although a complete answer could fill several pages, here are four important determinants.

First, the number of ice-creams people will buy depends on the price of ice-creams; for example, at 20p each the quantity bought will be more than at a price of 50p. Second, the number depends on people's incomes; for example, if many people are unemployed and feeling pinched for funds, the number of ice-creams purchased will be less than if they are not. Third, the weather will have a major influence; cold and rainy days will see fewer ice-creams sold than hot and sunny days. Finally, people's tastes will matter; if ice-creams are popular, sales will be larger than if apples are thought to be tastier, and/or better for the health.

The first two determinants listed above, price and

income, are explained within the subject of economics. The last two, weather and tastes, are not. Weather is understood – if at all – by meteorologists, and tastes – if at all – by psychologists.

So we now have something that we wish to explain – ice-cream sales – and four possible determinants of those sales – price, income, weather, and tastes. How do economists proceed when some of the influences in which they are interested are explained within economics while others lie outside it? Simply, economists seek to explain the factors that lie within their expertise, such as price and income, and they take as *given* those that do not, such as weather and tastes.

When we say we take such things as weather and tastes as *given* we mean that, although we are interested in the *effects* of these things on what we are trying to explain, we are not, as economists, interested in what *causes* them to change. So when we say, for example, the state of the weather is given, we mean it has a particular state – say, a very warm summer – which we accept without trying to explain why it occurred. We are, however, interested in the question 'what will happen to the demand for ice-cream if the weather changes?', but we do not try to explain *why* such changes in the 'givens' occur.

Some terms to learn

A Variable: Throughout our study of economics we shall encounter magnitudes that are called variables. A VARIABLE is some quantity that can take on different values. We meet variables as the 'unknowns' in algebra. For example, in the equation $Y = 2 + 7X$, both X and Y are variables. In this particular case, *if* $X = 2$ *then* $Y = 16$ and *if* $X = 3$ *then* $Y = 23$ and so on. In the example considered earlier, the quantity of ice-cream sold per week is a variable. As yet we do not know its value, and its value may change from week to week. Other variables are the price of ice creams, people's incomes and the weather.

Endogenous and Exogenous Variables: Variables that are explained within our subject, such as prices and incomes, are called ENDOGENOUS VARIABLES while variables that are taken as given, because they are explained outside our subject, are called EXOGENOUS VARIABLES. Note two things about these terms. First, they are relative to the observer's point of view. For example, the weather is exogenous to economics but endogenous to meteorology. Second, exogenous does *not* mean unimportant; economists

are keenly interested in the effects on economic behaviour of changes in things that they take as exogenous.

ECONOMIC ISSUES

One main lesson to be learned from the above discussion of boundaries is that there are few problems whose complete solution lies within economics – or for that matter, within any one social science. For complete explanations of social phenomena, social scientists need to help each other. For example, to explain such 'economic' behaviour as the sales of ice creams *completely*, economists need help from specialists in other subjects. Psychologists study how tastes are formed and changed. Sociologists study the influence of such institutions as the family. Social and economic historians help to put contemporary matters and tastes into a longer-term perspective. Many specialists in subjects outside the social sciences may also contribute to the understanding of so-called economic issues – for example, accountants, philosophers, meteorologists, and engineers.

The above discussion helps with the question: What is economics? A useful definition, that will serve us well enough for the moment, is that 'economics is what economists do'. This will be sufficient, provided we understand that what economists do is to study questions that can be handled with their own expertise.

When all of the jargon and technical apparatus has been stripped away, what economists are really interested in is people's living standards – i.e. in their material well-being. Economists assume that people have certain wants. They then study how particular societies are organized so as to satisfy people's wants. In doing so they ask such questions as: Is one way of organizing the economy more efficient for satisfying wants than another? Can government intervention improve the society's ability to satisfy wants?

One key aspect of wants is that, for all practical purposes, they are unlimited. Most of us want rising living standards; most of us would like some goods we do not now have and more of those we do have – better living accommodation, more holidays, faster and more comfortable cars, more rock concerts or visits to the theatre, possibly just more or better food; indeed, the list is endless.

The country's ability to satisfy wants depends on

- how much is produced,
- how many people are there to consume what is produced, and
- how the production is divided up among those who wish to consume it.

The nation's total output measures how much is produced. What is produced are called commodities. These are divided into two broad categories – physical GOODS, such as TV sets, handbags and cars, and SERVICES, such as permanent waves, pop festivals, and theatrical performances. Goods and services together are referred to as COMMODITIES.

Total output divided by the number of people available to consume it determines average output per person, which is usually called output per head (or sometimes *per capita* output). It determines the country's *average* standard of living.

How evenly output is divided up determines whether there are great or small divergencies between the amounts going to the 'better-off' and the amounts going to the 'worse-off' members of the population. This concerns the distribution of living standards among the people in society.

Economic Resources

The first question in the above list is 'how much is produced?' The answer depends on the resources available to produce commodities which satisfy wants and on how efficiently the resources are used. Economists find it useful to divide resources into four categories which they call LAND, LABOUR, CAPITAL, and ENTREPRENEURSHIP. Collectively these are referred to as *factors of production.*

Land: Land includes everything commonly called natural resources. It includes the surface of the earth itself, in the condition that nature provided it, and all the other resources provided by nature such as minerals, waterfalls, and trees.

The nation's total endowment of land, as we have broadly defined it, is inherited from the past. This inheritance can be used now and/or passed on to the future. Some resources are *non-renewable*. If they are used now, they will not be available in the future. Examples are oil and coal deposits. Other resources are *renewable*. They can be used today and, under appropriate circumstances, can also be used in the future. Examples are forests and fish. The current interest in such issues as conservation and pollution is centred on the *use* of non-renewable resources and

the *destruction*, by over-exploitation, of resources that would otherwise be renewable.

Notice that renewable resources are living things that will reproduce themselves naturally, while non-renewable resources are inanimate things that, once removed, will not reproduce themselves.

Labour: The term labour refers to all human resources that could be used in the production of goods and services. The basic determinant of the amount of the nation's labour is its population. The size of the population is itself determined by three factors: (i) birth rates, (ii) death rates, and (iii) the balance of migration movements into and out of the country.

Of course, the whole population is not available for use in production. First, only those of working age – roughly identified as those between 16 and 65 – are currently available as a productive resource. Second, many of those who are of working age do not choose to work. This latter group includes, for example, those who stay on at school beyond 16, those who choose to retire early, and those who stay at home to look after their families.

Those who are available for work are referred to as THE LABOUR FORCE, or THE WORKING POPULATION, and the fraction who are in the labour force defines what is called the ACTIVITY RATE, or the PARTICIPATION RATE. For example, about one-half of the women between 16 and 25 are in the UK labour force, so the participation rate of that group is about 0.5.

Capital: Capital refers to man-made aids to further production. Factories and equipment are capital. So also are the tools that any workers use, as well as word-processors and computers used by office staff. Capital is a produced factor of production. Its production requires effort; the pay-off to such effort comes because much more can be produced with capital than without it.

Capital can take either of two forms, fixed or circulating. FIXED CAPITAL is mainly plant and equipment. All of a country's stock of factories, warehouses, machine tools and equipment are a part of its fixed capital. CIRCULATING, or WORKING, capital circulates through the production process. Stocks of raw materials that a firm is waiting to use, all goods in the process of being produced and all stocks of finished goods waiting to be sold are part of a country's circulating capital.

Fixed capital provides a stream of services to the firm during its lifetime. Circulating capital consists of goods in the process of production. For example, a dress manufacturing firm would regard its factory and its dress-making machines as fixed capital, while its circulating capital would consist of stocks of cloth waiting to be processed, of partly finished dresses, and of stocks of completed dresses waiting to be sold.

Notice, therefore, that 'fixed' does not necessarily mean 'bolted to the floor'. It means instead, equipment that can be used over and over again in the production of many units of output. Considering our dress manufacturing firm again, needles are part of its fixed capital even though they are mobile in an everyday sense.

The basic meaning of capital is clear enough, but the concept can be a tricky one, as is shown by the following two issues.

First, when resources are used to preserve, or improve, the productivity of land, this is correctly regarded as increasing capital rather than land. When resources are used in education to improve the productivity of labour, this is also correctly regarded as increasing the amount of the nation's capital. Such capital is so important that a special term, HUMAN CAPITAL, is used to describe it. This refers to the skills that labour acquires through education and training (both on and off the job) as opposed to abilities that are inherited.

Second, in ordinary speech, people refer to money as capital. A wealthy widow with £1 million in the bank (waiting to be invested in some profitable enterprise) might refer to that sum as her 'capital'. In economics, however, capital refers to the real assets (factories, etc.), and the skills that exist to aid further production. It does not refer to sums of money, although we may value capital in money terms just as we do with output.

Entrepreneurship: Managers are employees, though usually well-paid ones. Therefore, management is a part of labour as defined above. In a well-established firm where years of experience in producing and selling some standard product have been acquired, managers may have little more to do than supervise routine tasks. When a new venture is being contemplated, however, risks arise. They involve the unknown future. Will a new product appeal to consumers? Can it be effectively marketed? Will its cost of production turn out to be as predicted? And so on.

Someone must bear these risks and make judgements about whether or not to undertake them in the first place and, if so, how best to meet them. The people who do so are called ENTREPRENEURS, and economists usually treat their services as a separate factor of production called ENTREPRENEURSHIP. (When this is not done, economists include entrepreneurs under labour.)

Often in the past, and sometimes today, such single, colourful individuals as Lord Nuffield or Helena Rubinstein initiate new products or new ways of producing old ones. Today, institutions often act as entrepreneurs. People's Express, the US airline which introduced cheap transatlantic fares after the collapse of Laker Airways, was the brainchild of a group of New York businessmen, not any one individual. On the other hand, Virgin Airways, the second cheap carrier to enter the transatlantic market in the 1980s, was largely the inspiration of one man, Mr Richard Branson.

Factor Services: So far we have talked about the factors of production themselves – land, labour, capital, and the entrepreneur. Each of these factors is owned by someone. For example, workers are, of course, owned by themselves (except where slavery exists). The owners of factors provide the services of their factors to firms. Workers, for example, provide work effort to the firm that hires them; they do not sell themselves. Landowners provide the services of their land to tenant farmers (or to themselves if they farm their own land). For this reason, we speak of *factor services* being sold on markets. These services are sold *by* those who own the factors *to* the firms that wish to use them in production.

Figure 1.1 summarizes our discussion of the four factors of production and shows how they may be used to produce goods and services that go to satisfy some of the unlimited wants of consumers.

RESOURCE ALLOCATION

What is often called 'the central economic problem' is the allocation of resources to satisfy human wants. The problem exists because of three characteristics of our society.

- Wants are, for all practical purposes, unlimited.
- The resources of land, labour and capital that are available to produce goods and services to satisfy these wants are limited.
- Most resources have alternative uses: land can be

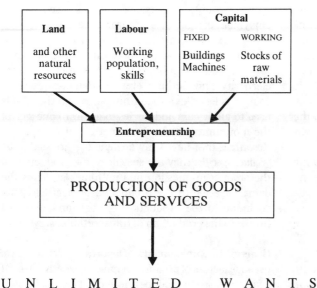

FACTORS OF PRODUCTION

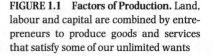

FIGURE 1.1   Factors of Production. Land, labour and capital are combined by entrepreneurs to produce goods and services that satisfy some of our unlimited wants

used to grow wheat, rye or barley, or as a site for a factory, or for a block of flats; labour can be employed on a farm, or in a factory, or in a pop band, and so on.

The first two of the above characteristics give rise to the basic economic problem of SCARCITY: there are not enough resources to satisfy all of the people's wants for goods and services to consume. Scarcity, in conjunction with the third characteristic noted above, gives rise to the basic need for CHOICE: how are resources to be allocated among their competing uses? How much labour, for example, should go into producing wheat, how much to eggs, how much to assembly-line work, and how much to pop bands?

Following on this discussion, 'the central economic problem' is often defined as *the allocation of scarce resources among competing uses for the satisfaction of consumers' wants.*

Opportunity Cost

A sacrifice is involved in choosing to use scarce resources to produce one thing *rather than another* – for example, certain amounts of land, labour and capital that could have made 20 pocket calculators can be used instead to make a word-processor. The sacrifice in making the word-processor is thus 20 pocket calculators. Consider a second example. We might plant more tomatoes in our kitchen garden, cutting back on runner beans to create the needed space. The sacrifice is then of runner beans. Note that we cannot avoid this choice by deciding to have more tomatoes *and* more runner beans. Our kitchen garden has limited space that is already fully used. So the decision to grow more tomatoes implies, therefore, a decision to grow less of something else, and that reduction in the output of the 'something else' can be regarded as the cost of the extra tomatoes.

To capture this basic idea of choice, economists use the concept of OPPORTUNITY COST, which measures the cost of something that one attains measured in terms of the sacrifice of the next best alternative. Thus, in our kitchen garden, the opportunity cost of tomatoes is measured in terms of the runner beans that we could have had instead. In precise terms, the opportunity cost of a pound of tomatoes might be $\frac{3}{4}$ of a pound of runner beans. In our other example, the opportunity cost of a word-processor was 20 pocket calculators.

Measuring opportunity cost

Notice two important things about opportunity cost.

First, opportunity cost is measured in physical, not monetary, units. Indeed, it is sometimes called *real* opportunity cost to distinguish it from money costs. For example, you might ask what is the cost of one more personal computer. To be told that it is £500 is not revealing unless you know what else £500 would purchase. Of course, we state costs in money terms constantly, but this is meaningful only because we know other prices and hence can make real, opportunity-cost comparisons implicitly, as soon as we hear a money price. Thus, if you feel £15,000 is a high cost for a particular car, it is because you know other prices and realize that to spend £15,000 on the car would imply the sacrifice of what you might otherwise have bought with the £15,000.

Second, notice that opportunity cost normally involves giving up some positive amount of one commodity in order to get more of another. We therefore describe this cost as being *positive*.

Can opportunity cost ever be zero?

We have said that opportunity cost is normally positive in the sense that to have more of one commodity requires giving up some positive amount of some other commodity. There are, however, three important exceptions. These arise when there are free goods, or single-use factors, or general unemployment of all factors of production.

Free Goods: There are a very few things that nature provides in such abundance that no opportunity cost is involved in their use. In many rural areas, wild fruit grows on moors and in hedgerows. The fruit is there for the picking. Since it does not grow on cultivated land that could be used for other purposes, its 'production' by nature implies no sacrifice of alternative crops (though the actual picking does involve opportunity cost: if I spend time picking fruit, I give up watching television, for example). Oxygen is another example. There is no real cost in breathing it, for (at least at present) there is more than enough for everyone to breathe with plenty left over for the filling of oxygen cylinders. Note, however, that a good may be free at one time, but not free at another. For example, fresh drinking water was once a free good but is now costly to produce in most areas; oxygen, now a free good, may cease to be one if depletion of the world's forests reduces the natural production of oxygen so much that we have to use scarce resources to produce it artificially.

Single-use Factors: Positive opportunity costs occur when resources have alternative uses. Where such alternatives do not exist, there is no opportunity cost.

For example, a scenic site in the Scottish highlands may have only one use: either it is used for the enjoyment of sightseers or it is not used at all.

Such examples are most often encountered with capital equipment, which does often have only one use. For example, a hydroelectric plant can produce electricity and nothing else; a coalmine produces coal, or is left idle; a road tunnel through the Alps is used to allow cars and lorries to get from one side of the mountain to the other, or it is not used at all. Resources that have only a single use are said to be *product specific*; they are specific to the production of the product in question and nothing else. Thus the dam is specific to the production of electricity, the coalmine to the production of coal, and the road tunnel to the production of transportation services.

General Unemployment: Opportunity cost exists because factors of production have alternative uses. If a factor is used to produce one good, it cannot be used to produce another. Thus, if factors that were building schools are now used to build hospitals, the opportunity cost can be measured as so many schools forgone per hospital built. For much of the last 40 years, something close to full employment of resources existed. In these circumstances, opportunity cost certainly was positive: producing more of one thing required taking resources away from producing something else. At some times, however, there are unemployed supplies of all resources and, at such times, opportunity cost may be zero. If, for example, there are unemployed building labourers, cranes, building supplies, and everything else needed in the building trade, it may be possible to build more hospitals without having to build fewer schools – or fewer of *anything* else.

Such situations of zero opportunity cost occur during periods of heavy unemployment of *all* resources, but not at other times. Note the condition that there be general unemployment of *all* relevant factors. If there is unemployed labour, but no unemployed equipment, then the decision to build more hospitals would not require that labour be taken from any other job (since the unemployed could be put to work), but it would require that the equipment be moved from some other use and production would have to fall in the use from which the equipment was withdrawn. Thus, positive opportunity cost requires that there be full employment of at least one, but not necessarily all, of the factors of production needed to make the commodity whose output is to rise.

In the first half of this book, we shall assume that opportunity cost is positive. This applies in either of two cases. First, full employment of at least some resources may exist, as it often has in the past and does in some parts of the UK today. Second, the government may decide, as a matter of policy, to maintain a certain level of unemployment of resources. (This could be part of its macroeconomic policy, to be discussed in Parts 4 and 5 of this book.) If so, the resources needed to produce more of something will have to be drawn from other lines of employment. Opportunity costs will then, in effect, be positive in spite of the existence of unemployed resources.

Production Possibility Curves

We are now going to illustrate our discussion using a graph. Graphs are used extensively in elementary economics, both to display information and, more importantly, as a reasoning device. A facility with graphs is thus a necessity for any student of economics. Since we know that some of you will have had trouble with geometry, and possibly not learned as much of it as you were supposed to, we have prepared an appendix telling you what you need to know about the use of graphs in order to read this book. This appendix starts on page 563. Everyone should look at it by way of review, and those who find they do not already know some of the things covered in the appendix must study it with care.

Several aspects of the important concept of opportunity cost can be illustrated with the aid of a graph. In Figure 1.2, we show the way in which resources can be deployed in an ultra-simple economy, one in which the nation is capable of producing only two goods, jeans and kebabs, abbreviated to *j* and *k*.

On the vertical axis we measure the number of kebabs produced. On the horizontal axis we measure the number of jeans. We will soon portray on the graph all the combinations of jeans and kebabs that the economy is capable of producing when all of its resources are fully employed in the most efficient manner.

Suppose that the possible combinations of output are those listed in Table 1.1. This Table tells us that, when all resources are devoted to kebab producton, the maximum total output is 350*k*. It also tells us that, when all resources go to jean production, output is 50*j*. These two points appear on the graph and are labelled *a* and *f*. They lie on the two axes.

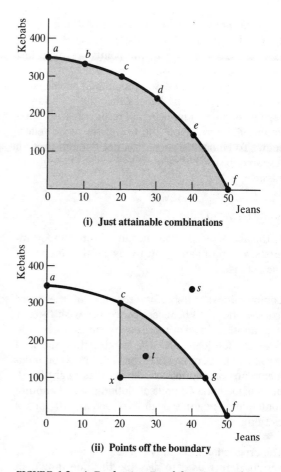

FIGURE 1.2   A Production Possibility Curve. This curve shows all of the combinations of commodities that can be produced by fully, and efficiently, employing all available factors of production

TABLE 1.1 Alternative Production Combinations of Kebabs and Jeans

Kebabs	Jeans	Reference letter
350	0	a
330	10	b
300	20	c
250	30	d
150	40	e
0	50	f

Next we plot the intermediate points corresponding to the other four combinations of outputs shown in the Table. In these cases, factors of production are used to produce some of both goods. These points are the *combinations* (*b*) 330*k* and 10*j*, (*c*) 300*k* and 20*j*, (*d*) 250*k* and 30*j*, and (*e*) 150*k* and 40*j*.

As a next step we join the points we have just plotted with a line. This line is called a PRODUCTION POSSIBILITY CURVE. It describes all the possible combinations of jeans and kebabs that the economy is capable of producing, using all resources with maximum efficiency.[1] Note the use of the word 'efficiency'. To be on the curve it is not enough that all resources be used, they must be used as efficiently as possible.

Some terms to note

In the above section, we introduced some important terms. We must pause now to say a little more about each of these.

Combinations: First, note the use of the word 'combinations'. Whenever economists wish to refer to quantities of two or more commodities, such as 30 pairs of blue jeans *and* 250 kebabs, they speak of COMBINATIONS, or BUNDLES, or BASKETS of commodities. Thus one bundle of commodities might be 20 units of food and 40 units of clothing, while another combination might be 30 units of food and 10 units of clothing.

The Production Possibility Curve: Second, note the various terms used to describe the line drawn in Figure 1.2. We have called it a 'production possibility curve'. In practice, a bewildering number of terms are used to describe this simple construction. Look first at the last word that we use. We use the term 'curve'. We might also have said 'boundary'. Both of these words can be used to indicate the line or curve shown on the diagram.

The term 'boundary' emphasizes that the points on the curve are maximum points. It is always possible to produce at points *within* the curve by not employing some factors of production, or by using them inefficiently. (We shall investigate this possibility in more detail below.)

Now look at the first part of the term. We have used the words 'production possibility', but the term 'transformation' is also used. The idea behind the

term 'transformation' is that you can transform one commodity into another by moving resources from the production of one commodity into the production of the other. The idea of transforming one commodity into another stresses the idea of opportunity cost.

You can make up four terms by combining the words listed below. All four terms mean the same thing:

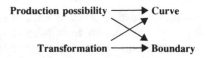

Aspects of production possibilities

Figure 1.2 can be used to illustrate some important features of the economy's production possibilities. We shall look at four of these: inefficient output combinations, unattainable combinations, the representation of opportunity cost, and the representation of changes in the economy's production possibilities.

Inefficient Output Combinations: If it is possible to produce combinations shown by points *on* the curve, it is also possible to produce combinations shown by points *inside* the curve (i.e. in the shaded area of part (i)). Such a point would indicate less of both goods than can be produced at some points on the curve. Production inside the curve occurs if one or more factors of production are either being used inefficiently or not being used at all (i.e. unemployed labour, idle machines, or half-used factories).

Consider, for example, point *x* in Figure 1.2 (ii), representing the output combinations 100*k* and 20*j*. It is clearly possible to produce more jeans or kebabs without having less of the other good. To see this on the diagram, draw lines from point *x* horizontally and vertically to meet the production possibility curve at *c* and *g*. This defines the shaded area enclosing all combinations of output which are greater than that at *x*, either in jean production (e.g. point *g*), in kebab production (e.g. point *c*), or in both jean and kebab production (e.g. point *t*).

Unattainable Output Combinations: All output combinations represented by points lying outside the shaded portion of Figure 1.2(i) are unattainable. Society's resources are insufficient to allow, for example, the production of 350*k* and 40*j* indicated by point *s* in Figure 1.2(ii). If 350 kebabs are produced there are no resources free to make jeans; while if 40

---

1 Strictly speaking, our decision to draw a smooth line through the points implies also that all possible combinations of j and k outputs between the six listed in Table 1.1 are attainable – e.g., 45*j* and 100*k* and 4½*j* and 339*k*.

jeans are produced, there are only enough resources to make 150 kebabs.

The Graphical Representation of Opportunity Cost: Opportunity cost itself can be represented on the production possibility boundary. To see what is involved, we reproduce the curve of Figure 1.2 in Figure 1.3. Suppose the economy is producing only kebabs, i.e. is at point *a* on its production possibility curve. Output is 350*k*. We then decide to produce 10 jeans. What is the opportunity cost of doing so? It is the kebabs given up as a result of this decision. From the Table we know that kebab output must fall from 350*k* to 330*k*. So the opportunity cost of 10 jeans is 20 kebabs: 10 jeans *cost* – i.e. require the sacrifice of – 20 kebabs. If we want to find the opportunity cost *per pair of jeans*, we need to divide the 20 'lost' kebabs by 10 – the number of jeans 'gained'. This gives us the opportunity cost of each pair of jeans, i.e. 2 kebabs.

The graphical expression of the opportunity cost of the first 10 jeans produced is simply the vertical drop in kebab production of 20*k*. As we move from *a* to *b* on the production possibility curve in Figure 1.3, this drop is the distance *aw*, which we can read off the vertical axis as equal to 20*k*. If we increase jean production further and so move downwards further along *ab* to point *c*, we produce another 10 jeans (20*j* in total). The opportunity cost of these extra jeans is the reduction in output of kebabs from 330*k* to 300*k*. This is again given by the vertical distance, *bv*, which equals 30 kebabs.

Shifts in the Production Possibility Curve: Changes in the efficient allocation of resources are represented by *movements along* the production possibility boundary; e.g., from point *b* to point *c* in Figures 1.2 or 1.3. Changes in productive capacity of the economy are reflected in *shifts* of the production possibility curve. Such shifts could be caused by rises (or falls) in the supplies of factors of production, or by changes in their productivity. An increase in productive capacity pushes the production possibility curve outwards (i.e. upwards and to the right). An example is shown by the shift from *af* to *a′f′* in Figure 1.4. Some things that could cause such a shift are an increase in the size of the working population, a rise in labour productivity, and technological advance. A decrease in productive capacity pushes the production possibility curve inwards (i.e. downwards and to the left). An example is shown by the shift from *af* to *a″f″* in Figure 1.5. Some things that could cause such a shift are a fall in

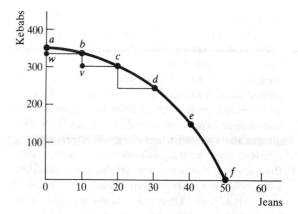

FIGURE 1.3   **The Representation of Opportunity Cost.** The curve shows how much of one commodity must be sacrificed to get specific amounts of the other commodity

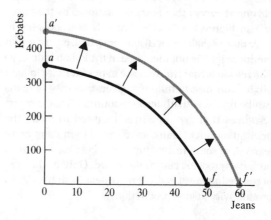

FIGURE 1.4   **An Outward Shift in the Production Possibility Curve.** It is now possible to have more of both commodities

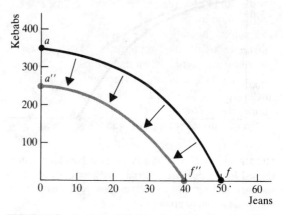

FIGURE 1.5   **An Inward Shift in the Production Possibility Curve.** Less of both commodities is now available

the size of the population, a drop in worker efficiency, or depletion of a non-renewable resource, such as oil.

The new curves $a'f'$ and $a''f''$ in Figures 1.4 and 1.5 have been drawn in a particular way. They show a change in productive capacity of the economy that is proportionately the same for the outputs of both jeans and kebabs; i.e. if j output rises by 10 per cent, k output rises 10 per cent as well. This is not, however, always the case. Changes often affect productivity relatively more in the production of one commodity than another. Suppose, for example, a new machine were introduced into the jean industry which raised productivity there. There is no reason to suppose that it would affect productivity in the kebab industry. In such a case, the new production possibility curve would not be parallel to the old curve. Both would start from exactly the same point, a, on the kebab axis. But the new curve would be to the right of the old one at every other point, as is shown by the curve af''' in Figure 1.6. Notice that it is now possible to have more kebabs, as well as more jeans, even though productivity has not increased in the kebab industry? The reason is that the increase in productivity in jean production means that any given quantity of jeans can be produced with fewer resources. If some of the resources that are no longer required to make the original output of jeans, are devoted to making more jeans and some to making more kebabs, output of both commodities can be increased. Only in the case of zero jean output is there no benefit from the rise in productivity in jean production.

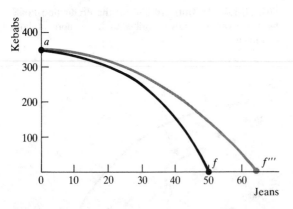

FIGURE 1.6   A Shift of the Production Possibility Curve Caused by an Increase in Productivity only in the Jean Industry. As long as some jeans are produced, more of both commodities can be produced

THREE BASIC ECONOMIC QUESTIONS

Earlier in this chapter, we said that economics was about what determines people's living standards. We can now take our study of the determinants of living standards a step further by asking three key questions that relate to how the economy does determine these living standards.

Question 1: Will the economy use its resources so that production takes place somewhere on, rather than inside, the production possibility curve? This question entails two subsidiary ones. (i) Will all resources be employed or will some lie idle? and (ii) Will factors of production be used efficiently? (We shall deal with unemployment in great detail later in this book; in the meantime, on the principle of one thing at a time, we shall confine ourselves to the issue of the efficient use of those resources that are employed in production.)

Question 2: Which of the combinations of outputs represented by all the points on the production possibility curve is to be selected? Choosing one particular point means producing one particular bundle of goods and this, in turn, implies one particular allocation of resources among their competing uses. Choosing another point means producing another bundle of goods which, in turn, implies another allocation of resources.

Question 3: How are the chosen outputs to be divided among all the members of society? This question involves consideration of the distribution of income among the nation's inhabitants.

When we look at these questions in terms of the production possibility curve, it is natural to ask them in the order listed above. In the next chapter, however, it is simpler to reverse the order of questions 1 and 2. Having done this, we can then restate the three basic questions as follows:

> *What* to produce? (question 2 above)
> *How* to produce it? (question 1 above)
> *Who* gets it? (question 3 above)

This is the form in which we shall encounter these three basic questions in the next chapter.

SUMMARY

1 Economics is one of a group of subjects known as the social sciences which study the behaviour of human beings in society.

2 Economists seek to explain the behaviour of variables such as prices and incomes which lie within their expertise. They take as 'given', variables such as the weather and tastes, whose explanation is outside of their field of study. The former are called endogenous variables, the latter are exogenous variables.

3 A nation's resources are termed its factors of production. There are three main groups: land, labour, and capital. Land includes everything commonly called natural resources; labour refers to human resources; and capital refers to man-made aids to production. A fourth factor, entrepreneurship, referring to the undertaking of business risks, is also sometimes distinguished.

4 What is often called the central economic problem is the allocation of resources to satisfy human wants. It arises from the scarcity of factors of production, which have alternative uses. Since resources are limited and wants are infinite, choices have to be made on how to allocate the scarce resources.

5 The opportunity cost of producing a commodity is the sacrifice involved in NOT using the required resources in the next best alternative line of production.

6 Opportunity cost is normally positive. It may, however, be zero in three special cases: (i) where there is abundant supply in nature, (ii) where a factor of production has only a single use, and (iii) where there is general unemployment.

7 The production possibility curve is a graphical expression of all the combinations of goods and services that can be produced when all resources are fully and efficiently employed.

8 Three basic economic problems are:
- What assortment of goods and services should be produced?
- How should the economy use its resources so that output is at a maximum?
- How should output be divided up among all the members of society?

Basic Questions and Answers

In the previous chapter we listed three of the basic questions of economics. Just by looking around us we can see examples of these questions every day.

THE THREE QUESTIONS IN EVERYDAY LIFE

What to produce?

Travel to your nearest shopping area and you will see an enormous variety of goods and services available for purchase. Breakfast cereals are sold (and hence must be produced) in very large quantities, while herrings are sold (and hence must be produced) in smaller quantities. Many shops offer to style your hair, while only a few offer to repair your shoes.

What would your grandparents have noticed if they had also been asked to make such observations? First, they would tell you that, when they were young, there were no supermarkets, and, in the grocery stores of their day, you would not have found the current vast array of prepared breakfast foods – but you would have found herrings. Also there were, they would tell you, far fewer hairdressing establishments and far more shoe repair shops then than now. These observations, and a myriad others like them, illustrate the WHAT question: What goods and services are to be produced and in what quantities?

How to produce it?

Read any newspaper, or visit any factory town, and you will hear of factories closing and, in some towns at least, of new factories being built. The new ones will almost always use production techniques that differ from those used in factories about to close.

Talk to the careers officer at any school. You will quickly learn that the skills required of school leavers change dramatically from decade to decade. Before the invention of the typewriter and the desk calculator, the ability to add long columns of figures rapidly and accurately, and to write clearly, was essential for an office worker (who, in the words of W. S. Gilbert, could 'rise to the top of the tree' by merely 'copying all the letters in a hand so free'). With the invention of the typewriter and the desk calculator came a need for different skills. No one then gained rapid promotion for penmanship or for prodigious feats of dreary calculations which the new machines could do faster and more accurately than people. Today, with the advent of the word-processor and the computer, an ability to communicate with the computer in its own language is becoming more important for office staff than are the more conventional office skills.

These observations illustrate our economy, giving changing answers to the HOW question: By what method is the nation's output of goods and services to be produced?

Who gets it?

Now walk around your home town and see some people living in large houses and others in small ones; some people driving large new cars, others small old ones, and yet others walking; some people buying a share of the expensive luxuries available on supermarket shelves, others confining their purchases to bread-and-butter items; some people taking skiing holidays in Switzerland as well as Mediterranean cruises in the summer, while others make do with a whizz down the hill of the local heath, if snow comes in winter, and with staying home to tend to the garden during the summer.

If you had made the same observations at the beginning of the century you would still have seen different expenditure patterns for different income groups. You would have observed, however, much larger differences between amounts of money spent by skilled and unskilled workers and between factory managers and foremen then than you would today.

In all of these observations we see the economy dealing with the WHO question: Who receives larger, and who receives smaller, proportions of the economy's total production (i.e. how is that production distributed among the population)?

Notice that the set of observations just given highlights people's tastes as well as their incomes. On the one hand, while a rich person can take many expensive holidays abroad, which many do, some others choose not to because they do not like foreign travel. On the other hand, while poorer persons find foreign holidays stretching their meagre means, some like foreign travel so much that they stint on other lines of expenditure in order to be able to afford an occasional trip abroad. Thus, while the market economy determines people's purchasing power – by determining their incomes – it leaves everyone free to spend the income that they do receive according to their own tastes, and hence, to decide on the 'bundle' of goods that will best satisfy their own wants.

Aggregate observations

When we look around us, as we have just imagined doing, we see illustrative details of how our economy provides answers to the three basic questions. We can also see how these questions are answered by examining economic data.

Figure 2.1 shows what is produced. The current allocation of resources in the UK is such that about 22 per cent of the total output is manufactured goods, 16 per cent is the services of banking and finance, 9 per cent is education and health, and so on, as shown in the figure. Finer breakdowns are available so that we could show, for example, how resources were allocated to produce outputs of ten different groups within the manufacturing sector.

Part of the answer to the question 'How is it produced?' is illustrated in Figure 2.2. It shows for each major British industry the proportion of total

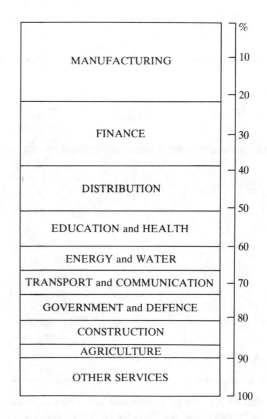

FIGURE 2.1   Gross Output by Industry, 1985
(*Source*: United Kingdom National Accounts)

expenditure accounted for by capital and labour. The ratio of the shaded area to the total area of each circle therefore represents the ratio of capital services to labour services used in that industry. We see from the diagram that the relative amounts of capital and labour vary greatly among industries. Energy and water use most capital per unit of labour followed by chemicals, while textiles and construction use least.

Figure 2.3 shows part of the answer to question 3: 'Who gets what is produced?' It tells us that *before-tax* income is far from equally distributed in the UK. A few very rich have very high incomes, more have very low incomes (these include retired persons, part-time employees, etc.). For example, the top 20 per cent of households received nearly half of total pre-tax income.

Coverage of the three questions

Virtually all of the basic issues that concern economists are covered by the three questions that we have just illustrated. This may not, however, always

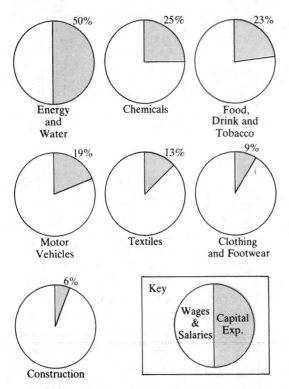

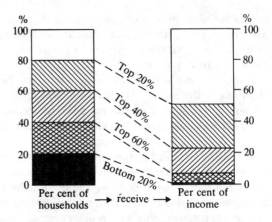

FIGURE 2.3   Distribution of Household Income (Before Tax), UK, 1984 (*Source*: *Social Trends*, 1987)

FIGURE 2.2   **Capital Expenditure and Wages and Salaries as Proportions of the Total for Each Industry, UK, 1984** (*Source*: Census of Production, Business Monitor PA1002)

be obvious. 'Where', for example, you might ask, 'does unemployment fit in?'

In fact, it clearly comes under question (1). Other things being equal, the higher unemployment is, the lower will be the nation's total output of goods and services.

'Well, then, what about economic growth – isn't it ignored?' In fact, growth involves all three questions! Economic growth usually involves an increased total output of goods and services, changes in the methods of production, and changes in the distribution of income (since there are almost always winners and losers from the process of growth).

ECONOMIC SYSTEMS

An economic system is a distinctive method of providing answers to the three basic economic questions. In its entirety, each country's economic system is a very complex engine. It includes laws – such as

those relating to property rights – rules, regulations, taxes and subsidies, and everything that governments use to influence what is produced, how it is produced, and who gets it. It includes firms, both large and small, both publicly and privately owned, those that are owned domestically and those that are foreign controlled. It includes consumers of every sort, both young and old, both rich and poor, and both working and non-working. It also includes customs of every conceivable kind, and the entire range of contemporary mores and values.

Social organization is a particularly important part of any economic system because it can influence the use of resources. Three of its aspects need to be distinguished. One relates to *ownership*, the second to *control*, and the third to the *objectives* of those who do exercise control.

Consider, for example, the factor of production, land. Its *ownership* may be in the hands of the state or of private individuals. In the latter case, there may be a few large landowners, numerous small peasant farmers, or anything in between. *Control* of the current uses of the land may lie with the owners or be devolved onto tenant farmers. *Objectives* (often also called *goals*) of those who have control over the land may vary enormously. Some people may be very money-conscious and cultivate crops that yield the largest return. Others may grow mainly for their own consumption. Some may go for immediate return at the expense of the long-term fertility of the land, while others may be concerned to preserve its productivity.

So, the idea of an economic system encompasses many different institutional arrangements and behaviour patterns. It is helpful, however, to suppress many of the details of particular systems in order to distinguish three major types, called *traditional*, *command*, and *market*.

Traditional Economic Systems

The first method of allocating resources consists of continuing with the behaviour of the past, following traditional patterns. A few small, isolated, self-sufficient communities still retain many traditional features. In earlier times, however, when tribal groups predominated, traditional systems were much more widespread.

The characteristics of traditional systems are fairly obvious. Young men follow their fathers in choice of occupation: hunting, fishing, fighting, etc. Women do what their mothers did – typically cooking and labouring. There is little change in the pattern of goods produced from year to year, other than those imposed by the vagaries of nature. The techniques of production also follow traditional patterns, except when the effects of an occasional new invention are felt. Finally, production is allocated among the members according to long-established traditions of hierarchy or communality. The answers to the economic questions of what to produce? how to produce it? and how to distribute it? are based on tradition.

Such a system works best in an unchanging environment. Prehistoric studies show that the systems did change, but only occasionally, and usually only when large external shocks made some form of adaptation unavoidable. A climatic change, the introduction of a new crop, or the invention of a new tool, are obvious examples. But where conditions are static, a system that does not continually raise problems of choice may be efficient on economic, as well as on social, grounds.

Command Economies

In command economies, questions about resource allocation are decided by some *central* authority, which makes all the necessary decisions on what to produce, how to produce it, and who gets it. Such economies are characterized by the *centralization* of decision-taking. However, since centralized decision-taking requires plans for the desired outcomes, the terms *command economies* and *centrally planned economies* are used to refer to the same type of economic system.

Planning

Central planning of all economic decisions in a large, modern industrial nation is an extremely complex business. Planners need to know the entire range of technological possibilities for production and to have full details of the supplies of all factors of production with their characteristics. On the basis of this information, the planners must settle on their choice of goods and services to be produced and how to produce them. Planning the allocation of commodities may be done by decree; e.g. by rationing. However, planners often use prices for distribution. In this case they set the prices of consumers' goods and leave individuals to buy what they wish at the state-controlled prices. Even then, however, the planners must predict the pattern of consumers' demands in order to issue the correct production orders. Whenever they get the quantities wrong, there are queues for some scarce goods and unsold surpluses of others.

The sheer quantity of data required for central planning of an entire economy is enormous, and the task of analysing it to produce a fully integrated plan can hardly be exaggerated. Moreover, the plan is not once-and-for-all. It must be a rolling process, continually changing to take account, not only of current data, but also of future trends in labour supplies, in technological developments, and in tastes of the population for different goods and services. Doing so involves the planners in *forecasting* – a notoriously difficult business, not least because of the unavailability of all essential accurate and up-to-date information.

Realizing plans

Once plans are drawn up, they must be put into effect. For this there are several *instruments* to which the planners can turn. Policies that help governments achieve their goals are called *policy instruments* (or often just *instruments* for short). These include direct controls, such as direction of labour to different industries and parts of the country, and directives setting targets for both the inputs used and the outputs produced by firms. Some are set in physical units – e.g. so many dresses produced each month – others are set in financial terms – e.g. target rates of profit.

Production: One major problem with this type of planning is incentives. How can management and labour be induced to carry out the plan? Solutions vary from the 'carrots' of profit and wage incentives to the 'sticks' of fines (or even prison sentences) for non-fulfillment.

Fulfilling the plan in terms of numbers is not enough. Quality is a continual problem in centrally planned economies. If firms get credit solely for fulfilling physical output quotas, they have little incentive to maintain the quality of their products. Complaints about the low quality of consumers' goods, and exhortations designed to persuade producers to do better, are one of the recurrent themes, for example, in official Soviet publications.

Distribution: When it comes to distributing the national output among the community this could also, in principle, be done centrally by rationing – allocating a bundle of goods to each person. The method would be to issue ration coupons permitting each person to obtain specified amounts of each commodity. There are two compelling reasons why, in practice, this method is rarely resorted to in normal times. First, it requires an enormous administrative apparatus. Second, it makes no allowance for differences in tastes. Some people would find themselves with more coupons than they wanted for good X and not enough for good Y. Others would be in the opposite situation. People would probably have to waste large amounts of time trading coupons so as to get closer to their personally preferred consumption bundles.

Central planners have always realized the great advantage of decentralizing consumption decisions. Thus, in virtually all centrally planned economies, consumers receive an income which they are then left largely free to spend as they wish. The size of the income, and hence the size of the 'bundle' available to each consumer, is determined by the state – often partly with work incentives in mind – high incomes for occupations the planners wish to encourage, and low incomes for the occupations they wish to discourage. Individual consumers are then left free to determine the composition of their own consumption bundles by spending their incomes as they wish.

They do this within constraints of price and availability that are laid down by the planners. Some commodities are priced cheaply – sometimes below their cost of production – while other commodities are priced expensively. For example, in many Eastern bloc countries, food and vodka have low prices while consumers' durables such as TV sets and automobiles have high prices. There is also the question of availability. For some goods, demand exceeds supply and queues, or long waiting lists, are common. For other goods, supply exceeds demand and unsold surpluses tend to pile up. The system is to this extent inefficient in allocating resources.

Full planning

If we have conveyed the impression that fully centralized planning of all economic decisions in an advanced country involves an almost impossibly complex set of arrangements, this was intended. Indeed, the Soviet literature is itself full of discussions of the difficulties inherent in such a system. As a result, there have been significant changes since the early days of central planning to decentralize some forms of decision-taking. For example, firms are left to take many decisions themselves, guided by the prices that are set by the planners. In spite of these moves to decentralize some decisions, most of the key choices – such as the proportion of the nation's scarce factors of production to allocate to the production of consumers' goods or investment goods – are still made by the central planners.

Central planning is valued in socialist economies because it allows the state to determine production and distribution according to social values (at least as they are perceived by the planners). Moreover, central planning is not confined to fully planned economies; it is also found to some extent in the mixed economies that we shall soon consider.

Market Economies

In the third type of economic system to be considered, the decisions about resource allocation are made without any central direction but, instead, as a result of innumerable independent decisions taken by individual producers and consumers; such a system is known as a *market economy*.

Decentralized decision-taking

In a market economy, decisions relating to the basic economic issues are decentralized. They are nonetheless co-ordinated. The main co-ordinating device is the set of market-determined prices – which is why the free-market system is often also called a PRICE SYSTEM. Much of our study in this book will be of how prices are determined and of how they act to co-ordinate decentralized decisions.

A MARKET is an institution defined as any convenient arrangements whereby persons can communicate with each other in order to buy and sell goods, services, or factors of production. Markets are sometimes located physically in particular buildings or streets. The Stock Exchange in Throgmorton Street and the London Metal Exchange in Fenchurch Street, both in the City of London, are specialized markets where buyers and sellers of shares in companies, and of non-ferrous metals respectively, meet to deal with each other. Petticoat Lane in the East End of London, and the Bull Ring in Birmingham, are popular street markets where many stallholders offer a range of goods from antiques and bric-à-brac to vegetables.

The term 'market' is not, however, confined to particular sites. We speak of the 'foreign exchange market', which has no more specific location than the international telephone network and computer hook-ups, *by which dealers buy and sell pounds, dollars, francs, yen and other currencies*. Markets may indeed use all conceivable means of communication including the press, as in the case of the markets for many second-hand goods such as motorcars. If you have a car to sell, or want to buy one, you will discover that 'the market' comprises the local press, specialized magazines such as *The Motor* and *Exchange and Mart*, as well as the showrooms of used-car dealers.

Market economies are characterized by two key features:
   (i) specialization in production, accompanied by freedom to exchange what is produced among individuals; and
   (ii) market-determined prices.

Specialization and exchange

Small, isolated, traditional societies in the pre-agricultural stage of history were (and where they now occur, are) self-sufficient. Such societies are characterized by a

'relative simplicity of material culture, the lack of accumulation of material wealth and mobility. . . . Subsistence requirements are satisfied by only a modest effort – perhaps two or three days a week by each adult: . . . Such features set hunters and gatherers apart from more technologically developed societies whose very survival depends upon their ability to maintain order and to control property.'[1]

1 *The Times Atlas of World History* (Maplewood, NJ: Hammond, 1979), p. 39.

The societies referred to in the above quotation are those few nomadic societies that survive today. They were, however, typical societies about 10,000 years ago, before the first agricultural revolution which put an end to wandering self-sufficiency. This revolution, which came when man learned how to plant and cultivate crops, brought with it surplus production: the new farming methods meant that farmers could produce substantially more than they needed in order to survive. As a result, some of the population was freed from the need to work on the land. New occupations then appeared: artisans, soldiers, barbers, entertainers, priests, and government officials. The age of specialization had begun.

Specialization must be accompanied by trade. People who produce only one thing must trade most of it to obtain all of the other things that they require. Early free-market economies used BARTER, the trading of goods directly for other goods. But barter is costly in time spent searching out satisfactory exchanges. If a farmer has wheat and wants a hammer, he must find someone who has a hammer and wants wheat. A successful barter transaction thus requires what is called a *double coincidence of wants*.

To avoid the cumbersome nature of barter, another institution, known as money, evolved. Money eliminates barter by separating transactions. If a farmer has wheat and wants a hammer, he does not have to find someone who has a hammer and wants wheat. He merely has to find someone who wants wheat. The farmer takes money in exchange, then finds another person who wishes to trade a hammer, and gives up the money for the hammer. Money becomes the medium of exchange. *By eliminating the cumbrousness of barter, money greatly facilitates trade and specialization.*

Specialization by individuals in the production of only one commodity was accompanied by a tremendous increase in productivity. Rising output was also aided by another aspect of specialization generally known as the *division of labour*: the specialization on the single task within the making of one commodity. The most efficient way of building a house is not to employ a dozen who share all the necessary tasks, *each* doing some bricklaying, some plastering, some painting and decorating, some electrical wiring, some plumbing, and so on. It is, instead, to employ bricklayers, plasterers, painters and decorators, electricians, plumbers, etc. Skilled craftspeople are more effective if each chooses the occupation in which he or she has some natural advantage and then concentrates on the skill in which continual practice and experience raises efficiency.

The combination of specialization and division of labour proved to be the most powerful instrument of economic progress that the world has ever seen. Its power reached unprecedented heights during the industrial revolution which began in the early eighteenth century.

Market-determined prices

We have seen that an economic system in which people specialize in the production of goods and services necessitates the exchange of commodities. Perhaps the most remarkable feature of the market system is that it requires no planning authority, no bureaucracy, to allocate resources. The price mechanism works as a result of millions of decisions made by individual producers and consumers acting in their own self-interest. The key to the whole process is to be found in the role of prices, which perform the crucial function of providing signals that help to determine the allocation of resources. That they do it remarkably well (though not without some deficiencies, to which we shall return later) is clear because what some groups want to sell usually matches what other groups want to buy.

A Co-ordinator of Decisions:　Every day, millions of people independently make millions of decisions concerning production and consumption. Most of these decisions are not motivated by a desire to contribute to the social good, or to make the whole economy work well, but by considerations of self-interest. The price system co-ordinates these decentralized decisions, so that the whole system is sensitive to wishes of the individuals who compose it.

The basic insight into how this system works is that decentralized private decision-takers, acting in their own interests, respond to *signals*, which are the prices of what they buy and sell. Economists have long emphasized price as a signalling agent. When a commodity such as oil becomes scarce, its price tends to rise. Firms and households that use it are led to economize on it and to look for alternatives. Firms that produce it are led to discover more of it and bring higher-cost sources, such as tar sands, into production. This system works best, as we shall see, when prices are flexible and determined in markets where there are many buyers and many sellers. The prices that give signals about scarcities and surpluses are then set by the impersonal forces of demand and supply and are acted on by individuals.

Lack of Conscious Direction:　The market economy fulfils its function of co-ordinating decisions without anyone having to understand how it works. For example, the dairy farmer doesn't need to know how many people eat butter and where they live, how many people drink milk, how many other dairy farmers there are, or whether more money is spent on beer than on milk. What he needs to know includes the prices of different kinds of fodder, the characteristics of different cows, the price of milk, the cost of hired labour relative to that of farm machinery, and what his net earnings might be if he sold his cows and raised sheep instead.

By responding to such public signals as the costs and prices of what he buys and sells, the dairy farmer helps to make the whole economy fit together, to produce what people want, and to provide it where and when they want it.

Laissez-faire:　The ability of impersonal market forces to co-ordinate economic decisions led early economists to speak of a policy of *laissez-faire*. This French expression indicates a belief that the nation's commerce functions best when it is free from government intervention and left to be governed by what the great eighteenth-century Scottish economist Adam Smith called the 'hidden hand' of market forces.

In later times, the term *laissez-faire* came to be used to describe a callous policy of ignoring all concerns about social welfare. Originally, however, it merely described the belief that the market economy would perform most efficiently if left free from government intervention.

How Markets Work

We shall consider two situations which serve to illustrate the way in which market systems allocate resources. These are a change in tastes, and a change in costs.

A Change in Tastes:　First consider how markets react to a change in consumers' tastes. Assume that at the outset, producers find it equally profitable to produce Wensleydale or Cheddar cheese, and consumers are prepared to buy the quantities of each that are being supplied at prevailing market prices.

Now suppose that consumers experience a greatly

increased desire for Wensleydale and a diminished desire for Cheddar cheese. The reason could be discovery of the delicious flavour of Wensleydale following on holidays in Yorkshire, establishment by the medical profession of the fact that eating Wensleydale while smoking cigarettes reduces the risk of contracting dandruff, or a particularly effective advertising campaign by Saatchi and Saatchi.

What will be the effects of this change? First, consumers will buy more Wensleydale and less Cheddar. With production unchanged, a shortage of Wensleydale, and a glut of Cheddar, will develop. In order to unload their surplus Cheddar, merchants will reduce its price on the principle that it is better to sell it for less than not to sell it at all. In contrast, merchants will find that they cannot keep Wensleydale on their shelves. It has become a scarce commodity. People will be prepared to pay more for it and its price will rise. As the price rises, less Wensleydale will be bought as people buy less expensive Cheddar instead. Thus, the quantity demanded will be adjusted to the available supply.

The price changes brought about in the shops will filter through to cheese factories. They will reallocate their resources from Cheddar to Wensleydale production since, provided costs of production have not altered, it will be profitable to do so. Thus, the change in consumer tastes, working through the price mechanism, causes resources to be reallocated to meet the change.

A Change in Costs: For our second example, consider a change originating, not with consumers, but with producers. Begin, as before, with a situation in which producers find it equally profitable to produce Wensleydale and Cheddar, and that consumers are prepared to buy, at prevailing market prices, the quantities of these two cheeses that are supplied. Now imagine that a technological change occurs: an improved Wensleydale-making process is developed and this lowers costs of Wensleydale production. Since costs fall, Wensleydale production becomes more profitable. Everything else is unchanged, including consumers' tastes and the costs of making Cheddar cheese.

What will happen now that Wensleydale production is relatively more profitable than it used to be? Clearly, if they are at all interested in increasing their profits, producers will begin to switch resources from Cheddar to Wensleydale. Soon the quantities of the two cheeses coming on to the market will change. A

shortage of Cheddar and a glut of Wenslydale will result. The price of Cheddar will start to rise and that of Wensleydale to fall. As the former becomes more expensive, less of it will be bought by consumers. The opposite will happen with Wensleydale. The lower price will entice consumers to buy and eat more of it. At the same time there will be an incentive for producers to move back into Cheddar production as its price rises relatively to that of Wensleydale.

The functions of prices

The price mechanism operates to allocate resources in such a way as to answer the three basic questions of what is to be produced, how it will be produced, and how it will be distributed among the population. Prices do so by acting as *signals* to consumers and producers in two sets of markets:
- (i) markets for goods and services (often called GOODS MARKETS for short)
- (ii) markets for factors of production (often called FACTOR MARKETS for short).

Markets for goods and services

Goods markets are a major determinant of the answer to our first question: 'What is to be produced?' We described the functioning of the price mechanism in the market for Wensleydale and Cheddar cheeses. These two goods, chosen for illustrative purposes, may be regarded as typical of the markets for *all* goods and services. The signalling function of prices in the goods market was implicit in our explanation of the ways in which changes in production and consumption of Cheddar and Wensleydale cheese responded to movements in their prices. *Prices signal to producers which goods are the most profitable to produce. Prices signal to consumers which goods give most value for the money they must pay to purchase them.* Resources are rechannelled in new directions following price changes brought about by changes in tastes, or in costs of production.

Markets for factors of production

We now need to look at the part played by factor markets in answering the three basic questions: What is produced? How is it produced? and Who gets it?

The operation of the price mechanism in factor markets closely parallels that in goods markets already described. The services of each factor – land, labour, capital, and entrepreneurship – are bought and sold, just as are goods and services for consumption. The price of labour is the wage rate that is paid for employing it. The price of land is its rent, and so on. The price of any factor of production is influenced by two forces: the amount offered for sale on the market, and the amount firms wish to purchase.

What is Produced?   This question, as we have seen, concerns the allocation of resources. Are more resources allocated to producing Cheddar or Wensleydale cheese and similarly for all other products? We have seen that part of the answer to this question comes from goods markets, where signals go to consumers and firms.

If firms are to respond to a signal to produce more of one product and less of another, resources must be released from the firms who are contracting production and persuaded to move to firms who wish to expand production. A major signal for such reallocations of resources comes from changes in factor prices. These prices are set in factor markets.

A rise in the demand for factors in some productive use, or geographical area, will tend to raise the prices of the factors in that use or area. A fall in the demand for factors in other productive uses, or other geographical areas, will tend to lower the prices of factors in those uses or areas. The owners of factors – workers, capitalists, and landowners – respond to these price signals by moving their factors out of uses where prices are falling and into uses where prices are rising.

When a factor responds to changing price signals by moving from one use to another, that factor is said to be *mobile*. Mobility relates to movements between occupations, industries, or regions. A rise in wage rates, for instance, acts as an incentive for labour to move. The relative strength of demand for accountants since the 1970s has led to higher earnings for accountants, which in turn has encouraged increasing numbers of school leavers to train for the accountancy profession. The fact that wage rates are, on average, higher in London than in Birmingham or Glasgow helps to cause a southward migration of labour. These movements are responses to the signals provided by prices. Factors move as long as it pays them to do so. The movement of factors, however, tends to reduce the disparities between factor prices in different regions, in different occupations, and in different industries.

How is it Produced?   Consider next how factor markets help to answer the second basic economic question: 'What methods of production are to be used?' Because factors of production are to some extent interchangeable, there is usually more than one way in which a given output can be produced. Labour, capital and other factors can be combined in different proportions. Some industries use relatively large amounts of one factor, such as labour, and are described as *labour-intensive*, while others use relatively large amounts of capital and are described as *capital-intensive*. Figure 2.2 illustrates differences in factor proportions. It shows some relatively capital-intensive industries such as energy and water, some relatively labour-intensive ones, such as construction, and others in between. Why should these differences exist?

The answer has two strands, one technical and one economic. A simple example will illustrate. How does a farmer decide the best method of producing a given quantity of cauliflowers? We assume he only uses three inputs – land, labour and fertilizers.

Consider, first, the technical side of the matter. The farmer knows from experience how the productivity of his land changes as he varies the amounts of labour and fertilizers he employs. If all these factors of production were free, he would clearly use all the labour and fertilizer needed to secure the maximum possible yield from his land. The farmer would be looking for only technical efficiency. He would be trying to maximize the yield from every square foot of his land. He would do this without regard to how much labour and fertilizer he uses because all he wanted of these inputs was freely available.

Labour and fertilizers are not, however, free factors. They are scarce and have alternative uses. Each commands a price which is influenced by market forces. Because the most *economically* efficient combination of factors produces the given quantity at minimum cost, regard must be given to input prices. Farmers who are trying to run their businesses as profitably as possible, will consider the prices of the factors that they use.

To see how changing factor prices affect farmer Brown's choice of production techniques, imagine that, after he has selected his minimum-cost method, the price of one of the factors alters. Suppose, for instance, that fertilizers fall in price because of technical progress in the chemical industry, while the price of labour remains the same. Brown will rethink his situation, recalculate his costs of different production methods, and will substitute fertilizers for labour. He does this by using less labour but more fertilizer to produce cauliflowers. If, in contrast, the price of labour falls because of an influx of farm workers from overseas, he will substitute labour for fertilizers. In all this, he is reacting to the signals he receives of relative prices, and he is adjusting his input combinations to minimize his production costs. Because he is trying to make as much profit as he can, he reacts in a predictable way to price changes.

The Significance of Cost Minimization: We have seen that factor prices influence producers in their decisions on what methods of production to adopt. But what is the significance of this for the whole economy? The answer is that cost minimization when factor prices are set by demand and supply tends to lead to *efficient production.* Let us see how this comes about.

The prices of factors of production tend to reflect their relative scarcities. In a country with a great deal of land and a small population, for example, the price of land will be low while, because labour is in short supply, the wage rate will be high. In such circumstances, firms producing agricultural goods will tend to make lavish use of (cheap) land and to economize on (expensive) labour; a production process will be adopted that is land-intensive. On the other hand, in a small country with a large population, the demand for land will be high relative to its supply. Thus, land will be relatively expensive and firms producing agricultural goods will tend to economize on it by using a great deal of labour per unit of land. In this case production will tend to use labour-intensive methods of cultivation.

In general, abundant factors will tend to have prices that are low relative to the prices of factors that are scarce. Firms seeking their own private profit will then be led to use much of the factors with which the whole country is plentifully endowed, and to economize on the factors that are in scarce supply.

This discussion provides an example of how the price system co-ordinates decentralized decision-taking. No single firm need be aware of national factor surpluses and scarcities. Prices determined on the competitive market tend to reflect these, and individual firms that never look beyond their own private profit are nonetheless led to economize on factors that are scarce in the nation as a whole.

We should not be surprised, therefore, to discover that methods of producing the same commodity differ in different countries. In the United States, where labour is highly skilled and very expensive, a steel company may use very elaborate machinery and economize on labour. In China, where labour is abundant and capital very scarce, a much less mechanized method of production may be appropriate. The Western engineer who feels that the Chinese are way behind because they are using methods abandoned in the West as inefficient long ago, may be missing the truth about economic efficiency in the use of resources.

The price system tends to produce an efficient use of resources. The common sense of this is that *any* society interested in getting the most out of resources should take account of relative scarcities in deciding what productive process to adopt, which is what the price system leads individual producers to do.

Who Gets It? The final basic question of resource allocation – how the output of goods and services is divided up among the population – is also answered by a market system. This is the question of the distribution of income, and we must now see how factor markets provide the answer.

The prices of factors of production fulfil a twofold signalling function on the demand and on the supply side. On the demand side, users of factors are induced by considerations of profit maximization to economize on expensive factors and, wherever possible, to make more use of cheap factors. On the supply side, a high price for a factor encourages an increase in the supply of that factor while a low price encourages a decrease. For example, high prices for computer programers and low wages for file clerks will encourage people to stay on in school to train as computer programers rather than to leave school early to become file clerks.

As a result of the interaction of demand and supply, factors get priced. The income earned by any factor depends on the price paid for it: wages for labour, rent for land, etc. Those factors which command high prices for their services will also be able to earn high incomes. For instance, workers with scarce skills in strong demand tend to be paid more than other less-skilled workers for whose services demand is weak and the market price is low. Owners of land in city centres earn higher rents than owners of marginal hill farms. Prices play their part in the determination of individual incomes. Thus the pricing of factors of production helps to determine the distribution of income going to the owners of factors.

Mixed Systems

So far we have discussed three pure types of economic system: traditional, command, and market. Our discussion of the command system made it clear that no pure command system exists. For example, consumers are not commanded to consume a certain bundle of goods; instead they are always left some substantial freedom to decide for themselves on the bundle of goods they will consume. 'Socialist' nations which prohibit private ownership of capital can, and do, make some use of the price mechanism, especially for the distribution of national output. Most such countries allow prices of consumer goods and services to be influenced by market forces. Information about rising and falling prices can help planners decide what commodities should be produced. Even decisions on how to produce may be decided by the price mechanism. For example, state factories may be set profit targets and left to make their own decisions rather than being given directives on what to produce and how to organize production. Yugoslavia, for instance, relies quite heavily on this kind of planning.

If a complete command economy does not exist, neither does a pure *laissez-faire* market system. Governments intervene with a host of policies from laws and directives to taxes and subsidies. Also, in every country some production activities are run by the government. Moreover, even in relatively free-market economies, a degree of central planning is sometimes useful. It has been widely adopted during periods of large-scale war, when the overriding national aim is to bring hostilities to a successful conclusion. Priority to military needs is then generally accepted as being of prime concern and consumer interests take second place. At these times, rationing of essentials such as food and clothing may be introduced without popular complaint.

Central planning is also useful in achieving major and rapid structural changes in the economy. Planning has been used in an attempt to bring about speedy industrialization of poor agricultural countries in the Third World – though such nations tend to have fewer reliable sources of statistical data of the kind needed for efficient central planning. Partial planning, comprising centralized decision-taking for a limited number of sectors of the economy which are regarded as of key importance, is also common in many countries. Some governments take on the role of central planners, organizing production in a few industries such as coal, railways and postal services,

as is done in the UK. The reasons for state intervention differ from industry to industry and will be considered at length in a later chapter.

Thus, although it is helpful to study pure types to gain insight into various issues, it is important to remember that *all real economies are mixed economies.* Each country differs only in the proportion of the mix between reliance on markets to co-ordinate decentralized decisions, and reliance on centralized decision-taking using the command principle. What differentiates the economies of such countries as the USSR and the US is not the complete absence of markets in the former and the complete absence of government intervention in the latter. Instead, it is that there is much more central planning and much less use of markets in the USSR than in the US. The UK lies between the two countries in the degree of its mix between reliance on planning and on markets but on balance it is closer to the US than to the USSR.

THE ECONOMY AS A WHOLE

So far we have discussed individual markets, such as those for labour or for wheat. We are now in a position to discuss how these markets all fit together into a broader picture.

The Circular Flow of Income

In Figure 2.4, all *producers* of goods and services are grouped together in the lower circle labelled producers. All *consumers* of goods and services are grouped together in the upper circle labelled consumers. Of course, most individuals have a double role. As buyers of goods and services, they play a part in consuming output; as sellers of factor services, they play a part in producing that output.

The interactions between producers and consumers take place through two kinds of markets.

Goods Markets: The outputs of commodities flow from producers to consumers through what are usually known as goods (or product) markets. Note the plural in 'product markets'. Just as firms produce many products, so are there many markets in which products are sold. Individuals constitute one major group of consumers – indeed the largest, by amount consumed. They buy, for their own use, goods and services such as food, clothing, train journeys, record albums and automobiles. Other 'consumers' are firms who purchase capital goods produced by yet other firms, and foreigners who purchase our exports. For the time being, we concentrate on the first group.

Factor Markets: Most people earn their incomes by selling factor services to firms. Exceptions are people receiving payments from pension plans and unemployment and supplementary benefits; they receive an income but not in return for providing their factor services to aid in current production.

Most of those who do sell factor services are employees. They sell their labour services to firms in return for wages. Some others own capital and receive interest or profits for providing it. Others own land and derive rents from it. Buying and selling of these factor services takes place in factor markets. The buyers are producers, who use the services to produce goods that are sold to consumers.

What we have just described involves a circular *flow*. Money flows to producers as a result of selling goods and services to consumers, and to consumers as a result of their selling factor services to producers.

This concept of a circularity in economic relations is a critical one. It helps us to understand how the separate parts of the economy are related to each other in a system of mutual interaction. For example, what producers do affects households, since the wages they pay affect people's incomes. What households do affects firms, since the goods they buy affect the sales revenues of firms.

The circular flow can be examined at various levels. The first is what is called the MICROECONOMIC aspect. This is what we have been doing so far in this chapter and what we will do in the first half of this book. The microeconomic view stresses the details of the flows within and between the myriad individual markets that form the entire economy.

The second level is termed the MACROECONOMIC aspect. We shall briefly consider this below, and it is the subject of the second half of this book. The macroeconomic level is painted with a broad brush; it aggregates flows in individual markets to consider flows between various very broad 'sectors' of the economy.

We now consider each view of the circular flow.

The microeconomic view of the circular flow

In microeconomics, which is the subject of Parts 2 and 3 of this book, we focus on the economy's many individual markets and on the interrelationships among them. When doing so, we pay attention to prices and quantities as signalling agents. Most consumers have to accept market prices as *given* – by which we mean that the prices are determined by forces beyond their control so that there is nothing they can do to change them. These prices provide the *signals* to which consumers respond. Many producers also face *given* market prices – prices that are set on markets over which they have little or no control. They respond as best they can to these *given* prices. Other producers set their own prices, and they respond to the amounts that they are able to sell at the prices that they set.

In their purchasing decisions, consumers respond to prices in goods markets. In so doing, the aggregate behaviour of all consumers affects those prices. Prices in goods markets also serve as signals to producers, telling them what products they can profitably provide to the market. Given their techniques of production, and the prices of factors of production, producers must choose among (1) the products they could produce and sell, (2) the various ways of producing these products, and (3) the various quantities they could produce. By so doing, the aggregate behaviour of all firms also affects product prices.

In their purchasing decisions, producers respond to factor-market prices. The total amount of factor services that they buy depends on how much they intend to produce, but the *proportions* in which they use factors are influenced by factor prices. Firms will try to use less of factors that are particularly expensive and more of factors that are particularly cheap. By demanding various amounts of different factors, producers, in the aggregate, help to determine factor prices. Those persons who supply factor services to firms make their decisions as to how much to offer on the market partly on the basis of the factor prices that they face. These choices determine the supplies of factor services that are available and, in the aggregate, help to determine factor prices.

The macroeconomic view of the circular flow

Macroeconomics suppresses the details of the many markets through which the circular flow works. In doing so, attention is concentrated on the total flows shown in Figures 2.4 and 2.5. Macroeconomics deals with broad aggregates, and may therefore be described as *aggregate economics*. Microeconomic analysis depends on some aggregation of the behaviour of individuals. For example, when we study the behaviour in a single market, we are interested in the total amount that *all* the purchasers in that market want to buy and in the total amount that *all* the sellers want to sell.

Macroeconomics operates at a much higher level of *aggregation.* In macroeconomics we study such things as the total number of people employed (the aggregate amount of labour flowing through all of the labour markets in the economy), and the total sales of all consumers' goods (the aggregate amount of all goods and services for consumption flowing through all of the economy's relevant markets).

Money Flows: Dealing with such aggregates immediately poses an important measurement problem: how do we add up the various amounts to get the total flows that are to be studied in macroeconomics? We can measure total output of wheat in tonnes, of shirts in numbers and of electricity in kilowatts. But what is the total output of all three taken together? To answer this question, we need a common denominator that we can use to add up such diverse outputs as wheat, shirts and electricity.

The common denominator that we use is money. Almost all goods and services have money values, which are simply the prices paid to purchase them. The total money *value* of all output is, thus, a meaningful, and a convenient, way of measuring the *volume* of the economy's total, or aggregate, output.

Income Flows: The way in which we look at the totals that flow through the economy's markets, using the measuring rod of money, is shown in Figure 2.5. The two Figures, 2.4 and 2.5, are alternative ways of looking at the same transactions. Every market transaction is an exchange. It has two sides, in the sense that, for every sale, there is a purchase and, for every seller, there is a buyer. The buyer receives goods or services and parts with money; the seller receives money and parts with goods or services.

Figure 2.4 concentrates on the flows of goods and services through markets. These are seen flowing, anti-clockwise, from consumers to producers and from producers to consumers. Figure 2.5 concentrates on the corresponding money flows. Money flows are seen going, clockwise, in the opposite direction. Money flows from producers to consumers to pay for factor services purchased, and from consumers to producers for goods and services purchased.

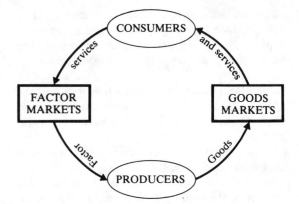

FIGURE 2.4 The Circular Flow of Goods and Services. Factor services flow from consumers to producers, while goods and services flow from producers to consumers

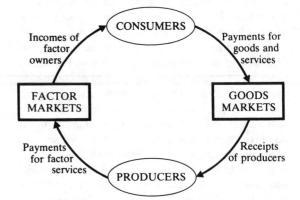

FIGURE 2.5 The Circular Flow of Income. Payments flow from consumers to producers in return for goods and services bought by consumers; payments flow from producers to consumers in return for factor services bought by producers

To distinguish these two sets of flows, each of which is the counterpart of the other, the flows in Figure 2.4 are called *real flows* while those in Figure 2.5 are called *money or nominal flows.*

Macroeconomics deals with the money flows that are shown in Figure 2.5 (and many other similar flows that we shall encounter later). When we talk of total output, we refer to the right-hand flow in Figure 2.5: the total value of goods and services produced and flowing through goods markets to purchasers. When we talk of the total amount of factor services used, and of the total incomes earned by the owners of factors of production, we refer to the left-hand flow in the Figure: to the total value of all factor services flowing through factor markets from the suppliers of factors to producers.

The Eighth Wonder of the World?

The allocation of resources through a market system has many attractive features which were extensively praised by eighteenth-century economists. As we remarked earlier, the great Scottish economist Adam Smith wrote in his classic *Wealth of Nations*, published in 1776, of 'the invisible hand' guiding resources into their most profitable and socially effective uses. He called the hand invisible because it was, and still is, precisely that. Decisions taken by millions of individual producers and consumers match each other as a result of the working of the price mechanism.

Without any centralized planning, the efforts of private individuals to maximize their own satisfaction and their profits causes the quantity of each good and service to match the quantity that people want to buy. All this is brought about by price movements responding to changes that occur in conditions prevailing in the market, such as changes in consumer tastes or in costs of production. The price system is, moreover, an automatic, flexible and self-regulating device which provides, with no conscious overall direction, answers to the basic question of how to allocate resources among competing uses. It appealed to Smith and many of his contemporaries because of the prevailing philosophy of the time and, in particular, because it relegated the role of government to a relatively small number of matters such as defence of the realm and the administration of justice. Perhaps, then, the market economy should be regarded, as is suggested by the title to this section, as the eighth wonder of the world? In this book we will look at that question in some detail.

Capitalism and the market system

It is not a matter of chance that the market system has reached its heights under the organization known as capitalism. The main feature of a capitalist system lies in the institution of private property and, in particular, the private ownership of capital by persons, or organizations, called capitalists.

Early economists saw that capitalists' pursuit of profits might be beneficial, not only to the capitalists themselves, but also to the rest of the community. Their self-interested profit-seeking led them to produce those goods and services wanted most by consumers. The historical association of markets with private property led many people to consider the latter to be an essential ingredient of the former.

Ownership, however, is a side issue. The price mechanism can, and does, operate in many economies where ownership is collective rather than private; i.e., where firms belong to the state but the managers respond to the price signals provided by the market. The National Coal Board, for example, has been owned since 1947 by the British government. Yet the production of coal is very much influenced both by its price, and also by the prices of the various factors of production that are used in the production of coal.

Shortcomings of the market system

The merits of the price system have not gone unchallenged by social observers. Your study of economics has not yet gone far enough to allow you to appreciate the strength of the arguments on either side, let alone to form a judgement on the balance between them. We shall attempt to help you to do so throughout this book. We should even now, however, mention briefly some of the more important criticisms that can be levelled at the price system. At the same time we must emphasize that it is a lot easier to criticize one system than to show that another could perform better. No one seriously believes that any society has yet evolved a system which is anywhere approaching the perfect.

Criticisms of a *laissez-faire* market system are about micro and macroeconomic performance. Here we deal with the main criticisms about its microeconomic performance, which concern equity and efficiency.

Equity or Fairness: The price mechanism ensures the production of goods and services that consumers want to buy. But people's ability to buy things depends on their incomes. A market system may be likened to an election in which votes are cast, not for political candidates, but for goods and services. The 'votes' are not ballot papers, but notes and coins. Consumers 'vote' for a good by spending money on it, and producers pocket the money when they provide the goods people are willing to buy. However, unlike parliamentary elections, where everyone has one vote, in market 'elections' votes are distributed unequally. Those with high incomes have more votes than those with low incomes.

Thus, in a *laissez-faire* market system the distribution of income affects the allocation of resources. If the distribution of income is inequitable (meaning unfair, which is not the same thing as unequal), the allocation of resources will be regarded as unsatisfactory. If the distribution of income is regarded as equitable (meaning fair), the allocation may be regarded as satisfactory. Equity is, however, an ethical question on which opinions differ. We cannot, in our role as economists, settle the question of the fairness of the distribution (althouth we can study the consequences of attempts to change it). We cannot, therefore, settle the question of the extent to which the allocation of resources is satisfactory insofar as it is influenced by the distribution of income.

Efficiency: The second criticism of *laissex-faire* is that the market economy may fail to allocate resources efficiently. Later in this book we shall consider several cases in which this may be true. Suffice it to mention three here.

Collectively Consumed Commodities. There are certain goods and services that, if produced, are available to the community as a whole. Remember that producers supply goods that individuals want to buy, and that can be sold to the users. So it is not surprising that no private suppliers would supply the Metropolitan Police Force, which benefits everyone (except criminals) by its very existence, and whose benefit cannot be denied to someone who is not willing to buy its services. Neither would private suppliers produce and offer for sale the street lighting in Glasgow, which again, by its very existence, benefits all Glaswegians.

Even the earliest supporters of the market system recognized that there were goods of this sort, which economists call *public goods*. Hence, there are very few who deny the need for some state intervention in the production of goods and services to provide those goods that benefit all but which cannot be sold by private producers to private consumers. Opinions differ, however, on how important such goods are quantitatively.

Sluggish Markets. The second possible cause of inefficiency in a market system is that it may take 'too long' to achieve a satisfactory allocation of resources. If producers and consumers respond quickly to needed changes, the system works better than if responses are sluggish. There is no doubt that markets take time to work. The real question is whether other systems would respond to the need for change faster and more effectively. State intervention may sometimes speed up the process of adjustment, for example by the provision of education and

training for needed skills, and by running job centres to which workers may go in search of jobs. In other cases, markets are extremely adaptable and produce adjustments to actual or anticipated changes much faster than do centrally planned economies.

Concentration of Power. The final criticism of the *laissez-faire* market system that we mention here is that it often appears to result in the building up of significant economic power in the hands of a relatively small number of large organizations. This is a particularly relevant consideration in the UK, where almost half of all output in manufacturing is in the hands of a mere 100 giant producers.

The consequences of the concentration of economic power are important both politically and economically. This power has significant implications for the extent to which producers compete with each other, and it affects the allocation of resources. We shall return to this issue later in the book. We shall also deal with other criticisms, such as the existence at times of massive unemployment, after we have studied macroeconomics in the last half of the book.

Concluding Remarks

The above suggests that it may be wrong to conclude that the *laissez-faire* market system functions so perfectly as to be the eighth wonder of the world. But a wonder it surely is. What kind of rating it should get – should it be 8 out of 10, or some much lower mark? – is something on which we hope to help you to form your own judgement in the course of reading this book.

Because few people are willing to give the *laissez-faire* market system 10 out of 10, there are no completely free-market systems in the world – any more than there are any completely planned economies. In reality, all economies are mixed economies where market forces and state intervention both play a part in the allocation of resources. Different countries differ in the degree of the importance given to these two forces in determining the allocation of resources. Even within any one country, there are swings in public opinion on what is the best mix. In the UK we can distinguish two distinct periods since the end of the Second World War. From 1945 to 1951 the Labour government that was then in power pushed the mix strongly in the direction of more state determination of the allocation of resources. In 1979, a Conservative government that was dedicated to pushing the mix strongly towards market determination of resource allocation, came into power. Economists are to be found that support each of these positions. None of them believe in total *laissez-faire* or in the total state determination of all economic decisions. But they do differ on which way they think the current mix should be moved. We shall have a good deal more to say about the economic aspects of this issue later in this book.

SUMMARY

1 The three basic questions of economics – what to produce? how to produce it? and who gets it? – can be answered in several ways. The term economic system refers to a distinctive set of social and institutional arrangements within which answers are provided by determining how resources are allocated.

2 Three major types of economic system are traditional, command and market economies. Traditional economies allocate resources according to traditional patterns. In command economies, resources are allocated by decisions taken by central planners. In market economies the allocation of resources is determined by decentralized decisions co-ordinated through the price mechanism.

3 A market comprises any institution through which buyers and sellers can communicate with each other. Markets are characterized by free exchange, decentralized decision-taking, specialization and the division of labour.

4 Market prices of goods and services determine *what* is produced. Prices of factors of production determine how they are produced and how output is divided up among all the members of society.

5 In reality, there are no pure market or pure command economies. All real economies are mixed economies, with varying degrees of reliance on markets and central planning in different countries.

6 In a market system, money flows in a circular fashion linking markets with each other. The circular flow has a microeconomic aspect, focusing on the interrelationship between individual markets, and a macroeconomic aspect, focusing on flows of income and expenditure among broad groups of producers and consumers. The macroeconomic circular flows run from producers to consumers in payment for the services of factors of production, and back from consumers to producers in payment for the goods and services purchased for consumption.

7 The price mechanism appealed to eighteenth-century economists because it mobilized the self-interest of individuals in an automatic, flexible and self-regulating system, which operated with minimal government intervention. The capitalist system is based on the price mechanism and private ownership of property, though the latter is not a necessary precondition for a pricing system. The main shortcomings of the market system are that it may sometimes be unfair or inefficient. Inefficiency can arise from such factors as the existence of collectively consumed goods, the sluggishness of market forces and the concentration of market power.

3

How Economists Work[1]

Economists are often asked to give advice on a variety of problems. If you glance through a newspaper, listen to the radio or watch television, you will almost certainly find some economists' opinions being reported. Perhaps it is on the prospects for unemployment or inflation, on the merits of an investment project such as the Channel Tunnel, on the case for privatization or nationalization of an industry, on the efficiency of the National Health Service, or some other topic.

A distinctive feature of the advice that economists offer is that it can differ substantially from one economist to another. Why is this? The reason why economists differ in their policy recommendations arises from the nature of our subject and the methods we adopt when tackling problems. In this chapter we describe our methods.

SCIENTIFIC METHOD

To assist in solving problems, economists must be able to understand how the economy works – how, for example, prices and incomes are determined in the world in which we live. Thus, economics is, at least partly, what is known as an empirical subject, based on factual observation of behaviour in the real world. But this is not the whole story. Economics is also a theoretical subject. Economists develop theories about human behaviour based on some basic assumptions about human motivation.

---

1 Students may omit this chapter without immediate loss of understanding, but should return to it at a later stage when they can relate it to the economics they will have learned by then.

For example, it is known that consumers tend to buy fewer quantities of goods and services when their prices rise, or when the incomes of consumers fall. These observations led economists to propose theories about the nature of the relationship between quantity demanded and prices and income. Insofar as they turn out to fit the facts that we already know, and allow us to predict things we do not yet know, they are useful theories.

Economics shares some things in common with the natural sciences. Both try to develop theories that explain behaviour. In the case of physics, the behaviour is that of inanimate physical matter. In the case of economics, the behaviour is social, or human. Both seek to identify consistent behaviour patterns of the kind we have mentioned. Both employ what is known as *scientific method*.

A great deal has been written on the question of whether or not economics is a fully-fledged science. We shall not enter into the controversy because it would not be profitable at this stage of your studies. If we understand a science to be a subject which relates theory to evidence in a *systematic way*, then economics is a science. In economics the evidence in which we are interested is that of human behaviour – how men and women react to changing circumstances.

Experimental and Non-experimental Sciences

Much work in economics consists of the collection of empirical evidence about human behaviour, the propounding of theories based on that evidence, and the testing of theories against new evidence. The two main purposes of economic theories are: (1) explaining observed behaviour, and (2) predicting as yet unobserved behaviour.

To understand how economists go about their jobs, we must first deal with a major distinction between *experimental* and *non-experimental* sciences. In such fields as physics and chemistry, laboratory experiments are used to generate observations against which to test a theory. Such sciences employ what is known as the *experimental method.*

Economists, in common with most other social scientists (other than some psychologists) and astronomers, are denied the luxury of experimentation. This is a notable disadvantage. (Indeed, this is one reason why some people have contended that economics is not even a science.) The ability to conduct experiments carries two outstanding advantages, replication and control.

The advantage of laboratory experiments

Experiments can be Repeated: A physical scientist may continue to repeat his experiments over and over again – no first result is convincing until he has repeated it enough times to be satisfied with it. Furthermore, other scientists who are sceptical can, and will, replicate the experiment. Generally, no new result gains wide acceptance until many independent scientists have verified it.

Experimental Conditions can be Controlled: The behaviour of many substances is liable to be affected by a number of influences. Laboratory conditions can often be used to create conditions which isolate a single determinant of behaviour. Consider, for instance, an example from the field of biology. The rate at which a plant grows may be affected by several factors, including the amount of sunlight received, the moisture and the nitrogen content of the soil. Suppose we desire to ascertain the importance of nitrogen content. We can create conditions in a greenhouse (laboratory) in which the amount of sunlight and moisture in the soil is held constant. We can do so by using two sets of plants. Both sets are given the same amount of sunlight and water. However, one set has more nitrogen than the other set, which is used as a 'control'. We may then attribute any observed differences in plant growth to the only difference between them – the nitrogen content. We have ourselves created the difference in our laboratory. One of the reasons why scientists want to duplicate experiments before accepting a

result is the worry that, no matter how hard they tried, the original experimenters may have failed to hold constant all of the factors other than the one they were consciously varying.

The inapplicability of laboratory experiments in economics

The reasons why economists cannot use experimental methods fall into two categories, non-controllability and the purposeful nature of human behaviour.

Non-Controllability: The determinants of human behaviour are complex. Consider how to design an experiment to isolate the determinants of investment decisions made by businesspersons. Suppose that we suspect (rightly, as it happens) that the amount of investment that businesses undertake depends, among other things, on their expectations of the profitability of their investment and on the rate of interest that they have to pay on money they borrow to finance the investment. How can we possibly generate conditions in a laboratory wherein we incarcerate a number of business executives and hold constant everything else while we vary the rate of interest and observe how much they spend on investment?

The answer is that we cannot. We might try to get them to play a game like Monopoly with 'pretend' money. But we would be rash to imagine that, in the complex real world, they would behave as they do when playing games. In a word, we cannot usually generate laboratory conditions that simulate the real world sufficiently well to derive useful results from our experiment.[1]

Human Behaviour is Consciously Determined:
Human beings differ from inanimate objects and plants in that their reactions to stimuli are *consciously* thought out. We are not lumps of matter that will react identically to identical circumstances. You can bombard a set of atoms using a linear accelerator, and the atoms will just 'sit there' while their neighbours are smashed one by one. But try doing the same using

---

1 There are a few areas in economics, such as the attitudes of individuals to risk and uncertainty, that have been investigated by laboratory experimentation. Opinion in the profession is divided on the usefulness of such experiments in understanding the behaviour of people to risk in the real world.

a weapon from a concealed position on a group of humans. The first person 'smashed' might seem like a mystery to the others and cause little movement from the rest. But smash a few, and very soon the rest will *deduce* the presence of a malevolent force – even though they cannot see it – and they will take evasive action.

Moreover, individuals may react differently to the same stimulus. For example, if you put a match to a dry piece of paper the paper will burn. If you try to extract vital information from human beings by torture, some will yield it while others will not. More confusingly still, the same individual may react differently at different times. While the response of inanimate objects to stimuli is consistent, that by human beings may appear to be less so.

A Science of Human Behaviour

The fact that economics is not able to use the method of controlled, and repeatable, laboratory experiments does not mean that it cannot make use of scientific method. All it does mean is that other methods of confronting theories with evidence have to be used.

Economists have no data generated in controlled experiments. But of course they do have data. A mass of data about human behaviour is generated naturally in the real world. Every day, for example, consumers are comparing prices and deciding what to buy. Firms are comparing prices and costs of production and deciding what to offer for sale. All these acts can be observed and recorded. They then provide the observations against which to test theories about the effects of different prices on the amount bought by consumers and on the amount offered for sale by producers.

Peculiarities of economic behaviour

The difficulty of conducting laboratory experiments is one characteristic that makes life difficult for economists. There are two others: the variability of human behaviour, and the complexity of the determinants of social behaviour.

The Variability of Human Behaviour: It is often argued that social science is impossible because it attempts to deal with people who have free will and cannot be made subject to inexorable laws. Such a view implies that it is impossible to develop laws which will determine *precisely* how an individual will

always react to any situation. There is a strong element of truth in this view. This does not mean, however, that human beings behave in a totally capricious and unpredictable way. It may be hard to say when, or why, any particular person will buy an ice-cream, but we can observe a stable response pattern from a large group of individuals: the higher the number of people visiting the beaches, the greater the sales of ice-cream.

Many other examples come to mind, where we cannot predict the behaviour of any one individual but can do so with remarkable accuracy for a *group* of individuals. No one can predict with accuracy when Betty Smith will die, or whether James Jones will have a motoring accident. But for large groups of men and women, we can know with a remarkable degree of certainty how many will die in any particular year and how many will have car accidents. Moreover, the larger the number of people in our group and the more information we have about them, the greater the accuracy with which we can make predictions.[1]

The Complexity of the Determinants of Social Behaviour: The second problem arises from the large number of factors that can affect human behaviour and in the ways in which they can interact with each other. Consider, for example, the hypothesis that one's health as an adult depends upon one's diet as a child. Clearly, all sorts of other factors affect the health of adults – heredity, conditions of childhood other than nutrition, age, sex, exposure to infections, and other environmental factors. The complexity of the determinants of social behaviour means that we should not be too ambitious about developing 'laws' about all types of behaviour. We must also be prepared to accept partial explanations of behaviour which may work better at some times than at others. They will usually be better than nothing, but they will always be subject to some significant degree of error.

The Nature of Economic Theory

Economists develop their theories in an effort to understand and predict the behaviour we see around us. Because of the complexity of the determinants of

---

1 This is because of the properties of what is known as the 'law' of large numbers. See R. G. Lipsey, *An Introduction to Positive Economics* (Weidenfeld & Nicolson, 6th edn 1983, 7th edn 1989). All subsequent references to this book are made to 'IPE'.

economic behaviour, it is impossible to work with all possibly relevant considerations.

The method used by economists is to construct what is described as a 'model' of the economy, or of that part of it which they wish to study. The model is no more than a simplified representation of what are believed to be the major factors influencing the behaviour in question. Economists are basically no different from workers in other disciplines in their use of models. For instance, civil engineers use models of bridges to study such factors as metal fatigue and the effects of wind on structural stability; car manufacturers work with models of new designs, to study various performance characteristics. The word model as used here has the same meaning as theory, or hypothesis.[1] Models deliberately ignore some factors in order to concentrate on others. Thus, an economic model of the determinants of the savings made by the population of the UK might concentrate on things such as the level of income, the rate of interest that may be earned on savings, and the total amount of savings accumulated in the past. The model might exclude other potential determinants of savings, such as the age distribution of the population, the expectation of life, the rate of inflation, and people's existing wealth.

When economists exclude some matters that might affect the subject they are studying from their model, we say that they are abstracting from reality. Abstraction is acceptable because a model is not intended to be a duplication of the real world but a useful simplification of it.

The variables listed in the theory are assumed to be the important ones, while the many omitted variables are assumed to be unimportant. Since any theory must abstract from the potentially infinite number of influences, the inclusion of a small number of variables and the exclusion of many is necessary. The test of whether or not all the important variables are included and only unimportant ones are excluded is whether the theory correctly predicts events that are yet to be observed. Consider, for example, the demand for carrots. If the important determining variables have been included in the behavioural relation, then virtually all observed variations in demand for carrots will be associated with these variables. If important

influencing factors have been omitted, then variations in demand for carrots will occur that cannot be associated with the variables included in the behavioural relation.

Components of economic models

All economic models contain three elements: (i) at least one variable whose behaviour is to be explained; (ii) at least one variable that provides the explanation; (iii) behavioural assumptions that explain how the dependent variable is related to the independent variables.

The meaning of each of these elements of an economic model can best be explained with the use of an example. For our example we choose one basic component of all economic theories, a so-called *behavioural relation.* Such a relation shows the variable in which we are interested as depending upon a specified set of other variables that are assumed to influence the first. (Despite our earlier emphasis of the complexity of the determinants of economic behaviour, it is convenient to use a very simple example here.) The illustration we use is the determinants of saving behaviour. To make the model – or behavioural relation – as simple as possible, we assume that there is only a single determinant of savings – the level of consumers' income. Our theory, or model, of savings is therefore that the level of income determines the amount of savings.

Consider how to identify the three elements in that model. First, take the variable to be explained. In this case it is savings. The variable that does the explaining is income because income is the variable on which savings depends. Finally there is the behavioural assumption. In this case, we assume that savings and income are positively related – i.e. an increase in income leads to an increase in savings.

Properties of a good economic model

There are two characteristics that are desirable in any model: (i) the variables are clearly defined; (ii) the relationships in the model are quantifiable.

Definitions: Ambiguity in the meaning of a theory is clearly undesirable. Failure to define all terms accurately can only lead to confusion.

Consider again our model, which states that savings depends positively on income. Both variables in the model are capable of many different interpret-

---

1   Note that some economists reserve the word model to describe certain more complicated kinds of relationships that interact with each other in a complete system. Our use of 'model' includes these interactive models, but also includes simpler theories and individual behavioural relations.

ations. What exactly is meant by savings? Savings might be money people put in the bank or in building societies, or even banknotes they store under the bed. Alternatively, savings might be thought of as the sums accumulated over an individual's lifetime, including not only the money kept in the bank but also accumulations of assets, such as stocks and shares and perhaps a house or flat. Alternatively, again, savings could mean the difference between the income people receive and the amount of that income they spend on goods and services for their consumption.

The variable 'income' could also mean many things. Income could refer to the total national income, to the total income of persons (i.e. excluding the income of institutions such as the government), or it could refer to the incomes of factors of production (the sum of wages, rent, and interest on capital).

Quantification: An economic model can simply state that one variable depends positively or negatively on another. But quantification of an economic model tells us the extent of the influence. Let us return yet again to our savings model. The form in which it has been expressed so far is not quantified. It becomes quantified when we state by *how much* savings change when income changes. For example, if we state that savings are always 20 per cent of income, we quantify the income-savings relationship. Such a model yields more information than one which is not quantified.

Alternative expressions

There are four ways in which a model or behavioural relation may be expressed: (i) verbal statement; (ii) illustration by schedule (i.e. table); (iii) mathematical statement (i.e. using algebra); and (iv) geometrical statement (i.e. using graphs).

Verbal Statement: With a verbal statement, the dependence of one variable on another is expressed in words. This is the only form that we have used so far.

Consider the savings model that we are using for purposes of illustration. In a quantified form, the verbal statement of the theory might be: 'Savings depend on income in such a way that 20 per cent of income is always saved'. This statement gives us enough information to enable us to calculate the level of savings *given* the level of income. For example, if income is £100, savings are 20 per cent of £100, i.e.

£20. If income is £200, savings are 20 per cent of £200, i.e. £40, and so on.

Schedules: Economists sometimes present the information relating to theories in the form of tables or schedules. For example, our savings model can be illustrated in tabular form as in Table 3.1.

TABLE 3.1 The Relation Between Income and Savings

Income (Y)	Savings (S)
100	20
200	40
300	60
400	80

Such tabulations, or *schedules*, are less complete than other ways of expressing a model because they present only a select number of observations of the variables.

Mathematical Statement: Students are sometimes frightened by mathematical expressions. Mathematics, however, is only a language. It uses symbols to make statements much as written languages use words to make sentences, and it does so very economically.

Using the symbols S for saving and Y for income, our model of savings behaviour can be expressed concisely as:

$$S = 0.2Y$$

This statement is in the form of an algebraic equation. It gives us exactly the same information as the verbal statement of the theory. We can calculate S for every level of Y. For example, if $Y = 100$, $S = 20$; if $Y = 200$, $S = 40$, and so on.

Geometrical Statement: The fourth method of expressing an economic model is by the use of graphs, which are commonly used in this book. You must fully understand graphical methods if you are to read, and appreciate, major parts of later chapters. We assume here that you are able to use and interpret graphs. (If you are not, you should study the appendix to Chapter 1 carefully.)

Figure 3.1 is the graphical representation of our savings model, which is expressed verbally as *savings are 20 per cent of income*, and algebraically as *$S = 0.2Y$*. The vertical axis in the graph measures

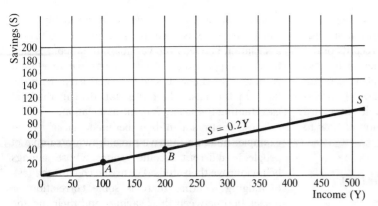

FIGURE 3.1   **A Graphical Expression of a Relationship Between Savings and Income.** The specific relationship is that savings are always 20 per cent of income

savings, and the horizontal axis measures income. Any *point* on the graph represents the value of savings that is associated with a particular value of income. For instance, point *A* represents savings of 20, associated with income of 100. The line marked *S* on the graph joins all points where savings are 20 per cent of income ($S = 0.2Y$). It is thus the graphical expression of our model.

Choice of formulations

We have described four ways in which a relation between two variables can be expressed: verbal, tabular, mathematical and geometrical. All have their uses. In this book we shall rely heavily on graphical expressions, which are especially convenient in elementary economics. A major disadvantage of geometry is that it is normally confined to dealing with relationships between two (or at the most three) variables.

In the real world, however, relationships are rarely restricted to two or three variables. In their more advanced theories, economists often need to work with numerous variables and this is why much professional work uses mathematical models. Mathematics is essential for the analysis of complex situations. But we shall not employ it often in this book. When we introduce a few very simple mathematical models later on, we shall explain them fully.

TESTING ECONOMIC MODELS

We have seen that economists construct theories and then seek to test them against facts. We have already discussed the construction of theories and we turn now to their application to empirical evidence.

Economic Statistics

Modern statistical analysis has been developed to test economic theories when evidence is generated in a haphazard fashion. To some extent, statistical techniques used by economists are common to those used in other scientific subjects. However, there are also problems peculiar to economics, for which a special branch of statistics has grown up. It is called *econometrics*.

Testing theories by confronting them with evidence is a procedure with the following steps:
1. State the theory in a testable form – i.e. one which gives predictions of the response of one variable to changes in one or more others.
2. Collect relevant data.
3. Compare the predictions from the theory with the evidence.
4. Ask if there is reason to believe that the associations discovered are causal.

These steps may be illustrated by applying them to our model of savings behaviour.

Step 1. State the theory in a testable form

It will help if the theory is quantifiable. Our expression that savings is a constant 20 per cent of income is in such a form. It allows us to predict savings from a knowledge of income.

Step 2. Collect data to test the theory

For our test we need observations of past savings behaviour at different income levels. It is obvious that we cannot obtain data about all past income-savings relationships for all people for all time. Hence we select some data which we believe to be representative of the total. Such partial data is known as a sample (of the total population). To test our savings theory we could, for example, obtain records of the savings of persons of different income levels. If those we selected were representative of people in general, we would be satisfied we could draw general conclusions about the population as a whole. Standard statistical theory deals with the question of how to choose a representative sample.

Step 3. Compare the predictions of the theory with the evidence

Statistical theory has well developed procedures for deciding whether the evidence is consistent with the facts. Since nothing can ever be certain in our world of experience, these statistical tests give probabilities that the theory is correct *given* the observations that have been made.

Statisticians use the term *statistical association* (or *correlation*) to describe the extent to which a theory they are testing is consistent with the facts. Consider a theory that says two variables are positively associated. If the observed facts show no statistical association between the variables, the theory is said to be not supported by the test. If a positive correlation is shown, the theory is said to be consistent with the facts. In this case, there are statistical methods of ascertaining the strength of the association.

These matters can best be made clear by an example. Imagine that we have drawn a sample of people in different income groups whose savings behaviour we then study. We are faced with the task of judging whether there is some correlation or association between their savings and their income levels. One of the most useful starting points is to plot the observations on a graph to give a visual representation of the relationship between the two variables. Such a graph is called a *scatter diagram*. (Another example is shown in the appendix to Chapter 1.)

In Figure 3.2 we show two scatter diagrams based on hypothetical data related to the savings and income of two different groups of people. Let us ask whether we can detect any statistical association in

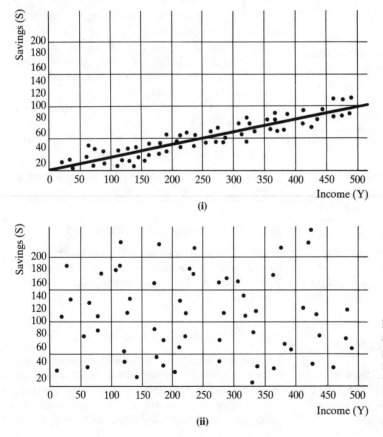

FIGURE 3.2   Alternative Sets of Observations on Savings and Incomes. Each dot gives the income earned and the savings made by a particular household: in part (i), there is a close positive association between savings and income; in part (ii), there is no discernible association between savings and income

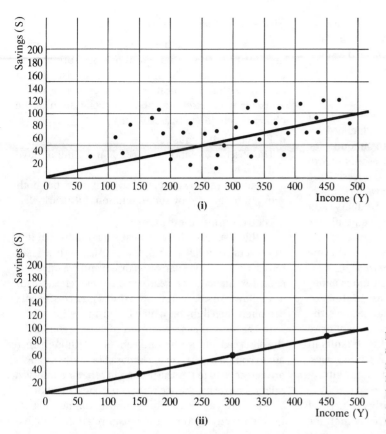

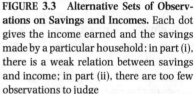

FIGURE 3.3 **Alternative Sets of Observations on Savings and Incomes.** Each dot gives the income earned and the savings made by a particular household: in part (i), there is a weak relation between savings and income; in part (ii), there are too few observations to judge

either case, and how much confidence we would have in any correlation we observed.

To see whether there is an association, we need to look at the graphs for any clear pattern. If we do so, we find a distinct pattern in one case and not in the other. In Figure 3.2(i) the points on the graph are scattered close to one another around a line that we have drawn which represents the average relationship between income and savings of all the people in the sample.[1] In contrast, there is no obvious pattern in the scatter of points in Figure 3.2(ii). At any given level of income, we find savings that vary over a very wide range.

The correlation we observe in part (i) of the diagram suggests a definite *quantitative* relationship between income and savings. It shows not only that incomes are positively correlated with savings but that savings are, on average, 20 per cent of income.

The line drawn through the points in the diagram shows the average relationship between the two variables. All the points on the line describe exactly this – i.e., when incomes are 100, savings are, on average, 20; when incomes are 200, savings are, on average, 40; and so on.

Having established the existence of a statistical association between income and savings in Figure 3.2(i), we need also to ask whether that association is strong or weak. The answer depends on two considerations: the variability of the observed behaviour and the number of observations on which the association is based.

To illustrate these points compare Figure 3.2(i) with the two parts of Figure 3.3. In neither of these latter two cases would one have as much confidence in the association as in Figure 3.2(i), despite the fact that the average relationship between income and savings is the same in all three cases. In Figure 3.3(i) there are as many observations as in Figure 3.2(i), but the variability around the line is much greater. In Figure 3.3(ii), there are only three observations. Despite the fact that savings are exactly 20 per cent of

[1] The line representing the average relation between any two variables can be found precisely by using well-known statistical procedures – the simplest of which is known as 'least-squares regression analysis'.

income for the three people shown, one would hesitate to draw the general conclusion that income and savings were positively related from such a small sample. The result could all too easily be a matter of chance.

Chance and Confidence: Because the results of testing for statistical association are influenced by chance, statisticians have devised techniques for assessing the probabilities involved. Descriptions of these techniques belong in statistics courses. They are, however, based on the two characteristics of sample data already mentioned – variability and sample size. The application of the techniques allows test conclusions to be expressed in terms of the probability of any discovered relation, such as the line shown in Figure 3.1(i), being due to chance.

Not only do economists need to be cautious about accepting the existence of a statistical association for the reasons already discussed, but also because the data may be unreliable. Errors of measurement arise in any scientific work. They may be due to faults in recording apparatus, human error in reading scales, or in tapping a keyboard to send data into a computer.

Economists have to cope with another source of errors of observation. This is because we do not, for the most part, generate our own data but rely on that gathered by others, often for purposes other than for the testing of economic theories. Consider as an example the data on personal savings, such as would be used to test the savings model we have discussed in this chapter. Total savings, which are published by the government Central Statistical Office, happen to be one of the most unreliable of all our published statistics. Without going into detail on the reasons, the extent to which the reported figures are revised for years after they are first published, tells us that they are subject to large errors of measurement.[1]

Working economists must assemble the best data available, and apply the most efficient statistical techniques for establishing whether or not associations exist between the variables in which they are interested. What they are then able to decide is the probability that the association really exists given the observations that have been made.

---

[1] For a discussion of some problems of data reliability, see C. Harbury and R. G. Lipsey, *An Introduction to the U.K. Economy*, 2nd edition (Pitman, 1986), Chapter 7. Hereafter, references to this book are given as 'Harbury and Lipsey, Chapter X'.

Step 4. Consider causality

Let us say we have a theory that X is the cause of Y, and our tests show that variations in X are accompanied by variations in Y. The data is consistent with our theory of causation, but it does not prove it. Consider what else might be the explanation of the observed relation between X and Y.

- Y might be the cause of X.
- The observed relation between X and Y might have arisen by chance.
- X and Y might be unrelated to each other but both might be affected by some common third variable.

Let us consider these in turn.

In the first case, there is a causal relation, but it is the reverse of what we think it is. Although we can never be certain, we can often discover if we have our causal sequence reversed. For example, effects usually follow causes. So a study of the sequence of events can often shed light on which is causing what.

In the second case, there is no causal relation, so the observed relation arose by chance. Although once again complete certainty is impossible, statistical tests are designed to tell us the probability that an observed relation arose by chance rather than by causation.

The third case is one of the most common causes for incorrectly assuming a causal relation. To illustrate what is involved, consider a very simple case. If you look at the statistics of the number of marriages and the numbers of suicides per annum for the UK since the turn of the century, you will find evidence of a strong statistical association (for example, the numbers of suicides rose from 3,481 to 5,118 between 1911 and 1948, while the numbers of marriages also rose substantially between the same years from 274,000 to 450,000).

Should we attribute causality to the association – that marriages *cause* suicide? In this case, the reason for the observed statistical *association* is really that between the years 1918 and 1948 the whole population of the UK went up from about 42 million to about 50 million. Hardly surprisingly, therefore, the numbers of both marriages and suicides went up. We should have been surprised if they had not.

Causation is difficult to prove. What we observe in the world is a sequence of events. Causation is something we impose on the events, and we explain this causation with theories. We are more likely to accept the hypothesis that X causes Y if we can predict this causal relation from a theory that has also been successful in predicting other relations.

POSITIVE AND NORMATIVE STATEMENTS IN ECONOMICS

The success of modern science rests partly on the ability of scientists to separate their views on *what does, or is likely to, happen* from their views on *what should, or what they would like to, happen*. For example, until the nineteenth century almost everyone believed that the earth was only a few thousand years old. Evidence then began to accumulate that the earth was thousands of millions of years old. This evidence was hard for many religious people to accept since it ran counter to a literal reading of many religious texts. Those people did not want to believe the evidence. Nevertheless, scientists, many of whom were religious, continued their research because they refused to allow their feelings about what they wanted to believe to affect their search as scientists for the truth.

Distinguishing what is true from what we would like to be, or what we feel ought to be, depends partly on being able to distinguish between what are called *positive* and *normative* statements. Normative statements depend on *value judgements*. They involve issues of personal opinions, which cannot be settled by recourse to facts. Positive statements, in contrast, do not involve value judgements. They are statements about what is, was or will be, statements that are about matters of fact. Many, but not all, positive statements are testable. A testable statement is one that is, in principle, refutable.

Let us consider some examples.

- The statement that unemployment is such a bad thing that governments should try to reduce it to zero at all costs, is a normative statement depending on our value judgements.

- The statement that there is an association between the rate of inflation and the rate of unemployment such that increasing inflation will reduce unemployment is a positive and a testable statement.
- The statement that at some time in human history there will exist a society with zero unemployment is a positive statement, since it does not depend on value judgements, but it is irrefutable. No matter how much time passes without the advent of the zero-unemployment society, true believers can say 'just wait, it is around the corner'. Not until the last second of human history could we say the statement had been refuted – and then it would be too late, since there would be no one around to know about it.

It is important to appreciate that testability refers to testability *in principle*. All we mean by saying a statement is testable is that it is possible to *design* a test which, if it could be perfectly carried out, could disprove it.

To make sure you fully understand the distinction between positive and normative, consider the ten statements listed below.

All five statements listed below as positive, assert things about the nature of the world in which we live. Indeed, all five are not only positive statements, they are testable statements. Given enough evidence, the probability of their being false could be established. In other words we could design tests, collect evidence and decide if the statements were wrong.

Statement A, for example, could be tested by collecting data to see whether, in the past, high rates of interest were associated with high saving and vice versa. (In fact existing evidence tends to support the statement.) In contrast, statement B can in no way be tested by recourse to facts. It is 'correct' if saving is 'a

	POSITIVE		NORMATIVE
A	Raising interest rates encourages people to save.	B	People should be encouraged to save.
C	High rates of income tax encourage people to evade paying taxes.	D	Governments should arrange taxes so that people cannot avoid paying them.
E	Rising wage rates cause people to work harder.	F	Firms should raise wage rates to encourage people to work harder.
G	Lowering the price of coffee causes people to buy less of it.	H	The government should put a tax on coffee so that people will consume less coffee.
I	Given a choice, people prefer to live in a world of inflation than of unemployment.	J	The government ought to be more concerned with reducing unemployment than inflation.

good thing', otherwise not. But whether or not saving is good in itself is a question which depends on a value judgement about the desirability of saving. It is clearly a matter on which opinions can differ from one person to another. Therefore the statement is a normative one.

We leave the reader to analyse the remaining eight statements to decide precisely why each is either positive or normative. Remember to apply the two tests: (1) Is the statement one of fact? If so, it is a positive one. (2) Are value judgements necessary to assess the truth of the statement? If so, it is normative.

Several points need to be noted about the positive/ normative distinction. First, positive statements need not be true. Statement G is almost certainly false. Yet it is positive, not normative. Second, the inclusion of a value judgement in a statement does not necessarily make the whole statement normative. Statement I is about the value judgements that people hold. It is possible to try to find out whether people really do prefer unemployment to inflation. One can ask them and one can observe how they vote. There is no need to introduce a value judgement in order to establish the validity of the statement itself.

Third, not all statements are necessarily classifiable into positive or normative. There is an important class of statements, called *analytic*, which involve conditional theorizing and are neither factual nor require value judgements. For example, the statement 'if all men are immortal and if you are a man you are immortal' is true by the rules of logic. It involves no value judgement to assess its truth. Nor is it a statement about the real world. It is a conditional statement which is logically unfalsifiable. Such statements often occur in economic reasoning.

Can Economics be Scientific?

It has only been in this century that the systematic testing of economic theories against bodies of evidence has been popular. Many economists had unreasonable expectations of advances that could be made by the application of scientific, quantitative methods to economics. Although some of these extreme hopes have been dashed, virtually all debates on economic issues take place today in the light of, and constrained by, a large body of observed facts. The demand that economic theory be consistent with what we know about the world stops it from degenerating into pure scholasticism, and helps theorizing to be focused on real issues about real behaviour.

Many people have argued that positive economics is impossible because economists cannot be purely objective. Scientists are human beings. They hold personal opinions, and it is difficult to be certain that these do not interfere with their research work. For example, in the late 1940s, when called upon to advise on the feasibility of building a hydrogen bomb, Dr Robert Oppenheimer undoubtedly let his moral abhorrence of the device cloud his professional judgement on its feasibility. Today, some scientists feel so strongly that genetic engineering is morally wrong that they refuse even to engage in research involving it. Occasionally, too, the work of a scientist is discredited because he or she actually went so far as to manipulate evidence in order to support certain conclusions.

Economists cannot be completely above suspicion of designing their research to influence their results, though one hopes, and expects, that they rarely do so consciously. But, as we observed earlier, unconscious bias is likely to be much more frequent. Most economists care which way the data points, and they are likely to let this influence their choice of techniques, their choice and assessment of data to study, and so on.

Fortunately, the fact that individual scientists can seldom, if ever, be purely objective calculating machines does not make positive science impossible. Science has been successful in spite of the fact that individual scientists have not always been totally objective. Individuals may passionately resist the apparent implications of evidence. But the rule of the game, that facts cannot be ignored and must somehow be fitted into the accepted theoretical structure, tends to produce scientific advance in spite of what might be thought of as unscientific, emotional attitudes on the part of many scientists.

But if existing protagonists succeed in changing the rules of the game by encouraging economists to ignore inconvenient facts or define them out of existence, this would be a major blow to rational enquiry in economics.

SUMMARY

1 Economics is a science in the sense that it is a subject in which theories are related to evidence in a systematic way.

2 Experimental sciences such as physics and chemistry can test theories under laboratory conditions in which all but the variable being studied are held constant. Non-experimental sciences such as economics and astronomy must wait for the passage of time to throw up evidence that is relevant to their theories, and such evidence will arise from situations in which more or less everything is changing at once.

3 Economics is a science concerned with human behaviour, which is variable and adaptive, and hence more complex to understand than many simple natural processes.

4 Theories, models or hypotheses, as they are variously called, contain at least one variable whose behaviour is to be explained, at least one variable that does the explaining, and behavioural assumptions that link the two types of variables together causally.

5 Relations assumed in theories are called behavioural relations; they may be stated verbally, mathematically or geometrically, or illustrated in schedules.

6 Major steps in testing economic theories are (i) state the theory in testable form; (ii) collect relevant data; (iii) confront the theory's predictions with evidence (using various statistical techniques); and (iv) ask if there is reason to believe that the associations observed in the evidence are causal ones. Causality can never be proved from the fact that variables are associated, but it is more likely to be present when a causal theory is successful in predicting, and explaining, a wide range of observed associations.

7 Positive statements are about matters of fact. They are testable if refuting evidence could in principle be found. Normative statements involve value judgements and cannot even in principle be settled by a mere appeal to the facts.

8 Scientific enquiry proceeds even when individual scientists are not fully objective. The appeal to reproducible evidence and procedures of analysis means that the subject can develop in spite of biases, and unconscious deceptions, on the part of individual investigators.

Preface to Parts 2, 3, 4 and 5

When a professional golfer arrives at a golf course that he has never played on before, he is well advised to make a tour of the course to give himself an impression of its general nature before studying the detailed problems posed by each of the eighteen holes.

Before you started to read this book, you were probably in a position similar to the golfer. You are unlikely to have had very much idea of what the subject of economics was all about. Now, however, you have made your general survey of the ground and are ready to embark on a detailed study of its constituent parts. You should not worry if you feel you have not fully understood all of the material you have read so far. Students commonly feel like this early on in the study of economics. Also it may reassure you to know that you will meet virtually everything you have read so far again, somewhere in the rest of this book – often many times. When you have read to the end of the last chapter, you will find that the material in the first three chapters makes a lot more sense to you than it may now do. At that time you will find it helpful to reread those chapters, when you will be able to supplement the few examples we selected with many others that you will have studied.

Economics is conventionally divided into what is called *microeconomics* and *macroeconomics*, though there is no clear-cut line between them. However, there is a general principle underlying the distinction. Its nature can be gleaned from the meanings of the Greek words *micro*, which means small, and *macro*, which means large.

Microeconomics is the name given to the part of economics which studies economic behaviour 'in the small'. It looks at the detail of the economy, and at the relationships among its constituent parts. In microeconomics, we are concerned with such matters as prices, costs and quantities in thousands of individual markets for goods, services and factors of production. It is as if we are looking at parts of the economy through a microscope.

There is no such instrument as a macroscope, the opposite of a microscope. However, if you could see through a microscope from the 'wrong' end, you would get a macroscopic view. If you were looking at the economic system, you would not see any of the details. You would be looking at broad features which stand out – the forest rather than the trees, as it were. In macroeconomics, we ignore the interrelations among individual markets and among individual prices, and study instead such matters as the course of the average level of prices, total output and total employment, in the economy as a whole.

Our treatment of each of two branches of the subject is divided into an elementary and an intermediate portion. Thus the remainder of our book is organized as follows:

Part 2 Elementary microeconomics
Part 3 Intermediate microeconomics
Part 4 Elementary macroeconomics
Part 5 Intermediate macroeconomics

You cannot, of course, read and understand either intermediate section before its corresponding elementary section. But, given that constraint, there are still several routes that you can take. All of them start with Part 1. *Route 1*: Parts 2, 3, 4, 5. *Route 2*: Parts 2, 4, 3, 5. *Route 3*: Parts 4, 2, 3, 5. *Route 4*: Parts 4, 2, 5, 3. *Route 5*: Parts 4, 5, 2, 3.

However, since modern macroeconomics relies so heavily on micro foundations we would recommend either Routes 1 or 2. Also, since Part 5 uses demand and supply curves, no one should attempt that Part without having studied the material on demand, supply and elasticity from Part 2.

Part 2

ELEMENTARY MICROECONOMICS

Demand and Price

In Chapter 2, we described how a market system allocates resources among alternative uses. Buyers and sellers interact in markets where goods and services are bought and sold. The prices at which these transactions take place help to determine the allocation of resources, and movements in these prices help to stimulate the reallocation of the resources.

Part 2 of this book is about the determinants of quantities of goods bought and sold and the prices at which these sales take place (markets for factors of production are considered separately in Chapters 20 and 21). This chapter is the first of two which is devoted to a study of demand – the behaviour of buyers. It is followed by a chapter on supply – the behaviour of sellers. Finally we look at how supply and demand come together in markets to determine actual quantities and prices.

CONSUMER DEMAND

Consider those who buy goods and services for their own consumption – in economics they are called consumers. (They are sometimes also called buyers, purchasers or households.) The quantity of a good that consumers want to buy per period of time is referred to as their *demand* for that commodity. What are the main determinants of consumers' demand for a commodity?

When outlining the theory of demand, it is important to define all our terms carefully.

Consumers: These are the people who make decisions about buying goods and services. Some consumers are individuals acting for themselves alone; others are members of households buying on behalf of their group. (Because we are not yet considering businesses' demand for factors of production, we neglect purchases by firms of outputs that they intend to use in their production processes.)

Consumer Motivations: We assume that consumers seek to allocate their expenditures among all the goods and services that they might buy so as to gain the greatest possible satisfaction. We say that consumers try to *maximize their satisfaction, or their utility*. When they succeed we say that they have achieved an OPTIMUM position (using the Latin word meaning the best possible result).

Goods and Services: We have earlier drawn a distinction between goods and services. Another distinction is also important. Some goods are only used once. They are consumed and are of no further use – a lamb chop or a baby's disposable nappy for example. Many other goods are durable and are useful over an extended period of time. This book, a television set, and a ballpoint pen are examples of such durable-use goods. The former type of goods are called NON-DURABLES while the latter are called CONSUMER DURABLES or sometimes DURABLE CONSUMER GOODS.

Time: To describe consumers' behaviour we need to know how much they wish to purchase – how many bottles of wine, concert tickets, etc. – per period of time. This means that demand is a *flow*, it is expressed over the passage of time and it is measured as so much *per period of time*. The unit of time chosen is merely a matter of convenience. After all, it means exactly the same thing to say that a consumer buys oranges at a rate of *one per day* , or *seven per week*, or *365 per year*.

Effective Demand: Demand theory is about the quantities of a good that consumers *desire to buy* over a period of time. The phrase 'desire to buy' is critical. It is not just 'desire' in the sense of 'would like to have', it is 'desire *to buy*' in the sense of 'prepared to spend the necessary money to make the purchase'. Thus, demand means *effective* demand, in the sense of being able and willing to buy.

Price-taking Behaviour: At the outset we consider markets that contain a large number of buyers. There are so many of them that no one of them can have an appreciable effect on the market by altering his or her own behaviour. Each consumer buys so small a fraction of the total being sold, that an increase, or a reduction, in the quantity each purchases, would go unnoticed. Clearly, many real world markets are like this. Even complete withdrawal by any one buyer from the market has no noticeable effect.

We shall consider markets in which buyers have significant influence later in this book. For now, we confine ourselves to situations in which buyers are so numerous that they must take the market price as they find it, being unable to influence it. We say such buyers are *price-takers*.

WHAT DETERMINES QUANTITY DEMANDED?

How much of some commodity will consumers be willing to buy, say, per month? This amount will be influenced by many variables including: the commodity's own price, the prices of all related commodities, average consumers' income and its distribution among them, tastes, expectations, the size of the population, and social and psychological factors.

We can neither develop a simple theory, nor understand the separate influence of each variable, if we start by trying to consider what happens when everything changes at once. Fortunately, there is an easier way. We can consider the influence of the variables one at a time. To do this, we hold all but one of them constant, i.e. we make the assumption that they do not change. For example, when examining the relationship between quantity demanded and price, we assume that consumers' incomes, tastes, and *all the other determinants* of quantity demanded, are unchanged. We then let price vary, and study how it affects quantity demanded. We then do the same for each of the other variables in turn. In this way we are able to understand their importance by studying their influences one at a time. Once this is done, we can aggregate the separate influences of two or more variables to discover what would happen if several things changed at the same time – as they often do in practice.

Holding all other influencing variables constant is often described by the words 'other things being equal' or by the equivalent Latin phrase, CETERIS PARIBUS. When economists speak, for example, of the influence of the price of wheat on the quantity of wheat demanded, *ceteris paribus*, they refer to what a change in the price of wheat would do to the quantity demanded, if all other factors that influence the demand for wheat do not change.

In this chapter, we discuss exclusively the relationship between the quantity demanded of a good and one of these variables – its own price, which is referred to as OWN PRICE. We return, in the next chapter, to consider the other variables.

DEMAND BY A SINGLE CONSUMER

Holding all other influences constant, how do we expect the quantity of a particular commodity demanded to vary as its own price varies? *In the case of almost all commodities, this quantity increases as the price of the commodity falls* – all other influences being held constant, by our *ceteris paribus* assumption.

To illustrate the relation between price and quantity demanded, we consider a particular good, lamb

TABLE 4.1 Alan's Demand for Lamb Chops

Reference letter	Price (£s per lb.) (i)	Quantity demanded (lbs. per month) (ii)
a	2.50	0
b	2.00	2
c	1.50	4
d	1.00	6
e	0.50	8
f	0.00	10

chops. Table 4.1 presents data showing the quantities in column (i) that one consumer, whom we call Alan, would be prepared to buy per month at 6 selected prices. The Table is called a demand schedule. It shows, for example, at a price of £2.00 per lb. his quantity demanded is 2 lbs. per month; at a price of £1.00 his quantity demanded is 6 lbs. per month and so forth. Each of the price-quantity combinations in the table is given a letter for easy reference.

The data in Table 4.1 can also be presented in the form of a graph. In Figure 4.1, we measure price on the vertical axis and quantity on the horizontal axis. We choose our scales in order to accommodate the numbers in the table and then plot each point, one at a time. The first point labelled *a*, represents 0 lbs. of lamb chops at a price of £2.50 per lb. It conveys identical information to that of the top line in the Table. Point *b* represents 2 lbs. of lamb chops demanded per month at a price of £2.00 per lb. Points labelled *c*, *d*, *e* and *f* on the graph correspond to the price-quantity combinations shown in the corresponding rows in the Table. Point *f* tells us how many lamb chops Alan would consume per month if they were totally free.[1]

A Demand Curve

We now draw a continuous line through all these points. This is then called a *demand curve* for lamb chops. It is more general than the schedule in the table, which shows only six price-quantity combinations. The demand curve shows the quantities demanded not only at *all* the prices in the table, but also at all intermediate prices. For example, to find quantity demanded at a price of £1.75 per lb., we locate the price £1.75 on the price axis and follow that price over to the demand curve. We then run down to the quantity axis to find that the associated quantity is 3 lbs. per month. We can do this for any price. For example at a price of £0.75, quantity demanded is 7 lbs. per month. The DEMAND CURVE describes the complete relationship between price and quantities demanded.[2]

---

1   Note that the point *f* does not tell us what he would do if the price fell to zero for a short while – presumably he would buy enough to stock up the deep freeze. Each point on the demand curve tells us what the consumer would buy if he expected the indicated price would persist indefinitely.

2   Geometrically, a demand curve may take the shape of either a curved or a straight line. By convention, the demand relation is referred to as a demand *curve* in either case.

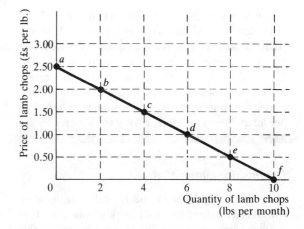

FIGURE 4.1   Alan's Demand Curve For Lamb Chops. The curve shows the amount Alan would buy at each price

The Slope of the Demand Curve

The demand curve in Figure 4.1 is consistent with the statement made earlier that the quantity of any commodity that is demanded increases as its own price falls. To put it the other way, quantity decreases when its own price rises. This type of relationship is known mathematically as a *negative relationship*. It means simply that the two variables, price and quantity, move in opposite directions to each other.

Why should this be so? One reason is that when a good's own price falls, the good becomes cheaper, relative to other goods. It is, therefore, easier for the good to compete against those other goods that are substitutes for it. At £0.50 a lb., lamb chops are cheap relative not only to steak and chops but relative to minced beef and other low-priced meats. At £2.00 a lb., lamb chops look expensive, relative to these other kinds of meat, and Alan will mainly buy these other kinds instead of lamb chops. Do not forget that our *ceteris paribus* assumption means that all other influences, including the prices of other kinds of meat, do not change.

Utility

A somewhat deeper explanation of the negative slope of demand curves is given by what is called utility theory. The satisfaction that consumers derive from the goods they buy is called their UTILITY. We use this concept, although consumers may never have heard of it, because it enables us to construct a theory of consumer behaviour.

Consider the utility that one consumer, call her Kate, derives from purchases of a good such as ice-cream. If only one ice-cream is consumed each week, it will be enjoyed greatly, the second perhaps a little less, the third, fourth, fifth and subsequent ice-creams will each give less pleasure still. Indeed, once a dozen or two are consumed each week, Kate may have had her fill and want no more, even if the ice-creams are free.

Diminishing marginal utility

The relationship between utility and quantity consumed is formalized by a well-known principle – that of *diminishing marginal utility*. In order to explain this principle we must make an important distinction between the *total utility* derived from the consumption of all of the goods consumed over some period of time and the *marginal utility* of an additional unit of the good consumed over that period of time. MARGINAL UTILITY is defined as the difference in utility arising from a change in the rate of consumption per period of time. If TU_{n+1} stands for the total utility from consuming $n+1$ units of a good and TU_n stands for the total utility from consuming n units of the good over the period of time in question, then marginal utility is the difference, TU_{n+1} minus TU_n.

The more of a good that any individual consumes, per time-period, the greater the TOTAL UTILITY that he or she enjoys. But consider what happens to marginal utility, i.e. the *increases* in total utility that occur as consumption increases. Suppose Kate's

consumption rises from one ice-cream per week to two. Total utility from two ice-creams will be greater than from one. Suppose a third ice-cream is bought each week. Total utility rises again, but the *extra* or *marginal utility* from the third ice-cream is less than that from the second, which is less again than that from the first.

The principle of diminishing marginal utility (from consumption of ice-creams in this case) states that, while total utility rises with consumption, marginal utility, in contrast, falls. In other words, the *extra* satisfaction obtained from eating more and more ice-creams leads to *smaller and smaller* rises in satisfaction. To put this point yet another way, the rate at which total utility is rising is diminishing as consumption increases. If all this sounds forbidding, read on and soon you will find the idea becoming quite clear.

Utility schedules and graphs

Table 4.2 sets out hypothetical data illustrating the assumptions that have been made about utility. Column (ii) of the table shows Kate's total utility rising as the number of ice-creams she eats each week rises. Everything else being equal, the more ice-creams she eats each month the more satisfaction she gets – at least over the range shown in the table.

Now consider the marginal utility, shown in column (iii) of the table – for example, the marginal utility of 40, shown against an increase in consumption from 1 to 2 ice-creams per week. This arises because total utility increases from 60 to 100 – a difference of 40 – with the second ice-cream. The marginal utility of 2, shown in the last row of the table, arises because total utility rises only from 196 to 198, when consumption rises from 9 to 10 ice-creams per month. Marginal utility is associated with the *change* from one unit of the good to another. To indicate this, the figures are recorded between the rows. When plotting marginal utility on a graph, it is plotted at the midpoint of the interval over which it is computed.

Now, notice that although total utility is rising as the number of ice-creams Kate consumes each week rises, her marginal utility associated with each extra ice-cream consumed per month is falling.

The same data can also be shown graphically, as in Figure 4.2. Note that the curve showing total utility rises continuously. But the amount of the rise is less and less as more and more ice-creams are consumed. Thus the marginal utility curve is declining: *each*

TABLE 4.2 Kate's Total and Marginal Utility Schedules.
Total utility rises but marginal utility declines as Kate's consumption increases

Number of ice-creams eaten per week (i)	Total utility (ii)	Marginal utility (iii)
0	0	
		60
1	60	
		40
2	100	
		30
3	130	
		20
4	150	
		16
5	166	
		12
6	178	
		8
7	186	
		6
8	192	
		4
9	196	
		2
10	198	

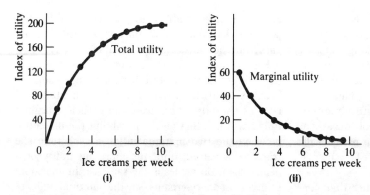

FIGURE 4.2 Kate's Total and Marginal Utility Curves. The total utility curve rises but the marginal utility curve falls as the quantity consumed rises

successive ice-cream adds to total utility but each adds less than its predecessor.

Four issues now need to be considered.

Can Marginal Utility Reach Zero?   With many commodities there is some maximum consumption beyond which additional units give no additional utility. If the individual were forced to consume more, the additional units would actually reduce total utility.

Cigarettes are an obvious example. Even for heavy smokers, at some point long before consumption has reached the point of chain-smoking from the instant of awakening to the moment of falling asleep, smoking additional cigarettes would cease to add to utility. Indeed it would almost certainly begin to subtract from it. At that point, additional cigarettes would have a negative marginal utility (or, as it is sometimes called, a marginal disutility), although, of course, the individual would not voluntarily continue to consume cigarettes, or any other commodity, when marginal utility became negative. The same is true of many other commodities such as food, alcoholic beverages and most recreation. (Although a few fanatics might be happy to play golf from dawn to sunset for all their leisure hours, most of us would not.)

How Universal is the Principle of Diminishing Marginal Utility?   This is a question of fact. (A question of fact is often called an EMPIRICAL question.) Experiments have been devised to test it in various situations. Although such tests are difficult to design, the evidence from consumer behaviour suggests that the principle is widely applicable.

Of course, it would not be plausible to assume that diminishing marginal utility applies to every single commodity for everybody in the world. There are bound to be exceptions. Addictive drink and drugs may provide examples of such exceptions. It is quite possible that the second or third drink, or fix, per day gives users more satisfaction than the first. But, sooner or later, the point of diminishing marginal utility will occur as further amounts bring less and less satisfaction. After all, if you drink too much it will, sooner or later, make you ill.

Variety in Uses of a Good: Many commodities can be used for several purposes. The demand for them is known as COMPOSITE DEMAND. Moreover, the principle of diminishing marginal utility is related to the number of uses to which a good can be put. This varies from commodity to commodity. For example, consider champagne. It can be used for several purposes. The most obvious is for drinking on special occasions, such as weddings. Champagne can also be drunk as an aperitif like sherry; it can also be served as a table wine with a meal. One can even think of uses for champagne other than drinking it. Ships have been launched by breaking bottles over their bows. Film stars have even been known to bathe in it!

All these uses of champagne have some value for the person buying it. But some uses have more value than others. The diminishing values of uses, helps to explain why the demand curve for champagne (and virtually all other goods) slopes downwards. When the price of champagne is around £15 a bottle, it will be bought principally for celebrating special occasions. When the price is a little lower, some may be bought to serve friends calling round for 'drinks'. When it is lower still, it may be used more widely as a table wine. At a lower price some may even bathe in it. The variety of uses to which champagne can be put reinforces the tendency for marginal utility to fall as consumption rises. This is because, as its price falls, it may be used for less valued uses while also encouraging its further use for the more valued purposes.

Because this point is important, a second example

may be worth considering. Instead of the 'luxury good', champagne, consider the 'necessity good', water. Some minimum quantity of drinking water is necessary to sustain life, and people would, if necessary, give up all of their incomes to obtain that quantity. The marginal utility of that quantity is extremely high. Much more than this bare minimum can be drunk, but the marginal utility of successive glasses of water drunk over some time period will decline steadily. Hence the demand curve for water is negatively sloped.

Water has, however, many uses other than for drinking. For this reason, too, the demand curve for water slopes downward. Water is used for baths, for brushing one's teeth, watering the kitchen garden and the lawn, washing the car, etc. To any individual the importance of all these uses will vary. But some are certainly more important than others at any particular time. We may therefore expect that water will be put to more and more 'lower utility uses' as its price falls.

We may summarize the arguments of this section as follows: demand curves slope downwards because successive units consumed of a commodity in any one use have diminishing marginal utility, and because most commodities have multiple uses that confer different utilities.

Derivation of a Demand Curve from Marginal Utility: The argument so far has been intuitive. Now we consider how to derive a demand curve for a product, doing so formally from a knowledge of a consumer's marginal utility for that product.

Consider Table 4.2, which shows Kate's total and marginal utility schedules for ice-creams. Given some price of ice-creams, say 40p each, how many would she buy?

To answer this question, we recall our assumption that Kate, and all other consumers, seek to maximize their total utilities from consumption. *The principle for doing so is that they should distribute their expenditures among all available commodities until the last penny spent on each commodity yields the same marginal utility.* This has an immediate appeal to common sense. If the last penny spent on ice-creams yielded more utility than the last penny spent on apples, then total utility could be increased by transferring a penny of expenditure from apples to ice-creams. Say, for example, the last penny spent on ice-creams yielded 100 units of utility, while the last spent on apples yielded only 70. By spending a penny less on apples, 70 units of utility are lost; by spending that penny on ice-creams, 100 units are gained. The net gain from the transfer is thus 30 units of utility.

Let us suppose that Kate is in this situation, and that she starts reallocating her spending as suggested. As she buys less apples, their marginal utility will rise; as she buys more ice-creams, their marginal utility will fall. She goes on, gaining the difference between the two marginal utilities each time she transfers a penny, until the marginal utility of a penny spent on apples is the same as the marginal utility spent on ice-creams. Say the marginal utility of ice-creams has fallen to 90, while that for apples has risen to 90. There is now nothing to be gained from further reallocations of expenditures between the two products.

The condition for dividing expenditures between apples and ice-creams can now be stated in an equation. We do this by letting *MU* stand for marginal utility, calling apples 'good A' and ice-creams 'good B'. Now we can write:

$$MU \text{ of 1p spent on } A = MU \text{ of 1p spent on } B. \quad (1)$$

Next we ask: 'how do we know the marginal utility of a penny spent on any commodity, say ice-creams, when all we are given is the marginal utility of a unit of the commodity?' Table 4.2, for example, tells us that the marginal utility of the third ice-cream is 30. What, however, is the marginal utility of a penny spent on ice-creams when consumption goes from two to three? The answer depends on how much ice-creams cost. If the third ice-cream costs 30p and yields 30 units of utility, then the utility per penny is 30/30p = 1 unit of utility per penny spent. If ice-creams cost only 15p, then the marginal utility per penny spent is 30/15p = 2; if the price is 60p, then the marginal utility per penny spent is 30/60p = 0.5.

In general, then, the marginal utility of a penny spent on some commodity is the marginal utility of that commodity divided by its price. Now we can rewrite equation (1), the condition of maximizing utility, into a new form:

$$\frac{MU \text{ of } A}{\text{price of } A} = \frac{MU \text{ of } B}{\text{price of } B}. \quad (2)$$

Now let us consider the demand for one of these products, commodity A. Rearrangement of (2) produces the following result:

$$\frac{MU \text{ of } A}{MU \text{ of } B} = \frac{\text{price of } A}{\text{price of } B}. \quad (3)$$

Equation (3) tells us that in equilibrium the consumer will adjust her purchases of any two goods until their marginal utilities are proportional to their prices. This is not a new condition, it is just another way of putting the point made in (2). The consumer wants the same marginal utility per penny spent on *A* and on *B*. This means that, if a unit of *A* costs twice as much as a unit of *B*, she must get twice the marginal utility from the last unit of *A* as from the last unit of *B*.

We can now see why the demand curve for *A* has a negative slope. Holding other things constant, which in this case means holding the price and consumption of commodity *B* constant, let the price of *A* fall. The consumer restores equilibrium by consuming more *A* until its marginal utility falls in the same proportion as its price has fallen. For example, if the price of *A* falls by 10 per cent, the consumer increases her purchases of *A* until the marginal utility of *A* falls by 10 per cent. Then the ratio given in (3) will be re-established.

This demonstrates the negative slope of the demand curve for *A*, and by a similar argument for every other commodity. Notice that the consumer adjusts her purchases of *A* until its marginal utility changes in proportion to the change in its price. This does not mean changing the quantity of *A* in that proportion. If the marginal utility of *A* falls quickly, only a little more *A* will be bought; if the marginal utility of *A* falls slowly, then a lot more *A* will be bought.

Simplified versions of this analysis often say that the marginal utility of *A* is equated with the price of *A*. This applies only if the marginal utility and price of *B* are set equal to unity. What is correct is that, for given prices and quantities of all other commodities, the quantity purchased of any commodity will be positively associated with its price

MARKET DEMAND

So far we have looked at a single consumer's demand for a good. To explain market behaviour we need to know the *total demand* for a good from all consumers.

To obtain the market demand, we add together the demands of all individuals. To illustrate, we take a simple case where there are only two consumers, Alan and Jill. Alan's demand schedule and demand curve we have already encountered. We repeat it in column (ii) in Table 4.3 and in Figure 4.3 (i) below,

TABLE 4.3 Individual and Market Demand Schedules for Lamb Chops

PRICE	QUANTITIES DEMANDED		
(£s per lb.)	Alan (lbs. per month)	Jill (lbs. per month)	Market demand (lbs. per month) (Alan *plus* Jill) (ii) + (iii)
(i)	(ii)	(iii)	(iv)
4.00	0	0	0
3.50	0	$\frac{3}{4}$	$\frac{3}{4}$
3.00	0	$1\frac{1}{2}$	$1\frac{1}{2}$
2.50	0	$2\frac{1}{4}$	$2\frac{1}{4}$
2.00	2	3	5
1.50	4	$3\frac{3}{4}$	$7\frac{3}{4}$
1.00	6	$4\frac{1}{2}$	$10\frac{1}{2}$
0.50	8	$5\frac{1}{4}$	$13\frac{1}{4}$
0.00	10	6	16

adding Jill's demand schedule in column (iii) of the table, and putting her demand curve alongside Alan's in Figure 4.3(ii).

Market Demand Schedule

Let us deal, first, with the market demand *schedule*. This is obtained by adding the quantities demanded by Alan and Jill at each price to give a total quantity demanded in column (iv). Since Jill likes lamb chops more than Alan, we see that when price is between £2.50 and £3.50 per lb., only Jill buys them. Since Jill is then the only consumer in the market, the market demand schedule corresponds exactly to Jill's schedule at these high prices. As soon as price falls below £2.50 per lb., however, Alan wants to buy lamb chops too. The market demand at these prices is, therefore, the sum of both person's positive demands. For example at a price of £2.00 per lb. the demand is 2 lbs. from Alan plus 3 lbs. from Jill, which equals 5 lbs. for the two of them. When price is £1.00 a lb. the market demand is 6 plus $4\frac{1}{2} = 10\frac{1}{2}$ lbs., and so on.

Market Demand Curve

Now consider the derivation of the market demand *curve*. This can, of course, be constructed by plotting the market demand schedule in column (iv) of Table 4.3, which we derived in the previous paragraph. The geometrical equivalent of this is to add horizontally, the demand curves of the two individuals. This

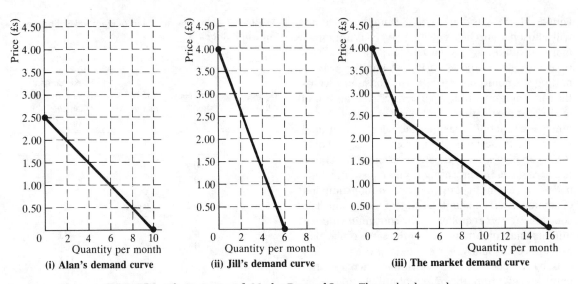

FIGURE 4.3   The Derivation of a Market Demand Curve. The market demand curve
is the horizontal sum of the demand curves for all of the consumers in the market

process is illustrated in Figure 4.3. By taking a common price on each curve, and adding the corresponding quantities, we discover the total quantity demanded at each price. For example at a price of £1.50 a lb. the two curves tell us that Alan will demand 4 lbs. while Jill will demand $3\frac{3}{4}$ lbs. This makes a total of $7\frac{3}{4}$ lbs. which is plotted as the total market demand associated with a price of £1.50 per lb.

In practice, we seldom obtain market demand curves by summing the demand curves of individual consumers. Our knowledge of market demand is usually derived by observing total quantities directly. We have shown the way to do it here, because we wish to understand the relationship between curves for individual persons and the market curve. Of course, market demand curves express the demands for many more than two people – in some cases it is millions of people. We have used two persons merely to illustrate the procedure.

Distinctive features of total market demand

Predictability: Individuals are not perfectly predictable machines. They sometimes do erratic things that we are unable to explain in rational terms. As long, however, as this behaviour is random, it will tend to cancel out when each individual's behaviour is aggregated to obtain the market demand curve. If, for example, some individual for no apparent reason decides to increase his purchases of lamb chops this week, a second individual may, equally inexplicably, decide to reduce her purchases. Thus, occasional erratic behaviour on the part of any one or another person will not upset the normal systematic relations between market demands and the factors that influence them. As long as this erratic behaviour is unrelated across consumers (i.e., everyone does not do the same erratic thing at the same time), the market as a whole will be observed to behave normally.

Price and Quantity Demanded: Because the extra satisfaction consumers derive from consuming additional units of a commodity tends to fall as more of it is consumed, people will only buy more of a commodity (*ceteris paribus*), when its price falls. Thus, a fall in price stimulates individuals already buying a good to buy more of it. This is the explanation of the downward sloping demand curve for individual consumers. But when we consider the whole market, we must also note that a fall in price *encourages new consumers to enter the market*. We saw this in the hypothetical demand curve for lamb chops which we drew in Figure 4.3. When price falls from £3 to £2 Jill increases her consumption from $1\frac{1}{2}$ to 3 lbs. per week. However, Alan, who bought no lamb chops when the price was £3, decides to enter the market when the price drops to £2. He buys 2 lbs. at the lower price. Market demand (Jill plus Alan) rises, therefore, by the $1\frac{1}{2}$ lbs. extra consumption by Jill *plus* 2 lbs. new consumption by Alan. His entry into the market provides a reason additional to each consumer's diminishing marginal utility for quantity demanded to increase when price falls.

Consumer Surplus

Consider an individual buying strawberries. Call him Harold. Table 4.4 shows part of his demand schedule. Suppose that market price is 60 pence per pound and that Harold maximizes his satisfaction when he buys 5 lbs., costing him £3.00.

Now let us ask what is the money value of the total satisfaction that Harold enjoys when he consumes 5 lbs. of strawberries? Harold's demand schedule can provide us with the answer, because we can deduce from it the marginal utility of each additional pound of strawberries. If we add together the marginal utilities of all 5 lbs., we end up with their total utility.

The marginal utility of the first pound must be worth 80 pence to Harold, because he would be prepared to pay that amount for it. The marginal utility of the second pound, by similar reasoning, is worth 75p, that of the third is worth 70p, and so forth. The total utility derived by Harold from 5 lbs. is made up of the sum of the marginal utilities of the 1st, 2nd, 3rd, 4th and 5th lbs. – i.e. $80 + 75 + 70 + 65 + 60p = 350p$.

As we observed, however, 5 lbs. of strawberries do not cost Harold 350p, but only 300p. The difference between Harold's total outlay of 300p and his total satisfaction of 350p is known as CONSUMER SURPLUS. It is made up in this example of a surplus of 20p on the first pound (80–60) plus surpluses on the second, third and fourth pounds of 15, 10 and 5p. Of course there is no consumer surplus on the fifth pound, which Harold values at 60p which is also the market price paid.

The concept of consumer surplus defined as the difference between total utility and total outlay can be applied to a whole market as well as to a single

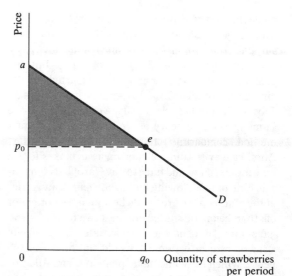

FIGURE 4.4 Consumer Surplus for an Individual. Consumer surplus is total utility less total outlay (aep_0).

individual; and it may be depicted graphically. In Figure 4.4 we show a market demand curve for strawberries. Suppose that market price is p_0 and the quantity bought is q_0. Total consumer outlay is given by the area Op_0eq_0, representing price times quantity. Total utility is represented by the area under the demand curve, $Oaeq_0$, showing the sum of the marginal utilities,[1] derived from q_0 strawberries. The difference between these two areas, which is the shaded area aep_0, is the consumer surplus which accrues to all consumers, variously as individuals depending on how much each values intra-marginal units of strawberries.

A helpful way of thinking about consumer surplus is to describe it as the difference between the amount that a consumer *actually pays* when he buys a number of units of a good, and the *maximum amount he would be prepared to pay* if he could be charged a different price for each unit. In Harold's case in Figure 4.4, one might imagine charging him 80p for one pound of strawberries. This is the value he places on the first pound consumed. After Harold has bought one pound, you then offer him a second. How much would he pay for that? The answer is 75p when 2 lbs. are bought. So one could go on, charging Harold a price equal to the value that he places on each unit. The total you extracted from him would be the full

TABLE 4.4 Harold's Demand for Strawberries

Price (pence per lb.)	Quantity demanded (lbs. per month)
80	1
75	2
70	3
65	4
60	5

---

1 See Appendix to Chapter 1.

value that he places on his total consumption. And, of course, he would not be left with any consumer surplus. You would have drained it all away, by charging him differential prices per unit. But the difference between the amount you extracted and the amount he would have had to pay if he had bought all 5 lbs. at the market price of 60p, would add up to the same figure of 50 pence as we obtained by our first method, comparing total utility and total outlay. Another way to think of consumer surplus is to ask how much you would have to pay Harold to compensate him for not allowing him to buy *any* strawberries at the market price. He would be no worse, nor better off, than before he started buying strawberries, if you gave him 50 pence to compensate for complete strawberry deprivation. He would still have the 300 pence, which he would have spent on them. Add this to the 50 pence compensation, and Harold has 350 pence altogether, which is equal to the total utility he would have gained.

The Paradox of Value

The notion of consumer surplus has many uses in economic analysis. One is to explain what is known as the paradox of value. It was noticed by Adam Smith, more than 200 years ago, that some 'useful'

commodities, such as water, had very low values in exchange, while other less 'useful' ones, such as diamonds, had much higher exchange values.

There is little doubt that the emotional reaction of many people to goods reflects a certain unease which is related to the paradox which Smith pointed out. Yet there is really nothing paradoxical about his observation. The high value that people put on water refers to the total utility that is derived from it, not to its marginal utility.

A good such as water has a high total utility and hence consumers gain a large consumer surplus from it. A good such as diamonds has a lower total utility and hence consumers gain a lower consumer surplus from it. If you doubt this, compare the amounts of money consumers would accept to persuade them to give up their total consumption of water and of diamonds. Since water is a necessity of life itself, a vast – even infinite – sum would not be enough to compensate most people for giving up all water.

But water is plentiful and cheap, so it is consumed to the point where its marginal utility is low. Diamonds are scarce and expensive, so consumers stop buying them when their marginal utility is still high. Thus there is no paradox in a good with a high total utility having a low price and marginal utility as long as it is plentiful.

SUMMARY

1 The theory of demand is concerned with the quantities of a good or service that consumers wish to buy per period of time. In the elementary theory of demand, consumers are assumed to be price-takers.

2 The quantity demanded of a good depends on many factors. It is helpful to consider them one at a time, holding the others constant.

3 One important determinant of demand is own price. The relationship between own price and quantity demanded is represented graphically by a demand curve.

4 Demand curves for individual consumers have a negative slope showing that price and quantity demanded vary in the opposite direction. One explanation of their slope is diminishing marginal utility, whereby the total utility derived from increased consumption of a good rises at a diminishing rate. The fact that many goods have

multiple uses also contributes to the negative slopes of demand curves.

5 A market demand curve is derived by the (horizontal) summation of the demand curves of all individuals in the market. Market demand is more predictable than individual demand. An additional reason why market demand curves have a negative slope is that new consumers enter the market when price falls.

6 Consumer surplus refers to the excess of total value that a consumer places on the consumption of a good over the total outlay by consumers on it. It may also be thought of as the difference between what the consumer actually pays for the quantity he purchases, and the maximum he would be prepared to pay faced with the choice of having nothing or having the amount he is presently consuming.

5

Demand, Income and Other Determinants

This chapter continues our discussion of the determinants of the quantity of a good that consumers wish to buy. In the previous chapter, we concentrated on the influence of the commodity's own price (which we agreed in Chapter 4 to call the *own price*) on its demand. In the first part of this chapter, we consider other determinants of demand first from the viewpoint of the individual consumer, and afterwards for the market as a whole.

Determinants of Demand Other than the Own Price of a Commodity

To consider other determinants of quantity demanded, the *ceteris paribus* clause must now include the good's own price. In what follows, therefore, we assume a certain fixed price for the good in question. The influences we shall then discuss are: (1) income, (2) prices of other goods, (3) expectations, and (4) other factors.

Remember that quantities demanded are still to be regarded as so much *per period of time*. We shall continue to label diagrams 'per period' on the quantity axis in this and the next chapter until it becomes second nature for you to think of demand in this way. Later we shall take this as understood.

Income

Consider, first, the effect of changes in income on quantity demanded.

Normal Goods: Usually, we would expect an individual to buy more of a good when his or her income rises, and to buy less of it when his or her income falls. This positive association between price and income is common, and the goods which obey this rule are called NORMAL GOODS. Two possible exceptions need to be noted.

Goods Subject to Satiation: The first is where the quantity demanded remains unchanged once the consumer's income reaches some critical level. This is the case for commodities for which the desire is completely satisfied after a certain level of income has been reached. For example, the demand for salt is not much affected by an increase in a consumer's income from £15,000 to £16,000 per annum or by a decrease within the same range (though the demand for salt might conceivably fall if a consumer's income sank to £500 per annum).

Inferior Goods: The second exception to the rule, that income is positively associated with quantity demanded, relates to goods where the association is *negative*, i.e. a rise in income is associated with a fall in quantity demanded, and vice versa. Goods which fall into this category are known as INFERIOR GOODS. They are often those which are regarded as cheap but inferior substitutes for other commodities. In many countries, potatoes, margarine and black bread provide examples. As incomes rise above some critical level, consumers switch to more expensive vegetables, to butter and to white bread. A black and white television set is also an inferior good for those persons who replace it with a colour set when their incomes rise. Notice that *inferiority is relative to income*. Goods that are inferior at some levels of income will be normal at some lower incomes.

In Figure 5.1 we show the relationship between income and the demand for a good under the assumption that all factors other than income remain constant. Note that the axes used here are not the same as for the demand curve of Figure 4.1 in the previous chapter. We now measure quantity demanded on the *vertical* axis, and we measure *income* on the *horizontal* axis.

Quantity demanded and income are positively related with normal goods and negatively related with inferior goods. Curve 1 illustrates the case in which an increase in income brings about an increase in purchases at all levels of income. Such a commodity is normal at all income levels.

Curve 2 illustrates the case in which the commodity is a normal good up to some level of income, here y_1, while, for higher levels of income, demand does not respond at all as income varies. The same quantity, q_1, is demanded at income levels y_1 and y_3, for example.

Curve 3 illustrates the case in which a commodity is an inferior good after a certain income level is reached, here y_2. Until that income is attained, the good is a normal one. However, increases in income beyond y_2 are associated with decreases in quantity demanded. For instance q_3 is demanded at income y_2, but only q_2 at income y_3. You can now see why a good cannot be inferior at *all* levels of income. If you try to draw the curve for such a good it will lie below the quantity axis. This would mean a negative quantity consumed, which makes no sense.

The prices of other goods

When the price of one good changes, this may affect the demand for other goods, because of a change in their *relative* prices.

There are three possible relations between the demand for a commodity and the prices of other commodities. A fall in the price of one commodity may lower the quantity demanded of another; it may raise it; or it may leave it unchanged. Goods involved in these three possibilities are called: (1) substitutes, (2) complements, and (3) unrelated.

Substitutes: If a fall in the price of one good causes a fall in the quantity demanded of another good, the two goods are said to be SUBSTITUTES. The relationship is the one shown in Figure 5.2(i), where goods X and Y are substitutes. A rise in the price of good X leads to an increase in the purchases of good Y as people switch purchases from the increasingly expensive good X to its substitute that has not risen in price.

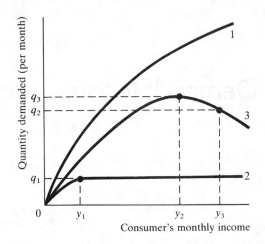

FIGURE 5.1 Income and Quantity Demanded. For normal goods, quantity demanded increases as income rises; for inferior goods, quantity demanded decreases as income rises

Examples of substitutes are butter and margarine, carrots and cabbage, cinema tickets and theatre tickets, bus rides and taxi rides. It is important, however, to realize that substitutability need not be as close or as obvious as with these examples. Whenever a consumer weighs up the relative merits of buying two goods, they are potential substitutes for that consumer. If a rise in the price of food leads a poor family to spend less on entertainment, because it must spend more on food, then, for that family, food and entertainment are substitutes. Do not be confused by the fact that sausages and visits to the cinema are not substitutes in the conventional sense of the word.

Complements: If a fall in the price of one commodity raises the demand for another commodity, the two are said to be COMPLEMENTS. When the price of one such commodity falls, more of it is consumed and more of other commodities that are complementary to it are also consumed as illustrated in part (ii) of the figure. Here, when good X falls in price the demand rises for good Y, which is complementary to it.

Goods that are complements are those which tend to be consumed together. Examples are skis and ski boots, strawberries and cream, needles and sewing thread, and cameras and film. These goods are sometimes said to be in JOINT DEMAND or to be jointly demanded. All this means is that if you decide to have more of one, this usually implies wanting more of the other.

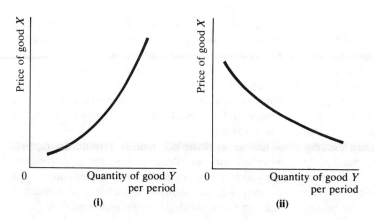

FIGURE 5.2 Substitutes and complements. If a rise in the price of X increases the quantity demanded of Y the two goods are substitutes; if it reduces the quantity demanded of Y the two goods are complements

Expectations

We have seen that changes in prices and changes in incomes cause consumers to change the quantities that they demand of the various goods. If these changes happen unexpectedly, people cannot react until the change has occurred. But sometimes the changes are foreseen. Then people can, and often do, react to the expectation that changes in prices or incomes will occur in the future. If people expect some price to rise, they may rush to buy now while the commodity is still cheap, relative to what they expect it to cost in the future. If people expect their incomes to rise in the future they may borrow and spend now, intending to repay the loan out of the increase of income that they expect in the future.

Other factors

Many other factors affect the demand for a good. We have grouped them into four subgroups.

Sociological and Demographic Factors: Here we include age, sex, marital status, health, education, social class, place of residence (particularly whether urban or rural) and moral and religious values whether induced by family, peer group or political allegiance.

Psychological Factors: This head covers all the influences, inherited and acquired, that affect personality and therefore *tastes*. Also included are fads, fashions and other taste phenomena that influence economic variables, but are not influenced by them.

'Acts of God': This term describes such factors as the weather, earthquakes, the incidence of disease of man, beasts or crops. This category also includes strikes, war, riots, etc which insurance companies call acts of God, but which are, in fact, acts of man.

Acts of the State: Government legislation can affect the demand for a commodity in a great variety of ways. Rules compelling the wearing of seatbelts in cars, controlling the advertising of cigarettes, banning the sales of heroin, and regulating the emissions from car exhausts are examples of ways in which the government can affect the demand for different goods.

Market Demand

As in the previous chapter, we must point out certain distinctive features which apply to market demand rather than to the demand of any one individual.

In the first place, our earlier remarks about predictability are equally applicable to the determinants of quantity demanded other than the price of the good. Erratic behaviour from some individuals tends to cancel out in aggregate market demand. For example, a large number of people may find their incomes rising and decide to buy a few more lamb chops. Some may, however, decide to reduce their purchases for all sorts of individually applicable reasons. Others might even decide to buy no meat except lamb chops for reasons that seem good to themselves. But the erratic behaviour of these few consumers will tend to cancel out, and the market as a whole will show a stable relation, with the demand for lamb chops increasing moderately as incomes rise.

In the second place, when considering market as opposed to individual demand we need to take certain distributional factors into account. Two are of particular importance – the distribution of income, and the distribution of the population.

Distributional Aspects – Income: Income, which influences individual demand, gets an extra dimension when we are considering market demand. The new dimension is distributional. Even if total income is constant, a change in the distribution of that income can shift the demand curves for many products.

Consider, for example, two societies with the same total income. In one society there are quite a few very rich households, many very poor ones, but hardly anyone is in the middle income range. In the second society most households have incomes that do not differ much from the average income for all households. Income distribution is unequal in the first society, relative to that in the second.

Even if the influence of all other factors affecting demand is exactly the same in the two societies, they will have different patterns of demand for goods and services. In the first, there will be relatively large demands for goods bought by the rich, such as solid silver cutlery, and also for goods bought by the poor, such as plastic knives and forks. In the second society, demand for both these types of good will be relatively small, but there will be larger demands for goods bought by middle-income households, e.g. stainless steel cutlery. In other words, the pattern of demand for particular goods will change if the distribution of income changes.

Now consider a change in income distribution of a different kind – one between young and old. Suppose that retirement pensions are raised, and that this is financed by means of increased taxes on single persons (who tend also to be young). There will be an increase in demand for goods and services bought by elderly people, such as hearing aids and large-print books, and a fall in the demand for things bought by young, single persons, such as tennis balls and recorded pop music. Note, that these changes come about without any change in the overall level of income – only its distribution changes.

Distributional Aspects – Population: Any shift in the populations between groups that have different tastes and needs will tend to alter the pattern of demand for different goods and services. One example is a change in the age distribution of the population, such as might be brought about by a decline in the birth rate, accompanied by fall in the death rate of people over 60. This might result in precisely the same type of changes in the demand for goods and services as that described in the previous paragraph. In this case, however, the changes are a direct result of a change in the age distribution of the population rather than in income distribution.

Two other examples arise in the proportion of the population living in the towns rather than in the country, and a fall in the proportion of married couples in the population, such as may occur with a rise in the divorce rate.

Insofar as townsfolk tend to buy different goods from country dwellers, and single and divorced persons buy different goods from married couples, the pattern of market demand will change as a result of this distributional shift in the population.

Shifts in Demand Curves and Movements Along Them

It is important to distinguish between a movement along a demand curve and a shift of the whole curve. The distinction is, in principle, straightforward, but be warned that even quite experienced students sometimes have difficulty in putting it into practice. To help the distinction in your mind, remember that the demand curve shows the relationship between own price and quantity demanded on the assumption of *ceteris paribus* – that is to say that all influencing

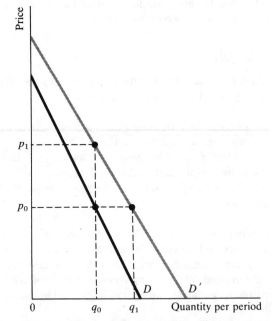

FIGURE 5.3 **Shifts of a Demand Curve.** Changes in the conditions of demand shift the demand curve to the right if demand increases and to the left if demand decreases

TABLE 5.1 The Terminology of Demand Curves

Change	Terms Used to Describe the Change
(A) A change in the price of the good causes a MOVEMENT ALONG a demand curve	
1. Price of the good rises.	1. *A decrease, fall or reduction in the quantity demanded.* A contraction in demand.
2. Price of the good falls.	2. *An increase, or rise, in the quantity demanded.* An extension of demand.
(B) A change in any of the other influences causes a SHIFT OF a demand curve	
1. A rise in income, if the good is normal. A fall in income, if the good is inferior. A rise in the price of a substitute. A fall in the price of a complement. A change in tastes in favour of the good.	1. *A rightward,* upward or northeasterly *shift of the demand curve.* *An increase in demand.* An improvement in the conditions of demand.
2. A fall in income if the good is normal. A rise in income if the good is inferior. A fall in the price of a substitute. A rise in the price of a complement. A change in tastes against the good.	2. *A leftward,* downward or southwesterly *shift of the demand curve.* *A decrease in demand.* A deterioration in the conditions of demand.

Note: The terms we employ most commonly in this book are italicized.

factors other than own price do not change. These other factors cannot, of course, cause quantities demanded to alter unless they themselves change.

It follows, therefore, that *the effect of a change in price on quantity demanded is to be read off a demand curve.* Discovering the effects of movements in price involves moving along the demand curve to ascertain the effect on quantity demanded. Such movements are also sometimes described as EXTENSIONS or CONTRACTIONS of demand. An extension is a downward movement to the right along a demand curve in response to a fall in price; a contraction is an upward movement to the left along the demand curve in response to a rise in price.

In contrast, *the effect of a change in any factors other than price on quantity demanded, involves a shift in the demand curve itself*: at any given price the quantity demanded changes; a different quantity is bought because something else has changed. The 'something else' will be any of the determinants of demand other than price. A change in income, or in its distribution, in the prices of other goods, in expectations or in sociological factors cause the whole demand curve to shift. Such changes are often referred to as changes in the CONDITIONS OF DEMAND. For example, consider the demand for lamb chops discussed in Chapter 4. If Alan's income rises he may buy more lamb chops even though their price is unchanged.

Changes in the conditions of demand shift the demand curve – to the right if demand increases and to left if demand falls – showing different quantities demanded at every price.

This is illustrated in Figure 5.3, which shows the two demand curves D and D'. A shift in the demand curve from D to D' indicates an increase in demand; more is demanded at each price. For example at price p_0 quantity demanded rises from q_0 to q_1. A fall in price causes a movement downwards along a single demand curve, i.e. an increase in the quantity demanded. For example, when the demand curve is D', a fall in the price from p_1 to p_0 increases the quantity demanded from q_0 to q_1.

Now let the original demand curve be D'. A shift in the demand curve to D indicates a decrease in demand; less is demanded at each price. For example, at price p_0 quantity demanded falls from q_1 to q_0. A rise in price causes a movement upwards along a single demand curve, i.e. a decrease in the quantity demanded. For example, when the demand curve is D', a rise in price from p_0 to p_1 reduces the quantity demanded from q_1 to q_0.

Some Terminology to Learn: Economists have no universally accepted terminology to distinguish between the two types of change we have described. In particular the phrases 'increase in demand' and 'decrease in demand' are sometimes used to refer to a movement along a curve and sometimes to refer to a shift of a curve. This is unfortunate. Moreover, there are several terms that are used to describe shifts in the demand curve. These include (1) shifts to the right or left, (2) upward or downward shifts, (3) shifts to the North East or to the South West. The first refers to the fact that a different quantity is bought at each price; the second refers to the fact that each quantity is associated with a different price; the third draws an analogy with a map where a journey upwards and to the right on the map is a journey towards the N.E. while a journey downwards and to the left is a journey to the S.W., and vice versa. Sometimes one term is more descriptive than another. In this book we shall avoid the use of the compass directions of NE and SW, and stick mainly to leftward and rightward shifts.

All of the terminological distinctions are summarized in Table 5.1, which covers most of the important factors affecting demand.

Time and Demand

Note that the response of demand to a change in price can vary as the time period over which the response can take place is lengthened.

One reason is that most of us are to an extent creatures of habit. Hence, the fall in price of a good that we are unaccustomed to buying may not have any immediate impact on our spending behaviour. However, if the price fall persists, we may in time reconsider the relative merits of the good compared to others. Take, for example, the case of trout. Some years ago a pound of trout cost at least double that of a pound of cod. Today the two fish cost about the same. When the price of trout fell, relative to that of cod, many people did not even consider it as an alternative fish. The lower price has, however, persisted. In consequence, the demand for trout has grown, though it has taken time to do so.

A second reason why demand may respond slowly to price changes is that we are not always as price-conscious as we might be. We do not immediately realize that changes in relative prices have occurred, but only after they have lasted for a longish period. This is particularly likely to be the case in the kind of inflationary world that we have lived in for many years. When all prices are tending upwards, changes in relative prices may be difficult to discern. When

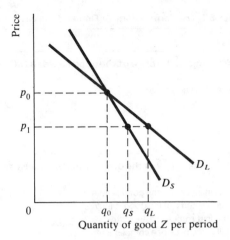

FIGURE 5.4   Short- and Long-run Demand Curves. The longer the time allowed, the greater the probable response of quantity demanded to a price change

they are discerned, quantities demanded will increase when relative prices have fallen, and decrease when relative prices have risen.

The greater response of quantity demanded to a price change, the longer the period under consideration is illustrated in Figure 5.4, which shows two demand curves for a product, Z. D_S is a short-run demand curve, while D_L is the demand curve for the same product when time is sufficient for people to make a full adjustment to a price change. If price falls from p_0 to p_1, the quantity demanded increases only to q_S in the short term, but to q_L in the longer term.

The Law of Demand and Exceptional Demand Curves

The tendency for the quantity demanded of any good to vary in the opposite direction to that good's own price, and its graphical expression in the negatively sloped demand curve, is sometimes called the LAW OF DEMAND.

There are cases where the law of demand does not hold, in the sense that more is demanded at high prices than at low. We deal with four of the most common types, though we shall show that the first is not so much an exception to the law as a confusion of movements along a demand curve with shifts of the entire curve. They are: (1) speculative demand, (2) snob demand, (3) judging quality by price, and (4) Giffen goods.

Speculative Demand: The first alleged exception to the law of demand occurs when the price of a good rises, but that rise is expected to be followed by a further rise. We may observe an association of rising price with rising quantities bought in such cases. However, the real reason for the rise in demand is not the rise in price, but the new expectation that a further rise will follow. As we explained earlier, if there are such expectations, the demand curve *shifts*, temporarily, to the right as people rush to buy now in the belief that the good is cheap, relative to what it will soon become. So what we observe is not a movement along a perverse, upward-sloping curve, but a shift of a normal, downward-sloping curve.

Snob Demand: The second alleged exception to the law is of a good which is wanted, not for the satisfaction it intrinsically gives, but because it is expensive. Goods in this category are sometimes said to have snob appeal. When the price of such a good rises, it becomes more desirable only in order to show off. Purchasers value it because of its price. Hence, when the price rises they demand larger quantities.

Assume, for example, that a consumer's satisfaction depends not only on how much is consumed of some commodity, but also on the price he or she has to pay for it. Some consumers may, for example, buy diamonds not because they really like diamonds, but because they wish to display their wealth in an ostentatious, but socially acceptable, way. These consumers value diamonds precisely because they are expensive; thus, a fall in price might lead them to stop buying diamonds and switch to a different object for ostentatious display. No doubt there are some consumers of this type. They have positively sloped individual demand curves for this particular good: the lower the price, the fewer they will buy. This is a genuine exception to the law of demand for particular groups of consumers and it occurs because the utility derived from the good rises when the price rises, and vice versa.

But what of the demand curve for the market as a whole? If enough consumers act similarly, the market demand curve for diamonds would slope upwards as well. But an upward-sloping market demand curve for diamonds, and other similar products, has never been observed. Why? The most obvious explanation is that most existing and potential purchasers do not buy diamonds just for their snob value but because they like them. The behaviour of the masses of lower-income consumers who would buy diamonds if they were cheap enough would swamp that of the minority of consumers who buy for ostentatious display. Hence, the demand curve for the market as a whole slopes downwards, and the exceptional snob-based demand is a rarity, if it exists at all.

Judging Quality by Price: Another reason why demand curves may slope upwards for some individuals is that they may mistakingly judge quality by price. When the price of one good falls, consumers may incorrectly assume that its quality has fallen as well, and switch to other, more expensive, close substitutes. This behaviour will show up as an upward-sloping demand curve: when the price falls less, rather than more, is bought.

The same comment applies here as to snob-goods. It is quite easy to imagine some consumers behaving in this way but, for the market to do so, these consumers must be in the majority. What is more likely is that the normal behaviour of the majority will swamp the behaviour of the smaller group who judge quality solely by price. Note that the above argument applies only to consumers who incorrectly assume that quality has changed because price has changed. There is, however, evidence – for example from *Which?* magazine, published by the Consumers' Association – that cheaper goods *tend* to be of lower quality than more expensive goods of the same type. If the quality of a good does change then it is not quite the same good and its demand curve will shift. Thus the observation that a fall in price is accompanied by a fall in quantity demanded of a good whose quality has changed is not an observation of two points on one positively sloped demand curve. Instead it represents two points on two different demand curves.

Giffen Goods: Another genuine exception to the downward-sloping demand curve for a commodity is called a 'Giffen good', after the Scottish economist, Sir Robert Giffen, who is alleged to have observed such a case in the nineteenth century. This case can occur when an inferior good that is a staple rises in price. If the poor spend a high proportion of their incomes on this good, they may be so impoverished by the price rise that they must severely cut down on their few luxuries and buy even more of the staple in order to get sufficient sustenance to keep alive. This rare exception to the law of demand is further discussed in Part 3 after we have developed the theory needed to understand it more deeply.

SUMMARY

1 The principal determinants of each consumer's demand for a good, other than its own price, are the consumer's income, the prices of other goods, and expectations.

2 Normal goods are those where quantity demanded is positively associated with income. Inferior goods are those where the association is negative.

3 Two goods are substitutes if a change in the price of one leads to a change in the opposite direction in the quantity demanded of another. Two goods are complements if a change in the price of one leads to a change in the same direction in the quantity demanded of the other.

4 Changes in consumers' expectations of future prices, incomes or other variables may affect quantities demanded at a given price.

5 Non-economic factors affecting demand include social, demographic and psychological factors as well as 'acts of God'. Economists are prepared to analyse the effects of changes in such determinants, but not their causes.

6 Market demand – the aggregate demand of all consumers – is affected by the distribution of the population and by the distribution of income among the population.

7 Movements along a demand curve must be sharply distinguished from shifts in the curve itself. Movements along a demand curve show the effects of price changes on quantity demanded, *ceteris paribus*. Shifts in the demand curve are the effect of a change in any determinant of demand other than own price (i.e. *ceteris non-paribus*).

8 Demand tends to respond more to a change in the price of a good as the time-period lengthens.

9 The Law of Demand is the tendency for quantity demanded to vary in the opposite direction to the price of a good.

10 Exceptions to the Law of Demand include cases of speculative demand, snob demand, the incorrect judgement of quality by price, and Giffen goods. The conditions necessary for a Giffen good are an inferior good with no close low-priced substitutes that takes up a high proportion of total household expenditure.

Supply

In the two previous chapters, we outlined the elementary theory of the demand for a good. We now turn to the supply side of the market to present a parallel elementary theory of supply. Our treatment of supply is shorter than that of demand because much of the discussion concerning supply is broadly similar to what we have already said about demand, and does not need to be repeated in full.

The Nature of Supply

This chapter is about business behaviour – in particular about the quantities of a good that suppliers wish to produce and offer for sale. We describe the elementary theory of supply in a manner similar to that of the previous chapter on demand. We explain first who the suppliers are, the kind of goods they are supplying and the forces determining their behaviour.

Suppliers: The organizations which make decisions about how many goods to supply are variously known as suppliers, sellers, producers, businesses and enterprises. These terms are often used interchangeably, although it is not always correct to do so. The word 'producer', for example, usually describes someone who makes a product such as a motorcar. It is not strictly applicable to second-hand car dealers – although both are suppliers. Some of the terms, such as producers and enterprises, have technical meanings which will be explained in Chapter 13. For present purposes we employ the words seller, supplier, or producer when we wish to refer to the organizations responsible for supply.

Who actually makes decisions to produce? This is an important question to which we return in Chapter 13. For now, we ignore it, and assume that each supplier makes decisions as if these decisions were made by a single individual. This allows us to take the supplier as the basic unit of behaviour on the supply side of markets, just as the consumer is treated as the basic unit of behaviour on the demand side.

Sellers' Motivation: We assume, to start with, that suppliers make their decisions with respect to a single goal or objective – to make as much profit as possible. When a supplier reaches a situation where profits are maximized, that position is said to be *optimal* from the supplier's point of view. This goal of PROFIT MAXIMIZATION is analogous to the consumer's goal of utility maximization. There is a difference, however: although consumer satisfaction cannot be directly observed and measured, a seller's profits can be.

Goods and Services: Parallel to the decision taken with demand, we confine ourselves in this chapter to supplies of goods. We thereby exclude other areas of supply, such as that of factors of production, which are dealt with in Chapters 20 and 21.

Time: As with demand, the theory of supply is concerned with the quantities offered for sale *per period of time*. Thus quantity supplied is always to be taken as a *flow*, so many lamb chops *per month* or ice-creams *per week*, etc. In all the diagrams in this chapter, we shall continue to label the quantity axes 'per period'. For the rest of the book, to avoid cluttering diagrams, we shall assume that this is understood and that we do not need to write it every time.

Price-takers: We deal at this stage with markets that contain many sellers. We assume that there are so many of them that no one of them can have any appreciable effect on the market price. No alteration in one producer's own behaviour, even by withdrawing from the market completely, will affect the market price of what the producer sells. Many real-world markets are of this type. For example, one more or less supplier would scarcely be noticed in most retail shopping areas and in most agricultural markets. Within manufacturing, however, this is not the case. There are only a few car manufacturers and makers of household detergents. Each is quite large. One more or less in either industry would cause a very noticeable change that would appreciably affect the car and detergent markets, as would a significant change in the output of one or more of them. For the moment, however, we shall confine ourselves to situations where the sellers are so numerous that they must take the market, including the price, as they find it, and cannot influence it. We say such sellers are *price-takers*. In Part 3, we shall extend our study to producers who can influence the price of the products.

WHAT DETERMINES QUANTITY SUPPLIED?

How much of some commodity will each producer be willing to make and offer for sale per period, say per month? The amount will be influenced by the following variables.
- The own price of the commodity.
- The prices of other goods.
- The costs of production, which depend on
    (i) The prices of factors of production.
    (ii) The state of technology.
- The goals of producers.
- Producers' income.
- Expectations of the future.
- Other relevant factors.

Supply and the Own Price of the Commodity

To keep our study simple to begin with, we concentrate on a single major influence determining supply: the price of the good itself, its own price. We therefore adopt the assumption to which you should by now have become accustomed, of *ceteris paribus*, i.e. we

assume that all other possible influences on the producer's output decision do not enter the picture. They are assumed unchanged. Thus, for the moment, we concentrate on the first influence from the above list.

Our basic hypothesis on the supply side is that the quantity that a producer will supply is positively associated with the commodity's own price: quantity rises when price rises and falls when price falls. This hypothesis is derived formally in Chapter 15. In the meantime, we can note its commonsense appeal: the higher the price of a good, the greater are the prospects for making profits and thus the greater the incentive to produce more and offer it for sale. Exceptions are important; they will be mentioned later (and considered at length in Part 3).

We illustrate the relationship between price and quantity supplied with hypothetical data for a producer of lamb chops. The data can, as we know from our earlier consideration of the demand side of this market, be presented either in the form of a schedule or graphically. Table 6.1 is a supply schedule. It shows in column (ii) the quantities supplied at each price shown in column (i). For example, the producer will offer 300 lbs. for sale each month when the price is £1.00 a lb. If the price rises to £1.50 a lb., 600 lbs. will be supplied, and so forth. Each of the price-quantity combinations in the schedule is given a letter for easy reference.

The data in Table 6.1 can be presented in the form of a graph, exactly as the demand schedule was so presented (see pp. 46–7).

The graphical presentation is given in Figure 6.1 where, as in Figure 4.1 when we drew a demand curve, price is plotted on the vertical axis and quantity on the horizontal axis, and the scales are chosen to accommodate the numbers in the table. For example, point v on the graph corresponds to the

TABLE 6.1 A Producer's Supply Schedule for Lamb Chops

Reference letter	Price (£s per lb.) (i)	Quantity supplied (lbs. per month) (ii)
t	0.50	0
u	1.00	300
v	1.50	600
w	2.00	900
x	2.50	1,200
y	3.00	1,500
z	3.50	1,800

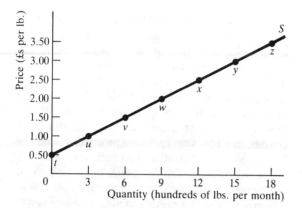

FIGURE 6.1   A Producer's Supply Curve. The higher the price, the larger the quantity supplied

third line of the table. Both indicate that 600 lbs. will be supplied each month when the price is £1.50 a lb. Similarly, we plot points t, u, w, y and z on the graph corresponding to the combinations with the same labels shown in the table.

Note that the supply curve cuts (or INTERCEPTS) the vertical price axis at a positive price (i.e. a price above zero). This positive intercept is the geometrical expression of a basic property of the production of most goods. Some minimum price is needed to call forth any supply at all; below that minimum price, quantity supplied is zero. In the present case, nothing at all is supplied at a price of £0.50 or less. A price in excess of 50p is needed to bring forth any output. The supplier could not even cover its costs if it had to sell for £0.50 (or less), so it would rather produce nothing.

We now draw a smooth line through the points t to z. This line is the producer's SUPPLY CURVE. It shows the quantity offered for sale at every price in the table *and at all intermediate prices*. For example, to find the quantity supplied at a price of £2.75 per lb., we locate £2.75 on the vertical axis, run over to the curve at that price, then drop vertically down to the quantity axis and discover that the quantity associated with a price of £2.75 is 1,350 lbs.

What lies behind the supply curve?

The justification for drawing an upward-sloping supply curve, such as the one shown in Figure 6.1, is that sellers are likely to feel they can profitably offer more of a good for sale the higher is its price. This parallels the justification that we initially offered for the downward-sloping demand curve: that people are inclined to buy more of a good the lower is its

price. Both arguments seem plausible, but they are not theoretically tight explanations.

In the case of the demand curve, we were able to derive its downward slope from the theory of diminishing marginal utility, combined with the hypothesis of utility maximization. The utility-maximizing consumer, faced with the market price of a commodity, buys that quantity at which the marginal utility of the last unit purchased is equal to its price. A parallel theory explains the upward-sloping supply curve. Whereas the consumer is assumed to seek to maximize utility, the producer is assumed to seek to maximize profits. By virtue of the assumptions of price-taking made earlier, both the producers and consumers face a market price that they are unable to influence. To complete the story, all we need is the producer's counterpart of diminishing marginal utility. This is the concept of *increasing marginal cost*, which we must now explain.

Each level of output that could be produced implies some level of total cost. No one will be surprised to hear that, the greater the producer's output, the greater will be its total costs of production. To produce more requires more labour and more of all other factors of production, all of which must be paid for. Thus total costs rise as output rises (just as the consumer's total utility rises as total consumption of some product rises). But how fast do costs rise as output is increased? To answer this question we need the concept of *marginal cost*, which is analogous to the concept of the consumer's marginal utility.

The MARGINAL COST (MC) of producing an extra unit of output is defined as the *increase* in total costs incurred by the producer as a result of producing an extra unit of output. Say, for example, that to produce 10 units of output costs £200, and to produce 11 units costs £225. Then, the marginal cost of producing the 11th unit of output is £25 (i.e., £225–£200). In more general terms, if the total cost of producing n units of output is TC_n and the total cost of producing $n+1$ units (i.e. one more than n) is TC_{n+1}, then the marginal cost of the $n+1$th unit is $TC_{n+1} - TC_n$.

So now we know what marginal cost is, the next thing to ask is, how does marginal cost behave as output varies? The answer is given in much more detail in Chapter 14, where it is shown to depend on a famous law called the Law of Diminishing Returns. All we can do at this stage is to assert the result, and offer an intuitive explanation for it. The basic result is that, given the size of producer's plant, *the marginal cost of producing extra output rises*. In other words, each unit produced adds more to total costs than did each preceding unit produced. To illustrate using our previous example, the producer might decide to produce a 12th unit and find that costs rose to £255. Since 11 units cost £225, the marginal cost of the 12th unit is £30 (£255–£225). Thus marginal costs are rising since the marginal cost of the 11th unit was only £25. The intuitive reason for rising marginal cost is that production becomes less and less efficient the more output is squeezed from its existing plant and equipment.

So now we have a producer trying to maximize profits, faced with a given market price and a marginal cost curve which rises as output increases. How much should be produced? The answer can be presented in the form of a rule which must be followed if profits are to be maximized. The rule is that production should be at that level of output for which *marginal cost (MC) is equal to price (p)*:

$$MC = p$$

The logic behind this rule is similar to the logic behind the rule that the utility-maximizing consumer should equate marginal utility (*MU*) to price (*p*): *MU* = *p*. Both are maximizing rules. Let us see how the *MC* = *p* rule works in the case of the producer.

First, say that, at the present level of output, marginal cost is *less than* price. This means that an extra unit can be produced at a cost less than it can be sold for. Its production will thus add to profits so that the unit should be produced. *Whenever, at the present level of output, marginal cost is less than price, output should be increased.*

Now assume that, at the present level of output, marginal cost *exceeds* price. This means that the last unit produced adds more to costs (its marginal cost) than it adds to the producer's revenue (the price at which the unit is sold). Thus there is a loss on producing the last unit of output, and it should not be produced. *Whenever, at the present level of output, marginal cost exceeds price, output should be reduced.*

Since output should be increased when *MC* is less than price, and should be reduced when *MC* is greater than price, *it follows that only when marginal cost equals price is there no profit incentive to alter output.*

We have now discovered how to derive the producer's supply curve. Since the profit maximizing level of output is where marginal cost equals price, the producer's marginal cost curve *is* his supply curve. Going back to our previous example, the marginal cost of the 11th unit of output was £25 and

the marginal cost of the 12th unit was £30. If the price of the product is £30, the producer should produce 12 units of output. Thus as soon as we know the producer's marginal costs, we know what will be produced at each market price. It follows that the supply schedule shown in Table 6.1 is also the producer's marginal cost schedule. For example, the marginal cost of producing the 1,200th unit must have been £2.50. Otherwise the producer would not have produced 1,200 units when the price was £2.50.

We will return to this discussion in Chapter 16. In the meantime, all that you need to remember is that any producer who is seeking to maximize profits will produce that level of output where marginal cost equals price. *And since we are assuming that marginal cost increases as output increases, this explains why supply curves are upward-sloping.*

Other Determinants of Supply

We studied the relationship between the quantity of a good supplied and its own price using the assumption that all other influencing forces were held constant. We now examine the influence of each of the factors listed on page 64, by letting them change one at a time on the assumption that all other influencing forces, including the product's own price, are held constant.

Prices of Other Goods: Prices must be viewed *relative* to one another. When the price of *x* falls, while the price of *y* remains the same, *x* has become *relatively* cheaper while *y* has become *relatively* more expensive. As relative prices change, what matters on the supply side is substitutability *in production*.

When considering the effect of a change in the price of other goods on the supply of a product, therefore, we consider price changes of those other goods which can most easily be produced with the resources at the firm's disposal. For example, a manufacturer of steel roof-racks for cars could probably switch production to steel frames for chairs without too much difficulty. If the price of such chairs were to rise, while the price of roof-racks was unchanged, there might well be a reduction in the desired output of racks, accompanied by a rise in the output of chairs.

Commodities which, for technical reasons, are produced in association with each other – i.e. one is a by-product of the other – are said to be in JOINT

SUPPLY. Examples are beef and leather, oil and petrol, and gas and coke. For example, a rise in the price of beef will increase the quantity of leather supplied because the quantity of skins available for tanning into leather increases automatically as the output of meat increases. They are *jointly supplied.*

Costs of Production: We have seen that firms will offer goods for sale so long as the extra revenue received is greater than the marginal cost of production. Thus any change in production costs will, *ceteris paribus*, affect quantity supplied.

To illustrate, return to Table 6.1 on p. 64, where the supply schedule may now be understood as a marginal cost schedule. Suppose marginal cost rises by 50p at all the output levels shown in the table – possibly because some input has become more expensive. The quantities offered for sale now fall. For example, 300 units would now be supplied only if the price were £1.50 instead of at £1.00, 600 would be supplied at a price of £2.00 instead of at £1.50, and so forth.

We now study two important reasons why production costs may change: changes in the prices of factors of production and changes in technology.

Changes in Factor Prices. If the price of a factor of production rises, costs of production must rise. If the market price of the good produced by the factor of production is unchanged (as it is under our *ceteris paribus* assumption), its output becomes less profitable, and less will be produced. A fall in the price of a factor of production has the opposite effect.

The State of Technology. Costs of production depend not only on the prices of the factors of production, but also on their productivity. At any given moment of time, productivity may be taken as given – determined by the state of technology (or 'the state of the arts', as it is sometimes called). Over time, however, technology advances. Indeed, the enormous increase in production per worker in industrial societies over the last 200 years is largely due to improved methods of production. Discoveries in chemistry have led to lower costs of production of well-established products such as paints, and to a large variety of new products such as plastics and synthetic fibres. The modern electronics industry based on the microchip has revolutionized production in television, hi-fi equipment and computers. Nuclear energy may be used to produce fresh water from saltwater. At any time, what is produced, and how it is produced, depends on what is known. Over time, knowledge changes and so therefore do the costs of producing and, hence, the supplies of commodities.

Sellers' Goals: Earlier in this chapter we noticed that individual suppliers may strive after various goals. We start by assuming that the prime objective is to maximize profits, and we postpone alternative hypotheses until a later chapter. For the present it is sufficient to indicate the nature of some of them.

A supplier may aim, for example, at a high growth rate for its sales as well as profitability. A business may be run by an individual who enjoys taking big risks for big returns, or by someone who is very cautious. A small supplier, in particular, may be under the control of a man or woman whose personal lifestyle exerts an influence over its activities – e.g., the local record shop may be closed every Wednesday so that the owner can play squash. Some businesses may be run on Scrooge-like principles, others with worker satisfaction playing a dominant role. We proceed no further at this point with the consequences of different hypotheses about the goals at which a producer may aim. *Here we only note that quantity supplied is affected by the producer's goal.*

Producers' Income: A producer's net income is his profits. Thus, income enters as a determinant of supply through the assumption of profit maximization.

It may be worth noting, however, that the owners of some small businesses may have target incomes. If the prices of the goods they sell rise, *ceteris paribus*, the producers' incomes also rise. They may elect, instead of producing more, to produce and sell less. By doing so they maintain their target income, and reduce the amount that they have to work.

Expectations of the Future: .Supply can be affected by changes in expectations. If there is an unexpected change in any of the determinants of supply, producers will react after the change has occurred. If, however, the change is foreseen, producers may react to the expectations of the change. Many changes in supply can only be understood as responses to an expected change in one of the variables that influence supply.

'Acts of God': Such forces as disease and weather, which are largely outside the control of man, can sometimes be of immense importance to supply. For example, *ceteris paribus*, a drought will reduce the supply of corn while excellent growing weather will increase it.

Acts of the State: Government regulation can affect supply conditions in a variety of ways. Rules relating to smoke pollution, for instance, control the types of boilers that may be used; while laws prescribing working conditions affect the productivity of labour. Many government policies, such as taxes and subsidies, influence supply decisions by affecting costs of production. Such taxes and subsidies affect quantities supplied by changing the sellers' marginal costs.

Social and Psychological Factors: Under this heading, we include all influences on producer behaviour not elsewhere mentioned, e.g. the state of business confidence, political considerations, etc.

MARKET SUPPLY

To obtain market supply, we need to add together the supplies of all producers in an industry. Let us take a simple case where there are only two producers. We shall call them producer A and producer B. Both producers supply lamb chops.

Suppose the supply schedule and the supply curve of one producer, A, are those shown in Table 6.1 and Figure 6.1 above, which are repeated again now in Table 6.2 and Figure 6.2 together with a second

TABLE 6.2 Individual and Market Supply Schedules

PRICE	QUANTITIES SUPPLIED		
(£s per lb.)	Producer A (lbs. per month)	Producer B (lbs. per month)	Market supply (lbs. per month) (ii) + (iii)
(i)	(ii)	(iii)	(iv)
0.50	0	0	0
1.00	300	0	300
1.50	600	150	750
2.00	900	300	1,200
2.50	1,200	450	1,650
3.00	1,500	600	2,100
3.50	1,800	750	2,550

schedule and curve comprising hypothetical data relating to another producer, B. Note that the minimum price required before producer B will provide anything to the market is higher than that for A.

The derivation of the *market supply schedule* is by simple addition of quantities supplied at each price by the two producers. We see, therefore, that market supply when price is £1.00 per lb. is identical with supply by producer A. At this low price, producer B (which presumably has higher production costs than producer A) does not offer any lamb chops for sale at all. However, at the price of £1.50 a lb., producer A supplies 600 lbs. and producer B supplies 150 lbs. Market supply is therefore 600 + 150 = 750 lbs. The market supply at each of the prices in the table is the sum of columns (ii) and (iii).

Consider next the *market supply curve*. This, of

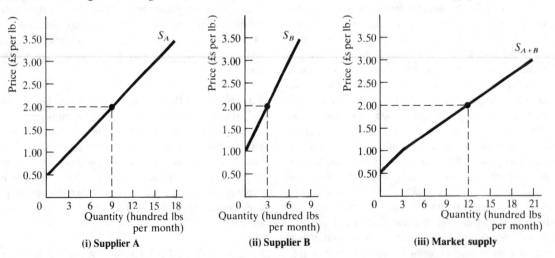

FIGURE 6.2   Derivation of a Market Supply Curve. The market supply curve is the horizontal sum of the supply curves of all sellers in the market

course, can be plotted directly from the combined supply schedule in column (iv) of Table 6.2. But we can also use the geometric method explained in connection with the construction of the market demand curve (see Chapter 4, pp. 51–2). Just as we added, horizontally, the demand curves of two consumers to get the market demand curve, so we can add, horizontally, the supply curves of two producers to get the market supply curve. As the two methods are identical, we shall not repeat the explanation in full. Consider, however, market supply at the price of £2.00 per lb. This is the sum of the 900 and 300 for producers A and B respectively. To find the appropriate point on the market supply curve at the price of £2.00 we mark off a distance equal to the sum of these two quantities, i.e. 1,200, and plot it against £2.00 in the Figure. Repeating the exercise for other prices and joining up the points yields the market supply curve, S_{A+B}.

Shifts in Supply Curves and Movements Along Curves

The supply curves with which economists mainly work are those relating quantity supplied to price. As with demand curves, it is important to make the same distinction between a movement along a curve and a shift of the entire curve. *A change in quantity supplied resulting from a change in price is read as a movement along a supply curve. A change in supply resulting from a change in anything else involves shifting the whole curve.* The shift means that a new and different quantity is

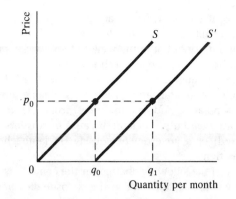

FIGURE 6.3 Shifts of the Supply Curve. A change in the conditions of supply changes the quantity offered for sale at every price

supplied at each market price. Such shifts, arising from changes in one or more of the *ceteris paribus* assumptions, are often referred to as changes in the CONDITIONS OF SUPPLY.

Little further needs to be said in explanation of movements along a supply curve. They are simply readings of quantities supplied at different prices *ceteris paribus*. But it may be helpful to provide a few illustrations of causes of shifts in supply curves, and to explain also the *direction* of the shifts.

Figure 6.3 shows two supply curves for lamb chops, labelled S and S'. S is the original curve. The curve S' implies that larger quantities are supplied at each and every price. For example, at price p_0, the quantity goes from q_0 to q_1.

TABLE 6.3 The Terminology of Supply Curves

Change	Terms Used to Describe the Change
(A) A change in the price of the good causes a MOVEMENT ALONG a supply curve	
1. Price of the good rises.	1. *An increase or rise in the quantity supplied.* An extension of supply.
2. Price of the good falls.	2. *A decrease, fall or reduction in the quantity supplied.*
(B) A change in any of the other influences causes a SHIFT OF a supply curve	
1. A rise in the price of a substitute product. A fall in the price of a factor of production. An improvement in the state of technology (a rise in productivity).	1. *A rightward, downward or southeasterly shift of the supply curve.* An increase in supply. An improvement in the conditions of supply.
2. A fall in the price of a substitute product. A rise in the price of a factor of production. A deterioration in the state of technology (a fall in productivity).	2. *A leftward, upward or northwesterly shift of the supply curve.* A decrease in supply. A deterioration in the conditions of supply.

Note: The terms we use most commonly are italicized.

Any of the following changes in conditions of supply could explain the shift to S': a fall in the price of any input, e.g. a fall in the wage rate of workers in sheep farming; a change in technology, e.g. a cheaper method of slaughtering lambs is introduced; a fall in the price of an alternative product, e.g. if pork chops lose popularity and fall in price, producers may increase their output of lamb because pork is less in demand; or a government subsidy on lamb chop production.

Any of the following changes in the conditions of supply could explain shift in the opposite direction, from S' to S, implying fewer lamb chops supplied at each and every price: a rise in the wages of shepherds; a decline in productivity of workers in abattoirs; a rise in the price of pork chops; spreading of sheep tick disease; or government quotas restricting the output of lamb chops.

The terminology used to describe shifts of supply curves and movements along them by economists is no more standard than in the case of demand. Table 6.3 summarizes the main terms used, and covers the most important factors affecting supply.

Time and Supply

Our only reference to time, so far, in this chapter on supply was when we pointed out that economists think of supplies as *flows* taking place over a period of time. That is why the diagrams containing supply curves had axis labels saying quantity *per period*.

We must recognize, however, that the length of time under consideration can have important implications for the response of suppliers to changes in the price of a good. In general, the longer the time that passes, and the longer a change is expected to last, the greater the likely response.

Note, too, that the time pattern of response may vary from one good to another. In cases where factors of production can be easily switched to alternative outputs, less time is needed for a substantial change than where it is difficult to do so. An example of easy switching is a producer of carrots, who can use his land to grow other crops (though the time between sowing and harvesting provides a lower limit to the time needed for output to change). An example of difficult switching is an aircraft manufacturer. He would have so much specialist equipment that it would probably be many years before he could switch into the easiest alternative type of production.

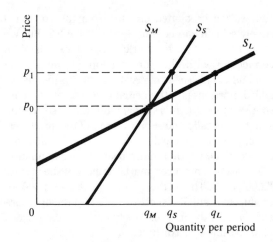

FIGURE 6.4　Supply Curves over Different Time-periods. Momentary, short-run and long-run curves

Three conventional time-periods

The responsiveness of quantity supplied to a change in price increases steadily as time passes. To capture this in a useful but simplified way, economists use three conventional time-periods. They are called momentary,[1] short run and long run.

The first of these, the MOMENTARY period, refers to situations when there is insufficient time to alter production. Although the term 'momentary' is used to describe it, you should notice that the momentary period may cover quite a bit of calendar time. For example, in agriculture it may take up to a year for output to be altered, as a new, larger or smaller crop is planted, grown, harvested and brought to market. The second, the SHORT RUN, refers to a period over which production can be varied within the confines of the producer's productive facilities. A farmer will have a fixed size of farm and a manufacturer fixed plant and equipment. It is possible for producers to take on or lay off labour, and to buy more or less materials. But production is constrained by the given productive facilities. The third, the LONG RUN, refers to a period long enough to change everything that producers wish to change in response to a change in price. New factories can be built, land can be brought

---

1　This period has been given various names over the years, including momentary period, market period or instantaneous period. We have chosen 'momentary' because it seems to be the most commonly used term today.

in from other uses, and more or less labour and other factors of production may be employed. (These distinctions will be discussed in more detail in Chapters 14 and 15.)

Figure 6.4 illustrates the different shapes of the supply curve over these three periods. The curves S_M, S_S and S_L are the momentary, the short-run and the long-run supply curves. Assume that we start with a market price of p_0. The quantity supplied is q_M in all three cases. All three curves go through the present price-quantity combination because they are meant to describe reactions over various periods of time starting from the existing situation.

Consider, now, how quantity supplied varies over time in response to a change in price, resulting perhaps from a switch in consumers' tastes in favour of the commodity. Suppose the new price is p_1. In the momentary period, supply cannot be changed. The quantity offered for sale remains at q_M, so that the supply curve is the vertical line S_M. In the short run, the quantity can be changed somewhat. S_S is the appropriate supply curve and the quantity offered for sale rises from q_M to q_S. In the long run, S_L is the relevant supply curve. Sufficient time is available for the producers to make a full response to the price change. A further increase in supply takes the quantity supplied from q_S to q_L.

Exceptional Supply Curves

We concluded our discussion of the elementary theory of demand in the previous chapter with a section on exceptional demand curves that did not slope downwards as do most demand curves. We conclude this chapter on the same note, with a mention of supply curves which are exceptional in the sense that they do not slope upwards as do all the supply curves that we have drawn so far.

This section is much briefer than that in the previous chapter. The reason is that while upward-sloping supply curves based on rising marginal cost curves are very common in the short run, other slopes are possible, and do indeed occur. In the long run, costs do not always rise as output rises. Indeed, they may remain constant, or even fall, when producers have made full adjustments to their outputs in response to changes such as a rise in demand. In such cases, long-run supply curves will not slope upwards. We deal at length with several possible shapes of all supply curves in Chapter 15.

SUMMARY

1 The theory of supply is concerned with the quantities of a good or service that producers wish to offer for sale per period of time. In the elementary theory of supply, sellers are assumed to seek to maximize their profits and to be price-takers.

2 The quantity supplied of a good depends on many factors. The relationship between own price and quantity supplied, other influencing factors held constant, is represented graphically by a supply curve.

3 A profit-maximizing seller will offer more for sale as price rises if the marginal cost increases as output increases, which leads to a positively sloped supply curve.

4 A seller maximizes profits by producing that level of output for which marginal cost is equal to price.

5 The principal determinants of the supply of a good, other than its own price, are the prices of other goods, the prices of factors of production, the state of technology, the goals of producers, producers' incomes and expectations.

6 Goods are substitutes in production if a change in the price of one good leads to a change in the opposite direction in the supply of another good. Goods are said to be in joint supply if a change in the price of one good leads to a change in the same direction in the supply of another good.

7 Costs of production depend on the prices of factors of production and on their productivity, reflecting the state of technology.

8 Non-economic factors affecting supply include 'acts of God', acts of the state, and social and psychological factors. Economics can analyse the effects of changes in such determinants, but not their causes.

9 A market supply curve is derived by the horizontal summation of the supply curves of all individual sellers in the market.

10 Movements along a supply curve must be sharply distinguished from shifts in the curve itself. Movements along a supply curve show the effects of price changes on quantity supplied, *ceteris paribus*. A supply curve shifts when any determinant of supply other than the price of the good changes (i.e. *ceteris non-paribus*).

11 Supply tends to respond more to a change in the price of a good as the time-period over which adjustment is allowed lengthens. Three time-periods can be distinguished: momentary supply – when there is insufficient time to alter production – short-run supply and long-run supply.

Elasticity of Demand and Supply

Smoking can damage your health. The government has tried to discourage cigarette smoking by banning television advertising and requiring warnings to be printed on cigarette packets. What about trying to use the price mechanism? What about a swingeing increase in the tax on cigarettes? How effective would it be? What would happen to consumption, market price and government revenue?

The government could easily raise tobacco tax to any level it desired. However, the effectiveness of such a measure would depend on the responsiveness of demand to price rises. If smokers continued to smoke nearly as much as before, the only impact would be a large rise in government tax revenue. In contrast, if the price rise led smokers to cut cigarette consumption drastically, the government would achieve its purpose. Between the two rather extreme cases just described, there might be *some* fall in consumption and *some* rise, or fall, in government revenue. Obviously, the government would like to estimate the likely outcome before introducing such a measure. What the government needs to know in order to predict the outcome of its tax is the *elasticity of demand* for cigarettes. Let us see what is involved.

Economists have a special measure for the response of one variable, such as quantity demanded, to changes in another variable, such as price. It is called *elasticity* and it has many uses, as we shall find out in this chapter and beyond. In the present chapter we deal with the responses of two main variables, quantity demanded and quantity supplied, and we refer to these as demand elasticity and supply elasticity.

DEMAND ELASTICITY

We have seen that a large number of variables influence quantity demanded. The response to change in each influencing variable is measured by a separate elasticity concept. We start with the most commonly encountered of all elasticities, price elasticity of demand.

Price Elasticity of Demand

One of the most common applications of the concept of elasticity is to measure the responsiveness of the quantity demanded of some good to changes in its own price. This measure is known as PRICE ELASTICITY OF DEMAND, though we shall follow normal practice and drop the word price when no ambiguity is involved. The first part of this chapter is devoted to explaining this measure.

A formal definition

Price elasticity of demand, sometimes symbolized by the Greek letter η (spelt eta and pronounced eeta), is defined by the following formula:

$$\eta = \frac{\% \text{ change in quantity demanded}}{\% \text{ change in price}}$$

This formula tells us that the elasticity of demand is calculated by dividing the percentage change in quantity demanded by the percentage change in price which brought it about.

To see what is involved, consider two examples. In the first case, the price of product X *falls* by 2 per cent and the quantity demanded *increases* by 4 per cent. The elasticity of demand for product X is thus $4\%/-2\% = -2$. In the second case, the price of product Y also falls by 2 per cent while the quantity demanded *rises* by only 1 per cent. The elasticity of demand for product Y is thus $1\%/-2\% = -0.5$. We see that (ignoring the negative sign for the moment) product X's elasticity of 2 is higher than product Y's elasticity of 0.5. This tells us that the demand for X is more responsive to this particular price change than is the demand for product Y.

The negative sign of elasticity as measured above arises because that price and quantity demanded are negatively associated (i.e. the slope of demand curve is negative). If prices rise then quantity demanded falls, and the value of the denominator in the elasticity formula is positive, while the value of the numerator is negative. If price falls quantity demand rises, and the denominator is negative, while the numerator is positive. In both cases, elasticity is negative, since the change in price and the change in quantity have opposite signs.

In practice, the sign is often ignored and elasticity is treated as a positive number. We shall follow this common practice. (Note, however, that when numerical estimates of actual elasticities are reported elsewhere, they often have their negative signs attached.)

There are some other important aspects of the formula to which we shall shortly return. First, however, let us familiarize ourselves with the concept itself. The formula for elasticity is a fraction: the percentage change in quantity demanded *divided by* the percentage change in price that brought it about. If the value of the fraction is one, then percentage changes in price and quantity are equal. If the percentage change in quantity demanded is greater than the percentage change in price, the fraction will have a value greater than one. If the percentage change in quantity demanded is less than the percentage change in price, the numerical value will be less than one.

Demand curves which have an elasticity greater than one are called ELASTIC. Those which have a value less than one are called INELASTIC. Those which have a value of elasticity exactly equal to one are called UNIT ELASTIC, or are said to have an elasticity of *unity*.

If a demand curve has an elasticity of, say, 2, that means that the percentage change in quantity is double the percentage change in price. If elasticity is $\frac{1}{2}$, the percentage change in quantity is half the percentage change in price. If the elasticity is 1, the percentage changes in price and quantity are of the same magnitude (although, as always, they have opposite signs).

Elasticity of demand and changes in total outlay

Money spent in purchasing a commodity is received by the sellers of the commodity. The total amount spent by purchasers is, thus, the gross revenue of the sellers. How does total amount spent on purchases of biscuits, for example, or, what is the same thing, total gross revenue received by biscuit sellers, react when the price of a product is changed? The simplest example will show that total expenditure (expressed in monetary units, not percentages) may either rise or fall in response to a decrease in price. Suppose 100 units of a commodity are being sold at a unit price of £1. The price is then cut to £0.90. If the quantity sold rises to 105 units, the total revenue of the sellers falls from £100 to £94.50. But if quantity sold rises to 120 units, total revenue rises from £100 to £108.

What happens to total outlay is related to the price elasticity of demand. If elasticity is less than unity (that is, less than one), the percentage change in price will exceed the percentage change in quantity. The price change will then dominate, so that total outlay will change in the same direction as the price change. If, however, elasticity exceeds unity, the percentage change in quantity will exceed the percentage change in price. The quantity change will then be dominant, so that total outlay will change in the same direction as quantity changes, and in the opposite direction to the change in price. When elasticity is exactly unity, the two changes in price and quantity cancel each other out. If price falls, for example, by 5 per cent while quantity demanded rises by 5 per cent, total outlay remains unchanged.

This discussion illustrates the following general relationships:

- If demand is elastic, a fall in price increases total outlay and a rise in price reduces it.
- If demand is inelastic, a fall in price reduces total outlay and a rise in price increases it.
- If elasticity of demand is unity, a rise or a fall in price leaves total outlay unaffected.

The results of this section are summarized in Table 7.1.

TABLE 7.1 Total Outlay with Different Elasticities of Demand

Description	Elasticity Value	Total Outlay
Elastic	Greater than 1 ($\eta > 1$)	Rises for a price fall; falls for a price rise
Inelastic	Less than 1 ($\eta < 1$)	Rises for a price rise; falls for a price fall
Unity	Equal to 1 ($\eta = 1$)	Unchanged as price rises or falls

A technical problem

In order to explain the meaning and significance of elasticity of demand, we have deliberately avoided a small technical problem associated with the calculation of percentages. We must now face that problem.

When we calculate a percentage change we must define the change as a percentage of something. Consider the data in Table 7.2. Let the price of sausages fall from £1 to 50p. We could show this as a change of 50 per cent by calculating the change as a percentage of the original price of £1: $(0.5/1.0 \times 100 = 50$ per cent).

However, we could just as well have been considering the effects of a rise in price from 50p to £1. The original price would then have been 50p. In this case the 50p *change* in price would have emerged as 100 per cent $(50/50 \times 100 = 100$ per cent) of the price of 50p.

The problem arises with percentage changes in quantity as well as in price. The quantity demanded rises by 100 lbs. when price falls from £1 to 50p per lb. This quantity may be taken as a percentage of quantity demanded at the higher price (10,000) or of the amount demanded at the lower price (10,100). The former would give a percentage rise of 1 per cent $(100/10,000 \times 100 = 1$ per cent). The latter would give a percentage change of 0.99 per cent $(100/10,100 \times 100 = 0.99$ per cent).

None of this is very satisfactory, since it makes the elasticity between any two points on the demand curve depend on the direction of movement. To avoid this problem, we take the price changes as percentages of the *average* of the higher and the lower price; and we take the quantity changes as percentages of the *average* of the higher and the lower quantities. This gives us a single value of elasticity of demand between any two points on a demand curve.

We are now able to calculate the elasticity of demand for sausages between the price of £1.00 and £0.50 from the data given in Table 7.2. Note first that the *average* price is £0.75, while the price change is £0.50. This makes the percentage change in price $(0.5/0.75)100 = 66.7$ per cent. Similarly, the change in quantity is 100 units and the *average* quantity is 10,050, making the percentage change in quantity $(100/10,050)100 = 0.995$ per cent. Now, dividing the percentage change in quantity by the percentage change in price yields 0.01 (i.e. 0.995/66.7). This shows the demand for sausages is highly inelastic over the price range between £1 and £0.50, i.e. it has a value well below unity. Notice, also, that since the demand is inelastic, we expect a fall in price to reduce total expenditure on the product. The calculations in the last column of the table confirms this. Total outlay at the lower price is barely more than half of total outlay at the higher price.

Arc elasticity of demand

Our formula for elasticity is now seen to be a fraction, in which the numerator is the change in quantity *as a percentage of the average quantities at the higher and the lower price*, and the denominator is the change in price *as a percentage of the average of the higher and the lower prices*. Writing this in symbols, the formula defines what is known as the ARC (or AVERAGE) ELASTICITY OF DEMAND. To do this, we let p_0 and q_0 stand for the original price and quantity, and p_1 and q_1 for the new price and quantity:

$$\text{Arc } \eta_d = \frac{\dfrac{q_1 - q_0}{\dfrac{q_1 + q_2}{2}} \times 100}{\dfrac{p_0 - p_1}{\dfrac{p_0 + p_1}{2}} \times 100}$$

TABLE 7.2 Two Price–Quantity Points on a Demand Curve for Sausages

Price (£s per lb.)	Quantity (lbs.)	Total outlay (i) × (ii) (£s)
(i)	(ii)	(iii)
1.00	10,000	10,000
0.50	10,100	5,050

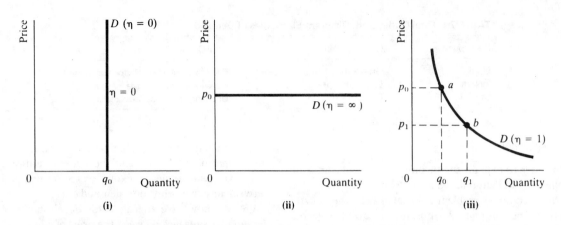

FIGURE 7.1   **Three Cases of Demand Elasticity.** The only two straight-line demand curves with a constant elasticity are vertical and horizontal

The formula for arc elasticity of demand now looks rather complicated. We can simplify it considerably in three steps.

First, we use the commonly employed symbol of the greek letter Delta, Δ, instead of 'change in'. Also, we write P and Q to stand for the average price and the average quantity respectively. This gives us

$$\eta = \left(\frac{\Delta q}{Q} \times 100 \right) \div \left(\frac{\Delta p}{P} \times 100 \right),$$

which can also be written

$$\eta = \frac{\dfrac{\Delta q}{Q} \times 100}{\dfrac{\Delta p}{P} \times 100}.$$

Second, we cancel out the 100s from the denominator and the numerator. This tells us that the *ratio* of proportionate changes is the same as the corresponding ratio of percentage changes:

$$\eta = \frac{\dfrac{\Delta q}{Q}}{\dfrac{\Delta p}{P}}.$$

Third, we invert the denominator so that we can multiply by it. To do this we multiply the numerator and the denominator by $P/\Delta p$ to obtain:

$$\eta = \frac{\Delta q}{Q} \times \frac{p}{\Delta p}.$$

Now, since the order in which we write terms is of no consequence, we can rewrite the above to obtain

$$\eta = \frac{\Delta q}{\Delta p} \times \frac{P}{Q}.$$

This last is our final formula for the calculation of elasticity of demand. It has the same meaning as the formula on page 73 of this chapter, and we shall find it a convenient form for considering the meaning of elasticity when looking at graphs of demand curves.

Elasticity of demand is a measure so widely used in economics that you should make sure that you have mastered the technique of calculating it. Let us give you another example of how to do so, using the above formula, and letting P and Q stand for the average price and the average quantity respectively.[1]

Suppose two points on a demand curve are (i) price £10, quantity sold 550 and (ii) price £9, quantity sold 590. To find the value of the arc elasticity of demand, apply the formula

$$(\Delta q / \Delta p)(P/Q)$$

Δq is the change in quantity, which is 590–550 = 40.

---

1 Note that the formula can be used to calculate not only the elasticity of demand, but also the effects of a change in price for a given elasticity, if sufficient other information is also provided. Thus, suppose you are told that a certain good has a demand elasticity of 2 and that price is lowered by 1 per cent. You can use the formula to find the new quantity demanded, provided you are given the old quantity. If elasticity of demand is 2, the percentage change in quantity is double the percentage change in price, i.e. two times 1 per cent equals 2 per cent. So quantity demanded increases by 2 per cent when price falls by 1 per cent. If you are given the old quantity demanded, you can calculate the new quantity demanded. Say the old quantity is 50; the new quantity at the lower price will be 50 plus 2 per cent of 50, which is 54.

Δp is the change in price, which is £10 − £9 = £1.

P is the average price, which is the average of £10 and £9 = £9.50.

Q is the average quantity, which is the average of 550 and 590 = 570.

Putting the numbers into the formula we get

$$\eta = (40/1)(9.5/570) = \tfrac{2}{3}.$$

The elasticity of demand is therefore $\tfrac{2}{3}$.

Graphical interpretation of price elasticity

As long as demand curves do not have positive slopes, the value of elasticity can vary between zero and infinity. It is convenient to approach the graphical interpretion of elasticity from the viewpoint of these limiting cases.

Elasticity of Demand is Zero ($\eta = 0$):   Figure 7.1 (i) depicts a demand curve where the same amount q_0 is demanded at all prices. Since the percentage change in quantity is zero whatever the percentage change in price, elasticity calculated from our formula will always be zero. Such a demand curve is called PERFECTLY or COMPLETELY INELASTIC.

Elasticity of Demand is Infinite ($\eta = \infty$):   Figure 7.1 (ii) depicts a demand curve where consumers are prepared to buy all they can obtain at the market price of p_0, while the smallest possible rise in price above p_0 causes demand to fall to zero. Put the other way around, the smallest possible fall in price from just above p_0 increases demand from nothing to an indefinitely large amount. This demand curve is called PERFECTLY or COMPLETELY ELASTIC at the price p_0. (This rather unlikely sounding case turns out to be important when, later in the book, we come to study the behaviour of suppliers under conditions called perfect competition.)

Elasticity of Demand is Unity ($\eta = 1$):   A third key case is where demand is neither elastic nor inelastic, but equal to unity. Here total outlay by consumers is the same at different prices because changes in price are exactly offset by equal proportionate changes in quantities bought.

We make use of this property to draw a demand curve of unit elasticity throughout its length. Total outlay is price times quantity. In graphical terms, price is a length and quantity is a length and total outlay, price times quantity, is therefore an area. In

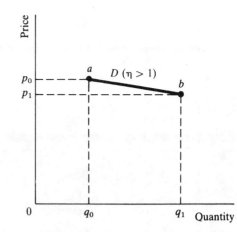

FIGURE 7.2   Relatively Elastic Demand. Total expenditure is higher at the lower price

Figure 7.1 (iii), we draw a demand curve of unit elasticity. Consider the point on this curve labelled a. At price p_0 quantity demanded is q_0. Total outlay is $p_0 \times q_0$, which is the area Op_0aq_0. Since, by definition, unit demand elasticity implies equal total outlay at different prices, the area Op_1bq_1, which represents the total outlay at price p_1, must equal the area Op_0aq_0. The two areas must be equal, not only to each other, but also to areas representing total outlay at every other price. (The demand curve is known mathematically as a rectangular hyperbola, which means that the areas of all rectangles enclosed by dropping perpendiculars from any point on the curve to the two axes are equal.)[1]

Elastic Demand: The argument to explain the nature of a demand curve of unit elasticity can be extended to intermediate cases, where elasticity lies between 0 and 1, and between 1 and ∞. Figure 7.2 shows a portion of a demand curve the elasticity of which is greater than unity, but less than infinite. It is an elastic demand curve over the range between points a and b. You will remember that an elastic demand is one where the proportionate change in quantity is greater than the proportionate change in price which brought it about. This means too, as we explained, that the total outlay by consumers is greater at the lower price. Total outlay at price p_0 is

---

1 The equation for a rectangular hyperbola is $pq = C$, where C is a constant equal to total outlay on the product, and p and q are price and quantity.

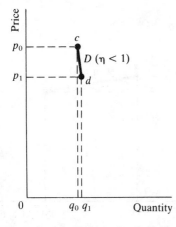

FIGURE 7.3   Relatively Inelastic Demand. Total expenditure is lower at the lower price

Op_0aq_0, whereas total outlay at the lower price p_1 is Op_1bq_1. Op_1bq_1 is greater than Op_0aq_0; hence the demand curve is relatively elastic between the prices of p_0 and p_1.

Inelastic Demand: The final case to be considered is one where demand elasticity lies between 0 (perfectly inelastic) and unity. The demand curve shown in Figure 7.3 is inelastic between the points c and d. The proportionate change in quantity demanded here is less than the proportionate change in price. Total outlay by consumers is, therefore, greater at the higher price than at the lower. Total outlay at the higher price p_0 in Figure 7.3, is Op_0cq_0. This is greater than total outlay at the lower price, p_1, which is Op_1dq_1.

Measuring the elasticity of a demand curve

The careful reader will have noticed that in the previous two sections we did not refer to the demand *curves* as being relatively elastic and relatively inelastic but to *portions* of demand curves *between the two prices* we were considering. This is because the elasticity of demand normally varies between different points on one demand curve.

Linear Demand Curves: The above point is easily illustrated by showing that the elasticity of a straight-line (called a LINEAR) demand curve is different at all points along it.

Consider the elasticity formula $\eta = \Delta q/\Delta p \times P/Q$. The first term, $\Delta q/\Delta p$, is the reciprocal of the slope of

the demand curve. (The slope itself is $\Delta p/\Delta q$.) Since the demand curve is a straight line, the slope of the curve, and hence its reciprocal, must be the same all along it. Thus the slope $\Delta p/\Delta q$ in Figure 7.4 is the same when price goes from p_0 to p_1 (and quantity from q_0 to q_1) as when price goes from p_2 to p_3 (and quantity from q_2 to q_3).

The elasticity of demand is *not*, however, the same everywhere on the curve. Recall that the formula is $\Delta q/\Delta p(P/Q)$. It is true that the *first term* in the formula *is* constant along the demand curve, but there is a second term, P/Q, price divided by quantity. This term varies along the demand curve. Near its upper end, P is high and Q is low so the ratio P/Q is large. Near the lower end, P is low and Q is high, so the ratio P/Q is small. It follows that *elasticity falls as we move downwards to the right along a linear demand curve*. Finally, consider the two end-points of the curve. Where it cuts the quantity axis P is zero, so P/Q is zero, so elasticity is zero. Where it cuts the price axis Q is zero, so P/Q is infinite, so elasticity is infinite.[1] We conclude that the elasticity of a straight-line demand curve varies from infinity, where the curve cuts the price axis, to zero where it cuts the quantity axis.

Figure 7.4 shows the sections of the demand curve

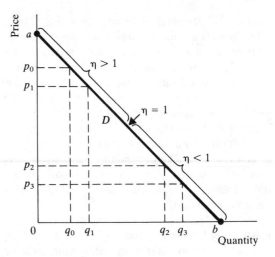

FIGURE 7.4   Elasticity on a Linear Demand Curve. Along a linear demand curve, the higher the price the higher the elasticity

---

1 Strictly speaking, division by zero is an inadmissible operation. But as q-gets smaller and smaller, the ratio p/q increases without limit – which is what we mean when we say loosely that its value is infinite when q is zero.

labelled with their corresponding elasticities. Notice that at the mid-point along the curve, demand elasticity is exactly unity.[1] Below that point, demand elasticity varies between 0 and 1; it is relatively inelastic – marked in Figure 7.4 as $\eta < 1$ (meaning less than unity). Above that point, demand elasticity varies between 1 and ∞; it is relatively elastic, marked in Figure 7.4 as $\eta > 1$ (meaning greater than unity).

The intuition of the variable elasticity is that the constant slope of a straight line indicates a constant absolute reaction of quantity (Δq) to a constant absolute change in price (Δp), while the elasticity refers to percentage changes. If we move down the demand curve making equal absolute changes in price and quantity, these represent small percentage changes in P and large percentage changes in Q near the top of the curve (elasticity high) and large percentage changes in P and small percentage changes in Q near the bottom of the curve (elasticity low).

Curvilinear Demand Curves: If you draw a non-linear demand curve at random, it will very probably also have an elasticity that varies over its length. There are, however, non-linear curves that have constant elasticities over their whole lengths. We already know one. The demand curve when elasticity is equal to unity is a rectangular hyperbola, with the equation $PQ = C$.

The method of calculating elasticity on non-linear curves involves drawing a tangent to the curve in order to find the slope at a point, which gives the first term of the formula. We do not go into this method more fully here.[2]

Determinants of demand elasticity

The size of the elasticity of demand differs from commodity to commodity and is an empirical matter, i.e. it is a question of fact about the real world. We can, however, make some generalizations about the determinants of elasticity. We do so under two main heads: the nature of the good, and the length of time under consideration.

The Nature of the Good: There are three aspects that need consideration under this heading: availability of substitutes, the definition of the good and income effects.

(i) *Availability of substitutes.* Undoubtedly the most important is the availability of close substitutes. Some commodities, such as margarine, cabbage, pork and Ford cars have quite close substitutes – butter, cauliflower, beef and Datsun cars, for example, A change in the price of such commodities, *the prices of substitutes remaining constant,* will cause quite substantial substitutions. A fall in the commodity's price will lead consumers to buy much more of the commodity in question, and much less of the substitute; a rise in the commodity's price will lead consumers to buy much less of the commodity, and much more of its substitute. Demand is, therefore, quite responsive to price changes, and elasticity is high. Other commodities, such as salt, housing, and all vegetables taken as a group, have few, if any, satisfactory substitutes. A rise in their prices will cause a smaller fall in quantities demanded than if close substitutes had been available. In these cases, demand is relatively unresponsive to price changes and elasticity of demand is, therefore, low.

Note that the argument about the availability of substitutes has not been couched in terms of a division of commodities into two sets called 'luxuries' and 'necessities'. This is partly because studies of demand do not in practice show groups of commodities falling clearly into these two categories. Instead there is continuous spread of values of measured elasticities, running from the very low to the very high. Moreover, the definition of 'luxury' and 'necessity' varies tremendously from one individual to another, and it is quite closely associated with income. In consequence, there are many goods which could be loosely termed 'luxuries' but which may have low elasticities of demand. Rolls Royce cars, for example, are certainly 'luxury' items for most of us, but, for the relevant (high) income groups who buy them, a rise in their price may not discourage purchases by a large amount.

(ii) *Definition of the good.* The elasticity of demand depends on how closely a good is defined. The reason for this is related to the question of the availability of substitutes, just discussed. Consider, for instance, the examples we used to illustrate goods with relatively elastic demands – cabbages and cauliflowers. Compare them with all vegetables taken as a group, which we cited as illustrative of inelastic demand. What this

---

1 For those who would like to see it, a proof of this proposition is given in the Appendix to this Chapter.
2 See, however, Appendix to Chapter 1, p. 566, and IPE.

comparison illustrates is the narrower the definition, the more likely it is that a good will have close substitutes and, therefore, will have a relatively elastic demand. For example, elasticity of demand is very high for 1 litre black Mini Metros. Substitutes include all other-colour Mini Metros, other-engine-size Mini Metros, and all other makes of car. The elasticity of demand for 1 litre Mini Metros of all colours, taken as a group, must be less than that for 1 litre black Mini Metros because the closeness of substitutes is less – other-colour Mini Metros are no longer possible substitutes. The elasticity of demand for Mini Metros of any engine size or colour must be less still, because other-engine-size Metros are also excluded from the possible substitutes. You can continue the chain at your will, defining the commodity more and more widely, with the effect that you reduce the elasticity of demand. You may end up considering the elasticity of demand for all cars, which will be lower than the average elasticity for all sub-groups of cars. Why? Because there are fewer close substitutes of cars in general than for any single model.

We are not just inventing distinctions for their own sake. How widely or narrowly a good is defined depends on the problem at hand. For example, a general blight that destroys all vegetable crops will make its effects felt against a relatively inelastic demand for vegetables. But a cauliflower worm that attacks only that vegetable will make its effects felt against a relatively elastic demand for that one vegetable.

(iii) *Income effects*. It is sometimes argued that the smaller the percentage of a consumers' income spent on a good, the less the elasticity of demand. Examples are then chosen of goods such as matches and salt to illustrate the supposed truth of the statement. The impression is given that demand is largely unaffected by price changes because no one notices price changes with commodities that take up little of one's expenditure.

The examples chosen do happen to have low elasticities. But the reason is the one already given: they have few, if any, satisfactory substitutes. There is no reason to assume, however, that such goods have low elasticities *merely because* they take up little of a consumer's income. In the case of matches, some substitutes do exist (e.g., gas lighters), but they are few and not very satisfactory for all purposes. That is why the elasticity of demand for matches taken as a whole is relatively low. However, the elasticity of demand for any one brand of matches, expenditure on which is an even lower proportion of consumers' total expenditure, is likely to be high, because consumers can switch to other brands of matches. Consider another example. Polo mints undoubtedly take up a very small proportion of consumers' expenditure. But does anyone doubt that a significant rise in their price would lead to a large fall in purchases as mint suckers switched to other less expensive types of sweet? (Evidently the producers of Polo mints do not think they face a very low elasticity! If they did, they would increase their price and enlarge their profits, since their revenues would rise if the elasticity of demand really was less than unity.)

Time and Elasticity: In Chapter 3 we pointed out that the longer the period of time under consideration, the greater we would expect the effect of a change in the price of a good to be on the quantity demanded. All we need to do now is to couch this same discussion in terms of elasticity. We suggested several reasons why demand responds more in the long term than in the short term. First, news of price changes takes time to percolate through the whole community. Second, habits take time to be broken. Third, the commodity itself may be durable, so that the full reaction does not occur until all of the existing stock has been replaced. Fourth, full adjustments require a lot of time whenever the commodity in question is used along with a durable complement (as, for example, petrol is with cars). These reasons cause elasticities of demand for many goods to be greater the longer the time-period considered.

For example a large fall in the price of imported cars will not make everyone discard their domestic-made cars immediately, but as these cars are replaced, more buyers may switch to imported cars. The result may be a small response to the price reduction over a month, quite a large response over a year and a massive response over five years.

Other Demand Elasticities

The concept of elasticity of demand can be broadened to measure the response of quantity demanded to *any* of the factors that influence demand. Besides the price of the good itself, we often need to know how changes both in income and in the prices of other commodities affect quantities demanded.

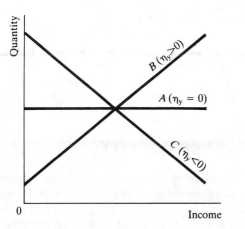

FIGURE 7.5   Income Elasticity of Demand for 3 Goods. Three goods with positive, zero and negative income elasticities

Income elasticity of demand

As incomes rise, consumers increase their demands for many commodities. In richer countries, the demand for food and basic clothing does not increase with income nearly as much as does the demand for many durable goods and many kinds of service.

The responsiveness of demand to changes in income is measured with a concept called the INCOME ELASTICITY OF DEMAND, denoted by η_y and defined as

$$\eta_y = \frac{\%\ \text{change in quantity demanded}}{\%\ \text{change in income}}$$

Normal and Inferior Goods: Income elasticity varies from plus infinity to minus infinity. For most commodities, increases in income lead to increases in quantity demanded. You may remember from Chapter 4 that they are called 'normal' goods in contrast to

'inferior' goods where demand falls as income rises. The principal subdivisions of income elasticity of demand are related to these two categories. Normal goods have positive income elasticities; inferior goods have negative elasticities. The boundary between them is zero income elasticity, corresponding to the case where a change in income leaves quantity demanded unchanged. Figure 7.5 shows the relationship between income and quantity demanded for the three types of good.

(Note these are *not* the familiar demand curves relating quantity to price. Income is measured on the horizontal axis, and quantity on the vertical axis.) Good A has zero income elasticity of demand. Good B is a normal good with a positive income elasticity ($\eta_y > 0$). Good C is an inferior good with a negative income elasticity ($\eta_y < 0$).

Normal goods are much more common than inferior goods. Notice, however, that a good does not have to be in the same category at all levels of income. This is illustrated in Figure 7.6. Four stages are shown for an income elasticity which might be typical of the relationship between income and the demand for cheap table wine. At low incomes, less than y_0, no wine is demanded. Income elasticity of demand is zero over this range of income. As income rises between y_0 and y_1, the quantity demanded increases as consumers buy more of it. Income elasticity of demand is positive over this range of income. At income levels between y_1 and y_2, income elasticity returns to zero as consumers buy no more despite rising income. At income levels greater than y_2, the cheap wine becomes an inferior good. Income elasticity is now negative, because consumers substitute better vintage wines for the cheap, table variety.

This example helps to emphasize that income

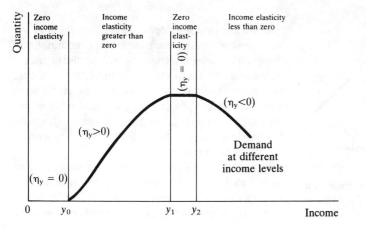

FIGURE 7.6   Income Elasticity of Demand Varies as Income Varies. The demand curve drawn shows income elasticity of zero, greater than unity and less than unity as income rises

elasticity is related to standards of living. As incomes rise in Third World countries, therefore, one expects to find the demand for such goods as television sets, cars and refrigerators moving into the range of high positive income elasticities of demand; while in rich countries, the demands for the same goods have become relatively income inelastic.

Consider also the relationship between income elasticity of demand and total outlay by consumers. When income elasticity is positive, total outlay rises with income, regardless of the numerical value of elasticity. When income elasticity is negative, total outlay falls as income rises.

Cross Elasticity of Demand

We have already seen that the quantity demanded of a good can be affected by changes in the price of other goods. The responsiveness of demand to changes in the price of *another* good is known as the CROSS ELASTICITY OF DEMAND. It is denoted by η_{xy} and defined as

$$\eta_{xy} = \frac{\% \text{ change in the quantity of good } X}{\% \text{ change in the price of good } Y}$$

The value of cross elasticity of demand can vary between minus infinity and plus infinity. Goods which are substitutes for each other have positive elasticities. Goods which are complements to each other have negative elasticities. One would, therefore, expect butter to have a positive cross elasticity of demand with respect to changes in the price of margarine, because a fall in the price of margarine would lead consumers to substitute it for butter. The

relationship would be as in Figure 7.7 (i). As the price of margarine falls, the demand for butter falls too. In contrast, the cross elasticity of demand for ski boots with respect to the price of skis is likely to be negative. A fall in the price of skis would lead to an increase in demand for ski boots, as in Figure 7.7 (ii).

SUPPLY ELASTICITY

Just as elasticity of demand measures the response of quantity demanded to changes in any of the factors that influence it, so *elasticity of supply* measures the response of quantity supplied to changes in any of the factors that influence supply. Because we are focusing mainly on the commodity's own price as the factor influencing supply, we shall be concerned mainly with *price elasticity of supply*. We follow the usual practice of dropping the adjective 'price' and referring simply to 'elasticity of supply' wherever there is no ambiguity in this usage.

Supply elasticities are very important in economics. We shall devote less space to the elasticity of supply than we have to elasticity of demand, however, because they have much in common, as will soon become clear.

A Formal Definition

ELASTICITY OF SUPPLY is defined as the percentage change in quantity supplied divided by the percentage change in price which brought it about. Letting the Greek letter epsilon, ϵ, stand for elasticity of supply, its formula is

$$\epsilon = \frac{\% \text{ change in quantity supplied}}{\% \text{ change in price}}$$

With the upward-sloping supply curves that we have used so far, the numerator and denominator of the fraction both have the same sign – a rise in price is associated with an increase in quantity supplied, and vice versa. The value of elasticity of supply in such cases is therefore positive. As with demand, it is best to calculate percentages on the average of higher and lower prices and quantities, and to use the concept of arc elasticity (see above, p. 76).

Note that the relationship between elasticity and total outlay which we observed in the case of price elasticity of demand does *not* apply to supply curves which are positively sloped. Such supply curves show

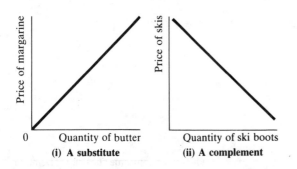

(i) A substitute   **(ii) A complement**

FIGURE 7.7   **Quantity Demanded at Varying Prices of a Substitute and a Complement.** Cross elasticity of demand for substitute goods is positive and for complements is negative

that price and quantity are positively associated, i.e. when price rises quantity also rises; when price falls quantity also falls. It follows that sellers' total receipts (i.e. prices times quantity) must always rise when price rises, and vice versa, whatever the value of the elasticity of supply. However, total receipts rise more, for a given change in price, the greater is the elasticity of supply.

Graphical Interpretation of Elasticity of Supply

Figure 7.8 illustrates the two limiting cases of supply elasticity. The vertical supply curve (labelled $\epsilon = 0$) is perfectly inelastic, i.e. has zero supply elasticity. The same quantity q_0 is offered for sale regardless of price. The horizontal supply curve (labelled $\epsilon = \infty$) has infinite elasticity. Suppliers would be prepared to offer an unlimited amount at the price p_0 – but even the smallest fall in price would reduce the quantity supplied to zero. Such a curve is often described as being perfectly (or completely) elastic.

Figure 7.9 shows four supply curves. The two labelled $\epsilon = 1$ have unit elasticity, as do *all* straight-line supply curves passing through the origin. This is because the proportionate change in price and quantity are the same at all points on such curves. The curve labelled $\epsilon > 1$ is relatively elastic, as is any straight-line supply curve intersecting the price axis. The curve labelled $\epsilon < 1$ is relatively inelastic, as is any straight-line supply curve which would, if projected, intersect the quantity axis.[1]

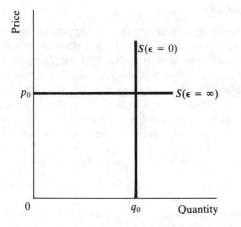

FIGURE 7.8 Perfectly Elastic and Perfectly Inelastic Supply Curves. If $\epsilon = \infty$, the amount supplied at price p_0 is infinite; if $\epsilon = 0$, the same amount is supplied at every price

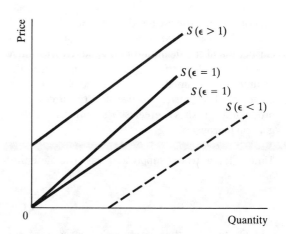

FIGURE 7.9 Relatively Elastic, Inelastic and Unit Elastic Supply Curves. If $\epsilon = 1$, the supply curve passes through the origin of the graph; if $\epsilon > 1$, the supply curve cuts the price axis; if $\epsilon < 1$, the supply curve cuts the quantity axis

Determinants of Elasticity of Supply

As we explained in Chapter 6, upward-sloping supply curves are based on the assumption of rising marginal costs. We emphasized that there are important exceptions to this upward slope (to be considered in Chapter 15). We confine ourselves here to pointing out the relevance of two aspects of elasticity of supply that are similar to the case of elasticity of demand. They are the nature of the good and the relevance of the time-period used for estimating elasticity.

The Nature of the Good: As with demand elasticity, the principal determinant under this head is the availability of substitutes. There is, however, an important distinction between the interpretation of the word 'substitutes' for supply and for demand. In the case of supply, substitute goods are those to which factors of production can most easily be transferred, not those goods which are substitutes in the minds of consumers. For example, a producer may easily move from producing spanners to producing screwdrivers, even though consumers will not regard these products as close substitutes. Mobility of factors of production is also relevant. The more easily factors can be transferred from the production of one good to

---

1 As drawn in Figure 7.9, the intersection of the supply curve ($\epsilon < 1$) with the quantity axis at a positive quantity implies that such an amount is supplied, as it were, 'free', but that a positive price must be paid to call forth supplies greater than this. See IPE.

that of another, the greater the elasticity of supply.

Exactly the same point may be made about supply elasticity and the definition of a good, as was made about demand elasticity. The more narrowly the commodity is defined, the greater the elasticity. For example, it is easier to transfer resources from producing red skirts to green skirts than from skirts in general to trousers.

Time: It is as true of supply as it was of demand that

elasticity tends to be greater the longer the time-period over which it is measured. The longer the period, the easier it is to shift factors of production among products, following a change in their relative prices. This argument has particular force for many agricultural products, because of the natural time-lag between planting and harvesting of crops. The argument is also strong when long-lasting and costly capital equipment may continue to be used after a fall in demand, but not replaced when it wears out.

SUMMARY

1 Elasticity is the economist's measure of the response of one variable, such as quantity, to changes in another variable, such as price.
   The price elasticity of demand is defined as percentage change in quantity demanded divided by percentage change in price.

2 Demand elasticity varies between zero (called perfectly inelastic) and infinity (called perfectly elastic). When elasticity of demand is equal to unity, a given percentage change in price is associated with a percentage change in quantity demanded of the same magnitude.

3 When demand is elastic (value greater than unity), consumers' total outlay changes in the opposite direction to a change in price. When demand is inelastic (value less than unity), consumers' total outlay changes in the same direction as a change in price. When demand is unit elastic, consumers' total outlay does not change when price changes.

4 Two problems in calculating elasticities with numerical data are encountered: (1) although technically elasticity of demand is a negative number, the minus sign is usually ignored in elementary treatments, and (2) to avoid ambiguities in calculating percentages, the arc elasticity formula is used, in which percentages are calculated on average prices and average quantities.

5 The value of elasticity varies at every point on a linear demand curve, other than the case of perfectly elastic demand curves, which are horizontal lines, and perfectly inelastic demand curves, which are vertical lines; unit elastic demand curves are rectangular hyperbolae.

6 The elasticity of demand for a commodity tends to be greater the more good substitutes there are for it, the more narrowly the commodity is defined, and the longer the time-period.

7 The income elasticity of demand is defined as percentage change in quantity demanded divided by percentage change in income. It varies between plus and minus infinity. It is positive for normal goods and negative for inferior goods.

8 The cross elasticity of demand between any two goods x and y is defined as percentage change in quantity of good x demanded divided by percentage change in price of good y. It varies between plus and minus infinity. Substitute goods have positive cross elasticities, while complements have negative elasticities.

9 The elasticity of supply is defined as percentage change in quantity supplied divided by percentage change in price. It varies between plus and minus infinity.

10 Elasticity of supply may be interpreted graphically. It may be estimated at any point of a supply curve. The value of elasticity of supply varies at every point of a supply curve. The value of elasticity of supply varies at every point on a linear supply curve, other than perfectly elastic supply curves, which are horizontal lines, perfectly inelastic supply curves, which are vertical lines, and unit elastic supply curves, which are straight lines through the origin of the graph.

11 The elasticity of supply for a commodity tends to be greater the more good substitute commodities there are to which factors of production can be transferred, the more narrowly a commodity is defined, and the longer the time-period.

Market Price Determination

In the first part of this book we gave an intuitive description of how the pricing system allocates resources. In this part we have been going over the same ground, only in a more formal and elaborate manner. Now, in this chapter and the two which follow, we are ready to put supply and demand together and see how they interact in markets.

All of the definitions and assumptions introduced in the previous two chapters still hold. In addition we need to remind you of two concepts previously encountered, that of a market and *ceteris paribus*.

The Market: The key concept in this chapter is the market. This is any kind of institutional arrangement whereby buyers and sellers communicate with each other to buy and sell a commodity. The market is our stage. The players on the demand side are consumers who wish to buy goods and, on the supply side, are producers who offer goods for sale. We have already made the key assumptions about the behaviour of these two groups. Consumers aim to maximize the satisfactions that are derived from their purchases, while producers attempt to maximize their profits. We have also assumed that both groups are price-takers, being unable, individually, to affect market prices by changing the quantities they supply or demand.

Ceteris Paribus: The analysis uses the *ceteris paribus* assumption, that everything that affects the quantity of a good demanded and supplied is held constant except the price of the good itself. We have called this the 'own price' of the commodity. Later we shall drop the assumption, so that we can study the effect of other influences.

PRICE DETERMINATION

In Chapters 4 and 6 we derived market demand and supply curves by adding together the curves of two consumers, and of two suppliers.

Table 8.1 sets out hypothetical data for market demand and market supply for bottles of table wine. This is a market that contains thousands of buyers and scores of sellers, no one of whom is important enough to influence the market price by altering his or her own behaviour.

Notice that if table wine costs only 40p per bottle, consumers in this market would drink 19 thousand bottles each month. As the price of table wine rises over the range shown, the quantity that people buy falls continuously.

On the supply side, no one will offer any table wine for sale until the price is at least £1 per bottle. As the price rises above that amount, over the range shown, more and more bottles of wine are offered for sale.

Equilibrium Price

First consider the price £1.80 in the table. At that price the quantity demanded is 12 thousand bottles per month; the quantity supplied is also 12 thousand bottles per month. At this price the quantity that consumers wish to buy is exactly the same as the quantity that producers wish to sell. Notice, also, that there is no other price shown in the table at which this is the case.

This price is known as the *equilibrium* price, and the quantity bought and sold at that price, 12,000 bottles

TABLE 8.1 Demand and Supply Schedules for Bottles of Table Wine

PRICE (£s per bottle)	QUANTITIES	
	(Thousand bottles per month)	
	Demanded	Supplied
(i)	(ii)	(iii)
0.40	19	0
0.60	18	0
1.00	16	4
1.40	14	8
1.80	12	12
2.00	11	14
2.50	8.5	19
3.00	6	24
3.50	3.5	34

0.60, 1.00, 1.40 } Excess demand

1.80 Demand equals supply

2.00, 2.50, 3.00, 3.50 } Excess supply

plotted from columns (i) and (iii), which together show how much is supplied at each of the prices. (If you are in any doubt about how to plot these curves from the data in the table, refer back to Chapter 4, page 47, which explains how to do it in detail.)

The equilibrium price and the equilibrium quantity occur at the *intersection* of the demand and supply curves. At the intersection point, the quantity demanded, which is read off the demand curve, is the same as the quantity supplied, which is read off the supply curve. Thus, *graphically, the equilibrium price is the price at which the demand and the supply curves intersect.* When the market price is equal to the equilibrium price, there will be neither unsatisfied demanders nor unsatisfied suppliers in the market.

per month in this example, is known as the *equilibrium* quantity.

EQUILIBRIUM *occurs when supply and demand are balanced, when the quantity suppliers want to offer for sale balances the quantity consumers want to purchase.* At this price there are no unsatisfied buyers or sellers. The market is exactly *cleared.*

Now look at Figure 8.1, which plots both the demand and the supply data from Table 8.1. The demand curve is plotted from columns (i) and (ii), which together show how much is demanded at each of the prices covered in the table. The supply curve is

Disequilibrium Prices

The *equilibrium price* is the price at which demand equals supply. It is the price at which there are neither unsatisfied buyers nor unsatisfied sellers. The *market price*, which is sometimes also called the *actual price*, is the price that actually rules at any point in time. The equilibrium price does not change unless the demand or supply schedules shown in Table 8.1 change. But the actual market price can change continually. Thus, for example, given the schedules in Table 8.1, the equilibrium price remains at £1.80. The actual market price may, however, be above the

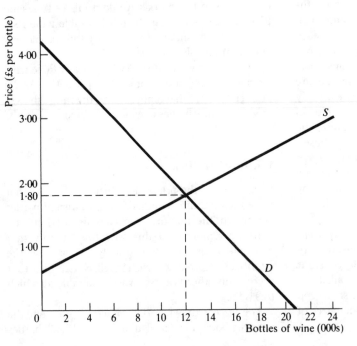

FIGURE 8.1 The Demand and Supply Curves for Bottles of Table Wine. The equilibrium price is found at the intersection of the supply curve and the demand curve

equilibrium price – in which case there will be excess supply – or it may be below the equilibrium price – in which case there will be excess demand.

Now consider what happens when the market price does *not* equal the equilibrium price. Looking at the data in Table 8.1 or the curves in Figure 8.1, it is clear that, when the market price is above the equilibrium price, the amount demanded is less than the amount supplied. For example, at a price of £3.00, both the table and the diagram indicate a quantity of 6 thousand bottles demanded, and a quantity of 24 thousand bottles supplied. In such circumstances, the quantity sellers offer for sale exceeds the quantity consumers wish to demand. Graphically, the supply curve lies to the right of the demand curve at that price. Notice, also, that at market prices below the equilibrium price, both the table and the diagram indicate that the quantity demanded exceeds the quantity supplied. Graphically, the demand curve lies to the right of the supply curve at those prices.

To repeat, only at the equilibrium price does the quantity demanded equal the quantity supplied so that the market is cleared. Graphically, this is the price at which the demand and supply curves intersect.

When the quantity demanded is greater than the quantity supplied, there is said to be EXCESS DEMAND. This the case for all prices below £1.80 in both Table 8.1 and Figure 8.1. When the quantity supplied is greater than the quantity demanded, there is said to be EXCESS SUPPLY. This is the case at all prices above £1.80 in both the figure and the table.

The working of market forces

We now consider the forces that will be acting on the market price when it is not the equilibrium price. On the one hand, when there is excess demand, consumers will not be able to buy all they wish to buy. There simply is not enough supplied for them to be able to do so. On the other hand, when there is excess supply, suppliers will not be able to sell all they wish to sell. Demand is insufficient for them to be able to do so.

In the cases of excess demand and excess supply, therefore, some people are not able to do what they would like to do. We would expect some action to be taken as a result. That action is described as the working of market forces.

Excess Demand: Suppose, first, that market price is *below* the equilibrium price of £1.80. Say market price is £1.00 in Figure 8.2. The quantity demanded is 16 thousand bottles per month, while the quantity supplied is 4 thousand. Thus, *excess demand* of 12 thousand bottles develops. What will then happen?

Market price will begin to rise. On the one hand, some consumers, finding themselves unable to buy as much as they wish to buy, offer higher prices in an attempt to get more of what is available for themselves. On the other hand, suppliers, finding themselves easily able to sell all of their total production, begin to ask for higher prices for the quantities that they have produced. Thus market forces – the response by producers to the competition among

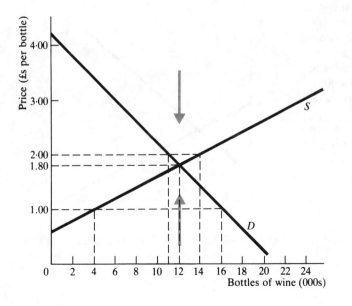

FIGURE 8.2   Excess Demand and Supply. Market forces drive price towards equilibrium

consumers for goods – tend to force price to rise. These market forces are illustrated by the upward-pointing arrow in Figure 8.2, indicating an upward pressure on the market price whenever it is below the equilibrium price of £1.80.

Excess Supply: Suppose now that market price is *above* equilibrium. Say it is at £2.00 in Figure 8.2. Quantity supplied is now 14 thousand bottles, while quantity demanded is only 11 thousand. Thus, *excess supply* of 3 thousand bottles develops. Market price will now fall. Suppliers will find themselves unable to sell all of their output. As a result they will begin to ask lower prices for what they sell. Buyers will observe the glut of unsold output and will begin to offer lower prices in response. Both of these pressures, coming from sellers and from buyers, will push the market price down. This market pressure is illustrated by the downward-pointing arrow in Figure 8.2, indicating a downward pressure on the market price whenever that price is above the equilibrium price of £1.80.

Summary of market-price determination

The theory just outlined explains why price in the market for bottles of table wine tends towards equilibrium at the point of intersection of the supply and demand curves. At prices above equilibrium, market forces tend to push price down, with the consequence that excess supply is eliminated; and, at prices below equilibrium, market forces tend to push price up, with the consequence that excess demand is eliminated. Only when market price is at its equilibrium value is the market exactly cleared in the sense that consumers *want* to buy exactly the same amount that producers *want* to sell. The equilibrium price is, therefore, sometimes called the MARKET CLEARING PRICE or the price that clears the market, leaving no unsatisfied buyers or sellers.

This equilibrium price is also the price at which there are no market forces – brought about either by excess demand or by excess supply – to cause the price to change.

WHAT EQUILIBRIUM IS *NOT*

We have said something about the nature of equilibrium. It is equally important to be clear that equilibrium does *not* imply certain things.

- Equilibrium is not the only price at which the quantity actually bought is equal to the quantity actually sold.
- Equilibrium is not necessarily desirable.
- Equilibrium is not necessarily ever achieved.
- Equilibrium is not necessarily stable.

Equilibrium and the quantity bought and sold

Our first point to make about equilibrium is that it is not the only position where the quantity bought is equal to the quantity sold. Indeed, these two quantities are equal *at every other price.* You cannot buy from me more (or less) than I sell to you. By the same token, all that is bought by purchasers must have been sold by sellers.

To drive the point home, consider Figure 8.3, which shows a market for onions. The equilibrium price is p_0 and the equilibrium quantity is q_0. Suppose, however, that the current market price is p_1, putting the market in disequilibrium. At p_1, suppliers would like to sell q_2 but buyers are only willing to buy q_1. How much will be bought and sold? What no one will buy cannot be sold. So actual sales will be the same as actual purchases, q_1, and the excess supply will remain unsold. Thus, the actual quantity bought and sold are equal even though, in this case, the market price of p_1 exceeds the equilibrium price of p_0. Desired sales of q_2, however, exceed desired purchases of q_1.

What distinguishes p_1 from p_0 is *not* any difference between the *actual* quantity bought and the *actual* quantity sold. The points *are* distinguished by whether the quantity consumers *want* to buy is equal

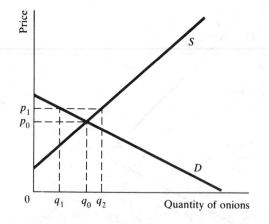

FIGURE 8.3 Desired and Actual Quantities. At price p_1, actual quantities bought and sold are both q_1, while desired purchases and desired sales are unequal at q_1 and q_2 respectively

to the quantity that suppliers *want* to sell. It is only in equilibrium that the wants of suppliers and consumers are simultaneously, and fully, met, so that there are neither unsatisfied buyers nor unsatisfied sellers.

What is actually bought and sold is also referred to as the realized (or the *ex post*) quantity. Realized purchases and sales are necessarily always equal to each other by virtue of the two-sided nature of transactions: what is bought by someone must have been sold by someone else. What buyers want to buy and what sellers want to sell are referred to as desired, planned, or *ex ante* quantities. These are equal only in equilibrium and are unequal at all other prices.

Desirability of equilibrium

The word equilibrium is sometimes thought to carry an overtone of desirability. The meaning of equilibrium, however, is purely technical – the price and quantity towards which market forces tend. Whether equilibrium is desirable is a question that can only be settled by bringing in additional considerations, including value judgements. For example, it might be important to know whether the distribution of income is satisfactory or not.

We discussed briefly in Chapter 2 (see pp. 27–8) some unsatisfactory aspects of market systems. We shall consider them at greater length in Chapter 9. For the present we only emphasize that there is nothing *necessarily* 'good' about equilibrium.

Achievement of equilibrium

Our explanation of the means by which equilibrium was reached, in the market for bottles of table wine, was based on a simple model of a market where price was determined by supply and demand. We should not jump to the conclusion that all markets in the real world behave like that one. Although some markets work in a very similar fashion, others do not. There are many reasons for this, which we shall consider in Part 4 of this book. Two are worthy of mention now.

First, market forces do not work instantaneously. It takes time for excess supplies and/or excess demands to stimulate quantity adjustments to price movements. In some cases, the time-lags are considerable.

Second, the world is a place where many things are continually changing. Market forces may tend towards equilibrium but, as conditions change, the equilibrium itself may change before it is reached.

Thus equilibrium may never actually be reached. Instead, market behaviour may be a perpetual chase towards an ever-moving target.

Stability of equilibrium

A market equilibrium is said to be STABLE if any movement of the market price away from the equilibrium price is self-restoring, i.e. market forces are set up which return market price to equilibrium price.

For an equilibrium to be stable, two conditions are necessary.

(1) When the market price is not equal to the equilibrium price, forces should be set up to push it back *in the direction of* the equilibrium price.

(2) These forces should not be so strong as to continually push the market price *past* the equilibrium, thus setting up a series of gyrations in which, although the price is pushed towards the equilibrium, it *overshoots* each time and never gets to its equilibrium value.

If both these conditions are fulfilled, the market may be stable in much the same way as was one of those old-fashioned toy clowns with a weighted bottom (known to connoisseurs as Kelly toys). You cannot knock the clown over: however hard you push it, it always comes back upright – its behaviour is stable.

If either of these conditions is not fulfilled, the market is said to be UNSTABLE because if an equilibrium is disturbed, market forces will not restore that equilibrium. There are two types of unstable equilibrium, depending on which of the above necessary conditions for stability are not fulfilled. We leave the discussion of the case where the second condition is not fulfilled until the next chapter. Here we discuss the simple case where the first condition is not fulfilled.

An analogy may help to clarify the distinction between a stable and unstable equilibrium that arises when condition (1) is not fulfilled. Imagine two bowls, one the right way up and the other upside down. Now, place a marble in the bottom of the first bowl, and balance another on the top of the second. Both are in equilibrium. However only the first is in *stable* equilibrium. If you push it away from the bottom of the bowl with your finger, it will always roll back. But if you push the marble balanced on top of the upside-down bowl in any direction, it will not return to the top. It is (or rather it was) in an *unstable* equilibrium, before you disturbed it.

The first condition for equilibrium was fulfilled by our wine market. To illustrate, look again at Figure 8.1. Assume the price in equilibrium is at £1.80. *Any* fall in price would create excess demand and set up market forces pushing price back up again towards the equilibrium price. Conversely, any rise in price above the equilibrium value would cause quantity supplied to exceed quantity demanded. The excess supply would then set up market forces pushing price down towards equilibrium.

The market shown in Figure 8.4, however, does not meet this necessary condition for stability. The intersection of the supply and demand curves produce an equilibrium price, p_0, and an equilibrium quantity, q_0. At this price, desired purchases and desired sales are equal.

So far this is all very familiar. Now consider, however, what would happen if price rose above p_0, say to p_1. The rise in price reduces the quantity demanded to q_2, but it reduces the quantity supplied, by even more, to q_1. Thus, *excess demand* of $q_2 - q_1$ develops. Excess demand pushes the market price upwards. But that leads price *away* from its equilibrium value, so that market forces here do not restore equilibrium, as they did for the market shown in Figure 8.2.

It is beyond the scope of this book to probe far into the conditions that are sufficient for market equilibrium to be stable. But we wonder if you can spot a crucial difference between Figures 8.4 and 8.2. One difference is that in Figure 8.2 the supply and demand curves have their normal slopes, while in Figure 8.4

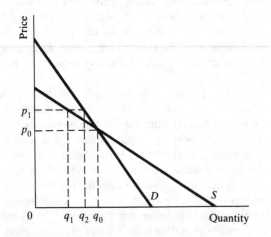

FIGURE 8.4   **An Unstable Equilibrium.** Excess demand occurs at prices above equilibrium, while excess supply occurs at prices below equilibrium

the demand curve has the same (negative) slope as Figure 8.2, but the supply curve also slopes downward.[1]

SHIFTS IN DEMAND AND SUPPLY

So far in this chapter, we have looked at how markets work when the only factor that influences demand and supply is the price of the good being studied. To do this, we used the *ceteris paribus* assumption to hold all other factors which influence demand and supply constant. We are now ready to drop that assumption, in order to see how to handle changes in the conditions of supply and demand.

We repeat, yet again, that changes in the conditions of demand or supply cause *shifts* in the entire demand or supply curve. Both curves can be shifted in either of two directions. A *rightward* shift means that more is demanded, or supplied, at every market price. A *leftward* shift means that less is demanded, or supplied, at every market price.

Four 'Laws' of Supply and Demand

Two curves that may shift in either of two directions give rise to four cases. These cases are so important that they are sometimes even called 'laws of supply and demand'. These laws are derived for markets of the type that we have been considering – i.e. where supply curves slope upwards, demand curves slope downwards, and buyers and sellers are both maximizers and price-takers. Whenever these conditions hold, the laws are applicable; where the conditions are not applicable, the laws may not hold.

A rise in demand

We start by considering a rise in demand. In Figure 8.5 the original demand curve is D and the original supply curve is S. The original equilibrium price is p_0.

---

1   A bit of experimentation will show you that a negative slope on the supply curve is not, by itself, sufficient to cause instability. Try yourself with S and D curves which both slope downwards, but with an S curve steeper than the D curve at the point of intersection. For instability, it is necessary that there be excess demand at prices above equilibrium and excess supply at prices below it. If both the D and S curves are negatively sloped, this requires that the S curve be *flatter* (i.e. less steep) than the D curve.

The original quantity supplied and demanded is q_0.

Assume now a change in the conditions of demand, say a rise in consumers' income. This increases the quantity that consumers wish to buy at every price. The demand curve shifts to D'. As a result, excess demand develops, because at the original price of p_0 the quantity demanded is now q_2. There is excess demand of $q_2 - q_0$, which sets up market forces which raise the equilibrium price. The process continues until price rises from p_0 to reach a new equilibrium p_1. Quantity sold rises from q_0 to reach the new equilibrium level of q_1.

This analysis establishes our first conclusion:

(1) *A rise in the demand for a commodity (a rightward shift of the demand curve) causes an increase in the equilibrium price and quantity.*

A fall in demand

Next consider the effects of a fall in demand. Assume a change in the conditions of demand, which leads consumers to want to buy smaller quantities at every price. For example, there might be a fall in the price of a substitute for the good in question.

The fall in demand shifts the demand curve leftward. To study the effects, let D' in Figure 8.5 be the original demand curve and D the new lower demand. The original equilibrium price and quantity are now p_1 and q_1. When the demand curve shifts to D, however, *excess supply* of $q_1 - q_3$ develops. Market forces push price downwards towards the new equilibrium price of p_0. The new equilibrium quantity bought and sold is q_0. This gives our second conclusion:

(2) *A fall in the demand for a commodity (a leftward shift of the demand curve) causes a decrease in the equilibrium price and quantity.*

A rise in supply

Let the original demand and supply curves be D and S in Figure 8.6. This yields an equilibrium price and quantity of p_0 and q_0. Now consider a change in the conditions of supply which increases the quantities that producers are prepared to offer for sale at every price. Say, for example, that there is an increase in the productivity of factors of production following from a technological advance, which lowers costs of production. The supply curve in Figure 8.6 shifts rightward from S to S'.

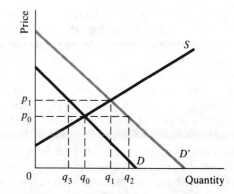

FIGURE 8.5   The Effect of a Shift in the Demand Curve. A rightward shift raises equilibrium price and quantity. A leftward shift lowers equilibrium price and quantity

On this occasion, the increase in supply causes excess supply to develop at the old equilibrium price. At that price the quantity demanded is still q_0, but suppliers now offer q_2 for sale. The excess supply of $q_2 - q_0$ sets up market forces which depress price. Price continues to fall until the new equilibrium price of p_1 is reached. At that new price the quantity supplied and demanded are equal, at q_1. This gives our third conclusion:

(3) *A rise in the supply of a commodity (a rightward shift of the supply curve) causes a decrease in the equilibrium price and an increase in equilibrium quantity.*

A fall in supply

Reasoning parallel to that of the previous paragraph can be applied to the effects of a fall in the supply, such

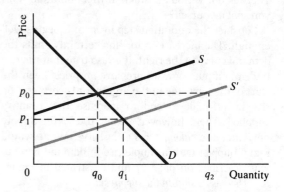

FIGURE 8.6   The Effect of a Shift in the Supply Curve. A rightward shift lowers equilibrium price and raises equilibrium quantity. A leftward shift raises equilibrium price and lowers equilibrium quantity

as might result from a rise in the price of a factor of production, or any other appropriate change in the conditions of supply. This would lead producers to offer smaller quantities for sale at every price. It is illustrated in Figure 8.6 by letting S' be the original supply curve, yielding an equilibrium price and quantity of p_1 and q_1. Now let the supply curve shift leftward to S. At the old equilibrium price of p_1, excess demand is the entire quantity demanded, q_1, because the quantity supplied is now zero while q_1 is still demanded at the old equilibrium price of p_1. Market forces now push price upwards until the new equilibrium price p_0 is reached, at which price the quantity supplied and demanded are equal at q_0. This leads to our fourth and final conclusion:

(4) *A fall in the supply of a commodity (a leftward shift in the supply curve) causes an increase in the equilibrium price and decrease in equilibrium quantity.*

Shifts versus Movements along Curves Again

In previous Chapters we stressed the difference between shifts of curves and movements along curves. We warned that it is easy to confuse the two. The mistake is common, so we devote a little space here to illustrate the trap. Someone who fell into it, wrongly wrote in an answer to an examination question:

'An increase in income causes demand to rise. The rise in demand causes an increase in price. The increase in price causes an increase in supply, which pushes price back towards its original level.'

There is one serious mistake in this quotation. Can you spot it yourself?

Consider the quotation step by step. It begins well enough. The increase in income certainly shifts the demand curve to the right. It is also true that the rise in demand puts upward pressure on price. Even the start of the next step in the argument is correct. The rise in price does tend to increase the quantity supplied. Then, however, comes the error. Supply only increases *along the supply curve*. What would really happen with a simple rise in demand is what was described on page 91 and illustrated in Figure 8.5. *There is no shift in the supply curve.*

The mistake lies in confusing a movement along the supply curve, as a result of a change in price, which does happen, with a shift in the supply curve, which does not happen. The confusion led the

student to argue as if the increase in price shifts the supply curve upwards. Compare the student's incorrect statement with the following *correct* version of the effects of a change that occurs *only* in the conditions of demand, the conditions of supply being unchanged.

'An increase in income causes demand to rise. The rise in demand induces an increase in price. The increase in price induces an increase in the quantity supplied. Price settles at a new equilibrium level above the old price, where the quantity consumers want to buy equals that which producers want to sell.'

Are these laws?

As previously stated, it is common to refer to the four conclusions printed in italics on the previous pages as the 'laws of supply and demand'.

Economic laws, insofar as they exist at all, are *scientific* laws.[1] At this point it may be helpful to say something about such laws. Scientists until the eighteenth century, and laymen even today, often think of scientific laws as truths proven once and for all, an example being Newton's law of gravity. As scientific method was applied to test such 'proven laws', however, scientists began to realize that some did not always fit the facts and some had to be amended or even occasionally discarded. Even the great laws of Newton himself were challenged after 200 years and found to express relations that were only approximately true over 'small portions' of the universe.

As a result, scientific theories are no longer accepted as statements of truths that must apply everywhere and for ever, but as hypotheses, which although useful may, sooner or later, be discovered to be in conflict with evidence. They may then be replaced by superior hypotheses, which can provide fuller and better explanations of all existing observations.

With these points in mind, let us ask what we should understand from the laws of supply and demand. The conclusions that we have established

---

1 They are not moral laws, which tell us what must be done according to a particular ethical code, such as the Ten Commandments, nor are they like laws which prescribe the criminal code or the rules of the game of cricket.

from the theory of price can be looked at in two ways. First, in terms of their internal consistency as theories; second, as predictions which are intended to fit the facts of the world.

Looked at in the first way, we are only interested in logical consistency. Do the propositions follow logically from the assumptions of the theory? For example, we may say: '*if* the demand curve for cars slopes downwards, and *if* the supply curve slopes upwards, *then* an increase in the demand for cars will raise their equilibrium price.' This sentence is logically correct. The *then* conclusion follows from the two *ifs*. Obviously, we want our theories to be logical (and therefore internally consistent). Not all economic theories have always been so impeccable, and, at the advanced stages of the subject, there is sometimes doubt as to whether or not a given proposition follows from a given set of assumptions.

The second way to look at conclusions described as 'laws' is to view them as making predictions about real-world behaviour, and to ask whether they help both to explain what we have already observed and to predict behaviour in the future. This requires that the theories be tested against evidence drawn from real-world behaviour. If the theories do not allow us to explain and to predict what we observe in the world around us, then they are of little, if any, value,

irrespective of whether or not they are logically consistent (i.e. what they assert is derived logically from the theory's assumptions).

So-called economic laws are subject to continued testing every time they are applied to some real-world case. If they repeatedly fail to predict the consequences of changes in the conditions of demand or supply, they must be amended or discarded in favour of more successful alternative theories. We stress 'repeatedly' since the world is too uncertain, and our observations too subject to error, for us to be upset by a single conflict between any theory and real-world observations.

Advanced statistical techniques have been developed to aid testing. They usually require a large amount of data, and their interpretation is a difficult task. A great deal of knowledge has been acquired about economic behaviour in the real world, and about the ability of economic theory to explain and predict it. Every time one thing is learned, however, new unsolved problems seem to arise, so that the vision of a fully tested, accepted theory seems to be an unattainable dream. But, although perfection may elude us, the acquisition of knowledge through quantitative research is a reality, and those who wish to learn more about real-world behaviour can, at least, be thankful for that small mercy.

SUMMARY

1 A market is in equilibrium when price is such that the quantity consumers wish to buy is equal to the quantity that sellers wish to offer for sale. The equilibrium price is that which exactly clears the market. Graphically, the equilibrium price is found at the intersection of the supply and demand curves.

2 When market price is above equilibrium, excess supply exists, which leads to a downward pressure on price as a result of competition among sellers. When market price is below equilibrium, excess demand exists, which leads to an upward pressure on price as a result of competition among buyers.

3 The equilibrium price is not the only price at which the quantity actually bought is equal to the quantity actually sold. The equilibrium price is not necessarily desirable; it will not necessarily be

reached; and it is not necessarily a stable price, in the sense that movements away from equilibrium are self-restoring.

4 A rise (or fall) in the demand for a commodity causes an increase (or decrease) in the equilibrium price and an increase (or decrease) in the equilibrium quantity bought and sold.

5 A rise (or fall) in the supply of a commodity causes a decrease (or increase) in the equilibrium price and an increase (or decrease) in the quantity bought and sold.

Economic laws, insofar as they exist, are scientific laws. Insofar as they are logically consistent, they are valid deductions from a set of assumptions. Insofar as they fit the facts of the real world, they are helpful in understanding and predicting economic events.

Market Equilibrium

In this chapter we complete our analysis of the workings of the price mechanism in simple market situations. There are three main topics to be considered: the influence of time, market interactions, and market efficiency.

TIME AND MARKET FORCES

There are two important ways in which time enters into the analysis of supply and demand in the marketplace. One is an application of something we learned earlier about supply and demand in the short and long run. The other is new, and relates to a time-lag between price changes and changes in quantity supplied.

The Effects over Time of a Shift in Demand or Supply

We first apply what we know about the effects of shifts in demand and supply curves to emphasize differences that may be expected in the short and in the long run. In Chapters 4 and 5, we concluded that the longer the period of time under consideration, the greater the expected response of both supply and demand to a price change. We can now apply these conclusions to market-price determination.

Figure 9.1 reproduces the three supply curves corresponding to the three different time-periods we met previously and showed in Figure 6.4. S_M is the momentary supply curve, when supply is fixed and cannot be increased, nor decreased, regardless of what happens to market price. S_S is the short-run supply curve, where time is allowed for some re-sponse to price changes. S_L is the long-run supply curve, which permits full adaptation to price movements. The original equilibrium price is p_0, which means that whatever supply curve we are considering must have intersected the demand curve, D, at that point.

A shift in demand

Suppose now there is a change in consumer tastes in favour of the good in the figure. This involves a rightwards shift of the demand curve to D'. Observe, now, the different effects as the time-period varies. In the momentary period, supply is fixed. Quantity cannot change and price rises from p_0 to p_1. In the short run, when S_S is relevant, the quantity supplied increases but only from q_0 to q_2. The price rise is, in

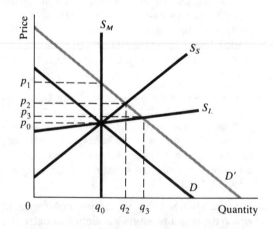

FIGURE 9.1 **The Effects of Demand Shifts over Various Time-periods.** The longer the time that passes, the greater the change in quantity and the less the change in price

consequence, moderated and the new price is p_2. In the long run, supply curve S_L comes into play. Quantity offered for sale increases more with the passage of time, to reach q_3. The price increase over its original level, p_0, is less than in either of our other cases. Price now settles at p_3.

This analysis can be generalized to give a set of four further conclusions to be added to the four 'laws' of supply and demand that we developed in the previous chapter.

(5) *The longer the time-period allowed, the less price will rise and the more quantity will increase following an increase in demand.*

A similar proposition may be derived concerning a fall in demand. We think you might be bored if we were to reproduce the argument in full since it is largely a repetition of the analysis leading up to 'law 5' stated above. So we suggest you do so for yourself. Here is how to do it.

Redraw the three supply curves and the original demand curve, D, from Figure 9.1. Now draw a new demand curve, this time *to the left of* the original demand curve (*not to the right of* the original curve, as it was in Figure 9.1). Locate the same original equilibrium position. Now locate the three new equilibrium positions resulting from the intersection of the new demand curve with the three supply curves applying to the three different time-periods. This will show you that:

(6) *The longer the period allowed, the less price will fall and the more quantity will decrease following a fall in demand.*

A shift in supply

Consider, next, two further propositions concerning, this time, the effects of a change in *supply* over different time-periods. Now, we need to use a diagram which has different *demand curves* for each time-period. In Figure 9.2 we show two demand curves, D_S and D_L, which are similar to the curves in Figure 5.4. We have added two supply curves, S and S'. S is an original supply curve which intersects the two demand curves at the point at which they intersect each other. S' is the curve to which supply shifts. D_S and D_L have the same meaning as before. D_S shows how demand responds to price changes when only enough time has passed for people to have made a partial adjustment. The curve D_L shows how demand re-

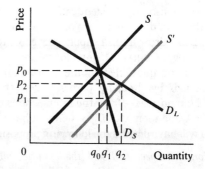

FIGURE 9.2 The Effects of Supply Shifts over Different Time-periods. The longer the time that passes, the greater the change in quantity and the less the change in price

sponds to a price change when sufficient time has passed for people to have made a full adjustment.

Recall, from the discussion in Chapter 5, that a full adjustment to a price change may take a very long time. For example, when the price of oil rose substantially in the 1970s, the demand fell somewhat over a fairly short time, as people economized on their use of petroleum products using their existing equipment. Over a longer period, which in this case was five years or more, demand fell quite substantially as full adjustments were made – for example the design and sale of more petrol-efficient cars, particularly in the United States, and the design and construction of factories that used alternative sources of energy.

The original equilibrium price and quantity are p_0 and q_0. Now suppose a fall in the costs of production. This shifts the supply curve to the right, to S' in Figure 9.2, as more is produced and offered for sale at each price. Now, observe the different effects over the two periods of time. In the shorter period, the new equilibrium price and quantity are p_1 and q_1. In the longer period, the curve D_L is relevant and the equilibrium price and quantity are p_2 and q_2. Comparing the two new equilibrium positions shown in the Figure, we can conclude that, over the longer period, the fall in price is less, and the rise in quantity bought and sold is more, than in the short period. This result for a rise in supply can be added to our earlier 'laws of demand and supply':

(7) *The longer the period allowed, the less price will fall and the more quantity will increase following a rise in supply.*

A further result can be derived for a decrease in

supply. The reasoning is identical, and again we suggest that you do it yourself. You can do so using Figure 9.2. Just draw a third supply curve, S'', to the left of the original curve, S. Now, locate the equilibrium prices and quantities for the shorter and the longer periods by dropping perpendiculars to the price and quantity axes from the intersections of S'', first with D_S and then with D_L. When you have done this, you will have derived the following proposition:

(8) *The longer the period allowed, the less price will rise and the more quantity will decrease following a fall in supply.*

Various elasticities

The four propositions, developed in the previous two sections, refer to the different effects of shifts in demand and supply curves when the period of time allowed for adjustment varies. The same analysis can also be used to study the effects of shifts in demand and supply curves when elasticities vary, to yield yet two more 'laws' of supply and demand.

First, reconsider Figure 9.1. The three supply curves, S_M, S_S and S_L, have different elasticities at price p_0. The elasticity is zero in the momentary period, positive, but not too large in the short period, and larger in the long period. We can, therefore, reinterpret these curves as being three alternative supply curves applying to the same moment in time but having different elasticities. This immediately gives us another important result:

(9) *The greater the elasticity of supply, the less price will change and the more quantity bought and sold will change in response to a rise or a fall in demand.*

Now reconsider Figure 9.2. The two demand curves, D_S and D_L, are curves having different elasticities at price p_0. At the price p_0 the steeper curve, D_S, has a lower elasticity than has the flatter curve, D_L. We can, therefore, reinterpret these two curves as being two alternative demand curves applying to the same moment in time but having different elasticities. This immediately gives us our last result:

(10) *The greater the elasticity of demand, the less price will change and the more quantity bought and sold will change in response to a rise or a fall in supply.*

Stated in these forms, the propositions have a more general applicability than they were given in the previous section. This is because the elasticities of both demand and supply depend on more than just the time-period under consideration. The availability of good substitutes, for example, influences elasticity. If we were comparing the effects of a rise in supply on market price and quantity for two commodities, we could identify in Figure 9.2 the demand for the good with more and better substitutes with the curve D_L, and the good with fewer and poorer substitutes with the curve D_S. Our conclusion would then be that, for any given time-period, an increase in supply would cause price to fall less, and quantity to rise more, for the good with many close substitutes than for the good with few such substitutes.

The Attainment of Equilibrium

In the previous section, we compared the equilibrium market situations in different time-periods. We were, then, comparing equilibrium prices. We did not ask about the course taken by price as it changed between one equilibrium and another. Nor did we ask if the equilibrium would ever be achieved. If we want to deal with these questions, we must do *dynamic analysis*, which takes account more fully of *time-lags* in the adjustment of supply to demand. As we do so, we will be reconsidering the question of the stability of equilibrium that we discussed in the previous chapter (see pp. 89–90). There, we considered only one of the conditions for market stability – that market forces should push the actual price back in the direction of equilibrium if it should, temporarily, diverge from the equilibrium price. Now, we discuss a second condition – that market forces should not set up a series of perpetual price oscillations around its equilibrium value.

Consider, now, the case shown in Figure 9.3 which shows the supply and demand curves for potatoes. The demand curve is the one we are used to. It shows how the quantity of potatoes demanded varies with their current market price. It is downward-sloping, indicating that the lower the current market price of potatoes, the greater will be the quantity currently demanded. The supply curve, S, is the short-run supply curve for potatoes. It also has the familiar shape, indicating that more potatoes will be produced and offered for sale the higher is their price. However, the curve differs in one very important way from the ones we have considered so far. It explicitly takes account of a time-lag in adjusting supply to the current market price. We assume that, if farmers wish to vary the quantity of potatoes that they produce and

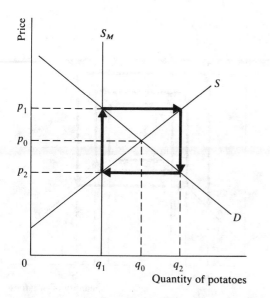

FIGURE 9.3   A Stable Cobweb. Price and quantity fluctuate repeatedly around the equilibrium

offer for sale, it takes a year for the new crop to be planted, harvested and brought to market. Thus, the supply curve relates the quantity produced in any one year to the price ruling *in the previous year*. This year's output of potatoes was planted last year and thus depends on last year's price.[1] Putting the same point in another way, next year's quantity of potatoes depends on *this year's price*.

The equilibrium price and quantity are determined in the usual way at p_0 and q_0. If the price p_0 has ruled for several years, farmers will plant q_0 potatoes each year and, when the crop comes onto the market the following year, it will be sold at a price of p_0. This price will clear the market and will lead farmers to plant the same quantity for the following year. Unless something happens to disturb it, equilibrium will continue unchanged from year to year.

Now, suppose that something new does happen. Assume, for example, that, as a result of a severe but temporary epidemic of potato blight, this year's output falls to q_1, which is below the equilibrium quantity. What will happen? As a result of the blight, this year's crop is fixed at q_1. The momentary supply

curve (which in this case persists for a year until a new crop comes onto the market) is S_M, which is perfectly inelastic at quantity q_1. To find the price at which the quantity q_1 will be bought, we go to the temporary equilibrium at the intersection of S_M with the demand curve. This tells us that the price that clears the market, i.e. the price at which the output q_1 will be sold, is now p_1. As a result of the shortage of potatoes, the market price rises.

How might the market return from its temporary equilibrium at p_1 to its equilibrium of demand and supply at p_0? If the quantity produced were to expand slowly and continuously from q_1 to q_0, as it would in many markets, the price would fall slowly and continuously from p_1 to p_0. However, this is not the case in our potato market.

The 'momentary' equilibrium price persists for a year, i.e. until next year's crop is planted, raised and harvested. While it does persist, farmers know only the current market price at which the present crop is being sold, but they must now make their plans for how many potatoes to plant for sale next year. The signal they see is a rise in the market price from p_0 to p_1. Their supply curve tells us that at p_1 the amount they would like to supply is not q_1 but q_2. If they behave as we described earlier, relating their current plantings, and hence next year's output, to the current price, they will plan to produce q_2 the following year.

What happens the following year when q_2 potatoes comes on the market? There is then another momentary supply curve which is vertical at the new output of q_2. At the old price of p_1, there is, now, an excess supply of potatoes q_2-q_1. This will bring potato prices plummeting down. Price does not, however, fall to its equilibrium value of p_0. Instead, there is a momentary equilibrium price which clears the market. Price must fall all the way to p_2 (which is the intersection of the demand curve and the new momentary supply curve which is vertical at the current output of q_2). This, then, becomes the new momentary equilibrium that persists until another new crop comes onto the market. But, at the new price p_2, farmers will only want to produce q_1. Say they plant that amount. When q_1 comes onto the market in the following year, excess demand recurs at the price of p_2 and the market is cleared at a momentary equilibrium of p_1 and q_1. Farmers respond now again to the price p_1, by producing q_2 next year; but when this comes onto the market, price falls to p_2 and so on. . . .

Thus, a series of temporary equilibria recur with

price oscillating around its equilibrium value. This is because the quantity coming onto the market next year is the response to the price ruling, while that price is determined by the demand curve and the momentary supply on the market this year, which was determined by last year's price. The case shown in Figure 9.3 is called a *stable* cobweb because the fluctuations go on repeatedly, without increasing or decreasing in magnitude.

What we have just described is a model, or theory, of the behaviour of a market where supply adjusts to price with a very specific time-lag. This model is usually referred to as THE COBWEB THEOREM.

Two observations may be made about the cobweb theorem. First, the reason for the 'cobweb' part of its name may now be understood. Figure 9.3 looks a little like a cobweb, and Figures 9.4 and 9.5 look much more so. Second, and more importantly, we conclude that with some kinds of time-lag on the supply side, market forces may not tend towards equilibrium, even in theory. In the language which we used on p. 89 of the previous chapter, equilibrium may be unstable, in that a departure from equilibrium is not self-restoring, i.e. changes in quantities supplied and demanded do not lead us back to equilibrium.

Convergent and divergent cobwebs

In Figures 9.4 and 9.5 we show two more versions of the cobweb theorem. Each shows behaviour which differs from the repeated, steady oscillations of the stable cobweb in Figure 9.3.

Convergent Cobwebs: Consider the case of Figure 9.4, which is described as a *convergent cobweb*. We shall not retrace each step of the argument. The process is similar to that described in the previous section. If you are not clear about it, we suggest you read the earlier description again before proceeding. We start as before, with a crop failure which takes the momentary supply to q_1 in the diagram and the momentary equilibrium to point 2, where the price p_1 clears the market. Price and quantity movements follow the pattern shown in the diagram, going in the direction of the arrows from points 2 to 3, to 4, etc. Just to remind you, position 3 occurs when farmers supply q_3 in response to price p_1; but this forces price down until position 4 is reached; but then when output contracts, position 5 is reached, and so on.

The distinguishing feature of Figure 9.4 is that the oscillations become smaller and smaller every period.

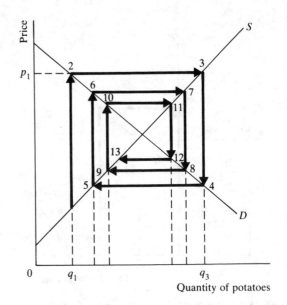

FIGURE 9.4   **A Convergent Cobweb.** Price and quantity converge on the equilibrium

Price and quantity do not cycle repeatedly and steadily around equilibrium as they did in Figure 9.3. In Figure 9.4 the oscillations get smaller each year and gradually approach the equilibrium. This version of the cobweb theorem is described as convergent, which means that the oscillations converge on the equilibrium price and quantity.

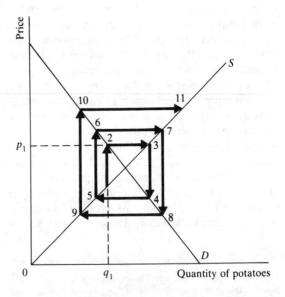

FIGURE 9.5   **A Divergent Cobweb.** Price and quantity diverge further and further from the equilibrium

Divergent Cobwebs: Consider finally Figure 9.5. Starting once more with a crop failure that reduces output temporarily to q_1 and produces a momentary equilibrium at point 2, we follow the price and quantity movements represented by points 2, 3, 4, 5 and so on, in the direction of the arrows. Note that on this occasion the oscillations become greater and greater every period. This is the divergent case. The process is explosive.

Evidence on cobwebs

We need not bother you with the precise nature of conditions which lead to the different cobweb cases.[1] You may perhaps wonder, though, whether there is any basis in fact for this cobweb-type behaviour or is it just a piece of abstract economic theory without any supporting empirical evidence?

The cobweb theory was first propounded in the 1930s by an American economist called Mordecai Ezekial. He noticed price oscillations in the hog (pig) market in Chicago and developed the theory to explain it. Today, cobweb tendencies are still sometimes observed. They are, however, rather less pronounced than might be suggested by the crude theory given here. The main reason is that producers learn, by experience, not to link supplies *mechanically to past prices*. Such intelligent learning from experience is no more than we would expect. Such learning explains, for instance, why explosive cobwebs do not persist indefinitely. Producers do not ignore historical patterns in the price of the good they produce. Nonetheless, to look ahead and anticipate cobweb-type fluctuations is much more sophisticated behaviour than merely reacting to current prices. Furthermore, whenever the conditions of demand or supply change, the nature of the potential cobweb fluctuations will change, thus rendering past experience, to an extent, obsolete. But because producers cannot perfectly anticipate market forces, many agricultural products do exhibit cycles, with periods of low output and high prices alternating with periods of high output and low prices. Because producers can par-

tially anticipate market forces, explosive or even stable cobwebs do not persist for ever.

MARKET INTERACTIONS

The major purpose of supply and demand analysis is to understand the way in which a market system allocates resources. Yet most of the analysis so far in this chapter has been concerned with behaviour in a single market.

Partial and General Equilibrium

The study of behaviour in markets taken one at a time is known as PARTIAL EQUILIBRIUM ANALYSIS, because it deals with only a part of the economic system. It is based on *ceteris paribus* assumptions. One of these is that prices in markets other than the one under consideration are unchanged (i.e. the prices of other goods are held constant). In order to see the full working of a market system, however, we must look at interactions among markets and follow the ways in which the forces of supply and demand push prices towards equilibrium in all markets. The study of such reactions is known as GENERAL EQUILIBRIUM ANALYSIS.

The theory of general equilibrium is an advanced subject. It employs complex mathematical techniques and cannot be fully explained by the use of two-dimensional diagrams showing supply and demand in individual markets. We can, however, take you a little way along the road to understanding it.

Interactions in markets for two goods

Consider, for purposes of illustration, two goods: boots and shoes. The goods are, incidentally, carefully chosen. They are *related* to each other on both supply and demand sides, i.e. they are substitutes in both production and consumption. Changes in relative prices can lead both consumers to switch purchases, and producers to switch production, between boots and shoes. Let us now consider the effect of a single disturbance on the equilibrium of both markets.

These effects cannot be *fully* explained with supply-demand diagrams. We can, however, observe something of what is involved with the aid of a diagram. In Figure 9.6 we show the original supply and demand

---

1 If you want to know, supply and demand curves with the same absolute slopes give the continuous oscillation of Figure 9.3. If the supply curve is steeper than the demand curve, you get convergent oscillations as in Figure 9.4. If the reverse is true, you get divergent oscillations as in Figure 9.5. For a discussion of the factors lying behind these differences and a fuller discussion of the cobweb theorem, see IPE, Appendix to Ch. 10.

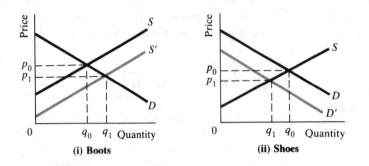

FIGURE 9.6   Market Interactions. Price changes in one market can cause shifts in supply and demand curves in related markets

curves in the market for shoes and in the market for boots. Both are in initial equilibrium with prices p_0 and quantities bought and sold q_0.

Next, imagine that some change takes place to disturb the equilibria. It could be a change in any one of several supply or demand influences that are held constant by the *ceteris paribus* assumption. Suppose it is a change in the state of technology, lowering the production costs of boots.

We can show the immediate impact of the change in Figure 9.6(i) by a rightward shift in the supply curve for boots from S to S'. The result is a downward movement in the price of boots towards a new equilibrium of p_1 and an increase in the quantity bought and sold, tending towards q_1.

However, boots and shoes are substitutes for consumers, and the demand curve for shoes is drawn on the assumption that the prices of other goods are constant. Since the price of boots has fallen, the conditions under which the demand curve for shoes was drawn are no longer applicable. Shoes are now relatively more expensive compared to boots, so consumers demand fewer at every price of shoes. In other words, the demand curve for shoes shifts from D to D', as shown in Figure 9.6(ii). This change will have the effect of depressing the price of shoes, which moves towards the new equilibrium price of p_1.

Chain reactions

This is not the end of the story. The fall in the price of shoes just referred to, means a change in the conditions under which the demand curve for boots was constructed. We should therefore draw a new demand curve for boots, lower than the old one. We refrain from doing so because the process we have started to describe is a chain. Every time there is a change in the price of boots, the demand curve for shoes shifts; every time there is a change in the price of shoes, the demand curve for boots shifts.

Moreover, we have not yet mentioned the possibility of shifts on the supply side. They are likely to happen as well. Supply curves are also drawn on the *ceteris paribus* assumption that the prices of other goods to which resources might shift are constant. Factors of production making shoes could, without too much difficulty, be transferred to boot production, and vice versa. When the price of boots changes relatively to the price of shoes, therefore, resources would be attracted from the production of one good to that of the other. When the price of boots falls relative to the price of shoes, for example, suppliers produce more shoes. The supply curve for shoes shifts rightwards.

You may now appreciate why we said that supply and demand curves cannot track the whole process by which equilibrium is reached even in two markets. Our diagrams would become immensely complicated as we drew shifting supply and demand curves every time there was a change in the price of a related good. As the number of markets we consider rises, such a procedure is completely out of the question. That is why mathematical techniques are essential for the general equilibrium analysis of all the markets in the economy.

It is beyond the scope of an introductory book on economics to develop further the theory of market interactions. We can, however, say something about the conclusions that would be reached if we could.

When either the supply or demand for a good changes, the appropriate curve shifts and leads to a change in the price *in the market for that good*. Buyers and/or sellers respond to the price change by moving along their supply or demand curve.

The new equilibrium price in one market, however, alters prices of that good relative to those of other goods. When relative prices change, supply and demand curves *in related markets* shift in the manner we have explained. Such shifts lead to price changes in other related markets. Buyers and sellers then respond to the price changes by moving along their supply or demand curves, in the usual manner. Quantities demanded tend to increase for goods the prices of which have fallen. Quantities supplied tend to increase for goods the prices of which have risen. The extent of the changes in prices and quantities depend on the elasticities of supply and demand. Chain reactions are set up which continue until general equilibrium is established. This occurs when the relative prices of all goods are such that there are no economic forces at work encouraging changes in quantities supplied or demanded of any commodities. This is when, in every market, prices are equal to marginal costs for producers, and prices are equal to marginal utilities for consumers.

MARKET EFFICIENCY

In Chapter 2, we outlined some of the reasons why the market system may produce an efficient allocation of resources. We also outlined some of the criticisms that have been levelled at a *laissez-faire* market economy. Now that we have some tools of economic analysis at our disposal, we can review both sets of arguments. We must do so within the framework we have so far used, in which buyers and sellers are price-takers. We shall take a final look at the market system in Chapters 23 and 24, when we shall be able to drop the price-taking assumption.

We must, first, be more explicit about what we mean by an inefficient and an efficient allocation of resources. The current allocation of resources is said to be INEFFICIENT if it is possible to reallocate resources in such a way as to make *everyone* better off.[1] The allocation of resources is said to be EFFICIENT if this is not possible, i.e. if any reallocation of resources that makes someone better off must make at least one other person worse off.

Note also that an efficient resource allocation is often referred to as an OPTIMAL ALLOCATION. Although the word optimal comes from the Latin

word which means 'best', it does not have that embracing significance when used in context. An optimal allocation of resources means only an *efficient* allocation, in the sense in which that term has been defined. It does *not* mean an allocation which is necessarily best from all conceivable points of view.[1]

The Case for *Laissez-faire*

We begin with a restatement of the case for *laissez-faire*. This may now be put in a more rigorous form than the intuitive argument of Adam Smith's 'invisible hand' that we studied in Chapter 2.

An important aspect of the formal case for allowing the free market to determine the allocation of resources is that, given certain important conditions, it will produce an allocation that is efficient in the sense defined above. Let us see first how this case is developed, and then look at the nature of the conditions that are needed to make it work.

The General Case: Buyers are assumed to maximize their satisfactions and sellers to maximize their profits. In doing so, they adjust their demands and supplies of goods and services in response to signals produced by changing market conditions. The signals that they react to are the market prices of the goods they buy or sell.

Recall that buyers maximize their satisfactions when the last unit of each good that they buy yields as much satisfaction as it costs. In other words, the marginal utility (*MU*) of each commodity that they purchase is equal to its price. Recall also that suppliers maximize their profits when the last unit of any good that they produce yields as much revenue as it costs to produce the good. Since the revenue that price-taking suppliers receive from the sale of each unit of a good is the price for which that unit sells, profit maximization requires that price is equal to marginal cost (*MC*).

We have also seen that market forces produce equilibrium situations where price is equal to marginal utility for each consumer and to marginal cost for each producer. It is but a small step, therefore, to conclude that, if all markets are in equilibrium as a

---

1 This is sometimes expressed in the alternative form 'to make at least one person better off without making any other person worse off'. But, given perfect divisibility of goods, this is the same as what we have said in the text. If there are n persons altogether, and one person is given x more while everyone else has unchanged amounts, then all n persons could have been made better off, for example, by giving each x/n more.

---

1 Efficiency in resource allocation, in the sense defined above, is sometimes referred to as *Pareto-efficiency*, after the great Italian economist, Vilfredo Pareto, who first worked out the conditions required to achieve this type of efficiency.

result of the working of the price mechanism, marginal utility for each and every consumer must be equal to marginal cost for each and every producer in each and every market – since both MC and MU are equal to price. Thus, when equilibrium is reached in all markets, the marginal utility of bread, for example, is equal to the marginal cost of bread, the marginal utility of lamb chops is equal to the marginal cost of lamb chops, and so on for every good and service.

Next, consider the meaning of the term 'cost' in the sense used by economists. This we have seen to be real opportunity cost. The opportunity cost of producing a good is the sacrifice of another good that could have been produced with the same resources. If all resources used to produce a good are valued by producers so as to reflect their true opportunity costs, we can measure marginal opportunity cost in money terms. This means that in equilibrium – when marginal costs are equal to prices – an extra pound spent by a producer of one good correctly measures the market value of the other goods that this pound's worth of resources could have produced instead. Since marginal utilities are equal to prices, it follows that these market values also measure the marginal utilities that consumers attach to the goods.

All of this tells us that the equality of marginal utility and marginal cost, brought about by the price system, has a special significance. It means that the extra utility that consumers derive from an additional unit of a good is equal to its opportunity cost, measured by the sacrifice of not having extra quantities of other goods in its place. If this condition holds in the markets for all commodities, the allocation of resources is efficient in the sense defined above.

An Illustration: So far the discussion has been rather abstract. We can give it more intuitive appeal by considering an example using only two goods. We shall call them food and clothing. The markets for these goods are shown in the two parts of Figure 9.7. When the two markets are in equilibrium, the price and quantity of food are p_0 and q_0, while the price and quantity of clothing are P_0 and Q_0. (To distinguish the prices and quantities in the two markets, we use lower-case letters for the food market, and capital letters for the clothing market.)

The best way to show the efficiency of this equilibrium situation is to show the *inefficiency* of any alternative allocation of resources between the two markets. To do this, let us assume that *more* than the equilibrium quantity of resources is allocated to *food*, and *less* than the equilibrium quantity is allocated to *clothing*. Say, for example, that the output of food is q_1 while that of clothing is Q_1. If people are consuming q_1 of food, the marginal utility of food must be p_1 (since the demand curve tells us that p_1 is all that people would be prepared to pay to purchase q_1 units of the commodity). However, if producers are producing q_1 units of food, the marginal cost of producing the last unit is p'_1. Thus, *in the food market, marginal cost exceeds marginal utility*; it costs more to produce the last unit of food than the value consumers put on it (as shown by the amount they would be prepared to pay for it).

Now consider the clothing market. Here the reverse situation holds. Output is only Q_1, which is less than the equilibrium output of Q_0. Since consumers are consuming only Q_1 of clothing, its marginal utility must be P_1 (since the demand curve tells us that P_1 is what they would be prepared to pay for it). Producers, however, have a marginal cost of only P'_1 (which is read off the supply curve at the quantity Q_1).

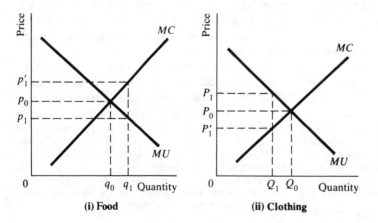

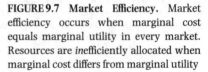

FIGURE 9.7 **Market Efficiency.** Market efficiency occurs when marginal cost equals marginal utility in every market. Resources are *inefficiently* allocated when marginal cost differs from marginal utility

Thus, *in the clothing market, marginal utility exceeds marginal cost*; it would cost less to produce another unit of clothing than the value that consumers would put on that unit.

Next, consider transferring £1's worth of resources from food to clothing production. On the one hand, the extra utility of the additional clothing production is worth more to consumers than the extra cost of producing it. On the other hand, in the food industry, the lost utility from reduced food production is worth less than the marginal cost of producing the food – whose reduction in production released the resources for the additional clothing production. So there is a gain in transferring these resources: all consumers can be made better off by this transfer since *every* consumer values the lost food at *less* than its marginal cost, and *every* consumer values the additional clothing at *more* than its marginal cost. Indeed, efficiency can be continually improved if resources are transferred from food to clothing, as long as the marginal cost of food exceeds its marginal utility, while the marginal cost of clothing is less than its marginal utility.

Thus, when free-market equilibrium is not achieved, it is always possible to transfer resources from industries where marginal cost exceeds marginal utility into industries where marginal cost is less than marginal utility, and make all consumers better off. The source of this gain is the extra value that can be created by moving resources from uses where marginal utility is less than marginal cost and into uses where marginal utility is greater than marginal cost.

When equilibrium does exist, in these two markets (and in all others) there is no further gain in transferring resources. Consumers now value the forgone production in the market that loses the resources the same as they value the additional production in the market that receives the resources. There is no way that resources can be transferred among markets to make everyone better off. Since there is no reallocation that will create extra value, it is not possible to make a reallocation that has the potential of making everyone better off. (Since additional value cannot be created for everyone by reallocating resources, the only way to make some people better off is by taking income from others who are, therefore, made worse off.)

The argument in previous paragraphs is a restatement, using the technical tools now at our disposal, of the intuitive reasoning in the section called 'Eighth Wonder of the World' in Chapter 2. We explained there why the 'invisible hand', as Adam Smith described the price mechanism, had its great appeal. He saw it as an automatic, flexible and self-regulating device which provides, with no conscious overall direction, answers to the basic question of how to allocate resources among competing uses. Moreover, we are now able to describe the allocation of resources brought about through the market system as optimal, in the strict sense of efficient, as we have defined that term at the beginning of this section.

The price mechanism is sometimes also said to result in an allocation of resources in line with 'consumer sovereignty', to imply that the consumer is 'king' and calls the tune as far as resource allocation is concerned. We prefer to avoid the use of that term, which is only half of the truth. A market system gives sovereignty to two groups – producers as well as consumers. Both supply *and* demand determine prices and, therefore, the quantities supplied of different goods and services.

Reservations about the Market System

The criticisms that can be levelled at a *laissez-faire* market economy were also outlined intuitively in Chapter 2. Now we can reconsider them, using our new tools of economic analysis. (Note that, as before, we limit our discussion to microeconomic issues of resource allocation, leaving such 'macroeconomic issues' as economic growth and general unemployment to be dealt with in Part 5 of this book.)

We continue to use a threefold classification for criticisms of market allocations – equity, efficiency and concentrations of economic power. However, since all our analysis up to this point has been based on the assumption that buyers and sellers are price-takers, we are not yet in a position to discuss the consequences of economic power being concentrated in large organizations. We deal here, therefore, only with considerations of equity and efficiency. (In Part 3 we shall take up the question of how far concentration may weaken the case for *laissez-faire*; see Chapters 19, 23 and 24.)

Equity or fairness

The price system allocates resources efficiently (given the assumptions we have made so far). But *efficiency* is not the same thing as *equity* (and equity, you will recall, is not the same thing as equality – equity means fair while equality means equal). It is possible to have an efficient allocation of resources in a society in which there are a few very rich citizens and the rest are very poor. It is also possible to have an efficient allocation in a society in which most of the people have incomes close to the average. All that efficiency guarantees is that it is not possible to make some people better off without making some others worse off. *Given the distribution of income*, there is an advantage in avoiding an inefficient allocation – because when allocation is inefficient *everyone* can be made better off by an appropriate reallocation of resources. But what can we say about two societies, both of which have efficient allocations, but very different distributions of income. To judge between the two, we need to bring in value judgements about these different distributions.

When we first discussed this issue in Chapter 2, we likened the market-place to an 'election' for goods and services, with notes and coins representing 'votes'. Because those with high incomes necessarily have more votes than those with low incomes, the results of 'elections' are bound to be influenced by the distribution of income. If people regard the distribution as inequitable (meaning unfair, not, we would remind you, unequal), the allocation of resources may not be regarded as *satisfactory*, even if it is *efficient*.

We are now ready to take the argument a little further. Recall what we said in Chapter 2 under the heading 'Who Gets It' (see pp. 14–15): the working of the *laissez-faire* market system *determines* the distribution of income. People earn their incomes by selling on the market either the services of the factors of production that they own or the goods that they produce. When the market determines the prices and quantities of these goods and factor services, it also determines the incomes of those who sell them. People who sell goods and factor services that the market values highly will tend to earn large incomes, and people who sell those that have low market values are likely to earn low incomes. We shall have a lot more to say about this aspect of the working of the market in Chapters 20 and 21. In the meantime, we merely note that allowing the *laissez-faire* market mechanism to determine the allocation of resources, also means allowing it to determine the distribution of income.

The second point to consider is that the collection of goods produced will differ between societies with different distributions of income. Consider a society that produces only two goods, caviar and hamburgers, and assume that the workings of the free market produces a very unequal distribution of income. Most of the income is concentrated in the hands of the few rich, and much less finds its way into the hands of the many very poor citizens. As a result there will be a large demand for the caviar that the rich can afford to consume and a smaller demand for the hamburgers that are the fare of the poor. In response to this pattern of demand, caviar production will be high and hamburger production low. As long as the market works efficiently, so that marginal cost is equated to marginal utility in both the hamburger and the caviar industries, the allocation of resources will be efficient: it will be impossible to make any citizen better off without making at least one other citizen worse off.

Most citizens are unlikely, however, to judge such a distribution of income as equitable. Let us suppose that in response to such judgements, a government is elected on a platform of egalitarianism. It uses the tax and expenditure system to reduce income inequalities; the rich are made less rich and the poor less poor. Now the demand for caviar falls and the demand for hamburgers rises. Production will respond so that more hamburgers and less caviar will be produced than in the pre-election situation. Once again, however, as long as the market works efficiently so that marginal cost is equated to marginal utility in both industries, the allocation of resources will be efficient: it will be impossible to make any one citizen better off without making at least one other citizen worse off.

Since resources are efficiently allocated in both the pre- and the post-election situations, there is no way of choosing between the two output combinations on efficiency grounds alone. We can only make such a choice on the basis of our value judgements about which distribution of income is preferable.

This example illustrates the important proposition that efficiency in resource allocation and equity in income distribution are quite distinct concepts. The desire for efficiency is a desire to avoid waste, to avoid situations where everyone could be made better off. The desire for equity is a desire for fairness. We might have a fair distribution of income with resources allocated inefficiently, and we might have an unfair distribution of income with resources allocated efficiently. Of course, the ideal situation is one in which the distribution of income is judged equitable and resources are allocated efficiently.

In conclusion it is important to note that the argument so far has assumed that income can be redistributed without affecting efficiency. Usually this is not the case. The very taxes and expenditures that are used to redistribute income tend to upset the efficiency conditions, making it impossible to achieve an efficient allocation of resources. Thus by redistributing the economic pie (i.e. total output) we tend to make the pie smaller. This means that it is usually necessary to trade off efficiency considerations against equity considerations. Few of us approve of the distribution of income that would result from the completely unhindered working of the market, so we all accept some redistribution of income by the government. Even if we thought a completely equal distribution of income was the most equitable distribution, however, we would hesitate to go that far with government redistribution policies because the effects of such policies in reducing efficiency would shrink the available economic pie too drastically. The important, but very complex, issue of the interrelation between redistributive policies and efficiency is taken up briefly in a later chapter.

Efficiency

The argument of the previous section showed that the allocation of resources in a market system may be efficient without being satisfactory, because the distribution is not regarded as satisfactory. We now take account of the fact that, sometimes, the market system may not even lead to an efficient resource allocation.

Externalities: The idea behind the first reason why market allocations may be inefficient was illustrated in Chapter 2 with the discussion of commodities described as PUBLIC GOODS. Private producers supply goods that they can sell on the market to individual consumers who are prepared to pay for them. But there are goods that are consumed *collectively*, in the sense that if these are provided for one person's benefit, other persons benefit automatically. For example, if lights are provided for a city centre, the lights benefit all who pass beneath them, whether or not the passers-by 'demand' them. The same is true for the police force and many other public goods. Such goods are unlikely to be provided by private suppliers in a *laissez-faire* market system because there is no way to prevent a person who refuses to pay for the good from consuming it anyway. Cinemas can

be provided privately because it is easy to exclude those who will not pay. A lighthouse cannot, because there is no way a private owner can exclude all those who pass by from benefiting from the light whether or not they pay him for providing it.

Public goods are an example of a type of good that the market will not provide. There are other goods that the market may provide, but not in the appropriate quantities to ensure economic efficiency. These are goods which generate what are called *spillover effects* or EXTERNALITIES. Their production, or consumption, indirectly affects persons *other than those who produce or consume them*.

Inoculations, for example, benefit *directly* individuals who have them. But they also *indirectly* benefit others because the reduced risk of contracting infectious disease spills over, from the persons who have been inoculated, to the rest of the community. The benefits accruing to society *as a whole* are, therefore, greater than the benefits accruing to the individuals who obtain them directly. Economists say that *social values* exceed *private values*. In such cases, markets do supply these services for the people who want to buy them for their own benefit. But markets will not supply as much as is needed for an efficient allocation of resources, from *society's* point of view. This is because the persons buying them take no account of the favourable spillover effects on others.

In the above example, *social benefits exceeded private benefits*. In other cases, however, *private benefits exceed social benefits*. These cases occur when the externalities are detrimental to, or impose costs on, other individuals. Free markets supply such goods in overlarge quantities compared to what is needed to achieve economic efficiency from a social point of view.

There is force to the criticism of a *laissez-faire* market system, based on the existence of externalities. The market may *underprovide or overprovide*, compared to the outputs that would be socially optimal. Underprovision occurs where social benefits exceed private benefits – health, education, and the arts, for examples. Overprovision occurs where social costs exceed private costs – pollution and traffic congestion are examples.

Sluggish Markets: There is another sense in which the market mechanism may be said to be inefficient. Market forces may be sluggish and take 'too long' to achieve a satisfactory allocation of resources. There is little to add here to what we said on this subject in

Chapter 2, except to observe that we can now illustrate this possibility with the cobweb theorem, which showed price and quantity oscillations around equilibrium. In this case equilibrium is achieved, if at all, only after much time has passed. We should, however, warn you that economic adjustments take time under any system. The real issue, therefore, is whether markets perform more or less satisfactorily than alternative systems, and whether or not market performance can be speeded up by some forms of policy intervention that cost less to administer than the benefits that they confer.

Concluding Remarks

We ended our preliminary critical consideration of resource allocation under a *laissez-faire* market system in Chapter 2 with the suggestion that it was premature to attempt an assessment of the balance between the advantages and disadvantages of mar-

kets. We end this chapter with the suggestion that it is still premature.

There is much more that we have to learn about market behaviour in the next Part of this book. After that, our final tentative assessment of the performance of the *laissez-faire* market system will come in Chapters 23 and 24. We again say tentative because even the assessment in those later chapters must be 'premature' since much of the economic theory and evidence that is relevant for such an assessment is beyond the scope of an introductory book.

Notice, also, that we have said very little about policies intended to improve the workings of the market system. In later chapters, we shall outline some of these policies and also raise the question of *their* efficiency. It is easier to point out a market inefficiency than it is to design an effective system for removing it. Thus, care must be taken lest, as can sometimes happen, the cure is worse than the 'disease' it is designed to alleviate.

SUMMARY

1 The longer the time-period allowed: (1) the less price will rise and the more quantity will increase following an increase in demand, and (2) the less price will fall and the more quantity will decrease following a decrease in demand.

2 The longer the time-period allowed: (1) the less price will fall and the more quantity will increase following a rise in supply, and (2) the less price will rise and the more quantity will decrease following a fall in supply.

3 The greater the elasticity of supply or demand, the less price will change, and the more quantity will change, in response to a shift in demand or supply.

4 When there is a lagged response of quantity supplied to price, a series of temporary equilibria may ensue. The Cobweb Theorem shows that such equilibria may gradually diverge away from, or converge towards, the equilibrium where the supply and demand curves intersect, or they may oscillate around it.

5 The study of the behaviour of individual markets is known as partial equilibrium analysis. The study of interactions among individual markets is known as general equilibrium analysis. A shift in

any supply or demand curve sets up chain reactions as other supply and demand curves shift in response.

6 The allocation of resources is said to be efficient if it is impossible to make anyone better off without making at least one person worse off by a reallocation of resources.

7 Subject to the presence of certain conditions, a free-market system will result in an efficient allocation of resources, since for each and every consumer and producer the equality of marginal utility and marginal cost is brought about through the equality of each with market price in each and every market. The price mechanism achieves an efficient allocation of resources as a result of the pursuit by consumers of the maximization of utility and by producers of the maximization of profits.

8 Market allocations are not necessarily always desirable. Market shortcomings include: (1) the allocation of resources may be regarded as inequitable (unfair); (2) the market may over- or under-supply goods and services where private and social benefits (or costs) diverge because of externalities; and (3) markets may be sluggish in operating.

How to Use Supply and Demand Analysis

The tools of supply and demand described so far in this book are simple but powerful. If you have understood them, you can apply them to novel situations. In this chapter we show you how to do so. We suggest a 5-step procedural framework to help ensure that you deal with all relevant aspects of any problem (provided, of course, that it does not call for more advanced economic analysis not yet discussed).

THE A-F FRAMEWORK – A 5-STEP PROCEDURE

First, we summarize the 5 steps in the procedure, which can easily be remembered as the alphabetical sequence AB, C, D, E and F. Second, we explain each step in a little more detail. Last, we illustrate how to use the framework with a sample of problems.

The A-F Procedure in Outline

The 5-step procedure we propose is intended to deal with market allocations which start from an equilibrium situation. Some change is then introduced which disturbs that equilibrium. For example, there may be a change in the conditions of demand, or some change may prevent equilibrium being attained. The five steps are labelled

- AB   Appropriate Because
- C   Causes
- D   Direction
- E   Effects
- F   Finale.

AB stands for *appropriate because*. Although we have used only certain elementary tools of analysis in Part 1 of this book, they can be applied to many real-world problems. We must first check that our tools are appropriate to the problem to be studied.

C stands for *causes*. Identify the causes of the changed situation. We distinguish two different causes, which we call Types C_1 and C_2, each of which requires a slightly different treatment in our procedure.

D stands for *direction*. Decide whether the direction of the initial change is positive or negative, e.g. whether demand curves shift to the right or to the left.

E stands for *effects*. This step is usually the longest in the sequence. It involves tracing through the consequences of the change, having regard to prices and quantities over different time-periods.

F stands for *finale*. This is the final step in our procedure, where comments on steps A to E are made. Such comments are on the efficiency of resource allocations, and often also on their equity, as well as more general comments on other relevant issues.

The A-F Step-by-Step Procedure in Detail

The procedure suggested is now discussed in more detail. Our discussion is fairly full and designed to cover the major kinds of analytical question that may be involved. Not every single step, or substep, is necessarily needed in every problem.

Step AB (Appropriate Because)

The elementary supply-demand analysis described in the previous chapters cannot be applied to all problems – only to those for which it is appropriate. The analysis can certainly be applied if all the assumptions of the elementary theory of price hold. These are that demand curves slope downwards, supply curves slope upwards, buyers and sellers try to maximize satisfaction and profits respectively, and buyers and sellers are price-takers. If these assumptions hold, a free-market equilibrium, of the type we have already studied, exists, and you have the green light to proceed to the next step, C.

You would not be able to move on if any of the assumptions are significantly violated,[1] except in one special case described in the next paragraph. In particular, if sellers are price-makers and control output in order to influence prices, the tools of analysis you have so far learned are inadequate. You have to wait until you have read some of the intermediate analysis in Part 3 of this book before you can correctly analyse such situations. (Monopoly theory, for example, is in Chapter 17.)

The major exception to the rule that all the assumptions should hold is where sellers set an *arbitrary* price, which prevents the attainment of a free-market equilibrium. An example would be where the price of tickets for the Wembley Cup Final are set below free-market equilibrium – as everyone knows they are. Sellers are not then price-takers; the price they set is an arbitrary one which differs from what it would be in equilibrium. The elementary tools of supply and demand *are* adequate, however, for comparing the free-market equilibrium with the resource allocation that accompanies arbitrary prices. Hence, you *can* use the A-F framework for such cases.

The problems we have chosen to illustrate the A-F procedure in this chapter are all assumed to pass step AB, so you will not have to worry about this matter now but can concentrate on learning how to use the other steps.

---

1 The qualification 'significantly violated' is important. Theory is always an abstraction from reality, so its assumptions rarely hold exactly. For example, consider the assumption that sellers are all price-takers, which is violated in many retail stores whenever a seller shades his price in order to get your business (most common with consumer durables). However, such price variations are limited and insufficient to render the analysis, based on price-taking assumptions, inapplicable. Unless we were prepared to accept minor departures of reality from theory, we could seldom analyse real-world situations. The acid test of whether a departure is or is not significant is whether economic analysis helps understand the situation to which it is applied.

Step C (Causes)

There are a great many causes of changes in market situations. Step C asks you only to distinguish between two different causes, which we call type C_1 and type C_2.

Type C_1. Equilibrium Changes: The first type of change is one that will cause a market, previously in equilibrium, to move towards a new equilibrium. Anything which causes either the supply or the demand curve to shift is liable to have this effect. For example, a rise in productivity will shift the supply curve to the right, leading to a new and lower price and an increase in the quantity bought and sold in a new equilibrium.

Type C_2. Equilibrium Prevented: The second type of change is one that prevents the attainment of equilibrium. For example, state intervention stipulating a maximum or minimum price for a commodity will usually have this effect, as will the above-mentioned setting of an arbitrary price by sellers.

For correct analysis, it is essential to appreciate the distinction between changes of type C_1 and C_2. The former involve shifts in curves, following changes in the *ceteris paribus* assumptions on which they were drawn. The latter, type C_2, involve analysis of movements along curves.

Step D (Direction)

Step D requires you to determine the direction of change. This is a straightforward application of the principles outlined in Chapters 4 to 9. The precise procedure needs, however, to be varied slightly for the two types of cause, C_1 and C_2, described in Step C.

Type C_1 Changes: For changes involving shifts in either the supply or the demand curve, you must decide not only which curve shifts, but also which way it moves. Thus, for example, a fall in the price of a good which is a substitute for the good under consideration will shift the demand curve to the left; a rise in factor productivity will shift the supply curve to the right, and so on.

Type C_2 Changes: For changes which do not involve shifting curves, but which make equilibrium unattainable, you must first note whether the change is in price or quantity. (The examples we consider here are of the imposition of disequilibrium prices.)

But quantities may also be controlled arbitrarily, as for example when output is restricted by the imposition of quotas while price is left to be determined on a free market.

In the case where a disequilibrium price is imposed, you must then decide whether price is above equilibrium, in which case there will be excess supply, or below equilibrium, in which case there will be excess demand. Thus, for example, state legislation setting a commodity's maximum permitted price below its equilibrium price will cause excess demand; a minimum price set above the equilibrium price will cause excess supply.

In taking Step D, two pairs of concepts which you have learned will be particularly useful: substitutes and complements, and normal goods and inferior goods. For example, to determine the effect of a change in the price of one good on the price of another good, you must decide whether the goods are substitutes or complements in order to find out the direction of change. Or, to determine the effect of a change in consumer income on market price, you must decide whether the good is normal or inferior to find out the direction of change.

Step E (Effects)

This step is normally the longest in the procedure. In it, you should attempt an assessment of the effects of changes, the directions of which were identified in Step D. Usually, such assessment will include the size of the effects, whether due to shifts in supply or demand curves, or to the presence of excess demand or excess supply.

Three substeps that we suggest as guides to the kind of analysis required when considering effects are discussed below:

Effects on Prices and Quantities: An attempt should be made to examine the likely effects on the following variables:
   (a) the own price of the good (p)
   (b) the quantity of the good bought and sold (q)
   (c) total revenue and total outlay on the good (pq)
A major determinant of these effects are the relevant elasticities – price and income elasticities of demand, and elasticities of supply. You might wish to refer back to Chapter 7 to refresh your memory on the determinants of these elasticities when you come to a particular problem.

In the case of type C_2 changes, you should try to quantify the amount of excess demand or supply. (Here again elasticities are relevant.) Since excess demand or excess supply mean that some people cannot succeed in buying or selling all that they wish to at the prevailing price it may also be important for you to determine which consumers actually do succeed in buying, and which suppliers actually do succeed in selling, the good in question. If the forces of demand and supply do not actually allocate commodities in a market system, other mechanisms must be at work. There are several such mechanisms which we discuss when we come to the second illustrative application of the procedure (see below, pp. 115–16).

Effects Over Time: It will sometimes be relevant to consider whether effects, of the kind described above, differ as time passes. It will often be helpful to employ the three categories – momentary, short run and long run (see p. 70).

Primary and Secondary Effects: With some changes, it will be necessary to examine not only *direct* effects on the primary market, but also *indirect* effects on related, or secondary, markets. For example, suppose you are faced with the problem of examining the effects of the introduction of a tax on sales of good x. Our procedure suggests that you should examine, first, the effects of the tax on the price, quantity and total outlay on good x. You should then consider the effects on *related* markets. For example, if x is ballpoint pens, you should consider what will happen in the market for *pencils* when ballpoints are taxed, as well as what will happen in the market for ballpoints. Exactly the same considerations will arise in secondary markets – i.e. elasticities and time-periods – and you would be well advised to think about cross elasticities (see Chapter 7, p. 82) when discussing secondary markets.

Step F (Finale)

As a final step, you are often asked to comment on the results of applying economic analysis, particularly if a question of economic policy is involved – for example, maximum-price control. Two types of comment are called for, in recognition of the two major goals of policy – efficiency and equity. Efficient resource allocations are those (*on* the production possibility curve) where it is not possible to make any one person better off without making at least one other person worse off. Equitable resource allocations are fair ones.

Fairness is a subject which calls for the exercise of personal opinions or value judgements, i.e. normative, rather than positive, issues. Some policies get closer to the goal of efficiency or of equity than to the other. Choosing among them requires, then, a ranking of goals – another matter that calls for value judgements.

You may well be asked to comment on the desirability of particular market allocations. The advantages and disadvantages of market allocations (discussed in Chapter 9) should guide you here. The prime advantages of market allocations follow from the signalling functions of prices, which bring about the equality of marginal utility and marginal opportunity cost. The possible disadvantages of markets, with which we have dealt so far, are related to the distribution of income, the difference between private and social costs and benefits (the presence of externalities), and the sluggishness of markets in some situations.

Moreover, we should stress that when you are asked to comment on a particular policy measure, you should do so in the light of the expressed object of the measure, i.e. how well does it achieve its target? That should not preclude you from commenting on any side-effects. For example, if asked to comment on the desirability of rent controls for accommodation in order to protect tenants, you should consider both whether tenants are protected and also relevant side-effects, e.g. the effects of rent control on the supply of houses and flats for rent. You might also ask, on grounds of equity, why tenants should be singled out for special treatment.

Finally, whenever you are faced with a particular policy proposal, you should always consider, in principle, whether there are alternative policy measures which might be more efficient in achieving a stated objective. There may not be time to make a complete analysis of all possible policy alternatives in every case you come across, but one should never make a final judgement on any one proposal without considering alternative policy measures.

Summary procedure

We now illustrate the 5-step procedure outlined above, fairly fully in two typical cases and more briefly in two others. But we won't take you through Step AB (Appropriate Because) in every case because, as previously stated, we have selected only problems for which the framework is appropriate for analysis.

APPLYING THE A-F PROCEDURE

We shall now illustrate the procedure by taking you through two problems in some detail. Those we have chosen require the application of most of the steps in the procedure in full. That is why we chose them. But when you come to tackling problems of your own, it is important to appreciate that all steps may not be necessary. It depends on the nature of the problem. For example, you might be asked to analyse the effects of a government subsidy on potatoes *on the price of potatoes*, or of the effects of a tax on sugar *on government tax revenue*. These are *limited* questions, and you would only be expected to use the appropriate parts of the A-F framework to do your analysis. It would be quite wrong to use the parts of the framework which deal, for example, with redistributive effects. They would be irrelevant. The framework is not intended to be applied, totally and indiscriminately, for all purposes; you must think of it as your servant, not your master.

Our first application of the A-F framework relates to the imposition of a tax on the sales of a commodity, and it involves a C_1 type change. The second application is the imposition of a maximum price for a commodity, and it involves a C_2 change.

Application No. 1: The Imposition of a Tax on Sales of a Commodity

Governments impose taxes on many goods and services, and for many reasons – e.g. to raise revenue, to redistribute income, or to reduce consumption of a particular good. Suppose we are invited to analyse and comment on a proposal to place a tax of 10p a tube on glue. Let us apply our A-F procedural steps.

Step AB (Appropriate Because)

We assume the procedure is appropriate because the AB conditions discussed earlier in this chapter apply in this case.

Step C (Causes)

This step calls on us to decide whether the imposition of the tax will lead the market towards a new equilibrium or merely prevent the attainment of equilibrium. A good way to decide is to ask whether or not the initial disturbance, here the tax, causes the supply or demand curve to shift. If either (or both) curves shift, we are probably dealing with a type C_1 problem. As a check, ask yourself if there is anything about the initial disturbance that will prevent the attainment of a new equilibrium in which the quantities demanded and supplied are equal. If there is, then you are dealing with a type C_2 change.

Let us suppose that the machinery for imposing the tax is to require sellers of glue to pay the government 10 pence for every unit sold. This must surely affect the quantity sellers will wish to supply at every market price. Hence, the supply curve will shift.[1] Thus, we have a type C_1 change to analyse.

Step D (Direction)

On this step, we must determine the direction of the shift of the supply curve. To find this, note that the 10p tax must be paid to the government on every tube of glue sold. It may be regarded as an increase in the marginal costs of production. As well as paying all their factor costs that went to determine the supply curve, S, producers must pay an additional 10 pence per unit to the government. Hence, the tax shifts the supply curve upwards and to the left. This is illustrated in Figure 10.1. The original supply and demand curves are labelled S and D. The effect of the tax is to shift the supply curve upwards, and hence to the left, to $S+T$. The vertical distance between the two curves is equal to the tax that has to be paid.

To understand this, consider, for example, point c on the supply curve S. This point tells us that q_1 will be offered for sale if suppliers receive a price of p_2. If the tax, bc (equals $p_1 p_2$), is added to the price that sellers receive, they will, in fact, supply q_1. This is because consumers will pay p_1 for q_1 units. Sellers, of course, must pass bc per unit to the government, leaving them with p_2. Hence, a *market* price of p_1 induces sellers to supply q_1 and, thus, point b must be on the new supply curve $S+T$.

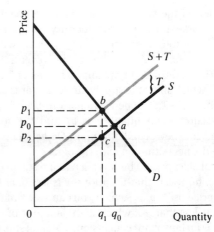

FIGURE 10.1 The Effects of a Tax on the Sales of a Commodity. In general, price rises by less than the full amount of the tax (see Figure 10.2 for exceptions)

Note that b lies above c by an amount exactly equal to the tax per unit. All other points on the new supply curve also lie vertically above the old supply curve by an amount equal to the tax. Hence $S+T$ is parallel to S. (Had the tax been a percentage tax, the new supply curve would lie to the left of the old supply curve, but the vertical difference between them would have been a constant percentage of the price received by sellers. It would lie a constant percentage above the original supply curve and therefore by an increasing absolute amount.)

Step E (Effects)

Now we come to the meat of the analysis, and ask the question what happens to market price, quantity bought and sold, and total outlay. Remember, relevant considerations include the elasticities of demand and supply and the time-period.

It is sometimes helpful to consider the effects in four limiting cases of elasticities of both demand and supply, where each is equal to zero and to infinity. This allows you to draw conclusions about intermediate cases: the higher the actual elasticity, the closer will the result be to the infinite elasticity case and the lower the actual elasticity, the closer the result will be to the zero-elasticity case. First, however, let us analyse the typical case where the elasticity of both supply and demand are greater than 0 and less than ∞, as in Figure 10.1.

The Typical Case: The original equilibrium is at the

---

1 Note, it would be perfectly satisfactory to analyse this problem by shifting the demand curve rather than the supply curve. If we deduct the tax from the demand curve then both the D and S curves indicate the after-tax price received by sellers. If we add the tax to the supply curve, then both the D and the S curve indicate the pre-tax market price paid by buyers. Deducting the tax from the demand curve would indeed be the more obvious way of approach if the state were to collect the 10p tax directly from consumers instead of from sellers. Some textbooks analyse tax incidence in this fashion (drawing a new demand curve net of tax). The results are the same regardless of approach. You can test this for yourself by trying the alternative method *after* you have read to the end of the section.

intersection of the supply curve S and the demand curve D; market price is p_0, the quantity bought and sold is q_0 and total consumer outlay (which when there are no taxes is also the sellers' revenue) is Op_0aq_0. The government now imposes a tax of T per unit sold, which shifts the supply curve upwards and to the left, to $S+T$. The new equilibrium price is p_1, the new equilibrium quantity is q_1 and the total outlay at the new equilibrium, is Op_1bq_1. Let us compare the new situation with the old.

First, consider price. This has risen as a result of the tax. Note, however, that *the price rise is less than the tax*. The price rise is p_0p_1, which you can see from the diagram is less than bc, which is the amount of the tax. This is an important conclusion. We shall shortly examine special circumstances when the price change is equal to the tax, but in the case where *neither* demand *nor* supply has an elasticity of zero or infinity, sellers do not pass the full amount of a tax on to consumers. They cannot do so if market forces are allowed to work.

Consider, next, the change in quantity. This falls as a result of the tax from q_0 to q_1. This is a second general conclusion (though, again, we examine exceptions below in the next diagram). The imposition of a tax on a commodity lowers the quantity bought and sold. Finally, consider the change in total consumer outlay and sellers' revenue. Whether this

rises or falls depends, of course, on the value of the elasticity of demand. If the elasticity is greater than unity, the rise in price reduces consumers' total outlay; if it is less than unity, total outlay rises.

Total outlay by consumers is not, however, the same as total receipts by sellers because part of sellers' revenue must be passed over to the government. Sellers' total receipts, net of tax, are shown by the area Op_2cq_1. Government tax revenue is the new equilibrium quantity, q_1, multiplied by the tax, bc, which is the area, p_1bcp_2.

Extreme Cases: The conclusion that the imposition of a tax on a commodity causes market price to rise, but by less than the full amount of the tax, does not hold in four extreme cases, which are illustrated in Figure 10.2. That diagram is in four sections, two which show price rising by the full tax and two which show price unchanged despite the tax. *Price rises exactly as much as the tax if either demand elasticity is zero or supply elasticity is infinite*. These cases are illustrated in Figure 10.2(i) and (ii), and are self-explanatory.

The remaining sections of Figure 10.2 (iii) and (iv) show the cases where the tax does *not* affect market price. This occurs when *either demand is perfectly elastic or supply is perfectly inelastic*. Section (iii) of the diagram is again self-explanatory, but it is worth

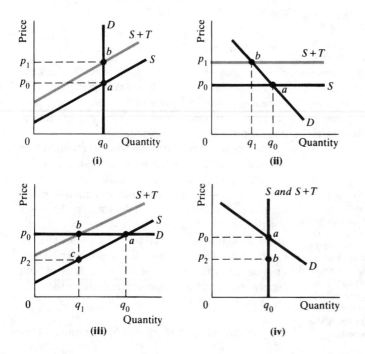

FIGURE 10.2   The Effects of a Tax on the Sales of a Commodity. Four extreme cases of demand and supply: (i) demand completely inelastic – price rise equals tax; (ii) supply completely elastic – price rise equals tax; (iii) demand completely elastic – price unchanged by tax; (iv) supply completely inelastic – price unchanged by tax

pointing out the reason why there is only one supply curve in the case of section (iv) because it may not be immediately obvious. The reason is that, when supply elasticity is zero, sellers offer the same quantity for sale regardless of the price they receive. Hence, there is only one supply curve, which is labelled both S and $S+T$. The quantity q_0 is offered for sale before and after the tax, though sellers' total receipts are, of course, different in the two cases. Without any tax, total receipts are Op_0aq_0 (which is equal to total outlay by consumers). With the tax, however, sellers only retain Op_2bq_0. The remainder, p_0abp_2, is handed over to the government as tax revenue.[1]

There is one more question to ask about these exceptional cases. How does quantity bought and sold after the tax compare with quantities in the original equilibrium? In the typical case (i.e. when the elasticities of supply and demand are greater than 0 and less than infinity), quantity falls after the tax is introduced. This conclusion holds also in two of the exceptional cases – when either the demand or the supply curve is perfectly elastic, as in sections (ii) and (iii) of Figure 10.2.

In the two other exceptional cases, the conclusion does not hold. If either the demand or the supply curve is perfectly inelastic, the quantity bought and sold does not change after the tax is introduced (see Figure 10.2 (i) and (iv)). It is not difficult to understand why this is so. If changes in price leave either quantity supplied or demanded unaffected, it is not surprising that market equilibrium pre- and post-tax shows the intersection of the supply and demand curves at the same quantity.

Effects in Different Time-periods: Recall that our Step E requires consideration of what happens when we vary the time-period under consideration. We can make certain generalizations about such differences using Figures 10.1 and 10.2. We use the threefold classification of time-periods – momentary, short and long run – in this analysis.

(i) *Momentary period*. The instantaneous market situation is that of Figure 10.2 (iv) – supply is perfectly inelastic.

(ii) *Short run*. Compared to the momentary period,

in the short run both demand and supply tend to be more elastic; hence Figure 10.1 may better represent the situation than Figure 10.2 (iv).

(iii) *Long run*. In the long run, both demand and supply tend to be even more elastic than in the short run. The limiting cases are where supply is perfectly elastic, as in Figure 10.2 (ii), and where demand is perfectly elastic, as in Figure 10.2 (iii). As we shall see when we come to study costs of production (Chapter 15), the former case is quite common in the long run, when costs of production are constant with changing output, leading to a perfectly elastic supply curve. The latter case, in contrast, is exceptional, even in the long run. Elasticity of demand equal to infinity is rarely found. Figure 10.2 (iii) might, however, come close to representing the effects of a tax on a commodity such as red bicycles, for which almost perfect substitutes – black, green and purple bicycles – exist. Consumers would switch their purchases to bicycles of other colours, leaving market price of red bicycles almost unchanged, and bringing in little tax revenue to the government. (Even in this case, however, we would not expect demand to be perfectly elastic. If people have colour preferences we would expect them to be willing to pay some amount to exercise those preferences.)

The four limiting cases illustrated in Figure 10.2, and the general case shown in Figure 10.1, show the very different effects a tax can have on market price, sellers' receipts and tax revenue as demand and supply elasticities differ. In a real problem, it would be useful to obtain some empirical evidence on the values of supply and demand elasticities over various time-periods.

Secondary Market Effects: So far in Step E, we have concentrated on effects in the primary market – i.e. the market for glue – on which the tax was levied. In principle, one should next look to see whether there are any secondary markets closely related on the demand and/or the supply side. This is the point at which cross elasticities are relevant.

Sometimes the effects on secondary markets are small enough to be safely ignored. At other times the effects are large and it would be dangerous to ignore them.

For an extreme example of the latter case, assume that initially the government is levying a tax on all new cars and that it then elects to double the tax on red cars only. The main primary result will be a large drop in sales of cars of that colour, without raising

---

1 You may like to notice that this case is not an exception to our rule that the tax shifts the supply curve vertically upwards by the amount of the tax. If you take any point on a vertical supply curve and shift it upwards by any amount, you will still get the same vertical curve.

much revenue for the government. If you looked only at the primary market, that would be the end of your story. But those who would have bought red cars will now buy cars of other colours. So there will be an increase in the demand for all other cars approximately equal to the fall in sales of red cars. Tax revenues will rise on the resulting extra sales. In this case an analysis of the effect on the government's revenue from the increased tax on red cars based solely on the demand and supply curves for red cars would have been hopelessly in error.

Step F (Finale)

In the final step of our procedure, we need to evaluate the potential success of the government's policy. We can, of course, comment generally on the efficiency and equity aspects of the resource allocation. To relate our analysis towards the specific criteria, however, we need to know the government's objective in imposing the tax. Because we have not been told what it is, we must now consider a number of alternative objectives – raising revenue, discouraging consumption and redistributing income.

If the main purpose of the tax is to raise revenue for the state, the conclusion is clear. A given unit tax will produce more income for the government the less elastic is demand or supply (e.g. Figure 10.2 (i) or (iv)). If, in contrast, the prime purpose is to discourage consumption (perhaps because, for example, of health hazards from sniffing glue), the answer is equally clear, though different. The fall in the quantity bought and sold is greater the greater is the elasticity of demand or supply (see Figure 10.2 (ii) and (iii). If the government's aim is redistributive, the analysis is much more complex, and we cannot consider it in detail here. Suffice to say that we should need to know whether the objective is to give most help to the buyers or the sellers of glue. If we are told this, we can attempt an assessment of the redistributive effects of the tax by reference to whether the facts of the situation were such as to cause the tax to fall more heavily on the one or the other group (though it is pretty obvious that a tax on glue is a very poor instrument for redistribution from rich to poor).

If there are no reasons to suspect the existence of externalities or sluggish markets (as is probable in the case of glue), there remains only one final observation to make in our commentary. This simple, though important, conclusion concerns the efficiency of resource allocation: if there is reason to believe that resource allocation was efficient before the tax was imposed, then we should be more content with the tax if market conditions resembled those of Figure 10.2 (i) or (iv). These are the cases where either supply or demand are perfectly inelastic, because in neither of them is there any change in the quantity bought and sold. Hence, if resource allocation was efficient before the tax, it will remain efficient after the tax. Having said that, one should be warned that it does not follow that taxes on goods in highly inelastic demand or supply are always to be preferred to taxes on other goods. There are other considerations to be taken into account. We discuss some of these in Chapters 23 and 24.

Application No. 2: A Maximum Price for Bread

Many goals of economic policy have been pursued through the use of controls, of which one type is the setting of legal maximum and minimum prices. For our second illustration of the application of the A–F procedure, we shall analyse and comment on a hypothetical government proposal to introduce a price ceiling for bread. We are told, in this case, that the reason for the measure is redistributive – to help the poor. Let us apply our procedure, beginning at Step C, because, as previously stated, we assume that the problem has passed through Step AB, and that our framework is appropriate to use.

Step C (Causes)

In this step, we ask whether the introduction of a price ceiling is a type C_1 or a type C_2 cause. Type C_1 changes involve the market moving to a new equilibrium because of a shift occurring in either the demand or supply curve. Type C_2 changes prevent equilibrium being attained. Price controls do nothing to shift demand or supply curves. They affect price, but not quantities demanded or offered for sale at every possible price. Therefore, a type C_2 analysis is called for – equilibrium prevented.

Step D (Direction)

The third step in the procedure calls for an indication of the direction of change to be expected. For changes which do not involve any shifts in supply or demand curves but prevent equilibrium being attained, you

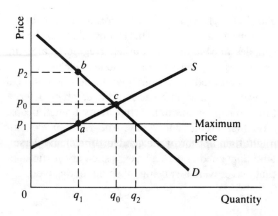

FIGURE 10.3   A Price Ceiling. A maximum price set below equilibrium creates excess demand

must decide whether excess supply or excess demand develops. In order to answer the question, a diagram may be helpful.

In Figure 10.3, the market for bread is depicted, with equilibrium price p_0 and equilibrium quantity bought and sold q_0. Notice that the imposition of a price control does not necessarily interfere with the operation of market forces. If the maximum price is set *at or above* the equilibrium price, there would be no reason why that price should not continue to prevail. There would, then, be no effect to be analysed, and we need not proceed any further. Equilibrium is attainable.

It would, of course, be rather pointless for the state to set a price ceiling at a level which had no current effect (though such a policy might be introduced to prevent price rising above existing levels in the future). More commonly, price ceilings are set below equilibrium market prices. In this case, we assume the legal maximum price for bread to be p_1 in Figure 10.3. We can see from the diagram that, at price p_1, consumers wish to buy q_2 bread, while sellers are only prepared to offer q_1 for sale. In the absence of the price control, market forces would tend to push price upwards. However, this is illegal and, provided the maximum price can be enforced (see below), there will be an excess of quantity demanded over quantity supplied. That is the direction of change, and we move to Step E to consider the effects that might follow the appearance of excess demand.

Step E (Effects)

We are now ready to take the biggest step in our

procedure and examine the effects of the excess demand for bread that follows the imposition of a price ceiling.

We ask, first, what happens to price, quantity and total outlay, according to the proposed framework for analysis. These questions cause little problem if we assume that 'policing' arrangements are completely effective, so that no bread is sold at prices above the legal limit. Price falls from p_0 to p_1, quantity bought and sold falls from q_0 to q_1, and consumers' outlay, and sellers' revenue, falls from $Op_0\,cq_0$ to $Op_1\,aq_1$.

When equilibrium is unattainable because of a price ceiling, however, there is a new and important question to be asked. This question is a direct result of the presence of excess demand, q_2-q_1. From Figure 10.3, we can tell that consumers would like to buy q_2 at the legal price, while there is only q_1 available. The question is, who is to get the supply q_1?

Economic theory does not offer a single answer to this type of question. There are several alternative ways in which the relatively small supply can be allocated when there is a legal maximum price.

We can consider them under five headings: (1) queues, (2) black markets, (3) rationing, (4) sellers' preferences, (5) random allocation.

Queues: The first possibility is that queues will develop for the product in relatively short supply. The length of the queue will be directly related to the amount of excess demand, q_2-q_1. In the case of a product such as the bread which we are examining, the probability is that the queues will take the form of physical lines of people outside bakers' shops and at bread counters in supermarkets. Note, however, that queueing can take other forms, one of the most common of which is the growth of waiting lists of those wanting to buy goods in short supply. If there are waiting lists, the length of time that one must wait one's turn to be supplied is directly related to the amount of excess demand, q_2-q_1. Queueing through waiting lists is often used with consumer durables, such as popular new-model cars, and with council flats and houses.

Black Markets: The second possibility is that the law will be broken and some bread sold on the black market at prices in excess of p_1. It is bound to be profitable for sellers to do this because, as we can see from Figure 10.3, consumers would be prepared to pay p_2 for the amount q_1.

Whether or not black markets develop, and what

proportion of total supply finds its way to them, are questions beyond the realm of economics. The answers depend on such matters as the strength of the incentive to break the law described in the previous paragraph, the efficiency of compliance measures taken by the government, including the severity of penalties imposed on offenders, and the willingness of consumers to pay black-market prices. It is unlikely that all the available output is ever put on the black market, but human nature appears to be such that some black-market activity is usual.

Rationing: The third possible way of allocating a short supply is by rationing. The government can issue ration books containing coupons which must be surrendered, as well as cash, to obtain bread. The state can control the supply of coupons to equal the available supply. Rationing by coupon was widespread in the UK during the war, when prevailing views were egalitarian – fair shares for all in the pursuit of victory. Rationing in peacetime is rare. It tends to be unpopular, and costly to administer. (Note, rationing does not defeat its egalitarian objective even if coupons are freely transferable. If the poor prefer to sell their coupons and use the proceeds to buy goods other than bread, they may be even better off than if everyone receives an identical supply of non-saleable coupons.)

Sellers' Preferences: The fourth possible means whereby limited supplies may be allocated is where the sellers decide whom to sell to. There are many ways in which they might do this. For example, shopkeepers might choose to sell on a first-come, first-served basis. Under such circumstances since sellers are not exercising their preferences, the allocation is that of the first alternative described on the previous page, namely by queues. Alternatively, sellers might store bread 'under the counter' and give preference to regular customers, for example, or to those who also buy their cakes and pastries. In the case of some commodities subject to price ceilings, sellers may opt to give preference to whomsoever they choose. Council dwellings, for instance, are allocated on a points' system, intended to reflect 'needs', by awarding points for family size and income, as well as other 'sellers'' preferences, e.g. length of residence in the area, for which points are usually given.

Random Allocation: For completeness, we should mention a fifth way in which supplies may be allocated, which we describe, for want of a better description, as random. This is most likely to occur if supplies appear on the market irregularly and the product is very perishable. Bread is a fair example of such a commodity, though it would be a better one if we were considering bread in France, which deteriorates so rapidly in quality that many French people buy their bread twice daily. The random element might then appear in the good fortune of any person who happened to pass a baker's shop at the moment that loaves were just being taken out of the oven.

Effects in different time-periods

In respect to the present case, economic analysis has little to offer on the question of different expected effects as the time-period under consideration lengthens. Any of the five allocative mechanisms described above may persist in the long term as well as the short. However, the short-run demand and supply curves may shift as a result of the enforced disequilibrium price. Consumers, deprived of the opportunity of buying as much bread as they would like, may decide to bake their own, or turn to substitutes for which they may acquire a taste. This means a leftward shift in the demand curve for bread. Sellers, faced with the low price of bread, began by cutting back on production to equate marginal cost with the new lower price. But a lower level of production means that there will be excess capacity in terms of too many bakers, too many ovens and too many shops in the bread industry. As time passes, thought will be given to alternative ways of utilizing underused resources. Some bakers will switch to other occupations and some equipment will not be replaced when it wears out. Thus, the supply curve of bread will shift to the left as the size of the bread industry shrinks. Supply-side forces, therefore, tend to increase the shortage as bakers switch to other occupations, while demand-side forces work to moderate the shortage as consumers switch their purchases to substitutes for bread. The net effect on excess demand cannot therefore be predicted in the absence of further quantitative knowledge.[1]

---

1 It may be worth noting a difference between supply and demand in this case. On the supply side, bakers can sell all they want so their responses are the ones we analysed in general terms in earlier chapters – more elastic the longer the time-span under consideration. Demanders cannot buy all they wish so their response is

Secondary-market effects

As suggested in the previous sections, the imposition of a price ceiling for bread might well have significant impacts on related markets. The legal maximum price for bread disturbs the previous equilibrium between that price and the price of bread substitutes. Sellers will be encouraged to turn to the production of goods such as cakes and other flour confections, by the relative price differential. Buyers, too, will turn to substitute products because of the shortfall in supplies of bread caused by the price ceiling. We cannot tell whether the end result will be that of a rise in the price of cakes, etc. That will depend on whether there is a larger switch on the demand or on the supply side. If the former exceeds the latter, the price of cakes will rise, and vice versa. But whatever happens, the allocation of resources will be different from what would occur under a freely working price mechanism.

If people spend less money on bakery products in general, then they will have more to spend on all other goods. Presumably much of this will go to buy other food products. The effect, however, is likely to be spread over the markets for so many products that the effect in any one will be negligible. If so this is a case where effects in secondary markets can be ignored.

Step F (Finale)

In this final step in our procedure, we comment on the efficiency and equity aspects of the resource allocation. In this case, we have been told that the object of the price ceiling was to benefit the poor, so we must consider if it does so and how effectively.

Consider, first, efficiency. Let us compare the new allocation of resources with that brought about by free-market forces. The equilibrium price, before the price control was introduced, cleared the market at an output which ensured the equality of marginal cost and marginal utility. The legislation removed that equality and led to an output at which marginal utility was greater than marginal cost (the difference between them being *ab* in Figure 10.3). We know, however, that market allocations are preferable only under certain conditions, one of which is that no

redistribution is considered to be worth the cost.[1] So although there may well be efficiency losses, these may be judged to be acceptable if they are small and the measure helps the poor enough. Let us proceed by asking two questions: (1) whether the price ceiling fulfils its purpose of helping the poor, and (2) whether there might be a better way of doing this.

Consider the first question which asks, in effect, whether redistribution of income in favour of those at the bottom of the scale results from the price ceiling. The answer depends on which of the five methods of allocation discussed in Step E are actually adopted. Let us consider them one by one.

Queues: Suppose, first, queues form outside bakers' shops. Will this achieve the objective of helping the poor? The answer can only be yes if the poor manage to be in the front of the queues. If, as may be the case, they have less time to spare for queueing, the answer will be no. Allocation by queueing gives preference to people with most time available for standing in queues, for example those households with retired and unemployed members. So, for example, rich families with retired parents living in or nearby will gain at the expense of single-parent families with children in school. Some rich people have even been known to pay others to stand in queues for them. In other words, redistribution may be haphazard by income or even perverse, in the sense that most of the cheap bread goes to the rich while the poor account for most of the unsatisfied demanders.

Black Markets: The second alternative we considered was allocation through black markets. If this were to happen, the objective of helping the poor would certainly be hindered. Insofar as the black-market price exceeds the free-market equilibrium price without a price ceiling, the poor are *less* able to afford bread than before, and there is less bread to go around as well.

Rationing: Thirdly, suppose the government sup-

---

something we have not analysed previously. Their demand curves are shifting in response to a new variable, the probability of being able to buy the good when they want it. When dealing with unhindered markets we did not need this variable because in equilibrium there were no unsatisfied demanders (or suppliers).

1 Market allocations can only be regarded, strictly speaking, as ideal if the distribution of income is fair and equitable. Since we are never likely to encounter such a situation in real life, the condition is stated as in the text. We do not inhabit an ideal world and the only useful consideration is this operational one. Market allocations may not be distributively fair, but if the cost of deviating from them is greater than the gain in equity, then they are preferable, or optimal; otherwise, not.

ports its price control with a coupon rationing scheme. What then? If rations are set to be equal per head of the population, the poor will certainly benefit in being able to buy cheaper bread, though probably less of it than they would wish to buy. Note, too, that the favourable income distributive effect (in terms of the stated objective of greater equality) is not frustrated by allowing coupons to be freely transferable. Indeed, the poor may be even better off if they can sell their ration coupons for cash, and use the money to buy things they value even more highly than bread.

Sellers' Preferences: Fourthly, allocation might be according to sellers' preferences. We cannot deal with all the possible outcomes here. They are as many as the different preferences that might motivate sellers. However, let us consider two examples, both possible. In the first case, assume bakers decide to ration supplies unofficially, and equally, to each of their regular customers. The effects would be rather similar to official rationing by the government, except in so far as the customers of bakers with relatively few regular customers do better than others. In contrast, if there are customers who are not regulars at any shop, they will get no bread at all. In the second case, assume that bakers favour customers who buy other goods from them – cakes, pastries, etc. In so far as these other goods are more expensive commodities, less affordable by the poor, the stated objective of helping lower income groups may be frustrated. Indeed bakers could raise the price of the cakes sold along with the bread, so that the total price of cakes plus bread was what it would have been in the absence of the price cutting.

Random Allocation: Lastly, allocation may be what we have called 'random', when the probability of some of the poor being assisted by the price control will be, by definition, a matter of chance. However, since some rich and some poor will be lucky, and other rich and other poor unlucky, the most likely outcome will be no redistribution, on average, among income groups – although there will be redistribution between the lucky and unlucky groups.

The only conclusion we can reach, therefore, on whether the price ceiling will achieve its goal of helping the poor must be that it depends on the actual way in which the shortfall in supply is allocated. Certainly, redistribution will occur, but without rationing it is unlikely to be from rich to poor.

There is, however, one other result that we reached in Step E to be taken into account. This concerns the probability of demand and supply switching to related markets. Let us reflect on this aspect briefly.

Secondary market implications may work in many ways. Let us for purposes of illustration consider just one. Suppose there is a bigger transfer of demand than of supply to one close substitute for bread – namely cakes – which causes the price of cakes to rise. Indeed, it is commonly found that price ceilings have the effect of pushing up the prices of substitute goods. This may frustrate, at least partially, the stated objective of the government, however effective are the measures used to enforce a fair allocation of the limited supplies of the price-controlled commodities. For example, during the war, 'meat' was strictly rationed, as well as being price controlled. One consequence was that those who could afford it bought unrationed poultry and game at high free-market prices. This is not to say that the system was completely ineffective, simply that it was not 100 per cent egalitarian in impact. Nor could it be. It is virtually impossible (as well as very costly) to control all prices and ration all goods and services.

So far, we have only considered the effects on consumers. Bakers will be affected as well as their customers. If the demand switches to substitutes made by bakers, they may not be seriously affected. But if the demand switches to other products, e.g. imported Norwegian biscuits, bakers lose sales and some may be driven out of business. Thus, bakers as a whole suffer, and it is important to include them in the redistributive effects. The final assessment, which includes the benefit to bread consumers and other redistributive effects discussed above, should include the effects on producers' incomes as well. If some bakers are poorer than their customers, the redistribution, on this account, could be from poor to rich.

When we outlined our A–F procedure for the application of supply and demand analysis, we stressed the importance of considering alternative policy measures for achieving a stated objective. Such a step is essential before forming a final judgement on a particular policy proposal, such as the imposition of a price ceiling for bread, which we have analysed.

Since the maximum-price control was designed to help the poor, we ought to compare our results with analyses of alternative policies having the same aim. To do so in full would be an enormous task simply because of the multitude of redistributive policies that can be adopted. We may, however, mention here two alternatives to a price ceiling on bread, for purposes of illustration. One method would be to allow a free market to operate for bread but to subsidize bread purchases by the poor. Coupons, valued at so much money when spent on bread, could be given to those below a certain income. (Bakers who accepted these could redeem them for cash from the government.) Such a measure would have two main advantages over the price ceiling. In the first place, the benefits would be restricted to the poor; and in the second place, there would be no decline in bread production. Another policy alternative would be to forgo all direct intervention in the bread market and give all poor people a straightforward income supplement, thereby increasing their purchasing power. There is a lot to be said in favour of this alternative, which benefits all poor people, regardless of how much they happen to like bread.

Further Applications

We have outlined what we call the A-F procedure for applying supply and demand analysis. We believe you should find it a helpful framework that can be used for any suitable problem that you come up against. We illustrated the procedure with only two applications. They were, however, carefully chosen to cover the two different types of situation that crop up – described as types C_1 and C_2 in Step C, *causes*.

You already have adequate tools in your toolkit for dealing with a wide range of problems similar to those analysed in the two illustrations given in this chapter. For example, the procedure for applying supply and demand analysis to state subsidies on a commodity would run along the lines of the tax illustration. The main difference would be that you would shift the supply curve to the right instead of to the left. You could use the same steps in your analysis for any change which caused a shift in the supply or demand curve – for example the requirement that petrol sold should be lead-free, which would shift the supply curve to the left because of the additional costs incurred, or the increase in the price of oil following the OPEC price shocks of 1973 and 1980, and the decrease in the price following the growth of non-OPEC supplies (the second is not unrelated to the first).

Similarly, you could use the analysis illustrated in the case of price ceilings for bread, for other problems which result in the creation of excess demands – for example the allocation of any commodity by means

other than market forces. Likewise, you could twist the procedure slightly to cope with problems of excess *supply*, such as result from the introduction of a *minimum* price above the equilibrium price, for a good or service. You will, in such a case, have to provide a set of alternative ways in which the excess supply is disposed of – though you should not find it too hard if you base your set on the categories used in the second application (see pp. 117–18). They will look a little different – i.e. the queues will be of frustrated *sellers* wishing to dispose of surplus supplies; the black markets will be where sellers *undercut* the legal minimum price; rationing will be some kind of system where sellers allocate quotas among themselves; sellers' preferences will be translated into *buyers'* preferences, as consumers choose where to make their purchases.

The rather special nature of supply and demand conditions in agricultural markets will require careful attention in Step D. These affect both supply and demand curves. On the supply side, price elasticity of supply tends to be low, especially in the short run. Once a crop has been planted, it is harvested in due course, though weather conditions and the incidence of disease may cause the actual quantities supplied to vary, sometimes very greatly, from year to year. Sudden large fluctuations in quantity supplied caused by forces other than price changes are one of the major reasons why governments intervene in agricultural markets. In addition, there are cases of lagged responses by farmers to price in previous periods, so that the cobweb theorem may be relevant. On the demand side, the price elasticity tends to be low also. In the case of foodstuffs, this arises from the fact that consumption tends to vary less with price changes than it does, say, for many manufactured goods. In the case of raw materials, such as timber, textile fibres and hides and skins, the prime determinant of quantity demanded is frequently the level of consumer income, which has the consequence that the *price* elasticity of demand is low (though the *income* elasticity of demand may be high).

Agricultural market conditions, with low price elasticities of both demand and supply, are associated with the large fluctuations in prices and quantities mentioned earlier. Draw a diagram with steeply sloping S and D curves. Let S shift to show a bumper harvest and a poor one, and note the effects on price. Then let D shift to show a rise and fall in consumers' income, and observe similar effects on price. Note, too, what happens to total revenue of farmers (and to total outlay by consumers). When the demand curve shifts, farmers' total revenue varies in the same direction as output. When the supply curve shifts, however, revenue varies *in the opposite direction to output* because of the low elasticity of demand. Thus, farm incomes tend to be high when the harvest is poor and low when there is a bumper harvest.

You are now ready to consider policy options. A price ceiling can be analysed in similar manner to that used in our example of a maximum price for bread (i.e. type C_2 cause). A price floor calls for parallel treatment, also involving a type C_2 cause. A subsidy to farmers when incomes are low calls for a rightward shift of the supply curve (and is a type C_1 cause). A buffer-stock policy is one where the government sets the price and enters the market, buying surpluses and selling from its own stockpiles when there is either excess supply or demand, respectively (i.e. the demand curve, or the supply curve, becomes perfectly elastic at the controlled price so the cause is type C_1).[1]

Allocation of a fixed supply

A common problem concerns alternative methods of allocating the supply of a commodity which is fixed, for example the supply of tickets for the Centre Court at Wimbledon, or of seats at Wembley Stadium for the Cup Final. A less hackneyed example would be a university with limited parking spaces for cars, relative to the number of staff who would like to use them. How should the available spaces be allocated?

One method is to charge the market-clearing price. This method is often rejected in favour of alternative ways of allocating the fixed supply. When this is done we have a type C_2 problem, because equilibrium is prevented. The alternatives could be analysed using our A-F framework. Under Step E, you might include the following possibilities: allocation by ballot, by seniority (i.e. rank) of staff, by length of service of staff, on a first-come, first-served basis, as a 'perk' for doing unpopular jobs, and by any other means you can think of. Sometimes a problem arises of choosing between different methods of allocation. For example, suppose a town has two squash courts. One sells time at a profit-maximizing price. The other allocates use at a price below free-market equilibrium, using an advance booking system. Suppose one of the courts is to close. Which should it be?

SUMMARY

This chapter sets out a 5-step A-F procedure for the application of elementary supply and demand analysis to solve problems you might face.

AB (Appropriate Because): The first step is to check that the procedure can be applied to the particular problem – i.e. that free-market equilibrium exists or is possible. This will be the case if the assumptions, that we have used thus far actually hold: (1) demand curves slope downwards, (2) supply curves slope upwards, (3) buyers and sellers are maximizers, and (4) buyers and sellers are price-takers. This will not be the case if some authority has imposed an arbitrary price which prevents the attainment of free-market equilibrium.

C (Causes): The second step is to identify the cause of change. Two types are distinguished – type C_1, where equilibrium changes (because of a shift in a supply and/or demand curve), and type C_2, where equilibrium is prevented (e.g., because of the imposition of a price control).

D (Direction): The third step is to decide on the direction of the change that will take place. For type C_1 causes, this means deciding on whether supply and/or demand curves shift, and whether to the right or the left.

For type C_2 causes, this means deciding on whether excess demand or excess supply will develop. Relevant concepts are substitutes/complements, and normal/inferior goods.

E (Effects): The fourth step calls for analysis of the size of the effects of the change on such matters as price, quantity, and total outlay. Relevant concepts are elasticities of demand and supply, and the time-period (momentary, short- and long-run). For type C_2 causes, the question of how excess supply or demand is allocated should be considered (e.g., whether by queues, black markets, rationing, sellers' preferences, or other means). Note also effects on the primary market and on secondary or related markets.

F (Finale): The fifth step is the most varied. Some problems call for consideration of economic policy, when the goals of efficiency and equity should be considered. A policy should usually be assessed against alternatives and positive and normative issues kept separate. Some problems call for comparison of market allocations with other means of allocating resources. Relevant considerations are the automatic, flexible and low cost of operation of markets; market shortcomings are concerned with equity, externalities, and possible sluggishness of market forces.

Part 3

INTERMEDIATE MICROECONOMICS

11

Indifference Curves

In the elementary theory of demand in Part 2, we began the study of consumer behaviour. In this and the next chapter, we delve deeper into the same subject, developing some new analytical tools here, and applying them in Chapter 12.

Our early discussion of demand was based on three assumptions. First, we assumed that consumers maximize their satisfaction. Second, we assumed that consumers are price-takers. Third, we assumed that consumers' marginal utilities diminish as their consumption of commodities increases (from which we derived the implication that demand curves slope downwards).

The first of these assumptions is also used in our intermediate theory.

The second assumption, that buyers are price-takers – i.e. that not one of them is large enough to affect market price by buying larger or smaller amounts – will require further consideration. Occasionally, the assumption is not fulfilled. To deal with cases of consumer power, we shall later develop a theory of what is called *monopsony*, which refers to a market in which there is only one buyer. For now, we maintain the assumption of price-taking which applies to most consumers most of the time.

The third assumption that we have used so far is that of diminishing marginal utility. In the present chapter, we deal with a theory of consumer behaviour that does not employ that assumption. Since our new theory does not assume that marginal utilities can be measured or compared, it is not based on the assumption of diminishing marginal utility (but on an alternative that produces similar results).

CHOICES FACING A CONSUMER

We begin by studying the behaviour of a single consumer, who has a given money income and is faced with the decision of how to allocate that income between *only two goods*, which we shall call eggs and bacon. (Later we extend the analysis to cover the case of many goods.) There are three pieces of information that are necessary before we can proceed. They are the consumer's income, the prices of the goods, and the consumer's tastes.

We may start by considering how to represent diagramatically the choices open to the consumer, whom we shall call Chris.

The Budget Line

We now construct what is called the consumer's *budget line*. This shows all the combinations of the two goods that Chris can purchase given her money income and given the prices of the goods that she buys. To illustrate, we assume that Chris's money income is £10 per day, that eggs cost 50p per dozen while bacon is £1 per lb.

Table 11.1 shows some of the alternative combinations of eggs and bacon that can be bought with Chris's £10 income. If all of it is spent on bacon, 10lbs. can be bought. If all of it is spent on eggs, 20 dozen can be bought. Alternatively, any of the combinations listed in the table can be purchased, e.g. 9 lbs. of bacon and 2 dozen eggs, 1 lb. of bacon and 18 dozen eggs, and so forth.

TABLE 11.1 Maximum Available Quantities of Goods for a Consumer with a Given Income

Reference point	Eggs (dozens) (i)	Bacon (lbs.) (ii)
a	20	0
b	18	1
c	16	2
d	14	3
e	12	4
f	10	5
g	8	6
h	6	7
i	4	8
j	2	9
k	0	10

The data in Table 11.1 are plotted in Figure 11.1. We measure quantities of eggs and bacon on the two axes. Each point in the diagram, labelled *a* to *k*, corresponds to a row in the table. If the customer is at point *a* all income is spent on eggs; at point *k* all income is spent on bacon; at point *b*, 18 dozen eggs are bought *and* 1 lb. of bacon, and so forth.

Next we join all the points in the figure with a straight line. The resulting line is called the consumer's BUDGET LINE (sometimes also called the CONSUMPTION POSSIBILITY LINE). It shows all of the combinations of the two commodities – those shown in the table and intermediate ones as well – that the consumer can buy by spending all of her income.

Attainable and Unattainable Combinations: But what about other points on the graph? Point *m*, inside the budget line, for example, shows an *attainable* purchase of 4 dozen eggs and 4 lbs. of bacon. However, at point *m*, Chris would not be using all her income. At the stated prices and assumed income, it would be possible to buy more of one or both goods.

Point *n*, beyond the budget line, on the other hand, shows an *unattainable* combination, 14 dozen eggs and 8 lbs. of bacon which Chris simply cannot purchase with an income of £10 a day when faced with the stated prices.

Changes in Income

What happens to Chris's budget line when income changes? We consider this question with the aid of Figure 11.2, where the line *AB* repeats the budget line in Figure 11.1. Suppose, for example, Chris's income falls from £10 to £5, *while prices are unchanged* – the quantities of the two goods that she can buy is cut in half. If she buys no bacon, only 10 dozen eggs can be bought. Alternatively, if she buys no eggs then she

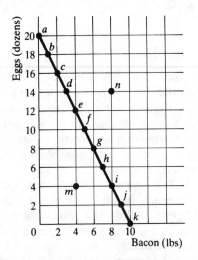

FIGURE 11.1   The Consumer's Budget Line. This line shows all the combinations of the two goods that can be purchased with given prices and income

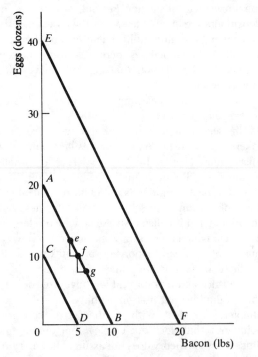

FIGURE 11.2   The Effect of Changes in the Consumer's Income. A rise in income shifts the budget line upwards, while a fall in income shifts it downwards

can purchase only 5 lbs. of bacon. All the new combinations of eggs and bacon now available to our impoverished consumer are given on the new budget line CD in Figure 11.2. Note that this line is *parallel* to the old budget line AB, but closer to the origin, O, of the diagram.

Now go back to Chris's original income of £10. If her income now doubles to £20, twice as much bacon and eggs are attainable. If only eggs are bought, at the unchanged price of 50p per dozen, 40 dozen are now in range. If only bacon is bought, 20 lbs. can be purchased. Indeed, any combination of the two goods shown by points on the new budget line EF are now available. Note again that EF is *parallel* to both AB and CD, but is further from the origin, O, of the diagram.

We conclude that variations in a consumer's income shift the budget line in a parallel fashion, downwards towards the origin when income falls, upwards away from the origin when income rises. For practice, you might like to draw budget lines for incomes of £4 and £8, with unchanged prices of eggs and bacon.

Changes in Prices

Consider, next, the representation of changes in prices, *while income remains constant*. We must distinguish two types of price change that can occur. The first is an equal proportionate change in all prices. The second is a change in relative prices.

Equal proportionate changes in all prices

The first is the easier to deal with. Suppose that, as a result of inflation, the prices of both eggs and bacon double, while Chris's income remains unchanged. The real purchasing power of her income of £10 is now halved, in consequence. At £1 a dozen, she can only afford 10 dozen eggs, even without any bacon. And at a price of £2 per lb. of bacon, only 5 lbs. can be purchased without any eggs. This causes the budget line to shift downwards from AB to CD in Figure 11.2, exactly as it did when income halved while prices remained unchanged.

This is not surprising. A doubling of prices with constant income has the same effect as a halving of income with constant prices. Both of these changes lower the real purchasing power of income to the same extent.

Changes in relative prices

The representation of changes in relative prices is no more difficult. However, it takes a little longer to explain.

You probably noticed our use of *italics* for the word *parallel* to describe the shifts in the budget line which we have so far considered. This emphasized that, whenever there is a change in income (or an equal proportionate change in all prices), the new budget line remains parallel to the former line. The reason is that the *slope of the budget line measures the relative price of one good in terms of the other*, while neither of the above changes affects relative prices. To see what is involved, we apply our concept of opportunity cost to view the price of a good in terms of the quantity of another good that is sacrificed if the good in question is bought.

Consider the matter in the light of the example we have been using. The price of eggs is 50 pence per dozen. The price of bacon is £1 per pound. So £1 will buy *either* two dozen eggs *or* a pound of bacon. If Chris spends £1 on one good, she sacrifices the opportunity of spending £1 on the other good. The opportunity cost of 2 dozen eggs is, therefore, 1 lb. of bacon. When we talk of the *price of eggs in terms of bacon*, we mean the sacrifice that must be made – the bacon given up when eggs are bought instead. It is clear that this depends on the *relative* prices of eggs and bacon. If eggs were 50 pence a dozen and bacon £4 per lb., the opportunity cost of a dozen eggs would be an eighth of a pound of bacon. If eggs cost 50 pence a dozen and bacon also cost 50 pence a pound, the opportunity cost of a dozen eggs would be a pound of bacon.

The opportunity cost of one good in terms of another is dependent only on their relative prices, and on nothing else. It is in no way affected by consumers' income.

We now need to show how the relative price of the two goods determines the slope of the budget line. Consider the budget line AB in Figure 11.2, which is based on the same data as Figure 11.1. The price of eggs is 50 pence per dozen. The price of bacon is £1 per lb. If, for convenience, we drop the words dozen and lbs., we could say that the relative price of the two goods is such that 1 unit of bacon costs 2 units of eggs, because the price of bacon (per lb.) is twice the price of eggs (per dozen). Now suppose that Chris was at point f on the diagram – buying 10 (units of, i.e. dozen) eggs and 5 (units of, i.e. lbs.) bacon. She can, of course, choose to spend her £10 in any way she chooses

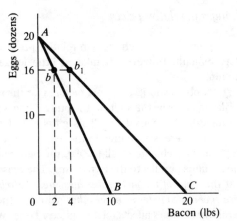

FIGURE 11.3   A Fall in the Price of Bacon: A change in the price of one good changes the slope of the budget line

along the budget line. If we imagine her wanting an extra lb. of bacon, this involves moving down the budget line to point g, sacrificing 2 eggs. Conversely, if she decides to buy 2 more units of eggs, she moves up the budget line to point e, sacrificing 1 unit of bacon. The slope of the line actually measures this opportunity cost. It depends only on the price of eggs relative to the price of bacon. It is the same all along the budget line.

A Fall in the Price of One Good: Consider, now, a situation where everything remains the same except for the price of bacon, which we assume falls to 50p per lb. How do we represent Chris's new budget line? Well, we know that her income of £10 still buys 20 eggs. However, it now buys 20 bacon, compared with only 10 before the price fall. The new budget line is AC in Figure 11.3. It cuts the egg axis at the same point (20 dozen) as the old one. However, the intersection of the budget line with the horizontal axis must be a point representing the 20 bacon which can now be obtained with an income of £10.

Notice that the slope of the new budget line is flatter than the old one, reflecting the fact that the cost of bacon in terms of eggs is lower. Imagine that Chris is currently consuming at point A on the graph, buying only eggs. Suppose she wants to change her consumption bundle, so that it includes some bacon. We describe this change in her consumption pattern by saying that she is 'exchanging' eggs for bacon because, as we already knew, she must give up buying some eggs in order to be able to buy some bacon. The rate at which she can make this 'exchange' is given by the slope of the budget line AC. Two extra bacon can be obtained for the sacrifice of 2 eggs, because their per-unit prices are equal. So, if Chris reduces her purchases of eggs by four, she can

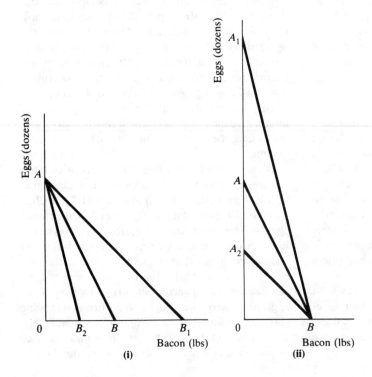

FIGURE 11.4 Shifts in the Budget Line Caused by Changes in Relative Prices. Changes in relative prices change the slope of the budget line:(i) changes in the price of bacon with the price of eggs constant; (ii) changes in the price of eggs with the price of bacon constant

move to point b_1, buying 16 eggs and 4 bacon. Previously, when bacon was £1 per pound so that the budget line was AB, she could only have moved to point b, consuming 16 eggs and 2 bacon, as can be seen from Figure 11.3.

Changes in the Price of Either Good: In Figure 11.3 we showed how to represent a fall in the price of bacon, while income and the price of eggs were unchanged. We can now deal generally with any changes in relative prices. Consider Figure 11.4 (i), which shows three budget lines. These are all drawn on the assumption that Chris's income and the price of eggs are both constant, while the price of bacon is varied. The original budget line is AB. A fall in the price of bacon takes it to AB_1, where B_1 is the quantity of bacon that can be bought at the lower price if all income is spent on bacon. A rise in the price of bacon takes the budget line to AB_2, where B_2 is the quantity of bacon that can now be bought at the higher price if all income is spent on bacon. Because, with a constant income, the same quantity of eggs can always be bought at their unchanged price, the budget line always starts at the same point A on the egg axis. But, because, as the price of bacon varies a different quantity of bacon can be bought, if all income is spent on bacon, the intersection of the budget line with the bacon axis changes. As the price of bacon rises, the budget line becomes steeper; as the price of bacon falls, the budget line becomes flatter.

Figure 11.4 (ii) also shows the effect of changing relative prices. The difference between it and Figure 11.4 (i) is that we now vary the price of eggs instead of that of bacon, which we hold constant together with Chris's income. The constant income always buys the same quantity of bacon, so all budget lines must start from the same point on the bacon axis. This is point B in Figure 11.4 (ii), which indicates how much bacon can be bought if all income is spent on that commodity. Start with a price of eggs which yields the budget line AB. A rise in the price of eggs takes the budget line to A_2B, where A_2 indicates the smaller quantity of eggs that can be bought if all income is spent on eggs. A fall in price of eggs takes the budget line to A_1B, where A_1 indicates the now larger quantity of eggs that can be bought if all income is spent on eggs.

Because the price of bacon (as well as income) is held constant, all the budget lines go through the same point on the bacon axis. Changes in the price of eggs change the slope of the budget line. A rise flattens it, while a fall steepens it. This is in contrast to the effect of a change in income, relative prices remaining unchanged, which is to shift the budget line without changing its slope (as in Figure 11.2).

Note, once more, that the slope of the budget line depends only on the relative prices of eggs and bacon. AB_1 in Figure 11.4 (i) is drawn with the same slope as A_2B in Figure 11.4 (ii). This indicates that relative prices are the same in the two cases. This means that the percentage fall in the price of bacon that took the budget line from AB to AB_1 in part (i) is the same as the percentage rise in the price of eggs that took the budget line from AB to A_2B in part (ii).[1] Both changes leave the relative prices unchanged, but they have different effects on the position of the budget line.

CONSUMERS' TASTES

In order to analyse consumer behaviour, we said that we needed to be able to deal with three pieces of information. We already know how to deal with two – income and relative prices. We now turn to the last of the three, the consumer's tastes.

In this treatment, we use the concept of indifference curves to display the consumer's tastes. This treatment has two advantages over the familiar demand curves.

(1) Indifference curves do not need to rely on all the *ceteris paribus* assumptions of demand curves. *Indifference curves* allow us to consider the behaviour of consumers when they are faced with 'collections' of several goods. These are usually referred to as BUNDLES OR COMBINATIONS OF GOODS. For example, one bundle might be 3 oranges and 5 apples, while another bundle might be 6 oranges and 2 apples. We start by considering two commodities simultaneously, and then find that we can consider the equilibrium of the consumer faced with numerous commodities.

(2) Indifference curve analysis avoids the need to measure the *absolute* value of utility obtained from consuming goods. The new method assumes only that consumers are able to *rank*, or *order*, the levels of satisfaction obtained from consumption of different quantities.

---

1 Recall from Chapter 7 that to avoid the ambiguity in defining percentages, all changes are calculated as a percentage of the *average* of the *new and old* prices, and the new and old quantities.

In order to understand the importance of this second point, we need to understand the distinction between *cardinal* and *ordinal* measures of utility.

Two measures of utility

A measure of utility that assumes the utility attached to alternative bundles can be *quantified*, and the *differences* in utility compared, is called a CARDINAL MEASURE OF UTILITY. With a cardinal measure, the consumer is assumed to be able to compare the *increases* in utility obtained from going, say, from the consumption of 1 orange to the consumption of 2 oranges, with the increase in going from the consumption of 2 oranges to 3. The consumer might tell us, for example, that his increase in utility in going from 2 oranges to 3 was less than his increase in going from 1 orange to 2. The utility theory that we used in Part 2 was based on such a cardinal measure of utility. The concept of diminishing marginal utility is a cardinal concept, since it assumes that the consumer can compare the extra utility he gains from successive additions to his consumption of oranges (or of any other commodity) and tell us that this extra utility is diminishing. For example, in Table 4.2 (on page 48), we were assuming that we had a cardinal measure of utility.

A measure of utility that assumes only that levels of satisfaction obtained from consuming alternative 'bundles' of goods can be ranked or ordered is called an ORDINAL MEASURE OF UTILITY. With an ordinal measure we assume only that the consumer can say he prefers, say, three oranges to two oranges, and two oranges to one orange. But we do not assume that he can say by *how much more* he prefers three to two, or two to one. Thus, the concept of diminishing marginal utility is not included in an ordinal measure. (We shall see later, however, that the two theories are quite compatible with each other.)

In previous chapters we assumed that we could measure utilities, and so say by *how much* utility was increasing as the consumption of one good increased. Since no known unit of measurement of direct satisfaction is yet available to man, we measured such satisfaction in monetary units. This is not entirely satisfactory. Hence, the ordinal measurement used in indifference theory is something of an improvement.

Indifference theory was first developed by the great Italian economist Vilfredo Pareto, and was later introduced into English-speaking economics in 1939 by Sir John Hicks (who later won the Nobel Prize) and the late Sir Roy Allen.

An Indifference Curve

Now let our consumer, Chris, have some quantity of each of the two goods, say 18 units of eggs and 10 units of bacon. (Recall that a consumption pattern that contains quantities of two or more distinct goods is called a *bundle* or a *combination* of goods.) Now offer Chris an alternative bundle of goods, say 13 units of eggs and 15 units of bacon. This alternative has 5 fewer units of eggs and 5 more units of bacon than the first one. Which bundle Chris prefers depends on the relative valuation that she places on 5 more units of bacon and 5 fewer units of eggs. If she values the extra bacon more than the forgone eggs, she will prefer the new bundle to the original one. If she values the bacon less than the eggs, she will prefer the original bundle.

There is a third alternative. If Chris values the extra bacon the same as she values the forgone eggs, she would gain equal satisfaction from the two alternative bundles of bacon and eggs. In this case, Chris is said to be *indifferent* between the two bundles.

Assume that, after much trial and error, a number of bundles have been identified, each of which gives equal satisfaction. These are shown in Table 11.2. The table shows that Chris gets equal satisfaction, and is thus indifferent, among bundle *a* (30 eggs and 5 bacon), bundle *b* (18 eggs and 10 bacon) and so on down to bundle *f*.

Now consider Figure 11.5. This shows points *a* to *f* plotted from Table 11.2. There will, of course, be combinations of the two commodities, other than those set out in the table, that will give the same level of satisfaction to the consumers. All of these combinations are shown in Figure 11.5 by the smooth curve

TABLE 11.2 Alternative Bundles Giving a Consumer Equal Satisfaction. These bundles all lie on a single indifference curve

Reference point	Eggs (dozens)	Bacon (lbs.)
a	30	5
b	18	10
c	13	15
d	10	20
e	8	25
f	7	30

that passes through the points plotted from the table. This curve is an INDIFFERENCE CURVE and it shows all *combinations* of goods that yield the same satisfaction to the consumer. In other words, a consumer is *indifferent* between the combinations indicated by all the points on one indifference curve.

Any points above and to the right of the curve show combinations of bacon and eggs that the consumer would prefer to combinations indicated by points on the curve. Consider, for example, the combination of 18 eggs and 20 bacon, which is represented by point *h* in the figure. Although it may not be obvious that this bundle must be preferred to bundle *f* (which has more bacon but less eggs), it is obvious that it will be preferred to bundle *c* because there is both less eggs and less bacon represented at *c* than at *h*. Inspection of the graph shows that *any* point above the curve will be obviously superior to *some* points on the curve in the sense that it will contain both more bacon and more eggs than those points on the curve. But since all points on the curve are equal in the consumer's eyes, the point above the curve must be superior to *all* points on the curve. By a similar argument, points below and to the left of the curve represent bundles of goods that are inferior to bundles represented by points on the curve.

Slope of an indifference curve

The indifference curve that we have drawn in Figure 11.5 has two basic characteristics. First, it slopes downward to the right – i.e. it has a negative slope. Second, its slope gets flatter and flatter as we move downwards along it to the right.

The slope was no accident. It reflects the two basic assumptions of indifference theory. To see these assumptions we must first define a new term.

Marginal Rate of Substitution: We have seen that all the points on one indifference curve indicate combinations of the two commodities that give the consumer equal satisfaction. If we now compare two nearby points on an indifference curve, we can answer another question: how much of one commodity could the consumer give up in return for an additional unit of the other commodity, while her level of satisfaction stays the same? The answer to this question measures what is called the marginal rate of substitution of eggs for bacon. The MARGINAL RATE OF SUBSTITUTION (MRS) is the amount of one commodity a consumer could give up to get one more

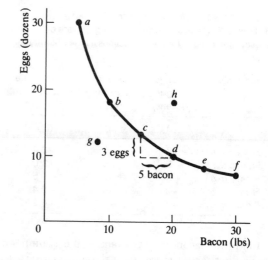

FIGURE 11.5   An Indifference Curve. This indifference curve shows combinations of bacon and eggs that yield equal satisfaction and among which the consumer is indifferent; its slope indicates the marginal rate of substitution between the two commodites

unit of another commodity and just leave the level of satisfaction unchanged.

The first basic assumption of indifference theory is that the MRS is always negative. This means that to gain an *increase* in consumption of one commodity, the consumer is prepared to *reduce* her consumption of a second. Graphically, the negative marginal rate of substitution is shown by the usual downward slope of indifference curves.

The Hypothesis of Diminishing Marginal Rate of Substitution: A basic idea of indifference theory is that the marginal rate of substitution between any two commodities depends on the amounts of the commodities currently being consumed by the consumer. Consider a case where the consumer has a lot of eggs and only a small amount of bacon. Common sense suggests that the consumer might be willing to give up quite a few of her plentiful eggs to get one unit more of very scarce bacon. Now consider a case where the consumer has only a few eggs and quite a lot of bacon. Common sense suggests that the consumer would be willing to give up only a few of her scarce eggs to get one more unit of already plentiful bacon.

This example illustrates the second main assumption of indifference theory, the assumption of the DIMINISHING MARGINAL RATE OF SUBSTITUTION. In

TABLE 11.3 The Marginal Rate of Substitution Between Eggs and Bacon. The marginal rate of substitution of eggs for bacon declines as the quantity of bacon increases

Movement	Change in eggs (dozens)	Change in bacon (lbs.)	Marginal rate of substitution (i) ÷ (ii)
	(i)	(ii)	(iii)
From a to b	−12	+5	−2.4
From b to c	−5	+5	−1.0
From c to d	−3	+5	−0.6
From d to e	−2	+5	−0.4
From e to f	−2	+5	−0.2

terms of our bacon-and-egg example, the assumption states that *the fewer eggs* (and the more bacon) *the consumer has already, the smaller will be the number of eggs she will be willing to give up to get one further unit of bacon.*

The assumption says that the marginal rate of substitution changes systematically as the amounts of two commodities consumed vary. Take any two commodities, A and B. The more A and the less B the consumer currently has, the less B that consumer will be willing to give up to get a further unit of A.

The assumption is illustrated in Table 11.3, which is based on the example of bacon and eggs in Table 11.2. When the consumer moves from a to b, she gives up 12 units of eggs and gains 5 units of bacon; she remains at the same level of overall satisfaction. The consumer at point a was prepared to sacrifice 12 eggs for 5 bacon, which is 2.4 units of eggs *per unit of bacon* obtained ($-12/5 = -2.4$). (Notice that the ratio is negative because the change in eggs is negative while the change in bacon is positive.) When she moves from b to c, she sacrifices 5 units of eggs for 5 units of bacon (a rate of substitution of 1 unit of eggs per unit of bacon). Column (iii) of the table shows the rate at which the consumer is prepared to sacrifice units of eggs per unit of bacon obtained. At first she will sacrifice 2.4 units of eggs to get 1 unit more of bacon, but as consumption of eggs diminishes and that of bacon increases, the consumer becomes less and less willing to sacrifice further eggs for more bacon.

Graphical Representation of the MRS: The graphical representation of the marginal rate of substitution is also shown in Figure 11.5. The figure plots points c and d from Table 11.2. It shows that, in moving from c to d, the consumer needs 5 bacon to

compensate for the loss of 3 eggs. Over this range, the rate at which the consumer will substitute eggs for bacon is 3/5 which, as Table 11.3 shows, is 0.6. In other words, she is prepared to give up 0.6 units of eggs for every additional unit of bacon that she gets over this range. This *MRS* is the average slope of the indifference curve over this range of consumption. Thus, the *MRS* is the slope of the line joining the two points in question.[1]

Now that you know that the marginal rate of substitution is given by the slope of the indifference curve, you may see that the graphical representation of the assumption of the diminishing marginal rate of substitution is that an indifference curve becomes flatter as the consumer moves downward to the right along the curve. In terms of the indifference curve in Figure 11.5, the *MRS* diminishes as the consumer moves down the curve because she is prepared to sacrifice fewer and fewer eggs to get one more unit of bacon. The gradually diminishing slope of the indifference curve reflects just this.

The Indifference Map

So far we have constructed a single indifference curve, a curve that relates to a particular level of satisfaction. To represent consumer tastes at higher and lower levels of satisfaction, we need other indifference curves. The whole range of tastes is expressed by a set (also called a 'family') of indifference curves known as an INDIFFERENCE MAP. On each curve, the level of satisfaction remains constant, but at a different level from every other curve. To be able to relate one curve to the other, we introduce the third basic assumption of indifference curve theory that *more of any good is always preferred to less of that good.*

Now let us see how indifference curves order the level of satisfaction associated with various consumption bundles. Consider, for example, point h in Figure 11.6, which represents a combination of e_0 eggs and b_0 bacon. Compare it with combination a on indifference curve I_1, which represents e_1 eggs and b_0 bacon. Combination a has more eggs and the same amount of bacon as combination h and, given our assumption

---

1 For a very small movement along the curve, the *MRS* becomes very close to being the slope of the curve. At any *point* on the curve, the *MRS* is the slope at that point. (See Appendix to Chapter 1, on tangents.)

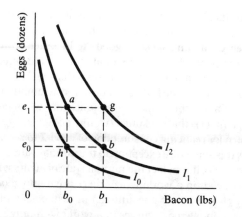

FIGURE 11.6   **An Indifference Map.** The further from the origin of the graph, the greater the level of satisfaction represented by an indifference curve

that more of any good is preferred to less, *a* must be preferred to *h*. Point *h* cannot be on the same indifference curve as *a*, and the indifference curve I_0 that does pass through *h* must represent a lower level of satisfaction than the curve I_1, that passes through *a*. Any points on I_0 represent combinations of eggs and bacon which yield the same satisfaction as any other points. They all yield less satisfaction than any points on I_1.

Consider, in similar fashion, point *g* in Figure 11.6, which represents e_1 eggs and b_1 bacon. Compare it with a point such as *b* on I_1. Clearly *g* is preferable to *b*, because it represents more eggs and the same amount of bacon as *b*. Therefore *g* must lie on a different, higher, indifference curve than I_1. We have drawn this preferred curve through *g* on the graph, and labelled it I_2. Each point on I_2 yields equal satisfaction to any other point on it. They all yield higher satisfaction than any points on I_1.

Inspection of the graph shows that any point above and to the right of any indifference curve will obviously be superior to some points on that curve, in the sense that it contains more eggs and more bacon than those points on the curve. But, since the bundles represented by all points on a curve are equal to each other in the eyes of the consumer, the point above the curve must be superior to all points on the curve. Hence, we may conclude that indifference curves represent higher levels of satisfaction the further they are from the origin of the graph. All points on I_2 are superior to all points on I_1, which are in turn superior to all points on I_0. Conversely, of course, indifference curves represent lower levels of satisfaction the closer they lie to the origin of the graph.

Characteristics of Indifference Curves

Now that we know how to represent a consumer's tastes by an indifference map, we need to look in more detail at some important characteristics of indifference curves.

Indifference curves cannot intersect each other

No two indifference curves can intersect (or touch) each other. In Figure 11.7, we draw two intersecting indifference curves. We have written WRONG over it, because it is an impossible situation.

The argument is brief. Point *g* on I_B is preferred to *h* on I_A by the assumption that more is preferred to less (*g* has more eggs and the same bacon as *h*). But *h* must give the same satisfaction as *f* (representing e_0 eggs plus b_0 bacon), since they are both on indifference curve I_A. However, *g* must also give the same satisfaction as *f*, since they are both on indifference curve I_B. It follows, therefore, that *g* and *h* should give the same satisfaction, since both give the same satisfaction as *f*. But we started by showing that *g* must be superior to *h*. So we have a contradiction: *g* cannot be both equal to, and superior to, *h*. Therefore, indifference curves cannot intersect because for them to do so would yield a result that some combinations of goods were simultaneously superior to, as well as equal to, other combinations.

Indifference curves when there are more than two goods

So far we have dealt with a world of two commodities – bacon and eggs in our example – which are easily

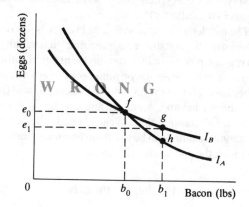

FIGURE 11.7   **Indifference Curves Cannot Intersect Each Other.** This Figure shows an impossible situation

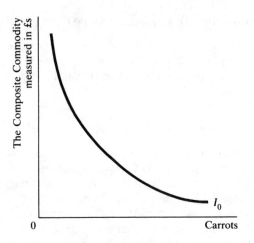

FIGURE 11.8   **Indifference Curves when there are more than Two Goods.** The vertical axis measures all goods other than carrots

represented on a two-dimensional graph. But consumers buy many commodities, and we want to be able to study their behaviour when they do so. This can be done mathematically by assigning a dimension to each commodity. But if we wish to draw a graph we cannot handle cases with many dimensions, so we introduce a new kind of indifference curve, based on the same *ceteris paribus* assumptions that are made when drawing ordinary demand curves.

Such an indifference curve is shown in Figure 11.8. It shows the combinations of carrots and the money value of *all other goods* on the market which yield the same satisfaction to the consumer. In this diagram, the vertical axis measures the money value of 'everything except' carrots instead of a second commodity. This 'everything else' is sometimes called the COMPOSITE COMMODITY.

The indifference curve in Figure 11.8 gives the rate at which the consumer is prepared to exchange carrots for money (which can be spent on all other goods) at each level of consumption of carrots and other goods. Given the money price of carrots and the consumer's income, a budget line can be obtained, showing all combinations of carrots and other goods that the consumer can buy with given money income and with the given price of carrots.

Indifference curves that cut the axis

Figure 11.9 shows an indifference curve that cuts the axis. The curve tells us (among other things) that the

consumer is indifferent between bundle (1), x_0 of good X plus g_0 of all other goods, and bundle (2), g_1 of all other goods and *none* of good X. In other words, whatever bundle the individual is now consuming, there is some amount of other goods that can be given to him to persuade him to cut out his consumption of good X altogether. This case assumes that when he is at point (1), the consumer would accept g_1-g_0 in return for reducing consumption of good X to zero.

Is this some rare exception to the normal pattern of tastes? No, it is in fact the normal state of affairs with most goods in a world where there are many goods, though it is rarely encountered in textbooks which explain indifference curves in a world with only two goods.

To see that this is not an unusual case, ask yourself two questions. First, how many existing goods do you *not* consume at all? (For most of you the list will include chainsaws; video cameras; all the brands of toothpaste, breakfast cereals and a list of other brand-name products, except your favourite brand; some or all kinds of cars, and so on – a trip around the local shopping centre will easily persuade you that the list is very long.) For each of these goods, your indifference curve must cut the axis. Otherwise you could not be in equilibrium consuming zero quantity of that good. Second, ask yourself how many goods you currently consume that you could be persuaded to do without in return for some large enough amount of money. Surely the answer is 'many of the goods you now consume'. For although you are currently consuming them, there are probably many that you

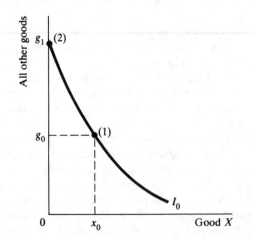

FIGURE 11.9   **An Indifference Curve Cutting One Axis.** Not every good is consumed by all people

could be induced to cut out entirely if you were offered a large enough compensation of other goods. Hence, your indifference curve must cut the axis for each of the goods that you would be prepared to cut out.

Now put the matter the other way around. If the indifference curve for X did *not* cut the axis, that would mean that not even an infinite amount of ability to consume other goods would persuade you to do without good X. This surely *is* the case for such absolute necessities as water and air, but for most of us it is not the case for sausages, pink hats, bicycles, visits to the cinema and a host of other items. The amount you would need to be paid to go without each of these commodities might be large, indicating that the indifference curve that you are on cuts the axis for the good in question very high up on the composite-good axis. For most non-necessities, and for most of us, however, indifference curves do cut axes somewhere.

Indifference curves with special shapes

Indifference curves are not the easiest of the concepts we have met in economics. To familiarize you with them, it may be helpful to consider some of the shapes that they may have in special circumstances. Figure 11.10 shows some possibilities.

(i) Perfect Substitutes: When two goods are perfect substitutes in the mind of the consumer, he or she will be prepared to trade one for the other at a constant rate. For example, drawing pins that came in yellow packages of 100 would be perfect substitutes for the identical pins that came in green packages of 100 for a colour-blind consumer, Joseph. He would be willing to substitute one type of package for the other at a rate of one for one because he was quite indifferent between the two packages. Joseph's indifference curves would thus be a set of parallel lines (with a

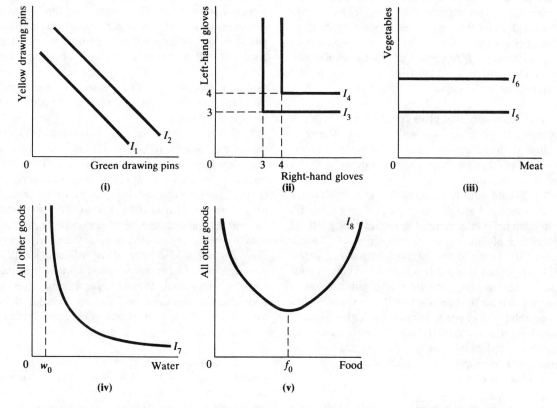

FIGURE 11.10   Indifference Curves with Special Shapes. Each special case of consumer's tastes gives rise to an indifference curve with a special shape: (i) goods which are perfect substitutes; (ii) goods which are perfect complements; (iii) one good (meat) gives zero utility; (iv) one good (water) is an absolute necessity; (v) one good (food) gives negative utility after a point

slope of -1). Two such curves I_1 and I_2, are shown in part (i) of the figure. Generally, it can be said that, *when two goods are perfect substitutes in the mind of the consumer, the indifference curves will be straight lines, the slopes of which indicate the rate at which one can be substituted for the other.*

(ii) Perfect Complements: If two goods are perfect complements, one of them is of no use without the other. Left- and right-hand gloves, left and right shoes, and a stick of dynamite and its detonator, are examples. In this case, the consumer requires the goods in fixed proportions and no additional amount of one would persuade him to give up any of the other. For example, if Stephen starts with three left- and three right-hand gloves, no additional offer of right-hand gloves would persuade him to part with one of his left-hand gloves (because, if he did, he would have only two usable pairs and a lot of useless odd gloves). Stephen's indifference curves for left- and right-hand gloves are illustrated in part (ii) of the figure. There is no rate at which he will substitute one kind of glove for the other when he starts with equal numbers of each. Of course, he prefers more pairs to less, so the curve I_4 represents a higher level of utility than does curve I_3. *Indifference curves for perfect complements are 'L-shaped'.*

(iii) A Commodity that gives Zero Utility: When a commodity gives no satisfaction at all, a person would be unwilling to sacrifice even the smallest amount of other goods to obtain any quantity of the good in question. Such would be the case for meat with Claudia who is a vegetarian. Her indifference curves for meat are shown in part (iii) of the figure. They are horizontal straight lines, indicating a marginal rate of substitution of zero for meat. Claudia would not be willing to substitute any of her vegetables to get any meat. When a good has no value for the consumer, the marginal rate of substitution of other goods for that good is zero. Since Claudia likes vegetables, the curve I_6 indicates a higher level of satisfaction than does I_5 but in both cases her satisfaction is not affected by the amount of meat she has (since, no matter how much she is given, she won't eat any of it).

(iv) An Absolute Necessity: In Figure 11.10 (iv), there is some minimum quantity of water, w_0, that is necessary to sustain life. No amount of other goods will persuade any consumer to cut his or her water

consumption below that amount. As consumption of water falls toward w_0, increasingly vast amounts of other goods are necessary to persuade the consumer to cut down on his water consumption even a little bit more. Thus, the indifference curve, I_7, becomes steeper and steeper as it approaches w_0. As a result, the marginal rate of substitution increases until, in the limit, it becomes infinite as the indifference curve becomes vertical at w_0. *The marginal rate of substitution for an absolute necessity reaches infinity as consumption falls toward the amount that is absolutely necessary.*

(v) A Good that Confers a Negative Utility after some Level of Consumption: Many goods would begin to confer a negative utility if they were consumed beyond some 'satiation' point. There is only so much of many foods, beverages, movies, plays, or cricket matches that most of us would want to eat, drink, or watch, even if they were free. Beyond a point, further consumption would yield negative utilities. This means that, beyond that point, the indifference curves begin to slope upwards, because the consumer would be willing to sacrifice some amount of other goods to be allowed to reduce his or her consumption of the offending commodity. In economic theory, we usually ignore these cases because we assume that the consumer can reject quantities of the good that are actually disliked.

To illustrate this situation, we show, in part (v), the case of a consumer, Ralph, who is *forced* to eat more and more food. At the amount f_0, he has all the food he could possibly want. At this point, his indifference curve, I_8, has a zero slope, indicating a zero marginal rate of substitution of other commodities for food. Beyond f_0, his indifference curve slopes upwards, indicating that he gets *negative* value from consuming the extra food, and so he would be willing to sacrifice some amount of other commodities to avoid consuming this extra food. When, beyond some level of consumption, the consumer's utility is reduced by further consumption, the indifference curves begin to slope upward.

This concludes our development of two key tools of analysis: budget lines, which tell us what consumers can do, and indifference curves, which tell us what consumers want to do. In the next chapter we bring these two together to study what the consumer does do, which means developing a theory of consumer behaviour.

SUMMARY

1 Indifference curves have two advantages over demand curves: (1) indifference curves can represent consumer tastes for a collection of any number of goods (although the limitations of geometry restrict our graphs to depicting two goods), and (2) indifference curves avoid the need for cardinal (absolute) measures of utility, since utility is measured only ordinally – i.e. a consumer merely ranks combinations of goods according to preference.

2 A budget line shows all combinations of two goods that can be purchased with a given money income and given prices of the goods. The slope of the budget line measures the relative prices of the goods. A change in a consumer's income with unchanged relative prices shifts the budget line outwards away from, or inwards towards, the origin of the graph while leaving its slope unchanged.

3 Consumer tastes at different levels of satisfaction can be represented by an indifference map, comprising a set of indifference curves. Each indifference curve shows all combinations of goods that yield the same total satisfaction. Indifference curves cannot intersect each other.

4 The marginal rate of substitution is defined as the amount of one good that a consumer would be prepared to give up in return for one more unit of another good, while retaining the same level of satisfaction. The marginal rate of substitution is measured by the slope of an indifference curve. It is negative and diminishing as consumption of a good increases.

5 The basic hypothesis of indifference theory is that of the diminishing marginal rate of substitution, and its graphical expression is the increasing flatness of each indifference curve as one moves along it downwards and to the right.

6 The notion of a composite commodity is used in indifference curve analysis to study consumer choice between a particular good and everything else.

7 Indifference curves for most goods are convex towards the origin of the graph, reflecting the 'law' of diminishing marginal rate of substitution. Despite this, many indifference curves intersect one axis, which implies that at some relative prices the individual will consume a zero quantity of the good in question.

12

Indifference Curves in Action

In this chapter we bring together the two parts of the theory we kept previously separate – indifference curves and the budget line – and set them into action. In our theory, consumers are assumed to seek to maximize their satisfactions. If there were no constraints on their consumption they would consume more and more of everything, moving further and further away from the origin of their indifference map and reaching higher and higher indifference curves.

But in our world such unconstrained consumption is impossible because one must pay for what one consumes. As a result no one, not even the richest person in the land, can consume an infinite amount of any good that commands a positive market price. So consumers seek to maximize their satisfactions subject to the constraint exercised by their incomes. When they have done this, we say they are in equilibrium.

CONSUMER EQUILIBRIUM

An indifference map describes the preferences or tastes of a consumer who would like to reach the highest possible indifference curve, thereby maximizing satisfaction or utility. The budget line provides a constraint on the consumer's consumption. Its position and slope depend on the consumer's income and the price that must be paid for each good, and it shows the maximum amounts of the goods that can be purchased.

Figure 12.1 brings together the tastes of our consumer as shown by her indifference map, and her consumption possibilities as shown by her budget

line. (We continue to assume that the only two goods available are eggs and bacon.) The budget line in Figure 12.1 assumes a weekly income of £10 and prices of 50 pence per dozen eggs and £1 per pound of bacon. Our consumer, who we continue to call Chris, can attain any point in the area bounded by her budget line and the two axes. However, we already know that points *inside* the area mean that she is not spending all her income.

Suppose Chris starts at point *a* in Figure 12.1, spending all of her income on eggs. Remember, all the points on her budget line are available to her. Imagine, therefore, that she considers buying some bacon and reducing her purchases of eggs. In the

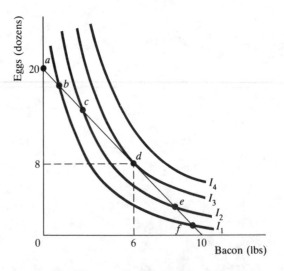

FIGURE 12.1 Consumer Equilibrium. The consumer maximizes satisfaction at the point where an indifference curve is tangent to the budget line

graph, this means she moves downward to the right along her budget line. Let us compare her levels of satisfaction at points *a*, *b*, *c*, *d*, *e* and *f*.

As Chris moves down her budget line she reaches higher and higher indifference curves which represent higher and higher levels of satisfaction until she reaches point *d*. If she moves beyond that point, to *e* for example, she arrives at lower indifference curves and hence achieves lower levels of satisfaction.

Utility Maximization

The highest attainable level of satisfaction is at point *d*. Graphically, this is the point where an indifference curve just touches but does not cut, i.e. is tangent to, the budget line. At this point, the budget line and the indifference curve have the same slope.

We saw in the previous chapter that the slope of the indifference curve measures the marginal rate of substitution between the two goods (see p. 129). Recall also that the slope of the budget is the ratio of the prices of the two goods (see pp. 125–6).

We may conclude, therefore, that Chris *maximizes her satisfaction at the point on the budget line where the marginal rate of substitution between eggs and bacon is equal to the relative price of eggs in terms of bacon.*

Expressed in this way the condition for consumer maximization may look formidable. We shall show it to be really no more than common sense. The best way of doing so is by using indifference curves on a diagram. However, before we show you this, let us set out the argument verbally. Do not worry if you do not follow it all at first reading. It is not easy. It should make complete sense after you have read the argument using a diagram. So come back and read it again if you need to.

The reason why satisfaction is maximized where the marginal rate of substitution between two goods is equal to their relative prices is as follows. The marginal rate of substitution measures the rate at which Chris *values* eggs in terms of bacon. The ratio of the price of eggs to the price of bacon measures the rate at which she *can obtain* eggs by giving up bacon (or vice versa). If she can obtain eggs in return for bacon given up at a lower rate than the rate at which she values eggs in terms of bacon, she will not be maximizing her satisfaction from the way she spends her income.

Consider an example. Suppose Chris's marginal rate of substitution of eggs for bacon is equal to unity (i.e. she is indifferent between her present bundle and

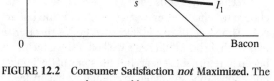

FIGURE 12.2   Consumer Satisfaction *not* Maximized. The consumer cannot be in equilibrium at any point where an indifference curve cuts the budget line

another containing one more egg and one less bacon). Suppose the price of eggs is 50p and the price of bacon is £1, i.e. the ratio of the price of eggs/price of bacon = 1/2. Then she is not maximizing her satisfaction. She could exchange bacon for eggs and be better off, for example she could give up one bacon and get two eggs in exchange. This must make her better off because, by assumption, she values one less bacon as worth one more egg (*MRS* = 1).

The example of the previous paragraph illustrates the result that a consumer will be better off exchanging bacon for eggs when the ratio of price of eggs/price of bacon is less than her marginal rate of substitution of eggs for bacon. It follows that the converse is true, that a consumer would be better off exchanging eggs for bacon if the price of eggs/price of bacon was greater than her marginal rate of substitution of eggs for bacon (e.g. if the *MRS* was equal to 1, as before, but each egg costs twice as much as each unit of bacon). We conclude that a consumer maximizes the satisfaction from a given income when the marginal rate of substitution of eggs for bacon is *equal to* the price of eggs in terms of bacon.

As promised, we now use a diagram to repeat the argument leading to the conclusion that consumer maximization occurs when the marginal rate of substitution (given by the slope of an indifference curve) is equal to the price of one good in terms of the other (given by the slope of the budget line).

Let us begin by showing situations in which Chris is not maximizing her satisfaction. For instance, suppose that she is at h in Figure 12.2. The slope of her indifference curve, I_1, at point h is different from the slope of the budget line. We know from Chris's indifference curve that she would be as well off if she gave up hk eggs and received km bacon in return. But we know from the budget line that she could obtain more than km bacon for hk eggs. She could *exchange* hk eggs for ky bacon – landing up at point y on the budget line. Hence, y must be on a higher indifference curve than h. Chris has raised her level of satisfaction by buying more bacon and less eggs than at point h.[1]

Alternatively, consider why Chris would not choose to remain at another point, n, on the budget line. The slope of her indifference curve through n tells us that she would be as well off if she gave up ns bacon in return for st eggs. But the slope of the budget line shows that she could exchange ns bacon for sv eggs, which is greater than st. Therefore, when Chris is at n, she would prefer to exchange bacon for eggs at the price available in the market.

It is only when *the rate at which Chris can exchange eggs for bacon in the market is the same as the rate at which she values eggs in terms of bacon that she cannot reach a higher indifference curve.* That is when the budget line is tangent to her highest attainable indifference curve.

When the consumer has chosen the bundle of goods that maximizes her satisfaction, she will continue to consume the goods in the proportions indicated by the point of tangency between the budget line and an indifference curve until something changes. The consumer is said to be in equilibrium.

Shifts in the Budget Line

We must deal now with the two changes which can affect the consumer's equilibrium position: a change in income and a change in relative prices.

A change in income

As we saw in the previous chapter, changes in income lead to *parallel* shifts of the budget line. For each level of income there will, of course, be an equilibrium position at which an indifference curve is tangent to the relevant budget line. Each such

---

1 This argument is an intuitive rather than a rigorous proof, which requires differential calculus, because the slope of any continuous indifference curve (such as I_1) varies at every point along it.

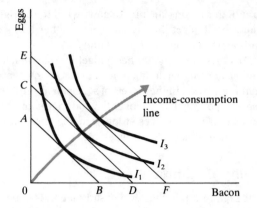

FIGURE 12.3   The Income-Consumption Line. This line shows how consumption changes as income changes with relative prices held constant

equilibrium position means that the consumer is doing as well as she possibly can for that level of income.

An example is shown in Figure 12.3. As Chris's income increases, the budget line moves outwards from AB through CD to EF. The combinations of eggs and bacon that she selects can be found by reading off the quantities of the two goods corresponding to the points of tangency of the budget lines and indifference curves. If we move the budget line through all possible income levels and join up all the points of equilibrium, we trace out what is known as an INCOME-CONSUMPTION LINE (or an INCOME-EXPANSION PATH). This line shows how consumption changes as income changes, with relative prices held constant.

The shape of the income-consumption line depends on the nature of the goods. In particular, it depends on whether a good is normal or inferior. Both cases are illustrated in Figure 12.4. In part (i) of the Figure, steak and turkey are assumed to be normal goods, so that consumption of each increases as income increases. For example, with an outward shift of the budget line from AB to CD, consumption of turkey increases from q_1 to q_2 (and consumption of steak increases also) as shown. In Figure 12.4(ii), we show the case of an inferior good, sausages, and the normal good, steak. The outward shift of the budget line from AB to CD in this case leads to a *fall* in the quantity of sausages purchased from q_3 to q_4. (In order to avoid cluttering the diagram with too many lines, we have not shown that steak is a normal good in Figure 12.4(i) and (ii). You should be able to do so by

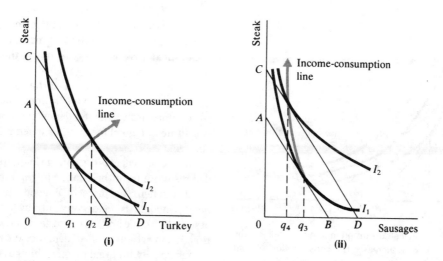

(i)   **(ii)**

FIGURE 12.4   Income-Consumption Lines for Normal and Inferior Goods. When both goods are normal, the income-consumption line slopes upwards to the right. In (i), both turkey and steak are normal goods over the range of income chosen; in (ii), steak is normal, but sausages are an inferior good over the range of income shown

dropping perpendiculars from the equilibrium positions to the vertical axes.)

Engel's Law: Over 100 years ago, the German statistician Ernest Engel (contemporary with, but not the same person as, Friedrich Engels, famous for his association with Karl Marx) studied the relationship between income and expenditure on certain classes of commodities. Engel's Law, named after him, states that the proportion of income spent on food tends to fall as income increases.

Curves that plot income on one axis and consumption of some commodity on the other are called ENGEL CURVES. Four such curves plotted from UK data are shown in Figure 12.5.

It is important not to equate Engel curves with income-consumption lines. Engel curves show the *proportions* (or percentages) of income spent on goods of different kinds. Income-consumption curves show the *absolute* quantities consumed with changes in income. The graphs on which they are drawn have, therefore, different axis labels. The two curves are, nevertheless, closely related. We can see, in Figure 12.5, that Engel's Law does apply to food (and to fuel, which is another basic necessity). Other items of expenditure, such as household durables, vehicles and services, tend to show rising proportions of income spent on them as people become more affluent up to a point. At the levels of income reached in the very richest economies today, the proportion of income spent on consumer durables is declining while the proportion spent on services is rising.

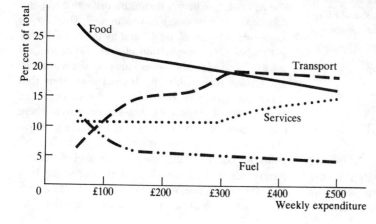

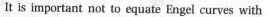

FIGURE 12.5   Engel Curves. Percentages of total household expenditure on selected commodity groups, UK, 1985 (*Source:* Dept. of Employment, *Family Expenditure Survey*)

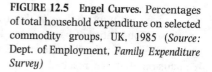

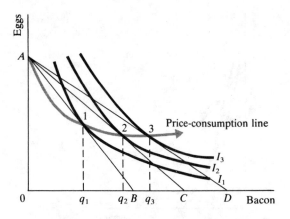

FIGURE 12.6   A Price-Consumption Line. A fall in the price of a commodity increases the consumption of that commodity

A change in relative prices

We saw in the previous chapter that a change in the relative price of two commodities changes the slope of the budget line. We illustrate a change in the price of bacon in Figure 12.6.

Assume the consumer has an income which allows the purchase of either A eggs and no bacon, or B bacon and no eggs. Given the budget line AB, the consumer chooses point 1 on the graph, buying q_1 bacon. Now allow the money price of bacon to fall, while income and the price of eggs remain unchanged. The budget line pivots, to AC. A further fall in the price of bacon pivots the line to AD. Two more points of equilibrium can be identified as tangents of AC and AD with indifference curves I_2 and I_3. The quantity of bacon consumed rises to q_2 and then to q_3 at these lower prices of bacon.

If we move the budget line through all possible prices of bacon and join up all the points of equilibrium, we trace out what is known as a PRICE-CONSUMPTION LINE. This line shows how consumption of bacon changes as the price of bacon changes, with income and the price of eggs held constant.

INCOME AND SUBSTITUTION EFFECTS OF A PRICE CHANGE

The price-consumption line in Figure 12.6 shows increasing quantities of bacon being bought as the price of bacon falls. This is consistent with the conclusion that we reached when explaining the

elementary theory of demand. Price and quantity are negatively associated in the vast majority of cases.

Our next task is to break down the effect of a change in the price of a good on the quantity demanded into what are called the substitution and income effects. The substitution effect reflects, straightforwardly, the tendency for consumers to substitute one good for another when relative prices change.

The income effect is the change in quantity demanded resulting from the change in *real* income that is implicit when the price of a good changes while *money* income is held constant (by *ceteris paribus* assumption). We are, of course, familiar with the idea that income changes affect demand. We need now to recognize only that real income changes when prices change while money income is constant, as well as when money income changes while prices are held constant.

We now employ our new technical apparatus to break down the effect of a price change into a substitution and an income effect. In Figure 12.7 we portray our consumer, Chris, faced with a budget line AB. Her equilibrium is at point 1 where q_1 of bacon is consumed. Now let the price of bacon fall, while money income and the price of eggs remain the same. Her new budget line is AC and her new equilibrium is at point 3 on indifference curve I_2, where q_3 bacon is purchased.

The Substitution Effect

We can isolate the pure substitution effect of the price change in the following manner. We hold Chris's real income constant, and see what she would do if just relative prices changed. If Chris's real income stays the same, she must remain on indifference curve I_1. She will not, however, maximize satisfaction at point 1, because relative prices have changed. They are no longer given by the slope AB, but by the slope AC. So, to find her best combination of eggs and bacon, we ask where on her indifference curve, I_1, she will settle. The answer is that she will choose the point on that curve where the new relative price of bacon in terms of eggs is equal to her *MRS*. As we know, this is where the indifference curve is tangent to the line representing the ratio: price of bacon/price of eggs. To find this point, we construct the line $A'C'$, parallel to AC, and tangent also to I_1. Since $A'C'$ and AC are parallel, they have the same slope; and, since the point of tangency of $A'C'$ with I_1 is Chris's equilibrium position, we can

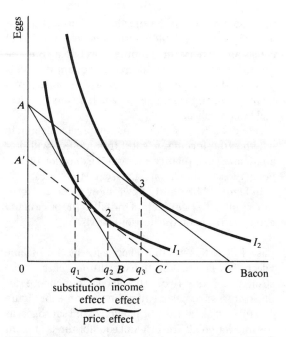

FIGURE 12.7   The Income and Substitution Effects of a Fall in the Price of Bacon (a Normal Good). Both effects cause the quantity of bacon to increase

say that she will maximize her satisfaction at point 2, buying q_2 bacon, if the price of bacon falls and her real income is held down. The difference between her consumption of bacon before the price fall, q_1, and her consumption after the price fall, q_2, is $q_2 - q_1$, which is the substitution effect of the price change.

The Income Effect

Since we know the full effect of the price change must be the sum of the income and substitution effects, we could deduce the size of the income effect immediately as $q_3 - q_2$ bacon, being the difference between the total increase in quantity $q_3 - q_1$ minus the substitution effect, of $q_2 - q_1$ bacon. However, it is important to understand how the income effect is derived. Conceptually, the pure income effect of a price change is the extent to which a change in real income affects quantity purchased, while relative prices are held constant.

When we isolated the substitution effect we held real income constant by confining Chris to her original indifference curve, I_1. Now we want to identify the income effect, we release her from this restriction and allow her to attain I_2. We want to observe her behaviour when we allow her income to

rise but no change occurs in relative prices, because we are now interested only in the income effect of the price change.

All we need to do to isolate the income effect is to observe the difference in Chris's consumption of bacon when the price of bacon is held constant, but her real income is allowed to rise as much as it would from the fall in price. This is done by holding the money prices of the two goods constant and raising her real income. In other words, we must compare her bacon consumption at point 3 with that at point 2, because the relative price of bacon is the same at both points, and only her real income has gone up from I_1 to I_2. We can see from Figure 12.7 that Chris increases her consumption of bacon from q_2 to q_3, when the price of bacon is held constant but her real income rises. So the income effect of the price change is $q_3 - q_2$.

The last few paragraphs have been rather technical. It may be useful to summarize them. The effect of a change in the own price of a good on the consumer's purchases may be *conceptually* divided into two parts. One part is due to a change in the purchasing power of the consumer's income caused by the price change with constant money income. The other part is due to the effect of the change in relative prices. The former effect is the income effect. It shows the effect on quantity demanded of a move from one indifference curve to another (representing the change in real income). The latter effect is the substitution effect. It shows the change in consumption that would occur if relative prices change, while real income is held constant. The sum of the income and substitution effects is equal to the full price effect.[1]

Price Effects with Inferior Goods

The explanation we gave of the breakdown of the effects of a fall in the price of bacon assumed that bacon was a normal, not an inferior, good. We did not

---

1 Income and substitution effects occur in practice simultaneously. It is only possible to isolate them conceptually. We have chosen to identify the substitution effect before the income effect, as do many textbooks. It is equally valid to reverse the process and show the substitution effect by comparing points of tangency at the new and the old relative prices on the indifference curve reached after the price change rather than on the initial indifference curve. Such a procedure would be likely to show some (small) difference in the relative sizes of the income and substitution effects, but not of the overall price effect. Neither approach is more correct than the other.

draw your attention to this fact before because we wanted to avoid complications in our first discussion of this subject.

Normal goods, you should remember, are defined as those for which the quantity demanded by a consumer rises when income rises, and falls when income falls. They are straightforward to deal with because both the income effect and substitution effect of a price change move *in the same direction.* If you refer back to Figure 12.7, you will see that bacon being a normal good, the fall in its price led the consumer to buy more of it as a result of the rise in her real income. The substitution effect also led to an increase in consumption.

In the case of inferior goods, income and substitution effects work in *opposite directions* to each other. This arises because of the sign of the income effect. The substitution effect always has the same sign, regardless of whether a good is normal or inferior. Holding real income constant, the consumer will always tend to substitute a good whose price has fallen for one whose price is unchanged. It is the income effect which may be positive or negative.

When we are dealing with an inferior good, we must allow for an income effect which operates in the

opposite direction to the substitution effect. If such a good falls in price, the substitution effect will still cause an increase in quantity purchased. But the income effect will cause a decrease in quantity. This is because the fall in price raises a consumer's real income which, for an inferior good, means that less will be demanded.

Economic theory alone cannot predict definitely whether the income or substitution effect will predominate. Their relative strength is a question of fact, not of theory. But we can analyse the two cases.

In Figures 12.8 and 12.9, we show income, substitution and full price effects of the fall in the price of the good referred to on the horizontal axis.

Case 1. The Substitution Effect exceeds the Income Effect: In Figure 12.8 the substitution effect is the stronger of the two. The goods we choose for illustrative purposes are the same as those for Figure 12.4(ii) – steak, as the normal good, and sausages, as the inferior good. The original equilibrium is at point 1. The consumer buys q_1 sausages. The price of sausages now falls, as indicated by the shift of the budget line from *AB* to *AC*. The substitution effect

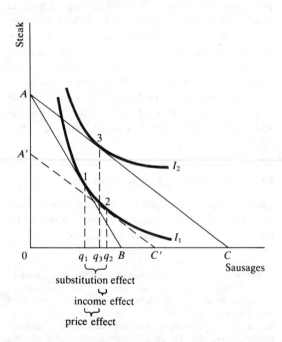

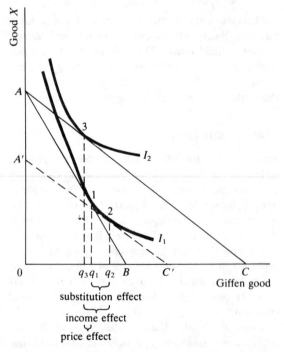

FIGURE 12.8   The Income and Substitution Effects of a Fall in the Price of an Inferior Good. The quantity of an inferior good demanded increases when its price falls, provided the substitution effect is larger than the income effect

FIGURE 12.9   The Income and Substitution Effects of a Fall in the Price of a Giffen Good. An inferior good becomes a Giffen good only if the income effect is larger than the substitution effect

then shifts the consumer from point 1 to 2. It results in an increase in the quantity bought of q_2-q_1. When the income effect is brought in, however, equilibrium moves from point 2 to point 3. Because sausages are assumed to be inferior goods, there is a decrease in quantity of q_2-q_3, as a result of the income effect alone. The full price effect is for an increase in quantity of sausages bought of q_3-q_1. This is made up of an *increase* of q_2-q_1 and a *decrease* of q_3-q_2. The substitution effect more than offsets the income effect.

Case 2. The Income Effect exceeds the Substitution Effect (Giffen Goods): Figure 12.9 illustrates the extreme case of an inferior good where the income effect is greater than the substitution effect. As forewarned in Chapter 5, there is a special name for goods in this category. They are called GIFFEN GOODS. The diagram is, as it happens, quite difficult to draw, but no more difficult to explain, than Figure 12.8. The original equilibrium is at point 1 with quantity q_1 consumed. The fall in price of the Giffen goods shifts the budget line from AB to AC as before. The substitution effect of the price fall, as it must, leads the consumer to buy more of it, q_2-q_1 in this case. However, the income effect on this inferior good, q_2-q_3 in this case, is so large that it more than offsets the income effect.

The full effect of the fall in the price of a Giffen good is, therefore, a fall in the quantity demanded. This was one of our examples of exceptions to the 'law' that demand curves slope downwards, that we discussed in Chapter 4. However, we should remind you that there is no evidence that Giffen goods are any more than extremely rare phenomena, if they exist at all. We include them here for theoretical completeness.

INDIFFERENCE CURVE ANALYSIS AND THE CONVENTIONAL DEMAND CURVE

You, the reader, could hardly be blamed if you were wondering what the analysis using indifference curves which we have taken you through has to do with the conventional demand curves that you studied in the elementary theory of Chapters 4 and 5. The answer is that these intermediate concepts provide insight into the forces operating, silently

offstage as it were, when we draw a demand curve. The two levels of theory are, however, perfectly consistent with each other. Indeed, it is not hard to show how ordinary demand curves for individual consumers can be constructed from their indifference maps.

In Figure 12.10 we derive the demand curve of our consumer, Chris, for a single commodity, bacon. In order to do this, we use the composite commodity that we first introduced in the previous chapter (see p. 132). We are interested, now, in the quantity of bacon demanded at different bacon prices, *the price of all other goods held constant.*

The upper portion of Fig. 12.10 contains Chris's indifference map, which is similar in all respects save one to the other diagrams in this chapter. The one difference is that, instead of measuring the quantity of

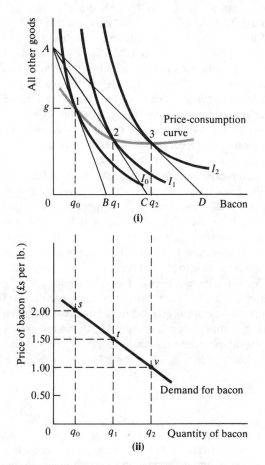

FIGURE 12.10 Derivation of the Demand Curve of a Consumer. All the data needed to draw a demand curve is implicit in the indifference curve diagram, where one price varies

eggs on the vertical axis, we measure the value of *all* other goods available on the market (the composite commodity). The budget line AB means that, with any given money income, Chris can buy either B of bacon and nothing else or A of other goods and no bacon. The quantity A can be thought of as representing the consumer's real income in terms of its purchasing power over all goods and services.

In the usual fashion, we can hold constant Chris's income and the prices of all goods, except that of bacon. This pivots the budget line around point A. If we then join all the points of tangency between the budget lines and an indifference curve, we trace the familiar price-consumption curve (see p. 140 above).

The relationship between the price-consumption curve and the conventional demand curve for bacon may now be shown. Each point on the price-consumption curve corresponds to one price of bacon and one quantity demanded. These are the two pieces of information that we require to plot the demand curve in the lower portion of the diagram. Note that the horizontal axis of Figure 12.10(ii) is exactly the same as that of Figure 12.10(i) – the quantity of bacon. The vertical axis is the one that differs. In the upper diagram we show the price of bacon by the slope of the budget line. In the lower diagram, we show the price measured directly on the axis.

The budget line AB, let us suppose, has a slope which represents a price of £2.00 per lb. for bacon. Chris finds her equilibrium at position 1 on the graph, where indifference curve I_0 is tangent to the budget line. At the given price, she uses Ag of her income to buy q_0 bacon (spending Og, therefore, on all other goods). To derive a point on Chris's demand curve, all we need to do is to plot point s in the lower part of the diagram, showing that q_0 bacon is demanded at a price of £2.00. To find other points on the demand curve, we pivot the budget line around A and read off the quantity of bacon demanded at different prices. For example, when the price of bacon is £1.50 per lb., the budget line is AC. At this lower price, q_1 bacon is demanded. We can then plot a second point, t, on the demand curve in the lower part of the diagram showing the price of £1.50 directly and the same quantity, q_1, on the horizontal axis. If we perform this exercise for all possible points on the price-consumption curve, we trace out the conventional demand curve, showing directly the relationship between prices and quantities demanded for bacon.

Note that the demand curve we derived in Figure 12.10 has the normal downward slope, showing increasing quantities demanded with falling price. Only in the rare Giffen good case, when the income effect of an inferior good is stronger than the substitution effect, would we trace out an upward-sloping demand curve relating price to quantity. This is an important conclusion. If you cannot immediately see that it is true, we suggest that you place a piece of blank paper below Figures 12.8 and 12.9 and derive the conventional demand curves in precisely the same way as we have done for goods measured on the horizontal axes. You will find an upward-sloping demand curve only in the Giffen good case, Figure 12.9.

Alternative theories of demand

Indifference curve analysis has, we hope, been shown to be a useful tool of economic theory. It is much employed in more advanced applications, beyond the scope of this book. It also has the two advantages over price-quantity demand curves mentioned at the beginning of the previous chapter – that it can show consumer choice between two goods on a two-dimensional graph, and that it does not require absolute, or cardinal, measurements of utility. It may, however, be said in criticism of indifference curve theory that such curves cannot be drawn for real persons. Although this may limit the theory's usefulness, it does not prevent the theory from giving valuable insights into the determinants of consumer behaviour.

SUMMARY

1 A consumer maximizes satisfaction by buying that combination of goods for which the budget line is tangent to an indifference curve – i.e. where the marginal rate of substitution between goods is equal to their relative prices.

2 An income-consumption line shows how consumption changes as income changes, relative prices being held constant. It is derived from the points of tangency of indifference curves and parallel budget lines.

3 A price-consumption line shows how consumption changes as the price of one good changes, while money income and the price of other goods are held constant. It is derived from the points of tangency of indifference curves with budget lines of varying slope, pivoted around the intersection of the line with the axis measuring the good with unchanged price.

4 The substitution effect of a price change is found by holding real income constant on a single indifference curve and examining the effect of changing relative prices by changing the slope of the budget line.

5 The income effect of a price change is found by holding relative prices constant and varying the position of the budget line with its slope constant.

6 The substitution effect of a price change causes a change in quantity bought in the opposite direction to the price change. The income effect of a price change causes a change in the quantity bought in the opposite direction to the price change in the case of normal goods, and in the same direction to the price change in the case of inferior goods. The price effect (income plus substitution effects) of a price change always leads to a change in the quantity bought in the opposite direction to the price change for normal goods and for those inferior goods where the substitution effect outweighs the income effect. In *theoretically possible exceptional cases*, the income effect of an inferior good outweighs the substitution effect, producing a Giffen good where price and quantity demanded are positively associated with each other.

Business Decisions

The previous two chapters took our theory of demand to the intermediate level. It is now the turn of supply, which we dealt with very briefly in the elementary theory in Part 2. This is the first of a set of three chapters extending our study of the behaviour of sellers. Now, we consider the background to business decisions, followed by a study of factor productivity and, in Chapter 15, costs of production. We shall then be ready to look at how economists analyse the behaviour of firms in different market situations.

The elementary theory of supply and demand in Part 2 of this book was built on simplifying assumptions. Because those assumptions proved reasonably satisfactory on the demand side, our intermediate theory of demand consisted mainly of obtaining a deeper understanding of the forces behind individual and market demand curves.

The same cannot be said on the supply side, where the simplifying assumptions have greatly limited the conclusions we were able to reach. Consider the nature of those assumptions, which were (1) sellers are price-takers, (2) supply curves slope upwards, and (3) sellers maximize their profits. There are indeed areas in the UK and other economies where these assumptions hold, at least approximately. However, there are other important sectors where they do not.

The intermediate theory of supply, to which the next chapters are devoted, includes a formal restatement of the theory of supply where the above assumptions hold, but also deals with the economic behaviour of businesses in the following conditions:

(1) Many sellers do not have to take market prices as given because they are large enough to be able to affect price by altering their output.

(2) Some supply curves slope downwards, rather than upwards. This condition is not as heretical as it might sound. We have seen that the quantity that a firm offers for sale depends, among other things, on the marginal costs of production. Thus when marginal costs rise as output increases, supply curves slope upwards. In some industries, however, economies of large-scale production give rise to decreasing marginal costs and hence to downward-sloping supply curves.

(3) Businesses seek to achieve goals other than the simple maximization of profits.

When we have mastered this theory we can deal in later chapters in this part of the book with a host of problems, of which the following are a few examples. What is the effect of various forms of competition or monopoly on the efficiency and level of production in an industry? Why do firms combine? What is the best way of using public policy to control monopolistic practices so that they are more in the public interest?

SELLERS' DECISIONS

Consider Figure 13.1. It portrays the different types of decision that have to be made by those who run businesses. Business decisions may be divided into two categories – those relating to outputs and those related to inputs. The upper portion of Figure 13.1 portrays these.

Output decisions

There are four interrelated matters to consider: (1) what goods to produce, (2) how many of them, (3) of what quality, and (4) what price to charge for them.

For a business engaged in producing more than one product, the first three of these are questions concerning the *mix* of quantities and qualities of products that should be produced. Most businesses in the real world make a range of products, and some of the most interesting questions on the supply side of economics relate to product mixes. Their analysis is, however, complicated and difficult to handle in non-mathematical terms. Hence, most of our discussion will deal with single-product businesses that make a product of given quality.

The fourth question, what price to charge, is one that we meet now for the first time, because we have so far assumed firms to be price-takers. We shall discuss price determination at length in a later chapter, but it may be said, now, that a seller's power to determine the price of its product is never un-limited. Even the strongest of monopolies is con-strained by the demand for its product. The price that it charges will be influenced by the amount that it wishes to sell. A firm that is not a monopolist is also constrained by its competitors' behaviour. What it can charge for its product depends, among other things, on what competing firms charge for theirs.

A further problem concerns how large a stock of its output the firm wishes to hold. The firm adds to its stocks by producing more than it sells; it reduces its stocks by producing less than it sells.

Input decisions

A separate set of decisions must be taken by busi-nesses about the inputs of factors of production that it uses. They include: (1) where to locate production, (2) how to raise capital, (3) how much labour, capital and land to use, (4) how much is to be spent on research and development (R & D), and (5) what stocks of raw materials to hold.

Consider, for example, a new business about to start production of electric guitars. One of the first decisions it must make is where to locate production. It will need to consider the advantages and disadvan-tages of alternative locations including the availa-bility of energy, raw materials and skilled and unskilled labour it will employ. It must also take account of the geographical distribution of markets in which it hopes to sell, and the costs of transporting its factors of production and its finished products.

Another step to be taken by our imaginary guitar producer is how to raise the finance to start its operations. (It must face the same question again if it wishes to expand its scale of operations.) Basically, it has a choice of two courses of action. Either it can raise funds from people who take a share in the

ownership of the business, or it can borrow money from people who are then added to its lists of creditors. (A *creditor* is someone who grants credit.)

The next set of decisions concern the amounts of each factor of production to use. These are often complex and interrelated. The firm must decide on its scale of operations. Will its output capacity be large or small? This will help to determine the amount of capital that it needs. The firm must also choose from among several different techniques of production that are usually available. Some are, for example, rela-tively labour-intensive, while others call for relatively large quantities of capital equipment. This question of *how* to produce a given output is one of the basic questions of economics, to which we referred as far back as Chapter 2. It has two distinct aspects.

One is purely *technological*. In these days of 'high technology', for example, computer-controlled robo-tics have introduced major new production possi-bilities. The other aspect of choice of technique is *economic*. Choices are influenced by the prices of various factors of production, which help to deter-mine costs of production. Factor prices tend to reflect factor scarcities. So, our guitar producer will have to decide on the best proportions of labour and machin-ery to use in the factory. Or, to take another industry to illustrate this important point, farmers will have to decide on the best proportions of land, labour and capital to employ in agriculture. It is no accident that one finds highly land-intensive techniques used in farming in land-rich countries such as Australia, Canada and the USA; while in land-scarce countries, such as the UK and the Netherlands, the available land is farmed more intensively, using relatively more labour which is relatively cheap. Such responses are encouraged by the price system, and it is no accident that crop yields *per acre* in the UK are among the highest in the world.

Businesses have other decisions to make regarding the use of inputs. Two are shown in Figure 13.1, how much to spend on research and development (R & D), and what stocks of raw materials and other inputs to hold. Expenditure on R & D is a form of investment, made in order to develop new products and/or more efficient techniques of production. Both may be important to attain, or retain, competitive advantage over other businesses. The best ratio of stocks of inputs to ouput is another important decision. The firm wishes to reduce the risk of hold-ups in produc-tion, while at the same time keeping the cost of capital tied up in stocks as low as possible.

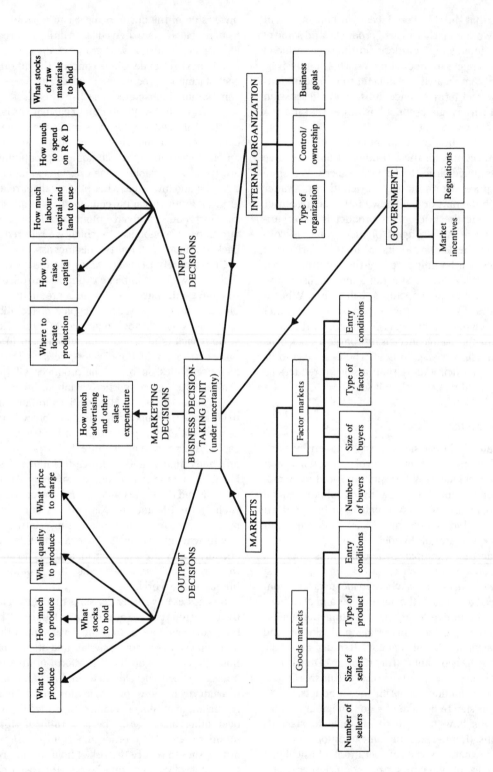

FIGURE 13.1   Types of Business Decisions and their Determinants

Next consider the firm's marketing decisions. Advertising, packaging, and other selling expenditures, and choice of markets, are different from the firm's other decisions in the sense that marketing decisions can affect the demand for a firm's products. Indeed, as we shall see, they may be used, as alternatives to changing price, to try to influence the strength of demand.

Business Decisions Under Uncertainty

Business decision-taking can be an exciting, even a nerve-racking, affair. Virtually all the issues on which decisions must be taken involve the uncertain future. Decisions about what to produce and how to produce it, even whether to produce at all, inevitably require that the producer take some view about the future course of events. For example, what will the demand for electric guitars be in a year or two's time, when a new factory gets rolling, what will competitors be doing, both at home and overseas, how much will it cost to employ labour in Telford, Tooting, Tonypandy or wherever?

Success in business is the result of efficient management coupled with reasonable prediction about demand and costs of production in the future. Sainsbury's supermarkets, for example, have performed outstandingly well in recent years, partly by anticipating demand for new product lines, such as home and garden centres. Disaster can, and often does, befall those who are unlucky, unfortunate or who perform poorly. For example, several travel companies were forced out of business in 1984 because they failed to anticipate the devaluation of sterling earlier in the year, and the rise in the price of fuel needed for charter-flight holidays.

All business decisions are taken in an atmosphere of uncertainty. There are modern techniques which can reduce some of the risks in certain kinds of ventures, but they can rarely be eliminated entirely. The reward for successfully undertaking business uncertainties is profits, that for failure is losses.

THE DETERMINANTS OF BUSINESS DECISIONS

The lower portion of Figure 13.1 illustrates schematically some sets of factors which affect the decisions that businesses take. The two most important are markets and internal organization. We deal with these influences in turn, touching finally on the influence of government.

Market Considerations

A business's ability to make any of the decisions we have discussed above depends on conditions prevailing in two kinds of markets – those in which it sells its product, and those in which it buys the services of factors of production, known as GOODS MARKETS and FACTOR MARKETS, respectively.

It would be, perhaps, too strong a word to describe the competition between businesses as battles for markets. But competitive forces can be cut-throat in the sense that losers may be forced out of business. Freedom for individual producers to manoeuvre depends, to a substantial extent, on the degree of competition that exists in the markets in which they operate. The strength of competition in turn depends on four characteristics depicted in the lower portion of Figure 13.1, which are (1) the number of sellers in the industry, (2) the size of sellers, (3) the type of product, and (4) entry (and exit) conditions. These market characteristics influence the firm's ability to make independent decisions on such matters as what price to charge for its product.

Goods markets

Consider, first, the importance of these four characteristics in the markets for the products of a business.

The Number of Sellers: This is, perhaps, the prime determinant of the freedom of individual businesses to make decisions. The smaller the number of sellers, the greater the chance that any one of them can choose exactly what it wants to do. In the extreme case, there may be industries where only a single firm operates. These are called *monopolies* (from the Greek for single seller) or *monopsonies* (single buyer). Pure monopolies are, as we shall see in a later chapter, rare in the real world. More common are markets, known as *oligopolies*, where there are a *few* sellers. If the number of producers is very large, the industry is likely to be very competitive and the freedom of manoeuvre for any one producer, in consequence, to be small.

The Size of Sellers: A very large number of sellers in an industry is not sufficient to ensure that one of them can influence market prices by its actions. If all sellers are to be price-takers, it is also necessary that no single seller should be large. Obviously, one giant business surrounded by a very large number of small ones is constrained more than if it were the sole supplier, since it may well have to consider what the other firms may do, before taking some actions itself.

Type of Product: The power of a seller to make decisions on the price charged for its product depends not only on the number and size of all the producers in the industry, but also on the nature of its product. It is usual to distinguish between two groups of products, called homogeneous and heterogeneous. In an industry where all firms are producing virtually identical products, these are described as HOMOGENEOUS (meaning of the same sort). Where products are differentiated, the term is HETEROGENEOUS (meaning of different sorts). For example, English-grown Granny Smiths apples are a homogeneous product. One trader's stock does not differ significantly from that of another. On the other hand, the car industry produces heterogeneous products since each model of car is different from every other model – although they all share a set of basic common characteristics that make them cars.

If a producer sells a good which is identical to that of every other producer, its price-setting freedom, for example, will be more limited than that of a producer whose product is differentiated from those of its competitors.

A greengrocer is constrained in the price he can charge for King Edward potatoes by prices charged by other greengrocers, whose King Edwards are regarded as identical to his own. On the other hand, restaurateurs are less constrained in the prices they can charge, because of differences in menus offered, quality of food, imagination of the chef, 'ambiance', location or other distinctive features. They cannot, however, get their prices too far out of line from those of other restaurants with similar menus and qualities. We shall deal, in Chapter 18, with some important features of markets where products are differentiated.

Entry Conditions: The final market consideration, affecting the ability of a business to make independent decisions, is entry conditions into the market. These determine the length of time that its power over the market lasts. A business may possess a degree of monopoly power in the short run, but as new producers (or new products) enter the industry, that

power will weaken and may disappear altogether. There are, however, *barriers to entry* of new producers. Barriers can be of many types – artificial or natural, legal, locational or related to cost conditions. They are of immense importance in deciding the long-run competitiveness of different industries. We discuss them further in Chapter 17.

Factor markets

We have described, at some length, the determinants of the degree of competition in the markets in which a business sells its product. A similar set of considerations determine the competitiveness of the factor markets in which businesses buy their inputs. We deal with them briefly (they are discussed at length in Chapters 20 and 21) under the same headings as those used for the markets for products (see Figure 13.1).

The Number of Buyers: This consideration parallels that of the number of sellers in the goods markets. Businesses are buyers of the services of factors of production and other inputs. The smaller the number of buyers, the greater the freedom of a single one of them to do what it wants to do. In the extreme case of a factor market where there is a single buyer, it is a *monopsonist*; where there are only a few buyers, they are *oligopsonists*.

The Size of Buyers: Just as we specified the need for all sellers to be small in the goods market (as well as the requirement for there to be a lot of them) in order that all should be price-takers of their products, so we add that no single buyer should be large in the factor market. One powerful purchaser in a particular factor market will not be constrained, even by a large number of other buyers, if they are all small.

Type of Factor: In goods markets, we noted that the freedom of sellers depends on whether or not their products are homogeneous, or differentiated from each other. In factor markets, a similar consideration arises – whether the factor is homogeneous or not. Some inputs are, of course, homogeneous – e.g., one lathe of any given size is the same as another; but the markets for the factor of production 'labour' are characterized by major sources of variation, such as the region where labour is located. We shall discuss several such aspects of factor markets in Chapter 21.

Entry Conditions: The final consideration affecting factor markets concerns entry conditions. Just as barriers to entry (and exit) in goods markets affect business decisions, so barriers of various kinds in factor markets have similar effects. Factor mobility is impeded by such barriers, which will be described in Chapter 21.

Internal Organization of the Business

Market considerations apart, the actual decisions taken by a business depend also on its internal structure and objectives. After all is said and done, decisions are made by persons (or committees) whose identity and objectives may affect the way they act. The extent to which decision-takers have freedom of manoeuvre, depends on many things. We distinguish three internal matters which may impinge on decisions taken by a business: (1) the type of business organization, (2) the identity of those who own and control the business, and (3) the business's goals.

Types of business organization

There are four principal forms of business organization in the private sector in the UK: (1) single proprietorships, (2) partnerships, (3) co-operatives, and (4) joint-stock companies. State-owned industries in the public sector are discussed in Chapters 19 and 24, and for a fuller discussion of all of these see Harbury and Lipsey, Chapter 2.

Single Proprietorships: As its name implies, this category covers businesses which are *owned* by a single person, whether run by that person or by a hired manager. The owner is personally responsible for everything done by the business. He gives the orders and, without consultation, can make all of the decisions we have so far discussed. The only constraints on his decisions are those dictated by what is technically feasible and by market forces, as discussed in the previous section. With a few notable exceptions, virtually all businesses in this category are small.

Partnerships: In a partnership, as its name implies, there are two or more joint owners of the business. Each of the partners is jointly, and personally, responsible for what is done by the firm. Often partnerships comprise members of the same family. Many partnerships are small, and the average size of

all UK partnerships is only a little larger than that of single proprietorships. Partnerships are common in certain professions, such as accountancy and the law.

Co-operatives: Some business activity, especially in the retail trade but also in farming, is organized on co-operative lines. There are two types of co-operative – those where production is organized by *workers* and those run by, or on behalf of, *consumers*. The distinctive feature of co-operatives is that any profits of the business are shared among workers, or consumers.

Consumer co-operatives can be traced back to 1844, when a small co-operative store was opened in Rochdale. They expanded during the following century but more recently have declined. Today co-operative societies account for less than 10 per cent of total retail trade, though they are still important in milk distribution. Worker co-operatives are less common, appearing from time to time when employees band together to rescue a business threatened with closure. The extent to which the co-operative form of organization restricts the freedom of action of the decision-takers varies from one case to another. The most important impact lies in the particular goals sought by a co-op. This aspect is discussed below (see pp. 154–5).

Joint-stock Companies: Joint-stock companies – known also as corporations – are firms which are owned by their shareholders. The corporation, however, is regarded in law as having an identity of its own, separate from owners who are not personally liable for anything done in the name of their company.

This form of business organization has grown to dominate most sectors of the UK economy, especially manufacturing industry, since the principle of limited liability was introduced in a series of Company Acts going back to the 1860s. LIMITED LIABILITY refers to the release from responsibility for the debts of the firm for owners, who are known as shareholders. Their liability is limited to the amount they have invested in the business.

Individuals wishing to acquire a stake in a company have only to buy shares in that company in the specialized markets for such financial assets known as the Stock Exchange. There are several different kinds of shares. Some promise a fixed rate of return, but the greatest interest attaches to so-called ORDINARY SHARES or EQUITIES, which give their owners a share in whatever profits are made, and provide also voting rights at company meetings. The issue of shares provides a major source of funds for new companies and for the expansion of existing corporations. Another major source of finance is the sale of securities, known as debentures. A DEBENTURE is a financial asset which promises a fixed annual income and, usually, the return of the original purchase price at the end of some stated period, at which time the debenture is said to be REDEEMED. Debenture holders are not owners of the business, and have no say in the way in which it is run.

There are hundreds of thousands of companies organized on a joint-stock basis in modern Britain. The vast majority are small private companies, similar in many ways to partnerships or to single proprietorships. They are organized as joint-stock companies for tax and other advantages, accruing from the fact that the company is a separate entity from its owners. While the majority of companies are therefore small, almost all large-scale business is in the hands of joint-stock companies. Some of these companies themselves own other companies, known as SUBSIDIARIES, which may, in turn, own subsidiaries of their own. The main parent organization may be called a HOLDING COMPANY, owning a pyramid of other companies which can number many hundreds. The Sears group, for example, operates in many different markets from shoes and jewellery to second-hand cars and betting shops through its ownership of Dolcis, Mappin & Webb, Selfridges and William Hill (Racing) Ltd. It is one of the 50 largest company groups in the UK, controlling more than 400 companies through five pyramidal tiers. (For a description of the Sears organization, see Harbury and Lipsey, Chapter 3.)

Special terms are used to denote the role of individual parts of such giant businesses. The whole entity of companies under one ownership (including ownership of a controlling interest in other companies) is called an ENTERPRISE. Subordinate companies within the empire are subsidiaries, which may operate one or more ESTABLISHMENTS or PLANTS, comprising individual factories on specific sites. Some of the very largest enterprises have interests in many countries in the world. They are known as MULTINATIONALS.

Very large businesses do not necessarily rely on highly centralized decision-taking made from head offices. Decentralization of the managerial structure can allow autonomy to divisions, and to even smaller segments of a business, especially where companies operate over a widely diversified product range. However, financial constraints are usually placed by Head Office of the 'primary company' on the use of capital by subsidiary companies.

It is among the giant corporations that we find oligopolists (and monopolists), for which the assumption that sellers are price-takers is particularly inappropriate. Giant enterprises are not, of course, necessarily free from competition from other giants, but their freedom of manoeuvre is usually different from that of small businesses in industries consisting of large numbers of small companies. Moreover, decision-takers in large enterprises may pursue somewhat different goals from those of small companies.

Mergers

Businesses grow in size in two distinct ways – by internal growth, and by MERGER or AMALGAMATION, when two or more separate businesses join up to become a single enterprise. Three types of merger are commonly distinguished: (1) horizontal mergers, (2) vertical mergers, and (3) conglomerate mergers.

When mergers are among companies producing the same product, they are termed HORIZONTAL MERGERS, for example between Dolcis and Saxone shoe retailers. Other mergers among businesses at different stages of the production process are termed VERTICAL MERGERS, which may be 'forward' or 'backward'. Forward integration involves merger towards the market in which the product is sold, e.g. the acquisition of public houses by breweries. Backward integration involves acquisition of suppliers of inputs to the firm, e.g. the purchase of a printing company by a publishing company. A third type of merger, known as CONGLOMERATE MERGER, is between firms without obvious common interests in production. In so far as lower costs result from conglomerate mergers, they are usually associated with managerial, marketing or financial economies or with risk reduction through diversification. Many conglomerate mergers are not motivated by production economies, but by the desire to increase the 'market power' of the amalgamating businesses. We shall discuss this further in the next chapter and in Chapter 18.

The concept of a firm

Economists use the general term FIRM to cover all

four types of business organization discussed above. The term therefore refers to *any* organization that makes decisions on how to organize factors of production so as to produce output. In other words, the firm makes all of the decisions listed in the top half of Figure 13.1 and is influenced by all of the forces shown in the bottom half of the figure.

Owners versus Controllers

In their attempts to explain the behaviour of businesses, economists construct various theories of the firm. To understand the ways in which firms behave, and to be successful in predicting how they react to changing circumstances, we need to know who actually controls the firm, as distinct from who formally owns it.

There is, usually, no difficulty on this matter in the case of single proprietorships, partnerships and small joint-stock companies, especially when the owners take an active role in running the business. Even when owners are inactive, differences between the decisions they would have made and those made by employed managers are unlikely to persist, since a manager can be replaced.

In giant corporations, in contrast, the situation may be quite different. The owners of joint-stock companies are the shareholders. They elect the Boards of Directors, who are answerable, in principle, to the shareholders at company meetings, especially at the annual general meeting (the AGM) when audited accounts for the past year, and forecasts for the future, are presented for approval. The directors, in turn, appoint salaried managers to run the business for them. The chief of these is usually the chairman (sometimes the managing director), of the company.

The power that the owners of a business have over directors may, however, be quite limited in practice. Many investigators of corporate behaviour hold the view that groups other than the majority of ordinary shareholders exert the determining influence. They support the hypothesis that a minority of shareholders exercise effective control over the decisions of the company.

Dispersion of share ownership

The power of small groups of shareholders depends, among other things, on the distribution of share ownership. It may be slight if ownership is widely dispersed. To understand why this is so, it is necessary to appreciate that each ordinary share normally carries one vote, which is cast at the company's annual meeting, either in person or by assignment of a *proxy* to others. Any individual or group owning 51 per cent of the voting shares clearly controls a majority of votes. But, suppose one group owns 30 per cent, with the remaining 70 per cent distributed so widely that few of the dispersed group even bother to vote. In this event, 30 per cent may be the overwhelming majority of shares *actually voted*. Often a small fraction of the shares actually voted may exercise the dominant influence at shareholders' meetings.

Dispersed ownership and minority control are common in giant companies. The separation of ownership and control was first pointed out in the United States more than 50 years ago by Berle and Means. They concluded that nearly half of the largest 200 US corporations were effectively under the control of managers because no individual or group owned as much as 25 per cent of voting shares. The tendency is even more marked today, partly because of a recent trend for large financial institutions to increase their stakes in company shares. Today, in the UK, institutional shareholders (especially insurance companies, pension funds and banks) own over half of ordinary shares, whereas thirty years ago the majority of such shares were owned by private individuals. Because financial institutions have shown themselves to be relatively uninterested in the day-to-day affairs of the firm whose ownership they share, this may give management more scope for independent action.

The power of directors is reinforced by their peculiarly favourable position for acquiring proxy voting rights. It is the directors who call the annual general meetings, and they usually include, in the mailing forms, offers to exercise proxy rights on behalf of shareholders who are unable or unwilling to attend company meetings. Hence, the divorce of ownership from control in many corporations leaves the Board of Directors in a strong position to exercise control.

The power of directors, even in companies where share ownership is widely dispersed, is not, however, unlimited, especially in the longer run. Apathetic shareholders may be roused to revolt by continual mismanagement. However, such occasions are rare.

A more common constraint on directors is the

threat of TAKEOVER from powerful, usually larger, companies. Mismanagement and poor performance by directors rarely goes unnoticed for ever. It is a spur to outside interests, which may seek to take over the firm by making offers to existing shareholders to buy their shares on favourable terms. If successful, the new owners can replace the directors and attempt to run the company more efficiently. Takeover bids are usually made on attractive terms, relative to the current market price of the shares. If the firm is not currently well managed, such prices can be offered in the expectation of being able to increase the firm's profits after the takeover has occurred. Often, in such cases, directors engage in a battle with the predators, as they see them, for control of the company. Shareholders receive letters from would-be takers-over, and from defending management, urging them to sell, or not to sell, their shares. The outcome can go either way. The important point, however, is that the threat of takeover actions is a constraint on manager-controllers, even when share ownership is widely dispersed.

Goals of the Firm

The third set of factors which rank high in importance in understanding the decisions made by a firm is the goals or objectives of those who control it.

In the elementary theory of supply in Part 2 of this book, we explicitly assumed that firms try to *maximize their profits*. The assumption has much to commend it, and there are many competitive markets where it motivates firms' behaviour. It is, however, not universally applicable. In practice, the extent to which individual firms can and do depart from the objective of trying to maximize profits depends on three circumstances: (1) the goals of owners, (2) the extent of divorce of ownership from control, and (3) market conditions.

The Goals of Owners: There is no reason for believing that all businessmen are interested in profitability as their sole aim. Some decisions in single proprietorships confirm this, e.g. the location of a factory close to agreeable surroundings despite higher production costs, or the decision to close down on Wednesdays to allow for a regular game of tennis. Co-operatives also have objectives other than profit maximization. Worker co-operatives generally seek maximum opportunities for employment, especially

where the occasion for the establishment of worker control has been the threat of the closure of an unprofitable business. Consumer co-operatives claim to operate in the interests of the customers, but co-operative societies in retailing in the UK happen also to be politically motivated and associated with the Labour Party, and this can affect some of their business decisions.

The Extent of the Divorce of Ownership from Control: Large joint-stock companies are often, as we have seen, characterized by the divorce of ownership of the company from control by directors and managers. Nonetheless, whenever directors and managers seek to make the company as profitable as possible they are serving the interests of shareholders.

Directors and managers, however, may have other objectives. The chief of these are probably job security and remuneration (i.e. salary and other 'perks'). Although, in the UK, company directors are required by law to be shareholders, for many of them their salaries are a more important source of income than their share of profits. The salaries of directors are related to the size of a business, whether measured in terms of its output, sales, employment or other variables. Hence, maximizing the growth of sales may loom large in the goals that boards of directors strive after. That is not to say that directors are likely to ignore profitability entirely. A sufficient level of profits to keep shareholders quiet, and/or keep takeover bidders at bay, must be a consideration. However, the goal of profit *maximization* may not be an appropriate assumption. In such cases it is sometimes said that the firm is SATISFICING, a term used by American economist and Nobel prize winner Herbert Simon, to describe behaviour aimed at achieving a certain *target* level of profits, but striving at other objectives such as the volume of sales, market share, or just an easy life.

Some large businesses may even seek (or proclaim that they seek) to include 'social responsibility' among their objectives. By social responsibility they usually mean having regard to the needs of the local community in which they operate, the wishes of their employees and even national targets, such as the avoidance of pollution. These so-called social objectives do not always conflict with profit maximization – for example, provision of good canteen and sports facilities for staff can aid productivity. Also, voluntary inclusion of national economic targets may pre-empt governments from forcing them on a firm.

Market Conditions: Our discussion of business goals has emphasized what decision-takers would like to do. The extent to which they are able to do what they would like depends substantially on market conditions and, in particular, on the degree of competition facing an individual firm.

All the four determinants of competitiveness discussed earlier in this chapter – number and size of firms, type of product and entry conditions – are here relevant. There is no need to go over them again. It is enough to appreciate that a firm possessing a great deal of market power is freer to depart from the aim of profit maximization than a small firm in a highly competitive industry, where maximum obtainable profits are kept low by competitive forces, and where the pursuit of other objectives may mean extinction. We should, however, be careful not to jump to the conclusion that large firms always have great market power. Strength depends on more than mere size. We shall discuss this subject at greater length in Chapter 19.

The Influence of Government

If you return for a final look at Figure 13.1, you will see that we have included government as a separate force that can influence business decisions. Indeed, we mentioned this possibility earlier when we commented on the activities of firms said to be seeking to adopt 'socially responsible' objectives.

The many and complex ways in which governments can impinge on business decisions are studied in Chapters 19, 23 and 24. In the meantime, we note that state intervention can take two main forms. The first is through direct controls, or regulations, for example the refusal of permission for a factory building, or the requirement that minimum safety standards be maintained for a product. The second is through indirect influence by offering incentives that encourage or discourage certain actions, for example by subsidizing production in areas of heavy unemployment or by taxing products deemed to be harmful. More, much more, will be said about these and other governmental influences in later chapters.

SUMMARY

1 Businesses make decisions with respect to their outputs and their inputs. Output decisions relate to the type, quantity, and quality of production, selling price, and stockholding. Input decisions relate to factor use.

2 Business decisions have to be made under conditions of uncertainty and are influenced by the type of market in which the business operates and by its internal organization.

3 Market considerations affecting business decisions include the number and size of buyers and sellers, whether the products and factors of production are homogeneous or heterogeneous, and entry conditions. All these affect the degree of competition in the market.

4 Internal considerations affecting business decisions include the type of business organization, the relationship between ownership and control, and the goals of the business.

5 The chief types of business organization are single proprietorships, partnerships, co-operatives, and joint-stock companies based on the principle of limited liability for shareholders (owners) of the business.

6 A business enterprise is an organization which makes decisions on how to organize factors of production so as to produce outputs. It may comprise one or more firms controlling one or more subsidiaries and one or more establishments (or plants).

7 Joint-stock companies are owned by shareholders and controlled by Boards of Directors formally appointed by the shareholders.

8 Ownership and control often diverge in giant corporations, especially where the number of shareholders is very great. In such cases the directors may have little regard for the interests of shareholders, though they may be influenced by the threat of takeovers from outside firms.

9 The goals of a business may include profit maximization, growth or sales maximization, and 'satisficing'. For any business, the goals actually selected are influenced by the extent of any divergence between ownership and control, by market conditions, and by government activities.

The Productivity of Factors of Production

This is the second of three chapters dealing with supply at an intermediate level. In the previous chapter we discussed the many decisions that must be made by a firm. For a theory of supply, our major concern is with the firm's decisions on the amount that it will produce, and the price at which it will offer its output for sale. For brevity, these are often referred to as the firm's price-output decisions.

A major determinant of the firm's price-output decision is its cost of production. The firm's costs, in turn, depend on two influences. The first is the technical relation of how outputs vary as inputs vary, i.e. factor productivity. The second is what it costs the firm to obtain its factor inputs, i.e. factor prices.

This chapter is devoted to a consideration of how output varies as inputs vary. The next chapter uses the conclusions from this one and deals with costs of production.

Factor Productivity

The ability of a factor of production to produce output is known as the factor's PRODUCTIVITY. It is a purely technological relationship, between what is fed into the productive apparatus by way of inputs of factor services and what is turned out by way of product. In stating this relationship it must be remembered that production is a flow: it is not just so many units; it is so many units *per period of time*. If we speak of raising the level of monthly production from 100 to 101 units, we do not mean producing 100 units this month and 1 unit next month, but going from a *rate* of production of 100 units each month to a rate of 101 units each month.

For the rest of this chapter we shall consider the relationship between factor inputs and output in a very simple example. We shall pretend that there are only two factors of production, labour and capital. Output of the firm's product, per period of time, depends on the quantities of these factors that are used by the firm. This simplification will not materially affect the conclusions we shall reach, but it will enable us to get quickly to the essential aspects of the problem.

Suppose now that the firm wishes to increase its rate of output. To do so it must increase the inputs of one or more factors of production. But the firm cannot usually vary both of its factors with the same ease. Labour, for example, can be taken on, or laid off, at fairly short notice (in a week or a month). But a longer time is needed to vary the quantity of some other factors, for example to install more capital.

To allow for different speeds with which different kinds of inputs can be varied, we think of the firm as making decisions within two time-periods, the short run and the long run.

The short and long runs

Any factor of production that cannot easily be varied over the time-period under consideration is called a FIXED factor. Any factor that can be varied over the time-period under consideration is called a VARIABLE FACTOR. The SHORT RUN is defined as the period of time when one or more factors of production is fixed.

In the real world, the factor that is fixed in the short run is usually an element of capital (such as plant and equipment) or land, but it might be the services of management or even the supply of skilled labour. As we are dealing with a simplified case with only two factors, we let capital be the fixed factor and labour the variable factor. If the firm wishes to vary its production in the short run, it can do so only by changing its labour input. *Since capital is fixed, this necessitates changing the proportions in which labour and capital are combined.*

The LONG RUN is defined as that period long enough for all factors of production to be varied, within the confines of given technology. All factors are variable.

The long run is the period that is relevant when a firm is either planning to go into business or to expand, or contract, its entire *scale* of operations. The firm can then choose those quantities of all factors of production that seem most suitable. In particular, it can opt for a new factory of any technologically feasible size. However, once the planning decision has been carried out – the plant built, machines purchased and installed, and so on – the firm acquires fixed factors and it is operating in the short run.

The boundary between the short and the long runs is not defined by reference to any particular period of calendar time, measured in months or years. It varies from industry to industry, and from one time to another, being defined only in terms of the fixity of one factor of production. In the electric power industry, for example, it takes three or more years to acquire and install a steam-turbine generator. Thus, an increase in the demand for electricity cannot immediately be met by increasing capital equipment. Existing machines must supply as much of the extra demand as they can. In contrast, a courier service can meet an increase in demand by acquiring an extra one or more motorcycles in a matter of days or even hours. The length of the short run is influenced by technological considerations, such as how quickly equipment can be manufactured or installed, and by economic matters, such as the price the firm is willing to pay for equipment.

We turn now to consider how the productivities of factors of production vary with output in the short and in the long run. As we shall explain, short-run productivity reflects changes in the proportions in which factors are combined. Long-run productivity reflects changes in the entire scale of operation.

RETURNS TO A VARIABLE FACTOR IN THE SHORT RUN

In the short run we are concerned with the behaviour of output as more units of a variable factor are applied in conjunction with a given quantity of a fixed factor.

We continue to assume that the firm we are using, for illustrative purposes, employs two factors of production – capital which is fixed, and labour which is variable.

Table 14.1 presents hypothetical figures for the behaviour of output as the amount of labour is varied. The same data are shown graphically in Figure 14.1. We can look at the effect of changing the quantity of inputs on total product, average product, and marginal product. These three are described in the three output columns – (iii), (iv) and (v) – in Table 14.1 and in Figure 14.1.

TOTAL PRODUCT (TP) means just what it says; the total amount produced during some period of time by all the factors of production employed.

AVERAGE PRODUCT (AP) is total product divided by the amount of the variable factor, which is labour in the present illustration. Letting L stand for the quantiy of labour, we can express average product as TP/L. This is total product *per unit of* labour.

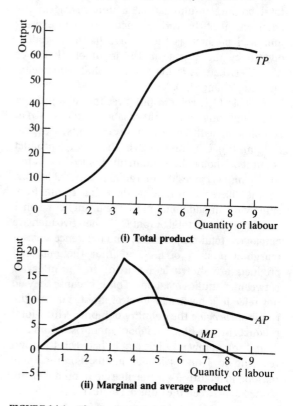

FIGURE 14.1   The Productivity of a Variable Factor Used in Combination with a Fixed Factor in the Short Run. *TP* rises, first at an increasing and then at a diminishing rate. When *AP* is rising, *MP* is greater than *AP*; when *AP* is falling, *MP* is less than *AP*

TABLE 14.1 The Relation Between Output and the Amount of a Variable Factor (Labour) used in Combination with a Fixed Factor (Capital)

INPUT OF		OUTPUT		
Labour	Capital	Total product	Average product (iii)/(i)	Marginal product
(i)	(ii)	(iii)	(iv)	(v)
1	10	4	4	4
2	10	10	5	6
3	10	21	7	11
4	10	40	10	19
5	10	55	11	15
6	10	60	10	5
7	10	63	9	3
8	10	64	8	1
9	10	63	7	−1

MARGINAL PRODUCT (MP) is defined as the *change* in total product resulting from a unit *change* in the employment of the variable factor. We can express marginal product as the change in total product divided by the change in the input of labour, or $\Delta TP/\Delta L$ (where Δ is the Greek capital letter delta, meaning 'change in').

In Table 14.1, column (iii) gives the total product from employing 1 to 9 units of labour (column (i)) in combination with a fixed quantity (10 units) of capital (column (ii)). Column (iv) gives the average product per unit of labour – i.e. column (iii) divided by column (i). Column (v) gives the marginal product of labour, i.e. the difference in total product that results from employing an additional man. For example, when 1 man is employed, total output is 4; when two men are employed, total output is 10. The difference gives a marginal product of 6. (Note that the marginal products are shown as occurring in the intervals between quantities of labour. This is because they do not refer to a particular level of input, but are the result of *changing* the quantity of inputs. Thus, total product rises by 19 when labour input rises from 3 to 4, and the number 19 appears in between the rows referring to 3 and 4 labour inputs. For the same reason, in Figure 14.1 the marginal products are plotted in between the units of labour.)

The 'Law' of Diminishing Returns

Although the data used for Table 14.1 and Figure 14.1 are hypothetical, the relationship shown between total, average and marginal products is widely applicable. We use the word 'law' to describe the relationship, in the same way as we used that term in connection with the 'laws of supply and demand' (in Chapter 8, pp. 90–92). The relationship would, of course, be more accurately described as a hypothesis, which is valid if consistent with the facts. However, it is sufficiently well tested for us to follow common practice and refer to the 'law of diminishing returns'.

The LAW OF DIMINISHING RETURNS *states that when increasing quantities of a variable factor are used in combination with a fixed factor, the marginal and average product of the variable factor will eventually decrease.* Another name for the law of diminishing returns is the LAW OF VARIABLE PROPORTIONS. In some ways it is a better descriptive title, as we shall later explain.

Consider the numbers in Table 14.1. Total product increases as the number of men working with the fixed amount of capital rises from 1 to 8. Average product increases until 5 men are employed. Thereafter, average product declines. Marginal product rises until 4 men are employed. Then it diminishes.

The Relationship Between Marginal and Average Product: Note that the marginal product curve cuts the average product curve at the latter's maximum point. This happens to be a mathematical property of any average and marginal series. So long as marginal product exceeds average product, the average product *must* be rising. Thus, only when marginal product falls below the level of average product does average product fall. Since *AP* rises when *MC* exceeds *AP*, while *AP* falls when *MC* is less than *AP*, it follows that when average product is at a maximum, it is equal to marginal product. (Note this cannot be seen in the table which does not show the absolute maximum average product, which lies between 4 and 5 labour inputs.)

For reasons that we do not fully grasp, generations of students have had difficulty in understanding the arithmetic of the last paragraph, but can follow the same argument if it is expressed in terms of cricket averages. So, we shall repeat the argument with a cricket analogy.

Consider a cricketer, Ian Botham perhaps. He goes in to bat every week, scoring a certain number of runs. His latest score is his marginal score. His average score is the total number of runs he has made to date, divided by the number of innings when he was batting (we ignore the possibility that he was 'not out', even though he probably would not like that!).

Suppose, then, that Botham has played in three matches so far this year and scored 25, 50 and 75 runs. His average is 50. In this fourth match he scores 62, i.e. his marginal score fell (from 75 to 62). However his average score is now 53. It is still rising, because his marginal score of 62 is above his previous average score of 50. Suppose, however, he goes on to score 53 in his fifth match. This is exactly equal to his average score, which does not then change. But if, in his sixth match Botham gets only 47 runs, his average now starts to fall (it is now 52), because his marginal score is less than his previous average score. This example illustrates the general proposition that when marginal values exceed the average value, then the average value must be rising, but when the marginal value falls below the average value that must drag the average value down.

The Basis of the 'Law':   In order to understand why the 'law' of diminishing returns operates, it is essential to remember that the application of varying quantities of one factor to a fixed quantity of another, *changes the proportions* in which the two factors are combined. Some factor combinations are more efficient than others. As we move towards the best combination, productivity tends to rise. As we move beyond it, diminishing returns set in. The reason lying behind the argument is that the best combination of factors is the one which gives the optimum scope for division of labour and specialization.

A common illustration of the law of diminishing returns is in farming. To explain it, we need to make a slight change in our assumptions. We continue to assume that there are only two factors of production, but the fixed factor is now land (rather than capital), which is worked with the aid of a variable factor, labour. Suppose a farmer has 10 acres of land, and consider the likely effects on output of employing additional men to work it. If he has only a single worker, the labourer will have to do all the tasks required. At harvest time he must cut the corn, gather it into piles, load them on to a cart, thrash the corn, fill sacks with the grain, dispose of the chaff, etc., etc. There is no opportunity for specialization. One worker must try to do everything.

Suppose the farmer now takes on a second worker. He can divide the different duties between the two men, increasing their skills, and reducing the time they must spend moving from job to job. Each man can, to an extent, perform specialist functions. When three men are employed, the possibilities for specializ-

ation increase again. Average product will again tend to rise, as a result of such specialization.

Why then, you may wonder, do diminishing returns ever set in? The answer is because the men are, by definition, being employed *in conjunction with a fixed amount of land*. With only 10 acres to farm, the opportunities for specialization gradually diminish as more men are employed. Division of labour is likely to be extremely effective when a second man is taken on – one drives the cart around while the other loads the corn. But as more and more men are working, the opportunities for efficient division of functions become less. Indeed by the time, say, 20 men have been taken on, each is already doing a single specialist task. The only work the farmer can think of for a 21st man might be to carry beer round to the others when they are thirsty. Hence, the scope for raising productivity by increasing specialization will be great when only a few are employed, but eventually a level of employment will be reached where 'diminishing returns' set in.

Indeed, if the farmer were silly enough to continue to add more and more workers to his 10 acres of land, the point would finally be reached when additional workers had a *negative* marginal product: they would cause total product to fall, because, for example, there were so many of them that they got into each other's way. Such a case is illustrated in Figure 14.1 where the total product curve turns down when 9 men are employed. Note that in the lower section the marginal product becomes negative, though average product remains positive. Such a situation is not, however, of any economic significance. No profit-maximizing producer would consider employing so many men.

The reason for diminishing returns is the presence of a fixed factor of production, with which the variable factors have to work.

If the farmer bought more acres of land whenever he hired more labour, the law would not be applicable. But we would no longer be considering the application of varying quantities of one factor together with a fixed factor. We would be varying both of them. So there is no reason to expect the law to apply. *The law of diminishing returns refers only to the effect of varying factor proportions.* It is for good reason that the law is also known as the law of *variable proportions*.

At the beginning of the chapter, we spoke of the productivity of a factor. It is now clear that we can speak either of the average or the marginal productivity of a factor. The first is total output divided by the number of units of the factor used. The second is the increase in total product resulting from the use of an additional unit of the factor.

The Consequences of the 'Law': The empirical evidence in favour of the hypothesis of diminishing returns is strong in many fields. Indeed, were the hypothesis false, there would be no need to fear that the growth in the world's population would cause food crises. As long as the marginal product of labour were constant, food production could be expanded indefinitely, merely by employing more people on the fixed amount of land in the world. As it is, a rise in the proportion of labour to land would be bound, eventually, to lead to diminishing returns – an inexorable decline in marginal product as additional labour was employed in farming. The quantity of land in the world is fixed. Hence, the only hope for preventing diminishing returns lies in new and better techniques of production. Without a continual and rapidly accelerating improvement in such techniques, the population explosion will eventually cause declining living standards over much of the world.

RETURNS TO A VARIABLE FACTOR IN THE LONG RUN

In the short run, the only way to change output is to alter the inputs of the variable factor, changing thereby factor proportions. The long run, however, is defined as a period long enough for *all* factors of production to be varied. When this is done, holding factor proportions constant, we talk about RETURNS TO SCALE. A firm might for example double the amount of labour used in production and double the amount of capital as well.

When the scale of operations is increased, or decreased, the law of diminishing returns simply does not apply. No factor of production needs to be fixed. Capital, land and all other factors may be varied in quantity. We may then find that returns to scale increase, decrease or remain constant.

Returns to scale are said to be *increasing* if an equal percentage increase in all inputs results in a larger proportionate change in output. To illustrate, consider a firm employing two factors of production, capital and labour. If the firm doubles its use of *both* labour and capital, and output more than doubles, there are increasing returns to scale. If the same

doubling of inputs causes a doubling of output, returns to scale are *constant*. If, finally, doubling inputs causes a rise in output that is less than double, then *decreasing* returns to scale are operating.

The three cases are illustrated in Figure 14.2. All three sections of the diagram show the short-run average and marginal product curves as variable amounts of labour are employed *in two plants of different sizes*. In the short run, the firm is restricted to one or other plant so that output changes can come only from changing the input of the variable factor, labour. In the long run, the firm can elect to operate either plant. Long-run changes, therefore, consist of moving from one set of short-run curves to another, which is done by altering the amount of capital. The short-run curves are labelled SAP_1 and SMP_1 for the smaller plant; and SAP_2 and SMP_2 for the larger plant, which is assumed to employ exactly twice the number of units of capital as the smaller plant.

Constant Returns to Scale: Figure 14.2(i) illustrates *constant* returns to scale. Suppose the firm is operating on SAP_1 at the point, c, at which average product is at a maximum, i.e. labour input is 1_1 and average output per worker is 1_1c. It then builds a new plant of double the size of the original plant, and double the amount of labour is also employed (i.e. 1_2 is double 1_1).

What happens to output? It doubles also. We can deduce from this that output per unit of input stays the same. Thus, in Figure 14.2(i) $1_1c = 1_2d$ and output changes in direct proportion to inputs: returns to scale are said to be constant.

Increasing Returns to Scale: Figure 14.2 (ii) shows *increasing* returns to scale. If we repeat the argument of the previous paragraph, this may be clear. We suppose the firm moves from the smaller plant to the larger plant, thereby doubling its amount of capital. It also doubles its input of labour from 1_1 to 1_2. This time, average product rises: 1_2h is greater than 1_1g. If average product per unit of labour rises when labour and capital inputs double, then total product must more than double. Returns to scale are increasing.

Decreasing Returns to Scale: Figure 14.2 (iii) shows *decreasing* returns to scale. The argument is precisely similar to that of the previous two cases. The only difference is that here, a doubling of the size of the plant and of labour input, lowers average product from 1_1n to 1_2m and hence less than doubles output.

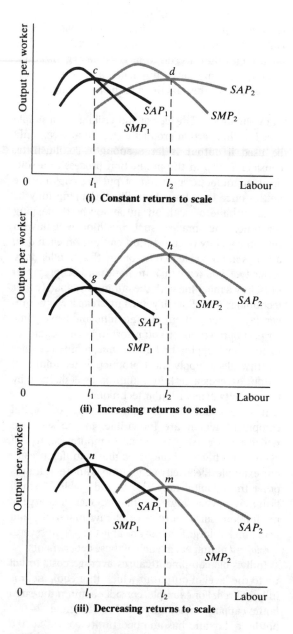

FIGURE 14.2   **Returns to Scale.** Output changes exactly in proportion to, more than, or less than input changes according to whether returns to scale are (i) constant, (ii) increasing, or (iii) decreasing

Diminishing returns to a variable factor and increasing returns to scale

Figure 14.2 shows that a firm may be subject both to diminishing returns to a variable factor, and increasing returns to scale. There is no inconsistency

TABLE 14.2 Various Outputs Resulting from Different Inputs of Labour and Capital

		UNITS OF CAPITAL		
		1	2	3
UNITS	1	100	120	135
OF	2	130	220	290
LABOUR	3	150	300	335

between these two relationships. The former relates merely to the short run when capital is fixed; the latter relates to the long run when capital can be varied. It is important to grasp this point. To avoid any possible confusion we offer a numerical example as a supplement to the diagram.

Table 14.2 shows total output that results from the use of different inputs of labour and capital. The table can be used to derive the marginal product of capital, the marginal product of labour and returns to scale.

Consider first the marginal product of labour. To derive this, we examine the behaviour of total output going down any of the *columns* in the table, which means increasing labour inputs with capital held constant. The first column can be used to calculate the marginal product of labour when 1 unit of capital is employed, the second column the marginal product of labour when 2 units of capital are used, and so forth.

The marginal product of capital is derived in a similar way. We now need to hold constant the quantity of labour and vary capital inputs. Hence we inspect the figures of output going across the *rows* of the table. The first row provides the basis for calculating the marginal product of capital working with 1 unit of labour; the second row for calculating the marginal product of capital working with 2 units of labour, etc.

Returns to scale can be calculated from the table by holding factor proportions constant. We therefore inspect the figures for total output in the cells forming the *diagonal* going from the top left to the bottom right-hand corners. The first cell of the diagonal shows output from 1 unit of labour and 1 unit of capital; the second shows the same for 2 units of capital and 2 units of labour, and so forth.

Let us illustrate what we have just said, by looking at some figures. First, let us find the marginal product of labour working with a fixed single unit of capital. To do so we read the figures of total output down the first column, which show it to be 100 and 130 for 1 and 2 units of labour respectively. The marginal product of labour is therefore 30 (130 minus 100). Now increase labour input by another unit, still holding capital constant at one unit. Output becomes 150. The marginal product of labour is therefore 20 (150 minus 130). Thus the *marginal product of labour is diminishing* (from 30 to 20).

Now consider returns to scale. For these we need to look at the figures in the diagonal cells. From them we see that output is 100 when 1 unit of capital and 1 of labour are employed. It is 220 when 2 units of capital and 2 units of labour are employed. In other words, inputs double and output more than doubles, from 100 to 220. *Returns to scale are increasing.* Now increase labour and capital again. This time raise them by 50 per cent, i.e. from 2 to 3. The table tells us that output goes from 220 to 335. In this case we have increased inputs by 50 per cent, while output rises by just over 52 per cent. *Returns to scale are still increasing.*

You do not need to spend too much time playing with the arithmetic in this table. You could, however, confirm for yourself that the marginal product of labour is also falling when capital is held at 2 units (or at 3 units); and, if you like, that marginal product of capital is falling when the quantity of labour is held constant at 1, 2 or 3 units of labour. The essential lesson to learn from this exercise is that exactly the same figures of the productivity of labour and capital can yield diminishing returns to each factor, but increasing returns to scale. *This is because the law of diminishing returns relates to varying of one input while holding the other constant, while the relations of returns to scale refer to the varying of both inputs.* It is this conclusion that you must grasp. Whether you do so as a result of verbal argument, arithmetic or graphs is of secondary importance.

The Determinants of Returns to Scale

Increasing, decreasing and constant returns to scale are found in many industries. We end this chapter by discussing some of the major reasons for each. We start with increasing returns, and end the chapter with the reasons why constant and decreasing returns are found.

The bases of increasing returns to scale

We deal here with two major sources of increasing returns to scale – the existence of *indivisibilities*, and

changes in production techniques. Both relate specifically to efficiency in production. There are other advantages that accrue to large-scale organization, relating to markets, financial and other considerations. We discuss them in the next chapter.

Indivisibilities: The idea of 'indivisibility' is a simple one. It is that certain productive techniques can only be used if output is large enough. To illustrate, consider a step in the production process of a soft-drink manufacturer – that of putting caps on the bottles once they have been filled. Capping may be done by hand or with an automatic bottle-capping machine. The smallest such machine will have a certain capacity of caps that it can put on each day, and it is not possible to have one with a smaller daily capacity. If you want an automatic bottle-capper, you must buy a machine with the minimum capacity that technology will allow. If you want to cap fewer bottles per day, either you buy the machine and leave it idle for part of the time, or you resort to labour-intensive methods of 'capping by hand'. Thus, it only becomes worthwhile to apply most production techniques if output exceeds a certain minimum level dictated by the capacity of a particular technique.

It is not difficult to find examples of capital equipment which are indivisible, in the sense in which we are using the term. Computer-controlled cylinder boring machines in engine manufacture are one example. Electricity generation is another. Inputs other than capital may also be indivisible. A small firm may have a single *general* manager in charge of production, sales, purchases of raw materials, and personnel. A large firm may be able to appoint several *specialized* managers in each of these departments.

Indivisible equipment causes average costs to fall up to the level of output at which that equipment is fully utilized. For example, consider a minimum-sized bottle-capping machine that can handle 24,000 bottles a day and has an opportunity cost of £600 a day. If only 6,000 bottles need to be capped each day, the cost is 10p per bottle, but as production rises the machine cost per bottle capped falls steadily until the machine is at full capacity yielding a cost of $2\frac{1}{2}$p per bottle (i.e. £600/24,000).

The Principle of Increased Dimensions: A particular example of an important kind of 'indivisibility' follows from what is known as the PRINCIPLE OF INCREASED DIMENSIONS. This is a purely technological phenomenon, best illustrated by containers. It is a fact of life that the capacity of a container increases more than proportionately to the quantity of material used to construct it.

To illustrate, imagine an oil tank 2 m. × 2 m. × 2m. The surface area of the 6 sides is 24 square metres. Compare it with another tank 4 m. × 4 m. × 4 m. The surface area of the 6 sides is 96 sq. m. So the quantity of material needed to make the large tank is about four times that of the small one. But now compare the capacity of the tanks. The capacity of the little tank is 8 cu. m.; that of the big one is 64 cu. m. A four-fold increase in material content raises capacity eightfold.

The principle of increased dimensions illustrates the idea that indivisibilities lie behind the existence of increasing returns to scale. Output volume has to be large enough to take advantage of specialized techniques, often capital-intensive, especially in the manufacturing industry where long runs of standardized products are involved.

The Bases of Constant and Decreasing Returns: In the previous section, we described some important reasons for the existence of increasing returns to scale. We look now at why constant and even decreasing returns to scale are sometimes present.

Our discussion can be brief, since the explanation of the appearance of constant and decreasing returns to scale lies simply in the exhaustion of the bases for increasing returns. Sometimes the cause may be purely technological – larger machines may be more efficient up to a certain point, but there is no reason why larger and larger machines will always be so. A point may come where they become unwieldy, without being more efficient. One of the most common explanations for eventually decreasing returns to scale, however, relates to management. Experience suggests that increasing the entire scale of operations creates problems of management co-ordination, so that efficiency declines when top management loses touch with all sections of a business.

CHANGES IN TECHNIQUES: THE VERY LONG RUN

In the long run, factor inputs are varied within the confines of given techniques. Over time, however, knowledge changes, so that capital (and labour) may become more productive. This means that the long-run product curves such as those in Figure 14.2 shift upwards, indicating that given amounts of labour *and* capital become more productive, as a result of the invention of new and superior techniques of production. The period of time over which these changes occur, sometimes called the VERY LONG RUN, is important when the rate of economic growth is being studied. Although economic growth is related to economic efficiency and is increasingly understood to be a microeconomic issue, it is traditionally considered part of macro rather than microeconomics, and is dealt with in Chapter 39 of this book.

In the meantime, we note that changes in the techniques of production are a very potent source of long-term increases in living standards. Indeed, in the last few decades the material standard of living of the typical family has risen substantially in all the world's industrialized countries. Much of this increase has been due to the invention of new improved ways of making products. It is, for example, rare for a firm to replace an existing piece of capital equipment with another which is exactly the same. The new equipment usually incorporates some technical advance, which may be of stupendous significance, as with high-speed computers, or relatively modest, as with improved internal combustion engines used in cars.

Productivity increases can stem from forces other than new advances in technology. Better raw materials, better trained labour and better organization of production can each account for rising productivity. New ideas can raise efficiency by being applied to new products. Imagination can design a better mousetrap, with no change in the quantity of any factors of production.

Inventions and innovations

Productivity increases can follow the discovery of new ideas and their application in productive processes. An INVENTION is defined as the discovery of something new, such as a production technique or a new product. An INNOVATION is defined as the *introduction of an invention* into use.

Little more can be said at this stage about innovation, except that it may result from the activities of the firm itself, through its own research and development, or from that of other firms or institutions, such as universities. The institutional framework may play a part in stimulating innovations. Patent laws, the tax structure and even forms of business organization can also be important influences.

SUMMARY

1 Factor productivity affects a firm's decisions on factor use. It is important to distinguish between productivity in the short run and in the long run.

2 In the short run, one or more factors of production are, by definition, fixed, while one or more are variable. In the long run, by definition, all factors of production can be varied.

3 The Law of Diminishing Returns applies to the short run, and states that when increasing quantities of a variable factor are used in combination with a fixed factor, the marginal and average products of the variable factor will eventually decrease. The law is based on the fact that the proportions in which factors are used necessarily changes in the short run.

4 Average product is defined as total product divided by the number of units of the variable factor. Marginal product is defined as the change in total product resulting from a unit change in the employment of the variable factor.

5 When the marginal product of a factor is equal to, greater than or less than the average product of that factor, then average product must be constant, rising or falling respectively.

6 The relationship between outputs and inputs in the long run is referred to as returns to scale. Returns to scale are said to be constant, increasing or decreasing when total output increases proportionately, more than proportionately or less than proportionately, respectively, to total inputs.

7 Diminishing returns to a factor of production in the short run are consistent with constant, increasing or decreasing returns to scale in the long run.

8 Increasing returns to scale may be attributable, among other things, to indivisibilities of factors of production and to productive techniques.

9 In the short and long runs, techniques of production are assumed to be given. In what is called the very long run, changes in techniques may occur as a result of the introduction into the production process (innovation) of new discoveries (inventions).

Costs of Production

This is the last of the group of three chapters dealing with supply at the intermediate level. It follows directly from the previous chapter where we considered the behaviour of output as the inputs of factors of production were varied. All the material there concerned physical quantities of inputs and outputs. The next step is to relate physical quantities of inputs to money values in order to provide information about how costs of production vary. In other words we need to know how much it costs a firm to use each of its inputs.

THE NATURE OF COSTS

The cost of each factor that the firm uses will usually be expressed in money terms. It is important, however, that the monetary values put on costs reflect real opportunity costs.

The idea of opportunity cost is one we met in the first chapter of this book. It was defined as the sacrifice of the next best alternative when one chooses to do something. In the context of business costs, the meaning of opportunity cost refers to resources that have alternative uses. If a firm purchases the services of a factor of production, the real cost of using that resource is the other factors of production that could have been purchased instead.

Do Money Costs Measure Opportunity Costs?

In some situations the money paid out by a business represents the true opportunity cost incurred. If a firm spends £10,000 a year employing an office manager, the same sum could have been used to hire a sales manager, or to buy office equipment or a host of other things. The £10,000 could then be regarded as a money measure of opportunity cost. However, there are situations where the amounts actually paid out by a firm are not representative of the real cost incurred. We discuss these in the next sections, starting from the extreme case where no money is paid out but the use of the factor does have a cost to the firm.

Imputed costs

No actual payments are made for the use of resources that are already owned by a firm. Yet a cost must be assigned to their use, if they could have been productively employed in other ways. Such costs are known as IMPUTED COSTS. They should be reckoned at values reflecting what the firm could earn by shifting them to their next best alternative use. The principle can be illustrated with three examples.

The Cost of Money: Consider a firm that uses £100,000 of its own money that could have been loaned to someone else, at 15 per cent interest per year. £15,000 should, therefore, be accounted for by the firm as the cost of funds used in production. If, for example, the revenue after paying for all other costs was £14,000, it should show a loss of £1,000. This is because the firm could have closed down, and loaned its money to someone else, yielding £15,000.

Special Advantages: Suppose a firm owns a valuable patent, giving it the sole right to use a new industrial process, or a highly desirable location, or that it makes a product with a popular brand-name, such as Coca-Cola, Nescafé or Seiko. Each of these involves an opportunity cost to the firm. Even if the patent or trademark was acquired free, the firm could always choose to sell, or lease, it to others rather than use it itself. Hence a real sacrifice is involved. Typically the value of assets such as these, differs from the cost at which the firm originally acquired them which is called HISTORICAL COST. The historical cost must be clearly distinguished from current opportunity cost.

Depreciation: The cost of using capital equipment, such as building and machinery, usually involves a cost, which is the loss in value of the asset. Such cost is called DEPRECIATION, or sometimes USER COST. It may arise simply because the asset wears out with use. However, depreciation may also occur because an asset becomes obsolete. To illustrate, successive generations of more powerful and efficient computers are replacing older ones, which lose their value even though working perfectly. The depreciation that should be allowed for is the reduction in the value of the assets, whatever the cause.

Depreciation should be calculated using the principle of opportunity cost. This principle requires careful consideration of the appropriate alternatives open to a firm. The precise nature of the asset, and the firm's intentions, are relevant to the calculation. However, as the following example will show, the historical cost of the asset is rarely an appropriate starting point.

Consider the case of Claire Vue, a window cleaner. Her only capital equipment is a ladder, which cost £150 when she bought it last year. Claire is a bit heavy on ladders and only keeps them for two years, when they are replaced. How much depreciation should Claire allow at the end of the first year? The answer is that the depreciation should be the *replacement cost of the ladder minus its second-hand price*. Say, for example, that new-ladder prices have held constant at £150 but that the market price of a one-year-old ladder is only £30. She should then charge herself £150 minus £30 = £120 depreciation for using the new ladder over its first year. Why charge £120? Why not just charge £75, on the grounds that she only half used up the £150 ladder, which she intends to use for two years? The reason is that, instead of buying a new ladder for £150 at the beginning of the year, she could have bought a one-year-old ladder on the second-hand market for £30 and used the remaining

£120 for other purposes. Her use of a new ladder for a year did indeed cost her £120, i.e. it entailed the sacrifice of £120 worth of other things.

Accounting versus opportunity costs

Accounting practices that are used to provide for depreciation vary. Some are conventionally based on historical costs. When this happens, two unfortunate consequences may ensue. In the first place, as we have shown, profits may be misstated. In the second place, serious errors may be made in the decisions a firm makes about its best course of action. This is because, as we have again seen, historical costs may not be the same as opportunity costs.

Some assets, for example, are of the kind described in Chapter 1 as 'single use' assets (see p. 8). Suppose a firm has just spent £100,000 on a set of machines used in the production of fishing rods. Suppose, too, that the machines cannot be used to produce anything other than fishing rods, that they have a negligible scrap value, and that they last 5 years. How much depreciation should be charged on the opportunity cost principle?

The answer is that the opportunity cost of the machines is *zero*. They have no alternative use and no scrap value. This is true, regardless of whether or not the firm continues to use the machines. Once bought, the firm is saddled with them. Even if the demand for fishing rods falls dramatically, so that the machines remain idle, there is no other use to which they can be put. Of course, the firm would not have bought the machines if it had known what was going to happen to the demand for fishing rods. But *once it has bought them*, the opportunity cost of using them is zero.

Suppose, however, that the fall in demand is such that sales revenues will just cover the labour and all other costs of production, but is insufficient to cover the full depreciation for the machines. Should they be used, or should the business be shut down? The answer is that the machines should indeed be used, as long as their use is profitable in the sense that they yield *any* net revenue over all variable costs. The machines exist and have no other use. The decision to install them may have been wrong, but historical costs are irrelevant to current decisions.

The principle illustrated by this example may be stated in the form of a general principle: *bygones are bygones and should have no influence on what is currently the most profitable thing to do.*

This principle has widespread implications in

economics, and outside. In a general sense, the principle of bygones being bygones simply means that, at any moment of time, the best course of action depends only on *current* alternatives. Past mistakes should have no bearing on current decisions. We have a very old friend who having inherited some money, decided to buy a small flat in London. It cost him £100,000. Unfortunately, he bought at the top of the property boom and could not let the flat at a rent which covered his out-of-pocket expenses. We suggested that he should consider selling the property if he could earn more on his capital by lending it elsewhere, for example to a building society. This he refused to contemplate because, he told us, the resale value of the flat was only £80,000 and he had paid £100,000 for it. He acknowledged freely that the purchase had been a mistake, but could not see the *irrelevance* of that *past* mistake for his current position – that bygones are bygones. So he held onto the property and made less money than if he had sold it and put £80,000 into a building society account. Our friend's behaviour shows his failure to appreciate the significance of the way in which economists calculate costs – that the best course of action always depends only on *current* alternatives. Past history is irrelevant. Bygones are bygones.

THE RELATIONSHIP BETWEEN COSTS AND OUTPUT IN THE SHORT RUN

We have argued that the cost for any given output must be based upon real opportunity costs, including imputed costs, where a firm uses resources that it owns, and allowing for depreciation with proper regard to the alternatives to which resources may be put. To discover which of its possible levels of output is the most profitable, a firm needs to know how costs vary with output.

From Productivity to Costs

We know from the previous chapter how the returns to a variable factor working with a fixed factor, vary in the short run, and how returns to scale vary in the long run. We now wish to derive short- and long-run cost curves for the firm. To do this we merely value all factors at their opportunity costs, according to the principles outlined in the previous sections.

To illustrate, let us reconsider the output data in Table 14.1 on page 158 which showed the variations in output from using increasing units of labour with a fixed quantity (10 units of capital). If we now assume that the price of labour is £20 per unit and the price of capital is £10 per unit, we can derive 2 sets of figures of costs of production. See Table 15.1.

Columns (1), (2) and (3) in Table 15.1 reproduce from the Table 14.1 details about inputs of capital and labour, and total output respectively. The remainder of the table shows the costs of producing the different levels of output. Costs are shown in three ways, (i) total cost, (ii) average cost, and (iii) marginal cost.

Total Cost (TC):   This is the total cost of producing any given rate of output. Total cost is divided into two parts: TOTAL FIXED COST (TFC) and TOTAL VARIABLE COST (TVC). *TFC does not* vary with output. 10 units of capital are employed at a price of £10 per unit. Therefore total fixed cost, which is the opportunity cost of using the 10 units of capital, is £50 at all outputs (see column (4)). Fixed costs are often referred to as OVERHEAD COSTS, and sometimes as INDIRECT COSTS or UNAVOIDABLE COSTS. (They are unavoidable because they exist even if the plant temporarily shuts down.)

All costs that vary directly with output are called VARIABLE COSTS, often known as DIRECT COSTS, as PRIME COSTS, and occasionally as AVOIDABLE COSTS. (They are *avoidable* because they do not have to be paid if the plant is temporarily closed down.) In Table 15.1, the only variable cost is that of using the variable factor, labour. Column (5) in the table is calculated by multiplying the inputs of labour (column (2)) by the price of labour (£20 per unit). So, in the top row of the table 1 unit of labour is used, giving a figure of £20 for total variable costs. In the second row, 2 units of labour give total variable costs of £40, and so on.

Column (6) in the Table is the sum of total fixed and total variable costs. It is calculated by simply adding the figures in columns (4) and (5).

Average Cost: The average cost of producing any given output is the cost of producing it divided by the number of units produced. AVERAGE TOTAL COST (ATC), sometimes known as UNIT COST, may be divided into AVERAGE FIXED COST (AFC), and AVERAGE VARIABLE COST (AVC).

Average fixed cost must always decline as output increases, since the fixed total is divided by larger and

TABLE 15.1 Short-run Cost Schedules. (The figures are based on output data in Table 14.1 valued at a price of labour of £20 per unit and a price of capital of £10 per unit)

INPUTS (units)		OUTPUT (total)	TOTAL COST			AVERAGE COST			MARGINAL COST[5]
Capital	Labour		Fixed (TFC)	Variable (TVC)	Total[1] (TC)	Fixed[2] (AFC)	Variable[3] (AVC)	Total[4] (ATC)	(MC)
(1)	(2)	(3)	(4)	(5)	(6)	(7)	(8)	(9)	(10)
									£5.00
10	1	4	£50	£20	£70	£12.50	£5.00	£17.50	
									3.33
10	2	10	50	40	90	5.00	4.00	9.00	
									1.82
10	3	21	50	60	110	2.38	2.56	4.94	
									1.05
10	4	40	50	80	130	1.25	2.00	3.25	
									1.33
10	5	55	50	100	150	0.91	1.82	2.73	
									4.00
10	6	60	50	120	170	0.84	2.00	2.84	
									6.67
10	7	63	50	140	190	0.80	2.22	3.02	
									20.00
10	8	64	50	160	210	0.78	2.50	3.28	

[1]Col. (4) + col. (5).   [4]Col. (6) ÷ col. (3) = col. (7) + col. (8).
[2]Col. (4) ÷ col. (3).   [5]Change in output from col. (3) divided by change in variable cost from col. (5).
[3]Col. (5) ÷ col. (3).

larger outputs. This is a process popularly known as 'spreading one's overheads'. In column (7) of Table 15.1, AFC is calculated by dividing TFC (column (4)) by total output (column (3)). In the top line of the table, the AFC of producing 4 units of output is £50 divided by 4 = £12.50. In the second row, AFC is £50 divided by 10 = £5, and so on.

Average *variable* cost may rise, fall or remain unchanged as output varies. As production grows, AVC will rise if TVC rises more rapidly than output, and vice versa. AVC will be constant if TVC rises at the same rate as output rises. AVC, shown in column (8) of Table 15.1, is calculated by dividing TVC (column (5)) by total output (column (3)). So, the top row in the Table shows AVC as being £5. This figure is the result of dividing £20 by the output of 4. In the second row, AVC is £40 divided by 10 = £4, and so on.

ATC, column (9) in the Table, is the sum of AVC and AFC, obtained by adding the figures in columns (7) and (8) (or by dividing the figures in column (6) by column (3)).

Marginal Cost (MC):   This is shown in column (10) in the Table and is defined as the difference in total cost resulting from a unit change in output. The

MARGINAL COST is, therefore, calculated by dividing the increase in total cost by the change in output. Looking at the Table, we see that an increase in output from 4 to 10 units results in an increase in total costs from £70 to £90. The difference in total cost is therefore £20. The change in output is $10 - 4 = 6$ units. Marginal cost is, therefore, £20 divided by 6, or £3.33, which is the figure in the last column of the table. When output rises from 10 to 21 units, total cost rises from £90 to £110. Marginal cost is then £20 divided by 11 = £1.82.

We have calculated marginal cost from the figures of total (fixed *and* variable) cost in column (6). We could equally have used the figures in column (5) of total variable cost alone. If you perform the calculations in the previous paragraph substituting column (v) for column (vi), you will find that they give exactly the same results. This is because *fixed costs do not enter into marginal costs.* They are fixed and do not change when output changes. In other words, *marginal fixed costs are bound to be zero, so that marginal costs are marginal variable costs.*

Marginal costs may rise, fall or remain constant as output varies. They are determined by the rate of change of total cost, as output increases or decreases one unit at a time.

The three measures of cost are merely different ways of looking at the same basic data. They are mathematically related as we have seen. Sometimes it is convenient to use one, and sometimes another.

(Note that in Table 15.1 marginal costs are recorded in the intervals between the other rows, because they are the result of changing output by the difference between two adjacent rows. The reason is exactly the same as that for showing marginal product in the intervals between rows in Table 14.1.)

Cost Curves in the Short Run

The cost schedules in Table 15.1 are represented graphically in Figure 15.1. Part (i) of the figure displays the *total* costs of producing different outputs. Part (ii) shows the *average and marginal* (i.e. the unit) cost of producing the same outputs. The scales of the two sections are, therefore, identical on the output (horizontal) axis, but differ on the vertical axis, which measures costs.

Figure 15.1(i) shows total fixed costs as a horizontal straight line at a figure of £50, because that cost is incurred at all outputs. The curves *TVC* and *TC* are parallel. The vertical distance between them is £50, which is *TFC*.

Figure 15.1(ii) shows *AFC* as downward-sloping, because total fixed costs are spread over larger outputs. Total fixed cost for any output is average fixed cost times the quantity of input, which is the area enclosed by dropping perpendiculars from a point on the *AFC* curve to the two axes. For example, when output is 20, *AFC* is £2.50 and *TFC* is 20 × £2.50 = £50; when output is 25, *AFC* is £2 and *TFC* is 25 × £2 = £50. These areas are equal because *TFC* is always £50. (*AFC* is, therefore, a rectangular hyperbola for the same reason as is a demand curve of unit elasticity – see Chapter 7, p. 77.)

There is an alternative way of showing *AFC* in the diagram. Since total cost is made up of fixed and variable cost, average fixed cost is also the *difference* between *AVC* and *ATC*. Since average cost is measured for any output as the height of the cost curve at that output, the vertical distance between *AVC* and *ATC* must measure *AFC*. Moreover, as *AFC* falls continuously as output increases, *AVC* and *ATC* must become vertically closer to each other as output rises.

Average variable cost, average total cost and marginal cost curves fall at first as output increases, reach minima, and then start to rise. They are

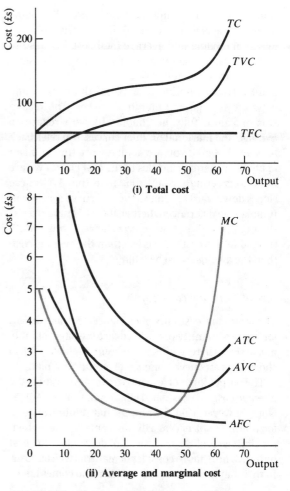

FIGURE 15.1 Short-run Cost Curves. Total Cost curves are everywhere positively sloped, while Average Variable Cost, Average Total Cost and Marginal Cost curves are all U-shaped

therefore sometimes described as U-shaped. Their shape is due to the 'law' of diminishing returns, which applies because these are short-run cost curves. If you turn back and compare Figure 15.1 with Figure 14.1 on page 157, you will notice a striking similarity between them. The one is an inverted image of the other. The cost curve is U-shaped, the product curve is ∩-shaped. Average product rises at first, reaches a maximum and starts to fall. Average cost falls at first, reaches a minimum and starts to rise. The common sense of this cost relation is that each new worker adds the same amount to cost, but a different amount to output. When output per unit of labour is rising, the cost per unit of output is falling, and vice versa. The same argument applies to the relationship between average total product and average total cost, and also to that between marginal product and marginal cost.

Notice that *MC* cuts *ATC* and *AVC* at their lowest points. This is another example of the relationship between average and marginal curves. The reason was explained fully in Chapter 14 with regard to average and marginal product curves. (*Do* refer back to pages 158–9, if you are at all unsure that you can apply the general principles to the cost curves we are now considering.) Note, too, that the *ATC* curve slopes downward as long as the *MC* curve is below it. It makes no difference whether the *MC* curve itself is sloping upward or downward. The reason is that, if the addition to cost (*MC*) is less than the average cost, then the average must be falling.

Size of plant and capacity

The short-run cost curves in Figure 15.1 are drawn for a given quantity of the fixed factor – say a plant of given size. There will be a different U-shaped set of short-run cost curves for each different-sized plant.

The output that corresponds to the minimum of the average cost curve is called FULL or PLANT CAPACITY. Note, however, that the output that minimizes costs for a firm is not necessarily the same as that which maximizes profits. In order to determine its best output, a firm has to consider demand as well as costs. In this chapter we discuss costs (demand comes later).

THE RELATIONSHIP BETWEEN COSTS AND OUTPUT IN THE LONG RUN

In the short run, at least one factor of production is fixed. Output can only be changed by adjusting the input of the variable factor. Thus, in the short run, once the firm has decided on its output, there is only one technically possible way of achieving it.

In the long run, however, all factors are variable. A firm, then, has an additional decision to make: by which of the various technically possible methods will any given output be produced? Should the firm adopt a technique which uses a great deal of capital and a relatively small amount of labour, or should it adopt one which uses less capital but more labour, for example?

Usually, there are many ways of producing a given output. Some are relatively more labour-intensive than others, some more capital-intensive, some more land-intensive, and so on. How should the firm decide on which is best?

Assuming that the firm's prime objective is to maximize its profits, the answer must be to choose the technique that incurs the lowest possible cost. This is called COST MINIMIZATION. In other words, as long as the firm is trying to maximize its profits, it will choose the least costly method of production open to it in the long run.

Long-run planning decisions affect tomorrow's profits. Today's variable factors are tomorrow's fixed factors, in that once a new factory is built or new expensive equipment installed, it is fixed – perhaps for a very long time to come. If the firm makes a mistake now it must live with the consequences. Long-run decisions are difficult, because the firm must anticipate what methods of production will be the most efficient in the years ahead. This depends on the future prices of labour, capital and raw materials and on the demand for its product. New products may emerge, and new production techniques may be developed. A firm that is shrewder in estimating future trends in costs and demand than others will reap the rewards of larger profits. The other firms, through bad judgement, bad luck, or a combination of both, will earn smaller profits. They may even make losses and be forced to close down.

Cost Minimization and Factor Prices

The alternative methods of production open to the firm in the long run involve different amounts of the inputs of labour, capital and other factors of production. The cost of each method will differ according to the quantities of the different inputs and of the prices of these inputs. Hence, the least-cost method requires a consideration of factor prices.

There is a general principle to guide the firm in its search for the minimum-cost method. It is that *the last pound spent on each and every factor of production should yield the same extra output.*

To illustrate the principle, let us apply it to a hypothetical situation. Assume, as we did previously, that a firm has two factors, capital costing £10 per unit and labour costing £20 per unit. Suppose, now, that the marginal product of capital is 100 units of output and that the marginal product of labour is 200 units of output. Since the last unit of capital yields 100 units and costs £10, its output *per pound* spent on it is 100/£10 = 10 units. Since the last unit of labour yields 200 units and costs £20, its output *per pound* spent on it is 200/£20 = 10 units. Both are equal. The condition is satisfied and costs minimized.

The Principle of Substitution: To demonstrate why the principle illustrated in the previous paragraph is necessary for cost minimization, let us consider the implications of a choice of techniques where the condition does not hold.

Assume, as before, that the prices of labour and of capital are £20 and £10 per unit respectively. However, we now assume that the marginal products of capital and labour are both 200. The last unit of capital employed costs £10 but yields 200 units of output. Therefore, the yield of the last pound spent on capital is 200/£10 = 20 units per £1 spent. The last pound spent on labour however remains, as before, 200/£20 = 10 units per £1 spent. Thus, each pound spent on labour yields only half the output of each pound spent on capital. In this case, the firm could lower the cost of producing the *same output*, by substituting capital for labour. It would pay the firm to switch to a more capital-intensive technique of production, so long as the productivity of capital *relative to price of capital* was greater than the productivity of labour *relative to the price of labour*.

We can now state the principle of equality of marginal products per pound spent on each factor more generally. What we did in the above example was to divide the marginal product of each factor by its price, and equate the results:

$$\frac{\text{MP of capital}}{\text{price of capital}} = \frac{\text{MP of labour}}{\text{price of labour}}$$

or writing K for capital and L for labour:

$$\frac{MP_K}{P_K} = \frac{MP_L}{P_L}$$

Expressing the condition for cost minimization this way emphasizes that the condition for cost minimization relates to the *ratios* of the various factors' marginal products, divided by their prices. Be careful not to make the common error of stating the principle for cost minimization as the equality of the marginal products. Marginal products are defined *in terms of physical inputs of factors of production*. The condition for cost minimization runs in terms of marginal products *per unit of money spent* on them.

Changes in Techniques of Production: The rule for cost minimization can be used to show how a profit-maximizing firm responds to changes in cost conditions. Such changes can arise in two ways – from changes in factor prices, or from changes in production techniques, which affect marginal products of factors of production.

Changes in any one of the following – the marginal product of capital, the marginal product of labour, the price of capital and the price of labour – affect the lowest cost technique whenever they alter the value of either of the fractions in the equation stated above. Thus it pays a firm to substitute labour for capital if the marginal product of labour rises, or the price of labour falls, relative to that of capital.

This proposition is central to the theory of the allocation of resources. It lies behind the arguments in Chapters 1 and 2 about the ways in which a market economy reallocates resources in response both to changes in the supplies of factors – which are reflected in changes in factor prices – and to changes in productivity – which reflect technical advance. Firms tend to use less of factors that become relatively expensive, in terms of their productivity, and more of those which become relatively cheap.

Cost Curves in the Long Run

There is a best, least-cost, method of producing each rate of output when all factors are free to vary. If factor prices and productivities are given, a minimum cost can be found for each possible level of output. If this minimum achievable cost is expressed as an amount per unit of output, we obtain the long-run average cost of producing each level of output. When this information is plotted on a graph, the result is the LONG-RUN AVERAGE TOTAL COST CURVE (LRATC CURVE). An example is shown in Figure 15.2.

LRATC is determined from the technology of the industry and the prices of the factors of production. LRATC may also be viewed as a boundary between attainable and unattainable levels of cost. Output q_0, for example, could not be produced at an average cost of c_0, nor at any unit cost less than c_1. Hence, all points in the area below the LRATC curve are unattainable. Output q_0 could, however, be produced at a cost of c_2, c_3 or at any higher level of unit cost. Hence, all points above the LRATC curve are attainable levels of cost. However, were a firm to produce in the long run at costs above the LRATC curve, it would not be cost-minimizing.

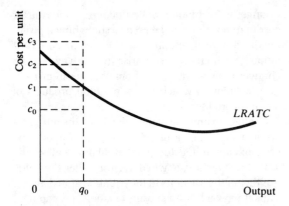

FIGURE 15.2   A Long-run Average Total Cost Curve. The *LRATC* curve shows the costs of producing different outputs when all factors are free to vary

Now we consider the relationship between the short- and long-run cost curves. We have just described the *LRATC* curve, and we described the short-run cost earlier as the curve that shows average costs for different outputs with a given size plant. It is the curve *AVC* in Figure 15.1, which we now rename the SHORT-RUN AVERAGE COST CURVE (SRAVC) to distinguish it from long-run curves. Notice that since all costs are variable in the long run, we do not need to distinguish between variable and fixed costs in the long run; so while in the short run there are several *SRAC* curves – *SRAVC*, *SRAFC* and *SRATC* – in the long run there is only one, the *LRATC* curve, and because there is no ambiguity, the *T* for total is often omitted.

A firm producing q_0 in Figure 15.2, at an average cost of c_2 is not necessarily failing to minimize its costs. An alternative explanation is that it is operating in the *short run* with a plant of a given size that precludes production q_0 with cost c_1. Its appropriate long-run decision is to build a larger plant that will

allow it to obtain the output of q_0 at an average cost of c_1.

If we let the firm choose between plants of many different sizes, we can derive the long-run average cost curve shown in Figure 15.3. The *LRATC* curve is sometimes described as the ENVELOPE curve that encloses the entire family of *SRATC* curves which just touch it (are tangent to it). Each *SRATC* curve shows how costs vary if output changes in the short run. For each such curve the amount of the fixed factor is that which is needed, when the plant being used is optimal. The *LRATC* curve shows how costs vary if output changes when all factors can be varied.

The shape of the long-run average cost curve

The long-run average cost curve that we drew in Figure 15.2 shows long-run average cost falling at first as output increases, reaching a minimum, and then rising. It is U-shaped, as are the short-run cost curves drawn throughout this chapter. It is important to appreciate, however, that the reason for the U shape of the short-run cost curves (the 'law' of diminishing returns to a variable factor used with a fixed factor) cannot explain the shape of the long-run average cost curve because, in the long run, all factors may be varied.

We can best approach the question of the shape of the long-run average cost curve by studying the three regions of the cost curve – i.e. that showing decreasing long-run costs, constant long-run costs and increasing long-run costs. Our procedure parallels closely the one we used in the case of short-run costs. We must examine the behaviour of productivities and attach prices to the factors of production used, thereby converting inputs of physical quantities of labour and capital into costs.

In the long run, average and marginal factor productivities do change not because of changing

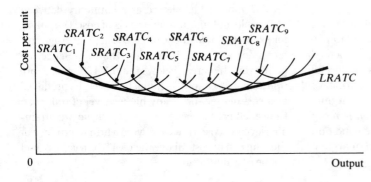

FIGURE 15.3 The Envelope Long-run Cost Curve. The *LRATC* curve shows how average costs vary with output when all factors can be varied

factor proportions, but because of changes in the scale of operations. If you recall the discussion of returns to scale (see pp. 160–2), you will know that these may be increasing, constant or decreasing. Translating into costs, they yield decreasing, constant and increasing costs, respectively.

Decreasing long-run costs

Consider a business enjoying increasing returns to scale in production. Assume, too, that the prices of the factors of production are not affected by the amount the firm buys. Then, the firm's long-run costs of production fall as output increases. A number of sources of falling costs can be noted, although the borderlines between them are not always clear-cut.

TECHNICAL ECONOMIES OF SCALE refer to the techniques of production itself. Included among them are the matters we described under the heading of increasing returns to scale (in Chapter 14). The chief source of such economies is the opportunity for increased specialization that arises because of indivisibilities, for example the fact that it is only worthwhile installing expensive, highly specialized and efficient machinery if the scale of production warrants it. The so-called principle of increased dimensions (see p. 162) is only one example of the technical advantages that can be reaped with increased size. Further examples abound in manufacturing industries.

Firms in many modern industries produce a wide range of different products. For example, a modern paper manufacturer may produce over 400 different types and grades of paper. Each product may have development costs and require some specialized types of machinery. These are fixed costs. The longer the production run of each product, the lower the average total costs because these fixed costs are spread over more and more units. Modern research has shown that in many many industries these PRODUCTION RUN ECONOMIES are a more important source of falling costs than the traditional scale economies referred to in the previous section.

The opportunities for division of labour and the employment of specialists apply as much to managerial skills as to those of the 'labour force' and give rise to MANAGERIAL ECONOMIES OF SCALE. A large firm will be able to provide full-time activity for those with specialist managerial skills such as accountants, lawyers, buyers, personnel, marketing, production and other managers.

MARKETING ECONOMIES OF SCALE arise because the principle of the employment of specialists can be extended to marketing arrangements on both the buying and selling sides. A large enough firm can use the services of specialized buyers of its raw materials – perhaps even a specialist for each raw material. It can also employ personnel trained in the peculiarities of the market, or markets, in which it sells its product. There are technical economies to be reaped in marketing, too (which could as well be included under our first heading). Bulk purchases or sales may be made at lower unit costs, as for example is the case with much packaging, invoicing, delivery and so on.

Most firms need to borrow from time to time to finance their activities, especially to increase their scale of operations. There are FINANCIAL ECONOMIES OF SCALE because the cost of borrowing is substantially lower, the larger the sums involved. This is because there are certain fixed costs incurred by financial institutions, and thus lower average costs if they are spread over larger amounts than over small ones.

A final scale effect, called RISK-BEARING ECONOMIES OF SCALE, arises from the well-established fact that larger firms are able to *diversify*, and spread their risks. To an extent, risk reduction is a cause of the lower cost of borrowing money, which we have already dealt with. There are, however, other cost advantages of diversification. A firm which is operating in many different markets is less vulnerable than another firm selling in a single market, to the possibility of catastrophic collapse, or mere slump, in any particular one. The argument applies to firms selling the same goods in different markets, say at home and overseas. It applies, too, to diversification in the number of types of goods that the firm produces – i.e. not keeping all one's eggs in one basket.

Learning by Doing: The discussion of economies of scale, as we have so far conducted it, has concerned the relationship between two variables – costs and output. But there is a variable other than the level of output that may cause costs to change. It is time itself.

Early economists placed great importance on a factor that we now call *learning by doing*. They felt that, as businesses specialize in particular tasks, workers and managers gradually become more efficient in performing them. As people acquire expertise, or know-how, costs tend to fall *as time passes, rather than because output grows*. Empirical research, moreover, suggests that this really does happen.

It is important to distinguish carefully the implications of learning by doing and of economies of scale for the cost curves of a firm. Changes in costs traceable to changes in the level of output, due, e.g., to technical, managerial and other economies of scale, involve *moving along* a downward-sloping long-run cost curve. Changes in costs that happen over time, as a result of learning by doing, cause the long-run cost curve to shift downwards.

Internal and External Economies of Scale:
Economies of scale are of two kinds, known as internal and external economies. The various sources of falling long-run costs that have been mentioned so far are known as INTERNAL ECONOMIES OF SCALE, because they are within the control of the firm itself. There are other, so-called EXTERNAL ECONOMIES OF SCALE which we must now consider. External economies are sources of cost reduction which are outside the control of the firm. They arise because of events *in the industry* in which the firm operates, or in related industries.

Expansion of the industry can lower the costs of each firm within it, for example by increasing the supply of labour with specific skills needed by the firm. This could reduce the costs incurred by the firm in training labour for itself. Some of the training may be done by other firms, and some part, at least, of training costs may fall on the government, as schools and colleges introduce courses in skills in vocational subjects.

As an industry expands, its firms may find their costs fall because firms *in related industries* are subject to increasing *internal* economies of scale. For example, aluminium production is subject to increasing returns to scale. An expansion of the aircraft industry, which is a consumer of aluminium, reduces the cost of producing aluminium, thereby lowering costs in the aircraft industry.

The two sources of external economies of scale described above – increased factor efficiency and lower costs of inputs supplied by other industries – are likely to have particular strength when an industry is highly concentrated geographically. Information spreads quickly within a locality, and this is conducive to efficiency. This is, incidentally, one reason why geographical concentration of industry is quite common – for example, motor-vehicle assembly and manufacture of vehicle parts in the West Midlands.

Constant long-run costs

The opportunities for specialization, division of labour, and the resulting falling production costs are not unlimited. When a firm reaches the size at which opportunities for economies of scale are exhausted, costs per unit cease to fall. The *LRATC* curve becomes a horizontal line, as illustrated in Figure 15.4. The level of output at which production costs cease to fall is called the *MES*, standing for MINIMUM EFFICIENT SCALE; it is shown by output q_0 in this figure.

It is useful to examine the *MES* in the context of the size of the industry as a whole, in order to know the maximum number of firms of minimum efficient size that the industry can accommodate. Evidence for the UK shows that there are many sectors where the *MES* is high as a proportion of total sales, especially in manufacturing.

For example, the ratio of *MES* to total industry sales is over 30 per cent for aluminium semi-manufactures, over 50 per cent for diesel engines and refrigerators, and 100 per cent or over for TV tubes and electronic calculators. In this last case, production at the lowest possible cost would require that the industry contain only one firm. Such a firm would be called a NATURAL MONOPOLY. We shall consider the implications of the existence of natural monopolies in Chapter 19.

Increasing long-run costs

The long-run average total cost curve shown in Figure 15.3 was U-shaped. The upward-sloping portion of the curve means that as output increases unit costs rise, even in the long run. It corresponds to the range of decreasing returns to scale.

The sources of rising long-run costs may be internal to the firm or external. Significant internal

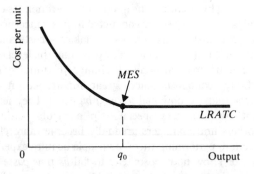

FIGURE 15.4   Minimum Efficient Scale. *MES* is the level of output beyond which costs cease to fall

diseconomies of scale tend to be associated with management or with geography.

It is hard to find firm evidence on the subject, but firms can get so large that managerial problems become excessive. Rising costs associated with such management problems may more than offset other potential economies of large-scale production, so that overall costs rise as output increases. However efficient a management may be, it may eventually lose touch when a business grows beyond a certain size. Delegation to subordinates and decentralization may give rise to problems of co-ordination and control. Transport costs per unit of output may increase as businesses spread further from head office. Moreover, industrial relations may deteriorate as firms reach giant size. Low morale and a feeling of alienation, not to mention more frequent industrial disputes, may lower productivity on the shop floor, thereby raising costs of production.

Diseconomies of scale external to the firm, refer to rising costs outside the control of the firm itself as the industry, or the region in which the firm operates, grows. The entire set of costs curves then shifts upwards, showing higher costs at every level of output. Of major significance among external diseconomies are those related to congestion, which push up transport costs in areas of heavy industrial concentration. There are also pressures which lead to increasing prices of factors of production as industries expand.

The continued existence of small firms

Both large and small establishments continue to exist in the UK economy. The former's existence is, doubtless, due substantially to economies of large-scale production. Indeed, we have become used to living in an economy where technological advance seems to favour large-scale production. But, although some small-scale production takes place in plants owned by large enterprises, small independent firms do persist in some industries. Several reasons need to be mentioned.

Cost Conditions: In the first place, it is a fact that in some industries costs rise sharply as output increases, thereby denying any advantage to large size.

Market Limits: The opportunities for specialization and division of labour are limited by the size of the market. The demand for tuning forks, for example, is hardly likely to be such that the production of the entire national demand would require a very large firm. Moreover, while costs of production may fall for standardized products, there is demand in many industries for variety. There are, however, costs involved in producing a range of products, and even very large firms may produce several individual products at high cost. This sometimes allows small firms producing one or a few differentiated products to survive alongside the large firms.

Product Cycles: New products appear continually, while others disappear. At the early stage of a new product, total demand is typically low, costs of production are high and many small firms are trying to get ahead of their competitors by finding the twist that appeals to consumers, or the technique that slashes their costs. Some new products never get past that stage. In other cases, the successful firms grow to dominate the industry, often eliminating their rivals by merging with them or by forcing them out of business. Eventually at the mature stage of the industry, a few giant firms may dominate the industry.

Sooner or later, however, new products appear that erode the position of the established large firms, which run into financial difficulties and/or switch over to other industries, including those where small firms are already present. The cycle starts again. At any moment of time, industries can be found in all phases, helping to explain, therefore, the persistence of small firms.

Non-profit Maximization: As we saw in Chapter 13, not every business tries to maximize its profits. In some cases, small firms do not grow because their owners prefer to keep them small for reasons not related to profit maximization. We should note incidentally that non-profit maximization may also work to *increase* the size of firms if they strive to grow beyond the most efficient size in pursuit of other objectives (see below, Chapter 18).

The discussion in this chapter, and the previous one, have been concerned with the cost conditions facing firms, and with reasons why both small and large firms persist in a market economy. In the next two chapters we shall put cost and demand conditions together to construct theories of the firm which can help explain their behaviour, especially with regard to the choice of output and price.

SUMMARY

1 The costs that are relevant to business decisions are opportunity costs, which may or may not be reflected in money costs. These include opportunity costs for the use of resources owned by a firm – e.g. money, special advantages and the user cost (depreciation) of existing equipment.

2 Accounting costs, if based on original or historical costs, may not reflect current opportunity costs. In assessing opportunity cost, bygones are bygones.

3 Short-run average total cost is divided into average fixed cost and average variable cost. Marginal cost is the difference in total cost resulting from a unit change in output.

4 When marginal cost is equal to, greater than, or less than average cost, then average cost must be constant, rising, or falling respectively. In the short run, cost curves are drawn for a given size plant (the fixed factor). Average and marginal cost curves are U-shaped, reflecting the law of diminishing returns.

5 In the long run, the firm has a choice of plant size. The long-run average cost curve is derived from the set of short-run cost curves for different size plants, and is an envelope curve.

6 The condition for long-run cost minimization for a firm is that it should employ factors of production up to the points at which the marginal products of every factor *per unit of money spent on them* are equal. This condition may alternatively be stated as that the marginal product of each factor should be proportional to its price.

7 In the long run, costs may be decreasing, constant or increasing. Decreasing long-run costs may be attributed to technical, managerial, marketing, financial, or risk-bearing economies of scale.

8 Economies of scale – which cause *LRAC* to fall – may be internal to the firm, i.e. within its control, or external to it, i.e. arising from conditions in the industry and outside the firm's control.

9 When long-run economies of scale are exhausted, the Minimum Efficient Scale (*MES*) of plant is reached. Beyond that output, long-run costs may be constant for some time, but sooner or later they are likely to begin increasing.

10 The continued existence of small firms in some industries may be attributed to rising costs (especially those associated with managerial diseconomies of scale and with geography), to market limits, to product cycles, and to the pursuit by firms of goals other than profit maximization.

16

Perfect Competition

The first five chapters in the intermediate micro-economic theory we have so far studied in Part 3 of this book, have dealt in turn with the demand and the supply side of the market. We now begin a set of three chapters which put the two together in an intermediate theory of price. This explains how firms behave when they operate in different market situations.

Because of the varied circumstances that can apply to firms, we need to develop a number of theories, each based on different circumstances. We shall develop a theory in this chapter which is applicable to one set of circumstances in which firms operate – where they are all price-takers. In the following two chapters we shall consider further sets of circumstances, in order to develop other theories.

CIRCUMSTANCES APPLYING IN ALL FIRMS

To begin, we need to establish some points that are relevant to all maximizing firms, regardless of the markets in which they sell their products.

Various Profit Concepts

According to economists' definitions, total costs include the opportunity cost of capital. If profit is then defined as total revenue minus total cost ($TR - TC$), profits are only those revenues in excess of *all* costs including the opportunity cost of capital. Businessmen, however, define profits as revenues minus all costs except the opportunity cost of capital. Thus they include the cost of capital in their profits, while the economist's definition of profits excludes it. To make

this distinction clear, profits defined as total revenue minus *all* costs are often referred to as ECONOMIC or PURE PROFIT.

In order to get closer to business procedures we follow a second commonly used set of definitions. We define NORMAL PROFIT as the profit that a firm could obtain by using its resources, not in their present, but in their next best use; i.e., their opportunity cost. We showed, in Chapter 15, that a firm should always state its costs in opportunity-cost terms. The cost curves of a firm are therefore drawn up to include normal profits. If a firm is earning less than normal profits, it is using its resources less profitably than it could, and should not therefore remain in its present line of business. Sometimes we shall observe firms making SUPERNORMAL or SUBNORMAL profits. These terms have parallel meanings, i.e. that profits are in excess of, or less than, the opportunity cost of employing resources elsewhere.

Since the different definitions of costs and profits can be confusing, we compare them visually in Figure 16.1. The vertical scale is measured in money units and various costs are marked off, starting with variable costs. Three usages are then compared by showing the costs and revenues to which they refer.

Various Revenue Concepts

The revenues of a firm are the receipts that it obtains from selling its products to buyers. These are identical to the outlays by the buyers. We can look at these revenues in three ways, just as we did with costs in the previous chapter.

TOTAL REVENUE (TR) means just what it says, the total receipts of money that the firm obtains from all

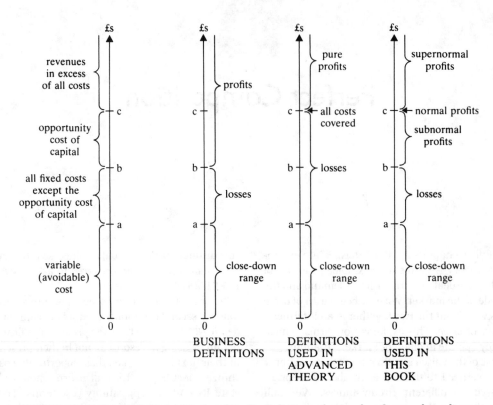

FIGURE 16.1   **Various Definitions of Costs and Profits.** Definitions of cost and profits vary depending on how the opportunity cost of capital is treated

its sales. Total revenue is also obviously equal to the quantity of goods sold multiplied by their selling price.

AVERAGE REVENUE (AR) is total revenue divided by the number of units sold. Average revenue is the same as the price of the product.

MARGINAL REVENUE (MR) is the *change* in total revenue resulting from a *change of one unit* in the rate of sales per period of time (say, per month). If the total revenue from the sale of 9 units per month is £15 and the total revenue from the sale of 10 units per month is £17, marginal revenue is equal to £17 − £15 = £2.

Two Points to Notice: Note first that marginal revenue is defined as the change in revenue resulting from the production and sale of *one more* (or *one less*) good. Sometimes, however, we only have data for changes covering more than one unit. In such cases, we have to strike an average over the range of output for which information is available. For example, if total revenue from the sale of 9 units per month is £15 and total revenue from sales of 11 units per month is £23, then marginal revenue is £(23−15)/(11−9) = 8/2 = £4. To accommodate such possibilities we de-fine MR as $\Delta TR/\Delta Q$, where Δ stands as usual for 'change in'.

The second point to note is that marginal revenue refers to different values of output *at the same period of time*. Do not think that 9 units are sold at one time, and 11 units at some later time. Marginal revenue refers to what would happen during any one period if different amounts were sold.

Two Rules for the Profit-Maximizing Firm

We now give two rules that any firm should follow if it is to produce the output which results in maximum profits. The rules answer two distinct questions. First, should the firm produce at all? Second, if it is profitable for the firm to produce, what is its best, or optimum, output?

Rule 1. The shut-down rule

The first rule states that output should be greater than zero only if total revenue is equal to, or greater than, total variable cost. If there is no output for which total variable cost is less than total revenue, output should be zero. This is often called the shut-down rule, because it shows when a firm that is currently producing should stop doing so. But it might just as well be called the start-up rule because it also tells when a firm currently shut-down should start producing again.

The reason for this rule is that the firm's variable cost can be avoided by ceasing production. Hence it only pays to produce if revenues at least cover these avoidable (i.e. variable) costs. We can state this condition in two ways. First, we can say that total revenue should exceed total variable cost $(TR > TVC)$. A second way of saying the same thing is that price (p), which is the TR divided by output, should exceed average variable cost, which is TVC also divided by output $(p > AVC)$.

Because different costs are avoidable in the short and the long runs, rule 1 has two applications, one relating to the short run, and the other to the long run. It is important to distinguish between them.

Shut-down Conditions in the Short Run: When a firm is considering whether or not to close down in the short run, its decision depends only on its short-run variable costs and is unrelated to its fixed costs, which are unavoidable since they have to be met even if the firm produces no output at all.

An example may clarify this important principle of the irrelevance of fixed costs. Consider a hotel business at a seaside resort. During the winter, demand is slack so that only a few rooms may be occupied every day. Should the hotel close down for the winter, or rub along trying to cover some of its costs?

The hotel has both fixed and variable costs. The unavoidable fixed costs may, for example, include rates payable to the local authority, interest on capital used to buy the hotel (or perhaps the annual rent on a lease that can not be cancelled at short notice). The variable costs include all avoidable expenses of running the hotel, such as wages, heating and lighting, laundering, etc. If the hotel cannot earn enough revenue to cover the variable costs of keeping open for the few guests that will come during the

winter, the most profitable course would be to shut down for that period.

Indeed many hotels do just this. However, some hotels may find that, by staying open, they can earn enough revenue to cover all their variable costs and make some contribution to their fixed costs. It then clearly pays them to keep going in the winter, in spite of the fact that they do not cover their total costs. They would be worse off if they closed down, *because they still have to meet their fixed costs.* That is why you will see some hotels in holiday resorts open in the winter. Many offer special low rates out of season, usually just enough to cover their variable costs, and make some contribution, however small, towards fixed costs.

Shut-down Conditions in the Long Run: Because in the long run all costs are variable, a profit-maximizing firm will stay in business in the long run, *only* if it can cover its total costs. Covering short-run variable costs is not sufficient. To return to our seaside hotel, it is only sensible to remain open in winter, just covering the variable costs of doing so, if the revenue in summer is sufficient to cover total costs *of the year as a whole.* If this is not possible, the firm should close down in the long run.

To illustrate these conditions, consider as an example a particular hotel, the Esplanade Hotel at Brightpool. Its revenues and costs of operating during the in-season and off-season periods are shown in Table 16.1. When charging the profit-maximizing price for its rooms, the hotel earns a return over its total variable costs of £24,000 during the in-season, as shown in the final column of the table. This surplus goes towards meeting the hotel's fixed costs of £26,000. The hotel discovers that, by charging lower prices during the off-season, it can let some of its rooms for a total revenue of £20,000 at a cost of staying open of £18,000, as shown in the second row of the table. This surplus, though relatively small, can go towards covering some part of the fixed costs. Therefore the hotel should stay open the whole year round. (Indeed, if it were to close in the winter, it

TABLE 16.1 The Esplanade Hotel, Brightpool. Total costs and revenues (£s)

	Total revenue (TR)	Total variable costs (TVC)	Net revenue (TR−TVC)
In-season	60,000	36,000	24,000
Off-season	20,000	18,000	2,000

Note. It is assumed that total fixed costs per annum are £26,000.

would have to close in the summer too, since it could not then cover its total fixed and variable costs.)

Now assume that the off-season revenue falls to £19,000 (everything else the same). The short-run condition for staying open, $TR > TVC$, is met in the in- and the off-seasons. But the long-run condition is not, since the excess of TR over TVC over the whole year of £25,000 is less than the fixed costs of £26,000. The hotel will remain open as long as it can do so with its present capital. But it will not pay the owners to replace the capital as it wears out.

The hotel will become one of those run-down hotels where guests ask 'why don't they do some-thing about this place?' But the owners' behaviour is sensible. They are operating the hotel as long as it covers its variable costs but they are not putting any more investment into it since it cannot cover its fixed costs. Sooner or later the fixed capital will become too old to be run, or at least to attract customers, and the hotel will be closed.

Rule 2. The rule for the best possible positive output

The second rule states that if a firm is to produce at all, the output at which profits are maximized is the output where marginal cost is equal to marginal revenue.

To see the reason for this rule, consider the profits of a firm which does *not* follow it. First, suppose a firm finds that, at its present level of output, the cost of making another unit per month (marginal cost) is less than the revenue that would be gained by selling that unit (marginal revenue). In this case, total profit could be increased by producing another unit of output. Next suppose the firm finds that, at its present level of output, the cost of making the last unit exceeded the revenue that was gained from selling it. Total profit could be increased by not producing the last unit each month. Thus, whenever a firm whose objective is maximizing profits, finds that, at the current level of output, marginal revenue exceeds marginal cost, output should be expanded; whenever marginal cost exceeds marginal revenue, output should be contracted. Its profit-maximizing output is, therefore, where *marginal cost* is neither greater nor less than *marginal revenue* but equal to it.

Optimum output

The output that maximizes a firm's profits is called its OPTIMUM OUTPUT. The two rules tell us how to find it.

If the condition set out in rule 1 is not fulfilled, the optimum output is zero; if that condition is fulfilled, then rule 2 tells us that the optimum output is where marginal cost equals marginal revenue.

PERFECT COMPETITION

An INDUSTRY is a group of firms that sells goods in a particular market. This means that all of the firms in an industry must produce a similar product. Our next step is to take account of the kind of market in which the firms in a particular industry operate. The characteristics of a market are called its MARKET STRUCTURE. We shall consider four different market structures: (1) perfect competition, (2) pure mono-poly, (3) monopolistic competition, and (4) oligopoly. The first is dealt with in this chapter; the others in Chapters 17 and 18.

The word 'perfect' in the term perfect competition does not carry a connotation of desirability. When used together with the word competition, perfect means the *complete* or *highest* degree of competition conceivable.

Perfect competition provides the theory that lies behind the supply curves we used in Part 2. Thus we are now going to do the first thing that we promised for an intermediate theory of supply: go behind the supply curve of Part 2 and explain the behaviour that gives rise to it.

A market is said to be PERFECTLY COMPETITIVE when all firms in that market regard themselves as price-takers – i.e., they can sell all they could conceivably produce at the going market price, and nothing at any higher price. A set of conditions that is sufficient to guarantee this result is sometimes known as the assumptions of perfect competition. These are (1) a homogeneous product, (2) many sellers, (3) perfect information, and (4) freedom of entry and exit.

A Homogeneous Product: A product which is the same for every firm in the industry is called a homogeneous product. One farmer's brussels sprouts are indistinguishable from those produced by any other farmer. They are homogeneous. By contrast, the Ford Motor Company's *Escort* model is distinct from car models of all other motor manufacturers, and from Ford's other models. It is differentiated.

Many Sellers: For firms to be price-takers, the

number of sellers must be large enough that no single firm, acting by itself, can exert any perceptible influence on the market price of its product by altering the quantity that it offers for sale. This is another key distinction between, for example, the car industry and the brussels sprout industry. Any one farmer's contribution to the total production of sprouts is a tiny portion of the total. He could double his production, or switch completely to some other crop, with no perceptible effect on the total market supply, and therefore the price of sprouts. In contrast, Ford's car output is a significant part of total car production. Ford does have the power to influence price by varying the number of cars it produces. Of course, the power is not unlimited, but it certainly exists.

Perfect Information: When buyers of the product are fully informed about the prices and qualities of goods offered for sale by sellers, we say that they have perfect information. An important consequence is that, if any firm raises the price of its (homogeneous) product above the prices charged by other producers, it will lose all its customers. This is because people will not buy a commodity from a firm at one price if they know that the identical commodity can be purchased at a lower price from another firm. Hence only one price can prevail.

Freedom of Entry and Exit: Assumptions 1, 2 and 3 relate to individual *firms*. The fourth assumption relates to the *industry* as a whole. Freedom of entry means that a new firm is free to start up production if it so wishes. There are no barriers to entry. There are no legal or other restrictions on entry. Freedom of exit means that any existing firm is free to cease production and leave the industry if it so wishes. There are no legal or other restrictions on exit.

The Equilibrium of the Firm under Perfect Competition

To develop a theory of the behaviour of a firm under perfect competition, our first step is to derive the demand curve facing the firm.

The demand curve for a firm under perfect competition

In perfect competition, the individual firm produces a product which is indistinguishable from the products of other firms. The firm is also too small to exert any perceptible influence on market price. Hence, each perfectly competitive firm is a *price-taker*. It faces a price that is determined by market forces that are beyond its control. The firm's problem is, then, to decide whether to produce at all, and, if so, on its profit-maximizing output.

The graphical expression of the demand curve for a firm which is a price-taker, is a horizontal straight line drawn at the going market price. In Figure 16.2 (i), we show the perfectly competitive firm's demand curve. We assume for the moment that price has been determined at p_0 by the market forces of supply and demand. The firm can sell any quantity it wishes at price p_0. If it tries to raise its price above p_0, its sales will fall to zero, since all its customers realize that they can buy the identical product elsewhere at price p_0. In other words the demand curve is *perfectly elastic* at price p_0.

A perfectly elastic demand curve has an important characteristic: the average revenue from the sales of all units will be equal to the marginal revenue from the sale of an extra unit. Average revenue, you will remember, is another word for the price at which the firm sells its product. Marginal revenue is the change in total revenue resulting from the sale of an additional unit of the product. Since the firm can sell as much or as little as it wants at the going price, marginal revenue must be equal to average revenue. Consider for example, a producer who faces a market price of 25 pence per pound for brussels sprouts. Since every pound of sprouts he sells brings in 25p, average revenue per pound of sprouts is 25p. Also, since price is *given* at 25p, each additional pound sold will bring in 25p, i.e. marginal revenue is also 25p. This illustrates the key point: *MR = AR for the firm under perfect competition*. The demand curve facing the firm is, thus, identical to both the average and the marginal revenue curves. All three coincide in the same straight line, showing that $p = AR = MR$. As far as the producer is concerned, all are constant regardless of the quantity of sprouts he offers for sale. The producer's *total* revenue is not, of course, constant. Since price is constant, total revenue rises in direct proportion to output, as shown in Figure 16.2(ii).

Optimum output of a firm under perfect competition

Earlier, we derived the shape of the cost curves that apply to any firm. Now we know the revenue curve

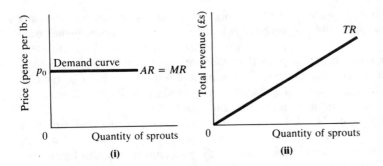

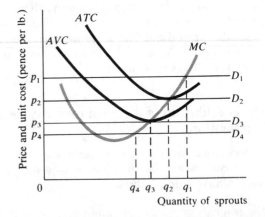

FIGURE 16.2   Demand Curve and a Revenue Curve for a Firm under Perfect Competition. In perfect competition, the firm is a price-taker and faces a perfectly elastic demand curve

facing any firm in perfect competition. If we put these cost and revenue curves together we can use the two rules developed earlier in the chapter to derive each firm's profit-maximizing, or optimum, output.

Consider, first, rule 2: if the firm is to produce at all, it should produce the output for which marginal cost is equal to marginal revenue. In the case of perfect competition, we know that $MR = AR = $ Price. So our rule becomes, *equate marginal cost to price*. Note, however, that this is a *special* form of the *general* rule, $MC = MR$, that applies *only* in perfectly competitive markets. We may use *either* form of the rule in this chapter, but we must remember to avoid the special form, $MC = $ Price, when we come to consider other market types in the following chapters.

Now look at Figure 16.3, which shows the cost curves of a firm in a perfectly competitive market. The diagram also shows four demand curves, which the firm might face. They are all perfectly elastic, i.e. they are horizontal straight lines. If the firm faces demand curve D_1, it can sell as much as it wants at price p_1; if the demand curve is D_2, it can sell as much as it wants at the price p_2, and so forth.

Rule 2 tells us that, if the firm is to produce at all, its optimum is the output corresponding to the point of intersection of the marginal cost curve with the demand curve, which shows the price at which output can be sold. Hence, if the demand curve is D_1, the optimum output is q_1; if the demand curve is D_2, the optimum output is q_2, and so forth.

Now we must apply rule 1 to determine whether the firm should produce at all under each of the different demand conditions obtained in the market or should close down. Consider, first, the demand curve D_1. When the firm sells q_1 at the price p_1 it is not just earning normal profits, since average revenue exceeds average total costs. It is earning supernormal profits, and should certainly not consider shutting down. Next, assume that the demand curve is D_2. Now the firm equates MC to price, and is just earning

normal profits. It is covering all its costs, though only just. Hence, the firm should stay in business in this case too. Now, consider the situation of the firm when faced with the demand curve D_3. Optimum output for the firm, q_3, puts the firm on the margin of indifference as to whether or not to remain in production. Average variable costs are just covered by average revenue, but the firm is earning nothing towards its fixed costs.

Finally, let the demand curve be D_4. The best that the firm can do if faced with a price of p_4 is to produce q_4, *if it is to stay in production*. But at q_4 output, the firm's average revenue is less than its average variable cost. The firm is not even covering its avoidable costs, so it would be better off shutting down completely. Its optimum output is zero.

The supply curve of a firm under perfect competition

We now wish to derive the firm's short-run supply

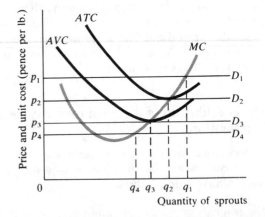

FIGURE 16.3   The Optimum Output of a Firm under Perfect Competition. Under perfect competition the profit-maximizing firm produces the output that equates marginal cost to price

curve under perfect competition. This is a simple matter since, as we shall soon see, we have really done everything that is required in the previous section.

A firm's supply curve shows the relation between the market price of the commodity and the firm's desired output. We saw in the previous section that a profit-maximizing firm producing under conditions of perfect competition produces the output which equates marginal cost to price. For example, in Figure 16.3 the firm produces output q_1 when price is p_1, output q_2 when the price is p_2, and output q_3 when price is p_3. It follows that the marginal cost curve of a perfectly competitive firm is that firm's supply curve.

Recall that at any price below p_3, such as p_4, the firm produces nothing, since if it did produce where $MC = P$, it could not even cover its variable cost. *Thus the MC curve is the supply curve only for prices at or above the minimum point on the firm's AVC curve.* The firm's short-run supply curve is shown in Figure 16.4 as the section of the marginal cost curve that starts at a (where $MC = AVC$).

We have now derived the supply curve for the firm under perfect competition in the short run. The curve is upward-sloping, because the law of diminishing returns causes marginal cost to increase as output increases.

Notice that the above remarks refer to the short-run supply curve of a firm. The long-run supply curve of a firm may be derived by application of the same principle of identifying the marginal cost of production in the long run. As explained in the previous chapter, a firm is able to vary its techniques of production in the long run, when all factors of production are variable. It can then choose among plants of different sizes. The long-run marginal cost is the cost of changing output by one unit using the most efficient plants for producing each output.

The Equilibrium of the Industry under Perfect Competition: The Long Run

So far, we have examined the equilibrium of an individual firm. Next we look at the industry as a whole.

In order to see what is happening in the market as a whole, we need market demand and supply curves. The market demand curve is the ordinary demand curve for a product, such as we used all through Part 2 of this book.

The market supply curve is scarcely more of a problem. We showed, in Chapter 6, how to derive the market supply curve by the horizontal summation of the supply curves of individual firms. We now know that each firm's short-run supply curve is the portion of that firm's marginal cost curve that lies above its AVC curve. *Hence if we sum these marginal cost curves horizontally, we get the industry supply curve.*

In Figure 16.5 we set the market supply and demand curves shown in part (ii), beside the cost curves for a typical firm shown in part (i), which is one of the many firms in this perfectly competitive industry. The vertical scales of the two parts of the diagram are identical – price per lb. of sprouts. The horizontal axes both measure quantities of sprouts. However, the horizontal *scales* are different. We have chosen to calibrate the quantity axis in the diagram for the individual firm in lbs.; while that for the industry has been calibrated in tonnes. The difference reflects the fact that each individual firm supplies only an insignificant part of the whole market. The firm in the diagram is taken as the typical firm in the industry. In particular it is typical in the sense that potential new entrants may expect to do about as well, or as poorly, as this firm does.

Long-run equilibrium

Figure 16.5 shows the firm's position when the industry is in long-run equilibrium. Equilibrium market price (p_0) is determined at the intersection of the *market* supply and demand curves, in part (ii) of the diagram. *At this price the demand curve facing the price-taking firm is perfectly elastic; it is the horizontal*

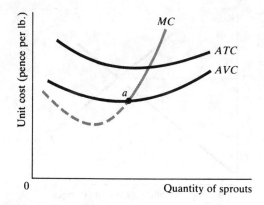

FIGURE 16.4   The Supply Curve of a Firm under Perfect Competition. The firm's supply curve is the section of its MC curve that lies above its AVC curve

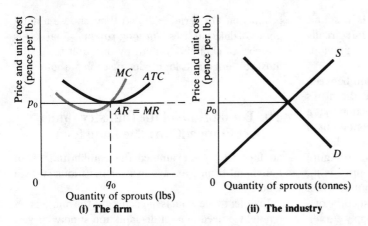

FIGURE 16.5   Firm and Industry in Long-run Equilibrium. The typical firm in the industry is just covering its total costs (including normal profits)

line labelled $AR = MR$ in part (i). The firm's maximum-profit output is where $MR = MC$, namely output q_0. At price p_0 and output q_0, the total revenue of the firm covers, and only just covers, its total costs, including 'normal profits'. This is shown in the diagram by the fact that $AR = ATC$. You will recall that normal profits are included in the cost curve, and must be earned if the firm is to remain in the industry.

Entry and Exit of Firms: The key to long-run equilibrium for a perfectly competitive *industry* is entry and exit. So long as firms are just breaking even, they are doing as well as they could if they employed their capital elsewhere. They have no incentive to leave the industry. Nor will there be any incentive for new firms to enter the industry. Long-run equilibrium has then been achieved. If, however, existing firms are earning supernormal profits after meeting all costs, including the opportunity costs of capital, new firms will enter the industry to share in these

profits. If existing firms are making subnormal profits, firms will leave the industry, because a better return can be obtained elsewhere in the economy.

Long-run disequilibrium

Figures 16.6 and 16.7 show industry in long-run disequilibrium. Both diagrams show the same typical firm as was shown in Figure 16.5. The difference between the three figures is that the industry demand curves are different; hence so are market prices. Let us consider them in turn.

In Figure 16.6, the intersection of the market supply and demand curves determines a market price of p_1. The perfectly elastic demand curve for the individual firm is at market price p_1. Profit-maximizing output for the firm is at q_1, where marginal cost is equal to marginal revenue. The firm's total revenue now exceeds its total cost – average revenue (AR) exceeds average total cost

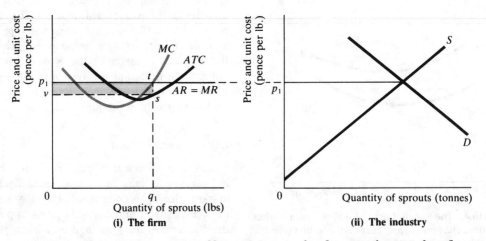

FIGURE 16.6   Industry in Long-run Disequilibrium. Supernormal profits attract the entry of new firms

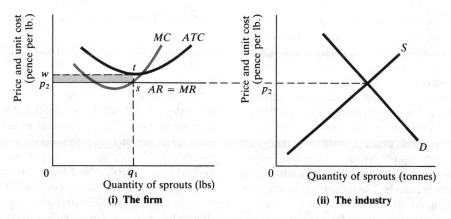

FIGURE 16.7   **Industry in Long-run Disequilibrium.** Subnormal profits lead to exit of firms

(*ATC*). The firm is, therefore, making supernormal profits of $p_1 v (= st)$ per unit. Over its whole output, supernormal profit is $p_1 v$ multiplied by output, which is shown by the shaded area $p_1 vst$ in the diagram.

This industry is not in long-run equilibrium; the presence of supernormal profits will attract new firms into the industry to share in these profits.

Before considering the way in which equilibrium is reached, consider Figure 16.7. This is similar to Figure 16.6 in every respect, except that market price of p_2 is such that the firm is not able to cover all its costs at its profit-maximizing output. It makes subnormal profits, equal to the deficiency of average revenue from average cost, i.e. w minus p_2 $(= ts)$ per unit, or a total deficiency of the shaded area $p_2 wts$.

Long-run shifts in the supply curve

The entry and exit of firms provides the mechanism by which an industry moves into equilibrium when super- or subnormal profits are present. Changes in output by any *one* individual firm cannot affect market price, but the entry or exit of *many* firms will do so.

The short-run supply curve is the summation of the cost curves of those firms that are currently in the industry. If new firms enter the industry because of the presence of supernormal profits (such as are shown in Figure 16.6), the *industry* supply curve will shift to the right. Market price will fall, which in turn causes a downward shift in the horizontal demand curve *facing each firm*. (Do not forget that the individual firm's demand curve is horizontal at the prevailing market price.) Both old and new firms will adjust their outputs to this new price.

Figure 16.8 shows this process in operation. The original disequilibrium situation is that of Figure 16.6.

Market price p_1, determined in the right-hand portion of the diagram, provides firms with supernormal profits. New firms enter the industry, and this

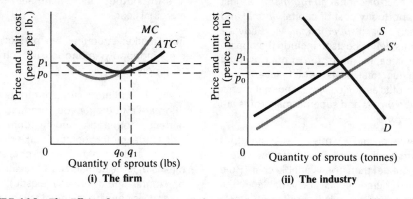

FIGURE 16.8   **The Effect of New Entrants on the Industry Supply Curve.** New entrants shift the industry supply curve to the right, which causes the market price to fall

shifts the supply curve, S, to the right, to S' in Figure 16.8(ii). Market price falls, lowering, thereby, the horizontal demand curve facing each existing firm, as well as each new entrant. Each firm adjusts output to new profit-maximizing positions, where marginal cost equals marginal revenue. Firms will continue to enter the industry so long as supernormal profits can be earned. Each new entrant increases market supply and lowers market price. Eventually, there are enough entrants to push the supply curve to S'. Price has now fallen back to its initial level of p_0, where only normal profits are made. The industry is in long-run equilibrium, similar to that in Figure 16.5.

The use of space in a textbook for one purpose has a real opportunity cost in that it cannot be used for another. We leave you to fill in the parallel argument to show how, when market price leads to subnormal profits, as in Figure 16.7, the *exit* of firms continues until a new long-run equilibrium is reached.

The equilibrating process summarized

The process by which long-run equilibrium is reached has been outlined in the previous section. It may be summarized as follows. Supernormal or subnormal profits in a competitive industry lead to the entry or exit of firms. On the one hand, an increase in demand, following a change in tastes for example, raises market price, lifts the demand curve facing individual firms, increases optimum outputs and the level of profits. New firms enter the industry to restore equilibrium (as in Figure 16.8). On the other hand, a reduction in demand lowers market price, shifts the demand curve facing individual firms downwards, reduces optimum outputs, and produces subnormal profits. Given free entry and exit, long-run equilibrium will occur where firms are just covering total costs, including normal profits, and there is no incentive for the size of the industry to change.

SUMMARY

1 Rules of the profit-maximizing output of any firm are based on its costs and revenues. Average revenue is defined as total revenue divided by the number of units sold. Marginal revenue is defined as the change in total revenue resulting from a unit change in sales.

2 The term profit is used in different ways by different groups. A business person refers to any revenues in excess of all costs excluding the opportunity cost of capital as profit. Some elementary treatments, including ours, use this definition and then call profits that less than cover the opportunity cost of capital *subnormal*, that just cover the opportunity cost of capital *normal* and that more than cover it *supernormal*. More advanced treatments define costs to include the opportunity cost of capital and pure profits as total revenues minus total costs, which means that subnormal profits are called *losses*, normal profits are called *zero profits* and supernormal profits are called *pure profits*.

3 The shut-down or start-up rule states that output should be greater than zero only if total revenue is equal to, or greater than, total variable cost (Rule 1). Because different costs are variable in the short and long runs, the rule has different effects in these two periods. The firm will only produce a positive quantity if its revenue exceeds its variable costs in the short run and if its revenue exceeds its total costs in the long run.

4 The rule for what to produce if revenues exceed variable costs is that marginal cost should be equal to marginal revenue (Rule 2).

5 The firm's profit-maximizing output is called its optimum output; it is zero when there is no output at which total revenue exceeds total variable cost, while if total revenue exceeds total variable costs it is the output where marginal revenue equals marginal cost.

6 Four market structures are perfect competition, pure monopoly, monopolistic competition and oligopoly.

7 A set of conditions sufficient for perfect competition are a homogeneous product, many sellers, perfect information, and freedom of entry and exit. Under perfect competition, price is set by the market and each firm is a price-taker, which means that the demand curve facing each firm is a horizontal line (perfectly elastic), and average revenue is equal to marginal revenue.

8 The equilibrium of the firm that is producing a positive output under perfect competition occurs where marginal cost is equal to marginal revenue (Rule 2), which is also equal to price. This means that each firm's supply curve is its marginal cost curve and that the industry's supply curve is the horizontal sum of the firms' marginal cost curves.

9 The long-run equilibrium of a perfectly competitive industry is where the total revenue of existing firms just covers their total costs, including normal profits, and there is no incentive for firms to enter or leave the industry. When total revenue is greater than total cost, existing firms enjoy supernormal profits. New firms are attracted into the industry, causing the supply curve to shift to the right and market price to fall. When total cost exceeds total revenue, existing firms make sub-normal profits. Some firms leave the industry, causing the supply curve to shift to the left and market price to rise.

17

Monopoly

In the introduction to the previous chapter, we said that we needed to develop a number of theories to explain business behaviour in different circumstances. We then described the theory of perfect competition, where all firms are price-takers. Now, for the first time in this book, we drop the price-taking assumption and study the market structure which is at the opposite extreme from perfect competition, and which is called pure monopoly.

What is a Monopoly?

We first define a MONOPOLIST as a firm that is the only seller in an industry. Hence, the demand curve for the industry is also the demand curve for the monopolist. The term *monopolist* refers to the firm; the term MONOPOLY describes a situation in which an industry has only one producer.

Can there in fact be a complete monopoly? This is a question that has worried some people. In one sense, the answer to the question is yes. One can imagine a single seller of a product, whose position as the only firm in the industry is maintained by some barrier to entry. In a second sense, however, the answer is no. Since all products compete for the consumer's limited income, no firm, even if it is the sole seller of one product, is without competition from the sellers of other products.

PROFIT-MAXIMIZING OUTPUT OF A MONOPOLIST

Any profit-maximizing firm, be it a monopolist or a firm in perfect competition, must follow the two general rules set out in Chapter 16 – the rule for the best positive output to produce, and the shut-down rule. The latter applies in a straightforward manner. The former requires a careful interpretation in the case of monopoly.

Under perfect competition, we saw that the general rule, $MC = MR$, could also be expressed as $MC = P$ because for any price-taking firm, average and marginal revenues are equal. This form of the rule does *not* apply to monopoly because, as we shall see below, a monopolist's price does not equal its marginal revenue. The profit-maximizing rule, $MC = MR$, is unchanged but its application becomes a trifle more complicated.

Marginal revenue under monopoly

We know that, in perfect competition, marginal revenue is equal to price. This is because an individual firm can sell as much or as little as it wishes at the going price. A monopolist is unable to do the same. Because it is the sole supplier of the industry's product, *the demand curve facing the monopoly firm is the same as the market demand curve of the industry*. Since market demand curves are downward-sloping, a monopolist that wishes to sell an extra unit of output must *lower* its price. The reduction in price applies to *all* units of output. Therefore, the *marginal revenue from the sale of an extra unit is less than the price* at which all units are sold.

An example will help to clarify this point. Suppose a monopolist is selling 3 units of output per week at a price of £6 each for a total revenue of £18. Suppose, too, that in order to sell 4 units per week, price must be lowered to £5 yielding a total revenue £20.

Marginal revenue, which is the difference in total revenue from selling 4 rather than 3 units, is thus only £2. This is less than the new price of £5 at which the increased sales of 4 units takes place.

Another way of looking at the reason for marginal revenue being less than price, is to consider the change in total revenue when sales rise from 3 to 4 units as being the result of two components. In the first place, there is an *increase* in total revenue of £5, resulting from the sale of one extra unit at the price of £5. In the second place, there is a *decrease* in total revenue, resulting from the lower price now charged on the 3 units that formerly sold for £6 each and now sell for only £5. The decrease in total revenue is therefore £3. We can now calculate marginal revenue as:

Increase in total revenue from 1 unit at £5	= +£5
Decrease in total revenue from 3 units at £1 *less*	= −£3
Net change in total revenue	= +£2

Table 17.1 sets out the average and marginal revenues for a monopolist at five different prices, at which it sells various quantities. Note that marginal revenue is less than average revenue throughout the table (except at output 1, where total revenue is the same as the increase in revenue between zero output and output one). Note, too, that marginal revenue becomes negative when output increases from 4 to 5 units. Total revenue at the higher output and lower price is less than total revenue at the lower output and higher price. If you recall the relationship between total revenue and elasticity of demand in Chapter 7 (see pp. 74–5), you will appreciate that this situation arises whenever elasticity of demand is less than unity.

TABLE 17.1 Average and Marginal Revenue for a Monopolist. Marginal Revenue is always less than Average Revenue wherever the demand curve is downward-sloping

Output	Average revenue (= price) (£s)	Total revenue (£s)	Marginal revenue (£s)
1	8	8	+8
2	7	14	+6
3	6	18	+4
4	5	20	+2
5	3	15	−5

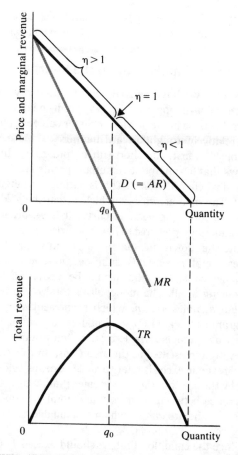

FIGURE 17.1 The Relation between Average, Marginal and Total Revenue under Different Elasticities of Demand. When demand is elastic, *MR* is positive and *TR* is rising. When demand is inelastic, *MR* is negative and *TR* is falling. When demand elasticity = 1, *MR* = 0 and *TR* is constant

Marginal revenue and elasticity of demand

The relationship between average and marginal revenues is portrayed graphically for a straight-line demand curve in Figure 17.1. We showed in Chapter 7 that the elasticity varies continuously along such a demand curve. We show, again, the elasticity of the different parts of the demand curve as we did in Figure 7.4 on page 78 (to which you should refer for a full explanation).

The diagram makes clear the two important characteristics of the marginal revenue curve of the monopolist.

(i) *MR* lies below *AR* for each level of output.

(ii) *MR* is negative whenever elasticity of demand is less than unity, because a price fall lowers total revenue. (*MR* is zero when demand has elasticity equal to unity, since total revenue is then constant.)

Monopoly Equilibrium in the Short Run

Now that we have derived the marginal revenue curve for a monopolist, the two profit-maximizing rules described in the previous chapter can be applied in a relatively straightforward manner.

Consider, first, the short-run output rule which shows that for any positive output, profits are maximized where $MC = MR$. This is output q_0 in Figure 17.2. The market price at which q_0 can be sold is determined by the demand curve. It is p_0, because consumers are prepared to buy q_0 at price p_0.

The shut-down rule for the short run states that, unless total revenue is sufficient to cover total variable costs, the firm would be better off not producing at all. The monopolist's total revenue is output, q_0, times price, p_0, which is represented on the diagram as the area Op_0sq_0. Total variable costs are given by average variable cost, a, times output, q_0. They are represented as the area $Oatq_0$. In this case, total revenue exceeds total variable costs, as evidenced by the fact that Op_0sq_0 is greater than $Oatq_0$. (The difference between total cost and total revenue is given by the area ap_0st, which is available to cover fixed costs and for profits.)

Since the condition that *TR* should exceed *TVC* is the same as the condition that $AR(= TR/q)$ should

exceed $AVC(= TVC/q)$, Rule 2 can be checked by a simple comparison of average variable cost, which is a on the figure, and average revenue (equals price), which is p_0 on the figure.

Monopoly Equilibrium in the Long Run

We may now apply the same two rules for a profit-maximizing firm to find monopoly equilibrium in the long run. Rule 2, which states that as long as output is positive, the profit-maximizing output occurs where $MC = MR$, produces the same results in the two time-periods: output q_0 and price p_0.

The application of Rule 1, however, leads to results that may differ in the two time-periods. While, in the short run, the rule requires that total revenue is sufficient to cover only total *variable* costs, in the long run the firm's total revenue must cover total costs. These total costs include those that are fixed, and those that are variable in the short run, since all costs are variable in the long run. To see whether this is the case, we need to inspect the total cost curve as well as the variable cost curve. This we do in Figure 17.3, which is identical to Figure 17.2, except for the addition of the total cost curve, *ATC*, which includes average fixed (and variable) costs.

Total revenue is obtained, as in Figure 17.2, by multiplying output q_0 by price p_0 – i.e. the area Op_0sq_0. Total costs, both fixed and variable, are obtained again by multiplying the average total cost a by

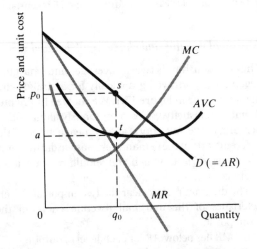

FIGURE 17.2   Monopoly Equilibrium in the Short Run. The monopolist produces the output at which $MR = MC$

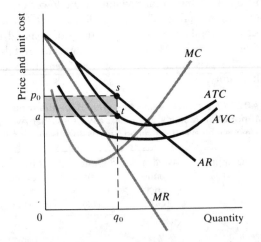

FIGURE 17.3   Monopoly Equilibrium in the Long Run. This monopolist is producing the output at which $MR = MC$, and earning supernormal profits because *AR* is greater than *ATC*

output q_0 to give the area $Oatq_0$. It may be seen that total revenue is greater than total costs. Therefore, the firm will be profitable in the long run, producing its profit-maximizing output q_0. The difference between TR and TC is the monopolist's supernormal profits (sometimes called its MONOPOLY PROFITS). They are represented in Figure 17.3 as the difference between Op_0sq_0 and $Oatq_0$, which is the shaded area ap_0st. (Another way of checking that the monopolist shown in Figure 17.3 should not shut down in the short run is to note that average revenue of p_0 exceeds average total cost of a.)

Barriers to Entry

Under perfect competition the presence of supernormal profits, such as ap_0st in Figure 17.3, would lead to entry of firms until long-run equilibrium of the industry was reached where only normal profits were earned by the typical firm.

Under monopoly, in contrast, there is only a single producer in the industry. If the monopolist is to retain its position as the only seller, there must be BARRIERS TO ENTRY, which are defined as any force which prevents other firms from entering the industry. Barriers to entry, thus, protect the monopolist's position from encroachment by other firms. They may be natural or man-made and each type can take several forms. Some of the more important barriers are discussed below.

Natural barriers

Three important sources of natural entry barriers are (1) cost advantages, (2) uniqueness, and (3) locational barriers.

Cost Advantages: In an industry subject to increasing returns to scale, (or, what is the same thing, falling long-run costs), the larger the firm the lower its costs. Any industry where there is room for only one firm producing at minimum efficient scale (MES) is called a NATURAL MONOPOLY. In such an industry, competition among firms will lead to the emergence of one large firm serving the whole market – since the largest firm always has lower costs, and hence can undersell any smaller competitors.

Uniqueness: A second natural barrier (which may be the prime cause of cost advantages described in the

previous paragraph) is uniqueness. A firm may possess sole access to the supply of a major input, such as a raw material; or it may have an exceptionally talented employee on its staff. For example, Alcoa Corporation of Canada owns the major areas of land beneath which aluminium is found; the Beatles were a unique group with exceptional talents; the Louvre museum in Paris owns the only painting of the *Mona Lisa* by Leonardo da Vinci, etc.

Locational Advantages: Particular locations often give the firms there special advantages and thus make it impossible for potential new entrants, who do not enjoy these special advantages, to compete on equal terms. Corner sites offer twice the window space of other sites; newsagents' shops adjacent to bus stops can expect larger sales than those more remote; and so forth. Note, however, that some locational advantages could be equally well classified under cost advantages. For example, proximity to a river lowers costs of waste disposal for firms located there, compared to other firms. We treat locational advantages as a special case because they are commonly encountered.

Man-made barriers

All the barriers to entry described so far have their source in natural causes. Man-made barriers are those deliberately created by human beings, both private and governmental. Here again we use a threefold classification: (1) barriers created by firms, (2) legal restrictions, and (3) barriers created by government.

Barriers Created by Firms: Firms can often establish barriers to restrict the entry of other firms. Many are related to marketing. Some arise from product differentiation – the creation of a product which is distinctive from others on the market. This important class of barriers is discussed again in Chapter 18.

Legal Barriers: The chief legal restrictions preventing the entry of new firms are patents on processes, and copyrights on publications. Flymo Ltd enjoyed a legal monopoly of lawnmowers based on the hovercraft principle in the UK for 16 years until the patent ran out in 1972. The D'Oyly Carte Opera Company enjoyed an absolute monopoly on commercial performances of Gilbert and Sullivan operas until the copyright ran out 50 years after Sullivan's death.

Barriers Created by Government: Akin to patent monopolies, governments can create monopoly situations by granting legal rights to single firms. For example, Acts of Parliament protect the remaining nationalized industries, to some extent, from competition from private firms. The state, or its agencies, may also grant monopoly status to private firms; e.g., the commercial radio and TV companies, or to single duty-free shops at airports.

The persistence of entry barriers

Barriers to entry are essential to the persistence of monopoly power. Some, such as cost advantages arising from economies of scale, endure for very long periods of time. Others such as patents, which run out, and differentiated products, which may be more or less copied, last for shorter periods.

The evidence, however, strongly supports the view that barriers to entry often exist for long enough for monopolists to earn large supernormal profits. This creates an incentive for other firms to enter the industry to challenge the existing monopoly and to share in monopoly profits. The greater the monopoly profits, the more powerful the incentive for new firms to try to enter an industry. In the view of the distinguished economist the late Joseph Schumpeter, no monopoly lasts for ever, precisely because the incentive of monopoly profits leads outside entrepreneurs to strive to share them. Firms outside a monopolistic industry strive to enter, and existing monopolists strive continually to create *new* monopoly situations as challenges from other firms gather strength. Schumpeter called this the process of 'creative destruction'. He saw the attempt of firms to seize the monopoly profits of existing firms, and to acquire their own monopolies by inventing new products and new, cheaper, ways of producing old products, as *the* great engine of growth in market societies.

Barriers to exit

For completeness, we should mention the existence of barriers preventing firms from leaving an industry, when profits fall below the opportunity cost of capital. Virtually all such exit barriers can be traced to government regulation, on behalf of consumers (e.g., postal services in remote country areas) or of workers, especially where heavy geographical concentration of an industry exists (e.g., support for British Leyland).

CONCLUSIONS

Four important conclusions can be drawn from the analysis of monopoly equilibrium.

A Monopolist can Control Price or Output: A monopolist has the power to set *either* price *or* output. If it chooses to set price, the quantity it will be able to sell is fixed by the demand curve. If it chooses to set output, the price at which that output can be disposed of, is also fixed by the demand curve. The monopolist cannot set *both* price *and* output.

A Monopolist will not Operate in the Range where the Elasticity of Demand is Less than Unity: The reason is clear from Figure 17.1. When demand elasticity is less than unity, marginal revenue is negative. Since costs are always positive, the intersection of MR and MC could not occur under such conditions.

A Monopolist does not Necessarily Earn Supernormal Profits: The analysis of monopoly equilibrium allows for the possibility of supernormal profits; it does not guarantee them. Figure 17.4 shows the optimum position of a monopolist who is earning only normal profits, because $ATC = AC$, at profit-maximizing output q_0. Whereas long-run equilibrium under perfect competition is *always* that equilibrium where only normal profits are earned, such an equilibrium would be a pure coincidence for a monopoly. The ATC and AR curves just happened to touch but not to intersect. A monopolist may also earn subnormal profits in the short run. This occurs if the ATC curve is

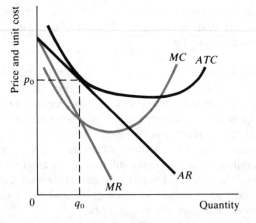

FIGURE 17.4   A Monopolist Earning only Normal Profits. ATC equals AR at profit-maximizing output and exceeds it at all other levels of output

everywhere above the *AR* curve. As long as variable costs are covered, the monopolist will remain in the industry for the short run. In the long run, however, it will exit and the product will no longer be produced.

A Monopolist need not Maximize Profits: Monopoly firms can often earn supernormal profits. However, they are under no obligation to *maximize* profits. There is even a common misconception that if such firms are not maximizing their profits, they must be making subnormal profits. This certainly does not follow. In Figure 17.3, for example, ap_0st supernormal profits are earned by a profit-maximizing monopolist. But a monopoly might choose to produce output other than q_0 and would still remain in business over the long run so long as total revenue was equal to, or greater than, total cost.

PRICE DISCRIMINATION

So far in this chapter we have assumed that the monopolist charges the same price for every unit of product, no matter to whom or where it is sold. But other situations are possible. Milk is often sold at one price if it is for drinking, but at a lower price if it is for making ice-cream or cheese. Some doctors in private practice, solicitors and other professionals vary their fees according to the incomes of their clients. Foodstuffs may be sold at prices in the home market that differ from the prices charged in overseas markets, as when the EEC sells grain to Eastern Europe below the prices within the Common Market.

All of these are examples of PRICE DISCRIMINATION, which is defined as the selling of the same product at different prices in situations where such price differences do *not* result from differences in costs. The above definition tells us that all price differences do not represent price discrimination. For example, when the price charged for goods sold in a distant market exceeds the price charged in a nearby market, this is *not* price discrimination. It is the result of differences in transport costs. But when EEC produce is sold to countries outside the EEC at lower prices than it is sold to EEC member states, this *is* price discrimination because the price differences have nothing to do with cost differences.

Types of price discrimination

There are two types of price discrimination. One type

involves the sale of different quantities of a good at different prices *to the same consumer*. Car-parking spaces, for example, are often charged at different rates for long and for short stays. Another example is where consumers pay different prices for units of gas or electricity according to their total consumption. This type of price discrimination often requires keeping close track of sales of each unit to individual consumers.

The second type of price discrimination involves the sale at different prices of identical products to *different* consumers. This may happen within one market, as when any professional charges his rich client more than his poor client for exactly the same services. It may also happen between markets as when EEC goods are sold at one price within the EEC countries and another outside it.

Conditions for price discrimination

There are two conditions which must hold before price discrimination takes place. One is to do with the *possibility* of discrimination, the other with its *profitability.*

First, the markets must be separate. Consumers in the market where price is relatively low must be *unable* to resell to consumers in other markets. Unless this condition holds, flows of goods between markets will erode any attempt to maintain different prices. Discrimination will not be possible.

Second, the demand curve in each market must be different.[1] To show that price discrimination is profitable as well as possible when this condition holds, consider the following illustration.

Suppose that a firm sells a single product in two markets, home and foreign. We show the average and marginal revenue curves in each market in Figure 17.5(i) and (ii). How should the profit-maximizing firm decide how much to sell, and at what price in each market?

To determine the profit-maximizing total output, the monopolist must equate marginal cost with marginal revenue. Marginal cost poses no new problem. The firm merely needs to know what an extra unit of production would add to its cost.

---

1   Strictly speaking if at each price chosen the elasticity of demand is the same on both demand curves, price discrimination will not be profitable. If the elasticities differ, then price will be higher in the market with the less elastic demand curve. For a full explanation of this proposition, see IPE.

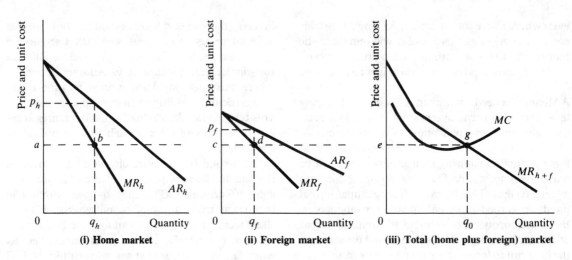

FIGURE 17.5   Price-Discriminating Monopoly. Optimum output is where *MC* equals the combined *MR* of home and foreign markets; price charged is higher in the market with the more inelastic demand

Marginal revenue, however, does pose a new problem. The firm is selling in two markets, home and foreign. What is its overall *MR*? The solution lies in realizing that the profit-maximizing firm will allocate any given output between the two markets so as to maximize its total revenue. Were this not done, so that *MR* were greater in one market than the other, it would be possible to switch sales of a given output between home and overseas and increase total revenue.

To discover the firm's overall marginal revenue we need to construct a marginal revenue curve for the two markets combined, MR_{h+f}. This curve is drawn to show the marginal revenue from the sale of all possible outputs, allocated in such a way that total revenue from sales is maximized by making the marginal revenue the same in the two markets. To find the overall marginal revenue that applies to each output, therefore, we merely sum the separate quantities in each market that correspond to each particular marginal revenue. If, for example, the 10th unit sold in the home market and the 15th unit sold in the foreign market both have marginal revenues of £1, then the marginal revenue of £1 corresponds to overall sales of 25 units. The overall marginal revenue curve, MR_{h+f}, is therefore derived by horizontal summation of MR_h and MR_f. At prices P_h and above, MR_{h+f} is identical to MR_h; at lower prices, MR_f has to be added to it.

Point *g* on the combined marginal revenue curve, for example, is constructed by measuring *eg* equal to *ab*+*cd*. (The procedure is similar to that used in Chapter 4 to construct the market demand curve from the demand curves of two individuals.)

Having derived the overall marginal revenue curve MR_{h+f} in Figure 17.5(ii), we find its point of intersection with the marginal cost curve.

The second step in the process of determining the equilibrium of the price-discriminating monopolist, is to divide total output optimally between home and foreign markets. To find the best allocation we apply the principle that *marginal revenues must be equal in the two markets.* Finding the split between markets involves, as it were, retracing the steps we took to construct MR_{h+f}. So, we move leftwards along the horizontal grid line drawn from *a* to *g*, selling q_h in the home market and q_f in the foreign market. This must ensure equality of marginal revenues in the two markets, and also, of course, that of marginal cost and marginal revenue.

To determine the price to be charged in each market, we move up from the points *b* and *d* to the demand curves. The quantity q_h will sell at price p_h in the home market; the quantity q_f will sell in the foreign market at the price p_f. These two prices are different, because the demand curves are different in the home and foreign markets.

Perfect Competition and Monopoly: A Preliminary Comparison

A detailed comparison of various types of market will be given in Chapter 19. In the meantime, we conclude by pointing out three important distinctions between perfect competition and monopoly.

- *Output* under profit-maximizing monopoly is less than under perfect competition for any given set of cost and demand conditions. This follows from the monopolist's power to restrict output in order to raise price.

- *Price* under monopoly is higher than under perfect competition for any given set of cost and demand conditions. This follows from the fact that MR is less than AR under monopoly, while $MR = AR$ in perfect competition.

- *Marginal cost* under perfect competition equals price, while under monopoly, MC is less than price.

SUMMARY

1 A monopoly is defined as an industry where there is only a single seller. The market demand curve for the industry's product is also the demand curve of the monopoly firm.

2 A monopolist can affect the price of its product by altering the quantity offered for sale. Marginal revenue is thus less than average revenue, which means that the marginal revenue curve lies below the average revenue (demand) curve. Marginal revenue corresponding to a particular output is positive, zero, or negative, according to whether the elasticity of demand for the product is greater than, equal to, or less than unity at that output.

3 The equilibrium of a profit-maximizing monopolist is where marginal cost is equal to marginal revenue. Providing total costs can be covered, the monopolist's equilibrium is the same in the long run as in the short run. If revenues are sufficient to cover variable costs, but are insufficient to cover total costs, output will be positive in the short run but the firm will close down in the long run.

4 Barriers to entry are essential to the persistence of monopoly. They may be natural barriers, i.e. uniqueness, cost or locational advantages, or they may be man-made, i.e. legal, marketing or government-created barriers.

5 Four important conclusions to be drawn from the analysis of monopoly are (i) a monopolist can control price or output, but not both together; (ii) a monopolist will not operate in the range where the elasticity of demand is less than unity; (iii) a monopolist does not necessarily earn super-normal profits; and (iv) a monopolist need not maximize profits.

6 Price discrimination occurs when the same product is sold at different prices for reasons other than cost differences. The conditions for price discrimination to be possible and profitable are that the markets are separate and that the demands are different. Profit-maximizing equilibrium is found where marginal revenues are equal in every market and are equal to marginal cost (and where, since demands are different in the different markets, prices are also different).

7 Three important distinctions between equilibrium under perfect competition and monopoly are: (i) output under monopoly is less than under perfect competition; (ii) price under monopoly is higher than under perfect competition; and (iii) marginal cost under perfect competition equals price, while under monopoly it is less than price.

Monopolistic Competition and Oligopoly

This is the final chapter in the group of three outlining various theories of the firm in different market situations.

The previous two chapters described the two extreme market structures of perfect competition and pure monopoly. Conditions in some real-world markets do approximate to perfect competition and monopoly. Basic raw materials and foodstuffs, for example, are sold on highly competitive world markets, while there a few products produced by a single firm, for example insulin and telephone services. (It is very rare that such monopolists are completely protected from all forms of competition, including that from overseas.) The two extreme market forms do not, however, cover important segments of the economic activity that we see today. Many firms involved in the production, distribution and retailing of consumer goods and services operate in markets which lie between the two extremes. The same is true of most firms which make capital goods. These firms do not operate under perfect competition because they are not price-takers. Nor are they monopolies because there is usually more than one firm in the industry. They lie somewhere between these two extremes. They are monopolistic, in the sense that they have power to set their own prices; they are competitive, in the sense that they actively compete with each other.

THE GROWTH OF CONCENTRATION

Eighteenth- and nineteenth-century capitalist development in Britain took place in an environment dominated by small businesses who often operated under conditions that approximated perfect compe-tition. The increasing importance of large corpor-ations began about a hundred years ago, helped by the legislation of limited liability and the appearance of joint-stock companies (see above, Chapter 13).

There are two ways of looking at the growth of concentration. The first examines trends in the *overall* share of output controlled by large companies; the second focuses on changes in individual industries in what is termed *market* concentration (otherwise known as industry, seller or sectoral concentration).

Overall Concentration

The modern large corporation typically produces a variety of goods and services spread over different industries. The share of total output in all industries in the hands of large businesses is a measure of OVERALL CONCENTRATION. (Other indices of concen-tration measuring shares of total employment, sales, and capital values, are also used.)

The one hundred largest corporations, commonly referred to as *giants*, now control a very substantial proportion of total output. Restricting ourselves to the manufacturing sector, where most applied re-search has been done, we can obtain a good idea of the level of overall concentration and of past trends from the share of the 'top 100' in total output. The number of companies of all sizes in manufacturing is close to 100,000, so the top 100 represent approxi-mately one-tenth of one per cent of the total. They include companies such as ICI, Unilever, General Electric, Marks & Spencer and Boots, as well as other less familiar names like Rio Tinto Zinc, Lohnro, Tate & Lyle and Bowater. Even the smallest of the top 100 employs nearly 20,000 workers and makes a profit of over £40 million per annum.

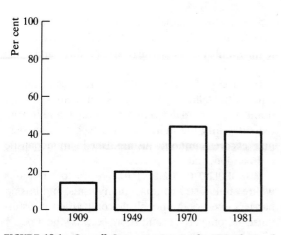

FIGURE 18.1   Overall Concentration in the UK: Share of the 100 Largest Enterprises in Manufacturing Industry (*Sources:* S. J. Prais, *The Evolution of Giant Firms in Britain* (Cambridge University Press, 1981) and P.E. Hart, 'Recent Trends in Concentration in British Industry', *National Institute of Economic and Social Research Discussion Paper No. 82,* 1985)

Figure 18.1 shows the share in total manufacturing output of the largest 100 enterprises since the first decade of the century. Their share rose from less than 20 per cent at that time, to over 40 per cent by 1970, since when it has more or less stabilised.

The growth of giant enterprises has followed the two paths laid out in Chapter 13 – internal growth, and amalgamation or merger.

Growth by merger became a matter of public concern in the 1960s with the first of a series of merger waves. Peak merger activity resulted in well over 1,000 amalgamations per annum, and since that time at least half of the increase in concentration has been due to mergers. Most mergers have been *horizontal*, i.e. between firms at the same stage of production process. A few have been *vertical* amalgamations between firms merging forwards with their customers or backwards with their suppliers. The most rapidly increasing type of merger in the 1960s and 1970s was, however, of the *conglomerate* type, involving diversification of interests. Conglomerate mergers have accounted for about a third of the total since 1980.

Market Concentration

One characteristic of giant companies in the UK economy is their widely diversified interests. The typical giant operates in several distinct markets. For example, the Sears group, mentioned earlier (see p. 152), has interests in shoe shops, betting shops, department stores, engineering, shipbuilding, etc., while the Pearson group controls Penguin Books, Royal Doulton China, *The Financial Times*, oil companies and Madame Tussauds, among many others.

To see the extent of concentration in particular markets in the hands of large company organizations, we have to look, therefore, at market shares. This is usually done through what are known as market CONCENTRATION RATIOS (CRs). These are the shares that the largest companies have in either output or employment. Often the shares of the 5 largest enterprises are used. This measure, called CR5, shows the proportion of total output or employment in the hands of the largest 5 enterprises.

In Table 18.1 we show statistics of CR5 for the percentages of total employment by the five largest enterprises in the UK in 1981. The wide variation that exists in the degree of concentration in British industry can be seen from the table. Thus 21 industries have very low concentration ratios, with the largest five enterprises employing 20 per cent, or less, of the total workforce in those industries; while 16 industries have CR5s of over 70 per cent, i.e. the largest five enterprises in those industries account for nearly three-quarters of total employment.

Table 18.1 shows the level of concentration at a single point in time, 1981. Trends in concentration over time are not easily measured, largely because industrial structure is not static: some industries are

TABLE 18.1 Concentration Ratios in Manufacturing Industry, UK 1981. (Shares of the largest 5 enterprises in total employment)

Range of CR (%)	Number of industries
1–10	1
11–20	20
21–30	12
31–40	18
41–50	13
51–60	14
61–70	9
71–80	6
81–90	6
91–100	4
	103

Source: P. E. Hart, 'Recent Trends in Concentration in British Industry', *National Institute of Economic and Social Research Discussion Paper No. 82,* 1985.

expanding and others contracting, while new industries replace old ones. Estimates suggest, however, that market concentration increased sharply until the 1970s, since when there has been very little change in most sectors. These results are based on the average change in all sectors taken together. There were some industries where concentration changed both more, and less, than the average.

The Implications of Concentration of Industry

High levels of concentration do not imply more than that perfect competition and pure monopoly are not representative of major sectors of the British economy. Even a particular numerical value of a concentration ratio does not carry with it a precise implication of the extent of power in the hands of any particular firm. For example, a CR5 of 76 says only that the 5 largest firms control 76 per cent of total output. Those 5 firms could all be of approximately equal size, or there could be a single giant and 4 much smaller 'largest firms', or anything else in between.

Remember, also, that overall concentration has been increasing during the present century. Much of this growth, as we have explained, is the result of giant firms diversifying – spreading their interests over several industries. The consequence is that we may find *the same* giant enterprises among the largest firms in more than one industry. These typical, multi-product, firms compete with each other in several markets. The result is a form of competition between giant companies which can become intense because of the enormous resources that are at their disposal.

Economic theories capable of analysing and predicting the behaviour of giant multi-product firms competing in several industries must necessarily be complex. They are still, moreover, being developed, and we cannot offer the reader at this stage, anything like a comprehensive coverage. Our approach, here, is to present a selection of the basic theories which have been put forward to deal with intermediate markets.

Types of Imperfect Market

Market structures which fall between perfect competition and pure monopoly are known generally as those of IMPERFECT COMPETITION. This term is used to describe markets where *any one* of the assumptions that give rise to perfect competition is not present. (See Chapter 16, pp. 180–1.) They relate in particular to the number of firms, the type of product, and entry conditions.

Under *imperfect* competition, there must be one or more of the following conditions – a relatively small number of firms, a differentiated product, and restricted entry into the industry. Two types of imperfect markets are commonly distinguished – monopolistic competition, and oligopoly.

MONOPOLISTIC COMPETITION refers to situations where an industry contains many firms, and has no barriers to entry. Monopolistic competition is distinguished from perfect competion, because the product of each firm is differentiated from those of other firms. The concept was developed in the 1930s by the American economist Edward Chamberlain, reacting to the inapplicability of the theories of perfect competition and monopoly to large sectors of the economy.[1]

OLIGOPOLY refers to a market where there are *few* sellers (the word oligopoly means precisely that in Greek).

MONOPOLISTIC COMPETITION

The major characteristics of monopolistic competition are: (i) a large number of firms, (ii) each firm has a distinctive, or *differentiated*, product, and (iii) there is freedom of entry into, and exit from, the industry.

The first characteristic, a large number of firms, is the same as under perfect competition. It means that each firm in a monopolistically competitive industry takes its decisions with no thought to causing reactions from other competing firms. Any one firm is just too small for its actions to be noticed by the others.

The second characteristic, the products of firms are differentiated from each other, means that although the products have enough in common to be grouped together as one commodity (e.g. ready-to-eat breakfast foods), they are sufficiently different from one another to be regarded by consumers as not perfectly

---

1 Reacting to the same phenomenon, the British economist Joan Robinson went in another direction by assuming that all industries were monopolies. Although her work greatly advanced the theory of monopoly, it did not prove useful in explaining the behaviour of the great range of intermediate markets.

substitutable for each other. Note that it does not matter if the products really are physically identical, so long as they are perceived as differentiated in the minds of consumers. Because the products of the firms in an industry are imperfect substitutes for each other, the typical monopolistically competitive firm is not a price-taker. It can raise price without losing all of its sales to competitors; and it can lower price in order to sell more. The demand curve facing the firm slopes downwards; it is not perfectly elastic, as in perfect competition.

The final characteristic of monopolistic competition, freedom of entry and exit, likens the industry to perfect competition rather than to monopoly. If excess profits are being earned by existing firms, newcomers will enter the industry. If losses are being made, firms will leave.

Short-run equilibrium

Assuming that firms are profit-maximizers, the short-run equilibrium of the firm in monopolistic competition is exactly the same as under monopoly. Maximum-profit output is found where marginal cost is equal to marginal revenue (so long as total revenue is equal to or greater than total variable costs). Figure 18.2 shows equilibrium output q_0 with market price p_0. Supernormal profits are given by the shaded rectangle ap_0st – price *minus* average total cost *times* output. Notice, incidentally, that the diagram is identical to that of Figure 17.2 in the previous chapter, except that we have drawn the demand

curve under monopolistic competition as flatter than the demand under monopoly, on account of the large number of substitutes available.

Long-run equilibrium

So far, we have seen that the short-run equilibrium of the firm under monopolistic competition is the same as under monopoly. Because of barriers to entry under monopoly, the equilibrium of a monopoly is the same in the long and short runs. This is not so under monopolistic competition because there is freedom of entry into the industry. If existing firms are making supernormal profits,[1] as in Figure 18.2, new firms enter the industry, attracted by these profits. Their entry adds to the total supply in the industry and depresses the general level of demand for the product of every firm. This shifts the demand curve of each existing firm to the left, as its market share is reduced. The process continues until the typical firm in the industry is making only normal profits. This occurs when the demand curve has shifted far enough to the left so that it is just tangent to the average cost curve at the most profitable output.

The long-run equilibrium of each firm under monopolistic competition is the same as was shown in Figure 17.4 on page 192 for a monopolist who was just covering its total cost. The only difference is that for a monopolist this result would be a sheer coincidence, while for a monopolistic competitor this result is made necessary in the long run by entry (wherever profits are supernormal) or exit (wherever profits are subnormal). In Figure 17.4 the most profitable output is q_0, where marginal cost equals marginal revenue. Market price is p_0. At output q_0 and price p_0, average revenue exactly equals average cost. The only profits are normal profits, which are included in the cost curve.

Excess capacity under monopolistic competition

Note, in Figure 17.4, that the equilibrium output of the firm is at output q_0 where average total costs are falling.[2] Average cost is minimized at the output

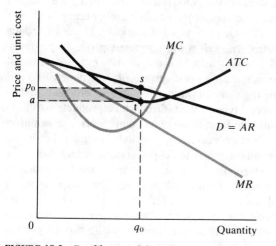

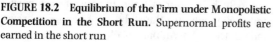

FIGURE 18.2   Equilibrium of the Firm under Monopolistic Competition in the Short Run. Supernormal profits are earned in the short run

---

1 If the demand curve intersects the *ATC* curve – as, e.g., in Figure 18.2 – supernormal profits can be made by producing anywhere in the range where the *AR* curve lies above the *ATC* curve.

2 The *AC* curve is tangent to the downward-sloping demand curve at output q_0. Therefore, as the two curves must have the same slope at that point, the *AC* curve must also be downward-sloping.

where the MC curve cuts the ATC curve. This is a larger output than q_0. In other words, firms under monopolistic competition do not achieve full productive efficiency, i.e. produce at minimum average costs, as is the case under perfect competition.

The difference between equilibrium output and minimum-cost output is called EXCESS CAPACITY. Such excess capacity is associated with long-run equilibrium under monopolistic competition, and was regarded for many years as a sign of the relative inefficiency of this market form. (Under perfect competition, in contrast, excess capacity can only occur in the short run.)

The modern view of the excess capacity argument is less critical of monopolistic competition. While not denying the existence of excess capacity, in the technical sense of higher than minimum average costs, it stresses the benefits to consumers of having a *variety* of differentiated products from which to choose. These benefits need to be offset against the higher average costs of producing a differentiated set of products instead of a single standardized one. It can be shown that, under certain circumstances, consumers would choose to have a wide selection of more expensive goods rather than a narrow choice of cheaper ones.

The Relevance of Monopolistic Competition

The theory, described in the previous paragraphs, refers to markets where a large number of firms compete to sell differentiated products. Developed in the 1930s, the theory has suffered a major blow, because of growing realization that such conditions are rarely, if ever, found in the economy.

At first sight, this may sound surprising. A visit to any department store or supermarket will reveal that there are many industries where a large number of slightly differentiated products compete for the buyer's attention. In most such cases, however, the industries contain only a few firms, each of which sells a large number of products. For example, you may easily find a dozen different brands of instant coffee on the supermarket shelves. But the number of different blends of coffee bean, of roasting processes and of packagings greatly exceeds the number of different companies producing instant coffee. Or take retail shopkeeping. In every city you will find a large number of shops selling a particular range of products. But any one individual store is not in *effective*

competition with *all* of them, only with those in fairly close geographical proximity. The boutiques in London's Kings Road compete with each other far more than they do with dress shops in Hampstead or Croydon. Moreover, several of the shops selling one line of goods may belong to a single business enterprise, e.g. Saxone, Dolcis and Manfield shoe shops, mentioned earlier.

In the view of present-day economists, therefore, the theory of monopolistic competition among *large numbers* of small firms producing differentiated products does not apply to any major sectors of the economy. Attention has shifted to competition among *small numbers of firms* which are in close competition with each other. They are the subject of the theory of oligopoly.

OLIGOPOLY

Oligopoly refers to market situations in which a few sellers compete with each other. The feature of oligopoly that distinguishes it from perfect and monopolistic competition, is that the number of sellers should be so few that each individual firm *is affected by the actions of its rivals* and when each takes its decisions it knows its rivals may react. This *rivalrous* behaviour distinguishes oligopoly from monopoly, where a single seller is protected from potential rivals by barriers to entry. In oligopoly, sellers are not price-takers, but price-makers, though the quantity each sells depends not only on how much a firm raises or lowers price, but also on whether such price changes spark off retaliatory actions by other firms.

There are two types of oligopoly. The first contains firms who sell a homogeneous group of products. Steel companies, for example, sell a range of commodities, but a piece of sheet steel of given dimensions will be the same no matter which firm produces it. The second type contains firms whose products are differentiated from those of its competitors. For example, Robertson's orange marmalade is similar, but by no means identical, to Cooper's orange marmalade.

Oligopoly is the most common market structure outside agriculture. It has been the subject of much theoretical and applied work in economics. The results are complex and, to an extent, still inconclusive. We shall concern ourselves with three aspects of oligopoly behaviour: (i) the nature of cost curves under oligopoly, (ii) the stability of oligopoly prices, and (iii) the indeterminacy of oligopoly equilibrium.

The Nature of Cost Curves under Oligopoly

Ever since economists began estimating firms' costs, they reported that average variable costs were flat, rather than U-shaped. The evidence is now overwhelming that in manufacturing, and some other industries, cost curves have the shape shown in Figure 18.3, with a long flat middle portion, and sharply rising sections at either end. Over the flat range, from q_0 to q_1, average variable and marginal costs are constant. At outputs below q_0, AVC is declining, so MC is below it. At outputs above q_1, AVC is rising, so MC is above it. Such cost curves are described as *saucer-shaped*. Minimum average cost under such conditions, occurs over a *range* of outputs, rather than at a single point, as with U-shaped cost curves. The firm, normally, hopes to operate at some output below output q_1 where unit costs start to rise. This might be output q_2 in Figure 18.3. Output q_1 is called FULL CAPACITY OUTPUT, while output q_2 is called NORMAL CAPACITY OUTPUT. The gap between q_2 and q_1 allows a margin of spare capacity on which the firm may draw in periods of peak demand, but does not use in periods of average or slack demand.

At first sight, the saucer-shaped short-run average variable cost curve might appear to violate the 'law' of diminishing returns (see Chapter 14). This 'law' formed the basis for the U shape that we previously encountered. There is, however, no contradiction. The explanation for the falling and rising portions of the AVC curve, given in Chapter 15, p. 169, was the presence of a fixed factor of production. The falling portion of the curve occurs because the fixed factor is less than optimally employed; the rising portion occurs because the fixed factor is more than optimally employed, i.e. there is not enough of the fixed factor to provide the optimal combination with the variable factor. The falling part of the short-run cost curve occurs, as we explained, because the fixed factor is *indivisible*, which means that all of it must be used all of the time.

In most industries the factor that is fixed in the short run is capital, while the variable factor is labour. In many industries, the fixed factor is *divisible*, *in the sense that all of it need not be used all of the time.*

Consider, as a simple example, a 'factory' that consists of 10 sewing machines in a shed, each of which requires one and only one operator. Whatever output is required, the best way of producing it is by using a combination of operators to machines of one-to-one. This implies that not all the machines will actually be employed if demand is below the full capacity of the plant, i.e. demand can be met by less than 10 sewing machines. Thus, at a time of low demand, only 6 machines may be used, and only 6 operators hired (rather than having, say, 6 operators dashing around trying to keep 10 machines working). Idle machines will only be brought into use when demand warrants it. When that happens, extra staff will be engaged, one for each extra machine used. Clearly, in such cases, the marginal cost of altering output will be *constant*. It is constant because the 'fixed' factor, capital (sewing machines in this case), is divisible. Thus, the ratio of *employed capital/employed labour* does not vary as output varies (at least over the range from zero to the normal output possible from 10 machines). Hence, there is no conflict between the law of diminishing returns, *which applies when factor proportions are varied*, and the saucer-shaped constant short-run average and marginal costs commonly found in manufacturing industries, *which applies when factor proportions are held constant.*

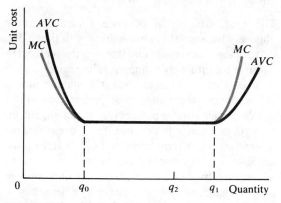

FIGURE 18.3   Saucer-shaped Average Variable and Marginal Cost Curves under Oligopoly. Average cost is at a minimum over a range of outputs

Price Stability under Oligopoly

A second finding about the behaviour of oligopolistic industries is that their prices tend to be 'sticky', in the sense that firms do not alter price every time either their costs or demand conditions change. While they do alter their prices, they do not do so as frequently as would be required by the conditions of short-run profit maximization that we have developed so far.

Like monopolists, oligopolists are price-makers,

because they face downward-sloping demand curves. However, being a price-maker does not necessarily imply changing price every time demand shifts. Oligopolists often adopt a policy of ADMINISTERED PRICES, holding their prices relatively steady, and becoming quantity adjusters in the face of short-term changes in demand. Why should this be so? Four possible explanations will be considered. The first suggests that firms are not short-run profit maximizers. The other three are consistent with short-run profit maximization and explain price stickiness by forces that are omitted from the simplest theories of the firm. We consider these four explanations in turn.

Full cost pricing

According to the ideas of Hall and Hitch, two pioneering Oxford economists writing in the 1930s, businessmen calculate the average total cost of operating at full capacity – which they call their 'full costs' – and then add a conventional 'mark-up' to determine price. They then sell whatever they can at that price, so that fluctuations in demand cause quantity, rather than price, to fluctuate.

Hall and Hitch explained full cost pricing as showing businessmen to be uninterested in profit maximization. Instead they were seen as creatures of habit, who added conventional mark-ups to costs calculated at their typical output and were then reluctant to change the prices that resulted from such calculations.

The cost of changing prices

What seems like full cost pricing behaviour may, however, be consistent with profit maximization. For example, the 'conventional' mark-up may correspond to the one that maximizes profits at normal output, and it may be costly to alter prices frequently. The first point is illustrated in Figure 18.4. Having built a plant, whose normal capacity is consistent with profit-maximizing output, q_0 in the diagram, the mark-up can be set to achieve maximum profits in normal times – i.e. p_0. Fluctuations in demand, e.g. to D' or D'', cause fluctuations in quantity sold, to q_1 or q_2, at the fixed market price of p_0.

The second point is that there is a significant cost involved when any modern industrial firm changes its selling prices. Such a firm often sells thousands of different products, and changing prices across the whole range is a costly affair. New price lists must be printed; price tags must be changed; salesmen must be informed; and other firms who buy from the firm in question must also make adjustments. The changes also require complicated bookkeeping each time they occur. There is also the worry an oligopoly firm must have about losing consumer goodwill, if it changes prices too often. If there were no cost of changing prices, profits would be maximized by altering prices every time demand shifted, no matter how short-lived the change was expected to be. If the cost of changing prices is great enough, the most profitable policy will be to set the profit-maximizing price for the average level of sales expected and then hold price constant as demand varies about that average in the short term.

Non-price competition

The next explanation of price stickiness under oligopoly has something in common with that of full cost pricing. Both rest, to an extent, on the real cost to a firm of continuously changing selling prices.

Given that a business finds it profitable not to change price, there are, in imperfect markets, a number of alternative policies that it can engage in, following a change in demand. These are embraced under the general term NON-PRICE COMPETITION. For example, a fall in demand can be met by increased advertising, by 'free gifts' of goods (e.g. glass storage jars, free bingo entry forms, etc.) or by differentiating the product. The choice of policies facing a multi-product oligopolist, with respect to price- and non-price-competitive methods, is usually great.

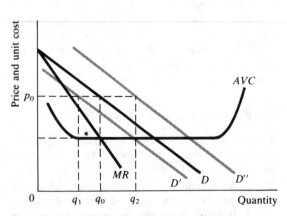

FIGURE 18.4 Full Cost Pricing. Firms charge a conventional mark-up to determine price, and change quantity, not price, when demand changes

Kinked demand curve

An alternative explanation of price stickiness under oligopoly, also developed in the 1930s, predicts price stability in the case of changing *costs* as well as changing demand.

The theory is known as that of the 'kinked demand curve' because it assumes that the demand curve facing the firm is 'kinked' at the current price-output combination, such as at point *a* in Figure 18.5. The kink arises because of two key assumptions. First, the firm is assumed to believe that, if it *cuts* its price, rival firms will follow suit. The firm's own sales will therefore expand slowly along the relatively steep portion of the demand curve below *a*. Second, the firm is assumed to believe that, if it *raises* its price, its rivals will *not* follow suit. Its own demand will, therefore, fall off rapidly along the relatively flat part of the demand curve above *a*.

The flat demand curve above the current price and the steep curve below it, mean that the curve facing the firm is kinked at the going price. As a result, a really major change in either cost or demand conditions may be necessary before the firm will consider changing its price.

The stickiness of price following cost changes may be demonstrated by inspecting the marginal revenue in the diagram. Because of the kink in the demand curve, the curve marginal to it is discontinuous. (This should be clear to those readers who also study mathematics.) The discontinuity may be explained by considering that the demand curve, *Baf* consists of portions of two distinct demand curves. One is the portion *Ba* of the demand curve *Bac*, and the other is the portion *af* of the demand curve *Eaf*. The two marginal revenue curves *Bgk* and *Emh* correspond to these two demand curves. The portions of those marginal revenue curves appropriate to the demand curve *Baf* make up the marginal revenue curve *Bgmh*, which is discontinuous between *g* and *m*.

The effect of the discontinuity in the marginal revenue curve at the current price-output combination is that a change in marginal cost, within the range q_0m and q_0g, has no effect on market price for a profit-maximizing firm. If the *MC* curve varies between *MC* and *MC'* in the diagram, for example, marginal cost remains equal to marginal revenue, *without any change in price (or output).*

Although the kinked demand curve explanation of price stickiness under oligopoly is intuitively plausible, it suffers from two major disadvantages. First, it denies not only price but also output fluctuations in response to cost changes, a stability unsupported by evidence. Second, the theory offers no explanation for how the current price (at which the demand curve is kinked) is arrived at.

Price stability in practice

Most modern industrial economists believe the short-run stickiness of industrial prices is consistent with profit-maximizing behaviour. The reasons are those we have covered: price changes are costly, and non-price methods of competition may be superior to price-cutting when conditions change temporarily. Under these circumstances, profit maximization requires only that price (which is another way of saying the mark-up over full costs) should be set so as to maximize profits at the firm's average levels of output and sales. Of course, when changes in demand or costs are permanent, oligopolists do change their prices; their prices are just sticky, not stuck.

Indeterminacy under Oligopoly

In perfect competition or monopoly, equilibrium is determinate, in the sense that the theories predict a unique price-output combination for profit maximiz-

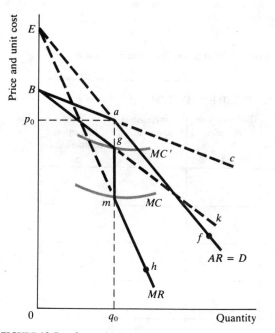

FIGURE 18.5 The Kinked Demand Curve under Oligopoly. Price and output are unchanged despite a change in *MC*

ation. In oligopoly, this is not necessarily the case. The firm has a range of alternative policies that it may pursue – price adjustment, product differentiation, advertising, etc. There may thus be more than one price-output combination for an oligopolist that will leave the firm unwilling to change its behaviour, because of variations in other policies.

In order to be able to predict precisely the behaviour of an oligopolist, economic theory must be supplied with much more information than is the case under perfect competition or monopoly. In particular, we need to know (1) the effect of changing price (in either direction), (2) the effect of advertising, product differentiation, (3) every other policy open to the firm, and (4) the response of rivals to all possible policies.

Because of the large number of variables to be considered, it is not surprising that there is no single economic theory of oligopoly, comparable to that of monopoly, which predicts the firm's behaviour. Theories range from those based on highly restrictive assumptions, to others based on elaborate assumptions that attempt to be general and are, in consequence, ultra-complex. A well-known example of the former is the DUOPOLY (two sellers) theory of Cournot. The restrictive assumptions of Cournot's theory are that there are only two firms, the product they sell is homogeneous, and they compete only on price (i.e. they do not engage in any non-price forms of

competition). Under such restrictive assumptions, Cournot was able to deduce a determinate outcome.[1]

When we take into account all the possible strategies open to oligopolists, however, economic theory becomes extremely complex. It is usually based on applications of what is known as the *theory of games*, which studies mathematical strategies in small-group situations.

We may illustrate the problem of developing a general theory of oligopoly with Table 18.2. Here, again, we assume that there are only two firms, but we give each a choice of five strategies – raise price, lower price, differentiate the product, increase advertising, and engage in other forms of non-price competition. Even with two firms and five strategies, it can be seen that the possible policy combinations amount to twenty-five. With three firms and five strategies, the number is 625. As we add to the number of firms and alternative strategies (e.g. various ways of changing the product), the number of possible outcomes reaches almost astronomical proportions. Hence, it is hardly surprising that there is no single well-developed theory of oligopoly that can predict behaviour patterns.

---

1 For a discussion of Cournot's duopoly theory, and more recent developments of it, see IPE.

TABLE 18.2 A Selection of Policy Options Available under Oligopoly. Two firms and several policies give rise to many possibilities

			STRATEGIES OPEN TO FIRM A			
		Raise price 1	Lower price 2	Differentiate product 3	Increase advertising 4	Other non-price competition 5
STRATEGIES OPEN TO FIRM B	Raise price 1					
	Lower price 2					
	Differentiate product 3					
	Increase advertising 4					
	Other non-price competition 5					

Goals of firms

The reasons for the absence of a single definitive theory of oligopoly should be clear from the complex nature of the decisions to be taken by individual firms, outlined in the previous section. However, the situation is even more difficult to analyse when one considers the possibility that firms may not even be trying to maximize their profits.

As we explained in Chapter 13 (pp. 153–5), the possibility of firms pursuing goals other than profit maximization arises out of the divorce of ownership from control in large joint-stock companies, where ownership of shares is widely dispersed. This is just the kind of circumstance which we might expect to find under oligopoly (or monopoly). And it adds yet another dimension of uncertainty about firms' behaviour.

Managerial Theories of the Firm: We cannot analyse all the possible results that would follow from different assumptions about firms' goals, partly because at least one of them, 'satisficing' (see p. 154), is essentially vague. However, there is a group of so-called MANAGERIAL THEORIES OF THE FIRM that try to explain behaviour of a business which pursues managerial goals rather than profit-maximization. To illustrate the different results that may be reached, consider a firm which seeks to maximize, not its profits, but its total revenue, subject only to the constraint of not making a loss. This firm will produce the output where its average total cost cuts the demand curve. At that price-output combination, price will just cover all costs. Inspection of any monopoly diagram where profits are earned will show the output is higher under sales maximization ($ATC = AR$) than under profit maximization ($MC = MR$). Look for example at Figure 17.3 on page 190; determine the sales-maximizing output, and compare it with the profit-maximizing output that is already shown on that figure.

Behavioural Theories of the Firm: A further set of theories – the so-called BEHAVIOURAL THEORIES OF THE FIRM – should also be mentioned. They provide different explanations of firms' behaviour. Such theories stress that a firm is not always run by either owners or managers, but represents a diversity of interests, all of which may play a part in some decisions that need to be taken. These interests include, of course, owners and managers, but also workers, customers, local inhabitants of the area where the firm is located, and others. Behavioural theories consider the bargaining processes which take place within the firm between all relevant interests, covering such activities as production, profits, growth, location and so forth.

Collusion

It should be clear that firms under oligopoly may have much to lose from the actions of their rivals and, therefore, much to gain from engaging in some form of collaboration with them. Collusion can be explicit, or implicit (i.e. tacit).

Explicit collusion occurs when a group of firms jointly decides on a fixed price for the outputs of all firms, in what is known as a CARTEL. Firms may collude on many matters. They may regulate output by quotas among themselves, refuse to supply customers (e.g. retailers) who stock the products of competing firms, and engage in many other types of restrictive practices. Most forms of such practices are illegal in the UK (see Chapter 19 for exceptions). That does not mean there is no collusion, but that if it occurs it must be covert.

Joint Profit-maximization: Collusion, whether overt or covert, leads to *joint* maximization of the profits of collaborating firms. But it is not the only road to joint profit-maximization. The same result can also follow from tacit collusion (sometimes called 'quasi-agreement') among firms which remain independent, but behave *as if* they were branches of a single firm. Firms may behave in this way, recognizing that they are interdependent and face a downward-sloping industry demand curve, so that joint profits depend on the price that each of them charges. This gives firms an incentive to charge the same price as would be charged by a single-firm monopolist. At the same time, each firm will realize that it might gain more from an aggressive policy of setting its own price below the monopoly level. Thus there are some incentives pushing the firm towards collusion and others pushing the firm away toward competition.

The likelihood of joint profit maximization by tacit collusion occurring varies from industry to industry. We can only touch on the subject here to emphasize two aspects of the market that are particularly relevant. First, joint profit maximization is more likely to occur in an industry where there is a single dominant firm, which may act as a PRICE LEADER, that other firms follow. Second, joint profit maximization is more likely if there are significant barriers to the entry of new firms. Barriers to entry were discussed at length in the previous chapter when we were discussing monopoly. To them should now be added 'predatory pricing' (i.e. below cost) by existing firms – sparked off perhaps by a price leader, to prevent newcomers entering the industry.

Joint profit maximization is in the collective interests of all the firms in an industry. As a group, they cannot do better than this. But it will generally be in the interests of any *one* firm to depart from the joint profit-maximizing behaviour, *as long as the other firms do not retaliate*. The departure by one firm lowers the group's *total profits*, but raises that one firm's *share* of the profits. This will bring gain to the firm that 'cheats', by departing from the joint profit-maximizing behaviour. But if all firms succumb to the same temptation, they all depart from the joint profit-

maximizing behaviour and the total pool of profits shrinks so much that all are probably worse off. All are now fighting a self-defeating battle to increase their shares of an ever-shrinking profit pool. (Such divisive forces have been evident in the OPEC countries in recent years. If one country sells more than its quota, it can increase its profits; but if all countries do the same, they cause the price to fall so much that they all lose.)

We can take this difficult subject no further here.[1] We have another task – to attempt some comparisons between the resource allocations under different market structures and to consider alternative policies that may be pursued to deal with inefficiencies. These are the subject of the next chapter.

---

1 See IPE, for a more detailed discussion.

SUMMARY

1 Most firms operate in imperfect markets that lie between the extremes of perfect competition and monopoly. Imperfect market structures are classified according to the number of firms in an industry, the type of product and entry conditions.

2 The degree of concentration in large firms in the UK varies from industry to industry. Concentration has also been increasing during the present century as a result of internal growth and by amalgamations – horizontal, vertical and conglomerate – among firms.

3 Under monopolistic competition, there is a large number of firms each of which produces a differentiated product, and freedom of entry into and exit from the industry.

4 The short-run equilibrium of a profit-maximizing firm under monopolistic competition is the same as under monopoly. The long-run equilibrium is different because of freedom of entry and exit, which, by shifting the demand curve facing each individual firm, in response to the existence of super- or subnormal profits, causes market price to be such that existing firms earn only normal profits in the long-run.

5 Excess capacity, defined as the difference be-

tween equilibrium output and cost-minimizing output, exists under monopolistic competition. As against this, consumers benefit from having a variety of differentiated products from which to choose.

6 Oligopolistic markets have only a few sellers, each of which is affected by the actions of its rivals. Oligopolists may produce homogeneous or differentiated products, but they are price-makers rather than price-takers.

7 Cost curves under oligopoly are typically 'saucer-shaped', containing a long middle section where they are flat, because average and marginal costs are constant.

8 Under oligopoly, prices tend to be stable, or 'sticky', despite the fact that firms are price-makers. There are several possible explanations for this. (i) Oligopolists may not be profit maximizers, and may set their prices by adding a conventional mark-up to cost in what is called 'full cost pricing'. (ii) The act of changing prices is itself usually quite costly. (iii) Oligopolists often compete with their rivals in ways other than by changing prices – e.g. by advertising or differentiating their products. (iv) The demand curve facing an oligopolistic firm may be kinked, as a result of which the marginal revenue curve is discontinuous and profit-maximizing price (and output) does not alter for every change in costs.

9 The theory of oligopoly does not predict a unique price-output combination for each firm. Indeterminacy arises partly from the many possible strategies open to any firm with which it may compete with its rivals, and partly because oligopolists may not be profit maximizers.

10 Several theories seek to explain why oligopolists might seek goals other than profit maximization: (i) in managerial theories, firms seek managerial goals – e.g. maximum growth of sales or output; (ii) in behavioural theories, firms seek compromise goals in the interests of owners, managers, workers, customers, local residents, and others.

11 Oligopolists may collude in search of joint profit maximization. Collusion may be explicit, as in a cartel, where price (and maybe output) is jointly fixed by member firms. It may also be implicit, when independent firms behave *as if* they were branches of a single firm – for example when there is a single dominant firm which acts as price leader.

Government and Industry

The bulk of this book has so far been devoted to explaining how a market system allocates resources among competing uses. In Chapters 2 and 10, however, we raised the issue of assessing how well the market does this job. There we used a fourfold classification – equity, efficiency, time-lags and concentrations of economic power. We discussed the first three issues, but postponed the fourth because we were then dealing with markets which contained large numbers of small firms, each of which was a price-taker. Now that we have studied the theory of imperfect markets, we can discuss the policy issues that are raised by concentration of economic power in imperfect markets.

Before proceeding, let us be clear that the existence of a case for intervention by the state is not to be taken as meaning that the state *should* always intervene. Market allocations are sometimes inefficient, but state intervention may, at times, lead to even greater inefficiencies. Each case should be decided on its merits. This can be a difficult process, involving comparisons of what is, with what might be, and includes political considerations. We shall return to these issues of state intervention in Chapters 23 and 24, when we review the entire scope of government economic activity in resource allocation.

Economic Efficiency and Market Structures

The concept of economic efficiency, used several times in this book, has two distinct aspects, ALLOCATIVE EFFICIENCY and PRODUCTIVE EFFICIENCY. We consider allocative efficiency first.

Allocative efficiency occurs when it is not possible to make any one consumer better off without, at the same time, making at least one other consumer worse off. The efficiency conditions are that marginal (opportunity) cost of production (MC) should be equal to marginal utility (MU) for each and every good in the economy. The conditions are fulfilled as long as consumers and producers are both price-takers. Consumers maximize utility by equating marginal utility to price (MU = p). Firms maximize profits by equating marginal cost to marginal revenue (MC = MR). In the case of perfect competition, firms are price-takers, so marginal revenue is equal to price (MR = p). In this case, profit-maximization equates marginal cost to price (MC = p). Since consumers and producers face the same price, the equality of marginal cost and marginal utility to price (MC = p = MU) entails fulfilling the efficiency condition that marginal cost equal marginal utility (MC = MU).

Allocative Inefficiency Under Monopoly

We saw in Chapter 17 that, under monopoly, marginal revenue is less than price. Thus when the firm equates marginal cost to marginal revenue it ensures that marginal cost will be less than marginal utility. Let us see how this works out in a figure. Monopoly equilibrium was described in Figure 17.3 and is shown again in Figure 19.1. We assume it shows the cost and revenue curves for a drug called Balium, of which there is a single producer.

As any other profit-maximizing firm, the monopolist depicted in Figure 19.1 is in equilibrium producing output q_m, at which marginal cost is equal to marginal revenue. The market-clearing price at which q_m is sold is read off the demand curve as p_m. This means that the valuation put by consumers on the last unit of Balium is worth p_m, in money terms.

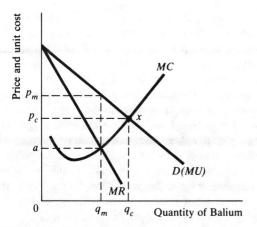

FIGURE 19.1 Monopoly Output Compared to Output Under Perfect Competition. Under monopoly, allocative inefficiency occurs because marginal cost is less than marginal utility; under perfect competition, output is efficient because marginal cost equals marginal utility

Notice, however, that the marginal cost of Balium, when q_m is produced, is only a. We may, thus, derive the important result that the marginal utility of Balium is greater than its marginal cost. This suggests that resource allocation could be improved if more Balium were produced. Consumers value it, at the margin, as being worth more than it costs to produce. And, since marginal cost, in real terms, means the opportunity cost of producing other goods, consumers would be better off if such other goods were produced in smaller quantities in order to produce more Balium.

Perfect Competition and Monopoly Equilibrium Compared

In the final section of Chapter 17, we briefly noted three differences between the equilibrium of an industry under perfect competition and that under monopoly. We focus on one of these: output is less under monopoly than under perfect competition. We are now in a position to appreciate the implications of that comparison from the viewpoint of the efficiency of a market system.

Look again at Figure 19.1, and ask what the output of Balium would be, *if that industry were perfectly competitive*. The answer is straightforward. It would be q_c – the output at which marginal cost is equal to marginal utility and, therefore, also equal to price. So, the comparison between monopoly and perfectly

competitive output can be made. Monopoly output is q_m, perfectly competitive output is q_c. Under monopoly, marginal utility is greater than marginal cost. Under perfect competition, marginal utility is equal to marginal cost. It follows, therefore, that profit-maximizing monopoly output involves allocative inefficiency, while perfectly competitive output does not.

Notice that allocative inefficiency under monopoly is defined solely in terms of output. It has nothing whatsoever to do with monopoly profits, if they exist. There may be arguments for income redistribution arising from the existence of monopoly profits, but they are a separate matter. Notice, also, that allocative inefficiency is different from productive inefficiency. Allocative inefficiency can arise despite the fact that a profit-maximizing monopolist minimizes costs for every level of output. There are issues related to costs under monopoly that will be discussed later in the chapter. They are relevant to productive inefficiency, not to allocative inefficiency.

The inefficiency described in this section does not occur only with pure monopoly, but whenever a firm faces a downward-sloping demand curve, and therefore, profit-maximizing output is less than it would be under perfect competition. For ease of exposition only, however, we shall follow the common practice of referring to monopoly policy rather than to the more cumbersome 'policy where competition is less than perfect'.

MONOPOLY OUTPUT AND GOVERNMENT POLICY

We now consider three policies that government can use to deal with the allocative inefficiency that arises when competition is imperfect: (1) policies using the price mechanism, (2) policies improving the price mechanism, and (3) extra-market policies.

Policies Using the Price Mechanism

The first set of policies retains the market system. Such policies aim to change the price signals faced by buyers and/or sellers, so that output departs less from the optimal. For example, we consider how the profit-maximizing monopolist might be induced to produce output q_c rather than q_m in Figure 19.1.

Since profit maximization occurs where $MC = MR$, the two main ways of achieving this result are to shift either the MC or the MR curve. We illustrate how this might be done, working through the price system.

Price control and monopoly output

One way of inducing a monopolist to produce the perfectly competitive output, q_c, would be to impose a maximum price at which the product could be sold. In Figure 19.1 we assume that the government rules that the maximum price that may be charged for the drug Balium is p_c. The effect of such a rule would be to change the demand curve facing the firm, for all outputs below q_c. If the firm cannot charge more than p_c for any quantity that it puts on the market, its demand curve becomes perfectly elastic at that price, for all quantities at which the firm would otherwise charge higher prices. For quantities of Balium, for which the firm would, in any case, charge prices below the legal maximum, the demand curve is unchanged. The new demand curve facing the monopolist, therefore, is shown by the dashed line in Figure 19.1, running from p_c to x and then following the original demand curve below and to the right of x. Note also that, since the demand or average revenue curve is horizontal up to output q_c, the marginal revenue curve is now the same as the demand curve up to that point.

Recall that, on a perfectly elastic demand curve, average revenue and marginal revenue are equal. It follows that the profit-maximizing output of the monopolist shifts to q_c, because this is now the output that equates cost with the new marginal revenue. The common sense of this result is that the monopolist restricts output below q_c in order to force up the market price of his product. If the market price cannot rise, there is no sense in restricting output.

Problems with this Policy: Problems involved in carrying out such a policy make it a less simple solution to allocative efficiency than it might superficially appear to be. To apply the policy the state needs to know the cost and demand curves for Balium. Without such information, the price ceiling needed to call forth optimum output cannot be calculated. If, through ignorance, the maximum price is set at a level other than p_c there could still be an improvement in resource allocation, so long as the firm produced more than q_m. This is not a necessary result, however. (Can you suggest a maximum price

which would result in an even less efficient output than that of a profit-maximizing monopoly? The answer is any price ceiling lower than the marginal cost of production at q_m output, because that would induce the monopolist to produce less than q_m.)

Moreover, the state's demand and cost information needs to be kept up to date, so that the price ceiling can be changed as circumstances change. For example, if either demand or costs increase, the controlled price should be raised. In practice, political and administrative reasons make it difficult for the controlled price to be varied frequently. Thus, the actual price is in danger of getting further and further away from the optimal price as time passes.

In short, the state has to know and establish the competitive equilibrium price – which change every time the conditions of cost and/or demand change. This puts an enormous burden on the government officials who are given the task of calculating and establishing what a competitive market would do automatically.

An output-related subsidy under monopoly

A second method of inducing perfectly competitive output from a profit-maximizing monopolist would be to change its marginal cost curve. This could be done by offering the firm a subsidy *related to the output which it produces*.

In Figure 19.2 we reproduce, once more, the cost and revenue curves for the monopolistic Balium producer. Now suppose that, instead of imposing a

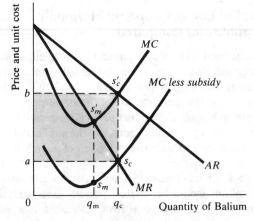

FIGURE 19.2   An Output-Related Subsidy. Monopoly produces optimum output when an output-related subsidy is introduced

price ceiling, the government offers the firm a subsidy *per unit of output*. The subsidy will shift the firm's supply curve in the manner of an output-related tax explained in Chapter 10 (see p. 111), *except* that the marginal cost curve with a subsidy *falls* by the amount of the subsidy (whereas with a tax, the curve *rises* by the amount of the tax). Suppose the amount of the subsidy is shown as the vertical distance between the firm's marginal cost curve and the new marginal cost curve labelled 'MC less subsidy'. In other words, the subsidy is equal to $s_m s_m'$ at output q_m, which is the same as $s_c s_c'$ at output q_c.

The new marginal cost curve has been drawn to intersect the (unchanged) marginal revenue curve at q_c, the optimal output. The monopolist's profit-maximizing output now shifts, from q_m to q_c. At q_c the monopolist incurs a marginal cost of $q_c s_c'$, but receives a subsidy of $s_c s_c'$ per unit, so that its net outgoings on the last unit produced are only $q_c s_c$, which is equal to marginal revenue at that output.

Problems with this Policy: This policy suffers from the two problems that we described in the case of price control in the previous section. The government may not know MR and MC at the time the subsidy is introduced, and MR and/or MC may shift over time.

There is also a third problem that does not occur with the price-control policy. The subsidy has the effect of increasing the monopolist's profits. This may well be regarded as undesirable on grounds of distributive justice – a matter which we discuss in a wider context in Chapter 24. It is relevant here, however, because it may appear to the general public as undesirable, if not noxious, and therefore be ruled out on political grounds. There is, however, a rather neat way of operating a policy of this kind which would avoid redistribution of income in favour of the monopolist. This is to impose a tax on the firm which *is not related to output*, but is equal to the total amount paid in subsidy, which *is* related to output.

The total cost of the subsidy to the government is the subsidy per unit multiplied by the output produced. In Figure 19.2 this is $s_c' s_c$ or the area $a b s_c' s_c$ (shaded in the diagram). If the state introduced legislation allowing Balium to be produced only under licence,[1] it could set a price on the licence at a figure exactly equal to the cost paid out in subsidy.

[1]   An alternative to selling licences is to tax *profits*. So long as firms do not regard a profits tax as affecting their variable costs, output is not affected by the tax.

Policies Improving the Price Mechanism

The second set of policies retain the framework of a market economy, but seek to change the *structure* of markets so as to move them in the direction of perfect competition.

Policies in this category seek to remove the bases of monopoly power. When outlining the theory of monopoly in Chapter 17, we emphasised the importance of barriers to entry to the continuance of monopoly power. If barriers can be removed and competition increased, there is some hope that industry output will move nearer to the perfectly competitive output.

Legal barriers to entry

One of the chief legal barriers to entry is the protection afforded by patent and copyright legislation. Patents can play an important role in stimulating innovative activity by firms. They guarantee freedom from early competition, so that the expectation of temporary monopoly profit, if an innovation is successful, may compensate for the costs and risks of innovating, which may be substantial.

The legal right to exclusive use of inventions in Britain can be traced back to the time of Queen Elizabeth I. Today, patents are still granted, normally for 20 years from the date of application. Although details concerning patents are available to the public, and licences may be granted by the patentor to other firms to produce a patented product, the existence of patent rights can be a powerful protective device for maintaining monopoly power. So, too, can the existence of copyrights, which extend the exclusive right to use of printed material to a period of 50 years after the death of the author.

It is clearly possible for changes to be introduced which reduce the power of patents to act as barriers to entry.

Two methods of doing so would be either to reduce the period of time for which patents were valid, or to force patentors to grant licences to other producers in exchange for a fee. The first alternative would reduce the innovation-stimulating effect of the patent system. It would, however, also run against recent trends, which have been in the direction of lengthening the life of patents. The second alternative would also encounter problems. For example, if the price set for compulsory licensing were left to free negotiations between firms, the monopoly could set so high a price that 'compulsory' licensing would be totally ineffective. A second problem would be to ensure that the information available to firms was sufficient to allow them to identify those patents that were profitable, and which they would like to manufacture, under licence. There is nothing to stop a firm taking out large numbers of patents in order to create a smoke-screen through which it is difficult to discern *the* patent actually being used. (Rank-Xerox were said to have done this in 1979.) Both problems could be, to an extent, overcome by the creation of bodies charged with their solution. The administrative costs of such bodies could well be high enough to exceed the benefits that resulted from their work. Here is an example of our oft-repeated warning that the existence of market shortcomings, even if proven, does not carry the implication that state intervention would necessarily improve efficiency.

Marketing barriers to entry

The principal barrier to entry under this head, to which we drew attention in Chapter 18, results from product differentiation. Where a firm produces a good with real quality differences from those of its competitors, there is little that the government can, or possibly should, do. However, some product differentiation is of a kind that could be described as 'imaginary', in that identical products are marketed under different brand names and consumers are misled into thinking they are choosing among genuinely different products.

Many products maintain distinctive brand images as a result of advertising expenditure by manufacturers. It has long been known that advertising performs two functions. The first is informative – to increase the flow of information, especially about new products on the market. The second function is a *persuasive* one, whereby a manufacturer tries to persuade consumers that its product is better than similar products offered by competing firms. The informatory function is generally regarded as performing a valuable service. Moreover, competitive advertising that seeks to persuade is a part of the competitive process. In so far as it leads to inter-firm competition, there is something to be said for it.

Most advertising is a mixture of the informatory and the persuasive. The case for having some state control, over and above the prohibition of blatantly false information, centres around the persuasive aspect of advertising, and the desirability of protect-

ing the individual from the results of his or her own actions. It is useful to distinguish between the advertising of products which are purchased repeatedly, and those of other, usually expensive goods, which are only bought *occasionally*, at long intervals.

With repeated purchases of commodities like frozen fish fingers, shoe polish or beer, the consumer can learn from experience and is unlikely to be long misled by trade puffs that proclaim, for example, that 'brand X beer is best'. There are, of course, some people who never learn (there is a 'sucker born every minute'), but opinions differ on whether it is the state's duty paternalistically to save such people from themselves.

With occasional purchases of expensive goods, such as cars and washing machines, however, consumers are at a disadvantage because they cannot learn rapidly from experience of repeated bad buys. The case for state intervention is stronger in such cases.

The value of advertising is a subject of debate. It takes a little less than 2 per cent of national resources. No one wants to ban it all; some, however, would try to reduce that part which creates allocative inefficiency. There is, however, no easy and cheap way of doing so.

The control of advertising in the UK takes many forms. Some are designed to improve the quality of information about goods and services, to enable consumers to make appropriate comparisons among claims of competing sellers. One example lies in the field of the cost of credit. Because there are so many ways in which the rate of interest charged for credit may be presented, the law requires the statement of what is called the APR or 'true' rate of interest in every case, so that consumers are not misled into believing that one firm's rate is lower than another's, simply because of the way in which it is calculated.

There are other laws directed at those advertisements which might be 'misleading' as well as those which are fraudulent, though the machinery for enforcing them is not costless. The advertising industry itself also operates its own 'code of conduct'. One of the main sources of improvement in consumer protection lies, we would suggest, in more compulsory information about the merits and demerits of different product brands. This is particularly important in the range of complex consumer goods, such as computers and Hi-Fi equipment, where it is difficult for consumers to know which brand to purchase to meet their special needs. In many countries, comparative testing of products is carried out by governments. In the UK, this function has been carried out, since 1957, by the Consumers' Association, an independent body whose regular reports in the magazine *Which?* have had some effect in reducing barriers to entry arising from product differentiation.

Other barriers to entry

Some entry barriers owe their existence, ironically enough, to the government protecting its own monopoly position by putting obstacles in the way of firms which might compete effectively with it. Examples are common. Many nationalized industries have been given statutory monopolies over the whole or part of the industry in which they operate – e.g. the Post Office, the gas industry, the National Coal Board, to mention a few. Some other barriers are based on locational advantages enjoyed by a single firm. Often the government is, again, directly or indirectly responsible for the protection afforded – for example by giving monopolies to those firms granted licences to operate at motorway service centres.

There may be powerful reasons for the state to grant monopoly status in particular cases. They may, for example, be helpful in pursuing policies of regional development in areas of the country which would otherwise be depressed. (See below, Chapter 24, pp.290–2.) They may, alternatively, be based on social considerations, e.g. to prevent rural communities being disadvantaged. If the Post Office had to compete with private businesses in the collection and delivery of mail in large cities, it would almost certainly have to raise the price of postage for letters to and from remote areas.[1] Or, again, statutory monopolies may be granted in the interests of industrial relations (one of the reasons given by the Sankey Commission – in 1919 – for the nationalization of the coal industry!).

One of the troubles with state-run monopolies is that they may operate inefficiently. Let us illustrate with an example – duty-free shops at airports.

Until recently airports in the UK were operated by a semi-government body, called the British Airports Authority. In each airport, there is a duty-free shop, which is permitted to sell to persons leaving the country, alcohol, tobacco and many other

goods, without tax. The prices of most goods on sale at duty-free shops in Britain have been, by and large, considerably in excess of the prices that would be paid at the most competitive retail outlets in the UK if no duty had to be paid on them. Why should this be so?

The answer is simple. Each duty-free shop enjoys a monopoly position in each airport. Each is protected by a barrier to entry which is the result of a local monopoly awarded to the firm given the sole contract to run the duty-free shop. The policy option available, in this case, for reducing allocative inefficiency, is no more complex than to offer contracts to provide this service to several companies. Provided collusion is prevented, the prices of most duty-free goods would come tumbling down, and allocative efficiency would be increased with the removal of a legal base for the monopoly power.

Entry barriers based on cost advantages

Our final category covers the entry barrier which arises when one firm is so efficient that its costs of production preclude the possibility of competition by other firms.

Consider the firm depicted in Figure 19.3. Its costs of production differ from those of the monopolist producer of Balium in Figures 19.1 and 19.2, in that they fall over the entire range of output for which demand is positive. These falling costs are associated with economies of large-scale production, discussed in Chapter 15.

These cost conditions create a barrier to entry that is not amenable to removal by government action. For, suppose that the state decided to encourage another firm to enter the industry – perhaps by offering a subsidy, to cover the initial capital costs. The result would be that the total cost of production of the two firms would exceed that of the single monopolist, at every level of output for which there is a demand.

To show this, imagine that an output of q_1 units is to be produced, and that we must choose between that output coming from one firm, which produces q_1 units alone, or from two firms of equal size, each of which produces q_0 units. The output q_1 will command a market price of p_1. We see from Figure 19.3 that a single firm's average costs of producing q_1 is c_1, which yields profits when the output is sold for p_1. But when each firm produces q_0, their average costs are each c_0, which is higher than the price at which total output ($2q_0 = q_1$) can be sold.

---

1 There is a viable alternative here. Competition could be allowed in cities and other areas where the market was large enough to sustain it, and mail delivery to remote areas could be subsidized.

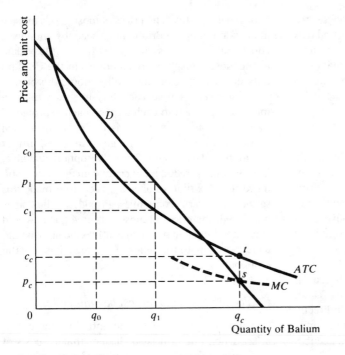

FIGURE **19.3** · **A Natural Monopoly.** Falling average total costs can give rise to a natural monopoly which must earn losses when price is set equal to marginal cost

Extra-market Policies

A single firm can produce the total output at a lower unit cost than can two or more firms sharing that output between them. This is bound to be true whenever an industry enjoys economies of scale over the entire range of output for which there is a demand. Production by a single firm is, therefore, the lowest cost method of production.

Since one large firm can produce cheaper than, and can thus undersell, two smaller firms, natural market forces based on profit-maximizing will lead to the emergence of one large firm. For this reason such an industry is sometimes referred to as a natural monopoly.

There is one important policy that does operate on the demand side. Barriers to international trade often isolate each country's market. When the local markets are too small, one local firm may enjoy a 'natural monopoly' in each country. If international trade barriers were lifted, a single, multi-country market would be created. This market may be large enough to support two or more competing firms. Thus, the removal of restrictions on international trade may be a way of eliminating natural monopolies and creating competition. There are difficulties, however, in implementing such policies, which involve international co-operation. We shall return to consider international economic policy in the next chapter.

Our final set of policies directed towards the reduction of allocative inefficiency under monopoly involves what we have dubbed extra-market policies. The feature which binds such policies together is that they involve partial or total abandonment of reliance on profit-maximizing behaviour by firms and consumers to achieve optimum outputs.

Nationalization

The most common extra-market policy is that of public ownership and control – nationalization. Many arguments have been advanced for state ownership. Not all are concerned with economic efficiency, as we shall see when we return to the subject in Chapter 24. For now, however, we discuss nationalization only as a policy aimed at avoiding of allocative inefficiency.

State ownership gives the government the power to decide on price and output for its industries. What price should be charged? The policy that is often suggested for nationalized industries to ensure that output is optimal, is that they should be instructed to equate marginal cost to price. This policy is known as MARGINAL COST PRICING.

This requirement for state-owned firms to charge a

price that equals marginal cost is based on the idea, with which we are familiar, that optimum output occurs under perfect competition, where price is equal to marginal cost. Turn back to consider again our Balium producer in Figure 19.1. Suppose the industry were nationalized and required to charge a price equal to marginal cost and to satisfy all demand at that price. How much Balium would be produced? The answer is q_c where the marginal cost cuts the demand curve. Only at output q_c can all demand be satisfied at a price equal to marginal cost. At a higher output there would be excess supply when price was set equal to marginal cost, while at a lower output there would be excess demand. We know that output q_c is the optimal output, which would be produced under perfect competition. Hence marginal cost pricing leads, in principle, to optimal resource allocation.

There are many practical problems that must be faced when implementing marginal cost pricing for nationalized industries. We deal here with two of the most important. The first is that of defining the marginal unit, the cost of which is to determine the price charged for all units. To take an extreme example, what is the marginal cost of an additional passenger on the railways? It could lie within a wide range from zero (or very close to it) if there were room on an existing train, to the cost of adding another carriage, or even running a second complete train. There are other less extreme examples to be found in industries such as gas and electricity. The usual approach to problems of this kind is to take some sort of 'average' of the marginal cost of using resources, in order to calculate the price to be charged. In the example of the passenger train, the price charged to all consumers is the cost of running the train divided by the total number of passengers – marginal cost 'averaged', so to speak, over users.

The second problem with implementing marginal cost pricing arises from differences between short- and long-run marginal costs, i.e. from changes in total costs in the short run and those in the long run, when the scale of operations is variable. Once again, the principle to be used is clear. At any point in time, marginal cost should reflect the real opportunity cost of using *existing* resources. Price should, therefore, be based on short-run marginal costs. Only these measure the current real sacrifice of other goods and services given up. Long-run, historical costs are of no relevance to current pricing decisions. This principle is founded in the early discussion we had on the

nature of opportunity cost (in Chapter 2 and developed also in Chapter 15).

The conclusion that price, at any moment of time, should be set to equal short-run marginal cost to ensure the optimum use of existing resources is all very well, but what happens if short-run marginal costs are different from long-run marginal costs? Do not long-run costs enter the decision-making process at all?

The answer is that *they do affect decisions about the size of plant that should be built in the long run*. But *they do not affect the output decision for a plant already in existence*. If, for example, short-run marginal cost is greater than long-run marginal cost, then, setting price equal to short-run marginal cost implies that long-run marginal cost is less than price. If that is the case, the proper procedure for the nationalized industry is to expand capacity – to build a larger plant, for instance. In other words, the fixed costs of new investment, which are part of long-run but not short-run marginal costs, should be taken into account at the moment that the decision to invest is made. But once that investment has been made (if shown to be profitable), no opportunity costs are incurred from the use of capital. Bygones are forever bygones. The price of output should be set equal to short-run marginal cost.

Nationalization and natural monopoly

Marginal cost pricing policies run into special difficulties if the nationalized industry happens to be a natural monopoly. To understand why this is so, consider Figure 19.3 once again.

In that figure, average cost is declining where it cuts the demand curve. This is sufficient to make the industry a natural monopoly because at any output that can be sold for a price that will at least cover costs ($AC \leqslant AR$), average costs are declining.[1]

If the firm were a profit-maximizing monopolist, output would be determined by the intersection of the marginal cost and marginal revenue curves. However, let us assume that the industry is nationalized,

---

1 A natural monopoly need not be one whose long-run costs are falling at its profit-maximizing output. For example, if the profit-maximizing output were at the minimum point on the long-run cost curve (or even somewhat beyond it), there would still not be room for a second firm to produce and sell as cheaply as the first firm. In the text we confine ourselves to the case where the cost curve is falling throughout its relevant range but this, to repeat, is not the only case of natural monopoly.

and is told to follow the marginal cost = price rule, so as to induce optimum output. This is output q_c where the MC curve (only a portion of which is shown) cuts the D curve. Consider the implications of such a directive.

Let us ask two questions about output q_c. First, what is the market-clearing price, i.e. at which price will q_c be sold? The answer is p_c ($= q_c s$). Second what are the average total costs of producing output q_c? The answer is c_c ($= q_c t$). The implications of directing the natural monopoly to produce the optimum output is, then, that price will not cover average costs; the industry will makes losses. This is always the case when average cost is falling, because marginal cost is then always less than average cost. Hence, *falling-cost firms always make losses if they are required to charge a price equal to marginal cost.*

The policy of nationalizing natural monopolies whose optimum output occurs in the range of falling costs suffers, therefore, from a difficulty. The industry will not be able to cover its total costs if directed to follow the marginal cost = price rule, or if it is set a price ceiling, equal to marginal cost. If the industry is to produce the optimal output it will earn subnormal profits, or it may even make losses that will have to be covered by a government grant.

Other policies face other difficulties. That of removing barriers to entry, for example, is ineffective in the natural monopoly case. The barrier here is extensive economies of large-scale production. And, as we saw above, the forced entry of a second firm results only in raising total production costs. (No second firm would voluntarily enter the industry, except in error.) However, if the natural monopoly is the result of barriers to international trade, their removal – effectively expanding the market from one country to the world – makes the natural monopoly much less likely.

There is one obvious course of action that can be taken in such cases. This is for the state to give a subsidy to the industry to cover the difference between total costs and total revenue at optimum output. Two objections may be raised to adopting this solution. The first is relevant if the natural monopoly is privately owned. It is, simply, a politically motivated reluctance on the part of many people to subsidizing private monopolies. This is one reason why such industries are often considered candidates for nationalization – so the taxpayer can feel that they are *publicly* accountable through Parliament, rather than only to their private shareholders.

The second objection to using a policy of a subsidy is the danger that an industry then has less incentive to minimize its costs. This is a question of productive rather than allocative efficiency and is discussed in detail shortly.

If the industry is nationalized, a direct subsidy will be needed only if the gap between revenues and total costs exceeds the opportunity cost of the industry's own capital. If it does not, all that happens is the industry earns a lower than normal return on its capital; if it does exceed this amount, a subsidy will be needed to help the industry meet some of its other costs.

Optimum Output and the 'Second Best'

Before leaving the question of allocative efficiency, we have one important matter still to deal with. To introduce it, let us remind you for one last time of the basis of the argument so far, which is that optimum output occurs when marginal cost is equal to marginal utility. We must now interpose a qualification. The argument is correct if, but only if, such equality obtains throughout the entire economy. It is not valid if there are some sectors where marginal cost differs from marginal utility.

To show this proposition, consider two sectors in an economy, illustrated in Figure 19.4, those producing films and toys. We assume that the film industry is monopolistic and the toy industry operates under conditions of perfect competition. (We also assume, as we have throughout Parts 2 and 3 of this book, that there is full employment.) The profit-maximizing monopolist, if left to itself, will produce q_m films (in the left-hand section of the diagram). Profit-maximizing, perfectly competitive firms produce q_c toys (in the right-hand section of the diagram). We may now ask whether the allocation of resources is efficient.

We should have no difficulty in saying that film production is not optimal. Marginal utility is greater than marginal cost in a monopoly equilibrium. But what about the efficiency of the toy industry? On the face of it, there would appear to be optimum resource allocation. The last toy produced yields exactly as much benefit as it costs to produce.

The superficial answer is, however, not the right one. Even in the toy industry, output is not optimal; instead it is *too large* relative to output in the film industry. To show this is true, imagine that resources are transferred gradually from toy production to film production and observe the effects on consumers.

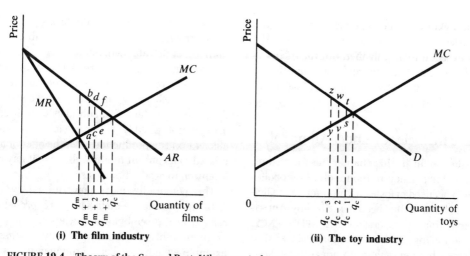

FIGURE 19.4   Theory of the Second Best. When one industry is producing less than optimum output, the optimum outputs for other industries are less than the perfectly competitive outputs

As the output of toys falls, by one unit, and that of films increases, by one unit, the quantities produced change from q_c to q_{c-1} in toys, and from q_m to q_{m+1} in films. Now, look at the relationship between marginal cost and marginal utility in the two industries. In the film industry, the marginal utility of films is still greater than the marginal cost, but the difference is less than it was when q_m films were produced. The excess of marginal utility over marginal cost is shown by the vertical distance *ab*.

Now, look at the toy industry. The reduction of output to q_{c-1} results in an excess of marginal utility over marginal cost measured by the vertical distance *st*. But, *the excess of marginal utility over marginal cost is less in toys that it is in films*. The transfer has improved resource allocation by adding more to utility than to cost – consumers have lost £*st* in toys, but have gained £*ab* in films. Gain and loss refer to net gain over an opportunity cost.

The conclusion to draw from this is that resource allocation is not optimal if price is equal to marginal cost in one industry, *unless the two are also equal in all other industries*. When perfect competition exists throughout the entire economy, or other circumstances ensure the equality of marginal cost and marginal utility in *every* industry, resources are efficiently allocated. This conclusion was first derived in Chapter 9 (see pp. 101–3). But if the condition does not hold in *every* sector of the economy, the best allocation of resources is where marginal cost is *not* equal to marginal utility in *any* sector. More can be gained by the transfer of resources from sectors where

marginal cost is equal to marginal utility, to those where marginal utility is greater than marginal cost. This result is an aspect of what is called the THEORY OF THE SECOND BEST.[1]

Second best theory has wider implications than are discussed in this section, which is restricted to allocative efficiency arising out of monopoly. We shall return to the subject in Chapter 23. Meanwhile, we may observe its impact on government policy aimed at achieving efficiency. It is pervasive. Stated briefly, it means that we need to reinterpret everything that has been said so far about optimum output and the varied ways that it may be achieved. The output guideline of marginal cost equated to marginal utility must be used only for the economy as a whole, or not at all. If marginal utility exceeds marginal cost in one sector (e.g. because of monopoly), then resources will be better allocated if marginal utility is greater than marginal cost in all sectors.

The new guideline is of considerable relevance in an economy such as that of the UK where, for a variety of reasons, there are sectors where marginal cost does not equal price. State intervention to 'correct' monopoly output, and to determine output for its own nationalized industries, should take this into account. Note, however, that this requires the

---

1 The general rule for such transfers (the proof of which is beyond the scope of an introductory text) is that marginal utilities should stand in the same proportion to marginal costs in all sectors.

government to know the demand and cost schedules in all industries. This is a formidable requirement. We should not expect it to be fully met. But the theory of the second best can indicate, at least roughly, the direction that state intervention, on efficiency grounds, should take.

Productive Inefficiency under Monopoly

The discussion so far in this chapter has focused on the allocative inefficiency of monopoly. Monopolies are also often accused of fostering productive inefficiency. Such behaviour has been described by American economist Harvey Lieberstein as X-INEFFICIENCY, by which he means the 'organizational slack' that exists in firms where managers do not strive to keep costs as low as possible.

Profit-maximizing firms, whether under perfect competition or monopoly, must be operating with efficient methods; otherwise their profits could be increased by reducing their costs of producing any given level of output. Hence, such firms use factors of production in the technically best ways available, given the state of technology; they also employ factors of production so that the ratios of the marginal products of the factors that they use, are the same as the ratios of the costs of those factors to the firm.

Monopolists are not, however, necessarily, profit-maximizers. If they are not trying to earn maximum profits, but seeking some goal such as 'satisficing' (see p. 154), they may not be doing everything possible to produce at minimum cost.

The presence of productive inefficiency provides a case for state intervention that is every bit as powerful as the case based upon allocative inefficiency. Indeed, the evidence from the real world suggests that losses due to productive inefficiency may be considerably higher than those due to allocative inefficiency. If true, this implies that consumers could be made considerably better off if the least efficient firms, in every industry, became as efficient as the least-cost firms.

The same forces that lead the management of a privately owned firm *not* to minimize costs, may also operate on the management of publicly owned firms. This case for nationalization requires the added assumption that there will be less productive inefficiency under public ownership than under private ownership. This assumption is widely disputed; indeed many people hold the opposite to be more likely. They believe that the absence of a group of owners

whose incomes depend on the firm's profits, leads to more productive inefficiency under public ownership than under private ownership.

Government policies directed at allocative efficiency may compete with those needed to improve productive efficiency. In particular, we should stress the inappropriateness of subsidies to unit costs. If a firm is not already cost-conscious enough to be efficient on the production side, the offer of a subsidy related to its output might well make it pay even less attention to production costs.

The potentially most powerful policy tools for reducing productive inefficiency are, probably, those related to the removal of barriers to entry and the promotion of competition already discussed. The example we gave earlier, of the way to improve the efficiency of duty-free shops, can illustrate this argument. In so far as monopolistic firms can earn profits easily because they are protected from competition, the incentive to minimize cost may be reduced. Similarly, policies to reduce obstacles to trade between nations, may subject domestically protected industries to foreign competition, and so force them to produce at lower cost. Certain measures taken by the Conservative government under the name of 'privatization' may also be effective in reducing the power of some state-owned industries, for example the partial removal of the Post Office's legal monopoly on the carriage of mail. Other aspects of privatization are discussed more fully in Chapter 23.

Imperfect Competition and State Intervention

The argument in this chapter has been concerned with the allocative and productive efficiency of monopoly compared to that of perfect competition. However, as pointed out in Chapter 18, there are large sectors of the UK economy where firms fall into intermediate categories between perfect competition and monopoly. Firms which are oligopolists, or operate in monopolistically imperfect markets, may also fail to produce efficiently.

Inefficiency is particularly likely to be present when such firms engage in collusion, in order to achieve joint profit-maximization, in the way that we discussed in Chapter 18. All the analysis and policy implications relevant to monopoly are, then, equally applicable to them.

One must be careful, however, not to jump to the conclusion that the presence of oligopoly, or of rising concentration within industry, necessarily calls for state intervention. Competitive forces may sometimes be strong even where there are only a few firms in an industry and where measured concentration (using concentration ratios) is rising. For example, consider an industry where CR3 rises from 60 to 90, indicating that the largest three firms raise their share of total output from 60 to 90 per cent. The original situation might be one where the largest firm in the industry controlled 55 per cent of total output, with the remaining 45 per cent divided among 100 small firms. At the later time, when concentration had risen, the three largest firms in the industry might each control 30 per cent of output. The later period is one when three large oligopolistic firms share the bulk of the market. It could also, however, be when effective competition was far greater than in the previous period which saw one dominant firm. In such circumstances, the case for any state intervention is almost certainly greater when the measured concentration is lower than when it is higher.

A final consideration that arises in imperfectly competitive markets is that large firms, especially if they are controlled by their managers rather than their owners, may be much nearer to being productively and allocatively efficient than are profit-maximizing monopolists. We saw in Chapter 18 that a firm striving to maximize sales, produces an output which is greater than that of a profit-maximizing monopolist (see p. 205). If entry barriers are low, there is reason to suspect that such a firm will also be striving to produce at minimum costs, so that allocative, and productive, efficiency might be much higher than would be suggested by the theory of monopoly.

In summary, oligopoly is an important market structure in today's economy because there are many industries where the minimum efficient scale is simply too large to support a large number of competing firms. In such cases, oligopoly will not, in general, achieve the allocative efficiency of perfect competition. Rivalrous oligopoly, however, may produce more satisfactory allocative results than monopoly. Oligopoly may also be effective in producing very-long-run adaptations that develop both new products and cost-reducing methods of producing old ones.

The defence of oligopoly as a market form is that it may be the best of the available alternatives when minimum efficient scale is large. The challenge to public policy is to keep oligopolists competing and using their competitive energies to improve products and to lower costs rather than merely to erect entry barriers.

THE BRITISH APPROACH TO COMPETITION POLICY

The conclusions that are suggested by the analysis of this chapter as a whole are that there is no simple policy rule to deal with efficiency in real world markets which are not perfectly competitive. The best policy in one case may be the worst policy in another. There is no reason to believe, moreover, that any policy involving state intervention necessarily results in an improvement in economic efficiency, in its widest sense, compared to a policy of *laissez-faire*. Intervention is rarely costless, and many people have political objections to giving more power than is necessary to the state. Totally different solutions to the problem of economic organization have been suggested to avoid both pure *laissez-faire* and complete state control. They include the reorientation of business goals away from profit-maximizing towards 'social responsibility' and workers' control; but it is beyond the scope of this book to discuss their advantages and disadvantages.

Moreover, we should remind you of the argument of Joseph Schumpeter, which we discussed in Chapter 17. Schumpeter saw the drive to enjoy monopoly profits as the main engine of economic growth in industrialized societies. This argument carries the greatest weight when monopoly strongholds are continually under attack, by competing firms seeking to establish new monopoly situations by inventing new products and finding new and cheaper techniques of production.

A pragmatic approach has, therefore, much to commend it. If each case of market imperfection is treated on its merits, one can take all relevant considerations into account. These include:
- whether inefficiency is, at root, productive or allocative and, if both are suspected, which is the more important;
- why the market is imperfect (e.g. are there artificial or natural barriers to entry);
- how strong the monopoly power is;
- what policy tools are available, and how effective they might be;
- what are the economic costs of alternative courses of action, and whether they are politically feasible.

The British approach to what has come to be known as COMPETITION POLICY (and used to be called monopoly policy) has much to commend it from the point of view of flexibility. We shall not describe the details of that policy in this book[1] but confine ourselves to pointing out its three main strands: (1) policy towards single-firm monopolies, (2) policy towards mergers among firms, and (3) policy towards practices engaged in by groups of colluding firms (called 'restrictive practices').

Three government-created agencies operate British competition policy. They are the MONOPOLIES AND MERGERS COMMISSION (MMC), the RESTRICTIVE PRACTICES COURT and the OFFICE OF FAIR TRADING (OFT). The first is charged with making recommendations on single-firm monopolies and mergers. The Court rules on cases of collusion, while the OFT, under its Director General of Fair Trading (DGFT) operates in all three areas. The DGFT plays a key role in deciding, in conjunction with the Secretary of State for Trade, which industries or sectors should be given priorities for investigation.

Single-firm monopolies

The MMC has two tasks to perform whenever it is required to review a single-firm monopoly. The first is to determine whether a monopoly exists. If satisfied on the first point, the MMC is then asked to make a judgement as to whether or not the industry is working against the 'public interest'.

Neither question is easy to answer. The first is directed at the degree of monopoly power held by a firm and the Commission is simply told to consider a firm to be a monopolist if it controls 25 per cent or more of the supply of a product. This apparently simple guideline does not, however, offer an unambiguous test for the existence of monopoly power, because the product has to be defined in each case. Because there are many potential substitutes for most goods and services, it is hard to know where to draw the line to define a particular market, and to identify an industry that supplies that market. For example, is mail-order trade a distinct industry, or is it part of the retail trade as a whole? According to the answer you give to this question, the largest mail-order firm in the UK will, or will not, be a monopoly.

The second question, whether or not an industry

has been operating against the public interest, involves profound difficulties. The Commission is given some guidance on the meaning of the public interest in the legislation. However, guidelines are difficult to formulate, and the discretion available to the MMC allows it great flexibility in making recommendations.

Mergers

The procedure for competition policy on mergers is, basically, similar to that on single-firm monopolies. Merger proposals, where large firms are involved and/or monopoly power is in danger of increasing, can be referred to the MMC for investigation and report. The criteria for deciding whether a merger comes within the scope of the law are either the same market share as for single monopolies or that the gross assets of the merged company would exceed a minimum amount (£30 million since 1984).

The main difference between single monopoly and merger references is that in the former case the MMC's approach has been generally neutral, while in the case of mergers there has been a tendency for the MMC to presume that mergers are *not* against the public interest, unless there is positive evidence to the contrary.

The guidance available to the Commission on mergers is, as with single-firm monopolies, flexible. The distinction we drew in the theory of imperfect competition between mergers of different types is sometimes helpful. Horizontal mergers (the most common type) and vertical mergers suggest, on the face of it, the possibility of increased economies of large-scale production. Conglomerate mergers suggest diversification as a likely objective of the merger.

Merger policy has stopped only a small proportion of mergers that come within the scope of legislation. This is partly because of the inherent difficulty of predicting adverse *future* effects of mergers which have not yet taken place. It is partly due, also, to the presumption, mentioned above, that mergers are not against the public interest unless there is positive evidence to the contrary. This last feature has led to some pressures to reverse the 'onus of proof', which would almost certainly result in the stopping of many more mergers, though some of them would be likely to be 'in the public interest'. The administrative costs of such a reversal could also be high.

---

1 See Harbury and Lipsey, Chapter 6, for a fuller discussion.

Restrictive practices

The third strand of competition policy concerns acts of *collusion by groups of firms* known as CARTELS. The policy approach here differs significantly from that of the other two strands. This is the only area where British policy takes the positive, and general, stand of outlawing certain kinds of collusive behaviour. The chief activities concerned are joint price-fixing agreements (including resale price maintenance, RPM, and agreements to exchange information) among firms, and supportive measures to enforce those prices, e.g. by collective boycott of other firms which do not adhere to the fixed prices. A number of types of behaviour by groups of firms have been specified by the government as 'restrictive practices' which are deemed to be against the public interest, and therefore unlawful, unless it can be shown that there are, on balance, benefits to the public. The Restrictive Practices Court was set up in 1956 to hear cases brought before it, and to consider granting waivers in specific cases. In making its decisions, the Court has been given certain guidelines, similar to, but not identical with, those given to the MMC. The guidance on restrictive practices provides a set of so-called 'gateways' through which a practice may pass to avoid being declared unlawful. In contrast to the effects of merger policy, the restrictive practices strand of competition policy has had a considerable impact. Only a very few collusive agreements have been allowed to continue (one of the most famous of such agreements being that for the price-fixing of books). Indeed, some people have drawn the inference that the merger waves of the 1960s could be traced, in part, to the success of the restrictive practices legislation in outlawing collusion among firms. It remained perfectly legal for a firm, formed by the merger of two or more businesses, to engage in some practices that would not have been allowed by agreement between them when they were separate entities.

It is beyond the scope of this book to make an assessment of British competition policy, and to mention all the other governmental bodies (such as the National Economic Development Council, 'Neddy', the National Enterprise Board, NEB, and the Industrial Reorganization Council, IRC) which have, over the years, played important roles in attempting to raise economic efficiency. You are advised to turn elsewhere to learn about their work.[1] But we hope we have provided you with an analytical framework to help you consider their effectiveness in reducing economic inefficiency.

Government and Industry in Context

We end this chapter with a cautionary word about what it has *not* tried to do. It has not been designed to include all aspects of the relationship between government and industry, but to discuss industrial problems from the viewpoint of economic inefficiency arising out of imperfect competition, including monopoly.

There are more reasons for questioning the workings of a *laissez-faire* market system than that of inefficiency due to market imperfections. We have ignored these because we will make a broader assessment of the market system in the two final chapters in Part 3, when we shall reconsider several issues such as nationalization and privatization, already dealt with from the narrow viewpoint of economic efficiency.

1 See, for example, Harbury and Lipsey, Chapters 2 and 6.

SUMMARY

1 The allocation of resources is said to be efficient when a given output is produced at minimum cost (productive efficiency) and when it is not possible to reallocate production to make any one person better off without at the same time making at least one other person worse off (allocative efficiency).

2 Allocative efficiency is satisfied in perfectly competitive markets by the equality of marginal cost and marginal utility, brought about through market price. It is not satisfied under monopoly or other imperfect markets where firms produce an output that is less than optimal.

3 Government policy towards monopoly can be any of three types: (i) policies using the price mechanism, (ii) policies improving the price

mechanism, and (iii) extra-market policies.

4 A marginal cost pricing policy runs into difficulties in the case of those natural monopolies which have falling average cost at equilibrium output. In this case, marginal cost is less than average cost, so that the industry will not cover its full costs. Either it will make subnormal profits or losses. In the latter case it will require a subsidy.

5 The output targets for individual industries to improve allocative efficiency should take account of what is known as the theory of the second best, which shows that optimum output is only identical to perfectly competitive output if applied to every sector of the economy. If some markets are producing sub-optimal outputs, the optimum output for the others will be less than the perfectly competitive.

6 Productive inefficiency (sometimes called X-inefficiency) occurs when firms are not cost-minimizers, as may happen when they are seeking goals other than profit-maximization. The most effective policies for reducing productive inefficiency are usually related to lowering barriers to entry and promoting competition.

7 Competition policy in practice should seek to remove the sources of both productive and allocative inefficiency while weighing the costs of doing so against the benefits. A high degree of concentration does not necessarily imply economic inefficiency – for example, economies of scale may be lost if firms are broken up, and the drive to enjoy short-run monopoly profits has been observed to act in the past as a stimulus to economic growth and development.

8 UK competition policy has three main strands – towards single-firm monopolies, towards mergers, and towards restrictive practices – some of which seek to weight costs and benefits in a case-by-case approach.

Perfectly Competitive Factor Markets

The focus of this book so far has been on the way in which *markets for goods and services* function. We turn now, in this chapter and the next, to the operation of *markets for factors of production*. This branch of economics is known as the theory of distribution. In this chapter, we study the functioning of factor markets under perfect competition. In the next chapter, we see how these markets work when they are imperfectly competitive or monopolized.

WHO GETS WHAT?[1]

Much of the information available to the public on the distribution of income comes from the income-tax returns made each year to the Inland Revenue. From this data, and other sources, we know that the top 10 per cent of the population receive about a quarter of total income, while the bottom half just over a fifth. The highest income groups are those receiving six-figure and even seven-figure incomes as executives of the major industrial companies and City finance houses, or those with investment incomes derived from the ownership of capital assets to the value of several million pounds. Their incomes are high, but they are few in number. At the same time there are many more people with average incomes, including here skilled and semi-skilled workers in offices and factories and some who are self-employed. There are still more people with below-average incomes, including lower-paid unskilled workers, young persons

and those who have retired, as well as a disproportionate number of females and non-whites.

There is a very wide spread of incomes, as we saw in Chapter 2 (see Figure 2.3). The theory of distribution attempts to explain why incomes differ. It is concerned, too, with whether the distribution of income has been changing, and if so, why. Have the poor been getting poorer and the rich richer, as Karl Marx predicted? Or, are the poor creeping out of poverty as educational opportunities spread, while the rich are becoming relatively less so, as the great nineteenth- and early twentieth-century English economist, Alfred Marshall, hoped they would?

As citizens, we want to know the answers to these and similar questions in order, perhaps, to do something about the distribution of income. If we want to change it or even to say whether or not we approve it, we should recognize that these are normative issues involving personal value judgements. But as economists, if we want to know why incomes are not evenly distributed, or to consider the effects on economic efficiency of trying to change the distribution of income, these are positive issues, which can in principle be settled by evidence.

The Functional and the Size Distribution of Income

At the outset we need to distinguish two interrelated ways of looking at the distribution of income: the functional (or factor) distribution and the size of distribution.

Income takes many forms – such as wages and salaries, rental income from property, interest and profits. When we classify income in this way, we

---

1 For more details of the distribution of income in the UK, see Harbury and Lipsey, Chapters 4 and 6.

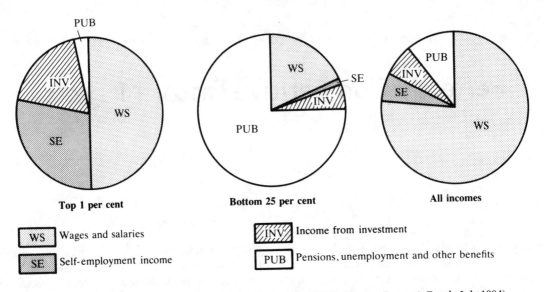

FIGURE 20.1   **Distribution of Pre-Tax Income by Source, 1981/2.** (*Source*: *Economic Trends*, July 1984)

are interested in the FUNCTIONAL (or FACTOR) DISTRIBUTION of income, i.e. in the amounts of income paid to the owners of various factors of production.

People may receive income from their ownership of several different factors of production. For example one man might earn income from such varied sources as his own labour services, the property he owns, and his holdings of shares in several joint-stock companies. When we classify income according to the size of individuals' incomes, irrespective of the sources of that income, we are dealing with the SIZE DISTRIBUTION of income.

The distinction we have just drawn can throw some light on why incomes vary. Some people have higher incomes than others because they have more *sources* of income. We see in Figure 20.1, for example, that about 20 per cent of the income of those in the top 1 per cent of the population came from investments, compared to about 7 per cent for the average person, whose main source of income was wages and salaries. Behind this explanation lies a high degree of inequality in the ownership of income-producing personal wealth. The top 1 per cent of the population currently receive about a quarter of all income from investment.

There are many reasons why the distribution of property is unequal. These include the institution of inheritance, and differences in saving habits among individuals. Although *wealth* distribution explains some of the inequality of *income* in Britain, it is not the

only cause. Within each functional share of the total income, there are also substantial variations. Ian Botham, Boy George and the chairmen of the major industrial and financial companies, receive incomes from their labour services greatly in excess of those of unskilled workers, especially if they are black, female and live in Northern Ireland, for example.

Sometimes it is said that people earn according to their ability. But note that labour incomes are distributed more unequally than any measured index of ability, such as IQ or physical strength. In what sense is Boy George twenty, thirty or more times abler than a promising new pop singer? In what sense is a lorry driver more able than a school teacher, or a football player than a boxer? If answers couched in terms of ability seem superficial, so are answers such as 'It's all luck,' or 'It's just the system.' Can economic theory explain income differences better than the above glib 'explanations'?

MARKET EXPLANATIONS OF INCOME DIFFERENCES

The services of factors of production are bought and sold in the market-place. Wages, salaries, rent, interest and profit are no more than the prices of factors of production. Hence, we would expect the forces of supply and demand for the various factors of production to play at least some part in determining their prices.

To explain the market determination of income, we merely apply to the case of factor services the principles we have learned about the operation of market forces. There are some key distinctive features of labour and other factor markets that we shall encounter later, but we can go quite a long way just using our existing demand and supply techniques.

Note that we should always talk of the prices of *services* of factors of production, not the prices of the factors of production themselves. This is because it is the services that are supplied and demanded. Firms, which actually own factors of production, buy them only for the services that they provide. Incidentally, the buying of a labourer, as opposed to just the buying of his or her services, implies the existence of a slave market! However, solely for convenience, we shall talk of the price of labour and the prices of other factors, when we really mean the prices of their *services*.

Factor Prices in Perfect Markets

The reader should be familiar enough, by now, with the practice of economists of starting to analyse problems with simple models. We make no excuse for doing so again. Our idea is to present a theory, based on extremely unrealistic assumptions, which would explain a world in which all incomes were equal. We shall then be able to see why the inapplicability of at least some of the assumptions helps to explain why incomes differ.

You may recognize our theory as resembling perfect competition. Suppose there is a factor of production, the price of which is determined by market forces. The factor could be land, labour, or capital, but we shall call it labour, and its price wages. We now make the following six assumptions:

- Buyers and sellers are price-takers.
- Labour is a homogeneous factor of production, i.e. there is no difference in ability, or in any other characteristic, between one worker and another.
- Every buyer and seller is fully informed about the price and quality of labour.
- Wages fluctuate so as to equate the demand for labour with its supply.
- There is perfect mobility of labour. This assumption parallels that of freedom of entry and exit of firms under perfect competition. It means that there are no barriers to movement of labour between regions of the country, occupations or industries.
- Finally we have our maximizing assumptions.

Employers seek to use labour in pursuit of profit-maximization. Workers seek to work in industries where wages are highest.

Given these assumptions, market forces will ensure that all workers earn the same wages, regardless of the industries in which they work. To illustrate, suppose there are two industries, employing homogeneous and perfectly mobile labour. Let us call them clothing and textiles. Assume that markets for both clothing and textiles are in equilibrium, and that the level of wage is the same in both industries. Assume, now, that the demand for clothing rises while that for textiles falls. The demand for labour will also rise in the clothing industry, and fall in the textile industry. The new demand conditions will have an immediate, but temporary, effect of raising wages of clothing workers, and of lowering wages of textile workers.

This wage difference cannot, however, persist. Textile workers, aware of the higher earning opportunities in the clothing industry, will pack up and move. This migration from one industry to the other will cause a shortage of textile workers which will raise wage rates in textiles. It will also increase the supply of clothing workers, causing their wage rates to fall. Labour will continue to flow between the two industries until there is no incentive for any workers to move from one to the other. This will be when wage rates are once again the same in clothing and textiles, but now there will be more workers in clothing and fewer in textiles than in the original equilibrium. The transitory difference in wages served the purpose of reallocating workers between the two industries but, in the final equilibrium, wage rates returned to equality.

The ultra simple model outlined above is not, of course, a mirror of the world in which we live. But market forces exercise a powerful influence on the distribution of personal incomes. In this chapter we investigate more closely the working of such market forces under perfect competition. In the next chapter, we shall study some of the forces leading to inequality in income distribution. Meanwhile let us examine, first the demand for, and second the supply of, some factor of production, in order to understand more about the way in which the market price of a factor is determined.

We have seen that we can study the behaviour of the prices of factors of production using a supply-demand framework, as we did with the prices of commodities. To go further we need to examine the determinants of factor supply and demand, distinguishing, as we proceed, any features peculiar to factor markets.

The Demand for a Factor

Firms require land, labour, raw materials, machines and other inputs to produce the goods and services that they sell. The demand for any input depends on there being a demand for the goods that it helps to make. We say that the demand is a DERIVED DEMAND. In other words, factors are demanded, not for themselves; instead, their demand is derived from the demand for the goods which they are capable of producing.

Obvious examples of derived demand abound. The demand for computer programmers is growing as firms turn increasingly to the use of electronic computers in production and for office work. The demand for shipyard workers declines as the ship-building industry declines, and so forth. Typically, one factor is used for making several goods rather than just one. Agricultural land is used in growing many crops; the services of carpenters are used to make many products. Total demand for a factor will be the sum of its derived demands in all of its productive uses.

The marginal product of a factor

In Chapter 15, we showed how a profit-maximizing firm decides how much to employ of the various factors of production available to it. The rule for the cost-minimization was expressed in the form that the last pound spent on each and every factor should yield the same extra output. That rule can be applied to each single factor of production: *A profit-maximizing firm will equate the marginal cost of a factor of production to the marginal revenue derived from using it.*

The principle applies to all profit-maximizing firms in perfect and imperfect goods markets. It is known as the MARGINAL PRODUCTIVITY THEORY. It asserts that a firm maximizes profits by employing units of each variable factor up to the point where the marginal cost of the factor to the firm, equals the addition to the firm's total revenue from the employment of the last unit of that factor. This latter concept is called the MARGINAL REVENUE PRODUCT (MRP) of a factor. It tells how much is added to the firm's total revenue by the use of one more unit of the factor.

So the general rule for deciding how much of a factor to employ is:

$$MC \text{ of factor} = MRP \text{ of factor}$$

If there were any factor for which this did not hold, the firm could increase its profits by varying the employment of that factor. If MC were greater than MRP, the firm should decrease its use of that factor, and vice versa.

Having explained the above rule, which holds in equilibrium for every factor employed by every profit-maximizing firm, our next step is to apply it to firms operating under different market conditions for their product.

Different market structures

In this chapter we are confining our attention to perfectly competitive *factor markets*. We need, however, to consider various types of *goods markets*. This is because the firm's demand for factors will be influenced by the type of market in which it sells its output. To demonstrate this, we show the derivation of the demand for a factor, first by a firm which sells its output in a perfectly competitive market, second by a firm which sells its output in a monopolistic market. Let us start with the perfectly competitive case.

Perfect Competition in the Goods Market: You will recall that firms selling their output in perfectly competitive markets are price-takers facing a perfectly elastic demand curve for their product. Under such circumstances, the demand curve for a factor can be directly derived from the curve of the factor's

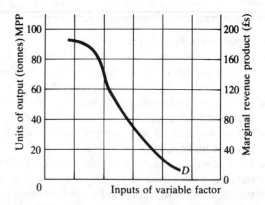

FIGURE 20.2   A Firm's Demand for a Variable Factor of Production. The firm's demand for a variable factor is derived from the marginal product of the factor

marginal product. Figure 20.2 shows *both* the marginal product of a variable factor and the firm's demand curve for labour! We put an exclamation mark after the previous sentence just to emphasize that we have not, by mistake, forgotten to draw one of them. There are, however, two scale markings on the vertical scale axis. The one on the left is marked in units of output in physical terms. This is the one that applies to the curve of marginal product, which is given the full name of MARGINAL PHYSICAL PRODUCT (MPP). This curve is drawn in exactly the same way as was the curve of the marginal product of a variable factor, in Figure 14.1 on page 157 of Chapter 14. You should refer back to the text there if you are in any doubt about it. The scale on the right is MPP multiplied by the price of the product (£2 per tonne in this case). It is thus just a constant multiple of the scale on the left.

Imperfect Competition in the Goods Market: If a firm is not operating in a perfectly competitive market for its product, it is a price-maker, not a price-taker. It faces a downward-sloping demand curve, so that, in order to sell additional units, it has to lower the price of its product. We explained at some length in Chapter 16 that, under these conditions, the marginal revenue from additional sales is less than the price of the product.

This divergence of price from marginal revenue for firms which are price-makers has important implications for the demand curve of such firms for a variable factor of production. This can be seen if we apply, to a simple example, the rule that a firm's demand for a factor is derived from the marginal revenue product of the factor.

Suppose a firm is producing 100 units of output which are sold at a price of £50 each. Total revenue of the firm is £5,000. Now assume that an extra unit of a factor of production is employed, and output increases by 4 to 104. Since the firm is not a price-taker, it must lower the price of its product in order to sell more. Say, the price at which 104 can be sold is £49 per unit.

First consider the VALUE OF (the extra factor's) MARGINAL PRODUCT (VMP). This is the extra 4 units produced multiplied by the £49 at which they are sold. This makes a value of £196.

Next consider the marginal revenue product (*MRP*). Total revenue from the sale of the original 100 units at £50 per unit was £5,000. The total revenue from the sale of the 104, at a price of £49, is £5,096.

The *change* in total revenue from the employment of an extra factor of production is therefore £96. This is the *marginal revenue product* of the extra unit of the factor. It is clearly less than the value of the marginal product of that unit of the factor.

There is no mystery about this. The value of the marginal product is merely the extra output multiplied by the price at which it is sold. This calculation takes no account of the cut in price that is needed to sell the extra output, and which reduces the revenue gained from all of the units that were already being sold. Thus, the contribution of an extra unit of a factor of production to increased revenue is equal to the extra revenue resulting from the sale of the additional amount it adds to output *minus* the loss in revenue resulting from the cut in price on units already being sold. This is simply the change in total revenue resulting from the employment of another unit of the factor of production.

This result holds whenever the firm faces a downward-sloping demand curve, so that more sales mean a lower price on all units sold. Under perfect competition, in contrast, the firm can sell all that it wishes at the going market price. There is no loss of revenue on units already being sold. It follows, therefore, that the value of the marginal product is the net addition to the firm's revenue, i.e. the marginal revenue product.

There are three summary points to this discussion:

(1) All profit-maximizing firms will hire each factor up to the point at which the marginal revenue product is equal to the cost of the factor.

(2) Under perfect competition, the marginal revenue product is equal to the value of the marginal product, so the price of the factor will in equilibrium be equal to the value of the factor's marginal product.

(3) Whenever the firm faces a downward-sloping demand curve for its product, the factor's marginal revenue product will be less than the value of its marginal product.

The industry demand for a factor

When we derived the market demand curve for a commodity in Chapter 4, we merely added horizontally the demand curves of all the individuals in the market. We cannot adopt such a simple procedure in the case of the demand for a factor of production. The reason is as follows.

When the price of a factor of production falls, a firm will use more of it. *But so will all other firms.* The result will be that the output of the product sold by *all* firms in the industry will rise, leading to a fall in the price of a product. This price fall will be reflected in a decline in the marginal revenue product for all firms in the industry. Hence, the industry demand curve cannot be derived by straightforward addition of the demand curves of each of the firms in the industry. It is a more complicated procedure, which we do not include in this book.[1]

Elasticity of demand for a factor of production

We conclude our general discussion of the demand for a factor with four propositions concerning the determinants of the elasticity of demand for a factor of production, i.e. the determinants of the responsiveness of the demand for a factor to changes in that factor's price.

(1) *The elasticity of demand for a factor will be greater the more elastic is the demand for the industry's output.* This follows from the fact that the demand for a factor is derived demand. So if the price of a factor falls, costs of production fall. The supply curve *of the product* shifts to the right. More of the product will be offered for sale at a lower price than before. If the demand for the product is relatively elastic there will be relatively large increases in sales and, hence, a relatively large increase in the demand for the factor of production itself.

(2) *The elasticity of demand for a factor will be greater the easier it is to substitute other factors for the one in question.* How easy this is to do depends on the technological conditions of production. In agriculture, for example, wheat and other crops may be produced by varying combinations of land, labour, machines and fertilizers. A substantial change in the price of one of these factors, relative to another, may, therefore, result in a considerable shift in the use of resources. Production may become more land-intensive, more labour-intensive or more capital-intensive, depending on relative factor price changes.

(3) *The elasticity of demand for a factor of production will be greater the longer the time-period allowed.* This is merely an extension of the very general conclusions we drew in Chapter 7 about elasticity of both supply and demand in the goods market. All we are saying here is that, the elasticity of demand for a factor will be greater the longer the time-period allowed for

demand to respond to a given change in the factor's price. The longer the time allowed, the easier substitution becomes among factors.

(4) *The elasticity of demand for a factor of production will be smaller the less the proportion of total cost accounted for by that factor.* The reason why this is so is not difficult to appreciate. When the price of a factor of production falls, for example, this lowers the marginal costs of production and shifts the supply curve to the right. With any given demand curve, the rise in output that follows depends on how large or small is the shift of the supply curve.

Consider, for example, the use of two factors of production, where expenditure on factor A accounts for 2 per cent of the total costs of production, while expenditure on factor B accounts for 50 per cent of total costs. Now, suppose there is a 1 per cent fall in the price of each factor. The fall in the price of factor A will shift the supply curve much less than the fall in the price of factor B. Therefore output, and hence the derived demand for the factor, will increase less when factor A's price falls, than when factor B's does. We may conclude that the elasticity of demand for a factor is smaller the less the proportion of total costs accounted for by that factor.

The Supply of a Factor

Note, first, that there are sometimes different determinants of supply of a factor at the local and at the national levels. Just as in the case of demand, where we distinguished between the firm and industry demand, so we should differentiate supply according to the level at which we wish to study it. In particular we distinguish: (i) *total* supply of a factor, (ii) supply of a factor *for a particular* use, and (iii) supply of an *individual unit of a factor.*

Total supply of a factor

When we talk of the total supply of a factor, such as land or labour, we mean the total quantity that is offered for sale at different prices, throughout the entire economy. At first glance, it may seem plausible to assume that the total supply of most factors is fixed. After all, there is only so much land in the country and, indeed, in the world as a whole. There is an upper limit to the number of workers. There is only so much coal, oil, copper and iron ore in the earth. These considerations certainly put absolute maxima upon the supplies of each factor. But, in virtually every

---

1 For details see IPE.

case, current use is not near the upper limits, and the determinants of the total *effective* supply of land, labour, natural resources or capital need to be considered.

Take land, for example. If by 'land' we mean the total area of dry land, then its supply is pretty well fixed. However high the price of land may rise, no more than a marginal increase can be obtained by reclamation of land from swamp or sea. The traditional assumption in economics has, therefore, been that the total supply of land is perfectly inelastic. However, if by 'land' we understand all the *fertile* land available for cultivation, then the supply of land is subject to large fluctuations. There is no doubt that a high return to land provides incentives for irrigation, drainage and fertilization schemes, that can greatly increase the total supply offered on the market. When, in contrast, the return to land is low, the *care and effort* needed to sustain its productive power is not always forthcoming, leading to a loss of fertility and a reduction in supply.

Labour supply offers a different illustration of the same point. In so far as the size of the workforce depends on the numbers of adults in the population, this, too, is fixed for longish periods. However, the total number of persons offering to work, the effective supply, or the labour force, is also variable with respect to the price of labour. ACTIVITY RATES (or PARTICIPATION RATES) are defined as the proportions of the total number of persons, in various groups, seeking employment. These proportions certainly vary with the level of wages and other factors, as is illustrated by the doubling of the activity rates for UK married women since 1950.

Supply of a factor for a particular use

Most factors have alternative uses. It would, therefore, still be necessary to allocate them among competing uses, even if they were absolutely fixed in total supply. A given amount of land, for example, can be used to grow a variety of crops; it can be subdivided for a housing development, given over to parkland, factory or airport construction, etc. A mechanic from Coventry can work in any one of a very large number of garages in almost any part of the country, and in many different industries which run their own transport.

It follows that the supply of factors of production to any particular use is likely to be more elastic than the total supply of that factor. Moreover, when we use the term 'particular use', we should think of it in a broad sense to refer to the supply to a particular firm, to a particular occupation, to a particular industry, or to a particular region in the country. The extent to which a factor responds to differences in the prices paid for its services in various uses is termed its FACTOR MOBILITY. If a factor is highly mobile, in the sense that owners will quickly shift from use A to use B in response to a small change in relative factor prices, then the supply will be relatively elastic. If, in contrast, factor owners are 'locked-in' to some use or other, and so do not respond quickly, the supply of the factor to a particular use will be relatively inelastic.

Mobility among factors of production is very much a question of the circumstances of time and place, and the specific factor under consideration. One of the few generalizations that can be made about factor mobility is that it is normally greater the longer the time allowed for movement to take place.

It is important to appreciate that the extent to which factor prices vary generally reflects the degree of factor mobility. If factors move easily and speedily in response to price differences, those differences will not last long. If factor mobility is low, factor price disparities will persist. Thus wage differences offered by different firms, for workers with a particular skill, will usually stimulate workers to move from firms offering low wages to firms offering high wages. The mobility of one type of labour among jobs tends, therefore, to reduce wage differences. In contrast, wage differences among different occupations tend to persist because the need for training to acquire new skills makes labour mobility relatively low.

Considerable interest attaches to the issue of the degree of factor mobility in the markets for labour, because of the implications this carries for the distribution of personal incomes arising from wage differences. We discuss labour mobility in the next chapter, where we consider further distinctive features of the supply and demand for labour.

The factor of land, although the least mobile factor of production *in a physical sense*, is highly mobile *in an economic sense*, i.e. it can be switched among uses. For example, land used for dwellings can be turned into motorways, or office space, as existing buildings come to the end of their lives, if not before. Agricultural land is highly mobile among competing uses. A farmer can easily switch his crops from one harvest time to another in response to changes in the relative prices of cauliflowers, wheat and other crops. The land can also be sold for urban development.

Individual supply of a factor

Finally, we consider the response of the individual owner of a productive factor to the price offered for its services. This analysis is in terms of labour, but could equally well apply to the supply of other factors.

The response that individual workers make to a change in the wage rate depends on the alternative uses of time that are available to them. This idea is, of course, none other than our old friend, opportunity cost. The opportunity cost of an hour's work is the leisure that is given up by working. Hence the supply of work, sometimes called THE SUPPLY OF EFFORT, is dependent on each individual's desire for leisure.

We can even put a price on leisure time. It is the cost to the individual of not working. The higher the available wage rate, the higher the cost of leisure, because more potential income has to be given up for idling away an extra hour. Consequently, a change in the wage rate implies a change in the price of leisure in terms of earnings given up. We can view the effects of a change in the wage rate *either* on the demand for leisure, *or* on the supply of effort. The one is simply the reverse of the other.

Let us imagine that there is a rise in the wage rate offered to a worker whom we shall call Mary, who is paid by the hour and can choose how many hours to work. How will Mary respond? The answer depends on the relative importance of two other 'old friends' – the income and substitution effects of a price change.

The substitution effect of a rise in the wage rate is the response to a change in the relative price of leisure. Work is now better rewarded. So leisure becomes more expensive. *Mary will therefore tend to supply more hours worked as a result of the substitution effect alone.*

Consider, however, the income effect of the rise in the wage rate. This is the change in hours worked that follows a rise in real income. The rise in real income comes about in the following way. When the price of labour rises while the prices of goods and services are unchanged, the real purchasing power of income received for every hour worked increases. Mary can now afford to buy all the goods she bought before, while working fewer hours, and so taking more leisure time. As long as leisure is a normal good (i.e. as long as people wish to have more of it as their income rises), *the income effect tends to work in the opposite direction to the substitution effect. A rise in the wage rate leads the worker to supply less hours' work as a result of the income effect alone.*

Say Mary is working 40 hours a week at £3 an hour. She earns £120 a week. Say her wage goes up to £4. She could still work 40 hours and earn £160. She could, however, elect to work only, say, 38 hours. She now gets an income of £152 and 2 more hours' leisure. In this case the income effect has predominated. On the other hand she might elect to take less leisure, since every hour of leisure now 'costs' her £4 compared to only £3 previously. If she works 42 hours she gets £168. In this case the substitution effect has predominated.

The total effect of a change in the price of the factor, labour, is the result of both the income and the substitution effects. Since they work in opposite directions, there is no presumption that either will be dominant. Standard economic theory, therefore, tells that workers may work longer, shorter or the same number of hours following a change in their wage rate.

Backward-sloping supply curves

It is useful to describe the appearance of the supply curve of a factor of production where either the income or the substitution effect predominates. In Figure 20.3 we show what is called a 'backward-sloping' supply curve of labour. The explanation of this somewhat unusual-looking curve is as follows.

In Figure 20.3 as the wage rate rises the number of hours worked increases up to a certain point h_1. Thus, at w_0 wage rate, h_0 hours are worked. At a higher wage rate w_1, hours worked increase to h_1. Thereafter, wage-rate increases lead to reductions in the

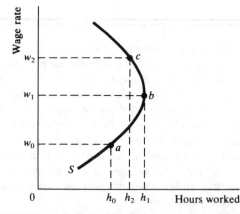

FIGURE 20.3   A Backward-sloping Supply Curve. Hours worked increase as the wage rate increases up to a point, after which they decrease

hours worked – e.g. at w_2 only h_2 hours are worked. We can explain the shape of the curve in terms of whether the income or the substitution effect predominates.

At a very low wage rate, the substitution effect is dominant. Consider, for example, a rise in the wage rate from w_0 to w_1. We see in Figure 20.3 that Mary works more hours, h_1 instead of h_0. Mary's income, which is represented on the figure as the *area*, hours worked multiplied by the hourly wage rate, rises from $0w_0ah_0$ to $0w_1bh_1$. At wage rates greater than w_1, however, the income effect dominates. A further rise in the wage rate, to w_2, lowers Mary's hours worked to h_2 as she takes more leisure. Mary's income continues to rise, however. This time it goes from $0w_1bh_1$ to $0w_2ch_2$.

Income and substitution effects

The relative sizes of the income and substitution effects of a change in wage rates can be shown using indifference curve analysis. The presentation is analogous to the description of these effects on the demand for a commodity given in Chapter 12. On the face of it, it may sound very different. It is less so than it might appear, because we can tell the supply of effort when we know the demand for leisure. Hence, we are looking at the income and substitution effects on the demand for leisure instead of on the demand for a good.

In Figure 20.4, we let Mary vary her hours devoted to work and leisure. Each day she has 24 hours to spend earning income or taking leisure. The rate at which she earns is given by the slope of the line AB. If Mary did no work, income would be zero and she would take OA (i.e. 24 hours) leisure time. If she worked 24 hours, OB income would be earned. Of course, no one can work 24 hours a day and most people divide their time between working and taking leisure.

How many hours will Mary choose to work? In order to answer that question, we must know Mary's indifference map. Each of the indifference curves in Figure 20.5 shows all combinations of income and leisure which yield the same total satisfaction. The *slope* of the indifference curve at any point tells us the marginal rate of substitution of leisure for income, i.e. the amount of extra income that just compensates for one less unit of leisure time (and vice versa).

Under the circumstances depicted in the diagram, Mary will maximize her satisfaction by selecting the best combination of income and leisure available. This will be where she reaches the highest possible indifference curve. Here, it is at point d, where indifference curve I_0 is tangent to the line AB. How does Mary get there? Well, she starts with 24 hours of time, at point A. She moves up the budget line, giving up leisure for income, until she reaches point d. She is then left with Oh leisure hours and she earns her income in return for hA hours of work.

A change in the wage rate

Consider, now, the effects of a change in the wage rate. Suppose it rises in Figure 20.5, so that OF, rather than OB, income can be earned in a full 24-hour day. The higher wage rate is reflected in the fact that the slope of AF is steeper than that of AB. Does Mary work more or less hours? The answer is exactly the same number, *because of the way in which we drew the diagram*. We can tell this by the new point of equilibrium, e, which is where the new price line AF is tangent to the higher indifference curve, I_1. Point e is directly above point d. Mary works the same number of hours and takes the same amount of leisure. But she now earns a higher income, he instead of hd.

The technique we use to separate, and quantify, the income and substitution effects of a change in the wage rate, is the same as that used for the same purpose for analysing the effects of a change in the price of a good or service. You might find it helpful to reread pp. 140–1 in Chapter 12, before proceeding.

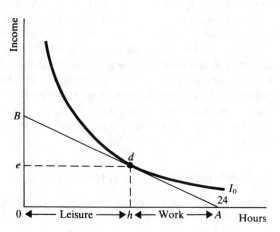

FIGURE 20.4   Hours Worked and Leisure Taken at a Given Wage Rate. The individual maximizes satisfaction by choosing the combination of work and leisure represented by the point of tangency between the budget line and an indifference curve

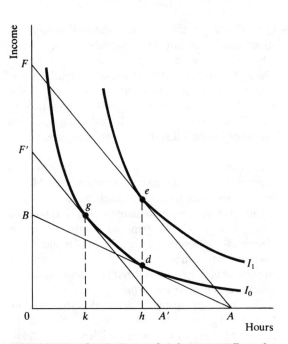

FIGURE 20.5 The Income and Substitution Effect of a Change in Wage Rates. A rise in the wage rate having no effect on hours worked because the income and substitution effects exactly offset each other

To find the substitution effect of the rise in the wage rate, we hold real income constant on I_0, and draw $A'F'$ parallel to the new budget line AF, and tangent to the indifference curve I_0, at point g. This point shows Mary's equilibrium if she faced the new higher wage rate (given by the slope of $A'F'$ and AF), but her real income were held at the level of I_0. In other words it shows the effect of the higher relative price of leisure, in terms of work which yields income. The substitution effect of the change in the wage rate is, therefore, found by examining the difference in hours' work (or leisure taken) at points d and g. We can see from the diagram that, as a result of *the substitution effect* alone, Mary works more hours and takes less leisure. Her hours worked rise from Ah to Ak, and her leisure falls, from $0h$ to $0k$. Thus the substitution effect of the wage rate rise is *plus kh* work.

Since we know the full effect of the change in the wage rate is the sum of the income and substitution effects, we can deduce the income effect immediately, as being the same size, but opposite in direction to, the substitution effect. This is because we know that at the new equilibrium, Mary is at point e, working the same number of hours and taking the same amount of leisure as before the change in the wage rate. Since

the substitution effect was shown to be *plus kh* hours' work (and therefore minus *kh* hours' leisure), the *income effect* must be minus *kh* hours' work (and plus *kh* hours' leisure). This result can be obtained directly, by observing Mary's behaviour as she moves from g to e, which is the pure income effect, because at e Mary has a higher real income (on I_1 instead of I_0), but there is no change in the wage rate (AF and $A'F'$ are parallel).

In the example we have been using, the income and substitution effects cancelled each other out ($-kh$ and $+kh$ respectively). *This is only because of the way we drew the diagram.* If we had wanted to show the substitution effect as being the stronger influence, we would have drawn I_1 tangent to AF at a point to the left of e. This would have meant that the rise in the wage rate increased the number of hours worked; i.e. it would indicate the upward-sloping part of the supply curve in Figure 20.3. Conversely, had we wanted to show the income effect as being the stronger, we would have drawn I_1 tangent to AF at a point to the right of e. This would have meant the rise in the wage rate reduced the hours worked; i.e. it would indicate the backward-sloping portion of the supply curve in Figure 20.3. But, as we stated earlier, there is no presumption from economic theory that either effect is dominant. There is evidence in support of both portions of the supply curve, affecting various groups of people at various times.

Notice two interesting applications of this analysis. First, raising people's wage rates will not always make them work more. They may elect instead to earn more income, and to take more leisure as well. Second, lowering the rate of personal income tax may not be an effective incentive for more work. A fall in the tax rate means a rise in the after-tax wage. Again, people may elect to take some of their extra earning potential in after-tax income, and some in more leisure (as, for example, when the after-tax wage rate rises by 10 per cent and they work 5 per cent fewer hours).

Equilibrium in Perfect Factor Markets

It may be useful at this point to consider what has been said about equilibrium in perfectly competitive factor markets, in the light of what was said about equilibrium in goods markets earlier in the book.

Consider Figure 20.6, which shows the supply and demand for a variable factor of production. The operation of market forces is broadly similar, in this

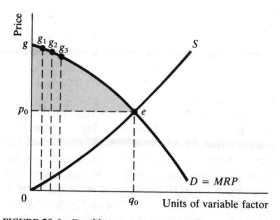

FIGURE 20.6 Equilibrium in a Perfectly Competitive Factor Market. An area below the equilibrium price is the earning of the factor; the shaded area above the price is the remaining revenue

case, to that in the market for goods. But recall that the demand curve for a factor is *derived* and should be interpreted as the curve of of the MRP of the factor (whether or not there is perfect competition in the *goods* market). The supply curve must be interpreted as the units of factor services offered for sale at different prices. Equilibrium market price is p_0 and equilibrium quantity is q_0. Sellers maximize profits at this price-quantity combination; buyers maximize satisfaction. Total factor earnings are equal to the area Op_0eq_0 (quantity of factor used times its price). The shaded area, p_0ge, represents the revenue remaining to the firm to pay for all other inputs, including profit. This, perhaps, needs a word of explanation.

The total revenue of a firm can be viewed as the sum of revenues it receives from selling each and every unit of output – i.e. the sum of all its marginal revenues. Equally, the total revenue from employing additional units of variable factor can be viewed as the revenue it receives from the employment of each and every unit of factor employed – i.e. the sum of all its marginal revenue products.

We can see how much the total revenue is from employing a given amount of the variable factor, in the diagram. To see this, let us mark out units of that variable factor on the horizontal axis of the graph. If we do, we can describe the total revenue from, say, 3 units of the factor as $g_1+g_2+g_3$ in Figure 20.6. Extending this approximation to the general case, we can find the total revenue from employing any number of units of a variable factor, as the *area under the demand curve for the factor*. Thus, in the present

case, when q_0 units are employed, total revenue is given by the area $0geq_0$. However, as we have already explained, $0p_0eq_0$ is the total paid to the variable factor. Therefore, the remainder, p_0ge, is the amount available for all other payments.

All the conclusions we reached in Part II of this book, on price determination in the market for goods, can be applied to the factor market. We strongly recommend you to refer back, at least to the summary pages of Chapters 8 and 9, to refresh your attention to the difference between movements along, and shifts of, the supply and demand curves. In the context of factor markets, the same principle remains as valid as in goods markets. If any change occurs in anything other than the price of a factor, then either the demand curve or the supply curve shifts. If price itself changes, this represents a movement along the relevant supply or demand curve. For example, an increase in labour productivity following training would shift the MRP, i.e. the demand curve for labour, to the right; immigration of workers from overseas would shift the supply curve of labour also to the right. Similar generalizations may also be made about the responsiveness of demand and supply to price changes, in the short- and long-run factor markets.

ECONOMIC RENT AND TRANSFER EARNINGS

Because of its importance in explaining income differentials, we make a distinction between two components that together comprise the total earnings of a factor of production. A part, called TRANSFER EARNINGS, represents the amount that any unit of a factor must earn in order to prevent it from transferring to another use. Thus, transfer earnings are essentially the opportunity cost of employing a factor in its present use. They are the *minimum* necessary to retain it. The second part of factor earnings is called ECONOMIC RENT. This is the *excess* over transfer earnings that a factor receives.

An example will help to illustrate this important point. Assume a machinist is earning £10 an hour in his present occupation, and could earn £8 in his next best occupation. His total earnings are £10 per hour, his transfer earnings are £8, and the £2 remainder is economic rent.

Let us return to re-examine Figure 20.6, which is reproduced in Figure 20.7 except that a different area

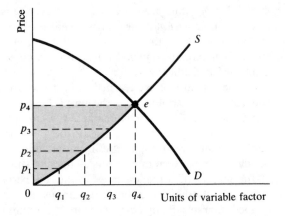

FIGURE 20.7   Economic Rent and Transfer Earnings. Total factor earnings are made up of transfer earnings and economic rent

is shaded. We know that the total income of all the units of the variable factor in Figure 20.7 is the price per unit, of p_4, multiplied by the quantity of q_4, which is the area $0p_4eq_4$. How much of that total is transfer earnings and how much is economic rent? The key to the answer is contained in the supply curve.

As we know, 4 units of the factor are employed in equilibrium. We can see from the supply curve how much each unit *needs to be paid* to attract it into the industry. The first unit required a price of p_1, the second unit a price of p_2, the third unit a price of p_3. Only the fourth and final unit actually needed to be paid the market price of p_4. Hence, we can conclude that the total earnings of the fourth factor unit is wholly transfer earnings, but there is an element of economic rent in the incomes of all the other three units. That element, in the case of the first unit, is the price of p_4 that it received, less its transfer earnings p_1. Thus its economic rent is $p_4 - p_1$. By similar reasoning the economic rents of the second and third units of the factor are $p_4 - p_2$, and $p_4 - p_3$, respectively. If we now assume that there is a smooth supply curve, we can partition the total factor income, of $0p_4eq_4$, into transfer earnings of $0eq_4$ (the area under the supply curve) and economic rent of $0p_4e$ (the area above the supply curve and below the equilibrium price of the factor).

Land and Economic Rent

The concept of economic rent was first developed by the great British economist of the early nineteenth century, David Ricardo. During the Napoleonic Wars both the rent that tenants had to pay landlords for agricultural land and the price of corn (the term used to describe all cereal grains) rose greatly. Were the high rents being paid for land, driving up the price of corn, or was the high price of corn driving up the price of the land?

Ricardo argued for the latter alternative – because corn was expensive, there was keen competition among farmers for land, which in turn bid up the level of farm rents. Thus, so went Ricardo's argument, farm rents were high because the price of corn was high. Ricardo thus rebutted the popular view of the time, that the high price of corn was the consequence of rapacious landlords profiteering from the war. The high rents followed the shortage of land, not vice versa.

Ricardo's argument assumed that land had only one use, the growing of corn, and that the amount of land available was perfectly inelastic. This is illustrated in Figure 20.8 where q_0 amount of land is assumed to be available, regardless of the price of land. Even if the price of land were zero, the same amount, q_0, would be supplied. When D is the demand curve for land, the price is p_0. Total earnings of landlords, $0p_0dq_0$, would consist of economic rent, because nothing was needed to be paid in order to attract the land into use. If the price of corn rises, and the derived demand for land rises, say to D', the new price of land, p_1, merely increases economic rent (by p_0p_1cd).

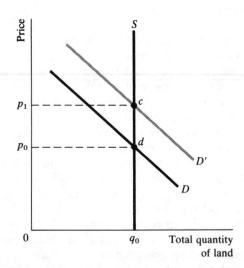

FIGURE 20.8   A Factor Earning Only Economic Rent. All income of a factor in completely inelastic supply consists of economic rent

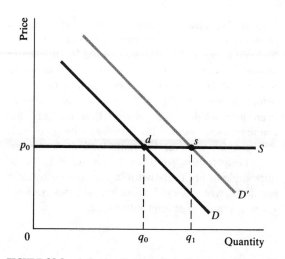

FIGURE 20.9 A Factor Earning Zero Economic Rent. All the income of a factor in perfectly elastic supply consists of transfer earnings

It is important to appreciate that Ricardo's argument cannot be used to explain all superficially similar historical events. It applied only where the supply of land is very inelastic. But as we have emphasized, the amount of land available *for any particular use* is, normally, highly elastic to relative price changes. Consider, for example, the supply of land for growing sugar beet today. There is plenty of land currently used for growing other crops which could be turned over to sugar beet if the price of that product were to rise relatively to other farm products. Indeed, the supply of land for sugar beet is probably close to perfectly elastic, as illustrated in Figure 20.9. A price of p_0 will call forth any quantity of land that is required, because land can easily be switched, from growing other crops, to sugar beet. The entire amount paid for the land by sugar-beet growers consists, therefore, of transfer earnings. An increase in the demand for land for growing sugar beet, shown by the rightward shift in the demand curve from D to D', raises transfer earnings from $0p_0dq_0$ to $0p_0sq_1$, and does not give rise to any economic rents.

The Modern View of Economic Rent

The modern view of economic rent is that it is a form of surplus payment *to any factor of production* over and above the minimum necessary to keep it in its current use. Indeed, we can say that economic rent forms a part of the income of every factor which is *not* in

perfectly elastic supply. The intermediate case is common and was illustrated in Figure 20.7.

Most factors earn some economic rent, at least in the short run. To illustrate, consider labour, in an industry which is experiencing an increase in the demand for its product. More workers are needed and, in so far as it is necessary to pay a higher rate of wages to attract extra workers, *existing* employees will also be paid more. To these existing workers, the rise in wages is an economic rent. They were already in the industry; hence they did not need any further inducement to work there. Of course, the new workers do not receive any economic-rent component in their income. The higher wages represent their transfer earnings, needed to attract them into the industry.

Quasi-rent

We may extend the concept of economic rent to the factor of capital. Many pieces of capital equipment have several uses and do not earn economic rent. The price that is paid for their employment in one particular use is the transfer earnings to keep them from moving to other uses.

Much equipment, however, has only one use. In this case any income that is made from its operation is economic rent. Assume, for example, that when some machine was installed it was expected to earn £5,000 per annum in excess of all its operating costs. If the demand for the product now falls off so that the machine can earn only £2,000 it will still pay to keep it in operation rather than scrap it. Indeed, it will pay to do so as long as it yields any return at all over its operating costs. It has no alternative use to which it can be put. Hence all the return earned by the machine, *once it has been installed*, is economic rent.

Machines, however, wear out eventually. When they do, they will not be replaced, unless they are expected to earn a return over their lifetime sufficient to make them worthwhile investments for their owners. Thus, in the long run (defined as the expected life of a machine) some part of the earnings of a machine are transfer earnings. If they are not earned, a machine will not be replaced when it wears out.

Whether a payment made to a depreciating factor of production, such as a machine, consists of economic rent or of transfer earnings, depends on the time-span under consideration. In the short run, once a machine which has a single use has been installed, all of its earnings are economic rent because no payment is needed to stop the machine from transferring to another use (it has none). In the long run, some (possibly even all) of it is transfer earnings because this amount must be earned or the machine will not be replaced when it wears out. Factor payments which are economic rent in the short run and transfer earnings in the long run are called QUASI-RENTS.

Implications of the existence of economic rents

Transfer earnings serve a function in allocating resources to uses where they are most productive. Economic rent serves no allocative purpose. It is a surplus. The idea of taxing the owners of factors of production which receive *only* economic rent once had great appeal. Such factors would be supplied at any price, so why not tax them? Supply will not be reduced. It lay behind the Development Land Tax before its abolition in 1985. No one has, however, been able to devise a scheme that can tax the economic rents, but not the transfer earnings, of such divergent factors as land, patents, football players and High Court judges. Until this can be done, it will be impossible to tax rents without also taxing transfer earnings, which would affect the allocation of resources among their alternative uses.

SUMMARY

1 The distribution of income has two interrelated aspects: (i) the factor, or functional, distribution, and (ii) the size distribution among persons. People have different incomes because they own different amounts of factors of production which provide them with different sources of income and because market forces set different prices for different factors.

2 In a perfect factor market – where buyers and sellers are maximizers and price-takers, the factor is homogeneous, its price equates demand and supply, and there is perfect information and perfect mobility of labour – the price of any factor will tend to equality in all its uses. The source of factor price differences is to be found in the inapplicability of one or more of these assumptions.

3 The demand for a factor is derived from the demand for the product that the factor produces. A firm will demand factors up to the point at which the marginal revenue from using the factor equals the marginal cost of employing it.

4 The marginal revenue from using a factor is called its marginal revenue product (MRP). Under conditions of perfect competition in the market for the product, the MRP is equal to the marginal physical product of the factor (MPP) multiplied by the price of the product (called the value of the marginal product, or VMP). Under imperfect competition in the goods market, MRP is less than VMP (because marginal revenue is less than price).

5 The elasticity of demand for a factor is greater (i) the greater the elasticity of demand for the industry's output, (ii) the easier it is to substitute the factor for others, (iii) the longer the time-period, and (iv) the greater the proportion of total cost accounted for by the factor.

6 The total supply of a factor is more variable than one might imagine. The proportion of all the land in existence, or of all the people in a country, that is offered in factor markets tends to vary with the prices the factors command.

7 The supply of a factor for a particular use depends on the mobility of that factor among different uses. It also tends to be more elastic than the total supply of the same factor.

8 The supply of an individual's effort depends on the alternative uses of time available to an individual worker. A change in the wage rate will have both an income effect and a substitution effect. These normally work in opposite directions, so that the total effect of change in the wage rate depends on the relative sizes of the two. If the latter predominates, the supply curve is positively sloped. If the former predominates after a certain level of income, the supply curve becomes backward-sloping (i.e. has a negative slope).

9 The total earnings of a factor can comprise two elements: (i) transfer earnings, which must be paid to attract the factor into its present occupation, and (ii) economic rent, defined as the

difference between transfer earnings and total earnings, which serves no allocative purpose.

10 The earnings of a factor in perfectly inelastic and perfectly elastic supply are all economic rent and all transfer earnings respectively. The income of a factor which has an upward-sloping supply curve, comprises part economic rent and part transfer earnings.

11 Factor payments for some items of capital equipment with only a single use, but which must be replaced in the long run, earn quasi-rents. This is the term for a factor payment that is an economic rent in the short run, but a transfer earning in the long run.

Labour and Capital

This is the second of the set of two chapters concerned with the theory of distribution – the study of markets for factors of production. In this chapter we study the causes of differences in personal incomes which stem partly from the fact that personal incomes are not identical to factor incomes, and partly from market imperfections. We shall be concerned, in particular, with the incomes of labour and capital, and shall take account of some important imperfections that were assumed away in Chapter 20:

- Buyers and sellers are not all price-takers. There are monopoly influences on the supply side, which take the form of workers banding together in trade unions to bargain with employers on wages. There are also monopoly influences on the demand side. These are described as *monopsony* influences (the parallel word to monopoly, but meaning a single *buyer*).
- Labour is not a homogeneous factor of production. Workers differ in ability, age, sex, training and other characteristics.
- Knowledge of the market is far from perfect.
- Labour is not perfectly mobile.

LABOUR

In one respect, labour is different from other factors of production. It is human. Although all factors are owned by people, the labour force itself consists of people. An important consequence is that our maximizing assumptions call for rather special interpretations. Workers do not always seek employment in industries which pay the highest wages, but this can still be interpreted as maximizing behaviour. The explanation is that workers care about more than just wages – working conditions for example. So when a worker chooses a job that maximizes the utility that he gets from it, he will not necessarily choose the job that maximizes the wage he will earn.

The Population Base[1]

The size of the labour force, sometimes known as the active or occupied population (or even by the sexist term manpower), depends on the size of the population itself. Nearly two hundred years ago, the Reverend Thomas Malthus, an economist, discussed the determinants of the size of the population in his *Essay on the Principle of Population* (1798). Malthus was living at a time when population growth was accelerating at an unprecedented rate. He took a pessimistic view of the prospects, and forecast that the rate of population growth would slow down as a result of disease, famine, war and other pestilence, unless steps were taken to keep it in check. The reasons for Malthus's gloom were his belief in an ever-widening disparity between the natural rates of growth of population and of the means of subsistence. He held, reasonably enough, that the supply of land in the world was limited, and that the 'law' of diminishing returns operated. As a result, he saw no way in which supplies of foodstuffs could keep pace with the accelerating population growth of the late seventeenth and early eighteenth centuries, which had had its roots in the control of disease and rising birth rates. He therefore advocated 'preventative

---

1 For more detailed information on the structure of the population of the UK, see Harbury and Lipsey, Chapter 4.

checks', especially the postponement of marriage, and the use of birth-control techniques (then in their infancy), to avoid impending disaster.

Malthus's pessimism has not been confirmed for countries in Western Europe, North Africa and other 'advanced' countries, largely because of massive improvements in the application of technology to agriculture, and of a natural fall in fertility rates (due at least partly to the spread of Malthus's own proposal for voluntary family limitation). His message retains substantial applicability today to some less-developed countries, many of which actively seek to discourage large families.

Forecasting future population trends is nowadays regarded as a subject for demographers, rather than for economists. We may note, however, that whoever does the job needs to predict birth rates, death rates and the balance of migratory movements. Birth rates depend on such factors as the typical age of marriage, and the typical number of children per family. Over long periods, these social forces are notoriously changeable. Over short periods, the number of births is easier to predict, since it is heavily dependent on the numbers of women of child-bearing age, which – immigration and emigration aside – is known for twenty or more years in advance, because all such women are alive now. Death rates depend, more than anything else, on the success of medical science. Over the past half century, the expectation of life at birth in Britain has risen from 59 to over 70 years for males, and from 63 to 76 for females. Future improvements in mortality rates will have to come from extending the lives of older people, now that most of us survive for so long. Migration movements are relatively small, because of governmental restrictions on immigration all over the world. At the present time, the UK loses roughly 50,000 persons per annum, *net*, and no reasons for any major departure from this trend are foreseeable today.

The labour force

The UK population in the mid-1980s stood at about 56 million, and the best estimates are for a slight increase as we near the end of the century. Of this total, we need to ask how many should be included in the factor of production called labour?

The size of the labour force expressed as a proportion of the total population, the activity rate, depends on a variety of economic, social and demographic factors. They may be grouped into two categories: (i)

the age distribution of the population, and (ii) the numbers of persons seeking employment.

The Age Distribution of the Population: This is the prime demographic determinant. At the present time, only about 70 per cent of the total population are in the age bracket from which the labour force comes. However, not all in that bracket choose to work, so that the UK labour force is only about 26 million.

The Numbers Seeking Employment: About 10 million people of working age do not enter the labour force for various reasons. The principal one is that many are married women, staying at home to raise families. A second important category comprises young persons continuing full-time education, and there is a small number of others who choose not to seek employment.

The overall activity rate reflects social attitudes, legal requirements and economic incentives, which are liable to change, so that the activity rate changes in consequence. The rate for married women, for example, has more than doubled in the past 30 years, as more and more wives have chosen to return to a job as soon as their children became old enough to attend school. The numbers in full-time education are directly affected by such matters as changes in the minimum school-leaving age, and by the size of funds allocated for tertiary education.

The social factors mentioned in the previous paragraph must be seen within an economic context, rather than in isolation. Many individuals in the DEPENDENT POPULATION (those *not* in the labour force) choose not to seek employment because the alternatives are more attractive. Thus, the incentive to work must be strong enough to encourage participation. Such incentives fall into two classes – the rate of pay and the job opportunities. Both tend to change in the same direction. In prosperous times, wage rates are relatively high and there are ample job opportunities. The reverse is true in times of depression. Economic incentives also affect those outside what is regarded as the 'normal' working age group, as people take early retirement when the economy is in recession, or may be induced to work above the age of 60 or 65 in periods when there are shortages in many occupations.

Characteristics of the labour force

The labour force, or the working population, consists

of individuals who differ from each other in a number of respects which can affect their earnings. The chief differences relate to (i) age, (ii) sex and race, (iii) ability and skill, (iv) attitude to work, and (v) location.

Age: A distinct pattern is to be found in the age-earnings profile for most workers. Earnings rise with age, reach a peak, and then decline. The peak is reached at different ages for different categories of workers. In the manual category, highest weekly earnings appear around the mid-thirties, when presumably physical productivity is greatest. In the top non-manual (professional) category, in contrast, earnings continue to rise until the age of about 60. This can reflect productivity rising with experience in managerial occupations.

Sex and Race: Women and non-whites have always earned less, on average, than white males in the UK and in many other countries. No one is entirely certain why.

One possible explanation of earnings differentials is, of course, to be found in differences in productivity. Women tend to leave the labour force for a time while raising families, and both women and non-whites are often less well trained, all of which can lower their marginal products relative to male white workers.

A further possible explanation is that women, and non-whites, are discriminated against in the labour market. DISCRIMINATION is said to exist when factors with equal productivity receive different rewards for their work. It requires the SEGMENTATION of the labour market into a number of different markets for different types of labour – for men and women, black and white, etc. Economic theory can then be applied to explain differences in wage rates, and levels of employment, in such markets, where equally productive labour is bought and sold.

A special case of segmented labour markets is where the market is divided into two – the so-called DUAL LABOUR MARKET HYPOTHESIS. According to this theory, there are PRIMARY and SECONDARY markets for labour.

The primary market is that for pleasant, well-paid jobs, with a high degree of job security, structured promotion, etc. The secondary market is that for low-paid, irksome work, with little job security. Wage differentials in the primary and secondary labour markets are resistant to market forces, because of institutional barriers to mobility between the two

markets. Since there are high proportions of blacks, women and unskilled workers to be found in secondary markets, and high proportions of whites, men and skilled workers in primary markets, the possibility must be considered that persistent differentials are due to discrimination, coupled with the difficulty for workers in the secondary market to move into the primary one.

Much research has gone into testing the validity of the dual labour market hypothesis, but with inconclusive results. Workers in the primary market are, in general, better educated and trained than those in the secondary market. They are also more likely to be in industries, or occupations, which are supported by strong trade unions. The problem for researchers, therefore, is to decide how much of observed income differences is due to these factors, and how much, if any, is the result of discrimination. Unfortunately, we can take the subject no further in this introductory book.

Ability and Skill: A third characteristic of the labour force which affects earning power, is ability and skill. There is no doubt that both genetically inherited ability, and skill acquired by training, are important determinants of work performance and pay. Assessing the relative importance of each of these is difficult, not to say highly controversial.

Economists have spent much time researching the influence on earnings of extended education and on-the-job training. This aspect lies more firmly within the scope of economic analysis, because people have some choice in the amount of education and training they will undergo, whereas they have no choice (as far as we know!) of their parents. Every individual is faced, in principle, with a decision to seek employment immediately after reaching the minimum school-leaving age, or to acquire additional qualifications through further education. A similar decision continues after starting paid employment – whether to forgo current earnings in the hope of raising future earning power by further training. The process involves the acquisition of what may be called 'human capital' and we discuss it in the second part of this chapter.

Attitudes to Work: We have already explained in the previous chapter that an individual is faced with a choice between earning income by working and taking leisure. Differences in attitudes towards work can explain a significant part of earnings differentials.

Although the opportunity for varying hours worked is not available to all individuals, there remains remarkable choice, in so far as some people can elect to 'moonlight' (to take a second job in their spare time), while others only want to work part-time, earning a minimum for their limited needs, or, in the extreme case, preferring to live on social security.

Attitudes to risk are a second source of income differences arising from distinctive personal attitudes. We are not referring here so much to the higher earnings of people such as steeplejacks and office-block window cleaners, as to the expected *variability* of earnings in different occupations. Some careers are relatively 'safe', carrying limited but relatively secure lifetime income prospects, including pension rights after retirement. Others offer much higher rewards for the really successful, matched by much lower prospects for others. Individuals differ in their preferences for undertaking risks of this kind. They may be said to have different degrees of *risk aversion*, or *risk preference*, and this may affect their earnings. Risk averters tend to seek employment in occupations which offer a high degree of job security, which is often accompanied by relatively low pay. Risk preferrers, who value the *chance* of well above average incomes more than they fear the chance of well below average earnings, tend to go into careers that yield a few high incomes despite the risk of earning low ones – e.g. in self-employment.

A third source of income differences, traceable to distinctive personal attitudes, is to be found in what are termed the NON-MONETARY or NON-PECUNIARY ADVANTAGES of different occupations. These are, as their name implies, advantages of a non-monetary kind, which attach to particular jobs and which make them more or less attractive than other jobs. Such advantages often appeal because they overlap with an individual's leisure interests, e.g. that of dancing instructors or sales assistants in hi-fi music shops, or because they involve work in congenial surroundings, e.g. in the open air. There are also jobs which have NON-PECUNIARY DISADVANTAGES, i.e. where the job is boring or dirty.

Individuals may differ in the extent to which they value the non-monetary advantages of different occupations. Those who place high values on such advantages often earn *monetary* incomes which are lower than those attached to jobs without such non-pecuniary advantages. Market forces tend to equate the *net* advantages, monetary and non-monetary, of different occupations – *ceteris paribus*, of course.

Location: A final characteristic of the labour force which affects earnings is its geographical location. Wage rates and earnings vary regionally to a considerable extent for workers with similar degrees of skill and in similar occupations. Average earnings of adult males in Greater London for example are about 20 per cent above those in Northern Ireland, to take the highest and lowest regional groups.

Were the geographical mobility of labour high, one might expect market forces to reduce, if not entirely remove regional earnings differences. Workers would move from areas where wages were low, to those where they were high. However, geographical mobility is distinctly limited, especially in the short run, more so in the UK than in some other countries. Labour mobility is impeded by two main types of barrier: (i) social and psychological barriers, and (ii) housing availability.

The social and psychological barriers call for little explanation. Most people are not like the nomads of the past, who moved with their tribes. They are, often, naturally reluctant to pack up and leave their family and friends, and take up new life-styles, particularly when they are no longer young.

The geographical distribution of the existing stock of housing is a second major barrier to mobility, and its influence is strengthened by the small amount of housing available for rent in the UK. The total stock of dwellings in the entire country is approximately 20 million, and annual additions to the total are approximately 1 per cent of this figure. The time it takes for houses to be built, severely limits the prospects of housing supplies quickly matching changes in the supply and demand for labour in different locations.

Moreover, the state of the housing market in the UK is far from conducive to labour mobility. There are long-winded rigmaroles of legal and institutional barriers to be overcome in the buying and selling of a house, barriers that are not present in other countries; there is a general shortage of accommodation to rent (largely due to the operation of rent controls); and people who live in council houses face loss of priority when they move, unless they can arrange 'swaps' with existing tenants elsewhere.

The difficulties surrounding geographical migration are not of course insurmountable. During the present century there has been plenty of movement, mainly from Scotland, Wales and the north of England towards the south. It has, however, been very much a long-term response to earnings differentials and job opportunities, and much of it has taken the form of new generations of young people moving away from home at the start of their adult lives, before settling down with their own families. Notice, however, that regional differences in earnings may be reduced without labour mobility, but as a result of firms choosing to locate themselves in low-cost areas of the country. Neither the mobility of labour nor of firms has been sufficient to prevent regional inequalities from developing. As a result, governments have for many years intervened in markets in an attempt to iron out these differences. We discuss these policies in Chapter 24.

Imperfect Labour Markets

Our discussion of factor price determination in the previous chapter was based on the assumption that buyers and sellers were all price-takers. We now drop this assumption and study labour markets where either employers, employees, or both, are able to exert some degree of monopoly power. First, we examine market power on the demand side.

Monopsony

A single firm which is the only buyer of labour in a particular market is known as a MONOPSONIST (from the Greek *mono*, one, and *opsonia*, purchase). In the same way as a monopolist can affect the price of the product that it *sells* by restricting the quantity offered on the market, a monopsonist can affect the price of the labour that it *buys* by restricting the amount that it purchases. (If you need to refresh yourself on the theory of monopoly, refer back to Chapter 17 before you read on.)

As we analyse the behaviour of a profit-maximizing monopsonist in the labour market, you will see how closely it parallels the behaviour of a profit-maximizing monopolist. Consider Figure 21.1, which shows the marginal revenue product curve (MRP) of a monopsonist buyer of labour services and the labour supply curve, S. We know that a firm in a perfectly competitive industry would go on hiring labour until the wage rate was equal to the MRP, i.e. it would employ q_c labour. The equilibrium wage rate would be w_c. At that wage rate the MRP of the factor is equal to the wage rate.

Competitive firms, however, are price-takers. When they wish to employ extra workers, they do not have to offer higher wage rates. A monopsonist is in a different position. If it buys more labour, it has to pay

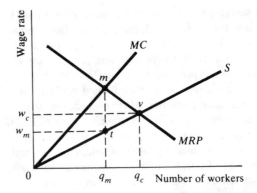

FIGURE 21.1 Monopsony and Monopoly in the Labour Market. The marginal cost to a monopsonist of using labour is greater than the average cost; employment and the wage rate are lower than under competition

a higher wage rate to every worker. If it buys less labour, the wage rate is driven down. It follows that *the marginal cost to a monopsonist employer is greater than the wage rate paid.* For example, if 10 workers are employed at a wage of £20 per day, the total cost is £200. If 11 workers are employed and the wage rate is driven up to £21 per day, the total cost becomes £231. The average cost *per worker* is £21, the wage rate; but the marginal cost to the firm of hiring one more worker is £31 (£231–£200). (The argument is similar to that which explains why marginal revenue is less than average revenue, or price, for a monopolist.)

All this is shown in Figure 21.1. The MC curve lies above the supply curve of the factor. The profit-maximizing monopsonist will equate the marginal cost of labour with its marginal revenue product. In other words, it will go on buying the factor until the last unit purchased increases total cost by as much as it increases total revenue. This is at point m in the figure, which gives an equilibrium quantity q_m. The price paid for q_m units is read off the supply curve. It is w_m. To achieve this equilibrium, the monopsonist offers a wage of w_m which produces a supply of q_m workers, who have an MRP of $q_m m$. The equilibrium price and quantity under monopsony can be compared with that under competition, which would be w_c and q_c. Therefore, monopsony results in a lower level of factor employment, and a lower wage rate, than under competition.

Monopoly trade unions

The counterpart to the monopsony power of employers is the monopoly selling power exercised by workers through trade unions. Early in the history of unions, their organizers perceived that ten or a hundred men acting together had more influence than one acting alone. The union was the organization that would provide a basis for confronting the monopsony power of employers with the collective (i.e. monopoly) power of the workers. But employers did not accept unions passively. Union organizers were sometimes sacked, physically assaulted and even murdered. The 'right' to organize was only effectively won as a result of a number of Acts of Parliament, beginning in the 1820s; after that the trade-union movement grew from strength to strength, though with some membership set-backs in years of depression (including the 1980s).[1]

The successful unions in the early years were of highly skilled specialist workers. There were two reasons for this. First, it was easier to control the supply of skilled workers than of semi- or unskilled workers. Organize the unskilled and the employer could find replacements for them. But the skilled workers – the coopers, bootmakers and shipwrights – were another matter. There were few of them, and they controlled access to their trade by controlling the conditions of apprenticeship. The second main reason was that a union of a small number of highly skilled specialists could attack the employer where he was most likely to give in, and thus would need fewer resources to withstand employer resistance than would unions of the unskilled. It is obviously difficult to find substitutes for highly skilled specialist workers, who also control entry to their trade.

Today, unions are successful over all the industrialized world. They have won the right to bargain with employers over wages and working conditions. Their negotiating power stems from their solidarity and the use of the STRIKE, the concerted refusal of the members of the union to work, backed by PICKETING, when lines of striking workers parade in front of the entrance to the workplace and attempt to dissuade other workers ('blacklegs') from entering. Unions also have political aims. Many are affiliated to the Labour Party; they often co-operate with the government of the day; and they offer educational and social benefits for their members.

Trade unions do many things to benefit their members. We concentrate on two prime objectives –

the levels of wages and employment. What unions accomplish depends partly on the institutional setting within which they operate. Of particular importance, in this connection, is the legal framework controlling wage bargaining, strike and picket actions, etc., which has undergone changes in recent years, restricting, on the whole, union power.

Economic analysis can be applied to union actions to secure wage rate increases and to affect the level of employment in their industry. Often these two aims may be in conflict with each other, with the union facing a choice between raising wage rates and lowering employment.

To analyse the exercise of trade-union power, we need to consider the conditions that operate in the labour market. Two market situations will be distinguished, (i) where employers are perfectly competitive in the market for labour, and (ii) where one employer acts as a monopsonist in the labour market.

Trade Unions versus Competitive Employers: A union enters the competitive labour market as shown in Figure 21.2, where the wage rate, w_c, is determined by the forces of supply and demand, with q_c workers employed. We assume that the union has the power to set the wage rate. This it does, at a rate of w_u, above the market rate of w_c.

The effect of setting this wage rate is to change the supply curve of labour. No worker is allowed to offer his or her services for less than w_u. Firms can hire up to q_m workers at this rate (i.e. the amount that will be voluntarily supplied at this rate). If they wish to employ more than q_m workers, they will have to pay higher rates, as shown by the supply curve of labour, S. The new supply curve to the industry is $w_u fgs$.

Since firms are free to employ as many, or as few, workers as they wish, they will choose to take on the number most profitable to them. As we know, the profit-maximizing level of employment is where the marginal revenue product of labour is equal to the marginal cost of labour. Since the union has set the wage rate at w_u, the employer must pay w_u to all the workers it employs. The supply curve $w_u fgs$ is, therefore, horizontal or perfectly elastic, up to point g, where q_m workers are employed.

The most profitable level of employment for any firm, as we know, is where the MRP is equal to the marginal cost of employing an additional worker. This is found at the intersection of the new supply curve with the curve of MRP at point f, where q_u workers are taken on. This result means that the

1 For more details on the structure of trade unions in the UK, see Harbury and Lipsey, Chapter 4.

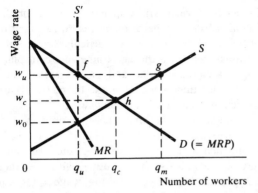

FIGURE 21.2   Wages and Employment Following Trade-union Action. A rise in the wage rate occurs at the cost of a fall in employment whether the wage is negotiated or supply is restricted

union has, indeed, succeeded in raising the wage rate, but only at the cost of reducing the level of employment, from q_c to q_u.

Notice that the number of workers who would offer their services at the union-fixed wage rate of w_u is q_m. Hence, there is an excess supply of $q_u q_m$ workers over the quantity demanded. Some of these workers would be prepared to work for a wage even below w_c, the old pre-union rate. It is clearly to the employers' advantage to hire some of these workers at less than the going rate and, given the chance, they will do so. This implies that the union can only succeed in effectively raising the wage rate if it can strictly enforce the set wage. If not all employees are parties to the collective agreement (i.e. if there are some workers who are prepared to work for less than the union rate), this will be difficult. If the union and employers agree to, and abide by, a rule that only members of the union may be taken on, it is easier to enforce the agreed wage rate. Hence, the importance attached to CLOSED SHOP, agreements which do limit employment to union members. They are widespread from coal mining to acting, but suffer considerable tension when unemployment in the economy as a whole is high, because there are many unemployed who would be willing to work at less than the union rate and many firms who would like to employ them.

Another point to notice is that the union could, in principle, achieve the same result if, instead of fixing the wage rate, it decided to restrict the supply of labour. Suppose in Figure 21.2 the union reaches agreement that only union members will be taken on by employers (i.e. a closed shop agreement), and the

union also restricts membership of the union to q_u workers. The effect will be that only q_u workers can offer themselves for employment. The supply curve to the firm now follows the original supply curve up to the wage w_o at which q_u workers would want employment. At that point the supply becomes perfectly inelastic, $q_u S'$, intersecting the demand curve at f to determine an equilibrium wage of w_u.

The method of restricting the supply of labour by the trade union secures an increase in the wage rate at the cost of a lower level of employment, exactly as does a directly negotiated rise in the wage itself. The only difference is that, when the wage is negotiated, there is excess supply of labour (fg in the figure) while, when supply is restricted, no excess need occur.

So far we merely assumed that the union decided to set wage w_u. But given a choice, what is the best wage for the union to set, assuming that the union wishes to maximize the total return to its members? To find out what wage will do this, we need to know the union's marginal cost and marginal revenue.

The supply curve of labour is the marginal cost curve to the workers. It tells the minimum amount that would induce an extra unit of labour to seek employment, and hence it is the marginal cost of that employment as seen by workers. The employers' demand curve for labour is derived from their marginal revenue product curves. From the point of view of the union, however, this demand curve is the average revenue curve. For any given amount of labour offered, the demand curve tells the wage rate (the average return to labour) that will clear the market. But if one more unit of labour is employed, that drives down the wage of all those already in employment. To find the net gain from increasing employment by one unit, we need the marginal revenue curve, the curve which shows the increase in total wages obtained by employing one more unit of labour taking into account the accompanying fall in the wage rate. This is the curve MR in Figure 21.2.

In that figure the MR curve that we have just derived intersects the marginal cost curve at quantity q_u. When that quantity is offered on a market with many competitive employers, the market-clearing wage will be w_u. Thus, faced with a group of firms hiring labour competitively, the maximizing union would seek to establish the wage w_u and employment q_u. It can do this either by setting that wage rate and letting the employers voluntarily decide to hire q_u workers, or by restricting the supply to q_u and letting the competitive market determine the wage of w_u.

Higher Wages versus Employment: Two conclusions may be drawn from the above analysis. The first is that unions often face a trade-off between wages and employment. They have a choice of going for higher wages or for maximum employment (though they cannot, of course, achieve a level of employment higher than the competitive equilibrium).

The second conclusion is that although the alternative policies of setting wages or controlling the labour supply result in the same total of unemployment, the *actual persons who lose their jobs may well differ.* When the union sets the wage rate, the employers decide whom to employ. When the union restricts the labour supply in order to raise the wage rate, it is the union that decides who will be employed.

Trade Unions versus a Monopsonistic Employer: So far, we have examined cases where competition is imperfect on either the supply or on the demand sides of the labour market. Monopolistic elements can, however, exist side by side in a market for labour, as when a union faces a monopsonistic employer. Such a situation is described as one of bilateral monopoly.

In Figure 21.1, we showed that a monopsonistic employer facing a competitive (i.e. non-unionized) labour supply will pay a lower wage rate and employ fewer workers than do perfectly competitive employers. We now show that the formation of a trade union in such circumstances can lead, rather surprisingly perhaps, to an increase in the wage rate *and* a rise in the level of employment. To see this, return to Figure 21.1, which shows monopsony equilibrium without a trade union.

We have seen that before the union is formed, the monopsonist is faced with a supply curve of labour, S, and a marginal cost curve of labour, MC, which lies above it. Optimum employment for the firm is found where MC equals MRP, q_m workers being employed at a wage rate of w_m. Suppose now that the trade union sets a wage rate of w_c. The supply curve facing the firm now becomes perfectly elastic at the set wage rate, i.e. it is given by $w_c v s$ in Figure 21.1. Moreover, since the supply curve is horizontal until q_c workers are employed, the marginal cost of employing additional workers becomes the same as the average cost (the wage rate). Hence, the monopsonist maximizes profits by employing q_c workers at the wage rate w_c, just as in the competitive case.

So far we have seen that a wage-setting union can raise wages and employment if it enters a market where the wage has previously been set by a monopsonistic buyer. What will happen, however, if a monopolistic union faces a monopsonistic buyer and both seek to determine the wage rate? Economic theory offers no simple answer.

We have seen that the wage-setting monopsonist would seek to establish the wage w_m in Figure 21.1 with employment q_m. We have also seen that the wage-setting union would seek to establish the wage w_u with employment q_u in Figure 21.2. An all-powerful union would obtain wage w_u; an all-powerful employer would obtain wage w_m. If both have some power, the wage will settle somewhere between these limits, being closer to the limit desired by the group with more power. This is as far as simple economic theory can take us.

Bargaining power of trade unions

So many factors come into the picture that generalization about the outcome of union-employer wage bargaining is difficult. All we shall do is to suggest the kind of circumstance which might favour one side or the other. We put our suggestions in the form of circumstances favouring unions, and leave you, the reader, to reverse the arguments to present them from the employers' point of view.

Trade-union bargaining strength will tend to be high under the following circumstances.

- *When there is little scope for substituting other factors of production for labour.* This gives doctors, for example, strong bargaining power, and unskilled labourers little clout.
- *When the demand for the product is relatively inelastic.* If this is the case, a rise in wages, and therefore, in costs of production, depresses the quantity demanded relatively little. For example, this gives electric power workers strength, but shopworkers in a single department store weakness.
- *When labour costs are a small proportion of costs.* If this is the case, a given rise in wages shifts the firm's marginal cost curve only by a small extent. Equilibrium output of the firm is, therefore, only reduced by a small amount, and there is little reduction in the demand for labour.
- *When the union itself is strong.* A union will tend to be stronger, the higher the proportion of workers in the industry that are its members; the greater the support of the membership; the higher the financial resources enabling it to withstand, if necessary, prolonged strike action; and the more a union can

count on the support of other unions in a struggle with employers.

- *When the employer earns substantial profits.* There is obviously little scope for unions to raise wages in industries which are on the margin of profitability. Where employers enjoy high profits, however, the unions' prospects for raising wages are better. This means that both employers and employees may gain if a firm can monopolize the market for its products.

- *When the union offers productivity 'deals'.* Many wage agreements have been satisfactorily reached as a result of unions agreeing to accept productivity improvements which they had previously opposed. In this age of rapidly advancing technology, such productivity changes frequently involve mechanisation and reduction in the industry's workforce. While unions are, understandably, reluctant to agree to the sudden unemployment of their members, they are often realistic enough to accept that they cannot stand for ever opposed to the introduction of new production techniques. Hence agreements on matters of this nature tend to be for a *gradual* phasing-in of new processes.

CAPITAL

To many Marxists, capitalists are villains. To many Conservatives, they are heroes, who steer the economy onwards and upwards to higher living standards. To an economist, capitalists are simply those who own capital, which we defined earlier as man-made aids to further production. If there are capital goods, someone must own them, though that someone may be private individuals or it may be the state.

Our interest in this chapter is not with the ownership of capital, but with its price, as a factor of production. A key characteristic of capital is that it is durable and yields a return over its useful life. This means that it has not one, but two, *prices*, although, as we shall see, they are closely related to each other.

The Two Prices of Capital

The two prices of capital are its *yield* (or rental value) and its *purchase price*. The yield is the price paid for the use of the factor's services for a period of time, say one year. The price at which a capital good is bought and sold, reflects the present value of the entire future flow of services that can be obtained from the good over its lifetime. The distinction is the same as between renting a house (paying, say monthly, for the flow of housing services it gives) and buying the house, thereby acquiring the right to all its future services. For this reason, the current yield on capital is called its *rental value*, while what the capital good will be bought for is called its *purchase price*.

The relationship between the yield and purchase price

Consider a machine that costs £100, if bought today. Suppose, if put to use to produce plastic toy soldiers, it yields a net revenue in a year's time of £110, at which time it reaches the end of its life and has to be scrapped. The yield of the asset may be expressed as a percentage, known also as the RATE OF RETURN ON CAPITAL:

$$\text{yield} = \frac{110}{100} = 10 \text{ per cent.}$$

Now look at the capital asset from a different viewpoint. Let us assume that we know only that it will yield a return of £110, one year from now. That yield must be worth something, even today, because the asset could be sold for cash to someone who wanted £110 next year. Whatever that person was prepared to pay for the asset gives us the PRESENT VALUE of the capital – its purchase price.

The present value of a capital asset, therefore, represents the purchase price that an individual will be prepared to pay to enjoy its yield in the future. Note, too, that this yield is something to be obtained, not now, but in the future. The benefits are postponed. Not unnaturally, therefore, future yields are worth less today than when they accrue. The *present value* of a future yield (even if quite certain) is less than the yield itself.

There is a standard method of finding the present value of a future yield. It involves what is called DISCOUNTING, by which is meant scaling down, by a factor which quantifies the sacrifice involved in postponement. For any individual the value he or she places on such a sacrifice depends on his or her preference for the present over the future, a subject we shall shortly discuss. It will suffice, for the present, to use the market rate of interest, which measures the market valuation of such sacrifices. For example, if the market rate of interest is 10 per cent, I can enjoy

£110 next year by lending out £100 today. I sacrifice £100 today, but get £110 in a year.

Returning to our example of finding the present value of £110 in a year's time, when the rate of interest is 10 per cent, we discount using the formula:

$$\text{present value (PV)} = \frac{\text{yield}}{1+r}$$

where r is the rate of interest expressed as a decimal fraction, rather than a percentage.

As the yield is £110 and r is 10 per cent (0.1), this gives

$$\text{PV} = \frac{110}{1.1} = £100$$

Compound interest[1]

Students of mathematics will recognize the formula at the end of the previous paragraph as that for simple interest. The compound interest formula for a stream of yields over t years is

$$P = \frac{A}{(1+r)^t}$$

where P stands for Principal, A for Amount, r for the Rate of interest expressed as a ratio, and t for the Time, in periods over which compounding takes place. In economic usage, the term P stands for Present Value and A for the Yield, while r and t have the same meanings as in the compound interest formula. Note, too, that the present value (P) is also sometimes called the Discounted Cash Flow (DCF). This word is particularly descriptive, since it conveys the idea that converting future yields to a present value involves discounting, by means of the rate of interest.

The reason why the rate of interest is used to convert future sums into values in the present, is that present amounts of money become greater if invested at the ruling market rate of interest. If, at a rate of interest of 10 per cent, £100 becomes £110 in a year's time, then the present value of £110 a year from now is £100. Or, using the formula to make this calculation:

$$\text{PV} = \frac{100}{(1+0.1)^1}$$

1 This section on compound interest may be omitted without loss of the main argument of the Chapter. For a fuller treatment, see IPE.

The example just given is of the present value of an asset which produces a yield for only a single year. The formula can be used to calculate the present value of an asset lasting any number of years. Suppose, for example, the asset lasts two years and yields £220 next year and £242 the year after. Assuming, still, that the rate of interest is 10 per cent, the yields must be discounted over the different periods, as follows:

$$\text{PV} = \frac{220}{(1+0.1)^1} + \frac{242}{(1+0.1)^2}$$

$$\text{PV} = \frac{220}{1.1} + \frac{242}{1.21}$$

$$\text{PV} = 400.$$

In other words the present value of £220 next year plus £242 the following year is £400.

Notice that the formula can be used to calculate any one of the four variables, P, A, r or t, given the other three – i.e. the present value of £x in t years' time at the rate of interest r per cent; the yield of £x in t years' time if it earns at the rate of r per cent; the rate of interest earned if a sum £x yields £y over t years; and how many years a sum £x will take to yield £y at r rate of interest.

Demand for Capital by a Firm

In what sense is capital productive? Rarely, if ever, do we make consumer goods directly with the aid of such simple tools as nature provides. Productive effort goes, first, into the manufacture of capital – tools, machines and other goods that are desired not in themselves, but only as aids to making other commodities. The capital goods are then used to make consumer goods. The use of capital renders the production process ROUNDABOUT. Instead of making what is wanted directly, producers engage in the indirect process of first making capital goods, which are then used to make consumer goods. The roundaboutness raises efficiency, in the sense that more consumer goods can be produced in future years by making capital goods in the current year.

When capital is productive, its use eventually yields a return over all other costs of production, though it is necessary to wait for this return to accrue.

It is convenient to think of a firm as having a stock of capital, which may be measured in physical units – so many machines, factories, etc. As with any other factor of production, there is an average and a marginal product of capital. The marginal product of capital is the contribution made to total output when the quantity of capital is increased by a single unit, the quantities of all other factors of production being held constant.

Marginal product is, then, a physical measure. We need, however, to obtain a measure of the value of the marginal product in money terms. To do so we value the output at its market price. The MARGINAL EFFICIENCY OF CAPITAL (MEC) gives the monetary return on each extra pound's worth of capital added, and since the amount of other factors are held constant, the *MEC* tends to fall, reflecting the law of diminishing returns, explained in Chapter 14.

A firm's *MEC* curve is shown in Figure 21.3. The horizontal axis measures the value of the firm's capital stock, while the vertical axis measures the money value of the product of capital, expressed in terms of percentage yields on that capital. The *MEC* curve slopes downwards, because of the law of diminishing returns. Thus, we can read from the diagram that the k_1th unit of capital has an *MEC* equal to r_1: the k_2th unit has an *MEC* equal to r_2, and so forth.

We must now explain why we have focused your attention on the *MEC* curve. It is because *the demand for capital by a firm is the marginal efficiency of capital of the firm*. In other words, its *MEC* curve *is* its demand curve for capital. This curve shows the amount of capital that a firm would choose to employ at different costs of employing it.

The reason for this is that the *MEC* curve is, effectively, the marginal revenue product curve for the factor of production, capital. To see why the *MEC*

curve is the firm's demand curve for capital, we need only consider how much capital the firm will demand at different prices, or yields, of capital. Recall, that the cost of capital is the rate of interest that has to be paid by a firm to borrow funds to acquire capital (or, for a firm that has funds of its own, the rate of interest that could be earned by lending them elsewhere).

Consider again Figure 21.3, and suppose the rate of interest (the cost of capital to the firm) is r_1. How much capital will the firm employ? It will certainly employ all capital up to k_1, because the marginal efficiency of capital is greater than its cost of capital to the firm. At the same time, it will not pay the firm to employ, say, k_2 capital because the *MEC* of the k_2th unit of capital is less than the rate of interest. Likewise, it will not be profitable for the firm to employ *any* capital in excess of k_1. Hence the optimum amount of capital for the firm is k_1, when the rate of interest is r_1. In other words, the *equilibrium amount of capital is that where the marginal efficiency of capital is equal the rate of interest*.

The important principle established above may be illustrated in another way. Consider the arithmetic example used on page 246, of a machine making plastic soldiers, which produced a yield of 10 per cent. If the firm faces a rate of interest of 10 per cent or less, it will be profitable to install the machine. If the rate of interest is more than 10 per cent, it will not.

The Supply of Capital

We looked at the demand for capital as a demand by firms to borrow money for the expansion of its capital stock. So, we can view one of the determinants on the supply side of the capital market, as the quantities of

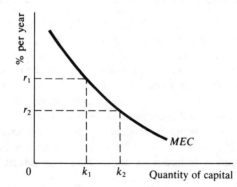

FIGURE 21.3   A Firm's Demand for Capital.   The demand curve for capital by a firm is the marginal efficiency of capital curve, which is negatively sloped

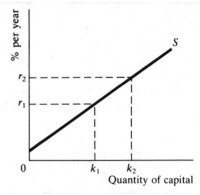

FIGURE 21.4   The Supply of Loanable Funds. The supply of loanable funds is greater at high rates of interest than at low rates

funds that are available for borrowing. This enables us to draw a supply curve in Figure 21.4.

In order to understand why anybody should offer any funds for lending, let us recall the discussion of the reason for discounting. The reason we gave for scaling down benefits to be received in the future in order to put a value on them in the present, was that people prefer a given sum of money to enjoy now, to the *same sum* tomorrow, or next year. By lending funds, people postpone their enjoyment; they sacrifice today's enjoyment for enjoyment in the future, when they are repaid.

It follows from the argument of the previous paragraph, that people can only be expected to lend a given amount now if they are repaid more than the sum lent later on. The precise extra amount that is needed to induce people to lend depends on what is known as their RATE OF TIME PREFERENCE, defined as the rate at which future goods are valued in terms of present goods. An example will help to make this clear. If someone values, say, £100 given up today, as being worth £110 at the end of the year, that person's marginal rate of time preference is 10 per cent. If the rate of interest that can be earned in the market is over 10 per cent, that person will be prepared to lend.

Thus, the supply of funds for lending will depend on the rate of interest (though it will also depend on some other important variables). What is more, the amount of funds offered for lending can be expected, *ceteris paribus*, to be greater the higher the rate of interest. The supply curve in Figure 21.4 is for this reason upward-sloping. At a rate of interest of r_1, k_1 funds are offered for lending. If the rate of interest is higher, at r_2, the supply of funds is k_2.

Our discussion in this section has been about the supply and demand for capital, and we have seen that both are dependent on the rate of interest. We cannot proceed further at this point to discuss the determinants of the rate of interest itself, because there are important monetary forces to be studied in macroeconomics first. So we must leave the question of interest-rate determination until then (see Chapter 34). Meanwhile, there is a distinctive type of capital to be dealt with.

Human Capital

While capital goods are usually discussed in terms of tangible assets such as buildings or machines, the notion of a capital asset as something that produces an increase in the stream of future outputs can be applied to labour. Consider, for example, three people, a 16-year-old who has enough education to get an unskilled job, an 18-year-old who has 3 good A-level passes, and a graduate who has completed a BSc degree in psychology. Each of the three could continue with further education – the 16-year-old to stay at school to take A-levels, the 18-year-old to go to university or further education, and the graduate to acquire a highly specialized qualification, say in educational or clinical psychology. All might improve their future earnings prospects if they underwent such additional training. We could regard doing so as a kind of investment in HUMAN CAPITAL, forgoing present income by staying in education instead of going to work now. Like any other type of investment, the yield comes later, in enhanced earning power, while the cost comes now in terms of current income forgone.

How should someone decide whether or not such investment in human capital is worthwhile on a purely monetary basis (we are ignoring any direct pleasure or pain that the education may involve)? This method is to compare the present value of the enhanced future earnings with the present cost, measured in terms of the amount of earnings sacrificed. If the former exceeds the latter, the educational expenditure pays off.

Interest on Capital, Risk and Profit

The part of this chapter devoted to the rewards to the factor of production, capital, has been written as if the productivity of capital is certain. In practice, the yield on capital investment cannot be known, only estimated. A machine is ordered today, or contracts signed for the construction of a new factory. But, there is a waiting time, not only before the machine arrives or the factory is built, but also for the duration of its life, before one can know whether the extra capital in fact yields as much as was hoped for. The same can be said about the uncertainty of the reward from investment in education and training.

The fact that there is an element of uncertainty about the future yield of capital investment means that such investment performs more than one economic function. The rate of return on capital provides the incentive for forgoing present consumption, but it also provides a reward for undertaking the risk that such investment may prove less profitable than hoped for. Part of the earnings of capital, therefore, is a reward for risk-taking.

No one knows precisely what the future will bring. Even if one thinks the *physical* productivity of a machine is certain at the time the decision is made to install it, events may reveal that one has been unduly optimistic or pessimistic.

Still greater uncertainty attaches to the profitability of investment *in money terms*. Not only must the physical productivity of the machine be estimated over its future life, but one needs also to forecast the prices at which the physical output of the machine can be sold.

We opened the section on capital in this chapter by referring to a view expressed by some people that capitalists ought to be regarded as heroes, because of the role they play in leading the economy towards higher living standards. In so far as the prospect of large profits and losses from investment induces owners of capital to make risky investments which promote economic growth, there is force in the contention that capitalists may well be, in a sense, 'heroes'. In so far, however, as the prime stimulus for economic progress comes from increases in the amount of capital investment of a relatively riskless nature, the heroic image weakens. There is plenty of evidence on this subject, but it is controversial and beyond the scope of this book.

Income Differences – a Summary Statement

A lot of ground has been covered in the two chapters on distribution. We set out to explain the reasons why incomes differ. The explanations are complex and have been introduced in a number of different places. We end by pulling together the principal reasons why individuals are observed to have different incomes.

Two underlying causes of income differences are factor ownership and factor prices.

The size of any person's income depends partly on the number of sources of income he possesses, i.e. on his ownership of factors of production. Even if all wages were equal and all returns on land and capital were the same, some people would earn higher incomes than others, unless everyone owned the same amount of land and capital (as well as labour). Indeed, the very considerable inequality in the ownership of personal wealth is a major cause of income inequality among persons.

Personal incomes also differ because the prices of factors of production differ. Even if everyone owned the same amount of land, labour and capital, some people would earn more than others because the prices of the factors they owned would be higher than those of the factors owned by others.

On page 225 of Chapter 20 we laid out the labour-market conditions which would lead to complete equality of labour incomes. These conditions suggest a convenient classification of the reasons why incomes would differ. The classification below is based on situations in which each of the assumptions listed on p. 225 does not hold in particular labour markets.

Imperfect Competition in the Labour Market: Many labour markets are characterized by monopolistic and/or monopsonistic elements. On the supply side, trade unions may be able to exercise monopoly powers, and we listed some of the chief determinants of union bargaining power earlier in this chapter. On the demand side, employers may be able to exercise monopsony powers. Different degrees of imperfect competition in individual markets, may, therefore, explain some income differences.

Imperfect Competition in the Goods Market: Some employers of labour are price-takers in the markets for their products; other are price-makers. Monopoly in product markets causes the value of the marginal product of labour to differ from its marginal revenue product and results in a wage below the competitive level. Some income differences, therefore, occur because some workers sell their labour to firms who sell their output in competitive markets while others sell to firms who sell in monopolistic markets.

Non-homogeneous Labour: The labour forces does not consist of identical clones. Individuals differ from each other in many ways, which affect their earnings. We emphasized the following characteristics as being important: age, sex and race, ability and skill acquired by training (human capital), attitudes, both towards work and leisure and towards risk.

Labour Immobility: There are many barriers to the movement of labour from areas of low pay to those of high pay. In addition to limited geographical and occupational mobility of labour, and where the notion of segmented labour markets is relevant, labour mobility is also restricted by social and psychological barriers.

We should not conclude that inequality in the distribution of income is either desirable or undesirable. We have been concerned in this chapter only with the positive side of income distribution – how market forces determine factor prices and how factor prices help to allocate factors to markets where they are most in demand. The normative side of the question involves personal value judgements about what distribution should be regarded as fair, as well as positive analysis about the consequences of moving towards greater fairness. For example, even if we all agreed that an equal distribution was the fairest, not everyone would agree to go for it if the result was

a 50 per cent reduction in total, and hence in average, income. Furthermore, not everyone agrees about how much equality is desirable, since many people feel that rewards should be related, at least partly, to effort.

We return to this subject in Chapter 24, when we examine government policy for income *redistribution*. We shall also consider labour markets in Parts 4 and 5 of this book, when we deal with the macroeconomic aspects of the general level of unemployment.

SUMMARY

1 The total supply of labour is affected by the size of the population, which depends on birth rates, death rates and the balance of migratory movements. The labour force, expressed as a proportion of the population (the activity rate), depends on the age distribution of the population and on the numbers seeking employment, which depend in turn on social attitudes, legal requirements, and economic incentives.

2 Individual differences in earnings can be attributed to personal characteristics, especially to age, sex and race, ability and skill, attitudes to work, and location. There is an age-earnings profile which varies among occupations.

3 Women and non-whites tend to earn less than men and whites. One explanation may be found in productivity differences, another is discrimination, and yet another is the existence of dual and separate labour markets with little mobility between them.

4 Earnings are related to genetically determined and acquired ability, and earnings potential can be raised by education and training. Some part of earnings differences may be attributed to choices made by individuals – e.g., on how long to work, or whether to seek a job with secure but relatively low pay or chance one with a high spread of earnings.

5 Wage rates vary regionally with supply and demand conditions, and these variations are maintained by limited geographical labour mobility.

6 The price of labour is likely to be different if the labour market is imperfectly competitive than if it is perfectly competitive. Imperfections may be

on the demand and/or supply sides. Under monopsony (a single buyer) in the labour market, both the wage rate and employment are lower than under perfect competition. Monopoly on the supply side of the labour market is usually exercised by trade unions seeking high pay and employment and good working conditions for their members.

7 If a union faces competitive employers, it may succeed in raising wages only at the cost of higher unemployment. If an employer was acting as a monopsonist before union action, however, wage rates and the level of employment may both be raised.

8 Negotiations between unions and employers are often a trial of strength with uncertain outcomes. The bargaining strength of a trade union will tend to be high if (i) there is little scope for substituting other factors of production for labour, (ii) the demand of the product is relatively inelastic, (iii) labour costs are a small proportion of total costs, (iv) the union itself is strong, (v) the employer enjoys substantial profits, and (vi) the union offers productivity 'deals'.

9 Capital as a factor of production has two prices, a yield and a purchase price. The latter reflects what someone would pay for the enjoyment of a stream of yields in the future.

10 The present value of a future yield is less than the yield itself and is found by the method of discounting, using standard (compound) interest formulae.

11 The use of capitalistic methods of production raises productivity. The marginal efficiency of

capital, defined as the rate of return to be expected from an additional unit of capital, is the firm's demand curve for capital. It slopes downwards, if other factors are fixed, by application of the law of diminishing returns and shows how much the firm would wish to borrow in order to invest at varying rates of interest.

12 The supply of capital depends, among other things, on the rate of interest obtainable for lenders. Since people tend to have a rate of time preference of present over future goods, a positive rate of interest is needed to induce lending and the higher the rate, the more lending may be expected.

13 Expenditure on education and training can be considered to be investment in human capital.

14 Income differences may be summarily attributed to factor ownership and factor prices, the latter being affected by the degree of competition in different factor markets, by the fact that labour is not a homogeneous factor, and by limited labour mobility.

International Trade

So far, we have studied the allocation of resources within the context of a single national economy. However, production and distribution are influenced by trading relations with foreign countries. This chapter is concerned with the question of what is gained by nations trading with each other, and with why obstacles are sometimes placed on international trade in goods and services. Later in the book, we shall deal with such other aspects of international economics as capital transactions and the balance of payments.

Interpersonal and Interregional Trade

Economists have long recognized that the *principles* governing the gains from international trade are the same as those governing trade within a single country.

In Chapter 2, we explained that the major source of economic growth and rising living standards throughout the world lies in the development of specialization and division of labour. Reaping the gains from specialization requires trade – trade among individuals, and trade among regions. Let us remind you of the argument.

First, consider trade among individuals. If there were none, each person would have to be self-sufficient, producing all the food, clothing, medical services, entertainment and other things that he or she required. It does not take much imagination to realize that living standards would be very low in such a self-sufficient world. Trade among individuals allows people to specialize in those activities they can do well, and to exchange their surpluses with other people, who specialize in different activities. Some

people, who are poor carpenters but good doctors, can specialize in medicine, providing physicians' services not only for themselves but also for persons who are good carpenters yet have neither the training nor the talent for medicine. Thus, trade and specialization are intimately connected. With trade, everyone can specialize in what they do relatively well, and all can gain.

Exactly the same principle applies to regional specialization. Without interregional trade, each region would have to be self-sufficient, producing all the agricultural products, manufactured goods and services that the people in the region require. With trade among regions, however, specialization is possible. Plains regions with suitable climates can specialize in growing grain crops; mountainous regions can specialize in timber and mining; cool regions can produce crops that thrive in temperate climates; hot regions can grow tropical crops such as coffee and bananas; regions with abundant power sources can specialize in manufacturing; and so on. With trade, each region can concentrate its efforts on what it does relatively well. And with exchange among specializing regions, all regions can gain.

Identical arguments apply to nations. International trade leads to specialization, and thus gain.

The Special Features of International Trade

Although identical principles apply to international, interregional and interpersonal trade, there are two characteristics that distinguish the first of these from the other two. They are barriers to movement, and national currencies.

Barriers to Movement of Factors of Production: International barriers to movement of factors of production tend to be stronger and more obvious between countries than between regions because of the existence of national frontiers. Not only do many nations have their own languages, they have different traditions and lifestyles, which impede factor mobility. For example, workers in Scotland face much more severe adjustment problems if, in search of higher wages, they consider migrating to Switzerland than if they contemplate moving to England. They not only need to understand one of the Swiss languages, they have to be prepared to change their diet rather drastically, not to mention not watching *Eastenders*.

Even if the Scottish worker is willing to make the adjustments involved in going to Switzerland, he may find legal restrictions on his international mobility. Indeed, most countries impose substantial restrictions on inflows of foreign labour seeking work.

National Currencies: Trading nations almost all have their own currencies – francs, dollars, pounds, yen, etc. As a result, an extra element of uncertainty is involved for a firm exporting to another country, compared to exporting to another part of its own country. For example, a Welsh firm selling in England sells its products for pounds sterling which are the currency unit in both Wales and England. But if it exports to Germany, it will be paid in deutschmarks, and there is an element of uncertainty about the rate at which deutschmarks will exchange for pounds, when payment is made.

National Economic Policies: The combination of the two distinctive features of *international* economic relations has the important consequence that national governments can pursue independent economic policies, designed principally for their own people. Such policies can affect economic conditions, including income and price levels within a country. They can also influence the exchange rate at which the domestic currency exchanges for the currencies of other nations (pounds sterling for US dollars, for example).[1] Indeed, domestic policies can be, and often are, deliberately directed at interfering with flows of imports and exports of goods and services. As we shall

---

1 Exchange rates are considered in Parts 4 and 5 in the macroeconomics part of this book. See Chapters 25 and 43.

see later in this chapter, governmental actions are one reason why international trade is sometimes at a much lower level than would otherwise occur.

THE GAINS FROM TRADE

We now look more closely at the sources of mutual gains from trade. These have three main sources: (i) specialization, (ii) economies of scale, and (iii) learning-by-doing.

The Gain from Specialization

To isolate the gains from specialization, we assume that costs of production are independent of the level of output – i.e. they are constant. To keep the analysis simple, we assume also that the world with which we are dealing consists of only two countries, that only two commodities are produced, and that transport costs are negligible. The conclusions that can be reached using this simple model have general applicability. Later, we shall refer briefly to some modifications to the theory that are necessary when it is applied to real world situations.

A special case: absolute advantage

Our first approach to demonstrating the gains that can result from specialization compares the amounts of two commodities that can be produced in each of two countries when both use the same quantity of inputs. One country is said to have an ABSOLUTE ADVANTAGE over the second country in the production of a commodity, say wheat, if the first country can produce more wheat using a given quantity of inputs than can the other. We first consider a case in which each country has an absolute advantage in the production of one of the commodities.

Table 22.1 provides a simple example, on the assumption that, with a given unit of resources, America (A) can produce *either* 10 bushels of wheat (w) *or* 6 yards of cloth (c); while the same quantity of resources in Britain (B) can produce *either* 5w *or* 10c. In this case America has an absolute advantage in wheat and Britain in cloth.

Row 1 in the table states the productivity of a unit of resources in A and B. If we further assume that each country has 10 units of resources available, we can show the gain from trade as follows.

TABLE 22.1 Gain from Specialization with Absolute Advantage

Row	(i)	Production		
		America	Britain	World (ii) + (iii)
		(ii)	(iii)	(iv)
1.	1 unit of resources	10w *or* 6c	5w *or* 10c	—
2.	*Self-sufficiency** (half resources used for w and half for c)	50w + 30c	25w + 50c	75w + 80c
3.	*Specialization** A produces only w B produces only c	100w + 0c	0w + 100c	100w + 100c
4.	*Gain from specialization**			25w + 20c

* Rows 2, 3 and 4 assume A and B each have 10 units of resources.

Suppose that, under self-sufficiency, A and B each devote half their resources to producing w and half to producing c. (The assumption of a fifty-fifty allocation is arbitrary, and does not affect the argument.) Total output in A is that shown in col. (ii) of row 2: 50w + 30c. Total output in B is that shown in col. (iii) of row 2: 25w + 50c. World output is the sum of the outputs of A + B and is shown in col. (iv) of row 2, namely 75w + 80c.

Row 3 of the table shows what happens if both countries specialize in the production of the good in which they have an absolute advantage. A produces 100w (and no c), while B produces 100c (and no w). World output becomes 100w + 100c, as shown in col. (iv) of row 3.

Row 4 of the table shows the gain from specialization as the difference in total world output under specialization from that under self-sufficiency, i.e. the difference between rows 2 and 3 of col. (iv). This is (100w + 100c) minus (75w + 80c). The gain from specialization is therefore 25w + 20c. There is both *more wheat and more cloth available* for world consumption when A and B specialize, and a potential gain from trade for both countries. This is hardly surprising. If one country can make more of one good than another, while the second country can make more of the other good, their joint production will increase if they specialize.

These gains result from specialization in the two countries. Note now that America is producing all of the wheat and Britain all of the cloth. If the inhabitants of each country are to consume a balanced bundle of both commodities, as they did when each country was self-sufficient, trade must take place. Britain must export cloth and import wheat while

America does the opposite.

Trade allows countries to specialize and the world to reap the gains from specialization. Thus economists tend to use the terms 'gains from trade' and 'gains from specialization' synonymously.

The general case: comparative advantage

What if one country has an absolute advantage in the production of *both* goods? Suppose, for example, that America is more efficient in both wheat and cloth production than Britain. This was the question that the English economist David Ricardo posed over 150 years ago, and in answer to which he developed his theory of the basis of the gains from trade.

Ricardo showed that a gain from specialization was still possible even if one country had an absolute advantage over another country in the production of all commodities, *provided that its margin of advantage was not the same in all lines of output.* This condition amounts to saying that a gain can result when one country has a relatively greater (or comparative) advantage in the production of some goods than of others. Ricardo's proposition is, therefore, known as the principle of comparative advantage (also, sometimes, as the principle of comparative costs).

We can demonstrate Ricardo's Principle of Comparative Advantage with the aid of another simple arithmetical example. In Table 22.2, we assume that American efficiency is greater than British in *both* wheat and cloth production. As shown in row 1, one unit of resources in A produces 20w *or* 10c, while in B the same unit produces only 10w *or* 8c. Britain no longer has an absolute advantage in the production of either commodity. You might imagine that efficient

TABLE 22.2 Gain from Specialization with Comparative Advantage

Row	(i)	America (ii)	Britain (iii)	World (ii) + (iii) (iv)
		Production		
1.	1 unit of resources	20w *or* 10c	10w *or* 8c	—
2.	*Self-sufficiency** (half resources used for w and half for c)	100w + 50c	50w + 40c	150w + 90c
3.	*Specialization** A uses 80% of its resources for w and 20% for c. B produces only c.	160w + 20c	0w + 80c	160w + 100c
4.	*Gain from specialization**			10w + 10c

* Rows 2, 3 and 4 assume A and B each have 10 units of resources.

America has nothing to gain from trading with such an inefficient partner as Britain. You would, however, be wrong. *Both* countries can gain from trade and it is important to see why.

In row 2 of Table 22.2 we can see, as in Table 22.1, the production that takes place if A and B are self-sufficient, and each devotes half its resources to cloth and half to wheat production. This assumption is again, of course, arbitrary. There must be *some* allocation of resources when each country is self-sufficient, and this one is as good as any other for purposes of illustration. Total production in A and B is shown in columns (ii) and (iii) respectively. A produced 100w + 50c, while B produces 50w + 40c.

Now let us see what happens to total production if each country specializes, at least to some extent, in the production of the commodity in which it has *comparative advantage*. The data in the table show that, although America has an absolute advantage over Britain in both wheat and cloth, her *margin* of advantage is not the same in the two goods. America can produce twice as much wheat as can Britain, using the same quantity of resources, but only twenty-five per cent more cloth. Therefore, we can say that America has a *comparative advantage* in the production of wheat (and a *comparative disadvantage* in the production of cloth), because Britain is *relatively less inefficient* than America in cloth than in wheat production.

In general a country is said to have a COMPARATIVE ADVANTAGE in the production of commodities whose costs of production are *relatively lower* than those of another country, and to have a

comparative disadvantage in the production of other commodities whose costs of production are relatively higher than those of the other country. In other words, comparative advantage exists, when one country's margin of advantage over another country is not the same for all commodities.

If we now allow America to devote more resources to wheat and Britain to specialize in cloth production, we can show the gain in total production of the two goods. Suppose Britain produces only cloth, while America increases its resources devoted to wheat[1] – allocating 8 out of its total 10 units of resources to wheat, and only 2 units to cloth production. A's output is then 160w + 20c. B's output is 80c. Total world output is, therefore, 160w + 100c.

Row 4 in Table 22.2 shows, in precisely the same way as in the case of absolute advantage, the amount of gain from specialization, i.e. the difference between world output in rows 2 and 3 of column (iv). The gain in this case is 10w and 10c. In other words, there is still *more wheat and more cloth* available for consumption with specialization, and a potential gain therefore, for both countries.

Comparative Advantage Summarized: Two important conclusions that can be drawn from the example we have been looking at are:

● The gains from specialization depend on the pat-

---

1 Note the difference between complete specialization by Britain and partial specialization by America. These are assumed only in order to simplify the exposition.

tern of comparative advantage, rather than on absolute advantage. World production can always be increased if trade takes place between countries which have different relative efficiencies in the production of any goods or services. If each concentrates on those commodities in which it is relatively more efficient, or relatively less inefficient, a gain is there for the taking.

- Without comparative advantage, there is no re-allocation of resources within countries that will increase total world production.

The second proposition follows directly from the first. There are no gains from specialization without comparative advantage, and no reallocation of resources within countries will increase total production of both commodities. For example, if one country is exactly twice or three times as efficient as another in every line of output, there will be no gain if they do specialize. To show this for yourself, construct a third table, similar to Tables 22.1 and 22.2, for the case where one unit of resources can produce 20w or 14c in A, or the same unit can produce 10w or 7c in B. Try as you may, you will find that world output of both commodities cannot be increased by specialization. In other words, comparative advantage is necessary, as well as sufficient, for gains from specialization to be possible.

Comparative advantage and opportunity cost

The principle of comparative advantage, as we have set it out, is expressed in almost exactly the same terms that were used by David Ricardo in 1817. We made use of the concept of a unit of resources, which could be equated across different countries in the world. However, techniques and factors of production differ so much among countries that the concept of a common measure of the real resource inputs is suspect.

Fortunately, however, the principle of comparative advantage can be stated without any reference to the real, or absolute, cost of resources, simply by using the more modern idea of opportunity cost, which all readers of this book are familiar with. To do this, return to the example of Table 22.2 and calculate the opportunity cost of wheat and cloth in the two countries. These are shown in Table 22.3. The calculations in the table are based on the original assumption that one unit of resources can produce *either* 20w *or* 10c in A, and *either* 10w *or* 8c in B.

Consider, first, the opportunity cost of a unit of wheat in the two countries. In A, the opportunity cost of 20w is 10c. So the opportunity cost of a single unit of w must be one-twentieth of that amount. In other words, the opportunity cost of 1w is $10c/20c = 0.50c$. In B, the opportunity cost of 10w is 8c. So the opportunity cost of 1w in B is $8c/10c = 0.8c$. The opportunity costs of 1w differ in the two countries. In A, one unit of w involves the sacrifice of 0.5c, while in B the sacrifice is 0.8c. The sacrifice is greater in B. Hence, A enjoys a comparative advantage in the production of wheat, while B has a comparative *dis*advantage in the production of that commodity.

Consider, next, the opportunity cost of a unit of cloth in each country. In A, the opportunity cost of 10c is the sacrifice of 20w given up. So, the opportunity cost of a single unit of c must be one-tenth of that of producing 10c. In other words the opportunity cost of 1c is $20w/10w = 2w$. In B, the opportunity cost of 8c is 10w. So, the opportunity cost of a single unit of c must be one-eighth of 10w. In other words, the opportunity cost of 1c is $10w/8w = 1.25w$. The opportunity costs are different in the two cases. In A, one unit of cloth involves the sacrifice of 2w, while in B the sacrifice is only 1.25w. This gives us the modern definition of comparative advantage: one country has a comparative advantage over another in the production of one commodity if its opportunity cost of producing that commodity is less than another's. In the above example, country B has a comparative advantage in the production of cloth, while country A has a comparative *dis*advantage in the production of that commodity.

The calculations in Table 22.3 show that comparative advantages differ in the two countries. Although America has an *absolute advantage* in the production of cloth *and* wheat (in that a unit of resources can produce more of either commodity in A than in B), the *margin* of advantage is greater in wheat than in cloth. A has a *comparative advantage* in wheat produc-

TABLE 22.3 The Opportunity Cost of 1 Unit of Wheat and 1 Unit of Cloth in Countries A and B

	Country A	Country B
1 unit of resources can produce *either*	20w *or* 10c	10w *or* 8c
Opportunity cost of 1w	$\dfrac{10}{20} = 0.5c$	$\dfrac{8}{10} = 0.8c$
Opportunity cost of 1c	$\dfrac{20}{10} = 2w$	$\dfrac{10}{8} = 1.25w$

tion. B has an *absolute disadvantage* in the production of cloth *and* wheat (in that a unit of resources can produce less of either commodity in B than in A). But B has a smaller margin of disadvantage in the production of cloth than of wheat. B has, therefore, a *comparative advantage* in cloth production. It is these differences in relative advantages and disadvantages that explain the gains which were shown in Table 22.2, as following specialization by each country in the production of the good in which it enjoys a comparative advantage.

It is important to appreciate that this conclusion rests on relative opportunity costs, and is *independent of the level of absolute costs*. Although we derived the figures of opportunity cost here from an example where we happened to know absolute costs, the gains from specialization arise from these opportunity costs, no matter what absolute costs lie behind them.

A graphic representation of the gains from specialization

The principle of comparative advantage is so important and powerful a tool of economic analysis that we shall restate it with the use of a diagram, which allows direct representation of opportunity costs.

The diagram we use, Figure 22.1, is basically similar to that of Figure 1.2 in Chapter 1. Part (i) shows the production possibility curve, *AA'*, for America, which can produce *either* 20w *or* 10c, or

indeed any combination of *c* and *w* on the curve. Part (ii) shows Britain's production possibility curve, *BB'*; B can produce *either* 10w *or* 8c, or any combination on its curve.[1]

As we have emphasized, world output can be increased by specialization because opportunity costs are different in the two countries – in the diagram the slope of the country's production possibility curves are not the same. A's curve is steeper than B's because A's opportunity cost of producing cloth (measured in terms of wheat forgone) is higher than B's. A has a comparative *advantage* in wheat and a comparative *disadvantage* in cloth.

Let us look at the gain from trade from the point of view of America and Britain, in turn. First America. Left to itself, a self-sufficient America could consume only at some point on its own production possibility curve. But suppose it were offered the chance of obtaining cloth by trading with Britain, at the British opportunity cost. We can show America's consumption possibilities by drawing a line on America's diagram, with the slope exactly the same as the British production possibility curve. We draw it here through point A, which implies that America pro-

---

1 Refer back to p. 11 if you have forgotten why the slope of the curve measures opportunity cost. Note, that the curves are straight lines because opportunity costs are here assumed constant; i.e. not to alter with output. This is different from Figure 1.2, where opportunity costs are increasing.

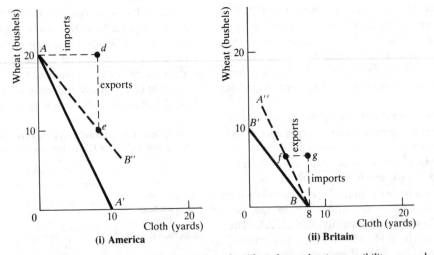

FIGURE 22.1   The Gains from Specialization and Trade. When the production possibility curves have different slopes in each country, world production can be increased by specialization, making use of comparative advantages

duces only wheat and exchanges it for British cloth. America's consumption possibilities are now enhanced. It can consume anywhere along AB''. For example, at point e, America would produce OA wheat, of which de would be exported in exchange for Ad cloth imported. The consumption level at point e is more favourable than at any point along AA', America's domestic production possibility curve. Clearly America has gained from trade and, though Britain has not done so in this illustration, it is no worse off, but has broken even.

By similar reasoning, it can be shown that Britain could gain from exchange, if it were offered the chance to trade at the American opportunity cost, in terms of cloth sacrificed. $A''B$ is drawn, with the same slope as AA', through point B on Britain's diagram, i.e. assuming Britain specialized completely in cloth production. Britain could then consume anywhere along BA'', such as point f, producing OB cloth, of which fg is exported in exchange for Bg imports of wheat. B's consumption level at f is more favourable than at any point on B's production possibility curve – the best available for B if it were to stay self-sufficient. Clearly, now it is Britain that gains from specialization and exchange.

This exercise has shown that A can gain if it trades at B's opportunity cost, and that B can gain if it trades at A's opportunity cost. In both cases, the second trading partner breaks even, so we may conclude there is a net gain to the world, i.e. to A and B taken together. Clearly both cannot happen at the same time. The rate at which A trades wheat for cloth must be the same as the rate that B trades cloth for wheat. This rate must lie between the opportunity cost ratios of the two countries, if *both* countries are to gain. The division of the gain between them depends on the actual rate at which trade takes place. The closer that rate is to the opportunity cost ratio of country A, the greater the gain will be for B, and vice versa.

The Gains from Large-scale Production

The second source of gain from trade is the reaping of economies of large-scale production made possible by the expansion of the market which trade permits.

In many lines of output, real production costs, measured in terms of resources used, fall as the scale of output increases. The bases of falling costs (or increasing returns to scale) were given in Chapters 14 and 15. If each country's resource costs fall as they specialize, the resulting increases in output when trade and specialization takes place will be larger than if costs were constant.

We may conclude that the potential gain from trade arising from large-scale production is likely to be greater for small countries such as Denmark and Israel, whose domestic markets are too small to allow the exploitation of the full economies of scale, than for countries such as the USA, which have domestic markets large enough for full realization of scale economies. In consequence, we should expect the cost of remaining self-sufficient to be particularly high for such small countries, while for large countries the gains from trade arise mainly from specializing in the production of goods in which they have a comparative advantage.

Learning-by-Doing

The discussion so far has assumed that costs vary only with output. However, as we know from Chapter 15, costs can vary not only with output but also over time. The tendency for firms to learn by doing, and acquire expertise as they specialize, applies equally to regions and to countries. This is our third source.

When learning-by-doing lowers costs, this means that the whole cost curve shifts downwards. If it occurred in the example of Table 22.2, it would mean that output of cloth per worker would rise in Britain, and that output of wheat per worker would rise in America, as each country specialized in the production of the commodity in which it had a comparative advantage.

Learning-by-doing suggests that existing patterns of comparative advantage must not be assumed to be immutable. The producers in a country may even learn enough by doing things in which they start with a comparative disadvantage to turn that situation into one of comparative advantage. This possibility has important policy implications, to which we return later in the chapter.

THE TERMS OF TRADE

The basis for increasing world production through trade has been shown to lie in the opportunities opened up for specialization and in the consequences of exploiting those opportunities. World output rises when countries specialize in the production of commodities in which they have a comparative advantage. The increased specialization, however, implies that countries are producing more of some goods and less of other goods than they want to consume, so trade must accompany specialization.

The total gain in world production is shared between A and B when they trade with each other. How much each country gains depends on the TERMS OF TRADE. The terms of trade are defined as the quantity of domestic goods that must be exported in return for a unit of imported goods. They depend, therefore, on the prices that a country has to pay for its imports and the prices it receives for its exports.

In Figure 22.1, we showed that Britain would appropriate all the gain from trade if she exchanged cloth for wheat at the American opportunity cost of wheat in terms of cloth (and that America would reap all the gain from trade if she exchanged wheat for cloth at the British opportunity cost of cloth in terms of wheat). If trade takes place at any rate of exchange (terms of trade) which lies *in between* the British and American domestic opportunity costs, the gain will be shared between the two countries. It is beyond the scope of an introductory textbook to show how the terms of trade are determined. We may, however, mention that the strength of demand for traded goods is a relevant factor.

Because actual international trade involves many countries and many commodities, the terms of trade is computed as an index number, itself consisting of two index numbers of prices – the price of exports and the price of imports:

$$\text{Terms of Trade (index)} = \frac{\text{price of exports (index)}}{\text{price of imports (index)}}$$

The terms of trade index rises if the price of exports rises *relative to* the price of imports. For example, if the price of exports rises from 100 to 120, while the price of imports falls from 100 to 80, the terms of trade index will rise from 100 in the first period to 150 (120 divided by 80). The terms of trade will also rise even though the prices of exports and imports both increase, providing that the former increases relatively more than the latter – e.g., if export prices rise by 50 per cent and import prices by only 25 per cent, the terms of trade index becomes 120 (150 divided by 125). In the opposite case, where import prices rise relatively to export prices, the terms of trade index falls – e.g., if the import price index is 160 while the export price index is 120, the terms of trade index is 0.75.

Rises in the terms of trade are commonly called *favourable* movements, and falls in the terms of trade

unfavourable movements. These adjectives have precise definitions, and should not be taken to mean more than these definitions, i.e. favourable movements in the terms of trade mean that more imports can be obtained per unit of exports, and vice versa.

Whether or not favourable movements in the terms of trade will bring social gain depends on the circumstances of each case. For instance, rising relative prices of exports may make them more difficult to sell abroad, and a favourable change in the terms of trade that results in pricing one's exports right out of foreign markets would hardly be regarded as desirable developments. But a favourable change that arose because one's exports were in increasing demand so that their prices rose would probably entail a net gain for the country.

International trading equilibrium

We take a step towards understanding how supply and demand determine prices, production and quantities traded, by looking at trade for a single commodity. Assume, as previously, a world with only two countries, this time France and Germany, abbreviated to F and G. The single commodity we shall call onions, which are produced under conditions of rising marginal costs in both countries. (This assumption differs from that lying behind our previous numerical examples, which assumed constant costs).

Part (i) of Figure 22.2 shows the domestic supply and demand curves for onions in France, and part (ii) shows them in Germany.

In the absence of trade, a self-sufficient France will produce and consume q_f onions; while a self-sufficient Germany will produce and consume q_g onions. The price of onions will be p_f and p_g in F and G respectively. Since the relative prices of onions in F and G reflect real opportunity costs, there is a clear potential gain to be reaped from specialization by G, which has the lower unit costs. Indeed, in the absence of governmental trade restrictions or prohibitive transport costs, profit-seeking businesses would spot the profit to be gained by buying onions in G and selling them in F.

Trade will be profitable so long as there is a difference between the price of onions in the two countries. But the opening up of trade will cause domestic prices in G and F to come closer together. As G exports onions, the quantity available on the domestic market falls, and the price of onions in G will rise. At the same time, as F imports onions, the

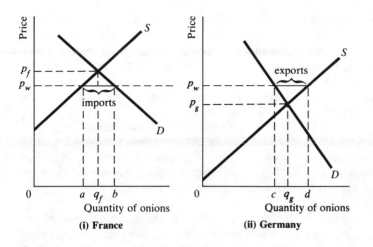

FIGURE 22.2 **The Equilibrium Level of Trade.** Under free trade, market forces equate domestic prices for traded commodities in the two countries' markets

quantity available in F's market (domestic production plus imports) rises, and the price of onions falls in F. Trade will continue until the domestic price of onions is the same in F and G. When that position is reached, trade is at an equilibrium level, and the quantity of onions that F wishes to import is exactly equal to the quantity that G wishes to export.

The equilibrium position may be seen in Figure 22.2. The price of onions is p_w in both F and G, and is, effectively, the world price. At the price p_w there is excess supply, cd, in Germany; while there is excess demand, ab, in France. Because $ab = cd$, imports and exports are equal. This is the trade equilibrium in the onion markets, *production* having risen in G (by $q_g d$) and fallen in F (by $q_f a$), while *consumption* has risen in F (by $q_f b$) and fallen in G (by cq_g).

The Case for Free Trade

The case for free trade rests on the principle of comparative advantage. When opportunity costs differ among countries, specialization leads to increased production and consumption on a world scale. There is abundant evidence, too, that significant differences in costs do exist in real life. Therefore there are large potential sources of gain. It is also clear that nations do not seek complete self-sufficiency. Trade not only exists, it has been growing faster than world production.

Free trade does not mean, however, that *everyone* is better off with trade than without. It only means that it is *possible* for everyone to be made better off. Usually, there are gainers and losers from trade. In the example of Figure 22.2, the gainers are German onion-growers and French onion-eaters. The im-

mediate losers are French onion-growers. German onion-eaters also lose, but they gain when they buy now-cheapened French goods. Of course, if comparative advantage exists, there will be further compensating benefits to be taken into account in a final reckoning. For example, displaced French onion producers will tend to move into the production of other goods in which France has a comparative advantage, and will therefore gain in the long run. Because trade creates gainers and losers, free trade does not appeal to the self-interest of everyone. The remainder of this chapter is devoted to a consideration of the case for interference in international trade, in order to find the balance between the advantages of more or less trade.

PROTECTIONISM

Methods of Protection[1]

Governments intervene in international trade for both economic and non-economic reasons. Such intervention is usually called *protection*. The available methods include measures to increase exports, but we shall be concerned mainly with those which hinder imports, and which are commonly called barriers to trade.

There are basically three means by which a country can try to reduce its imports of some goods.

---

1 For details of trade restrictions of the UK, see Harbury and Lipsey, Chapter 5.

They are: (i) tariffs, (ii) quotas, and (iii) non-tarrif barriers.

Tariffs: Taxes levied by the government on imports of a particular good are known as TARIFFS (or IMPORT DUTIES). A tariff may be either *specific*, i.e. so much money per unit of the good imported, or it may be *ad valorem*, which is calculated as a percentage of the price of the product. Tariffs bring revenue to the government, but we are concerned in this chapter with their objective of giving protection to domestic industry. This objective is achieved when the tariff raises the price of imported goods relative to the prices of competing domestic products.

Import Quotas: Limiting the quantity of a good that is allowed into the country over a period of time is done through IMPORT QUOTAS, which provide an upper limit to permitted imports over the given period.

Non-tariff Barriers: The term usually employed to cover all protective measures other than tariffs and quotas is NON-TARIFF BARRIERS. (Strictly speaking, quotas are non-tariff barriers.) Non-tariff barriers have provided the most important means of restricting imports since the early 1970s. There is a wide variety of devices that are employed, including the imposition by governments of quality restrictions on imports, or requiring importers to have special licences allowing them to buy goods from abroad.

Figure 22.3 compares the three methods of restricting imports. In each part of the diagram, D and S represent the domestic market demand and foreign supply curves of cars before protective measures are

introduced. We assume that foreign car producers are willing to supply, at the price p_0, all the cars that are demanded in the UK. Hence the supply curve of imports is perfectly elastic. Equilibrium is found at the intersection of the domestic demand and foreign supply curves. Price p_0 and quantity q_0 are the initial equilibrium values.

Now, suppose that the government wishes to restrict imports of foreign cars to, say, q_1. Part (i) shows the effect of doing so with a specific tariff; part (ii) shows the effect of a quota; and part (iii) the effect when non-tariff barriers are employed.

A Tariff: A tariff shifts the supply curve of imports upwards because it adds to the foreign producer's cost of every unit sold in the country imposing the tariff. If the tariff is t per unit, the new supply curve becomes S', horizontally above the original supply curve, by t, for all levels of imports. The intersection of the new supply curve with the unchanged demand curve identifies the new equilibrium position. Imports fall to the targetted q_1, while the domestic price of cars rises to p_1.

A Quota: If the government imposes a quota of q_1 cars which may be imported, the supply curve becomes vertical at that quantity. The market-clearing price for quantity q_1 is p_1, where the new supply curve, S'', intersects the unchanged demand curve.

Non-tariff barriers: The third method of restricting imports is to resort to one or other of a variety of non-tariff barriers which reduce the demand for imports. In part (iii), the effect of introducing a non-tariff

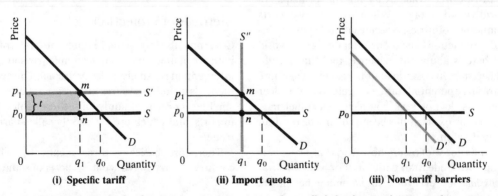

FIGURE 22.3 Methods of Restricting Imports. A specific tariff shifts the supply curve of imports upwards; an import quota limits the quantity of imports; non-tariff barriers lower the demand curve for imports

barrier is seen as shifting the demand curve to the left, from D to D'. Once again, quantity falls to q_1, but this time price stays constant at p_0.

Figure 22.3 shows that all three methods of protection succeed in restricting imports to the targetted amount, q_1. We should not, however, jump to the conclusion that all effects are the same. Indeed, there are two respects in which tariffs and quotas have very different effects.

Tariffs versus quotas

The first difference relates to the relationship between the domestic price of cars in the importing country and the price at which the reduced quantity of imports would be supplied by foreigners. Under a tariff, the difference between the prices p_0 and p_1 accrues to the government in the importing country, as revenue from the tariff. This is shown in Figure 22.3 (i) as the shaded area p_0p_1mn. Under a quota, however, the government receives no revenue. The shortage resulting from the quota restriction forces up the market price, so that foreign sellers are able to charge p_1 for q_1 cars (that they would have been willing to supply at price p_0). Our first conclusion from comparing a tariff and a quota is that the former benefits the Exchequer in the country imposing the tariff, while the quota benefits foreign suppliers.[1]

The second difference between a tariff and a quota concerns the effects of a change in either demand or supply conditions *after* the protection has been introduced. We illustrate with a change on the supply side. Suppose there is a reduction in costs of production affecting foreign suppliers of cars. Let us compare the effects when a tariff and a quota are in operation.

In Figure 22.4 we reproduce, in a single diagram, the tariff and quota of Figure 22.3(i) and (ii). The curves D, S, S' and S'' are the same in Figures 22.3 and 22.4. Both tariff and quota reduce imports from q_0 to q_1.

The reduction in costs of production affecting foreign suppliers now shifts the supply curve of imports down, to S_1, and the supply curve inclusive of

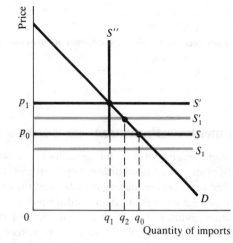

FIGURE 22.4 **Tariffs versus Quotas.** Tariffs maintain links between international prices, quotas remove them

the tariff shifts also down, to S_1' (also in grey). The intersection of the new supply curve S_1' with the demand curve identifies the new equilibrium with a tariff. Imports rise, despite the tariff, from q_1 to q_2.

Compare this result with that under a quota. The changed costs of production do not affect the relevant part of the supply curve. The quota made the supply curve vertical at quantity q_1, so no increase in imports follows the reduction in costs.

The second difference between the effects of tariffs and quotas can be summed up easily. Tariffs maintain links between international prices. Any change in supply and/or demand conditions can therefore affect trade flows. Quotas remove the links between international prices. The country imposing a quota insulates itself from the rest of the world, and, as in the example, consumers in that country fail to enjoy the benefits of technological advance elsewhere in the world.

If interference with free trade must occur, economists usually have a preference for tariffs over import quotas because the imposition of quotas prevents the price mechanism from performing its signalling functions. On the demand side, the severance of the links between international prices deprives consumers of the opportunity to buy more of goods whose costs of production fall. On the supply side, quotas tend to be allocated indiscriminately, e.g. on a first-come first-served basis, and so do not necessarily give any advantage to those producers with the lowest production costs.

Despite the foregoing arguments, tariffs are not

---

1 There are ways of using quotas which do not have this effect. For example, the government could decide to auction licences to import q_1 cars. Domestic importers would be prepared to pay the difference between the price charged by foreign suppliers (p_0) and the market-clearing price (p_1) for the right to sell q_1. The proceeds of the sale of licences would then be p_0p_1mn. The government would receive, in this case, exactly the same sum as under a tariff.

always preferred to quotas. The latter are, for example, usually more *certain* in their effects. The choice between methods must depend on the reasons why protection is regarded as desirable at all. It is to the arguments for protection that we therefore now turn.

Arguments for Protection

Two common arguments for protection concern objectives other than maximizing output – sometimes described as non-economic arguments – and the level of income seen from the narrow vantage point of an individual country, rather than from that of the world. Our discussion of arguments for protection runs in general terms and ignores the differences between tariffs and quotas just described. It ignores, too, the revenue-raising aspects of tariffs.

Non-economic arguments for protection

The citizens of a nation may rationally choose certain objectives other than maximizing national income and, therefore, choose to maintain policies which interfere with free trade. There are many reasons why they might choose to do so; we shall merely give a few examples. One reason might be to preserve a peasant farming community, even if it were inefficient. In support of such an aim, barriers might be imposed on the import of farm products which could be obtained more cheaply from other countries, i.e. as the EEC Common Agricultural Policy. A second example might be protection on grounds of national defence. It has been argued, for instance, that Britain needs an experienced merchant navy in case of war, and this industry should, therefore, be shielded from competition by more efficient foreign vessels, even in peacetime. A third example might be protection in order to diversify. A nation might have comparative cost advantages in a narrow range of commodities. The government, however, might decide that the risks of narrow specialization were undesirable. The use of tariffs to secure such non-economic objectives can be rational, because there are desirable objectives in life other than maximizing real income per head of population. Economists can still concern themselves with three aspects of such arguments for protection. First, they can try to see if the tariff does achieve the ends suggested. Second, they can calculate the cost of the tariff in terms of lost living standards. Third, they can check to see whether there are alternative

policies which might achieve the stated goal at a lower cost in terms of lost output.

Economic arguments for protection

Arguments for protection which have the objective of raising living standards are here described as economic. We deal with five such arguments. The first two are, to an extent, valid; the others have no validity whatsoever. The five arguments are: (1) protection to acquire comparative advantage: (2) protection to improve the terms of trade; (3) protection against low-wage foreign labour; (4) protection against 'unfair' foreign competition; and (5) other arguments.

(1) Protection to acquire comparative advantage

Foremost among the economic protectionist arguments for raising living standards, are those which assert that *existing* patterns of comparative advantage are not always the best guide to the best way of allocating resources in the long run. We explained earlier that economies of scale, and learning-by-doing, are important sources of gain from trade. It follows that a country which does not possess an efficient industry on a scale large enough, or in existence long enough, for it to have developed a comparative advantage in that sector, might nevertheless find it worthwhile to acquire that advantage deliberately, in order to enjoy the later benefits.

The best known variant of the argument for protection described in the previous paragraph is the INFANT INDUSTRY ARGUMENT. The argument applies to industries where costs are high when the industry is small and young, but fall as it grows. Protecting such a domestic industry from foreign competition may give it a genuine comparative advantage later on.

Three things should be said about the infant industry argument for protection. The first is that industries which are currently unprofitable but which will succeed in the long run, must be identified in advance. If the state must select such industries, we must ask why private businesses are not prepared to invest in them without government help. After all, businesses invest for *future* returns all the time – that is the nature of enterprise. The record of governments in picking future winners is not a very satisfactory one.

The second point is why private businesses are not

prepared to invest for future profits. The answer is that they would invest if the potential economies of scale are *internal* but not if they are *external*. Firms make planning decisions on the basis of costs and revenue as they see them. They do not take account of economies of scale which are *external to the firm* – i.e. *those related to the growth of the whole industry*. The infant industry argument for protection is therefore valid when there are external economies of scale.

The last point is that, in practice, it is often difficult to remove protection when the industry 'grows up'. All too frequently, the protected infant grows into a weak adolescent and feeble adult, requiring continued protection for survival. Overshielding young firms and industries from competition is one of the best ways of ensuring this does happen, so that protected industries remain backward and the anticipated comparative advantage never materializes.

(2) Protection to improve the terms of trade

A second argument for protection is to improve the terms of trade. This argument bears close similarity to the analysis of monopsony behaviour described in Chapter 21. Monopsonists are buyers who are price-makers rather than price-takers. They are able to force down the price of the goods or services that they purchase by restricting the quantities that they buy, just as monopolists force up the prices of their products by restricting the quantities they offer for sale. In similar fashion, a nation which has, for example, a monopsony position in world trade in a product, may be able to do best *for itself* by restricting its imports, thereby forcing down the price it has to pay – i.e. improving its terms of trade.

Notice three things about this protectionist argument. First, there is no conflict with the theory of comparative advantage. The reduction of world trade implies a loss of world output and forgone gains for the world as a whole. The benefit accrues entirely to the country imposing the tariff.

Second, in order to achieve the desired result, a nation must be in a monopsony position in world markets. This is generally rather rare, though it can happen, especially if importing nations act in collusion. The UK is the world's largest importer of tea, for example; so that if UK tea importers made an agreement with each other to restrict imports, they might well be able to force down the price of the tea they imported.

Third, if the terms of trade shift in favour of country A, they must, of necessity, move unfavourably for country B. This invites retaliation from B. Tariff wars may benefit none of the participants in the long run, as the volume of world trade shrinks with every retaliatory protective restriction.

(3) Protection against low-wage foreign labour

Probably the most common argument for protection put forward by industries suffering from competition by more efficient foreign producers, is based on the existence of low-wage foreign labour. It is, often, put in the form of job protection for workers in advanced countries from low-wage competition in the Third World. Although there are circumstances which can give a certain validity to such arguments, they are, in their typical form, fallacious, and deny the very basis for gainful trade – comparative advantage.

To appreciate the fallacy behind the argument, consider it first in a local, rather than in an international, context. Is it really impossible for a rich person to gain from trading with a poor one? Would the chairperson of a large corporation be better off if she did all her own typing, gardening and house repairs? No one believes that rich persons must lose by trading with poor ones.

It may, then, be argued, additionally, that poor countries price their goods 'too cheaply'. How on earth do consumers in the rich country suffer from that? Does anyone believe that consumers lose from buying a given good at a low rather than a high price? If, for example, Koreans pay low wages, and sell their goods cheaply, *Korean* labour may suffer, but we gain because we obtain their goods at a low cost in terms of the goods that we must export in return. (Incidentally, the Koreans would be *worse* off if we restricted imports from them.) The cheaper our imports are, the better off we are, in terms of the goods and services available for domestic consumption.

Providing protection against low-cost foreign producers implies denying consumers the opportunities of buying from the cheapest sources of supply. The only validity to the argument concerns the distribution of income within a country.

We emphasized earlier that the theory of comparative advantage demonstrates the possibility of universal gain, but does not assert that *everyone* gains. Within a country, some may gain, while others lose. The gainers from trade are consumers of imports and producers of exports. The losers are inefficient producers of all countries. If the British textile industry is a high-cost industry, tariff protection will harm textile consumers, but it will safeguard workers (and shareholders) in the textile industry in Britain. Is this a sufficient reason for accepting a tariff on textiles in the UK?

There cannot be an unequivocal answer to this question, because it involves judgements about the distribution of income. However, most economists are bold enough to assert that, in the long run at least, such arguments are very weak. They say this for two reasons. In the first place, it ought to be possible to redistribute income so that no one ends up worse off under free trade than under protection. In the second place, if there are legitimate reasons for protecting those who work in the textile industry, there are ways of protecting them which do not have the detrimental side-effects of tariffs.

One variant of this argument that has some short-run validity calls for *limited duration protection*, to allow time for workers displaced by efficient foreign competition to move, retrained if necessary, to other industries. However, the argument is not especially related to international trade. It applies equally to regions within a country which suffer from competition from other regions. It tends to be strongest when declining industries happen to be located in regions with few alternative occupations. We discuss industrial policy towards depressed areas in Chapter 24.

(4) Protection against 'unfair' foreign competition

Complaints are often heard from businesses that they are unable to compete with foreign firms, not because they are less efficient, but because the foreigners employ 'unfair' practices.

Two types of 'unfair' practice are involved. One is simply voluntary action by the foreign firm selling its goods below cost – so-called DUMPING. The second is government support, by way of subsidy or other means of help, which allows foreign firms to sell at artificially low prices.

Both arguments resemble that based on protection against low foreign wages. The same question can be raised as was raised there. Does anyone believe that consumers lose from buying a good at a low rather than a high price? The same answer can be given, while remembering that there are distributional aspects to be taken into account.

There are, however, additional considerations in the dumping case. One problem with dumping has always been to define it. Some countries define selling a commodity for a lower price in the export market than in the home market as dumping. Such a price could still be above average total costs. Other companies define it as selling below cost. But what cost? The cost that is relevant to the short-run decisions of the firm is marginal cost, but anti-dumping laws often refer to total cost. Determining a firm's average total cost when many of these are imputed, is no easy task. We cannot go into these issues in further detail, but enough has been said to show that even the *concept* of dumping is not a simple one.

Now consider the purpose of dumping. If the reason *why* foreign producers wish to price their products below their costs of production is that they are in receipt of government subsidies to protect labour in some depressed areas of their own, there is nothing further to be said. If, however, the dumping is a short-term tactic which is part of a long-term strategy aimed at increasing its scale of output, benefits should continue to accrue to consumers in the importing country as prices should remain low, though no longer below costs. There is, however, a third possible reason why dumping takes place, which has very different implications. This reason is one that also implies a short-term tactic as part of a longer-term strategy, but the long-term aim is to destroy the domestic industry. In such cases, the importing country can expect price to be raised after the collapse of the home industry, thereby removing the only source of benefit to consumers. In such cases, anti-dumping practices may well be justified.

(5) Other arguments for protection

Four major types of argument for protection have been discussed. There are numbers of others which are related to aspects of macroeconomics, including the balance of payments and the general level of unemployment. These are discussed in Chapter 44 in Part 5 of this book.

Alternative Policies for Protection

Several of the arguments for protection that we have examined contain a certain force. Before tariffs are proposed for such cases, it is important to ask whether the objective sought could not be attained by other means which were less costly. The answer to this question is, often, yes, there is a less costly alternative policy to a tariff.

We illustrate with two of the most common arguments for tariffs – the infant industry and the low-wage cost arguments. Let us assume that, in some situation or other, the arguments are accepted as valid and then compare the effects of tariff protection with protection by means of a direct subsidy to domestic producers.

You will recall that the main detrimental effect of the tariff to protect an industry from low-wage competition in another country falls entirely on consumers, while the beneficial effect is the safeguarding of workers in the domestic industry. If, instead of the tariff, the government grants a subsidy to the producers in that industry, the 'beneficial' effects can be retained. Note, however, that the detrimental effects of higher domestic prices have disappeared. There is, therefore, on the face of it, a case for preferring the subsidy to the tariff. Consumers of the product of the protected industry are not disadvantaged. Instead, taxpayers as a whole have to pay for the subsidy. The burden of protecting the industry is, thus, spread more widely.

In the case of the protection of the infant industry, the same argument can be applied, leading to the conclusion that consumers may enjoy low-price imports while the infant industry is growing up, protected by a subsidy rather than by a tariff on imports. There is, moreover, in this case an additional reason for preferring the subsidy. It is that the domestic industry will have to market its products in open competition with those of efficient foreign producers, who already have low cost levels.

Why, in the face of these considerations, are governments usually reluctant to indulge in much direct subsidization? The answer is that in order to pay out subsidies, the state needs revenue, and raising the general level of taxation is not the most popular of policies for a government with an eye on the electorate. Substituting a subsidy for a tariff means giving up a policy which actually yields revenue, for one that involves paying out. Someone always pays for the protection. In the case of a tariff, consumers pay through higher prices. In the case of a subsidy, taxpayers pay through the tax system. But the former burden may be less noticed and politically less costly, even if it is economically less efficient.

International Co-operation

This chapter has argued that, although individual countries may try to protect sectional interests, the gains from international trade are great. Attempts by a single country to gain a narrow advantage can so easily be offset by retaliatory action by others, that all countries have a common interest in trying to keep barriers to trade low. This is more easily achieved by joint action than otherwise, and the experience of the 1930s, when nation after nation indulged in protective policies that resulted in a downward spiralling of the volume of world trade, gave a strong stimulus after the end of the Second World War to collaborative action.

International collaboration takes place at two levels, global or regional. Global agreements to remove barriers to trade are those affecting all (or most) trading nations of the world. The organization dedicated to lowering existing tariffs, and making it difficult for countries to raise them, is known as GATT (the General Agreement on Tariffs and Trade). Its success in reducing tariffs since the Second World War has been dramatic, although more recently it has had little success in restricting the growing use of non-tariff barriers.

Customs unions

Regional co-operation is distinguished from global because it involves only a limited number of countries, which come together in a CUSTOMS UNION, defined as an area within which trade is free of restrictions, and a common external tariff on imports from non-members is agreed by all members of the union.[1] The best-known example of a customs union is the EEC (European Economic Community), of which the UK is of course a member.[2]

The benefits of customs unions are all the advantages associated with free trade among its members that have been discussed in this chapter – greater opportunities for specialization, greater scope for economies of scale, and greater competition to keep producers on their toes. There are, however, detriments to be considered.

To illustrate the source of the detriments, consider a world where there are three countries, A, B and C. Suppose that all three countries trade with each

---

1 A FREE TRADE AREA is similar to a customs union, except that members do not agree on a *common external tariff*, but maintain their own rates of protection on imports from non-members. The most important example is the European Free Trade Area (EFTA).
2 See Harbury and Lipsey, Chapter 5, for further details on GATT (and the EEC).

other, but maintain 10 per cent tariffs on imports, regardless of source. Let A and B now form a customs union, abolishing tariffs on each other's goods, but both retaining the 10 per cent tariff on imports from C.

Two effects can be expected. The first, known as TRADE CREATION effects, are those with which we are familiar. Free trade between A and B will improve resource allocation between them. Each will now import from the other some goods which were previously produced at home.

The second effect of the formation of the customs union is known as TRADE DIVERSION. In sharp contrast to the beneficial trade-creation effects, the trade-diversion effects involve a *less* efficient world allocation of resources. This happens because the customs union involves *discrimination* against imports from non-member nations, even when real costs of production are lowest outside the union.

An example may help to explain the nature of the trade-diversion effects. Suppose the real cost of soap per tonne is £150 in A, £130 in B and £120 in C. C is, thus, the lowest cost producer in the world. If, before the customs union was formed, all three countries imposed a 10 per cent tariff on imports on each other's goods, regardless of source, the cheapest source of supply of soap for A and B would be imports from C. In A, for example, the price, inclusive of the 10 per cent tariff, would be £132 for imports from C, £143 for imports from B, compared with £150 for domestically

produced soap. A would therefore buy its soap from C.

When the customs union is formed, A and B abolish tariffs on each other's goods, but maintain the 10 per cent tariff on imports from C. The price of soap in A now becomes £130 for imports from B, £132 for imports from C (and, of course, remains at £150 for domestically produced soap). The cheapest source of supply of soap in A is now from country B, its partner in the customs union. So A switches imports from the lowest cost producer, C, to imports from B, which no longer bear import duty. This result runs counter to comparative advantage. It follows solely from the fact that the customs union *discriminates against non-member nations*, and in favour of union trading partners. Exactly the same argument can, of course, be applied to country B, in other goods.

The conclusion to this does not conflict with the case for free trade based on comparative advantage. It merely calls for the general case to be qualified. *Complete* free trade throughout the world still leads to improved resource allocation. But *limited* free trade in a part of the world can have the effect of lowering efficiency.[1] What happens on balance depends on whether the trade-creating or the trade-diverting effects predominate.

---

1 The theory of customs unions is another example of the theory of the second best, described in Chapter 19, pp. 216–18).

SUMMARY

1 The theory of international trade is an extension of the theory of specialization and division of labour among individuals and among regions. The distinctive features of *international trade* are the relative immobility of factors of production and the existence of national currencies, which allow governments freedom to conduct independent economic policies.

2 A gain from trade is said to occur if total world production can be increased by the international specialization which trade permits.

3 One source of the gain from specialization is cost differences among countries. A country is said to have an absolute advantage in the production of a commodity if it can produce more than another country using a given quantity of resources.

4 A gain from specialization exploiting cost differences is possible even if a country has an absolute advantage over another in the production of every commodity, provided its *margin* of advantage differs from one commodity to another. This is the principle of Comparative Advantage, originated by Ricardo, the modern version of which is expressed in opportunity cost terms.

5 A second source of gain from specialization is through increased opportunities for large-scale production as the market expands. This includes falling long-run costs due to scale economies and so-called 'learning-by-doing', which can change patterns of comparative advantage over time.

6 The division of any gain from trade among

nations depends on the terms of trade, defined as the relative price of imports in terms of exports. The opening up of trade causes domestic prices of commodities to come closer together.

7 The case for free trade is an extension of the general argument about *laissez-faire* and free-market systems. Everyone in trading nations is not necessarily made better off by trade, because changes in the distribution of income within countries may prevent it.

8 Government intervention in international trade can be carried out with tariffs (taxes on imports), quotas (quantity restrictions on imports), or other non-tariff barriers. Tariffs are generally preferred to quotas because they maintain some limited international links between domestic prices and costs in different countries and allow some reaction to changing conditions of costs and demand.

9 Arguments for protection can be based on economic and non-economic grounds. Two economic ones which contain valid elements are protection to acquire comparative advantage (the infant industry and learning-by-doing argument), and protection to improve the terms of trade by the use of monopoly bargaining power.

10 Two fallacious economic arguments are protection against low-wage foreign labour, and against some kinds of 'unfair' foreign competition.

11 The common interest that most nations have in trade may be furthered by international co-operation through such organizations as the GATT. Partial free trade through regional customs unions has trade-creating effects, improving the allocation of resources among member countries, but also trade-diverting effects, worsening the allocation of resources between union members and the rest of the world.

Principles of Microeconomic Policy

In Chapters 23 and 24, the last two chapters of Part 3, we deal with microeconomic policy – the role of the state in the allocation of resources and the distribution of income. In this chapter we outline some general principles of economic policy; in the next, we apply these principles to some specific problems.

Efficiency and equity are the two major goals of economic policy.[1] We begin with efficiency and then go on to consider equity.

You should not expect us to round up this chapter with a conclusion that unfettered markets are invariably better, or worse, than other methods of allocating resources. All methods have their advantages and their deficiencies – which is why mixed economies are so widespread. Most economists feel that they are best decided case by case, rather than generally.

THE EFFICIENT ALLOCATION OF RESOURCES

The case for *laissez-faire* can be summarized as follows. Competitive market forces lead to equilibrium output in each market where supply and demand are balanced. Provided certain conditions prevail, those equilibria ensure that there is no social gain that can be achieved by transferring resources from any one line of production to another. This is because the opportunity cost of the last unit of output of any commodity is equal to the value consumers place on that unit.

---

1 These are microeconomic goals. The macroeconomic goals are considered in Parts 4 and 5. Although they are conveniently treated separately, there is a considerable overlap among them, which will be discussed in the closing chapters of Part 5.

We know that economic efficiency has two components. Productive efficiency ensures that production is on the production possibility curve rather than inside it. Allocative efficiency ensures that production is at the right point on the production possibility curve. All this is familiar, but we can gain some new insights by showing the conditions for allocative efficiency in a new way.

To see what is involved, consider Figure 23.1, which shows a production possibility curve similar to the curve in Figure 1.2(ii), together with two illustrative indifference curves which we assume represent levels of satisfaction derived from consumption of jeans and kebabs by all consumers. Indifference curve I_1 is tangent to the transformation curve JK at point e, where k_0 of kebabs and j_0 of jeans are produced and

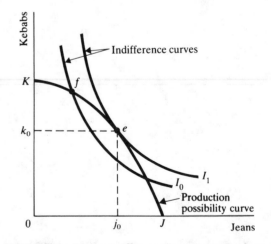

FIGURE 23.1   Economic Efficiency Once Again. Productive efficiency occurs at all points on the production possibility curve. Allocative efficiency occurs where the slope of the production possibility curve equals the slope of the indifference curve

consumed. This point gives the highest possible level of satisfaction to consumers. Compare it, for example, with point f which also lies on the production possibility curve (and is therefore also a point of production efficiency). The indifference curve which passes through f is I_0, which gives a lower level of satisfaction to consumers than I_1. Therefore, point e is preferable to point f, as it is to every other point on the graph. Point e is the point of allocative efficiency as well as productive efficiency. Note, too, that at e the marginal opportunity cost of kebabs in terms of jeans sacrificed, given by the slope of the production possibility curve, is equal to the marginal rate of substitution of kebabs in terms of jeans given by the slope of the indifference curve. In other words, at e the benefit to consumers of an extra kebab is equal to the extra cost of producing it. There is no other point on the diagram where this is true.[1]

Economic Efficiency and Market Forces

We know that both productive and allocative efficiency can result from the operation of market forces, without any state intervention, if all buyers and sellers are price-takers. We also know that the allocation of resources that would occur under a freely working market system may be regarded as unsatisfactory for four reasons, all of which have been mentioned many, many times before: (i) buyers and sellers are not always price-takers, (ii) externalities exist in some markets, (iii) markets may be sluggish, (iv) the distribution of income and wealth brought about by market forces may be regarded as inequitable.

We now come to a fifth reason which, although mentioned previously, has yet to be stressed. *Consumers may not always be the best judges of their own welfare.*

There may be a prevailing view that there are certain goods, called MERIT GOODS, that would benefit consumers, but which they would not choose to buy for themselves; and certain other goods, which would be bought by consumers but which would be detrimental to them. In such cases, the state may deem it desirable to take these goods out of the market system

altogether. This *paternalistic* attitude may apply to merit goods such as art galleries, so that they are supplied even if the private demand for them is negligible, and to goods such as addictive drugs so that they are not (legally) supplied even if the private demand for them is strong.

While most people would wish to make a distinction between government action to help those unable to help themselves (e.g., children) on the one hand, and telling adults what is in their best interests on the other hand, both types of governmental intervention are paternalistic in the sense that they pre-empt the rights of individuals to make choices for themselves. Decisions involving children are made in most societies by parents. However, the state is often given the power to ensure that certain minimum levels of education, and other goods, should be provided for children, regardless of the wishes of their parents.

OBJECTIVES AND METHODS OF STATE INTERVENTION

If any of the above reasons exist, there is a case for considering state intervention. No more than this can be said – certainly not that the state *must* intervene, because government inefficiency can be worse than market inefficiency. Each case for intervention must be considered on its individual merits.

There are literally hundreds of ways in which governments can, and do, intervene in the allocation of resources, in pursuit of the microeconomic goals of efficiency and equity. We now describe the chief methods of state intervention, which we shall apply to some illustrative problems of economic policy in Chapter 24.

Once again, we use the threefold classification introduced in Chapter 19: (i) policies using the price mechanism, (ii) policies improving the price mechanism, and (iii) extra-market policies.

To refresh your memory, policies using the price mechanism aim to change the price signals faced by buyers and sellers, e.g. by taxes and subsidies related to output. Policies for improving the price mechanism are designed to change the structure of markets, so that they function more efficiently, e.g. by competition policy, laying down safety standards, and introducing rules that outlaw discriminatory employment practices. Extra-market policies do not work through the price mechanism, but outside it, e.g. by

---

1 This conclusion is part of what is known as welfare economics, whose detailed exposition is a subject for intermediate rather than introductory courses in economics. The argument in this paragraph uses community indifference curves, without calling them by that name and without deriving them – a task left for more advanced treatments.

central planning and the setting of output quotas for particular industries.

In putting its policies into effect, the government has to choose between two kinds of policy instrument: (i) budgetary policies, and (ii) rules and regulations.

Budgetary Policies

One of the most notable features of the government's economic policy is the annual Budget which is presented for Parliament's approval by the Chancellor of the Exchequer. It sets out the sources of state income and expenditure for the coming financial year. Budgetary instruments aimed at the improvement of the efficiency or equity of the economy include taxes, subsidies and other items of income and expenditure. We deal here only with the chief categories on both sides of the government account and which are listed in Table 23.1.[1]

Government income

The left-hand side of the table lists the principal sources of government income. The first comprises taxes on income, often called DIRECT TAXES. These may be levied on persons, as in the case of Income Tax, or on corporations, as in the case of Corporation Tax on company profits. Taxes on income often have

1 For more details on the UK government's budget, see Harbury and Lipsey, Chapter 6.

the prime objective of changing the distribution of income. Taxes on expenditure, often called INDIRECT TAXES, may have different prime objectives. For example, the duties on alcohol and tobacco – known as EXCISE DUTIES, because they are levied by the Department of Customs and Excise – could be used to discourage consumption of these goods, although in practice rates are more commonly set so as to maximize the government's revenues from these taxes. Customs duties may also, as we saw in the previous chapter, be adopted to protect an industry from overseas competition. Taxes on capital are distinguished from those on income and expenditure because they are levied on the owners of wealth. Thus, Capital Transfer Tax is charged on transfers of capital from one individual to another. Capital taxes resemble income taxes, in that one of their prime purposes is often redistributory; simply raising money to finance state expenditure is of course their other main purpose.

The government can raise income by borrowing, as well as by taxing. The total of all government past borrowings, net of all repayments, is known as the NATIONAL DEBT. When the state increases the amount of borrowing, it adds to the size of the National Debt, and vice versa.

Whatever the main purpose for which taxes are levied, their effect can be, and often is, redistributive. It is usual to refer to taxes as falling into one of three groups, which are defined according to the proportion of income that is paid in tax. PROPORTIONAL taxes are those where the proportion of income taken

TABLE 23.1 Income and Expenditure of Central and Local Government

INCOME	EXPENDITURE
TAXES	TRANFER EXPENDITURES
on income (direct taxes):	Retirement pensions
Income Tax	Unemployment benefit
Capital Gains Tax	Supplementary benefit
Corporation Tax	Other social security benefits
National Insurance contributions	Interest on National Debt
on expenditure (indirect taxes):	EXHAUSTIVE EXPENDITURES
Value Added Tax	Education
Customs duties	Health
Excise duties	Housing
Petroleum Revenue Tax	Industry and agriculture
on capital:	(including regional aid)
Inheritance Tax	Environmental services (roads,
Rates (local authority)	parks, museums, etc.)
BORROWING	Miscellaneous (employment services,
	law and order, etc.)

in tax does not vary with the level of income. PROGRESSIVE taxes absorb a higher proportion of income as income rises. REGRESSIVE taxes are the opposite of progressive; they take a lower proportion of income as income rises. All three relations are shown in Figure 23.2. Progressive taxes, therefore, tend to move the distribution of income in the direction of equality, regressive taxes in the direction of inequality.

Note, too, that income taxes may be negative as well as positive. An income 'tax' which gives the poor an income subsidy is, effectively, a NEGATIVE INCOME TAX. We deal with subsidies below, under government expenditure.

Income taxes tend to be progressive in the UK, and expenditures taxes, especially VAT, which is levied at a flat rate on most goods, tend to be proportional, or regressive. Which category any tax falls into depends on the type of good taxed. Taxes on goods which form a higher proportion of the income of the poor than of the rich are regressive; those on goods where expenditure does not change as income rises, are proportional. Taxes on 'luxury goods' bought mainly by higher income groups are progressive.

A tax which is levied at a constant rate may, nevertheless, be progressive, in the sense in which that term has been defined. This will be the case if there is a minimum level of income that must be earned before tax liability is incurred. Consider the tax illustrated in Figure 23.3, which is levied at a constant rate on income in excess of the minimum level of y_0. The diagram shows that the tax paid on an income of y_1 is y_1a; while the tax on a higher income,

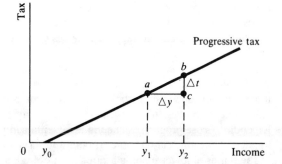

FIGURE 23.3   A Progressive Tax with a Constant Marginal Tax Rate and an Exemption Limit. Despite having a constant marginal tax rate, the average tax rate rises as income increases, if there is a minimum level of income below which no tax is paid

y_2, is y_2b. The proportion of income paid in tax, known as the AVERAGE TAX RATE (ATR), rises as income rises. For example, ATR at income y_1 is $ay_1/0y_1$; which is less than the ATR at income y_2, which is $by_2/0y_2$. Therefore the tax in Figure 23.3 is progressive.

Note that we define progressivity in terms of a rising *average* tax rate. The ATR must be distinguished from the MARGINAL TAX RATE (MTR), which is defined as the *change* in tax that accompanies a *change* in income, or $\Delta t/\Delta y$. The marginal tax rate is shown in the diagram by the slope of the tax line. When income rises, for example, from y_1 to y_2, tax paid on that extra income is bc. The MTR is, therefore, bc/ac (shown in the figure as $\Delta t/\Delta y$). If the MTR rises as income rises, the tax is progressive. However, a tax is also progressive, even if the MTR is constant, so long as the ATR rises. This will be the case if, as in Figure 23.3, there is an exemption limit, i.e. a minimum income, which must be reached before an individual is liable to pay any tax.

Government expenditure

The right-hand side of Table 23.1 lists the principal categories of government expenditure. There are two distinctive types, called transfers and exhaustive expenditures. TRANSFER PAYMENTS are payments not in return for any goods or productive services. They are thus one-sided transactions; the state gives money and gets nothing in exchange. The recipients can allocate the funds as they wish. EXHAUSTIVE EXPENDITURES are those on goods and services, where the state decides to claim the use of resources

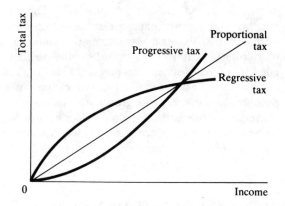

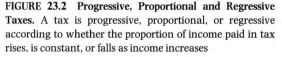

FIGURE 23.2   Progressive, Proportional and Regressive Taxes. A tax is progressive, proportional, or regressive according to whether the proportion of income paid in tax rises, is constant, or falls as income increases

for particular purposes, for example expenditure on roads, schools, etc. These are two-sided transactions where the state gives money and receives goods or productive services in return.

Both transfer and exhaustive expenditures affect the distribution of income, and may be considered as increasing or decreasing the progressivity of the government's budget in a way that is similar to taxes. Expenditures are progressive, i.e. have an equalizing impact, if they put relatively more goods and services in the hands of lower income groups than of higher ones. They are regressive in the opposite case. Most transfer payments in the UK are progressive. So are many kinds of expenditure, but some are proportional, i.e. when goods or services provided by the state benefit individuals in proportion to their incomes. Some are regressive when the goods or services are consumed mainly by higher income individuals.

Notice that the redistributive effect of the government's budget cannot be judged simply from the degree of progressivity of income taxes. The overall effect of the entire tax-expenditure system needs to be estimated. Although possible in principle, this is difficult to do accurately. This is mainly because there is no sure way of determining precisely how each and every burden, and benefit, in the budget falls on individuals and on income groups. There are also some collective benefits, such as defence and the judicial system, which can only be allocated among income groups on an arbitrary basis. The one safe generalization is that the expenditure side of the account has, in the UK, tended to promote equality more than has the taxation side.

Taxes and transfers have been discussed, so far, from the point of view of their redistributive effects. They are also used for improving the efficiency of resource allocation. For example, as we saw in Chapter 19, subsidies related to output can induce changes in the level of production by monopolistic firms. Taxes and subsidies can also be used to 'correct' for divergencies between private and social costs or benefits arising from the presence of externalities, and to encourage, or discourage, production and consumption of commodities that are thought beneficial or detrimental on paternalistic grounds.

Rules and Regulations

The second group of policy instruments available for the achievement of the goals of efficiency and equity, are rules and regulations. They do not involve expenditure by the government, other than the costs of administering the regulations.

Some rules and regulations are directed at improving the structure of markets, as we illustrated in Chapter 19 when we were discussing the effects of monopolistic practices. The examples we mentioned included price ceilings and the establishment of the Monopolies and Mergers Commission (though, whatever the intent, some of these actions may worsen the efficiency of markets). Other rules are directed paternalistically at the protection of individuals from themselves – e.g. the banning of sales of addictive drugs and street soliciting by prostitutes.

Regulations can be directed at the improvement of resource allocations arising from externalities. Examples are the introduction of 'smoke-free zones', and the requirement on drivers of motor vehicles to take out insurance for the benefit of innocent 'third parties' who may suffer in accidents.

Regulations may also be used in an attempt to influence the distribution of income directly. Examples are laws banning wage differences on grounds of sex or ethnic origin, and the provision of minimum-wage legislation. Notice that we speak of intent, which may differ from actual results. For example, minimum-wage laws, meant to raise the incomes of unskilled workers, may succeed instead in increasing unemployment among the young, the old and the disabled.

In each of the above cases, rules may be *prescriptive*, laying down minimum standards of quality, for instance, or *proscriptive*, for example banning pollution. A second division of rules according to whether they are automatic or discretionary is also often useful. An example of an automatic (or mandatory) rule is that which guarantees any student admitted to an *undergraduate* degree course in Britain, a subsidy to cover the costs of the education (and possibly also a maintenance grant). An example of a discretionary rule is that which provides awards to *postgraduate* students, since these are awarded at the discretion of the awarding body.

THE COSTS OF INTERVENTION

When the government intervenes in any way, costs are involved. Some are fairly obvious and have been

TABLE 23.2 State Intervention and Resource Allocation

Policy goals (i)		Reasons for intervention (ii)	Types of policy (iii)	Policy instruments (iv)	Costs of intervention (v)
Efficiency	M A R K E T S H O R T C O M I N G S	Income distribution	Policies using the price mechanism	Budgetary	Administrative
Productive Allocative		Externalities		Taxes Subsidies	Redistributive
		Concentration of economic power	Policies improving the price mechanism		New distortions
Equity		Sluggish markets	Extra-market policies	Rules and regulations	Government failure
		Paternalism			

mentioned already – for example, administrative costs borne by the state, and 'compliance' costs of coping with the tax laws, borne by taxpayer – others are more subtle, such as the effects of distorted market signals that arise when taxes and subsidies alter relative prices of goods in ways not related to costs of production. Any gain achieved by a government policy must be assessed in relation to the costs associated with that policy. Some of the less obvious but nonetheless potentially serious costs are listed in column (v) of Table 23.2, and are discussed below.

Equity versus efficiency

In a free-market system, the prices of factors of production – wages, rent, interest and profits – act as signals to the owners of those factors who respond by supplying different amounts according to the prices they receive. Attempts by the state to distribute income more equally than would the market may affect the incentives for supplying factor services. We illustrate with a few examples.

A progressive income tax may lead some people to work less hard, though we should remember that, as we saw in Chapter 20, the income effect of a fall in the effective wage rate (with an income tax) may just as easily lead to an increased willingness to work (see pages 230–2). The same argument may be applied to a high rate of unemployment benefit, as well as to any taxes, or benefits, which reduce the differential between the gain from working as against not working. As far as other factors of production are

concerned, a tax on profits, or intervention to hold down the rate of interest, will reduce the incentive for businesses to engage in profitable production, or reduce the incentive for people to save a part of their incomes. There is no presumption in any of these cases, however, that reduced incentives will lead to reductions in the amounts of services supplied. The income effect is still relevant. For example, it can cause businesses to strive harder for profitable activities, if the rate of profit falls; or it may stimulate people to save more of their income when the rate of interest falls, simply in order to prevent their income from investment from falling.

New distortions

A different type of cost, when the state intervenes to alter factor prices, concerns economic efficiency, both productive and allocative. The reasons why market forces lead to an allocation of resources that is efficient, subject to certain stringent conditions, were set out at the beginning of this chapter. Prices can only allocate resources when they reflect real opportunity costs. If the government intervention changes factor prices so that they no longer reflect opportunity costs, market forces will also no longer allocate factors of production efficiently.

It is not only productive efficiency which can be adversely affected by some state actions, but allocative efficiency as well. Moreover, choosing between alternative resource allocations may involve moral issues on which opinions differ. For example, supporters of income supplements generally favour allowing individuals to decide for themselves how best to allocate their expenditure, and rely on markets, in which prices reflect opportunity costs, to ensure efficient allocations. Supporters of subsidies on goods and services, such as food, heat, medical care and housing, feel that minimum quantities of such goods are basic requirements of a civilized life, and should be available to everyone, regardless of their real cost. Some are even in favour of goods of this type being provided free of charge when goods are consumed up to the point where their marginal utilities become zero. Such issues tend to be very controversial, and it is impossible to do justice to both sides of the arguments in a few pages.

Government failure

Issues such as those discussed in the previous section would exist even if the government had perfect foresight in defining goals, an unerring ability to choose the least costly means of achieving them, and intelligent and dedicated officials whose concern was to do those things – and only those things – that achieved the greatest possible economic efficiency. Government intervention usually falls short of such high standards. This is not because bureaucrats are necessarily worse than other people, more stupid, more rigid, or more corrupt, but because they are like others, with the usual flaws and virtues.

Here are six reasons why government intervention can be imperfect and fail to improve resource allocations.

Imperfect Knowledge or Foresight: Regulators may not know enough to set correct standards. For example, natural gas prices may, with the best of intentions, be set too low. The result will be too much quantity demanded and too little quantity supplied, with no automatic correction. Or officials may over-optimistically estimate the future demand for a long-term investment project, which turns out to be an inefficient use of resources (e.g., Concorde).

Rigidities: Regulatory rules and allocations are hard to change. Yet technology and economic circumstances change continually. Regulations, that at one time protected the public against a natural monopoly, may perpetuate an unnecessary monopoly after technological changes have made competition possible (e.g. in the delivery of mail). An outstanding example of government intervention in

the UK which has outlived, for over half a century, its original purpose, is rent control. This was introduced, as an *emergency* measure, during the First World War but gradually became more and more entrenched. Later in the decade, however, the government showed signs of rethinking its policy concerning rent controls.

Inefficient Means: Government may fail to choose the least costly means of solving a problem. It may decree a specific form of anti-pollution device that proves less effective, and more expensive, than another. A strict rule that proves all but impossible to enforce may be passed, when a milder one would have achieved higher compliance at lower enforcement cost.

Over-specialization: Regulation may become too restricted and too narrowly defined because the regulators are forced to specialize. Specialization may lead to expertise in a given area, but the regulators may lack the breadth to relate their area to broader concerns. Officials charged with the responsibility for a healthy railway industry (dating from the time when railways were the dominant means of transportation) may fail to see that expansion of road transport, even at the expense of the railways, may be necessary for a healthy transport industry as a whole.

Political Constraints: Political realities may prevent the 'right' policy from being adopted, even when it has been clearly identified. This is particularly true in a government based on checks and balances. Suppose a technically perfect tax (or tariff or farm policy) is designed by the experts. It will surely hurt some groups and benefit others. Lobbyists will go to work. The policy is likely to be modified, mutilated, rebuilt, and finally passed in a form the experts know is inadequate. Although Parliament may be aware of its flaws, it will be passed into law because it is 'better than nothing'. These events occur because the political process must respond to political realities. 'After all,' the MP may reason, as he yields to the demands of a particular lobby (against his best judgement about the public interest), 'if I'm defeated for re-election, I won't be here to serve the public interest on even more important issues next year.' (Next year he may support the same lobby, out of a sense of consistency!)

Decision-maker's Objective: Public officials almost always wish to serve the public interest. But they have their careers, their families, and their prejudices as well. Their own needs may not be always and wholly absent from their consideration of the actions they take. Similarly, their definitions of the public interest are likely to be influenced heavily by their personal views of what policies are best.

The proper balance

The above examples show that, just as markets can fail, so too can governments. It follows that a valid case for state intervention requires (i) that there is a market inefficiency or unsatisfactory distribution of income, (ii) that a perfectly functioning government could reduce the inefficiency, or redress the inequity, at a cost that is less than the benefit gained, and (iii) that government failure to function perfectly does not eliminate the gain otherwise available.

SUMMARY

1 Graphically, economic efficiency occurs when production is on the production possibility curve, not inside it, and when the production possibility curve has the same slope as consumers' indifference curves at the point of actual production and consumption. This ensures that the marginal rate of substitution between goods is equal to the ratio of their marginal costs.

2 The allocation of resources may be regarded as unsatisfactory if: (i) some buyers and/or sellers are price-makers; (ii) externalities exist in some markets; (iii) market forces are sluggish; (iv) the distribution of income resulting from market forces is regarded as unfair; and/or (v) there are merit goods which consumers would not choose to buy for themselves.

3 If market allocations are unsatisfactory, there is a case for state intervention to improve them in pursuit of the prime microeconomic goals of efficiency and equity, though intervention can worsen the allocation.

4 Three types of interventionist policies are: (i) those using the price mechanism; (ii) those improving the price mechanism; and (iii) extra-market policies.

5 Two sets of policy instruments are available for intervention: budgetary policies, and rules and regulations.

6 Budgetary policies refer to the income and expenditure of the government. The former includes taxes, which may be progressive, proportional or regressive, and related to income, expenditure, wealth, or other bases. Government expenditures may be transfers or exhaustive, and are capable of being as redistributive as taxes, depending on the incidence of each. Taxes and subsidies may also be used to 'correct' the allocation of resources if they would otherwise depart from optimal.

7 Rules and regulations may be of many kinds and do not involve government expenditures other than the cost of administration. They may be prescriptive requirements or proscriptive bans, as well as mandatory (automatic) or discretionary.

8 Assessments of economic policy in particular cases should have regard to (i) policy goals; (ii) market shortcomings; (iii) types of policy; and (iv) policy instruments.

9 Costs of intervention must also be considered. They include cost of administration, the costs of redistribution, distortions created, and other causes of government failure.

Problems of Microeconomic Policy

In this chapter, we illustrate the principles of micro-economic policy described in the previous chapter by applying them to four problems of current interest.

THE PROBLEM OF POLLUTION

We take pollution as our first policy problem to illustrate the pros and cons of state intervention. This familiar issue from everyday life is an illustration of the spillover effects or *externalities* which we analysed in Chapter 9.

We saw in Chapter 9 that where private and social costs diverge, market forces do not result in the socially optimum output. For example, if private producers exclude the costs imposed on other people from their cost and profit calculations, they will produce more than is socially desirable.

We now look at a case where a factory discharges effluent into a river and imposes costs on the inhabitants of a local town, who have to purify the river water which is used for drinking. We will look at the difference between private and social optimum output, and consider what, if anything, the government can do about it.

It will be helpful to consider this question in two stages. First, we enquire which category, or categories, of the market shortcomings and policy goals listed in Table 23.2 is relevant. Second, we compare alternative courses of action open to the state.

Policy Goals and Market Shortcomings

The primary source of market failure here is the existence of externalities which lead to non-optimal allocation of resources. The primary goal for the state is therefore that of efficiency.

There is, however, a secondary effect of the divergence between private and social values. This involves the distribution of income. In the illustration we are using, there are gainers and losers. The gainers include the producers and consumers of the output that causes the pollution; while the losers are the inhabitants of a town near the factory.

It is important to distinguish the allocative inefficiency of non-optimal outputs from their distributive consequences. Both commonly occur, and any state intervention affects both. Sometimes, a single state remedy may improve the allocation of resources without adverse distributive effects. At other times, however, there may be need for one action to improve efficiency, and another to correct the adverse distributive effects of the first action.

Private and Social Optimum Outputs Compared

In Figure 24.1 the pollution-creating output is measured along the horizontal axis, while monetary values associated with output are measured on the vertical axis. Two curves are drawn on the diagram. The curve labelled MR shows the marginal profit of the factory. MR slopes downwards since we assume that the margin of profit decreases as output increases. (This could be due to rising marginal costs, falling marginal revenues, or both.) The curve labelled BC shows the marginal loss to townsfolk as the pollution-creating output rises. BC is drawn as a horizontal line because we assume that the townsfolk's loss from pollution is directly proportional to output.

Consider the output that results when profit-maximizing producers take account only of their own (private) costs and revenues, and exclude from their reckonings the costs imposed on local townsfolk. Producers will continue to expand output until there is no net profit from doing so. They will, therefore, produce at point R. *This is the private maximum output, where the marginal gain from producing another unit is zero.*

Next, consider the socially optimum output, i.e. the output that the firm would produce if it took account of the costs imposed on the townsfolk, as well as its own private costs. Diagrammatically, we know that the former are represented by OB per unit of output. Therefore, we draw a curve, NS, parallel to MR, but exactly $MN (= tS)$ below it, to show the marginal gain to the firm *after deducting the loss to townsfolk.* This shows the marginal net social gain allowing for both the internal effects of production on the firm and the external effects on the townsfolk. Each unit produced up to S has a positive net social gain and so it adds to social value. Each unit beyond s has a negative social gain (i.e. a loss), so it subtracts from social value. It follows that S is the social optimum output. Note that marginal net social gain becomes zero at output S, which is also *the output at which the marginal profit to the producer is equal to the marginal loss to the townsfolk.*

The optimum degree of pollution

Notice that the output associated with socially optimal production described in the previous para-

graph is *not* zero. In other words, there is a positive level of pollution at the social optimum. This conclusion, which would surprise many people, should not surprise you, if you have understood the basic principles of economics which have been explained in this book. This positive level of pollution is socially desirable because it involves a greater gain to producers and consumers of the product than it does loss to townsfolk. This is true for all levels of output up to point S in Figure 24.1.

The optimum level of pollution is not zero because zero pollution could only be achieved at the cost of zero output. In the circumstances assumed here, the loss of all output would be socially undesirable, because some positive output brings gains greater than losses from pollution. (Note that this does not mean that the optimum level of pollution is *never* zero. There are several sets of circumstances which could lead to that result. One would be where the marginal loss from pollution was greater than the marginal gain to producers at every positive level of output.)

To emphasize that it is socially optimal to produce some pollution, consider a case in which, if the firm is to produce, it must compensate the townsfolk for their loss. The production of the first unit is worth OM to the firm and the townsfolk must be paid OB to compensate them for the pollution. The firm can do this and still gain, so there is net gain over the whole society. A similar argument applies to every unit up to s since the firm can pay OB compensation for each extra unit produced and still have some gain left.

What if the firm is tempted to produce beyond S? Say, for example, that output were q_1. At this output the townsfolk would continue to require $OB (= q_1v)$ to compensate them for the pollution brought by the last unit of production, but the production of that unit is only worth q_1w to the firm. Since the firm gains q_1w but must pay q_1v, there is a net loss from that unit.

The exercise emphasizes that the movement of production from zero to S is towards greater economic efficiency (see page 101) because someone can be made better off while no one is made worse off. A movement beyond S is not more efficient because someone must be made worse off (either the firm, if it has to pay full compensation, or the townsfolk, if the firm pays no more than its own gain).

Policies to Control Pollution

Having identified the socially optimum output and compared it with the output that would be produced

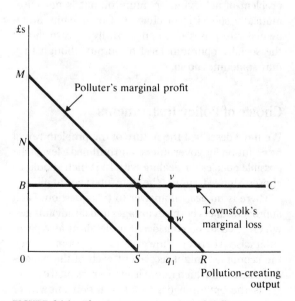

FIGURE 24.1   The Optimum Amount of Pollution

by profit-maximizing producers, who ignored the costs imposed on outsiders, let us turn to consider what the state might try to do to secure the social optimum. We may use the classification system described in the previous chapter – policies using the price mechanism, policies improving the price mechanism, and extra-market policies.

Policies using the price mechanism

The simplest device that falls into this category is a tax imposed on the firm and directly related to its output. If the tax was exactly equal to the costs of the pollution imposed on townsfolk, this would effectively make the offending firm include the costs imposed on outsiders in its calculations.

Consider the way in which a policy would work in terms of the diagram which we have been using, Figure 24.1. The cost of the pollution to townsfolk has been assumed to be constant and equal to OB. A tax of OB per unit would shift the curve of marginal profit to the producer downwards. Instead of MR, the new marginal profit curve, net of tax, would be NS, which is parallel to MR, but lies below it by an amount equal to OB at every level of output. The profit-maximizing firm will still continue to produce up to the point at which its marginal profit falls to zero. However, this point, net of tax, is now S, which happens to be the socially optimum output.[1]

Policies improving the price mechanism

When we were describing the optimum level of output from a social point of view, we explained it by asking how much the townsfolk would have to be compensated for accepting the pollution, and how much the firm would be prepared to pay. If the two parties affected by output – the firm and the townsfolk – were able to negotiate the bargain with each other, the socially optimum level of output could be reached without any state intervention being needed. Such bargaining can actually take place. It would be quite likely if the parties concerned were, for example, two independent companies – say a chemical works polluting a river upstream from a brewery.

One reason why such bargaining might be less likely in the case we have been examining is that there are many local inhabitants, and there might be no machinery through which they could negotiate with the factory owners. If that were the case, the justification for intervention by the government would be that the market system was not working efficiently, because of the absence of a market for 'purity' of water supplies, which only townsfolk value. The situation might be remedied if the state intervened merely to bring the two sides together, and left them to negotiate with each other.

Extra-market policies

Our final category of policies that a government can use is that of taking the problem outside the market system, rather than using it, or improving it. A large number of rules or regulations could be proposed, e.g. banning output which caused pollution, banning the use of techniques of production that caused the most pollution, forcing the firm to purify water discharged into rivers, etc. Such rules are not always easy to formulate, and they can be costly to enforce, the costs often falling not only on the taxpayer but also on the firm which must comply (compliance costs).

One extreme option which falls into this category is for the state to acquire ownership of the company causing pollution, i.e. nationalizing it. We deal separately with the problems of state provision of goods and services below. We might note, however, that the problem of achieving optimum output is not automatically solved by a change of ownership. State-owned enterprises are not necessarily likely to choose the socially optimum level of output, though they may sometimes do so.

Choice of Policy Instruments

We have described the nature of the problem raised by pollution for government, and outlined a few of the possible policies for dealing with it. Which should be chosen? Indeed, should the state intervene at all?

There is no *general* answer to this question. Each approach suffers both advantages and disadvantages, which need to be considered in detail in any particular case. There are, however, four questions which the economist might ask about each of the policies discussed and which might lead to a reasoned choice: (1) Is the optimum degree of pollution known, or unknown? (2) What are the costs of different policies?

---

1 There are, of course, many taxes which could induce the same output by reducing the firm's marginal profit to zero at point S. (Could you draw in the proportional tax which would achieve this?) Note, too, that a tax *related to the amount of pollution* might be more efficient than one related to output, if it induced the firm to change its production technique to one which led to less pollution.

(3) What are the distributive consequences of the policies? and (4) How flexible are the policies?

Let us consider the pros and cons of the alternatives we have considered, anti-pollution taxes, improving the market, anti-pollution rules, and non-intervention, in the light of these questions (also remembering, of course, that the policy alternatives we have considered are representative rather than comprehensive, and that there may be other questions to be asked in particular cases).

If the optimum degree of pollution is *not* known, there is a clear advantage of using a policy which facilitates negotiation between the parties, and which allows market forces to help find it. If the optimum degree of pollution is unknown, it is virtually impossible to design a tax or set of rules which would achieve it.

The costs of different policies

The costs that must be considered here are, of course, real costs involving the use of scarce resources with alternative uses. Such costs may be born directly by the government, e.g. cost of administering taxes or rules or setting up negotiating machinery. They may also be borne by firms, when they take the form of compliance costs which must be included in the assessment, since they equally involve the use of scarce resources.

The benefits of pollution prevention naturally vary from case to case, and may be difficult to quantify (see our discussion of cost-benefit analysis below). The greater the benefits, i.e. the greater the costs imposed on outsiders from pollution, the more worthwhile it is incurring the costs of controlling it. Indeed, if the benefits to be gained are high, the policy of control by regulation, or even complete ban, may be advantageous, providing the costs of enforcement are low enough. Otherwise, there is little that can be said of a general nature on this question. Careful estimates should be carried out for all options.

The distributive consequences of different policies

The distribution of income is likely to be affected by the application of the different policy measures adopted. The losers from pollution control probably include three sets of people – the owners of the firm which causes pollution, their workforce, and consumers of their product. The first of these suffer profit reductions; the workers suffer job losses and/or lower wages; while consumers suffer reduced output

and/or higher prices. The gainers from pollution control are the third parties; in the example we have been using, they are the local inhabitants.

If we assume that the optimum level of pollution is known, and can be achieved by any of the policies we have been considering, there may be much to be said in favour of encouraging negotiation over other policy options, because we know that the gainers will not pay the polluters more than they stand to win in terms of extra satisfaction. However, it must be appreciated that there may be a very broad band of possible negotiated settlements. If one of the parties holds a strong bargaining position, it may use a monopoly, or monopsony, position to achieve a particularly favourable outcome for itself. This might be the case if a single producer was negotiating with a large number of local residents (or if a single local authority was negotiating, on behalf of its constituents, with a large number of producers). Negotiated settlements might well be the preferred policy, on this count, if the two sides were fairly evenly balanced. If they were not, pollution control by means of regulations or tax incentives might be the best solution. The decision on how the proceeds of any tax should be spent needs to be taken into account when considering the distributive consequences of government policies.

The flexibility of different policies

Flexibility in the face of change is a very important consideration when choosing among policies. The costs and benefits of pollution control are liable to alter with the passage of time. So, too, in consequence, are the optimum level of pollution and of socially optimal output. One of the main reasons why control through rules and regulations is not favoured by many economists, is that they would need amending every time such a change occurs. Much the same argument applies to control via anti-pollution taxes. Of the policies we have considered, only one – bringing the parties together – allows for automatic adjustment. It would occur in this case through renewed negotiation. But such a policy might be undesirable on other grounds. It might, for example, have unfavourable distributive consequences.

Should the State Intervene?

In conclusion, it is necessary to ask also whether any intervention is desirable. We cannot just assume that the free-market output, inefficient though it may be, is less inefficient than whatever output would result from government intervention. After all, few state actions are costless. Therefore, before proposing or supporting a particular policy for pollution abatement, the costs and benefits of the best policy alternative need to be estimated, and compared with a non-interventionist situation. Do not misunderstand us. We are not saying that nothing should be done about pollution! What we are saying is that the optimum level of pollution is often not zero, and that the costs of reducing pollution should be taken into a reckoning of anti-pollution policy. So, too, should the benefits of pollution control, which are unquestionably high in some cases, for example the discharge of nuclear waste, and relatively small in others. After all, nature often takes care of pollution, as when rivers purify themselves. The problems arise when we overload nature. So, control of the mild pollution of a river at a particular point may bring very little benefit, while control of severe pollution may bring great gain.

THE PROVISION OF ROADS

Our second illustrative policy problem is the provision of roads, which is usually regarded as a function of central and local government. Some roads fall into a special class of goods called PUBLIC GOODS (also sometimes COLLECTIVE CONSUMPTION GOODS), in contrast with private goods that are the ordinary commodities we have considered so far in this book. The two distinguishing characteristics of public goods are that they are *non-rivalrous* and *non-excludable*.

Public Goods

We start by explaining the meaning of the two characteristics possessed by public goods, non-rivalrousness and non-excludability.

A public good is NON-RIVALROUS, because consumption of it by any one individual does not reduce the amount of it available for consumption by any other individuals. For example, if lights are provided in the centre of Cardiff, they shine as brightly when I enjoy their benefit as when 1,000 people pass beneath them. Compare this with a private good such as one tandoori chicken. If I eat it, no one else can!

A public good is NON-EXCLUDABLE, because when it

is provided for any one person, no one else can be prevented from consuming it also. To continue with the example of street lighting, there is no effective way of excluding everyone who walks the street at night from benefiting from it. Compare a private good such as a rock concert. The number of people that can attend a concert is limited by the size of the hall in which it is given. They can be excluded, by the simple expedient of charging for a ticket to enter the building.

'Pure' public goods are those which possess these two characteristics completely, and to achieve the optimal output *no price should be charged for the use of a public good*. Why should this be so?

The answer stems from the non-rivalrous characteristic of public goods, and from the general rule for optimum resource allocation that price should equal marginal cost so that the marginal utility from consuming it will equal the opportunity cost of producing it. When this rule is applied to pure public goods the result is that the correct price to be charged is nothing, because the marginal cost of providing another unit of the public good is zero. Since they are non-rivalrous, there is no less for you when I consume a public good; there is zero opportunity cost in its consumption by you, me or anyone else once the decision has been taken to provide it in the first place.

Now consider the second characteristic of public goods, non-excludability. If you cannot exclude people from benefiting from a public good by charging, the only price that can be charged is zero anyway!

Roads as public goods

Pure public goods are rare, but there are many goods which have a strong element of 'publicness' about them, i.e. that they are very nearly non-rivalrous or non-excludable, or have a high degree of these characteristics. Roads are a good example.

Consider the two characteristics. All roads are non-rivalrous, up to their capacity. As long as there is room for your car as well as mine, the fact that I am driving does not interfere with your doing so too. Moreover, once a road is constructed, there is little by way of extra cost of using it (other than a long-term need for repair, which we may assume is small enough to be neglected). The *marginal* cost of one more person using the road is therefore zero. (We deal below with problems arising from congestion on roads, which *do* involve real marginal costs of use.)

What about the characteristic of excludability? This question can be put in the form of asking whether it is possible, and practicable, to exclude persons from using it by imposing a charge for use. Expressed this way, the answer must be a mixed one. There are some roads where the principle of non-excludability does not apply. Inter-city motorways with limited access can be priced, and indeed many in the USA and on the continent of Europe are priced – with users being charged a toll for the use of sections between access points. Urban streets, in contrast, are to all intents and purposes non-excludable. Although it would be physically possible to charge motorists tolls every time they turned from one street into another, it would be difficult and prohibitively costly to do so.

If the provision of roads is not to be left to the market, which category of market shortcomings and policy goals, listed in Table 23.2, are involved? The primary source of market failure in the case of roads is, again, the existence of externalities, and the primary goal for the state is, therefore, also that of efficiency in resource allocation. Indeed, public goods may be thought of as an extreme case of externalities. We have seen that with a good where *some* of the benefits spill over to other people, a free market will not provide enough of it to maximize social benefit. In the case of a pure public good, the only difference is that because of non-exclusiveness *all* the benefits spill over to other people. A private supplier could collect nothing for providing the services of the good since he cannot exclude those who do not pay. Thus the market does not only underprovide, it does not provide at all.

State Intervention in Road Provision

There are three important questions to ask about state policy in the provision of roads:
- How much should be spent on roads (and how should that total be allocated around the country)?
- How should the finance for road construction and maintenance be raised, given that a price will not be charged for their use?
- Should the state itself provide the roads or simply pay for private firms to do so?

How much to spend on the roads?

In the case of any private good, the question of whether it should be supplied, and in what quantities, is determined in the market by the quantities that consumers want to purchase. In the case of a public good, the good should be provided if the total benefit people get from using its services exceeds the cost of producing the good. The benefit people derive from it can be measured in principle by seeing how much each would pay in order to have the service provided.

In the case of a road, if the sum of what each potential user would be willing to pay to have the roads available exceeded the cost of building the road, then building the road brings social gain.

The case of the road is complicated, however, by the fact that some of its benefits accrue to non-users. For example, a non-driving shopowner benefits from a road that allows his customers to reach his shop. This is a standard case of an externality, which has nothing to do with the road being a public good.

Because the optimal price of the use of the road is zero whether or not externalities are conferred, these raise no short-run problem. Where they matter with a public good is in the long-run decision of whether or not to produce it in the first place. If the total that the potential *road users* were willing to pay for the road fell short of the cost of building it, its construction might still be socially optimal. This would be the case if what *all those who benefit* – users *and* non-users – would be willing to pay exceeded the cost of constructing the road.

Cost-benefit analysis

One practical method of making these calculations of the social value of proposed investment is known as COST-BENEFIT ANALYSIS (sometimes with the word SOCIAL before the word Cost).

To illustrate what is involved, suppose the state is contemplating the construction of a hypothetical new motorway, linking Bradchester with Wigport. We assume that the construction costs of the motorway are known, and the problem is to quantify the benefits in monetary terms which can then be compared with the costs.

The first step in a cost-benefit analysis is to identify the benefits that should be included. The second step is to place a value on them. In the case of the proposed motorway, the benefits would include those *directly* accruing to users of the new road, and those *indirectly* accruing to others, for instance motorists who continue to use existing roads, which become less congested and retailers whose shops become more accessible. These benefits would consist, among other things, of cost savings of petrol consumption, and wear and tear on vehicle parts such as tyres, brakes and clutch. There would also be benefits of time saved, and possibly of reduced accidents, when the motorway is ready.

Some of the above benefits can be estimated with a fair degree of precision, though the extent to which traffic will switch from existing routes to the new route, and the volume of new traffic that will be generated, can only be forecast within a margin of error. Other benefits are even more difficult to evaluate in money terms. Of special interest, in the case of roads, are the values to put on savings of time and of reduced numbers of accidents.

The appropriate way to value time saved poses a particular problem, since it depends on the use to which time is put. If travellers decide to work longer hours, the proper figure to adopt is the marginal increase in income that can be earned. If the time saved is used for more leisure the value might be somewhat less than this, though exactly how much is difficult to say. In practice, in cost-benefit studies, average hourly wage rates are often used to value time.

The value to be placed on reduced accidents is also difficult to assess, though a minimum would be the cost of vehicle repair or replacement, plus the cost of medical resources needed for the injured, plus the income forgone before victims are able to return to work. The most difficult problem is how to value the lives that may be saved of those who would otherwise be killed in road accidents. Let us admit that there is no entirely satisfactory method of placing a monetary value on human life itself. For instance, one could assess the value in terms of the future earnings of the individual in question, the amount he or she would pay to remain alive, or the amount that other people would pay for the same thing. Profound moral questions are raised, which lie well beyond the boundaries of economics. Indeed, many people are inclined to say that the value of a human life is infinite. If you are one of them, let us point out that the logical conclusion of that premise is that *no* resources should be used for any purpose in the world other than the saving of life until there was not a single preventable death!

The best estimates of benefits from the new motorway will typically consist of a *stream* of benefits running over a period of years in the future. To compare motorway projects covering different time-spans, such benefits must be compared. The standard method calls for discounting future benefits, using a rate of interest. This yields a single present value for each project, in a manner basically similar to that described in Chapter 21 for decisions on the profitability of private investments. Finally, the present value of the stream of benefits from the motorway must be compared to its costs. If the benefits exceed the costs, the motorway should be built. If the costs exceeds the benefits, it should not, at least on grounds of economic efficiency (though there may be other considerations to override this conclusion, e.g. national security).

Cost-benefit analysis has come under attack in recent years. The basis for the attacks is largely a worry that it produces numerical valuations of costs and benefits which give spurious impressions of accuracy in matters where precision is inherently difficult. The claim made for cost-benefit analysis is that it faces up to the problems of valuation directly, i.e. there is no way of avoiding such value judgements without implicitly putting values on some things that you may think 'unvaluable'.

The critics of cost-benefit analysis argue that it is dangerous, because it tends to highlight the results of the calculations rather than the value judgements on which they are based. Our own feeling is that cost-benefit analysis is a useful tool (especially if estimates of some of the most intractable costs and benefits are made on a *range* of assumptions), though it can be misused – especially if all information on which calculations are based is not fully and clearly expressed.

How to finance road construction and maintenance?

The second question to ask about state provision of roads is how to finance them. The two main alternatives are charging for the use of the roads, and financing them out of general taxation. If the marginal costs of use of a particular road are zero, once it has been constructed the first alternative is ruled out on grounds of optimum resource allocation. However, this is not the case with all roads, and we now deal with state provision of those with positive marginal costs. For example, if maintenance or policing costs rise with each additional road-user, then the marginal cost of an additional unit of use is not zero.

In such cases, if it is feasible to charge road-users, and if the costs of administering tolls are not prohibitively high, road pricing may be the preferred choice. Such a method is common for inter-city motorways in many countries.

If tolls are used, the level at which they are set is a matter of some importance. Tolls should, of course, be related only to marginal costs, i.e. they should exclude costs of construction. Once a motorway has been built, construction costs are of historical interest only. Bygones are bygones. Marginal costs include only the costs of maintenance and repair properly attributable to road use.

In some cases, it may be right to charge users *more* than the marginal costs of maintenance and repair. This is when the road is a congested one, and the time taken for journeys rises for everybody when an additional driver joins the traffic, i.e. externalities are present. A congestion tax not only reduces the level of congestion, but also helps to ensure optimum use of the road, because each individual user is forced to take account of the costs imposed on other users.

In cases where the principle of non-excludability applies, charging is not a possibility, e.g. in urban streets. Where congestion is high, however, the government might charge a licence fee to those who want to drive in certain areas in city centres.[1]

In most urban roads, congestion is not a problem outside rush hours. In such circumstances, the obvious alternative to charging is for the state to cover its road costs by levying taxes not related to road use. If such taxes are paid by local residents in the region around the road, this has some advantages even over road pricing, since it covers all beneficiaries – not only road-users. However, long-distance travellers passing through a region also benefit. So may many people all over the country, as a result of lower distribution costs of any goods transported by lorry. Therefore, it would seem equitable to allocate a portion of the costs to the national exchequer. In most cases, however, there is no perfect way of allocating costs when public goods are being provided – only some ways which are worse than others.

Should the state itself provide the roads?

It should now be clear that government finance is

usually necessary to cover the construction costs, and at least some of the maintenance costs, of a national road network. Our last question is whether the state itself should actually build the roads as well as financing them, in whole or in part, or whether it should simply pay private firms to do so. This raises the issue of private versus public provision of goods and services, which is sufficiently large to have a whole section devoted to it. It is in fact the topic of our next section, which deals with nationalization and privatization.

The main issues involved in the question of state versus private provision of goods and services are those of ownership and of accountability. The first of these, ownership, refers to whether the providing firm should be owned by its shareholders or by the state (on behalf of the community at large). The second issue, of accountability, is related to the first. It is whether those who manage the firm's operations should report to the shareholders, or to some government organization, for example to Parliament.

Both of these issues carry heavy political undertones, and there is little point in trying to present the 'purely economic' aspects of the general case for, and against, state provision. We choose, instead, to look at the cases for nationalization and privatization, as they have been made; though, as we shall see, the word 'privatization', as currently used, carries wider implications than simply those of ownership and of accountability.[1]

STATE VERSUS PRIVATE OWNERSHIP

The two prime goals of microeconomic policy of equity and efficiency are useful in examining the case for nationalization.

Equity: The case of state ownership that rests on the question of fairness in the distribution of income and wealth, is a moral and political one. Advocating the abolition of private property in the *Communist Manifesto* in 1848, Karl Marx sought to deprive what he called the 'bourgeoisie' of the power to 'subjugate the labour of others by means of appropriation'. Marx's

---

1 As an interesting application of advanced electronic technology, we might mention the possibility of fitting metering devices to vehicles which can be used to charge motorists a fee for use of *blocks* of roads in city centres. Such devices have not (yet!) caught on in this country.

---

1 For further details on the nationalized industries and privatization in the UK, see Harbury and Lipsey, Chapters 1, 2 and 6.

motives were basically moral and ethical. His views, and those of the later Fabian socialists such as George Bernard Shaw, were not confined to such issues, but contained inefficiency arguments to which we shall shortly turn.

Modern political arguments for nationalization tend to rest on a narrower base than older ones, and are related to the distribution of income and wealth, i.e. to the degree of equality or inequality that citizens want to have. Although such distributive arguments can have a strong appeal, they suffer from the weakness that redistribution can usually be achieved by means other than state ownership.

Take, for example, the desire to ensure that monopoly profits are acquired for 'the community at large' rather than for the owners of a privately owned business. Nationalization could be a means of trying to bring this about. But it is also possible to devise taxes, rules and regulations that prevent a firm from earning a level of profits greater than that which the government considers desirable. Hence, the abolition of private property is not the only way of achieving a given distribution of income – unless the structure of what Marx called 'social power', which he saw as concentrated in the hands of capitalists, is so strong that redistributive policies are ineffective.

Efficiency: Efficiency arguments for nationalization may be based on any of the shortcomings of the market mechanism listed in Table 23.2. We met one such argument with the provision of roads in this chapter, and another with natural monopolies in Chapter 19. Such arguments were based on certain *allocative* inefficiencies of the market. In this section we discuss the more controversial question of the *productive* efficiency of private versus public ownership.

Whether state-owned enterprise is more or less productively efficient than privately owned enterprise is a question of fact, not of opinion. Nevertheless, many distinguished writers have held the view that because private enterprise is not always efficient, state enterprise must always do better. Almost half a century ago, for instance, George Bernard Shaw wrote, 'Any State railway service can be made punctual, efficient, solvent and profitable if the Ministry of Transport is determined to make it so.'[1] But assertions like this are expressions of faith that ignore

the body of evidence showing that the administrative and incentive structures under which decisions are taken can substantially affect the outcomes of those decisions.

What facts are there to support the view that state-owned production is more efficient than privately owned production? The answer is, very few. One reason is that the majority of nationalized industries in the UK have particular characteristics which make comparisons with private-sector industries difficult. First, many nationalized industries have been given social obligations which conflict with profitability, and, second, they are often industries which, like the Post Office, possess a degree of monopoly power. This power can allow nationalized industries to conceal inefficiencies, both productive and allocative. Sheltered from competitive forces, they may not strive to produce a given output at minimum cost. And they may engage in what is known as *cross-subsidization*, which means using profits in one part of their operations to cover losses in another. The divergencies of price from marginal cost that are involved in cross-subsidization lead to misallocations of resources, although such allocations may appear to be justified on social or distributive grounds – e.g. keeping rail fares below cost for passengers living in rural areas, by charging fares in excess of cost to those using urban routes. Is there, however, any special reason why the subsidy that is effectively paid to rural inhabitants should fall on urban rail-users rather than on the general taxpayer?

While profits are a good guide to economic efficiency in competitive private industries, this is not necessarily so with many nationalized industries. If such industries are monopolists, their profits may merely reflect exploitation of their power to fix prices. In so far as they have social objectives, such as the control of inflation, imposed upon them, their losses may be the result of the imposition of these other objectives. In the special case of natural monopolies, nationalized industries may be precluded from making profits at all if they charge the price that equals marginal cost, in order to achieve allocative efficiency.

In the absence of substantial factual evidence about the comparative costs of private and public enterprise working side by side, one is thrown back on faith or argument. There are those who believe, as Shaw did, that state enterprise can be made as, or more, efficient than private enterprise, and there are others who believe the opposite to be true. The latter

---

1 *Everybody's Political What's What?* (Constable, 1944), p. 254.

group worry about the rigidities of bureaucratic directors of nationalized industries, and that the political motives of their Ministerial masters may interfere with the efficient operation of the business.

It is not difficult to find substantial evidence of inefficiency in nationalized industry. Whether it is more widespread than in the private sector is a very difficult question to answer, because the issue is so very broad. It is easier, however, to compare the performance of specific industries before and after they were nationalized (or privatized), though even on this narrower question the evidence is not strong, one way or the other. The greater problem is with industries which remain in the public sector for a long time, such as the Post Office and coal, and which possess a certain degree of monopoly power. They are, of course, accountable to the government which, since 1957, has used a special House of Commons committee to scrutinize their activities. One hopes that the government acts in the interests of the nation in this matter. Supporters of nationalization must be more or less happy that it does. Opponents of nationalization are less so.

Privatization

Just as the case for nationalization has sometimes been associated with doctrinaire political arguments on the left of the political spectrum, so there has been an opposite doctrinaire view on the right, favouring private over public enterprise. Of course, there are also many moderates who have expressed cautious, non-doctrinaire, views in favour of one over the other, on balance.

Privatization is a term which has appeared in recent years to describe a number of measures designed to increase competition and strengthen the profit motive in areas where they have been weak in the past. The prime microeconomic objectives of supporters of privatization have rested on the belief that the profit motive, and increased competition, are the principal instruments for achieving economic efficiency. There are, however, other objectives of a more political nature, e.g. the desire to secure a wider spread of share ownership in British industry in pursuit of the ideal of 'a property-owning democracy'.

Denationalization, which means the sale of state-owned industries to private individuals, is one policy advocated by supporters of privatization. It may apply to whole industries, such as the sale of British Telecom, or to parts of them, such as the sale of

Jaguar (part of British Leyland), and the hotels owned by British Rail. The state may sell off the whole of its shareholding or a portion of it, as with British Telecom, where only 51 per cent was sold in 1984.

Apart from denationalization, the term privatization, as commonly used nowadays, includes a variety of other measures, such as the promotion of joint ventures between public and private enterprises (e.g. the creation of Allied Steel and Wire Ltd by the state-owned British Steel Corporation and GKN, a private company); subcontracting work by state enterprises to private firms (e.g. refuse collection by local authorities) and DEREGULATION, meaning the removal of previous regulatory restrictions (e.g. the opening up of the supply of spectacles to ordinary retailers).

Welfare services may be privatized, for example by the sale of council houses to tenants, or by introducing so-called 'vouchers' for education, which may be used by parents to 'buy' education in the schools of their choice for their offspring. Such measures are aimed at increasing consumer choice.

We have no space for an assessment of the various privatization policies undertaken in the UK, any more than we had for assessment of the nationalized industries. Which side of the privatization *versus* nationalization debate you come down on depends on both politics and economics.

Of course, one does not have to be wholly pro-nationalization or pro-privatization. Whether one is in favour of more or less state-ownership depends on exactly how much there is at any moment of time. Moreover, industries have particular characteristics, so that the arguments should be considered on their merits in each case. For example, there seemed to be stronger arguments for the privatization of Jaguar cars, where the profit motive can perform a fairly clear function in a competitive industry, than for the privatization of British Telecom, which has elements of a natural monopoly about it. However, political arguments are also relevant to an assessment, and we refrain from commenting on them.

THE REDISTRIBUTION OF INCOME AND WEALTH

The final policy problem that we use to illustrate government intervention, concerns the goal of equity in the distribution of income and wealth. It is not the job of the economist to pronounce on the issue of fairness. It is our business, however, to consider alternative ways in which the government might be able to change the distribution of income, *if that is what it wishes to do.*

Types of Redistribution

People are usually interested in the distribution of income seen from several points of view. We cannot deal at any length with all of them here. But we shall deal with income distribution by age, and by region. First, however, we shall consider the size distribution of income, because that is the one which is most talked about.

A convenient way of representing the data to show the degree of income inequality is in a LORENZ CURVE, which shows how much of total income is accounted for by different percentages of the population. Figure 24.2 shows such a curve for the UK based on pre-tax income in 1984. The axes measure the percentage of the total number of households and the percentage of total household income. Both percentages are cumulative. Hence we can read off the share of total income accounted for by different percentages of households. Thus, the lowest 20, 40 and 60 per cent of households had about 3, 6 and 24 per cent of total income respectively.

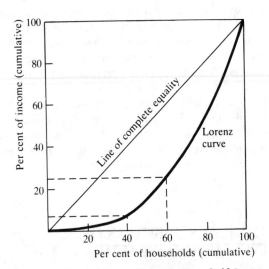

FIGURE 24.2 **Lorenz Curve Showing Household Income Distribution Before Tax, UK, 1984** (*Source: Social Trends,* 1987)

To form an idea of how equal or unequal the distribution of income is, we may compare the Lorenz curve with the 'Line of Complete Equality', also shown on Figure 24.2. This is the diagonal line making an angle of 45° with the axes. Every point on the line represents complete equality, because it shows that any given percentage of the population receives the same percentage of total income.

The Lorenz curve in Figure 24.2 shows that income is indeed distributed unequally in the UK. The degree of inequality depends on how far the Lorenz curve lies below the diagonal line of complete equality. We should be interested, too, in whether the degree of inequality is changing – i.e. in whether the Lorenz curve is shifting over time nearer the diagonal (indicating increasing equality) or further from it.

Policies for Income Redistribution

In this section we shall assume, for argument's sake, that the state's declared objective is to secure greater equality in the distribution of income. We shall consider the alternative policies that may be used, retaining the now-familiar classificatory system: policies using the price mechanism, policies improving the price mechanism, and extra-market policies.

Policies using the price mechanism

Under this head we include two types of policy. The first aims to influence the market price of factors of production. The second uses taxes and/or subsidies to raise the poor's income relative to that of the rich.

The first category includes measures such as the imposition of legal minimum wages for particular groups of workers who would otherwise be low-paid. Such government action is often considered appropriate for the protection of workers in industries where trade unions are weak. The effects of legal minimum wage rates are very similar, analytically, to the effects of trade-union action to fix the level of wages. We therefore refer you back to Chapter 21 (pp. 243–5), where these were fully discussed.

Taxes and subsidies are commonly used to change the distribution of income. The more progressive the tax, the greater the redistributive effects. Among British taxes[1], the income tax is progressive.

---

1 For a discussion of UK taxes in more detail, see Harbury and Lipsey, Chapter 6.

Although the marginal tax rate is the same for the vast majority of taxpayers, progressivity is built into the system because there is an exemption limit below which incomes are not subject to tax at all. The average tax rate, therefore, rises as income rises.

Of other taxes used for redistributive purposes, only one has any significant, though limited, progressive element – Inheritance Tax (IT). IT is levied on gifts and legacies of wealth. The rates run from 30 per cent on the estate of a person leaving property to the value of a little less than £100,000 to a maximum rate of 60 per cent on property worth about £350,000 and over. (Certain lifetime gifts are also liable to IT.) Capital taxes should, in principle, be effective redistributive instruments, because a relatively high proportion of the income of many of those in the highest classes is derived as a return on their wealth. However, there are many exemptions and devices that reduce their effective incidence.

Capital gains taxation (CGT) is another instrument of redistribution. CGT is levied on the *increase* in the value of assets owned by individuals between the dates of purchase and of sale. Although there are several exemptions, and CGT is levied at a flat rate (30 per cent), the tax is, to an extent, redistributive because higher income groups tend to have the most capital and therefore pay the most capital gains tax.

Most taxes on expenditure, e.g. VAT, petroleum, alcohol and tobacco duties, are, broadly speaking, proportional taxes and therefore not designed to redistribute incomes. Many tend even to be regressive towards the top of the income range, because higher income groups spend a lower proportion of their incomes than do other groups.

There has never been a shortage of new ideas for taxes to redistribute income or wealth. Among suggestions of special interest are a general expenditure tax and an annual wealth tax. The former, if substituted for the income tax, would impose a tax burden on people in relation to their consumption of goods and services, rather than in relation to their income, i.e. it would exempt that part of income which was saved. Supporters of a general expenditure tax, levied at progressive rates (unlike VAT), favour the idea of taxing a person for taking bites out of the national cake, rather than for helping to make it, as occurs when income is taxed. An annual wealth tax has been proposed in order to redistribute wealth more equally. So, too, have capital transfer taxes levied on *recipients* of gifts and bequests instead of on donors, as with the existing IT. This could encourage a wider spread of wealth, since the rich would pay less tax if they divided up their property in a large number of small parcels than in a small number of larger ones. There are, of course, moral and political objections to the new tax ideas described in this paragraph, and the administrative costs of introducing some of them would be high.

Tax Incidence: The effectiveness of any given tax in redistributing income does not depend on the progressivity of its impact, but on whom the burden of the tax ultimately falls, known as its INCIDENCE. The analysis of the incidence of taxes is a highly complex matter, beyond the scope of this book.

Although we cannot go into this subject in any depth here, we can give you some idea of its implications by reminding you of the analysis of the effects of a tax on the sales of a commodity in Chapter 10. There we saw that a tax could, at one extreme, raise the price of the good to consumers by the full amount of the tax, or at the other extreme, leave market price unchanged. Hence, taxes on some goods can be mainly passed on to consumers, while others cannot to any great extent.

Much the same is true of other taxes, such as those on income. For example, suppose James Jordon was earning £24,000 a year and taxed at a rate of 25 per cent. His income net of tax would be £18,000. If the government decided to redistribute income away from him by raising his tax rate from 25 to 40 per cent, he would certainly receive a smaller net income if his salary remained at £24,000. But if he managed to persuade his employers that they must pay him £30,000 in order to retain his services, he would receive the same net pay of £18,000 even at the higher tax rate. In this case, the tax system would have failed in its attempt to redistribute income.

Governments also use subsidies to redistribute income. These may be thought of as negative taxes, and they may be paid directly to persons, or to firms to encourage production of particular goods or services. The incidence of subsidies is as difficult to determine as it is for taxes.

Governments tend to rely more on subsidies than on taxes, for distributive purposes. Subsidies to persons, which are also called *transfer payments* – social security payments and unemployment benefits – are more effective instruments for redistributing income in the UK than are taxes. Income-related subsidies on sales of goods and services, e.g. rent rebates, are also more redistributive in an egalitarian manner, than those on health and education, which are closer to being proportional in their effects.

Policies improving the price mechanism

The second set of policies open to the government are those which try to improve the market mechanism. They focus on the causes of inequality in the distribution of income, particularly those related to departures from competition, barriers to labour mobility, and differences in the amount of education and training received by individuals (their human capital).

A great many measures used by the state fall into this category. We mention a few of them.[1] One group is directed to changing the structure of the market for labour, by introducing regulations which prohibit discrimination in pay or employment by sex or ethnic origin of employees. Other examples are to be found in the legislation which controls the power of trade unions and management, the provision of machinery for the settlement of industrial disputes on wages or conditions of employment, and the appointment of industrial tribunals to safeguard workers against unfair dismissal and to fix redundancy payments.

A second set of policies aims to diminish income disparities arising from differences in the human capital embodied in individuals. Examples are raising the school-leaving age, youth training schemes operated by the Manpower Services Commission, higher education in universities and polytechnics largely financed by the government, and local authority training schemes.

A third group of policies attempts to increase labour mobility, both directly by the provision of Job Centres which help workers find employment, and indirectly, for example by the construction, or subsidization, of houses in areas of high wages. These latter form part of a government's regional policy, which we treat separately. Training and retraining facilities also serve to increase labour mobility as well as encouraging individuals to acquire human capital.

Extra-market policies

Policies that work through the market, or seek to improve it, cover those most commonly employed in mixed economies such as the UK. In pure command economies, income distribution is, by definition, decided centrally, though in modern times, countries such as the USSR set wages partly for incentive reasons. Direct control of personal incomes is rare in mixed economies in peacetime. The nearest we come to it in the UK is the setting, by the government, of wages and salaries in the public sector; though even here market forces play their part in the final outcome of negotiations between the relevant trade unions and their state employers.

Other Aspects of Income Distribution

Having dealt at some length with income redistribution according to the size of income, we turn to examine the other aspects of distribution mentioned earlier.

Distribution of income by age

Concern is usually felt, not only about how many poor people there are in a country, but how many there are in different age-groups and especially how many are old.

As we know from Chapter 21, age is one of the personal characteristics that affects income, and age-earnings profiles exist at different points in different occupations. Little state action is usually called for to change these patterns. But the very substantial drop in income which affects almost everyone after they stop working is thought by most people to be a good reason for the government to intervene, to try and ensure that the incomes of those who have passed the age of retirement should not fall below a reasonable minimum level. Of course if the state did not provide a minimum pension on retirement, individuals would be likely to furnish themselves with the wherewithal to survive after they finish working – by saving some of their incomes while they were young. They might not do so, adequately enough anyway, because of myopia (short-sightedness), because they cannot know (nor even wish to know) how long they will live, or because they earn inadequate incomes while they are working.

Income distribution and regional policy

In Chapter 21 we drew attention to the wage differences that are associated with different regions in the country, and to the extent to which such differences are maintained by the regional immobility of labour. Regional policy is concerned with remov-

---

1 See Harbury and Lipsey, Chapters 4 and 6, for others.

ing, or at least reducing, disparities in income and in unemployment rates, and with other purposes to which we shall refer later. If the state wishes to intervene to reduce such disparities, there are two ways that it may approach the problem. It may seek to 'take work to the workers' or to 'take the workers to work'.

'Taking the workers to work' is another way of saying increasing labour mobility. This is no simple matter. Encouraging workers to move around the country confronts a range of physical, psychological and social problems. But the state can help by providing ample information about job opportunities and rates of pay in different regions, and by providing or subsidizing housing construction in places where the demand for labour, and therefore wages, are high. The alternative policy of 'taking work to the workers' also aims to reduce regional disparities. To understand why state action to influence the regional location of industry may be called for, we should ask, first, why industrial location is uneven in a country such as the UK.

The way in which market forces allocate resources regionally can be understood by application of the theory of comparative advantage explained in Chapter 22. Profit-maximizing firms will tend to locate themselves in regions where costs of production are lowest. Their choice of location will be the result of several forces pulling in different directions. Proximity to markets for products may pull one way, while access to, and prices of, inputs of factors of production-labour, raw materials, semi-finished products and power supplies – may pull in others. Transport costs will also influence the calculation of the lowest cost location.

Ceteris paribus, firms should be attracted to areas of low wages and high unemployment. Why does this not happen sufficiently to remove regional disparities in income and employment? Why are there relatively high wages and low unemployment in such places as London and the south-east of England, while wages are relatively low and unemployment high in others such as Scotland and the north of England?

There are no simple answers to these questions. But two answers may be suggested – the fact that market forces sometimes work sluggishly in evening out regional disparities, and the presence of externalities. There is little doubt that market forces can move very slowly in relocating industry because of what is called *industrial inertia*. The regional distribution of factories at any point of time, for example, is

the result of decisions taken in the past – perhaps up to a hundred years ago – when they were built. The locations of industrial buildings cannot be altered overnight as a result of a change in the profitability of different sites.

The second reason is the presence of externalities, which here take the form of what are called *conglomerating tendencies*. As a region becomes an attractive place for firms to settle in, it becomes more attractive for other firms, simply because of a build-up of an industrial background. The area becomes a place where there is plenty of skilled labour, know-how and supplies of other inputs, as well as markets for many firms' products. In other words, there are external economies of scale. Up to a point, the more firms there are in a particular part of the country, the more attractive it is for new firms to join them.

The result of these forces is that disparities in the prosperity of different parts of the country become pronounced, and that certain areas become depressed, suffering low incomes and high unemployment in particular.[1] State intervention may assist in arresting the decline of such areas in a variety of ways, which are covered by the phrase 'taking work to the workers'.

Policies can make depressed regions more attractive, and prosperous regions less so. Examples of the former include subsidies, cheap loans, tax advantages, and the provision of what is sometimes called INFRASTRUCTURE – roads, schools, hospitals, libraries and other basic services that make places attractive. The mere provision of information about existing advantages of locations may even be sufficient to attract businesses, which were formerly unaware of them.

Such policies can be particularly successful in attracting what are known as 'footloose' industries into regions requiring development. ('Footloose' implies the absence of any strong locational pulls.)

The alternative policies of making prosperous regions less attractive, can be pursued by means of high rates of taxation, or by rules and regulations. One of the most powerful locational policy instruments in the UK has been refusing permission for firms to locate new factories, or expand existing ones, in regions where further development is to be discouraged. Since 1947, the government has had the power to grant, or refuse, an Industrial Development

---

1 The regional distribution of industry and regional policy in the UK are discussed in Harbury and Lipsey, Chapters 3 and 6.

Certificate to businesses wishing to locate a factory. The policy has also been effective in dealing with problems of congestion in some very prosperous districts, such as London and the south-east. We already drew attention to the externalities involved in the conglomerating tendencies that influence industrial location. Where externalities are positive, movement of a new firm to the area lowers costs for existing firms. But 'conglomerating' can go too far. There comes a point where a district becomes so crowded that the costs of all firms are raised when a new one arrives.

We introduced the subject of regional policy in the context of income distribution, and we have come rather a long way from this matter. We make no great apology for doing so. Problems of economic policy can rarely be sorted into narrow compartments. Indeed, it is perhaps even fortunate that we should end our last illustration of a policy problem with a case of this kind. Regional policy is designed to change resource allocations brought about through market forces, on counts of both efficiency and equity. We concentrated, to start with, on the equity aspects, and showed how the distribution of income might be altered by various policy measures. But we also recognized, in passing, that market forces do not always secure an optimum location of economic activity.

AN APPROACH TO MICROECONOMIC POLICY

We have reached the end of this long chapter on microeconomic policy without, as we warned earlier,

discussing all the areas where the government might have a case to intervene in the working of a market economy. Our intention is to provide, by way of examples, a framework which could be used in most cases that arise. The framework is based on the contents of Table 23.2. Four separate steps are involved:

Step 1. Determine the cause of dissatisfaction with market allocations, using column (ii) in Table 23.2.

Step 2. Identify the primary goal of policy, and any secondary goals, using column (i) in Table 23.2.

Step 3. Consider the effectiveness of the alternative policy instruments available for achieving the policy goals, distinguishing (1) policies using the price mechanism, (2) policies improving the price mechanism, and (3) extra-market policies, as in columns (iii) and (iv) of Table 23.2.

Step 4. Weigh the best interventionist policy identified in Step 3 against the costs of intervention, as in column (v) of Table 23.2.

Using the procedure does not guarantee reaching simple conclusions on the best policy to be adopted. But it should, we hope, aid you to think logically, as an economist, about how to tackle problems you are faced with. One final word remains to be said. The policies we have discussed in this chapter have dealt with efficiency and equity. There are other goals with which the state is concerned that have so far been ignored. These are the goals of macroeconomic policy, and we discuss them in Parts 4 and 5 of this book.

SUMMARY

1 Pollution is an example of the existence of externalities. When private and social values diverge, private output is sub-optimal from a social point of view. The primary goal for intervention is therefore allocative efficiency.

2 Alternative policies for pollution control include those using the price mechanism (e.g. an output-related tax), those improving the price mechanism (e.g. introducing negotiating machinery for polluters and polluted to bargain),

and extra-market policies (e.g. banning or limiting pollution by law).

3 The preferred policy may depend on the following considerations: (i) Whether the social-optimum output of the pollution-creating activity is known or unknown. If unknown, policies using the price mechanism may help to find the optimum. (ii) The costs of alternative policies. These must be carefully estimated, including direct costs of administering policies, and com-

pliance costs borne by the private sector. (iii) The distributive consequences of alternative policies. There is a need to identify the gainers and losers from pollution and from alternative ways of controlling it. If a tax/subsidy solution is under consideration, the question of who pays for this is clearly relevant. (iv) Flexibility in the light of changing circumstances. Rules and taxes are generally less flexible than negotiated settlements in this type of problem.

4 The final policy choice calls for comparison of costs and benefits of all alternative policies, including that of non-intervention. The technique of cost-benefit analysis is designed to assist in making such comparisons.

5 The provision of roads raises questions of public goods, which are defined as non-rivalrous and non-excludable. Public goods involve zero marginal cost of providing for an extra unit of use, and their efficient price is also zero.

6 Roads are not pure public goods but have a strong element of publicness about them. The marginal cost of using them is zero up to capacity, and, though tolls can be charged on intercity motorways, the exclusion, by pricing, of users on individual urban roads is not a serious possibility.

7 The case for state intervention rests on the element of public goods in roads, implying that private provision would be sub-optimal. When a good is not, or cannot be, priced, decisions on its provision may be made in a cost-benefit analysis, in which costs are compared with all benefits, some of which are not easy to value in money terms (e.g. time saved and reduced accidents). The discounted present value of future benefits should exceed the costs if a road is to be built. At least part of the finance for road works usually comes from taxation, local and/or national. Such tolls should not cover full marginal costs, where benefits spill over to users of other less-congested routes. But there is a case for charging a congestion tax, reflecting costs imposed on others, where roads would otherwise be used beyond capacity.

8 When a case for state intervention is accepted, the question often arises whether the state should itself also provide goods and services or should pay private firms to do so. This concerns the issues of ownership and accountability, and carries heavy political overtones.

9 Arguments for nationalization are made on many grounds. Some involve equity in the distribution of income and wealth, and concern over the concentration of economic power in large private firms. Others concern efficiency, especially productive efficiency.

10 Whether privately owned or publicly owned businesses operate with more productive efficiency, is a controversial matter. It is difficult to make comparisons on the basis of profitability because several nationalized industries possess a degree of monopoly power, some have characteristics of natural monopolies, and others have social obligations placed on them.

11 Arguments for privatization rest partly on the assumption that the profit motive is a spur to efficiency. Privatization in the UK covers a range of measures designed to increase competition, including denationalization, but covering also such acts as deregulation and subcontracting government activities to the private sector.

12 The case for state intervention to redistribute income and wealth is based on market allocations being regarded as unfair.

13 Policies available are plentiful, and should be chosen after identifying the underlying reason for dissatisfaction with market allocations: (i) policies using the price mechanism include price controls (e.g. minimum wages) and taxes/subsidies; (ii) policies improving the price mechanism are often directed at removing barriers to labour mobility – e.g. by education and training; (iii) extra-market policies, involving state-regulated incomes, are rare in such countries as the UK in peacetime.

14 Regional policies are directed at reducing disparities arising from immobilities and conglomerative forces. Approaches can focus on taking 'workers to work' or 'work to the workers'.

15 A procedure for assessing economic policies comprises: (i) identifying the cause of dissatisfaction with market allocations; (ii) identifying the primary policy goal and any secondary goals; (iii) considering alternative policy approaches; and (iv) weighing the best interventionist policy against the costs of intervention.

Part 4

ELEMENTARY MACROECONOMICS

An Introduction to Macroeconomics

Inflation, unemployment, recession, economic growth, the balance of payments and the exchange rate are everyday words. Governments worry about how to reduce inflation and unemployment, how to prevent or cure recessions, how to increase the rate of growth, and how to achieve a satisfactory balance of payments. Firms are concerned with how inflation affects their earnings, how to increase their productivity, and how to insulate themselves from the consequences of recessions. Those firms that are engaged in foreign trade also worry about the value of sterling on the foreign-exchange markets. Workers are anxious to avoid the unemployment that comes in the wake of recessions and to protect themselves against the hazards of inflation. All of these issues relate to problems studied in macroeconomics.

WHAT IS MACROECONOMICS?

We saw in Chapter 2 that economics is customarily divided into two main branches, microeconomics and macroeconomics. Indeed, that earlier discussion is a necessary introduction to our present study and it is thus *essential* that you reread pages 25–6 now.

Because macroeconomics paints with a broad brush, it avoids much of the economy's interesting but sometimes confusing detail. In contrast, microeconomics deals with the detailed behaviour of individual markets, such as those for wheat, coal or strawberries.

The following example should help you to understand the difference between the two branches of economics.

A Microeconomic Problem: Explaining the behaviour of energy prices is a typical microeconomic problem. For decades, energy prices fell in relation to the prices of most other commodities. Then, beginning in the early 1970s, this trend was reversed with energy becoming increasingly expensive relative to most other goods and services. In microeconomics, we seek to understand the causes and the effects of such changes in *relative* prices.

A Macroeconomic Problem: Over the decades, as well as changing relative to other prices, energy prices have tended to follow the general trend for all prices to rise. Accounting for the average behaviour of all prices is a typical macroeconomic problem. This average is called the *general price level.* (Note, however, that the adjective 'general' is often dropped so that reference is made to 'the price level'.) Why does the price level rise slowly in some decades and rapidly in others? In macroeconomics we seek to understand the causes and effects of such changes in the general price level.

In this chapter we are going to introduce you to macroeconomics. We do this by considering the main variables, whose behaviour we shall be studying throughout Parts 4 and 5. In the course of the discussion, we define a number of important terms which will be used over and over again in the rest of this book. Because these terms are important, and because some of them will not reappear again for several chapters, we urge you to make a list of their names and definitions.

Six Macroeconomic Issues

Six major macroeconomic issues concern: (1) employment and unemployment, (2) inflation, (3) the trade cycle, (4) stagflation, (5) economic growth, and (6) the exchange rate and the balance of payments.

Most of these terms will probably be familiar to you. In any case, we shall explain their meaning below as we take a preliminary look at each of them in turn.

Employment and Unemployment: The 1980s saw high unemployment, as did the 1930s. Why did such decades see high unemployment, while other decades, such as the 1950s and the 1960s, saw relatively low unemployment? Indeed, why is there not always a job for everyone who would like to work? We have seen that all economies are characterized by *scarcity* – not nearly enough goods and services can be produced to satisfy everyone's wants. Why, then, should resources lie idle when what they could produce is very much wanted by consumers?

Inflation: Why did the pace of inflation accelerate during the 1970s to reach levels not seen before in peacetime in most advanced western nations? Why was inflation quite low in the late 1980s? Why should we worry about inflation in any case?

The Trade Cycle: The TRADE CYCLE refers to the tendency of output and employment to fluctuate over time in a recurring sequence of ups and downs. Boom periods of high output and high employment alternate with slump periods of low output and low employment, often referred to as recessions or, when they are extremely severe, as depressions. In boom periods, unemployment is low and the rate of inflation often accelerates. In periods of recession, unemployment is high and inflation often moderates. What is it about market economies that produces this cyclical behaviour? Why do such economies not settle into periods of stability where all markets are cleared at prices that produce full employment of all resources?

Stagflation: The alternating bouts of boom and recession have caused many policy headaches in the past. But the 1970s saw the emergence of a new economic ailment. Why were the recessions of that decade accompanied, not only by their familiar, and traditional, companion of earlier recessions – high unemployment – but also by an unexpected fellow traveller – rapid inflation? The new disease, called STAGFLATION, is the simultaneous occurrence of a recession (with its accompanying high unemployment) *and* inflation. Will it be a recurrent problem of free-market economies in the future?

Economic Growth: In spite of the short-term vari-

ations of output that are associated with the trade cycle, the long-term trend of total output has been upward for several centuries in all advanced industrial countries. The trend in the nation's total output over the long term is referred to as ECONOMIC GROWTH. Since rates of economic growth have typically exceeded rates of population growth in all advanced countries, there has also been an increase in per capita output – output per head of the population. Over recent centuries, the rise in per capita output has brought more or less continually rising living standards for the average person. Starting in the mid-1970s, there was a slowdown in worldwide growth rates which left per capita output stagnant. Does this represent a basic change in underlying trends, or is it just a reaction to the prolonged recessions of the 1970s and 1980s?

Much of the rise in per capita living standards that has occurred over the years has been the result of a rise in what is called PRODUCTIVITY. This is a measure of how much is produced per unit of resources used in production. If each unit of resources can produce more and more over the years, then it is possible to produce more output for everyone in the nation.

Of the various possible productivity measures, most interest is focused on LABOUR PRODUCTIVITY. This is total output divided by the labour used in producing it. In other words, it is output *per unit of labour*. Labour productivity may be calculated by dividing a measure of total output – either in one part of the economy or overall – by the total amount of labour used in producing that output. If total output is divided by the employed labour force, we get output per employed person. The problem with this measure, however, is that it will vary not just as labour gets more or less productive, but also as hours worked vary. For example, a decline in the average weekly hours worked from 48 to 40 hours per week would, other things being equal, lower measured labour productivity by over 15 per cent – even though labour was no less productive per hour worked. For this reason, a more satisfactory measure of the productive ability of labour is to divide total output by the total number of hours worked. The result is *productivity per hour of labour* actually spent on the job.

The Exchange Rate and the Balance of Payments: All international transactions are recorded in the country's balance-of-payments statistics. These transactions are influenced by the EXCHANGE RATE. This is the rate at which a country's own currency exchanges for foreign currencies. The trend in the value of the pound sterling in terms of many other currencies, including the US dollar, has been downwards in the last 50 years. Economists wish to discover the causes and consequences of such changes.

FOUR KEY MACRO VARIABLES

The key variables of macroeconomics are:

1. The overall level of employment and unemployment.
2. The total national product.
3. The general price level.
4. The balance of payments and the exchange rate.[1]

We hear about them on television; politicians make speeches about them; economists theorize about them. To discuss them in a reasoned fashion, we must first understand several things about them:

1. Precisely how are they defined?
2. Why are we concerned about them?
3. How have they behaved in the past?

Employment and Unemployment

Definitions: The EMPLOYED are those persons working for others and paid a wage or a salary, while the SELF-EMPLOYED are those who work for themselves. The UNEMPLOYED are those who would be willing to accept work if jobs were available – an easier concept to understand than to measure.[2] The WORKING POPULATION, or LABOUR FORCE, is the total of the employed, the self-employed and the unemployed, i.e. those who have a job plus those who are looking for work.

In the microeconomic analysis of Parts 2 and 3, we were concerned with employment and unemploy-

ment in individual markets, such as, for example, the market for mechanics in Coventry. In macroeconomics we are concerned with overall employment and unemployment in the whole economy.

The unemployed are often expressed as a percentage of the labour force. We will express it in this form and denote it by the symbol U. Thus

$$U = \frac{\text{number unemployed}}{\text{labour force}} \times 100.$$

Why Unemployment is a Matter of Concern: To understand the importance of unemployment, it is necessary to distinguish between voluntary and involuntary unemployment. VOLUNTARY UNEMPLOYMENT occurs when there is a job available but the employed person is not willing to accept it at the existing wage rate. INVOLUNTARY UNEMPLOYMENT occurs when a person is willing to accept a job at the going wage rate, but cannot find such a job. When we are concerned about the undesirable social effects of unemployment in terms of lost output and human suffering, it is involuntary unemployment that mainly concerns us. When we use the word *unemployment* hereafter, we mean involuntary unemployment, unless we say otherwise.

The social and political importance of the unemployment rate is enormous. It is widely reported in newspapers; the government is blamed when it is high and takes credit when it is low; it is often a major issue in elections; and few economic policies are formed without some consideration of their effect on it.

There are two main reasons for worrying about unemployment: it wastes economic resources, and it causes human suffering. The economic waste is fairly obvious. If a fully employed economy has 25 million people who are willing to work, their labour services must either be used now or be wasted. If only 22 million are used because 12 per cent of the labour force is unemployed, the potential output of three million workers *is lost for ever*. In an economy characterized by scarcity, with not nearly enough output to meet everyone's needs, any waste of the potential to produce that output is a serious matter.

In addition to economic waste, there is the human cost of unemployment. Severe hardship and misery can be caused by prolonged periods of unemployment. Not only do the unemployed lose the goods and services that they could have bought with their incomes from work, prolonged periods of unemployment have been observed to be associated with above

---

1 You may wonder why we earlier discussed six macroeconomic issues, and now identify only four main groups of macroeconomic variables. This is because all of the issues that were discussed earlier concern the behaviour of these four variables. Of the items that do not directly repeat the list of macroeconomic variables, the trade cycle and stagflation relate to the behaviour of employment, national product and the price level, while economic growth concerns the rate at which national product is growing.

2 Many of the definitions needed here were given in Chapters 19 and 20. We repeat those that are needed for macroeconomics, both for completeness and because some of you will be studying Part 4 before studying Part 3.

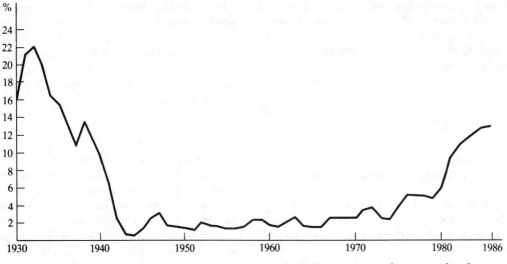

FIGURE 25.1   Unemployment in the UK. The figures show the average numbers unemployed as a percentage of the labour force in each year

average incidences of ill health, alcoholism and divorce among those without work.

Experience of Unemployment: Figure 25.1 shows the statistics for UK employment and unemployment since 1930. During the period between the two world wars, UK unemployment was *never* less than 10 per cent in any single year. The 1950s and 1960s provided a sharp contrast. Unemployment was always less than 3 per cent, and it was not until the early 1970s that it exceeded that figure. In the mid-1970s, however, unemployment rose steadily, reaching 5 per cent early in 1976. By 1981 the rate had passed the 10 per cent level – or what is sometimes called the 'two-digit level' – and it had reached 13 per cent by 1986.

There are several reasons why the UK's unemployment experience over the last two decades has been regarded as particularly serious. In the first place, there is a marked inequality of unemployment rates among regions. Northern Ireland and the north of England have tended to have rates around 50 per cent higher than those in the south-east. This is connected with the decline of the old staple industries that were concentrated in the north, and the rise of new, technologically based industries in the south-east.

In the second place, recent unemployment has been particularly high among the young. Many school-leavers find it impossible to obtain jobs. When this happens, they not only lose income, they miss the valuable on-the-job training that usually accompanies early job experiences.

In the third place, there is today the added phenomenon, particularly among youth, of those who draw unemployment or supplementary benefits but who do part-time work for cash (on which they pay no taxes). They might well prefer to have full-time, steady jobs, but for them unemployment is not the same serious problem that it was for the unemployed worker of the 1930s who usually had no means of earning extra income and who did not receive anything like the benefits that are available today to those without a job.

In the fourth place, experiences of unemployment are becoming much longer in duration. In the 1950s and 1960s the typical unemployed person was without a job for a fairly short period of time. In the late 1970s and the 1980s the average duration of a period of unemployment – the time between losing a job and finding a new one – increased significantly. Long-term bouts of unemployment are particularly upsetting to those who experience them. Also, the longer a person is unemployed the more difficult it becomes to re-enter the employed labour force.

Total National Product

Definitions: The nation's total output is loosely described as its *national product, national output* or *national income*. Precise measures and their definitions are discussed in the next chapter. In the meantime, we recall that, as we saw in Chapter 2, this total product is calculated by adding up the money values of all the goods and services that are produced in the economy over some period of time, usually taken as a year.

A serious problem arises when prices change due to inflation. To see the problem, consider an example. Say that, over one year, all prices remain unchanged while the quantities of all outputs increase by 10 per cent. In this case, the value of total output also rises by 10 per cent. Next, say that, over the following year, all quantities of output remain unchanged while the prices of everything that is produced rise by 10 per cent. In this case, the value of total output also rises by 10 per cent. But the two cases are very different. In the first case, the measured value of output rises by 10 per cent because the *quantities* of everything that is produced rise by 10 per cent. In the second case, the measured value of output rises by 10 per cent because *prices* rise by 10 per cent while quantities remain constant.

Methods exist to distinguish these two cases, and we shall shortly consider them. In the meantime, we merely note that national product can be calculated in two ways.

In the first method, output is valued each year at the market prices ruling in that year. It is then referred to as national product, *valued at current prices*, or as NOMINAL NATIONAL PRODUCT, or as MONEY NATIONAL PRODUCT. In this case, the measured value of national product changes from year to year as a result of both price and quantity changes. For example if, from one year to the next, all market prices *and* all quantities produced rise by 10 per cent, national product valued in current prices will rise by about 21 per cent.

In the second method, national product is valued at the prices ruling in some fixed year. It is then referred to as NATIONAL PRODUCT VALUED AT CONSTANT PRICES or as REAL NATIONAL PRODUCT. In this case, the prices used to value output do not change from year to year. Once the particular set of prices to be used is decided upon, the actual year is often then referred to as the BASE YEAR. If, for example, the base year is 1982 so that actual prices ruling in 1982 are used as the constant prices, the resulting output figure could be referred to as *national product at 1982 prices*. Because the prices used to value all the outputs are unchanged from year to year, changes in the measured value of output must be due only to changes in the quantities of output.

A further important output concept is POTENTIAL OUTPUT, or FULL-EMPLOYMENT OUTPUT. This refers to what the economy could produce if all resources were fully employed. When the economy is producing its potential or full-employment output, the production point is somewhere on the transformation curve shown in Figure 1.2 on page 9. When there are unemployed resources, so that production is less than potential, the production point is somewhere inside the transformation curve. Potential output is a very important concept, and you should be sure you remember both terms that are used for it.

Why Output is a Matter of Concern: Short-run fluctuations of national product around its potential level reflect the ebb and flow of economic activity, which we have referred to as the trade cycle. Policy-makers care about such short-term fluctuations because of their consequences for unemployment and lost output.

Long-run, trend changes in national product, valued at constant prices, have generally been upwards in recent centuries. We have already referred to this as the phenomenon of economic growth, and have noted that such growth is the major cause of long-term increases in living standards. The worst horrors of the early industrial revolution are no longer with us, mainly because economic growth has removed the necessity of fourteen-hour days worked in extremely harsh conditions. As long as growth continues, each generation can expect, on the average, to have substantially higher living standards than were enjoyed by preceding generations. Not surprisingly, therefore, policy-makers are greatly concerned with the nation's rate of economic growth.

Output Experience: Figure 25.2(i) shows the long-term trend of output, while Figure 25.2(ii) highlights the fluctuations from one year to another. (Output is measured by a particular statistic called the GNP, which stands for Gross National Product and which we shall study in Chapter 26.) The two parts are two ways of displaying the same output series. Part (i) shows the level of output each year from 1945 to 1986. Part (ii) shows by how much output has changed from one year to the next over the same period – i.e. the growth rate of output.

Slow British growth rates from 1945 to the early 1980s have moved Britain down the list of present EEC countries from the second highest per capita in 1960 to the second lowest in 1985. If the growth rates of output that have been typical over the last few decades persist to the end of this century, West

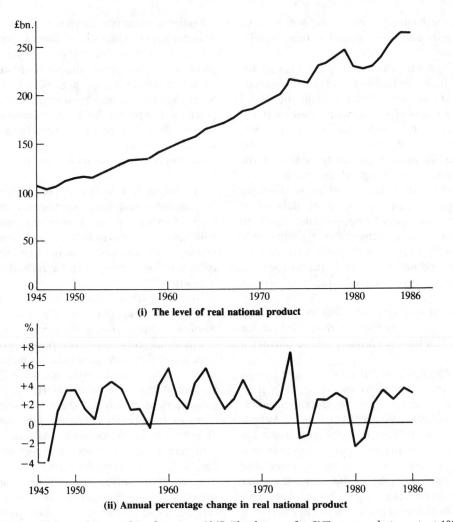

FIGURE 25.2　**Real National Product since 1945.** The data are for GNP measured at constant 1980 prices

Germany's per capita GNP will be six times Britain's. This is the same relative discrepancy as now exists between Britain and the South American Republic of Columbia. Recently, however, the UK's growth rate has risen and the key question is whether or not this is a change in the long-term trend or just the result of some transitory forces.

The General Price Level

Definitions

Changes in the Price Level: Macroeconomics uses the concept of the GENERAL PRICE LEVEL, the average level of the prices of *all* goods and services produced in the economy. In practice, we are not interested in the average level of all prices itself but in *changes* in this average. For example, you wouldn't be much the wiser if you were told that the average level of all prices ruling in the UK this year was £121.34. But you would be interested to know that the average level of all prices ruling this year was 7 per cent higher than the average ruling in the previous year. A rise in the price level is called an INFLATION, while a fall in the price level is called a DEFLATION.

Changes in the Value of Money: By definition, changes in the price level are reflected in changes in what is variously called the PURCHASING POWER OF MONEY or the VALUE OF MONEY. Both terms refer to *the amount of goods and services that can be purchased*

with a given amount of money. Inflation, which is a rise in the general price level, reduces the purchasing power of money, deflation increases it.

Say, for example, that all prices rise by 10 per cent. One pound sterling will now buy 10 per cent less goods and services than before the price level rose. Since each unit of money will now buy 10 per cent less than previously, we also say that the *value of money* (measured by what can be bought with it) has fallen by 10 per cent.

Now consider the opposite case. Assume that all prices fall by 10 per cent. Any given amount of money will now buy 10 per cent *more* than it previously did. Thus, this deflation raises the purchasing power (or the value) of money by 10 per cent.

These examples illustrate the general relation that *the purchasing power of money falls in inverse proportion to any rise in the price level, and rises in inverse proportion to any fall in the price level.*

Measuring Changes in the Price Level – Index Numbers: In practice, changes in the price level, and in the value of money, are measured by a PRICE INDEX which shows the average percentage change that has occurred in some group of prices over some period of time. The point in time from which the change is measured is called the BASE PERIOD (or base year), while the point in time to which the change is measured is called the GIVEN PERIOD. There are several aspects to the definition of any price index.

First, what group of prices should be used? This depends on the index. The RETAIL PRICE INDEX (RPI) covers prices of commodities commonly bought by households. Changes in the RPI are meant to measure changes in the typical household's 'cost of living'. The Wholesale Price Index measures a different group of commodities commonly bought and sold by wholesalers. The 'implied deflator for the GNP' is a price index that covers virtually all of the goods and services produced in the economy: it includes not only the prices of consumer goods and services bought by households but the prices of capital goods such as plant and machinery bought by firms.[1]

Second, what kind of average should be used? If all prices were to change in the same proportion, this would not be an important question. A 10 per cent rise in each and every price covered means an average rise of 10 per cent no matter how much importance we give to each price change when calculating the average. But what if – as is almost always the case – different prices change differently? Now it does matter how much importance we give to each price change. A rise of 50 per cent in the price of caviar is surely much less important to the average consumer than a rise of 40 per cent in the price of bread, and this in turn is surely less important than a rise of 30 per cent in the cost of housing. Why? The reason is that the typical household spends less on caviar than on bread and less on bread than on housing.

In calculating any price index, statisticians seek to weight each price according to its importance. Let us see how this is done for the RPI. Government statisticians periodically survey a group of households to discover how they spend their incomes. The average amount that households spend on each commodity group is calculated, and these become the weights attached to the price changes in each group. The price index is thus an average of the price changes in each commodity group, with heavy weight being given to commodities on which consumers spend much and light weight to commodities on which consumers spend only a little.

Third, the weighted increases are then converted into an index in which the base year is always given a value of 100. Each other year gets a value determined by the price increases calculated in the manner described earlier. The percentage change in the cost of purchasing the bundle is thus the index number minus 100. For example, an index number of 110 indicates a percentage increase in prices of 10 per cent over those ruling in the base year.

Some Difficulties with Index Numbers: An index number is meant to reflect the broad trend in prices rather than the details. This means that although the information it gives is valuable, it must be interpreted with care. Here are three of the many reasons why.

First, the weights in the index refer to an average bundle of goods. This average, although 'typical' of what is consumed in the nation, will not necessarily be typical of what each household consumes. The rich, the poor, the young, the old, the single, the married, the urban and the rural households typically consume bundles that differ from one another. An increase in air fares, for example, will raise the cost of living of a middle-income traveller while leaving that of a poor stay-at-home unaffected.

---

1 Be careful not to confuse a *deflator*, which is an index number designed to measure average price changes, and a *deflation*, which is a fall in average prices.

Second, households usually alter their consumption patterns in response to price changes. A price index that shows changes in the cost of purchasing a fixed bundle of goods does not allow for this. For example, a typical cost-of-living index for middle-income families at the turn of the century would have given much weight to the cost of maids and children's nurses. A doubling of servants' wages in 1900 would have greatly increased the middle-income cost of living. Today it would have little effect, for the rising cost of labour has long since caused most middle-income families to cease to employ full-time servants. A household that greatly reduces its consumption of a commodity whose price is rising rapidly does not have its cost of living rise as fast as a household that continues to consume that commodity in an undiminished quantity.

Third, as time goes by, new commodities enter the typical consumption bundle and old ones leave. A cost-of-living index in 1890 would have had a large item for horse-drawn carriages and horse feed, but no allowance at all for motorcars and petrol.

The longer the period of time that passes, the less some fixed consumption bundle will be typical of current consumption patterns. For this reason the government makes frequent surveys of household expenditure patterns and revises the weights. The base period is then usually changed to conform to the year in which the new set of commodity weights was calculated.

Why inflation is a matter of concern

The *level* of prices at which the economy's purchases and sales of goods and of factors of production occur is irrelevant to living standards. For example, no economist argues that the price level ruling in Britain in, say, 1785 was intrinsically better or worse than the one ruling in 1985.

The reason why one price level is just as good as any other price level is that, if all prices of goods, factors of production and everything else change in equal proportion, no relative prices have changed and there are no real consequences. For instance, if the amount of money you must pay for everything you buy doubles but the amount of money you receive also doubles, you are unaffected. You pay twice as much for everything you buy but, since your money income has also doubled, you can buy just as much as you could before prices rose.

It follows that *when all prices have been fully adjusted,*
a change in the overall level of prices has no effect. Another way of seeing this important point is to observe that changing the number of zeros on the prices at which all transactions take place has no real effect on anything.

The harm that inflation does occurs during the transition from one price level to another. While the price level is changing, some prices adjust faster than others. As a result, relative prices change and real effects occur. Those who find the prices of what they buy rising faster than the prices of what they sell, lose; while those who find the prices of what they sell rising faster than the prices of what they buy, gain. Thus, inflation causes haphazard redistributions of income. Those who are powerful and smart enough to keep up to, or even ahead of, the inflation do not lose and may even gain. Those without the necessary economic power, or the needed foresight, lose.

Fixed Money Income: The extreme case of the redistributive effects of inflation occurs when some people's incomes do not rise at all as prices rise. For example, if a retirement pension specifies an income as so many £s, a rise in the price level lowers the purchasing power of that income. Anyone who retired on a fixed money income in 1974 found the purchasing power of that income cut in half by 1979 and then by a further 35 per cent by 1983. This meant that the person could buy in 1984 only 32 per cent of what could be bought in 1974. For such people rapid inflation means great suffering.

Note that the problems only arise with pensions, and other payments, that really are fixed in money terms. State pensions in the UK were adjusted from time to time as the inflation proceeded. Many private pensions, however, remained fixed in money terms, so that their recipients saw the purchasing power of their incomes shrink steadily as the price level rose.

Indexing: Some of the redistributive effects of inflation can be avoided by what is called 'indexing' (or 'index linking'). Such indexing arrangements link the payments made under the terms of a contract to changes in the general price level. For example, a retirement pension might specify that it will pay the beneficiary £5,000 per year starting in 1990, and that the amount paid will increase each year in proportion to the increase in some specified index of the price level. Thus, if the price index rose by 10 per cent between 1990 and 1991, the pension payable in 1991 would be £5,500.

Foreseen Inflations: Indexation provides an automatic correction that does not require anyone to foresee future changes in the price level. However, even without formal indexation it is possible to allow for the effects of an inflation provided that the rise in the price level is *foreseen*. Wage and price contracts are major examples. If, say, a 10 per cent inflation is expected over the next year, a money wage that rises by 10 per cent over that period will preserve the expected purchasing power of wages. A money wage that increases by 13 per cent will provide for an expected 3 per cent increase in the purchasing power of wages (10 per cent more wages to preserve purchasing power in the face of the expected rise in prices and 3 per cent more to increase the real purchasing power of the wages).

So when an inflation is foreseen, many of its effects can be allowed for in contracts that take account of the expected rise in prices.

Unforeseen Inflations: The most harmful effects of inflation occur when the rise in the price level is unforeseen. Contracts freely entered into when the price level was expected to remain constant will mean hardships for some and unexpected gains for others if the price level unexpectedly starts to rise.

For example, consider a new wage contract that specifies wage increases of 3 per cent and that is made in the general expectation of a constant price level. Both employers and workers expect that the purchasing power of wages paid will rise by 3 per cent as a result of the new contract. Now assume that the price level changes unexpectedly. Workers lose if inflation occurs. If the price level rises by 10 per cent over the course of the wage contract, the workers' wages will buy less than they would before the wage increase was negotiated. (A 3 per cent increase in money wages combined with a 10 per cent increase in prices means a reduction in the purchasing power of wages of about $6\frac{1}{2}$ per cent.)[1]

The experience of inflation

Figure 25.3 shows the UK inflation rate for each year since 1930. Throughout the 1950s and the 1960s the rate, although low by current standards, was high enough to cut the purchasing power of the pound by more than half over those two decades and to be a worry to policy-makers and voters.

---

1 The purchasing power of wages is W/P where W stands for the money wage rate and P the price level. Letting the original real wage be W/P, the new purchasing power is $1.03W/1.1P = 0.936W/P$. Thus the new purchasing power is 93.6 per cent of the original. This represents a fall of 6.4 per cent in purchasing power.

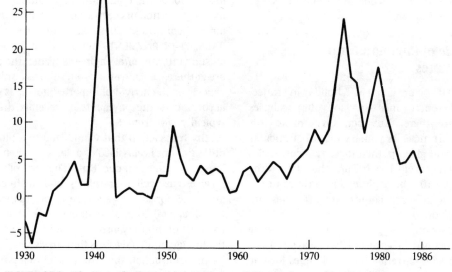

FIGURE 25.3   The Rate of Inflation in the UK since 1930. The figures show the percentage increase in the Retail Price Index from one year to the next

Then, in the late 1960s, the United Kingdom, together with the rest of the developed world, moved into a period of *accelerating* inflation. The rise in the inflation rate in the late 1960s was associated with two major forces. The first cause was an inflation in the US caused by that country's method of financing the Vietnam war. This inflation spread to the rest of the world. The second cause was what appears to have been a spontaneous wage explosion in the UK and in the countries of western Europe. From 1967 to 1971 the inflation rate rose steadily.

Then, after a slight deceleration in 1972, the rate rose dramatically in 1973–4. This further acceleration was associated with the large rise in the price of oil, and of numerous related products such as plastics, imposed by the members of the Organization of Petroleum Exporting Countries (OPEC). The inflation rate rose in many countries to levels never before seen during peacetime. By 1975 the annual rate of inflation reached a peak of approximately 25 per cent in the UK. (Had this rate continued for not much more than 3 years it would have halved the purchasing power of money!) The inflation rate did not, however, remain at that high level. Although prices continued to rise, the rate of inflation fell substantially until 1978. In 1979 it accelerated once again. During the early 1980s the rate fell again, and by 1987 it had fallen to less than 5 per cent.

The inflation rate over this extraordinary decade was such that a household retiring in 1972 with a comfortable income that was fixed in money terms saw 75 per cent of that income's purchasing power eroded over the next ten years.

The Balance of Payments and Exchange Rates

Definitions: If you are going on a holiday in France, you will need French francs to pay for your purchases while you are there. Any bank will make this exchange of currencies for you. If you get 10 francs for every pound you give up, then these two currencies are trading at a rate of £1 = 10F or, what is the same thing, 1F = £0.10. The exchange rate refers to the rate at which different countries' currencies are traded for each other.

The above example suggests that the exchange rate can be defined in either of two ways: (i) the amount of foreign currency that exchanges for one unit of domestic currency (10F for £1 in the above example), or (ii) the amount of domestic currency

that exchanges for one unit of foreign currency (10p for 1F in the above example). It is customary in the UK to express the sterling exchange rate in the former way. Thus the exchange rate between the pound sterling and the US dollar was £1 = \$1.80 at the beginning of 1988. This means that £1 would buy you \$1.80 or, what is the same thing, \$1 would buy £0.56.

Thus, in the UK the EXCHANGE RATE between sterling and any one foreign currency is defined as the amount of that foreign currency that must be given up to purchase one pound sterling, i.e. the price of sterling in terms of a foreign currency. Clearly there is a separate exchange rate between sterling and each other currency in the world. FOREIGN EXCHANGE is defined as foreign currencies (or claims to such currencies such as bank deposits, cheques and promissory notes payable in the foreign currency). The FOREIGN EXCHANGE MARKET is defined as the market where foreign exchange is traded (at a price which is expressed by the exchange rate).

If the exchange rate is left free to be determined on the foreign-exchange market by the forces of demand and supply, the country is said to have a FLOATING EXCHANGE RATE. If the country's central bank intervenes in the foreign-exchange market to hold the exchange rate at some pre-announced fixed value, the country is said to have a FIXED EXCHANGE RATE.

Now let us turn to the other important international concept that we need to consider at this point, the balance of payments.

In order to know what is happening to the course of international trade and international capital movements, governments keep account of the transactions among countries. These accounts are called the BALANCE-OF-PAYMENTS ACCOUNTS and they record all such international payments. When the accounts are gathered, each transaction, such as a shipment of exports or the arrival of imported goods, is classified according to the payments or receipts that would typically arise from it.

Any transaction that would lead to a payment to other nations is classified as a debit (–) item because it uses foreign exchange. British imports of goods and services, as well as outflows of British capital to purchase foreign assets, are debit items. (When British capital flows abroad, we speak of an *export* of capital, but this may also be thought of as an *import* of the foreign financial assets that the capital buys.)

Any transaction that would lead to a payment by foreigners to UK residents is classified as a credit (+) item because it earns foreign exchange. British exports of goods and services, as well as flows of foreign capital into the UK, are credit items. Note again that an inflow of foreign capital into the UK is called an import of capital but that this may also be looked at as an export of the financial assets that the money is used to purchase.

Consider some examples, first on the side of current transactions. When a British importer buys a Japanese personal computer to sell in the United Kingdom, this appears as a debit in the UK balance of payments because it uses foreign exchange – yen in this case. However, when a Japanese shipping firm insures with Lloyds of London a cargo destined for Alexandria, Egypt, this represents a credit in the UK balance of payments because when the insurance premium is paid, the shipping firm will have to give up yen in order to buy the sterling needed to pay Lloyds. This transaction thus earns foreign exchange. Of course a credit item to one country is a debit item to the other, and vice versa. Thus in the Japanese balance of payments, the transaction involving the personal computer is a credit while the insurance transaction is a debit item.

Now look at the capital side. If a British investor buys some shares in a Brazilian mining company, this appears as a debit item in the UK balance of payments because the transaction uses foreign exchange. When a Japanese citizen decides to buy shares in a British manufacturing firm, this is a credit item in the UK balance of payments because it earns foreign exchange. As with current items, so it is with capital items: what is a credit item for one country is a debit item for the other. Thus the sale of the shares is a credit item in the Brazilian accounts because it brings in foreign exchange, while the purchase of the shares is a debit item in the Japanese accounts because it uses foreign exchange.

Why Policy-makers are Concerned about Exchange Rates and the Balance of Payments: Unlike the other variables discussed above, such as unemployment and inflation, the exchange rate and the balance of payments do not provide obvious causes for concern. Most people agree that a *ceteris paribus* rise in either unemployment or inflation is undesirable. There is no reason, however, for feeling the same about a change in either the exchange rate or the balance of payments. Whether or not policy-makers need to be concerned about such changes depends on why the changes occurred. For this reason, it is best to postpone consideration of the reasons why policy-makers are sometimes concerned about these variables until we have studied them in more detail later in this book.

Experience: Figure 25.4 shows the exchange rate between the pound sterling and the US dollar since 1945. The long periods of stability are periods where the exchange rate was fixed. The sudden changes were periods when the rate was adjusted. Since 1972 the rate has been left to find its level on the free market, and this shows up as a continuously varying rate on the chart – i.e. a floating exchange rate.

Balance-of-payments experience can be understood only after you have learned more about the meaning of balance-of-payments figures. So we postpone looking at such data until a later chapter.

THE GOALS OF MACROECONOMIC POLICY

The two main goals of microeconomic policy concern efficiency in the allocation of resources and equity in

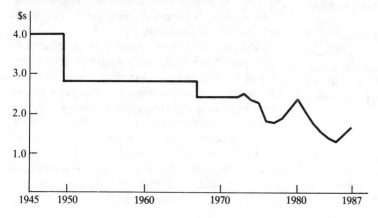

FIGURE 25.4   **The Sterling–US Dollar Exchange Rate.** The data show the average US$ price of £1 sterling during each year

the distribution of income. In the remainder of this book we shall be concerned with a further set of policy goals, which are related to the four key macro variables discussed above, employment, output, the price level, and the balance of payments. All of the issues raised here will be discussed again later in this book when we have developed the tools of analysis needed to consider them in detail. Do not spend too much time trying to understand what follows in every detail. It is a general survey of much of what we shall study in later chapters. The survey is included here to point the way, and to familiarize you with some important terms. If you return at the end of your study of macroeconomics to reread this chapter, you will then find that nothing here seems at all difficult.

Early Goals

Until the twentieth century, governments were assumed not to have any responsibility towards, or even any ability to influence, most of the macro variables we have listed above. The main government responsibility towards the economy was thought to be to provide a stable background of law and order, and security of contracts that would help private citizens to get on with the private economic activity on which the material wealth of the nation depended.

The one major exception was the price level. Early in the history of economics, it was realized that the amount of money and credit that was available to 'grease the wheels of commerce' was at least partially under the control of the government. It was also realized that mismanagement of the monetary system could, as we shall see in detail later, cause inflation. The government's responsibility was therefore understood to include management of the monetary system in such a way that there was enough money to satisfy the needs of trade, but not so much as to cause inflation.

The other macro variables were not, however, considered to be the responsibility of government policy. Good times and bad times seemed to follow each other – in the ebb and flow of the trade cycle – for reasons that were assumed, at the time, to be beyond government control.

Modern Goals

In response to the so-called Great Depression of the 1930s, and the decade of heavy unemployment that accompanied it, modern macroeconomic theory was born. Since that time, economists have understood that government policy can have a significant influence on the nation's overall level of economic activity, while governments have, for better or for worse, accepted a responsibility for influencing the behaviour of each of the major macro variables that we have discussed above. The policies with respect to each of these variables are usually stated as full employment, a satisfactory rate of growth of output, a stable price level, and a satisfactory balance of payments. We shall look briefly at each of these.

Full Employment: From 1945 onwards, the governments of most market-oriented, industrial countries accepted a responsibility for ensuring the existence of something close to full employment. In the UK, this objective was stated in the *White Paper on Employment Policy* (Cmd 6527), published in 1944 by the coalition government of that time.

Achieving the objective of full employment means holding national product at its potential, or full-employment, level. It does *not* mean achieving zero unemployment. Indeed, zero unemployment is an impossibility in any real economy, and here is why.

Any economy has a normal turnover of labour that arises both because people leave one job to take, or to look for, another, and because there are always some people leaving the labour force due to retirement, or death, and others entering it. As a result, there is always a pool of people who are unemployed because they are currently between jobs. Such unemployment, which is due to the normal turnover of labour, is called frictional unemployment. It is the amount of unemployment that exists when output is at its potential level. Thus, full employment does not mean having zero unemployment; instead it means having the amount of frictional unemployment that is associated with potential output.

The 1944 White Paper argued that the irreducible minimum was about 3 per cent in the UK. It therefore defined full employment as existing when the recorded unemployment rate was 3 per cent. For a decade or so, starting in 1950, unemployment rates of 2 per cent, or less, became common. Then in the late 1960s, and throughout the 1970s, the amount of unemployment associated with potential output rose steadily until, by the mid 1980s, it seemed to be somewhere between 6 and 8 per cent. The reasons for these changes will be discussed in Chapter 40.

A Satisfactory Rate of Growth of Output: We have seen that economic growth has been the major cause of long-term increases in living standards. Unfortunately, one of the least successful branches of economics has been the theory of growth. Economic theory does identify some factors, such as investment, and research and development, that are sometimes associated with high growth rates. No one, however, has been able to sort out causes and effects in these relations to the extent that governments can easily influence the growth rates of their economies. We shall discuss these matters further in Chapter 39.

Thus, although many UK governments have had growth targets, few have found the policy tools needed to influence the country's growth rate. Nonetheless governments do, as we shall see, continue to adopt growth policies.

Stable Prices: Governments still accept the responsibility, which was established centuries ago, for maintaining a stable price level, or, if that is not possible, for maintaining a low rate of inflation. Figure 25.3 shows that the UK government has had a mixed success in meeting this objective over the years. Mrs Thatcher's Conservative government undoubtedly gave high priority to this target, and by 1983 the rate of inflation had fallen well below the figure typical of the 1970s.

A Satisfactory Exchange Rate and Balance of Payments: Most governments feel that extreme, short-term fluctuations in the exchange rate are undesirable, while also feeling that long-term trends in the exchange rate cannot be resisted.

Governments differ on how they regard the balance of payments. Some countries have active policies, others leave the balance of payments to be determined by market forces, without any serious government intervention. Because the balance of payments presents no such obvious policy objectives as do employment, output and the price level, balance-of-payments objectives are sometimes said to be *secondary*, in contrast to the *primary* objectives of full employment, economic growth and price stability.

Policy Instruments

There are two major sets of macroeconomic policy tools available to the government. One set, called demand-side policies, works on the demand side of the economy's markets. These are called the policies of *demand management*. The other set, called supply-side policies, work on the supply side of these markets.

Demand-side policies

The major policies available to influence the demand side of markets are called fiscal and monetary policies.

Fiscal Policy: Fiscal policy attempts to influence the total level of economic activity in the country by influencing the *total demand for goods and services*. (This total demand is nothing other than the sum of all of the demands in the nation's individual markets that we studied in the micro half of this book.) An increase in total demand can be achieved through the government's budget. Either total government expenditure can be increased or total taxes can be decreased, or both. Reducing total demand requires reducing government expenditure, increasing taxes, or both.

An increase in government expenditure means that the government is demanding more of the goods and services to which it allocates its extra expenditure. This means that the government is directly causing an increase in total demand. Reducing taxes has a similar, though less direct, effect on total demand. If, for example, the rates of personal income tax are reduced, taxpayers will be left with more after-tax income to spend. When they increase their spending, they will add to total demand for the goods and services that they buy. Thus, cutting taxes adds to total demand indirectly, because it leaves more money in people's pockets and relies on them to increase total demand by spending some of this money.

Monetary Policy: Monetary policy seeks to affect total demand by influencing the amount of money and credit available, and the cost of that credit to borrowers (i.e. interest rates). Since business and households borrow to finance much of their expenditure, changing the availability, and the terms, of credit can influence total demand. By making more funds available to be borrowed, and by exerting a downward pressure on interest rates which lowers the cost of borrowing, the government seeks to increase total demand. By making fewer funds available to be borrowed, and by exerting an upward pressure on interest rates, the government seeks to lower total demand. How the Bank of England can accomplish these changes in the conditions of credit will be studied in detail in a later chapter.

Supply-side policies

As well as influencing total demand, the government can try to influence total national product by adopting what are called *supply-side policies*. These try to influence the total output that the private sector can, and will, produce. The possible policies are too numerous to outline here, but they will be discussed in detail later in this book.

Suffice it to say here that supply-side policies are designed to cause rightward shifts in the supply curves in many individual markets. Consider just two examples. First, let there be a reduction in the rates of personal income taxes. This *may* increase the amount of work that people wish to do. (This possibility is discussed in detail in Chapter 21.) If it does so, then the increased supply of labour will increase the economy's full-employment output. For a second example, let there be a large tax exemption for research and development. If this causes an increase in invention and innovation, there will be more output of those goods and services that are affected.

If enough individual supply curves are shifted, the aggregate supply of all goods will be significantly increased.

Macroeconomic Theories and Economic Policies

In this chapter, we have discussed the main variables of macroeconomics and some of the reasons why policy-makers are concerned about them. What determines the size of these variables, and the scope that governments have to influence them, is the subject-matter of macroeconomic theory to which we will soon turn our attention. First, however, we must look in more detail at the output and income variables of macroeconomics. This we do in Chapter 26.

SUMMARY

1 Macroeconomics studies the economy in terms of broad aggregates and averages such as total employment and unemployment, total national product, the overall price level and the balance of payments.

2 Six major issues concern: (1) the amount of employment and unemployment, (2) the rate of inflation (changes in the price level), (3) the trade cycle (fluctuations in output and employment), (4) stagflation (the combination of high unemployment and high inflation), (5) economic growth (long-term trend of output), and (6) the behaviour of the exchange rate and the balance of payments.

3 High unemployment is undesirable because of the lost output and human misery involved. High output is desirable because the size of the national product determines (along with the size of the population) the average standard of living of a country's residents.

4 Changes in the price level are measured by an index number of prices. The index shows the percentage change in the cost of purchasing a given quantity of commodities in any year, compared to a base year.

5 Three major problems concerning price indices are as follows: (i) the more an individual household's consumption pattern diverges from that of the 'typical' pattern used to weight prices in the price index, the less well does the price index reflect the average change in prices relevant to that household; (ii) a fixed-weight price index tends to overstate cost-of-living changes because it does not allow for changes in consumption patterns that shift expenditure away from commodities whose prices rise most and toward those whose prices rise least; (iii) a fixed-weight index makes no allowance for the appearance of new products nor for the declining importance of old ones in the typical household's consumption bundle.

6 Changes in the price level may be undesirable in so far as they cause the price mechanism to allocate resources less efficiently and/or less equitably than would otherwise occur. This tends to be more likely when inflation is unanticipated than when it is anticipated. Anticipated inflation

causes less disruption than does unanticipated inflation.

7 The major primary goals of macroeconomic policy are (1) full employment (which does not mean zero unemployment), (2) a satisfactory rate of growth of national product, and (3) a stable price level. A satisfactory balance of payments is usually regarded as a secondary policy goal, since it is not so obviously desirable in itself, but may inhibit attainment of the primary goals if it is not achieved.

8 Two sets of macroeconomic policy instruments are usually distinguished: (1) demand-side policies, which include fiscal and monetary policies; (2) supply-side policies, which attempt to influence total output.

The Circular Flow and National Income Accounting

Macroeconomics builds on the basic concept of the circular flow of income. This was first discussed in Chapter 2, and that discussion, on pages 24–6 which you have already been advised to reread, provides the starting point for our present study. Our discussion is divided into three parts. We first look at the major types of production in the economy. Then we study the three main ways of measuring the circular flow. Finally we raise a number of issues concerning the meaning and interpretation of these measures once they have been made.

Consumers and Households: A CONSUMER refers to a single individual who buys and consumes goods. A HOUSEHOLD refers to all people who live under the same roof and who make joint financial decisions about, among other things, the purchase and consumption of goods. In microeconomics we use the term consumer to refer to the basic purchasing unit. In macroeconomics we use the term household.

For some purposes, particularly when making detailed calculations based on real-world data, the difference between individual consumers and households can be important. At the introductory level, however, the distinction is unimportant. Thus we can use the two terms interchangeably to refer to those who purchase consumer goods and services. In what follows, we use the term 'household' to describe the basic purchasing unit for consumption goods because that is the term usually employed by macroeconomists. But for everything that matters in this book you can take the terms 'individual consumer' and 'household' as interchangeable.

MAJOR TYPES OF PRODUCTION

The circular flow diagrams on page 26 of Chapter 2 identified two main groups, producers and consumers. To avoid confusion, you should note that these groups are referred to by a variety of names. One is often called the *consumption sector*, or the *household sector*. The other is often called the *production sector*, the *firm sector* or the *business sector*.

To begin our study, we look at producers and divide their production into three main categories called consumption commodities, investment goods, and government production.

Consumption Commodities

The category of CONSUMPTION COMMODITIES includes the output of all goods and services for consumption by households (except for new houses). These are the economy's outputs of bread, beer, dresses, records, TV sets, haircuts, concerts, and a host of other goods and services that satisfy people's wants.

Notice three things about consumption commodities.

- First, the category includes only *currently produced* goods and services. For example, the output of new cars is part of the current production of consumption goods, but the purchase of a used car (produced in an earlier year) is merely a transfer of ownership of an existing asset. It is not a part of current car production. Thus the value of all second-hand goods transferred is not a part of the economy's current production.

It is worth noting before we pass on, however, that the value of the second-hand-car firm's contribution to the price of the used car *is* a part of current production. After all, the second-hand-car dealer is providing a current service that people are willing to pay for and which is a current output of a service. What does not count is the value of the car that goes to the former owner. Thus, if I sell my old car to a car dealer for £3,000, and he sells it to you for £3,500, current output is £500 – not £3,500, but not zero. The £3,000 is merely a payment that goes, in effect, from you to me in return for the transfer of a car that was manufactured at some time in the past. The £500, however, represents the value of the currently produced services of the second-hand-car dealer. He must pay his sales and office staff; he must also pay rent and advertising expenses; and he must earn a return on the capital that he has invested in the firm. This is where his £500 goes, and it will be reported as a current contribution to national product.

- Second, consumer goods and services are included in the measurement of production *when they are produced*, not when they are consumed. With non-durable goods such as haircuts and fresh strawberries, there is no significant difference between the time of production and of consumption, since these two points of time are very close to each other. Indeed with a service such as a haircut or a rock concert, consumption usually occurs at the same point in time as production. With durable goods, such as cars and TV sets, however, there is a marked difference. The good is produced at one time, but it is consumed over the good's lifetime, which may be many years. For example, a 1975 model refrigerator that lasted 10 years was produced in one year but was consumed over the 10 years that it was in service.
- Third, residential housing is the one exception to the general rule that the term consumption commodities refers to the output of all goods and services consumed by households. Housing is counted as investment and is considered below.

Investment Goods

INVESTMENT GOODS are the capital goods that we met in microeconomics plus residential housing, which is counted as an investment rather than a durable consumer good by the conventions of national income accounting. In macroeconomics, investment goods are divided into three main categories: fixed capital, circulating capital, and residential housing. The first two of these categories were discussed in detail in Chapter 21.

The *output* of these investment goods in any period is the amount of new capital goods, new additions to circulating capital and new residential housing produced over that period. The total output in these three categories is called total investment.

Fixed Capital: The current output of fixed capital includes currently constructed factories, and machinery and equipment currently produced. These fixed-capital goods may be used to replace other capital goods that have worn out or become obsolete, or they may be used to make a net addition to the nation's total stock of capital.

Circulating Capital: In the UK, circulating capital is called STOCKS, but the American term *inventories* is also used. It consists of (1) stocks of materials that firms hold for use in further production, (2) stocks of semi-finished goods in the process of production, and (3) stocks of finished goods ready for sale but not yet sold. Current output of these stocks consists not of the total stocks held, since much of this may be carried over from the past, but rather of the change in these stocks over the period in question. Letting I_s stand for current investment in stocks, we have:

$$I_s = \text{End-of-year stocks} - \text{Beginning-of-year stocks}.$$

If stocks held at the end of the year exceed those held at the beginning of the year, we say there has been an *accumulation of stocks* or *positive investment in stocks*. If stocks held at the end of the year are smaller than stocks held at the beginning of the year, stocks are being reduced. In this case, valuable things produced in the past have been used up in the current year and not replaced. Several equivalent terms are used to describe such a situation. We may say that there has been a *decumulation of stocks* or *destocking* or *negative investment in stocks*.

One final word of caution is in order. The word stock has two distinct, but related, meanings. First, it is used in the restricted sense just described: to denote circulating capital. Second, it is used in the more general sense to denote a quantity that does not have a time dimension. The quantity of circulating capital, the quantity of fixed capital, or the amount of money you have in the bank are all stocks in this more general sense, while the change in circulating capital per unit of time, the change in the quantity of fixed capital per unit of time, and the amount that you add to your bank balance per unit of time are all flows. A stock, in the restricted sense of the quantity of circulating capital in existence at any one time, is but one example of a stock in the more general sense.

Housing: A house is a very durable asset that yields its utility to its user slowly over the lifetime of the dwelling. For this reason, the nation's current output of new housing is treated as an investment item rather than as an item for current consumption.

Gross and Net Investment: The total production of investment goods that occurs during a period is called the economy's GROSS INVESTMENT. The amount of capital that wears out, or becomes obsolete, is called DEPRECIATION or THE CAPITAL CONSUMPTION ALLOWANCE. The amount necessary for the replacement of capital goods that have worn out, or have been discarded as obsolete, is called *replacement investment*. The remainder is called NET INVESTMENT:

Net Investment = Gross Investment − Depreciation.

A digression on stocks and flows

Before we go on to consider the third category of expenditure, which is governmment expenditure, we must pause for a moment to discuss at more length the important distinction between stocks and flows. This distinction arose in our discussion of investment, and it will arise in other important contexts later.

It is very easy to become confused between the nation's *stock* of capital and the *changes to* that stock which arise out of current production. The nation's current *stock* of capital – we are now using 'stocks' in the general sense – consists of all the fixed capital, all the circulating capital, and all the housing that has been produced in the past and is in existence today. The nation's *current output* of investment goods (capital goods) consists of additions to these stocks that are made in the current period. Thus only *additions* to fixed capital, and only *additions* to stocks of circulating capital, and only *additions* to the nation's stock of housing are counted as the *output* of *current* investment goods.

The possible confusion just mentioned is an

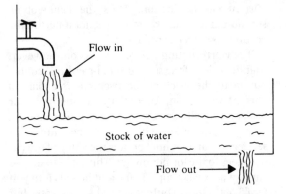

FIGURE 26.1   Stocks and Flows. The amount of water in the bath is a stock, the amounts entering through the tap and leaving through the drain are flows

example of a general problem of confusing *stocks* (e.g., the stock of capital) and *flows* (e.g., this year's addition to the stock of capital). To study the distinction, further consider, as illustrated in Figure 26.1, a bath half full of water with the tap turned on and the plug removed. You now have in mind a model similar to many simple economic theories. The level of water in the bath is a stock – an amount that is just there. We could express it as so many gallons of water. If we replaced the plug and turned off the tap, the stock of water currently in the tub would remain there indefinitely. Now consider the amount of water entering through the tap and the amount leaving down the drain. Both are flows. We could express them as so many gallons per minute or per hour. A flow necessarily has a time dimension – there is so much flow *per period of time*. A stock does not – it is just so many tonnes or gallons or machines.

The total amount of machinery in the country is part of the nation's *stock* of capital – analogous to the amount of water in the bath tub. The amount of depreciation is a flow that reduces the capital stock – analogous to the amount of water flowing down the drain. Finally, the amount of new capital goods produced, i.e. gross investment, is a flow that increases the capital stock – analogous to the flow of water coming from the tap into the bath.

Government Production

It is important at the outset to distinguish between two main types of government expenditure. The first type is expenditure which uses resources. This is expenditure on such things as road building and maintenance, national health, civil servants' salaries (which use the resource of labour), and defence. It is often called EXHAUSTIVE EXPENDITURE, and that is the term we shall use. All government exhaustive expenditure is counted as producing output of goods and services. Government output thus includes the activities of the police, courts of law, traffic wardens, Foreign Office employees, building inspectors, and a host of other activities at all levels of government.

The second type is expenditure which merely transfers purchasing power from one group to another. This is expenditure on such things as interest on the government's debt, retirement pensions, unemployment insurance benefits, disability payments, supplementary benefits, and a host of other payments made by the modern welfare state. This type of expenditure is usually called TRANSFER PAYMENTS. Such expenditures do not add to current marketable output; they merely transfer purchasing power from those who provide the funds – usually taxpayers – to those who receive them. Transfer payments made by the government are *not*, therefore, regarded as a part of the government's current output of goods and services. For the moment, we confine ourselves to exhaustive expenditures.

OUTPUT, EXPENDITURE AND INCOME IN THE CIRCULAR FLOW

Figure 26.2 is similar to the simple circular flow diagram which was Figure 2.5 on page 26 but with some of the explanatory labels omitted. To find out what is happening to the level of economic activity in the country, we need to measure the amount of this circular flow over some period of time, usually taken as a year. The diagram shows the three ways in which this can be done. These are called the output (or product) approach, the income approach and the expenditure approach. They are approaches to measuring the *total market value* of the nation's output. (Later we shall consider measures based on values other than market prices.) We discuss below how total output is measured using each of the three approaches. Figure 26.3 shows the major components of each of the three measures, and it can be referred to as the discussion proceeds.[1]

1 Much of the factual detail of the measures discussed here is given in Chapter 7 of Harbury and Lipsey.

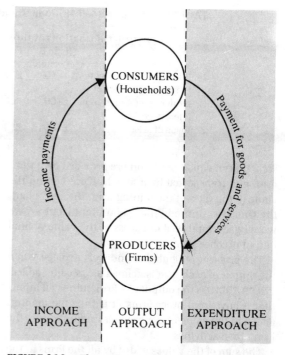

FIGURE 26.2   Three Approaches to Measuring the Value of the Nation's Output. The Output Approach looks directly at the value of what is produced; the Expenditure Approach looks at the expenditure needed to produce the nation's output; the Income approach looks at the incomes generated by the production of that output

The Output or Product Approach

The first approach is to go directly to producers and add up the values of all of their outputs. (We noted in Chapter 2, page 26, that we can add up the values of different types of production – tonnes of steel, megawatts of electricity, and kilos of strawberries – by adding up their money values.) This approach measures the circular flow at the point of production and it is shown by the middle, unshaded section of the diagram.

Double counting

When we measure the value of each producer's output, we encounter a problem which is called *double counting*. Because of the advantages of specialization, the output of virtually every commodity occurs over a series of stages, each stage being carried out by separate firms. Thus coffee spoons may be made by one firm, from stainless steel provided by a

TABLE 26.1 Value Added Through Stages of Production: An Example

Inter-firm transactions at three different stages of production				
	Firm B	Firm I	Firm F	All firms
1. Purchases from other firms	£0	£100	£130	£230 = Total inter-firm sales
2. Purchase of factors of production (wages, rent, interest, profits)	£100	£30	£50	£180 = Value added
3. Value of sales	£100	£130	£180	£410 = Value of total sales

second firm, which used iron ore provided by a third firm, and transported by a fourth. If we add up the value of the sales of the mining firm, the steel plant, the transport firm and the spoon manufacturer, we would get a total well in excess of the value of final output of coffee spoons.

The problem of double counting is avoided when the output of each firm is defined as its value added. VALUE ADDED is the output of a firm, minus all inputs that it buys from other firms. It is thus the amount added to the value of the product in question by the firm's own activities.

The sum of the values added by all the firms in the economy is the nation's total output, its national product. The worked example given in Table 26.1 develops this idea further. It uses a simple example in which production moves through three stages, begun by the basic producer, B, through the intermediate firm, I, and ending up with the producer of the final product, F. Firm B produces basic materials valued at £100; the firm's value added is £100. Firm I purchases these raw materials, valued at £100, and produces semi-manufactured goods (often called intermediate products) that is sells for £130 . Its value added is £30 because the value of the goods is increased by £30 as a result of the firm's activities. Firm F purchases these semi-manufactured goods for £130 and works them into a finished state, selling them for £180. Firm F's value added is £50. The value of final goods, £180, is found either by counting the sales of firm F or by taking the sum of the values added by each firm. This value is less than the £410 that we obtain by adding up the market value of the commodities sold by each firm.

The above illustration suggests another important distinction. INTERMEDIATE GOODS are goods and services that are sold by one firm to be used as inputs by another firm. FINAL GOODS are the end-product of economic activity; they are the economy's output. This final output includes all goods for consumption, all investment goods, and all goods and services produced by the government. Each firm's contribution to final output is measured by its value added.

The total value of output

The output approach measure the nation's output as the sum of all values added in the economy:

Total output = the sum of all values added.

The Expenditure Approach

The expenditure approach arrives at the nation's total output by adding up the expenditures needed to purchase all of the final output of the economy. This approach measures the flow around the right-hand part of the circuit shown in Figure 26.2. The main categories of expenditure are considered below.

Consumption: This includes the value of all consumer goods and services purchased over the year. *We give total consumption expenditures the designation C.*

Investment: This is the value of all capital goods produced over the year. It includes the value of all new, fixed capital, such as plant and equipment, all new housing, and any net changes in circulating capital. *We designate total investment expenditure by the symbol I.*

Government: When the government spends money to produce goods and services that are sold, the goods and services are valued at market prices. We have already observed, however, that many government exhaustive expenditures do not produce goods or services that are sold on the market. The value of the output resulting from such expenditures is taken to be the amount spent on them. In other words, valuation is at cost.

We have also observed that government expenditure on transfer payments is not a part of current

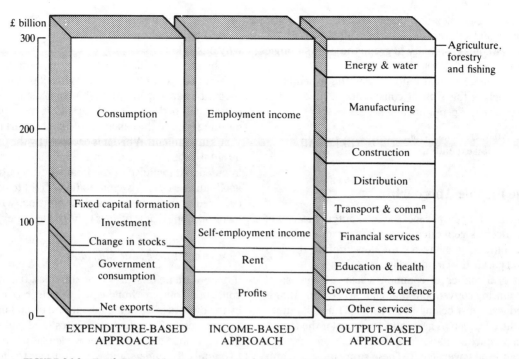

FIGURE 26.3   Total Output (Gross Domestic Product) Calculated from the Three Approaches. Total output is the same from all three approaches, but the breakdown is different in each case

output. Thus, *to get at the government's contribution to national income from the expenditure approach, we need to count only the government's exhaustive expenditures, which we designate by the symbol G.*

The total value of expenditure on output

A Closed Economy: A CLOSED ECONOMY is one that does not engage in foreign trade; an OPEN ECONOMY is one that does. In a closed economy, the expenditure approach measures total output as the sum of consumption, investment and government expenditure where investment *includes* changes in stocks, and government expenditure *excludes* government transfer payments. In symbols:

A closed economy's total expenditure $= C + I + G$

An Open Economy: Finally, we must allow for the fact that the economy of the UK is an open economy. Part of the expenditure in each of the categories so far considered – consumption, investment and government – goes to purchase commodities produced in other countries. For example, total expenditure on cars bought in the UK includes not only purchases of cars made in the UK but also purchases of cars produced abroad and imported into the UK. The

expenditure on imports creates incomes in the producing countries, not in the UK. Thus, to discover the output produced by the car industry in the UK, we must subtract from total expenditures on cars by UK residents the amount that goes to purchase imported cars. Similar considerations apply to all other categories of expenditure. Some expenditure on investment goes to buy equipment and materials imported from abroad. The same is true for government expenditure; e.g., when a Japanese computer is bought by a local authority, or a foreign selling agent is hired by a government department selling arms abroad.

So, to arrive at *national* output from the expenditure approach, it is necessary to subtract from $C + I + G$ the value of all expenditures on imports, which we designate as M.

Exports pose an analogous problem. When Italians, Swedes and Germans purchase British cars, this is expenditure on British production. So to calculate British national output from the expenditure approach, we must add in all expenditures by foreign residents on British exports. We give these the symbol X.

Net Exports: Now we have the two corrections that

are needed to allow for foreign trade: we must add exports and subtract imports. In symbols this is $+X$ and $-M$. It is customary to group these into a single term called NET EXPORTS $(X-M)$.

In summary, total output from the expenditure approach is the sum of consumption, investment, government expenditure and net exports:

$$\begin{array}{l}\text{An open economy's}\\ \text{total expenditure}\end{array} = C+I+G+(X-M).$$

The Income Approach

The income approach looks at total output in terms of the incomes generated in the process of producing that output. It measures the flow around the left-hand part of the circuit in Figure 26.2.

It is a matter of common sense, as well as of accounting convention, that all market value that is produced must belong to someone. Thus, all output produced is seen as generating income for the factors that produce it – plus, as we shall see, an amount that goes to the government. These sums must account for, and hence add up to, the total value of this output. The income may not actually be paid out until long after the output is produced, but whenever production does occur, some income simultaneously arises.

Major classes of measured incomes

Wages and salaries, which national income account-ants call income from employment, is by far the largest income share generated. This includes gross pay before income tax, social security and pension fund contributions are deducted. In total, these represent that part of the value of production attribut-able to labour. Next, in order of size, comes what are called gross trading profits (the incomes of privately and publicly owned producers who sell their outputs on the market), followed by the capital consumption allowance (which is also called depreciation). Smaller items include incomes of the self-employed and rent. The former is mainly the income of farmers, unincor-porated businesses, tradesmen, and professionals who work either on their own or in partnerships. The latter includes rents received by those owning pro-perty let to others, and what is called 'imputed rent' of owner-occupied dwellings.

This last term is new and requires some explan-ation. In general, to 'impute' means 'to attribute to'. In this case, a rental value of housing occupied by its owners is imputed to the owners' income even though no actual rent is paid or received. Let us see why this is done.

When a block of flats is built, the expenditure on it is part of this year's investment. When it is rented out, the rentals appear in national income as part of the gross profits of the owners of the flats. When a private dwelling is built, the expenditure on it is a part of this year's investment. When it is occupied by the owner, a rental value for the use of the housing services is imputed and included in the total value of output of goods and services. This imputation of rent to owner-occupied housing is needed if all housing, whether owner-occupied or rented, is to be treated similarly.

Government taxes and subsidies

If there were neither taxes nor subsidies, the market value of all output would equal the incomes earned by the owners of the land, labour and capital used in the process of production. Taxes and subsidies, however, introduce a kind of wedge between these two totals. To understand why, consider the follow-ing example.

If the government gives a subsidy to the producers of wheat of 50p per bushel of wheat produced, every bushel produced can generate 50p of income to farmers over and above its market value. Say, for example, that wheat sells for £4 a bushel but there is a subsidy to producers of 50p per bushel. Then, those factors used in producing wheat will earn £4.50 for every bushel produced.

Now consider taxes levied on the production or sale of goods and services, so-called indirect taxes. Say, for example, that there is no subsidy but instead a sales tax of 50p for every bushel of wheat sold. While the market value of each bushel produced remains at £4, the incomes earned by the factors used to produce that wheat will be only £3.50; the extra 50p goes to the government as an indirect tax.

The above examples illustrate the following im-portant conclusion. In the case of a subsidy, incomes earned by the factors of production (market value of production plus subsidies) exceed the total value of output. In the case of a tax, incomes earned (the market value of output minus taxes taken by the government) fall short of the total market value of output.

To allow for the effect of indirect taxes and subsidies, two adjustments are needed when we add up incomes generated by production in order to arrive at the total value of production *measured at market prices*. First, we must add the government's taxes on goods and services, since these are part of the market value of output that does not give rise to incomes going to land, labour or capital. Second we must subtract government subsidies on goods and services, since these allow incomes to exceed the market value of output.

In the national accounts, the effects of indirect taxes and subsidies are usually combined into one figure called *net indirect taxes*, which is total taxes minus total subsidies. Students are sometimes confused as to whether this amount should be added or subtracted. If you keep its purpose firmly in mind, you should not get confused. *If you have all factor incomes and want to get the market value of output, you must add in net taxes. If, however, you have the market value of total output and want to get factor earnings, you must deduct net taxes.*

The total value of income generated by output

The income approach measures the value of total output at market prices as the sum of all factor incomes generated by the process of production. This is the sum of all wages, interest, profits and rents, plus net indirect taxes.

Why the Three Approaches Yield the Same Total: The Identity of Output, Income and Expenditure

In all three approaches so far considered, the basic *overall* aggregate being measured is the total value of the nation's output at market prices. This can be looked at directly in terms of the output itself, O, or the expenditure required to purchase it, E, or the income it generates, Y. Although the details of each calculation give us independent information, the totals do not, since all three are defined so that they are identical:

$$O \equiv E \equiv Y.$$

(Notice the use of the *three-bar sign*, which is used to indicate and identify where the values on both sides of the ≡ sign are *necessarily* the same.)

The reason for the identity of Y and O is that Y does not measure incomes actually paid out during the course of the year, but instead measures the incomes generated by producing O (plus the amount that goes to the government as a result of net indirect taxes).

The identity of Y and O then follows from the accounting practice that the value of all output must belong to someone: what is not wages, interest and rent becomes either profits of the producers or goes to the government through indirect taxes.[1] Between them they must account for all output since someone must own the value that has been produced. Also, goods produced and not sold are valued at market prices, and the difference between their value and their cost of production is counted as profits and recorded as part of profit income even though this will not accrue until the goods are sold.

Now consider the identity between O and E. This follows because E measures the expenditure required to purchase the nation's output, which is the same thing as the value of that output. In calculating expenditure, national income accountants add up the amounts actually spent to purchase what is sold, plus the amount that would have to be spent if the output added to stocks had been sold instead; that is, firms are assumed to have purchased the inventories and to have paid the market price for them. This makes E the same thing as O.

The interest in having all three measures lies not in their identical total, which is purely a matter of definition, but in the breakdown of each. In the case of O, this is by industry, such as electricity generation and car production; in the case of E, it is by type of expenditure, such as consumption and investment; in the case of Y, it is by type of income, such as wages and salaries.

National income as the generic term

We have just seen that, when appropriately measured, output, income and expenditure are identical. They yield a single total that simultaneously measures the market value of total output, the incomes earned by producing that output (plus net government taxes), and the expenditure needed to purchase that output. It is important that you understand this point. Before reading on, you should reread the previous section if you feel in any doubt about it.

The usual term used to refer to this total in theoretical work is NATIONAL INCOME. It is given the symbol Y. Thus, when we refer throughout all subsequent chapters to the national income, we are

---

[1] If firms make losses, wages, interest, rent, etc. exceed the value of output and the losses must be subtracted from other incomes to get the value of output.

referring to the total value of income earned in the country over a year, as well as to the total value of output, as well as to the total value of the expenditure needed to purchase that output.

NATIONAL INCOME STATISTICS

In Chapter 28, when we come to the theory of how national income is determined, we shall see that expenditures are the most useful way of looking at national income. For this reason, we now study a series of expenditure measures. Each gives a somewhat different total, and each gives us useful and interesting information. The relation between them is illustrated in Figure 26.4 and discussed below.

Various Measures of Total Expenditure

We start with a measure that is the basis from which the most commonly quoted measures are calculated. TOTAL DOMESTIC EXPENDITURE (TDE) is the sum of all expenditure on final output that is made within a country irrespective of where the output was produced:

$$\text{TDE} = C + I + G.$$

Next comes TOTAL FINAL EXPENDITURE (TFE), which is the sum of all expenditure on final output that takes place within a country, irrespective both of the country in which the goods and services were produced, *and of the country in which they were consumed.* This is TDE plus exports:

$$\text{TFE} = C + I + G + X.$$

Next, we come to the most comprehensive measure of the national income. This is GROSS DOMESTIC PRODUCT (GDP) *at market prices.* It is defined as TFE minus imports. Subtracting imports reduces the value of TFE by the amount of expenditure that goes to purchase goods and services produced abroad:

$$\text{GDP (at market prices)} = C + I + G + (X - M).$$

Recall that it is customary to group exports and imports together into the single term $(X - M)$.

The GDP at market prices tells us the value of all final expenditure on the goods and services that are produced within the nation.

The next measure that we need to consider is called GROSS DOMESTIC PRODUCT *at factor cost.* This measures GDP at the cost of the factors used to produce it,

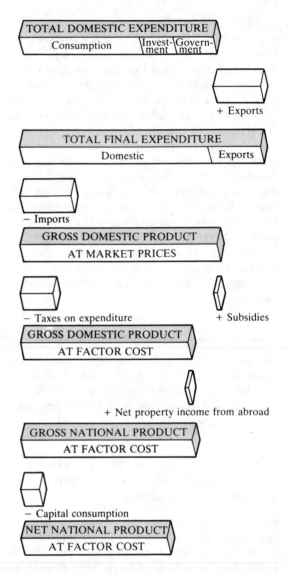

FIGURE 26.4 **The Relation Between the Various Expenditure Totals.** Of the totals shown, TFE is the largest and NNP is the smallest

and hence at the incomes earned by those factors. It differs from GDP at market prices by the correction for net indirect taxes. Spelling this out in detail, GDP at market prices must be changed by the *addition* of government subsidies on the production or sale of what is produced, and the *subtraction* of taxes on the production or sale of what is produced. Subsidies, as we have seen, allow factor incomes to exceed the market value of goods sold, while taxes on expenditure force incomes received to be less than the market value of goods sold because some of the proceeds derived from the sale of the product accrue to the government:

$$\text{GDP (at factor cost)} = \text{GDP (at market prices)} + \text{subsidies} - \text{taxes on expenditure.}$$

The next measure is GROSS NATIONAL PRODUCT (GNP) *at factor cost*. This is the sum of all incomes earned by UK residents in return for contributions to current production that takes place anywhere in the world. We get from GDP to GNP in two steps. First we *add* receipts of interest, profits and dividends received by UK residents from assets that they own overseas. These receipts are part of incomes earned by UK residents, but they are not a part of UK production. Second, we have to *subtract* interest, profits and dividends earned on assets located in the UK, but owned abroad, if we wish to arrive at income earned by UK residents. Although these are part of UK production, they are incomes earned, not by UK, but by *foreign*, residents. The total of these adjustments is called *net property income from abroad.*

$$\text{GNP (at factor cost)} = \text{GDP (at factor cost)} + \text{net property income from abroad.}$$

The next measure that we meet is called NET NATIONAL PRODUCT (NNP) *at factor cost*. This is GNP minus the capital consumption allowance (depreciation). NNP is thus a measure of the net output of the economy after deducting from gross output an amount necessary to maintain intact the existing stock of capital. The NNP measures the maximum amount that could be consumed by the private, and the government, sectors without actually running down the economy's capital stock. (In the UK National Accounts this is known as *net national income*.)

$$\text{NNP (at factor cost)} = \text{GNP} - \text{depreciation (or capital consumption allowance).}$$

We have illustrated the *net* concept by discussing NNP. But once we have the idea of deducting the capital consumption allowance to calculate a figure that is net of the amount needed to maintain the country's capital stock intact, we can make this subtraction from any of the 'gross' figures mentioned above. For example, if we take gross domestic product, GDP, and subtract the capital consumption allowance, we obtain *net* domestic product, NDP.

Other measures

All of the measures considered so far treat aspects of total output and total income. Now we consider two further concepts that are designed to measure important parts of national income.

The first measure is called PERSONAL INCOME. It is gross income earned by households, whether as factor payments or total outputs, as distinct from other income recipients, before allowance for personal income taxes. A number of adjustments to NNP (at factor cost) are required to arrive at personal income. The most important are (1) subtracting from NNP all income taxes paid by businesses (since these are part of the value of output that is not paid to persons); (2) adding to NNP all transfer payments (since these create incomes for persons that do not arise out of current production); and (3) deducting all undistributed business profits. These are incomes that are not paid out to persons because the firms retain the funds for their own purposes.

The second measure that we need to consider under this heading is called PERSONAL DISPOSABLE INCOME. This is a measure of the amount of personal income that households have available to spend or to save. It is calculated as personal income minus personal income taxes (including national insurance contributions).

INTERPRETING NATIONAL INCOME MEASURES

The information provided by measures of national income can be extremely useful, but unless carefully interpreted, it can also be seriously misleading. Furthermore, as we have been at pains to explain, since each specialized measure gives different information, each may be the best statistic for studying a particular problem.

We start with two variations on total national income, each of which gives us useful information.

Money Values and Real Values

We have already studied the important distinction between measures of national income that use current prices and those that use constant prices. (See pages 303–4.)

All we need to do here, therefore, is to summarize the significance of this important distinction. All national income data are valued either in current prices or in constant prices. When the valuation is in current prices, the result is called NOMINAL NATIONAL INCOME or MONEY NATIONAL INCOME. When valued in constant prices, the result is called REAL NATIONAL INCOME (sometimes also called CONSTANT-PRICE NATIONAL INCOME). These are terms you will encounter frequently from now on, and they should be memorized.

When nominal national income changes, we know that the market value of total output has changed. This may be the result of changes in either, or both, the *quantities* and the *prices* of final outputs. When real national income changes, we know that this must be the result of changes in the quantities of final output (since the prices at which outputs are valued remain unchanged).

Total Output and Per Capita Output

Both real and nominal national income are measures of aggregate, or total, income generated by the economy. For many purposes, totals are just what we require. For example, to assess a country's potential military strength, we need to know (among other things) the total output of which it is capable. Also if we wish to gauge the importance of a country as a market for our exports, we are interested in its total sales and purchases.

For other purposes, such as studying changes in living standards, we require *per capita* measures, which are obtained by dividing a total measure such as GNP by the population. Comparisons of living standards are often made by reference to per capita disposable income in constant prices. This measure allows for comparisons over time in a single country, and also for international comparisons, if disposable incomes are all measured in terms of the prices ruling in one country.

There are many useful per capita measures, and the division must be made by the appropriate 'population'. Dividing GNP by the total population gives a measure of how much GNP there is on average for each person in the economy; this is called PER CAPITA GNP. It is particularly useful in estimating living standards. Dividing GNP by the number of persons employed tells us the average output per employed person. This is called GNP PER EMPLOYED PERSON. Dividing GNP by the total number of hours worked measures output per hour of labour input. This is called GNP PER HOUR WORKED. These last two measures give us the estimates of overall labour productivity that we discussed in Chapter 25.

Measurement Problems

Next we raise some problems connected with getting accurate measures of national income. We will deal briefly with problems of classification, coverage and valuation.

Classification

Our first problem concerns how to classify those items that we agree are a part of total national income. There are many such problems of classification, and we illustrate them with the example of residential housing.

Earlier in this chapter, we saw that expenditure on new housing is classified as an investment expenditure, while expenditure on all other consumer durables, some of which last even longer than many houses, is classified as a consumption expenditure. The decision to do so is arbitrary but conventional.

Housing is regarded as an investment good because it lasts a long time. However, there are other durable goods that last for many years – for example, furniture. Housing improvements such as central heating, which are included in investment, may have lives shorter than many consumer durables such as dining-room suites.

Coverage

There is always room for disagreement on what items of expenditure do and do not form a part of national income. Although we know what we mean by national income in a general, theoretical way, no concept is perfectly clear at the margins. Precise definitions of what is, and is not, a part of national income tend to arise out of tough decisions as to whether or not to include an item. We will illustrate with the case of interest on the public (or national) debt.

Earlier in this chapter we observed that interest on private-sector debt is included in the national income while interest on public-sector debt is not. If a private firm borrows money and pays interest on its debt, this is counted as part of national income. The payment is understood to be in return for the service of private investors in providing productive capital to the firm. However, if the government borrows money to build a new nuclear power plant, the interest that is paid on this debt is counted as a transfer payment and hence not included in national income. In the case of the nuclear power plant, the distinction seems quite arbitrary. If the plant had been owned by a private firm, the interest on its debt would have been counted as a part of national income. But if the government owns the plant, and does exactly what the private firm would have done, the interest is not counted in national income.

The distinction between interest paid by private firms and by the government makes more sense in so far as the government's debt was accumulated to finance current, rather than capital, expenditures made in the past. Say, for example, that five years ago the government could not meet all of its unemployment benefits out of current tax revenue and borrowed money to enable it to make these payments. If the debt still exists, the government will be making current interest payments on it, and there will be no current output that is financed by these payments.

Many economists have argued that the government's accounts should be divided into a capital and a current account. Interest on money borrowed to finance capital expenditures would then be counted as part of current national income, just as it is for private firms. But interest borrowed to meet current expenses would not be counted as current national income. The accounting difficulties are, however, formidable, and this is not done.

The issue is currently resolved by counting all government interest payments as transfer payments – payments not associated with current output. This arbitrary decision probably reflects a judgement that government debt is undesirable because it is unproductive, while private debt is desirable because it is productive. If there is anything in this view, it must depend on a factual evaluation of what the government does with the funds that it borrows.

Valuation problems

Whenever a good is sold on the market, it can be, and is, valued at its market price. Major problems arise, however, with non-marketed output. We shall consider two categories of expenditure which present major valuation problems, government production and stock accumulation.

Consider government non-marketed production first. In many cases, the government's 'output' is not sold. This is the case, for example, with state education, defence and the services of fire departments. Since there is no market price at which to value these goods and services, they are valued 'at cost'. This means that whatever it costs the government to provide the service is taken as the value of the output

of the service. Thus, *the government's total production of goods and services is taken to be equal to the total of the government's exhaustive expenditures.*

There is no choice but to value non-marketed government services 'at cost'. Such a procedure does, however, have one curious consequence in that productivity may appear to rise when it has actually fallen, and vice versa. To see this, consider an example. If one civil servant now does exactly what two used to do, and the redundant worker shifts to the private sector, the government's measured output will fall. This happens in spite of the fact that the things the government does are actually unchanged, and productivity (output per employed civil servant) has risen. Suppose, however, that it now takes two civil servants to do exactly what one used to do, and an extra civil servant is employed for this purpose. The government's measured contribution to output will rise – even though the things the government does remain unchanged, and productivity has fallen.

Another valuation problem arises with stocks accumulated by the private sector. Since they are goods that have *not* been sold, they must be valued by some convention. They could be valued at cost or at current market prices. Valuation at cost means using the amount spent on them so far (net of the value of inputs purchased from other firms to avoid double counting). Valuation at market price means valuing them at what they could be sold for today, which is what has been spent to produce them *plus* the profit margin that will be added to costs to determine selling price. In the UK's official national income statistics, market prices are used to value stocks. (Accounting practices vary, however, among firms.)

Valuation of stocks at market prices causes its own problems. In times of unexpected slumps in sales, stocks of unsold goods may pile up in the storerooms of their producers. Because these are valued at market prices are used to value stocks. (Account-result, measured business profits will include the unrealized profits on these stocks. For this reason, an unexpected sales downturn, in which businesses may be in serious difficulty and be realizing few profits, is often accompanied by a high recorded level of profits in the national accounts.

Omissions from Measured National Income

Next we come to a series of undesirable omissions from all national income measures. These are not cases of omitting an easily measured magnitude such as interest on public-sector debt; rather, the omissions occur because of measurement difficulties.

Illegal activities

The GNP does not measure illegal production, even though many such goods and services are sold on the market and generate factor incomes. The production and distribution of soft and hard drugs are important examples today. As long as the income generated from such activities goes unreported, it is unlikely to show up in the national income statistics. If we wish to measure the total demand for factors of production in the economy, or the total marketable output – whether or not we as individuals approve of particular products – we should include these activities. The main reason for omitting illegal activities is that, because of their illicit nature, it is difficult to find the information needed to include them.

The Black Economy: An important omission from the measured GNP is the so-called *black economy*. Here the transactions are perfectly legal in themselves. The only illegal thing about them is that they are not reported for income-tax purposes. For example, an unemployed tiler repairs a leak in your roof and takes payment in cash in order to avoid tax. Such unreported transactions are unrecorded in the country's GNP. Thus, measured GNP statistics significantly understate the real values of output and income earned. If we could measure these transactions, they should be included in a measure of total market output.

The black economy seems to have grown rapidly in many countries during the last two decades. Probably the most important reason for this growth is income-tax evasion. But it also allows the evasion of a host of other taxes and regulations. VAT is not paid in the black economy. Safety regulations, minimum-wage laws, anti-discrimination regulations, and national insurance payments may all be avoided as well. Generally, the higher are tax rates, and the greater are the restrictions arising from rules and regulations, the greater the incentive to evade them all by 'going underground'. The growth of this economy has also been facilitated by the rising importance of services in the nation's total output. It is much easier for a window cleaner or TV repairman to pass unnoticed by the authorities than it is for a large manufacturing establishment, which is hard to hide. Another reason for the growth of this part of the economy is to help people to claim unemployment benefits while actually earning significant amounts of income.

Non-marketed economic activities

When a bank clerk hires a carpenter to build a bookshelf in his house, the value of the work done enters into the GNP; if the clerk builds the bookshelf himself, the value of his work is omitted from the GNP. In general, any labour service that does not pass through a market is not counted in the GNP. Such omissions include, for example, the services of the housewife, any do-it-yourself activity, and voluntary work such as canvassing for a political party or leading a Boy Scout troup.

Does the omission of these types of non-marketed economic activities matter? Once again, it all depends. For example, we may wish to account for changes in the opportunities for employment for those households who sell their labour services in the market. Here, we are not interested in changes in non-marketed activities, since these do not provide marketable employment opportunities. For this purpose, the omission of the services of the housewife, and unpaid political canvassing, is desirable.

If, however, we wish to measure the total flow of goods and services available to satisfy people's wants, whatever the source of the goods and services, then the omissions are undesirable and potentially serious. In most advanced industrial economies the non-market sector is relatively small, and it can be ignored even if GNP is used for purposes for which it would be appropriate to include non-marketed goods and services.

The omissions become serious, however, when one is using GNP figures to compare living standards in very different economies. Generally, the non-market sector of the economy is larger in rural than in urban settings and in less developed than in more developed economies. You should, therefore, be a little cautious in interpreting data from a country with a very different climate and culture from our own. When you hear that the per capita GNP of Nigeria is £200 per year, you should not imagine living in Britain on that income. Certainly the average Nigerian is at a low level of real income compared to the average resident of the UK, but the measured GNP figure does not allow for the fact that many of the things that are very costly to a UK resident are provided to the Nigerian by a host of non-marketed goods and services.

Living Standards: Factors Affecting Human Welfare but not Included in the Value of Output

Many things that contribute to human welfare are not included in the GNP. Leisure is an example. Although a shorter work week may make people happier, it will tend to reduce measured GNP. Furthermore, the GNP may not adequately reflect changes in the quality of products. A 1990 radio is a much superior product to a 1930 radio. It is more reliable and has better reception. But GNP measures do not reflect these changes in *quality*. Also, GNP does not allow for the capacity of different goods to provide different satisfactions. A million pounds spent on tanks, or a missile for an atomic submarine, makes the same addition to GNP as a million pounds spent on a school, a stadium, or sweets – expenditures that may produce very different levels of consumer satisfaction.

GNP does not measure the quality of life. To the extent that material output is purchased at the expense of such things as overcrowded cities and highways, polluted environments, defaced countrysides, maimed accident victims and longer waits for public services, GNP measures only part of the total of human well-being. These undesirable products are often called *bads* to distinguish them from *goods*, which are desirable products.

Finally, we should repeat here what we have noted in earlier sections: the GNP omits certain outputs, such as the illegal provision of products people want, non-marketed activities, and output in the black economy, some of which clearly add to people's living standards.

The philosophy of the national income statistician might be expressed in the observation: 'Man does not live by bread alone, but it is nonetheless important to know how much bread he has'. The national income figures do not measure everything that contributes to human welfare, nor were they intended to do so. But they are often so interpreted. For example an implicit assumption is often made that high levels, or fast growth rates, of national income per capita make for a better life.

Which Measure is Best?

To ask which is *the* best national income measure is something like asking which is *the* best carpenter's tool. The answer is 'It all depends on the job to be done'. *There are many related national income measures. There is no single true, or best, measure for all purposes. The advantages and disadvantages of each can be assessed only in relation to the particular problem for which it might be used.*

The use of several measures of national income, rather than just one, is common because each provides an answer to a different set of questions. For example, GDP provides the best answer to the question 'What is the market value of goods and services produced for final demand?' NNP answers the question 'By how much does the economy's production exceed the amount necessary to replace the capital equipment used up?' Personal disposable income answers the question 'How much income do households have available to allocate between spending and saving?' Additionally, real (constant-price) measures eliminate purely monetary changes, and allow comparisons of purchasing power over time; per capita measures shift the focus from the nation to the average person.

For yet other purposes, such as providing an overall measure of economic welfare, we may wish to supplement conventional measures of national income. We can do this by considering other welfare measures *alongside* GNP. For example, we might learn that the GNP measured at constant prices has risen but, because more is being spent on current investment and less on current consumption, a measure of welfare based on current consumption has fallen. What we learn from the combination of these two measures is that the nation's capacity to satisfy wants in the future is being increased by its large current investment expenditures, but at the cost of lower consumption standards now. Both pieces of information are important. We would judge the situation differently than if *both* GNP and a welfare measure were declining. In this latter case, there is no expectation of welfare being higher in the future to set against the decline in current welfare.

Even if better measures of welfare are developed, economists are unlikely to discard conventional national income measures. Economists and policymakers who are interested in the ebb and flow of economic activity that passes through markets, and in the variations in employment opportunities for factors of production whose services are sold on markets, will continue to use GDP as the measure that comes closest to telling them what they need to know.

SUMMARY

1 Production may be divided into four main categories: production for consumption, private-sector production for investment, production by the government, and production for export.

2 The category of consumption includes goods and services currently produced for use by households, with the exception of residential housing (which counts as investment). Investment covers new construction of fixed capital, residential housing and *changes* in stocks. Government production covers all the government's exhaustive expenditures but excludes its transfer payments. Exports include everything that is produced at home and then exported.

3 The output approach measures the total value of the nation's output by adding up the total value of final goods and services produced or the total of the *values added* by all producers in the economy.

4 The expenditure approach measures the total value of expenditure on final output in the categories of consumption, investment, government expenditure and *net* exports (exports minus imports).

5 The income approach measures the total value of incomes generated by production plus indirect taxes *net* of subsidies. The correction for *net* indirect taxes arises because the GNP at market prices exceeds the income going to factors of production by the amount of subsidies paid by the government, but falls short by the amount of indirect taxes levied by the government.

6 Because all three approaches measure the same

total, the three measures – total output, total expenditure and total income – should give identical values. Each of the separate measures is valuable because of the specific details of output, expenditure and income that it provides. In all the theory of the following chapters, this total is referred to as *national income* and it is usually measured from the *expenditure approach*.

7 Figure 26.4 summarizes the relations between total domestic expenditure, total final expenditure, gross domestic product at market prices, gross domestic product at factor cost, gross national product at factor cost and net national product at factor cost.

8 National income measured in current prices is called *money* or *nominal* income. It changes when prices and/or quantities change. National income measured in constant prices is called *real* national income. It only changes when the *volume* of output changes.

9 Many illegal, black-economy and do-it-yourself transactions are excluded from national income measurements because they go unreported. The first two types are market transactions that use scarce resources and generate income and should, therefore, be included in a measure of total marketed output.

10 GNP should not be thought of as a precise measure of current living standards because it includes much more than output to be used for current consumption, and because it excludes some things that do contribute to welfare such as leisure and others that lower living standards, such as pollution.

Consumption and Investment

Why does national income behave the way it does, exhibiting a short-term pattern of increases and decreases and a long-term rising trend? Why have there been long periods in the recent past when Britain's resources of land, labour and capital were more or less fully employed? Why have the 1980s seen long periods of heavy unemployment of resources in Britain (and in many of the other countries of Western Europe)?

To answer these and other similar questions, we need a theory to explain the behaviour of national income. Such a theory is called the THEORY OF INCOME DETERMINATION.

In the previous chapter we studied the national income accounting procedures that allow us to *measure* total national income and its components. It turns out that, of the three approaches studied in the previous chapter, the expenditure approach provides the categories most useful for the theory of income determination. We also saw in the previous chapter that the major categories of expenditure are consumption, investment, the government's exhaustive expenditures, and exports. In the next three chapters, however, we shall consider a very simple case in which the only categories of expenditure are consumption, which is made by domestic households, and investment, which is made by domestic firms. The group comprised of domestic households and the group comprised of domestic firms are often referred to as *sectors* of the economy – the firm sector and the household sector.

In this two-sector model of the economy, where the only two categories of expenditure are consumption and investment, there is no government and no foreign trade. (These are considered in later chapters.) Simple though this imaginary economy may be,

it allows us to study the nature of the forces that determine national income in any economy. Once we understand how these forces work, it becomes a relatively easy matter to allow for the government, and for foreign trade.

We develop this simple theory over three chapters. In this chapter we enquire into the determinants of the two expenditure flows of consumption and investment. In Chapter 28 we study the forces that determine the equilibrium size of national income, and in Chapter 29 the forces that cause national income to change.

Categories of Expenditure

We have already noted that, in the simple economy we are going to study, there are only two categories of expenditure:

(1) expenditure on investment goods, which we assume to be made solely by firms, and
(2) expenditure on consumption goods, which we assume to be made solely by households.

All *total expenditure*, both by firms and by households, accrues to firms in return for their sales of consumption and investment goods. Firms sell the consumption goods that they produce to households, and they sell the investment goods that they produce to other firms. Thus they have two sources of receipts: they receive payments from households for the consumption goods that they sell to them, and they receive payments from other firms for the investment goods that they sell to them.

All of *national income* goes to households as factor payments in the form of rent, interest, profits and wages. Households then decide how much they wish to spend on consumption and they save the rest.

Expenditure flows are real, planned, aggregate values

At the outset, we need to understand clearly three of the basic characteristics of all the expenditure flows that we will study.

Expenditures are Real (not Nominal):   Our theory is about *real*, not nominal, expenditures. We saw in Chapter 24 that total national income and its various components can be measured either in current, or in constant, prices. All the values of consumption and investment that we discuss in this chapter are measured in constant prices. Thus when the measured flow of consumption or investment changes, the real output of consumption or investment goods must be changing (since we are holding prices constant).

Of course, if the overall price level is constant, we get the same result whether we use current or constant prices (since prices are not changing). But when the overall price level does change, current and constant price measures will give different results. We choose the constant-price measure because we are concerned with changes in real outputs.

All Values are Planned Values: The term PLANNED EXPENDITURE refers to what people intend to spend; the term REALIZED EXPENDITURE refers to what they actually succeed in spending. The key point to remember is that when we refer to consumption and investment expenditure, we are referring to what households and firms plan to spend on purchasing consumption and investment goods. Realized expenditure will diverge from planned expenditure whenever plans are frustrated. For example, consumers' plans to spend on consumption goods may be frustrated by a strike that interrupts production of those goods. Note that planned expenditure is also described as *desired* or *ex ante expenditure*, while realized expenditure is often described as *actual* or *ex post expenditure*.

Expenditure Flows are Aggregate Flows: In macroeconomics, we are not concerned with the behaviour of individual households or firms, but with the aggregate behaviour of all households and all firms. Thus, when we talk about consumption expenditure, we mean the aggregate, i.e. the total amount that all households desire to spend on consumption; while investment expenditure also refers to the aggregate, i.e. the total amount that all firms desire to spend on investment.

Investment Expenditure

Since in the simple model of this chapter all investment is assumed to be made by domestic firms, we shall concentrate here on the reasons why firms make such investments. We shall also start by considering investment in plant and equipment. Later we shall study the determinants of other types of investment.

Profits provide the basic motive driving the investment decisions of private-sector firms. Firms will wish to spend money on investment if they expect the investment to yield a profit over all its costs. The factors that affect these expectations determine the amount of desired investment expenditure in the economy as a whole. We first list the main factors and then discuss how each influences investment decisions:
- the rate of interest,
- the price and the productivity of capital goods,
- expectations about the future demand for the machine's output and about the costs of producing the output,
- profits earned by firms and available for reinvestment, and
- the development of new techniques of production and of new products.

The Rate of Interest: The rate of interest measures the cost of capital to the firm. If the firm borrows money to spend on investment, it must pay the rate of interest to its creditors in return for these funds. If the firm uses its own funds, it must forgo the revenue that it could have obtained by lending out those funds to others and earning the rate of interest in return.

The lower is the rate of interest, the lower is the cost of borrowing money, so the lower is the cost of making investment, and the more investment firms will tend to make. To see this, think of the firm's opportunities for investing in new capital being arranged in order of profitability. There will be a few lines of investment that will offer very large returns. There will be further lines that will offer lower, but still quite substantial, returns. There will be yet more lines of investment that will offer moderate returns, and even more lines that will offer only quite modest returns. If the rate of interest is very high so that funds for investment are very expensive to the firm, the firm will only undertake the most profitable investments. If the rate is lower, there will be more investments that will offer a profit after the cost of the investment funds is deducted.

Consider a simple example. Let there be four investment opportunities, each involving spending £100 now and obtaining a single sum one year hence. The most profitable pays £120, the next £115, the next £110, and the least profitable only £105. At interest rates in excess of 20 per cent, none of these four will be profitable. At rates between 15 and 20 per cent, only the first will be profitable. For example, if the rate were 17 per cent, then the £100 could be borrowed at a cost of £17. In a year's time the investment would yield £120, allowing a profit of £3 after repaying the £100 borrowed and paying interest of £17. At rates between 10 and 15 per cent, the two best opportunities will be profitable. A rate below 10 per cent makes the third one profitable, while any rate below 5 per cent makes even the fourth opportunity profitable. Thus, as the rate of interest falls, first one, then two, then three, then all four opportunities become profitable, and desired investment expenditure rises from £100 to £200 to £300 to £400 on account of these four investment possibilities.

In general, the lower is the rate of interest, the greater the number of investment opportunities that will be profitable and, therefore, the greater the investment expenditure that firms will wish to make.

There is one exception to this rule. During very depressed times, investment opportunities are few or non-existent. At such times, changes in the rate of interest have little effect on investment decisions. In more normal times, however, a wide range of potentially profitable investment opportunities does exist. At such times, a change in the rate of interest shifts the line between what does and does not look profitable and hence affects the volume of desired investment expenditure. Countless empirical studies confirm that during normal times, not only do firms wish to spend more on investment as the rate of interest falls, they actually do so. Thus, *the volume of desired investment expenditure is negatively related to the interest rate, rising as the interest rate falls.*

The Cost and Productivity of Capital Goods: The cost of funds needed for investment expenditure has, as we have seen, an influence on the profitability of investment. So also has the price and productivity of the machines being purchased. A new process that reduces the price of capital goods will make any given line of investment more profitable because the interest costs involved will be reduced. For example, a machine costing £1,000 will have an interest cost of £100 per year at a rate of 10 per cent, but if the

machine's price falls to £800 its interest cost will only be £80 per year.

Also, any new invention that makes capital equipment more productive will make investment more attractive. For example, if the replacement of typewriters by word-processors makes a given amount spent on office equipment more productive, this will lead to a burst of investment expenditure to obtain the new capital equipment.

Expectations of the Future: Expectations of future demand conditions and future cost conditions exert a strong effect on investment decisions.

Expected demand conditions matter because the profitability of any investment depends on being able to sell the output of the capital goods, and to sell it at a favourable price. Investment expenditure made now, means producing goods for sale in the future. If firms have favourable expectations about the amount that they will be able to sell in the future and the price that they will be able to obtain, they will be inclined to invest now to create the capacity to sell in the favourable market that they expect in the future. If firms have low expectations about quantities they will be able to sell and about future market prices, they will be much less inclined to spend on capital equipment now.

Expected cost conditions also matter because profits, which are what motivate investment decisions, depend on market prices for output, and on the costs of producing that output. When a machine is bought now, the cost of the machine is known now. But the cost of the labour that will operate the machine, and the cost of the materials that will be used over the lifetime of the machine, depend on prices that will rule in the future.

On occasion, these expectations about the future can change dramatically and suddenly – these are what Keynes called the animal spirits of businessmen – and when they do change, desired investment will also change dramatically. A sudden swing from pessimism to optimism about the future can lead to a large increase in desired investment expenditure, while the opposite swing from optimism to pessimism can lead to a drastic curtailment of investment plans.

Profits: Investment is often financed by borrowed funds. But a great deal of investment is also financed by firms' own money. In this case, profits earned on past sales are retained – i.e. not paid out to the firms' owners – but instead are reinvested by the firms. Thus an important determinant of investment expenditure is current profits. If these are large, there is a large flow of funds that can be reinvested by the firms who made them. If profits are low or non-existent, there are few funds available from within the firm to finance new investment expenditures.

Process Innovations: New ways of producing old products are constantly being invented. These new ways are usually embodied in new equipment. For example, robotization has radically changed assembly-line processes. The installation of robots has accounted for large quantities of recent investment expenditures in manufacturing industries in advanced countries.

Product Innovations: When new products are developed, new investment is needed to produce the plant and equipment required to produce them. Sometimes existing plant and equipment can be modified, but only at the expense of some expenditure on modification and adaptation, while at other times whole new arrays of capital equipment are needed to make the new product.

Investment treated as a constant

In this chapter it is convenient to study how the level of national income adjusts to a fixed level of investment. To do this we assume that all of the factors that influence investment decisions, including those listed above, remain constant. For this reason, firms plan to make a given and unchanging amount of investment expenditure each year.

Later we shall drop this assumption. We shall let one or more of the above determinants change. This will cause firms to alter their investment plans. In the meantime we shall investigate the determination of national income under the assumption of a given, and unchanging, amount of desired investment expenditure. We shall also ignore investment in residential housing for the new few chapters. For the moment, therefore, we concentrate on investment spending by firms made to accumulate capital equipment and stocks.

Autonomous Expenditure: The above assumption makes investment what is called an AUTONOMOUS or an EXOGENOUS EXPENDITURE. These terms are used interchangeably to refer to expenditure flows that are determined by forces which are themselves unex-

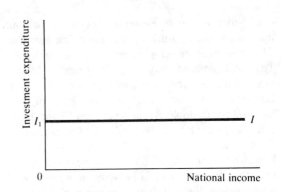

FIGURE 27.1   Investment Expenditure and National Income. Because investment is autonomous, its graph is a horizontal line showing no change as national income changes

plained by our theory. These forces remain constant as the things explained by our theory change. In the present case, our theory is being set up to explain changes in national income, and all of the forces that determine investment are currently unexplained by our theory. This means that investment does not vary as national income varies; instead, from the point of view of the theory we are currently building, it is an autonomous expenditure flow.

A Graphical Representation: Figure 27.1 plots national income on the horizontal axis and investment expenditure on the vertical axis. Because investment does not vary with national income, its graph is a horizontal straight line, labelled I in the Figure, showing the same amount of desired investment, I_1, at all levels of national income.

Note that in this type of graph all autonomous expenditures will be graphed by horizontal lines, showing that the expenditure in question does *not* vary as national income varies.

Consumption and Saving

Each household makes plans about how much to spend on consumption and how much to save. These are not, however, independent decisions. *The saving of households is defined as all household income not spent on consumption.* It follows, therefore, that households have to decide on a *single* division of their income between saving and consumption. For example, if households plan to spend £180 out of a weekly income of £200, they must, by definition, be planning to save the remaining £20.

The main incentives which influence aggregate household consumption and saving are the following:

- the level of income,
- the rate of interest,
- the tastes of households,
- the terms of credit,
- the level of wealth,
- the existing stock of durables,
- price expectations.

Not every household needs to be influenced by all of these factors, but each factor has an important influence on some households. As a result, all of the factors have an influence on aggregate behaviour.

The Level of Income: The higher is a household's income the more we would expect it to spend on consumption. If, for example, households always allocate 80 per cent of their incomes to consumption and save the rest, then households with higher incomes would also have higher consumption expenditures.

The Rate of Interest: The rate of interest provides a reward for saving. If a household saves £100 out of its current income, it will have £105 next year if the rate of interest is 5 per cent, £110 if the rate is 10 per cent, and so on. We would expect the decisions of households on how much to spend now and how much to lay aside for spending in the future to respond to this rate of interest.

The Tastes of Households: Household tastes determine savings attitudes in many ways. We mention two, *time preference* and the *bequeath motive*. If people are very impatient and unwilling to postpone present consumption in order to consume more in the future, they will save little; if people are willing to defer present consumption in order (by earning interest on their savings) to consume more in the future, they will save much. These attitudes are described as people's *time preference*. A second influence concerns the desire to pass on wealth to one's children and other heirs when one dies. The stronger is this desire, the greater the willingness to save.

The Terms of Credit: Many durable consumer goods are purchased on credit, whose terms may range from a few months to pay for a radio, to two or three years to pay for a car. If credit becomes more difficult or more costly to obtain, many households may postpone their planned, credit-financed purchases. If the typical initial payment required for goods purchased on hire purchase increases from 10 to 20 per cent, households that had just saved up 10 per cent of the purchase price would have to postpone their planned purchases until they saved 20 per cent of the purchase price. There would then be a temporary reduction in current consumption expenditures until these extra funds had been accumulated.

The Level of Wealth: Households save in order to add to their wealth.[1] If anything happens to reduce wealth suddenly, households may increase their rate of saving in order to restore their wealth. If something happens to increase their wealth suddenly, households may lower their rate of saving as they feel less need to add to their now-larger stock of wealth. So we may expect sudden changes in wealth to alter consumption decisions. By discouraging saving, and hence encouraging consumption, a rise in wealth may increase the amount of consumption associated with *each* level of income.

Existing Stocks of Durable Goods: Any period in which durables are difficult or impossible to purchase will be followed by a sudden outburst of expenditure on durables. Such a flurry of spending will follow a major war, when durables are unavailable, and a period of heavy unemployment, when many families have postponed buying durables.

The emphasis is on durable goods (e.g. cars and TV sets) because purchases of non-durable consumer goods (e.g. food and clothing) and of services (e.g. car repairs) cannot be so easily postponed. While expenditures on non-durables are relatively steady, purchases of durables are volatile and can be the source of sharp shifts in consumption expenditure.

Price Expectations: If households expect an inflation to occur, they tend to purchase now durable goods they would otherwise not have bought for another one or two years. In such circumstances, purchases made now are expected to be cheaper than purchases of the same good made in the future. By the

---

1 We have here the same stock-flow distinction that we earlier raised with respect to capital and investment. Saving is a flow, while wealth is a stock. In our bath analogy, wealth is the stock of water in the bath; saving is the flow of water from the tap into the bath.

same argument, an expected deflation may lead to postponing purchases of durables in hopes of purchasing them later at a lower price.

The consumption function

The term CONSUMPTION FUNCTION is used to describe the relationship between households' planned consumption expenditure and all of the forces that determine it. To develop a simple theory, we hold constant all but one of these forces. The one force that we allow to vary is income. We then study how consumption varies with income. This allows us to derive a simple relation between consumption expenditure and income. To describe this relation, we say that *consumption is a function of income*. When the other influencing forces change, they will shift the function relating consumption to income.[1]

Induced Expenditure: The assumptions just made have the effect of making consumption what is called INDUCED or ENDOGENOUS EXPENDITURE. This is expenditure that is influenced by, and hence varies with, the variable our theory is designed to explain – i.e., in this case, variations in consumption are explained by variations in national income.

The Aggregate Consumption Function: Every individual household has its own consumption function showing how its desired consumption expenditure varies with its income. In macroeconomics, we are interested in the aggregate behaviour of *all* households. The macro, or aggregate, consumption function shows how the total desired consumption expenditure of all households varies as national income varies.

The aggregate consumption function reflects the behaviour of typical households, with extremes cancelling each other out. To see what is meant by this, consider an example. When income rises, some households – especially very poor ones – may spend all of the extra income, while other households – especially very rich ones – may save all the extra income. But the great majority of households spend some of their extra income and save the rest. Thus the aggregate consumption function will show an increase in national income to be associated with an increase in *both* consumption and saving.

From now on when we speak of 'the' consumption function, we are referring to the aggregate function for the whole economy.

Characteristics of the Consumption Function: The following four characteristics describe how aggregate consumption behaviour is related to income in the short term.

(1) There is a *break-even level* of income, which is defined as the level of income at which households just plan to consume all of their income, neither more nor less.

(2) Below the break-even level, households plan to consume in excess of their current income. They do this by borrowing, or by spending out of their accumulated stock of wealth, which is known as *dissaving*. Clearly, such spending cannot go on forever because the stock of wealth is limited and people's ability to borrow eventually dries up. This is one reason why point (2) does not describe long-term behaviour – although it does describe behaviour that can go on for some time.

(3) Above the break-even level of income, households plan to consume only part of their income and to save the rest.

(4) Any change in income causes consumption expenditure to change, but by less than the change in income. For example, an increase in aggregate income of £1m per year might cause households to increase their consumption expenditure by £750,000 per year and to increase savings by £250,000 per year.

These are our four basic assumptions about the dependence of consumption and saving on income. Table 27.1 gives an illustration of this dependence that conforms with the four assumptions listed above. The schedule shown in the Table gives desired consumption and desired saving at each level of income.

The data in the Table are graphed in Figure 27.2. The line in that figure is obtained by plotting each national income from the first column of Table 27.1 against its corresponding planned consumption expenditure obtained from the second column of the Table. Let us notice some of the things that the Table and the Figure reveal.

Notice first that, unlike the investment function in Figure 27.1, the graph of the consumption function is *not* a horizontal line. Instead it slopes upward, indicating that as income rises so does consumption.

---

1 This is just what was done for demand curves in Part 2. All of the influencing forces except the good's own price were held constant, and a relation called a demand curve was established between the price and quantity demanded. When one of the other influencing forces changed, this *shifted* the demand curve.

TABLE 27.1 Planned Consumption and Savings Schedules (£ million). Both consumption and savings rise as income rises

National income (Y)	Planned consumption expenditure (C)	Planned saving (Y–C)	Reference letter
0	300	–300	a
400	600	–200	b
800	900	–100	c
1,200	1,200	0	d
1,600	1,500	+100	e
2,000	1,800	+200	f
2,400	2,100	+300	g
2,800	2,400	+400	h
3,200	2,700	+500	i

This is a graphical expression of an induced, or endogenous, variable. Changes in consumption are induced by changes in national income.

Notice second that, at an income of £1,200m, consumption expenditure is also £1,200m. This is the break-even level referred to in point (1) above. It is shown by point *d* on the Figure.

Notice third that, at an income of £800m, £900m is spent on consumption. At this level of income, consumption expenditure exceeds income by £100m. This extra expenditure must be financed by new borrowing or by the using up of past saving. This means that households in aggregate are *dissaving* – which is shown by a negative value in the planned saving column. This is an illustration of point (2) above. It is shown by point *c* in the figure.

Notice fourth that, at an income of £2,000m, desired consumption is only £1,800m (point *f* on the figure). This is an illustration of point (3) above.

Finally notice that, every time income rises by £400m, expenditure rises by £300m. This is an illustration of point (4) above. (We shall illustrate this point graphically later.)

Propensities to consume

Economists use two rather pompous terms to describe the relation between consumption and income. The AVERAGE PROPENSITY TO CONSUME (APC) is defined as total consumption expenditure, C, divided by total income, Y:

$$APC = C/Y.$$

(Many beginners have trouble remembering this and other related terms. It may help if you note that the word propensity comes from the Latin *propend*, meaning inclination towards.)

The MARGINAL PROPENSITY TO CONSUME (MPC) is defined as the change in consumption divided by the change in income that brought it about:

$$MPC = \Delta C/\Delta Y$$

(where, as usual, the Greek letter Δ means 'a change in').

Table 27.2 shows the calculations of the APC and

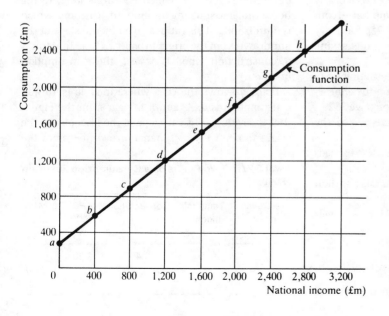

FIGURE 27.2   A Consumption Function. This function shows the relation between aggregate desired consumption expenditure and national income

TABLE 27.2 The Calculation of the Average Propensity to Consume (APC) and the Marginal Propensity to Consume (MPC). The APC measures the proportion of total income consumed, and the MPC measures the proportion of any change in income that is consumed

National income (Y) (i)	Planned consumption (C) (ii)	APC = C/Y (iii)	ΔY (Change in Y) (iv)	ΔC (Change in C) (v)	MPC = ΔC/ΔY (vi)
£m	£m		£m	£m	
0	300	—	400	300	0.75
400	600	1.50	400	300	0.75
800	900	1.13	400	300	0.75
1,200	1,200	1.00	400	300	0.75
1,600	1,500	0.94	400	300	0.75
2,000	1,800	0.90	400	300	0.75
2,400	2,100	0.88	400	300	0.75
2,800	2,400	0.86	400	300	0.75
3,200	2,700	0.84			

MPC from the consumption schedule of Table 27.1. It deserves careful study since it illustrates some very important concepts. Notice from the table that the APC in column (iii) exceeds unity below the break-even level of income (£1,200). This is because consumption exceeds income. Notice also that, above the break-even level of income, the APC is less than unity. This is because consumption is less than income. The last three columns, (iv), (v) and (vi), are set between the lines of the first three columns to indicate that they refer to *changes* in the levels of income and consumption.

In this example, the MPC is constant of 0.75 at all levels of income. This indicates that 75 per cent of any change in income is spent on consumption – consumption expenditure rises or falls by 75p for every increase or decrease of £1 of income – while saving changes by 25p.

For practice, we may use our new terminology to restate the four assumptions concerning the characteristics of consumption that we listed on page 332:

(1) At some positive level of income, called the break-even level, APC = 1.

(2) Below the break-even level, the APC exceeds unity (APC > 1).

(3) Above the break-even level, the APC is less than unity (APC < 1).

(4) The MPC is less than unity at all income levels (MPC < 1).

The graphical representation of the propensities

We now wish to illustrate these marginal and average propensities graphically. To make the graph as clear as possible, we consider two points on a *new* consumption function. These are shown as points x and y in Table 27.3 and graphed in Figure 27.3. (All figures are in £000m.) Note that in order to make the graph clear, we have taken quite unrealistic figures. (Most countries have MPCs between 0.75 and 0.95.)

Now consider how the two propensities that are calculated in the Table show up in the Figure. The APCs are shown in part (i). Point x shows the case where income is £5 and consumption is £4. The APC in this case is 4/5 or 0.80. Graphically, this is the ratio of the length of the vertical line showing the amount of consumption at x, which is 4 units long, to the horizontal line showing the amount of income, which is 5 units long. This ratio is given by the slope of the line drawn from the origin to point x. (Note that this is a construction line; it is *not* the consumption function.)

Point y shows the case where income is 10 and consumption is 6. Again, it is clear from the Figure that the ratio C/Y is the slope of the line joining the origin to point y which, when drawn, becomes the

TABLE 27.3 Two Points on a Consumption Function (£000m)

Reference point	National income (Y)	Consumption (C)	APC (C/Y)	MPC (ΔC/ΔY)
x	5	4	0.80	
				0.40
y	10	6	0.60	

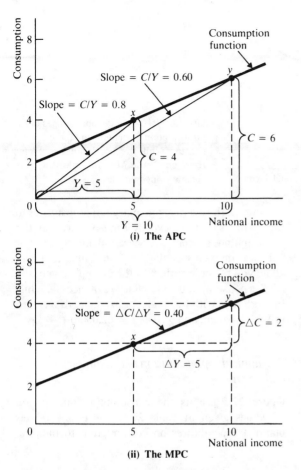

(i) **The APC**

(ii) **The MPC**

FIGURE 27.3 The Graphical Representation of the Average and Marginal Propensities to Consume. The *APC* is the slope of the line between the origin and the point in question, while the *MPC* is the slope of the line joining the two points in question

hypotenuse of the right-angle triangle whose other two sides have lengths given by the values of C and Y.

Now look at part (ii) of the Figure which illustrates the *MPC*. The *MPC* is the ratio of the change in consumption to the change in income, i.e. $\Delta C/\Delta Y$, measured over the change in income being considered. It is clear from the Figure that ΔC is the vertical distance separating points x and y, while ΔY is the horizontal distance between the two points. This makes $\Delta C/\Delta Y$ the slope of the line joining the two points in question. In other words, the *MPC is the slope of the consumption function between the two points in question*.

If the consumption function is linear, its slope is the same at all points between x and y. Real-world

consumption functions, however, are sometimes non-linear. We assert without proving that if the function is a curve – as shown, for example, in Figure 27.4 – then the *MPC* between two distinct points on the function must be understood as the average slope of the consumption function between the points in question.[1]

We have now derived two useful results relating to the graphical representation of these consumption propensities: *(i) the average propensity to consume at any one consumption-income point is measured graphically by the slope of the line joining that point with the origin; and (ii) the marginal propensity to consume between any two consumption-income points is measured graphically by the slope of the line joining the two points.*

Some possible consumption functions

The two parts of Figure 27.4 show two consumption functions that are consistent with the four basic hypotheses listed on page 332. The positive intercepts of both curves show that their *APC*s exceed unity at zero income. The positive slope of both curves shows that their *MPC*s are positive at all levels of income.

The consumption function C_0 is linear. This means that the *MPC* is the same at all levels of income. The *APC*, however, declines continuously as income rises along the line C_0. (To see this, draw lines from the origin to successive points further and further out on the consumption function and observe that their slopes fall continuously.)

The consumption function C_1 displays not only a declining *APC*, but also a declining *MPC*, as shown by the fact that the line C_1 gets flatter as income rises. Thus, successive increases in income cause smaller and smaller increases in consumption.

The saving function

We have seen that households have only one expenditure decision: how to divide their incomes between consumption and saving. It follows that, if we know the dependence of planned consumption on income, we also know the dependence of planned saving on income. Table 27.1 illustrates this. The figures in the third column are implied by the figures in the first two columns. Given the data for consump-

---

1 In fact the *MPC* defined as $\Delta C/\Delta Y$ is the slope of the chord joining the two points on the curve. (See page 569.)

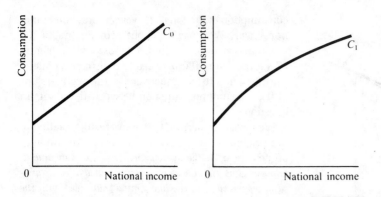

FIGURE 27.4   Two Possible Shapes of the Consumption Function. On C_0 the MPC is constant while the APC declines as income rises; on C_1 the MPC and the APC both decline as income rises

tion and income, the data for saving cannot be other than they are.

We may now define two saving concepts that are exactly parallel to the consumption concepts of APC and MPC already defined. The AVERAGE PROPENSITY TO SAVE (APS) is the proportion of total income devoted to savings. It is total saving divided by total income:

$$APS = S/Y.$$

The MARGINAL PROPENSITY TO SAVE (MPS) is the *change* in total saving divided by the *change* in total income that brought it about:

$$MPS = \Delta S/\Delta Y.$$

You can now go back to Table 27.1 and construct for yourself the average and marginal propensities to save. This is done in exactly the same way as the consumption propensities were calculated in that Table. Your own calculations from Table 27.1 will allow you to confirm that, in the example given, the MPS is constant at 0.25 at all levels of income, while the APS rises with income. (For example, APS is zero at $Y = £1,200m$, and 0.10 at $Y = £2,000m$.)

A graphical representation of consumption and saving

Figure 27.5 graphs the consumption and saving schedules given in Table 27.1. The C line relates planned expenditures on consumption to national

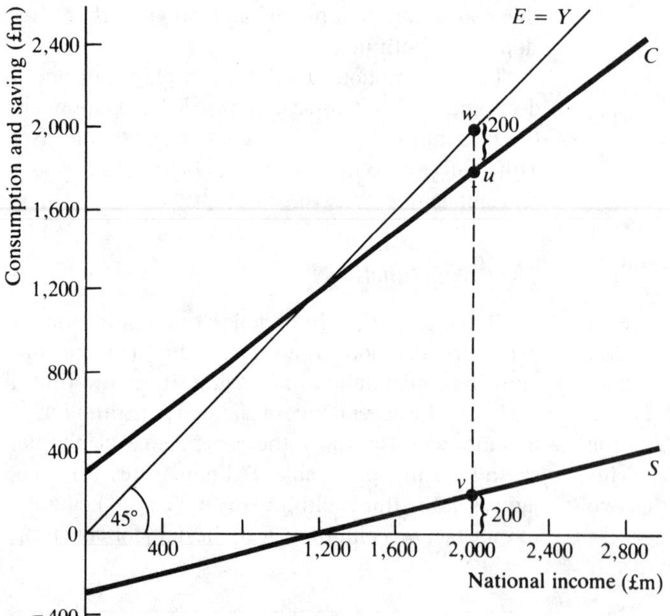

FIGURE 27.5   The Consumption and Saving Functions. Both consumption and saving rise as income rises

income. The S line relates planned saving to national income. Both rise as income rises.

Also shown in the Figure is a construction called the 45° line. This line does not plot any planned expenditures; instead it simply joins all those points at which the values measured on the two axes are equal. In other words, it joins all those points where expenditure equals income. To remind us of how it is constructed, the line is always labelled $E = Y$. Provided that we use the same scales on the two axes, the line has a slope of $+1$ or, what is the same thing, it makes a 45° angle with both axes. To remind us of its position, one of the 45° angles is usually shown.

The 45° line proves handy as a reference line. For example, it helps locate the break-even level of income at which planned consumption expenditure equals total income. Graphically, this is where the consumption line cuts the 45° line, telling us that this is the point on the consumption function where expenditure equals income. Notice also that the break-even level of income is where the saving line cuts the horizontal axis. This is because at the break-even level of income, saving is zero.

It is important to understand the relation between the three lines shown in the figure. Since saving is all income not spent on consumption, the vertical sum of the S and the C lines must, by definition, coincide with the 45° line. Or to put it another way, at any given level of income, saving is the vertical distance between the C line and the 45° line.

Consider an example. If income is £2,000m, planned consumption is £1,800m (point u), while planned saving is £200m (point v). Note that the £200m of saving is also shown by the gap between the consumption line and the 45° line (the distance from u to w). This is merely another way of saying that at each level of income, total income must by definition be the amount saved plus the amount consumed.

The Aggregate Expenditure Function

The only two kinds of output produced in our simple economy are consumption goods and investment goods. Thus, total desired expenditure on final goods must be the sum of desired consumption expenditure and desired investment expenditure. Letting E stand for total desired expenditure, we have

$$E = C + I.$$

We may now ask how changes in national income affect the total desired expenditure of households and

TABLE 27.4 Calculation of the Aggregate Expenditure Function (£m)

Y	C	I	$E = C + I$
(i)	(ii)	(iii)	(iv) = (ii) + (iii)
0	300	300	600
400	600	300	900
800	900	300	1,200
1,200	1,200	300	1,500
1,600	1,500	300	1,800
2,000	1,800	300	2,100
2,400	2,100	300	2,400
2,800	2,400	300	2,700
3,200	2,700	300	3,000

firms. The answer turns out to be quite simple. Aggregate expenditure in this simple model is the sum of desired investment and desired consumption expenditure. We have assumed for purposes of this chapter that investment is an autonomous expenditure that does not vary with national income. Hence, the answer is that aggregate desired expenditure varies with national income exactly as does desired consumption expenditure.

Table 27.4 illustrates the calculation of the aggregate expenditure function. The calculation is based on the consumption and income data in Table 27.1, along with the added assumption that investment is constant at £300 million. Column (i) together with column (iv) shows how desired aggregate expenditure varies with national income. These two columns define the AGGREGATE EXPENDITURE FUNCTION, which shows how much firms and households wish to spend on purchasing final output at each level of income. Since the aggregate expenditure function shows the total amount that households and firms wish to spend on the economy's output – i.e. how much output they demand – it is often called an 'aggregate demand function'. For the reason discussed in the footnote, however, we shall use the term *aggregate expenditure function*.[1]

---

1 In the past, the relation we have just described was usually called the aggregate demand function. In the last ten years, however, the term aggregate demand function has come to describe a different, but related, concept (which we shall ourselves study in Chapter 38). To avoid confusion, the relation we have just derived is now more usually referred to as the aggregate expenditure function. We shall follow this practice, since it is the usage that is becoming commonplace. Such changes in the meaning of terms occur very slowly, however, and in the meantime, there is nothing wrong with the practice of calling the function that relates aggregate desired expenditure to national income the aggregate demand function.

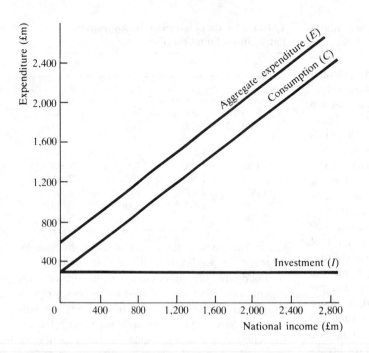

FIGURE 27.6　The Aggregate Expenditure Function. The function relates total desired expenditure to national income and is derived by vertically summing the functions for the separate components of desired expenditure

A graphical representation

Figure 27.6 graphs the consumption and investment function given in Table 27.4, together with the aggregate expenditure function. The Figure shows that geometrically the aggregate expenditure function is the vertical summation of the individual expenditure functions that make it up – in the simple case that we are considering here there are only two such functions, one for consumption and one for investment. Note that vertical summation of the $C + I$ curves is the geometrical equivalent of adding columns (ii) and (iii) in Table 27.4. In both cases we are finding the total amount of C and I associated with each level of income.

Shifts in the aggregate expenditure function

The aggregate expenditure function is the sum of the consumption and investment functions. Anything that shifts either of these individual functions will also shift the aggregate expenditure function.

Consumption: So far we have seen how consumption, and hence aggregate expenditure varies with national income. Earlier we observed that, to draw a stable relation between total desired consumption expenditure and total national income, we had to hold all of the other determinants of consumption

that we listed on page 331 constant. A change in any of these other determinants will shift the functions graphed in Figures 27.5 and 27.6. Let us now briefly consider such shifts.

First, consider upward shifts. Anything that increases the desire to spend on consumption, and hence reduces the desire to save, will cause an upward shift in the consumption function, and hence also an upward shift in the aggregate expenditure function.

This effect is shown in Figure 27.7(i). The initial consumption function is labelled C. The increased desire to consume shifts the function upwards to C', thus indicating a higher desired expenditure on consumption *at each level of national income*. This also shifts the aggregate expenditure function upwards by the same amount, from E to E'.

The reverse case of a reduced desire to spend on consumption (an increased desire to save) can also be shown on the same Figure. Let the initial consumption and aggregate expenditure functions be C' and E'. The fall in the desire to consume lowers the consumption function to C, and hence lowers the aggregate expenditure function to E.

Factors that can shift the consumption function upwards are shifts in any of the determinants of consumption that we listed earlier in this chapter and that we held constant in order to construct the simple relation between consumption and income. Among

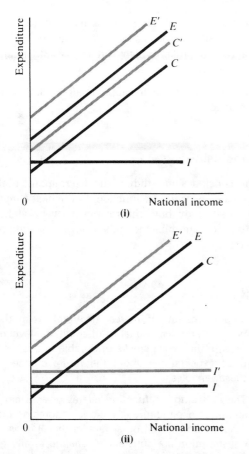

FIGURE 27.7   Shifts in the Aggregate Expenditure Function. Upward and downward shifts in the consumption and investment functions cause corresponding upward and downward shifts in the aggregate expenditure function

the most important are the following:

- A reduction in the thriftiness of the population.
- A fall in interest rates that reduces the reward for saving.
- Fear of a future inflation that encourages a psychology of 'buying now before prices rise'.
- An increase in wealth, so that people feel less urgency to save in order to add yet further to their wealth.

All of the above are forces that influence each individual household's consumption-saving decision and hence also influence their behaviour in the aggregate. Because the consumption function is the aggregate of the behaviour of all households, there is one further force that we must consider. This is a *redistribution of income among households*. Income

redistributions can shift the aggregate consumption function without shifting the consumption functions of the individual households.

Consider a redistribution that takes income away from a group of households whose marginal propensity to spend is 0.80. These households will cut their spending by 80p and their savings by 20p for every £1 that is taken from them. There are now three cases to consider.

First, assume that the income is transferred to a group of households whose *MPC* is 0.90. The households who gain the income spend 90p and save 10p out of every £1 that they receive. The net effect of this income transfer between the two groups is that an extra 10p is spent on consumption out of every £1 of income that is transferred.

Second, assume that the income is transferred to households whose *MPC* is only 0.70. Now the households who receive the income spend only 70p while saving 30p out of each £1 they receive. The net effect of this transfer is that 10p less is spent out of each £1 of income transferred.

Finally, assume that the income is transferred to households whose *MPC* is 0.80, the same as the *MPC*s of the households from whom the income was taken. Now the transfer has no effect on total consumption – those who lose income cut their spending by 80 per cent of the transfer, while those who gain income raise their spending by 80 per cent of the transfer. The net effect is zero.

We may conclude that *redistribution of national income will shift the aggregate consumption function, upwards if those gaining the income have higher MPCs than those losing it and downwards if those gaining the income have lower MPCs than those losing it.*

Investment: In this chapter we have assumed that investment is an autonomous expenditure flow. This is why the figures in column (iii) of Table 27.4 are constant and the *I* lines in Figures 27.1 and 27.6 are horizontal.

A change, however, in any of the forces that influence desired investment spending (see the list on page 328) will change the amount of such expenditure. This will change the figures in column (iii) of Table 27.4 and *shift* the investment function shown in the Figures.

An illustration is shown in Figure 27.7(ii). The initial investment, consumption and aggregate expenditure functions are *I*, *C* and *E*. A change in one of the determinants of investment will cause desired investment to change. If more investment expenditure is desired, the function shifts upwards, say to I', taking the aggregate expenditure function upward with it to E'.

The reverse case is shown by setting the initial functions at C, I', and E'. A reduction in desired investment expenditure shifts the investment function downwards to I, taking the aggregate expenditure function down with it to E.

From our earlier discussion, we can isolate the major changes that will cause the desired investment to increase:

● a fall in the rate of interest,
● a fall in the purchase price of capital goods,
● a rise in the productivity of capital goods,

● expectations of increased sales in the future,
● expectations of decreased costs in the future,
● a rise in profits which can be used to finance investment.

Opposite changes will cause a fall in desired investment.

Conclusion

This concludes our study of the determinants of the aggregate expenditure function. In the next chapter we shall study how the relations developed here interact to determine the equilibrium level of national income.

SUMMARY

1 All expenditure flows used in the theory of the determination of national income have several characteristics: (1) they are *real* flows, changes in which measure changes in *quantities*; (2) they are *planned*, or *desired*, flows showing what people want to spend or save, as distinct from *actual* or *realized* flows, that they succeed in spending or saving; (3) they are aggregate flows showing total desired expenditures added up over every unit wishing to make such expenditure.

2 In the elementary theory of income determination, investment is assumed to be autonomous which means that it does not vary with national income. When investment is plotted against national income, its graph is a horizontal line. Some of the important determinants of investment are the rate of interest, the price of capital goods, the productivity of capital goods, expectations of future sales, costs and profits, and innovations. Changes in any of these will shift the investment curve upwards if they encourage investment out of a given level of income, or downwards if they discourage it.

3 Households make a single decision on how to divide their incomes between consumption and savings. This decision is influenced by the level of income, the rate of interest, time preference, the bequeath motive, the terms of credit, the level of wealth, their own stocks of durable goods, and price expectations about the future course of these variables.

4 The consumption function relates desired consumption expenditure to national income on the assumption that all other factors that influence consumption are constant. A change in any of these other factors will shift the consumption function, upwards if it encourages consumption and downwards if it discourages it.

5 The average propensities to consume and to save are C/Y and S/Y, while the marginal propensities are $\Delta C/\Delta Y$ and $\Delta S/\Delta Y$ respectively.

6 In a simple model with no government and no foreign trade, the aggregate expenditure curve is the vertical summation of the consumption and investment curves. It shows the sum of these two desired expenditure flows at each level of income. It slopes upwards to the right because the consumption curve slopes upwards to the right, while the investment curve is horizontal.

7 A shift in either the consumption function or the investment function will shift the aggregate expenditure function.

Equilibrium National Income

In the previous chapters we developed assumptions about the two components of aggregate desired expenditure in our simple two-sector economy. According to that theory, investment is an autonomous, or exogenous, component while consumption is an induced, or endogenous, component. We are now ready to take the critical step of seeing how the equilibrium size of national income is determined.

When we considered the behaviour of prices and quantities in individual markets in Part 2 of the book, we found that they could be explained by the interaction of demands and supplies. Similarly, when we come to explain the behaviour of the nation's total output (i.e. its national income), we shall find that it depends on the economy's *total* demand and *total* supply.

The modern theory of the determination of national income began with the publication in 1936 of *The General Theory of Employment, Interest, and Money* by the great English economist, John Maynard (later Lord) Keynes. The theory that grew out of his work is a theory of the influence of total demand. It is particularly useful in explaining the short-term behaviour of national income. (To explain long-term behaviour, the influence of aggregate supply, which we shall study in later chapters, turns out to be more important than that of aggregate demand.)

Some Simplifying Assumptions

On the principle that it is easier to study things one at a time rather than all at once, we follow Keynes and concentrate first on aggregate demand. To isolate its influence, we make two key assumptions.

- The economy's *potential*, or *full-employment*, national income (defined in Chapter 25) is also the *maximum* output that can be produced with the existing resources of labour, land and capital.
- Firms will produce enough to satisfy all of the demand that is forthcoming at current prices until full-employment output is reached – i.e. there is no need for prices to rise in order to call forth further output, as long as firms have unused capacity available.[1]

These assumptions make the economy's total national output depend on total demand. If demand is sufficient to buy the whole of the economy's potential output, the economy's actual output will then be equal to its potential output. However, if there is only enough demand to purchase, say, 90 per cent of the economy's potential output, then actual output will only be 90 per cent of potential output.

The Concept of Equilibrium National Income

First, some points about the concept of equilibrium:

Equilibrium Income: National income is said to be in equilibrium when there is no tendency for it either to increase or to decrease. The national income thus achieved is referred to as the EQUILIBRIUM NATIONAL INCOME. When national income is changing because equilibrium is not currently established, we speak of a state of DISEQUILIBRIUM.

---

1 The second assumption means that firms have perfectly elastic supply curves up to potential output, after which the supply curves slope upward in the more usual fashion. Those who have already studied microeconomics will note that these *are not* the conventional, upward-sloping supply curves of perfect competition, but they *are* the short-run supply curves under oligopoly that we studied on pages 201–2.

Equilibrium Conditions: Anything that must be true when equilibrium is established is called an EQUILIBRIUM CONDITION. In what follows, we are going to study the equilibrium conditions for national income. We shall see that these can be stated in either of two ways:

- desired purchases equal actual output (the income-expenditure approach);
- leakages equal injections (the leakages-injections approach).

The Determination of Equilibrium Income: The determination of the equilibrium level of national income in our simple economy can be studied through either of the two approaches stated above. Both give the same answer, so they can be used interchangeably; each has different insights, so it pays to study both.

THE INCOME-EXPENDITURE APPROACH

We begin our study of the income expenditure approach by looking at Table 28.1, which repeats data from Table 27.1. Recall that, in our simple economy, all income generated by production, i.e. all national income, is paid out to households, so that household income is equal to the value of output.

The relation between expenditure and income

Now let us consider how much expenditure is planned at each level of national income. Assume, to begin with, that firms are producing an output of £1,600m. Household income is £1,600m and, according to Table 28.1, total planned expenditure by households and firms on consumption and investment is £1,800m at that level of income. *If firms persist in producing a current output of only £1,600m in the face of planned expenditure of £1,800m*, something must happen. In fact there are two extreme possibilities: either (1) production plans will be fulfilled and expenditure plans frustrated, or (2) expenditure plans will be fulfilled and production plans will be frustrated. Let us consider each of these extreme cases in more detail.

Unfulfilled Expenditure Plans: The first possibility is that households and firms will be unable to spend the £200m in excess of the value of current output that

TABLE 28.1 The Equilibrium of National Income Using the Income-Expenditure Approach. National income is in equilibrium where planned aggregate expenditure equals actual output (£m)

National income (Y)	Planned consumption (C)	Planned investment (I)	Planned expenditure (E = C + I)	
(i)	(ii)	(iii)	(iv) = (ii) + (iii)	
0	300	300	600	
400	600	300	900	
800	900	300	1,200	Pressure on income to increase
1,200	1,200	300	1,500	
1,600	1,500	300	1,800	
2,000	1,800	300	2,100	
2,400	2,100	300	2,400	Equilibrium income
2,800	2,400	300	2,700	
3,200	2,700	300	3,000	Pressure on income to decrease
3,600	3,000	300	3,300	

they plan to spend. Shortages of output and perhaps queues of unsatisfied customers will therefore appear. These provide signals to firms that they can increase their sales if they increase their production. When they do so, national income rises.

Unplanned Changes in Stocks: The second possibility is that households and firms will succeed in meeting their expenditure plans by purchasing goods that were produced in the past. Indeed, the only way people could fulfil their plans to purchase more than is currently being produced is by purchasing stocks of goods that are already in existence. In the present case, if plans to buy £1,800m worth of commodities are fulfilled in the face of current output of only £1,600m, then firms' stocks will be reduced by £200m. As long as stocks last, this situation can persist, with more goods being sold than are currently being produced. Sooner or later, however, stocks will run out. But long before that happens, firms will take steps to increase their output to meet the extra demand. The additional output will then allow extra sales to be made, without a further running down of stocks. Thus, in this case, as well as in the first case, the consequence of an excess of planned expenditure over actual output is a *rise* in national income.

Whether the excess of planned expenditure over current output manifests itself in queues of unsatisfied customers, as in the first case described above, or in unplanned reductions in the stocks held by firms, as in the second case described above, we may conclude that: *at any level of national income at which aggregate planned expenditure exceeds total output, national income will sooner or later rise.*

Now consider the national income of £3,200m shown in Table 28.1. At this level of income, households and firms wish to spend only £3,000m on consumption and investment goods. If firms persist in producing a total output of £3,200m worth of goods, £200m worth must remain unsold. Thus, stocks of goods in the hands of firms must rise. Firms will, however, be unwilling to allow stocks of unsold goods to rise indefinitely. Sooner or later, they will cut back on their output to bring it in line with their current sales. When they do so, national income will fall. Thus, *at any level of national income for which aggregate planned expenditure falls short of total output, national income will sooner or later fall.*

Equilibrium income

Now look at the national income of £2,400m in the Table. At this level, and only at this level, the planned expenditure of households and firms is exactly equal to national income. Households are able to buy just what they wish to buy without causing stocks to accumulate or to be depleted. Firms are just able to sell all of their current output, so that their stocks neither rise nor fall. There is no incentive for firms to change their total output. Thus, national income remains steady; it is in equilibrium. *The equilibrium level of national income occurs where aggregate planned expenditure is exactly equal to total output.*

The results just obtained are quite general and do not depend on the numbers chosen for this specific illustration. A glance at Table 28.1 will show that there is *always* a tendency for national income to be pushed in the direction of its equilibrium value. This is because aggregate planned expenditure is *less* than national income when income is above its equilibrium value, and *greater* than national income when income is below its equilibrium value. Only when aggregate planned expenditure is equal to actual national income do expenditure plans exactly match output. People plan to spend an amount equal to the value of what is produced. Since what people want to buy is equal to what is produced, there is no tendency for output to change.

Planned and actual expenditure

Before going on, we need to say a word about the relation between output on the one hand, and planned actual expenditure on the other hand. We saw in Chapter 26 that, as a matter of definition, the value of the nation's output is equal both to actual expenditure on that output and to actual factor incomes generated by the output. These are just different ways of looking at a single number, the value of total output produced.

But what matters for our theory is planned expenditure. We have seen above that *disequilibrium occurs when planned expenditure is not equal to total output.* There is no reason why the amount that households and firms *plan* to spend on purchasing total output should be equal to the value of total output. Indeed we have seen that, if these two magnitudes are not equal, national income must change.

We have also seen that *equilibrium occurs where planned expenditure is equal to total output.* The income-expenditure approach determines the equilibrium level of national income at that point. This means that people are just willing to purchase the total output that is produced.

THE LEAKAGES-INJECTIONS APPROACH

On page 315 we defined the circular flow of income as the flow of payments from households to firms (to pay for consumption goods) and from firms to households (to pay for factor services). Figure 26.2 (on page 315) depicts this flow. In the Figure the flow is closed, in the sense that nothing is added to it and nothing is subtracted from it.

The concept of leakages and injections

The circular flow is, however, not fully closed. Instead there are both leakages out of the flow and injections into it. A LEAKAGE, which is sometimes also called a WITHDRAWAL, represents payments received by firms or households that are *not* passed on through their spending. An INJECTION represents payments received by firms or households that do not arise from the spending of the other group. In other words, a leakage is an income receipt that *does not* cause further spending, while an injection is an income receipt that *was not caused* by household spending. Leakages are identified by looking forward to see where the income goes, while injections are identified by looking backwards to see where the income came from.

In the simple economy that we are currently considering, saving is the only leakage while investment is the only injection. Later we shall consider other leakages and injections. In the meantime let us see why savings are a leakage while investment is an injection.

Saving is a Leakage: Households do much of the saving in any real economy and, for simplicity in building our theory, we assume that households are the only savers. (This means that firms pay out all of their profits as dividends.)

Household saving is income received by households and *not* passed on to firms through household consumption expenditure. Saving thus represents a leakage from the circular flow. The sense in which saving is a leakage can be seen by considering an extreme case. The case is unreal, but pushing saving to extremes allows us to appreciate that, without doubt, it is a leakage. Assume that households suddenly go on a wild saving spree and save all of their incomes. All of the income received by households now leaks out of the circular flow; none of it is passed on to firms through consumption expenditure. Firms will receive no income as a result of the consumption spending of households because there is no spending. Being unable to sell anything to households, firms will sooner or later cut their production of consumption goods to zero.

Investment is an Injection: Investment creates income for the firms that make the investment goods. However, this income does not arise from the spending of households. It arises instead from the spending of those firms that purchase the investment goods. Investment thus represents an injection of income into the circular flow.

There is a possible source of confusion arising from the common usage in which a household says it *invests* in bonds or company shares when it buys them with its savings. This is *not* investment expenditure in the sense defined on page 313. All that the household is doing is passing funds over to the sellers of these shares or bonds – which in itself creates no output and no employment.

The relation between saving and investment

It is most important to note that *the decision to save is*

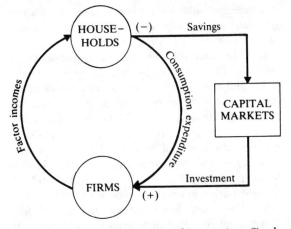

FIGURE 28.1   The Circular Flow of Income in a Simple Economy. Saving is a withdrawal from, and investment is an injection into, the circular flow of income between households and firms

made by one group, households, while the decision to invest is made by another group, firms. It is quite possible, for example, that firms may plan to increase their investment expenditure just at the same time that households plan to reduce their saving (in order to increase consumption). It is equally possible, however, that firms may plan to cut their investment expenditure just when households plan to increase their saving. So, although there are many financial institutions that help to channel savings into investment, the key point that matters for our theory is that: since saving and investment decisions are made by different groups, there is no automatic reason why the amount that households plan to save should be equal to the amount that firms plan to invest.

A Summary Using the Circular Flow Diagram: Figure 28.1 shows a circular flow diagram with expenditure flows going from firms to households (as income payments) and from households to firms (as consumption expenditure). It also shows the leakage of saving (marked with a '−') and the injection of investment (marked with '+'). Between the two lie financial institutions which operate in capital markets. Because *households* decide on the flow of leakages that they wish to make in the form of saving, while *firms* decide on the flow of injections that they wish to make in the form of investment, there is no reason why, at any moment of time, the flow of planned savings should equal the flow of planned investment.

The influence of saving and investment

We have seen that saving is income received by a household and not passed on by way of further spending. Not surprisingly, therefore, saving exerts a contractionary force on the circular flow of income. It reduces the flow around the income circuit just as a leakage at some point in your garden hose reduces the flow of water through the hose beyond that point.

We have also seen that an investment is revenue received by firms that does not arise out of the spending of households. In the case of investment goods, firms are both the buyers and the sellers. The firms that make and sell investment goods must employ factors of production. This, in turn, creates income for the households that supply the factors. Households can then, in their turn, spend this income on consumption goods produced by firms. Investment thus increases the flow of income just as a second garden hose that is joined to your first hose, and adds its volume of water to that hose, will increase the flow through the hose beyond the point at which the hoses join.

Equilibrium income

In view of the argument in the previous paragraph, we should not be surprised to find that the circular flow is in equilibrium – with national income neither rising nor falling – when the volume of leakages (caused in our present model by saving) is equal to the volume of injections (caused in our present model by investment). Let us see how this comes about.

Look now at Table 28.2, which repeats the data on planned saving and income from Table 27.1 and on planned investment from Table 28.1. To see how equilibrium national income is achieved through saving and investment, consider what would happen if the value of output were held at £1,600m. At this level of national income, households wish to save only £100m, while firms wish to invest £300m. Savings and investment plans are inconsistent with each other.

We have seen that there are two extreme possibilities if output is held at this level. Either production plans will be fulfilled and expenditure plans frustrated, or expenditure plans will be fulfilled and production plans will be frustrated.

Now consider each of the above possibilities. In the first case, households, which are unable to buy all that they wish to buy, end up by saving more than they planned to save. They are forced to save income

TABLE 28.2 The Equilibrium of National Income from the Withdrawals-Investment Approach.
National income is in equilibrium when firms plan to invest the same amount as households plan to save (£m)

National income (Y)	Planned saving (S)	Planned investment (I)	
0	−300	300	⎫
400	−200	300	⎪
800	−100	300	⎬ Pressure on income to increase
1,200	0	300	⎪
1,600	100	300	⎪
2,000	200	300	⎭
2,400	300	300	Equilibrium income
2,800	400	300	⎫
3,200	500	300	⎬ Pressure on income to decrease
3,600	600	300	⎭

that they planned to spend. Firms see that they could sell more, if only they were producing more.

In the second case, firms find their stocks of finished goods being depleted. They find, therefore, that they end up making less than the £300m total investment that they planned to make. They do spend £300m on capital goods but they also have an unplanned depletion of stocks. Actual total investment therefore is £300m minus the reduction in stocks. (Recall that total investment includes investment in fixed capital and changes in stocks.) If stocks fall by £200m – which is what must happen if plans to spend £200m more than current output are fulfilled – then while planned investment was £300m, actual total investment would only be £100m (since the reduction in stocks was unplanned and undesired). Since firms do not wish to deplete their stocks, they will increase their production in order to end this unplanned stock depletion.

In either of the two cases that we have just considered, there is a tendency for output to rise whenever households wish to withdraw less from the circular flow by saving than firms wish to add to it by investing. In other words, *whenever planned saving is less than planned investment, national income tends to rise.*

Now consider a level of national income above the equilibrium, say £3,200m. At this income, planned saving exceeds planned investment. If firms insist on holding output at £3,200m, they will be unable to sell all of it and stocks will rise. There will thus be unplanned investment in stocks. Firms will cut back their output in an effort to eliminate the unplanned increase in stocks. Thus national income will fall as a result of households wishing to withdraw more from the circular flow by saving than firms wish to add to it by investing.

When the level of national income is £2,400m, the plans of firms and households coincide so that both are able to save and invest just what they plan to save and invest at an unchanging level of income. Thus no one has any reason to alter their behaviour. This tells us that *national income is in equilibrium when planned saving equals planned investment.*

The above discussion may be summarized as follows. Below the equilibrium level of income and output, planned investment injects more spending into the circular flow than planned saving withdraws from it. This imbalance between the income-increasing forces of investment and the income-decreasing forces of saving tends to cause national income to rise. Above the equilibrium level of national income, planned investment is less than planned saving and the opposite imbalance between expansionary and contractionary forces tends to cause national income to fall.

Equilibrium income and potential income

It is important to remember that *equilibrium national income* is not the same thing as *potential national income*. The latter is the national income that the economy would produce if all resources were fully employed. The former is the national income at which there are no economic forces exerting pressure for income to change. The amount of unemployment in the economy will depend on the relation between the two: the further below potential income is equilibrium income, the more unemployment there will be at equilibrium national income.

THE EQUIVALENCE OF THE TWO APPROACHES

We have shown the determination of equilibrium national income by two different approaches. Both give the same answer, though offering different insights. It is important to assure ourselves that they really do come to the same conclusion. We do this first graphically and then algebraically.

A graphical demonstration

Figure 28.2 shows the determination of the equilib-

rium level of national income, first using the aggregate expenditure function in part (i), and then using the saving and investment functions in part (ii). The Figure is plotted using the data in Tables 28.1 and 28.2. The two graphs have the same scales. This allows us to compare desired expenditure and desired saving at any level of national income.

Look first at part (i) of the Figure. The aggregate expenditure function plots the data from columns (i) and (iv) of Table 28.1 and is labelled E.

Below the equilibrium level of income, the E line lies above the 45° line (labelled $E = Y$). This shows that planned expenditure exceeds income. When people wish to buy more than is currently being produced there is, as we have seen, pressure on national income to rise. This pressure is shown by the upward-pointing arrow to the left of income Y_e. Above equilibrium income, the E line lies below the 45° line, showing that planned expenditure is less than income. When people wish to spend less than the value of current production, there is pressure on income to fall. This pressure is shown by the downward-pointing arrow to the right of income Y_e.

Equilibrium occurs at the level of income Y_e, where the aggregate expenditure function, E, cuts the 45° line. At this point desired expenditure, measured on the vertical axis, is exactly equal to actual national income, measured on the horizontal axis.

Now look at part (ii) of the Figure. Below the equilibrium level of income, the investment curve lies above the saving curve, indicating that planned investment exceeds planned saving. Above equilibrium income, the saving curve lies above the investment curve, indicating that planned saving exceeds planned investment. Equilibrium occurs where the saving and investment lines intersect each other. At this level of national income, planned saving is exactly equal to planned investment.

We have already seen in Tables 28.1 and 28.2 that both the income-expenditure and the saving-investment approaches give the same solution for equilibrium income. This is also shown in the two parts of Figure 28.2, since the level of income, Y_e, where the aggregate expenditure curve cuts the 45° line, is the same as the level of income, Y_e, where the savings curve cuts the investment curve.

This is, of course, no accident. *Planned saving* is the difference between income and planned consumption expenditure, which, graphically, is *the vertical gap between the 45° line and the consumption line*. Aggregate planned expenditure is the sum of planned

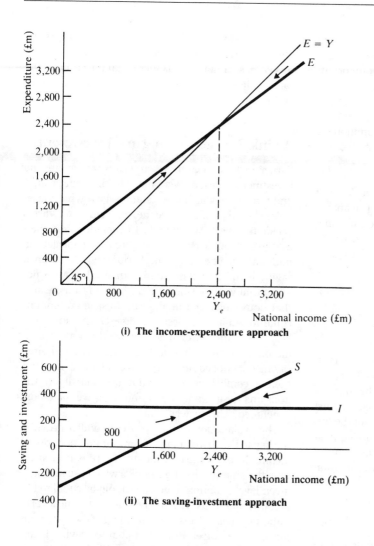

FIGURE 28.2 The Determination of Equilibrium. Equilibrium national income is the point where the aggregate expenditure curve intersects the 45° line and where the saving and investment curves intersect each other

consumption and planned investment expenditures, so that *planned investment is the vertical distance between the expenditure line and the consumption line.* Thus, when the expenditure line cuts the 45° line (i.e. planned expenditure equals income), the saving line must cut the investment line (i.e. planned saving equals planned investment). Put another way, in equilibrium households plan not to spend on consumption (leakages) an amount that is equal to the amount that firms plan to spend on investment (injections).

An algebraic demonstration

We have just shown the equivalence of the expenditure-income and the leakages-injections approaches using geometry. This section provides an alternative algebraic demonstration for those who

find it helpful. Others may skip the section. Those readers who are not worried by algebra may be interested to see a simple algebraic proof of something that may seem difficult and uncertain when argued in words or graphs.

When we determine equilibrium by the intersection of the 45° line and the aggregate expenditure curve, we are solving two simultaneous equations:

$$E = C + I \qquad (1)$$
$$E = Y. \qquad (2)$$

The first is the equation of the desired expenditure curve, and the second is the equation of the 45° line. Substitution of (1) into (2) tells us immediately that the equilibrium condition is:

$$C + I = Y. \qquad (3)$$

This says that, in equilibrium, desired expenditure (which is $C+I$ in this simple model) must equal actual income (i.e. actual output). This is the equilibrium condition from the income-expenditure approach.

We can now show the equivalence of the leakages-injections approach by recalling that households must allocate their income between consumption, C, and saving, S. Writing this in equation form gives us:

$$C+S=Y. \qquad (4)$$

We now take the equilibrium condition for the income-expenditure approach given by (3) above, and substitute into it the relation between income, consumption and saving given by (4) above, which we do by eliminating the common Y term. This gives us:

$$C+I=C+S. \qquad (5)$$

Subtracting C from both sides of equation (5) yields:

$$I=S, \qquad (6)$$

which is the equilibrium condition for the leakages-injections approach. This shows us that, if (3) is true, (6) must also be true. In other words, if the income-expenditure equilibrium condition is fulfilled, so must the leakages-injections equilibrium condition be fulfilled. It follows that the two approaches are equivalent because, fulfilling the equilibrium condition of one approach, implies that the equilibrium condition of the other approach is also fulfilled.

How General are the Results?

We have now developed a theory of the determination of equilibrium national income. We have done so, however, in the context of a simple model where there are only two expenditure flows, consumption and investment. Nonetheless, we have arrived at a general result that holds in more complex models. This is that national income is in equilibrium where aggregate planned expenditure is equal to actual output (i.e. actual national income). Graphically, this is where the aggregate expenditure line intersects the 45° line.

We have also seen that, in the present model, equilibrium occurs where planned saving equals planned investment. Graphically, this is where the S and I lines intersect. This is *not* a general result. The general result, using the leakages-injections approach, is that equilibrium occurs where the sum of desired leakages equals the sum of desired injections.

In the present special case, however, saving is the only leakage and investment is the only injection. In this case, saying that leakages equal injections is the same thing as saying that desired saving equals desired investment.

A Link Between Saving and Investment?

Earlier in this chapter we stressed that saving and investment decisions were made by different groups, and that there was no necessary reason why households should decide to save the same amount as firms decide to invest. We have just concluded, however, that in the simple economy we are now considering, national income is in equilibrium when planned saving is equal to planned investment. Does this not mean that we have found a mechanism that ensures that households end up desiring to save an amount equal to what firms desire to invest? The answer is 'yes', and the mechanism is in the changes in national income that are induced when desired saving does not equal desired investment. Is there not then a conflict between what we said about the decisions to save and invest and what we have now concluded? The answer is 'no'.

The explanation of the apparent conflict provides the key to the theory of the determination of national income in our simple economy. There is no reason why the amount that households wish to save at any given level of national income should be equal to the amount that firms wish to invest at that same level of national income. This is the meaning of the statement made at the outset. But when planned saving is not equal to planned investment, there are forces at work in the economy that cause national income to change until the two do become equal. This is the meaning of the later statement.

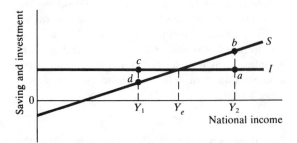

FIGURE 28.3 A Saving and an Investment Function. Planned saving equals planned investment only at the equilibrium level of national income

The argument of the above paragraph can be expressed graphically. That planned household saving does not have to equal planned investment by firms is shown graphically by the fact that the saving curve does not everywhere coincide with the investment curve. Where it does not, planned saving does not equal planned investment at the indicated level of income. The graphical expression of the point that planned saving will end up equal to planned investment is that the saving and investment lines do intersect somewhere, and the equilibrium level of income occurs at that intersection point.

For example, at income Y_2 in Figure 28.3, planned saving exceeds planned investment by the amount ab, while at income Y_1 planned investment exceeds planned savings by the amount cd. Both of these are disequilibrium situations and if national income is at either Y_1 or Y_2, it will move away from those levels. Only at Y_e is income in equilibrium, and only at Y_e is planned saving equal to planned investment.

In later chapters we shall consider other more elaborate models where there are injections in addition to investment and leakages in addition to saving. Although we shall then have to amend our results somewhat, the basic ideas developed in this chapter will not have to be altered.

Now we know the forces that determine equilibrium national income. Our task in the next chapter is to investigate the causes and consequences of changes in equilibrium income.

SUMMARY

1 In the simple theory of the determination of national income developed in Part 4, national income is demand-determined. (In Part 5 supply-side influences are introduced.) The influence of demand-side forces is isolated by the twin assumptions (i) that firms are willing to supply all that is demanded at current prices up to capacity output (also called potential, or full-employment, output), and (ii) that actual output cannot exceed capacity output.

2 Equilibrium national income occurs where there are no pressures for income to change.

3 According to the income-expenditure approach, equilibrium income occurs when aggregate desired expenditure equals actual output. For levels of income greater than equilibrium, desired expenditure is less than current output and output will be reduced. For levels of income less than equilibrium, desired expenditure is greater than current output and output will be increased.

4 According to the leakages-injections approach,

equilibrium income occurs when aggregate desired leakages equal aggregate desired injections. In the simple model of this chapter (i.e. in a closed economy without a government sector), this is where desired saving equals desired investment.

5 The two approaches are equivalent since, in our present simple model, the condition $E = Y$ implies the condition $S = I$.

6 If the level of national income is such that desired savings are not equal to desired investment, there will be pressures on income to change. In equilibrium, desired investment will equal desired saving. Thus, in the model of income determination used in this chapter, *the mechanism that equates desired saving to desired investment is fluctuations in national income.*

7 It is important to note that equilibrium income does not have to equal potential (or full-employment) income. When equilibrium income is less than potential income, there is unemployment of resources and wasted output.

Changes in National Income

In Chapter 28 we studied the conditions for national income to be in equilibrium, which is a state where there is no tendency for national income either to rise or to fall. Figure 25.2 on page 302 shows, however, that the national income of the UK does not remain in a position of unchanging equilibrium. Instead it changes continually, as do the national incomes of all countries.

In this chapter we use the theory of income determination to explain why national income changes. In Chapters 30 and 31 we go on to show how governments can intervene to alter the behaviour of national income.

As a preliminary to this study, we must emphasize the important distinction between movements along curves and shifts of curves. This is a crucial distinction, and failure to make it is a rich source of confusion. We recommend, therefore, that you study the next section with great care.[1]

MOVEMENTS ALONG CURVES AND SHIFTS OF CURVES

If planned consumption expenditure rises, it matters whether this is a response to a change in national income or to an increased desire to consume *at each level of national income*, including the present one. The former change is represented by a movement along the aggregate consumption curve. It is the response of

consumption to a change in income. The latter change is represented by a *shift* in the consumption curve. It means a change in the proportion of income that households plan to consume at each level of income and it occurs in response to a change in some variable other than income. For example, as we saw in Chapter 27, a rise in wealth may shift the consumption function upwards as people feel less need to save so as to add even more to their wealth.[1]

Figure 29.1 illustrates this important distinction. The lines in the Figure conform to our assumptions about how consumption, saving and investment are related to national income. The consumption and the saving curves slope upwards, indicating that households plan to consume and save more as income rises. Investment has, however, so far been assumed to be autonomous. Thus the investment line is horizontal, indicating that firms plan to make a constant amount of investment expenditure, I_0, whatever the level of national income.

Movements Along Curves: Each of the lines shows how the flows in question respond to a change in income. To illustrate, consider an example where national income rises from an initial value of Y_0 to a new value of Y_1. Figure 29.1 shows that at national income Y_0, consumption is C_0, saving is S_0 and investment is I_0. Now let national income rise to Y_1 in part (i) of the figure. Consumption expenditure now rises to C_1, while saving rises to S_1, but investment remains constant at I_0. These changes in saving and

---

1 Those of you who have already studied microeconomics will have encountered this distinction with respect to demand and supply curves. See Chapters 4 and 5.

1 Be careful here not to confuse wealth (a stock) with income (a flow), as is sometimes done in common speech. People often say they have become 'wealthier' when their income rises. But wealth refers to a person's *stock* of assets, not to his *flow* of income.

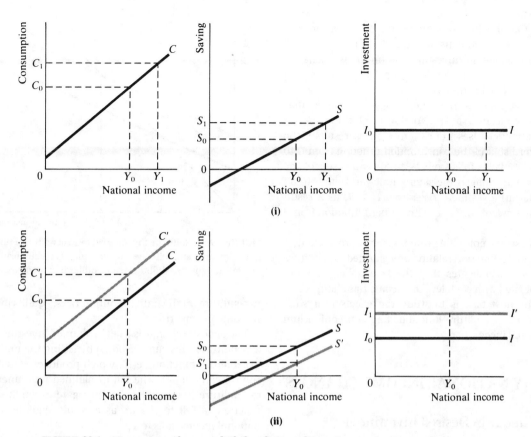

FIGURE 29.1   Movements Along, and Shifts of, Expenditure Curves. A movement along a curve occurs in response to a change in income; a shift of a curve indicates a different level of expenditure at each level of income

consumption represent the responses to a change in income.

This example illustrates a general proposition: the response of any flow, such as consumption, saving or investment, to a change in national income is shown by a movement along the curve relating that expenditure to income.

These responses are measured by the marginal propensities to save and consume that were defined on pages 333 and 336.[1] *A marginal propensity measures the change in some expenditure flow that results from a unit change in income.* Thus, marginal propensities relate to movements along curves and tell us how

much a particular expenditure flow responds to a change in income.

Shifts of Curves: So far we have studied how flows of expenditure respond to changes in income as indicated by movements *along* the appropriate expenditure function. However, expenditure flows can change for another reason: the curves themselves may shift, indicating a new level of expenditure that is associated with *each* level of national income. Such shifts are illustrated in part (ii) of Figure 29.1.

In each case, the curve shifts from the black to the grey line. This change is not a consequence of a change in income, but, instead, it represents a change in the whole relationship with income. The shift from C to C' is a rise in the consumption function – more is spent on consumption at every level of income, for example because a rise in wealth makes households less interested in saving more. The shift from S to S' shows a fall in the savings function – less is saved at

---

1 So far we have defined marginal propensities to consume and to save. But there can be a marginal propensity for any flow, X, defined as $\Delta X/\Delta Y$ and measuring the change of expenditure, X, that results from a change in income, Y. Thus in later chapters, when we distinguish other expenditure flows, we can define other marginal propensities.

every level of income, say, for the same reason that more is spent on consumption. The shift from I to I' shows a rise in investment – more is spent on investment at every level of income, say, because of a major fall in the interest rate.

To see what has happened, look at some particular level of income, say Y_0. At that level of income: (i) consumption rises from C_0 to C_1' as a result of the upward shift of the consumption function from C to C'; (ii) savings falls from S_0 to S_1' as a result of the downward shift in the saving function from S to S'; while (iii) investment rises from I_0 to I_1 as a result of the upward shift in the investment function from I to I'.

These examples illustrate a general proposition: a shift in the function relating any planned expenditure to income indicates that the level of expenditure associated with each level of income has changed.

Our next task is to study the effects that such shifts in expenditure functions have on equilibrium national income.

WHY NATIONAL INCOME CHANGES

A Change in Desired Investment

What will happen to national income if there is, say, an increase in the amount of investment expenditure that firms wish to make? For example, a new product may be invented and firms may decide to build new plants in order to serve the new market.

Just as we saw that we can describe equilibrium national income either by the condition that *desired expenditure equals national income*, or by the condition that *leakages equal injections*, so can we use either of these approaches to discover the effects of changes in planned expenditure flows, such as a rise in desired investment.

The income-expenditure approach

The rise in planned investment expenditure shifts the aggregate expenditure curve upwards, indicating that more expenditure is planned at each level of income. The effects are shown in Figure 29.2. In that figure, the initial expenditure function is E, and the initial equilibrium level of income is Y_0. An increase in planned investment now shifts the aggregate expenditure curve upward to E'. This raises equilibrium income to Y_1. Not surprisingly, if desired

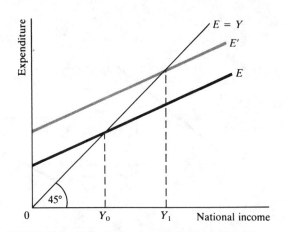

FIGURE 29.2　Shifts in the Aggregate Expenditure Function. Upwards shifts in the function increase equilibrium income; downward shifts decrease equilibrium income

expenditure on the nation's output rises, equilibrium national income rises.

The opposite change is a fall in planned investment expenditure. This can be shown by letting the initial expenditure function be E', which produces equilibrium income of Y_1. The fall in planned investment expenditure then causes the aggregate expenditure function to fall to E and, as a result, equilibrium national income falls to Y_0.

The leakages-injections approach

In Figure 29.3 the original saving and investment schedules are S and I. These curves intersect to produce an equilibrium national income of Y_0. Now let the investment schedule shift upwards to I'. There is more planned investment at each level of income and equilibrium income rises to Y_1 as a result.

We have derived two basic results:

- A rise in planned investment expenditure raises equilibrium national income.
- A fall in planned investment expenditure lowers equilibrium national income.

Let us now ask what economic forces are at work to cause the changes just studied? Since the saving curve is unchanged, the upward shift of the investment curve means that, at the initial level of income, Y_0, some decision-makers wish to inject more into the circular flow by way of investment than other decision-makers wish to withdraw through savings. This excess of planned investment over planned saving is shown by the distance ab in Figure 29.3.

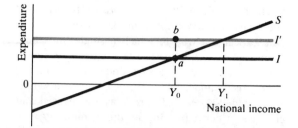

FIGURE 29.3   **The Effect on National Income of a Change in Investment.** An upward shift in the investment schedule increases equilibrium national income; a downward shift reduces it

As output is increased to meet this extra demand, national income rises. The rise in income causes the amount of desired savings to rise *in response to the change in income*. The rise in income continues until, at income Y_1, desired saving once again is equal to the (new and higher level of) desired investment. In other words, the upward *shift* of the investment curve has induced *a movement along* the savings curve until the flow of desired saving is again equal to the now-higher flow of desired investment.

It is important to remember that we are dealing with continuous flows measured as so much per period of time. An upward shift in the investment curve means that, *in each period*, desired investment is more than it was previously. It is also important to remember that we are dealing with real flows. Our curves relate real national income to real expenditure so they reflect the *quantities* of consumption and investment goods people wish to purchase at various levels of real national income.

A Change in Desired Consumption and Saving

Now consider the effect of an upward shift in the consumption function and, therefore, a downward shift in the savings function. Say, for example, that households in the aggregate decide to spend £500,000 more *at each level of income*. This means that they must save £500,000 less at each level of income.

The income-expenditure approach

We derive the effects using our two approaches in turn. The change in household behaviour is shown by an upward shift in the consumption function, and hence in the aggregate expenditure function, and by a downward shift in the savings function.

The income-expenditure approach has already been shown in Figure 29.2. The original aggregate expenditure curve is E, and the upward shift in the consumption function shifts the expenditure curve upwards to E'. This raises equilibrium income from Y_0 to Y_1. The reverse case of a fall in planned consumption shifts the aggregate expenditure curve downwards from E' to E, lowering equilibrium income from Y_1 to Y_0.

The leakages-injections approach

If households plan to spend more at each level of income, they must plan to save less, so the saving function shifts downwards. This is shown in Figure 29.4 where the initial curves of S and I intersect to produce an equilibrium national income of Y_0. The saving schedule then shifts downwards to S' and, as a result, equilibrium income rises to Y_1. Equilibrium is restored because the desire of households to save less, shown by a downward shift in the saving curve, causes income to rise until desired saving returns to its original level. This is shown by the movement *along the new saving curve* from point a to point b.

The reverse case of an increase in planned savings is shown by an upward shift in the savings schedule from S' to S. This lowers equilibrium income from Y_1 to Y_0. In this case, the desire of households to save more at each level of income, as shown by an upward shift in the saving curve, causes national income to fall until saving returns to its original level. This is shown by a movement along the *new saving curve* from point c to point d.

The above analysis leads to two further conclusions:

- A rise in planned consumption expenditure, which

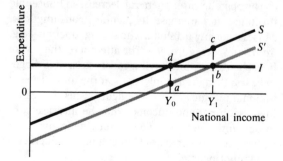

FIGURE 29.4   **The Effect on National Income of a Change in Saving.** A downward shift in the saving schedule increases equilibrium national income

is the same thing as a fall in planned saving, raises equilibrium national income.

- A fall in planned consumption expenditure, which is the same thing as a rise in planned saving, lowers equilibrium national income.

The paradox of thrift

The results just obtained have one rather surprising application. It appears that the macro behaviour of the economy contrasts with what we understand about individual behaviour. We all know that at the individual level, thrift normally leads to increased wealth and prosperity, while dissaving leads to eventual bankruptcy. But at the macro level, the outcome may sometimes be otherwise. Moreover, when *one* individual saves more, his or her savings rise. But when *all* individuals try to save more of their income, total savings may well not rise. This is why economists speak of the 'paradox of thrift'.

We have seen above what will happen if all households try simultaneously to increase the amount that they save – for example if the saving curve in Figure 29.4 shifts from S' to S. *The increase in thriftiness will decrease the equilibrium level of national income* – from Y_1 to Y_0 in the figure. The upward shift in the saving schedule causes planned saving to exceed planned investment at the initial equilibrium level of income. National income falls and this induces a decline in planned saving. Income continues to fall until saving is again equal to investment. But we are assuming that investment is constant. Therefore, saving must fall right back to its original level so that saving is, again, equal to the unchanged level of investment. *The attempts to save more are frustrated because income falls until everyone ends up saving just what they were saving initially.*

The opposite case, a general decrease in household thriftiness (an increase in planned consumption), causes a downward shift in the saving function – e.g. from S to S' in Figure 29.4. The attempt on the part of households to reduce saving causes desired leakages to be less then desired injections at the initial level of national income – Y_0 in the figure. This causes an increase in national income, and the increase continues until the actual volume of saving has been restored to its original level but at a new, higher level of national income.

The Paradox Explained:　The paradox of thrift is not really a paradox. *Rather it is a straightforward predic-* *tion that follows logically from the theory of the determination of national income.* It seems paradoxical to those who expect the way in which a single household should act if it wishes to raise its wealth and its future ability to consume ('save, save, and save some more') to be directly applicable to the economy as a whole. The paradox is resolved as soon as it is realized that changes in desired saving by the community as a whole *change the level of total demand* and, as a result, change the equilibrium level of national income (thereby also affecting the level of desired saving).

Applicability of the Paradox:　The validity of the paradox of thrift depends critically on the truth of two of the basic assumptions of the elementary theory of national income that we have accepted for the analysis of this chapter.

(1) National income is below its potential level. Thus, the available productive capacity will allow output to increase whenever demand increases. Conversely, anything that reduces total demand reduces output and employment. In other words, income is demand-determined. In this case, anything that lowers demand – e.g., an increased desire to save – lowers output.

(2) Plans concerning investment are assumed to be taken independently of plans concerning savings. There is no reason, according to the theory, why the amount that firms plan to spend on investment at any level of income should bear any relation to the amount that households plan to save. If the Smiths and the Greens *save* more, or save less, so the theory goes, that does not affect decisions by the National Coal Board or ICI on how much to spend on *investment*.

Let us now consider circumstances in which these assumptions are not correct, in which case the paradox will not apply.

(1) If actual national income is already equal to potential income, then the first assumption will not be correct. In such circumstances, a decrease in household saving, and an increase in consumption expenditure, will not cause an increase in real output and employment *since full employment already exists*. In such circumstances, the effect of the increase in spending will probably be (as we shall see in Chapter 41) to cause an inflation. An increase in saving, however, with its accompanying decrease in spending will tend to reduce output and employment.

(2) If the second assumption is invalid, none of the predictions of the paradox of thrift will hold. Assume,

for example, that the saving and the investment functions are linked together because changes in household saving *cause* changes in investment. In this case, there could be an offsetting shift in the investment function whenever the desire to save changes. An increase in the desire to save, for example, would shift the saving function upward but, by permitting more investment, it would also shift the investment function upward. As a result of these two offsetting shifts, no downward pressure on national income would emerge.

The predictions of the paradox of thrift, and most of the other predictions of the elementary theory of national income, depend critically, therefore, on the assumption that saving and investment decisions are taken to a great extent by different groups in society – savings decisions by households and investment decisions by firms – *and* that there is no mechanism whereby a change in the amount that households plan to save at a particular level of income will cause a change in the amount that firms plan to invest at the same level of income.

Such a possible mechanism does exist in the rate of interest, which exerts some influence on both savings and investment decisions. It is an important assumption of the paradox of thrift, therefore, that interest rates do not adjust smoothly and quickly so as to bring about an equality between planned savings and planned investment at each and every level of national income.

What is important about the paradox of thrift is the following insight: sudden shifts in consumer spending and saving *do* affect total demand and *do*, therefore, exert expansionary or contractionary demand pressures on the economy in the short term. As we shall see in Chapter 39, however, supply conditions, over the longer term, are more important in determining total output than are demand conditions. As a result, it is *not* correct that a reduction in planned savings will increase national income over the long term.

THE MULTIPLIER, OR HOW MUCH DOES NATIONAL INCOME CHANGE?

So far we have considered the direction of the change in national income caused by changes in planned expenditure flows. But what about the *magnitude* of these changes? If the annual flow of investment

expenditure changes by £1,000m, by how much will national income change?

The Definition of the Multiplier

A major prediction of national income theory is that a change in autonomous expenditure caused by a shift in any desired expenditure function will cause a change in national income that is greater than the initial change in expenditure. We first consider a change in investment expenditure, which gives rise to the well-known INVESTMENT MULTIPLIER (often given the symbol K). This is defined as the *ratio* of the change in national income to the initial change in planned investment expenditure that brings it about:

$$K = \Delta Y / \Delta I.$$

For example, if a change in investment of £2,000 causes a change in national income of £6,000, the multiplier is 6,000/2,000, which is 3.

Thus the multiplier is a ratio. Its value tells us the change in national income for each £1 change in investment. The value of 3 in the above numerical example tells us that for every £1 increase in desired investment expenditure there will be a £3 increase in equilibrium national income. So when investment increased by £1,000m, equilibrium income increased by £3,000m.

The Determination of the Multiplier

The importance of the investment multiplier in national income theory makes it worthwhile using more than one approach to develop it and to display its basic characteristics. We will explain the multiplier using an intuitive approach, then a numerical approach, then a geometric approach, and finally an (optional) algebraic approach.

The multiplier: an intuitive approach

What would you expect to happen to national income if there were a rise in firms' planned investment expenditure on new factories of £1,000m per year? Would national income rise by only £1,000m? The answer is 'No; national income will rise by *more than* £1,000m.' There will be an immediate, *direct* rise in income of £1,000m due to the rise in autonomous expenditure, but this will be followed by further rises as induced consumption expenditure will increase as a result of the increase in national income. In the end, the total rise in expenditure, and hence in national income, will be more than the rise in autonomous expenditure by the amount of the rise in induced expenditure.

This can be argued in either of two ways, remembering that we are dealing with flows of expenditure, so that a rise of £1,000m in planned investment on new factory construction means an extra £1,000m spent on new factories *each year*. First, we can say that the increase in investment expenditure of £1,000m per annum will induce further increases in consumption expenditure. The impact of the initial rise will be felt by the industries that provide the materials for the new factories and those that do the actual construction. Income and the employment of factors of production in those industries will rise by £1,000m as a direct and immediate result. But these newly employed factors will spend some of their new incomes buying food, clothing, shelter, holidays, cars, refrigerators, and a host of other products. This is the induced rise in consumption expenditure, and, when output expands to meet this extra demand, employment will rise in all of the affected industries. When the owners of factors that are newly employed spend their incomes, output and employment will rise further; more income will then be created and more expenditure induced. Indeed, at this stage we might begin to wonder if the increase in income will ever come to an end. This question is more easily answered if we look at the second way in which the process of income expansion can be described.

The initial rise in investment expenditure is a rise in injections. This will increase income, but, as income rises, the volume of leakages (in the form of new saving) will rise. Income will continue to rise until additional saving of £1,000m has been generated. At this point, desired saving will have risen by as much as the original rise in investment and, assuming we began from an equilibrium, we will be back in equilibrium, but at a higher level of income. For example, if 20 per cent of all income is withdrawn through saving, then the rise in income will come to a halt when income has risen by £5,000m. At this higher level of income an extra £1,000m in saving will have been generated, and since the rise in saving equals the initial rise in investment, income will no longer be rising.

Thus, the increase in income does come to a halt. In this example, it halts when national income has risen by £5,000m. The multiplier is 5, since a rise in

investment expenditure of £1,000m causes a rise in national income of £5,000m.

The multiplier: a numerical approach

Suppose that the economy just studied behaved in the following simple way: every time any household receives some additional income it promptly spends 80 per cent of it on consumption ($MPC = 0.8$) and saves the other 20 per cent ($MPS = 0.2$). This economy's marginal propensity to spend is 0.8, and its marginal propensity to save is 0.2.

Now suppose that injections increase in the form of the £1,000m of new investment spending. National income rises by £1,000m. But that is not the end of the story. The factors of production involved directly and indirectly in manufacturing the investment goods devote £200m to new saving, and spend an extra £800m each year. The recipients of this £800m in turn spend an extra £640m a year (80 per cent of £800m), which is a further addition to aggregate expenditure. And so the process continues, with each successive set of recipients of new income spending 80 per cent of their new income and saving the rest. Each additional expenditure creates new income and yet another round of expenditure. Table 29.1 carries the process through ten rounds. Notice that the sum of all of this new expenditure approaches £5,000m, which is five times the initial new injection of £1,000m of investment. This argument thus leads to the same

TABLE 29.1 A Numerical Example of the Multiplier. Where 20 per cent of any new income leaks out of the circular flow through new Savings

	Increase in income at each round (£m)
Round 1: Initial increase in investment expenditure	1,000.00
2nd round increase (80% of £1,000m)	800.00
3rd round increase (80% of £800m)	640.00
4th round increase (80% of £640m)	512.00
5th round increase (80% of £512m)	409.60
6th round increase (80% of £409.60m)	327.68
7th round increase (80% of £327.68m)	262.14
8th round increase (80% of £262.14m)	209.71
9th round increase (80% of £209.71m)	167.77
10th round increase (80% of £167.77m)	134.22
Sum of 1st 10 rounds	4,463.12
All subsequent rounds	536.88
Total	5,000.00

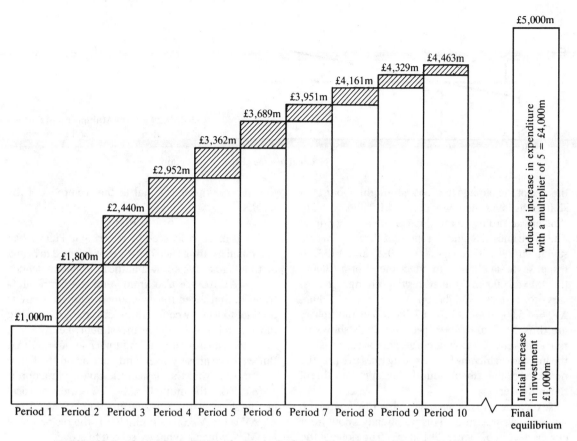

FIGURE 29.5   The Numerical Example Graphed. The total height of each bar shows the increase in national income over period zero as a result of an increase in investment expenditure of £1,000m

result as did the intuitive argument above. The multiplier is 5, given the numerical assumptions that we have made about consumption and saving.

The results of Table 29.1 are graphed in Figure 29.5. The white bar in each period shows the national income in the previous period. The shaded bar shows the increase in the present period, which is 80 per cent of the increase in the previous period. The total height of the two parts of each bar shows the total income in the period in question.

The multiplier: a graphical approach

In Figure 29.6, income is initially assumed to be in equilibrium at £80,000m.[1] Autonomous investment

is then assumed to shift upward from £30,000m to £31,000m because firms increase their spending on new factories. The shift in the investment curve by £1,000m from I to I' increases equilibrium income from £80,000m to £85,000m. This increase – which is shown as ΔY in the figure – is larger than the increase in investment – which is shown by ΔI – which caused the increase in income.

The *ratio* of the increase in income (ΔY) to the increase in investment that brought it about (ΔI) is the multiplier, K. In this case we have:

$$K = \Delta Y/\Delta I = £5{,}000\text{m}/£1{,}000\text{m} = 5.$$

Again this tells us that for every £1 increase in autonomous investment expenditure, equilibrium income rises by £5.

This much is simply definition: The multiplier is the ratio of the change in income to the initiating change in autonomous spending that brought it about.

Next consider Figure 29.7. In that figure we see that

---

1 Notice the break on each axis of the figure. This is to show that the scale does not run continuously back to zero. If we showed the whole range from 0 to 85,000, the changes in which we are interested, from 80,000 to 85,000, would be shrunk to such a small segment of the figure that they would be nearly invisible.

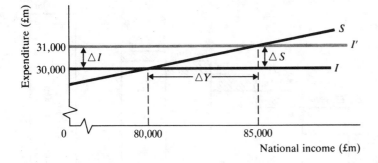

FIGURE 29.6   **The Multiplier and the Saving Function.** The value of the multiplier is the reciprocal of the slope of the saving function

the size of the change in income brought about by a shift in the investment function by £1,000m from I to I' differs according to the slope of the saving curve. The three lines S, S' and S'' represent three *alternative* saving curves with slopes of 0.40, 0.20 and 0.133. In response to a change in investment of £1,000m (i.e. ΔI = £1,000m), the respective changes necessary to restore equilibrium are ΔY_0 = £2,500m, ΔY_1 = £5,000m and ΔY_2 = £7,500m. The multipliers are thus 2.5, 5 and 7.5 respectively. This shows us that the *flatter* the saving curve, the larger must be the increase in income before saving rises to equal the new level of investment; thus the larger is the value of the multiplier.

Next we need to ask ourselves what the slope of the saving curve measures. This we already know from our discussion of Figure 29.1 above. The slope of the saving curve is the marginal propensity to save, *MPS* (i.e. $\Delta S/\Delta Y$). It measures the proportion of each new £1 of income that is saved. An *MPS* of 0.40 means that 40p of each new £1 of income will be saved.

So now we know that the multiplier is *larger* the flatter is the slope of the saving curve; i.e. the *smaller* is the *MPS*. This means that the value of the multiplier is negatively related to the *MPS*: the smaller the *MPS*, the larger the multiplier.

Finally, we wish to show that the exact relation is

that the multiplier is equal to the reciprocal of the *MPS*:

$$K = 1/MPS.$$

This is most easily seen by referring to Figure 29.6 again and locating each of the ratios referred to below on that Figure. We know that the multiplier is defined as $K = \Delta Y/\Delta I$. We also know, and the figure illustrates it, that when the economy has moved from its original to its new equilibrium, the change in saving must equal the change in investment; i.e. $\Delta I = \Delta S$. Thus we can rewrite the multiplier as $K = \Delta Y/\Delta S$. But we have already seen, and once again the figure illustrates it, that the *slope* of the savings function is $\Delta S/\Delta Y$. Thus the multiplier, $\Delta Y/\Delta S$, is the reciprocal of the slope of the savings function $\Delta S/\Delta Y$. Since $\Delta S/\Delta Y$ is the *MPS*, the multiplier is the reciprocal of the *MPS*, which is what we set out to prove.

We have derived two important propositions:

- The value of the multiplier is equal to the reciprocal of the *MPS* – i.e. the reciprocal of the fraction of the change in income that is saved, $K = 1/MPS$.
- Because *MPS* is less than 1, K must be greater than 1.

This completes our study of changes in equilibrium national income in our simple, two-sector model. In the next chapter, we go on to allow for the influence of government on national income.

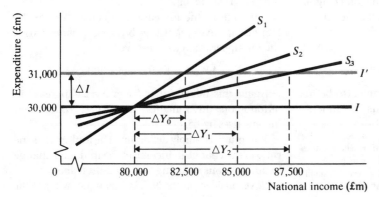

FIGURE 29.7   **The Multiplier and Various Saving Functions.** The flatter is the saving function, the higher is the value of the multiplier

SUMMARY

1 Expenditure may be either income-related, or autonomous (*not* income-related). Any change in autonomous expenditure shifts the aggregate expenditure curve, and causes equilibrium national income to change.

2 An increase in autonomous investment increases equilibrium national income, while a decrease reduces equilibrium national income.

3 A downward shift in the consumption curve (an upward shift in the saving curve) means less is spent at each level of national income and the effect is to reduce equilibrium national income. An upward shift in the consumption curve (a downward shift in the savings curve) means more is spent at each level of national income and the effect is to increase equilibrium national income.

4 The paradox of thrift states that, under certain specific conditions, an attempt to save more will merely reduce equilibrium national income and leave actual saving unchanged. By the same token, an attempt to save less will increase equilibrium national income and also leave actual saving unchanged. These results require (i) that actual equilibrium income is below potential income so that income is demand-determined, and (ii) that desired investment is unaffected by changes in desired saving.

5 The investment multiplier measures the change in equilibrium income that results from a change in autonomous investment expenditure. It is defined as the ratio of the change in income divided by the change in investment ($\Delta Y \Delta I$). The multiplier has a value greater than unity.

6 In the simple model of this chapter, the value of the multiplier is the reciprocal of the marginal propensity to save ($1/MPS$).

Government and the Circular Flow

Government spending adds to aggregate demand. Government taxes reduce aggregate demand by removing from households and firms income that they might otherwise have spent on purchasing goods and services. So total government taxing and spending activities have a major effect on the circular flow, and hence on the equilibrium levels of national income and employment. The government cannot avoid having these influences, since its mere size makes it one of the largest demanders of goods and services in the nation.

This chapter integrates the government into the model of the circular flow of income, showing how equilibrium national income is affected by the government's own revenues and expenditures. The following chapter investigates what is called FISCAL POLICY, which is the conscious use of the government's spending and taxing powers to influence the equilibrium level of national income.

Simplifying Assumptions

In the simple model used in Chapters 28 and 29, the only expenditures were consumption and investment. They were made by private households and firms, which together are described as the private sector. We are now going to add in government, or as it is often called, the public sector. (Until Chapter 32, however, we continue to deal with a closed economy with neither imports nor exports.)

Governments raise their revenues by many kinds of tax. The three main categories are taxes on income, taxes on expenditures (sometimes called direct and indirect taxes respectively) and taxes on capital assets, e.g. local rates which are levied on property values. We can simplify this introductory treatment without losing anything essential by dealing with only one type of tax, the income tax. This tax is, in practice, levied on both households and firms, but for simplicity of exposition we ignore the latter and assume that all income taxes are levied on households. As a result of personal income taxes, not all income that is earned by factors of production reaches their hands. Instead, part is taken by the government as tax revenue and only the remainder becomes personal disposable income.

THE INCOME-EXPENDITURE APPROACH

When we add the government to our model of income determination, we must alter the definition of aggregate expenditure to include all of the government's exhaustive expenditures. (If you have forgotten the distinction between exhaustive expenditures, which add directly to the demand for goods and services, and transfer payments, which do not, you should reread pages 314–15 of Chapter 26 now.) If we let G stand for exhaustive expenditures, as we did in Chapter 26, our new aggregate expenditure function is:

$$E = C + I + G.$$

This tells us that desired aggregate expenditure is the sum of desired consumption, desired investment and desired government expenditure.

The Behaviour of Desired Expenditure

Next we must consider the behaviour of each of these planned expenditure flows.

Investment: Planned investment is still assumed to be autonomous, just as in previous chapters. This is because we assume that investment is determined by factors other than national income and these factors are assumed, for the moment, to remain constant. Thus firms plan to spend a constant amount each year on investment in new plant and equipment, and to keep unchanged their holdings of stocks of materials and finished goods.

Government: For simplicity we start by assuming that planned government expenditure is also autonomous. This allows us to see how national income responds to a fixed level of government expenditure. Later we go on to see how national income is affected by changes in government expenditure.

Consumption: We continue to assume that consumption expenditure is related by the consumption function to households' income. There is, however, one important new consideration. In the earlier model, without a government, all national income accrued to households as their personal disposable income, and all of it was, therefore, available to them to spend or to save. Now, however, government income taxes introduce a gap, or what is often called a 'wedge', between total national income and disposable income.

We now need to use the distinction between national income, Y, and disposable income, Y_d, that was first introduced on page 321 of Chapter 26. National income is the total market value of all final goods produced. Disposable income is the income that is available to households to spend or to save. Disposable income is reduced below national income by tax payments but increased by transfer payments (described in Chapter 26, page 315). Thus, although transfer payments are not a part of government

demand for goods and services, they do affect demand by influencing household expenditure.

For present purposes it is convenient to assume that there are no transfer payments. This gives us a simple model with the following characteristics: (i) all saving is done by households, (ii) all taxes are income taxes on households, and (iii) there are no transfer payments. In these circumstances, disposable income is equal to national income minus the tax revenues raised by the government.[1]

All of the above matters because the consumption expenditure and the savings of households respond to their disposable income. For example, if national income remains constant, but the tax wedge is increased so that disposable income falls, both consumption expenditure and saving will fall.

We have seen that consumption expenditure depends upon disposable income. In our theory, however, all expenditure flows must be related to national income. To obtain this relation in the case of consumption we must now allow for the link between national income and disposable income.

To see what is involved, consider the example shown in Table 30.1. Here households are assumed to have a marginal propensity to consume *out of disposable income* of 0.8. This means that for every increase of £100 in their *disposable income*, they spend an extra £80 (and save the other £20). This defines basic household behaviour: they have a stable relation between changes in their disposable income and changes in their desired consumption. We call this the *MPC* out of disposable income, and measure it by the ratio $\Delta C / \Delta Y_d$.

We are interested, however, in how consumption

---

1 If we allow for transfer payments, we have $Y_d = Y - T + Q$, where T is total tax payments and Q is total transfer payments to households. In the present case, we let Q be zero for simplicity.

TABLE 30.1 The Marginal Propensities to Consume out of Disposable Income and out of National Income.
Columns (ii) to (vii) show the calculations of the two *MPC*s for cases (1), (2) and (3)

Assumed case	ΔY Change in national income	ΔT Resulting change in tax revenue	ΔY_d Resulting change in disposable income	ΔC Resulting change in consumption	$\Delta C / \Delta Y$ *MPC* out of national income	$\Delta C / \Delta Y_d$ *MPC* out of disposable income
(i)	(ii)	(iii)	(iv)	(v)	(vi)	(vii)
(1) Tax rate is zero	100	0	100	80	0.80	0.80
(2) Tax rate is 25%	100	25	75	60	0.60	0.80
(3) Tax rate is 40%	100	40	60	48	0.48	0.80

changes as national income changes, which we call the MPC out of national income, $\Delta C/\Delta Y$. The example illustrates how the two marginal propensities are related.

In the first case, shown in row (1) of the Table, taxes are zero. Thus national income is the same as disposable income and consumption expenditure rises by £80 for every rise of £100 in national income. In this case, the marginal propensity to consume out of national income (column vi) and the marginal propensity to consume out of disposable income (column vii) are both equal to 0.80.

In the case shown in row (2) of the Table, the tax rate is 25 per cent. Thus £25 out of every £100 of national income goes in taxes, so that only £75 becomes the disposable income of households. Now when national income rises by £100, disposable income will only rise by £75 and planned consumption will only rise by £60 (= 80 per cent of £75). In this case, the MPC out of national income is only 0.60 even though the MPC out of disposable income remains unchanged at 0.80.

Row (3) of the Table shows a case where the tax rate is 40 per cent. Thus £40 of each £100 of new national income goes in taxes, and only £60 reaches households as their disposable income. Now if national income rises by £100, disposable income only rises by £60, and consumption only rises by 80 per cent of that amount, i.e. by £48. In this case, the MPC out of national income is only 0.48 even though households continue to consume £80 out of each £100 of disposable income that they receive.

The effect of increasing tax rates on the consumption and aggregate expenditure functions is shown geometrically in Figure 30.1. Curve C_1 is consistent with the example in row (1) of the Table, curve C_2 with the example in row (2), and curve C_3 with the example in row (3). We see that the function relating consumption to national income shifts from C_1 to C_2 to C_3 as the fraction of income going to taxes is increased. This illustrates an important conclusion: *since increasing the tax rate reduces disposable income, it reduces the amount of consumption associated with each level of national income – i.e. it shifts the consumption function relating desired consumption to national income downwards.*

Anything that shifts the consumption function downwards also shifts the aggregate expenditure function downwards. So an increase in tax rates must lower the aggregate expenditure function.

The Aggregate Expenditure Function: Figure 30.2 shows the derivation of the aggregate desired expenditure function for the present model. Investment expenditure, shown by the I curve, is assumed constant at I_0. Government expenditure, shown by the G curve, is assumed constant at G_0. (Don't forget G_0 refers to the distance from the origin to G_0, *not* just the distance from I_0 to G_0.) Consumption expenditure, shown by the C curve, varies with national income in a way that is determined, as we have just seen, by the relation between consumption expenditure and disposable income (which depends on household behaviour) and the relation between disposable income and national income (which depends on the government's tax rates).

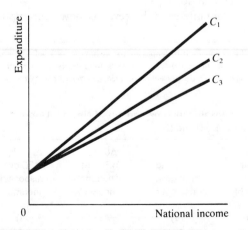

FIGURE 30.1　Changing Tax Rates Shift the Consumption Function. The higher the proportion of national income taken in taxes, the lower the curve relating consumption to national income

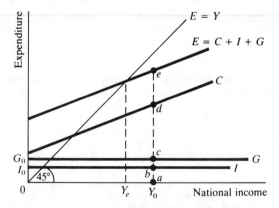

FIGURE 30.2　The Derivation of the Aggregate Expenditure Function with a Government Sector. The E curve is the vertical summation of the C, I and G curves

The aggregate expenditure curve is merely the vertical sum of these three curves. (We add the curves vertically because we want E to reflect the sum of I, G and C at each level of income.) For example at income Y_0, total desired expenditure is ae, which is the sum of ab (investment expenditure), ac (government expenditure), and ad (consumption expenditure).

Equilibrium National Income

If you look again at Figure 30.2, you will see the usual diagram for the determination of equilibrium national income by the intersection of the aggregate expenditure function and the 45° line (which indicates the equilibrium condition that planned expenditure should equal actual output). In the Figure, equilibrium national income is determined at Y_e.

There are two differences between the present model and the one developed in the previous chapters. First, the aggregate expenditure function now includes the government's exhaustive expenditure. Second, the consumption function (and hence the aggregate expenditure function) has been shifted by the presence of taxes in the manner discussed above.

This is all there is to the determination of equilibrium by the income–expenditure approach in our new model. Figure 30.2 is the same as Figure 28.2(i) in all its essential features. All that differs is what underlies the aggregate expenditure function (i.e. the addition of exhaustive government expenditures and the effect of taxes on the consumption function).

The Effects of Changes in Government Taxes and Expenditures

The government may change its taxing and spending policies for many reasons. Whatever the motivation, such changes will affect equilibrium national income. We first consider the changes that increase equilibrium income and then the changes that reduce it.

Fiscal Changes that Increase Equilibrium Income: Let us consider two changes in government policy that increase income. First, consider an increase in the government's exhaustive expenditure, *while tax rates are held constant*. The increase in spending adds to the amount of total desired expenditure in the economy that is associated with each level of income – i.e. the aggregate expenditure function shifts upwards. Second, consider a reduction in tax rates while *government expenditure is held constant*. This leaves

more disposable income in the hands of households (because the government's tax wedge is reduced). As a result, households increase the amount of their consumption spending that is associated with any given level of national income – the aggregate expenditure function shifts up.

We have already studied the effects of an upward shift in the aggregate expenditure function. If you turn to Figure 29.2 on page 352, you will see these effects summarized. The conclusion that we reached there needs only to be recalled here: an upward shift in the aggregate expenditure function raises the level of equilibrium national income. This leads us to our first major conclusion which relates to what are sometimes called *expansionary fiscal measures*: *an increase in government expenditure, or a decrease in tax rates, raises equilibrium national income.*

Fiscal Changes that Reduce Equilibrium Income: Now consider the opposite two changes in government policy – ones that will reduce income. First, a reduction in the government's exhaustive expenditures reduces the amount of desired expenditure associated with each level of income – it shifts the aggregate expenditure curve downwards.

Second, an increase in tax rates reduces the amount of national income that becomes households' disposable income. This means that households have less to spend on consumption, so that the amount of planned consumption associated with any given level of national income falls. The consumption function relating consumption expenditure to national income thus shifts downwards. Since the aggregate expenditure function is the sum of C, I and G, this shift in the consumption function also shifts the expenditure function downwards by the same amount.

Again, we already know the effects of a downward shift of the aggregate expenditure function; it lowers equilibrium national income (see p. 352). We have now developed an important further proposition concerning what are sometimes called *contractionary fiscal measures: a reduction in government expenditure, or a rise in tax rates, reduces equilibrium national income.*

THE LEAKAGES-INJECTIONS APPROACH

We now repeat the same analysis using the leakages-injections approach. Not only is the repetition good practice in such a key area; we will find some important insights that come from this approach.

We have several times had occasion to observe that government expenditure is an injection into the circular flow of income, while tax payments are a leakage from it. Let us recall the reasoning.

Government Expenditure is an Injection: Recall that injections (which we symbolize by J) are anything that creates income for households or firms that does not arise out of the expenditure of the other group. Government exhaustive expenditure creates incomes for the firms and households from which it buys goods and services. This income arises from the spending of government, not from the spending of either firms or households. It is clear, therefore, that government expenditure comes within our definition of an injection.

Tax Revenue is a Leakage: Recall that leakages (which we symbolize by L) are any income received by either households or firms that is not passed on to the other group by way of spending on goods and services. Income taxes create a leakage between the income claims that are created by the production of final goods by firms and the disposable income that is actually received by households. Instead of being received by households, the tax revenues go to the government. Clearly, therefore, tax revenues come within our definition of a leakage.

The Behaviour of Taxes and Expenditures

Government Expenditure: First, consider government expenditure. We have already made the assumption that planned government expenditure is autonomous – i.e. it is determined by factors other than Y. This means that our two injections are both constant; they do not change as Y changes. Expressing injections in symbols, we have:

$$J = I + G.$$

The graphs of investment and government expenditure, and hence the graph of the aggregate injection expenditure function $(I + G)$, are all horizontal lines, as shown in Figure 30.3. They indicate that planned injections do not change as national income changes. Note, in the Figure, that the aggregate injections are the sum of the two separate injections so that, at any level of national income, reading off the vertical axis,

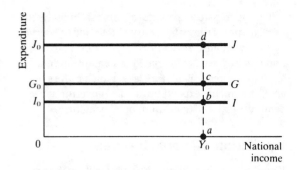

FIGURE 30.3　Injections with a Government. The injections function is the sum of investment and government expenditures

I_0 plus G_0 equals J_0. For example, at income Y_0 aggregate injections are ad, which is the sum of ab investment expenditure and ac government expenditure.

Tax Revenues: Next consider government tax revenues, which we continue to assume are all raised through personal income tax. If the government keeps its *rates of tax* constant, its actual *tax revenues* will rise as national income rises. For example, income taxes levied at a rate of 15 per cent take 15p out of every new £1 of income earned. They will thus yield an additional £150,000 for every £1,000,000 increase in national income. In general, therefore, provided that the government leaves its tax rates unchanged, its tax revenues will rise as national income rises.

The relation between the government's total tax revenues and national income with constant rates of tax is shown in Figure 30.4. At national income of Y_0, tax revenue is T_0. At national income of Y_1, tax revenue is T_1. In the diagram, the change in national income from Y_0 to Y_1 is indicated by ΔY, while the

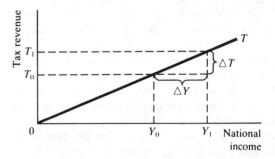

FIGURE 30.4　The Government's Tax Revenue Function. With constant tax rates, tax revenues rise as national income rises

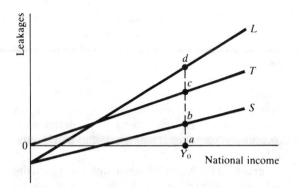

FIGURE **30.5 The Aggregate Leakage Curve.** In the present model, aggregate leakages are the sum of savings and tax revenues

change in tax revenues from T_0 to T_1 is indicated by ΔT. The slope of the tax curve is $\Delta T/\Delta Y$. This slope tells us the proportion of any increase in national income that goes to the government in the form of increased tax revenue. We refer to this as the MARGINAL PROPENSITY TO TAX (MPT).

Total Leakages: In Chapter 27 we studied the leakage of savings (S), drawing a savings function and defining the marginal and average propensities to save. We have now done the same for a second leakage, government tax revenue. The total of these two leakages gives us aggregate leakages in the present model:

$$L = S + T,$$

where T stands for total government tax revenue.

The derivation of the aggregate leakage function is shown in Figure 30.5. The aggregate leakage curve, L, is merely the vertical summation of the saving curve, S, and the tax revenue curve, T. Thus, for example, at income Y_0 aggregate leakages of ad are equal to the sum of ab savings and ac tax revenues.

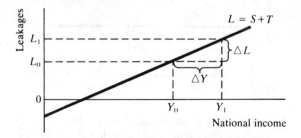

FIGURE **30.6 Calculation of the Marginal Propensity to Leak.** The MPL is the ratio of the change in leakages to the change in income

Figure 30.6 shows the calculation of the relation between changes in national income and changes in leakages. At a national income of Y_0, leakages are L_0. At national income Y_1, leakages are L_1. The change in income is indicated on the Figure by ΔY and the change in leakages by ΔL. The slope of the aggregate leakage curve is given by the ratio of these two changes, that is by $\Delta L/\Delta Y$. This slope shows the fraction of each £1 change in national income that leaks from the circular flow due to the aggregate of all leakages. But any change in aggregate leakages must be accounted for by a change in saving or in tax revenues. Thus $\Delta L//\Delta Y$ must be equal to the sum of the MPS and the MPT. All that this says is that the proportion of national income that leaks out of the circular flow must be the sum of the proportions that leak out through saving and through taxes. We need a term for this fraction. Although ugly, the most obvious term is the MARGINAL PROPENSITY TO LEAK (MPL).

In summary: the slope of the leakage curve shows the proportion of any change in income that goes in leakages, $\Delta L/\Delta Y$, and is called the MPL. Where the leakages are saving and taxes, it is also the sum of the MPS and the MPT out of national income.[1]

Equilibrium National Income

Part (i) of Figure 30.7 shows the determination of equilibrium income. The leakage and injection curves intersect to determine equilibrium national income at Y_0. This graph is similar to Figure 28.2(ii) on page 347 except that, in the present Figure, we allow for two leakages of saving and tax revenues and two injections of investment and government expenditure, whereas in Figure 28.2 the only leakage was saving and the only injection was investment.

The Effect of Changes in Government Taxes and Expenditures

Fiscal Changes that Increase Equilibrium Income: Let us first consider two changes in government policy that increase income. Figure 30.7 illustrates

---

1 A little algebra does wonders here! Leakages are $L = S + T$. This implies that $\Delta L = \Delta S + \Delta T$. Now divide through by ΔY to get $\Delta L/\Delta Y = \Delta S/\Delta Y + \Delta T/\Delta Y$. But the three terms are, in order, the marginal propensities to leak, to save and to tax. This is the same thing as $MPL = MPS + MPT$.

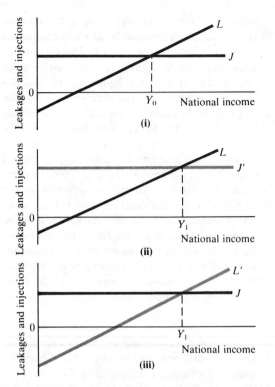

FIGURE 30.7　Equilibrium Income Through the Leakages-Injections Approach. Equilibrium occurs where the withdrawals and injections schedules intersect

two types of expansionary fiscal change. We have already observed that the initial injection function of J, and the initial leakage function of L, intersect to produce equilibrium income of Y_0 in part (i) of the Figure.

Part (ii) shows the effects of an increase in government expenditure with tax rates held constant. The injection curve shifts upwards to J' – i.e. by the amount of the additional planned government expenditure. This increases equilibrium income to Y_1.

To show the effects of a cut in tax rates, return to part (i) with the initial curves of L and J. Now a cut in tax rates causes less income to leak out of the circular flow in the form of taxes at each level of national income, and this causes the aggregate leakage curve to shift downwards to L', as shown in part (iii) of the Figure. Equilibrium national income rises from Y_0 to Y_1 as a result.

Fiscal Changes that Reduce Equilibrium Income: Now let us consider the opposite changes in government policy – ones that reduce income. The two

contractionary fiscal changes are shown in Figure 30.8. We can be brief, since by now we are covering familiar ground. The initial curves are J and L, for desired injections and leakages respectively. They intersect in part (i) of the Figure to produce an initial equilibrium national income of Y_0. Part (ii) of the Figure shows a downward shift of the injection function to J'', brought about by a decrease in government spending. It reduces equilibrium income to Y_2.

Part (iii) of the Figure shows an upward shift in the leakages function, to L'', brought about by an increase in tax rates. The rise in tax rates means that an increased amount of tax revenue is withdrawn from the circular flow at each level of national income. Equilibrium national income falls to Y_2 as a result.

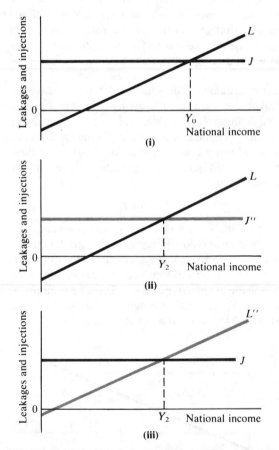

FIGURE 30.8　A Contractionary Fiscal Policy. A fall in government expenditure shifts the injections function downwards; a rise in tax rates shifts the leakages function upwards; both changes reduce equilibrium national income

Tax and expenditure changes compared

We drew Figure 30.7 to show that equilibrium national income is increased, both by an upward shift in the injections function and a downward shift in the leakages function. Note, however, that as we drew the curves, the rise in national income was the same with the tax cut as it was with the expenditure increase. Figure 30.8 was drawn to show that equilibrium national income is reduced, both by a downward shift in the injections curve and an upward shift in the withdrawals curve. Once again, however, we drew the curves so that the reduction in national income was the same with the tax increase as it was with the expenditure cut. The fact that we could do this shows that any desired change in equilibrium national income can be achieved either with expenditure changes or with tax changes.

These alternative policies will, however, have other effects that differ. So, although they are interchangeable in terms of their effects on national income, they are not identical in their other effects. We shall consider these other effects in Chapter 31.

THE MULTIPLIER WITH A GOVERNMENT SECTOR

Since aggregate injections are just the sum of the separate injections of I and G, it follows that aggregate injections are equally affected by a £1 change in either I or G. If the shift in aggregate injections is the same, so is the change in equilibrium income. So we do not need separate multipliers for each type of injection. Instead we re-define the multiplier to be the ratio of the change in equilibrium national income, ΔY, to the change in whatever injection brought it about, ΔJ. This makes our new multiplier formula:

$$K = \Delta Y/\Delta J.$$

There is nothing profound about this: if injections change only because of a change in I, then this multiplier will be the same thing as $\Delta Y/\Delta I$. To illustrate, consider an increase of £1m in private investment expenditure ($\Delta I = £1$m) with government expenditure held constant. This also means a £1m increase in total injections ($\Delta J = £1$m). Assume that, as a result, equilibrium national income increases by £3m. This makes the multiplier equal to 3, whether we calculate it as $\Delta Y/\Delta I$ or $\Delta Y/\Delta J$.

The Size of the Multiplier

We saw that, in the simple model of Chapter 29, the size of the multiplier depended on the *MPS*. We now wish to show that in the present model the size of the multiplier depends on the sum of the *MPS* and the *MPT*. Let us see why this is so.

The reason why the multiplier always exceeds unity is that any increase in income induces new spending, which further raises income and in turn induces further new spending through a series of rounds of new income and new spending. How much spending rises on each round depends on how much leaks out of the system. The higher the amount of leakages from each round of new income, the lower the induced new spending and the lower the final increase in national income.

For example, say that out of each £1 of new income 15p is saved, 25p goes to the government as new tax revenue, and the remaining 60p is devoted to new consumption expenditure. Now let there be £1,000m of new investment, just as we assumed in Chapter 29. This creates £1,000m of new income for those who supply the investment goods. According to our present assumptions, this will give rise to only £600m of new spending, as the rest will go to taxes and saving. This new spending creates new income, and this new income will in its turn create another £360m of new spending. And so the process goes on, with each new round of income creating a new round of expenditure of 60 per cent of the new income. Table

TABLE 30.2 A Numerical Example of the Multiplier.
Where 40 per cent of any new income leaks out of the circular flow through leakages

	Increase in income at each round (£m)
Round 1 : Initial increase in injections	£1,000.00
Round 2 increase (60% of £1,000m)	600.00
Round 3 increase (60% of £600m)	360.00
Round 4 increase (60% of £360m)	216.00
Round 5 increase (60% of £216m)	129.60
Round 6 increase (60% of £129.60m)	77.76
Round 7 increase (60% of £77.76m)	46.66
Round 8 increase (60% of £46.66m)	27.99
Round 9 increase (60% of £27.99m)	16.80
Round 10 increase (60% of £16.80m)	10.07
Sum of first 10 rounds	2,484.89
All subsequent rounds	15.11
Total	2,500.00

30.2 follows this process through 10 rounds of expenditure.

You should now compare this example with the one given in Table 29.1 on page 356. When you have done so, you will see that each new round of expenditure is less in the present case than it was in the previous one. This is because 40 per cent of each new increment of income leaks out of the income flow in the present case, while only 20 per cent leaked out in the case considered in the earlier chapter.

Figure 30.9 looks at this matter graphically. The initial curves of J and L intersect to give an initial equilibrium income of Y_0. The injections curve now shifts upwards to J', which yields a new equilibrium income of Y_1. The change in income from Y_0 to Y_1 is shown in the diagram as ΔY. The change in the injections that caused income to change is shown by ΔJ.

We already know that the multiplier is the ratio of the change in income to the change in injections that brought it about – i.e. $K = \Delta Y/\Delta J$. A look at Figure 30.9 reminds us of what we have already established: that the slope of the leakage function between Y_0 and Y_1 is $\Delta J/\Delta Y$. (This is because, to restore equilibrium, leakages must change by the same amount as did injections.) So the multiplier is the reciprocal of the slope of the leakage function.

We have already called this slope, $\Delta L/\Delta Y$, the marginal propensity to leak, MPL. So the multiplier is

$$K = 1/MPL. \qquad (1)$$

But we have already seen that, in our present model, the MPL is the sum of the MPS and the MPT. (This says nothing more than that the proportion of any income that leaks out of the system in total must be the sum of the proportions that leak out through the separate leakages caused by saving and taxes.) So we may also write the multiplier as:

$$K = 1/(MPS + MPT). \qquad (2)$$

The result in (1) is quite general and applies to any model of the type we are dealing with, no matter how many leakages are specified. The result in (2) is specific to this particular model, where there are only two leakages, S and T.

If all of this seems familiar stuff, it should be, because it is a repeat of the argument in Figure 29.5. The only difference is that, where we there spoke of investment and saving, we now speak of injections and leakages.

An Application

The above results may be used to throw light on one real-world issue. The fluctuations in income and employment since the Second World War have been much less in most countries than were the fluctuations before the First World War. (The period between the two wars was so disrupted that it is easier to leave it out of the comparison.) Many economists have wondered why this was so, and, during the 1950s and 1960s, many governments took credit for having brought about this greatly increased stability in their economies.

One important element in the explanation arises from what we have just established. After the Second World War, government expenditure grew to unprecedented heights in many countries, including the UK. To finance this expenditure, taxes also grew to take an unprecedented fraction of national income. Thus the marginal propensity to tax increased greatly. The theory we have just developed tells us that the multiplier would be reduced by this change. Thus, when the economy was hit by fluctuations in such injections as investment over which the government had no control, the induced changes in income and employment would also be correspondingly reduced. By lowering the value of the multiplier, the sheer increase in the importance of the government in the economy helped to reduce fluctuations in income and employment without any conscious stabilization policy on the government's part.

So an important contribution to the increased stability in many post-Second World War economies was the unplanned side-effect of the increased size of government taxes and expenditures. The consequent increase in the marginal propensity to tax reduced the values of each country's multiplier and so reduced the fluctuations in income and employment that accompanied shifts in expenditure functions.

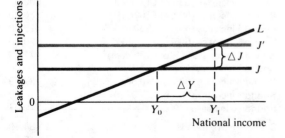

FIGURE 30.9   The Multiplier Once Again. The multiplier is the reciprocal of the slope of the leakages function

SUMMARY

1 To incorporate the government into the model of the determination of national income, allowance must be made for the effects of taxes and government exhaustive expenditures (as distinct from government transfers).

2 From the income–expenditure approach, government expenditures are an addition to the aggregate desired expenditure function, which becomes $E = C+I+G$. Taxes, which are for simplicity assumed to be only taxes on personal incomes, introduce a wedge between national income and disposable income. An increase in tax rates reduces household disposable income, and, with a given propensity to consume out of disposable income, the propensity to consume out of national income is reduced. Thus, an increase in tax rates shifts downwards the curve relating consumption expenditure to national income, while a decrease in tax rates shifts the curve upwards.

3 In the leakages–injections approach, government expenditure is an injection and taxes are a leakage.

4 Both approaches yield the key results that equilibrium national income is positively associated with government expenditure and negatively associated with tax rates.

5 In general, the multiplier is the reciprocal of the marginal propensity for expenditure to leak out of the circular flow: $1/MPL$. In the model without a government, this is $1/MPS$, but with a government it is $1/(MPS+MPT)$.

Income Fluctuations and Fiscal Policy

In the first half of this chapter we study the fluctuations in national income and employment that are known as the trade cycle. In the second half we consider how the government's fiscal policy can be used to offset some of these fluctuations.

TYPES OF FLUCTUATION

When national income, employment and other similar macroeconomic series are studied over time, a number of distinct variations can be disentangled.

Long-term Trend: The tendency for a series to change in the long term is called its secular or long-term trend. The long-term trend for income, output and employment has been upward over the last two centuries. Such upward trends are usually referred to as 'economic *growth*'.

Seasonal Variations: Many series show variations that take place within a single year. For example, retail sales tend to be high before and low after Christmas. Employment in construction tends to be relatively low during the winter months, when the weather impedes many outdoor construction jobs, compared to the rest of the year, when the weather is less of a hindrance.

The Trade Cycle: When both the long-term trend and seasonal variations have been accounted for, many economic series show further fluctuations of an up-and-down pattern. The most prominent of these fluctuations is called THE TRADE CYCLE or sometimes

THE BUSINESS CYCLE. Cycles lasting, on average, just under 10 years from peak to peak are clearly visible in the pre-1914 data for unemployment. More muted, and somewhat shorter, cycles in both output and employment are evident in the post-1945 data.

Stock Cycles: A shorter STOCK CYCLE of about 40 months' duration is sometimes observed. This cycle is associated with the alternating building up, and running down, of stocks held by firms. The desire to accumulate stocks raises the demand for output; the desire to reduce stocks lowers demand. The stock cycle is sometimes also called the *inventory cycle*, which is the American term for the same phenomenon.

Other Cycles: The Russian economist, Nikolai Kondratieff, thought he could identify long waves of 40 to 50 years associated with the introduction of major innovations. The existence of such long-wave cycles is highly controversial – although the depressed decade of the 1980s was 50 years after the depressed decade of the 1930s, which came 50 years after the depressed decade of the 1880s. Also, some economists have argued, as we shall see later in this chapter, that in many Western democracies there exists a political business cycle associated with the pattern of elections.

THE TRADE CYCLE

For the moment we concentrate on the trade cycle and start by considering its rich, and sometimes confusing, terminology.

The Terminology of the Trade Cycle

Although recurrent fluctuations in economic activity are neither smooth, nor follow a precise, regular pattern, a vocabulary has developed to denote their different stages. The two parts of Figure 31.1 show stylized cycles that will serve to illustrate some terms. Each diagram shows the economy's real GNP changing over time. The thick black curve shows the GNP at each point in time.

Part (i) shows the crudest distinction, that between boom and slump. When real GNP exceeds its *average performance*, we can talk of a boom; when real GNP falls short of its average performance, we can talk of a slump.

Part (ii) shows more detail and illustrates the more subtle vocabulary of cyclical fluctuations that is defined below.

Trough: The trough is, simply, the bottom. A trough is characterized by high unemployment of labour and low demand for final output. There is a substantial amount of unused capacity. Business profits are low or negative. Business confidence is lacking and, as a result, many firms are unwilling to risk new investments. If a trough is deep enough, it may be called a *depression*.

Expansion: The recovery of the economy out of a trough is called an expansion. One key influence is that the climate of business opinion swings from pessimism to optimism. The results of this change are many: worn-out machinery will be replaced; employment, income and consumer spending all begin to rise; investments that once seemed too risky may now be undertaken; as demand expands, production is expanded with relative ease merely by re-employing the existing unused capacity and unemployed labour. In the early stage, favourable business conditions and a good outlook for the future now encourage business activity.

Peak: The peak is simply the top. Sometimes the forces of expansion are weak and the peak occurs before GNP reaches its potential level. At other times the expansion is strong and GNP will reach or exceed its potential level at the peak.

When the peak is a high one, signs of 'overheating' may occur. Labour shortages may become severe, particularly in key skill categories; and shortages of raw materials may develop. Output cannot easily be increased because few resources remain unemployed. Output can be raised further only by means of investment that increases capacity. Because such investment takes time, further rises in demand are now met more by increases in prices than by increases in production. Costs rise, but prices rise also, and business remains generally profitable. Expectations of the future are favourable, and more investment may be made than is justified on the basis of current levels of prices and sales alone.

Recession: When the top of the peak is passed, the economy turns downward, into a period of recession or contraction. Demand falls off and, as a result, production and employment fall. As employment falls, so do household incomes; falling income causes demand to fall further. Profits drop, and many firms make losses. New investments that looked profitable on the expectation of continuously rising demand suddenly appear unprofitable. Investment plans are revised downward, and actual investment spending is reduced to a low level. It may not even be worth

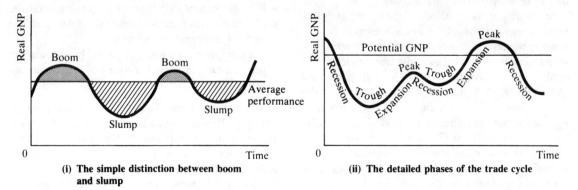

(i) **The simple distinction between boom and slump**

(ii) **The detailed phases of the trade cycle**

FIGURE 31.1 A Stylized Trade Cycle. While the phases of the trade cycle are described by a set of commonly used terms, no two cycles are exactly the same

replacing some capital goods as they wear out because unused capacity is increasing steadily.

Turning Points: The point at which a recession begins is called the *upper turning point*, while the *lower turning point* refers to the point at which a recovery begins.

Explanations of the Trade Cycle

Any explanation of the cycle needs to account for its two basic characteristics. First, there is the *cumulative* nature of economic activity: once started upwards, or downwards, the expansion, or contraction, tends to feed on itself. Second, there are the *turning points*: expansions eventually reverse themselves and become contractions; contractions eventually reverse themselves and become expansions. We shall consider these characteristics in turn.

Cumulative movements: the accelerator theory

An important explanation of the tendency of the economy to show periods of cumulative expansions and cumulative contractions is to be found in the combination of two forces: the multiplier, which we have already studied, and what is called the accelerator, which we must now study. To do this, we must look at the possibility that investment expenditure may be at least partially an induced (endogenous) expenditure rather than an autonomous (exogenous) expenditure, as we have regarded it so far.

Up to now, desired investment expenditure has been autonomous because it has not been related to national income. We are now going to consider a theory that makes investment an induced expenditure by relating it to national income.

Recall that gross investment has two components, replacement investment – what is needed to replace existing capital as it wears out – and net investment – investment to expand the productive capacity. According to the accelerator theory, usually just called THE ACCELERATOR, net investment is related to the *rate of change of national income*. When income is increasing, net investment is needed in order to increase the capacity to produce consumption goods; when income is falling, it may not even be necessary to replace old capital as it wears out, let alone to invest in net additions to the capital stock. Anything that changes the desired quantity of plant and machinery can generate investment ex-

penditure. The accelerator focuses on one such source of change, changing national income. This gives the accelerator its particular importance in connection with *fluctuations* in national income.

How the Accelerator Works: To see how the theory works, it is convenient to make the simplifying assumption that an industry has a particular capital stock needed to produce each given level of its output. (The ratio of the value of capital to the annual value of output is called the *capital/output ratio*.) Given this assumption, suppose that the industry is producing at capacity and that the demand for its output increases. If the industry is to produce the higher level of output, its capital stock must increase. This necessitates new investment.

Table 31.1 provides a simple numerical example of the accelerator. The table assumes that, in one particular industry, it takes £5 worth of capital to produce £1 of output per year. (This industry's capital/output ratio is 5.) The industry's sales, which are recorded in the second column of the table, are constant at first. Thus in years 1 and 2, there is no need for new investment. In year 3, however, a rise in sales of £1 requires investment of £5 to provide the needed capital stock. In year 4, a further rise in sales of £2 requires new investment of £10 to provide the needed new capital stock. When the increase in sales tapers off in years 7–9, investment declines. When, in year 10, sales no longer increase, new investment falls to zero because the capital stock of year 9 is adequate to provide output for year 10's sales. A comparison of columns (3) and (5) shows that the amount of new investment is proportional to the *change* in sales.

This example suggests three conclusions:

- Rising sales tend to induce investment expenditure.
- For investment to remain constant, sales must rise by a constant amount per year.
- The amount of new investment will be a multiple of the increase in sales because the capital/output ratio is greater than one.

The data in Table 31.1 were given for a single industry. If many industries behave in this way, aggregate new investment will bear a similar relation to changes in national income. This is what the accelerator theory tells us.

Note the difference in the influence of national income on consumption and on investment. According to the Keynesian theory of the consumption

**TABLE 31.1 An Illustration of the Accelerator
Theory of Investment**

(1) Year	(2) Annual output	(3) Change in output	(4) Required stock of capital, assuming a capital/output ratio of 5	(5) New investment: increase in the required capital stock
1	£10	£0	£50	£0
2	10	0	50	0
3	11	1	55	5
4	13	2	65	10
5	16	3	80	15
6	19	3	95	15
7	22	3	110	15
8	24	2	120	10
9	25	1	125	5
10	25	0	125	0

function, the amount of desired consumption depends on the size of national income. Thus the level of C is related to the level of Y. According to the accelerator theory, the level of desired investment expenditure is related to changes in national income.

Limitations of the Accelerator: The accelerator assumes that for each firm new investment is rigidly related to changes in sales (and thus, over the whole economy, to changes in national income). The actual relation is more subtle than that. Let us see why.

(1) Changes in sales thought to be temporary will not necessarily lead to new investment. It is usually possible to increase the level of output for a given capital stock by working overtime or extra shifts. This may be preferable to investing in new plant and equipment that would lie idle after a *temporary* spurt of demand had subsided. Thus *expectations* about whether changes in national income will be short-lived, or sustained, lead to a much less rigid response of new investment to changes in national income than the accelerator suggests.

(2) A further limitation of the accelerator is that it relates only to the investment in additional capacity that is similar to what is already in existence. It says nothing about the new types of investment needed to install new production processes, or to produce new products. Both of these types of investment may occur even though there is no increase in demand for existing products, the first because it helps to lower costs and the second because it helps to produce new products.

(3) The accelerator does not allow for the fact that investment in any period is likely to be limited by the capacity of the capital-goods industries, so that actual investment expenditure may fall short of desired investment as a result of capacity constraints in the capital-goods industries.

(4) It does not allow for the fact that the accelerator can have different values at different stages of the cycle. In slumps there is much excess capacity. A rise in demand may thus be met mainly by putting existing capital back to work and only slightly by adding to new capacity. In booms there is little excess capacity, and a rise in demand will have to be met mainly by increasing capacity, if it is to be met at all.

For these reasons, the accelerator does not, by itself, give anything like a complete explanation of variations in investment in plant and equipment. You should not be surprised, therefore, to learn that, taken rigidly on its own, the accelerator theory provides a relatively poor *overall* explanation of changes in investment. *Yet accelerator-like influences do exist and they do play a role in the variation of investment over the trade cycle.*

Cumulative movements: the multiplier-accelerator mechanism

The combination of the multiplier and accelerator-type influences can make upward or downward movements in the economy cumulative. We shall first illustrate this with an upward movement, and later show how the same process applies in reverse to downward movements.

Imagine that the economy is settled into a trough with heavy unemployment. Then, for some reason, a revival of investment demand occurs. Orders are placed for new plant and equipment, which creates new employment in the capital-goods industries. A multiplier process is now set up. The newly employed workers spend most of their earnings, and this creates new demand for consumer goods. The spending of the incomes newly created in the consumption-goods industries induces further increases in demand.

Once existing equipment is fully employed in any industry, extra output will require new capital equipment – and the accelerator theory takes over as an important determinant of investment expenditure. This investment will increase demand in the capital-goods sector of the economy. The resulting rise in expenditure creates new incomes in that sector, and the spending of this new income sets up further multiplier effects. So the process goes on, with the multiplier-accelerator mechanism continuing to produce a rapid rate of expansion.

Turning points

The combination of the multiplier and the accelerator, often referred to as the MULTIPLIER-ACCELERATOR THEORY, can also help to explain turning points.

Output 'Ceilings' and Upper Turning Points: A very rapid expansion out of a slump can continue for some time, but it cannot go on forever. A *ceiling* is something that restrains or halts the rise in output. The most important ceilings stem from supply limitations on the firm's inputs of labour and materials. For example, when the labour force is fully employed, firms cannot increase output simply by taking on previously unemployed workers.

At this point the accelerator again comes into play. A slowing down in the rate of increase of output leads to a decrease in the investment in new plant and equipment. To see this, look again at Table 31.1. Between rows 7, 8 and 9, output is still *increasing* but by ever smaller amounts. As a result of this *declining rate of increase*, the volume of new investment *decreases*. This decline in investment expenditure can cause a turning point to occur. After that, national income starts to fall.

Output 'Floors' and Lower Turning Points: A contraction, too, is eventually brought to an end. Anything that restrains the fall in output is called a *floor*. Let us see some of the main reasons why such floors exist.

First, as aggregate disposable income falls, households will spend a larger and larger fraction of their falling incomes. Second, government spending does not fall in proportion to the fall in government tax revenues. Government expenditures on most programmes will continue even if tax revenues sag to low levels. Third, even investment expenditures, in many ways the most easily postponed component of aggregate expenditure, will not fall to zero. Industries providing basic products such as food and clothing will still have substantial sales and will need to replace existing capital as it wears out. Even in a deep depression, the majority of people are still employed and they will buy new, attractive products if they come on the market. Furthermore, major new inven-

tions that reduce costs will be worth investing in as long as the cost reduction is large enough. Taken together, the minimum levels of consumption, investment and government expenditure will assure a minimum equilibrium level of national income that, although well below the full-employment level, will not be zero. There is a floor below which desired expenditure, and hence equilibrium national income, will not fall.

Sooner or later, an upturn will begin. If nothing else causes an expansion of business activity, there will eventually be a revival of replacement investment because, as existing capital wears out, the capital stock will eventually fall below the level required to produce current output. At this stage new machines will be bought to replace those that are worn out.

The rise in the level of activity in the capital-goods industries will then cause, by way of the multiplier, a further rise in income. Now the economy has turned the corner. An expansion, once started, will trigger the sort of cumulative upward movement already discussed.

Alternative Explanations of Turning Points: We have relied on floors and ceilings as an explanation of turning points. In fact, a large range of other factors can cause turning points to occur. A sudden change in businessmen's confidence about the future can do so. Falling confidence may lead to a fall in new investment, which causes the onset of a recession; rising confidence may lead to a rise in investment, which takes the economy through a lower turning point into a period of recovery. A sudden rise in costs for an important input such as oil, or for borrowed funds brought about by a rise in the interest rate, may lead to a fall in investment and an upper turning point. Reductions in input costs, and interest rates, have the opposite effect and can lead to a lower turning point. In the past, a financial panic brought on by a major bank failure has caused an upper turning point as sources of investment funds dried up.

Given the tendency of expansions or contractions to become cumulative once they have begun, any severe shock such as those that have been discussed above may be sufficient to cause the economy to turn from the expansion to contraction or vice versa. The fact that so many different shocks can do the job is one reason why different cycles have different durations.

Conclusion

Economists once argued long and bitterly about the best explanation of the recurrent cyclical behaviour of the economy. Today most economists agree that there is no single cause of trade cycles.

In an economy that has tendencies for both cumulative and self-reversing behaviour, any large shock, whether from without or within, can initiate a cyclical swing. The list of possible disturbances is long. Indeed the characteristic cyclical pattern involves many outside shocks that sometimes initiate, sometimes reinforce and sometimes dampen the cumulative tendencies that exist within the economy.

Cycles vary for other reasons as well. In some, full employment of labour may be the bottleneck that determines the peak. In others, high interest rates and shortages of investment funds may nip an expansion and turn it into a recession at the same time that the unemployment of labour is still an acute problem. In some cycles, the recession phase is short; in others, a full-scale period of slump sets in. In some cycles, the peak develops into a severe inflation; in others, the pressure of excess demand is hardly felt, and a new recession sets in before the economy has fully recovered from the last trough. Some cycles are of long duration; others are very short.

We have suggested reasons why an economy that is subjected to periodic shifts in aggregate expenditure will tend to generate fluctuations as cumulative forces first come into play, to be followed by self-reversing influences. In the next section, we study how governments seek to influence the cycle and remove some of its extreme fluctuations through the use of fiscal policy. As a preliminary to this study, you must reread pages 307–10 of Chapter 26 now. That earlier section discusses the broad macroeconomic goals of government policy.

FISCAL POLICY

Not so many years ago, it was generally accepted that a prudent government should always balance its budget. The argument was based on an analogy with what seems prudent behaviour for the household. It is a foolish household whose current expenditure consistently exceeds its current revenue so that it goes steadily further into debt. It was then argued that if avoiding a steadily rising debt is good for the individual, it must also be good for the nation.

But the paradox of thrift, discussed in Chapter 29, suggests that the analogy between the nation and the household may be misleading. When a government follows a balanced budget policy, as most governments tried to do even during the Great Depression of the 1930s, it must restrict its expenditure during a recession because its tax revenues will necessarily be falling. During a recovery, when its revenue is high and rising, it will increase its spending. In other words, it will roll with the economy, raising and lowering its expenditure in step with everyone else, thus helping to accentuate cyclical fluctuations in expenditure.

By the end of the 1930s, largely because of the lead taken by Keynes, many economists had concluded that the government could stabilize the economy by doing just the opposite of what everyone else was doing – by increasing its demand when private demand was falling, and lowering its demand when private demand was rising. This policy, which came to be known as Keynesian fiscal policy, sought to stabilize aggregate demand, even though its individual components were fluctuating.

When Milton Friedman – American Nobel Prize winner and leader of a group of economists called Monetarists – said in 1960, 'We are all Keynesians now,' he was referring to the general acceptance of the view that the government's budget is much more than just the revenue and expenditure statement of a very large organization. Whether we like it or not, the sheer size of the government inevitably makes its budget a powerful tool for influencing the economy.

In the rest of this chapter, we are going to look at the use of fiscal policy to influence the behaviour of national income and employment. But first, we must look at three important concepts – the deflationary gap, the recessionary gap and the inflationary gap.

Three Gaps

Figure 31.2 shows the economy in two alternate situations. In both cases potential, or full-employment, national income is indicated by Y_F. In part (i) of the Figure, where the desired expenditure function intersects the 45° line to produce an equilibrium income of Y_1 that falls short of the economy's potential income, the economy is in a period of slump. In part (ii), where the desired expenditure function intersects the 45° line at a level of income, Y_2, that is greater than potential income, the economy is in a period of boom.

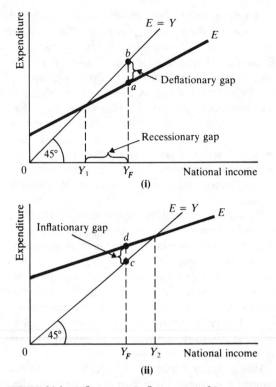

FIGURE 31.2   **Inflationary, Deflationary and Recessionary Gaps.** The recessionary gap is the horizontal distance between equilibrium income and potential income; the inflationary and deflationary gaps are the vertical distances between the desired expenditure and the 45° line at potential income

Part (i) illustrates two important concepts. The DEFLATIONARY GAP is the amount by which aggregate desired expenditure would fall short of income *if* full-employment income were achieved. It is thus the amount by which the expenditure function would have to shift upwards if equilibrium income were to coincide with full-employment income. This gap is indicated on the Figure by the vertical distance, *ab*, between the E curve and the 45° line at full-employment income, Y_F.

The second gap can also be seen in part (i) of the Figure. It is the RECESSIONARY GAP, defined as the difference between full-employment national income and actual national income. This is shown as the horizontal distance between Y_F and Y_1. The recessionary gap is a measure of the output that is lost when actual national income falls short of potential income. The recessionary gap is sometimes also called the *GNP gap*.

Notice that the deflationary gap measures the *cause*

of the economy's unsatisfactory performance, the amount by which aggregate expenditure falls short of what is needed to produce full-employment income. The recessionary gap measures the *consequence* of this shortfall, the amount by which equilibrium income falls short of potential, or full-employment, income.

Now consider part (ii) of the Figure. The difference between parts (i) and (ii) lies in the position of the aggregate expenditure function. In part (i) the E curve intersects the 45° line to produce an equilibrium income, Y_1, that is below potential income. In part (ii), the E curve intersects the 45° line to produce an equilibrium income, Y_2, that is above potential income. The resulting gap is called the INFLATIONARY GAP. It is defined as the amount by which aggregate desired expenditure exceeds income *at potential income*. In the Figure, it is shown as the vertical distance, *cd*, between the 45° line and the E line at Y_F. The inflationary gap is the amount by which the aggregate expenditure line would have to shift downwards if equilibrium income were to equal potential income.

In part (ii), we do not define a horizontal gap between actual and potential income, as we did in part (i) of the Figure. The reason is that the national income, Y_2, *cannot* actually be achieved, since to produce that much real output would require more resources than the nation has available. Thus, if the economy's curves are those shown in part (ii), actual real income will be held at Y_F by the unavailability of the resources needed to produce further output. The economy is thus in a situation of *disequilibrium*, and the inflationary gap measures the amount by which desired expenditure exceeds actual output at the existing level of income, Y_F. In other words, this gap is a measure of the amount of aggregate *excess demand*.

In this situation, demand will exceed supply in most of the economy's individual markets and prices will be rising as a result. If most individual prices are rising, the average of all prices – i.e. the general price level – will also be rising. Hence the term inflationary gap is a good one. Inflations associated with inflationary gaps are often called *demand inflations*, which means a rise in the general price level caused by the existence of general excess demand.

The Government's Budget

If the government is to vary its spending and taxing policies with a view to reducing inflationary or deflationary gaps, it must be willing to let the balance between these two change as necessary. To see what is involved, we look first at the budget balance. The government's BUDGET BALANCE is the difference between all of its current receipts and all of its current disbursements.

$$\text{The budget balance} = \begin{array}{l}\text{Government current}\\ \text{receipts} - \text{Government}\\ \text{current disbursements}\end{array}$$

The government's CURRENT RECEIPTS are everything that it takes in from taxes, and from revenues earned on anything that it sells. They do not, however, include funds that are raised through borrowing. The government's CURRENT OUTLAYS include all the funds that it spends, both for exhaustive and transfer expenditures.

If this balance is positive, we say that the budget is in surplus. If this balance is negative, we say that the budget is in deficit. If receipts are exactly equal to disbursements, we say that the budget is in balance, and we speak of a balanced budget.

Every year in the spring the Chancellor of the Exchequer introduces a Budget for the following year. (These days there is usually a supplementary 'Mini-Budget' in the autumn.) The government is concerned with how much revenue it expects to receive and how much money it expects to pay out, and with the expected balance between the two. Notice that, since they refer to the coming year, all of these figures are based on estimates. Not surprisingly, these estimates are subject to errors, which are often quite large.[1]

The debt implications of the budget balance

Now let us consider the influence that the current budget balance has on the national debt, i.e. on the total amount of debt accumulated by the government. New borrowing adds to the national debt, while the paying off of old borrowing reduces the national debt.

---

[1] There is an interesting point here relating to errors on the difference between two estimated magnitudes. Let us say that revenues are estimated at £1,000 and expenditures at £1,100, giving a deficit of £100. Estimating any magnitude with a 5 per cent error is quite a good result. But this can lead to much larger percentage errors on the budget balance. If revenues turn out to be 5 per cent lower than estimated, and expenditures 5 per cent more, the figures will be £950 and £1,205. This makes the balance between the two £255, which is over *twice* as much as the original estimate of £100, even though each side of the balance – revenues and expenditures – had only a 5 per cent error.

A Deficit: If the government's budget is in deficit, the shortfall must be made up by borrowing funds. Thus a deficit is matched by an equivalent amount of government borrowing. This new borrowing adds to the country's national debt.

The government may borrow funds from two main sources. First, it may borrow from the private sector. Both households and banks lend money to the government by buying government bills and bonds. Second, the government may borrow money from the central bank, the Bank of England. The financial implications of borrowing from these two main sources are quite different. We shall study these in detail in later chapters when we discuss the country's financial institutions.

A Surplus: In the opposite case, the government has a budget surplus, its receipts exceed its disbursements. Surplus is used to pay off some existing debt and, thus, to reduce the size of the national debt.[1]

The public-sector borrowing requirement

In the latter part of the 1970s, it was realized that the fiscal influence of the government spreads beyond the confines of its own budget. Public-sector spending includes not only the spending of the central government, but also that of local authorities, and the nationalized industries. A significant proportion of British industrial output was in the hands of nationalized industries (though the proportion was reduced by the privatization movement of the 1980s). Nationalized industries often borrow large sums, both for programmes of capital expansion and also to meet deficits of their current expenditures over their current revenues. The government is ultimately responsible for such debts, since it owns these industries.

To assess the total impact of government fiscal activities through government revenues and expenditures, as well as through the nationalized industries, the practice grew up of looking at the budget balance of the whole public sector. This 'public sector' is the government at the national and local level, plus the nationalized industries. The balance between current receipts and current disbursements over the whole public sector is called the

---

[1] A surplus necessarily reduces the net national debt whether the government uses it to pay off debt, which it usually does, or to invest in other assets, which it usually does not do.

PUBLIC-SECTOR BORROWING REQUIREMENT (the PSBR). This is nothing more than the government's budget balance that we discussed above, where the concept of the government is extended to include all levels of government and their nationalized commercial enterprises.

The Goals of Fiscal Policy

From 1945 to the mid-1970s, all UK governments took the suppression of substantial inflationary and deflationary gaps as major objectives of policy. Preventing deflationary gaps was designed to keep the economy operating at close to full employment. Preventing inflationary gaps was designed to prevent the outbreak of demand inflations.

Such a policy is called STABILIZATION POLICY, for the obvious reason that it attempts to stabilize the aggregate expenditure function at levels that would not give rise to large deflationary or inflationary gaps. The policy is also called DEMAND MANAGEMENT, since it seeks to manage the total demand for output – i.e. aggregate desired expenditure.

In this chapter we study how demand management works through fiscal policy. A second tool of demand management, called monetary policy, is studied in a later chapter.

Eliminating fixed gaps

A relatively easy problem faces the makers of fiscal policy when private-sector expenditure functions for consumption and investment are *given and unchanging*. What is needed in such circumstances is a once-and-for-all fiscal change to remove any inflationary or deflationary gaps. The policies are shown in the two parts of Figure 31.3.

In part (i), the expenditure function is E', yielding the equilibrium level of national income Y_1. Thus the economy is currently operating at less than full employment, with a deflationary gap of $Y_F - Y_1$, and a deflationary gap which is shown by the vertical distance between the E curve and the 45° line at Y_F. A policy that shifts the aggregate expenditure curve upwards to E, so that it intersects the 45° line at Y_F, will remove the deflationary gap, returning the economy to full employment. We saw in Chapter 30 that a shift of the desired expenditure function, such as the one from E' to E, can be achieved by a cut in tax rates or by an increase in government expenditure.

In part (ii) of the Figure, the aggregate expenditure

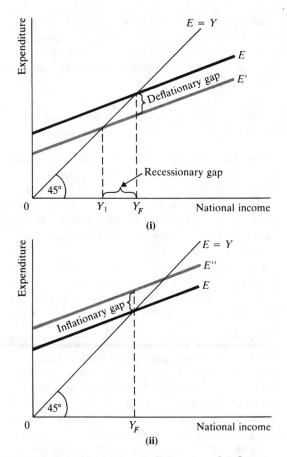

FIGURE 31.3   **Eliminating Deflationary and Inflationary Gaps.** A deflationary gap can be removed by fiscal policy that shifts the desired expenditure function upwards; an inflationary gap can be removed by fiscal policy that shifts the desired expenditure function downwards

curve is E''. National income is at its potential level, Y_F, and there is an inflationary gap, shown by the vertical distance between the aggregate expenditure curve and the 45° line at Y_F. A policy that shifts the aggregate expenditure curve from E'' to E, so that it intersects the 45° line at Y_F, will remove the inflationary gap without reducing national income below its potential level. We saw in Chapter 30 that the shift of the aggregate expenditure line from E'' to E can be accomplished by an increase in tax rates or by a decrease in government expenditure.

Eliminating variable gaps

So far, we have seen how the government can eliminate a given inflationary or deflationary gap. In this case, the government could identify a *stable* inflationary or deflationary gap and take steps to eliminate it for *once and for all*. Unfortunately, the more or less *continual shifts* in private expenditure functions that occur in reality make stabilization policy much more difficult than it would be if stable gaps were all that had to be dealt with. What can the government reasonably hope to achieve when private-sector expenditure functions are continually shifting?

Fine-tuning

The policy that was popular over the first two and a half decades following 1945 is called FINE-TUNING – which means trying to adjust fiscal policy so as to offset every fluctuation in the desired expenditure function.

In this case, fiscal policy must be altered continuously in an effort to stabilize national income at its potential level. The 1950s and the 1960s were a period of optimism about a fine-tuning-through-stabilization policy. Fiscal policy was to be altered frequently, and by relatively small amounts, to hold national income close to its potential or full-employment level. Careful assessment of the results of fiscal stabilization policies in the 1950s and 1960s have shown that its successes, if any, fell far short of what was hoped. The basic reasons lay in the complexity of any economy and the time-lags with which policy has to operate.

Complexity: Economists, and policy-makers, can usually identify broad and persistent trends. They do not, however, have detailed knowledge at any moment in time of all the forces that are operating to cause changes in the immediate future, nor of all the short-term effects of small changes in the various government expenditures and tax rates.

The economy is a very complex mechanism. Economists know quite a bit about what makes it work, and how it reacts to policy changes. But they do not know everything. Because of this complexity, economists are better at predicting long-term trends – caused or influenced by strong and persistent forces – than they are at predicting turning points, especially short-term twists and turns resulting from minor, often transient, forces. This makes fine-tuning difficult because the effects of small, short-lasting changes in fiscal policy are much less certain than the effects of major, and long-lasting, changes.

Time-Lags: Time-lags pervade all aspects of economic policy. Even our understanding of the economy's current position is subject to time-lags. Lags are of various sorts, as we shall see below.

Lags in Knowledge: By the nature of economic statistics, policy-makers only know where the economy was at some point in the past when the statistics were collected. Some statistics are reported with only a short lag, others with lags of many, many months. So policy-makers are in the position of a car driver whose only vision is through his rear-view mirror – he only knows where he was in the past, not where he is at present, let alone where he will be in the future. To compensate somewhat for this disadvantage, economists are able to make use of *leading indicators*. These are particular variables which tend to change ahead of most other variables and hence give advance notice of where the whole economy is going.[1]

Lags in Policy: Any policy change takes time to make its effects felt. This can mean that changes designed to remove one gap finally take effect when the economy is suffering from the opposite gap. For example, the building of a new motorway, decided on as an expansionary measure to remove a deflationary gap, may not get into full swing for several years. By the time it does, private expenditure may have recovered to such an extent that the economy's current problem is an inflationary, rather than a deflationary, gap. In this case, the 'stabilization policy' will actually destabilize the economy by increasing, rather than decreasing, the gap from which it is currently suffering.

Of course, if the fluctuations in the economy were perfectly regular, and fully known, the lags could be allowed for without further problems. We have already observed, however, that no two cycles are the same. Thus there is always the danger that either a contractionary or an expansionary fiscal policy, that looked stabilizing when initiated, will be destabilizing when it takes effect, because the economy will have unexpectedly gone through a turning point.

The conclusion to be drawn from the research in several countries is that efforts at fine-turning often have done as much to encourage minor fluctuations

---

1 Further discussion of leading indicators can be found in Harbury and Lipsey, Chapter 9.

in the economy as to remove them. In other words, they have often been destabilizing. As a result of such experience, few economists any longer believe that, given the present state of knowledge, fiscal policy can fine tune the economy to hold it at, or very near to, its full-employment level, preventing the emergence of either inflationary or recessionary gaps.

A Policy-Induced Cycle

The critics of fine-tuning have sometimes suggested that governments have deliberately used fiscal policy for political ends, and that this has had the effect of creating cyclical fluctuations rather than eliminating them. Why should the government cause such potentially disturbing expenditure shifts?

A Political Trade Cycle: Early in the development of the Keynesian theory of stabilization policy, the Polish-born economist Michael Kalecki warned that, once governments had learned to manipulate aggregate demand, they might engineer an election-geared business cycle. In pre-election periods they would raise spending and cut taxes. The resulting expansionary pressures would create rising output and employment that would cause voters to support the government. But the inflationary gap that would ensue would lead to a rising price level. So, after the election was won, the government would depress demand. This would remove the inflationary gap and also provide some slack for expansion before the next election.

This theory invokes the image of a cynical government manipulating employment and national income solely because it wants to stay in office. Few people believe that governments do this all the time, but the temptation to do it some of the time, particularly before elections, may prove irresistible.[1]

A Stop-Go Cycle: One variant of the policy-induced cycle does not require a cynical government and an easily duped electorate. Instead, both sides need only be rather shortsighted. This is the theory of the STOP-GO CYCLE.

In this theory, when there is a recession and relatively stable prices, the public and the government identify unemployment as the primary economic problem. The government then introduces an expansionary fiscal policy through some combination of tax cuts and spending increases. This, plus such natural cumulative forces as the multiplier-accelerator, expands economic activity. Unemployment falls, but, once an inflationary gap develops, the price level begins to rise.

At this point, the unemployment problem is declared cured. Now inflation is seen as the nation's number one economic problem. A contractionary policy is then introduced. The natural cumulative forces again take over, causing a recession. The inflation subsides but unemployment rises, setting the stage once again for an expansionary policy to reduce unemployment.

Many economists have criticized British government policy over the last few decades as sometimes causing fluctuations by alternately pushing expansion to cure unemployment and then contraction to cure inflation.[1]

Discretionary and Automatic Policies

So far, we have been speaking of deliberate government attempts to remove gaps by altering expenditures or taxes. Such policies are called *discretionary policies*. The government identifies a gap and then makes a conscious decision to alter its policies in an effort to reduce the gap. Discretionary stabilization policy is subject to all of the problems we have just discussed.

Stabilizers

Fortunately, the government's stabilization policy is made much easier than it otherwise would be by the presence of what are called AUTOMATIC, or BUILT-IN, STABILIZERS: 'automatic tools' of fiscal policy which influence government spending or tax yields without the need for the conscious exercise of government discretion. For example, if a recessionary gap opens up, a stabilizer may *automatically* increase government expenditure or reduce tax revenues and so help to reduce the gap.

---

1 In the American system, where elections occur on a fixed timetable, the temptation to manipulate booms to coincide with elections is particularly great. In British and European systems, where the timing of elections is at the discretion of the government in power, there is a tendency to manipulate elections to coincide with naturally occurring booms, giving rise to the possibility of an 'economic election' cycle.

---

1 In the UK, the stop-go cycle was also associated, in the past, with balance-of-payments problems in ways that we will study in Chapter 44.

In general, a built-in stabilizer may be regarded as anything that reduces the value of the multiplier. We have already observed that private expenditure functions shift frequently. Any shift in a private expenditure function has its effects on income and employment magnified through the successive rounds of expenditure, that are induced by the initial change, and whose full effects are summarized by the value of the multiplier. For example, fluctuations in investment expenditure of £1,000m around its average value will lead to fluctuations in national income of £5,000m around its average value when the multiplier is 5, but of only £2,000m when the multiplier is 2.

Thus, anything that reduces the value of the multiplier lessens the magnitude of the fluctuations in national income that are caused by shifts in autonomous expenditure. Most importantly, they do so without the government's having to react consciously to each change in private-sector spending as it occurs.

Note that the government may make a conscious decision to introduce some built-in stabilizer. The important point, however, is that, once put in place, the stabilizer adjusts government expenditures or tax revenues automatically as inflationary or deflationary gaps emerge.

The two principal built-in stabilizers are tax revenues and government transfer payments.

Taxes: Tax revenues are a leakage from the circular flow. Revenues that vary directly with income cause leakages to increase as income rises and to decrease as income falls; this dampens the fluctuations in income that are caused by fluctuations in autonomous expenditure. (On page 367 we saw that the higher the marginal propensity to tax, the lower the multiplier.) Progressive income taxes have a stronger dampening effect on fluctuations than do proportional taxes. They cause the *proportion* of income leaking out of the flow to rise as income rises and to fall as income falls.

Government Transfer Payments: Although transfer payments are not themselves a part of current national income, they do enter into households' disposable income and hence they affect current consumption expenditure. Many government transfer payments act as built-in stabilizers. They do so by stabilizing disposable income in the face of fluctuations in national income.

Unemployment and supplementary benefits are the main transfer payments that have this effect. If there were no such benefits, then every fall of £1 in after-tax wage income earned through work would mean a fall of £1 in disposable income. But because of transfer payments, people who become unemployed, and hence lose their wage income, find that their disposable incomes, and hence their ability to spend on consumption, is to some extent maintained. If, for example, a rise in unemployment causes the after-tax earnings of labour to fall by £1,000m, but unemployment and other social security benefits give £600m to the newly unemployed, then disposable income only falls by £400m.

The reverse effect occurs in booms. When income and employment rise, people are put back to work. If they had received no disposable income prior to going to work, their incomes and expenditures would rise greatly. Instead, however, their incomes only rise by the difference between their previous transfer payments and their new wage incomes. Their consumption expenditures will then only rise by a correspondingly smaller amount.

Because of transfer payments, variations in national income cause smaller variations in disposable income than in factor income earned from employment. As a result, fluctuations in consumption expenditure are correspondingly reduced.

Discretionary fiscal policy once again

Built-in stabilizers do an important job in reducing fluctuations in income and employment. Such stabilizers, however, cannot be expected to eliminate all fluctuations in income and employment. They work by producing stabilizing tax and expenditure reactions to changes in income that have already occurred. For example, until people become unemployed they cannot receive unemployment benefits. So this stabilizer, like all others, is only activated by a change in income and employment.

Short-term fluctuations that are not removed automatically by built-in stabilizers cannot, given present knowledge, be consciously removed by fine tuning the economy. However, larger and more persistent gaps sometimes occur. For example, there was a severe inflationary gap throughout much of the 1970s, and a severe deflationary gap throughout the first half of the 1980s.

Gaps such as these persist long enough for their major causes to be studied and understood, and for fiscal remedies to be fully planned and executed.

Many economists who do not believe in fine-tuning do feel that fiscal policy can aid in removing such persistent gaps. Others believe that, even with persistent gaps, the risks that fiscal policy will destabilize the economy are still too large to be worth taking. They would have the government abandon stabilization policy altogether. Instead, the government would set its taxes and expenditures solely in relation to such long-term considerations as the desirable size of the public sector, and the need to obtain a satisfactory long-term balance between its revenues and expenditures.

Other stabilization policies

In this chapter we have dealt with two major tools of fiscal policy, personal income tax rates and government expenditures. In conclusion, we should note a few other points.

Any tax rate can be varied to alter equilibrium national income. For example, a rise in the VAT rates will increase the leakage between the expenditures of households and the receipts of firms. This will lower equilibrium national income. In the same way, a fall in the VAT rates will raise equilibrium income.

Hire-purchase regulations can also be altered. If the legally required initial payment is raised, people will be forced to postpone some of their purchases until they have saved the higher amount now required. This will cause a temporary downward shift in the consumption function and in equilibrium national income.

Also, direct controls can be exercised, particularly on capital expenditures. Any control that decreases investment expenditure lowers equilibrium national income.

Furthermore, fiscal measures are not the only tools of stabilization policy. As we shall see in later chapters, monetary policy may also be used to shift the aggregate expenditure function.

Why Not Full-Employment Policy Now?

During the first half of the 1980s, unemployment rose steadily in the UK, from under 7 per cent in 1980 to over 13 per cent in 1986. Furthermore, there are, as we shall see in Chapter 40, good reasons to believe that this was a serious understatement of the number of persons able and willing to work if jobs had been available. Why then did the government not adopt an expansionary fiscal policy to bring equilibrium national income at least closer to its full-employment level? No British government would have hesitated to do so at any time during the period from 1945 to 1975, if they had been faced with similar levels of unemployment.

If this seems a mystery – maybe even a perversion – to you now, it is an incentive to read on. We cannot properly analyse British economic policy in the 1980s until we have learned more about inflation, stagflation and the 'supply side' of the economy. At this point, however, the case appears simple. If we had already learned all there was to know about the economy, there would be no reason, other than perversity, why fiscal policy would not have been made more expansionary in the first half of the 1980s. After all, the theory we have developed so far predicts that this would have increased equilibrium national income, employment, output and living standards. Why then was such a policy not adopted? Have patience and we shall see.

SUMMARY

1 Many economic time series show seasonal variations, cyclical fluctuations and long-term trends.

2 Cyclical fluctuations in national income are called the trade cycle. The upper half of the trade cycle is called a boom and the lower half a slump. More specifically, the trade cycle runs from a trough, through a lower turning point, to a period of expansion, to a peak, through an upper turning point, to a period of contraction called a recession (or a depression if very severe), and back to a trough.

3 The key force in the cyclical behaviour of the economy is the tendency for self-reinforcing upward and downward movements. One explanation of these lies in the multiplier-accelerator process. The accelerator theory relates new investment to changes in national

income. It interacts with the multiplier process. For example, as income recovers from the trough, the rise in income encourages investment. The income generated by this new investment sets up rounds of multiplier-induced consumption expenditure which, in turn, cause new investment. Similar considerations relate to cumulative downswings.

4 The accelerator provides part of the explanation of investment expenditure. The accelerator is determined by the capital/output ratio (i.e. the required stock of capital per unit of output). It is incomplete, however, because (i) changes in sales that are thought to be temporary do not set off an accelerator increase in investment; (ii) it says nothing about investment needed to install new production processes or to produce new products; (iii) it does not allow for the fact that investment will be limited by the capacity of the capital-goods-producing industries to produce capital goods; (iv) it takes no account of any existing unused capacity in the industries whose sales rise; and (v) it does not account for replacement investment.

5 Stabilization policy refers to attempts by the government to iron out fluctuations in economic activity – stabilizing the rate of growth of national income, through the budget of the public sector (comprising the central government, the local authorities and the nationalized industries).

6 The excess of public-sector spending over its income is called the Public Sector Borrowing Requirement. A deficit (outlays exceed revenues) increases the size of the national debt, a surplus (revenues exceed outlays) reduces it.

7 When equilibrium national income is less than potential income, two gaps can be identified. The deflationary gap measures the amount by which aggregate desired expenditure falls short of income at potential income. It is the vertical distance from the E curve to the 45° line at Y_F. The recessionary gap measures the amount by which equilibrium income falls short of potential

income. It is the horizontal distance between equilibrium Y and Y_F. These are two ways of indicating the fact that aggregate desired expenditure is insufficient to ensure full employment. The elimination of one gap implies the elimination of the other.

8 An inflationary gap occurs when aggregate desired expenditure exceeds potential income. In the simple model of Part 4 of this book, actual income will equal potential income, and the gap will be the vertical distance from the 45° line to the E curve at Y_F.

9 A fixed recessionary gap may be removed by any appropriate combination of increased government expenditure and reduced tax rates. Inflationary gaps are removed by any appropriate combination of decreased government expenditure and increased tax rates.

10 In the real world, however, recessionary gaps are rarely, if ever, fixed. Expenditure functions shift frequently. This makes stabilization policy more difficult than if expenditure functions were stable. Fine-tuning the economy exactly to offset shifts in expenditure functions by discretionary fiscal changes is no longer regarded as possible, both because of the complexity of the economy and because of time-lags before policy changes take effect.

11 Cyclical fluctuations can be induced by fiscal policy. Two possibilities are the political trade cycle, where booms are generated before elections and restrained afterwards, and the stop-go cycle, where alternating concern with unemployment and inflation induce fiscal policies which result in alternating bouts of expansion and recession.

12 Automatic stabilizers exert contractionary pressure as national income rises, and expansionary pressure as national income falls. These help to stabilize the economy without the problems associated with discretionary changes in taxes or government expenditure.

Foreign Trade and National Income

So far we have studied the behaviour of equilibrium national income in a closed economy, one that does not engage in foreign trade. We must now extend our analysis to an open economy, one that does engage in foreign trade. You should now review pages 306–7 of Chapter 26 concerning the balance of payments and the exchange rate, since the terms defined there will be used throughout this chapter.

INTERNATIONAL PAYMENTS AND EXCHANGE RATES

Our first task is to consider how international payments are recorded in the 'payments accounts' and how they are effected through foreign-exchange markets.

The International Payments Accounts[1]

First, we examine in some detail the accounts that are used to keep track of international payments. In Chapter 28 we studied the national accounts that are used to record the nation's output, income and expenditure. The other major set of accounts that we must now study are the international payments accounts, which are also called the *balance of payments*. These accounts are a record of the payments made as a result of the international transactions of a country's residents. Table 32.1 shows the UK payments accounts for 1986. Note that the accounts are

---

1 For a more detailed discussion of the issues raised here, see Harbury and Lipsey, Chapter 7.

divided into three main categories, the current account, the capital account and the official financing account. We shall now study each of these in turn.

Current account

The CURRENT (or income) ACCOUNT records payments arising from trade in goods and services and from income in the form of interest, profits and dividends earned on capital owned in one country and invested in another. This account is divided into the two main sections that are discussed in the two following paragraphs.

The first of these two main sections is variously called the TRADE ACCOUNT, the VISIBLE ACCOUNT, or the MERCHANDISE ACCOUNT. It records payments and receipts arising from the import and export of tangible goods (as distinct from services) – e.g., computers, cars, wheat and shoes. British imports require the use of foreign exchange and, hence, are entered as debit items. British exports earn foreign exchange and, hence, are recorded as credit items on the visible account.

The second main section is called the INVISIBLE ACCOUNT or the SERVICE ACCOUNT. It records payments arising out of trade in services and payments for the use of capital. Trade in such services as insurance, shipping and tourism is entered in the invisible account, as are payments for capital – interest, dividends and profits – owned in one country but used in another. Those items that use foreign exchange, such as purchases by UK residents of foreign insurance or shipping services, travel abroad by UK residents, and payments to foreign residents of interest, dividends and profits earned in the UK, are entered as debit items. Those items that earn foreign

TABLE 32.1 Balance of Payments of the UK, 1986 (£ million)[1] (*Source: Annual Abstract of Statistics*)

Current Account	
Visibles:	
Exports	72,843
Imports	81,306
Balance of visibles	−8,463
Invisibles:	
Credits	76,188
Debits	68,581
Balance of invisibles	+7,607
Current account balance	−856
Capital Account	
Overseas investment in the UK:	
Direct	5,420
Portfolio	8,202
Bank	64,049
Other inflows (net)	14,230
UK investment overseas:	
Direct	11,386
Portfolio	22,870
Bank	53,898
Official Financing	
Reserves (increase)	2,891

exchange, such as foreign purchases of British insurance or shipping services, foreign travel in the UK, and payments to UK residents of interest, dividends and profits earned abroad, are entered as credit items. Beware of the common error of assuming that credit items are good and debit items are bad. No such judgement is implied.

Capital account

The second main division in the balance of payments is the CAPITAL ACCOUNT, which records transactions related to international movements of financial capital. In the UK accounts, the capital account is referred to as 'Investment and Other Capital Transactions'. All exports of capital from the UK are entered as debit items because they use foreign exchange; all imports of capital into the UK are entered as credit items because they earn foreign exchange.

It may seem odd that, while the export of a good is a credit item, the export of capital is a debit item. To see

---

1 The balance of payments does not balance exactly because of errors in certain reported totals.

that there is no contradiction in the treatment of goods and capital, consider the export of British funds to purchase a German bond. The capital transaction involves the purchase, and hence the *import*, of the German bond, and this has the same effect on the balance of payments as the purchase, and hence the import, of a German good. Both items involve payments to foreigners and both use foreign exchange. They are thus debit items in the UK's balance of payments.

The capital account often distinguishes between movements of short-term and of long-term capital. Short-term capital is money held in the form of highly liquid assets, such as bank accounts and short-term Treasury Bills. If a non-resident merchant buys sterling and places it in a deposit account in London, this represents an inflow of short-term capital into the UK, and it will be recorded as a credit item on short-term capital account. Long-term capital represents funds coming into the UK (a credit item) or leaving the UK (a debit item) to be invested in less liquid assets such as long-term bonds or physical capital such as a new car-assembly plant.

The two major subdivisions of the long-term part of the capital accounts are direct investment and portfolio investment. *Direct investment* is the item in the balance-of-payments accounts that records changes in non-resident ownership of domestic firms and in resident ownership of foreign firms. Thus direct investment in the UK is capital investment in a branch plant or subsidiary corporation in the UK in which the investor has voting control. Alternatively, it may be in the form of a takeover in which a controlling interest is acquired in a firm previously controlled by residents. *Portfolio investment*, on the other hand, is investment in securities or a minority holding of shares that does not involve legal control.

Official financing account

The final section in the balance-of-payments account is called the OFFICIAL FINANCING ACCOUNT, and it covers transactions in the *official reserves* held by the country's central bank in the form of gold, in foreign exchange – claims on various major foreign currencies, in particular the US dollar – and an international currency called SDR (which we study in Chapter 43).

The Bank of England, operating on behalf of the government, has one of its functions to intervene in the market for foreign exchange to influence the sterling exchange rate. If, for example, the Bank intervenes to prevent the price of sterling from falling, it must buy sterling. This means it must sell gold or foreign exchange. It can only do so if it holds reserves of these media. When the Bank wishes to stop sterling from rising in value, it enters the market and sells sterling. In this case, the Bank buys foreign exchange which it adds to its reserves.

The Balance of International Payments

We have seen that the trade statistics show the total of receipts of foreign exchange (called credit items) and payments of foreign exchange (called debit items) on account of each category of payment. It is also common to calculate the *balance* on separate items or groups of items. The balance of payments on particular parts of the payments account refers to the difference between the credit and the debit items on that part of the account. As a carry-over from a long-discredited eighteenth-century economic doctrine called Mercantilism, a credit balance on current account – receipts exceed payments – is called a FAVOURABLE BALANCE, while a debit balance – payments exceed receipts – is called an UNFAVOURABLE BALANCE. For the moment, all you need to do is to note these terms. Later on we will see why 'favourable' and 'unfavourable' are inappropriate descriptions for these balances.

The concept of the balance of payments is used in different ways. These can be confusing, so we must approach this issue in several steps.

Desired and Actual Payments: Notice that the trade statistics and the balance-of-payments accounts record *actual* payments, not *desired* payments. At some exchange rate between sterling and yen, for example, it is quite possible for holders of yen to want to purchase more sterling in exchange for yen than holders of sterling want to sell in exchange for yen. In this situation, the quantity of sterling demanded exceeds the quantity supplied. But holders of yen cannot actually buy more sterling than holders of sterling actually sell; every yen that is bought must have been sold by someone, and every pound sterling that is sold must have been bought by someone.

The balance of payments must balance

It follows from what we have just said that the total receipts of foreign exchange arising from current-account transactions, capital-account transactions and the Bank of England's official settlements must be exactly equal to the total payments of foreign exchange arising from current-account transactions, capital-account transactions and the Bank of England's official settlements. Since the value of all payments must equal the value of all receipts, the balance of payments minus receipts must be zero.

This relation is so important that it is worth going to the trouble of working it out symbolically. We let C, K and F stand for current account, capital account and official financing account, and use a subscript P for payments (a debit item) and R for receipts (a credit item). Now we can write

$$C_R + K_R + F_R \equiv C_P + K_P + F_P. \qquad (1)$$

This says, what we have already argued, that if we add up across all transactions, they must balance in total.

Although this is necessarily true, it often worries students who feel that it need not be so. To help to clarify the issue, let us consider an alleged exception.

Say that the sole international transaction by a small country called Myopia was an export to the UK of Myopian coconuts worth £1,000 sterling. The Myopian central bank issues its local currency, the stigma, but does not operate in the foreign-exchange market, so there is no official financing, and this year its self-sufficient inhabitants want no imports. Surely, then, you might (wrongly) think, Myopia has an overall favourable balance of £1,000, which is a current-account receipt (C_R) with no balancing item on the payments side? To see why this is wrong, we must ask what the exporter of coconuts did with the sterling he received for his coconuts. Say he deposited it in a London bank. This transaction represents a capital export from Myopia. Myopians have accumulated claims to foreign exchange which they hold in the form of a deposit with a London bank. Thus there are two entries in the Myopian accounts – one a credit item for the export of coconuts (C_R = £1,000) and the other a debit item for the export of capital (K_P = £1,000). The fact that the same firm made both transactions is irrelevant. Although the current account is in credit, the capital account must exactly balance this. Hence, looking at the *balance of payments as a whole*, the two sides of the account are equal. The balance of payments has balanced – as it always must do.

Consider now a slightly more realistic case which would arise if the coconut exporter wants to turn his

£1,000 into Myopian stigmas so that he can pay his coconut pickers in local currency. To do this, he must find someone who wishes to buy his sterling in return for Myopian currency. But we have assumed that no one in Myopia wants to import, so there is no one wanting to sell him Myopian currency for current-account reasons. Assume, however, that a wealthy Myopian landowner would like to invest £1,000 in London by buying shares giving him ownership of a British firm. To do so, he needs £1,000, which he gets from the exporter. The coconut exporter sells his £1,000 to the landowner in return for stigmas. Now he can pay his local bills. The landowner sells stigmas to the exporter and takes sterling in return. Now he can buy his British shares.

Once again the Myopian balance-of-payments figures will show two entries, equal in size but opposite in sign. There will be a credit item for the export of coconuts (the sale of coconuts earned foreign exchange) and a debit item for the export of capital (the purchase of British pounds used foreign exchange).

Payments on parts of the accounts do not need to balance

Although the overall set of payments must equal the overall set of receipts, this does not have to be true on sections of accounts. We now look at such balances, first in relation to particular countries and then in relation to particular sectors of the account.

Country Balances: In the above example, Myopia had what is called a bilateral payments balance with the UK, which means that its payments to, and receipts from, the UK were equal. In general, the *bilateral balance of payments* between any two countries is the balance between the payments and receipts flowing between the two countries. If there were only two countries in the world, their payments would have to be in bilateral balance. But this is not true when there are more than two.

Suppose that next year Myopia again sells £1,000 worth of coconuts to the UK, that the landowner does not wish to invest further in the UK, but that the Myopian people wish to buy 10,000 yen's worth of parasols from Japan. (Assume also that on the foreign-exchange market £1 trades for 10 yen.) Finally, assume that a Japanese importer wishes to buy £1,000 worth of singles recordings from a London record company.

Now what in effect happens is that the Myopian coconut exporter sells his £1,000 to the Japanese record importer for 10,000 yen, which the coconut dealer then sells to the Myopian parasol importer in return for Myopian stigmas. (In the real world the exchanges are all done through banks, but the above is what happens in effect.) Now the Myopian payments statistics will show a £1,000 bilateral payments surplus with the UK – receipts of £1,000 from the UK, and no payments to the UK – and a 10,000 yen (which is equal to £1,000) bilateral deficit with Japan – £1,000 of payments to Japan, and no receipts from Japan. But when all countries are considered, Myopia's multilateral payments are in balance.

In general, the MULTILATERAL BALANCE OF PAYMENTS refers to the balance between one country's payments to, and receipts from, the rest of the world. It follows from what we have said earlier that, when all items are considered, every country must have a zero multilateral payments balance with the rest of the world – although, as the Myopian example has just illustrated, it can have bilateral surpluses or deficits with individual countries.

Sectoral Balances: Let us now look at the balance of payments on individual sectors of the payments accounts.

The *balance* on visible account refers to the difference between the value of UK exports of goods and the value of imports of goods. A surplus, or 'favourable balance', occurs when exports of goods exceed imports of goods, while a deficit, or 'unfavourable balance', occurs when imports exceed exports. The balance on invisibles refers to the difference between the value of receipts on invisibles and the value of payments for invisibles.

The balance of payments on current account is the sum of the balances on the visible and invisible accounts. It gives the balance between payments and receipts on all income-related items.

The balance on capital account gives the difference between receipts of foreign exchange and payments of foreign exchange arising out of capital movements. A surplus, or 'favourable' balance on capital account, means that a country is a *net* importer of capital, while a deficit, or 'unfavourable' balance, means that the country is a *net* exporter of capital.

Notice that a deficit on capital account merely indicates that a country is investing abroad. For a rich country to invest abroad and accumulate assets that will earn income in the future may be a very desirable situation. So once again we observe that there is nothing necessarily unfavourable about having an 'unfavourable' balance on any of the payments accounts.

A credit balance on official settlements account means that the Bank of England has bought more gold and foreign exchange than it has sold. This adds to its reserves of foreign exchange. A deficit balance means that the Bank has sold more gold and foreign exchange than it has bought. This reduces its foreign exchange reserves.

The relation between various balances

Since payments must balance on an overall basis, it is clear that when the phrase a balance of payments 'deficit', or 'surplus', is being discussed, it must be the balance on some part of the payments account that is being discussed. Note, too, that, because of the necessity for the balance of payments to balance overall, a deficit or surplus on one *part* of the accounts implies an offsetting surplus or deficit on *the rest* of the accounts. Two particular relations are important.

Current and Capital Balances: To make the relation between current and capital balances clear, let us assume that the Bank of England does not engage in any foreign-exchange transactions. This means that both F_R and F_P in equation (1) above are zero.

Now it follows that any deficit or surplus on current account must be matched by an equal and opposite surplus or deficit on capital account. For example, if a country has a credit balance on current account, the foreign exchange earned must appear in the capital account. The foreign exchange may be used to buy foreign assets, or merely stashed away in foreign bank accounts. In either case, there is an outflow of capital from the UK. It is recorded as a debit item because it uses foreign exchange.

We can see this clearly if we return to equation (1) above and set F_R and F_P equal to zero to indicate no transactions by the Bank of England. This gives us

$$C_R + K_R \equiv C_P + K_P. \tag{2}$$

Now subtract C_P and K_R from both sides of the equation:

$$C_R - C_P \equiv K_P - K_R. \tag{3}$$

This expresses, in equation form, what we have just argued verbally: a surplus on current account must be balanced by a deficit on capital account (i.e. an

outflow of capital), while a deficit on current account must be matched by a surplus on capital account (i.e. an inflow of capital).

One important implication concerns capital transfers. A country that is exporting capital has a deficit on capital account and so it *must* have a surplus on current account. Also, a country that is importing capital has a surplus on capital account so it *must* have a deficit on current account.

If we allow for Bank of England transactions, the above relations do not need to hold exactly. They can diverge by the balance on official settlements account $(F_R - F_P)$ but, since this balance is usually small relative to net payments on current and capital account, the relation between the two major accounts shown in equation (3) is usually approximately true.

The relations just discussed are important, and we shall be making frequent use of them in later chapters.

Official Financing and the Rest of the Accounts: When people speak of a country as having an overall balance-of-payments deficit or surplus, *they are usually referring to the balance of all accounts excluding official financing.* A balance-of-payments surplus means that the Bank of England is adding to its holdings of foreign-exchange reserves. A balance-of-payments deficit means that the Bank of England is reducing its reserves.

The Exchange Rate

Although we shall study the determination of exchange rates in detail in Chapter 43, we need to say a little about this subject now. We saw in Chapter 27 that the exchange rate for sterling gives the price of a unit of sterling in terms of some foreign currency. For example, if the exchange rate between sterling and US dollars is $1.25, then it costs $1.25 to buy £1 or, what is the same thing, its costs 80p to buy $1 $(1/1.25 = 0.80)$.

The exchange rate is like any other price. Its free-market value is set by demand and supply.

The demands and supplies for foreign exchange arise from the transactions that are recorded in the payments accounts. Holders of foreign currencies demand sterling in order to be able to buy exports of goods and services from the UK, to make payments of interest, profits and dividends to UK residents, and in order to move money into the UK to buy short- or long-term British assets that must be purchased with sterling. Holders of sterling demand foreign exchange in order to buy UK imports, to pay interest, profits and dividends to foreign residents, and to move funds into foreign countries in order to buy short- or long-term foreign assets.

On a free market, the exchange rate will move to equilibrate these demands and supplies, just as the price of carrots moves to equilibrate the demand and supply for carrots.

The only other thing we need to note is the effect of a change in the exchange rate on the international payments that people will desire to make.

First consider a rise in the sterling exchange rate. This means that foreigners will have to give up more of their currency to get each £1 that they buy, and UK residents will be able to get more foreign currency for each £1 they offer. For example, if the sterling-dollar rate moves from $1.25 to $2.00, holders of dollars will find it costs them $2.00 instead of $1.25 for each pound that they buy. This will make buying anything whose price is set in sterling more expensive to holders of foreign money. British exports of goods and services will cost more, as will a holiday in Britain. Also it will cost more for any foreigners to buy British assets such as Treasury Bills or shares in British Telecom. This will discourage such purchases and the number of pounds sterling demanded in order to buy British goods and services will fall. On the other hand, it will now cost less for holders of sterling to buy foreign currency. When the exchange rate is $1.25, $1 costs 80p, while when the rate rises to $2.00, $1 costs only 50p. When the exchange rate rises, goods, services and assets priced in foreign currency will appear cheaper to holders of sterling. This will encourage British imports of goods and services.

If you have understood all this, you should be able to work out the opposite case for yourself. If the exchange rate goes from $2.00 to the pound to $1.25, British goods and services will seem cheaper to foreigners and they will tend to buy more of them. At the same time, foreign goods and services will be more expensive to holders of sterling, who will tend to buy less of them.

This discussion leads us to an important general conclusion. *A rise in the price of sterling on the foreign-exchange market will tend to discourage UK exports and capital imports and encourage UK imports and capital exports, while a fall in the price of sterling will have the opposite effect.*

FOREIGN TRADE IN THE THEORY OF INCOME DETERMINATION

In the second half of this chapter, we extend our theory of income determination to cover foreign trade. As a first step, we must study the forces that influence a country's exports and its imports.

The determinants of exports

The foreign demand for UK exports depends on two main forces:

- the *level of income* in the rest of the world, and
- the *relative prices* of UK and foreign goods; these relative prices, in turn, depend on:
  (a) the *price levels* in the UK and in the rest of the world, and
  (b) the *exchange rate.*

Our first task is to explain how each of these forces work.

We saw in Chapter 29 that consumption expenditure depended on income. When foreign incomes rise, foreigners buy more domestically produced goods, and more imported goods. This increases UK exports. As a result, UK exports are positively associated with foreign income.

In the micro economics of Part 2 of this book, we saw that relative prices influence consumers' demands for commodities. If UK prices rise relative to the prices of competing foreign goods, foreigners will buy fewer UK goods. If UK prices fall relative to the prices of competing foreign goods, foreigners will buy more UK goods. Thus UK exports are negatively associated with the relative prices of UK goods – the higher their relative prices the fewer will be bought.

The prices of UK goods relative to the prices of foreign goods depends on the price levels ruling in the UK and abroad, and on the exchange rate. First, consider the effect of price levels. If we hold the exchange rate constant, a rise in the UK price level, relative to foreign price levels, makes UK exports relatively more expensive and reduces the quantity that will be sold. A fall in the UK price level, relative to foreign price levels, makes UK goods relatively less expensive, and increases the quantity that will be exported.

Second, consider the effect of the exchange rate. If we hold price levels constant, the effects are those that we studied in the previous section. A rise in the

TABLE 32.2 Causes of Changes in Imports and Exports

FORCES THAT WILL INCREASE UK EXPORTS	FORCES THAT WILL INCREASE UK IMPORTS
1. A rise in foreign income	1. A rise in UK income
2. A fall in the UK price level relative to foreign price levels	2. A rise in the UK price level relative to foreign price levels
3. A fall in the sterling exchange rate	3. A rise in the sterling exchange rate

sterling exchange rate raises the price of UK exports and reduces the quantity sold. A fall in the UK exchange rate reduces the price of UK exports and increases the quantity sold.

For the moment it is convenient to assume that all of these influences remain constant so we can treat exports as autonomous. This does not mean that exports never change, only that for the moment we are holding constant *all* factors that influence UK exports – in particular, we are assuming that price levels, the exchange rate and the level of foreign income are all constant.

The determinants of imports

Not surprisingly, the same general forces that influence UK exports also influence its imports, income and relative prices. What matters now, however, is income in the UK, not foreign income.

UK imports depend on UK demand. We have already seen that UK consumption expenditure varies directly with UK national income. We now make the parallel assumption that UK imports vary directly with UK national income: as UK income rises, firms, households and governments spend more, both on domestically produced goods and on foreign goods.

UK imports also depend on the relative price of UK goods and foreign goods, which in turn depend, as we have seen, on relative price levels and the exchange rate. Because we are dealing with imports, however, the effect of changes in relative prices is reversed. Anything that raises the price of UK goods relative to the prices of foreign goods – a rise in the UK price level relative to foreign price levels, or an increase in the exchange rate – will tend to increase British imports. Anything that reduces the price of UK goods relative to the prices of foreign goods – a fall in the UK price level relative to foreign price levels, or a fall in the exchange rate – will tend to reduce UK imports.

The forces that increase imports and exports are summarized in Table 32.2. A fall in UK exports will be induced by the opposite of the changes listed in the first column. A fall in UK imports will be induced by the opposite of the changes listed in the second column of the table.

The Theory of Income Determination

Initial assumptions

We start by assuming that price levels and the exchange rate are constant. This removes the influence of changes in relative international prices by holding them constant. We also treat *foreign* national income as exogenous. It is not affected by anything within our model of the determination of our own country's national income. These assumptions make exports exogenous – they are unaffected by anything in the model of income determination.

Since relative prices are constant, these cannot influence UK imports. But UK national income cannot be held constant, since it is UK national income we are determining. Thus imports are not exogenous; instead they vary with UK national income: the higher is national income, the higher are imports.

Import Propensities: In earlier chapters we defined marginal and average propensities to consume, to save and to tax. We can now define similar propensities with respect to imports, M. The average propensity to import, the APM, is total imports divided by total income, i.e. M/Y. The marginal propensity to import, the MPM, is the proportion of any *increase* in national income that is spent on imports, i.e. $\Delta M/\Delta Y$ (where, as usual, the symbol Δ means a change in the variable to which it is attached).

Table 32.3 illustrates the calculation of the average and marginal propensities to import using an

TABLE 32.3 Calculation of the Average and Marginal Propensities to Consume

(1)	(2)	(3)	(4)	(5)	(6)
		$(2) \div (1)$	Change	Change	
Income	Imports	APM	in Y	in M	MPM
(Y)	(M)	(M/Y)	(ΔY)	(ΔM)	$(\Delta M/\Delta Y)$
100	20	0.20			
			100	16	0.16
200	36	0.18			

TABLE 32.4 A Net Export Schedule. The schedule assumes that exports are exogenous and that the *MPM* (and the *APM*) are 0.10

(1) National income (Y)	(2) Exports (X)	(3) Imports (M)	(4) Net exports (X − M)
1,000	240	100	140
2,000	240	200	40
2,400	240	240	0
3,000	240	300	−60
4,000	240	400	−160
5,000	240	500	−260

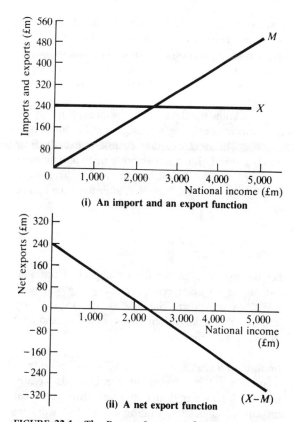

FIGURE 32.1   The Export, Import and Net Export Functions. When exports are assumed constant and imports are positively related to national income, the net export function is negatively related to national income

example where an increase in income from 100 to 200 causes imports to increase from 20 to 36.

The Net Export Function: Our assumptions about exports and imports are illustrated in the hypothetical example given in Table 32.4. Exports are autonomously determined at a value of £240m. Imports rise with income, and the Table uses an example where both the marginal and average propensities to import are constant at 0.10 – i.e. 10 per cent of income is always spent on imported goods and services.

Net exports are the difference between exports and imports, i.e. X − M. Because X does not change with income, while M *rises* as income rises, *net* exports *fall* as income rises. For low levels of income, *net* exports are positive; while for high levels of income, *net* exports are negative.

Figure 32.1 graphs the data from Table 32.4. Part (i) shows how exports and imports vary with national income, part (ii) shows how *net exports* vary with national income. The graph shows that as income rises, exports are unchanged (the X function is horizontal), imports rise (the M function is positively sloped) and net exports fall (the X − M function is negatively sloped).

We now wish to see how imports and exports fit into our theory of the determination of national income. We look first at the income-expenditure approach and then at the leakages-injections approach.

The expenditure approach

In the model used in Chapters 30 and 31, aggregate expenditure has three components: consumption, C, investment, I, and government expenditure, G. To put exports and imports into the aggregate expendi-

ture function, we merely recall our discussion in Chapter 26 (see page 320) where we showed that, in an open economy, the aggregate expenditure on UK output was equal to what it would be in a closed economy, C + I + G, plus net exports, X − M:

$$E = C + I + G + (X - M). \qquad (1)$$

From this point on, the argument proceeds exactly as it did in the earlier chapters. The only difference is that the desired expenditure curves in such Figures as 28.2 (p. 347) and 29.2 (p. 352) contain an added term for net exports.

Since exports add to aggregate demand while imports subtract from it, equilibrium income is increased by a rise in autonomous exports or a fall in *the propensity to import* which lowers imports. By the same reasoning, equilibrium income will be lowered by a fall in exports or a rise in the propensity to import. Note that, since exports are autonomous, we can speak of a rise or a fall meaning that they change from one constant amount to another. But since imports are a function of income, we must speak of a shift in the whole import function, indicating a change in the amount of imports at each level of income.

So we know the direction of the change in equilibrium income caused by a change in either imports or exports. The next question to ask is exactly how much a given change in imports or exports causes equilibrium national income to change. This question is better studied, however, after we have looked at the leakages-injections approach.

The leakages-injections approach

Let us now look at the determination of national income in an open economy using the leakages-injections approach. The first step is to see why imports are a leakage from the circular flow and why exports are an injection.

Imports as a Leakage: When a UK resident buys a commodity that was made abroad, this creates income for foreign firms. Imports thus represent income of domestic spending units that was not passed on to domestic firms through the purchases of domestically produced commodities. Imports, therefore, withdraw expenditure from the domestic circular flow. For example, if households reduce their expenditure on domestically produced consumption goods in order to buy more foreign-produced goods, leakages will rise just as they would if the consumption expenditure had been reduced in order to save more.

Exports as an Injection: When a foreign household purchases a good manufactured in the UK, it creates income for a UK firm and thus for the factors of production that the firm employs. So exports represent incomes earned by UK firms that do not arise from the spending of UK households. Exports, therefore, inject expenditures into the domestic circular flow.

In our closed-economy model we had two leakages, savings and taxes, and two injections, investment and government expenditure. We now amend that model to allow for the extra leakage of imports and the extra injection of exports. For leakages, we now have

$$L = S + T + M,$$

and, for injections,

$$J = I + G + X.$$

Equilibrium Income: Equilibrium in the circular flow occurs when aggregate desired leakages equal aggregate desired injections, i.e. $L = J$. Spelling this out in terms of the components of both L and J gives as the condition for equilibrium:

$$S + T + M = I + G + X. \qquad (2)$$

The equilibrium is shown in Figures 32.2 and 32.3. Because I, G and X are assumed to be autonomous, the total injection line is horizontal, showing that injections are the same at all levels of national income. Because imports rise with national income, just as do savings, the total leakage line remains upward-sloping.

Assuming that the original injection and leakage curves are J and L, equilibrium income is Y_1 in both figures. At Y_1 the sum of savings, tax revenues and imports equals the sum of investment, government expenditure and exports.

Changes in Exports and Imports: Figure 32.2 also shows the effect of changes in exports and imports. A rise in exports increases the level of injections associated with all levels of national income and so shifts the injections function upwards. This is shown by the shift from J to J' in the Figure. As a result, equilibrium income rises from Y_1 to Y_2. A fall in the export function can be shown by a downward shift in the injection function, taking it from, say, J' to J. As a result, equilibrium income falls from Y_2 to Y_1.

Figure 32.3 shows the effects of a change in the import function. An increased desire to import at each level of national income shifts the import

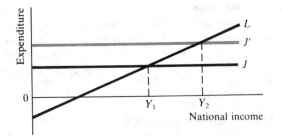

FIGURE 32.2   The Determination of Equilibrium National Income and the Effect of a Rise in Exports. A rise in exports shifts the injections function upwards and raises equilibrium national income

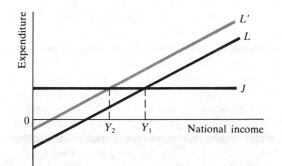

FIGURE 32.3   The Determination of Equilibrium National Income and the Effect of an Upward Shift in the Import Function. A rise in the import function shifts the aggregate leakages function upwards and reduces equilibrium national income

function upwards, and hence shifts the whole leakage function upwards. In the figure, the leakage function shifts from L to L' and equilibrium income falls from Y_1 to Y_2. A decreased desire to import can be shown by a downward shift in the leakage function from, say, L' to L. As a result, equilibrium income rises from Y_2 to Y_1.

Except for the introduction of a new injection and a new leakage, the analysis of the leakages-injections approach is identical to that given in earlier chapters. A change of £1 in one type of injection expenditure has a similar effect on aggregate expenditure, and hence on equilibrium national income, as a change of £1 in any other type of injection. Similarly with leakages, an increase in the leakage function reduces equilibrium income, whether the expenditure leaks out through new saving, new tax revenue or new imports, and vice versa.

The Size of the Multiplier

We saw on page 358 that the value of the multiplier is given by the reciprocal of the slope of the leakage function, $1/MPL$, where MPL stands for the marginal propensity to leak. This is a general result in the present type of model.

All we need to do now is to note that the increase in total leakages *when income rises by £1* is equal to the sum of the amount of new saving, as measured by the MPS, the amount of new tax revenue, as measured by the MPT, and the amount of new imports, as measured by the MPM.[1] Stating this in symbols gives for an open economy:

$$MPL = MPS + MPT + MPM. \qquad (3)$$

All that this equation says is that the *total leakages* per £1 increase in national income must be equal to *the sum of the individual leakages.*

The multiplier, $1/MPL$, can now be rewritten as:

$$K = 1/(MPS + MPT + MPM). \qquad (4)$$

This tells us that the *value of the multiplier in an open economy is equal to the reciprocal of the sum of the marginal propensities to save, tax and import, all expressed as propensities out of national income.* The expression also tells us that, *ceteris paribus*, the larger is the marginal propensity to import, the smaller will be the multiplier. Again, there is nothing surprising about this. We saw by comparing Tables 29.1 and 30.2 on pages 356 and 367 that the larger were the leakages out of each round of induced expenditure, the smaller was the final increase in income when the multiplier process had worked itself out completely. Since imports are a leakage, this result applies directly to imports.

For relatively open economies such as the UK, the MPM is quite large. Thus the value of the multiplier is much smaller than it would be if there were no foreign trade (in which case MPM would be zero).

Now we know that a £1 change in any injection – investment, government expenditure or exports – will increase national income by the amount given in equation (4). Let us illustrate with an example using figures that are probably somewhere near those of the UK economy. (The exact estimation of these propensities is, however, a difficult matter.) Let the figures be $MPS = 0.05$, $MPT = 0.40$, and $MPM = 0.25$. This makes the marginal propensity to leak 0.70 and yields a multiplier of $1/0.7$ which is 1.43. Thus, in this example, an increase in investment, government, or export expenditure by, say, £1m would increase equilibrium national income by £1.43m.

The International Transmission of Income Changes

The foreign-trade multiplier can be used to show that the fates of various economies are intertwined. So far

---

1 It is important to remember that all of these propensities are propensities to spend *out of national income* and, hence, show the response of savings, tax revenue and imports to a change in national income. (For the distinction between the MPC out of disposable income and out of national income, see page 361.)

in this chapter we have assumed that imports and exports are totally independent of each other, but this is a simplification that is not exactly correct.

If the UK suffers a fall in national income for some purely domestic reason, UK imports will fall. British residents will reduce their purchase of such things as German Volkswagens, Irish tweed jackets, Swiss watches, Japanese cameras, and Austrian skiing holidays, as well as many types of raw materials. As a result, the exports, and hence the national incomes, of these countries will fall. Then they, in turn, will buy fewer imports from all countries including the UK. The reduction in British exports further reduces the UK's national income.

Thus, the national incomes of various countries are linked together: any change in income in one country tends to cause the incomes of other countries to change in the same direction, and the changes in the incomes of other countries tend to reinforce the initial change in the first country.

The extent to which changes in income in one country affect incomes in other countries, and the extent to which these changes reinforce the initial change, depends on their marginal propensities to import. In many countries, such as Canada, Japan and the United Kingdom, the marginal propensities to import are high, and fluctuations in income in one of these countries are easily transmitted into fluctuations in the incomes of other countries. As a result, both booms and slumps are internationally infectious. A boom or a slump in one major trading country is easily communicated to other trading countries.

IMPORTS AND EXPORTS: GOOD OR BAD?

It is commonly argued that exports are 'good' because they raise equilibrium national income, whereas imports are 'bad' because they lower equilibrium income. When we say exports raise national income, we mean that they add to total expenditure and raise equilibrium income. But they do not add to the value of domestic consumption. In fact, exports are goods that are *produced* at home but *consumed* abroad, while imports are goods that are produced abroad and consumed at home.

The view that exports are beneficial and imports harmful goes back at least as far as the eighteenth

century, to a group of economists called Mercantilists. The issues involved are important, and we shall approach them indirectly by thinking not of exports and imports, but of a farm family that sells its produce to the city ('exports') and buys goods from the city ('imports'). Suppose the farm family sells everything it can grow, but buys nothing. The money will roll in, but the family will get hungrier, their car will run out of petrol, their clothes will become tattered; and their TV set will eventually stop working. Clearly, they could be better off if they used some of their income to buy needed goods. Although this is an extreme case, it is not without some modern international parallels.

The standard of living of a person, or of all persons in a country, depends on the goods and services that they consume, not on what they produce. The *average* material standard of living of the residents of a country may be thought of in terms of the following equation:

$$\begin{array}{c} \text{Average} \\ \text{standard} \\ \text{of living} \end{array} = \frac{\text{total goods and services consumed}}{\text{number of people}}$$

If exports are really good and imports really bad, then a fully employed economy that obtains an increase in its exports without any corresponding increase in its imports ought to be made better off. This change will, however, result in a reduction in current standards of living because, when more goods are sent abroad and no more are brought in from abroad, the total goods available for domestic consumption must fall.[1] The importance of exports is that they permit goods and services to be imported. This two-way international exchange is valuable whenever more goods can be imported than can be obtained if the same goods were produced at home.

An Economy with Unemployment: An Exception?

What about an economy with substantial amounts of unemployment, such as the UK economy in the 1980s, or the 1930s? Assume that the UK government

---

1 Those of you who have read Chapter 22 will recall that the gains from trade depend on the ability to import goods at a lower opportunity cost than they could be produced at home. In this view, the gains from trade depend on the terms of trade and the *volume* of trade, not on the *balance* of trade. The more a country exports and imports the more it is taking advantage of the gains from trade.

gave a subsidy to exporters and put tariffs and quotas on imports, or depreciated the exchange rate to encourage exports and discourage imports. As we saw earlier in this chapter, both the rise in exports and the switch in domestic expenditure from imports to home goods would reduce the recessionary gap and hence increase equilibrium national income as well as employment. Surely, in a time of recession, this can be regarded as a 'good thing'.

Two points need to be made about such a policy. In the first place, the goods being produced by the newly employed workers in the export sector are not available for domestic consumption and so do not raise domestic standards of living. Would it not be better if, instead of encouraging exports, the government encouraged the production of goods for the home market, so that the initial rise in employment would also contribute to a rise in domestic living standards? Or if the public objected to the government subsidization of private firms, then the government could create new employment by building more roads, schools and research laboratories. Again, income and employment would go up, but, again, there would be something more tangible to show for it than the smoke of ships bearing the subsidized exports to foreign markets disappearing over the horizon.[1]

The second point to be made concerns the effects on other countries of such a policy of fostering exports and discouraging imports in a situation of general world unemployment. Although the policy raises domestic employment, it will have the reverse effect abroad – it will lower incomes and create unemploy-ment abroad. Foreign countries will suffer a fall in their equilibrium national incomes because their exports will fall and their imports rise. They cannot be expected to sit idly by. If they seek to protect their domestic employment by encouraging their exports and discouraging their imports, this will reduce other countries' national incomes. If all countries adopt such a policy, the net effect will be a fall in the volume of international trade without any rise in the level of employment in any country.

This was indeed what happened in the Great Depression of the 1930s, and also to some extent in the last half of the 1980s. Many countries adopted policies of encouraging exports and discouraging imports. Taken together, the policies were self-defeating because they cancelled each other out. They did nothing to increase equilibrium income and employ-ment. They did, however, switch domestic demand in each country from imports to home-produced goods and, as a result, they greatly reduced the total amount of international trade. Because the inter-national specialization that is a major source of the gains from trade was reduced when the volume of trade fell, world living standards were reduced – the policies had no effect on *total* world employment, but they did cause resources to be less and less efficiently allocated internationally.

Such policies are often called BEGGAR THY NEIGHBOUR POLICIES because a country tries to deal with its unemployment problem by buying less from, and selling more to, other countries, which raises unemployment in these other countries. One country can operate such a policy successfully if other coun-tries do not retaliate. But as we have seen, if all countries try to 'beggar their neighbours', the em-ployment effects cancel out but the loss of inter-national efficiency implies that each country has ended up 'beggaring' itself.

---

1 We are here considering the effects of the *initial* rise in employ-ment in either the export or the investment industries. Of course there would be multiplier effects of an increase in exports, and these could contribute to an increase in domestic living standards.

SUMMARY

1 Flows of expenditures in respect of international transactions are recorded in the balance of pay-ments, which is divided into three sections: the current account, the capital account and the official financing account. The current account is further subdivided into visibles and invisibles.

2 Taking all transactions into consideration, the balance of payments must balance: every bit of foreign exchange earned (credit items) must be used for some purpose (debit items).

3 In a world of many countries and many items, there may be a positive or a negative balance between two countries and/or on some part of the account. The terms balance-of-payments sur-

plus or deficit usually refer to the balance on current plus capital account (which must be matched by a balance of the opposite sign on the official financing account).

4 Exports (regarded as autonomous) depend on foreign national income and international relative prices. Imports depend on domestic national income and international relative prices. International relative prices in turn depend on price levels and the exchange rate.

5 The determination of equilibrium national income in an open economy by the expenditure approach requires only that net exports (i.e. X minus M) be added to the aggregate desired expenditure function: $E = C + I + G + (X - M)$. For the leakages-injections approach, exports are added as an injection, $J = I + G + X$, and imports as a leakage, $L = S + T + M$.

6 Equilibrium income (where $E = Y$, and $J = L$) is increased by a rise in autonomous exports or by a downward shift in the import function. It is decreased by the opposite changes.

7 Foreign trade reduces the size of the multiplier, $1/MPL$, by adding another leakage. The multiplier then becomes $1/(MPS + MPT + MPM)$, (where all marginal propensities are out of national income).

8 Foreign trade links the national incomes of various countries in that a rise in income in one country raises its imports which, being another country's exports, raise income elsewhere.

9 Foreign trade benefits participating countries. Policies of trying to raise domestic income by increasing exports and reducing imports are self-defeating. When followed by many countries, they tend to lower living standards in all countries.

Money and the Price Level

One of the most quotable quotes in the English language is that 'the love of money is the root of all evil.' But just what is money, and what part does it play in the economic process that we have studied throughout this book? How in particular is it related to national income, to prices and the price level? We discuss these general issues in this chapter. In subsequent chapters we consider the more important aspects of money in greater detail.

MONEY

To understand the place of money in the economy, we must understand what money is and the functions that it fulfils. At the outset it is natural to ask: What is money?

Anything that serves as money usually fulfils several related functions, all of which we study below. The most important function that distinguishes money from everything else is its use as a medium of exchange. Indeed MONEY may be defined as any generally accepted medium of exchange – anything that will be accepted by virtually everyone in exchange for goods and services.

The Functions and Characteristics of Money

Four of the most important functions of money are to act as:

● a medium of exchange,
● a store of value,
● a unit of account, and
● a standard of deferred payments.

We shall discuss these in turn. Money must also have several characteristics if it is to be fully satisfactory. It must be:

● acceptable,
● portable,
● divisible, and
● difficult to counterfeit.

It is best to discuss these characteristics along with the functions of money because they are best understood in terms of the ability of money to carry out each of its functions.

A Medium of Exchange: Where money does not exist, goods must be exchanged through BARTER, the direct exchange of one good for another. If a wheat farmer wants a winter coat, he must seek out someone else who both has a winter coat and also wants wheat. This need for both sides in a barter transaction to want the good the other has to trade is called the need for a *double co-incidence of wants*. Clearly, locating such double co-incidences can be difficult and time-consuming, and sometimes impossible. As a result, under barter, most people are forced to be relatively self-sufficient – to make both their wheat and their winter coat and, indeed, almost everything else that they consume.

The great advantage of money is that it separates the two sides of the barter transaction. Let us see what this means in the case of the wheat farmer who wants a winter coat. Money allows the farmer to sell his wheat to anyone who wants it, whether or not the purchaser has anything that the farmer wants. Instead, the farmer takes money in exchange for his wheat and then seeks out someone else who has a winter coat for sale, secure in the knowledge that the seller of the coat will accept money in exchange.

A high degree of specialization requires that most of what one produces goes to others, and most of what one consumes comes from others. This requires an extent, and efficiency, of exchange of products that is quite impossible under barter. Without money, therefore, our complicated economic system, based on specialization and the division of labour, would be impossible.

To serve as an efficient medium of exchange, money must have the following characteristics.

(i) *It must be readily acceptable*, for if one is to take money in exchange for what one wants to sell, one needs to know that others will, in their turn, take the money in exchange for what one wants to buy. This is, of course, the fundamental characteristic that money must have.

(ii) *It must be easily portable*, which requires that it must have a high value for its weight, for it would otherwise be a nuisance to carry around.

(iii) *It must be divisible*, for money that comes only in large denominations is useless for transactions having only a small value.

(iv) *It must not be easy to counterfeit*, for money that can be easily duplicated by anyone will quickly lose its value.

All of these are characteristics that are found in virtually all types of modern money.

A Store of Value: Many goods, and all services, cannot be stored up for future needs. Money, however, allows us to store purchasing power: you can sell your goods today and store the money. This gives you a claim on someone else's goods that you can exercise at some future date.

To be a fully satisfactory store of future purchasing power, money must have a stable value in terms of the things that it can buy. If prices are stable, one knows how much command over goods and services has been stored up when a certain sum of money has been accumulated. If there is uncertainty about future prices, one does not know how many goods an accumulated sum of money will command when one comes to spend it.

Thus, aside from the characteristics listed above, the most desirable one for the store-of-value function is that *the purchasing power of money remains stable over time*. This has *not* always been a characteristic of modern money. Later in this chapter we study in more detail how inflation changes the value of money.

A Unit of Account: Money may also be used purely for accounting purposes, without having any physical existence. For instance, a village commune might say that each person had so many 'roubles' at his or her disposal each month and might then establish these as credits on the books of the village's only shop. Goods would be given prices and purchases would be recorded. Each consumer would be allowed to buy the desired goods until his or her supply of roubles was exhausted. The money would have no existence other than as entries in the shop's books, but it would be serving as a perfectly satisfactory unit of account.

A Standard of Deferred Payments: This is a fourth function that is sometimes distinguished, although it is really implied by the other three. Acting as a standard of deferred payments means that a payment to be made in the future can be denominated in money terms in just the same way as can a payment to be made today. Here, money is acting as a unit of account with the added dimension of time.

The History of Money

A surer understanding of what money is, and what it does, can be gained by studying some of the highlights in the history of money.

Metallic money

All sorts of commodities have been used as money at one time or another, but gold and silver proved to have great advantages. They had a high and stable price, both because their supply was relatively limited and because they were in constant demand by the rich for ornament and decoration. They had the additional advantages that they do not easily wear out, and are divisible into extremely small units. They were also easily recognized and generally known to be commodities that would be readily accepted – their acceptability, of course, being the key characteristic they needed to develop as money.

Before the invention of coins, it was necessary to carry precious metals around in bulk, and to weigh the amount required for each transaction. The invention of coinage eliminated this need. The government made a coin using a fixed quantity of gold or silver for value, mixed with base metals to give the coin durability. It then affixed its own seal to guarantee the amount of precious metal contained in the coin.

This system worked well as long as the government played its part. From time to time, however, the temptation to cheat proved overwhelming. When the government had debts that it could not pay, it could *debase* the coinage. Gold and silver coins would be melted down and coined afresh, but, between the melting down and the recoining, further inexpensive base metal was added. If the coinage were debased by adding, say, one ounce of new base metal to every four ounces of old coins, five coins could be minted for every four melted down. With these extra coins the government could pay its debts.

The result was inflation. When the government paid its bills, the recipients of the extra coins would spend some or all of them, and this would cause a net increase in demand. The extra demand would bid up prices. Debasing the coinage thus led to a rise in the general price level. Such experiences led early economists to propound the *quantity theory of money and prices*. They argued that a change in the quantity of money would lead to a change in the price level in the same direction. (We shall have more to say about this theory later in the chapter.)

Gresham's Law: The early experience of currency debasement led to a famous economic 'law' that has stood the test of time. The law states that 'bad money drives out good' and is called GRESHAM'S LAW after the Elizabethan financial expert, Sir Thomas Gresham, who first explained its workings to Queen Elizabeth I. Monarchs before Elizabeth had severely debased the English coinage. Seeking to help trade, Elizabeth minted new coins containing their full face value in gold. But as fast as she fed these new coins into circulation, they disappeared. Why? Suppose that you possess one new and one old coin, each with the same face value but different gold contents. Now you have an account to settle. Which coin would you use? Clearly, you would pay with the debased coin and keep the undebased one. You part with less gold that way. If you wanted to obtain a certain amount of gold bullion by melting down the gold coins (as was frequently done), which coins would you use? Clearly, you would use new undebased coins because to get a given amount of gold you would part with less 'face value' that way. The debased coins would thus remain in circulation and the undebased coins would disappear. Whenever people got hold of an undebased coin, they would hold on to it; whenever they got a debased coin, they would pass it on. Hence the bad money stayed in circulation and drove the good money out of circulation.

Gresham's law has many modern applications.

Here is one for illustration. Until about 25 or 30 years ago, most countries used some silver content in many of their coins, but the market value of silver content was much less than the face value of the coin. Then in the 1960s, the price of silver soared. The value of the silver in the coins exceeded the face value of the coins and when this became known, they became 'good' money. True to Gresham's law, they quickly disappeared from circulation. People melted them down and sold their silver content for more than the face value of the coin.

Paper money

Paper money came into use in many ways. One was through the practice of storing gold for safekeeping with goldsmiths – craftsmen who worked with gold. The goldsmiths issued receipts promising to hand over the gold to the bearer of the receipt on demand. These receipts soon became a medium of exchange. A buyer needed only to transfer a goldsmith's receipt for so much gold to a seller, who would accept it, secure in the knowledge that the goldsmith would pay over the gold whenever it was needed. As the receipts became *acceptable* for settling market transactions, they *became* money. The convenience of using easy-to-carry pieces of paper instead of gold is obvious.

Thus, when it first came into being, paper money was a promise to pay on demand so much gold, the promise being made first by goldsmiths and later by banks. Early banks, too, undertook to store gold and issued their promises to pay that gold on demand. These promissory notes were called BANK NOTES. As long as the institutions were known to be reliable, their pieces of paper would be 'as good as gold'. Such notes remained an important part of the money supply until the early part of the twentieth century. When a country's money is *convertible* into gold, the country is said to be on a GOLD STANDARD.

Fractionally Backed Paper Money: Such was the convenience of paper money that most people were content to use it for most of their transactions and only occasionally did they demand to convert their notes into gold or silver. At any one time, therefore, some of the bank's customers would be withdrawing gold, others would be depositing it, and the great majority would be using the bank's paper notes without any need, or desire, to convert them into gold. For this reason, the bank was able to issue *more* money, redeemable in gold, than the amount of gold held in its vaults. This was good business, because the banks could use the money to make interest-earning loans. In such a situation, we say that the currency is *fractionally backed* by the reserves.

In the past, the major problem of a fractionally backed currency was to maintain its convertibility into the precious metal by which it was backed. The imprudent bank that issued too much paper money found itself unable to redeem its currency in gold when the demand for gold was even slightly higher than usual. This bank would then have to suspend payments, and the holders of its notes would suddenly find that no one would accept them because they could not be converted into gold.

The prudent bank, which kept a reasonable relation between its note issue and its gold reserve, found that it could meet the normal everyday demand for gold without difficulty. But if the public lost confidence and *en masse* demanded redemption of their bank notes, even prudent banks could find themselves unable to honour their pledges. Banks were sometimes ruined by sudden, 'panic-induced' runs on their reserves.

Central Banks: A central bank was a natural outcome of the fractionally backed currency system. Where were ordinary banks to turn when they had good investments but were in temporary need of cash? If these banks provided loans to the public against reasonable security, why should not some other institution provide loans to them against the same sort of security?

In response to such needs, central banks evolved as private institutions acting as banker to the other banks. In time, central banks throughout the world became the main institutions permitted to issue notes. Central banks in turn became governmental institutions.

The English central bank, the Bank of England – commonly known as 'the Bank' – was founded as long ago as the seventeenth century. Although it developed close associations with the government and eventually became an arm of government policy, it remained technically a private institution until its nationalization in 1946. To distinguish the central bank from all other banks, the others are commonly referred to as commercial banks. The Bank of England is studied in detail in Chapter 37.

Fiat Currencies: Originally, central banks issued currency that was fully convertible into gold. The gold

supply thus set some upper limit on the amount of paper money that the central bank could issue. But the central bank could issue (as banknotes) more currency than it had gold because only small amounts of the currency would be presented for redemption at any one time.

During the period between World Wars I and II, virtually all the countries of the world abandoned gold convertibility – the UK did so in 1931. From that time on, paper money has depended for its value on nothing more than its general acceptability – and the fact that the government has ordered it to be accepted. Inconvertible paper money that is declared by government order (or fiat) to be legal tender for settlement of all debts is called FIAT MONEY.

Modern Money

Most of the terms referring to various kinds of money have been introduced already. In view of the large number of terms in use, some of which mean the same thing, it is worth pausing to recapitulate.

Coins refers to all metallic money. Examples are the 10p and 50p coins in your pocket. *Notes* refers to paper money. In England, virtually all paper money in circulation consists of notes issued by the Bank of England. In Scotland, notes issued both by the Bank of England and the Bank of Scotland are in common circulation. (The Bank of Scotland is the central bank of Scotland). Examples are the £5, £10 and £20 notes that you carry around to make everyday purchases. Taken together, notes and coins are commonly referred to as *cash* or *currency*. *Deposit money* or *bank money* refers to deposits held at banks. Which types of bank deposits are properly regarded as money is discussed later in the chapter.

Legal tender is money that must be accepted if offered in payment for a purchase or settlement of a debt. In the UK, legal tender consists of coins (up to certain maximum amounts) and notes. Cheques drawn on bank deposits are not legal tender, although they are commonly used in purchases and in the settlement of debts.

Money is said to be *convertible* if it can be converted into some other form of money that is legal tender. In the UK, bank deposits are convertible money since they are convertible into legal tender – and they are so converted every time a customer withdraws currency from his bank account.

Convertible money is said to be *backed* by the legal tender into which it can be converted. It is *fully backed* if, for every unit of convertible money outstanding, a unit of whatever backs it is held in reserve. Convertible money is said to be *partially backed* or *fractionally backed* if the reserves held to back it are only a fraction of the amount of convertible money outstanding. Money that is not convertible into anything is said to be *fiat* or *inconvertible* money.

Modern Fiat Currencies: Today, all notes in circulation are fiat money, as is our coinage. Modern coins, unlike their predecessors, contain a value of metal that is characteristically only a minute fraction of the face value of the coin. Modern coins, like modern paper money, are merely tokens. Nonetheless, they function satisfactorily as money. Since they are acceptable, they are a medium of exchange; since their purchasing power remains relatively stable in normal times, they are a satisfactory store of value; and since both of these things are normally true, they will also serve as a satisfactory unit of account and a standard of deferred payments.

Modern Deposit Money: Early in the twentieth century, most private banks lost the authority to issue *bank notes*. Yet they did not lose the power to create *money*. Let us see how banks create money in the modern world.

Banks' customers frequently deposit coins and paper money for safekeeping, just as in former times they deposited gold. Each deposit is recorded as an entry on the customer's account.

Customers who wish to pay debts might come to the bank to claim their money in notes and coins, and then pay the money to another person. This person might then redeposit the money in a bank. Like the gold transfers, this is a tedious procedure, particularly for large payments. It is more convenient to have the bank transfer claims to the money they hold on deposit. The common 'cheque' is an instruction to the bank to make the transfer. As soon as such transfers became easy and inexpensive, and cheques became widely accepted in payment for commodities, bank deposits on which cheques could be drawn became a form of money called DEPOSIT MONEY. In the UK this type of bank deposit is called a SIGHT DEPOSIT or a CURRENT ACCOUNT DEPOSIT. The deposit can be transferred to others by means of cheque and it can be converted into cash on demand.

Cheques are in some ways the modern equivalent of old-time bank notes issued by commercial banks. The passing of a bank note from hand to hand transferred ownership of a claim against the bank. A cheque on a bank account is similarly an order to the bank to pay the designated recipient money credited to the cheque writer's account. Unlike bank notes, however, cheques do not circulate freely from hand to hand. Thus cheques themselves are *not* money. The balance in the bank deposit is money; the cheque transfers money from one person to another. Because cheques are easily used, and because they are relatively safe from theft, they are widely regarded as being virtually as good as the currency they stand for.

Thus, when banks lost the right to issue notes of their own, the form of bank money changed, but the substance did not. Today's banks hold reserves to back the convertibility of their deposit money, just as their predecessors did. Some is held as currency in their vaults, but the bulk is held as deposits made by the commercial banks with the central bank. These deposits are *claims* to currency that the commercial banks know the central bank will always honour, so they are as good as cash – indeed, they are often referred to as part of their 'cash reserves'.[1]

It is true today, just as in the past, that most bank customers are content to pay their bills by passing among themselves the bank's promises to pay money on demand, which they do by writing cheques. Only a small proportion of the transactions made by the bank's customers is made in cash. Thus today, just as in the past, banks can create money by issuing more promises to pay (deposits) than they hold as reserves to pay out. The details of how this works are laid out in Chapter 35.

Near Money: The term NEAR MONEY refers to assets that fulfil some of the functions of money but not all of them. Specifically, near money is anything that fulfils the store-of-value function, and is readily *convertible* into a medium of exchange, but is *not* itself a medium of exchange.

As long as all sales and purchases do not occur at

---

1 Note the possible source of confusion here. 'Cash' strictly means notes and coins. Although the reserves that commercial banks hold on deposit with the Bank of England are called 'cash reserves', they are not cash. They are only entries on the Bank of England's books. But they are convertible into cash on demand. Furthermore, since the Bank of England is responsible for issuing notes and coins, there is no doubt about its ability to honour the commercial banks' deposits whenever the commercial banks wish to withdraw cash.

the same moment, everyone needs a temporary store of value between the act of selling and the act of buying. Whatever serves the function of a medium of exchange can be held, and thus can also fulfil the function of a temporary store of value. But other assets can also be used for this store-of-value function.

Consider, for example, a deposit account – often also called a *time deposit* – at a bank or building society. With such an account you know exactly how much purchasing power you hold (at today's prices). But this deposit is not a medium of exchange because you cannot write cheques on it. However, given modern practices, you can turn your deposit into a medium of exchange – cash, or a sight deposit – at short notice. Additionally, your time deposit will earn some interest during the period that you hold it.

Why then does everybody not keep their money in deposit accounts instead of in sight deposits or currency? The answer is that the inconvenience of continually shifting back and forth between sight and time deposits may outweigh the interest that can be earned. One week's interest on £100 (at 12 per cent per year) is less than 25p, not enough to cover the time and money costs in transferring money needed in a week into an interest-earning account now, and back out again next week.

Money Substitutes: Near moneys are assets that are not themselves media of exchange, but which can be easily converted into such a secure rate (£1 in a time deposit can always be converted into £1 in a sight deposit). MONEY SUBSTITUTES, on the other hand, are things that serve as temporary media of exchange but are not stores of value. Credit cards are a good example. With a credit card, many transactions can be made without either cash or a cheque. But the evidence of credit, in terms of the credit slip you sign, is not money because it cannot be used to effect further transactions. Furthermore, when your credit card company sends you an account, you have to use money to pay that account which is, in effect, a delayed payment for the original transaction. The credit card serves the short-term function of a medium of exchange by allowing you to make purchases even though you have neither cash nor a positive bank balance currently in your possession. But this is only temporary; money remains the final medium of exchange for these transactions when the credit account is settled.

Operational definitions of money

What is an acceptable medium of exchange has evolved over time. Furthermore, new monetary assets are continuously being developed to serve some, if not all, of the functions of money, and these 'near monies' are more or less readily convertible into money.

Economists who wish to measure the quantity of money in existence now find it necessary to distinguish several concepts of money. In the UK the most important of these are:

● M0: notes and coins, plus bank reserves held on deposit with the Bank of England. M0 is also called *high-powered money* or *the monetary base*;
● M1: notes and coins, plus sterling sight deposits of the private sector against which cheques can be drawn;
● STERLING M3 (called £M3): notes and coins, plus all sterling sight and time deposits of the private sector;
● M3: this is £M3, plus deposits of UK residents held in other currencies such as marks or francs.

M0 is the narrowest money aggregate and includes all of the reserves of the commercial banking system which they must hold to maintain convertibility of their deposit liabilities. The full importance of M0 can only be understood after we study the creation of deposit money by the banking system in Chapter 35. The M1 definition concentrates on the medium-of-exchange function of money. £M3 is a broader monetary aggregate[1] and incorporates time as well as sight deposits of the banks. M3 also includes, in addition to everything included in £M3, deposits held in foreign currencies that can quickly be converted into deposits held in sterling.

The Supply of Money: Economists use the terms SUPPLY OF MONEY, and MONEY SUPPLY, to refer to the total amount of money available in the entire economy (defined in one of the ways just outlined). It is a relatively easy matter to collect statistics on the total amount of notes and coins in circulation (since they are issued by the central bank), and the total of bank deposits (since banks must publish their balance sheets). Thus, we can know with a reasonable degree of accuracy what the money supply is at any moment of time.

---

1 The broadest of all measures is known as PSL$_2$, which includes deposits with building societies as well as banks. For a complete current list, see the latest *Bank of England Quarterly Bulletin*.

As we shall see in Chapter 37, the Bank of England has direct control over MO. By deciding how much deposit money to create, the commercial banks exert strong control over any of the broader concepts of money such as M1 or £M3. Since MO includes all of the reserves of the commercial banks, the Bank of England can try to exert some influence over supplies of deposit money by altering the quantity of MO. This is one of the major tools of the Bank's monetary policy which we shall study in Chapter 37.

The Nominal and the Real Money Supply: It is also useful to distinguish the nominal from the real money supply. The NOMINAL MONEY SUPPLY is the money supply measured in monetary units. The REAL MONEY SUPPLY is the money supply measured in purchasing-power units and expressed in constant prices – prices that were ruling in some base year. To obtain the real money supply, the nominal money supply is deflated by an index of the general price level.

For example, the nominal supply (as measured by M1) was £10,500 million in 1970 and £50,620 million in 1984. The real money supply, measured in 1970 prices, was £10,500 million in 1970 and £8,000 million in 1984. The latter figure is found by dividing the nominal money supply of £50,620m by the index of retail prices for 1984 of 430 (1970 = 100) and then multiplying by 100. Thus, although the nominal money supply increased by nearly three and a half times between 1970 and 1984, the real money supply – the purchasing power of the existing money supply – actually fell over the period in question.

In everything that follows in this book, we shall deal with the nominal money supply. We mention the distinction because it is often encountered. But for our purposes, all we need is the nominal money supply.

MONEY VALUES AND RELATIVE VALUES

Money is our measuring rod in most economic activities. We value our wealth, our incomes, what we buy, and what we sell, all in money terms. When we think of a commodity's market value we usually think of its money price. 'What', we might ask, 'is the value of this refrigerator?' 'It costs £X' might go the reply. 'Is this refrigerator worth more than this hi-fi set?', is another type of value question we frequently

ask. Assuming the hi-fi set costs £200, the answer is 'yes' if the refrigerator is priced at more than £200 and 'no' if it is priced at less.

'Have I saved enough money this winter to afford a week's holiday in Spain next summer?' is another common type of question. The answer depends on comparing the amount you have saved now with what you *expect* the Spanish trip to cost you. If you are sure that prices will not change, you can answer the question now by comparing what you have saved with the currently quoted price of a package holiday. But if prices change between now and when you actually book your tour, the answer may be different because what now looks like enough money may be insufficient when the time comes to travel.

Money prices are our measure of economic value. Money prices allow us to compare different values at any point in time, as with the refrigerator and the hi-fi set. They also allow us to compare values over time, as with the amount saved now and the package holiday to be taken later.

Money as a Veil

One of the great insights of the early economists was that any one money value is not important in itself. The value of money is always relative. A single money price is meaningless unless it can be compared to the price of something else. What matters, therefore, is *the comparison of two or more money values.*

For example, you might tell a man, newly arrived from Patagonia, that the price of a refrigerator is £200. If he knows no other sterling values, this would convey no useful information to him.

But let us say that he entered Britain with £2,000. Now he knows his funds are sufficient to buy 10 refrigerators. He has compared two money values: the market value of the refrigerator and the value of the funds he has brought in with him.

But is the £2,000 he has with him a little or a lot? Now he needs to know the prices of all the things he might want to buy, either individually or expressed as an average. Here he is interested in the general purchasing power of his funds. This requires that he relate the amount of his funds to the *general level* of prices.

Consider a further example. How much meat, beer and travel can we buy for a day's wages? Such 'exchange rates' – between the labour that we sell and the goods that we buy – are what determine our living standards. If a worker sells his labour for £40 a day and buys a suit for £120, then what matters is that it costs him three days' work to buy the suit. If instead he only received £20 a day while a suit only cost him £60, the *real* exchange rate would be unchanged at three days' work to obtain the suit.

Adam Smith, writing in 1776, saw what the above examples illustrate, that individual sums of money, and individual money prices, each looked at in isolation, convey no useful information. Instead, the comparison of two or more monetary values is what conveys significant information. Such comparisons allow us to look behind individual money prices to find real opportunity costs: how much of one thing must be given up to obtain something else.

The great insight is that value is *relative*; the monetary unit in which values are expressed is irrelevant. If, for example, wheat is worth twice as much as is barley per bushel, it does not matter, as far as their exchange rate is concerned, whether wheat is £2 and barley £1, or wheat £4 and barley £2 or wheat £100 and barley £50. Early economists thus talked of money as a veil behind which real economic relations occurred and were reacted to.

In summary, the monetary unit in which commodity prices are measured (and the number of zeros on this unit) are not relevant to the determination of real values. The only thing that is relevant for real values is the relation between values measured comparably.

The neutrality of money

Out of this realization grew the doctrine of the *neutrality of money*. Correctly stated, this doctrine is that the units chosen to measure values have no effect on 'real values' – real values are 'relative values', and it is relative values that affect behaviour.

In Britain, the currency units are pounds and pence. So if wheat costs £4 and barley £2, wheat has twice the value of barley. But the basic unit might have been something else. Suppose the basic unit had been called the 'Brit', abbreviated to 'B' and made to be worth 50p. Given the prices in the above example, wheat would then have cost 8B and barley 4B, but the relative value would have been unchanged: one bushel of wheat is equal to 2 bushels of barley, whether the prices are denominated in pounds or 'Brits'.

It follows from the doctrine of the neutrality of money that, if we change *all* monetary values by the same proportion, nothing real happens. No economic effects can be expected.

The real and the monetary parts of the economy

The doctrine of the neutrality of money leads to a conceptual division of the economy into two parts. In the 'real part', *relative prices*, quantities and the allocation of resources are determined by such things as consumers' tastes, production technology, and the degrees of competition among buyers and sellers. In the monetary part, the *absolute level of prices* is determined by monetary forces.

Thus, for example, the relative price of wheat and barely might be determined in the real part of the economy at 1 bushel of wheat = 2 bushels of barley, their outputs at 3 and 5 million tonnes, and the resources of land and labour allocated to each at 1 and 2.5 million hectares and 10 and 20 thousand person hours respectively. These are determined by the real forces of tastes and production possibilities operating through the markets for commodities and for factors of production. The monetary part of the economy would then set the price level at which transactions would take place. For example, wheat might be priced at £4 and barley at £2 a bushel, and agricultural wages at £3 an hour; or wheat at £8 and barley at £4 and wages at £6. *Both* of these levels of absolute prices yield the same *price relatives*.

The neutrality of money is most easily seen with a currency reform, such as the one instituted in France by President Charles de Gaulle in the 1950s. By taking two zeros off the prices of all commodities, all factors of production and all contracts, nothing real was changed. Everyone's money incomes were reduced by a factor of 10, but so were the money values of all debts, and all other contracts, as well as all money prices. As a result, everyone's real position, income and wealth, was unchanged. No new value was created and no existing value was destroyed. The change was solely in the 'monetary part' of the economy.

The Process of Price-Level Changes: Will changes in the price level always leave real (relative) values unaffected? The answer is 'yes' when all adjustments have been fully made, but 'no' until then – and 'until then' may be a very long time. To see why, compare de Gaulle's monetary reform with a change in the price level that comes about through the normal workings of the market.

The French currency reform was carried out overnight by the stroke of a pen, and hence had virtually no real effects – the new long-run equilibrium set of money prices was established instantaneously. All prices, and all wealth holdings, were adjusted by legal decree at the same instant.

In most real-world situations, however, a major change in the price level is spread over a great deal of time – sometimes years and even decades. Consider a case in which a rapid doubling of the quantity of money leads to an eventual doubling of the price level. It may take years for this new price level to be achieved through the operation of normal market forces. Some prices will adjust quickly, others will take time. At the outset, all existing contracts – wage contracts, mortgages, loans, orders to buy output not yet produced, etc. – will reflect the old price level. New contracts reflecting the new price level will be written as old ones expire. But many contracts last for years, so it will take years for the full adjustment to be completed. For example, one farmer may have a long-term contract to supply wheat for three years at £4 a bushel which looked satisfactory at the old price level. But now that prices are rising, he will want to rewrite his contract to £8 a bushel, but he must wait for 3 years to do so. Long-term leases on flats, houses and factories may have decades to run and their adjustment must wait till a new lease is written. Thus, we see that, in the process of adjusting the price level, real changes in relative prices occur and, hence, the process of inflation has real effects.

The doctrine of the neutrality of money holds as a long-run equilibrium concept: it does not hold in transitory situations when the price level is changing.

Relative and Absolute Prices: It is important to realize that we are contrasting changes in relative prices with changes in absolute prices. The micro-economics which we studied in Parts 2 and 3 of this book is exclusively concerned with relative prices. Since we assume, however, that all money prices except the one being studied remain constant, all changes in money prices were changes in relative prices. A rise in the money price of a hamburger, for example, also raises its relative price *if all other prices remain constant.*

Now that we are doing macroeconomics, we must consider changes in the general level of all prices. Determination of changes in relative prices is a bit more difficult, however, if the general level of prices is rising. Now a rise in the relative price of a hamburgers requires that its price rise faster than other prices. Thus the same real forces of demand and supply that would cause the price of hamburger to rise by 10 per cent in the context of a stable price level will cause its price to rise by 21 per cent if the price level rose by 10 per cent at the same time. (No, this is not a printer's error. A 10 per cent rise over and above a 10 per cent rise, adds up to 21 per cent.)

THE RELATION BETWEEN MONEY AND PRICES: THE CLASSICAL QUANTITY THEORY OF MONEY

The real side of the economy dictates our living standards. Total output of real goods and services divided by the total population determines the average living standards attained in the country. Money prices merely determine the absolute value at which transactions take place.

What then determines the average level of prices at which these real exchanges occur? We observed earlier in this chapter that the relation between money and the price level suggested very early in the history of economics was given by the so-called QUANTITY THEORY OF MONEY. This theory predicts that the general price level is *positively related* to the quantity of money in such a way that changes in the price level are proportionate to changes in the quantity of money. Thus, for example, a doubling of the quantity of money would lead to a doubling of the price level.

The Demand for Money: Before developing the quantity theory of money, we need to define a further concept. The DEMAND FOR MONEY is the amount of money the public wishes to hold, as notes and coins and as bank deposits. Like any other demand, the demand for money is a planned, or desired, concept – i.e. it tells us how much the public wishes to hold. If that much money is not available, they will not succeed in holding as much money as they wish to hold.

The last sentence suggests a second concept – the *realized* or actual holdings of money is the amount the public actually ends up holding. As we have already observed, the planned holdings of money will not necessarily equal the realized demand.

The 'Equation' of Exchange

One way to introduce the quantity theory is through the so-called *equation of exchange* that was made famous by the late American economist Irving Fisher.

Although called an equation, it is in fact a definitional identity, which means something which is true simply by virtue of our definition of the terms involved.

Here are the four terms that appear in the 'equation'.

Y is real national income, i.e. the physical volume of output.

P is the average level of all prices. (Thus PY is the money value of national income.)

M is the quantity of money, i.e. the supply of money.

V is what is called the VELOCITY OF CIRCULATION, which means the average number of times that the typical unit of money must change hands, in order to accomplish all the sales and purchases involved in producing and selling the national income.

We are already familiar with the concepts of real national income, Y, the price level, P, and money national income, PY. We have also discussed the concept of the supply of money, M, earlier in this chapter. For purposes of this theory, M can be thought of as M1. The only new thing we need to notice about M is that, since every unit of money in existence must be owned, and hence held, by someone – either in the form of cash or a bank balance – we can call M *the total money balances held by the public.*

Only the last term in the above list, V, has not already been discussed in this book. So we must consider it here. First, consider a simple example. Say in an imaginary economy with only two £1 notes, there are £4's worth of income-creating transactions. In this case, the velocity of circulation is *two* since the two £1 notes must have been used twice on average to effect £4's worth of transactions. If next period's income-creating transactions rise to £8, then the velocity of circulation must have risen to four in order that the £2's worth of money could be used in £8's worth of transactions. This use of the term velocity in effect defines it as PY/M, which is a measure of the average amount of work that a typical £1's worth of money must do to create a money national income of PY.

We can now set out the 'equation' of exchange:[1]

$$MV \equiv PY. \tag{1}$$

What this tells us is that the quantity of money multiplied by its velocity of circulation must be identical to the money value of national income. So if, for example, money national income is £10 billion while the quantity of money is £2 billion, then velocity must be 10/2 which is 5. In other words the average £1 unit of money must have been used five times to create £10 billion worth of national income.

Because this relation is a *definitional identity* (i.e. true by definition), it tells us nothing about the real world. But it does provide a useful insight into the working of economic forces, as well as a framework for classifying real-world data. When we see national income measured in current prices rise, we can ask how much of this is accounted for by an increase in the quantity of money and how much by an increase in velocity. For example, if we observe PY to rise by 10 per cent while M only rises by 5 per cent, then there must also have been a rise in velocity of about 5 per cent.

From the Equation of Exchange to the Quantity Theory

The equation of exchange can be turned from an identity into a theory in two steps. First, we must define V independently of P, Y and M. Second, we must make empirical assumptions about the behaviour of all four variables.

First divide equation (1) through by V to obtain the following:

$$M \equiv \frac{PY}{V}. \tag{2}$$

Now define k as $1/V$ and substitute into (2) for k:

$$M \equiv kPY. \tag{3}$$

So far, (3) is still an identity but let us see what k means. We have defined k to be the reciprocal of V. (You will recall from school algebra that the reciprocal of any number x is $1/x$.) k is also the proportion of money national income actually held as money balances in the whole economy, i.e. $k = M/PY$. For example, in the case considered above, PY was £10 while M was £2. This makes k equal to 2/10, which is 0.2. This tells that the amount of money balances held by everyone in the economy was, in this example, 1/5th (i.e. 20 per cent) of the money value of national income – which is the same thing as saying that the velocity of circulation of money is 5 in that economy.

What k does is to express the realized quantity of

---

1 The symbol T, standing for the volume of transactions, is sometimes used instead of Y. The 'equation' is then $MV \equiv PT$.

money actually held in the economy in terms of the proportion of PY that people actually hold as money balances. Now to turn what we have into a theory, we redefine k in *planned* or desired terms. We now define k as the proportion of PY that people *wish* to hold in terms of money balances. The amount of money balances that people wish to hold, which we denote by M_D and call the demand for money, is now given by:

$$M_D \equiv kPY. \qquad (4)$$

Expression (4) says that the demand to hold money balances will be some proportion, k, of money national income, PY. To make sure you understand (4), consider an example. Say k is 0.2. This means that the public as a whole wishes to hold an amount of money balances equal to 20 per cent of their income-creating transactions. Now say the money national income is £15bn. Then (4) tells us that the public will wish to hold money balances equal in value to £3bn (i.e. £15bn times 0.2).

But is there any reason for assuming that the demand to hold money balances is related in this way to PY; or indeed, that it is related in any way to PY? To answer this question we must look at what is called the transactions motive for holding money balances.

The transactions motive

We saw earlier in this chapter that money is a medium of exchange. People and firms who use it as such must hold money balances in the form of cash and bank deposits to facilitate their exchanges. Let us see why such balances need to be held.

First, consider a firm. If that firm's payments and receipts were perfectly synchronized, so that every time it had to pay someone, someone else paid it, the firm would not need to hold transactions balances. But payments and receipts are not perfectly synchronized for any firm. As a result, the firm, like everyone else in the economy, must hold balances of money. When its customers pay, the firm's money balance is increased. When the firm settles its accounts, its money balance is diminished. At times when receipts are large, the firm's money balance will rise; at times when payments are large, its money balance will fall.

Similar considerations apply to households. They receive their income in periodic payments – usually every week or every month. They hold these receipts as money balances – currency and, for many, a bank balance as well – in order to finance their payments

until the next payday.

We may conclude from the above discussion that, given the way in which payments and receipts are timed, the public – people and firms – need to hold money balances in order to be able to receive and pay out money according to their needs. The amount of money that people wish to hold for these reasons is called the TRANSACTIONS DEMAND FOR MONEY.

On what does the size of this demand depend? The answer is that it mainly depends on the demander's money income. If your income and your expenditures double, you will find yourself holding about twice as much money to finance your purchases between paydays. Similarly, if a firm's business doubles, it will need to hold larger amounts of cash in order to be able to meet its now-doubled volume of payments as they fall due. If we add up this behaviour over all firms and individuals in the economy, we find that *the public's transactions demand for money is positively related to the level of national income measured in current prices*.

This tells that the demand for money balances, M_D, varies directly with PY. But this is exactly what equation (4) above says. The fraction of their annual income transactions that the public wishes to hold as money balances is given by k.

We shall study the demand for money in greater detail in Chapter 34. All we need to note here is that the transactions motive is the only motive for holding money recognized in the simple quantity theory of money described here, which is known as the Classical theory.

Other assumptions

We have now seen the reasoning lying behind the demand for money given in equation (4) above. Next, let us briefly outline the other assumptions of the theory.

- The amount of money is exogenous. It is determined by the banking system, including the central bank, but does not vary as P, Y or k vary.
- k depends on institutional factors, such as the frequency with which payments are made and received. Since these do not vary greatly from one year to the other, k can be taken as a constant.
- P rises when there is excess demand for output and falls when there is an excess supply.
- Since we are dealing with long-term trends, departures from full-employment income can be ignored. Y will therefore be assumed to be constant at its full-employment, or potential, level.

Note that the last two assumptions represent a major change in the assumptions we have used so far in Part 4. Up to now, we have assumed that the price level, P, was constant while real income was variable. In these circumstances, changes in aggregate desired expenditure caused real national income (and employment) to change. These were suitable assumptions for short-run analysis. To study long-run behaviour, however, we reverse these assumptions. We assume that, in the long run, actual national income will be equal to potential income (more precisely, that short-run deviations of Y from potential income can be ignored when studying changes over long-run periods of time). We also assume, however, that the price level can change – which we know it does do over long periods of time. In these circumstances, variations in aggregate desired expenditure will offset the price level but not real income.

The assumptions set out above are the assumptions about the variables in the theory. We now need to make some assumptions concerning what happens when the demand to hold money balances is not equal to its supply.

- When the demand for money balances is less than the supply – i.e. the public has excess money balances – an attempt is made to spend the excess on the purchase of current output. In other words, the aggregate desired expenditure curve shifts upward.
- When the demand for money balances is greater than the available supply – i.e. there is a shortage of money balances – the public will attempt to add to its balances by reducing its purchases of current output. In other words, the aggregate desired expenditure curve shifts downward.

Implications

What happens when the demand for money does not equal its supply, i.e. when the public wishes to hold an amount of money balances different from the amount that is available to be held? We have already seen that when there is an excess supply of money balances, aggregate desired expenditure on current output increases. Because Y is fixed at its potential level, the upward shift in the aggregate expenditure curve opens up an inflationary gap and the price level rises. As P rises with Y constant, PY rises and so, therefore, does the quantity of money that is deman-

ded. (See (4) above.) The price level goes on rising until all the excess money balances are willingly held.

Now consider what happens when there is a shortage of money balances. People try to add to their balances by reducing their expenditure, which means that the aggregate desired expenditure curve shifts downward, creating a recessionary gap. But unlike the theory we have considered in earlier chapters, the price level is now assumed to be flexible in a downward direction. Thus Y stays at its full-employment level and the price level, P, falls. As PY falls, less money is demanded to finance the falling value of money income. (See (4) above.) The price level goes on falling until the demand for money balances has fallen to equal the available supply.

Only when the demand for money balances equals the available supply, so that there is neither a surplus nor a shortage of money balances, will equilibrium be reached and the price level remain stable.

Let us show what is happening in equation form. Equation (4) above gives the demand for money. Equation (5) below expresses the equilibrium condition just discussed, that the demand for money, M_D, should equal its supply, M:

$$M_D = M. \tag{5}$$

Note that (5) is an equation, not an identity. It does not hold as a matter of definition. Indeed, it only holds in equilibrium. Out of equilibrium either M_D will exceed M – an excess demand for money – or M_D will be less than M – an excess supply of money.

Now we substitute (4) into (5) to get:

$$kPY = M. \tag{6}$$

Equation (6) expresses the equilibrium condition that the demand for money equals its supply just as does equation (5). The only difference is that (6) spells out what determines the demand for money; i.e. kPY.

Next, we divide (6) through by kY to get

$$P = \frac{M}{kY}. \tag{7}$$

This is the famous equation of the quantity theory of money. In it, both k and Y are assumed to be constant. Although the quantity of money is exogenous (which means it is unaffected by any of the variables in our theory, k, P and Y), it can be changed by the monetary system. The equation tells us that the equilibrium price level will vary in the same direction as M. Furthermore the equation also implies that M and equilibrium P will vary in direct proportion with each other. For example, a 10 per cent increase in M will cause a 10 per cent increase in P.[1]

Conclusion

These, then, are the predictions of the Classical quantity theory of money – which is sometimes also called the naïve quantity theory. We shall see that modern theories of the relation between money and the price level are not quite as simple as this one. Most modern quantity theorists rely on a more sophisticated version of the quantity theory than the one outlined above. Nonetheless, to understand the theory laid out in this chapter is to understand the fundamentals of the relation between the quantity of money and the price level.

Modern economists continue to accept the Classical insight that the quantity of money is closely related to the general level of prices. It is also worth noting that many more complex and satisfactory theories also predict the direct proportionality result of the simple quantity theory.

In Part 5 we continue our study of the modern theory of money by looking in much more detail at the demand for money in Chapter 34 and at the supply of money in Chapter 35.

---

1 That P and M vary in the same direction as each other is obvious from inspecting equation (6): holding k and Y constant, an increase in M must increase P. As an exercise in simple algebra, you might like to try to prove for yourself the proportionality result; i.e. that $\Delta P/P = \Delta M/M$ as long as kY is constant.

SUMMARY

1 The major functions of money are to act as a medium of exchange, a store of value, a unit of account and a standard of deferred payments. To act as a satisfactory medium of exchange, money should be generally acceptable, portable, divisible and not easy to counterfeit. To act as a satisfactory store of value, money should also maintain a stable value over time.

2 Many commodities, including precious metals and convertible paper, have been used as money in the past. Today the principal forms which money takes are metallic coins, bank notes (fiat paper) and certain deposits held in banks. The total amount of money in existence is called the money supply or the quantity of money.

3 Banks hold deposits in sight accounts, which are chequable, and in deposit accounts, which count as 'near money', but which pay interest to the deposit-holder. Other money substitutes include credit cards.

4 There are several measures of the money supply, used for different purposes. All may be expressed in *nominal* and in *real* terms, the latter allowing for changes in its purchasing power.

5 Real values are relative values which determine the rate at which different goods and services exchange for each other. The doctrine of the neutrality of money is a long-run equilibrium proposition that the quantity of money determines the price level, but has no effect on real (relative) values. The neutrality does not necessarily hold in disequilibrium situations where the price level is changing. This is the sense in which money is said to be neutral.

6 The equation of exchange $MV = PY$, forms the basis for the Classical quantity theory of money, which predicts that, in long-run equilibrium, a given percentage change in the quantity of money will cause an equal percentage change in the price level.

Part 5

INTERMEDIATE
MACROECONOMICS

The Demand for Money

This chapter begins Part 5, which contains a more advanced treatment of macroeconomics and money than Part 4. Chapter 34 is the first in a series of four that are designed to integrate monetary forces into the theory of the determination of national income. In this chapter we study the demand for money. In Chapter 35 we study how the commercial banking system creates deposit money and thus helps to determine the supply of money. Then, in Chapter 36, we study what is called the monetary transmission mechanism. This is the mechanism that links the demand and supply of money to aggregate desired expenditure and, through aggregate expenditure, links monetary forces to equilibrium national income and the price level.

Finally, in Chapter 37 we study how the Bank of England seeks, through its monetary policy, to control monetary forces and thus to influence equilibrium income and the price level.

Readers are warned that Part 5 uses tools of analysis that are developed in Part 2. For this reason Part 5 should not be attempted without studying demand, supply and elasticity from Part 2.

BONDS, BILLS AND THE RATE OF INTEREST[1]

In order to understand the nature of the demand for money, it is essential to appreciate that people have a choice between holding money and holding some other kinds of financial asset. To start with, we

---

1 For a fuller discussion of debt instruments, see Harbury and Lipsey, Chapter 8.

consider only 2 such assets, *bonds* and *bills*; and we must immediately introduce the idea of the rate of interest that financial assets may yield.

What is a Bond?

A bond is a particular kind of financial asset that is created when some types of loan are made. It is rather like an IOU that a person who borrows money gives to the person who lends the money. In other words, it is evidence of a debt.

If a firm wishes to borrow money on the open market, it will issue bonds which it offers for sale to the public. Those who buy these bonds are loaning their money to the firm.

To illustrate, consider a bond issued by D.G. Harsey & Co. on 30 December 1989 that is repayable on 31 December 1999 for £100. This bond is offered on the open market and bought by R.C. Lipbury for £100. In effect, Lipbury has lent Harsey & Co. £100. What has Lipbury got in return? Well, he has a piece of paper called a bond. Cutting through all the smokescreen in the small print on the bond, what it says, in effect, is the following:

> We promise to pay to the bearer
> the sum of £100
> on 31 December 1999
> and also £5 annually on 31 December until that date.
>
> ....
> (signed) D.G. Harsey – Treasurer

Notice three features about this bond.

First, the bond promises to pay a certain sum in the future. This is called its FACE VALUE.

Second, the date at which that sum will be paid is specified – 31 December 1999 in this case. This is called the MATURITY DATE. When that date arrives, that bond is said to be redeemed, or to have *matured*. It is a *redeemable* bond. The length of time that the bond has to run until its maturity date is called the TERM of the bond.

Third, the borrower promises to pay a specific sum each year until the bond matures. This sum, which is a *flow* of future income, is called the INTEREST that the bond pays. To facilitate comparisons of the attractiveness of different bonds having different face values, the interest paid is usually expressed as a percentage of the value of the bond. This is called a RATE OF INTEREST. In this case, the rate of interest is 5 per cent, since the £5 interest paid each year is 5 per cent of the £100 face value of the bond.

The Market Value of a Bond

Now let us say that on 31 December 1990, Lipbury wants his money back. He cannot go to Harsey & Co. and demand that his loan be repaid because a bond is evidence of a term loan – one that will be repaid at some specific future date – not of a demand loan – one that is repayable on demand. What Lipbury can do, however, is to find someone else – let us call her A. Student – who has money to lend, and sell his bond to her. When he does this, Harsey & Co. are unaffected. They still owe £100, which must be paid on 31 December 1999 and are obligated to pay £5 a year until then. But Lipbury now has his money back, and Student has assumed the position of being Harsey's creditor.

Now come the critical questions: how much would Student be willing to pay, and how little would Lipbury accept, for the Harsey bond? Let us assume there is no doubt that Harsey will meet his obligation and repay the loan on redemption day. Would Student ever consider paying anything more than £100 for the bond? Would Lipbury ever consider taking anything less? The answer is yes to both questions. The price they will both willingly agree on for the sale of the bond may be more or less than £100, depending on the current market rate of interest.

The Market Rate of Interest

Just above, we encountered a new term, THE MARKET RATE OF INTEREST. This is the rate of interest that can currently be earned on new loans – in other words, it is what borrowers are currently willing to pay to obtain loans.

Let us now see how this relates to Lipbury's sale of the bond to Student. On the one hand, if newly issued bonds and other loans are offering 10 per cent, then the bond will not be worth £100. This is because £100 used to purchase a newly issued bond would earn £10 per year, so no one would invest £100 in a bond that pays a mere £5 a year. On the other hand, if the market rate of interest were only 3 per cent, the bond that Lipbury has will be worth more than £100. This is because £100 used to purchase a new bond would earn only £3 per year, so *everyone* who has money to lend would like to buy the bond that Lipbury has for £100 and earn £5 rather than invest £100 in a new bond and earn only £3.

This example illustrates an extremely important proposition: *The value of an existing bond is negatively related to the market rate of interest. The higher the market rate, the lower the value of the bond. In future whenever we write of a fall in the rate of interest you must immediately realize that this also means a rise in the price of bonds.*

This relation often seems mystifying at first sight, so let us pause over it for a moment. Remember first what a bond is. It is a promise to make a certain set of money payments over some future time-period. These payments are often referred to as a *stream of future payments*, and looked at from the point of view of the bond owners they are a *stream of future incomes*. How much it is worth paying now to obtain such a promise depends on how much must be invested elsewhere to earn an equivalent stream of income. The market rate of interest tells you how much you can earn from £1 invested elsewhere. The higher is the market rate of interest, the *less* must you invest in order to earn some fixed stream of interest payments. Thus, the higher the market rate of interest, the *less* is the value of a bond which pays a fixed stream of interest.

Present Value

The PRESENT VALUE of a stream of future payments is the amount that stream is worth now. We have seen that this amount depends on the market rate of interest. But exactly *how much* is the future stream promised by a specific bond worth, and exactly *how much* does this value change as the market rate of interest changes?

In the case of the Harsey bond, and any other bond that promises a lump-sum repayment of its face value on redemption date, the calculation of the exact answers to these questions is a little complex. This is because of the need to put a present value, not only on the stream of interest payments, but also on the principal that will be repaid on redemption day. We can, however, discover much of what we need to know now by looking at a slightly different type of bond.

A Consol: The type of bond that we now look at is one that has no maturity date. It is a promise to make a specified payment each year forever, but not to repay any face value at a specified maturity date. You might think that no one would be willing to 'lend' money to anyone who stated categorically that he would never repay the loan. You would, however, be wrong. After all, you would surely be willing to pay some sum to obtain the right to receive £1,000 each year forever. Indeed the UK government has obtained money from the public by issuing some such bonds, the best known of which are called CONSOLS (short for Consolidated Stock), which it stated originally might never be repaid. People bought them *because of the interest that they were guaranteed* to receive each year. The study of this type of bond will tell us much of what we need to know about bonds in general. After we have completed this study, we can finalize our treatment of redeemable bonds with relative ease.

Let us ask what is the present value of a bond, such as a Consol, *which promises to pay £100 per year indefinitely*. We can now forget about the face value of the bond. It does not have one, because it will never be redeemed. The present value of this bond depends only on how much £100 per annum is worth to investors. This depends solely on the market rate of interest.

Suppose, for example, that this rate is 10 per cent. This means that borrowers will pay 10p in interest each year for each £1 that is currently lent to them. At this rate £1,000 must be lent out to earn £100 in interest per year.

Now we must look at the value of the existing bond in terms of what an investor would pay for it and what the existing holder would sell it for. First, let us look at an investor. If £1,000 can earn £100 per year on current loans, then investors will be willing to pay £1,000 for the existing bond, but no more. Second, look at what the existing holder would accept. If £1,000 can be borrowed for interest of £100 a year,

the existing bond holder would accept £1,000 and no less. Say, for example, he was only offered £900. Instead of selling his Consols, he could keep them and borrow £1,000 at an interest payment of £100 per year. The £100 he earned on his bond would then just pay the £100 interest on his loan so that he would end up with the use of £1,000, instead of only the £900 that he would have had if he sold his Consols. Since buyers would pay £1,000 and no more, and since the seller would accept £1,000 and no less, the market price of Consols will be exactly £1,000.

When the price of the Consol that pays £100 per year is exactly £1,000, people will be willing to hold it because its rate of return, of 10 per cent, is the same as can be earned on new loans. If the price exceeds £1,000, no one will want them, so they cannot be sold. If the price is less than £1,000, everyone will want them, so this cannot be an equilibrium price for Consols.

Now, suppose there is some change in market conditions so that the market rate of interest falls to 5 per cent. In this situation it takes £2,000 to earn £100 per year at the market rate of interest. The present value of the Consol that pays £100 per year will now rise to £2,000. If anything more is asked for them, no one will want to hold them when 5 per cent can be earned at the market rate of interest. If anything less is asked for them, everyone will rush to buy them, since they offer a rate of return greater than the market rate of interest.

This discussion leads to the conclusion that the present value of Consols will be that sum of money which, if invested at the market rate of interest, would earn the stream of payments that is offered by the bond. Since the higher the interest rate, the lower the sum of money that must be invested to yield a specific flow of interest payments, the lower is the present value of Consols that offer a fixed stream of future interest payments. This illustrates the conclusion we have already reached: the higher the interest rate, the lower the present value of any bond.

All of this is no unsupported theory. A glance at the investment pages of any newspaper will show you bond prices falling when interest rates are rising, and rising when interest rates are falling.

Redeemable Bonds: The value of ordinary bonds which, as we have already mentioned, have a maturity date at which their face value will be repaid, is similarly related to the rate of interest. The calculation of present value is a little more complicated in this case, however, because the present value of such bonds becomes increasingly dominated by the fixed, face-value payment as its maturity date approaches. To illustrate, take an extreme case. The present value of a bond that is redeemable for £1,000 in a week's time will be very close to £1,000 no matter what the interest rate. Thus its value will not change much, even if the rate of interest leaps from 5 per cent to 10 per cent during that week. This illustrates a second important conclusion: *The sooner is the maturity date of a bond, the less the bond's value will change with any given change in the rate of interest.*

Capital gains and capital losses

Because changes in the interest rate cause the price of bonds to vary, they confer gains and losses on the current holders of bonds. If the market rate of interest *falls*, the market value of all existing bonds rises. Holders of existing bonds then gain increases in the value of their wealth. Such gains are called CAPITAL GAINS. They increase the value of all bond-holders' wealth while not changing the flow of income they get from their bonds. If, on the other hands, the market rate of interest *rises*, the market value of all existing bonds falls. The holders of existing bonds then suffer reductions in the value of their wealth. Such losses are *negative* capital gains, and they are sometimes called capital losses. They lower the value of all bond-holders' wealth, while not changing the income streams that they get from their existing bonds.

Bills

We need to mention another type of financial asset that is created when a loan is made. This is called a BILL (which is short for a bill of exchange). A bill is like a bond in that it is a promise to repay a definite sum of money at some fixed date in the future. Unlike a bond, however, it carries no explicit interest payments. Interest arises from a bill because the investor buys it for less than its face value. Thus, for example, if a bill promising to pay £105 in one year's time is purchased for £100 now, the purchaser, in effect, earns an interest rate of 5 per cent on his investment. Furthermore, the issuer pays 5 per cent because he gets £100 now, but promises to pay £105 in a year's time. When a bill is purchased at its time of issue for less than its value at maturity, the bill is said to have been DISCOUNTED.

Bills are used for short-term debts, usually of less than a year (typically 3 months, as with Treasury Bills used by the UK government), while bonds are used for long-term debts (terms of 20 years or more are not uncommon).

If the holder of a bill that has some time to go to maturity wants his money now, he is in the same position as a holder of a bond. He must find someone who will buy it from him. The price that will be paid will depend on the interest rate and the time to go to maturity. When the bill is resold, it is said to have been REDISCOUNTED. To see what is involved, consider an example.

Say that a bill, payable on December 31st for £105, was bought for £100 on January 1st of the same year. This implies an interest rate of 5 per cent. Now assume that the holder wants his money back on July 1st of that year. If the interest rate is unchanged, he will be able to sell his bill for £102.50. This will yield him £2.50 on an investment of £100 for six months, which is an annual rate of interest of 5 per cent. The purchaser pays £102.50, holds the bill for six months, and then redeems it for £105, which is also an annual interest return of 5 per cent.

Now assume, however, that just before the sale on July 1st, the interest rate rose unexpectedly to 10 per cent. Now the owner of the bill can only sell it for a price that will yield an interest rate of 10 per cent to its purchaser. This price is £100. The bill will yield £5 in six months' time, which is a 5 per cent yield over 6 months, making an annual rate of 10 per cent. Now the seller has received no return on his investment in the bill that he has held for six months. He bought the bill for £100 on January 1st, and sold it for £100 on July 1st. So the unexpected rise in the interest rate has wiped out the gain he expected to get when he bought it.

The Concept of Liquidity

A liquid asset is one that can be turned into money quickly and without significant risk of capital loss. Money, therefore, is the perfectly liquid asset, since nothing need be done to turn it into money. An irredeemable bond that could not be sold (but did yield a stream of interest payments) would be a perfectly illiquid asset – it cannot be turned into money. In between, there are various assets with different terms to maturity. The shorter the term of the bill or bond, the more liquid it is for two reasons: first, the less the time its holder needs to wait to get it redeemed into a fixed sum of money, and second, the less its market price will fluctuate as the market rate of interest fluctuates. Thus, 30-day bills are more liquid than 90-day bills, which are more liquid than 2-year bonds, which are more liquid than 20-year bonds.

Notice also that the liquidity of an asset depends not on its term and when it was issued, but on how far away its maturity date now is – what is called its *term to maturity*. For example, a 10-year bond that was issued 9 years, 11 months ago has a 1-month term to maturity and hence is now more liquid than a 90-day Treasury Bill issued 10 days ago and therefore with an 80-day term to maturity.

This completes our preliminary study of interest rates, bond and bill prices, and the relation between them. With these essential concepts understood, we are now able to move to the main subject of this chapter, which is the demand to hold various financial assets in general, and money in particular.

MONEY AND WEALTH

At any moment in time, households and firms have a given stock of wealth. This wealth can be held in the form of many different kinds of assets, and it is helpful to group these diverse assets under three main headings.

Kinds of Assets

The first group of assets are those that serve as a medium of exchange and a store of value – i.e. coins, paper money and chequing deposits. As we saw in Chapter 33, such assets are called money.

The second group includes all evidences of debt, such as short-term bills and longer-term bonds, which earn a rate of interest and which usually yield a fixed money value at maturity. These are often called debt instruments.

The third group includes all forms of *ownership* of capital goods, either directly in the form, say, of a family business or indirectly in the form of shares in a company. (In the latter case, the shareholders own the company, and the company owns the capital.)

The first two types of assets are often called *financial assets* to distinguish them from the third group, which are called *real assets*.

Money and Bonds

To simplify our discussion of the determinants of the demand for money, it is helpful to ignore real assets and to consider only two kinds of financial asset: money and bonds. By money we shall for now mean any medium of exchange as defined in Chapter 33; and by 'bonds' we shall mean all other assets. Money, therefore, includes currency and all deposits that can be transferred by cheque. Bonds include all interest-earning debt instruments *plus* real capital. *Each individual's total wealth is now made up of the sum of his or her holdings of money and bonds.*

THE DEMAND TO HOLD MONEY AND BONDS

By summing everyone's wealth over the whole economy, we can obtain the total stock of wealth in existence. We can think of that wealth being held in a *portfolio* of various assets. The decision on how to divide one's wealth between the various available assets is called a *portfolio balance decision* concerning the allocation of wealth. When wealth-holders hold the portfolio of assets that they wish to hold, we say that they are in equilibrium with respect to their portfolio of asset holdings. When wealth-holders have too much of some assets and too few of others in their current portfolios, they are in portfolio disequilibrium.

The first step in studying portfolio balance is to look at the demand for one particular asset that virtually all wealth-holders hold, money. The amount of wealth everyone in the economy wishes to hold in the form of money balances is called the DEMAND FOR MONEY.[1] We now study what determines this demand.

---

1 Students sometimes have difficulty with the concept of the demand for money because they fail to appreciate that it is unlike the demands for goods and services that we considered in Parts 2 and 3, which were *flow* demand curves describing the amount of some commodity that people wish to buy and to consume *in each period of time*. The demand for money describes the demand to hold a given *stock* of money. Once the stock is achieved, no further additions to or subtractions from it will be made – at least until there is a change in one of the conditions that determines the demand for money.

Note first that, because we have grouped all forms of wealth into only two classes called money and bonds, the part of their wealth that households do not hold in the form of money, they must hold in the form of bonds. It follows that households have only one decision to make on how to divide their given stock of wealth. For example, if a group of households having wealth of £5 billion demand to hold £1 billion worth of money, their demand to hold bonds must be for £4 billion worth. If the demand for money rises to £2 billion, the demand for bonds must fall to £3 billion. In this case, people will be trying to reduce their holdings of bonds by £1 billion – by selling them on the open market – and increasing their holdings of money by £1 billion – by adding the proceeds of their bond sales to their money holdings. It also follows that, if households are in equilibrium with respect to their money holdings, they must be in equilibrium with respect to their bond holdings. They cannot, for example, feel that their current wealth is held in just the right amount of money and too many bonds. If too much of their wealth is held in bonds, then too little must be held in cash, since there is, by definition, no other way in which wealth can be held.

Because bonds yield an interest return to their owners while money held in the form of currency does not, holding wealth in the form of money involves an opportunity cost. *The opportunity cost of holding money is the rate of interest that could have been earned by holding bonds instead.*

If wealth can be held in the form of bonds which earn interest income, why hold it in the form of money which does not? Three reasons for doing so are important. They are called the transactions, the precautionary, and the speculative motives for holding money. As we shall learn, the first two relate to the function of money as a medium of exchange, while the third relates to the function of money as a store of wealth.

The Transactions Motive

The first motive for holding money is the one that we studied in connection with the Classical quantity theory of money, and pages 405–9 of Chapter 33 should be reread at this time. Let us recall what we learned in that chapter.

The amount of money that the public wishes to hold in order to finance their transactions is called their TRANSACTIONS DEMAND FOR MONEY. The need to hold such transactions balances arises because payments and receipts are not exactly synchronized. The transactions demand for money is positively related to the level of national income measured in current prices.

In the simplest theory, the transactions demand for money is proportional to nominal income:

$$M_D = kPY,$$

where M_D is the transactions demand for money, Y is *real* national income, P is the price level, so that PY is nominal national income (i.e. valued at current prices) and k is the fraction of national income that is held as transactions balances. It follows that *the transactions demand for money will be increased by either an increase in real national income with prices constant, or an increase in the general price level with real national income constant, or any combination of the two.*

The only reason for holding money in the Classical quantity theory is the transactions motive, and the resulting demand is related solely to PY. In the rest of this chapter, we go beyond the Classical quantity theory of money by studying other influences on the transactions motive and also other motives for holding money.

The transactions demand and interest rates

The modern view of the transactions demand for money makes it depend not only on income but also on interest rates. This view was first put forward in two important articles by the American Professors William Baumol and James Tobin.

The Theory: The key to these theories lies in the opportunity cost of holding money balances which, as we already know, is the interest rate. Because of the interest that is forgone when money balances are held, people and firms are motivated to reduce their transactions balances to a minimum. One way this can be done is to make frequent switches between money and other assets.

Consider a man who is paid a salary each month and who spends all of it in a steady flow of payments over the month. Just after getting paid, his money holdings will equal his monthly salary. After that, his money holdings will steadily diminish as he spends his income, and will reach zero just before he receives his next salary payment. Throughout the month he will, therefore, be holding some unspent income. He might choose to hold this income in a sight deposit on current account at his bank, in which case he will hold on average over each month (and hence over the year) transactions balances equal to half his monthly salary. By dividing each month into two fortnights, he could, however, keep only half of his salary in money at payday in order to finance the first fortnight's expenses. The other half of his salary he would invest in bonds. Then, at the start of the second fortnight, he would cash in the bonds that he bought on payday and obtain enough cash to finance the second fortnight's expenditure. In this way he reduces his average transactions holding to one-quarter of a month's income (compared to the one-half before). At the start of each half of the month, he has one-half of a month's income as a balance and at the end of the half he is down to nothing. Hence he correspondingly increases his average holding of interest-earning assets.

A similar line of argument could be used to show that if the same man made *daily* transfers of funds, he could reduce his transactions balances yet further. But obviously the most profitable arrangement will depend on how much interest can be earned and how costly it is (in terms of such things as time spent making trips to the bank, inconvenience and the cost of buying and selling assets) to switch assets. The higher the rate of return on interest-earning assets, the greater is the inducement to invest available funds rather than to hold transactions balances. But in order to hold a smaller quantity of transactions balances, an individual must make more frequent switches between money and other assets and incur higher costs. The modern theory of transactions balances predicts that these costs will be less of an inhibition the higher is the rate of interest, and thus that the amount of money held in transactions balances will be lower the higher is the rate of interest.

The Experience: This theory remained a relatively unimportant adjunct to the theory that the transactions demand depended on income until the late 1970s. Then interest rates soared from rates under 10 per cent to rates well over 20 per cent. At these new higher rates, it paid firms, especially big ones with large transactions balances, to devote much attention to reducing their balances. After all, if a large firm could reduce its average balances by £1 million over the year, this is an extra £250,000 earned, at a 25 per cent interest rate. That sum would pay the salary of a full-time cash-management official and still leave a profit for the firm.

This kind of thing happened on a grand scale in the 1970s with large firms lending out unwanted balances, sometimes for periods of no more than a few hours at a time. As a result the average transactions balances fell dramatically.

The Precautionary Motive

We have seen that the transactions need for cash arises because the timing of receipts and payments are not perfectly synchronized. The precautionary need arises also from money's function as a medium of exchange, but it arises because the timing and size of receipts and payments is *uncertain*. As with the transactions motive, both firms and households have precautionary motives for holding money which are broadly similar.

To see what is involved, assume that a firm knows for certain that all of its receipts for goods sold during the week will come in on Friday, and that all of its payments for everything it purchases will be made in equal amounts on each day of the week. In this case, a firm would have a large money balance on Friday just after it received its payments. It could then let its money balances run down as it paid its bills on each day of the following week until its balances reached zero just before it received its payments the following Friday.

Now assume that the firm is *un*certain about the exact timing of its receipts. Possibly on one Friday all its customers may not settle their accounts. Unless the firm has some additional cash balances, it will be unable to meet all its payments over the following week. Or, to take another case, although it receives all it expects on Friday, the following week there are some extra unexpected payments it has to make. Again, if its money balances were only what it received last Friday, it could not make these extra payments.

As a precaution against unexpectedly high payments, or unexpectedly low receipts, firms (and individuals) often hold more than the minimum balances that they need to accommodate their ordinary, expected flows of receipts and payments. The desire to hold money to accommodate such unexpected fluctuations in receipts and payments is called the PRECAUTIONARY MOTIVE FOR HOLDING MONEY. The precautionary demand for money arises out of uncertainty about the exact timing, and size, of payments and receipts.

Just as with the transactions need, the precautionary need varies directly with the level of money income, which is its prime determinant. If a firm does only £10,000 worth of business each week, it will need to hold, say, an extra £500 to guard against receipts that are 5 per cent below normal or payments that are 5 per cent above normal. But if the firm does £100,000 worth of business each week, it will need to hold £5,000 to guard against the same percentage fluctuations in its receipts and payments. *Thus the precautionary demand for money responds to the same influence as does the transactions demand for money. It varies directly with national income valued in current prices; the higher the level of money income, the larger the money balances that will be needed for transactions purposes.*

The Speculative Motive

The first two motives for holding money relate, as we have seen, to the function of money as a medium of exchange. The third motive, which we shall now study, relates to the function of money as a store of wealth. We have seen that money has an opportunity cost in the form of forgone interest. This provides an incentive for firms, and individuals, to hold no more money than the minimum they need to satisfy their transactions and precautionary motives. We might expect, therefore, that any surplus wealth would be held in the other form that is available, bonds.

The problem with holding wealth in the form of bonds is that the price of bonds may vary. As we saw earlier in this chapter, the price of bonds is negatively related to the interest rate: high interest rates mean low bond prices, while low interest rates mean high bond prices.

This variability in the price of bonds means that bond holders can make capital gains by buying when the price is low (i.e. the rate of interest is high) and selling when the price is high (i.e. the rate of interest is low). The motive that leads the public to vary their money balances in anticipation of changes in the value of bonds is called the *speculative motive*.

We shall see below that the speculative motive leads to the important result that the demand to hold money varies negatively with the rate of interest – the higher the rate of interest, the lower the demand to hold money, and vice versa. This negative relation between the demand for money and the rate of interest is well established empirically and it has, as we shall see in a later chapter, very important implications for the theory of income determination.

We must now look at two theories that attempt to explain the speculative demand for money. The first is due to Keynes, and the second to Tobin.

Keynesian theory of the speculative motive

Keynes' theory, which was published in 1936, refers to the amount of money held over and above what is necessary to satisfy the transactions and precautionary motives. He assumed that each wealth-holder has an *expectation* of the *normal* rate of interest, i.e. the rate that he or she expects to rule, on average, over the near future. Since bond prices are directly related to interest rates, an *expected* rate of interest implies an *expected* price of bonds. Whether the individual will hold his or her wealth in money or bonds depends, according to this theory, on the relation between the *expected* rate of interest and the *actual* rate currently ruling.

To see what behaviour is implied by this theory, assume first that the actual market rate of interest lies below the expected normal rate. This means, using the relation between interest rates and bond prices, that the price of bonds lies above their expected normal price. In such a case the wealth-holders could sell bonds now at their high price and hold the proceeds as money, intending to re-purchase bonds when their price fell to normal – i.e. when the rate of interest rose to normal. By so doing, they would make a capital gain.

Second, assume that the rate of interest lies above the rate people regard as normal. This means that the price of bonds is below normal. In this case, wealth-holders could use all the money available (above minimum transactions and precautionary needs) to buy bonds. They would be sold to replenish money holdings when the price of bonds rose to normal (the rate of interest fell to normal). This transaction would yield a capital gain.

This theory predicts that individuals will want to hold money rather than bonds when the rate of interest is low relative to the normal rate (the price of bonds is high and expected to fall), and bonds rather than money when the rate of interest is high relative to the normal rate (the price of bonds is low and expected to rise).

Key Features of the Keynesian Theory: The Keynesian theory of the speculative demand for money predicts a negative relation between the interest rate and the demand for money. When it was first stated, it was revolutionary. By making the demand for money depend on the interest rate, as well as on income, it broke out of the straitjacket of the Classical quantity theory of money. This had far-reaching implications, which we shall study in later chapters.

Nonetheless, the theory has some unsatisfactory features. We shall lay them out first and then show why they are unsatisfactory.

- If you are sure bonds are above their normal price, it will pay you to sell all your bonds now and hold only cash. You would then buy bonds again when their price falls back to normal. There would be no reason to hold *any* bonds. Similarly, if you are sure that bonds are below their normal price, it will pay you to put all the money you can spare into bonds now and sell some to replenish your cash balances when bond prices rise back to normal. Thus, on Keynes' explanation, an individual investor would either hold *all* of his or her available wealth in money – or *all* in bonds (over and above the minimum needed for transactions and precautionary purposes).
- In order to explain why *both* money *and* bonds are voluntarily held at any one time in the economy as a whole, Keynesian theory assumes that different people have different expectations about what is the normal rate of interest. Thus, if the current market rate of interest is 9 per cent, all those who believe that the normal rate is above 9 per cent will be holding bonds, while all those who believe that the normal rate is below 9 per cent will be holding money. Thus, over the whole economy, both money and bonds will be held.

Criticisms of the Keynesian Theory: There are two major criticisms that can be levelled at the Keynesian theory of the speculative demand for money.

- Individuals are not observed to hold all of their wealth *either* in money *or* in bonds, nor to switch completely from one to the other as the actual rate of interest passes through some critical value (their own expected rate of interest).
- The Keynesian theory does not explain how people form their expectations about the normal rate of interest. Therefore the theory assumes what it sets out to explain; in order to explain the rate of interest it assumes the existence of a normal rate about which the actual rate gravitates.

Although no longer accepted as the theory of the

speculative motive for holding money, Keynesian theory was an important advance when it was first put forward. Even today, it is useful in emphasizing the role played by expectations about the future rate of interest in helping to determine the current demand for money.

Tobin's theory of liquidity preference

In 1958, James Tobin published a more satisfactory theory of why the demand to hold money balances varies with the rate of interest. Tobin's article was path-breaking in creating an entire new branch of theoretical and empirical work that explains the mixture of assets in which wealth will be held. In 1981 he was awarded the Nobel Prize in economics for, among other things, his fathering of what is now called the 'portfolio balance theory'. *The basis of Tobin's theory is to combine the precautionary and the speculative motives for holding money.*

Let us now see how this theory works. Households and firms who hold bonds will have to sell some of their bonds if some temporary excess of payments over receipts exceeds their current money holdings. (Don't forget that 'bonds' stand for all assets other than money.) At one extreme, if a household or a firm holds all its wealth in bonds, it will earn interest on all that wealth, but it will have to sell some bonds the first time its payments exceed its receipts. At the other extreme, if a household or firm holds all of its wealth in money, the money will earn no interest, but the household or firm will never have to sell bonds to meet excesses of payments over current receipts. Wealth-holders usually do not adopt either extreme position; instead, they hold part of their wealth in the form of money and part in the form of bonds.

A household or a firm that holds some bonds and some money still runs the risk that an unexpected gap between its receipts and its payments will force it to sell some bonds. Anyone who may have to sell bonds to meet a need for money takes a risk. This is the risk that the price of bonds may be unexpectedly low at the time it must sell them. Of course, if the seller is lucky, the price may be unexpectedly high. But because no one knows in advance which way the price will go, firms and households must accept a risk whenever they hold some of their wealth in the form of bonds. Many firms and households do not like risk, in which case they are said to be *risk averse*. This leads them to hold more money than they otherwise would in order to reduce the risk of having to sell bonds in the future at a price that cannot be predicted in advance.

An important force acting on the decision of how to divide wealth between bonds and money is the cost of holding money. The reduction in risk involved in holding more money also carries cost in terms of interest earnings forgone. According to Tobin's theory, *the speculative motive leads households and firms to add to their money holdings until the reduction in risk obtained by the last pound added is just balanced (in each wealth-holder's view) by the cost in terms of the interest forgone on that pound.*

Because the cost of holding money balances is the interest that could have been earned if wealth had been held in bonds instead, the demand to hold money will vary inversely with the interest rate. When the rate of interest falls, the cost of holding money falls. This leads to more money being held, both for precautionary motives (to reduce risks caused by uncertainty about the flows of payments and receipts) and for speculative motives (to reduce risks associated with fluctuations in the market price of bonds). When the rate of interest rises, the cost of holding money rises. This leads to less money being held for speculative and precautionary motives.

Tobin's theory (of which we have given only the barest outline here) leads to the key prediction that variations in the interest rate will lead wealth-holders to change the proportion of their wealth that they hold in bonds (and, therefore, the proportion that they hold in money). Specifically, *the higher the rate of interest, the lower the demand for money balances.*

Tobin's theory also predicts that wealth-holders will hold both bonds and money, and will adjust the balance between these two assets continuously as the rate of interest changes; i.e. they do not suddenly move their wealth all into money or all into bonds as the rate of interest passes through some critical value. (Of course people with small amounts of wealth may hold no bonds at all, but most money balances are held by households and firms with large amounts of wealth, and they are observed to adjust their portfolios between money and bonds – and a host of other financial assets – as the interest rate varies.) Furthermore, Tobin's theory does not make the demand for money depend critically on the difference between the current market rate of interest and some expected future rate. Indeed, the theory works even if everyone expects the current market rate to persist. All that is needed is that they do not hold their expectations with perfect certainty. Some degree of uncertainty

about future interest rates, some uncertainty about the future need for cash, plus some amount of risk aversion, will lead people to hold amounts of money that will vary with the rate of interest.

The Total Demand for Money: A Recapitulation

Although Tobin and Keynes provide different explanations, both of their theories predict a negative relation between the demand for money and the rate of interest. For our purposes, this is all that matters.

The demand for money is defined as the total amount of money balances that everyone in the economy wishes to hold. Our discussion of the motives for holding money leads to the conclusion that the demand for money, which is the demand to hold a stock of money balances, varies *positively* with national income valued in current prices and *negatively* with the rate of interest.

Figure 34.1 shows the influences of money national income and the rate of interest on the quantity of money demanded. Note that since Y stands for real national income, we must multiply it by the average level of money prices, P, to obtain money national income, PY.

In part (i) of the Figure, the demand for money is shown as varying directly with money national income, along the curve T. As money national income rises from PY_0 to PY_1, firms and households increase their demand for money from M_0 to M_1. In part (ii), the demand for money is shown to vary inversely with the rate of interest, along the curve L. As the rate of interest falls from r_1 to r_0, firms and households increase their demand for money from M_2 to M_3.

Liquidity preference for a given level of national income

The function that shows how the total demand for money varies with the rate of interest is called the LIQUIDITY PREFERENCE (LP) FUNCTION. It shows the public's demand to hold the liquid asset money, rather than the illiquid asset bonds. Note that the liquidity preference function is also often called the DEMAND FOR MONEY FUNCTION. In the first of these terms, 'liquidity preference' refers to the choice being made: people are expressing their preferences between holding the liquid asset, money – which usually earns no interest – and the illiquid asset,

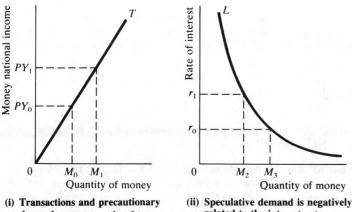

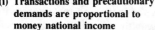

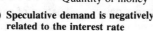

(i) Transactions and precautionary demands are proportional to money national income

(ii) Speculative demand is negatively related to the interest rate

FIGURE 34.1 The Demand for Money as a Function of the Interest Rate and Income. The quantity of money demanded varies negatively with the rate of interest and positively with national income valued in current prices

bonds – which does earn interest. In the second of these terms, 'demand for money' is a straightforward reference to the amount of money balances that the public wishes to hold.

In subsequent chapters of this book we shall be showing only the function relating the demand for money to the rate of interest, i.e. the liquidity preference function. Since the demand for money actually depends on both the rate of interest, r, and money national income, PY, any given LP function must be drawn for a *given level of PY*. Changes in PY thus shift the LP function. This important point is

illustrated by relating what we have already studied in Figure 34.1 to Figure 34.2.

Let money national income be constant at PY_0 in part (i) of that figure. The demand for money that depends on income is then M_0. When the rate of interest is r_0 in part (ii) of Figure 34.1, the demand for money that depends on the rate of interest is seen to be M_3. The total demand for money is then the sum of M_0 and M_3 in parts (i) and (ii) of Figure 34.1, which we plot as M_4 in Figure 34.2. As the rate of interest varies, the total demand for money varies along the line LP_0 in Figure 34.2. For example, if the interest rate rises to r_1, the demand for money falls to M_5, which is the sum of M_0 and M_2 shown in the two parts of Figure 34.1.

Now, however, let national income increase to PY_1 in Figure 34.1 (i). The demand for money that depends on income rises to M_1, as shown in Figure 34.1 (i). Now more money is demanded at each rate of interest. This causes the LP function in Figure 34.2 to shift rightwards by the amount $M_1 - M_0$ to LP_1. For example, at interest rate r_0 the total demand for money is now M_6, which is the sum of M_3 and M_1 in parts (i) and (ii) of Figure 34.1.

It is important to understand the distinction between movements along and shifts of the LP function. The function itself relates the demand for money to the interest rate. Changes in the interest rate cause changes in the quantity of money demanded, which are shown by movements along the curve, since it is drawn for a given level of money national income. Changes in money income shift the curve: a rise in income shifts the curve rightwards, while a fall in income shifts it leftwards.

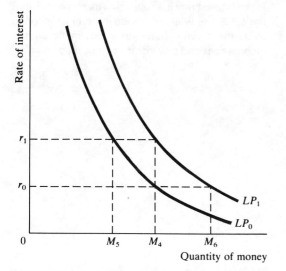

FIGURE 34.2 The Liquidity Preference Curve. This curve shows how the total demand for money varies with the rate of interest; it is drawn from a given level of nominal national income

Conclusion

The theory of the demand for money has a long history. It is important because, as we shall see in the next chapter, the demand for money provides one of the key links in the causal chain that joins the stock of money to the flow of national income. Although you have studied many issues in this chapter, all that you need to know for what follows is that *we expect people to wish to hold more money the higher is the money value of national income, which creates their need for it, and the lower is the interest rate, which is the opportunity cost of holding it.*

SUMMARY

1 A bond is an evidence of a debt. A redeemable bond is a promise to repay a fixed principal at a given redemption date and a fixed interest payment in the interim. An irredeemable bond (e.g. a Consol) has no redemption date.

2 A bill is also an evidence of debt. It is a promise to pay a stated sum at some future date. Interest arises because the bill is purchased at a price less than its future redemption value, in which case the bill is said to be discounted.

3 The market value of any bond or bill, which is called its present value, varies inversely with the rate of interest. When the rate of interest rises, the market value of bonds falls and their holders suffer capital losses. The opposite changes confer capital gains on bond-holders.

4 The demand to hold money depends on the transactions, precautionary and speculative motives. The demand is positively associated with nominal national income (*PY*) and negatively associated with the interest rate.

5 Keynes and Tobin developed somewhat different theories to explain the dependence of money on the interest rate. In the Keynesian theory, wealth-owners hold their wealth in bonds – in anticipation of capital gains on bond holdings – when the rate of interest is above their normal expected rate and hold their wealth in money – in expectation of capital losses on bond holdings – when the rate of interest is below their normal expected rate.

6 In Tobin's theory, people balance the risk in holding bonds, whose prices may change, against the interest forgone by holding money. The higher the interest yield, the greater the proportion of their wealth people will hold in bonds and, hence, the lower the demand for money.

7 The *liquidity preference function*, also called the *demand for money function*, relates the demand for money to the interest rate. It is drawn for a fixed level of nominal national income. A change in the interest rate is shown by a movement along the *LP* curve, while a change in nominal income shifts the curve – outwards if nominal national income rises and inwards if nominal income falls.

Banks and the Supply of Money[1]

In Chapter 34 we studied the demand for money. In this chapter we study the influence that the financial system has on the supply of money.

The main institutions of the UK banking system are the commercial banks, the building societies, the merchant banks, the discount houses, finance houses, overseas banks, and the Bank of England. The Bank of England is considered in detail in Chapter 37 where we deal with monetary policy, so we say little about it here. In the first part of this chapter, we deal with the commercial banks and with the influence they exert on the money supply by their ability to create deposit money. In the second part, we discuss the other main institutions of the banking system.

THE COMMERCIAL BANKS

To ordinary people, the most visible units in the present-day banking system are the COMMERCIAL BANKS, which are privately owned banks that deal with the public. These banks have a number of main functions:

- they accept deposits;
- they transfer certain kinds of deposits among both their customers and other banks, when ordered to do so (usually by cheque);
- they make loans to customers, called ADVANCES, charging them interest in return;
- they invest some of their funds by purchasing interest-earning assets on the open market.

---

1 Further details of UK banking institutions are given in Harbury and Lipsey, Chapter 8.

The most important of the commercial banks are the so-called London clearing banks, located in England and Wales, and the clearing banks of Scotland and Northern Ireland. (They are called clearing banks because they are members of a clearing house, which institution we discuss in the next section.)

The four largest London clearing banks dominate the system in terms of value of deposits held. They have numerous branches throughout the country. For this reason the UK system is called a 'branch banking' system as opposed to the American system, which is a 'unit banking' system and which contains many individual banks (over 15,000 in 1986), each with relatively few branches.

A unit banking system, by encouraging the existence of many banks, tends to result in more competition than does a branch banking system with its few large banks. However, the great advantage of a branch banking system over a unit system is its ability to spread risks. A crop failure in Nebraska could drive a local American bank into insolvency as the farmers who were its major customers found themselves unable to repay their loans. A crop failure in Somerset could not, however, seriously threaten the solvency of any British bank, since its customers in that county account for only a minute fraction of its total customers.

Commercial banks are in business to earn profits. They thus have a strong incentive to invest in assets that earn a high return. Generally, however, assets that earn the higher returns tend to be relatively illiquid. This creates a conflict with the bank's need to hold adequate reserves to meet its depositors' demands for cash. To meet these needs, the bank must hold reserves of cash in its vaults or on deposit with the Bank of England, or in very liquid 'near money' assets, such as short-term securities that can easily be redeemed for cash. So one of the arts of bank management is to obtain the best balance in the bank's portfolio of assets between revenue and liquidity.

Types of Financial Assets

The main assets held by the banks are shown in Table 35.1. Notes and coins held in their premises and their clearing balances on deposit with the Bank of England (called balances), which can be turned into currency on demand, are perfectly liquid assets. These assets earn no interest. Notice that, although deposits with the Bank of England are not cash, they are as good as cash, since the Bank will turn them into currency on demand. Thus the banking system's deposits with the Bank of England are often loosely referred to as their 'cash reserves'.

The remaining assets held by the banking system earn a return but are somewhat less liquid than its cash reserves. The most liquid of these are loans either for very short terms or 'at call', the latter term meaning repayable on demand. These short-term or call loans are called 'market loans'. The next most liquid assets are various types of bills, all of which will have terms of less than a year. By far the most important asset, however, is advances to customers. These are loans and overdrafts that may be repayable on demand or after a fixed term. Other longer-term, less liquid assets are also held. Of these, bonds and securities issued by commercial establishments (called investments), and by the government, comprise a significant proportion of the banking system's total assets.

Table 35.1 also shows the banks' major liabilities. Deposits are a liability of the banks, since they are promises to pay currency to any customer who wishes to withdraw his deposit. Some of these liabilities are denominated in sterling while the rest are denominated in a variety of foreign currencies. When you make a deposit at your local bank, you receive a credit denominated in sterling. Other depositors, however, may bring in foreign exchange payable in some foreign currency and they receive a credit denominated in that foreign money unit (say, so many German marks, or so many US dollars). Thus the liabilities of the UK's commercial banks are partly denominated in sterling, and partly in the currencies of other countries.

By far the largest of all liabilities are sight and time deposits denominated in foreign currency and held by overseas depositors. The largest sterling liabilities are time deposits, followed by sight deposits. The enormous size of deposits denominated in currencies other than sterling is an indicator of the internationalization of the world's banking system that has taken place in the last two decades. Ordinary banks now do a substantial amount of their business in foreign currencies, accepting deposits and withdrawals denominated in these currencies.

The Bankers' Clearing House

When a depositor in Bank A writes a cheque in favour of someone whose account is with Bank B, Bank A now owes money to Bank B. The cash flow is exactly the same as when one individual withdrew cash from Bank A and gave it to the second individual, who deposited it in Bank B. When the transaction is done

TABLE 35.1 Liabilities and Assets of UK Banks. December 1985 (millions of £s)

Liabilities		Assets	
Notes outstanding	995	STERLING ASSETS	
STERLING DEPOSITS		Notes and coins	2,313
Sight deposits	66,231	Balances with the Bank of England	750
Time deposits	129,524	Market loans (call & very short term)	71,363
Certificates of deposit	12,818	Bills (Treasury & local authority)	300
OTHER CURRENCY DEPOSITS		Bank and other bills	3,684
(SIGHT AND TIME)		Advances	131,994
UK monetary sector	92,656	Net lending to central government	574
Other UK	19,019	Investments	7,171
Overseas	323,730	Other	12,474
Certificates of deposit	64,125	OTHER CURRENCY ASSETS	478,474
	709,097		709,097

Source: Annual Abstract of Statistics, 1987.

by cheque, however, the banks, rather than the individuals, transfer the money. Multibank systems settle interbank debts through a CLEARING HOUSE, where interbank debts are cancelled.

In England, the clearing house is owned and operated by the commercial banks. At the end of the day, all of the cheques drawn by Bank A's customers, and deposited in Bank B, are totalled and set against the total of all the cheques drawn by Bank B's customers, and deposited in Bank A. The two banks then only need to settle the difference between these two sums. All of the customers' cheques used to be passed through the clearing house back to the bank on which they were drawn so that each bank could adjust its depositors' accounts by a set of book entries. Today, the operation is computerized, though the result is the same. Payments from one bank to another are unnecessary unless there is a *net* transfer of deposits from the customers of one bank to those of another.

The Creation of Money by the Commercial Banks

Our main concern in this chapter is with the supply of money. From that point of view, the most important aspect of the banking system is its ability to create and destroy deposit money. Banks have this ability because all customers do not try to convert their deposits into notes and coins at the same time. At any one time, some customers will be withdrawing cash from their accounts while others will be depositing cash to the credit of their accounts. Because these two amounts do not exactly balance, banks must keep reserves to accommodate their customers when withdrawals exceed new deposits. But because in normal times the net amount of withdrawals is far less than the total of customers' deposits on their books, the reserves that are required are only a small fraction of total deposits.

The behaviour summarized above is the basis of the fractional reserve system that we first encountered in Chapter 33. In turn, it is the fractional reserve system that allows banks to create money. We must now look into this process of money creation in more detail.

Some simplifying assumptions

To focus on the essential aspects, assume that banks can hold only two kinds of assets, cash and advances

to customers. Further assume that there is only one kind of deposit, a sight deposit, which earns no interest and can be withdrawn on demand. The other assumptions listed below are provisional. Later, when we have developed the basic ideas concerning the bank's creation of money, these assumptions will be relaxed.

Fixed Reserve Ratio: We have seen that commercial banks hold their cash reserves partly as notes and coins on hand to meet the day-to-day needs of their depositors and partly as reserves held on deposit with the Bank of England. (Note that some of these reserves are not cash as we defined it on page 400. But deposits with the Bank of England can be converted into cash on demand and so are counted as part of cash reserves.) Dividing total cash reserves by total deposit liabilities gives what is known as the RESERVE RATIO. For example, if a bank has deposit liabilities of £10m and reserves of £2.5m, its reserve ratio is 2.5m/10m, which is 0.25. This figure indicates that reserves held are sufficient to cover 25 per cent of all deposit liabilities.

For purposes of illustration, we shall assume that all banks have a desired reserve ratio of 20 per cent; that is, that banks decide to have at least £1 of reserves for every £5 of deposits. Reserves in excess of their desired reserve ratio are called *excess reserves*.

No Cash Drain from the Banking System: We further assume that the public wishes to hold a fixed, and unchanging, amount of currency. Thus, any changes in the money supply will take the form of changes in deposit money.

Deposit creation

We give below the balance sheet of a hypothetical bank. This bank's assets consist of reserves of £200, held partly as cash on hand and partly as deposits with the central bank, and £900 of loans to its customers. Its liabilities are £100 to those who initially contributed capital to start the bank, and £1,000 to current depositors. The bank's actual ratio

Balance Sheet 1. The initial position

Liabilities		Assets	
Deposits	£1,000	Cash and other reserves	£200
Capital	100	Loans	900
	1,100		1,100

of reserves to deposits is $200/1,000 = 0.20$, exactly equal to its assumed desired reserve ratio.

Now imagine that an immigrant arrives in the country and opens an account by depositing £100 in cash with the bank. This is a new deposit for the bank, and it results in the revised Balance Sheet 2.

Balance Sheet 2. Position after a cash deposit of £100

Liabilities		Assets	
Deposits	£1,100	Cash and other reserves	£300
Capital	100	Loans	900
	1,200		1,200

As a result of the immigrant's new deposit, both the bank's cash assets *and* its deposit liabilities have risen by £100. More importantly, its *actual reserve ratio* has increased to $300/1,100 = 0.27$. The bank now has excess reserves. With its present level of reserves of £300, it could support £1,500 in deposits and just maintain its desired ratio of 0.20 ($300/1,500$). This is £400 more in deposits than it now has.

A one-bank system

If this bank were the only bank in the banking system, it would know that any loan that it made would give rise to new deposits of an equal amount *all held at that bank*. It would then be in a position to say to the next person who comes in for a loan, 'We will lend you, or your firm, £400 at the going rate of interest.' Assuming that the person is a representative of a firm, the bank would do so by adding that amount to the firm's deposit account. The result is the new Balance Sheet 3.

The immigrant's deposit initially raises cash assets and deposit liabilities by £100. The new loans to firms then create an additional £400 of deposit liabilities. This restores the reserve ratio to its desired level ($300/1,500 = 0.20$). There are no longer any excess reserves and no further expansion of deposit money will occur. As the bank's customers do business with each other, settling their accounts by cheques, the *ownership* of the deposits will be continually chang-

Balance Sheet 3. Position after making £400 of new loans

Liabilities		Assets	
Deposits	£1,500	Cash and other reserves	£300
Capital	100	Loans	1,300
	1,600		1,600

ing. But what matters to the bank is that its *total* deposit liabilities, and its *total* reserves, will remain constant.

We conclude that the extent to which a single bank can increase its loans, *and thus its deposits* (which are part of the money supply), depends on its reserve ratio. Because, in this case, the ratio is 0.20, the bank is able to expand deposits to five times the original acquisition of money.

Many banks

Deposit creation is more complicated in a multibank system than in a single-bank system, but *the end result is exactly the same*. It is more complicated because, when a bank makes a loan, the recipient of the loan may pay the money to people who deposit it not in the original bank but in other banks. How this works is most easily seen under the extreme assumption that every new borrower in every bank writes cheques on his new deposit in favour of people who deposit the cheques *in other banks*.

We now assume that the bank illustrated in Balance Sheet 1 is one of many banks in a multibank system. Once again the bank receives a new deposit that puts it in the position shown in the Balance Sheet 2. With its new level of deposits at £1,100, the bank needs only £220 of reserves ($0.20 \times £1,100 = £220$). Since it has £300 in reserves, its excess reserves amount to £80. It cannot immediately create £400 worth of new deposits, as did the monopoly bank, because these will be drained off to other banks. Instead, all it can do in the first instance is to lend out the £80 of excess reserves that it now has on hand. According to our assumption, this £80 finds its way into other banks – as the recipient of the loan pays cheques to people who deposit them in other banks. The bank will then suffer a cash drain to these other banks. The result is Balance Sheet 4 and the bank once again has a cash reserve ratio of 0.20.

Balance Sheet 4. Position of a single bank in a multibank system after it has loaned its excess reserves

Liabilities		Assets	
Deposits	£1,100	Cash and other reserves	£220
Capital	100	Loans	980
	1,200		1,200

So far, deposits in the bank have increased by only the initial £100 of the new immigrant's money with which we started. (Of this, £20 is held as a cash reserve against the deposit and £80 has been lent out.) But *other* banks have received new deposits of £80 because the people receiving payments from the firm which borrowed the £80 deposited those payments in their own banks. The receiving banks (sometimes called *second-generation banks*) receive new deposits of £80, and when the cheques clear, they have new reserves of £80. Because they require an addition to their reserves of only £16 to support the new deposit, they have £64 of 'excess' reserves. They now increase their loans by £64. After this money is spent by the borrowers and has been deposited in other (third-generation) banks, the balance sheets of the second-generation banks will have changed as shown in Balance Sheet 5.

Balance Sheet 5. Position of 'second-generation' banks after receipt of new deposits

Liabilities		Assets	
Deposits	+£80	Cash and other reserves	+£16
		Loans	+64
	+80		+80

Note that Balance Sheet 5 only records *changes* in the balance sheets of the 'second-generation' banks, and it records them *after* the banks have (i) received new deposits of £80, (ii) lent out £64 (keeping the remaining £16 as reserves), and (iii) suffered a cash drain to 'third-generation banks' of £64.

The third-generation banks now find themselves with £64 of new deposits. Against these they need hold only £12.80 in reserves, so they have excess reserves of £51.20 that they can immediately lend out.

Thus immigrants' new deposits set up a long sequence of new deposits, new loans, new deposits, and new loans. The stages are shown in Table 35.2. The series in the Table should look familiar, for it is similar to the sequence we met when dealing with the investment multiplier (see Table 29.1 on page 356).

Now consider what has happened. Each bank manager can say 'What, me *create* money? Good gracious no! All I did was invest my excess reserves. I can do no more than manage wisely the money I receive.' Yet the banking *system* as a whole has created new deposits and thus new money.

If *r* is the reserve ratio, the ultimate effect on the deposits of the banking system of a new cash deposit will be $1/r$ times the new deposit. This is the same result reached in the single-bank case. (Although the

TABLE 35.2 Many Banks, a Single New Deposit. The banking system as a whole can create deposit money whenever it receives new reserves

Bank	New deposits	New loans	Additions to desired reserves
Original bank	£100.00	£80.00	£20.00
Second-generation bank	80.00	64.00	16.00
Third-generation bank	64.00	51.20	12.80
Fourth-generation bank	51.20	40.96	10.24
Fifth-generation bank	40.96	32.77	8.19
Sixth-generation bank	32.77	26.22	6.55
Seventh-generation bank	26.22	20.98	5.24
Eighth-generation bank	20.98	16.78	4.20
Ninth-generation bank	16.78	13.42	3.36
Tenth-generation bank	13.42	10.74	2.68
Total first 10 generations	446.33	357.07	89.26
All remaining generations	53.67	42.93	10.74
Total for banking system	500.00	400.00	100.00

'first-generation' bank that received the initial deposit cannot increase its deposits by that amount.)

Many deposits

The two cases discussed above, the introduction of a new deposit first in a single-bank system and then in a multibank system, show that under either set of extreme assumptions, the result is the same. So it is, too, in intermediate situations. A far more realistic picture of deposit creation is one in which new deposits accrue simultaneously to all banks because of changes in the monetary policy of the government. (We shall see in Chapter 36 how monetary policy does this.)

Say, for example, that the banking system comprises five banks of equal size, and that each receives a new cash deposit of £100. Now each bank is in the position shown in Balance Sheet 2 above, and each can expand deposits based on its own £100 of 'excess' reserves. (Each bank does this by granting loans to customers.)

Now consider what happens to any one bank – call it bank A. Because each bank does one-fifth of the total banking business, an average of 80 per cent of bank A's newly created deposits will find its way into other banks as A's customers pay other people in the community by cheque. However, 20 per cent of the new deposits created by the other four banks will find their way into bank A. The net result is no cash drain from bank A. As it is with bank A, so it is with the other four banks. So what happens is that all banks receive new cash and all begin creating deposits simultaneously, and no bank suffers a significant cash drain to any other bank.

Thus all banks can go on expanding deposits without losing reserves to each other; they need only worry about keeping enough reserves to satisfy those depositors who will occasionally require cash. The expansion can go on, with each bank watching its own ratio of reserves to deposits, expanding deposits as long as the ratio exceeds 0.20 and ceasing when it reaches that figure. The process will come to a halt when each bank has created £400 in additional deposits, so that for each initial £100 cash deposit, there is now £500 in deposits backed by £100 in cash. Now *each* bank will have entries similar to those in Balance Sheet 3 for the monopoly bank after it had expanded deposits on the basis of its new cash deposit.

The destruction of deposit money

The 'multiple expansion of deposits' that has just been worked through applies in reverse to a withdrawal of funds. Deposits of the banking system will fall by a multiple of $1/r$ times any amount withdrawn from the bank and not redeposited at another. We leave it to the reader to work through the previous examples assuming that, instead of a deposit, the initial disturbance is a withdrawal. Instead of having excess reserves, the banks will then have deficient reserves and will have to react by cutting their loans.

The creation of deposit money reviewed

A single bank could immediately expand deposits when it received a new cash deposit because it knew it would suffer no cash drain. Individual banks in a multibanking system cannot do this because they know they may suffer a cash drain to other banks. But the banking system as a whole suffers no cash drain; what is withdrawn from one bank ends up in another. Thus the banking system as a whole does what no single one of its banks can do: produce a multiple expansion of deposit money on the basis of an initial deposit of new cash arriving from outside the system. Similarly for a withdrawal, the single-bank system would require a multiple reduction of deposits when it suffers a cash withdrawal and the multibank system would end up with the same result after the effect worked through all the banks in the system.

The bank-deposit multiplier

The examples we have given make it clear that the amount of deposit expansion that occurs depends on the reserve ratio that banks keep. This relationship is easily seen if we use a few lines of simple algebra.

If r is the bank's reserve ratio, the reserves must be r times the amount of deposits. Letting R stand for reserves, and D for deposits, we can write this as:

$$R = rD. \tag{1}$$

If, for example, r is 0.20, as in the previous example, and banks have deposits of £1,000, the reserves must be 0.20 multiplied by £1,000, which is £200.

Now look at changes. If equation (1) is true, the following must also be true:

$$\Delta R = r\Delta D. \tag{2}$$

All this says is that any change in deposits must be matched by the appropriate change in reserves – which is r times the change in deposits.

Now all we do is divide equation (2) through by r to obtain:

$$\Delta D = \frac{1}{r}\Delta R. \tag{3}$$

The right-hand side of equation (3) is the so-called BANK DEPOSIT MULTIPLIER, which is defined as the amount of deposits which result from each £1 of new cash reserves.[1] Equation (3) above tells us what we have seen illustrated in the earlier examples: any change in reserves brings about a multiple change in deposits by an amount that depends on the reserve ratio r. What we have now proved is that the exact multiplier is $1/r$. Thus, if r is 0.20, the deposit multiplier is 5: every £1 of new reserves supports £5 of new deposits. If r is 0.10, the deposit multiplier is 10, and so on.

A complication: cash drains from the system

So far we have worked with the simplifying assumption that the public is willing to hold, in the form of deposits, all the new money that is created. A more realistic assumption is that the public wishes to

---

1 Notice that the bank deposit multiplier, also sometimes called the 'money multiplier,' the 'deposit multiplier' and the 'bank multiplier', must be carefully distinguished from the investment multiplier that links changes in national income to changes in investment.

maintain *a constant ratio* between the two kinds of money, deposits and currency. In this case, if £100 of *new money* is created, most will be held as new deposits, but some will be held as new currency. Assume, for example, that the ratio in which the public wishes to hold cash and deposit money is 1:9. Now when £100 of new money is created, the public will hold £90 in deposits and £10 in cash.

The important change in this case is that, when the banking system creates new deposit money, the system will suffer a cash drain as the public withdraws some of this new money to hold as cash. Now the story of deposit creation after the banking system receives new cash deposits becomes slightly more complicated. To illustrate how it works, assume that the public always wishes to hold 5 per cent of its money in cash and 95 per cent in deposits.

When the *whole system* receives new cash deposits, each bank starts creating deposits and suffers no significant cash drain to other banks. But because approximately 5 per cent of all newly created deposits is withdrawn to be held as cash, each bank suffers a cash drain to the public. The expansion continues, with each bank watching its own ratio of cash reserves to deposits. Each bank expands deposits as long as the cash reserve ratio exceeds 0.20 and ceases when the ratio reaches that figure. Because the expansion is accompanied by a cash drain, it will come to a halt with a smaller increase in deposits than when there was no cash drain.

When the process is finished, each bank's balance sheet will look as in Balance Sheet 6 (assuming each received an initial new cash deposit of £100):

Balance Sheet 6. Deposit expansion of each bank in a multibank system with a cash drain to the public

Liabilities		Assets	
Deposits	£1,395.80	Cash and reserves	£279.17
Capital	100.00	Loans	1,216.63
	1,495.80		1,495.80

Compare Balance Sheet 6 with Balance Sheet 3, which showed the position in a single-bank system. We now see that instead of ending up with £1,500 in deposits, the banking system now has just less than £1,400. Deposit expansion is less because of the cash drain. The banks have created a little less than £400 of new deposit money, and a little less than £20 of reserves – i.e. 5 per cent of the new deposits – has been withdrawn by the public to circulate as currency.

OTHER INSTITUTIONS IN THE UK FINANCIAL SYSTEM

In addition to the clearing banks, which we have already discussed, the UK banking system contains other, more specialized, banks: retail banks, overseas banks, and merchant banks (see Harbury and Lipsey, Chapter 8, for further details).

Retail Banks

Retail banks are defined as those banks that have networks of branches throughout the country and/or participate in a bankers' clearing house. They thus include the clearing banks as well as the Trustee Savings Bank, the National Giro, and a few other more specialized institutions.

There are two large savings banks, the National Savings Bank, operated by the Post Office, and the Trustee Savings Bank. These banks were originally intended as a repository for the deposits of small savers. Money could be deposited and withdrawn but not transferred by cheque. Now, however, the Trustee Savings Bank does offer chequing facilities.

Overseas Banks

This class of banks includes branches of foreign banks operating in the UK. The growing importance of foreign trade, and of international capital movements, has led to a steady increase in the number of such banks.

Merchant Banks

These banks, which are also called accepting houses, grew up in the nineteenth century to finance the country's international trade. They still do much of their business in international trade, but they also engage in other specialized work such as managing investment portfolios for other institutions, providing financial advice to companies, handling the issues of new shares and arranging mergers, and dealing in very large deposits with a term of over one year.

Non-Banking Financial Institutions

The UK financial system also includes a number of institutions that are not banks but which play an important part in financial markets.

Discount Houses: The DISCOUNT HOUSES are specialized institutions which are peculiar to the UK. They borrow money at 'call' (i.e. repayable on demand) from banks and other lending institutions. They use this money to purchase short-dated financial assets such as Treasury bills, which are special bills of exchange issued by the UK government (see Chapter 34). Since they borrow money that is repayable on demand and lend it out for terms of up to a month or more (as they do when, for example, they buy a Treasury bill that has 30 days to run to maturity), they are in the exposed position of 'borrowing short' and 'lending (relatively) long', though they can always turn to the Bank of England for loans in an emergency. This forms part of monetary policy and will be discussed in Chapter 37. The advantage to the regular banks of this arrangement is that they can earn interest on their cash reserves. (Loans to the discount houses are repayable at call and hence are as good as cash.)

The discount houses provide a good example of the division of labour. They are specialists in the short-term money market. Institutions that specialize in other forms of loans do not find it worth their while to acquire detailed knowledge of the short-term market. They lend those funds that they can commit only for short terms to the discount houses who, guided by their specialist knowledge, can lend them profitably.

Financial Intermediaries: Most banking systems also have a variety of other specialized institutions. Some of these accept time deposits from the public and lend money out on a longer-term basis. One of the most important is building societies. These financial institutions, originally engaged in lending money on mortgage for house purchases, have been becoming more and more similar to banks in recent years – because their deposits have been regarded by the public as being almost as liquid as bank deposits.

SUMMARY

1 The commercial banks are the most obvious part of the UK banking system. They accept deposits from the general public; they provide chequing facilities to their customers; they make advances to their customers; and they invest in various interest-earning assets such as bills and bonds. The bankers' clearing house allows banks to settle inter-bank debts that arise from cheques written on accounts in one bank and deposited in another bank.

2 Commercial banks create money by lending out any 'excess reserves'. Their ability to do so depends on the fractional backing of their deposit money – cash reserves need only be a small fraction of their outstanding deposit liabilities.

3 The bank deposit multiplier gives the value of new deposits that can be created for every £1 of new reserves that becomes available to the commercial banking system. With no cash drain to the public, this multiplier is $1/r$, where r is the commercial banks' desired reserve ratio. If the public wishes to hold some fraction of new money as currency, the expansion of deposits will be accompanied by a cash drain to the public and the deposit multiplier will be less than in the no-cash-drain case.

4 The major institutions in the UK banking system are the retail banks, which include the clearing banks, the savings banks, overseas banks, which are branches of foreign banks operating in the UK, acceptance houses, and such non-bank financial institutions as the discount houses, finance houses and building societies.

Money, Interest and National Income

In Part 4 we saw that equilibrium national income changes whenever the aggregate expenditure function shifts. This can be caused by a shift in any of its components – C, I, G or (X−M). Consider each of these in turn. The consumption function shifts whenever there is a change in households' propensity to spend and save out of disposable income, or whenever there is a change in tax rates that alters the relation between disposable income and national income. Desired investment shifts whenever there is a change in any of the variables that influence it. Government expenditure shifts whenever there is a change in the government's spending. The net export function shifts whenever there is either a change in the propensity to import or an autonomous shift in exports. (Recall that 'propensity' and 'desire' are used interchangeably in this context.)

In this chapter we show how the aggregate expenditure function can be shifted by monetary forces. We do this by bringing the rate of interest, which was formerly an exogenous variable, into our theory. This, in turn, has the effect of making investment, which is influenced by the interest rate, into an endogenous variable – one that is explained within our theory.

THE LIQUIDITY PREFERENCE THEORY OF INTEREST

Money Demand and Money Supply: To start the development of the theory that makes the interest rate endogenous by explaining how it is determined, recall what we have already learned about the demand for, and the supply of, money.

On the demand side, the key point was established in Chapter 34, where we saw that the demand for money depends on the level of national income and on the rate of interest. (See Figure 34.2.)

On the supply side, it is convenient to begin our study with the assumptions that the commercial banks have a given level of reserves, and that they have created all the deposit money that they regard as prudent on the basis of these reserves. As a result, the money supply is an autonomous (or exogenously determined) variable. It is unaffected by anything explained within our theory (being determined by the cash reserves of the banking system and the size of the money multiplier) and it remains constant unless changed by some force outside of our theory (such as new cash deposits received by the system as a whole). In Chapter 37 we shall see how the government attempts to change the money supply through its monetary policy.

Monetary Equilibrium: Next we need to define what is called MONETARY EQUILIBRIUM. This occurs when the demand for money equals the supply of money. In Chapter 8, we saw that in a competitive market for some commodity, that commodity's price adjusts to ensure an equilibrium where the quantity demanded equals the quantity supplied. We now ask, what does the same job for money? The answer is that *the rate of interest does the job of equating the quantity of money demanded to the available supply; i.e. it does the job of producing monetary equilibrium.*

In Figure 36.1, we see how the interest rate produces monetary equilibrium. The money supply is fixed exogenously at the quantity M_o. Because (by assumption) the money supply does not change with the rate of interest, the supply curve of money, M_s, is

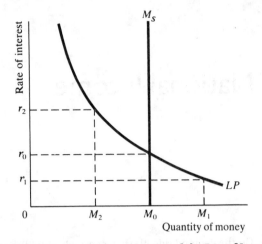

FIGURE 36.1 **Monetary Equilibrium and the Rate of Interest.** The interest rate rises when there is an excess demand for money and falls when there is an excess supply of money

shown as completely inelastic at the quantity M_0. The curve marked LP is the liquidity preference function that we first met in Figure 34.2. It shows how the demand to hold money varies with the rate of interest, and it is drawn for a specified level of money national income. Monetary equilibrium occurs at the interest rate r_0, where the LP and the M_S curves intersect. At that interest rate, everyone in the economy – households and firms – is just willing to hold all of the money that is available to be held.

Monetary Disequilibrium: Now let us ask what happens if the current interest rate is not r_0. First, let the rate be below its equilibrium value. For example, at the interest rate r_1 in the Figure, the demand for money is M_1 while the supply remains fixed at M_0 by assumption. Thus there is an excess demand for money of $M_1 - M_0$. As we saw in Chapter 34, an excess demand for money causes people to offer bonds for sale in an attempt to increase their money holdings. This will force the rate of interest upwards, and it will only stop rising (bond prices stop falling) when the interest rate reaches r_0. At that interest rate, the quantity of money demanded is equal to the available supply of M_0 and people will no longer be trying to turn bonds into money; instead, they will be content to hold the quantities of money and bonds that are currently in existence.

Second, consider what happens if the rate of interest is above the equilibrium rate. For example, at the interest rate r_2, the quantity of money demanded

is M_2, while the supply still remains fixed at M_0. Thus there will be an excess supply of money, $M_0 - M_2$. As a result, everyone will be trying to buy bonds with their excess money balances. This behaviour will force the rate of interest down (the price of bonds rises) until it reaches r_0, at which point the quantity of money demanded will have risen to equal the fixed money supply of M_0.

Conclusion: The important conclusion is that *the condition for monetary equilibrium is that the rate of interest will be such that everyone is just willing to hold the existing supply of money.*

In the previous chapter, we described the *liquidity preference theory of the demand for money.* We have now developed what is called the LIQUIDITY PREFERENCE THEORY OF INTEREST-RATE DETERMINATION. It is also called the PORTFOLIO BALANCE THEORY. The first term alludes to Keynes' theory of the demand for money as a function of the interest rate, while the second term alludes to Tobin's theory of the same phenomenon. (See Chapter 34, pages 420–22.) In either case, the mechanism at work is people's decisions on how to divide their portfolios between the two available wealth-holding assets, money and bonds. We have seen that both Keynes and Tobin developed theories to explain the reason why the demand for money is negatively related to the interest rate. Both of these theories are compatible with everything we have said in this chapter so far. The difference between the two lies solely *in the explanations that they give of what lies behind* the downward-sloping LP curve. They do not need to concern us here because all that matters for the rest of this chapter is that the demand for money is – for whatever reason – negatively related to the interest rate.

THE MONETARY TRANSMISSION MECHANISM

Now that these important preliminaries are behind us, we can turn to the main subjects of this chapter: the relationship between the supply of money and the aggregate desired expenditure function, and how *changes* in the money supply affect national income.

The link between the supply of money and aggregate expenditure is called the MONETARY TRANSMISSION MECHANISM. This term refers to the mechanism by which monetary changes – changes in the demand and/or the supply of money – are transmitted into changes in desired expenditure and, therefore, come to affect the equilibrium level of national income.

An Increase in the Supply of Money

There are several links in the transmission mechanism. To study these we first deal with the case of an increase in the supply of money.

Link 1: From money to the interest rate

The first link in the transmission mechanism is based on the liquidity preference theory of interest which we have just studied. To see how it works, we study what happens to the interest rate when there is a change in the supply of money. Money is still assumed exogenous – i.e. unaffected by anything within our theory – but we now allow for an exogenous change in the money supply.

This is one example of what is called a *monetary shock*. In general, a SHOCK is anything that disturbs an equilibrium. In the discussion of this chapter, a *monetary* shock is any *monetary* change that disturbs *monetary* equilibrium. (This modern term has come to replace words such as 'an autonomous change in an exogenous variable', which we have used so far in this book.)

In Figure 36.2 (i) the original supply of money is M_0, yielding an equilibrium interest rate of r_0. Now let the amount of money increase from M_0 to M_1. The supply curve of money shifts from M_S to M'_S, and, at the existing rate of interest r_0, there is excess supply of money. People still wish to hold only M_0 of money

balances, but M_1 is now available. What will happen?

In an effort to eliminate their excess stocks of money, everyone attempts to buy bonds. But *everyone* cannot simultaneously buy bonds, for no one is trying to sell them. The result of the attempt to turn money into bonds is that the price of bonds rises (and we know that this is exactly the same thing as a fall in the rate of interest.) When the interest rate has fallen to r_1, the quantity of money demanded will have risen to equal the available quantity supplied at M_1. Monetary equilibrium is thus re-established, though at a lower rate of interest.

Link 2: From the interest rate to investment expenditure

The second link in the transmission mechanism is the one that relates interest rates to desired investment expenditure. On pages 328–9 of Chapter 27 we saw that desired investment expenditure is negatively related to the interest rate: the lower the interest rate, the higher is desired investment expenditure, and vice versa. (This important discussion must be reread now.) This relation is shown in Figure 36.2 (ii). The curve in that Figure is called a *marginal efficiency of investment curve* (or just a *demand for investment curve*). It shows that the lower the rate of interest, the larger will be the number of investment opportunities that will show a profit and, hence, the larger the volume of investment expenditure that firms wish to undertake.

It is extremely important to understand that what we call investment expenditure really stands for *all* interest-sensitive expenditure. As interest rates rise, not only does investment expenditure tend to fall, but all other expenditure that is financed by borrowed

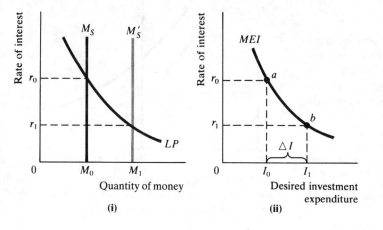

FIGURE 36.2   The Effects of Changes in the Money Supply on Desired Investment Expenditure. An increase in the money supply reduces the rate of interest and increases desired investment expenditure; a reduction has the opposite effect

funds – such as hire-purchase expenditure – tends to fall as well. Long-term investment may be sluggish in responding to changes in the interest rate, but other kinds of expenditures, such as purchases of houses on mortgages and of new cars on hire purchase, do respond.[1]

Note that, because both parts of Figure 36.2 have the interest rate on the vertical axis, the interest rate can be compared between the two parts. Both parts show an initial equilibrium with the quantity of money of M_0 (shown by the inelastic money supply curve M_S), and an interest rate of r_0. This gives rise to a level of desired investment expenditure of I_0 in part (ii) (point a).

Now when this equilibrium is disturbed with a monetary shock such that the money supply increases to M_1 (shown by the money supply curve M'_S), the rate of interest falls to r_1. Part (ii) of the Figure tells us that the fall in the interest rate from r_0 to r_1 increases desired investment expenditure from I_0 to I_1 (point b). This increase is marked ΔI in the Figure, and it is the effect on investment expenditure of the increase in the money supply shown in part (i).

Link 3: From investment expenditure to aggregate expenditure

So far, we have seen that an increase in the money supply leads to a fall in the interest rate which, in turn, leads to an increase in desired investment expenditure. We know from previous chapters (see e.g. figure 27.7 on page 339) that an increase in desired investment expenditure causes an upward shift in the aggregate desired expenditure curve. The amount of the shift is the ΔI shown in Figure 36.2 (ii).

Other Monetary Changes

A Reduction in the Money Supply: So far we have considered the effect of an increase in the money supply. A reduction in the money supply does everything in reverse. When we say this we are discussing the direction of the change and the final

---

amount of the change. We shall see later that the time taken by the economy to respond to a reduction in the money supply may be very much more than that taken to respond to an increase.

In Figure 36.2 let the original money supply be M_1. This produces a rate of interest of r_1 in part (i) of the Figure and investment expenditure of I_1 in part (ii). Now let the money supply fall to M_0. This causes a shortage of money at the interest rate r_1. People try to sell bonds to replenish money balances. This pushes the price of bonds down, which means a rise in the interest rate. When the rate has risen to r_0, people are content with holding the smaller money supply and monetary equilibrium is thus restored. The rise in the interest rate to r_0 lowers investment by ΔI in part (ii) of the Figure from I_1 to I_0. The fall in desired investment expenditure by the amount ΔI shifts the aggregate expenditure curve, downwards by that amount.

A Fall in the Demand for Money: The initial cause of the monetary disequilibrium has no effect on any of the subsequent links in the chain. So far we have looked at shocks arising from changes in the *supply of* money. Equivalent disequilibria can be caused by shocks arising from changes in the *demand for* money. On the one hand, a fall in the demand for money – a leftward shift in the liquidity preference function – creates an excess supply of money, just as does a rise in the supply of money. On the other hand, a rise in the demand for money – a rightward shift in the LP function – creates an excess demand for money, just as does a fall in the supply of money.

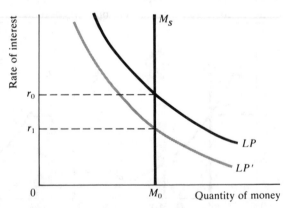

FIGURE 36.3   Changes in the Demand for Money Cause Changes in the Interest Rate. A fall in the demand for money lowers interest rates; a rise does the reverse

Figure 36.3 shows the effects of a decrease in the demand for money. The money supply is held constant at M_0 and the initial demand for money is given by the curve LP. The equilibrium interest rate is r_0. Now let the demand for money fall, taking the LP curve to LP'. This creates an excess supply of money, which people try to eliminate by purchasing bonds. The effect is to raise the price of bonds, which means a fall in the interest rate. When the rate falls as low as r_1, the public is willing to hold the existing stock of money and monetary equilibrium is restored. The fall in the interest rate sets the monetary transmission mechanism going. Desired investment expenditure rises, and this raises aggregate desired expenditure as well.

We see from this that a fall in the demand for money has the same effect as a rise in the supply of money. Both create a monetary disequilibrium that

reduces interest rates and, by increasing desired investment, shifts the aggregate desired expenditure curve upwards.

A Rise in the Demand for Money: A rise in the demand for money means a rightward shift in the liquidity preference function. The results are shown in Figure 36.3, where the liquidity preference function shifts from LP' to LP. The shortage of money causes the price of bonds to fall as people try to replenish their money balances by selling bonds. The rate of interest rises from r_1 to r_0, thus restoring monetary equilibrium. This causes desired investment expenditure to fall, thus shifting the aggregate desired expenditure curve downwards.

We see that a rise in the demand for money has the same effect as a fall in the supply of money. Both create a monetary disequilibrium that raises interest

THE TRANSMISSION MECHANISM FOR AN EXPANSIONARY MONETARY SHOCK

THE TRANSMISSION MECHANISM FOR A CONTRACTIONARY MONETARY SHOCK

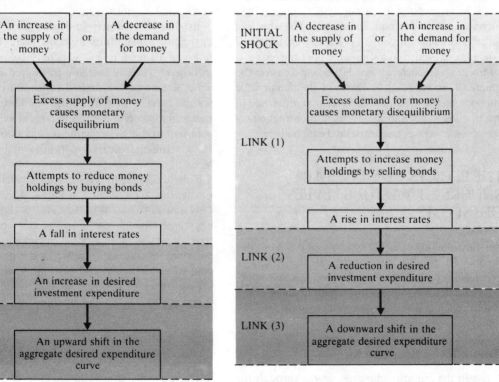

FIGURE 36.4   The Monetary Transmission Mechanism for an Expansionary Monetary Shock. An increase in the supply of money or a decrease in the demand for money sets an expansionary process in train

FIGURE 36.5   The Monetary Transmission Mechanism for a Contractionary Monetary Shock. A decrease in the supply of money or an increase in the demand for money sets a contractionary process in train

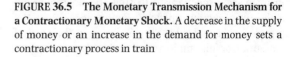

rates and, by lowering investment, also lowers aggregate desired expenditure.

The Monetary Transmission Mechanism Summarized

The transmission mechanism provides a connection between monetary forces and real expenditure flows. It has three links – it works (1) from a change in the supply of, or demand for, money, to a change in bond prices and interest rates, (2) through a change in investment expenditure, (3) to a *shift* in the aggregate desired expenditure curve. Increases in the supply of money and decreases in the demand for money shift the aggregate expenditure curve upwards; reductions in the supply of money and increases in the demand for money shift the aggregate expenditure curve downwards.

The mechanism is so important that it is worthwhile summarizing it schematically. The sequence of events summarized in Figure 36.4 is set in motion either by an increase in the supply of money or by a decrease in the demand for money. The shock is called *expansionary* because it raises aggregate desired expenditure. Figure 36.5 shows the opposite case of a *contractionary monetary shock*. Either a decrease in the supply of money or an increase in the demand for money sets up the sequence of events summarized in the Figure. The shock is called contractionary because it lowers aggregate desired expenditure.

THE EFFECTS OF MONETARY SHOCKS AT VARIOUS LEVELS OF INCOME

We can now get some substantial payoff from our theory. To do this, we investigate the effects of expansionary monetary shocks, first when equilibrium national income is below potential income and, second, when it is equal to potential income.

Unemployed Resources

A rise in the quantity of money works through the transmission mechanism to shift the aggregate expenditure function upwards. Figure 36.6 shows the upward shift and adds the 45° line and the level of potential, or full-employment, national income, Y_F. A

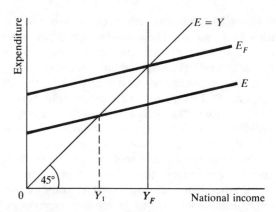

FIGURE 36.6   Monetary Expansion may Increase Equilibrium National Income. A rise in the money supply works through the transmission mechanism to increase aggregate desired expenditure and, if income is below potential, to increase equilibrium national income

vertical line is drawn through Y_F to indicate the resource constraints on further output: real national income cannot exceed Y_F because sufficient factors of production are not available.

In the case shown in Figure 36.6, the initial aggregate expenditure function is E. Equilibrium national income is Y_1, which is below potential income of Y_F. The increase in desired expenditure shifts the aggregate desired expenditure curve upwards, thereby increasing the equilibrium level of national income. If the rise in desired expenditure is sufficient to shift the expenditure function all the way to E_F, actual income rises to its full-employment level of Y_F.

This is nothing more than an application of the results that we obtained in Part 4 of this book; the only difference here is in the cause of the shift in the aggregate expenditure function. Our conclusion is that, when actual national income is less than potential income, an increase in the money supply can, by reducing interest rates and raising desired investment expenditure,[1] increase equilibrium national income and employment.

Full Employment

The analysis so far assumes that an increase in aggregate expenditure can increase the level of real

---

1 Do not forget what we reminded you of earlier in this chapter: 'investment' stands for all *interest-sensitive expenditure*.

national income. But what if equilibrium national income is already at Y_F? This case reveals some interesting aspects of the economy's behaviour. We analyse it in three steps: initial equilibrium, the creation of an inflationary gap, and the elimination of the inflationary gap.

The Initial Equilibrium: Consider Figure 36.7. Initially the money supply is M_0 in part (i) of the Figure, which gives a money supply curve of M_S. The original liquidity preference curve is LP, which intersects with M_S to establish an interest rate of r_0. In part (ii) of the Figure, we see that the interest rate r_0 induces investment expenditure of I_0. This amount of investment, added to consumption, government expenditure and net exports, yields an aggregate desired expenditure curve that we assume takes the position E_F in part (iii) of the Figure. This means that *equilibrium is initially at potential income, Y_F.*

The Creation of an Inflationary Gap: Now let us see

what happens when the money supply increases, starting the sequence outlined in Figure 36.4.

What happens is analysed in Figure 36.7. First, the money supply is assumed to increase to M_1 in part (i) of the Figure, shifting the money supply curve to M_S'. Since the demand for money is still given by the curve labelled LP, the interest rate falls to r_1 and desired investment expenditure rises by ΔI to I_1. This shifts the aggregate desired expenditure function upwards to E' in part (iii) of the Figure.

If resources were available to produce more output, national income would rise to Y_1 and that would be the end of the story. But in the case we are considering, equilibrium income is initially at the full-employment level. As a result, real national income remains at Y_F and the shift of the aggregate expenditure function to E' opens up an inflationary gap, shown by the distance ab in the Figure. The excess demand causes the general price level to rise.

The Removal of the Inflationary Gap: The next step

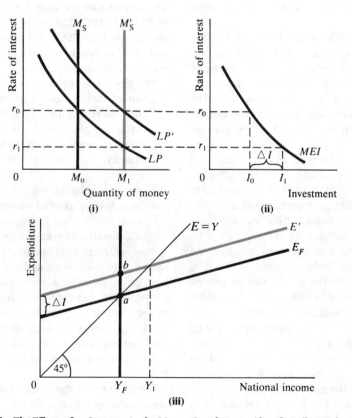

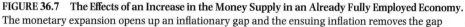
FIGURE 36.7   The Effects of an Increase in the Money Supply in an Already Fully Employed Economy.
The monetary expansion opens up an inflationary gap and the ensuing inflation removes the gap

in the sequence of events is an extremely important one; it is the reason why *single* monetary shocks cause the price level to rise but *not* forever or without limit.

The rise in the price level caused by the inflationary gap raises the money value of national income, and hence raises the money value of all transactions in the economy. As we saw in Chapter 34, more money will now be demanded at each rate of interest for transactions purposes. This shifts the *LP* curve to the right in the way that we analysed in Figure 34.2 on page 423.

At the existing rate of interest, there is now an excess demand for money. This starts the monetary adjustment mechanism in motion according to the sequence outlined in Figure 36.5 for a contractionary monetary shock. The interest rate rises, desired investment expenditure falls, and the aggregate expenditure curve starts to shift downwards again. This contractionary process will continue until the inflationary gap has been eliminated completely – because, as long as there is such a gap, the price level will be rising and the *LP* curve will be shifting to the right.

The final outcome can be seen in Figure 36.7. *When we last looked at the Figure*, the money supply was M_1, the interest rate r_1, investment I_1 and aggregate expenditure E', yielding an inflationary gap of ab. Now, however, as the price level rises, the *LP* curve shifts to the right, indicating a larger demand for money at each interest rate. The price level goes on rising and the liquidity preference curve goes on shifting to the right until it reaches LP' in part (i) of the Figure. At that point, the curve LP' intersects with the money supply curve M_S' to yield an interest rate of r_0. This restores desired investment expenditure to its original level of I_0 and, hence, shifts the aggregate desired expenditure function back to E_F.

It is worth pausing a moment to consider the behaviour that is implied when changes of this kind occur. The rise in the price level increases the money value of national income, which creates a need for more money for transactions and precautionary purposes. In an attempt to increase their money balances, wealth-holders try to sell bonds. But everyone cannot sell bonds at the same time, and the attempt to do so drives the price of bonds downwards, which means a rise in the rate of interest.

This process goes on as long as any inflationary gap exists. So as long as the aggregate expenditure curve lies above E_F in Figure 36.7, the price level and

interest rates will go on rising, and desired investment will go on falling. The process will come to a halt only when the expenditure curve has returned to its original position E_F. This happens because interest rates and desired investment expenditure have returned to their initial levels of r_0 and I_0. *The rise in the money supply has ended up having no effect other than raising the price level.*

This is the long-run neutrality of money that we first studied in Chapter 33: *Starting from a position of full-employment equilibrium, an increase in the quantity of money does have real effects during the period of disequilibrium, altering interest rates and desired investment expenditure. When equilibrium is restored, however, interest rates, and each of the components of desired expenditure, will have returned to their original levels. Real national income is unchanged and the only permanent effect of a change in the quantity of money is a change in the price level.*

The monetary adjustment mechanism

The process that we have just outlined is called the MONETARY ADJUSTMENT MECHANISM, which is a mechanism that eliminates any inflationary gap, no matter what its initial cause, *provided that the money supply remains constant.*

The process works as follows:
1. an inflationary gap causes the price level to rise;
2. this increases the level of nominal national income;
3. this increases the transactions demand for money, thus shifting the LP function to the right;
4. this raises the interest rate;
5. this lowers desired investment expenditure, thus shifting the aggregate expenditure curve downwards and reducing the inflationary gap.

This self-correcting monetary mechanism is the reason why price levels and the money supply have been linked for so long in economics. We shall see in Chapter 41 that many forces can cause the price level to rise. Yet, whatever the cause, *unless the money supply is expanded*, the increase in the price level will itself set up forces that will remove any initial inflationary gap and so will bring the inflation to a halt.

We have twice stated the absolutely key qualification to the operation of the self-correcting, monetary adjustment mechanism: *the money supply must remain constant.* To see why this is such an important provision, let us see how the monetary adjustment mechanism can be frustrated.

Frustration of the monetary adjustment mechanism

The self-correcting mechanism for removing an inflationary gap can be frustrated *if* the money supply is increased at the same rate that prices are rising. Say that the price level is rising at 10 per cent a year under the pressure of an inflationary gap. Demand for money balances will then also rise at about 10 per cent per year – i.e. the *LP* curve will be shifting outwards to the right at that rate. If the money supply is held constant, the interest rate will be rising steadily.

Now suppose that the Bank of England also allows the money supply to rise at 10 per cent per year. (Remember we are assuming throughout this chapter that the money supply is fixed, exogenously, by the central bank.) This possibility is shown in Figure 36.8. The initial curves are *LP* and M_S (money supply M_0). The initial interest rate is thus r_0, which is assumed to give rise to an inflationary gap. The resulting rise in the price level shifts the liquidity preference function to *LP'*. If the money supply is held constant, the interest rate rises to r_1. Instead, however, let the money supply be increased to M_1 at the same time as the *LP* curve shifts to *LP'*. No excess demand for money now develops at the interest rate r_0, since the extra money needed to meet the rising demand is forthcoming. The interest rate will *not* rise to reduce desired aggregate expenditure and so the inflationary gap will not be removed.

An inflation is said to be *validated* when the money supply is increased as fast as the price level is

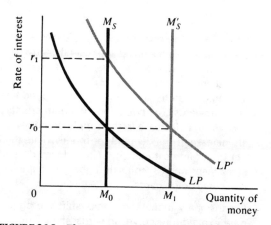

FIGURE 36.8 The Frustration of the Monetary Adjustment Mechanism. A rise in the supply of money that parallels a rise in demand for money can prevent interest rates from rising and so leave real expenditure unchanged

increasing so that the monetary adjustment mechanism is frustrated. A validated inflation can go on indefinitely although, as we shall see in a later chapter, possibly not at a constant rate.

Conclusion

Now that we know how changes in the supply of money affect aggregate desired expenditure and hence national income, we understand why policymakers are so concerned about the size of the money supply. Our next task is to see how the central bank tries to change the money supply in a conscious attempt to influence aggregate expenditure. We do this in the next chapter.

SUMMARY

1 The rate of interest is viewed here as equating the demand for and the supply of money.

2 The equilibrium condition for the liquidity preference (or portfolio balance) theory of interest rates is that wealth-holders are just content to hold the existing amounts of bonds and money. If wealth-holders feel that they have too many bonds and too little money, their attempts to sell bonds will drive down the price of bonds (drive up the rate of interest) until everyone is no longer trying to add

to their money balances. If wealth-holders feel they have too few bonds and too much money, their attempts to buy bonds will drive up their price (drive down the rate of interest) until everyone is no longer trying to reduce their money balances.

3 The transmission mechanism links monetary shocks to shifts in the aggregate desired expenditure curve. The initiating expansionary shocks are either an increase in the supply of money, or a reduction in the demand for money. In step (1), the monetary shock drives interest rates down. In step (2), the fall in the interest rate increases desired investment. In step (3), the rise in desired investment shifts the aggregate expenditure curve upwards. The two initiating contractionary shocks are a decrease in the supply of money, or an increase in the demand for money. This then (1) drives interest rates up, (2) reduces desired investment, and (3) shifts the aggregate expenditure curve downwards.

4 Expansionary monetary shocks shift the aggregate expenditure curve upwards and, if unemployed resources exist, increase national income. Contractionary monetary shocks reduce national income.

5 If full employment of resources already exists, an expansionary monetary shock will open up an inflationary gap. The price level will then rise until the inflationary gap is removed. In the final equilibrium, the increase in the quantity of money will have driven up the price level but restored national income and the interest rate to their original levels.

6 The force that removes the inflationary gap is called the monetary adjustment mechanism, which lets the rising money value of transactions increase the demand for money, which increases the interest rate and reduces aggregate desired expenditure. The monetary adjustment mechanism requires that the money supply be fixed. If the money supply is increased at the same rate as prices are rising, the monetary adjustment mechanism is frustrated because no money shortage develops to drive interest rates upwards. An inflation that is allowed to continue because the money supply is increasing as fast as the price level is increasing is said to be *validated*.

The Bank of England and Monetary Policy[1]

We saw in the previous chapter how changes in the demand for, and the supply of, money affect aggregate desired expenditure. In this chapter we study MONETARY POLICY, which is defined as conscious attempts to influence the behaviour of the economy by changing the money supply and/or the conditions of credit. Monetary policy is conducted by the central bank on behalf of the government.

Many Financial Assets: In order to study the monetary transmission mechanism in its simplest form in Chapter 36, we grouped all financial assets into two categories – money, and everything else, which we called bonds. Now, in order to study the details of how monetary policy works, we need to distinguish several different financial assets that can be held by the public. First, there is currency and non-interest-

bearing financial assets such as some sight deposits. Then there is a range of assets running from higher to lower levels of liquidity and from lower to higher rates of interest. Included are interest-bearing deposits at banks and building societies, bills of exchange and Treasury bills, medium- and long-term securities – ending with Consols, which are of infinite term.

THE BANK OF ENGLAND

Before we study monetary policy, we must first learn a bit about how the Bank of England works. Most countries have central banks which are responsible for the operation and control of their banking systems and their monetary policies. In the UK, the central bank is the Bank of England, often referred to as just 'the Bank' (and even as 'the old lady of Threadneedle Street', where it is located).

The Bank's activities are divided between two

---

1 Descriptive material related to the subject matter of this chapter is to be found in Harbury and Lipsey, Chapter 8.

TABLE 37.1 Bank of England Balance Sheet. December 1985 (£million)

ISSUE DEPARTMENT			
Liabilities		*Assets*	
Notes in circulation	13,540	Government securities	1,522
Notes in Banking Department	10	Other securities	12,028
	13,550		13,550
BANKING DEPARTMENT			
Liabilities		*Assets*	
Public accounts	76	Government securities	632
Special accounts	0	Advances and other accounts	722
Bankers' accounts	960	Premises, equipment, etc.	1,080
Reserves and other accounts	1,409	Other	11
	2,445		2,445

Source: Annual Abstract of Statistics, 1987.

departments, the Issue Department and the Banking Department, whose balance sheets are shown in Table 37.1.

The Issue Department is responsible for controlling the issue of notes and coins (although the actual manufacture of currency is in the hands of the Royal Mint). Notes and coins are put into circulation in return for securities obtained from the Banking Department. These appear as assets on the Issue Department's balance sheet, while the notes and coins appear as its liabilities.

The Banking Department acts as banker to the government and to the commercial banks. Deposits of the government (called public deposits), and of the commercial banks, appear as liabilities on this department's balance sheet. Other liabilities are deposits of nationalized industries, local authorities and the central banks of other countries. Assets of the Banking Department are government bonds (called securities) and bills (called Treasury Bills), loans to the banking system (called advances), and other assets such as bonds issued by local authorities and ordinary firms.

Functions of the Bank of England

The Bank's most important functions are given in the following list and are then discussed below:

- banker to the government;
- banker to the commercial banks;
- controller of the currency supply;
- agency for the government's policy with respect to the exchange rate;
- to support the financial system;
- agency for the government's monetary policy.

To be a banker to the government

Governments need to hold their funds in an account into which they can make deposits and against which they can draw cheques. Such government deposits are usually held by the central bank.

The Bank also 'manages' the National Debt. When the government issues new bonds, the Bank arranges their actual sale. The government's debt is also redeemed through the Bank. When a debt issue reaches maturity, the Bank will take in the bonds and pay out money to the bond-holders on behalf of the government.

The Bank also smooths over the effects that might otherwise ensue from uneven borrowing and lending requirements. The Bank purchases any part of new issues of the national debt that is not taken up by other lenders on the day of issue, at what the Bank deems to be a reasonable interest rate. If it has judged the market correctly, the Bank will be able to sell the remaining part of the new debt over the next week or so. If it has guessed incorrectly, it may end up holding some of the new debt indefinitely. The Bank also enters the market if there is a large issue of government debt due for early redemption. The Bank buys up this issue over a period of time, thus preventing a sudden large accretion of cash to the public on redemption date.

The Bank also makes the interest payments on the government debt on behalf of the government. When interest must be paid on outstanding bonds, the Bank issues the cheques that go to the bond-holders. Finally, the Bank holds substantial amounts of the National Debt itself. These are bills and bonds that the Bank has purchased from the government, paying with a credit added to the government's account held at the Bank.

To be a banker to commercial banks

The Bank of England acts as banker to the commercial banks. It holds most of their reserves against their outstanding deposit liabilities held on deposit at the Bank. The Bank will, on order, transfer commercial banks' deposits from one bank to the other. In this way the Bank provides the commercial banks with the equivalent of chequing accounts, and with the means of settling debts among themselves. The Bank also ensures that the banking system is able to obtain funds when it is temporarily short of cash. The Bank does this either by lending funds to the system directly or by buying bills from the system in the open market in return for the needed funds.

We shall see later in this chapter that these activities provide the Bank with the channels through which it operates its monetary policy.

To control the country's currency

In most countries the central bank has the sole power to issue banknotes. In England this is done by the Issue Department of the Bank of England.[1] The Bank

---

1 Certain Scottish banks are allowed to issue banknotes, but the operation of monetary policies is solely in the hands of the Bank of England.

makes no attempt, however, to control the quantity of coins and banknotes in circulation. This is determined by the tastes of the public for holding money as deposits or as cash.

The public does not decide the size of the whole money supply, as measured, say, by M1. What it can, and does, decide however, is the *proportion* of M1 that will be held as notes and coins and the *proportion* that will be held as deposits. For example, if the public decides permanently to withdraw some of its deposits in the form of currency, the commercial banks will be faced with a cash drain to the public. To meet this, they will draw their deposits with the Bank of England. The Bank will print new banknotes and give these to the commercial banks, reducing their deposits with the bank by the corresponding amount.

The accounts are balanced by the Banking Department transferring financial assets to the Issue Department, which issues currency against them. Thus, when the commercial banks withdraw £X cash from their deposits at the Bank, the Banking Department reduces its deposit liabilities to commercial banks by £X and its holdings of interest-earning assets by the same amount. The Issue Department increases its holdings of interest-earning assets and increases its note liabilities by £X.

In contrast, if the public wants permanently to hold less currency than previously, people will bring the currency to the commercial banks and accept deposits in return. The commercial banks will deposit the notes and coins with the Bank. The Banking Department of the Bank will credit the deposits of the commercial banks with that amount and will hand the cash over to the Issue Department in return for securities that it holds. The Issue Department will then retire the currency from circulation.

To operate in the exchange market

The Bank carries out the government's policy with respect to the exchange rate. It holds the country's official reserves of gold and foreign exchange, and it intervenes from time to time on the foreign-exchange market to influence the exchange rate between sterling and other currencies. These policies are discussed in detail in Chapter 43.

To support the financial system

The next function is often referred to as the Bank's SUPPORT FUNCTION, and it arose from the Bank's operation as a lender of last resort to the commercial banks. Today, the support function relates to the whole of the financial system and it consists of so managing the system as to avoid financial crises that could lead to failures of banks and other institutions that are in a basically sound position.

The two main aspects of the support are to provide financial institutions with sufficient liquidity and to prevent them then from being put into difficulties by very rapid shifts in interest rates.

Many financial institutions are in the position of 'borrowing short' and 'lending long'. This means that they are obliged to pay their depositors and other creditors on demand, or on short notice, but they lend money out for longer terms. Thus if too many depositors demand their money, the banks cannot immediately raise the required funds by recalling loans. This puts the system in temporary need of liquidity. To provide the needed cash the bank can make loans to the system or provide the cash by buying up assets held by the system. Later in the chapter we shall study in detail how this is done.

If interest rates rise quickly, the banks, building societies, etc., will have to pay their depositors (other than those with sight deposits) more interest immediately to prevent them from taking their money elsewhere in search of higher rates. But they can raise the interest that they charge on many loans only as old loans mature and new loans are made.[1] Thus a rapid rise in interest rates may put some financial institutions in financial difficulties. Rather than let this happen, the central bank may try to slow down the rise in interest rates. To do this, the bank enters the open market and buys bonds, thus preventing their prices from falling as much as they otherwise would.

We shall see later in this chapter that in its efforts to protect the financial system by controlling both the level and speed of change of interest rates, the Bank necessarily varies the reserve base of the commercial banks. As we shall shortly see, changes in these reserves are an essential component of monetary policy. However, the changes required for the support and monetary policy functions may conflict with each other.

The support function was one of the prime motives of the Bank's activities in the 1950s and 1960s. It tried

---

1 This problem does not arise on loans, such as mortgages, where the interest rate is not fixed at the outset, because building-society interest varies as the market rate varies.

to 'lean against the wind', slowing down changes in the interest rate in either direction. Today this motivation is somewhat less important, although the Bank still is the ultimate protector of the monetary system.

To carry out monetary policy

The Bank is responsible for carrying out the government's monetary policy. One aspect of monetary policy concerns the manipulation of the commercial banks' cash reserves. By deciding how much of the government's debt to hold itself, and how much to sell to the public, the Bank can, as we shall see, influence the money supply. A second aspect of monetary policy is via the Bank's function as a 'lender of last resort' to the rest of the system. The Bank will lend on short term to the financial system whenever there is a short-term need for liquidity.

MONETARY POLICY IN A CLOSED ECONOMY

We now turn to a detailed discussion of how monetary policy works.

Targets and Instruments

In discussing any economic policy, we need to distinguish three types of variables: instrumental variables (usually just called instruments), intermediate (or target) variables and policy variables (often called policy goals).

The INSTRUMENTS of monetary policy are what the Bank can directly manipulate in an effort to achieve its goals. The main instruments are: (1) the reserve base of the commercial banks (see page 401), and (2) interest rates.

The Bank manipulates these instrumental variables using the following techniques:

(1) the purchase and sale of financial assets (government securities, in fact) in the open market – so-called open-market operations,

(2) the lending rate at which the Bank will offer credit to the banking system, and

(3) various rules and regulations that the Bank uses to regulate the behaviour of the financial system.

The INTERMEDIATE TARGETS of monetary policy are the variables that the Bank monitors, and reacts to. When an intermediate target variable attains a value outside of the range that the Bank targets for it, the Bank will use its instruments in an attempt to get the variable 'back on target'. The two main intermediate target variables that have at one time or another been used in monetary policy are:

(1) the money supply as measured either by M1 or one of the broader aggregates listed on page 402, and

(2) interest rates.

We have not made a mistake in listing interest rates both as instruments and as intermediate targets. At different times, interest rates have been one or the other (as we shall see later in the chapter).

POLICY VARIABLES, or GOALS, or TARGETS are the ultimate objectives of policy. There is, as we shall see, some controversy as to what these goals should be. Traditionally, the goals of monetary policy have been to achieve:

(1) full employment,

(2) stable price level, and

(3) a satisfactory balance of payments

(4) a healthy financial system.

The first two are the primary goals of *stabilization policy*; the third is a secondary stabilization goal, because the balance of payments may at times interfere with the achievement of the primary goals. We ignore the balance of payments throughout this chapter by assuming we are dealing with a closed economy – one in which there are no international transactions. Later, in Chapter 42, we return to this matter. The fourth and final policy goal is called *support policy*, which refers to the Bank's role of supporter of the monetary system. In the bulk of this chapter, we concentrate on the goals of stabilization policy. At the end of the chapter, we briefly discuss the goals of support policy.

We now look at each of these three categories of variables in some detail.

The Instruments of Monetary Policy

We have observed that the two main instruments of monetary policy are the reserve base supply and interest rates. In studying these we first look at the three main methods available to the Bank to manipulate these instruments – open-market operations, loans to the financial system, and rules and regulations.

Open-market operations

Probably the most important method of manipulating instrumental variables is for the Bank to purchase and sell financial assets in the open market, activities which are referred to as OPEN-MARKET OPERATIONS. We shall see that these operations directly affect both interest rates and the reserve base. Recall from page 401 that the commercial banks' reserve base, which is also called the *cash base*, is defined as (i) the notes and coins in the hands of the public, plus (ii) the reserves of the commercial banks on deposit with the Bank of England.

Why are these two magnitudes grouped together? The answer is that the total of the currency in the hands of the public and the reserves of the commercial banks is determined by the central bank's holdings of securities. We shall see below that the Bank can increase or decrease the reserve base by selling or buying bonds in the open market. The public can decide how much of this reserve base is held as cash and how much is held as reserves by the commercial banks (see discussion on page 445), but the total reserve base is under the control of the central bank.

To see what is involved, we study in detail the monetary changes that occur first when the Bank purchases, and then when it sells, assets on the open market.

Purchases from the Public: Assume that the Bank enters the open market and purchases bonds. The immediate effect of these purchases is to force up the price of bonds, which means a fall in the interest rate. A more subtle effect, however, relates to the size of the reserve base. To see this effect, let us follow out the consequences of the bank's purchase of a single £100 bond from a household that maintains an account with one of the commercial banks.

The Bank pays for the bond by making out a cheque drawn on itself, payable to the seller. The seller deposits this cheque in its own bank. The commercial bank presents the cheque to the central bank for payment. The central bank makes a book entry increasing the deposit of the commercial bank at the central bank. At the end of these transactions, the central bank has acquired a new asset in the form of a bond, and a new liability in the form of a deposit by the commercial bank. The household will have reduced its bond holdings and will have raised its cash holdings. The commercial bank will have a new

TABLE 37.2 Changes resulting from the Purchase by the Central Bank of a £100 Bond from a Household

BANK OF ENGLAND

Liabilities	Assets
Deposits of commercial banks +£100	Bond +£100

COMMERCIAL BANKS

Liabilities	Assets
Deposits of households +£100	Deposits with central bank +£100

PRIVATE HOUSEHOLDS

Liabilities	Assets
No change	Bonds −£100
	Deposits with commercial banks +£100

deposit equal to the amount paid for the bond by the central bank. Thus the commercial bank will find its cash assets, and its deposit liabilities, increased by the same amounts. The balance sheets of the three parties concerned will show the changes indicated in Table 37.2.

A commercial bank will now be in the position that was originally illustrated by Balance Sheet 2 on page 428 of Chapter 35. It will have received a new deposit of £100 against which it holds £100 of reserves. In Chapter 35 we assumed that the new cash deposit reached the banking system when an immigrant deposited his money in some bank. Now we can see how such new deposits usually arise. They result from open-market purchases by the Bank of England. Whatever its source, however, the new deposit gives the commercial banking system reserves in excess of the minimum it wishes to hold, and thus allows banks to engage in the multiple expansion of deposits that we studied earlier.

Notice that everything has been accomplished by a set of book transactions. The commercial banks have extra reserves to their credit on the books of the central bank. The household has new deposits recorded to its credit on the books of the commercial banks. No new coins or banknotes will be created unless, and until, the public wishes to hold some of its new money in the form of cash.

Sales to the Public: Second, let the central bank enter the open market and sell £100 worth of bonds to the public. The immediate effect is to lower the price of bonds, which means a rise in the interest rate. Once again, however, there is a more subtle effect on the

TABLE 37.3 Changes resulting from the Sale by the Central Bank of a £100 Bond to a Private Household

CENTRAL BANK

Liabilities	Assets
Deposits of commercial banks −£100	Bond −£100

COMMERCIAL BANKS

Liabilities	Assets
Deposits of households −£100	Deposits with central bank −£100

PRIVATE HOUSEHOLDS

Liabilities	Assets
No change	Bonds +£100
	Deposits with commercial banks −£100

reserve base. To see this, follow through the resulting set of transactions. The central bank sells a bond to a household that maintains an account with a commercial bank. The Bank hands over the bond and receives in return the household's cheque drawn against its deposit at its own bank. The central bank presents this cheque to the commercial bank for payment. The payment is made merely by a book entry reducing the commercial bank's deposit at the central bank.

Now the central bank has reduced its assets by the amount it receives for the bond it sold, and has also reduced its liabilities in the form of deposits standing in the favour of the commercial banks. The household has increased its holdings of bonds, and reduced its cash on deposit with its own bank. The commercial bank has reduced its deposit liability to the household, and reduced its cash assets (on deposit with the central bank) by the same amount. The balance sheets of the three parties concerned will initially show the changes indicated in Table 37.3.

The important result is that the sale of bonds (or any other financial asset) by the Bank decreases the reserves of the commercial banks. The banks will then have to make a multiple contraction of deposits in order to restore their desired reserve ratio.

Open-Market Operations in an Inflationary World: Open-market sales designed to force commercial banks actually to reduce the amount of deposit money are rare in modern times. In a world where national income is rising year by year – due both to economic growth of real output and inflationary increases in prices – the Bank is usually expanding

the cash base continually. But by varying the rate at which it purchases bonds, the bank can vary the *rate* at which the reserve base expands, and hence the rate at which new reserves become available to the banking system.

Transactions with the Government: In the examples we have used so far, the Bank dealt with private individuals. But *any* open-market purchase or sale by the central bank has the effects just analysed. For example, if the Bank buys bills and bonds directly from the government, this equally, though less directly, increases the reserve base and allows a multiple expansion of deposit money. In the first instance, it is the government's account with the central bank that gains the new credit balance. But as soon as the government spends the money, writing cheques to households and firms, the money will find its way into the commercial banks, who then obtain new deposits that increase both their reserves and their deposit liabilities by an equal amount. This permits a multiple expansion of deposit money.

Purchase of bonds from the government can occur if the government is unable, or unwilling, to finance the whole PSBR by borrowing from the private sector. The government then sells its bonds to the Bank. This has the same effect as any other open-market purchase: it puts new reserves into the hands of the commercial banks, who can then engage in a multiple expansion of deposits. This is what is loosely referred to as *printing press finance*. Although it is all done by book entries, the effect is the same as if the government had printed pound notes in its own cellars and used them to settle its debts. That part of new debt that is sold to the Bank, rather than to the public, is financed by creating new money.

Loans to the financial system

We have seen that the Bank acts as a lender of last resort. Financial institutions often have sudden needs for funds with which to pay their debts – either to their depositors or to others from whom they have borrowed money. One way of getting the required funds is to borrow them from the central bank. Indeed, one of the major reasons for the early development of central banks was to lend funds to financial institutions that had sound investments but were in temporary need of funds. These activities of the Bank have the effect of altering the reserve base of the commercial banks.

Loans to the Discount Houses: In many countries, commercial banks borrow directly from the central bank. In the UK, however, the discount houses stand between the commercial banks and the Bank of England. If the banks find themselves in need of cash, they recall some of their demand loans made to the discount houses. Because (as we saw in Chapter 35) the discount houses use their borrowed money to buy short-term financial assets, they cannot repay the banks out of their own cash reserves. Instead, they must obtain the money by borrowing from the Bank of England. They put up approved financial assets (mainly short-term Treasury Bills) as security, and they pay interest on these loans. In these circumstances, the discount houses are said to be 'in the Bank'.

The rate the Bank charges the discount houses used to be set in advance and announced every week by the Bank of England. It was first called Bank Rate, and then the *Minimum Lending Rate* (MLR). Now, however, the rate is usually determined by the Bank from day to day, though the Bank has the power to set MLR if it chooses to do so. (It did so, for example, in 1984, when the exchange rate was under special pressure.)

Direct Purchase of Bills and Bonds: There is a second way in which the Bank can provide assistance when the banking system needs cash. Instead of lending to the discount houses, it can engage in open-market operations to buy bills and bonds directly. If commercial banks try to sell bills and bonds on the open market, the prices of these assets will be forced down. But if the central bank enters the market and buys all the bills and bonds offered at their present prices, this allows any institution that is in need of cash to obtain it by selling its financial assets. In the mid-1980s the Bank of England let it be known that it now favoured this method rather than the method of lending money directly to the discount houses.

Rules and regulations

Other techniques of monetary policy have been used from time to time. Ceilings have been placed on bank advances, and informal requests to banks to restrict lending have been employed in a procedure sometimes referred to as *moral suasion*. A system was also in use between 1973 and 1980 whereby the banks were set target rates of growth for their deposits and were penalized if they overshot them. (This was the so-called *supplementary deposit scheme*, otherwise known as the 'corset'.) Also in the 1970s, the Bank imposed a minimum liquid assets ratio on the commercial banks. As well as having their own desired ratio of cash to deposits, they were also forced to keep a minimum ratio of liquid assets – cash plus short-term bills – to deposits.

Finally we should mention the introduction in 1960 of *special deposits*. These are 'frozen' deposits of the commercial banks held at the Bank of England. These special-deposit requirements can be raised or lowered as a means of influencing the commercial banks' liquidity. Special deposits have not, however, been required since July 1980.

The world's banking system has become vastly more international, and vastly more competitive, over the last decade. Computers move funds around the world with ease. Would-be borrowers who cannot get funds in London can quickly turn to Paris, New York or Tokyo. As a result, all of these special restrictions are out of favour. They tend to hurt the competitiveness of one country's banks without really curtailing borrowing.

Announcement effects

The techniques reviewed so far work through the transmission mechanism which we studied in Chapter 36. However, since people's expectations are a major determinant of their spending decisions, the monetary transmission mechanism can sometimes be short-circuited. Assume, for example, that the Bank announces a tightening of monetary policy – in the past, it would have raised the MLR; today it might let it be known that it intends to enter the open market and drive up interest rates. If the announcement is taken seriously, people may expect contractionary forces to be felt in the near future and, as a result, may cut their expenditure plans now. For example, investment plans may be curtailed in anticipation of a future fall in national income. There is then a contractionary effect on aggregate expenditure that is felt before the restrictive monetary policy actually creates a money shortage and drives interest rates upwards.

Of course, if the Bank did not usually follow up on its announcements by instituting the expected policy, the announcements would soon cease to be believed. But as long as the Bank usually does what it says it is going to do, it can often get very quick effects that operate through changed expectations that alter planned expenditures and hence shift the aggregate desired expenditure function.

Choice of policy instrument

So far we have studied the mechanism by which monetary policy works to influence the Bank's instrumental variables. But which instrument should the Bank use, the money supply or interest rates? Although the two are related, as we shall see later, most central banks have found it necessary to choose to concentrate on one or the other. At different times and in different countries central banks have made different choices between them.

The Bank of England has, usually, opposed using the cash base as its main instrument because it feels such attempts may conflict with its function as lender of last resort. If the banking system is in need of liquidity the Bank must support the system by providing the needed funds (either by lending to the discount houses or buying up their bills in the open market). It is difficult to do this and stick to rigid targets for the size of the reserve base.

In 1981 the Bank announced that its policy would be to try to exercise its monetary policy by stabilizing interest rates within a narrow band. This band would be changed from time to time, whenever the Bank estimated that the liquidity preference schedule had shifted or the money multiplier had changed. We have already noted that the target rate is not stated publicly in advance. The Bank hopes that uncertainty about the interest rate that the financial system will have to pay to obtain funds will make the commercial banks more cautious in creating new deposit money. After all, if the system gets short of reserves and has to borrow from the Bank, it may be charged a very high rate – usually referred to as a penal rate – that would cut drastically into profits.

More importantly, the Bank removed virtually all required reserves of the clearing banks. They now operate with the minimum balances they need to finance their day-to-day clearings of interbank transactions. They also know that, if they run into difficulties, the Bank of England would have to make cash available to them rather than permit widespread failures among financial institutions.

This means that the Bank must use interest rates rather than reserves as its primary monetary instrument. It watches the various money supply figures; it watches the behaviour of real national income and the price level, as well as a host of international indicators, such as the balance of payments and the exchange rate. If it wishes to tighten monetary policy it enters the market and sells bills, seeking to drive the interest rate upwards. This moves the economy upwards to the left along its liquidity preference curve. If it wishes to be more expansive in its monetary policy, it enters the market and buys bills, seeking to drive the interest rate down. This moves the economy downwards to the right along its liquidity preference curve.

The Intermediate Targets of Monetary Policy

We have already observed that intermediate targets are the variables that the Bank monitors and reacts to. The Bank will normally have a target range for its intermediate variables and will use its instruments in an attempt to keep these variables within their target ranges.

Requirements for a satisfactory target

If this attempt is to be successful in meeting the Bank's ultimate objectives of influencing its policy variables in the desired manner, two conditions need to be fulfilled.

(1) The target variables need to be fairly quickly influenced by the Bank's instruments.

(2) The target variables must be closely related *in a stable manner* to changes in the policy variables in which the Bank is ultimately interested. If they were not, then there would be no point in the Bank adjusting its instruments with respect to the behaviour of the intermediate target variables. The circumstances under which this second condition is fulfilled are discussed later in this chapter.

Notice that we have italicized the phrase 'in a stable manner' in the previous paragraph. This is an important qualification. Because of the trade cycle, many economic variables are loosely correlated with each other, rising more or less together on the upswing and falling more or less together on the downswing. These variables will tend to move together, even when there is no direct causal link between them. As a result, many economic variables will show some correlation with national income and the price level, which are the ultimate targets of monetary policy. But most of these other variables will not make good intermediate targets because changes in them do not cause changes in income and prices. Consider an example. The number of loaded goods trains leaving London is correlated with UK's national income, but it would not be a good intermediate target. If the Bank tried to change this number with a view to affecting national income, it would find that the relation ceased to be a stable one. If, in order to restrain a boom, steps were taken to lower rail shipments (the assumed intermediate target), it is very unlikely that the boom would be restrained. Instead, alternative means would be found for shipping goods.

This leads to an important conclusion. To be a satisfactory intermediate target,

(1) a variable must be linked to national income by a causal chain so that changes in the variable cause national income to change; and

(2) the causal relation must be strong and *stable* enough that, when the intermediate target is changed by policy, the ultimate target continues to react in the way it always has done. This may sound rather abstract now, but the point will be illustrated with a specific example later in this chapter.

Actual targets

The main intermediate targets that have been used by central banks throughout the world are various measures of the money supply and interest rates.

The Money Supply: Controlling the money supply as measured by one of the various definitions listed on page 402, means controlling the supply of credit. Deposit money is created when commercial banks make loans to their customers. If commercial banks do not have sufficient reserves, they cannot expand the supply of new loans, and hence cannot expand the supply of new money, no matter how urgently their customers may want to borrow from them.

Interest Rates: Controlling the interest rate controls the demand for credit. The amount that firms will wish to spend on investment, and hence the amount they will wish to borrow to finance such expenditures, will, as we have seen, vary with the rate of interest. Thus high rates of interest will be associated with small demands for new borrowing, and hence new money creation, while low rates of interest will be associated with large demands.

The Relation Between the Money Supply and Interest Rates: Because of what we have just said about interest rates and the money supply, one might think of the bank having two policies, one influencing the supply of money and the other influencing the interest rate. This, however, would be a mistake. The reason is that interest rates and the quantity of money are linked to each other through the liquidity preference function. The Bank cannot set independent targets for the quantity of money *and* the interest rate. If it sets a target for one of these variables, it must be content with the value of the other that will allow it to meet its target. Thus, if there is a *stable* demand for money – i.e. an *LP* schedule that is not continually shifting – the Bank really only has one decision to make: what combination of interest rate and money supply – i.e. what point on the *LP* schedule – to aim at.

Which intermediate target?

It follows from what has just been said that, in a world of perfect stability and perfect certainty, it would not matter whether the Bank chose the quantity of money or the interest rate as its intermediate target variable. If the Bank knew exactly the location of the *LP* curve shown in Figure 37.1 and if the curve never shifted, then the Bank could decide on an intermediate target of either an interest rate of r_0 or a money supply of M_0, and both decisions would produce identical results. Both functions are shifting and their exact positions are uncertain; however, it does matter which variable the Bank chooses as its intermediate target. We cannot go into all of the reasons here, but we can look at some.

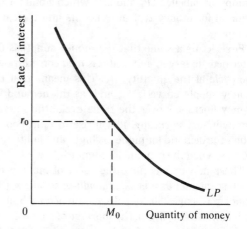

FIGURE 37.1   The Rate of Interest and the Quantity of Money as Intermediate Targets. Choice of a value for either one of the two intermediate variables implies a value for the other

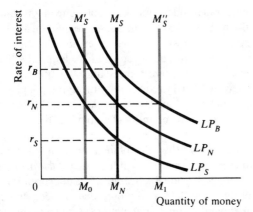

FIGURE 37.2   Alternative Stabilizing Policies when the *LP* Function is Shifting. Policies that stabilize interest rates lead to wide fluctuations in the money supply; policies that stabilize the money supply lead to wide fluctuations in interest rates

Shifts in the Demand for Money: The first thing to notice is that the demand for money varies cyclically. The *LP* schedule drawn in Figure 37.1 is drawn for a given national income. As national income rises in a boom, and then falls in a slump, so the *LP* function shifts to the right and then to the left. (The *LP* curve shifts in the manner studied on pages 422–3 because national income varies over the trade cycle.)

An example of such shifts is shown in Figure 37.2. The *LP* function that exists at potential income is labelled LP_N, which stands for the normal demand for money. The *LP* functions that exist in booms and in slumps are labelled LP_B and LP_S, which stand for the demand for money typical of booms and typical of slumps.

First, let us assume that the money supply is the intermediate target, and that it is held constant over the cycle at the quantity M_N. This means that the money supply curve is M_S and, as the demand for money fluctuates over the trade cycle, the interest rate will vary cyclically. It will rise to r_B in booms, when the demand for money is high, and fall to r_S in slumps, when the demand for money is low.

These movements have the effect of making the interest rate act as a *monetary built-in stabilizer*. (See Chapter 31, page 380, for a discussion of *fiscal* built-in stabilizers.) In the boom, the shortage of money forces up interest rates and thus tends to reduce interest-sensitive expenditure, and so reduce the high desired aggregate expenditure that is causing the boom. In the slump, the low interest rates tend to encourage

interest-sensitive expenditure, and hence to increase desired aggregate expenditure above the low levels that are causing the slump.

Second, assume that the interest rate is the intermediate target, and that it is held constant over the cycle. This means that the Bank must vary the money supply pro-cyclically in order to hold interest rates constant in the face of fluctuations in the demand for money. In Figure 37.2, the money supply must vary from M_0 in the slump, through M_N at potential income, to M_1 during the boom.

The net effect of this is that the built-in stabilizing effect of a fixed money supply is lost. During the boom the increased demand for money puts upward pressure on the interest rate and the Bank must expand the money supply to prevent interest rates from rising. The money supply curve is shifted to M_S'', in combination with LP_B. This yields an equilibrium interest rate of r_N. As a result, there is no monetary mechanism operating to restrain expenditure and so reduce the strength of the boom. During the slump, the decreased demand for money puts downward pressure on the interest rate and the Bank must contract the money supply to prevent interest rates from falling. The money supply curve is shifted to M_S' as the money demand curve falls to LP_S. As a result, the equilibrium interest rate remains at r_N, so there is no monetary mechanism operating to increase expenditure and so reduce the magnitude of the slump.

Uncertainty: In drawing Figure 37.2, we had to assume that we knew the exact positions of the M_S and the *LP* curves. But certain knowledge is never given to any policy-maker – nor, unfortunately, to any other person. The Bank does not know exactly where the *LP* function is at any time, nor does it know exactly what its open-market operations will do to the money supply. It was argued strongly during the 1960s and 1970s that, in the face of this uncertainty, monetary policy would have a more stabilizing effect on cyclical fluctuations if the money supply, rather than the interest rate, was taken as the intermediate target variable.

The evolution of the debate over intermediate target variables

From the end of World War II to some time in the 1970s, most of the world's central banks used interest rates as their intermediate target. Then, during the 1970s, one central bank after another, including the

Bank of England, went over to using some measure of the money supply as their intermediate target. It was hoped that using the money supply as an intermediate target would give the Banks more consistent control over aggregate desired expenditure than was obtained by using the interest rate.

The switch to the money supply as the intermediate target gave rise to a number of new issues, which are discussed below.

Which Money Supply as a Target?   In Chapter 33 we discussed several measures of the money supply, but in the analysis of the monetary transmission mechanism in Chapter 36 we assumed that there is a unique money supply. In fact, however, there is a continuous spectrum of monetary assets ranging from notes and coins, over sight deposits in current accounts of the commercial banks at one extreme, which are perfectly liquid and usually bear no interest rates, through time deposits in deposit accounts at banks, deposits at building societies, Treasury Bills maturing tomorrow, bills maturing in 30, 60 or 90 days, bonds with years to run to maturity, and finally to Consols that pay interest, but have no redemption date. Just where to draw the line between money and short-term liquid assets that are not money will always be an arbitrary decision. After all, the reason the government wants to control the money supply is because it wants to control the volume of bank lending. So what is important to know is what the banks regard as a safe set of reserve money and near-money assets. There *is no doubt* that money matters. There *is doubt*, however, about the existence of a unique group of assets that the central bank should use as its intermediate target.

Can the Money Supply be Controlled?   If the money supply – however defined – is to be the target variable, the Bank must be able to use its instruments to control that supply fairly closely.

There is no doubt that M0 (the high-powered money supply) can be so controlled. (Indeed it is so closely under the Bank's control that it is correctly referred to as an instrument rather than as a target.) But what about the various other measures of the money supply defined on page 402 – M1, £M3, etc.? A group of economists called Monetarists believe that the demands for these assets are stable enough that any group of them can be controlled through the high-powered money supply. That is, they believe in a *stable deposit multiplier*. (See page 430.)

Many critics of monetary targets have taken the view that the supply of money is determined, not exogenously by central bank policy, but endogenously by forces from within the economic system. They believe that if more money is demanded, the banking system will be able to generate more money of one type or another within very broad limits independently of what the central bank does to M0. It is often argued that this is especially so with the British system, whose particular institutions prevent the Bank of England from achieving the close control of the money supply that the American central bank is able to achieve.

Notice the effect of this view on the operation of the monetary adjustment mechanism that we studied on pages 440–41. The mechanism eliminates any inflationary gap because price-level increases cause a money shortage which drives up the interest rate and reduces desired investment expenditure. But if more money is always created whenever it is needed, no money shortage will appear. There will then be no monetary adjustment mechanism to remove an inflationary gap.

This possibility has already been discussed in the section entitled Frustrating the Monetary Adjustment Mechanism, on page 441. There is one difference, however. In our earlier discussion, the Bank of England consciously frustrated the adjustment mechanism by increasing the money supply in line with the rise in the price level. Now we are considering the possibility that the commercial banks can increase the money supply in the course of their ordinary operations without effective restraint from the Bank's monetary policy. In this case the monetary adjustment mechanism is frustrated without anyone making a conscious decision to do so.

This is an example of what is often called *Goodhart's Law*, which states that 'if policy-makers rely on a relation between two variables, the relation will change or even disappear.' Thus if x and y are related and policy-makers manipulate x seeking to influence y, the relation between x and y will change or disappear. The reason is that relations result from human behaviour and when policy-makers start to manipulate x, human behaviour will change, thus altering the relation between the two variables.

The Money Supply and the PSBR: Many critics have suggested that the existence of a large public-sector borrowing requirement makes it difficult if not impossible for the Bank to pursue a money-supply target. Let us see what is involved here.

The PSBR measures how much the public sector is spending in excess of its current revenues and, therefore, how much it needs to borrow. The effects of such public borrowing depend on whether the lenders to the government are the public or the Bank. If the requirements are met by borrowing from the public, there is no significant effect on the money supply (or on aggregate expenditure). Private-sector saving, which would have been lent to firms to finance private-sector investment spending, merely goes to finance public-sector spending. If, however, the requirements are met by borrowing (directly or indirectly) from the Bank, this means an increase in the money supply. The Bank has then engaged in an open-market purchase of securities and we know that such purchases increase the money supply.

Thus, there is no necessary relation between the size of the PSBR and any increase of the money supply. People who worry about such a relation worry that the larger is the PSBR the less likely is it that the requirements can be met by borrowing from the public and thus the more likely is it that the Bank will have to step in and, by providing funds to the market, bring about a monetary expansion. This has happened in the past when large PSBRs were financed by inflationary increases in the money supply. That such inflationary finance is more likely to occur the larger is the PSBR is an empirical judgement that may well be correct. It is important to understand, however, that it is no more than a judgement. It is important to consider the implications of any change in the PSBR in the context of the time, since there is nothing in economic theory to say that, whenever the PSBR rises, the rate of monetary expansion must rise as well.

Should Some Measure of the Money Supply be the Intermediate Target? Throughout the world, central banks have tried a variety of money-supply targets in an effort to find the one that bears the closest relation to national income and the price level, which are the policy variables that ultimately interest them. Critics say that there are so many different kinds of liquid assets, and such a high degree of substitutability between them, that no long-term relations will be found that relate any sub-group called 'money' to aggregate expenditure and hence to national income and the price level. Thus they argue that targeting on some measure of the money supply is unsatisfactory.

Those who advocate monetary targeting say that such stable relations do exist. Because they believe that the rate of growth of the money supply is the ultimate determinant of the inflation rate, they say that monetary targeting is the best way in which central banks can fulfil their function of controlling the price level.

There is no serious debate about the insight gained hundreds of years ago that money and the price level are closely related in the long term. The debate is instead on whether or not there is some group of monetary assets that is suitable for central banks to use as their intermediate target in pursuit of their ultimate policy goal of stabilizing the price level in the short or medium term.

POLICY VARIABLES

We have already observed that three goals are traditionally set for monetary policy. The first is to assist in stabilization policy designed to ensure full employment. The second is to ensure a relatively stable price level. The third is to support the financial system.

Stabilization Policy

The traditional view is that monetary policy can work along with fiscal policy to help to stabilize the economy. Let us see how this was supposed to work out.

When the economy was suffering from a recessionary gap, an expansionary monetary policy would be followed. The Bank would enter the open market and buy bonds. This would force down interest rates and expand the reserve base. Given a stable money multiplier, the actions of the commercial banks would expand the money supply by a predictable amount. The expansionary effects would then work through the monetary adjustment mechanism in the manner laid out in Figure 36.4 on page 437.

When the economy was suffering from an inflationary gap, a contractionary monetary policy would be followed. The Bank would sell bonds, forcing the interest rate up and contracting the reserve base. The resulting decline in the money supply would cause the monetary adjustment mechanism to operate in the contractionary manner outlined in figure 36.5 on page 437.

The use of monetary policy as a tool of stabilization policy has been criticized along two lines. One line of criticism, stemming from Keynesians, has been that monetary policy is often too weak in its effects to be a useful stabilization device. The other, stemming from Monetarists, has been that monetary policy is too strong in its effects to be a useful stabilization device! In discussing these arguments, we assume that the money supply can be controlled by the Bank, and study the results of being able to exercise such control. We will deal with the first criticism here, but postpone consideration of the second criticism until Chapter 42.

The strength of the effect of monetary policy

The factors that influence the strength of monetary policy are illustrated in Figure 37.3. In both parts of

that Figure, the money supply is originally M_0. This quantity and the liquidity preference function, labelled LP in the Figure, combine to yield an interest rate of r_0. The interest rate of r_0 combines with the marginal efficiency of investment (MEI) curve to yield a desired investment expenditure of I_0. (You will recall that the MEI curve relates desired investment expenditure to the rate of interest.)

A monetary expansion then increases the money supply to M_1. This lowers the interest rate to r_1 and increases desired investment expenditure by the amount ΔI to I_1.

This is the by-now-familiar operation of the monetary transmission mechanism. We shall now see, however, that the strength of the effect that works through that mechanism depends critically on the slopes of the LP and MEI curves – that is to say, on the magnitudes of the effects of changes in the money

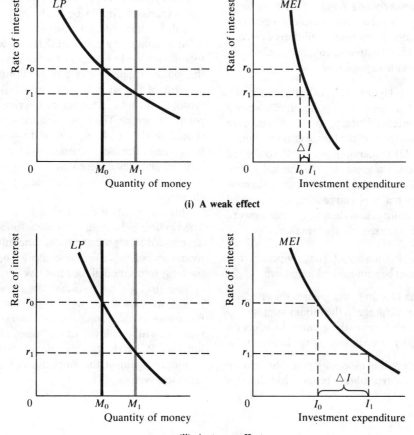

(i) A weak effect

(ii) A strong effect

FIGURE 37.3   **The Strength of Monetary Policy.** The magnitude of the effects of changes in the money supply depend on the slopes of the LP and the MEI curves

supply on the rate of interest, and changes in the rate of interest on the volume of investment.

A Weak Effect: Part (i) of the Figure illustrates the case of a weak monetary effect. The *LP* function is fairly flat so the interest rate does not fall by much as a result of the increase in the money supply. Also the *MEI* function is steep, so desired investment does not respond much to any fall in the interest rate that does occur. Taken together, the effect of the expansionary monetary policy is a small increase in desired investment expenditure, and hence only a small upward shift in the desired expenditure function.

The Liquidity Trap: An extreme case arises when there is a perfectly elastic *LP* curve. This is called the case of a *liquidity trap*: an increase in the money supply leaves the interest rate unaffected and, therefore, has no effect at all on desired investment and hence no effect on aggregate desired expenditure. This case is an unlikely one – indeed, there is some doubt if such a case has *ever* actually occurred. Nonetheless, it does show that conditions are conceivable where, at one extreme, monetary policy has no effect on aggregate expenditure.

A Strong Effect: Figure 37.3 (ii) illustrates the opposite case where monetary policy has a strong effect. The *LP* function is steep, so the interest rate falls quite a bit as a result of the increase in the money supply. Also the *MEI* function is fairly flat, so desired investment responds a great deal to the fall in the interest rate. Taken together, the effect of the expansionary monetary policy is a large increase in desired investment expenditure and, hence, a large upward shift in the aggregate expenditure function.

Summary: The influences of the shapes of the relevant curves can be summarized as follows.

● The steeper the *LP* curve, the greater the effect on interest rates of a change in the money supply.
● The flatter the *MEI* curve, the greater the effect on investment of any given change in the interest rate.

Those who believe that monetary policy has strong effects on aggregate expenditure believe that changes

in the money supply cause large changes in interest rates, which in turn cause large changes in desired investment expenditure. Those who believe that monetary policy has weak effects on aggregate expenditure believe that changes in the money supply cause small changes in interest rates, and that changes in interest rates cause only small changes in desired investment expenditure. Monetarists have often been associated with the view the monetary policy is strong, while some Keynesians have often been associated with the view that monetary policy is weak.

The Long-Term Behaviour of the Price Level

Those who believe that monetary policy is not an effective short-term stabilization device often advocate control of the price level as the sole goal of monetary policy. They believe that the *rate* of monetary expansion should be set in such a way as to provide for the needs of a growing economy but not so as to validate any inflation. This view often leads them to advocate a constant trend rate of growth of the money supply – a rate of growth that takes no account of the short-term fluctuations in national income but that is set equal to the rate of growth of potential income. The idea is that the supply of money should be allowed to grow as fast as what the long-term trend increase in the demand for money would be if the price level were steady. We shall have more to say about this simple monetary rule in later chapters.

This represents a major shift in policy variables. The cyclical behaviour of national income is to be abandoned as a policy variable; the full attention of monetary policy is to be concentrated on influencing the long-term trend of the price level.

Now that we have studied the Bank's monetary policy, we can move on to a further study of the behaviour of the economy, concentrating on long-term growth, employment and unemployment, and inflation. When this has been done, we shall return to look once again at the workings of both monetary and fiscal policy.

SUMMARY

1 The Bank of England is the controller of the currency supply, it acts as banker to the government and to the commercial banks, it carries out government policy with respect to the exchange rate and monetary policy, and supports the financial system.

2 An open-market purchase of securities increases the cash reserves of the banking system and leads to a multiple expansion of deposit money. An open-market sale lowers reserves and leads to a multiple contraction of deposit money.

3 The Bank provides funds when the banking system is in need of liquidity, operating as a so-called lender of last resort. These funds are either provided by lending, possibly at a penal rate, or by entering the open market and buying bills and bonds so that the banking system can obtain the needed liquidity without borrowing from the Bank. The terms on which the Bank will provide liquidity have an effect on the commercial banks' willingness to create deposit money.

4 The Bank also makes rules and regulations that govern banking practices and that may require different sorts of deposits to be made by the commercial banks with the Bank.

5 In the past the Bank's major intermediate target of monetary policy was the interest rate, but more recently it has been the money supply. The Bank seeks to control the money supply by setting a band within which it controls interest rates by its open-market operations. If the money supply is off target, the band of interest-rate control will be changed. If the money supply is growing faster than target, interest rates will be raised; while if the money supply is growing slower than target, interest rates will be lowered. *This means that the interest rate is the instrumental variable while the money supply is the intermediate target.*

6 Stabilizing the money supply helps to stabilize the economy because free-market interest rates then vary pro-cyclically, and this helps to dampen down booms and mitigate slumps. Stabilizing interest rates removes the stabilizing force of pro-cyclical variations in interest rates and thus tends to accentuate cyclical swings in the economy.

7 The extent to which the Bank can exercise close control over the money supply is debated by economists. They also debate which money supply should be the intermediate target. Successful use of the money supply as an intermediate target requires that the money supply be controllable without overly long lags by the Bank's policy instruments, and that the money supply maintains a fairly stable relation to the Bank's policy goals.

8 The strength of monetary policy depends on the slopes of the liquidity preference and the marginal efficiency of capital curves. A given change in the money supply will have a small effect if the *LP* curve is interest-elastic while the *MEI* curve is interest-inelastic; it will have a large effect if the *LP* curve is interest-inelastic while the *MEI* curve is interest-elastic.

9 The Bank's goal of supporter of the financial system can lead it to slow down changes in interest rates which cause changes in the money supply that may conflict with the intermediate targets for money growth that arise from its stabilization policy.

38

Aggregate Demand and Aggregate Supply

This chapter introduces two new tools of analysis, the aggregate demand curve and the aggregate supply curve. They will help us greatly in the studies of growth, unemployment and inflation that we undertake in the following three chapters. First, however, we need to review the main tool of analysis that we have used in macroeconomics so far.

The 45° Diagram

So far our study of equilibrium national income has used the famous Keynesian '45° line diagram'. This is the diagram that combines the aggregate desired expenditure curve with the 45° line, and determines equilibrium at their intersection. The model of the determination of equilibrium national income whose graphical expression is the 45° diagram provides a very valuable tool of analysis. But it can only get us so far.

One of its major disadvantages is that it cannot deal with any cause of inflation other than an inflationary gap at full employment. The analysis runs in terms of income, output and expenditure, which are *directly* measured on the diagram's axes. Implications for the price level are only deducible *indirectly* – and then only for cases where a change in the price level is caused by an inflationary or a deflationary gap – i.e. inflations which come from the demand side.

The model cannot explicitly handle any inflation that starts from the cost side, such as would result from increases in the prices of imported raw materials or increases in wages that are not themselves the result of an inflationary gap. For this reason it provides no explanation, for example, of the important phenomenon of *stagflation* – rising prices at times of *high* unemployment.

The Crisis of Stagflation: When stagflation first became a serious problem in the mid 1970s, it seemed such a mystery that numerous commentators proclaimed the end of conventional, Keynesian economics. In response to the challenge of new and surprising observations, theoretical and empirical work on stagflation proceeded at a hectic pace. Within a very few years an understanding of the problem was developed. Although this understanding did not overthrow Keynesian economics, it did establish two points: (1) the conventional Keynesian 45° analysis has to be amended to take account *explicitly* of the effects of changes in the price level on equilibrium national income; and (2) conventional Keynesian theory related almost exclusively to aggregate demand and paid insufficient attention to aggregate supply.

Of course, the full explanation of the events of the 1970s and 1980s is complex. But the essence of the explanation is so simple that it is now incorporated into elementary textbooks. It is to this revision and extension of the theory of income determination that we now turn our attention.

THE DEMAND SIDE OF THE ECONOMY

What is now called THE AGGREGATE DEMAND CURVE in most modern economic literature is a curve relating the price level plotted on one axis and *equilibrium national income* plotted on the other. The equilibrium national income plotted in this new diagram is determined by the intersection of the aggregate desired expenditure curve and the 45° line.[1]

Equilibrium National Income when the Price Level Changes

Figure 38.1 shows the by-now familiar determination of national income in the 45° diagram. The initial aggregate desired expenditure curve is $E(P_0)$ and equilibrium national income is Y_0. (We will shortly explain why the P_0 is there.)

Now we ask a key question: what does a change in the price level do to the aggregate desired expenditure curve, given that the money supply is held constant? This question does not require further study, for we have already answered it in Chapter 36 when we discussed the monetary adjustment mechanism. Let us review that discussion now.

The rise in the price level increases the demand for money for transactions and precautionary purposes. This creates an excess demand for money that sets the monetary transmission mechanism in motion along the lines described in Figure 36.5 on page 437. (Since it is critical to everything that follows in this chapter, it is essential that you turn back to pages 434–8 and 440–1 now and review the workings of the monetary transmission and monetary adjustment mechanisms.) The key result is so important that it deserves restating: *a rise in the price level, with the money supply held constant, increases the demand for money, which drives the interest rate up, which lowers desired investment expenditure, which shifts the aggregate desired expenditure function downwards.*

In Figure 38.1 the rise in the price level from P_0 to P_1 shifts the aggregate desired expenditure curve downwards from $E(P_0)$ to $E(P_1)$ and lowers equilibrium national income from Y_0 to Y_1.

A fall in the price level has the opposite effects. Because the money value of transactions falls, so also does the transaction demand for money. This causes a monetary disequilibrium and sets in train the events outlined in Figure 36.4 on page 437. The key result is: *a fall in the price level reduces the demand for money, which drives the interest rate down, which increases*

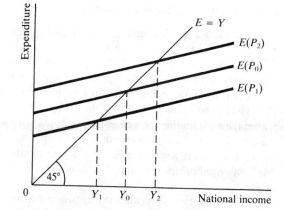

FIGURE 38.1 Determination of Equilibrium National Income when the Price Level is Changed. A rise in the price level shifts the aggregate desired expenditure curve downwards and thus lowers equilibrium income

desired investment, which shifts the desired expenditure curve upwards.

A fall in the price level from P_0 to P_2 shifts the aggregate desired expenditure curve upwards in Figure 38.1 from $E(P_0)$ to $E(P_2)$ and raises equilibrium national income from Y_0 to Y_2.

Because a change in the price level shifts the aggregate expenditure curve, each such curve must be related to a specific, and constant, price level. We did not have to worry about this in Part 4 because we were *assuming* a constant price level. Now, to remind us of this assumption, we state in parentheses after each aggregate expenditure curve's label the price level to which it relates.

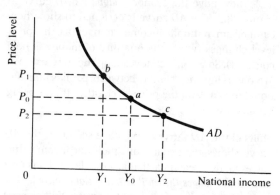

FIGURE 38.2 The Aggregate Demand Curve. The aggregate demand curve is negatively sloped because the higher the price level, the lower is equilibrium national income, *ceteris paribus*

---

1 Economics is a developing subject and so terminology is never fully agreed at any moment of time. Some economists use the term *macro demand curve* to refer to what we have just defined as the *aggregate demand curve*. They then use this latter term to refer to what we have called the aggregate desired expenditure curve.

Derivation of the aggregate demand curve

To derive the aggregate demand curve we merely plot in Figure 38.2 each equilibrium national income as determined in Figure 38.1 against the price level that determined it. Thus income Y_0 is plotted against price level P_0 to yield point a, income Y_1 against price level P_1 to yield point b and Y_2 against P_2 to yield point c. If we imagine changing the price level continuously, we can plot out a continuous curve in Figure 38.2, each point relating a specific price level to the specific level of equilibrium income with which it is associated.

The curve so derived is called the *aggregate demand (AD) curve* and it relates each price level to its associated level of equilibrium national income. The curve is negatively sloped because, *ceteris paribus*, the higher the price level the lower the level of equilibrium national income. It is important to remember the qualification of *ceteris paribus*. In particular it is the money supply that is being held constant. The rise in the price level creates a money shortage that drives up the interest rate and lowers interest-sensitive expenditure; that is why equilibrium income falls.

Movements along, and shifts of, the AD curve

We now come to the one point on which you must take special care: do not confuse movements along the *AD* curve with shifts of that curve.

Movements Along the *AD* Curve: We have seen that the *AD* curve plots equilibrium national income against the price level. Although changes in the price level *shift* the aggregate expenditure curve in Figure 38.1, they move the economy *along* its *AD* curve in Figure 38.2. The *AD* curve is designed to show how equilibrium national income changes as the price level changes (when the quantity of money is held constant). So when we move along the *AD* curve, we are observing the relation between equilibrium national income and the price level, other things being equal.

Shifts of the *AD* Curve: We have seen that the *AD* curve shows *the* equilibrium national income that corresponds to each particular price level. Thus any force that *changes the equilibrium national income that is associated with a given price level* must shift the *AD* curve. Examples are shifts in desired expenditure on consumption, investment, government exhaustive purchases, and net exports. Increases in any of these

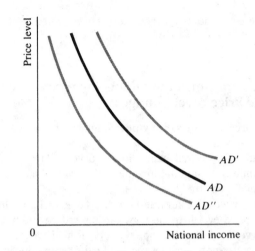

FIGURE 38.3   A Shift in the Aggregate Demand Curve. A rightward shift in the *AD* curve indicates a higher level of equilibrium national income is associated with each price level

will raise aggregate desired expenditure (at any given price level), increase equilibrium income, and hence shift the *AD* curve outwards to the right. Thus, *anything other than a change in the price level that shifts the aggregate desired expenditure curve, and so alters equilibrium national income at a given price level, also shifts the AD curve.*

The above analysis allows us to restate the conclusions we reached in Part 4, as follows. *A rise in the amount of desired consumption, investment, government, or net export expenditure associated with each level of national income shifts the AD curve to the right. A fall in any of these desired expenditures shifts the AD curve to the left.*

Such shifts are shown in Figure 38.3. The original curve is *AD*. A rise in any component of desired expenditure shifts the curve to the right, say to *AD'*. A fall in any component of desired expenditure shifts the curve to the left, say to *AD''*.

THE SUPPLY SIDE OF THE ECONOMY

Everything to do with aggregate demand is referred to as being on the 'demand side' of the economy, while everything to do with aggregate supply is referred to as being on the 'supply side'. We now pass to a consideration of what is called the supply side of the economy.

In doing so, our first step is to remove an unrealistic assumption that we have used to simplify all of the macroeconomic theory that we have studied so far. Up until now, we have assumed that income could not exceed Y_F. Thus an inflationary gap left income at Y_F but caused the price level to rise. Now we will allow an inflationary gap – desired expenditure exceeds income at Y_F – to cause income to rise above Y_F temporarily as well as causing prices to rise. Whenever actual income exceeds potential income there must be an inflationary gap – if equilibrium Y exceeds Y_F, the aggregate desired expenditure curve must lie above the 45° line at Y_F.

Our first step is to define a new curve. The AGGREGATE SUPPLY CURVE (AS) shows the total output (i.e. the real national income) that all the firms in the economy will be willing to produce at each price level. It turns out that we need to distinguish a short- and a long-run aggregate supply curve. We first consider the short-run curve and then, later in the chapter, we study the long-run curve.

The Short-Run Aggregate Supply Curve

The SHORT-RUN AGGREGATE SUPPLY CURVE (SRAS) shows how much will be produced and offered for sale at each price level *on the assumption that the firm's input prices* – labour, raw materials, etc. – *are fixed*. Two such curves, labelled SRAS and SRAS', are shown in Figure 38.4. For the moment, let us concentrate on the curve drawn with a solid line and labelled SRAS.

The Slope of the SRAS Curve: The SRAS curve is upward-sloping indicating that, other things being equal, the higher the price level, the greater will be the total quantity that will be produced, and the lower the price level, the less will be the total quantity produced. *It is important to remember that the other things that are held constant along a SRAS curve include the prices of all inputs.*

Let us now investigate the reasons for this overall upward slope. Suppose that, because of an increase in aggregate expenditure, firms wish to increase their current production. Even when the *prices* of all of the firms' inputs remain constant, this does not necessarily mean that firms' unit costs will remain unchanged. Increasing output may require that less efficient standby machines and plants are used, less efficient marginal workers are employed, and the existing workers put in overtime. Thus, even with the

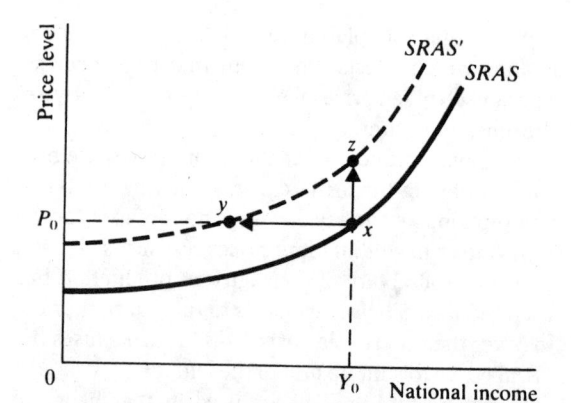

FIGURE 38.4 Two Short-Run Aggregate Supply Curves. SRAS curves slope upward to the right

restriction that prices per unit of input remain constant, higher output is associated with increased costs per unit of output because it requires the use of more, and more costly, methods of production.

This increase in *cost per unit of output* is referred to as *rising unit costs*. Since expanding output implies such higher unit costs, firms will only produce extra output if that output can be sold at higher prices. Thus, as the economy moves to the right along the SRAS curve, higher output tends to be associated with higher output prices.[1]

Now consider what happens when firms wish to reduce their output. The forces just discussed then work in reverse. There will be cost savings as the least efficient labour is laid off first, and the least efficient capital is put on standby. Thus, the lower output will be associated with somewhat lower unit costs and with lower output prices.

In summary, *the upward-sloping, short-run aggregate supply curve shows that, with input prices constant, higher output is associated with higher output prices because unit costs of production vary directly with output.*

Shifts in the SRAS Curve: As the next step in our study, we consider shifts in the SRAS curve. Such shifts are often called SUPPLY-SIDE SHOCKS. The short-

---

1 We are assuming, as is true for most of manufacturing, that firms do not sell their products in perfectly competitive markets. Instead they are price-makers who sell in oligopolistic markets and we assume that a rise in unit costs will lead the firm to increase the price that it charges for its output. The micro behaviour that lies behind this key assumption is discussed in IPE.

run aggregate supply curve will shift if there is *any* change which affects the output that firms offer for sale at each given price level. Here we consider two of the most important.

We have assumed so far that input prices are held constant along the SRAS curve. If we now drop this assumption, we can see one important reason for the SRAS curve to shift. If input prices rise, firms will find that the profitability of their current production has been reduced. Their response is to raise output prices to cover their increased costs. This in turn causes the SRAS curve to shift up and to the left.

Using the terminology we used in the theory of price in Part 2, an upward shift in the SRAS curve is referred to as a *decrease in supply* because at any given price level, less output will be willingly produced. Putting the same point another way; for any given level of output to be willingly produced, an increase in price will be required. This is illustrated in Figure 38.4.

In the Figure, the initial SRAS curve is shown by the solid curve. An increase in input prices shifts the curve upward to the dashed line, SRAS'.

Because the SRAS curve is positively sloped, this upward shift also moves the curve to the left. For example, suppose the price level is initially at P_0 and output is arbitrarily assumed to be Y_0 (point x). Following an increase in factor prices that reduces profitability, firms could maintain prices and reduce output, thus moving from point x to point y. They might, instead, maintain output but increase prices, thus moving from point x to point z. Or they could have some combination of price increases and output reductions, moving them to some point between y and z. The point to which the firms actually move depends, as we shall see, on the shape of the AD curve. But what is important is that SRAS' lies above and to the left of the original curve, SRAS.

EQUILIBRIUM OF AGGREGATE DEMAND AND AGGREGATE SUPPLY

Our next step is to bring the AD and the SRAS curves together to determine the short-run equilibrium values for national income and the price level.

Figure 38.5 does this. Equilibrium of aggregate demand and aggregate supply occurs where the AD and SRAS curves intersect. This yields the price level of P_0 and the real national income of Y_0 in the Figure.

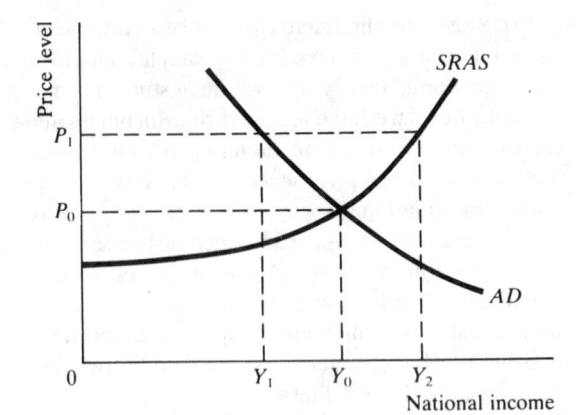

FIGURE 38.5 The Determination of National Income and the Price Level. The aggregate demand and the aggregate supply curves together determine the economy's price level and its total output

At higher price levels, aggregate supply exceeds aggregate demand; at lower price levels, aggregate demand exceeds aggregate supply. For example, if the price level were P_1, national income would be in equilibrium at Y_1 but producers would wish to make and sell Y_2. The resulting surplus would then force prices down from P_1 to P_0.

Shifts in the AD and SRAS Curves

Next consider what happens when either the AD or the SRAS curve shifts, i.e. when the economy is hit with either a demand or a supply-side shock.

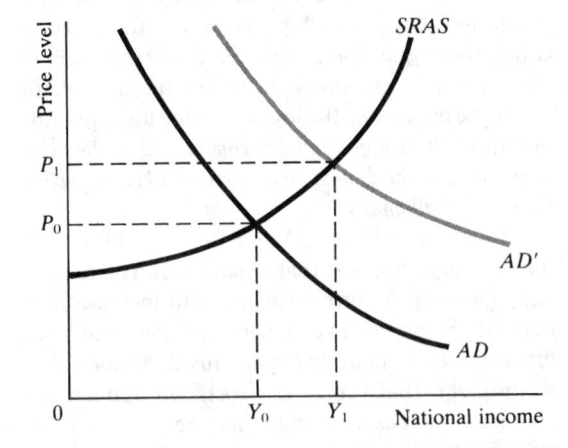

FIGURE 38.6 Aggregate Demand Shocks. Shifts in AD cause the price level and real national income to move in the same direction

Aggregate Demand Shocks: Figure 38.6 illustrates the effects of an increase in aggregate demand on the price level and real output. As previously explained, the increase could have occurred because of an increase in any type of autonomous spending – i.e. spending not resulting from a change in income. Examples are increased investment, increased government spending, or greater net exports. For now, we are not concerned with the source of the increase; we are interested in its implications for the price level and real output.

A demand shock now hits the economy in the form of a shift in the aggregate demand curve from AD to AD'. The price level rises from P_0 to P_1, and real national income rises from Y_0 to Y_1. Because the increase in aggregate demand causes the AD curve to shift to the right, the new equilibrium entails a movement along the $SRAS$ curve so that both the price level and the quantity of real output increases.

A decrease in aggregate demand causes AD to shift from, say, AD' to AD. As a result, the price level falls from P_1 to P_0 while real national income falls from Y_1 to Y_0.

Let us summarize what we have now established: *because the SRAS curve slopes upward, aggregate demand shocks cause the price level and real national income to change in the same direction, both rising or both falling together.*

Aggregate Supply Shocks: Figure 38.7 shows the effect of a supply shock consisting of a shift in the $SRAS$ curve to the left. This might have been caused by a change in costs of production – for example, by a rise in the price of imported raw materials or in the wage rate paid to labour. The upward shift from $SRAS$ to $SRAS'$ causes the equilibrium price level to rise from P_0 to P_1 while national income *falls from Y_0 to Y_1.*

An increase in aggregate supply caused, say, by an increase in productivity, causes the curve to shift downwards. This can be shown by assuming the initial aggregate supply curve is $SRAS'$ in Figure 38.7, and then letting it shift to $SRAS$. National income then *rises* from Y_1 to Y_0, while the price level *falls* from P_1 to P_0.

The cases we have just studied are caused by shifts in the $SRAS$ curve and movements along the AD curve. They lead to the following important conclusion: *aggregate supply shocks cause the price level and real national income to change in opposite directions, one rising and the other falling.*

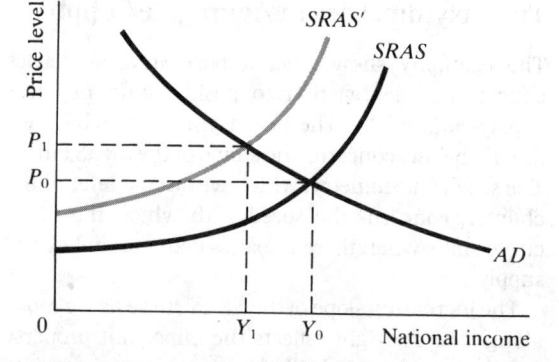

FIGURE 38.7   Aggregate Supply Shocks. Shifts in $SRAS$ cause the price level and real national income to move in opposite directions

The Slope of the *SRAS* Curve Further Considered

So far we have merely said that the $SRAS$ curve is upward-sloping. We must now consider a somewhat less obvious, but in many ways more important, property of a typical $SRAS$ curve: its slope *increases* as output rises. It is relatively flat to the left of potential output and relatively steep to the right. Why?

Below potential output, firms will typically have unused capacity – some plant and equipment will be idle. When firms are faced with unused capacity, only a small increase in the price of their output may be needed to induce them to expand production, at least up to normal capacity. Indeed, some firms may be willing to produce and sell more at *existing prices* if only the demand were there. (This is the case where the firm's short-run supply curve is perfectly elastic and output is determined by its intersection with a downward-sloping demand curve.)

Once output is pushed very far beyond normal capacity, however, unit costs tend to rise quite rapidly. Higher-cost capacity may have to be used. Bottlenecks appear in more and more stages of the production process. Overtime and extra shifts may have to be worked. These expedients raise the cost of producing a unit of output more and more as output expands. Many more costly productive techniques may also have to be adopted. These higher-cost methods will not be used unless selling prices can be raised to cover them. Furthermore, the more output is expanded beyond normal capacity, the more do unit costs tend to rise and hence the larger is the price rise associated with each further increase in output.

Two Asymmetries in Aggregate Supply

The economy shows two important asymmetries concerning the reaction to positive and negative supply-side shocks. The first asymmetry, which we discuss below, concerns the shape of the *SRAS* curve. The second asymmetry, which we discuss later in the chapter, concerns the speed with which the *SRAS* curve shifts when there is excess demand and excess supply.

The increasing slope of the *SRAS* curve as we move along it to the right reflects the important property which we refer to as the first asymmetry of the supply side of the economy: *below potential national income, changes in output are accompanied by relatively small changes in the price level; above potential national income, changes in output are accompanied by large changes in the price level.*

Now that we have learned more about the general slope of the *SRAS* curve, we can be a little more specific than we were about the effects of shifts in the *AD* curve when we first studied them in Figure 38.6.

Figure 38.8 shows an *SRAS* curve that is upward-sloping over its whole range. Its slope gets steeper the further to the right we move along it, being rather flat to the left of Y_F and rather steep to the right of Y_F.

The consequences of this slope are shown by combining the *SRAS* curve with various aggregate demand curves shown in the Figure. The curve *AD* produces equilibrium at income Y_0 and price level P_0. An increase in demand to *AD'* raises national income by a large amount to Y_1 and increases the price level only slightly to P_1. A further increase to *AD''* takes

national income to Y_F and the price level to P_2, again a large increase in income and a relatively small increase in the price level. Once potential income is passed, however, the responses of Y and P change rapidly. As aggregate demand rises from *AD''* to *AD'''*, and finally to *AD''''*, the increase in national income (from Y_F to Y_3 and Y_4) get smaller, while the increases in the price level (from P_2 to P_3 and P_4) get larger.

This leads to an important conclusion: the further is equilibrium income *below* potential income, the more will national income change and the less will the price level change for any given shift in the aggregate demand curve; and the further is equilibrium income *above* potential income, the less will national income change and the greater will be the change in the price level for any given shift in the aggregate demand curve.

AGGREGATE SUPPLY IN THE LONG RUN

So far we have concentrated on the short-run aggregate supply curve – a curve that assumes the prices of all inputs used by the firm are constant. Now we need to look at the behaviour of aggregate supply over a longer period of time. The key to understanding the *long-run* aggregate supply curve is to see how changes in aggregate demand eventually *induce* shifts in the *short-run* aggregate supply curve. Thus we will study induced shifts in the *SRAS* curve for the next several sections. When we fully understand these, we will be able to derive, and appreciate the significance of, the long-run aggregate supply curve.

Effects of an Increase in Aggregate Demand on the *SRAS* Curve

To see the long-run effects of an increase in aggregate demand, we assume that the economy starts off in the happy position of full employment and a stable price level, as pictured in Figure 38.9. In that Figure the initial curves are *AD* and *SRAS*, which produce an equilibrium level of income equal to the economy's potential level, Y_F, and a price level of P_0. A rise in autonomous expenditure, perhaps caused by an investment boom, shifts the aggregate demand curve to *AD'*. The immediate effects are that the price level rises to P_1 while real income rises above its potential level to Y_1.

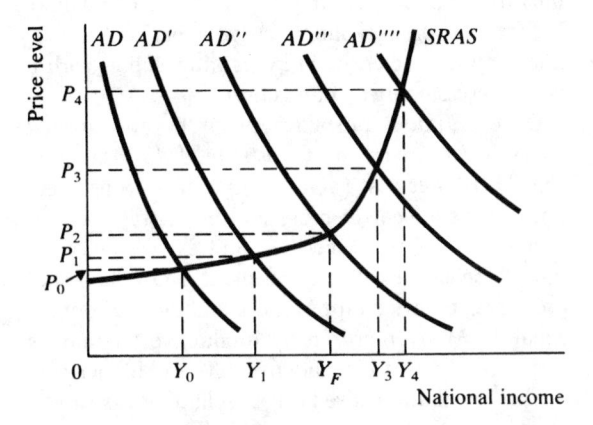

FIGURE 38.8   Shifts in the *AD* Curve with an *SRAS* Curve of Varying Slope. Given shifts in *AD* cause large changes in Y and small changes in P when Y is below Y_F, but small changes in Y and large changes in P when Y is above Y_F

Firms will now be producing beyond their normal capacity output, so there will be an excess demand for all factor inputs, including labour. Here we concentrate on the cost of labour to the firm, although analogous arguments apply to other factors. Workers will be demanding wage increases to compensate them for the higher cost of living caused by the increase in the price level. Thus the boom generates a combination of conditions – higher profits for firms, greater demand for labour, and a desire on the part of labour for wages to catch up with the price rises – that is, a recipe for increases in wages. Indeed, this sequence is just what past experience of the economy tells us will happen.

Increases in wages mean increases in costs. These, as we have already seen, lead to upward shifts in the SRAS curve as firms pass on their increases in unit costs by increasing their output prices. For this reason, the rise in the price level from P_0 to P_1 and real output from Y_F to Y_1 in Figure 38.9 is *not the end of the story*. The upward shift of the SRAS curve causes a further rise in the price level, but this time the price rise is associated with a fall in output. The cost increases, and the consequent upward shifts in the SRAS curve go on until income returns to its potential level. Only then does the excess demand for labour disappear. At this point, the short-run aggregate supply curve has shifted to SRAS' in Figure 38.9, taking equilibrium income back to Y_F and the price level yet higher to P_2.

Starting from full employment and a stable price

level (point *a* in Figure 38.9), the sequence of events following a demand shock can now be summarized.

(1) A rise in aggregate demand raises the price level and raises income above its potential level as the economy expands along a given SRAS curve (to point *b* in Figure 38.9).

(2) The expansion of output beyond its *normal* capacity level puts pressure on factor markets; factor prices then begin to rise, shifting the SRAS curve upward.

(3) The shift of the SRAS curve causes output to fall along the given AD curve; this process continues *as long as* actual output exceeds potential output. Therefore, actual output eventually falls back to its potential level. The price level will, however, now be higher than it was after the initial impact of the increased aggregate demand, but inflation will have come to a halt (when the economy reaches point *c* in the Figure).

The above reasoning shows that it is misleading to assume that there is a fixed and unchanging upward-sloping aggregate supply curve. The ability to increase output beyond the economy's potential output (point *b*) is only a short-term success. Achieving real income greater than Y_F sets up inflationary pressures that tend to push national income back to Y_F.

Effects of a Decrease in Aggregate Demand on the SRAS Curve

Let us return to that happy economy with full employment and stable prices that we considered

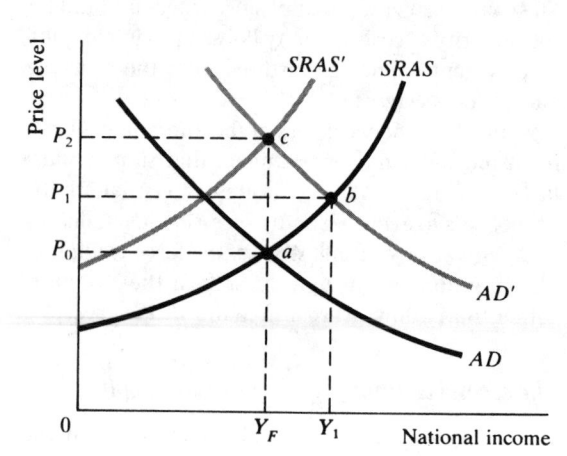

FIGURE 38.9   The Short- and Long-Term Effects of a Rise in Aggregate Demand. An upward shift of the AD curve first raises price and output along a given SRAS curve and then induces a shift of SRAS that further raises the price level but lowers output along the AD curve

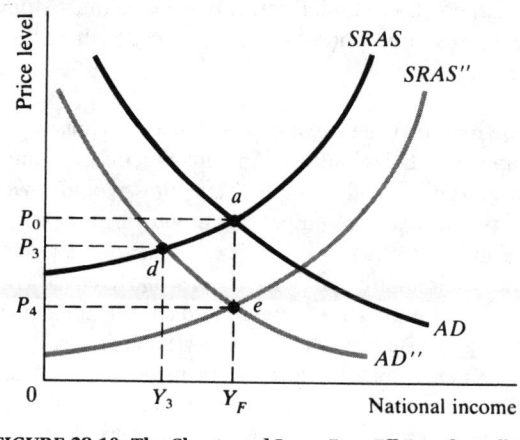

FIGURE 38.10 The Short- and Long-Run Effects of a Fall in Aggregate Demand. A downward shift of the AD curve first lowers the price level and output along the SRAS curve, and then induces a (slow) shift of SRAS that further lowers prices but raises output along the AD curve

above. It appears again in Figure 38.10, which duplicates the initial conditions of Figure 38.9. The initial curves are *AD* and *SRAS*, giving rise to full employment income of Y_F and a price level of P_0 (point *a*).

Now assume a *decline* in the aggregate demand curve from *AD* to *AD''*, perhaps due to a major reduction in investment expenditure.

The impact of this decline is a fall in income to Y_3 and some downward adjustment of the price level to P_3, as shown in the Figure (point *d*). As output falls, unemployment will rise. The resulting recessionary gap is $Y_F - Y_3$.

The importance of the labour market

In the previous section we assumed that excess demand in the labour market caused money wages to rise. There is ample evidence that this is the case in the real world. Now, however, we are considering a case in which there is excess supply in the labour market; there are insufficient jobs to employ everyone who would like to work at the going wage rate.

If the labour market were perfectly competitive, money wages would fall in the face of excess supply of labour so as to clear the market. But trade unions exert substantial monopoly power in the labour market and are often able to resist downward adjustment in wages. At most, wages fall very slowly in the face of excess labour supply; at worst, they do not fall at all. In other words, unemployment has, *at most*, a weak and sluggish downward effect on wages and, *at worst*, no effect at all. For this reason we must study two cases – one where wages fall and one where they do not.

Downward Wage Flexibility: Consider what would happen *if* the resulting unemployment did cause wage rates to fall. Falling wage rates would lower costs for firms, and competition among firms to sell in a depressed market would lead them to cut prices, once their falling costs gave them scope to do so. This in turn would cause a downward shift in the short-run aggregate supply curve. As a result of the shifting *SRAS* curve, the economy would move along its fixed *AD''* curve with falling prices and rising output until the *SRAS* curve reached *SRAS''* in Figure 38.10 and full employment was restored at potential national income, Y_F, and a lower price level, P_4 (point *e*).

We conclude that *if* wages were to fall whenever there was unemployment – a condition called down-

ward flexibility of wages – the resulting fall in the *SRAS* curve would restore full employment. In other words, downwardly flexible wages would provide an automatic adjustment mechanism that would push the economy back toward full employment whenever output fell below potential.

Wages that are flexible in both an upwards and a downwards direction make the economy's adjustment to increases and decreases in demand symmetrical. On the one hand, a rise in demand opens up an inflationary gap and the ensuing rise in wages eliminates the gap, returning national income to its full-employment level. On the other hand, a fall in demand opens up a recessionary gap and the ensuing fall in wages eliminates the gap, returning income to its full-employment level.

Downward Wage Inflexibility: Unfortunately, the symmetrical world in which flexible wages eliminate both inflationary and deflationary shocks with equal effectiveness does not exist in reality. Instead, the economy's behaviour is asymmetric, in the sense that wages respond rapidly to excess demand but only sluggishly to excess supply. Therefore, although the adjustment mechanism described in Figure 38.9 can act very quickly to remove excess demand, the adjustment mechanism described in Figure 38.10 is, *at best*, weak and slow-acting in its removal of excess supply.

Raw material prices, many of which are competitively determined, fall in recessions. This will push the *SRAC* curve downwards. But since wages account for the majority of costs in many lines of production, full employment cannot be restored from the cost side alone unless wages fall.

Notice that the weakness of the automatic adjustment mechanism does not mean that slumps must last indefinitely. All that it means is that, if the economy is to avoid a lengthy recession in conditions of downward wage inflexibility, the force leading to recovery must be an upward shift in the *AD* curve rather than a downward drift in the *SRAS* curve.

The second asymmetry of aggregate supply

We have now arrived at what may be called the second asymmetry of the supply side of the economy. (The first is the slope of the *SRAS* curve, flat below Y_F and steep above Y_F.) The second asymmetry runs as follows: *boom conditions, with severe labour shortages, do cause wages to rise rapidly, thereby causing upward shifts of the SRAS curve; but slump conditions, with heavy unemployment, do not cause wages to fall with a corresponding speed and, hence, do not cause the SRAS curve to shift down rapidly.*

The second asymmetry of aggregate supply behaviour explains two key characteristics of our economy. First, unemployment *can* persist for quite long periods without causing large decreases in wages and prices (which would, if they did occur, help to remove the unemployment). Second, booms, with labour shortages and production beyond normal capacity, *cannot* persist for long periods without causing large increases in wages and prices.

The Long-Run Aggregate Supply Curve

So far our analysis has concentrated on the interaction of *AD* and *SRAS* curves. Now we must consider what happens in the long run. Although, as we have seen, the downward adjustment of wages may not remove recessionary gaps fast enough to be acceptable to policy-makers, the *possibility* of automatic adjustments gives rise to an important theoretical concept called the LONG-RUN AGGREGATE SUPPLY (LRAS) CURVE. This curve relates the price level to equilibrium real national income *after all input costs, including wages rates, have been fully adjusted to eliminate any excess demand or supply.* It thus shows the national income that would occur *if* wages were flexible enough in both directions to eliminate any excess demand or excess supply of labour. Full employment would then prevail and output would be at its potential level, Y_F.

Thus, when all input prices are fully adjusted, the aggregate supply curve becomes a vertical line at Y_F, as seen in Figure 38.11. This is called the *long-run aggregate supply curve* because it refers to adjustments that require a substantial amount of time. Along the *LRAS* curve, the prices of *all outputs* and *all inputs* have been fully adjusted to eliminate excess demands or supplies in all markets. Points on the *LRAS* curve thus refer to situations where the prices of *all* outputs and *all* inputs have changed equi-proportionately (i.e. the same percentage change in each price).

Equal proportionate changes in money wages and in the price level (which, by definition, will leave real wages unaltered) will also leave equilibrium employment and output unchanged. The key concept is this: if the price of absolutely everything (including labour) changes in the same proportion, then nothing real changes. (We discussed this in detail on

pages 403–5 of Chapter 33.) When the prices of everything bought *and* sold change, everyone's real position is unchanged and, hence, no one has any incentive to alter behaviour. Output, therefore, is unchanged. The level of output will be what can be produced in the economy when all factors of production, including labour, are utilized at their 'normal' levels of capacity. It follows that the long-run equilibrium level of output is unaffected by the price level.

Equilibrium output and price level in the long run

Figure 38.11 shows the long-run equilibrium output and price level determined by the intersection of the *AD* curve and the vertical *LRAS* curve. The initial aggregate demand curve is *AD*, which intersects the long-run aggregate supply curve to produce the price level P_0. When the aggregate demand curve shifts upwards to *AD'*, *long-run* equilibrium income stays at Y_F but the price level rises to P_1.

One important implication of this analysis is that if the *LRAS* curve is vertical, output is determined solely by conditions of supply in the long run, and the role of aggregate demand is simply to determine the price level.

Note we are here discussing only long-term tendencies. To see the short-term impact of demand and supply shocks, we need to use the short-run aggregate supply curve. The vertical *LRAS* curve is really nothing more than an expression of the long-run neutrality of money (see Chapter 33, page 404). It says that a full-employment equilibrium of the economy *can* be achieved at any price level. The extent to which the *LRAS* curve is useful for applied analysis of the

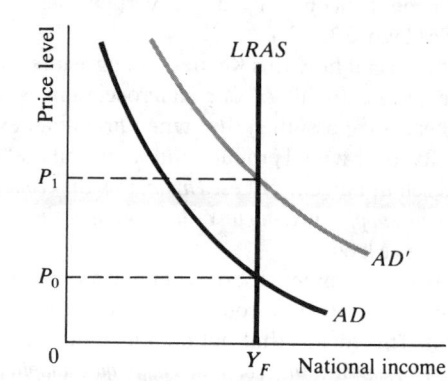

FIGURE 38.11   Long-Run Effects of Shifts in *AD* and *LRAS* Curves. When *LRAS* is vertical, aggregate supply determines *Y* and aggregate demand determines *P*

real world is quite another matter. For example, downward pressures on the price level are slow to act. For this reason, the *LRAS* curve is usually a poor guide to practical policy when the *AD* curve shifts left.

Note the sharp difference between the long-term and short-term results that we have obtained. Aggregate demand shocks exert an influence on real income only in the short run. When national income is already at full employment, real income cannot be permanently increased by raising aggregate demand. What is needed to do this job is a rightward shift of the *LRAS* curve, and a major source of such shifts is investment. Many early Keynesians paid little attention to the long-run effect of investment on aggregate supply. Although not an unreasonable thing to do when analysing the severe recessionary conditions of the 1930s, the neglect is serious when the economy is operating at or near full employment. These matters are discussed in detail in the next chapter. First, however, it may be helpful to relate what we have learned in this chapter to the aggregate supply curve that was implicit in everything we did in Part 4 of this book.

The Keynesian aggregate supply curve

In Part 4 (and in Part 5, up to this chapter) we used an aggregate supply curve that was so simple that we did not need to draw it. This *Keynesian aggregate supply curve* underlies the simple Keynesian model we have been using prior to the present chapter. (It is also sometimes called the 'J-shaped' or the 'reverse L-shaped' aggregate supply curve because it resembles a J and the mirror image of an L.) It is composed of a horizontal segment for national incomes up to full-employment income, Y_F, and a vertical segment at Y_F. (See Figure 38.12.)

Let us recall how this Keynesian aggregate supply curve arises. In all of our macroeconomics until Chapter 38 we assumed that when firms had excess capacity, they would produce and supply all that they could sell at current prices. *This makes the economy's aggregate supply curve up to Y_F horizontal at the current overall price level.*

We also assumed that, when firms reach full-capacity output, they could not produce any more output. This means that national income can never exceed Y_F, so that *the economy's aggregate supply curve is vertical at Y_F.*

Let us now examine the Keynesian aggregate supply curve which is shown by *KAS* in Figure 38.12,

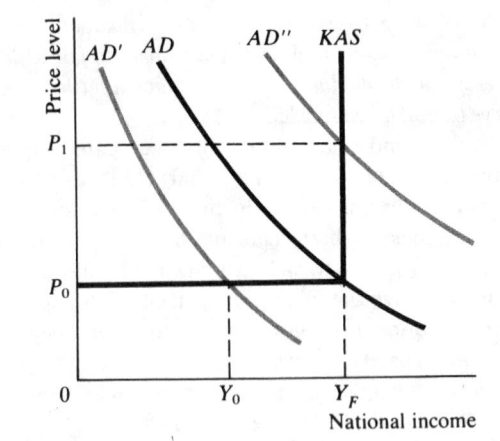

FIGURE 38.12   Shifts in the *AD* Curve with a Keynesian Aggregate Supply Curve. Below potential income, fluctuations in *AD* cause fluctuations only in national income; at potential income, increases in *AD* cause increases only in the price level

as a limiting case of the more general *SRAS* curve shown in the Figure 38.4. The Keynesian curve arises when the flattish portion of the *SRAS* curve below Y_F becomes perfectly flat (horizontal), and the steep portion above Y_F becomes as steep as possible (vertical).

Shifts in *AD* with the Keynesian *AS* Curve: Figure 38.12 shows a Keynesian *AS* curve, together with several aggregate demand curves. Fluctuations in the *AD* curve between *AD* and *AD'* will cause national income to fluctuate between Y_0 and Y_F while leaving the price level constant at P_0. This is the case we studied throughout Part 4 of this book. The *AS* curve was horizontal, the price level was fixed, and equilibrium national income was determined by aggregate demand.

Note also in the Figure that an increase in aggregate demand from *AD* to *AD''* raises the price level from P_0 to P_1 while leaving national income constant at Y_F.

The Keynesian aggregate supply curve was useful in our earlier chapters, but, for a detailed study of the relation between output and prices it represents an over-simplified view of the economy. First, changes in national income below the level of Y_F are often observed to be accompanied by changes in *both* real income *and* the price level. The horizontal Keynesian *AS* curve denies this possibility. Second, potential income is not an absolute constraint on output. At the micro level, firms can, and often do, produce beyond their normal capacity output, although the further they try to push output beyond normal capacity, the more costly it usually becomes to do so.

At the macro level, the economy is sometimes observed at a level of income in excess of potential or full-employment income. (This gives rise to a situation sometimes called *over-full employment*.)

SUMMARY

1 The 45° diagram is not suited to studying inflation because it can cope with inflation coming from the demand, but not from the supply, side. Although it can implicitly analyse demand inflations, because it does show the inflationary gap, it cannot handle cost-side inflations.

2 The aggregate demand curve plots the relationships between the general price level and equilibrium national income. Increases in the price level lower the equilibrium income because of the monetary adjustment mechanism. Thus the aggregate demand curve is negatively sloped.

3 Anything that shifts the aggregate desired expenditure curve upwards – other than a fall in the price level – shifts the aggregate demand curve to the right. Anything that shifts the aggregate expenditure curve downwards – other than a rise in the price level – shifts the aggregate demand curve to the left.

4 The short-run aggregate supply curve is positively sloped, indicating that, because unit costs rise with output, so does the price level rise with output. The *SRAS* curve is relatively flat to the left of potential income and relatively steep to the right of it. A rise in input prices shifts the curve upwards while a fall in input prices shifts it downwards.

5 Aggregate demand shocks cause national income and the price level to change in the same direction, rising or falling together. Aggregate supply shocks cause national income and the price level to change in opposite directions, one rising while the other is falling. An upward shift in the *SRAS* curve may cause a stagflation, with income falling and the price level rising.

6 With flexible wages, the initial effects on income of aggregate demand or aggregate supply shocks are reversed and any final effect is only on the price level. An expansionary aggregate demand shock increases income and the price level in the short run as equilibrium moves along the fixed *SRAS* curve. In the long run, the inflationary gap causes wages to rise. This shifts the *SRAS* curve upwards and income falls back to its potential level, while the price level rises further as equilibrium moves along a fixed aggregate demand curve.

7 The *LRAS* curve relates income to the price level on the assumption that all prices have been fully adjusted to remove excess demands or excess supplies from all markets. It is perfectly inelastic. This indicates that, in the long run, national income is solely determined by aggregate supply, while aggregate demand only determines the price level.

Economic Growth[1]

The term *economic growth* refers to the increase in the economy's potential or full-employment national income; it is measured as the growth in the nation's potential national income at constant prices – i.e. the growth in real, full-employment national income. It may be shown graphically in either of two ways: (1) by an outward shift in the economy's long-run aggregate supply curve, and (2) by an upward shift in the production possibility curve that we first saw in Figure 1.4. The former is a macroeconomic, the latter a microeconomic concept, reflecting as you will see, the fact that the determinants of economic growth are every bit as much micro as macroeconomic in origin. This will become clear as you read on, finding several references back to the microeconomic parts of this book. Indeed this whole chapter would be no less at home in Part 3 as here in Part 5.

Growth and Living Standards

In the circumstances facing most countries, the most important single force leading to long-run increases in living standards is economic growth. To see this, let us compare the effects of growth with policies that increase economic efficiency or redistribute income.

Increasing efficiency by pushing the economy closer to its production possibility curve (e.g. from point *x* to point *t* in Figute 1.2 (ii) on page 9) can increase national income somewhat. But a once-and-for-all increase of 5–10 per cent would be an extremely optimistic estimate of what could be obtained by making all possible reductions in economic inefficiencies.

Redistributing income can make some people better off at the expense of others; but increasing the incomes of the bottom 20 per cent of the people by, say, 10 per cent, would be an optimistic prediction of what could be done with further redistribution policies. In any case, without growth, the magnitude of the income gains that can be achieved for lower-income groups through redistribution is limited by the size of national income.

Economic growth, however, can go on raising national income for as long as it continues at a faster rate than population is growing, which can be for centuries on end. Provided the population is constant, even the modest rate of growth of 2 per cent per year takes a little less than 5 years to raise everyone's income by the 10 per cent, and just over 9 years to raise the living standards of the poor (and everyone else) by 20 per cent. The 2 per cent growth rate doubles average living standards about every 35 years, so that, if there is no change in economic efficiency or the distribution of income, everyone's living standards will increase by 300 per cent over one biblically allotted lifetime of three score years and ten.

Total and Per Capita Growth: The above discussion has made use of an important distinction which we now make explicit. Economic growth as we have defined it refers to the growth of total (potential) national income. What happens to living standards depends not only on the growth of total income, but also on the growth of the number of people among whom this income must be shared. To measure the growth in a country's average material living standards, we use PER CAPITA ECONOMIC GROWTH, which is the rate of growth of per capita national income (national income divided by the population).

1 Further descriptive material related to the subject of this chapter will be found in Harbury and Lipsey, Chapter 9.

The Cumulative Nature of Growth

The cumulative effects of growth rates are further illustrated in Table 39.1. It compares the real incomes of five different countries that experience five different growth rates. Again assuming a constant population, these growth rates may be taken also as indicators of rising living standards. In 'year zero' they all have national incomes of 100.

The effects of even small growth rates on living standards can be seen by looking down any column. For example, assuming a constant population, a 3 per cent growth rate doubles real national income in about 24 years, and at the end of 70 it has raised national income by over 700 per cent!

The effects of differences in growth rates can be seen by comparing across any row, showing national incomes in one particular year at various growth rates. Although all the countries illustrated start with the same real income at 'year zero', by 'year ten' they have very different real incomes. For example, the country with a growth rate of 1 per cent has a real income of 111, while the country with a growth rate of 7 per cent has a real income of 201! A 7 per cent growth rate doubles real income in 10 years, while a 1 per cent rate only increases it by 10 per cent!

The Continued Importance of Efficiency and Redistribution: Do not misunderstand us when we say that, over the long term, by far the most potent force for raising living standards is economic growth rather than reducing inefficiencies or redistributing income. We are *not* asserting the unimportance of policies designed to increase economic efficiency, or to redistribute income.

Consider efficiency first. If at any moment of time we could get a larger national income by removing certain inefficiencies, such gains would be valuable. After all, any increase in national income is welcome in a world where many wants go unsatisfied. Furthermore, inefficiencies may themselves serve to reduce the growth rate. For one example, we shall see in Chapter 40 that the policy of rent control, which can be criticized for violating efficiency conditions in the housing market, may also be criticized for reducing the geographic mobility of labour that is necessary if economic growth is to continue.

Now consider redistribution. It may be some consolation for the poor to know they are vastly better off – due to economic growth – than they would have been if they had lived 100 years ago. But this does not make it any the less upsetting if they cannot afford basic medical treatment for themselves, or schooling for their children, that is available to higher-income citizens. After all, what people *see* is how they compare with others in their own society, not how they compare with their counterparts at other times or in other places. Because we care about relative differences between people, we continue to have policies to redistribute income, and to make such basic services as health and education available to everyone, at least at some minimum acceptable standards.

Nonetheless, over the long term, the potential of economic growth for raising living standards of the poor, the middle-income groups, and everyone else, vastly exceeds the potential achieved by removing inefficiencies or redistributing the existing national income.

Interrelations Among the Policies: One important implication of the above discussion is that policies to

TABLE 39.1   Real National Incomes Over Time at Alternative Growth Rates.* Small differences in national growth rates can cause enormous differences in national incomes

YEAR	GROWTH RATES				
	1%	2%	3%	5%	7%
0	100	100	100	100	100
10	111	122	135	165	201
30	135	182	246	448	817
50	165	272	448	1,218	3,312
70	201	406	817	3,312	13,429
100	272	739	2,009	14,841	109,660

* The figures in the body of the table show real national income at alternative growth rates after the elapse of time shown in the first column.

reduce inefficiencies, or redistribute income, need to be examined carefully for any effects they may have on economic growth. Any policy that reduces the growth rate may be a bad bargain, even if it increases the immediate efficiency of the economy, or creates a more equitable distribution of income. Consider, for example, a hypothetical redistributive policy that raises the incomes of lower-income people by 5 per cent but lowers the rate of economic growth from 2 to 1 per cent. In 10 years, those who gain from the redistribution will be no better off than if they had not received the redistribution of income while the growth rate had remained at 2 per cent (and, of course, everyone who did not gain from the redistribution would be worse off from the beginning). After 20 years, those who had gained from the redistribution would have 5 per cent more of a national income that was 12 per cent smaller than it would have been if the growth rate had remained at 2 per cent. Thus, as a result of the lower growth rate, *everyone* will be substantially worse off than if the redistributive policy had not been followed.

Of course, not all redistribution policies have unfavourable effects on the growth rate. Some may have no effect, and others – by raising health and educational standards of ordinary workers – may raise the growth rate.

TWO KINDS OF 'GROWTH'

When you are told that real national income rose by 4 per cent last year, does this mean the country's potential income grew at 4 per cent? The answer is 'not necessarily'. To understand the reasoning behind this answer, we must first distinguish two reasons why national income can change (assuming of course that it is accurately measured): (1) because a recessionary gap is being eliminated so that national income is increasing towards its potential level; and (2) because potential income is itself increasing. This important distinction is illustrated in the two parts of Figure 39.1.

A Rise in Income that Removes a Recessionary Gap: In part (i) of the Figure, the original curves are AD, SRAS and LRAS. (Recall that the LRAS curve is drawn vertical at potential income, Y_F.) The aggregate demand and short-run aggregate supply curve intersect to yield equilibrium national income of Y_0.

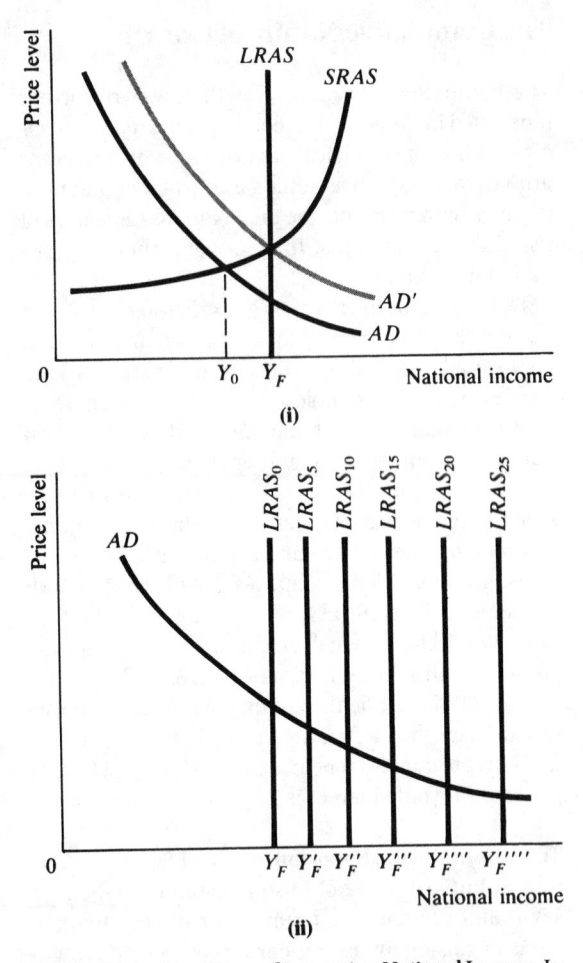

FIGURE 39.1   **Two Ways of Increasing National Income.** In the long term, shifts in aggregate supply exert a larger influence than do shifts in aggregate demand. In part (i) a rise in aggregate demand can raise income rapidly if an output gap exists. In part (ii) when output is at its potential level, the main source of increases in income is shifts in the aggregate supply curve

Since potential income is Y_F, there is a recessionary gap of $Y_F - Y_0$. A rise in aggregate demand to AD' will increase equilibrium national income to Y_F by removing this gap. The diagram shows a recessionary gap which is 20 per cent of potential income. This is an extremely large gap by historical standards, one that would be found only in the depths of the severest depressions.

Quite rapid increases in real national income can be achieved when there are recessionary gaps. Aggregate demand can increase rapidly and unemployed resources can be quickly put back to work in response. For example, if the output gap in Figure 39.1 (i) were eliminated over two years, there would be a 10 per cent growth rate of national income over each of these years. *But once national income reaches its full-employment level, further increases in aggregate demand cannot bring further permanent increases in real national income; instead they will only cause the price level to rise.*[1]

Increases in Potential Income: Part (ii) of the Figure shows the effects of economic growth. Increases in supplies of capital and labour and increases in factor productivity – more produced *per unit of factor employed* – raise the economy's potential income and thus shift the *LRAS* curve outwards to the right. The diagram gives an accurate representation of the effects of a 3 per cent growth rate on potential income over 25 years. Each vertical *LRAS* curve shows potential income 5 years after the *LRAS* curve that is located to its left (the subscript on each curve therefore refers to the number of years after the initial year, called year zero). Notice that at the end of 25 years, potential income has more than doubled.

Growth in Potential Income and the Reduction of Recessionary Gaps: The removal of a typical, large recessionary gap might cause a once-and-for-all increase in national income of 10 per cent. This is not to be disdained because it will reduce unemployment, which is a good result in itself, as well as raising output and, hence, average living standards. Yet a growth rate of 3 per cent per year raises potential national income by 10 per cent in just over 3 years – and then goes on to *double* real income in 24 years. Thus, over any long period of time economic growth, rather than variations in aggregate demand, exerts the major effect on real national income.

The Short- and Long-Run Effects of Investment on National Income

The theory of income determination that we studied in Part 4 is a short-run theory. It takes potential income as constant and concentrates on the effect of

investment expenditure on aggregate demand and thus on variations of actual national income around a given potential income. This short-term viewpoint is the focus of Figure 39.1 (i).

In the long run, by adding to the nation's capital stock, investment raises potential income. This effect is shown by the continuing rightward shift of the *LRAS* curve in Figure 39.1 (ii). The theory of economic growth is a long-run theory. It ignores short-run fluctuations of actual national income around potential income and concentrates on the effects of investment in raising potential income – i.e. increasing aggregate supply.

The contrast between the short- and long-run aspects of investment is worth emphasizing. In the short run, any activity that puts income into people's hands will raise aggregate demand. Thus the short-run effect on national income is the same whether a firm invests in digging holes and refilling them or in building a new factory. In terms of growth, however, we are concerned only with that part of investment that adds to a nation's productive capacity.

The Short- and Long-Run Effect of Saving on National Income

The short-run effect of an increase in saving is to reduce aggregate demand, because when households elect to save more they must spend less. The resulting downward shift in the consumption function lowers aggregate demand and thus lowers equilibrium national income.

In the longer term, however, higher savings tend to produce higher investment. Savings, both by firms and households, provide the funds out of which investment is financed. Firms usually reinvest their own savings, while the savings of households pass to firms, either directly through the purchase of shares or indirectly through financial intermediaries. If full employment is more or less maintained in the long run, then the volume of investment will be strongly influenced by the volume of savings. The higher the savings, the higher the investment – and the higher the investment, the greater the rate of growth due to the accumulation of more and better capital equipment.

It follows from this discussion that *in the long run there is no paradox of thrift; societies with high savings rates have high investment rates and, other things being equal, high growth rates.*

---

1 As we saw in Chapter 38 (see Figure 38.9), they may bring transitory increases by raising income above its potential level. But when the rise in money costs shifts the *SRAS* curve so as to remove the inflationary gap, income will fall back to its potential level.

THEORIES OF GROWTH

We now pass to a discussion of the causes of economic growth.

A Classical View: Growth Without Learning

Nineteenth-century economists viewed growth as a long-run process which consisted of the growth of the labour force and the growth of the capital stock taking place in the framework of fixed (or at least very slowly changing) technical knowledge. We shall see below how the law of diminishing returns would then operate to bring the growth process to an inexorable halt.

To gain some idea of what is involved, assume that the supply of land and labour is fixed, while the capital stock grows.[1] Also assume that there is a known and fixed stock of investment projects that might be undertaken. Suppose also that nothing ever happens to increase the supply of such projects. Whenever the opportunity is ripe, some of the investment opportunities are utilized, thereby increasing the stock of capital goods and depleting the reservoir of unutilized investment opportunities. Of course, the most productive opportunities will be used first.

Such a view of investment opportunities can be represented by the fixed *marginal efficiency of capital* curve shown in Figure 39.2. It relates the stock of capital to the productivity of an additional unit of capital. The productivity of a unit of capital is calculated by dividing the annual value of the additional output resulting from an extra unit of capital by the value of that unit of capital. Thus, for example, a marginal efficiency of capital of 0.2 means that £1 of new capital adds 20p per year to the stream of output.

The downward slope of the *MEC* schedule indicates that, with knowledge constant, increases in the stock of capital bring smaller and smaller increases in output per unit of capital. That is, the rate of return on successive units of capital declines. This shape is a consequence of the law of diminishing returns. If,

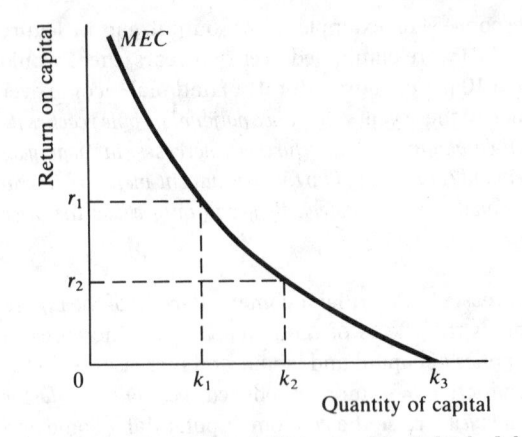

FIGURE 39.2   The Marginal Efficiency of Capital Schedule. A declining *MEC* schedule shows that successive additions to the capital stock bring smaller and smaller increases in output

with land, labour and knowledge constant, more and more capital is used, the net amount added by successive increments will diminish and will eventually reach zero.[1]

As capital is accumulated in a state of constant knowledge, the society will move down its *MEC* schedule. For example when the capital stock is k_1 in Figure 39.2 the marginal return on new capital is r_1, while when the capital stock has grown to k_2, the return on new capital will have fallen to r_2. When the capital stock finally reaches k_3, the marginal return to capital will have reached zero.

In such a 'non-learning' world, where new investment opportunities do not appear, growth in output will occur but, for a given rate of capital accumulation, the rate of growth of output will fall as the contribution of successive increments of capital falls. Eventually, when the capital stock reaches k_3, no further growth is possible.

So far we have discussed the *marginal* efficiency of capital. The *average* efficiency of capital refers to the average amount produced in the whole economy per unit of capital employed – i.e. total output divided by the total capital stock (Y/K). If each unit of new

---

1 Nineteenth-century economists were also interested in the consequences of the growth of population, but what we need for our purposes can be shown in the simple case in which capital is the only factor whose supply is increasing.

---

1 In some cases, curves of marginal returns have an upward-sloping portion. We ignore this possibility because (1) our assumptions about investment opportunities have ruled it out, (2) no competitive economy can be in equilibrium in the upward-sloping portion, and (3) even if it existed, we are not interested in it, since our concern is with what happens when growth has encountered diminishing returns.

capital adds less total output than did each previous unit, the average amount of output per unit of capital – i.e. the average efficiency of capital – must be declining.

In the theory of growth it is common to use the reciprocal of the average efficiency of capital (K/Y) and to call this new ratio the *capital-output ratio*. In a world without learning, the average efficiency of capital is declining and hence the capital-output ratio is increasing.

Since ratios can be very confusing, it may help to consider an example. Assume that in 'year one' an economy has an output of 1,000 and a capital stock of 5,000. In this case, the average efficiency of capital is 1,000/5,000, which is 0.20, while the capital-output ratio is 5,000/1,000, which is 5. All that these ratios tell us is that, on average, every £1's worth of capital produces 20p worth of output per year (the average efficiency of capital) and that the value of the capital stock is 5 times the value of annual output (the capital-output ratio). Next, assume that some years later, the economy's capital stock has grown to 6,000, while it's annual output has grown to 1,100. Now the average efficiency of capital has fallen to 1,100/6,000, which is 0.183, and the capital-output ratio has risen to 6,000/1,100, which is 5.455. Thus each unit of capital now produces on average less than it did before, and, what is the same thing, there are more units of capital per unit of output than there were before. This numerical example is consistent, therefore, with growth in a world without learning.

A Modern View: Growth With Learning

Modern economists look at the process of growth more optimistically than did economists of the nineteenth century. The main reason lies in the recognition of the importance of *changes*: changes in the nature of factor inputs, changes in the nature of outputs, and changes in the technology that links inputs to outputs. Experience has taught economists that models of the long-run growth process based on a fixed technology are not very helpful in understanding the dynamic world in which we live. Instead, modern growth is seen to take place in a context of the very long run, where the influences of the changes referred to above are pervasive.

The very long run

Those of you who have read Chapter 15 will recall

that in the long run, all factor inputs can be varied, but the firm must do the best it can within the confines of known technology – i.e. the production function is fixed. The best the firm can do is to be on, rather than above, its long-run cost curve.

The VERY LONG RUN is defined as a period of time over which the techniques of production, the nature of factors of production, and the products that can be produced, all change. Changes in production techniques cause downward *shifts* in long-run cost curves. Increases in the *quality* of factor supplies increase the output that can be obtained from given quantities of inputs. These two forces, along with the development of new products, are the major sources of economic growth. All three need to be considered in more detail.

New Techniques: First, consider changes in the techniques available for producing existing products. Over an average lifetime in the twentieth century, such changes have been dramatic. Eighty years ago, roads and railways were built by gangs of workers using buckets, spades and draft horses. Today bulldozers, steam shovels, giant trucks and other specialized equipment have banished the workhorse from construction sites and to a great extent have displaced the pick-and-shovel worker.

Increases in productive capacity can be either of two types, known as embodied and disembodied technical change. Those that are the result of changes in the form of particular capital goods in use are called EMBODIED TECHNICAL CHANGE. The historical importance of embodied technical change is clearly visible: the assembly line, automation, computerization and robotization transformed much of manufacturing, the aeroplane revolutionized transportation, and electronic devices now dominate the communications industries. These innovations plus less well-known but no less profound ones – for example improvements in the strength of metals, the productivity of seeds and the techniques for recovering basic raw materials from the ground – all create new investment opportunities.

Less visible, but nonetheless important, changes occur through what is called DISEMBODIED TECHNICAL CHANGE, which concerns changes in the organization of production that are not embodied in specific capital goods. One example is improved techniques of managerial control.

Changes in the Quality of Factors: The quality of

labour and capital has changed greatly over the years. A given value of capital, say a £1's worth, is much more productive today than it was in 1900 (where the values are measured in constant prices). This is mainly due to the kind of embodied technological progress referred to above, so we say no more about it here.

Increases in the quality of labour are reflected in increases in the productivity of labour. One cause of such increases is improvements in health standards. Of course, better health is desired as an end in itself, but it also increases productivity per worker-hour by cutting down on illness, accidents and absenteeism.

A second cause is the accumulation of human capital that we discussed in Chapter 21. Education and technical training, from learning how to operate a machine to learning how to be a scientist, have added to human capital. Training is clearly required to invent, operate, manage and repair complex machines. More subtly, there are general social advantages to an educated population. Productivity improves with literacy and, in general, the longer people are educated, the more adaptable they are to new and changing challenges – and thus, in the long run, the more productive.

New Goods: Finally, consider the changes in outputs. Television, polio vaccine, nylon, pocket calculators, quartz watches, personal computers and even ballpoint pens did not exist two generations ago. Other products are so changed that the only connection they have with the 'same' commodity produced in the past is their name. A 1988 Jaguar automobile is very different from a 1938 Jaguar. The European Airbus is revolutionary compared with the DC–3, which itself barely resembled the Wright Brothers' original flying machine which flew on its historic flight within living memory. All such new products are a major source of economic growth in the very long run.

Large firms, small firms and the product cycle

The very-long-run changes discussed above are all found in an important characteristic of a growing economy which is called the *product cycle*. The motto of a growing economy could be 'nothing is permanent'. New products appear continually, while others disappear. At the early stage of a new product, total demand is fairly low, costs of production are high, and many small firms are each trying to get ahead of their competitors by finding the twist that appeals to consumers or the technique that slashes costs. Sometimes new products never get beyond that phase. They prove to be passing fads, or else they remain as high-priced items catering to a small demand.

Others, however, do become items of mass consumption. Successful firms in growing industries buy up rivals, merge with, or otherwise eliminate, their less successful rivals. Simultaneously, their costs fall due to economies of large-scale production. Competition drives prices down along with costs. Eventually, at the mature stage, often, although not invariably, a few giant firms control the industry. They become large, conspicuous and important parts of the nation's economy.

Sooner or later further changes bring up new products that erode the position of the established giants. Demand falls off, and unemployment occurs as the few remaining firms run into financial difficulties. A large, sick, declining industry appears to many as a national failure and disgrace. At any moment of time, however, industries can be found in all phases, from new industries with many small firms to declining industries with a few ailing giants. Declining industries are as much a natural part of a healthy growing economy as are small growing ones.

Growth with a shifting MEC curve

The steady depletion of growth opportunities in the Classical case occurred because new investment opportunities never occurred, by assumption. We have just seen, however, that new investment opportunities are created continually. This causes the *MEC* schedule to shift outward over time as illustrated in Figure 39.3.

Such outward shifts can be regarded as the consequences of learning either about investment opportunities or about techniques that create such opportunities. When learning occurs, what matters is how rapidly the *MEC* schedule shifts relative to the amount of capital accumulation. Three possibilities are shown in the Figure.

In each case, the economy's capital stock grows by the same amount, from k_0 to k_1 to k_2. In each case, learning shifts the *MEC* curve outwards. The cases differ by the speed at which the *MEC* curve is shifting. In case (i), the shift from *MEC* to *MEC'* to *MEC''* is slower than the rate at which capital is accumulating, and the return on new capital follows the declining arrow. In case (ii) the *MEC* is shifting just as

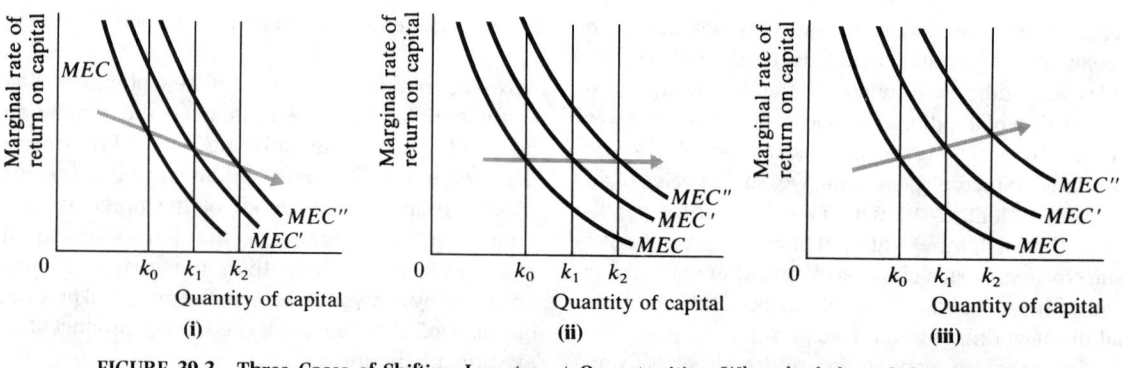

FIGURE 39.3   Three Cases of Shifting Investment Opportunities. When both knowledge and the capital stock grow, their relative rates of growth determine the actual marginal efficiency of capital. In (i), new investment opportunities are developed slower than old ones are used up. In (ii), new investment opportunities are developed at the same speed as old ones are used up. In (iii), new investment opportunites are being developed faster than old ones are being used up

fast as capital is being accumulated, and the return on new capital holds constant along the horizontal arrow. In the third case, the *MEC* shifts faster than new capital is being accumulated, and the return on new capital follows the upward-sloping arrow.

Gradual Reduction in Investment Opportunities: In Figure 39.3 (i), investment opportunities are created, but at a slower rate than they are used up. There is then a falling rate of return and an increasing ratio of capital to output.

This Figure illustrates a slightly more subtle version of the Classical theory of growth than the 'no-learning case'. No longer are investment opportunities unchanging because of an absence of any learning. Instead, learning occurs but not at a fast enough rate to counteract the decline in the marginal productivity of capital due to the growth in the capital stock.

Constant or Rising Investment Opportunities: Parts (ii) and (iii) of Figure 39.3 show cases where invention and innovation create new investment opportunities – seen as an outward shift of the *MEC* curve – as fast, or faster, than these opportunities have been used up through new investment – seen in a movement downwards along any given *MEC* curve. The Figures show that in a world with rapid innovation, the capital-output ratio may be constant or decreasing and, despite large amounts of capital accumulation, the marginal efficiency of new capital may remain constant, or even increase, as new investment opportunities are created.

The historical record suggests that modern economies have been successful in generating new investment opportunities at least as rapidly as old ones were used up. As a result, modern economists devote more attention to understanding the *shifts* in the *MEC* schedule over time and less to discovering its shape in a situation of static knowledege.

Additional Factors Affecting Growth Rates

We have seen so far that an economy's growth rate is influenced by

- the rate at which capital is accumulated,
- the rate at which new technologies are put in place,
- the rate at which the quality of the labour force increases, and
- the rate at which new products are brought into production.

There are, however, some additional forces that now need to be considered. These are:

- the quantity of labour.
- the size of the population.
- structural changes.
- the country's institutions.

The quantity of labour: population theory

Clearly, for any given state of knowledge and supplies of other factors of production, the size of the population can affect the level of output per capita. Thus, from an economic point of view, it is meaningful to speak of overpopulated or underpopulated economies, depending on whether the contribution to production of additional people would raise or lower the level of per capita income. Because population size is related to income per capita, we can conceive of an OPTIMAL POPULATION, which is defined as the population that maximizes national income per capita. We start by assuming a closed society with what we may call a 'balanced' age distribution between children, adults of working age, and old persons.

The optimum population, under these circumstances, is illustrated in Figure 39.4. For given technology and given supplies of land and capital, too small a population will not provide scope for the most efficient division of labour nor for the full exploitation of economies of scale in the nation's industries. Thus, as the nation's population increases, each new citizen adds more to total output than did each previous citizen. Thus the marginal contribution to national income of additional citizens is increasing. As the population goes on increasing, however, all of the opportunities for improving the division of labour and for exploiting scale economies will eventually be exausted. From that point on, further new inhabitants will add less to total production than did each previous addition to the population. Now the marginal product of further additions to the population will fall. In Figure 39.4, falling marginal product sets in after the population has reached N_1.

Eventually, the falling marginal product of new inhabitants will cause a fall in the average product of all the population. In the Figure, the average product per person begins to fall when the population reaches

N_2. The population that maximizes output per person is N_2.

Notice that, from the point of view of maximizing living standards, it pays to increase the population beyond the point of diminishing *marginal* returns. It does not matter if each new inhabitant raises income by less than did any or all of the previous new inhabitants. What matters is that a new inhabitant raises income by more than the *average* income produced by everyone – i.e. that the marginal product of a new inhabitant exceeds the average product of all existing inhabitants.[1]

Notice that the optimum population is defined for a particular stock of land and capital and given technology. The very-long-run changes that we have already studied will cause *upward shifts* in the average and marginal product curves shown in Figure 39.4. This will certainly increase the size of per capita income when the population is optimal, but it may or may not also increase the size of the optimum population by shifting the maximum point of the *AP* curve to the right.

We now drop the assumption of a closed economy with what we called a 'balanced' age distribution. This raises two issues.[2]

First, the balance of the population between the non-working (the young, housewives, and the old) and the working population influences the optimum size of the population. Total output depends on the size of the working population while real income depends on total output and the size of the whole population. On the one hand, if the birth rate is rising, a rising proportion of the population will be young and not yet in the labour force. They will consume while not producing, and so tend to lower per capita living standards, even if the working population is unchanged. On the other hand, if the birth rate is declining, the proportion of the population over retirement age will be rising. Again, this increases the proportion of people who are consuming without

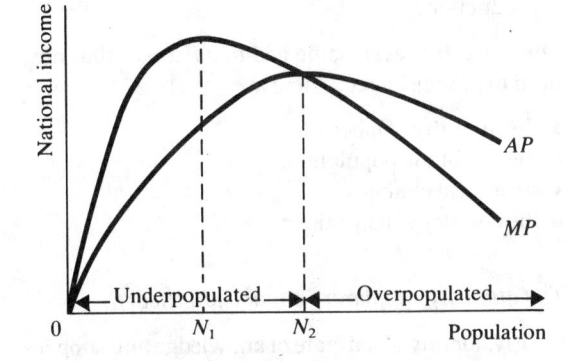

FIGURE 39.4   Optimum Population. The optimum population is the one that maximizes per capita national income

1 Notice that the theory of the optimum population is nothing more than an application, at the macro level, of the law of diminishing returns that is discussed in the microeconomic sections of this book (see Chapter 14). In the earlier chapter we considered adding more labourers to fixed amounts of land and capital in a particular firm and studied the average and marginal changes in output that resulted in that industry's output. Now we are considering the effects of more population being added to a whole country's fixed stock of land and capital and studying the average and marginal changes in national income that result.

2 For further discussion see Harbury and Lipsey, Chapter 4.

currently producing and tends to lower current per capita living standards.

Second, what do policy-makers do if they perceive their current population is far different from the optimum? If the population is too low, various inducements can be given for the size of families to be increased. After a long time, the working population will rise, but for nearly two decades after the birth rate rises, the net effect of such a policy will be a rise in the proportion of the population who are below working age. During this period, the pressure is for per capita living standards to fall. A more immediately effective policy is to encourage immigration. Through immigration, the population can be increased rapidly, and it is also possible to increase it in a 'balanced' way with children, working adults, and older persons all entering the country. Immigration policies sometimes go further by favouring people who are of working age and who have significant skills. This increases the relative size of the working population and gives a twofold upward pressure on living standards: first, as the working population gets closer to the optimum level, the average product of the working population rises and, second, as the proportion of non-working people in the population falls, each working person has, on average, fewer non-working dependent persons to support.

Many countries have had conscious population policies. North America in the nineteenth century sought immigrants, as did Australia until very recently. Germany under Hitler paid bonuses for the birth of additional Aryan children and otherwise offered incentives to create Germans. Greece in the 1950s and 1960s tried to stem emigration to Western Europe. All are examples of countries that believed they had insufficient population, though the motives were not in every case purely economic. In contrast, many underdeveloped countries of South America, Africa and Asia desire to limit population growth in the belief that they are at or above their optimum populations. The Chinese People's Republic, in particular, has strong economic incentives to limit the number of children to one per family.

We can summarize the effects on per capita growth rates as follows. A country's growth rate will be higher:

- the more rapidly its working population is growing if it is currently below the optimum;
- the more rapidly its working population is shrinking (or the less rapidly it is growing) if it is

currently above the optimum; and
- the more rapidly is the working population growing relative to the dependent population.

Structural change

Changes in the structure of the economy's output can cause changes in its measured growth rate. On the one hand, a decline in such low-productivity sectors as distribution and an expansion in such high-productivity sectors as manufacturing, will temporarily boost the measured aggregate growth rate as labour moves from the declining to the expanding sectors. On the other hand, a decline in the high-productivity manufacturing sector, and a rise in the size of the lower-productivity service sector, will lower the measured rate of growth while the movement is occurring. The first (growth-increasing) shift was typical of the 1950s and the 1960s, while the second (growth-reducing) shift was typical of the 1980s.

For example, when one type of energy (say, solar) supplants another type (say, oil), much existing capital stock specifically geared to the original energy source may become costly to operate and will be scrapped. New capital geared to the new energy source will be built. *During the transition*, gross investment expenditure is high, thus stimulating aggregate demand. But there is little if any increase in the economy's potential national income because the old capital goods have been scrapped. Similarly, new pollution control laws will affect investment expenditure but will not lead to growth in capacity. (The reduction in pollution may nonetheless be socially desirable.)

A rise in the international price of *imported* energy will also lower productivity. The higher-priced imported energy means that domestic *value added* falls, and with it GNP per worker. Although the same volume of goods can be produced with a given input of labour, a smaller portion of the output's value is now earned as income by domestic workers and firms, while a larger proportion is used to pay for the energy imports. These changes show up in the statistics as a decline in productivity and a temporary fall in growth rates.

These are some of the many factors that were operative throughout the world in the late 1970s and early 1980s. They worked to depress growth rates for some considerable period of time. But they are not permanent factors. When the structural adjustments are complete, their depressing effects will pass.

Institutional considerations

Almost all aspects of a country's institutions can encourage or discourage the efficient use of a society's natural and human resources. Social and religious habits, legal institutions, and traditional patterns of national and international trade are all important. So, too, is the political climate.

BENEFITS AND COSTS OF GROWTH

In the remainder of this chapter, we shall outline some of the costs and benefits of growth. We start by looking in the next four sections at benefits. Then we go on to consider costs.

Benefits of Growth

Growth and Living Standards:　We observed at the beginning of this chapter that in the circumstances facing most countries, the most important single force leading to long-run increases in living standards is economic growth. This point is so fundamental that we chose to make it at the outset. So under the present heading we have only to remind you of it and then pass on to some of the other advantages of growth.

Growth and Income Redistribution: Economic growth makes many kinds of redistribution easier to achieve than when national income is static. For example, if a static national income is to be redistributed, someone's standard of living will actually have to be lowered. However, when there is economic growth, it is possible, by redistributing some of *the increment* in income, to reduce income inequalities without actually having to lower anyone's income. It is thus much easier for a rapidly growing economy to be generous toward its less fortunate citizens – or neighbours – than it is for a static economy.

Growth and Lifestyle:　As well as producing more of what we already consume, growth changes consumption patterns and lifestyles in more profound ways. A family often finds that a big increase in its income can lead to a major change in the pattern of its consumption – that extra money buys important amenities of life. In the same way, the members of society as a whole may change their consumption patterns as their average income rises. Not only are more cars produced, but the government is led to produce more highways and to provide more recreational areas for its newly affluent (and mobile) citizens. At yet a later stage, a concern about litter, pollution and ugliness may become important, and their correction may then begin to account for a significant fraction of national income. Such 'amenities' usually become matters of social concern only when growth has assured the provision of the basic requirements for food, clothing and housing of a substantial majority of the population.

Growth and National Power:　When one country is competing with another for power or prestige, rates of growth are important. If our national income is growing at 2 per cent, say, while the other country's is growing at 5 per cent, the other country will only have to wait for our relative strength to dwindle. Moreover, the faster its productivity is growing, the easier a country will find it to bear the expense of an arms race, or a programme of foreign aid.

Costs of Growth

The benefits discussed above suggest that growth is a great blessing. Some of the consequences can, however, be a curse. Some of these less desirable effects were considered in Chapters 23 and 24, under the headings pollution and externalities.

Social and Personal Costs of Growth: Industrialization can cause deterioration of the environment. Unspoiled landscapes give way to highways, factories and billboards; air and water become polluted; and in some cases unique and priceless relics of earlier ages – from flora and fauna to ancient ruins – disappear. Urbanization tends to move people away from the simpler life of farms and small towns and into the crowded, sometimes crime-ridden life of urban areas. Those remaining behind in the rural areas find that rural life, too, changes. Larger-scale farming, the decline of population, and the migration of children from the farm to the city all have their costs. The stepped-up tempo of life brings joys to some but tragedy to others. Accidents, ulcers, crime rates, suicides, divorces and murder all tend to be higher in periods of rapid growth and in more developed societies. To what extent the latter is the cause of the former remains uncertain, but the association is unmistakable.

When an economy is growing, it is also changing. Innovation leaves obsolete machines in its wake, and it also leaves partially obsolete people. No matter how well trained you are at age 25, in another 25 years your skills may well be partially obsolete. Some will find that their skills have become completely outdated and unneeded. A rapid rate of growth requires rapid adjustments, which can cause much upset and misery to the individuals affected.

It is often argued that costs of this kind are a small price to pay for the great benefits that growth can bring. Even if that is true in the aggregate, personal costs are very unevenly borne. Indeed, many of those for whom growth is most costly share least in the fruits of growth. Yet it is also a mistake to see only the costs – to yearn for the good old days while enjoying higher living standards that growth alone has made possible.

The Opportunity Cost of Growth: In a world of scarcity, almost nothing is free. Growth requires investments of resources in capital goods and education. These investments absorb factors of production that could otherwise be used to produce goods and services for current consumption – hence current sacrifice. When, after a time, the new capital goods come into use, or the better-educated people enter the labour force, the economy's potential income will rise – hence future gain.

In a market economy, individuals decide how much current sacrifice will be made. They do this by deciding how much of their current incomes not to spend on current consumption. This part of their income is saved and can be made available for current investment.[1] In command economies, governments make the decisions by deciding how many of the nation's factors of production will be allocated to producing investment goods and how many to producing output for current consumption.

Many less-developed countries are using such planned approaches today. The shift of resources from consumption to investment is particularly important when growth rates are very small (say, less

than 1 per cent), for without some current sacrifice there is little or no prospect of a significant amount of growth in the lifetimes of today's citizens. Yet, at the same time, the sacrifices are great when per capita national income is low. The very lowest growth rates are frequently encountered in the very poorest countries. This creates a cruel dilemma called the VICIOUS CIRCLE OF POVERTY: the country needs investment to raise its living standards but its current living standards are so low that a diversion of resources from consumption to investment goods will cause major suffering.

Growth as a Goal of Policy: Do the Benefits Justify the Costs?

Do the already developed countries need yet more growth? Most people think they do. Poverty is now a solvable problem in many of the richer western European countries as a direct result of its enhanced average living standards. Clearly, people in the top quarter of the income distribution in any industrialized country have more opportunities for leisure, travel, culture, fine wines and gracious living than have persons with much lower incomes. Most of those now in the bottom half of the income distribution would like these opportunities too. Only growth can provide the national income needed to give these opportunities to them all.

Today, many countries that have not yet experienced sustained periods of economic growth are urgently seeking to copy those that have done so in order to obtain the benefits of growth despite its costs.

How seriously people rate the costs of growth depends in part on how many of the benefits of growth have already been achieved. With mounting population problems, the poorer countries are increasingly preoccupied with creating growth. With mounting awareness of pollution, the richer countries are devoting more resources to overcoming the problems caused by growth – at the same time that they are understandably reluctant to give up further growth.

Indeed, a similar conflict can often be seen within the same country at one time: a relatively poor community fights to acquire a new paper mill for the employment and income it will create; another, relatively affluent, community deplores the ruin of its beaches and its air by an existing mill.

---

1 Households make such decisions directly when they save and buy bonds or equities. If they put their savings in a financial institution, they have made the savings decision themselves but have left the investment decision to the financial institution. Firms also make these decisions (on behalf of their owners) by deciding to withhold some of their profits (savings) and spend the funds on capital equipment (investment).

SUMMARY

1 In the long run, economic growth is a more potent force for raising living standards than is increasing efficiency or the redistribution of income. Redistribution and efficiency policies are, nonetheless, important.

2 Growth of national income can result from the removal of a recessionary gap through a rightward shift in the *AD* curve. This can be at a rapid rate, but it must come to a stop when the gap is eliminated. Growth of national income can also result from an outward shift of the *LRAS* curve. This type of growth can go on indefinitely.

3 In the short run, investment increases aggregate demand while, in the long run, it increases aggregate supply as measured by potential income. In the short run, savings decrease aggregate demand while, in the long run, by providing the funds needed for investment, savings help to increase aggregate supply. In the long run, therefore, there is no paradox of thrift.

4 In a world of static technology, the accumulation of capital is the main source of growth. As capital accumulates, however, the capital-output ratio rises while the marginal return on capital falls towards zero, at which point growth will stop completely.

5 In a world of improving technology, the marginal efficiency of capital curve will be shifting outwards. If it shifts outwards as fast as the capital stock is growing, the return on capital will not fall, and the capital-output ratio will not rise. Such growth can go on indefinitely without any fall in the marginal return to new capital, creating a world dominated by 'very-long-run' changes in production techniques, the quality of factors of production and the development of new products.

6 The major factors affecting the growth rate are the rate at which capital is accumulated, the rate at which new technologies are put in place, the rate at which the quality of the labour force increases, the rate at which new products come into production, the growth of both the population and the labour force, and structural changes in the economy.

7 The optimum population maximizes output per capita in the economy. *Ceteris paribus*, growth of population raises living standards when the present population is less than the optimum, but lowers living standards if the present population is above the optimum.

8 The major benefits of growth are rising average living standards, easier redistribution of income, beneficial changes in lifestyle, and its contribution to growing national power. The major costs of growth are all of the costs associated with rapid change, including the rapid obsolescence of human skills, and the direct opportunity cost in forgone present consumption necessary to free the resources needed for growth-creating investment. Although growth has costs, most people appear to believe that the benefits outweigh the costs most of the time.

Employment and Unemployment[1]

In the early 1980s worldwide unemployment rose to very high levels, higher than during some of the years of the 1930s although not as high as the peak unemployment rates of that earlier 'Great Depression'. Not only was the overall level of unemployment wastefully large, the structure of unemployment was extremely varied – in Britain in 1985 the unemployment rate was about 25 per cent among males under 25 and 5 per cent among women over 55. Regional disparities were significant, although not so large as they were a decade or two before. Currently, the most serious problem of localized unemployment seemed to be the very high rates among the mainly unskilled residents of the decaying inner cores of large industrial cities.[1]

Economic conditions as well as social and economic policies instituted since the 1930s have no doubt made the economic consequences of short-term unemployment less serious than they were in earlier times. But the effects of the current high unemployment, especially for the long-term unemployed in terms of disillusioned groups who have given up trying to succeed within the system, many of whom sow the seeds of social unrest, is a matter of serious concern to those concerned with the long-term health of the society.

KINDS OF UNEMPLOYMENT

For purposes of study, the unemployed can be classified in various ways. We can distinguish among

categories of persons unemployed – e.g. youth, women, adult men – among age, sex, occupation, degree of skill, and even by ethnic groups. We may distinguish by location – e.g. unemployment in the South East, the North West, and Scotland. We may also distinguish by the duration of unemployment between, say, those who are out of jobs for long periods of time and those who suffer relatively short-term bouts of unemployment. Finally, we may distinguish the reasons for the unemployment.

In the present chapter we concentrate on the reasons for unemployment. Although it is not always possible to attach a specific cause to each unemployed person, it is often possible to gain some idea of the total numbers of people unemployed for each major cause. Different economists find it convenient to identify different causes, and there is no right or wrong about any system of classification. In what follows we take one common scheme for classifying unemployment by types:

- frictional unemployment
- structural unemployment
- real-wage (or Classical) unemployment
- demand-deficient unemployment.

Frictional Unemployment

The term FRICTIONAL UNEMPLOYMENT refers to the unemployment that is associated with the normal turnover of labour. People leave jobs for many reasons, and they take time to find new jobs; old persons leave the labour force and young persons enter it, but often new workers do not fill the jobs vacated by those who leave. Inevitably all of this movement takes time and gives rise to a pool of

1 Details of employment and unemployment in the UK may be found in Harbury and Lipsey, Chapters 4 and 9.

persons who are 'frictionally' unemployed while in the course of finding new jobs. This unemployment would occur even if the occupational, industrial and regional structure of employment were unchanging.

Structural Unemployment

Structural changes in the economy can cause unemployment. As economic growth proceeds, the pattern of demands and supplies changes constantly. Some industries, occupations and regions suffer a decline in the demand for what they produce, while other industries, occupations and regions enjoy an increase in demand. These changes require considerable economic readjustment. STRUCTURAL UNEMPLOYMENT occurs when the adjustments are not fast enough, so that severe pockets of unemployment occur in areas, industries and occupations in which the demand for factors of production is falling faster than is the supply; it is defined as the unemployment that exists because of a mismatching between the unemployed and the available jobs in terms of regional location, required skills or any other relevant dimension. In Britain today, structural unemployment exists, for example, in Wales, in the motorcar industry, and among machine-tool operators.

Structural unemployment can increase because either the pace of economic change accelerates or the pace of adjustment to change slows down. Natural forces and social policies that discourage movement among regions, industries and/or occupations can raise structural unemployment. Policies that prevent firms from replacing some labour with new machines may protect employment in the short term. If, however, such policies lead to the decline of an industry because it cannot compete with more innovative foreign competitors, they can end up causing severe pockets of structural unemployment.

Real-Wage Unemployment

Unemployment due to too high a real wage is called REAL-WAGE UNEMPLOYMENT. It is sometimes also called *Classical unemployment* after the many economists who held that unemployment in the 1930s was due to too high a real wage and whom Keynes called 'Classical economists'. Their remedy for unemployment was to reduce wages. Keynes argued that the unemployment of the 1930s was caused by deficient aggregate demand rather than by excessively high real wages.

The Keynesian view of the causes of the Great Depression eventually prevailed. But the debate of the thirties aroused such strong emotions that many modern economists have refused to believe that *any* significant amount of unemployment could be caused by real wages that were too high. There is concern, however, that some of the unemployment occurring in Britain and Europe during the 1980s is traceable to high real wages. The issue is by no means settled. The theory of real-wage unemployment is now well understood, and economists accept its possibility.

We can distinguish two types of real-wage unemployment, one associated with relative wages among different groups of labour and one associated with wages in general. The former involves microeconomic issues of resource allocation that we discussed in Chapters 20 and 21. We were there concerned especially with unemployment caused by setting the wage rate above the free-market equilibrium. We outlined the circumstances under which government policies or trade-union actions in support of wage-rate rises could create unemployment in a particular industry.

Disequilibrium relative wages

Typical microeconomic causes of unemployment are minimum floors to wages, union agreements that narrow wage differentials, nationally agreed wage structures that take no account of local market conditions, and equal-pay laws where employers perceive unequal marginal-value products among the groups concerned.

Consider, for example, a minimum-wage law. Figure 40.1 shows the effect of such a law on the market for unskilled labour. This is the only group that will be affected, since semi-skilled and skilled workers will earn wages above the minimum in any case. Under competitive conditions the forces of supply and demand produce a wage of w_c and employment of q_c. A minimum wage of w_m is now imposed. As a result, wages rise to w_m but employment falls to q_1. Now the conflict of interest becomes apparent. The q_1 workers who keep their jobs are benefited by the law: they can earn higher wages. But the $q_c - q_1$ workers who lose their jobs are harmed by the law: they must join the ranks of the unemployed. Also, a further $q_2 - q_c$ workers would now like employment at the higher wage, but they cannot find work.

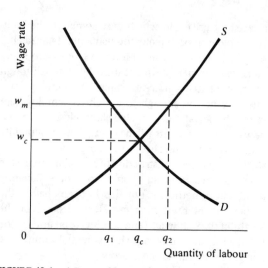

FIGURE 40.1   A Disequilibrium Relative Real Wage. A real wage that is held above its free-market level causes unemployment in that market

There is evidence that minimum-wage laws cause unemployment of new entrants to the labour force. Young, inexperienced workers tend to have a lower marginal productivities than do experienced workers and their low starting wages reflect this. But the young tend to learn quickly, so as they gain experience, their marginal productivities, and hence their free-market wages, rise. If a high minimum wage makes it hard for them to obtain their first job, they are delayed in gaining the work experience that would lift their market-determined wage above the minimum.

To see what is involved, consider an inexperienced school-leaver who would accept £X for her first job. A potential employer is willing to pay this, but the minimum is £1.5X. So the employer hires someone overqualified for the job on the grounds that, if he has to pay more than he needs to, he might as well get something extra in return.

Similar results tend to follow from wage structures that raise any group's wages above what their market wage would be. These structures set up a conflict of interest between those who obtain jobs at the higher wage, and are thus better off, and those who would like to work at that wage but cannot, and hence are worse off. This is true whether the higher wage is imposed by government intervention or agreed to in a union-negotiated contract.

So, having wages above their equilibrium level in some markets can cause unemployment in those

markets. This unemployment adds to the overall level of unemployment in the whole country. Next, we turn to the possibility that wages may be above their equilibrium levels in *all* labour markets.

A disequilibrium average real wage

So far in this book, we have used the term *the real wage* to refer to the purchasing power of money wages. This can be measured by deflating the money wage by the retail price index. Now we introduce a second type of real wage: the REAL PRODUCT WAGE, which is the money wage earned in a particular industry deflated by the value of that industry's product. For example, if labour costs £300 a week and each week produces an output whose market value is £400, then the real product wage is £300/£400, which is 0.75. What this means is that 75p out of every £1 of sales goes to pay for labour inputs.

Note that, since it is *labour costs* in which we are interested, the wage is the full cost to the employer of hiring a unit of labour, which includes the pre-tax wage rate, any extra benefits such as pension-plan contributions, and such government payroll taxes as employers' contribution to national insurance.

The real product wage can affect employment through forces operating both in the short run and in the long run. We shall consider each of these time-periods in turn.

Before we do, a few terms must be defined or recalled from earlier chapters. The CAPITAL-LABOUR ratio is merely the ratio of the amount of capital to the amount of labour used to produce any given output. If that ratio is high, indicating the use of a lot of capital relative to the amount of labour used, the production is called CAPITAL INTENSIVE. If the ratio is low, indicating relatively little capital per unit of labour used, the production is called LABOUR INTENSIVE.

First consider the short run, where the amount of capital is fixed. Past technological changes that are embodied in existing plant and equipment means that, at any moment in time, an industry will have an array of plants, running from those that can do little more than cover their variable costs through to those that make a handsome return over variable costs. Now assume that the real product wage rises by, say, 15 per cent. This will mean that some plants can no longer cover their variable costs and they will close down. If, for example, a plant originally had wages of 64p and other direct costs of 30p in every sales £1,

production would be worthwhile, since 6p of every £1 of sales would be available as a return on already invested capital. If the product wage rose by 15 per cent to 73.6p in every £1 of sales, then the plant would immediately be shut down, since it would not even be covering its variable costs, which would be 103.6p in every £1 of sales. The plant's employees would then lose their jobs.

Now consider the long run, when the amount of capital can be changed. It is usually the case that, at the design stage, more or less capital can be spread over a given labour force, thus varying the capital-labour ratio by any desired amount. It is also often the case, however, that, once built, the ratio in which capital and labour are used is embodied in the equipment and cannot be significantly varied. For example, you can design highly automated capital-intensive, or quite simple labour-intensive, textile plants and so vary the capital-labour ratio on the drawing board. Once a capital-intensive automated plant is built, however, you cannot profitably return to a labour-intensive method of production by applying masses of labour to the automated machinery.

Let us now consider the consequences of a large increase in the real product wage, when capital is of the type described in the previous paragraph. We have already noted that, in the short run, some plants would close down. In the long run, when new plants were being built, their designers would seek to substitute relatively cheap capital for relatively more expensive labour. So a given volume of output would employ less labour (and more capital) than before.

When plants that are too labour-intensive at the new, higher real product wage are being replaced by plants that are more capital-intensive, unemployment will develop. But although this may last for several years, it is nonetheless a transitional phase. The final result depends on whether or not the real product wage is too high to encourage sufficient investment. Two general cases need to be distinguished.

First, the real product wage may be raised so high that no new plants that can be built with existing technology are profitable. Then, old plants that cannot cover variable costs will be closed down, no new plants will be built, and an alleviation of the unemployment (assuming the real product wage is not lowered) must await the very long run, when technologies that are profitable at existing relative prices are invented.

Second, capital-intensive plants may be profitable at existing prices, in which case some will be built. While older, more labour-intensive plants are being scrapped and new capital-intensive ones are being built, severe unemployment may develop. Although the new plants will create some new employment, this may not be enough to match the employment lost as the old labour-intensive plants close down. But how many new plants will be built? If the profitability of investment diminishes at the margin as the capital stock grows, then construction of new plants will stop when further units of capital are not sufficiently profitable. Whether or not this happens before the whole labour force is put back to work depends on the height of the real wage (and capital costs) and on the speed with which returns to investment decline at the margin as the capital stock grows.

Demand-Deficient Unemployment

Unemployment that occurs because there is insufficient total demand to purchase all of the output that could be produced by a fully employed labour force is called DEMAND-DEFICIENT UNEMPLOYMENT.

Demand-deficient unemployment is the main subject of the national-income theory that we have studied throughout the macro part of this book. This theory seeks, among other things, to explain the unemployment that is caused by variations in the total demand for the nation's output – as shown by variations in both the aggregate desired expenditure curve and the aggregate demand curve.

National-income theory seeks to explain the causes of, and cures for, unemployment in excess of frictional and structural unemployment. Indeed, when we speak of 'full employment' we do not mean zero unemployment, but rather that all unemployment is frictional or structural.

Consider Figure 40.2. When aggregate demand is given by AD, short- and long-run equilibrium is at a national income of Y_F. At that level of income, there is no demand-deficient unemployment. If the aggregate demand curve shifts to AD', equilibrium income falls to Y_0. A recessionary gap shown in the diagram by $Y_F - Y_0$ opens up. The accompanying unemployment is called demand-deficient unemployment. It can be eliminated by raising aggregate demand to AD without setting up any inflationary pressures due to excess demand, in the sense that the price level will be no higher than it was before the fall in aggregate demand.

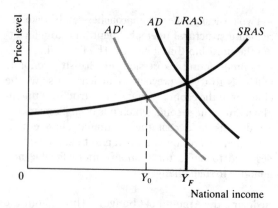

FIGURE 40.2 **Demand-Deficient Unemployment.** Demand-deficient unemployment occurs when the aggregate demand curve cuts the *SRAS* curve at a level of national income below potential income

Now consider the amount of unemployment that does exist at Y_F. It must be due to frictional or structural causes and it is sometimes called the NATURAL RATE OF UNEMPLOYMENT, defined as the level of unemployment at which the demand for and supply of labour are equal, so that the labour market is in equilibrium. Thus this amount of unemployment is sometimes also said to be *voluntary*. Many people object to this name because it seems to imply that that amount of unemployment is acceptable. In fact, all that can be said about the unemployment that occurs at Y_F is that it cannot be reduced permanently by raising aggregate demand (since we saw in Chapter 38 that national income cannot be raised above Y_F without setting up pressures to move it back to Y_F).

'Full employment' generally refers to a situation in which there is no demand-deficient employment. When the economy is fully employed, all remaining unemployment is frictional or structural and cannot be reduced, except temporarily, by the tools of demand management. Because the volume of structural and frictional unemployment changes from time to time, so also does the amount of unemployment regarded as full employment. Thus the changes in the natural rate of unemployment occur for any of the reasons discussed above under the headings of frictional and structural unemployment.

The brevity of our discussion of demand-deficient unemployment does not reflect any judgement that it is unimportant. Having studied it throughout macroeconomics, however, there is little more that needs to be said about it at this point.

THE MEASUREMENT OF UNEMPLOYMENT

There are two main problems of measurement that need to be addressed: the measurement of the overall rate of unemployment, and the measurement of different types of unemployment.

When we measure the overall rate of unemployment, what we would like to discover is the extent of *involuntary* unemployment. Problems arise both because we may not count some of those who are involuntarily unemployed, and because we may count some who are voluntarily unemployed and others who are actually working.

The number of persons unemployed in the UK is estimated from a monthly count of those who are eligible to claim unemployment benefits.[1]

There are reasons why this measured figure for unemployment may not reflect the number of people who are truly unemployed in the sense that they would accept the offer of a job for which they were qualified. On the one hand, the measured figure may *understate* involuntary unemployment by missing people who are genuinely willing to work at going wage rates. For example, some people who have worked in the past are not eligible for unemployment benefits and, therefore, are not counted. Also, those who have not worked before are not eligible for benefits. School-leavers and housewives who would work if a booming economy offered them jobs, will not show up on the statistics as unemployed. In contrast, the measured figure may *overstate* unemployment by including people who are not truly unemployed in the sense we have just defined. Some people cheat on the system by collecting unemployment benefits when they are employed. Some people do not really wish to work because the difference between their unemployment benefits and what they can earn in work is not sufficient to compensate them for the disutility of work. These people have voluntarily withdrawn from the workforce, but they register as unemployed in order to collect their benefits. Others, for reasons of age or disability, are unemployable but register in order to receive benefits.

---

1 Prior to 1982, the count was of those persons registered for work at Job Centres. The changed basis causes an apparent fall of nearly $\frac{1}{4}$ million in the numbers of jobless.

CURES FOR UNEMPLOYMENT

Frictional Unemployment

The labour turnover which causes frictional unemployment is an inevitable part of the functioning of the economy. There will always be some turnover as people of all ages change jobs for any reason. Furthermore, some frictional unemployment is an inevitable part of the learning process. One reason why there is a high turnover rate, and hence high frictional unemployment, among the young is that one has to try jobs to see if they are suitable. New entrants – whether the young or older women who have just decided to take a job rather than stay at home – typically try several jobs before settling into the one that most satisfies, or least dissatisfies, them.

Insofar as frictional unemployment is caused by ignorance, increasing the knowledge of labour-market opportunities may help. But such measures have a cost, and it is not clear how much is to be gained by further expenditure at the margin here.

Demographic and behavioural changes are expected to lead to a national decline of frictional unemployment over the next decade. First, population figures suggest that the proportion of the labour force made up of youth will decline. Since they have high rates of frictional unemployment, this change will cause a fall in such unemployment. Similarly, the long-term upward trend in female participation rates must slow down, if not come to a halt. This means that the proportion of female workers who are recent entrants to the labour force will also decline and, with that, frictional unemployment among female workers will decline.

Finally, policy changes that make it easier for youths to find jobs from which they can learn, and hence raise their productivity, could help. Youth training, and schemes aimed at subsidizing the wage rate for young workers, have also helped.

Structural Unemployment

The changes in the structure of the economy that cause short-term bouts of structural unemployment are an inevitable result of economic growth which is the main cause of long-term increases in average living standards. Although this does not make structural unemployment any the less unpleasant, it does put such unemployment into some perspective.

Two basically different approaches can be taken to reducing structural unemployment, and to alleviating the hardship that it causes. The first, which has sometimes found expression in British economic policy, is to try to prevent, or at least to slow, the changes in the economy that cause structural unemployment.[1] The second, which has been pioneered in Sweden, is to accept the economic change that accompanies economic growth and to adopt policies designed to make the economy more flexible and adaptive to such change.

Reducing the Amount of Change: Throughout the centuries many governments and workers have sought to combat the threat of structural unemployment by preventing, or slowing, structural changes.

One way in which this has been done in the past is through *manning agreements*. These seek to prevent people from being declared redundant, and thus becoming structurally unemployed, because of new innovations. For example, the replacement of coal by diesel in railway engines thirty years ago made firemen who shovelled coal into the boiler unnecessary, but existing firemen were kept on by agreement between British Rail and the firemen's union. A second way is through the support of declining industries by public funds. For example, if the market would support an output of X but subsidies are used to support an output of 2X, then jobs are provided for the 50 per cent of the industry's labour force who would otherwise become unemployed and then have to find jobs elsewhere.

Both of these policies will be attractive to the people who would otherwise become unemployed. It may be a long time before they can find other jobs and, when they do, their skills may not turn out to be highly valued in their new industries. If such policies are used to manipulate the rate at which jobs disappear in particular categories or in whole industries, they can be successful. If, however, they are used to resist change indefinitely, they will not in the end be sustainable. Manning agreements raise costs and hasten the decline of an industry threatened by competitive products. An industry that is declining due to market forces but supported by government subsidy, becomes an increasingly large charge on the public purse as the market becomes less and less

---

1 This has been sometimes attempted by UK regional policy – see Harbury and Lipsey, Chapter 6.

favourable to its success. Sooner or later, public support is withdrawn and an often precipitous decline in output and employment then ensues.

In assessing the above remedies for structural unemployment, it is important to realize that, although not viable in the long run for the economy, they may be the best alternative for the affected workers. Thus, there is often a real conflict between those threatened by structural unemployment, whose interests lie in preserving their old jobs, and the general public, whose interests lie in encouraging economic growth.

Increasing Adaptability to Change: The conflict just stated can be at least partly reduced by adopting a different set of policies. The decline of some industries and the destruction of some jobs, as well as the rise of other industries and the creation of other jobs, that accompany economic growth and change can be accepted and policies then designed to reduce the costs, and increase the speed, of the adjustments that must be made by those who are affected.

For example, retraining and relocation grants can make it easier for labour to move among jobs and between geographic areas. They can also reduce the hardship involved in making these movements. Such policies have the advantage of helping the economy adjust to inevitable change and, by speeding up the change, of reducing the pool of people who are structurally unemployed at any one time.

Policies that inhibit adjustment can be avoided, and policies that encourage it can be adopted.

British housing policy is a good example of a policy that inhibits the geographic reallocation of labour and hence increases structural unemployment. Rent controls discourage the private construction of rental accommodation in expanding areas. By thus contributing to a housing shortage, they make it harder for people to move. Geographic movement is also discouraged by the provision of council housing at low rents accompanied by an inadequate supply of such housing in expanding centres. To leave a declining area often means giving up cheap, and available, council housing in return for nothing more than a place on a long waiting list in the expanding area.

Unemployment and supplementary benefits sometimes make the margin between the income from unemployment in contracting areas and the income from employment in expanding areas less than the costs, and risks, of moving. Such benefits discourage geographic mobility and so contribute to structural unemployment. This is not to say that policies that reduce the suffering from involuntary unemployment are undesirable. But if they are designed with no concern about their potential for increasing structural unemployment, they can be self-defeating in the long run. Some countries require that those on benefits enter training schemes that will fit them for new jobs. Others give strong incentives to move to expanding areas, and disincentives to stay in contracting ones in the form of movement bonuses to those who move and reduced payments to those who do not.

Demand-Deficient Unemployment

We do not need to say much more about cures for this type of unemployment since its control is the subject of demand management which we have studied in several earlier chapters. A major recession that occurs as a result of the operation of market forces can be countered by monetary and fiscal policy to reduce demand-deficient unemployment.

It is worth noting, however, that a new situation arose in the 1980s: policy-induced, demand-deficient unemployment. This resulted from a policy-induced recession designed to cut inflation. We will discuss this policy at length in the next chapter. (See the section on breaking an entrenched inflation.) In this case, demand-deficient unemployment was accepted as the price of reducing inflation. In these circumstances, the only way to reduce the unemployment is to find ways of first reducing inflation so that policy-makers will then be willing to raise aggregate demand.

Real-Wage Unemployment

Whenever this type of unemployment exists, it is not easy to cure. Basically what is required is a fall in the real product wage, combined with measures to increase aggregate demand so as to create enough total employment. But the cure is a slow one, requiring enough time to build the new labour-using capital. The steps would run as follows.

First, the real product wage would be cut substantially. Possibly there would be some form of 'social contract' whereby unions, employers and the government agree to allow this to occur, or possibly the real wage would fall slowly as money wages rose less fast than the price level. Alternatively, employers'

contributions to unemployment insurance or to employees' pensions schemes could be cut, thus reducing the overall labour cost of producing each unit of output. The reduction would provide the incentive to create more employment by using more labour-intensive methods of production.

Second, since wages determine disposable income, and disposable income determines consumer demand, the cut in wages will tend to reduce aggregate demand and hence reduce equilibrium national income. One would then have to try to counter this deflationary force using fiscal and monetary policy to restore sufficient aggregate demand.

Third, it must be accepted that unemployment is likely to remain relatively high until new capital capacity is built to employ the surplus labour. Any attempt to push aggregate demand beyond the capacity output of the current capital stock will re-create the conditions for a demand inflation.

Conclusion

Most economists agreed that, throughout most of the 1980s, there was significant demand-deficient unemployment. This unemployment was accepted by government policy-makers as a necessary, although unfortunate, consequence of their anti-inflationary policies and their drive to reduce the public-sector borrowing requirement. Some economists felt that these policies were not worth the price that was entailed in terms of unemployment. They called for expansionary demand-management policies to eliminate the demand-deficient unemployment.

Most economists agreed that there was more structural unemployment in the UK in the 1980s than there had been at any time since the end of the Second World War. Many called for policies to increase the adaptability of the economy and reduce inhibitions to the movement of labour. Others were more attracted by government intervention, mainly in the form of moving work to the places where unemployment was highest. Grants to encourage unemployed persons to start regional service-oriented industries had a bit of both approaches in them.

Whether or not real-wage unemployment was a serious problem in Britain and Europe throughout the 1980s was probably the most contentious issue concerning unemployment. Advocates of the real-wage explanation argued that British real wages were some 10–15 per cent too high in the early 1980s and, as a result, significant amounts of capital were being scrapped. They also pointed out that the first sign of such an unhappy situation is a rise in recorded labour productivity such as occurred in the early 1980s. Since the least efficient plants are scrapped first, the average output per head of those remaining in employment will rise steadily. But a rise in productivity that results from destroying the capital that provides employment for a significant fraction of the labour force in manufacturing is hardly a desirable change. Economists who held this view argued that the unemployment could not be eliminated until the real product wage fell significantly – as it did in many American industries in the early 1980s.

Opponents argued that the great bulk of unemployment in the 1980s that was not structural was due to demand-deficient unemployment. They rejected the idea of an incomes policy to reduce real product wages. Instead they advocated an end to tight monetary policy, followed by an expansionary demand-management policy to restore full employment.

This is a debate that will no doubt go on until that happy day when something like full employment is once again restored in the UK.

SUMMARY

1 Unemployment normally refers to those who are involuntarily unemployed – i.e. willing to work at the going wage rate but unable to find a job. Unemployment is traditionally divided into four categories: frictional, structural, real wage, and demand-deficient unemployment.

2 Frictional unemployment is the irreducible minimum amount of unemployment due to labour turnover as new people enter the labour force and look for jobs and existing workers change jobs. Structural unemployment occurs because changes in the regional, occupational and industrial structure of the demand for labour are not matched by equivalent changes in the structure of the supply of labour.

Real-wage unemployment occurs when the real product wage is so high that firms close down and hence leave labour unemployed. Demand-deficient unemployment is due to a lack of sufficient demand to raise equilibrium income to potential income.

3 The measured unemployment rate overstates unemployment because some people may be eligible to claim unemployment benefits while having withdrawn from the labour force, and because others claim benefits while working surreptitiously. It understates true involuntary unemployment by recording only those eligible for unemployment benefits rather than all those who would be willing to work at the going wage rate if jobs were available.

4 Frictional unemployment can be reduced by reducing the amount of time taken between jobs.

5 Structural unemployment can be reduced by measures that increase the degree of labour mobility between regions, occupations and industries. Measures that attempt to reduce structural unemployment by reducing the amount of structural change in the economy are self-defeating in the long run.

6 Real-wage unemployment can be removed by lowering the real product wage, adopting expansionary fiscal and monetary policies to offset the expenditure-decreasing effects of lower wages, and waiting until new plants are built to employ a higher ratio of labour to capital.

7 Demand-deficient unemployment can be removed by using the tools of demand management to raise equilibrium national income to its potential level.

Inflation

This chapter deals with the important topic of inflation. As a preparation, the introductory material in Chapter 25 on the price level that begins on page 302 must be reread.

The analysis of this chapter builds on what you learned in Chapter 38 on aggregate demand and aggregate supply. Indeed, much of the early analysis of the initial effects of demand and supply shocks repeats what we studied in that earlier chapter. We repeat it here, rather than merely referring you back, because the review should be helpful and because the later analysis of sustained inflations builds on the study of isolated demand-side and supply-side shocks that we first cover.

Definition of Inflation

Any increase in the general price level can be called an INFLATION, and any decrease a DEFLATION. Two types of change can be distinguished. First, there are once-and-for-all shocks that cause a temporary burst of inflation as the general price level changes from one equilibrium level to another. Second, there are sustained shocks that cause the price level to change continually, giving rise to a sustained inflation. The distinction is important; the choice of words used to describe it are only a matter of convenience. We call all increases in the price level inflations, and distinguish between *once-and-for-all* or *transitory* bursts of inflation, and *sustained* inflation.[1]

---

1 Other economists have reserved the term inflation for sustained changes in the price level and have used other words, such as a *rise in the price level*, to refer to once-and-for-all changes. As long as one understands the distinction, the choice of words used to describe it is not a substantial matter.

Causes of Inflation

We first take a detailed look at the various possible causes of inflation. These are classified under two main headings, demand-side causes and supply-side causes. To begin our study of these we need to make some important distinctions.

Some important distinctions

Anything that tends to drive the price level upwards is often referred to as an inflationary shock, while anything that tends to drive the price level downwards is often referred to as a deflationary shock. We start by making three important distinctions concerning these shocks.

- Inflations that are caused by shifts in aggregate demand – which are referred to as demand-side shocks – must be distinguished from inflations that are caused by shifts in aggregate supply – which are referred to as supply-side shocks.
- Isolated demand- or supply-side shocks must be distinguished from repeated shocks.
- Increases in the price level that take place when the money supply is held constant must be distinguished from those that take place when the money supply is being increased at the rate at which the price level is rising. When an increase in the money supply accompanies supply-side shocks, the resulting inflation is said to be ACCOMMODATED by the monetary expansion; when a money supply increase accompanies demand-side shocks, the resulting inflation is said to be VALIDATED by the monetary expansion.

We first consider supply-side shocks and then go on

to consider demand-side shocks. We consider supply-side causes first because we shall need some of what we learn about the supply side in order to analyse demand-side causes completely.

Supply-Shock Inflation

When an inflation is caused by supply-side shocks, it is called a *supply-shock inflation*, a *supply-side inflation* or, most commonly, a COST-PUSH INFLATION. Such an inflation is defined as any rise in the price level originating from increases in costs *that were not brought about by excess demands in the markets for factors of production*. Examples are a rise in the cost of imported raw materials, and a rise in wage rates caused by the exercise of union power in the absence of any excess demand for labour.

Once-and-for-all supply shocks

The initial effects of a single cost-push shock were already analysed in Figure 38.7 on page 463.[1] Since these effects are important, we repeat the analysis in Figure 41.1. The original curves are *AD* and *SRAS*, which produce an equilibrium income and price level of Y_F and P_0. A rise in costs now occurs – say, a general increase in wage rates achieved by a particularly aggressive round of union bargaining. This shifts the short-run aggregate supply curve upwards from *SRAS* to *SRAS'* in the Figure. As a result, equilibrium income falls from Y_F to Y_1, while the price level rises from P_0 to P_1.

Thus, we note once again that the initial effect of a supply-side shock is to cause stagflation: the price level rises while national income falls. What happens next depends on how the monetary authorities react. Do they accommodate the supply-shock inflation or do they not?

No Monetary Accommodation: In this case the money supply is held constant, so that the aggregate demand curve remains at *AD*. What then happens

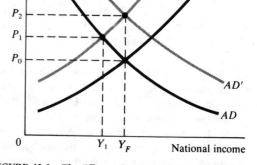

FIGURE 41.1 The Effects of a Supply-Side Shock. Initially equilibrium income falls while the equilibrium price level rises

depends on the behaviour of costs of production.

We have seen that the supply-side shock increases the price level and lowers equilibrium income. If wages and other costs do not fall, even in the face of excess supply – i.e. if there is complete downward inflexibility of costs – that is the end of the story. The economy remains in the equilibrium given by the curves *AD* and *SRAS'* in Figure 41.1.

The case of some downward flexibility of money wages, and other money costs, has already been analysed in Figure 38.11 on page 467. Again, however, we repeat it here because of its importance. If there is some downward flexibility of money wages and other money costs, the output gap of $Y_F - Y_1$ in Figure 41.1 will cause these costs to fall. This shifts the *SRAS* curve downwards, increasing equilibrium income while reducing the price level. As long as wages and other costs fall whenever there is excess supply, this continues until the *SRAS* curve has been restored to its initial position. Then equilibrium income is returned to Y_F and the price level to its initial value of P_0. *Given the fact, noted in Chapter 38, that money wage costs fall only slowly (if at all) in the face of excess supply, the recovery to full employment will take a very long time.*

Monetary Accommodation: Now let us see what happens if the money supply is changed in response to the isolated supply shock. This takes us beyond what we have previously studied.

The initial supply-side shock established the short-run equilibrium of Y_1 and P_1. Now suppose the Bank

---

1 Notice that we have stylized the *SRAS* curve by giving it a nearly constant upward slope. This makes the Figure easier to follow than if we had given it the more accurate slope shown in Figure 38.4. We can do this because all that matters in the subsequent analysis is the upward slope. If we wished to analyse the *proportions* in which Y and P were changing in response to various shocks, we would need to use a more accurate *SRAS* curve that was quite flat below potential income and quite steep above it.

of England reacts to the recessionary gap by increasing the money supply. We know that such an increase works through the monetary transmission mechanism to shift the aggregate desired expenditure curve to the right. (This process is outlined in Figure 36.4 on page 437.) This increases the equilibrium level of national income associated with any given price level and thus shifts the aggregate demand curve to the right.

The rise in aggregate demand causes both the price level and output to rise, as equilibrium moves along the fixed aggregate supply curve *SRAS'*. A sufficiently large increase in the money supply will shift the *AD* curve to *AD'*. This eliminates the output gap completely by restoring full-employment income Y_F, but it also further increases the price level to P_2. We have now reached an important conclusion: *monetary accommodation of an isolated supply shock can restore full employment, but at the cost of a further increase in the price level* (from P_1 to P_2 in Figure 41.1). Nonetheless, the monetary authorities might decide to accommodate the supply shock because, if they rely on wage deflation, an extended slump will ensue.

Repeated supply shocks

So far we have considered the effects of a single supply-shock inflation, distinguishing between the case in which the shock is, and is not, accommodated. We now consider the case of repeated supply shocks. Let us assume that powerful unions are able to push up money wages year after year, even when there is a recessionary gap. Since the cost push is due to wage increases, this case is often referred to as WAGE-COST-PUSH INFLATION.

What happens next depends on how the Bank reacts to this behaviour.

No Monetary Accommodation: The case in which the Bank does not accommodate these shocks is shown in Figure 41.2. Just as in Figure 41.1, the initial supply shock shifts the *SRAS* curve to *SRAS'*, and this lowers equilibrium income from Y_F to Y_1 while raising the price level from P_0 to P_1.

If unions continue to negotiate increases in wages, subjecting the economy to further supply shocks, the aggregate supply curve will rise to *SRAS''*, then to *SRAS'''*, and so on. This takes equilibrium upwards along the fixed *AD* curve in Figure 41.2, with income falling to Y_2, Y_3 and so on, while the price level rises to P_2, P_3 and so on. In other words, the stagflation

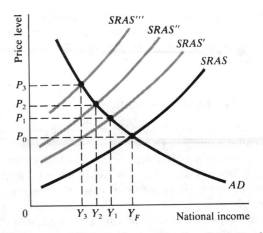

FIGURE 41.2   A Repeated, Non-Accommodated Supply Shock. The price level rises continually in the face of a growing output gap

continues with the price level rising while national income is falling.

If unions continue with their wage-cost push, *and the AD curve remains fixed*, the process will eventually drive national income towards zero. Long before this happens, however, everyone will come to realize that the rising wages in the face of unchanging demand are the cause of the falling employment. In other words, unions face a trade-off between wages and employment – they can have more of one only if they accept less of the other.

Might not really powerful unions continue to force wages up despite this realization? As long as they do so, the output gap will go on growing until, finally, unemployment reaches 100 per cent. Of course, this will not happen because, long before everyone is unemployed, unions will cease forcing up wages in order to maintain jobs for those who are still employed.

Once the wage-cost push ceases, there are two possible developments. First, the unions may succeed in holding onto their high wages, although they do not push for further increases. The economy then comes to rest with a stable price level and a large output gap. If, for example, the wage-cost push ceased when the *SRAS* curve had reached *SRAS'''* in Figure 41.2, the economy would come to rest at national income Y_3 and a price level of P_3. Second, the persistent unemployment may eventually erode the power of the unions, so that wages begin to fall. In this case, the supply shock is reversed, and the *SRAS* curve starts to shift downward. If money wages

continue to fall as long as an output gap exists, the SRAS curve will shift to SRAS'', then to SRAS', and finally back to SRAS. At that point, full employment has been restored and the price level has returned to its original value of P_0. Once again, it should be noted that the very slow pace with which wages fall, even in the face of very heavy excess supply, means that this adjustment process would at best take a very long time – and at worst it might never be completed.

The conclusion is that unaccommodated supply-shock inflations caused by wage-cost push have natural correctives, both in the restraining pressures of rising unemployment on further wage push and in the possible erosion of the power of unions to hold wages above the level that would produce full employment. But these correctives may take a very long time to operate and, hence, a wage-cost push can cause a long and sustained inflation and recession.

Monetary Accommodation: Now suppose that the Bank accommodates the initial supply shock with an increase in the money supply, thus shifting the aggregate demand curve to the right. This is just what we showed in Figure 41.1. There the initial equilibrium was at Y_F and P_0; the shift in the supply curve to SRAS' took equilibrium to Y_1 and P_1; and the monetary accommodation took equilibrium income and the price level back to Y_F and to P_2. This case is shown again in Figure 41.3, which duplicates the curves SRAS, SRAS', AD and AD' from Figure 41.1.

In the new full-employment equilibrium of Y_F and P_2 (point a in the Figure), both money wages and money prices have risen. The rise in money wages has been fully offset by a rise in prices. Workers are no better off than they were originally at Y_F and P_0 – although those who remained in jobs were better off in the transition period, after wages had risen but before the price level had risen from P_1 to P_2.

The stage is now set for the unions to try again. If they succeed in negotiating a further increase in money wages, they will hit the economy with another supply shock. If the Bank again accommodates the shock, full employment is maintained but at the cost of a further round of inflation. If this process goes on continuously, it can give rise to a continuous wage-cost-push inflation. The wage-cost push tends to cause stagflation, with rising prices and falling income. Monetary accommodation tends to reinforce the rise in the price level to offset the fall in income.

This process is illustrated in Figure 41.3. The

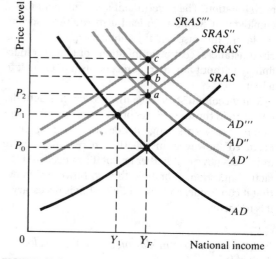

FIGURE 41.3 A Repeated Cost-Push Accommodated by Monetary Expansion. The price level rises continuously while income holds constant

second round of wage-cost push takes the aggregate supply curve to SRAS'', while the second round of monetary accommodation takes the aggregate demand curve to AD''. The next round of wage push takes the aggregate supply curve to SRAS''' while the accompanying round of monetary accommodation takes the aggregate demand curve to AD'''. If this process continues, with the monetary accommodation more or less synchronized with the wage-cost push, the inflation can go on indefinitely with national income remaining at its full-employment level. Successive equilibrium points are at a, b, c, and so on.

So now we know the two things that are required for wage-cost-push inflation to continue. First, powerful unions must ask for, and employers must grant, increases in money wages, even in the absence of excess demand for labour and goods. Second, the central bank must accommodate the resulting inflation by increasing the money supply and so prevent the falling income that would otherwise occur.

Is wage-cost-push inflation a real possibility?

As far back as the 1940s, early Keynesians were worried that, once the government was committed to maintaining full employment, much of the discipline of the market would be removed from wage bargains. They felt that the scramble of every group trying to get ahead of other groups would lead to a wage-cost-

push inflation. The government's commitment to full employment would then lead it to engineer accommodating increases in the money supply. In these circumstances, cost-push inflation could go on indefinitely without any market mechanism to bring it to a halt.

Many economists believe this process has actually occurred in those countries of Western Europe where unions are very strong. It does not seem to have occurred, however, in the US where unions have much less power. Whether or not it has occurred is a factual question. Economic theory, however, shows that it can occur, and also shows what is necessary if it is to occur.

Is monetary accommodation of supply shocks desirable?

Once started, the spiral of wage-price-wage increases can be halted only if the Bank stops accommodating the shocks. The longer it waits to do so, the more ingrained will be the expectations that the Bank will continue to accommodate. Many economists believe that these firmly held expectations will make wages more resistant to downward pressure arising from unemployment. Thus, if the government ever stops accommodating the wage-cost-push inflation, the *AD* curve will stop shifting upwards but the *SRAS* curve will continue to do so as unions carry on with their customary behaviour. Now we enter a phase analysed in Figure 41.2, with rising prices and rising unemployment. If the wage-cost-push habit is firmly entrenched, a very deep recession may have to develop before it ceases so that the *SRAS* curve can be stabilized.

Hence, the argument runs, it is best never to let the process of an accommodated wage-cost-push inflation get started. One way to ensure this is to refuse to accommodate any supply shock whatsoever. *To some people, caution dictates that no supply shocks be accommodated lest a wage-price spiral be set up. Others would be willing to risk accommodating obviously isolated shocks in order to avoid the severe and prolonged recessions that otherwise accompany them.*

At the conclusion of Chapter 31 we posed the question: why would any government that could control aggregate demand voluntarily accept anything less than full-employment income? We now have one reason. A government may be committed to controlling inflation and be worried about the outbreak of wage-cost-push inflation as a result of a

commitment to full employment. In these circumstances, it may refuse to accommodate supply-side shocks lest it set up the process shown in Figure 41.3. Because of the refusal to accommodate, the economy may come to rest at a position such as Y_1 and P_1 in Figure 41.3. Only if the output gap forces money wages down will full employment be established.

We may or may not agree with this policy – our assessment of it will depend, among other things, on our judgements about the relative social and economic costs of inflation and unemployment – but at least we can now understand part of its rationale.

Demand-Shock Inflation

When an inflation is caused by demand shocks, it is called a *demand-shock inflation*, or a *demand-side inflation*. The two most commonly used terms, however, are DEMAND-PULL INFLATION or, more simply, DEMAND INFLATION. It is defined as any inflation that is caused by general excess demand in the economy's markets for final goods and for factors of production. Demand inflation occurs when a demand shock causes aggregate demand to exceed aggregate supply at full-employment income.

The initial phases of a demand inflation were analysed in Figure 38.9 but we repeat the analysis in Figure 41.4 because of its importance. The original curves are *AD* and *SRAS*. They produce an original

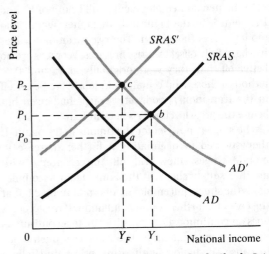

FIGURE 41.4 A Non-Validated Demand-Side Shock. Initially, national income and the price level rise; then the price level rises further while income returns to its potential level

equilibrium at the point labelled a, with income of Y_F and a price level of P_0.

The aggregate demand curve now shifts to the right. This shift could have occurred for either of two quite distinct sets of reasons. First, it may have been caused by an autonomous increase in aggregate desired expenditure. The desired amount of expenditure on consumption, investment, government purchases, or net exports that is associated with each level of national income may have increased. Second, there may have been an increase in the money supply. As we saw in Chapter 36, an increase in the money supply works through the monetary transmission mechanism – excess supply of money, higher price of bonds, lower interest rates, increased investment expenditure – to shift the aggregate desired expenditure curve, and hence the aggregate demand curve, upwards.

The demand shock shifts the aggregate demand curve in Figure 41.4 from AD to AD'. The initial effect of this shift is for equilibrium national income to increase to Y_1 and the price level to rise to P_1 (point b).

But this is not the end of the story. The rise in the price level to P_1 is a reaction of the goods market to the excess demand created when the aggregate demand curve shifts from AD to AD'. The $SRAS$ curve is, however, based on a given set of factor prices. The excess demand associated with income Y_1 will cause wages to rise, and this will shift the $SRAS$ curve upwards. Note that the rise in wage costs is not now the result of an exogenous wage-cost push. Instead, it is a rise of wage costs as a result of general excess demand. The rise in wages and other costs, in the face of general excess demand, begins to shift the $SRAS$ curve upward. What happens next depends on whether or not the demand shock is validated.

No Monetary Validation: The upward shift in the $SRAS$ curve raises the price level above P_1. As long as the Bank holds the money supply constant, the rise in the price level brings the monetary adjustment mechanism into play: the economy moves upward to the left along the fixed aggregate demand curve AD'. This rise in the price level acts to reduce the inflationary gap. Eventually the gap is eliminated as equilibrium is established at a higher, but stable, price level, with income returned to its potential level. In this case, the initial period of positive inflation is followed by further inflation that lasts only until the new equilibrium is reached.

This is shown in Figure 41.4 by the upward shift in

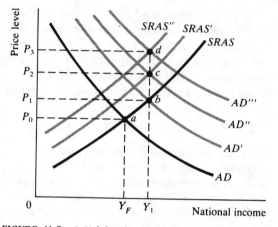

FIGURE 41.5 **A Validated Demand-Shock Inflation.** The inflationary gap persists while the price level rises continuously

the $SRAS$ curve to $SRAS'$, which takes equilibrium income back to Y_F and the equilibrium price level further upwards to P_2 (point c).

Monetary Validation: Next suppose that, following a demand shock that created an inflationary gap, the Bank frustrates the monetary adjustment mechanism by increasing the money supply when output starts to fall. Two forces are now brought into play. The wage increases that are fuelled by excess demand cause the $SRAS$ curve to shift upward. The monetary expansion causes the aggregate demand curve to shift upward. As a result, the price level rises but income need not fall. Indeed, if the shift in the aggregate demand curve exactly offsets the shift in the $SRAS$ curve, the inflationary gap will remain constant.

This process is shown in Figure 41.5. As before, the initial equilibrium is at a and the initial demand shock takes the short-run equilibrium to b. But now, as the $SRAS$ curve starts to shift upwards, the validating increase in the money supply means that the AD curve is shifted to the right, frustrating the monetary adjustment mechanism. When the $SRAS$ curve has reached $SRAS'$, the money supply is increased sufficiently to take the AD curve to AD''. Equilibrium is then at c. When the $SRAS$ curve reaches $SRAS''$, AD is shifted to AD'''. Equilibrium is then at d, with income still at Y_1, but with a price level of P_3. This takes the economy on the path of a continuously rising price level and a persistent inflationary gap. In other words, there is a sustained inflation.

We have now reached a very important conclusion: validation of an initial demand shock turns what would have been a transitory inflation into a sustained inflation fuelled by monetary expansion. The subsequent shifts in the *AD* curve that perpetuate the inflationary gap are caused by monetary forces.

Inflation as a Monetary Phenomenon

There has sometimes been heated debate among economists about the extent to which inflation is a monetary phenomenon with purely monetary causes – i.e. changes in the supply of (or demand for) money – and purely monetary consequences – i.e. only the price level is affected by inflation. One slogan by economists who have taken an extreme position on this issue is that 'inflation is *everywhere* and *always* a monetary phenomenon'.

In order to consider these issues, let us summarize what we have learned. First, look at the *causes* of inflation:

(1) We have seen that many forces can cause the price level to rise. On the demand side, anything that shifts the *AD* curve to the right will cause the price level to rise. This covers the expenditure changes of an autonomous increase in *I* and *G* (and an upward shift in the *C* and $(X-M)$ functions) and the monetary changes of an increase in the supply of money, or a decrease in the demand of money, on the monetary side. On the supply side, anything that increases costs of production will shift the *SRAS* curve upwards and cause the price level to rise.

(2) We have also seen that such inflations can continue for some time without being validated or accommodated by increases in the money supply.

(3) Furthermore, we have seen that the rise in prices must eventually come to a halt unless monetary expansion occurs.

Points (1) and (2) provide the sense in which a temporary burst of inflation need not be a monetary phenomenon. It need not have monetary causes, and it need not be accompanied by monetary expansion. Point (3) explains the sense in which a sustained inflation must be a monetary phenomenon. If a rise in prices is to go on continuously, it must be accompanied by continuing increases in the money supply. This is true regardless of the cause that set it in motion.

Second, let us look at the *consequences* of an inflation:

(4) We have seen that, in the short run, a demand-shock inflation tends to be accompanied by an increase in national income above its potential level.

(5) We have seen that, in the short run, a supply-shock inflation tends to be accompanied by a decrease in national income below its potential level.

(6) We have also seen that, when all adjustments are fully made so that the relevant supply-side curve is the *LRAS* curve, shifts in *AD* or *SRAS* leave national income unchanged and only affect the price level.

Points (4) and (5) provide the sense in which inflation *is not*, in the short term, a purely monetary phenomenon. Point (6) provides the sense in which inflation *is*, in the long run, a purely monetary phenomenon. We have now reached some important conclusions.

- Without monetary accommodation, supply shocks cause temporary bursts of inflation accompanied by recessionary gaps. The gaps are removed if and when wages fall, restoring equilibrium at potential income and at the initial price level.

- Without monetary validation, demand shocks cause temporary bursts of inflation accompanied by inflationary gaps. The gaps are removed as wages rise, returning income to its potential level but at a higher price level.

- With an appropriate response from the Bank, an inflation, initiated by supply or demand shocks, can continue indefinitely: an ever-increasing money supply is necessary for an ever-continuing inflation.

Some Confusions Resolved

The distinction between changes in aggregate demand and in aggregate supply as causes of inflation allows us to resolve some persistent confusions. Let us consider two.

Price Rises do Choke off Excess Demand, *Ceteris Paribus*:   The proposition just stated is sometimes denied. The denial is usually based on the argument that rises in the general price level do not choke off excess demand because labour's reaction is merely to demand higher wages, which means higher incomes, which means higher demand. Let us see what is wrong with this idea.

Assume that there is an inflationary gap such as is shown by point *b* in Figure 41.4. A rise in wages, as well as in all other money incomes, shifts the *SRAS* curve upwards. As long as the money supply is held

constant, the equilibrium moves along the fixed aggregate demand curve, AD', until it reaches point c. At that point, the excess demand has been eliminated.

Thus the removal of excess demand through a rise in the price level does not depend on what happens to wages and prices, but on what happens to the money supply. If the money supply is held constant, the rise in the price level brings the monetary adjustment mechanism into play. The transactions demand for money rises, interest rates rise, interest-sensitive expenditure falls and aggregate desired expenditure falls. This reduces equilibrium national income, as shown by a movement upwards, and to the left, along a fixed AD curve.

Raising Interest Rates is a Part of Most Successful Anti-Inflation Policies: This proposition is frequently denied, whenever a tight monetary policy is instituted. It is noted that, although rising interest rates may reduce demand, they also increase costs and hence drive up prices, and it is then asserted that the two effects offset each other.

To see what is wrong with this argument, consider a continuing inflation such as the one illustrated in Figure 41.5. Costs are rising and driving the $SRAS$ curve leftwards. But the inflation is being validated by a monetary expansion so that the AD curve is shifting rightwards. The two shifts are offsetting each other, so that the price level is rising and the inflationary gap is holding constant at $Y_1 - Y_F$.

Now, when the economy is at point c, let the Bank institute a tight monetary policy. For purposes of illustration, say it holds the money supply completely constant. This fixes the aggregate demand curve at AD''. The tight monetary policy will indeed cause a money shortage as the price level rises further, and this will indeed drive interest rates upwards. The rising interest rates are a sign that the monetary validation has stopped and must be expected, therefore, to accompany any successful policy aimed at slowing inflation.

If interest rates enter into current costs of production, this will in turn help to drive the $SRAS$ curve upwards. But because the AD curve is being held constant, the rising costs shift the equilibrium upwards *and to the left* along a fixed aggregate demand curve. The result is that the excess demand is eliminated. The rise in interest rates confers a *once-and-for-all* increase in costs and therefore a *once-and-for-all* upward shift in the $SRAS$ curve. But they also are a necessary accompaniment to the tight mone-

tary policy that stops the AD curve from shifting upwards *continuously*, since a one-time upward shift in the $SRAS$ curve that permits the ending of a continual upward shift in the AD curve is indeed anti-inflationary.

The key point to understand in both of the above fallacious arguments is that it does not matter how much the $SRAS$ curve shifts upward as long as the AD curve does not also shift upwards. As long as the AD curve can be held constant (or allowed to shift upwards by less than the $SRAS$ curve shifts), excess demand will be reduced.

Inflation, Savings, and Investment

Before we move on to the second part of this chapter, we need to digress for a moment to consider the relation between inflation, savings and investment. One of the things we have learned in Part 4 and Part 5 is that the effects often differ greatly between the short run, when aggregate demand exerts the dominant force on income, and the long run, when aggregate supply is the dominant force. This general lesson turns out to be applicable to both saving and investment.

Saving

We saw in Chapter 39 that, in the short run, saving tends to reduce national income by reducing aggregate expenditure while, in the long run, it tends to increase national income whenever those savings find their way into productive investment.

Saving Affects Inflation: An increase in savings tends to reduce the pressure of inflation in the short run by reducing desired aggregate expenditure and thus shifting the aggregate demand curve to the left. In the long run, it also has an effect on reducing inflationary pressures if it results in investment that shifts the $LRAS$ curve to the right.

Inflation Affects Saving: But what of the reverse influence – i.e. that of inflation on saving? The dominant influence here is that inflation reduces the value of all wealth that is denominated in money terms. For example, a bond with a £1,000 redemption value would lose half of its real value in terms of purchasing power if the price level should double. So inflation reduces the real value of that part of people's wealth that is denominated in money terms. If people

try to maintain their real wealth in the face of this inflationary erosion, they will increase their savings. This is one of the reasons why the volume of saving usually rises as the inflation rate rises.

Investment

Investment Affects Inflation: On the investment side, similar considerations apply. An increase in investment adds to aggregate demand in the short run and, hence, tends to add to inflationary pressures. But in the long run, investment adds to productive capacity and, by shifting the *LRAS* curve outwards, tends to alleviate inflationary pressures.

Inflation Affects Investment: As with saving, inflation tends to influence the amount of investment expenditure. For instance, when income-tax laws allow depreciation only on the historical rather than the replacement cost of capital, inflation acts as a tax on real capital unless offset by other compensating measures. If, for example, the price level doubles, a firm must put aside twice as much money just to replace its existing capital stock as it wears out. But tax laws usually allow depreciation to be deducted as a cost only on the basis of the orginal money price of the capital equipment. Therefore, the additional sums needed just to maintain capital must first be reported as profits, then taxed, then saved. So inflation, by taxing capital, tends to reduce real profits and makes less available for investment.

Because of inflation, recorded investment must be increased just to hold one's own against shrinking real values. As a result, a lot of what is really replacement investment shows up in the national accounts as new investment, merely because some accounting procedures do not easily handle changes that inflation causes in the real value of assets denominated in monetary units.

The above are only two of the links between investment and inflation. Depending on other provisions in the tax laws, inflation may exert other pressures to increase or decrease investment. All we seek to establish here is that inflation certainly does influence investment, but in different ways at different times.

This concludes our study of the basics of inflation. In the rest of this chapter, we go behind the *SRAS* curve to study the speed with which that curve shifts in the face of inflationary or recessionary gaps. We do this by studying a remarkable relationship called the Phillips curve.

THE PHILLIPS CURVE, OR HOW FAST DOES THE *SRAS* CURVE SHIFT?

We have seen that when the short-run equilibrium level of national income is not at its potential level, the *SRAS* curve tends to shift due to changes in input prices. When there is an inflationary gap, demand pressures in factor markets tend to push up input prices and shift the *SRAS* curve upwards. When there is a recessionary gap, demand pressures in factor markets tend to push input prices down and shift the *SRAS* curve downwards.

We have also stated that input prices can rise very rapidly when there is excess demand but that they tend to fall only very slowly when there is excess supply. On page 466 we called this the second asymmetry in the behaviour of aggregate supply. (The first asymmetry is in the shape of the *SRAS* curve, flat to the left of Y_F and steep to the right of it.)

The Nature of the Phillips Curve

In the 1950s, the late Professor A.W. Phillips was doing research on stabilization policy. He was interested in the question of the speed with which input costs responded to excess demand and excess supply. To study this question, he looked at the rate of change of money wage rates in the UK over a period of 100 years. By relating these wage changes to the level of unemployment, he discovered a remarkable relationship that came to be known as the Phillips curve.

The PHILLIPS CURVE refers to a graphed relationship between the rate of change of money wage rates and the rate of unemployment. The level of unemployment is plotted on the horizontal axis and the rate of increase in money wage rates on the vertical axis. Thus, any point on the curve relates a particular level of unemployment to a particular rate of increase of money wages. (It is important to understand that the vertical axis of the Phillips curve measures increases in *wage rates* and not increases in the general *price level* of goods and services; the two are, of course, related and we explain the relevance of each below.)

A numerical example of a Phillips curve is shown in Figure 41.6. We stress that the numbers on the Figure are hypothetical – although they are not totally unrealistic.[1] This is a new and unfamiliar type

---

1 See Harbury and Lipsey, Chapter 9, for some real data on the Phillips curve relationships.

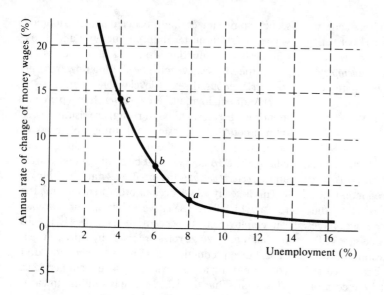

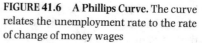

FIGURE 41.6   **A Phillips Curve.** The curve relates the unemployment rate to the rate of change of money wages

of curve, so a numerical example may help you to understand what it shows the first time you see it. In this example, point *a* on the curve shows that an 8 per cent unemployment rate is associated with an increase in money wages of 3 per cent per year.

The Phillips curve must be carefully distinguished from the *SRAS* curve. The *SRAS* curve has the price *level* on the vertical axis. The Phillips curve does not have the *level* of money wages on the vertical axis; instead its vertical axis plots the *annual rate of change* of money wage rates.

The shape of the Phillips curve

A Negative Slope: Note first that the Phillips curve has a negative slope, showing that the lower is the level of unemployment, the higher is the rate of change of money wages. This should not surprise us, since low rates of unemployment are associated with boom conditions when excess demand for labour will be bidding money wages up rapidly. High rates of unemployment, on the other hand, are associated with slump conditions when the slack demand for labour will lead to low increases in money wages, or possibly even to decreases.

A Flattening Slope: Moving along it from left to right, the Phillips curve gets flatter. This shape of the curve is a reflection of the second asymmetry of the behaviour of aggregate supply that we mentioned above – namely that input prices change more rapidly upwards than downwards. Let us see why.

First, assume that a growing boom is increasing the excess demand for labour. As the boom develops, the unemployment rate will decrease towards, but never reach, zero (there will always be *some* frictional unemployment). At the same time, the growing excess demand for labour will be bidding up wage rates more and more rapidly. This behaviour is shown when the Phillips curve gets very steep and lies far above the axis at its left-hand end. The further is the curve above the axis, the faster are wages rising. In Figure 41.6, a fall in unemployment from 8 to 6 to 4 per cent increases the rate at which wages are rising from 3 to 7 to 14 per cent (points *a* to *b* to *c*). By the time that unemployment has fallen as low as 4 per cent, wages are rising at a very rapid rate of 14 per cent per year, and it is clear that further small cuts in unemployment will increase the rate of wage inflation very much. The steepness of the curve in this range shows that even a very small reduction in unemployment will lead to a large increase in the rate of wage inflation.

Second, consider a growing recession that raises unemployment. This recession restrains wage increases. As a result, the Phillips curve comes closer and closer to the horizontal axis, indicating less and less upwards pressure on wages at higher and higher levels of unemployment. If the curve fell below the axis, then money wages would actually be falling at the associated levels of unemployment. We do not show this case in the Figure but assume that, as unemployment gets very large, the increase in money wages approaches zero but never becomes negative.

As unemployment rises from 8 to 10 to 12 per cent in the Figure, wages go from a 3 to a 2 to a $1\frac{1}{2}$ per cent annual rate of increase. *The flatness of the curve over this range shows that it takes a larger rise in unemployment to reduce the rate of wage inflation even slightly.*

The Phillips curve and unit labour costs

We have seen in earlier chapters that increases in costs of inputs increase unit costs of production and thus cause the SRAS curve to shift upwards. To see what is happening to unit costs of production, we need to relate the increase in wage rates to the increase in labour productivity (which we have earlier defined as output per unit of labour employed). For simplicity in the rest of the discussion, we will assume that labour is the only variable factor used by the firm. This allows us to associate the labour costs of each unit of output with total variable costs per unit of output. (We could equally well assume that all input prices change at the same rate as does the price of labour.)

What happens to unit costs of production now depends only on the *difference* between what labour costs the firm and what labour produces for the firm. Let us see why.

Assume, for example, that labour is *paid* 10 per cent more per hour but that it also *produces* 10 per cent more per hour. In this case, the firm's costs of production per unit of output – its unit costs of production – are unchanged. In general, unit costs of production rise if wage rates rise faster than productivity is rising, and fall if wages rise more slowly than productivity is rising. Thus, for example, a 5 per cent increase in money wage rates combined with a 3 per cent increase in labour productivity means a 2 per cent increase in unit costs of production, while the same increase in productivity combined with only a 1 per cent increase in money wage rates means a 2 per cent *decrease* in unit costs of production.

To illustrate what is involved, we repeat in Figure 41.7(i) the Phillips curve from Figure 41.6 and add to it a horizontal line labelled *g*, for growth in output per hour of labour input, which shows the rate at which labour productivity is growing year by year. In the hypothetical example of the Figure, we have assumed that productivity is rising at 3 per cent per year.

The intersection of the Phillips curve and the productivity line at the point *x* now divides the graph into an inflationary and a deflationary range.

(1) At unemployment rates lower than the inter-

section point – lower than 8 per cent in our example – wages are rising faster than productivity and, thus, unit costs of production are rising. If unit costs are rising, the SRAS curve must be shifting upwards and so, *ceteris paribus*, the price level will be rising.

(2) At unemployment rates greater than 8 per cent, money wage rates, although rising, are rising slower than productivity is rising and, thus, unit costs of production are *falling*. If unit costs of production are falling, the SRAS curve must be shifting downwards, and so, *ceteris paribus*, the price level must be falling.

This is really all we need in order to determine the rate at which the SRAS curve is shifting. For example, if unemployment is 6 per cent, then Figure 41.7(i) tells us that money wage rates are rising by 7 per cent per year. Since productivity is rising at 3 per cent, unit costs are rising at approximately 4 per cent per year. This means that the SRAS curve is shifting upwards at that rate. To take a second example, let unemployment be 12 per cent. Now money wages are rising at $1\frac{1}{2}$ per cent. Combined with a 3 per cent increase in labour productivity, this means a $1\frac{1}{2}$ *decrease* in unit

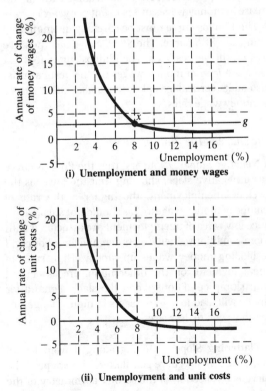

(i) Unemployment and money wages

(ii) Unemployment and unit costs

FIGURE 41.7 The Rate of Change of Money Wages and the Rate of Change of Unit Costs. Unemployment is negatively related to changes in wages and to changes in unit costs

costs of production. This means that the *SRAS* curve will be shifting downwards at that rate.

Notice that, although we have assumed downward inflexibility of money wages, this does *not* imply complete downward inflexibility of prices. As long as money wages rise less than productivity rises, then unit costs of production will be falling, and the *SRAS* curve will be shifting downwards. Complete downward inflexibility of prices – and thus the total absence of the equilibrating mechanism that comes from downward shifts in the *SRAS* curve – requires more than the downward inflexibility of money wages; it requires that money wages *never* rise by *less than* the increase in productivity, so that unit costs of production can never fall.

From a Phillips Curve to a Unit Labour Cost Curve[1]

The above is all we need to see how fast the *SRAS* curve is shifting and to see why it can shift upwards very quickly but downwards only slowly. Nonetheless, it may be worthwhile deriving from the Phillips curve a new curve that expresses in a Figure the verbal argument that we have just given. Let us see how this can be done.

First, we plot in Figure 41.7(ii) a new curve that relates the rate of unemployment not to the increase in money wage rates but to the increase in unit output costs. The new curve still measures unemployment on the horizontal axis, but it now measures the rate of increase in unit output costs on the vertical axis. Since the rate of increase in unit costs is merely the rate of increase in wage rates *minus* the rate of increase of productivity, the new diagram is just the same as Figure 41.7(i) except that the origin on the vertical axis has been shifted by the rate of productivity increase (3 per cent in this case). In other words, the only difference between the two parts of the Figure is that the Phillips curve has been shifted downwards by the rate of productivity growth – 3 per cent in this case.

To show the relation between the two curves, they are plotted one under the other so that they can be compared. It is clear, for example, that the level of unemployment where the Phillips curve cuts the productivity line in part (i) – wage increases equal productivity increases – is the same as when the rate

of change in unit costs curve cuts the horizontal axis – unit costs are neither rising nor falling.

The new curve tells us the rate at which unit costs of production are changing – and thus the rate at which the *SRAS* curve is shifting upwards – at each level of unemployment. But we are still plotting unemployment on the horizontal axis, while the *SRAS* curve plots national income. To get a curve that relates the change in unit costs of production to the level of national income, we merely observe that unemployment tends to be negatively related to the level of national income. As national income rises, unemployment tends to fall.

To make the relation precise, we assume that the labour force remains constant. Now, any short-run increase in national income, which means more labour is employed, must mean that less labour is unemployed. In this case, any *increase* in national income must mean a *decrease* in unemployment.

As a result of the relation just described, we can transform Figure 41.7(ii), which plots the rate of increase in unit costs of production against the *unemployment rate*, into a new relation, shown in Figure 41.8, which plots the same rate of increase in unit costs of production, but now against the level of national income. Since national income and unemployment vary negatively with each other, the curve in Figure 41.8 has the opposite slope to the curve in Figure 41.7(ii).

The upward shift in the SRAS curve explained

Figure 41.9 draws the familiar aggregate demand– aggregate supply diagram in part (i). Part (ii) shows the curve relating the rate of change of unit

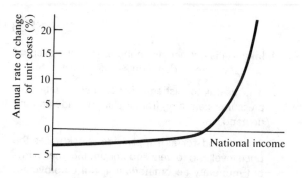

FIGURE 41.8   The Rate of Change in Unit Costs Related to National Income. Unit costs rise when national income exceeds potential income and fall when national income is less than potential income

costs to national income. Both parts have national income on their horizontal axes, and by lining these up we can compare one with the other.

Let the economy begin with the curves AD and $SRAS$, which produce long-run equilibrium with a stable price level, P_0, and full-employment income Y_F. The economy is also on its $LRAS$ curve.

Now let the aggregate demand curve shift to AD', taking national income to its new short-run equilibrium of Y_1. Part (ii) shows us that at income Y_1 unit costs will be rising at a rate of c_1 per cent per year. This means the $SRAS$ curve will be shifting upwards at that rate (not shown in the Figure). As it does, equilibrium moves upwards to the left along AD' in part (i). The economy also moves downwards to the left on the curve in part (ii). Thus unit labour costs rise at a slower and slower rate until the $SRAS$ curve has shifted to $SRAS'$, returning equilibrium to Y_F in part (i) and taking the economy to the point where the unit labour cost curve cuts the axis in part (ii).

All that the curve in part (ii) tells us is how fast the $SRAS$ curve in part (i) is shifting upwards. It is an explanation of the dynamic behaviour by which equilibrium income is returned to its potential level.

Conclusion

The Phillips curve, although much misunderstood when it was first introduced, is an integral part of the model of income determination. In particular, it explains the speed at which the $SRAS$ curve is shifting when actual income does not equal potential income. We have introduced this relation in this chapter. In Chapter 42 we see that we need to augment it to take

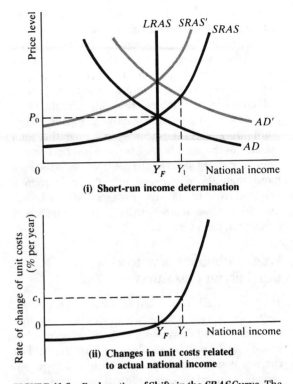

(i)   Short-run income determination

(ii) Changes in unit costs related to actual national income

FIGURE 41.9   Explanation of Shifts in the *SRAS* Curve. The intersection of the aggregate demand and the *SRAS* curves determines equilibrium income in part (i); equilibrium income then determines the rate of change of unit costs in part (ii); the change in units costs then determines the rate at which the *SRAS* curve is shifting in part (i)

account of some additional inflationary forces that we have not yet included in our analysis of the Phillips curve.

SUMMARY

1 Inflation is defined as an increase in the average price level, and a deflation as a decrease.

2 It is useful to distinguish between inflationary pressures stemming from the supply side and the demand side.

3 A once-and-for-all supply-side shock raises the price level and lowers equilibrium income. Without monetary accommodation, full employment will be restored only if costs fall sufficiently to restore the pre-shock position. With monetary accommodation, the *AD* curve can be shifted

sufficiently to the right to restore full employment but at the cost of a further increase in the price level.

4 Repeated supply shocks without monetary accommodation cause continued rises in the price level and falls in national income. With monetary accommodation, repeated supply shocks can cause a steady inflation at a constant level of national income.

5 A once-and-for-all demand shock leads in the short run to a rise in the price level and a rise in

output. If the rise in the price level is not validated by a corresponding increase in the money supply, the inflationary gap will cause factor prices to rise, shifting the *SRAS* curve upwards and pushing equilibrium national income back to its potential level.

6 If the rise in the price level following a demand shock is validated, the increases in the money supply frustrate the monetary adjustment mechanism and provide the shocks needed to sustain the inflation – the inflationary gap causes the *SRAS* curve to shift left, but the repeated increases in the money supply cause the aggregate demand curve to shift right, so that the net effect is a continually rising price level without any fall in equilibrium national income.

7 Increases in real expenditure functions can cause the price level to rise. Without monetary validation, the rise in the price level will cease once the monetary adjustment mechanism comes into play. Increases in costs can cause the price level to rise, but this will be accompanied by a continual fall in income. A sustained inflation at a constant level of national income requires an increase in the money supply at the same rate that prices are rising. In this sense, sustained inflation is a monetary phenomenon.

8 In its original form the Phillips curve relates the rate of change of money wages to the level of unemployment. (i) The rate of change of money wages minus the rate of growth of productivity determines the rate at which unit costs are increasing, which in turn determines the rate at which the *SRAS* curve is shifting upwards. (ii) The level of unemployment is negatively related to the level of national income. Using these two relations, the Phillips curve can be transformed into a curve determining the relation between national income and the rate of change of unit labour costs. This curve explains the speed of the dynamic adjustment whereby shifts in the *SRAS* curve push the short-run equilibrium level of national income back towards potential income. The Phillips curve can be used to determine the rate at which unit costs are rising and hence the speed at which the *SRAS* curve is shifting upwards.

Macroeconomic Policy in a Closed Economy

In this chapter we are going to draw together much of what you have studied in the earlier chapters on macroeconomics. Chapters 30, 31, 37 and 41 are particularly important. Although we shall review some of the main results of these chapters, we must assume that you understand what is in these earlier discussions.

Our main concern here is with stabilization policy in the context of a closed economy. (International complications are discussed in Chapter 44.) In the first half of this chapter, we consider fiscal and monetary policies of demand management. In the second half of the chapter, we look at the operation of demand-management policies in relation to their two main goals of maintaining low rates of both inflation and unemployment, ending with an assessment of policy limitations. A final section examines supply-side policies.

DEMAND MANAGEMENT

Demand management relates to all policies that seek to shift the aggregate demand curve. These include both fiscal and monetary policies.

Fiscal Policy

We studied the working of fiscal policy at some length in Chapter 31. Here we merely summarize its workings by outlining what may be called *the fiscal transmission mechanism*: how fiscal changes are transmitted into changes in (equilibrium) national income.

The fiscal transmission mechanism

The fiscal transmission mechanism is outlined in the left-hand half of Figure 42.1. (The right-hand half of the Figure is discussed later.) The two major instruments of fiscal policy are the government's exhaustive expenditures, G, and its tax rates, t.

Government expenditures, shown by G in the Figure, increase aggregate desired expenditure, E (as indicated by the plus sign). Aggregate desired expenditure in turn helps to determine the aggregate demand curve AD. An increase in G raises aggregate demand while a decrease in G lowers aggregate demand, operating in both cases through the linkages shown in the Figure.

Tax rates, shown by t in the Figure, determine, in combination with the level of national income, the size of the government's tax revenue, T. This revenue reduces aggregate expenditure (as shown by the minus sign). Once again aggregate desired expenditure helps to determine aggregate demand. An increase in tax rates reduces aggregate demand, while a reduction in tax rates increases aggregate demand – in both cases through the linkages shown in the Figure. Aggregate demand and aggregate supply interact in the manner discussed in Chapter 38 to determine real national income, Y, and the price level, P.

Crowding Out: There is a further effect of fiscal policy, one that works through the monetary sector. It is called the crowding-out effect, and here is how it works. The increase in national income caused by the expansionary fiscal policy increases the demand for transactions balances. This increased demand for money sets up the sequence of events summarized in

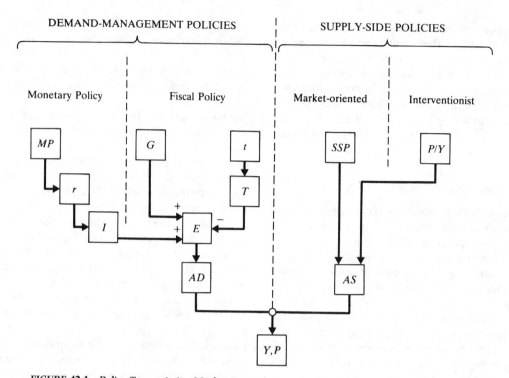

FIGURE 42.1   Policy Transmission Mechanisms. The two fiscal instruments of expenditures and tax rates affect aggregate desired expenditure and, through *AD*, real income and the price level. Supply-side policies act via *AS*

Figure 36.5 on page 437, which should be reviewed at this point. The increased demand for money drives up interest rates and exerts a *contractionary* effect on income that partially offsets the fiscal expansion. We shall say more about this effect below.

Alternative tools of demand management

So far in our discussion of demand management, we have emphasized the role of direct changes in income-tax rates and government expenditures. It is also possible for the government to use fiscal incentives to influence specific types of expenditures. A prime example is investment incentives, the most common of which are called investment (or depreciation) allowances. These can take various forms but they usually work by the government sacrificing some current tax revenues by giving favourable tax treat-ment to private investment expenditures in the hope of greatly increasing that expenditure.

A typical example is accelerated depreciation. If firms are allowed to write off their capital investments quickly against what would otherwise have been taxable profits, they can postpone paying taxes. Once the capital is fully depreciated, taxes will then have to be paid, but in the meantime the firm will have had the use of money it would otherwise have had to pay in taxes.

To see this point, consider an example using a rate of depreciation of 10 per cent of the purchase price of a machine each year. Assume that a firm made a new investment and expected to show net revenues before depreciation of £10m for the next ten years and after-depreciation profits of £8m after £2m of depreciation has been deducted. Now assume that accelerated depreciation allowances permit the firm to write off the entire £20m investment expense in the first two years. Its profits for tax purposes are zero in those two years and then £10m for each of the remaining eight years. Over the ten years, the total depreciation allowance has not changed but, since money has an opportunity cost, the firm is better off postponing its tax payment because it then has the use of the money for longer. The accelerated depreciation thus makes investment more attractive, especially when such measures are first introduced.

Many other policies may shift desired expenditure functions. For example we observed in Chapter 27

that wealth and consumption tend to be positively related. It follows that a once-and-for-all tax on wealth, by reducing households' present wealth, may reduce their desired consumption expenditure as households save more in order to recoup their lost wealth. A continuing tax on wealth reduces the after-tax return to saving – since part of the savings get taxed away by the wealth tax – and so will have a similar effect as a fall in the interest rate.

Tax changes versus expenditure changes

Let us assume that a persistent output gap exists, and that the government has decided to try to reduce it by adopting an expansionary fiscal policy.

An important issue now arises: since the expansionary policy can take the form of reductions in tax rates or increases in government expenditures, which should be chosen, and why? Four of the main considerations relevant to the answer that we discuss below are the size of the changes needed, the location of the effects, the duration of any time-lags, and the change in the role of the government in the economy.

The Size of the Changes: A given change in national income can be achieved either by cuts in tax rates or by increases in exhaustive expenditures. However, the magnitudes of the changes required by these two policies are different, because the multiplier effects differ.

First consider an increase in government expenditure. If the government spends an extra £1,000m, this much is added directly to aggregate demand. If the multiplier is 2, then the final increase in equilibrium national income is £2,000m.

Next consider a tax cut. First assume that the government cuts its tax rates in such a way that, at the initial level of national income, its revenues fall by £1,000m. This leaves an extra £1,000m in the hands of the private sector. But aggregate expenditure will rise by less than £1,000m, because part of that new disposable income will be saved. Say, for example, that the marginal propensity to spend out of disposable income is 0.75. In this case, the first impact of the tax cut of £1,000m will be to increase income-creating expenditure by only £750m. Combined with a multiplier of 2, this means a final increase in equilibrium income of £1,500m.

Thus we see that, with an increase in government expenditure or an equal reduction in tax revenues, the rise in income is greater with the expenditure increase than with the tax cut. This can be put slightly differently as our first important comparison: *bringing about given increase in equilibrium national income through fiscal policy requires a larger reduction in tax revenue than an increase in government expenditure.*

The Location of the Effects: The *impact effect* of any fiscal change refers to where the effects are initially felt. The full effect refers to what happens once adjustments to it have worked themselves out.

The impact effects of tax cuts, such as for example a cut in income-tax rates, tends to be spread over the whole economy. All taxpayers get an increase in disposable income and the demands for most consumer goods increase as a result. This is an advantage if the slump is a general one affecting the whole economy. However, if the slump has severely localized characteristics, with a few areas or industries being particularly hard hit, expenditure increases have some advantage. Their initial impact effects can be localized by the decisions on how the money is to be spent. Expenditure can be concentrated in particular areas or on particular industries. For example, if the construction industry has been particularly badly hit, then new expenditures on roads, schools and hospitals may be appropriate. Of course, the induced multiplier effects will spread out over the whole economy, but at least the impact effects can be partially localized in the construction industry.

The amount that £1's worth of government expenditure in a region adds to regional income is measured by a REGIONAL MULTIPLIER. Most regional multipliers tend to be *less than one*. How could this be? There are two main reasons.

First, only a part of each £1 spent in a region adds initially to regional income. For example, of each £1 spent on roads in some region, well over 50p may go for materials made in other regions and, hence, will create incomes in those other regions. Only the amount that goes to local labour and local contractors increases local incomes. The second reason is that there are leakages out of a region at each and every round of induced expenditure. For the *regional* multiplier, imports are all expenditures made on goods and services produced in other regions, and in most modern industrial economies these regional import leakages are large. So, in summary, only a fraction of each £1 of expenditure creates income in the region, and the multiplier that is applied to this fraction tends to be smaller the smaller the region.

Our second point of comparison, then, is: *expendi-*

ture increases have some advantage over income-tax cuts if it is desired to localize some of the effects of the expansionary fiscal policy.

Time-Lags: Discretionary fiscal policy, which is involved with tax and expenditure changes, is subject to at least two 'policy lags'. First is a *decision lag*. The problem must be identified, studied, and appropriate action decided upon. These lags can be long for both tax cuts and expenditure increases.

Once the measure has been authorized, there is an *execution lag*. For example, after funds have been allocated for a new road-building programme, some considerable time will pass before substantial income payments are made to private firms and households. Routes must be surveyed, land must be acquired, public protests must be heard, bids must be called for and contracts let. All of this takes time, a very long time for certain types of expenditure programmes.

Some expenditures, however, are not subject to such long lags. Funds can often be released quite quickly for education and health expenditures. Also cash limits placed on certain expenditures can operate with dramatic suddenness.

The execution lag for tax cuts is mainly due to the fact that Parliament normally enacts tax changes only once or twice a year, at budget times. Once Parliament has agreed to cuts in personal income-tax rates, however, households will very soon find themselves with more disposable income.

So our third point of comparison is: *certain forms of tax cuts and expenditure increases have advantages over others because they have a much shorter lag between the time when action is decided upon and when the effect is felt on aggregate expenditure. No general presumption exists, however, favouring tax cuts over expenditure increases or vice versa; instead, each measure must be judged on its merits as far as lags are concerned.*

The Change in the Role of the Government in the Economy: Many people have strong feelings about the size of the government sector. One measure of the importance of the government's use of productive resources can be obtained from the ratio G/Y, i.e. the ratio of government exhaustive expenditure to national income. Some would like to see this ratio reduced, while others would like to see it increased.

The policy that is adopted will certainly affect this ratio. If the government chooses the expenditure-increasing policy, then it will increase the amount of the nation's resources whose allocation is decided by the government. If the government chooses the tax cut, the government will hold constant the amount of the nation's resources whose allocation is determined by the government's exhaustive expenditure (G).

Our final point of comparison, then, is: *tax cuts leave the amount of the nation's resources whose allocation is determined by the government's exhaustive expenditures unchanged; expenditure increases raise this amount.*

Limitations of fiscal policy

We now consider a number of problems that arise with the use of fiscal policy. The problems arise from the crowding-out effect, the permanent-income effect, the need for policy to be reversible, and lags and forecasting errors. We shall study these below. Note that some refer to both expansionary and contractionary policies, others to only one and not the other.

The Crowding-Out Effect: The first limitation applies only to expansionary fiscal policy. When we discussed the transmission mechanism of fiscal policy earlier in this chapter, we noted that it had an added effect that worked through monetary forces. The increase of national income following a fiscal expansion tends to create a money shortage due to increased transactions demand for money. This money shortage then puts upward pressure on interest rates. The rise in interest rates tends to reduce interest-sensitive expenditure and partially offsets the expansionary effect of the increases in expenditure brought about by the initial tax cuts or government expenditure increases. This force is called the CROWDING-OUT EFFECT, and it is defined as an offsetting decrease in private-sector expenditure caused when an expansionary fiscal policy increases interest rates.

Critics of fiscal policy have made much of this effect. Although the strength of crowding-out tendencies will vary from case to case, depending on the state of the economy, there is no doubt that, *ceteris paribus*, a fiscally induced expansion does put upward pressure on interest rates, particularly as the economy nears full employment.

The problem need not detain us longer, however, since there is no need for the other things to remain equal. In particular, all that is needed to avoid the crowding-out effect is for the Bank to accompany the fiscal expansion with a sufficient monetary expansion to prevent interest rates from being driven up. If the

money supply is increased at about the same rate as the demand for money is increasing, the crowding-out mechanism does not operate.

The Bank must be careful, however, not to bring about so much monetary expansion that an inflation breaks out. Since we are discussing accommodating only the increased demand for money that accompanies an expansion in real income when a large output gap is reduced, the *appropriate* monetary expansion will not cause an inflation.

The Permanent-Income Hypothesis: The theory of the consumption function that we have used throughout this book, and which is basically due to Keynes, relates current consumption expenditure to current national income. However, an alternative theory of the consumption function, called the *permanent income theory*, relates consumption to what people regard as their 'permanent' income. It states that people form expectations about the long-run trend in their incomes, and then make their consumption decisions on the basis of these expectations. They do not let *short-term* fluctuations in their current incomes affect their consumption. According to this theory, if people find themselves with temporarily low incomes, they either reduce their current savings or borrow, in order to maintain their expenditure on current consumption. If they find themselves with temporarily high incomes, they add the extra to their current savings.

This theory has been used to question the effectiveness of short-term tax changes to act as a fiscal regulator. According to the theory, cuts in personal income-tax rates that are expected to be temporary, because they are perceived as part of short-run fiscal policy designed to provide temporary stimulus, will give rise to temporary increases in income that will be mainly saved. Thus consumption expenditure will not rise as much as the theory which relates consumption to current income predicts. Similarly, temporary tax increases, meant to reduce a transitory inflationary gap, will be paid mainly out of savings with little reduction in consumption.

Evidence suggests that consumers sometimes behave in this way. But the effects on consumption may not be as small as a simplistic reading of the permanent-income theory might suggest. For one thing, many people have neither sufficient liquid assets, nor the borrowing power to maintain consumption in the face of a temporary fall in their disposable income, even though they might want to

do so. For another thing, many people 'save' their temporary increases in income by 'investing' in durable consumer goods that they will 'consume' over subsequent years. Although such purchases count as saving in the permanent-income theory, they are, nonetheless, expenditures on currently produced goods which add to current aggregate demand.

The Need for Reversibility: A policy that is not easily reversible can easily turn out to have perverse effects. To see what is involved, consider Figure 42.2. There we *assume* that the average, or normal, position of the aggregate expenditure function is E_N. This implies that, on average, national income will be at its full-employment level, Y_F. Now assume, however, that a *temporary* slump in private investment shifts the aggregate expenditure function downwards to E_S, thus opening up a large deflationary gap (ab in the Figure). Equilibrium income falls to Y_S. Assume, furthermore, that the gap persists for some time.

Now assume that for one reason or another – possibly concern about the political effects or a careful assessment of the economic losses – the government finally decides to take action. Its expansionary fiscal policy shifts the expenditure function back to E_N, thereby restoring full employment.

But the slump in private investment spending is, by assumption, only temporary. When private invest-

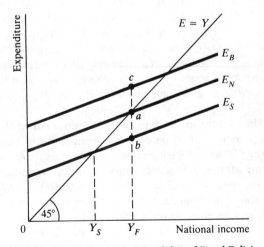

FIGURE 42.2   The Need for Reversibility of Fiscal Policies. Fiscal policies designed to remove temporary gaps will open up gaps if they are not quickly reversed when private expenditure returns to a more normal level

ment expenditure recovers, the desired expenditure function shifts upwards and, unless the government responds quickly, an inflationary gap will be opened up. The government has already shifted the expenditure curve up to E_N and, if nothing else is done, the revived investment expenditure will shift the expenditure function up to E_B, thereby opening up an inflationary gap (*ac* in the Figure).

To avoid this, the government must reverse its expansionary policy when investment expenditure recovers, allowing the reduction of the government's expenditure to offset the revived private expenditure. Done perfectly, the expenditure function will be held at E_N, with the government's contribution to aggregate expenditure diminishing as the contribution of private investment increases. This, however, is no easy task.

The above analysis leads to a very important conclusion: *Fiscal policies designed to remove inflationary or deflationary gaps resulting from temporarily high or low levels of private expenditure will lead to overshooting when Y moves back towards Y_F unless the policies can be rapidly reversed once private expenditure functions return to their more normal levels.*

Lags and Forecasting Errors: Finally recall that fiscal policy acts with lags – just as does monetary policy. These lags, combined with the difficulty in forecasting what private-sector aggregate demand will be when the fiscal measures take effect, raise the possibility that stabilization policy will actually destabilize the economy. These possibilities were discussed in Chapter 31, which material is relevant here.

Monetary Policy

We now move to a brief discussion of monetary policy. This tool of demand management has already been analysed in detail in Chapter 37. First let us recall the transmission mechanism of monetary policy.

The monetary transmission mechanism

The transmission mechanism that works for monetary policy is outlined in detail in Figures 36.4 and 36.5 on page 437. The mechanism works by putting pressure on interest rates. The contrasting effects with fiscal policy are important when in the next chapters we consider the issues that arise in the context of an open economy. On the one hand,

expansionary fiscal policy causes an increase in the transactions demand for money and thus puts upward pressure on interest rates, while expansionary monetary policy increases the supply of money and thus puts downward pressure on these rates. On the other hand, contractionary fiscal policy causes a reduction in the transactions demand for money and thus puts downward pressure on interest rates, while contractionary monetary policy reduces the supply of money and thus puts upward pressure on such rates. The broad outlines of this policy are also summarized in Figure 42.1 by the monetary policy tool, *MP*, affecting interest rates, *r*, which feeds through onto investment, *I* (which stands for *all* interest-sensitive expenditure) and thence onto aggregate desired expenditure.

Interest-rate changes with a recessionary gap and full employment

We have seen that the transmission mechanism of monetary policy works through the interest rate, lowering it in the case of an expansionary policy and raising it in the case of a contractionary policy. If the economy has unemployed resources, this mechanism works as we have described it.

Some observers have drawn from a correct appreciation of the monetary transmission mechanism the erroneous conclusion that an expansionary monetary policy can lower interest rates, even in times of full employment. Indeed, whenever interest rates rise, the call can be heard for the government to take steps to lower these rates by adopting an expansionary monetary policy.

In Chapter 36 we studied an increase in the money supply in a fully employed economy. The increase puts transitory downward pressure on interest rates, but the ensuing rise in the price level returns interest rates to their original level. So the sole effect, once equilibrium is re-established, is a rise in the price level. (See page 439.) This result is one aspect of the long-run neutrality of money that we studied in Chapter 33: in a fully employed economy, the rate of interest is *independent* of the quantity of money as long as the price level is at its long-run equilibrium value.

But what if the policy-makers seek to maintain the disequilibrium by creating new money as fast as prices rise in an attempt to maintain the lower interest rates induced by the initial monetary expansion? They will then be creating a fully validated inflation and the economy will be in the state

illustrated in Figure 41.5 on page 497. The initial monetary expansion creates an inflationary gap, and the subsequent monetary expansions frustrate the monetary adjustment mechanism, thus maintaining the gap. To study this possibility further, we need to make the important distinction between real and nominal interest rates.

Real and Nominal Interest Rates: The rate of interest, like many of the other variables we have been considering in this book, can be measured in real or in nominal values. The NOMINAL or MONEY INTEREST RATE is the one we have been considering so far. It is the annual money value of interest paid, divided by the principal of the loan. Thus, for example, a monetary asset that pays £5 per year on an investment of £100 yields a nominal interest rate of 5 per cent.

The REAL INTEREST RATE is the rate of interest earned after deducting an amount necessary *to maintain the purchasing power of the principal invested.* When an inflation is occurring, the real purchasing power of any money is falling at the rate of inflation.

For example, the purchasing power of £100 falls by 5 per cent each year in the face of a 5 per cent inflation. Thus it will take £105 next year to buy what £100 will buy this year. If £100 invested only yields £5 over the year, all of that sum is needed just to maintain the purchasing power of the principal. In this case the real interest rate would be zero, while the nominal rate was 5 per cent. To see why, note that if the investor saves the entire 5 per cent interest and adds it to his principal, he will have just maintained its purchasing power. If the money rate of interest had been 7 per cent, he could have deducted 5 per cent to maintain the purchasing power of his principal and had 2 per cent left over as a real return on his investment. In this case, the money rate is 7 per cent while the real rate is 2 per cent. Finally, consider an example in which the money rate of interest is only 3 per cent in the face of a 5 per cent inflation. If the investor saves the whole 3 per cent interest and adds it to the principal, his principal will be eroding at about 2 per cent per year. He will have received a negative real return; the real rate of interest will be −2 per cent in this case.

> The real rate of interest $=$ the nominal rate of interest *minus* the rate of inflation

Notice that, if the rate of inflation is zero, the nominal and the real rates are the same. Because if there is no inflation, there is no need to make a deduction to maintain the purchasing power of the principal. This is why we did not need to distinguish the real and the nominal rates up until now. But, when we suffer from a continuing inflation, the distinction becomes important.

Rational investors are concerned with the real, not the nominal, rate of interest. They want to know, before parting with their money, how much they will earn after maintaining the purchasing power of the amount lent. If investors expect a negative real rate, they would be better off not lending at all. Rather, they could buy some physical asset, such as a piece of land, or a machine, whose money value is expected to rise along with all other prices – to rise, that is, at the general rate of inflation. In that case, they would be obtaining a zero rate – instead of a negative rate – since the market value of the assets would, by assumption, rise at the same rate as the price level, thus preserving the purchasing power of the sum invested.

The real forces in the economy, such as the willingness of people to borrow and lend, tend to determine the real rate of interest. The nominal rate then becomes the real rate *plus* the expected rate of inflation. It follows that an inflation generated by policy-makers in an attempt to lower interest rates will end up *increasing* money interest rates by the amount of the inflation that they create.

We have now reached two very important conclusions:

● In a fully employed economy, a once-and-for-all increase in the money supply will have no effect on the real rate of interest or real income, only on the price level *once equilibrium is re-established.*

● In a fully employed economy, a continuing expansion of the money supply will increase the nominal interest rate *once the ensuing inflation is expected to continue*: it will, however, have no effect on the real interest rate, *once full adjustment to the expected inflation has taken place.*

Limitations of monetary policy

We now pass to a brief consideration of some of the limitations of monetary policy. These include problems associated with controlling the money supply, deciding on the right targets and indicators of monetary policy, and coping with the lags in the working of the policy.

Difficulties of monetary control

Short-Term Control of the Money Supply: One of the major limitations of monetary policy is the difficulty of controlling the money supply on a short-term basis. This important topic has already been discussed in Chapter 37, so we need only mention the issues here. The first reason follows from the fact that financial assets form an almost continuous spectrum from the most liquid to the least liquid. The central bank can control what is variously called the high-powered money supply, or the cash base. But all the other assets – from demand deposits, through time deposits at commercial banks and deposits with building societies, through commercial bills of exchange, to long-term bonds – are created by private-sector financial and commercial institutions. Although the whole edifice depends in the final analysis on convertibility into currency, this is a tenuous link in the short term.

The second reason why short-term control of the money supply is difficult follows from the fact that the Bank also has a function as supporter of the financial system. Hence, for example, it cannot suddenly deprive the system of liquidity if this would lead to a rash of bank failures.

Institutional arrangements are important in determining the degree of control that any central bank can exert over the money supply over various time-periods. It is generally agreed that the Bank of England has less short-run control over the money supply than the central banks of some other countries. The American central bank, for example, has had a high degree of success in controlling the money supply since it started to try to do so in the mid-1970s. The Bank of England's problems are partly due to its lender-of-last-resort function, which inhibits the Bank from exerting close control over the money supply to meet some monetary growth target independently of the monetary system's need for liquidity. For this reason, The Bank of England pays much more attention to interest rates. It takes steps to force interest rates up when it feels a more restrictive monetary policy is necessary, and to force interest rates down when it wants a more expansionary policy.

Short-Term Control of Aggregate Demand: There can be no doubt that, given a tough enough monetary policy, central banks can reduce the level of validation of inflation, thus slowing down the rate at which the aggregate demand curve is shifting right-wards, and so slow down the rate of inflation itself. The central banks of many industrialized countries succeeded in doing just this in the late 1970s and early 1980s. The degree of precision in this control is greater for long-term trends than for short-term fluctuations because so much of the money supply is only indirectly controlled by central banks.

We know that the transmission mechanism works from the money supply *through interest rates* to aggregate expenditure. It follows that as long as the Bank can succeed in driving up interest rates, by whatever method is available to it, and is willing to drive them up far enough, it can exert contractionary pressure on aggregate demand. No matter how loose is their control over the money supply, most central banks are able to use their tools of monetary control to create a sufficient money shortage to drive up interest rates, thereby curtailing interest-sensitive expenditures. Recall that such expenditures include hire-purchase expenditures, expenditures on houses purchased on mortgages and investment expenditures (although the latter may not be seriously affected unless the rise in interest rates is expected to persist for quite some time).

Long-Term Control of Money and the Price Level: The whole banking system does ultimately depend on the cash base to maintain its solvency. Thus, in the long run, the Bank does have the ultimate control on the whole spectrum of financial assets which include money narrowly, or broadly, defined. The Bank does, therefore, in the long term have the responsibility for whether the money supply, however defined, is expanding rapidly or slowly to validate a rapid or a slow inflation.

Intermediate monetary targets

The problem of intermediate targets, such as various measures of 'the' money supply, arises because the Bank is interested in controlling aggregate demand and, through that, national income and the rate of inflation, but, as we saw in Chapter 37, the linkages between what the Bank can control – the cash base (MO), and short-term interest rates – and national income and the price level take a long and a variable time to work out. For this reason, central banks have sought to identify an intermediate target that responds fairly quickly to MO and interest rates, and that correlates with their ultimate targets of national income and the price level.

The major problem is that no intermediate monetary target seems to maintain a stable relation with income and the price level over a long period of time. One reason is associated with the rapid changes in the nature of financial institutions over the last decades that we discussed in Chapter 37. These changes have allowed households and firms to reduce the transactions balances that they must hold. This means that neither M1, nor any of the other measures of the money supply, have held a stable relation to the central banks' ultimate targets.

Time-lags

Another very severe limitation on the use of monetary policy for short-term stabilization purposes is the long and variable lags with which the monetary transmission mechanism works. These were discus-

sed in detail in Chapter 37. Whenever any policy works with long time-lags, there is a serious risk that it will destabilize rather than stabilize if used in an attempt to reduce short-term fluctuations.

Fiscal *vs.* Monetary Policy

Depending on the circumstances, fiscal policy may be more or less potent than monetary policy. Let us see what these circumstances are. In Chapter 37 we saw that the strength of monetary policy depended on the slopes of the liquidity preference and the marginal efficiency of capital curves. An elastic LP curve, and an inelastic MEI curve, makes fiscal policy very potent, while an inelastic LP curve, and an elastic MEI curve, makes it relatively impotent.

Figure 42.3 shows that similar considerations apply to fiscal policy, because the slopes of the MEI

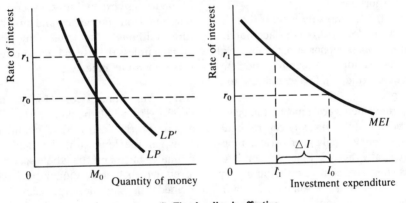

(i) Fiscal policy is effective

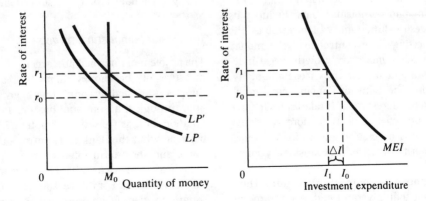

(ii) Fiscal policy is ineffective

FIGURE 42.3   The Strength of Fiscal Policy. An elastic LP curve and an inelastic MEI curve makes fiscal policy very effective; the reverse elasticities make it ineffective.

and *LP* curves determine the magnitude of the crowding-out effect. The left-hand sides of parts (i) and (ii) show monetary forces determining the interest rate. The original money supply is M_0 and the demand curve for money is *LP*, yielding an interest rate of r_0. An expansionary fiscal policy increases national income and hence increases the transactions demand for money. We know from Chapter 34 that this shifts the *LP* function to the right, say to *LP'* in the Figure. The additional demand for money, in conjunction with a fixed supply, causes the interest rate to rise to r_1 in the Figure. This then reduces investment (and all other interest-sensitive expenditure). This is shown by the fall in investment of ΔI, from I_0 to I_1 in the right-hand sides of both parts of the Figure.

In part (i), the *LP* function is inelastic, so the interest rate is driven up a lot. Also the *MEI* function is interest-elastic, so investment falls a lot. The crowding-out effect is large and much of the original fiscal stimulus will be offset.

In part (ii), the *LP* function is interest-elastic, so the interest rate does not rise much. Also the *MEI* function is inelastic, so the rise in the interest rate does not reduce investment by much. The crowding-out effect is small, so that the original fiscal stimulus will not be much reduced.

We now see that the same combination of elasticities that makes monetary policy relatively impotent makes fiscal policy relatively potent, and vice versa:

- the effect of a given fiscal stimulus is weaker and the effect of a given monetary stimulus is stronger: (i) the more inelastic is the *LP* function, and (ii) the more elastic is the *MEI* function;
- the effect of a given fiscal stimulus is stronger and the effect of a given monetary stimulus is weaker: (i) the more elastic is the *LP* function, and (ii) the more inelastic is the *MEI* function.

FULL EMPLOYMENT AND STABLE PRICES

In this second main section we assume that, by one means or another, policy-makers can manipulate aggregate demand, and we look at the problems that they then face in pursuing the two major goals of short-term stabilization policy in the context of a closed economy. These goals are traditionally described as achieving *full employment* and *stable prices*.

When UK full-employment policy was first adopted as a primary goal by the coalition government of 1944, total unemployment was thought to be divided between frictional and demand-deficient unemployment. Any demand-deficient unemployment could, it was widely believed, be dealt with by demand-management policy, and the remaining frictional unemployment seemed small enough to be acceptable. The 1944 White Paper on *Employment Policy* (Cmd. 6527) set a 3 per cent unemployment rate as a 'full-employment' target, by accepting 3 per cent as the minimum unavoidable amount of frictional unemployment. Experience over the next two decades suggested that even this figure was unduly pessimistic, since the unemployment rate in the 10 years after 1947 was below 2 per cent in all but a single year. Under these circumstances, the conduct of short-term stabilization policy seemed relatively simple.

Stabilization Policy with a Keynesian Aggregate Demand Curve

The J-shaped, Keynesian aggregate supply curve, first discussed on pages 468–9, was thought at the time to be a reasonable description of reality. It is shown again in Figure 42.4. Given such a curve, the problem of stabilization policy is to achieve point *x* where full employment and stable prices occur simultaneously. This is done by keeping the aggregate demand curve in the position shown by the curve labelled AD_F. First, assume that aggregate demand is too low, say at *AD'*; there is a recessionary gap of $Y_F - Y_1$, in the Figure. If aggregate demand is increased to AD_F, full employ-

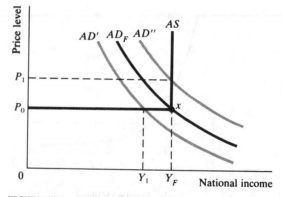

FIGURE 42.4   Stabilization Policy with a Keynesian Aggregate Supply Curve. By stabilizing aggregate demand at the appropriate level, full employment and stable prices could be achieved

ment and stable prices are restored. Second, assume that aggregate demand is too high, say at AD'' in the Figure. If nothing is done, an inflation will take the price level to P_1. However, if a contractionary policy can be introduced fast enough, the aggregate demand curve can be shifted back to AD_F, thus eliminating the inflationary gap and restoring full employment and stable prices.

So stabilization policy was designed to hold the aggregate demand curve at AD_F, thereby assuring full employment and a stable price level, with no more than 2–3 per cent of the labour force unemployed for frictional reasons.

Stabilization Policy with a Phillips Curve

The Keynesian aggregate supply curve describes a world where inflationary pressures only develop at full employment. Thus, either there is demand-deficient unemployment or there is inflationary pressure, but *never* both at the same time. In such a world, policy-makers know for sure whether aggregate demand is currently too low or too high. The development of the Phillips curve was a major step in upsetting this simple view of the world.

The Phillips curve describes a world where less unemployment can be obtained at the cost of more inflation, and less inflation can be obtained at the cost of more unemployment. When it came to be believed that the Phillips curve was a better description of reality than the Keynesian aggregate supply curve,

the possibility of a 'trade-off' between unemployment and inflation came to dominate stabilization policy. This domination continued for more than a decade. Today, economists no longer believe that such a trade-off exists in the long run, but it clearly does exist in the short run and this greatly complicates stabilization policy. Let us see what is involved in the 'trade-off issue'.

A Trade-Off Between Inflation and Unemployment?

One of the key points about the Phillips-curve view of the world is that potential income ceases to be the maximum attainable level of income. Figure 42.5 shows a wage-Phillips curve and a unit-cost inflation curve similar to the one drawn in Figures 41.6 and 41.8 on pages 501 and 503. The former curve relates the rate at which money wages are changing to the level of unemployment, the latter curve relates the rate at which unit costs are changing to the level of national income.

In the diagram we indicate two levels of national income. The first is Y_F. This is the level of income that is produced when the economy is operated at normal rates of capacity utilization; it is the economy's potential income. The amount of unemployment that is associated with Y_F is designated by U_N; it is often called the *natural rate of unemployment*. We defined it in Chapter 40 as the level of unemployment at which the demand for and supply of labour are equal, so that

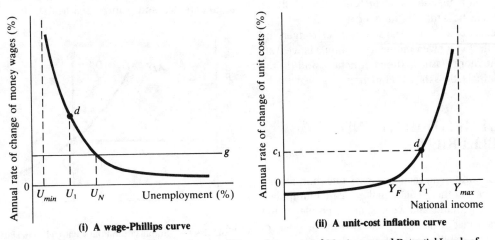

FIGURE 42.5 Minimum and Natural Rates of Unemployment and Maximum and Potential Levels of National Income. The natural rate of unemployment occurs when income is at its potential level and the minimum rate of unemployment occurs when income is at its maximum level

labour markets are in equilibrium and the only unemployment is frictional and structural. It is plotted in part (i) of the Figure.

The second level of national income is Y_{max}, the maximum level of national income that can be achieved by working the economy flat out. The level of unemployment associated with Y_{max} is called U_{min} and is also plotted in part (i) of the Figure. This is the economy's minimum achievable level of frictional unemployment; it occurs when there are so many job vacancies that job leavers can find a new job almost immediately. A national income of Y_{max} is what economies achieve during such emergencies as major wars, when people are patriotically motivated to work for long hours at demanding jobs and all available capital equipment is pressed into use.

Finally, note that any national income between Y_F and Y_{max}, and hence any unemployment rate between U_N and U_{min}, require that firms operate at more than normal-capacity output. The labour needed to produce more than Y_F comes from a fall in frictional unemployment as people take less time between jobs, and by an expansion of the labour supply as people are attracted into the labour market by both the ease of finding work and the rapidly rising wage rates.

The recognition of a range between Y_F and Y_{max} presented policy-makers with what looked like a possibility not allowed for by the older J-shaped AS curve. They could attempt to run the economy in the situation given by some point such as d in each part of the diagram. At that point, national income of Y_1 exceeds Y_F so that unemployment of U_1 is below U_N but unit costs are rising at the rate of c_1 per period.

As a result of the rising unit production costs, the SRAS curve will be shifting upwards. As we saw in Figure 41.1, this will tend, other things being equal, to eliminate the inflationary gap and reduce national income to Y_F and increase unemployment to U_N.

With the Phillips curve, however, a new policy option seemed to be open. The monetary authorities could ensure that other things do not remain equal. They could validate the inflation by increasing the money supply at the same rate that prices are rising. This frustrates the monetary adjustment mechanism. (This is the case we analysed in Figure 41.3 on page 495 and if you are in any doubt about it, you should review that discussion now.)

By following such a policy, a trade-off would have been made between inflation, on the one hand, and national income and unemployment, on the other. Instead of trying to stabilize national income at Y_F

with U_N unemployment and zero inflation, the policy-makers have accepted a positive inflation rate as the cost of lowering unemployment to U_1 and raising national income to Y_1.

Throughout the 1960s, this type of trade-off decision was made by many governments. Then in the 1970s something happened. Instead of being associated with a constant rate of wage inflation, a given level of unemployment came to be associated with an ever rising rate of wage, and hence unit-cost, inflation. In other words, the curve shown in Figure 42.5 began to shift upwards. As a result, the inflation rate began to accelerate in spite of there being no obvious increase in the inflationary gap or decrease in the level of unemployment.

To explain this acceleration of inflation we must first study a phenomenon called expectational inflation.

Expectational inflation

An *expectational inflation* is one that continues, and even accelerates, because of expectations of price and wage increases. Wage- and price-setters in both the markets for commodities and for labour (and other factors of production) form expectations about what the general price level will be over the lifetime of any contract currently being negotiated. They then seek to set their own price or wage in relation to the price level they expect to persist over this time-period.

Suppose, for example, that *both unions and firms* expect that a 10 per cent inflation will occur next year. Unions will tend to start negotiations from a *base* of a 10 per cent increase in money wages (which would hold their real wages constant). They will argue that firms will be able to meet the extra 10 per cent on the wage bill out of the extra revenues that will arise because product prices will go up by 10 per cent. *Starting from this base*, unions will then negotiate in an attempt to obtain some desired increase in their real wages. Firms will also be inclined to begin bargaining by conceding at least a 10 per cent increase in money wages, since they expect that the prices at which they sell their products will rise by 10 per cent. The bargaining between unions and employers will thus centre on how much money wages will be increased in excess of 10 per cent.

The conclusion is important and needs emphasis. *If both workers and employers expect an inflation of x per cent, their behaviour in wage- and price-setting will tend*

to bring that rate of inflation about, whatever the state of monetary and fiscal policy.

Accelerating inflation

Expectational inflation proved to be a major part of the explanation of the acceleration of world inflation throughout the 1970s. To see how it explains the problem, look at Figure 42.6. The curves labelled P in part (i) and C in part (ii) reproduce the curves from Figure 42.5. They tell us the increases in wage rates and unit costs due to demand pressure in labour markets *on the assumption that people expect the price level to remain constant.*

Now assume that the government has chosen a trade-off indicated by point d in the Figure. A high level of national income, Y_1, *and a correspondingly low level of unemployment, U_1, has been selected as well as its associated cost inflation of c_1* per cent per year. This rate of inflation is then validated by the appropriate rate of monetary expansion.

After a while, however, firms and unions will come to expect this inflation to continue. As a result, all wage- and price-setters raise wages and prices by c_1 per cent, just to hold their relative prices and wages constant. The result is to shift the P and C curves upward by the expected inflation rate, as shown by the curves P' and C'. At unemployment U_1 and national income of Y_1, the rate of cost inflation has accelerated to c_2 – point e in both parts of the Figure.

But after a further lapse of time, the new rate of price inflation will come to be expected and that rate

of wage increase will occur, just to 'hold one's own' against the general inflation. The curves then shift upwards to P'' and C'', causing inflation to accelerate once again. To keep the economy located at income Y_1 and unemployment U_1, a very rapid rate of monetary expansion is needed to validate the inflation now driven by the rate of increase of unit costs of c_3 per year – point f in the Figure.

Of course if the policy-makers are determined to maintain national income at Y_1 and unemployment at U_1, they must increase the rate of monetary expansion every time the two curves shift upwards. This is necessary in order to validate an ever-increasing rate of inflation.

This is one way of looking at the theory of accelerating inflation when national income is held above its potential level and any ensuing inflation is validated. The result is important, so it is worth reiterating what is happening.

When national income is held above its potential level, excess demand persists in goods and factor markets and the inflation continues *because of the demand pressures*, as shown by the original curve in Figure 42.5. When the inflation comes to be expected, people will seek to raise wages and prices by the expected inflation rate just to hold their own against the rising price level. Thus, an expectational inflation is added to the already-existing demand inflation. But the expectational inflation by itself will always tend towards the existing rate of inflation. Since demand pressures add to expectational inflation, the actual rate due to expectations *and* demand pressures will

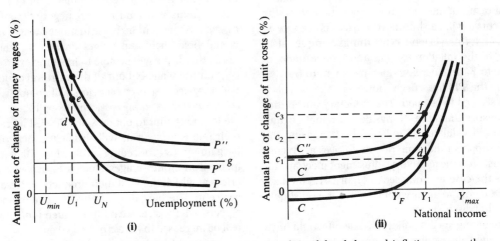

FIGURE 42.6 Accelerating Inflation. The persistence of a validated demand inflation causes the inflation rate of wages and unit costs to accelerate, as the continual upward revision of expectations cause the Phillips curve and the unit cost curve to shift upwards continually

tend to accelerate. A stable rate of inflation is impossible because expectational inflation will tend to approach the existing inflation rate *as that rate comes to be expected*, but the actual rate is always expectational inflation *plus* the inflation due to demand pressures. Like the dog chasing its tail, the accelerating spiral continues with expectations chasing the actual rate, but the actual rate being above the expected rate by the amount of demand inflation. All of this can only occur, of course, as long as the accelerating inflation is validated by an ever-increasing rate of monetary expansion.

Breaking an Entrenched Inflation

Faced with an accelerating inflation that had been validated for some time, government after government in the industrial countries finally decided in the late 1970s and early 1980s that the inflation rate had to be brought down. If inflation depended only on excess demand, there would be no problem. All policy-makers would do is to use the tools of demand management to eliminate the excess demand. A problem arose, however, because the inflation had continued so long that expectations that it would continue were firmly held. This is what is meant by an *entrenched inflation*, an inflation with firmly held expectations on the part of wage- and price-setters that it will continue.

Once the inflationary gap has been removed, expectations of inflation still drive wages upward. The Bank now faces a dilemma. Either it validates the inflation, in which case full employment can be maintained, or it continues with its tight monetary policy and allows unemployment to develop. If it is determined to break the inflation, it holds the rate of monetary expansion below the rate of inflation thus reducing aggregate demand. As demand falls, income falls and unemployment rises in the process analysed in Figure 41.2 on page 494. Sooner or later the resulting recession becomes severe enough that people no longer expect inflation to continue. They cease marking up wages and prices in expectation of general inflation, and the actual inflation falls. Once the inflation reaches zero, or some low acceptable rate, the authorities can then cautiously increase demand to take the economy back towards full employment – being careful, however, not to overshoot and allow inflationary pressures to start up once again.

Prices/Incomes Policies

Over the years, many economists have recommended prices and incomes policies and many governments have experimented with them. A PRICES AND INCOMES POLICY is defined as an attempt by the government to influence directly the setting of wages and prices. These are shown schematically by the box labelled P/Y in Figure 42.1 on page 507. Because these policies attempt to act directly on prices and/or wages, they operate through the aggregate supply curve. There is a wide range of possible measures.

First, the government could simply set voluntary guidelines for wage and price increases. By stating such guidelines, the government hopes to influence wage- and price-setting decisions.

A slightly more 'activist' form of incomes policy is consultation on wage and price norms among unions, management and government. The more centralized a country's wage- and price-setting mechanism, the more easily such consultation is accomplished. An even more activist approach is compulsory controls on wage and/or price increases. A more recent and as yet untried proposal is TIPs (tax-related incomes policies), which introduces penalties or rewards that operate through the tax system in an attempt to induce desirable wage- and price-setting behaviour.

If we are to evaluate these additional methods of controlling inflation, we need to distinguish the various circumstances in which they might be used. We can distinguish three main uses of prices and incomes policies: (i) to suppress a demand inflation, (ii) to break an expectational inflation, and (iii) to control a persistent wage-cost-push inflation.

Applied to demand inflations

One reason why incomes policies have bad reputations throughout the world is that they have often been used in futile attempts to stop demand inflations. To see why such attempts are futile, consider the situation shown at b in Figure 41.4 on page 496, where there is an inflationary gap of $Y_1 - Y_F$. If nothing else is done, the inflationary gap will cause wages to rise, shifting the *SRAS* curve upwards to *SRAS'*. The price level will then rise to P_2 and the inflationary gap will be removed. Direct government intervention could, however, be used to hold the price level at P_1. But once the intervention ceases, the excess demand will cause prices to rise. Thus, in the

face of an inflationary gap, prices/incomes policies can postpone an inflation, but, once they are removed, the price level will rise to the value it would have attained had the intervention never occurred.

Applied to expectational inflations

When there are firmly entrenched expectations that an existing inflation will persist, prices and incomes policies provide a possible way of forcing the inflation rate down and helping to lower expectations of future inflations. Such policies may be used in conjunction with a reduction in the rate of growth of the money supply to what is compatible with the target rate of inflation. The hope is that they would reduce the depth and duration of the recession that must occur until expectations fall.

Once a stable price level is achieved, the incomes policy can be removed. If everyone then expects the new low rate of inflation to persist, expectations will have been broken while the recession that follows from the use of monetary restraint alone will have been avoided.

Supporters of incomes policies contend that such policies can break an expectational inflation. Opponents disagree, offering several arguments.

1. *The policies are discredited because they did not work at other times and in other places.* But in the past, incomes policies have often been used alone to repress a *demand* inflation, rather than in conjunction with restrictive monetary policy to break an expectational inflation. Not surprisingly, they have failed in these circumstances.

2. *After the policies are removed, people will expect a resurgence of inflation, and so incomes policies merely postpone inflation.* This depends on whether or not the Bank's accompanying tight monetary policy convinces people that inflation will not break out again, and on there being no inflationary gap when the controls are removed.

3. *Incomes policies are unnecessary because inflationary expectations will be adjusted downwards as soon as an anti-inflationary policy is adopted.* Some economists have argued that inflationary expectations would adjust quickly once the Bank stopped validating the inflation. But the worldwide experience of 1980–83 showed that although the recession that normally accompanies the breaking of an entrenched inflation did not last as long as some pessimists had predicted, it lasted quite long enough to be very costly.

4. *Prices and incomes policies themselves would do much damage by inhibiting the operation of the price system.* This is a valid point, whose importance grows the longer the policies remain in force. A temporary bout of incomes policies lasting for a year or two, however, need not do long-term damage to the efficacy of the price system.

5. *Prices and incomes policies are unenforceable.* Individual unions and individual firms each have an incentive to violate these policies. In boom conditions, the policies hold wages down and create excess demand for labour. Workers would like to get higher wages, and firms would be willing to pay these to obtain scarce supplies of labour. When both sides of the market have an incentive to violate any price- or wage-setting rule, it is very expensive in terms of enforcement costs to try to maintain the rule, which may in the end become unenforceable.

Applied to permanent wage-cost push

The third and final use of prices and incomes policies is to deal with an alleged permanent wage-cost push. Some economists contend that upward pressure on wages will constantly shift the *SRAS* curve upwards even when there is no inflationary gap. Unlike expectational forces, this wage-cost push will not be eliminated, even if the inflation rate is held at a very low level for several years. Instead, inflationary pressure will always be present when the economy is anywhere near full employment. These economists thus advocate *permanent* prices and incomes policies as the only way to achieve anything approaching full employment and relatively stable prices.

Here the problem of interfering with the price mechanism becomes serious. Whereas a bout of administered price- and wage-setting by governments may not do too much harm for a year or two, its harmful effects grow the longer it persists because administered prices and wages get further and further away from the equilibrium prices and wages. The signalling functions of prices and wages are thus upset, which has serious long-run effects on the efficient functioning of the economy.

LIMITATIONS OF DEMAND MANAGEMENT

In this third main section we discuss the limitations of demand-management policies. Demand manage-

ment is undoubtedly an important part of the policy-makers' armoury for controlling the macro behaviour of the economy. Whether fiscal or monetary policy is used, however, demand management has severe limitations in that *many variables in which policy-makers are interested do not respond to variations in aggregate demand.* We conclude this chapter with a discussion of some of the major limitations of demand management, pointing out the fact that there are often goal conflicts.

Limitations in Fine Tuning

This case has been fully explored for fiscal policy in Chapter 31, pages 378–85, and analogous reasons apply to monetary policy.

Limitations in Achieving Full Employment

The Full-Employment Goal: Providing a job for everyone who wishes to work is a goal that most people accept. The problem is, however, providing a job *at what wage rate?* For example, in the 1980s, the UK had heavy unemployment in many sectors and many vacancies for lower-skilled, lower-paid jobs. Guaranteeing everyone the jobs for which they were trained is an impossible goal in a world of change. Guaranteeing everyone jobs at high real wages is also impossible, since the average real wage that can be paid is a real variable depending on the employed labour force and total national output.

So although most people accept some form of a full-employment goal as important, there has been substantial rethinking of what precisely is meant by such a goal.

Structural and Frictional Unemployment: Demand management can remove demand-deficient unemployment but it is an ineffective tool for dealing with the remaining level of unemployment – often called the 'natural' rate of unemployment. This natural rate is made up of structural and frictional unemployment and it may be disturbingly high. What can be done about it?

Structural unemployment is, as we saw in Chapter 40, the result of economic change and the slowness of labour and product markets to bring about the necessary adjustments to that change. This type of unemployment, which seems to have risen in most

countries over the last two decades, arises because micro markets do not work well enough and it therefore requires micro policies for its cure. Policies to increase labour mobility are one example. Reform of labour-market institutions is a second.

If an attempt is made to reduce such unemployment by increasing aggregate demand, labour will not be in the right places with the right training to meet the extra demand. Inflation will then ensue because the increased demand cannot be matched by increased output.

Limitations in Achieving Price Stability?

Insofar as inflation is caused by demand pressures, it can be controlled by demand management. This is a powerful tool for inflation control. Many people doubt that aggregate-demand tools can produce full employment and stable prices even under conditions where demand can be quite precisely regulated. The main concern is with cost-push inflation.

Insofar as there is an upward push on wage costs that does not respond to the state of aggregate demand, there is an inflationary pressure that does not respond to demand management. This gives rise to the behaviour of the economy analysed in Figures 41.1 and 41.2 on pages 493 and 494.

Such wage-cost-push inflation presents demand-management policy-makers with a cruel dilemma. Either they accommodate the resulting supply-side inflation, and produce something close to full employment, or they refuse to do so and accept a high, and possibly a rising, level of unemployment.

Wage-cost-push inflation can only be dealt with by removing the cost push. The two major alternative reforms that have been suggested are either to change bargaining practices so as to make wage costs more responsive to conditions of demand and supply, or to have an incomes policy that seeks to control wage inflation by state intervention, which bypasses market forces.

The first reform is technically possible. For example, American wage-bargaining practices differ greatly from those of the UK. Since there is no strong evidence of long-term, wage-cost-push inflation in the US, while there is such evidence in the UK, the suggestion is that the difference is due to the difference in the bargaining process. American unions are organized on an industrial basis, while British unions are mainly on an occupational basis. As a result, an American firm usually has only a single union to deal

with, while a large British firm typically has to deal with many. Also, closed shops, which give unions monopoly power, are much less common in the US than in the UK. Furthermore, American wages are more dependent on business conditions than are British wages. Since profits respond to the state of the market, so also do wages under the 'profit-sharing' schemes that are gaining popularity in the US. Many economists feel that gearing wages to profits would not only weaken the force of any wage-cost push, it would also reduce cyclical fluctuations in employment. (On pages 466–7 we showed that complete wage flexibility in response to market pressures in both an upwards and downwards direction would eliminate both inflationary and recessionary gaps.)

The second reform is a non-market one. Prices and incomes policies have been tried many times and have never proved a long-term success, although they have often been successful for short periods of time. Supporters of such policies say we should try harder. Detractors say they will never work in the long term unless they are the techniques of a command economy and have all of the attendant rigidities and inefficiencies.

Limitations in Influencing Economic Growth

In Chapter 39, we observed the importance of economic growth as a long-run determinant of living standards. The long-term growth rate does not seem to respond greatly to short-term demand-management techniques. People who are concerned with growth emphasize what are called supply-side policies to shift the long-run aggregate supply curve to the right. If the aggregate demand and the aggregate supply curves were independent of each other, then demand-management policies and supply-side policies could be carried out independently of each other. But many economists who emphasize the supply side maintain that many demand-management policies can be detrimental to growth. We shall consider this controversy further in the last chapter.

SUPPLY-SIDE POLICIES

The issue of growth just raised takes us to the final section of this chapter, *supply-side policies*. These policies are mainly long term in effect and they seek to influence national income by shifting the long-term aggregate supply curve. We have earlier discussed one supply-side measure, price/incomes policy. That measure, however, is short term in its effects and interventionist in its philosophy. It is also an adjunct to demand-management tools. It is supply side only because it works through the aggregate supply curve.

The supply-side policies that we now discuss are market oriented in their philosophy and look to long-term gains in increasing the rate of economic growth. (See Figure 42.1.)

The origin of the modern interest in supply-side policies lay in the increasing realization that economic growth is influenced by microeconomic, as well as macroeconomic, forces. At the macro level, the overall amounts of saving and investment are undoubtedly important. At the micro level, however, a key factor affecting growth is entrepreneurial activity, both to develop new techniques for producing old products and to produce new products. So also is the ability of the economy to adjust to the inevitable changes caused by growth. If relative wages cannot change to reflect excess demands in some sectors and excess supplies in others, and if labour cannot – or will not – move from jobs, industries and geographic areas that are declining to those that are expanding, the overall growth process will be inhibited. Tax policy, education policy, housing policy, labour-market policy and a host of other microeconomic policies that once were looked at only from the point of view of static efficiency and equity in income distribution, are increasingly being scrutinized for their effects on long-term growth rates.

Supply-side economics is not new. Indeed it's what Adam Smith's *Wealth of Nations* was all about. In its modern version, like many general but catchy terms, it sometimes means all things to all people. Basically, however, as a growth policy it means putting emphasis on pushing the long-run aggregate supply curve rightward rather than on manipulating aggregate demand. The motto here might be, 'It is more important to increase full-employment national income than to try to reduce the temporary output gaps that the market economy produces.'

Many of the measures advocated for shifting the aggregate supply curve rightwards have been discussed elsewhere in this book. Four of the most important are:

- to encourage saving,

- to encourage labour-force participation and mobility,
- to encourage business risk-taking, and
- to channel effort into productive activities instead of tax avoidance (by simplifying the tax system).

There is little doubt that many current government policies do have output-restricting effects. Thus some policy changes could do some of the things alleged by supply-side economics. If even a small increase in the growth rate of full-employment income could be achieved, the long-term effects on living standards would be enormous. (See Table 39.1 on page 471.) The supply-side agenda includes making the following changes in policies.

Ending Support for Declining Industries: The policy of supporting declining industries reduces resource mobility. Resources that could be more productively employed elsewhere leave the industry more slowly than they would under free-market conditions. Most economists agree that such policies are costly, harmful to growth and, in the end, self-defeating. There is room, however, to disagree on how much transitional adjustment help should be given to labour and capital in declining industries. *Laissez-faire* advocates tend to worry that transitional aid will become *de facto* permanent aid and thus cause the necessary adjustment to be postponed. Others feel that reasonable help could be given to those whose lives are disrupted by the changes associated with growth without inhibiting the growth process itself. (These issues are discussed at greater length in Chapters 19, 23 and 24.)

Ending Policies that Encourage Monopolies and Discourage Competition: Most economists tend to agree with this recommendation, although there is disagreement over how much competition is desirable, and possible, in certain industries. For example, advocates of *laissez-faire* tend to support complete deregulation of fare- and route-setting by airlines, while interventionists tend to worry that cut-throat competition may reduce airline quality and safety.

Ending the Taxing of Income rather than Consumption: Consider a woman in the 40 per cent tax bracket who earns an extra £1,000 and pays £400 income tax. If she spends her after-tax income, she will be able to buy £600 worth of goods. If she saves the income instead, she will be able to buy a £600

bond. If the bond pays, say, a 4 per cent real return, she will earn £24 interest per year. But a 40 per cent tax must then be paid on the interest earnings, leaving only a £14.40 annual income. This is a 1.44 per cent after-tax return on the original £1,000 of income earned. *Laissez-faire* advocate allege that this 'double taxing' is a serious disincentive to saving. They advocate taxes on consumption, not on income, so that any income saved would be tax-free. A tax would be levied only when the interest earned on the savings was spent on consumption.

Ending High Rates of Income Tax: Supply-side advocates allege that high taxes discourage work. But depending on the relative strengths of the substitution and the income effects, high taxes may actually make people increase *or* decrease the amount that they work. Theory is silent on which is more likely, and no hard evidence has yet shown that lowering current tax rates will usually make people work harder. (The effects of any tax-reducing policy on the distribution of income needs also to be considered.)

Ending 'Double Taxation' of Business Income: Business income is taxed first as the income of firms when it is earned and, second, as the income of households, when it is paid out as dividends. This, and other policies that reduce business profits, and hence diminish the return to investing in company shares, are alleged to discourage households from saving and investing in growing but risky businesses that are the mainspring of economic growth.

A CONCLUDING WORD: POLICY TRADE-OFFS

People often ask: Is one policy goal more important than another? This question is interesting only in so far as there are conflicts among the various policies – if they are unrelated to each other, all may be pursued simultaneously. In so far as conflicts exist, so that getting closer to one objective implies getting further from another, the question is interesting. There can, however, be no final answer to the question of relative importance, since any answer depends on both factual judgements about the effects of each and on value judgements about various goals.

Where there are important trade-offs between

goals, choices must be made. Most economists today accept a short-run trade-off between inflation on the one hand and output and employment on the other. A reduction in inflation is usually bought at the cost of a temporary fall in output below its potential level. A temporary rise in output above its potential level can be bought at the cost of a rise in the price level. Many economists also believe, however, that there is no long-run trade-off. They believe that potential income, which is the maximum sustainable level of income, is independent of the economy's rate of inflation. Other economists, however, believe that cost-push forces create a permanent conflict between achieving full employment by demand-management techniques and maintaining a stable price level. They believe that a choice must be made between full employment and stable prices as long as demand management is the only available tool.

Most economists also believe that there is a relation between full employment and growth, but that no choice is required in this case. Low levels of income, employment and capacity utilization are not conducive to the savings and investment which are an important determinant of growth. High levels of income, employment and capacity utilization are. So with full employment and growth, we can have our cake and eat it too! Getting closer to the former tends to give us more of the latter.

Probably one of the most serious trade-offs, and one that as yet we know too little about, is between equity and growth. It is clear that some measures introduced for reasons of equity, such as rent controls and high unemployment benefits, inhibit the adjustments needed for a high growth rate – rent controls by discouraging geographic mobility of labour, and high unemployment benefits by reducing the incentive to move to, or train for, new jobs when old jobs disappear.

To make an intelligent choice on trade-offs, where they do exist, we need much more positive knowledge than we now have about just how much each policy affects growth. Then each of us needs to exercise our value judgements to decide how much reduction in growth it is worth accepting – if this proves necessary – to get a given increase in equity.

There are many ways of classifying macroeconomic policies. We have chosen in this chapter to focus attention on demand-management (fiscal and monetary policies) and on supply-side policies. An alternative classification would be to group policies on more political criteria – whether they tend to be interventionist or market-oriented in character. We shall consider such a classification in Chapter 45. Meanwhile, however, we need to consider the complications that arise in an open economy, and that we have assumed away in this chapter.

SUMMARY

1 The first major tool of demand management is fiscal policy. An expansionary fiscal policy puts upward pressure on interest rates; a contractionary fiscal policy applies downward pressure on interest rates.

2 When initiating an expansionary fiscal policy, a key issue is whether to increase expenditure or to cut taxes. This choice is influenced by such considerations as the size of the change – the expenditure increase needed to obtain a given rise in equilibrium national income is smaller than the necessary tax-revenue decrease – the location of the impact effects, the time-lags involved, and the effect on the size of the government in the economy.

3 Some major limitations of fiscal policy are the following: (i) the crowding-out effect, which

occurs when an expansionary fiscal policy increases interest rates and the resulting reduction in investment partially offsets the initial fiscal stimulus; (ii) the permanent-income hypothesis, which suggests that temporary changes in disposable income may cause savings to change and leave consumption expenditure relatively unaffected; (iii) an expansionary or contractionary policy must be rapidly reversed when private expenditure functions resume their more normal positions.

4 The second major tool of demand management is monetary policy. This works through interest-rate changes and then onto interest-sensitive expenditures. An expansionary monetary policy puts downward pressure on interest rates, while a contractionary policy applies upward pressure.

5 When there is a recessionary gap, interest rates can be forced down by an expansionary policy and real income increased as a result. When national income is at its full-employment level, the long-run effects of an expansionary monetary policy are to raise the price level but to leave income, employment and real interest rates unchanged. In a fully expected inflation, the nominal interest rate will exceed the equilibrium real interest rate by the amount of the inflation.

6 Stabilization policy is difficult to operate using monetary policy because the money supply is hard to control precisely in the short run, and because there are long and variable lags between changes in the money supply and changes in national income and the price level.

7 The major goals of short-run stabilization policy in a closed economy are full employment and a stable price level.

8 With a Keynesian aggregate supply curve of the J-shape, the problem of stabilization policy appears easy: stabilize the aggregate demand curve to achieve full employment and a stable price level.

9 The Phillips curve suggests a relation where inflationary pressure rises continually as national income increases (unemployment falls). The rate of increase of money wages minus the rate of growth of productivity yields the rate of change of unit (wage) costs. Demand pressures make this positive when there is an inflationary gap (unit costs rise), and negative when there is a recessionary gap (unit costs fall).

10 A stable Phillips curve seemed to offer policy-makers a trade-off between inflation on the one hand and unemployment and national income on the other hand. This trade-off appears, however, to have been illusory in the long run. An attempt to hold unemployment below the natural rate, which means income above its potential level, leads to an accelerating inflation

rate as the Phillips curve shifts upwards continually.

11 An entrenched inflation is difficult to break because expectations of continuing inflation can push the SRAS curve upwards in spite of the absence of an inflationary gap.

12 An additional anti-inflationary policy is a prices and incomes policy. Such a policy, which works through the aggregate supply curve, is unable to suppress a demand inflation indefinitely, but it could shorten the recession that accompanies the breaking of an entrenched inflation. Some economists feel that such a policy is needed as a permanent check to wage-cost-push inflation without which full employment and stable prices would prove incompatible.

13 Limitations of demand-management policies, whether operated through monetary or fiscal forces, are the following: (i) demand management cannot stabilize income completely because time-lags and other uncertainties make fine-tuning potentially destabilizing; (ii) demand management cannot eliminate frictional, structural or real-wage unemployment; (iii) demand management cannot deal with permanent wage-cost-push inflation if it exists; and (iv) economic growth is mainly influenced by micro supply-side rather than macro demand-management policies.

14 Supply-side economics seeks to achieve economic gains by long-term measures designed to raise the rate of growth by shifting the long-run aggregate supply curve to the right. Some specific policies are designed to encourage saving, raise mobility and labour-force participation, and encourage entrepreneurial activities.

15 Where genuine trade-offs occur, no policy can achieve all our goals, and choices have to be made between them.

Exchange Rates and Exchange Regimes

In Chapter 32, we integrated foreign trade into the model of income determination. (Pages 390–94 of that chapter should be reviewed now.) We observed that the main determinants of imports and exports are national income and international relative prices. In that earlier discussion, we held international relative prices constant by assuming each pair of countries' price levels to be unchanged, as well as the exchange rate between their two currencies. This leaves income as the only variable that can maintain equilibrium in international payments. A change in exports causes the home country's national income to change in the same direction, while a change in that country's import function causes its national income to change in the opposite direction: an upward shift in the import function leading to a reduction in equilibrium national income, and vice versa.

We are now ready to see how prices exert influences on the values of exports and imports. To do this, we first allow the exchange rate to change and then we allow international price levels to change as well. When we have done all this, we will find that the main variable that changes to restore equilibrium in international payments is the exchange rate – i.e. changes in relative prices rather than changes in national income do the main job.

To see intuitively what is involved, consider the case in which the home country suffers an exogenous fall in its exports, which means the same fall in its *net exports*. (If X falls with M constant, then X − M falls by the same amount.)

We already know from Chapter 32 that, *ceteris paribus*, a fall in net exports will reduce the home country's national income. But the fall in exports will also mean less demand for the country's currency on foreign-exchange markets. This will tend to cause its

exchange rate to fall which, as we shall see, encourages exports and discourages imports through a relative price effect. These changes increase net exports and tend to offset the initial effect of the exogenous fall in exports. If the fall in net exports is reduced because of the exchange-rate changes, then the fall in national income needed to restore equilibrium is less than it would have been if the exchange rate had been fixed.

What we are going to study in the first part of this chapter is the detailed workings of this exchange-rate mechanism. In the second half of the chapter, we consider the regimes for determining exchange rates that have been used by the world's trading countries at various times during the twentieth century. Then, in Chapter 44, we take both income and price changes into account to complete the study of how international equilibrium is restored after it is disturbed by various shocks, and to make a final reconsideration of fiscal and monetary policies.

Two Important Distinctions

At the outset we need to introduce two important distinctions that we will need at various points over this and the next chapter. We distinguish between small and large open economies, and between tradeable and non-tradeable commodities.

Large and Small Open Economies: A LARGE OPEN ECONOMY is one whose imports and exports are so large in relation to the total volume of trade in those commodities that it can affect their prices by changing the quantities that it buys or sells. A SMALL OPEN ECONOMY is one whose imports and exports are too small in relation to the total volume of trade in those

commodities to affect their prices by changing the quantities that it buys and sells. A small open economy must accept the internationally determined *prices* of the goods that it trades and adjust the *quantities* that it trades in response to *given* prices. The UK comes closer to fulfilling the conditions of a small, rather than a large, open economy, and we therefore make that assumption about the UK's trading position.

Tradeable and Non-Tradeable Commodities: We can conceptually divide all commodities into two types. TRADEABLES are goods and services that enter into international trade, such as motorcars and wheat. For a small open economy such as the UK, the prices of tradeables denominated in foreign currency are given, whether it is the country that imports them, or exports them, since these prices are set on international markets. NON-TRADEABLES are goods and services that are produced and sold domestically but do not enter into international trade, such as haircuts and gravel.[1] Their prices are set on domestic markets by domestic supply and demand and these prices are unaffected by market conditions for the same products in other countries.

EXCHANGE RATES

With these preliminaries settled, we can begin our study of exchange rates.

---

1 Sixty years ago, many goods were too perishable or too costly to transport to be traded internationally. Today, with refrigeration and high-speed, low-cost transport, there are relatively few goods that do not routinely move across international borders. The majority of non-traded commodities are now services which must be consumed where they are produced. Many services, however, are also traded – e.g., banking, insurance and shipping.

When British producers sell their products, they require payment in pounds sterling. They need this currency to meet their wage bills, pay for their raw materials and reinvest or distribute their profits. If they sell their goods to British purchasers, there is no problem, since they will be paid in sterling. However, if British producers sell their goods to Indian importers, either the Indians must exchange rupees to acquire sterling to pay for goods, or the British producers must accept rupees – and they will accept rupees only if they know they can exchange the rupees for the sterling that they require. The same holds true for producers in all countries; they must eventually be able to receive payment in the currency of their own country for the goods and services that they sell. *In general, trade between nations can occur only if the currency of one nation can be exchanged for the currency of another.*

International payments, that require the exchange of one national currency for another, can be made in a bewildering variety of ways but, in essence, they involve exchange between people who have one currency and require another.

The Mechanism of International Transactions

An illustration of how transactions in foreign exchange are carried out is given below and summarized in Table 43.1. Suppose that an American firm wishes to purchase a British sportscar to sell in the US. The British firm that produced the car requires payment in pounds sterling. If the car is priced at £10,000, the American firm will go to its bank and ask for a cheque for £10,000. How many dollars the firm must pay to purchase this cheque will depend on the exchange rate between US dollars and pounds sterling. Let us suppose the firm is required to pay

TABLE 43.1 Changes in the Balance Sheets of Two Banks as a Result of International Payments

	UK BANK			AMERICAN BANK	
	Liabilities	*Assets*		*Liabilities*	*Assets*
(1)	Deposits of car exporter +£10,000	No change	(1)	Deposits of car importer −£14,000	No change
(2)	Deposits of computer importer −£10,000	No change	(2)	Deposits of computer exporter +£14,000	No change
(3)	Net change	0	(3)	Net change	0

$14,000. In other words, the exchange rate for this transaction is $1.40 to the pound (14,000/10,000), or, what is the same thing, £0.714 to the dollar (10,000/14,000). The American purchaser will send the cheque to the British car firm, which in turn will deposit the cheque in its bank.

Now assume that, in the same period of time, a British firm purchases seven American personal computers for sale in the UK. If the computers are priced at US $2,000 each, the American seller will have to be paid $14,000. To make this payment, the British importing firm goes to its bank and writes a cheque on its account for £10,000 and receives a cheque drawn on an American bank for $14,000. The cheque is sent to the US and deposited in an American bank.[1]

The American import of a British car reduces the deposit liabilities of the American bank to American residents and increases its deposit liabilities to British residents. The two transactions cancel each other out, and there is no net change in international liabilities. No money need pass between British and American banks to effect the transactions; each bank merely increases the deposit of one domestic customer and lowers the deposit of another. Indeed, as long as the flow of payments between the two countries is equal (Americans pay as much to British residents as British residents pay to Americans), all payments can be managed as in these examples. There will be no need for a net payment from British banks to American banks. What in effect has happened is that the American personal computer manufacturer received the dollars the American car purchaser gave up to get a British-made car, while the British car manufacturer received the sterling that the computer importer gave up.

Two ways of expressing the exchange rate

In our discussion so far, we have compared magnitudes measured in different currencies. These comparisons are made using the exchange rate. As a first step in studying such exchange rates we look at the two ways in which any exchange rate can be expressed.

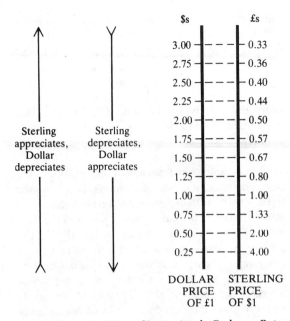

FIGURE 43.1   Two Ways of Expressing the Exchange Rate. The exchange rate between sterling and US dollars can be expressed as the dollar price of one pound sterling or the sterling price of one US dollar

The exchange rate of £1 = $1.50 expresses the *dollar price of £1* – i.e. it costs $1.50 to buy £1. The same information can also be expressed by quoting the *sterling price of $1*. If it costs $1.50 to buy £1, it also costs £0.667 to buy $1 (1/1.50 = 0.667).

In what follows it is necessary to move back and forth between these two ways of expressing the exchange rate. Because this can be confusing, we show their equivalents in Figure 43.1. On the left-hand scale, we give the exchange rate as it is normally expressed in the UK, the price of one unit of sterling in terms of some foreign currency – the US dollar in this case. On the right-hand scale, we give the reciprocal of this rate, the sterling price of one US dollar.[1]

A fall in the exchange rate – say from £1 = $1.50 to £1 = $1.25 – is called a DEPRECIATION of sterling. It takes fewer American dollars to buy £1. Looked at the other way around, the dollar has become more

---

1 The whole set of transactions can be done without even having cheques issued. Instead, the banks can telegraph to their correspondents in the other country with orders to pay. This would give rise to the same set of book entries as those shown in Table 43.1.

1 Although equal distances indicate equal price changes in the left-hand scale, they do not do so on the right-hand scale. This is because the figures on the right-hand scale are the reciprocals of the figures on the left-hand scale. (Because the figures on the right-hand scale are derived from those on the left-hand one, they do not all come out even, and they are quoted correct to two decimal places.)

expensive, in terms of sterling. In the case just considered, instead of costing £0.67, a US dollar now costs £0.80. This means that the relative value of sterling has fallen, while the relative value of the dollar has risen.

A rise in the exchange rate – say from £1 = $1.25 to £1 = $1.50 – is called an APPRECIATION of sterling. It takes more US dollars to buy £1. Looked at the other way around, the dollar has become cheaper relative to sterling. In this case, it now takes only £0.67 to buy a dollar instead of £0.80. As a result, the relative value of home currency has risen while the relative value of foreign currency has fallen.

The direction of changes in the prices expressed in both ways, when sterling appreciates or depreciates, is shown in Figure 43.1. Moving up the page on both scales indicates an appreciation of the sterling exchange rate, while moving down the page on both scales indicates a depreciation. Of course, the situation looked at from the point of view of the US dollar is the other way around. Whenever sterling appreciates relative to the dollar, the dollar depreciates relative to sterling. Whenever sterling depreciates relative to the dollar, the dollar appreciates relative to sterling.

For practice, let us follow through one further movement along both scales. If the pound is worth three dollars (as it was, not too many years ago), then the scale tells us – reading across – that the dollar is worth 33p. If the pound now falls to $2.50, the scale tells us – again reading across – that the dollar is worth 40p. The arrow now tells us that, since we are moving downwards along the scale, sterling is depreciating (it is worth fewer dollars), while the dollar is appreciating (it is worth more sterling).

Internal and External Value of a Currency: The exchange rate describes what is called the EXTERNAL VALUE of a country's currency, which means how much the currency is worth *in terms of the currencies of other countries*. For example, a rise in the exchange rate from $1.50 to $1.75 to the pound sterling means that the external value of sterling has risen. The external value of a currency must be clearly distinguished from what is called its INTERNAL VALUE, which means how much the currency is worth *in terms of purchasing power*. For example, an inflation that doubles the UK price level would cut the internal value of sterling in half because each unit of currency would only buy half as much as it did previously.

The Determination of the Exchange Rate

The theory that we develop here applies to all exchange rates, but for convenience we shall deal with the example of trade between the US and the UK, and with the determination of the rate of exchange between their two currencies, dollars and pounds sterling. To make the treatment general, the US can be thought of as *all foreign countries* and the US dollar as *all foreign exchange*. Since the UK is assumed to be a small open economy, all tradeable commodities – both UK imports and exports – have prices fixed in foreign currency, in this case US dollars.

We start with an important relation with respect to the market for foreign exchange. *Because one currency is traded for another on the foreign-exchange market, it follows that to desire (demand) dollars implies a willingness to offer (supply) pounds, while an offer (supply) of dollars implies a desire (demand) for pounds.*

For example, if at an exchange rate of £1 = $1.50, a British importer demands $6.00, he must be offering £4.00. If an American importer offers $6.00 at that exchange rate, she must be demanding £4.00. For this reason, the theory of the foreign-exchange market can be expressed in either of two ways: (i) we can deal either with the demand for, and the supply of, dollars, *or* (ii) with the demand for, and the supply of, pounds sterling. Both need not be considered. Because we are interested in buying and selling foreign exchange, we shall conduct the argument in terms of the supply, demand, and price of the dollar, which is foreign exchange from the point of view of the UK.

In our two-country world, there are only two groups of private traders on the foreign-exchange market: people who have sterling and want dollars, and people who have dollars and want sterling. *We shall assume, just for the moment, that the Bank of England does not intervene in the foreign-exchange market, and that there are no capital account transactions.*

The Demand for Dollars: The demand for dollars arises because holders of sterling wish to make payments in dollars. It thus arises from imports of American goods and services into the UK.

The Supply of Dollars: Dollars are offered in exchange for sterling because holders of dollars wish to make payments in sterling. The supply of dollars on the foreign-exchange market arises, therefore, because of British exports of goods and services to the United States.

The Exchange Rate Determined Graphically

We now wish to draw demand and supply curves of foreign exchange that will allow us to study the market determination of exchange rates. To do this, we must express the exchange rate *as the sterling price of a unit of foreign exchange* (the US dollar in this case). This is done in Figure 43.2. Note that the vertical axis measures the sterling price of $1. (Figure 43.1 shows how to translate these data into the dollar price of sterling.)

Until one gets familiar with this kind of diagram, these ratios can be confusing, so it is worth emphasizing what is being plotted on this Figure. As we move *upwards* on the vertical axis, the numbers on the axis tell us that the sterling price of a US $1 is rising. Looked at the other way around, this means that the dollar price of sterling is falling. In other words, relative to each other, the dollar is becoming more expensive while sterling is becoming cheaper. So when we move upwards on this axis, sterling is *depreciating* while the dollar is *appreciating*. (This is indicated by the left-hand arrow in the Figure.)

Conversely, when we move downwards on the vertical scale, the numbers on the axis tell us that the sterling price of the dollar is falling. Looked at the other way around, the dollar price of sterling is rising.

This means that, relative to each other, sterling is rising in value while the dollar is falling – i.e. sterling is *appreciating* while the dollar is *depreciating*. This is indicated by the right-hand arrow in the Figure.[1]

The slope of the demand and supply curves for dollars

Next we must determine what the slopes of the demand curve and the supply curve for dollars will be when we plot them on a diagram such as Figure 43.3. We have seen that the demand and supply of currencies on the foreign-exchange market arise out of imports and exports. To determine the slope of the demand and supply curves, we must first see what a change in the exchange rate does to the quantities of imports and exports and then to their values in terms of the foreign currency.

The Demand for Foreign Exchange: First consider imports. Table 43.2 illustrates the effects using hypothetical data. Because the UK is a small open economy, the price of its exports is fixed exogenously in foreign currency. We assume the foreign price is $10 for each unit of exports. In what we call Case 1, a US dollar costs £0.80. In Case 2, to be considered shortly, a US dollar costs £0.57. In the former case, this good must sell for £8 on the UK market. (When the sale price of £8 is converted to US dollars at that exchange rate, the world selling price of $10 is obtained.) We assume that 170 units of the good are imported, making a dollar cost of $1,700. Thus $1,700 is demanded on the foreign-exchange market in order to pay for these goods. Turning now to Case 2, when the exchange rate changes to make a US dollar cost £0.57, the sterling price of this good falls to £5.70. We assume that, in response to the fall in the sterling price, 240 units are now imported into the UK. This means that $2,400 must now be demanded in order to pay for more imports at an unchanged dollar price.

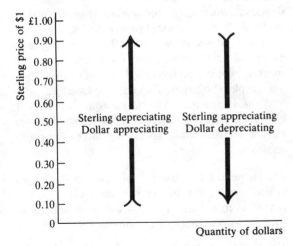

FIGURE 43.2 The Market for Foreign Exchange. The quantity of dollars is on the horizontal axis and the sterling price of one US dollar is on the vertical axis; sterling depreciates when the sterling price of a US dollar rises; sterling appreciates when the sterling price of one US dollar falls

---

1 You may wonder why we did not plot the dollar price of sterling on the horizontal axis, so that an upward movement would be an appreciation while a downward movement would be a depreciation of sterling. Less confusing? But if we did that, the demand curve for dollars would be upward-sloping while the supply curve would be downward-sloping! This would be even more confusing. So we have chosen the lesser of two evils. By quoting the prices in such a way that an appreciation is a downward movement and a depreciation an upward movement, the demand and supply curves have their normal shape.

TABLE 43.2 The Effect on the Demand for Foreign Exchange of Changes in the Exchange Rate

Case	US dollar price of UK import	Sterling price of US$1	Sterling price of UK import	Quantity of import	Dollar value of import (= demand for US dollars)
1	$10	£0.80	£8.00	170 units	$1,700
2	$10	£0.57	£5.70	240 units	$2,400

The appreciation of sterling has led to an increased demand for dollars on the foreign-exchange market.

Now let us state in more general terms what is happening. When the sterling price of a dollar falls (the pound appreciates), the sterling price of imports falls in the UK market. Thus, more imports will be purchased. Since their price is fixed in US dollars (because the UK is a small open economy) and a larger quantity is purchased, more dollars must be spent on them. Thus, the demand curve for US dollars – i.e. for foreign exchange – slopes downwards in Figure 43.3.

The Supply of Foreign Exchange: Now consider UK exports. A numerical example is shown in Table 43.3. The price of a unit of these goods is fixed in US dollars (because the UK is a small open economy). At a sterling price for the dollar of £0.80 (Case 1), each unit of this exported good will be priced at £4.00 in the UK. (At this price, producers are willing to sell the good at home – for £4 – and abroad – for $5.) We assume that 560 units are sold, making a dollar value of $2,800 for UK exports. This many dollars are supplied to the foreign-exchange market in order to pay for the UK goods.

Now let the sterling price of $1 fall to £0.57 (Case 2) and the price of the UK exported good fall to £2.85 in the UK market. The fall in the sterling price of exports has two effects: UK producers will make less of it (assuming a normal upward-sloping supply curve)

and UK consumers will buy more of it. So if less is made and more is bought at home, there must be less available for export. In the Table we assume the quantity exported falls to 320 units. The US dollar value of these exports is now $1,600. This is the amount of dollars that will be supplied to the foreign-exchange market to buy British exports.

The appreciation of sterling has led to a diminished quantity of US dollars supplied on the foreign-exchange market.

Now let us state what is going on more generally in this case. When the sterling price of the dollar falls (the pound appreciates), the price of UK exports falls in terms of sterling. Less is produced and more is consumed at home, so exports fall. Since their dollar price is unchanged, the dollar value of UK exports must fall. As a result, fewer dollars are supplied to the foreign-exchange market in order to buy UK goods.

The foreign-exchange market

Figure 43.3 plots the sterling price of dollars on the vertical axis and the quantity of dollars on the horizontal axis, just as did Figure 43.2. To familiarize you with this diagram, we plot a numerical example. The four points labelled a, b, c and d in the Figure are plotted from Tables 43.2 and 43.3. Each point plots an exchange rate against a quantity of dollars demanded or supplied. Point a is from Case 1 of Table 43.2 and point b is from Case 1 of Table 43.3. They show the

TABLE 43.3 The Effect on the Supply of Foreign Exchange of Changes in the Exchange Rate

Case	US dollar price of UK export	Sterling price of US$1	Sterling price of UK export	Quantity of export	Dollar value of exports (= supply of US dollars)
1	$5	£0.80	£4.00	560 units	$2,800
2	$5	£0.57	£2.85	320 units	$1,600

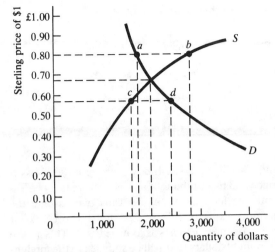

FIGURE 43.3 The Foreign-Exchange Market. The exchange rate is determined by the demand and supply curves in the foreign-exchange market

quantities of dollars demanded and supplied at a price of £0.80. Points *c* and *d* are from Case 2 in Tables 43.3 and 43.2 respectively. They show the quantities supplied and demanded at a price of £0.57.

The other portions of the two curves follow the general rules we have established. The negatively sloped demand curve indicates that, as sterling appreciates, more dollars are demanded to buy imports from the US. The positively sloped supply curve indicates that, as sterling appreciates, fewer dollars are supplied to buy UK exports.

Now look at how the market will determine the equilibrium exchange rate. Where the two curves intersect, which is at the price of £0.67 in Figure 43.3, quantity demanded equals quantity supplied at $2,000, and the exchange rate is in equilibrium. The equilibrium exchange rate is at $1 = £0.67 (which also means that £1 is worth $1.50). To show why this is the equilibrium exchange rate, we need to do no more than we did in the early microeconomics chapters; we follow the consequences of the exchange rate being at any other level.

Assume first that the current price of the dollar is above equilibrium – say it is £0.80 in the Figure. In this case the demand for dollars of $1,700 falls short of the supply of $2,800. The dollar will be in excess supply, so that some people who wish to convert dollars into pounds will be unable to do so. The price of dollars will fall. As a result, fewer dollars will be supplied and more will be demanded.

Now let us see what will happen if the current price

of the dollar is below equilibrium, say £0.57. At this exchange rate the demand for dollars is $2,400 while the supply is only $1,600. Since demand exceeds supply, some people who require dollars to make payments to the US will be unable to obtain them, and the price of dollars will be bid up. The rise in the value of the dollar is the same thing as a fall in the value of sterling. In other words, the sterling exchange rate will depreciate. This rise in the price of dollars reduces the quantity of dollars demanded and increases the quantity of dollars supplied.

Causes of Changes in the Exchange Rate

We may now use the theory we have just developed to understand the effects of several important changes in the conditions that determine exchange rates.

Price-level changes

A Change in the Price Level of One Country: Consider, for example, the case of a localized inflation in the UK. A local British inflation will raise the price of all non-traded goods and services and of all factors of production in the UK. But until the exchange rate changes, the sterling price of *importables* and *exportables* will not change. (Their dollar price is unchanged and if the exchange rate is unchanged, their sterling price will also be unchanged.) What will this do to the quantities of *imports* and *exports?* Since nontradeables rise in price, *imported* goods will now be relatively cheaper than they were, and more imports will be bought. As far as *exports* are concerned, there will be two effects. On the supply side, the rise in factor prices will raise costs and reduce the quantity of *exports* supplied at each price (because the supply curve will shift to the left). But exportables whose prices are unchanged, will look cheap relative to nontradeables, whose prices have risen and, as a result, more will be consumed at home; thus, there will be a smaller quantity of exports.

This leads us to an important conclusion. *A local British inflation raises the quantity of imports and lowers the quantity of exports.* Since international prices are unaffected by the localized British inflation, the demand for dollars to buy increased imports at a given dollar price must rise. Similarly, the supply of dollars to buy fewer British exports at an unchanged dollar price must fall.

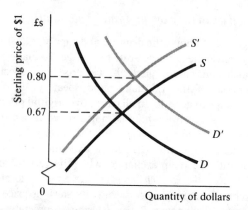

FIGURE 43.4 The Effect of a Localized Inflation. An inflation that raises the UK price level relative to other countries' price levels, causes a depreciation of sterling

The effects are shown in Figure 43.4, where we drop the numerical example and use letters to indicate quantities of dollars demanded and supplied at various exchange rates. As a result of the forces just considered, the demand curve for dollars will shift to the right – from, say, D to D' – while the supply curve shifts to the left – from, say, S to S'. The equilibrium price of dollars must now rise. *In other words, the pound depreciates.* In the Figure, the price of a dollar rises from £0.67 to £0.80. This rise in the value of a dollar means a fall in the value of the pound from being worth $1.50 to only being worth $1.25. (Don't forget that Figure 43.1 is there to help you turn any of these rates around the other way.)

An Equal Percentage Change in the Price Level in Both Countries: Now the prices of UK non-tradeables and UK factors of production rise by the amount of the inflation, but so do the prices of importables and exportables (whose prices are set on world markets) rise because the price level rises abroad as well as at home. These changes are exactly offsetting, and there is therefore no change in imports or exports.

The equal inflation in Britain and abroad leaves the relative prices of non-tradeables, importables and exportables all unchanged in the British market and hence has no effect on the pattern of trade. There is no reason to expect any change in the UK's demand for imports or its supply of exports at the original exchange rate, and hence no reason to expect any shifts in demands and supplies of foreign exchange. *Equal inflations in the two countries leave the equilibrium exchange rate unchanged.*

Differing Rates of Inflation in the Two Countries: Consideration of the last two cases of changes in the price levels, shows that what matters is the relative rates of inflation between any two trading countries. Differences in the inflation rates will cause changes in imports and exports and hence changes in demands and supplies on the foreign-exchange market. Thus the exchange rate between the two currencies will change.

The conclusion that follows from a simple extension of the two cases just studied is important: *If the price level in one country is rising faster (falling slower) than that of another country, the first country's exchange rate will be depreciating (ceteris paribus, of course).*

Structural changes

'Structural change' as we use it in this chapter, has a rather specialized meaning. It is an omnibus term for anything that affects the patterns of international competitiveness, such as changes in cost structures and the invention of new products. For example, a country might become less dynamic than its competitors, so that at the initial set of prices, consumers' demand shifts slowly away from that country's products and towards those of foreign countries. This would cause a slow trend depreciation in the home country's exchange rate.

Dramatic changes, such as major shifts in OPEC pricing policies, will have similar effects, except that they may occur suddenly over a space of months rather than gradually over a space of years.

The general conclusion from what has been established so far is an important one. *Long-term changes in exchange rates can be accounted for mainly by the relative inflation rates and structural changes.*

Capital movements

Finally, we must consider the effects of capital flows on exchange rates. First, consider UK capital imports. If holders of US dollars wish to transfer funds to the UK for any reason, they will be suppliers of dollars to the foreign-exchange market. This is equally true whether they wish to buy UK goods and services or UK financial assets. So capital imports, whether to put money into UK (sterling-denominated) bank accounts, to buy short-term Treasury or commercial bills, longer-term bonds, shares in joint-stock companies, or to build factories in the UK, all add to the demand for pounds, and the supply of dollars on the foreign-exchange market. It follows that increased

capital exports into the UK will increase the supply of dollars and cause their price to fall on the foreign-exchange market and hence cause sterling to appreciate.

Now consider UK capital exports. When holders of sterling wish to invest their funds abroad for any of the reasons listed in the previous paragraph, they become demanders of foreign exchange – US dollars in our sample case. This adds to the demand for dollars. It follows that, *ceteris paribus*, an increase in capital exports from the UK will increase the demand for dollars and hence bid up their price, causing sterling to depreciate.

This statement is true for short-term and long-term capital movements. However, since the motives that lead to capital movements often differ between the short and long terms, each needs to be considered.

Long-Term Capital: Long-term capital movements are mainly related to different prospects for earnings on capital in various countries. A country that offers persistently high returns on capital will attract inflows of long-term capital. Expectations of long-term earnings also depend on the expectations that conditions will continue to be favourable to such earnings in the future. Thus expectations about the general political and economic stability of a country will influence its long-term capital flows.

Short-Term Capital: The owners of capital that moves from country to country for short periods are not interested in the long-term outlooks of various countries. Instead their main concerns are short-term interest rates and expectations of movements in exchange rates over the short term. If exchange rates are not expected to change over the short term, capital will tend to search out the highest short-term interest rates. A rise in one country's rates will, *ceteris paribus*, tend to cause an inflow of short-term capital (and hence an appreciation of the value of its currency on the foreign-exchange market).

Expected changes in exchange rates will also exert an influence. An expected fall in the country's exchange rate will mean capital losses when short-term capital is eventually moved out of a country, and this will tend to cause an exodus of short-term capital immediately. An expected rise in the exchange rate will mean capital gains when the capital is moved out of the country after the exchange adjustment occurs. This will tend to cause an influx of short-term capital so that its owners can be holding the country's currency when its value rises.

Changes in the exchange rate: a summary

Figure 43.5 shows the demand and supply shifts that can cause the exchange rate to change. To make our conclusions more general, we drop the specific example of the US dollar and speak of foreign exchange in general. In all cases, the original price is p_0, the curve that shifts is indicated with a prime mark, the higher price is p_1, and the lower price is p_2. In each case, the horizontal axis measures the quantity of foreign exchange, while the vertical axis measures *the sterling price* of one unit of foreign exchange. Part (i) shows that the sterling price of foreign exchange will rise (sterling depreciates) if there is an increase in the demand for foreign exchange. Part (ii) shows that the same exchange-rate change can be caused by a decrease in the supply of foreign exchange. Parts (iii) and (iv) show that a fall in the sterling price of foreign exchange (sterling appreciates) can be brought about by either an increase in the supply of foreign exchange or a reduction in the demand for it.

The Trade-Weighted Exchange Rate

We have seen how to calculate the exchange rate when we consider only two countries. When we consider foreign exchange in general, how do we calculate the appropriate exchange rate for sterling? One answer is to use what is called A TRADE-WEIGHTED EXCHANGE RATE. This rate is an average of the exchange rate between sterling and each of the UK's major trading partners, with each rate being weighted by the amount of trade between the UK and the country in question. As a result, a movement in the sterling exchange rate with a major trading partner has a big effect on the trade-weighted exchange rate, while the equivalent movement with a minor trading partner has only a little effect.

The Effective Exchange Rate

Changes in the trade-weighted exchange rate are valuable indicators of changes in a country's international price competitiveness, but they do not tell the whole story. To illustrate, note that Sweden does little trade with Canada, so changes in the Swedish kroner–Canadian dollar exchange rate will have little effect on the Swedish trade-weighted exchange rate. But Sweden and Canada compete strongly in the sale of a number of commodities, such as pulp and paper,

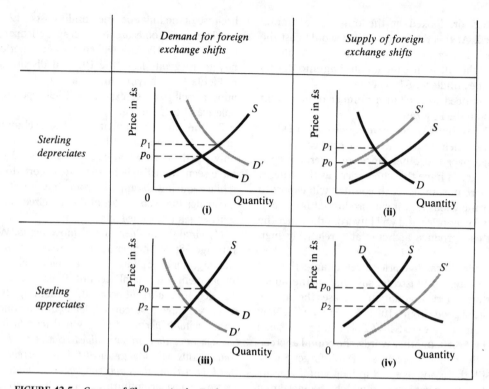

FIGURE 43.5   Causes of Changes in the Exchange Rate. Sterling is depreciated by an increase in the demand for, and/or a decrease in the supply of, foreign exchange; sterling is appreciated by a decrease in the demand for, and/or an increase in the supply of, foreign exchange

to the United States. If the kroner depreciates against the Canadian dollar, Swedish exports to the US will gain a price advantage over Canadian exports.

The International Monetary Fund calculates a series called the effective exchange rate. This attempts to weight changes on individual exchange rates by their importance in influencing competitiveness against each other's products and against those from other countries. Thus a change in the Swedish kroner–Canadian dollar rate would be weighted by the importance of Swedish sales to Canada *and* of Swedish sales to other countries that are made in competition with Canadian products.

What Determines the Value of the Exchange Rate in the Long Run?

So far in this chapter we have shown how demand and supply determine exchange rates. We have also shown how various forces can shift demands or supplies on the foreign-exchange market and so cause exchange rates to change.

We now ask why is the average value of the exchange rate taken over several years what it is, rather than something else? Why, for example, was the average sterling-dollar exchange rate, around $1.50 between 1980 and 1986, well down from what it had been a decade and a half previously?

The simple answer is that the relevant demand and supply curves intersected at a sterling price of around US$1.50 in that period, but at higher prices in earlier decades. But why did these curves intersect at those prices rather than at other very different ones? One theory that tries to answer this question seeks to explain the long-run trend around which the actual market rate fluctuates. It is called the PURCHASING POWER PARITY (PPP) THEORY, and the long-term rate predicted by this theory is called the PURCHASING POWER PARITY (PPP) EXCHANGE RATE.

The PPP rate is the one that equates the costs of purchasing a representative bundle of traded goods and services between any two countries. Thus, if a representative bundle costs $100 in the US and £62.50 in the UK, the PPP exchange rate is

$1 = £0.625 or, looked at the other way around £1 = $1.60. At this exchange rate, it would cost the same for a holder of sterling to buy the bundle for £62.50 in the UK or to convert sterling into dollars and buy the bundle for $100 in the US.

We now need to explain a number of important points about the PPP rate.

(1) If the exchange rate between two countries is at the PPP rate, neither will have an overall competitive advantage over the other since, on average, each country's goods have the same prices as the other's. In these circumstances, each country will export to the other the goods that it can produce at home at a relatively lower price and will buy from the other the goods it can produce at home at a relatively high price.[1]

(2) Changes in relative price levels change the PPP exchange rate. To illustrate, say that in the above example an American inflation increases the price of the bundle of goods from $100 to $125 in the US. Now the PPP rate changes to $1 = £2 or, what is the same thing, £1 = $0.50. In other words, the pound appreciates and the dollar depreciates. (Don't forget Figure 43.1 is still there on page 528 to help you if you are bothered by these ratios or by which changes are a depreciation and which are an appreciation.) Notice that, if the actual rate follows the PPP rate, the American inflation does not put it at a competitive disadvantage. The rise in the US price level raises all of its costs and prices, but the depreciation of the exchange rate exactly offsets this so that the prices of the bundle of commodities remain the same in both countries. Indeed, the PPP rate has the effect of holding the relation between the price levels of the two countries constant when they are measured in a common currency.

(3) *If the external value of a country's currency is overvalued relative to its PPP rate, that country will tend to have a deficit on the balance of trade while, if it is undervalued, the country will tend to have a surplus.* Assume in the previous example that, although the cost of purchasing the representative bundle in the US rose from $100 to $125, the actual US exchange rate remained constant at $1 = £0.625. Now the US dollar is overvalued relative to its PPP rate. Converting the cost of the representative bundle from £62.50 to US dollars at the existing exchange rate yields $100 but,

because of the inflation, the bundle costs $125 in the US. The same goods are, on average, cheaper in the UK than in the US. This will encourage Americans to buy more goods from the UK and discourage UK residents from buying American goods. American imports will rise and exports will fall, opening up a balance-of-trade deficit.

By the same argument, the UK exchange rate undervalues sterling relative to its PPP rate. (£1 is still only worth $1.60 when its PPP value is $2.) As we have seen, the UK will increase its exports to the US while reducing its imports from that country. This illustrates the second part of the italicized statement with which we opened this section.

(4) Finally, consider capital movements. We saw on page 388 of Chapter 32 that when a country is a net importer of capital (i.e. has a 'favourable' balance of payments on capital account) it also has a matching deficit on current account. Combining this with what we have just learned, leads to the conclusion that *capital-importing countries will tend to have exchange rates that are overvalued relative to their PPP rates – this will produce the deficit on current account needed to balance the surplus on capital account.*

Now consider countries that are net exporters of capital. Such countries have a deficit on capital account, which must be balanced by a surplus on current account. We have seen that surpluses are generated by having the country's actual exchange rate below its purchasing power parity rate. It follows that *countries that are net exporters of capital will tend to have exchange rates that are undervalued relative to their PPP rates.*

EXCHANGE-RATE REGIMES

A system for determining exchange rates is called an EXCHANGE-RATE REGIME. Although the nations of the world have tried many different regimes, no system has proved fully satisfactory.

Among the principal payments regimes, two extremes can be distinguished. The first is called a regime of FIXED EXCHANGE RATES or sometimes PEGGED EXCHANGE RATES. In it, exchange rates are fixed at pre-announced 'par' values that are only changed deliberately as an act of government policy. When this does happen, a fall in the official par value is called a DEVALUATION and a rise is called a REVALUATION.

The second is called a regime of FLOATING or

---

[1] Those of you who have read Chapter 22 will recognize this as the workings of the law of *comparative* advantage.

FLUCTUATING EXCHANGE RATES. It is a regime where exchange rates are determined by market demands and supplies in the absence of government intervention. Under this regime, the exchange rate is free to change continually as the demands and supplies of foreign exchange change; a rise in the exchange rate is then called an APPRECIATION and a fall a DEPRECIATION.

Between these two extremes is a third regime, called a MANAGED FLOAT or sometimes a DIRTY FLOAT. In this regime, the central bank seeks to have *some* stabilizing influence on the exchange rate, but does not try to fix it at a publicly announced par value. This regime is really a combination of the other two.

We study the two extreme cases of fully fixed and freely fluctuating rates for two reasons. First, understanding them is a prerequisite to understanding the managed float which is nothing more than a mixture of the two systems. Second, we wish to discuss the reasons why each of the three regimes has appealed to economists at one time or another.

Twentieth-Century Regimes

The world has worked under several exchange regimes in the present century. In this section, we briefly outline them, after which we study the theory that explains the behaviour of each type of regime.

When the twentieth century began, the world had been working for more than a century under a payments system called the GOLD STANDARD. In this system, each country tied its own national currency to gold by guaranteeing that holders of a unit of its paper currency could convert it on demand into a stated amount of gold. The gold convertibility of different national currencies established a fixed rate of exchange between them. For example, in 1914 the British pound was convertible into 0.257 standard ounces of gold, while the US dollar was convertible into 0.053 ounces. This established a rate of exchange between the two currencies of US$4.86 per £1 sterling, because US$4.86 was worth exactly as much gold as was £1.

The gold standard broke down under a series of crises that rocked the world's financial systems during the 1920s and early 1930s. Country after country dropped the gold convertibility of their currencies and thus removed the force that fixed the exchange rates between them. The gold standard finally came to an end when, in September 1931, the

UK, then the world's most important trading nation, suspended the gold convertibility of sterling. There followed a period of fluctuating exchange rates. Some countries pegged their rates to the currencies of one of their major trading partners. The currencies of most of the major trading countries, however, fluctuated freely on foreign-exchange markets where their rates were determined by the demands and supplies of foreign exchange.

With the outbreak of the Second World War in 1939, virtually all of the world's trading nations pegged their exchange rates and regulated foreign-exchange markets so as to use funds earned from exports for their war efforts. In 1944, representatives of the allied countries, who were by then obviously winning the war against Germany and Japan, met in the town of Bretton Woods in New Hampshire, USA to design the postwar payments regime. The system that emerged was one of fixed rates, but rates that could be adjusted in the face of what was called a fundamental disequilibrium (i.e. *persistent* excess demand or supply). Because the rates were pegged but were allowed to be changed occasionally, the system was dubbed an ADJUSTABLE PEG SYSTEM. It was also called the BRETTON WOODS SYSTEM after the town where it was born. This was the world's first payments system to be designed wholly by conscious acts of policy. The earlier gold standard arose because each country made its domestic currency convertible into gold and the fixed rates followed as a consequence. The regime of fluctuating rates that followed arose without central design and, instead, currencies were allowed to find their own levels on free markets.

The functioning of the Bretton Woods system was helped by a new international organization, the International Monetary Fund (IMF). This organization was designed to provide assistance to countries who were having difficulty maintaining their exchange rates in the face of fluctuations in demand and supply that, although severe, were thought to be temporary. The Bretton Woods system served the world well for two decades. Then in the late 1960s, financial markets were once again rocked by a series of crises and the regime of fixed exchange rates became increasingly difficult to defend. Finally, in the early 1970s, the system was abandoned as country after country announced that it would no longer defend a fixed par value for its exchange rate.

A period of freely fluctuating exchange rates followed. However, fluctuations turned out to be more extreme than had been expected, and slowly,

central banks in many countries increased their degree of intervention into foreign-exchange markets. As that happened, the payments system evolved from something close to freely floating rates, to one of managed floats. We will have more to say about these various payments systems later. But this preliminary survey is sufficient to provide the background to a study of the theory of how each system works.

A Regime of Fixed Exchange Rates

In a regime of fixed exchange rates, each country's central bank intervenes in the foreign-exchange market to prevent that country's exchange rate from going outside a narrow band on either side of a stated 'par value'.

Having picked an exchange rate for their currency against, say, the US dollar, each foreign central bank must then manage matters so that the chosen rate can actually be maintained. In the face of short-term fluctuations in market demand and supply, each central bank can maintain its fixed exchange rate by entering the exchange market and buying and selling foreign exchange as required. To do so, it must be prepared to offset imbalances in demand and supply by its own sales or purchases of foreign exchange.

To do this, the central bank has to hold reserves of acceptable foreign exchange. When there is any abnormally low demand for its country's currency on the market, the bank keeps the currency from falling in value by selling foreign-exchange and buying up domestic currency. This depletes its reserves of foreign exchange. When there is an abnormally high demand for its country's currency on the foreign-exchange market, the central bank prevents the currency from appreciating in value by selling domestic currency in return for foreign exchange. This augments its stocks of foreign exchange.

As long as the central bank is trying to maintain an exchange rate that equates demand and supply on average, the policy can be successful. Sometimes the bank will be buying and other times selling, but its holdings of foreign exchange (i.e. its reserves) will fluctuate around a constant average level.

If, however, there is a long-lasting shift in demand or supply of a nation's currency on the foreign-exchange market, the long-term equilibrium rate will move away from the pegged rate. It will then be very difficult to maintain the pegged rate. For example, if there is a major inflation in the UK while prices are stable in the United States, the PPP value of the sterling-dollar exchange rate will fall. In a free market the pound would depreciate and the US dollar would appreciate. But a fixed exchange rate is not a free-market rate. If the Bank of England persists in trying to maintain the original exchange rate, it will have to meet the excess demand for US dollars by selling from its reserves. This policy can persist only as long as it has sufficient reserves of its own, or that it can borrow from the IMF or other central banks. These reserves must be used to hold the exchange rate above its long-run equilibrium level. The central bank cannot do this indefinitely. Sooner or later the reserves that it has, and those that it can borrow, will be exhausted.

Advantages of fixed exchange rates

Advocates of fixed exchange rates feel that a regime of fixed rates has many advantages.

- They feel that secure knowledge of what rates will be encourages international trade.
- They also wish to prevent speculation, which they fear would destabilize rates under a regime of floating rates, as speculators rushed alternately to buy and sell a currency as a result of waves of optimism and pessimism about what was going to happen to its market value.
- They worry that nations will try to gain competitive trading advantages over each other by engaging in bouts of self-defeating devaluations and counter-devaluations of their currencies. They feel that fixed rates, with only occasional changes in the face of a clear disequilibrium, would prevent such beggar-thy-neighbour policies from breaking out again as they had in the 1930s. (See Chapter 31, pages 394–5.)

Problems with fixed exchange rates

The fixed-exchange-rate system has three characteristic problems. These were amply illustrated by the experience of the Bretton Woods fixed-exchange-rate regime that lasted from 1945 to the early 1970s, and we draw our examples from that experience.

The Provision of Reserves: With a free market, fluctuations in current- and capital-account payments cause the exchange rate to fluctuate. To prevent such fluctuations when rates are fixed, the central bank buys and sells foreign exchange in the necessary amounts. These operations require the authorities to hold reserves of foreign exchange,

without which they cannot maintain the pegged rate.

In the past, when exchange rates have been fixed, reserves have been held in the form of gold and such currencies as sterling and dollars. National currencies serve well enough as reserves as long as these reserve currencies have a stable value. The devaluation of a reserve currency, however, reduces the value of the reserves of that currency held by the central banks of all other countries. Fear that a devaluation will occur, destroys the acceptability of a currency as a means of holding reserves.

The problem of providing reserves, although serious, should not be insurmountable in any future system of fixed rates. After all, a balanced portfolio composed of some holdings of all currencies could be held as reserves. For whenever one currency falls in value against a second currency, the second currency rises in value against the first.

Coping with Long-Term Disequilibria: With fixed exchange rates, long-term equilibrium can be expected to develop because of lasting shifts in PPP exchange rates. There are three important reasons for such shifts. First, different trading countries have different rates of inflation. Second, changes in the demands for, and supplies of, imports and exports are associated with long-term economic growth. Third, structural changes, such as major new innovations or a change in the price of oil, cause major changes in imports and exports.

The associated shifts in demand and supply on the foreign-exchange market imply that, even starting from a current-account equilibrium with imports equal to exports, there is no reason to believe that equilibrium will exist at the same rate of exchange 5 or 10 years later. Indeed, the rate of exchange that will lead to a balance-of-payments equilibrium will tend to change over time; over a decade the change can be substantial.

Governments may react to long-term disequilibria in at least three ways. First, the exchange rate can be changed whenever it is clear that difficulty in maintaining the existing pegged exchange rate is the result of a long-term shift in the PPP exchange rate, and not the result of some transient factor. Second, the country's overall price level can be changed to make the present fixed exchange rate become the equilibrium rate. To restore equilibrium, countries with overvalued currencies need to have deflations and countries with undervalued currencies need to have inflations. But countries with overvalued currencies

find deflations difficult and costly to accomplish – e.g. reductions in aggregate demand intended to lower the price level are likely to raise unemployment. Countries with undervalued rates often have explicit policies of avoiding inflation. Third, restrictions can be imposed on trade and foreign payments. Imports, and foreign spending by tourists and governments can be restricted, and the export of capital can be slowed or even stopped. (This is what the UK did from 1940 to 1979.)

Since restrictions on trade and foreign payments are undesirable in a world economy characterized by large-scale international trade and foreign investment, and since deflations of the price level are difficult and costly to bring about, most countries want to preserve the possibility of making occasional changes in their exchange rates even when fixed rates are an object of policy.

Coping with Speculative Crises: The most important reason for speculative crises is that, over time, equilibrium exchange rates get further and further away from any given set of fixed rates. When the disequilibrium becomes obvious to everyone, traders and speculators come to believe that a realignment of rates is due. There is a rush to buy currencies expected to be revalued and a rush to sell currencies expected to be devalued. Even if the authorities take drastic steps to maintain rates at their current pegged values, there may be doubt that these measures will work before the exchange reserves are exhausted. Speculative flows of funds can reach very large proportions, and it may be impossible to avoid changing the exchange rate under such pressure.

As the PPP value of a country's exchange rate changes over time, possibly under the impact of high inflation, it becomes obvious that the central bank is having more and more difficulty holding the pegged rate. So when a crisis arises, speculators sell the country's currency. If it is devalued, they can buy it back at a lower price and earn a capital gain. If it is not, they can buy it back at the price at which they sold it and lose only the commission costs on the deal. This asymmetry, with speculators having a chance to make large profits by risking only a small loss, was what eventually destroyed the Bretton Woods system.

A Regime of Flexible Exchange Rates

Under a system of flexible exchange rates, demand and supply determine exchange rates without any

government intervention. Since the foreign-exchange rate varies to ensure that the demand and supply of foreign exchange is always equal, governments can turn their attention to such domestic problems as lowering inflation and unemployment, leaving the exchange rate and the balance of payments to take care of themselves – at least so went the theory before flexible rates were introduced.

Unfortunately, this optimistic picture did not materialize when the world went over to flexible exchange rates in the early 1970s. Free-market fluctuations in exchange rates were far greater – and hence potentially more upsetting to the performance of national economies and to the flow of international trade – than many economists had anticipated. As a result, central banks have felt the need to intervene quite frequently and extensively to stabilize exchange rates.

Actual exchange-rate experience

We saw earlier in the chapter that the long-run trend value of a country's actual exchange rate is predicted by the PPP theory to follow the PPP exchange rate. Research shows that actual exchange rates do follow their PPP rates quite closely, but only as a long-term trend. Fluctuations around the PPP rate are large in the short term. Indeed the actual rate can, and often does, diverge by large amounts for periods of up to several years.

Speculative Behaviour: During the Bretton Woods period of fixed exchange rates, the advocates of floating rates argued that speculators would stabilize the actual rate within a narrow band around the PPP rate. The argument was that, since everyone knew the equilibrium exchange rate was the PPP rate, deviations from that rate would quickly be removed by speculators seeking a profit when the rate returned to its PPP level. To illustrate, suppose the PPP rate is US$2.00 = £1.00 and that the actual rate falls to $1.90 = £1.00. The argument was that speculators would rush to buy pounds at $1.90, expecting to sell them for $2.00. when the rate returned to its PPP level. This very action would raise the demand for sterling and help push its value back towards $2.00. Such behaviour is called *stabilizing speculative behaviour.*

Such behaviour could be relied upon to stabilize the exchange rate near its PPP value *if* speculators could be sure that the deviations would be small and short-

lived. But as we have noted, the swings around the PPP rate have been wide and have lasted for long periods. Under these circumstances, speculation can no longer be relied on to stabilize the exchange rate at, or near, its PPP rate.

To understand this last point, consider an example. Assume that sterling fell to US$1.90 when its PPP rate was $2.00. If speculators knew that deviations were short-lasting, they would rush to buy sterling hoping to sell it back at $2.00 for a profit. However, when experience showed that rates could deviate from their PPP rates a great deal, and for long periods of time, speculators came to understand that the rate could go far below $1.90, possibly as low as $1.60, and that it could stay there for quite a while before returning to $2.00. In that case it might be worth speculating on a price of $1.80 next week rather than a price of $2.00 in some indefinite future. This would lead speculators to sell sterling and thus drive its price down even further. This is destabilizing speculative behaviour.

The extremely important conclusion is that *the wide swings in exchange rates that occur show that speculative buying and selling cannot always be relied on to hold exchange rates very close to their PPP values.*

A Regime of Managed Floats

As a result of the early experience with floating exchange rates, and the discovery that speculation could not be relied on to hold actual rates near their purchasing power rates, most countries quickly adopted a system of managed floating rates.

A major difference between the system of managed floats and the Bretton Woods system is that central banks no longer publicly announce par values for exchange rates that they are committed in advance to defend even at heavy cost. Central banks are thus free to adjust their exchange-rate targets as circumstances change. Sometimes they leave the rate completely free to fluctuate, and at other times they interfere actively to alter the exchange rate from its free-market value.

Some countries have opted for what is called a *currency bloc* by pegging their exchange rates against each other and then indulging in a joint float against the outside world. The best-known currency bloc is the European Monetary System – the EMS. Under this arrangement, most of the countries of the EEC maintain fixed rates among their own currencies but allow them to float as a bloc against the dollar.

Some countries maintain stable values for their

currencies in terms of another major trading currency, such as the US dollar, the British pound, and the French franc, especially if one of these is a major trading partner. Their rates then fluctuate against those of the other two major currencies.

Although central banks do intervene in the foreign-exchange market in an effort to reduce some of its fluctuations, they have not had sufficient reserves to stop major exchange-rate overshootings of the type discussed above. Of course, they could never hope to resist a shift in the PPP rate permanently. So the current exchange regime of managed floats has the advantages and the disadvantages of the regime of fully flexible rates, with the added advantage that the authorities can iron out some of the shorter-term speculative fluctuations. Many people are, however, concerned about the degree of fluctuations in current exchange rates and the long periods over which exchange rates deviate from their PPP rates. These worries guarantee that the debate over changes in the exchange regime will continue over the next decades.

SUMMARY

1 Large open economies can influence world prices of the tradeable goods that they import and export; small open economies must accept these world prices as given.

2 Exchange rates are the price of one national currency in terms of another. They are determined by demands and supplies in the foreign-exchange market. The demand for foreign exchange arises from the importing of goods and services and the exporting of capital. The supply of foreign exchange arises from the export of goods and services and the import of capital.

3 The equilibrium exchange rate between two countries' currencies changes when one country inflates at a different rate from the other country; when their relative patterns of competitiveness change; and when there is a change in net capital flows.

4 The long-term trend value of the exchange rate is determined by purchasing power parity: the exchange rate will change so as to hold constant between countries the price of a bundle of internationally traded commodities expressed in a common currency. A country's exchange rate will be depreciated by a rise in its relative price level, by structural changes that make it harder to export, and by the export of capital. The opposite changes will appreciate its rate.

5 Major advantages of an exchange regime of fixed rates are greater short-run security of international values and the avoidance of some speculative capital movements that cause foreign-exchange rates to diverge far from the PPP rate. The disadvantages are the need to adjust domestic policy to maintain external balance, the difficulty of providing adequate reserves, the difficulty of making adjustments of the rate when the PPP rate begins to diverge significantly from the pegged rate, and the enormous speculative movements of capital that occur when people come to feel that the pegged rate must be changed.

6 Major advantages of flexible rates are that policymakers do not have to subjugate domestic policy to the needs of external balance; most of the time, gradual adjustment of actual rates occurs as the PPP rate changes, and exchange controls and other restrictions on people's ability to spend money abroad are unnecessary. The major disadvantage is that the actual rate can diverge greatly from the PPP rate because of capital movements that are either purely speculative or in response to interest-rate changes due to domestic monetary policy (which can cause exchange-rate overshooting).

7 Managed floats attempt to get some of the best of both worlds by allowing the exchange rate to vary so as to achieve a payments balance (and so freeing domestic policy for domestic objectives) while maintaining enough intervention to stop the most extreme of speculative swings in exchange rates.

Macroeconomic Policy in an Open Economy

In Chapter 32 we saw how shifts in the values of imports and exports could cause national income to change in order to restore equilibrium. In Chapter 43 we concentrated on the equilibrating effects of relative price changes operating through the exchange rate. In the present chapter we combine income and price changes into a more general view of how the international equilibrating mechanism works, and of the problems it causes for policy-makers. Consideration of the openness of the economy introduces some new policy goals that may be in conflict with policy goals arising solely from domestic considerations. In the following section, we begin our study by considering these potentially conflicting goals.

Internal and External Balance

Internal objectives refer to conditions that the macroeconomic policy-makers are seeking to achieve within the domestic economy. External objectives refer to conditions that the policy-makers are seeking to achieve with respect to the balance of payments and the exchange rate. The former are, as we have previously stressed, primary goals in the sense that full employment and price stability are seen to be desirable in their own right. The latter are, in contrast, secondary, because the balance of payments and the exchange rate may pose problems which interfere with one or both primary goals.

Internal Balance: INTERNAL BALANCE occurs when policy-makers have achieved their goals with respect to the domestic economy. In the short run, these goals are to achieve low rates of unemployment and inflation. In discussing these objectives, it is important to notice what policy-makers cannot, as well as what they can, hope to accomplish.

In this discussion we shall ignore the possible problem of wage-cost-push inflation because there is nothing particularly special arising from moving from a closed to an open economy to be said about it. Supply-side and prices/incomes policies were discussed in the previous chapter and are referred to again in the next. From a demand-management point of view, anti-inflationary policy can only seek to avoid *demand* inflations, which means avoiding inflationary gaps. As far as unemployment is concerned, the long-term goal is to achieve a level of unemployment that is consistent with the absence of an inflationary gap. If significant structural and frictional unemployment still exists at that level of unemployment, other (mainly micro labour-market) policies are needed.

Thus the internal goal of demand management that we assume in this chapter may be summarized as trying to achieve the full employment, or potential level, of national income. It must also be added that, if a major inflation currently exists, the temporary goal of macro policy may be to produce a deflationary gap, with current income below potential income, in order to break the existing inflation.

Internal balance now refers to a situation in which the policy-makers' target level of national income has been achieved. This will normally be full-employment income, but it may temporarily be a lower level of national income, if current policy is directed to reducing an entrenched inflation through demand-management policies. (Recall that an entrenched inflation means one in which expectations that it will continue are firmly held and are not easily changed.)

External Balance: The term EXTERNAL BALANCE refers to a situation in which policy-makers' targets with respect to the balance of payments and exchange rates have been achieved. With respect to

external conditions, policy-makers will, depending on the conditions in which they operate, be concerned with the balance of payment on various accounts and the exchange rate. Here are some of the possibilities.

- If the country is on a fixed exchange rate, policy-makers will need to obtain an approximate balance of payments at that rate so that the pressures to change the rate do not become irresistible.[1]

- If the country is a long-term importer or exporter of capital (see page 388 above), policy-makers will wish to target for the appropriate deficit or surplus on the current-account balance of payments.

The above are no more than illustrations of the goals of external balance that policy-makers may have. For the analysis of this chapter, all that matters is that policy-makers have some reasons leading them to adopt a goal for the balance of payments on the current account.

For this reason, we focus in this section on the current account of the balance of payments as the external policy target. You will recall from Chapter 32, that the current account has two parts: the visible account – which comprises trade in goods – and the invisible account – which comprises trade in services, and payments for the use of capital in the form of interest, dividends and profits. Trade in goods and services responds to relative international prices, which in turn depend on price levels and exchange rates. Interest, dividends and profits depend on capital already invested at home and abroad. In the present discussion, we will concentrate on the trade (visibles) account. What we say, however, is equally applicable to the traded services part of the invisible account.

INTERNAL AND EXTERNAL BALANCE WITH A FIXED EXCHANGE RATE

For the first part of this chapter, we assume that the exchange rate is fixed. The analysis also applies to the type of managed float that we studied in Chapter 43. As long as the central bank has some reason for wishing to hold the exchange rate steady over the

time-span that we are considering, then its problems under a managed float can be studied by assuming a fixed rate.

Later in the chapter we shall study the complications that arise when the capital account, and a flexible exchange rate, are allowed for.

Internal and External Balance: The General Case

The conditions for internal and external balance are illustrated in Figure 44.1. On the horizontal axis, we plot national income and, on the vertical axis, we plot net exports $(X - M)$.

In the graph we give an example of the general case in which the targets for income and the balance of payments may take on any values. The target for real national income that defines internal balance is indicated by the vertical grid line drawn at Y_t. Normally this will be full-employment national income, Y_F, but to allow for the possibility that the target might be some other level of income, we use the symbol Y_t for the target.

The target for external balance is indicated by the horizontal grid line drawn at a trade balance of B_t. In the Figure, this target is a small current-account surplus, which is consistent with a desire to finance some capital exports. The level of the target is, however, unimportant for anything that follows. We might just as well have drawn B_t on the horizontal axis, indicating a target of zero current-account balance, or below the axis, indicating a target of a

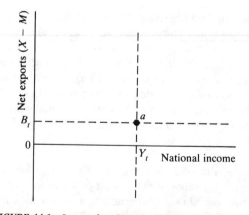

FIGURE 44.1   Internal and External Balance. Internal and external balance are simultaneously attained at only one combination of national income and the balance of payments

1 When we speak of an overall payments balance, we are referring to the balance of payments on current and captial account *but excluding the official settlements account.* See pages 385–8.

current-account deficit that would be consistent with a desire for capital imports. All that matters is that there should be some target for the current-account balance.

The two lines intersect at a, which indicates the only combination of income and balance of payments that simultaneously achieves both targets which we call internal and external balance.

Internal and External Balance: A Specific Case

For simplicity, we now make the assumption that the target level of real national income is potential income (which makes Y_t equal to Y_F), and that the target for the trade account is a zero balance. Hence, we can identify the initial situation relative to the targets simply in terms of the sign of the trade-account balance and the difference between actual income and potential income.

Achieving External Balance: Look at the line labelled $(X-M)$ in each of the four parts of Figure 44.2. It relates net exports to national income. It is downward-sloping because with a fixed exchange rate, the relationship is dominated by imports which rise as national income rises while exports are exogenous and constant. Under these circumstances, the difference, $X-M$, falls as national income rises. (We first encountered this relationship in Chapter 32 and if you have forgotten it, you should re-read pages 391–2 now.)

Achieving Internal Balance: The problems of using fiscal and monetary policy to change aggregate demand and thus to change equilibrium income were discussed in Chapter 41. Here we assume that the policy-makers are capable of altering equilibrium national income by using their instruments of fiscal and monetary policy. We then focus on what further problems arise in terms of seeking the twin goals of internal and external balance.

The Relation Between the Two Goals: It follows from the net export function that policies designed to change equilibrium national income will also influence the trade balance by causing a movement along the negatively sloped, net export function. Thus, as the Figure shows, rising income is associated with a declining trade balance.

One Instrument, Two Goals: The problem we now discuss arises because policy-makers have only one variable they can manipulate in order to reach two goals. This variable is equilibrium national income. Internal balance is approached by moving actual income in the direction of potential income. External balance is approached by moving actual income towards the point where the net export function cuts the horizontal axis – i.e. the level of income at which the balance of trade is zero.

Conflict or Harmony: The two goals are in harmony if a change in equilibrium national income moves the economy closer to internal and to external balance. This requires that if there is a recessionary gap, so that current income is too low, there should also be a trade surplus, so that raising income would move the economy towards external balance. It also requires that if there is an inflationary gap, so that current income is too high, there should be a trade deficit, so that lowering income also moves the economy towards a trade balance.

The two goals are in conflict if a change in equilibrium income needed to move the economy towards potential income increases the trade deficit. This occurs if a recessionary gap is combined with a trade deficit, or an inflationary gap with a trade surplus.[1]

A graphical analysis of conflict and harmony

Four of the possible cases are shown in Figure 44.2. In all four parts of the Figure, potential income is at the same level, indicated by Y_F. In each part of the Figure, the net export function is shown by the line labelled $(X-M)$ while current equilibrium income is at Y_0. The Figures differ from each other in the position of the net export curve and in the value of current equilibrium national income, Y_0. In parts (i) and (iii) of the Figure, there is a current-account deficit of b_1, while in parts (ii) and (iv) there is a current-account surplus of b_2.

Case 1: In part (i) of Figure 44.2, the economy's current income of Y_0 is assumed to be greater than its potential income of Y_F. Thus the economy is suffering

---

1 In the text we confine ourselves to conflicts with respect to small changes in national income. With large changes, it is clearly possible that one goal will be overshot before the other is achieved, in which case a conflict will arise where one did not exist originally.

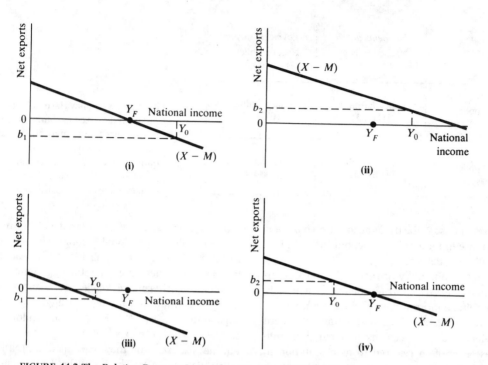

FIGURE 44.2 **The Relation Between Internal and External Balance.** The goals are in harmony when
each calls for a change in income in the same direction; the goals are in conflict when each calls for a
change in income in opposite directions

from an inflationary gap, measured by $Y_0 - Y_F$ in the
Figure. There is also a balance-of-payments deficit,
measured by b_1. In this case, there is harmony
between the two objectives since reducing the inflationary gap and reducing the payments deficit both
call for contractionary policies to reduce equilibrium
national income.

Case 2: In part (ii) of the Figure, actual income is
again assumed to be above potential income so that in
the initial position at Y_0 there is an inflationary gap,
$Y_0 - Y_F$. This time, however, there is a trade-account
surplus of b_2. Now there is a conflict, since a
contractionary policy designed to reduce the inflationary gap will increase the trade surplus, while an
expansionary policy designed to reduce the trade
surplus will increase the inflationary gap.

Case 3: In part (iii) there is a recessionary gap
because current income, Y_0, is less than potential
income, Y_F. There is also a trade deficit of b_1 at the
current level of income, Y_0. In this case, there is a
conflict. An expansionary policy of increasing national income to remove the recessionary gap will
worsen the payments deficit, while a contractionary

policy of reducing national income to remove the
payments deficit will increase the recessionary gap.

Case 4: In part (iv) there is also recessionary gap of
$Y_F - Y_0$. This time, however, there is a trade surplus
at current income. Now the current situation combines a deflationary gap, $Y_F - Y_0$, with a balance-of-
trade surplus of b_2. In this case there is no conflict. An
expansionary policy designed to raise income will
also reduce the payments surplus. As we have drawn
the Figure, the expansion of the economy can proceed
until both internal and external balance are achieved
at Y_F.

The four possible cases are set out in Figure 44.3.
Harmony arises when an inflationary gap is combined with a trade deficit, and a recessionary gap with
a trade surplus. Conflict arises when an inflationary
gap is combined with a trade surplus, and a deflationary gap with a trade deficit.

Conflict cases

In Case 3, the trade-account deficit calls for a decrease
in national income, but the recessionary gap calls for

	Payments deficit Needed policy: reduce Y	Payments surplus Needed policy: increase Y
Inflationary gap Needed policy: reduce Y	Policy harmony (Case 1)	Policy conflict (Case 2)
Deflationary gap Needed policy: increase Y	Policy conflict (Case 3)	Policy harmony (Case 4)

FIGURE 44.3   Policy Harmony and Policy Conflict under Fixed Exchange Rates. Harmony occurs when internal and external balance require that national income changes in the same direction; conflict occurs when the two balances require changes in the opposite direction

an increase. In Case 2, the trade-account surplus calls for an increase in national income, but the inflationary gap calls for a decrease.

Case 3 has traditionally attracted the most attention, perhaps because a trade deficit is generally viewed as being a more serious problem than a trade surplus, and – at least in the past – unemployment was considered a more serious problem than inflation. Case 3 is often referred to as a situation in which there is a 'balance-of-payments constraint' on domestic full-employment policy.

Case 3 described Britain's position during much of the period from 1950 to 1970, while fear of Case 2 strongly influenced German policy-makers during most of the 1960s and 1970s. As a result, not only did each country face its own conflict between internal and external balance, it also faced a political conflict between the policies that each country urged on the other.

EXPENDITURE-CHANGING AND EXPENDITURE-SWITCHING POLICIES

The conflicts that we have just considered arise because there was only a single instrument for achieving two goals. This instrument involves adopting policies to change equilibrium national income. The objectives are internal and external balance.

The conflicts arise because changes in national income designed to achieve internal balance also cause movements along the net export function. One resolution of such conflicts calls for policies that shift the net export function.

The policies that we have considered so far are

those that change aggregate desired expenditure and hence equilibrium national income. They are called EXPENDITURE-CHANGING policies. They lead to an increase, or a decrease, in total aggregate desired expenditure. Alternative policies are, however, available. These maintain the level of aggregate desired expenditure, $C+I+G+(X-M)$, but influence its composition between expenditure on domestic output and net exports, and they are called EXPENDITURE-SWITCHING policies. These policies leave aggregate desired expenditure constant but either increase $C+I+G$ and reduce $(X-M)$, or reduce $C+I+G$ and increase $(X-M)$.

Expenditure-Changing: Let us put what we already know into this new terminology. An expenditure-increasing policy increases domestic claims on domestic output by increasing G if government expenditures are increased, increasing C if tax rates are cut, or increasing all interest-sensitive expenditures, including I, if monetary policy is used to reduce interest rates. An expenditure-reducing policy reduces domestic claims on domestic output by reversing the above policies.

Expenditure-changing policies involve shifting the aggregate expenditure curve and so changing equilibrium national income. This in turn involves moving along a given net export function, which means that the trade balance and national income must change in the opposite direction to each other. If the initial situation calls for the trade balance and national income to move in the same direction, the use of expenditure-changing policies, on their own, necessarily involves a conflict.

Expenditure-Switching: An expenditure-switching policy shifts the net export function, so that for any given total of aggregate expenditure and national

income more or less goes to net exports. As we shall see, such policies can be used to make the trade balance and national income change in the *same* direction.

Expenditure-switching policies include devaluation or revaluation of the exchange rate, restrictions on international trade such as tariffs and quotas, and measures designed to change the domestic price level relative to foreign price levels. In this discussion, we shall concentrate on changes in the exchange rate. We speak of devaluations and revaluations because our analysis assumes a fixed exchange rate. The results apply, however, to a managed float where the Bank must decide whether to hold the existing exchange rate or allow either a depreciation or an appreciation.

It is important to notice, however, that changes in the exchange rate have *both* expenditure-switching and expenditure-changing effects. Devaluations increase net exports by encouraging exports and discouraging imports. They also tend to increase aggregate demand as expenditure is switched from imports to home-produced goods. Revaluations tend to reduce net exports by discouraging exports and encouraging imports. They also tend to reduce aggregate demand by switching expenditure from home-produced goods to imports.

Now we can discuss combinations of expenditure-changing and expenditure-switching polices needed to remove the policy conflicts that we earlier analysed. We take deficits first and refer to cases summarized, each of them numbered above.

A Trade-Account Deficit

Case 1. A Deficit Combined with an Inflationary Gap, No Conflict: If the economy already has an inflationary gap, an expenditure-reducing policy is needed to reduce national income. The trade-account deficit indicates that domestic expenditure is above the current level of national output and above the full-employment level of national income. To eliminate the deficit, expenditure must be lowered. In other words, if net exports are to rise, the resources needed to produce the necessary export goods must be released through a reduction in domestic usage. This calls also for expenditure-reducing policies. No conflict for expenditure-changing policies arises in this case, because the reduction of expenditure both reduces the inflationary gap and improves the trade

account (the latter by inducing a movement along the net export function).

Case 3. A Deficit Combined with a Recessionary Gap, Conflict: When national income is below its potential level, achieving internal balance calls for expenditure-increasing policies to raise national income. But an increase in national income, with a given net export function, will worsen the current account. So expenditure-increasing policies run into a conflict between internal and external balance. What is needed is a switch of domestic expenditure away from foreign goods (thus reducing the trade deficit) and towards domestic goods (thus reducing the recessionary gap).

This can be done using expenditure-switching policies. If expenditure can be switched from foreign goods – thus reducing imports – to domestic goods – thus increasing domestic expenditure – the payments deficit can be reduced and national income increased.

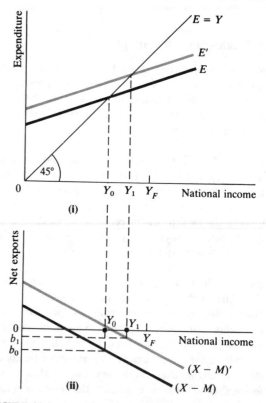

FIGURE 44.4   A Trade Deficit and a Recessionary Gap. A policy to switch expenditure away from foreign goods and toward domestic goods can be used to resolve the conflict posed by a trade deficit combined with a recessionary gap

These policies are shown in Figure 44.4. The initial aggregate expenditure curve is labelled E in part (i) of the Figure. This yields an equilibrium national income of Y_0. Since potential income of Y_F exceeds current income, there is a recessionary gap. In part (ii) of the Figure, the initial net export function is labelled $(X-M)$. At equilibrium income of Y_0, there is a payments deficit of b_0.

Now assume that an expenditure-switching policy is adopted in the form of a devaluation of the exchange rate. This increases the exports and reduces the imports associated with any given level of national income. The net export function thus shifts upwards, say to $(X-M)'$ in part (ii) of the Figure. The expenditure-switching policy also raises aggregate expenditure, since exports increase while imports decrease. Say that the curve shifts to E' in part (i) of the Figure. The new equilibrium level of national income is Y_1 and the current-account deficit is now b_1. Both the recessionary gap and the current-account deficit have been reduced.

A Trade-Account Surplus

Now let us look at cases involving a payments surplus, which are Cases 2 and 4 outlined above. In these cases, an increase in equilibrium national income will cause a move toward external balance by reducing net exports.

Case 4: In Case 4, where there is a recessionary gap, there is no conflict between internal and external balance. Expenditure-increasing policies will lead to movement toward both targets. By raising national income, they will move the economy towards Y_F and, by lowering the payments surplus, they will move the economy towards a zero trade balance.

Case 2: In Case 2, there is an inflationary gap combined with a payments surplus, and a conflict does arise. Achieving external balance calls for expenditure increases, but achieving internal balance calls for expenditure reductions. What is needed is a switch in expenditure away from domestic goods (thus reducing the inflationary gap) and towards foreign goods (thus reducing the trade-account surplus).

The necessary policies are illustrated in Figure 44.5. The initial expenditure function is E. Equilib-

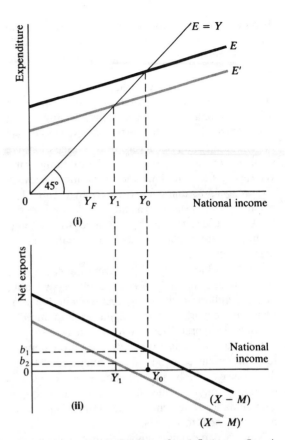

FIGURE 44.5 A Trade Surplus and an Inflationary Gap. A policy to switch expenditure away from domestic goods and toward foreign goods can be used to resolve the conflict posed by a trade surplus combined with an inflationary gap

rium income is Y_0, which exceeds potential income, Y_F. Thus there is an inflationary gap. Given the net export function of $(X-M)$ in part (ii) of the Figure, there is a trade-account surplus of b_1.

Now assume that the authorities adopt an expenditure-switching policy in the form of a revaluation of the exchange rate. This will shift expenditure from domestic to imported goods and hence will lower net exports at each level of income – i.e. the net export function shifts downwards to $(X-M)'$. The policy also lowers aggregate expenditure because less is spent on home-produced goods and more on imported goods. Thus the aggregate expenditure curve shifts downwards, say to E'. The equilibrium national income falls to Y_1 and at that lower income, the trade balance falls to b_2. Hence both the inflationary gap and the trade surplus are reduced.

A general statement

We have now seen the difference in the effects of the two types of policies in an open economy. The important point is that *to achieve internal and external balance, some appropriate combination of expenditure-changing and expenditure-switching policies is required.*

Here are the key policy implications concerning expenditure-switching policies that are suggested by the previous discussion.

- Expenditure-switching policies should be directed towards the policy of external balance.
- Expenditure-switching policies should be combined with the appropriate expenditure-changing policies that focus on internal balance.
- In particular, starting from potential income and an external imbalance, a devaluation designed to remove a payments deficit should be accompanied by expenditure-reducing policies designed to prevent the emergence of an inflationary gap, and a revaluation designed to reduce a payments surplus should be accompanied by expenditure-increasing policies designed to prevent the emergence of a recessionary gap.

MACROECONOMIC POLICY AND THE CAPITAL ACCOUNT

We start our study of the influence of capital flows with two important background matters: the target of external balance and the effects on the money supply of intervention in the foreign-exchange market.

An alternative target for external balance

So far in this chapter, external balance has meant achieving a target balance on the current account. We now consider extending this target to incorporate the capital account. To do this we now specify external balance in terms of a target level of the overall balance of payments which, as we saw on page 388, means the balance on current and capital account, *excluding the official settlements account.* For simplicity, we take this target to be a zero overall balance of payments, which leaves the Bank's foreign-exchange reserves constant. Any other target would do just as well for our study. What matters is that the authorities have some target that can be expressed in terms of a value for the overall balance of payments.

The balance of payments and the money supply

We shall see below that, once we allow for capital movements, we must distinguish sharply between the effects of fiscal and monetary policies. Because of this, we must study the effect on the money supply of open-market purchases of foreign exchange made by the Bank.

Suppose that the UK experiences a balance-of-payments deficit, and that the central bank intervenes in the foreign-exchange market to prevent a fall in the exchange-rate value of sterling. The central bank will be selling foreign currency in exchange for pounds, thereby running down the stock of official reserves. This is an open-market operation, and its effects are exactly the same as if the bank had bought domestic bonds. Because we have analysed open-market operations in detail in Chapter 37, we can be brief here.

The effects of a purchase of foreign exchange is summarized in Table 44.1. A balance-of-payments deficit of £100 leads to an excess demand for foreign exchange of £100, which is met by a sale of some of the central bank's official reserves by that amount. When the central bank receives payment in the form of a cheque drawn on a commercial bank, central bank reserves fall by £100. There will then be a multiple contraction of deposit money through the process analysed in Chapter 35.

We conclude that, if there are no offsetting transactions, a balance-of-payments deficit will lead to a decrease both in bank reserves and in bank deposits equal to the amount of foreign exchange sold by the central bank.

A surplus will have the opposite effects. Stated briefly, the bank will buy foreign exchange, paying with cheques drawn in domestic currency. When these cheques clear, the commercial banks will find themselves with new deposits and new reserves equal to the amount of the central bank's open-market purchases.

Sterilization: We have seen that a balance-of-payments deficit tends to cause a contraction of the money supply. The central bank has the option, however, of preventing this from happening by undertaking offsetting transactions. The decrease in bank reserves shown in Table 44.1 can be offset by an

TABLE 44.1 Balance Sheet Changes Caused by a Sale of Foreign Currency by the Central Bank. The money supplied is reduced when the central bank sells foreign currency

NON-BANK PRIVATE SECTOR		
Assets	*Liabilities*	
Foreign currency	No change	
(equivalent) value in		
domestic currency)	+100	
Deposits	−100	

COMMERCIAL BANKS		
Assets	*Liabilities*	
Reserves (deposits with	Demand	
central bank)	−100	deposits	−100

CENTRAL BANK		
Assets	*Liabilities*	
Foreign currency	−100	Deposits of	
		commercial	
		banks	−100

open-market purchase of domestic bonds, which will have the effect of increasing bank reserves. The increase in bank reserves that would result from a balance-of-payments surplus can be offset by open-market sales of domestic bonds, which decreases bank reserves. (A payment surplus requires that the Bank buy foreign exchange and this open-market operation lowers bank deficits and reserves.) This procedure of insulating the domestic money supply from the effects of balance-of-payments deficits or surpluses is known as STERILIZATION.

Fiscal and Monetary Policy Compared

In discussing the trade account in the first part of this chapter, we did not distinguish between the effects of monetary and fiscal policy, since both have similar effects on income. However, when we come to the capital account, we must distinguish between the two policies, since they have opposite effects on interest rates. We saw this in Chapter 42. In a closed economy, expansionary monetary policy exerts its influence on income by *reducing* interest rates. However, fiscal policy influences aggregate demand directly, and fiscal-policy-induced increases in national income create an excess demand for money, which increases interest rates.

Fiscal Policy and the Capital Account: The effects of fiscal policy on the capital account of an open

economy operate via changes in interest rates. For example, an expansionary fiscal policy tends to cause interest rates to rise in a closed economy. In an open economy, a rise in interest rates attracts short-term capital. So the capital-account sequence is: an expansionary fiscal policy will put upward pressure on interest rates, and this will lead to an inflow of foreign capital, thereby moving the capital account toward a surplus. A contractionary fiscal policy will have the opposite effects: domestic interest rates will fall, capital will flow out, in search of higher returns elsewhere, and the capital account will move towards a deficit.

Monetary Policy and the Capital Account: Since monetary policy influences interest rates in a closed economy, it will influence the capital account in an open economy. An expansionary monetary policy will put downward pressure on interest rates and lead to an outflow of short-term capital. This will move the balance of payments on the capital account toward a deficit. A contractionary monetary policy will put upward pressure on interest rates and cause an inflow of short-term capital. This will move the balance of payments on the capital account towards a surplus.

So the effects of the two policies on the capital account are the opposite of each other. Expansionary fiscal policy tends to cause a capital-account surplus, while an expansionary monetary policy tends to cause a capital-account deficit. Contractionary policies have the opposite effects.

Fixed exchange rates

We now consider the implications of these capital-account forces for fiscal and monetary policies, first with fixed, and then with flexible, exchange rates.

Monetary Policy: Monetary policy is extremely limited in its effects under a fixed exchange rate. Consider the following sequence of events. Suppose British interest rates are at levels similar to those in the rest of the world, and that there is equilibrium in international capital markets. Suppose now that the central bank, faced with a large recessionary gap, seeks to stimulate demand through an expansionary monetary policy. The Bank buys bonds in the open market, thereby increasing the money supply and reducing interest rates.

The lower interest rates, however, induce an

outflow of capital and thus cause a deficit on the capital account. To the extent that national income rises, the induced movement along the net export function creates a deficit on the trade account. Thus the overall balance of payments moves into deficit. To maintain the fixed exchange rate, the Bank will have to intervene in the foreign-exchange market and sell foreign currency. This open-market operation in foreign exchange will have the effect of reducing the money supply and thus reversing the increase brought about by the initial open-market operation.

If no other transactions are initiated by the Bank, national income and the money supply will fall and domestic interest rates will rise until they all return to their initial levels. Thus the induced balance-of-payments deficit will be self-correcting, and the Bank's expansionary policy will be nullified.

Suppose now that the Bank attempts to sterilize the impact on the money supply of the balance-of-payments deficit. The difficulty with this strategy is that it can be continued only as long as the Bank has sufficient reserves of foreign exchange. If capital flows are highly sensitive to interest-rate changes, as a great deal of evidence suggests is the case, these reserves will be run down at a rapid rate, and the Bank will be forced to abandon its expansionary policy.

This leads to an important conclusion. *Under a fixed exchange rate, there is very little scope for the use of monetary policy for domestic stabilization purposes because of the sensitivity of international capital flows to interest rates. The Bank will be forced to maintain domestic interest rates close to the levels existing in the rest of the world, and it will not be able to bring about substantial changes in the domestic money supply for expenditure-changing purposes.*

Fiscal Policy: Consider now the effectiveness of fiscal policy under fixed exchange rates. Suppose again that British interest rates are in line with those in the rest of the world when an expansionary fiscal policy is introduced, aimed at reducing a large recessionary gap. The fiscal expansion tends to raise the level of domestic interest rates and national income.

Higher interest rates stimulate an inflow of short-term capital, thereby leading to a surplus on the capital account. If the capital flows are large, the surplus on capital account will exceed the current-account deficit arising from the increased national income. Hence there will be an overall balance-of-payments surplus.

To maintain the fixed exchange rate, the Bank will have to intervene in the foreign-exchange market and buy foreign exchange. This will have the effect of increasing the money supply, thus reinforcing the initial fiscal stimulus.

This leads to another important conclusion. *Under a fixed exchange rate, interest-sensitive international capital flows stabilize the domestic interest rate and enhance the effectiveness of fiscal policy.*

Combining Monetary and Fiscal Policy: Consider an attempt to increase national income with expansionary monetary policy intended to reduce interest rates and thereby stimulate investment and other interest-sensitive expenditures. The decline in domestic interest rates causes short-term capital to move abroad to be invested at more attractive rates in foreign financial centres. This worsens the balance of payments on the short-term capital account. Of course, if the expansionary policy succeeds in raising income, there will also be a movement towards deficit on the current account as a consequence of the increased expenditure on imports caused by the rise in income.

In principle the conflict can be removed by an appropriate combination of monetary and fiscal policy. Consider a country that has full employment combined with a balance-of-payments deficit. The country could eliminate the deficit by following a tighter monetary policy to increase domestic interest rates and attract short-term capital. At the same time, the contractionary effect of tight money on domestic expenditure and employment could be offset by raising government expenditures or cutting taxes. Thus both goals can be achieved through a combination of tight monetary policy and expansionary fiscal policy.

The Temporary Nature of the Strategy: This strategy is unlikely to be a satisfactory solution to a persistent current-account deficit. Such a country will find it increasingly difficult to maintain its exchange rate by importing short-term capital.

Short-term international capital flows are extremely volatile, *and they are particularly sensitive to shifts in expectations concerning exchange rates.* If investors lose confidence in a country's ability to maintain its existing exchange rate, capital outflows will build up and ultimately a devaluation will be required to reduce the deficit and restore confidence.

Flexible exchange rates

A major advantage of a flexible exchange rate is that it removes any conflict between domestic stabilization objectives and the balance of payments, because balance-of-payments deficits or surpluses tend to be automatically eliminated through movements in the exchange rate.

Fiscal Policy: Suppose the government seeks to remove a recessionary gap by expansionary fiscal policy. An increase in government expenditures and/or a reduction in taxes will increase income through the multiplier effect and reduce the size of the recessionary gap. This will also tend to cause a movement along the net export function, leading to a deterioration of the trade account. This, however, is not the whole story, for there will also be repercussions on the capital account and the exchange rate.

Capital Flows and the Crowding-Out Effect: In a closed economy, an expansionary fiscal policy causes domestic interest rates to rise. This causes interest-sensitive private expenditures to fall, thus partially offsetting the initial expansionary effect of the fiscal stimulus. As we saw in Chapter 42, this crowding-out effect can play an important role in the analysis of fiscal policy in a closed economy. In an open economy, the crowding-out effect will operate differently, due to international capital flows.

Higher domestic interest rates that result from an expansionary fiscal policy will induce a capital inflow and cause the exchange rate to appreciate. If capital flows are highly interest-elastic, there will be a large capital inflow, which will cause the exchange rate to rise substantially. This will reduce aggregate demand by discouraging exports and encouraging the substitution of imports for domestically produced goods. (So the switch in expenditures reduces net exports, $X - M$, and reduces aggregate desired expenditure.) The initial fiscal stimulus will be offset by the expenditure-switching effects of currency appreciation.

We have now reached another important conclusion: *under flexible exchange rates, a fiscal expansion will crowd out net exports and this reduces its effectiveness.*

It is possible, however, to eliminate the crowding-out effect by supporting the fiscal policy with an accommodating monetary policy. Suppose that the central bank responds to the increase in the demand for money, induced by the fiscal expansion, by increasing the supply of money so as to maintain domestic interest rates at their initial level. There will then be no capital inflow, and no tendency for the currency to appreciate. Income will expand by the usual multiplier process.

The conclusion is as follows: *the effectiveness of fiscal policy under flexible exchange rates can be maintained by use of an accommodating monetary policy.*

Monetary Policy: We have seen that there is little scope under fixed exchange rates for the use of monetary policy for domestic stabilization purposes. Under flexible exchange rates, the situation is reversed; monetary policy becomes a very powerful tool.

Suppose the Bank seeks to stimulate demand through an expansionary monetary policy. The Bank buys bonds in the open market, thereby increasing the reserves of the commercial banking system. This in turn increases the money supply and puts downward pressure on interest rates. Lower interest rates will cause an outflow of capital and thus tend to open up a deficit on the capital account.

Under a fixed rate, we saw that the Bank may be forced to reverse its policy in order to stem the loss of foreign reserves. Under a flexible rate, however, the exchange rate can be allowed to depreciate. This will stimulate exports and discourage imports so that the deficit on the capital account will be offset by a surplus on the current account.

National income will be increased not only by the fall in interest rates, but also by the increased demand for domestically produced goods brought about by a depreciation of the currency. The initial monetary stimulus will be reinforced by the expenditure-switching effects of currency depreciation.

This leads to one further conclusion. *Under flexible exchange rates, monetary policy is a powerful tool for stabilizing domestic income and employment. If capital flows are highly interest-elastic, the main channel by which an increase in the money supply stimulates demand for domestically produced goods is a depreciation of the currency.*

Conclusion

The main message of this chapter is that stabilization policy looks very different when viewed from the perspective of an open rather than a closed economy, especially if the overseas sector is large. Under fixed

exchange rates, problems arise because use of the major tool of expenditure-switching – changes in the exchange rate – is sometimes ruled out. Conflicts of policy goals then arise when achieving internal balance calls for changing national income in one direction while achieving external balance calls for changing it in the other direction. When exchange rates are changed to get the benefit of their expenditure-switching effects, then their expenditure-changing effect must be allowed for as well – depreciations tend to increase domestic expenditure while appreciation tends to reduce it. If these changes move the economy away from internal balance, it is always open to try to offset their effects by appropriate expansionary or contractionary demand-management policies.

Under flexible exchange rates, a policy package that includes monetary and fiscal policy changes, aimed at internal balance, and exchange-rate changes, aimed at external balance, can normally achieve internal and external balance simultaneously.

SUMMARY

1 Internal balance occurs when the target level of national income has been achieved; external balance occurs when the target level on the balance of payments has been achieved.

2 A fixed exchange rate prevents one of the major expenditure-switching tools – exchange-rate variations – from being used. If only expenditure-changing tools are available, internal and external balance objectives may be in harmony, or in conflict. Harmony occurs when a recessionary gap is combined with a payments surplus or an inflationary gap is combined with a payments deficit. Conflict occurs when a recessionary gap is combined with a payments deficit or when an inflationary gap is combined with a payments surplus.

3 Irrespective of where the goods and services were purchased, a trade-account deficit means that total expenditure on consumption, investment and government ($C + I + G$) exceeds current output, a surplus means that $C + I + G$ is less than current output. If both expenditure-changing and expenditure-switching measures are available, expenditure-changing techniques can be used to make equilibrium income equal to potential income (internal balance), and expenditure-switching policies can be used to shift the net export function so that the desired balance-of-payments target is achieved (external balance) at potential income.

4 Although changes in the exchange rate are an expenditure-switching policy, they also have expenditure-changing effects: depreciations increase domestic expenditure, and appreciations reduce it. A pure expenditure-switching effect – no change in aggregate expenditure – requires that the expenditure-changing effects of an alteration in the exchange rate be offset by the expenditure-changing effects of fiscal and monetary policies.

5 When significant international capital movements can occur, the relative effectiveness of fiscal and monetary policy must be reconsidered. On a fixed exchange rate, monetary policy is relatively impotent while fiscal policy is potent. On a flexible exchange rate, monetary policy is potent while fiscal policy is relatively impotent.

Macroeconomic Controversies

How well do markets work? Can government improve market performance? In various guises, these two questions are the basics of most disagreements over economic policy. We shall see that, although they are microeconomic questions, the different answers that are given to them imply big differences in macroeconomic policy prescriptions as well.

In this, the last chapter of our book we shall review two extreme positions on the state of the economy. In doing so, much of what we have learned in earlier chapters will be reviewed.

ALTERNATIVE VIEWS

We have seen that macroeconomics is mainly concerned with employment (and unemployment), the price level and the rate of economic growth. Broadly speaking, we can identify a non-interventionist and an interventionist view with respect to each of these policy goals. The non-interventionist view says that the unaided market economy can best achieve the goal. The interventionist view says that government policy can improve the economy's performance regarding that goal. Since one can take a non-interventionist or an interventionist position with respect to each of these three goals, there are six different possible policy combinations.[1]

Consider two extreme policy stances. For lack of

better names we will identify these extremes as 'laissez-faire' and 'interventionist'. Advocates of pure laissez-faire are non-interventionist on every issue, while pure interventionists support government intervention in all cases. A few people may actually be pure laissez-faire or pure interventionist in this sense. Most, however, would find themselves favouring intervention on some issues and opposing it on others. They might still, however, identify themselves as being, on overall balance, laissez-faire or interventionist because they were more often on one side than the other.

It is popular to identify Monetarist with laissez-faire and Keynesian with interventionist. It is true that many Monetarists are on the laissez-faire side, while many Keynesians are on the interventionist side. But this is not always so. It is, for example, quite possible to be Keynesian in accepting the Keynesian macro model as a reasonable description of the economy's macroeconomic behaviour, but laissez-faire in believing that, in the absence of major externalities, the unaided market usually does the best job of allocating resources at the microeconomic level.

The laissez-faire view

Advocates of laissez-faire believe that the free-market economy performs well when left to itself. They believe that the economy is inherently self-equilibrating, and that the adjustment forces are strong enough to eliminate both inflationary and recessionary gaps fairly quickly and fairly completely – as long as the government does not adopt policies that frustrate these forces.

While all manner of unexpected changes may impinge on the system from time to time, they are, in

---

1 Since each of the three issues breaks up into hundreds of different sub-issues, there are thousands of different policy stances available on one side or the other of each major issue. Considering these two extreme cases is useful in identifying issues but does not necessarily identify two major groups.

this view, followed rather quickly, and often relatively painlessly, by the equilibrating adjustments dictated by the market system. For example, relative prices in booming sectors rise, drawing in resources from declining sectors or regions. As a result, whenever the market is allowed to work, resources (and particularly labour) usually remain fully employed, so there is no need for interventionist, full-employment policies. Heavy unemployment is blamed on poor interventionist policies. The *laissez-faire* solution is to remove the intervention, not to intervene more effectively.

Of course, few but the most extreme advocates of *laissez-faire* believe that the unaided market system would function perfectly, thereby ensuring *continuous* full employment. But the view is that the market system works well enough to preclude any role for government economic policy.

In addition, many believe that the available instruments of fiscal and monetary policy are so crude that their use is often counter-productive. A policy's effects may be so uncertain, with regard to both strength and timing, that it may impair, rather than improve, the economy's performance.

In a modern economy some government presence is generally regarded as inevitable because of public goods, major externalities and the need for regulation of certain economic activities such as mergers and bank lending. Thus a stance of *no* intervention is impossible; so we may reinterpret our extremist *laissez-faire* policy as one of *minimal* direct intervention in the market system. This involves little more than government's bearing responsibility for providing a *stable environment* in which the private sector can function.

The provision of a stable environment function is important in the *laissez-faire* programme, and it needs some explanation. The belief is that private decision-takers, risking their own or shareholders' money, will provide the best guarantee of rising living standards through economic growth in the long run as well as something close to full employment in the short run. These beneficial results will only occur, however, if economic activity takes place in the context of a stable environment where contracts are enforceable and enforced, where theft and other crimes against persons and property are minimized, where tax rates are reasonable and not subject to capricious changes, where failure is punished by loss of investment (that is not then refunded by the state) and success is rewarded by profit (that is not then confiscated by the

state), where the country is secure against aggressive foreign powers, where the transportation routes are secure for foreign trade, and where the price level is relatively stable. It is providing all of this backdrop, against which private initiative can get on with the job of achieving economic prosperity, that the advocates of *laissez-faire* see as the important functions of the government.

The interventionist view

Interventionists believe that the functioning of the free-market economy is often far from satisfactory. Sometimes markets show weak self-regulatory forces and the economy settles into prolonged periods of heavy unemployment. At other times, markets tend to 'overcorrect', causing the economy to lurch between the extremes of large recessionary and large inflationary gaps.

This behaviour can be improved, argue the interventionists. They believe that, even though interventionist policies may be imperfect, they are often good enough to improve the functioning of the unaided market with respect to all three main goals of macro policy.

DIFFERENT DIAGNOSES

The economy's performance is, of course, often less than perfectly satisfactory. Serious unemployment has been a recurring problem. Inflation was a serious problem throughout the 1970s and early 1980s. Throughout most of the same period, growth rates have been low in many of the industrial countries of Western Europe and North America. Interventionists and non-interventionists differ in diagnosing the causes of these economic ills.

The Trade Cycle

We saw in Chapter 31 that cyclical ups and downs can be observed as far back as records exist. Monetarists and Keynesians have long argued about the causes. *For purposes of the debate about the trade cycle, as well as about inflation, Monetarists can be identified with laissez-faire and Keynesians with interventionists.*

Monetarist Views: Monetarists believe the economy is inherently stable because such private-sector

expenditure relations as the consumption and the investment functions are relatively stable. In addition, they believe that shifts in the aggregate demand curve are mainly due to policy-induced changes in the money supply.

The view that trade cycles have mainly monetary causes relies heavily on disputed evidence concerning a relation between changes in the money supply and changes in real activity. A strong correlation does seem to exist, at least for the United States, between changes in the money supply and changes in the level of business activity. Major recessions have been associated with absolute declines in the money supply and minor recessions with the slowing of the rate of increase in the money supply below its long-term trend.

The correlation between changes in the money supply and changes in the level of business activity appears to be supported by the experience of many countries. There is controversy, however, over how this correlation is to be interpreted; do changes in money supply *cause* changes in the level of aggregate demand and hence of business activity? Is the association merely statistical, or is there (as many believe) a much more complex causal chain, or even, does the causal chain turn the other way around, with the changes in aggregate demand causing changes in the money supply. Also given the problems mentioned earlier in measuring the money supply, it is hardly surprising that economists are able to hold (and hold strongly) different views about what is apparently a question of fact.

Some Monetarists maintain that changes in the money supply cause changes in business activity. They argued, for example, that the severity of the Great Depression was due to a major contraction in the money supply that shifted the aggregate demand curve far to the left. This led them to advocate a policy of stabilizing the growth of the money supply. In their view this would avoid policy-induced instability of the aggregate demand curve.

Keynesian Views: The Keynesian view on cyclical fluctuations in the economy has two parts. First, it emphasizes variations in investment as a cause of trade cycles and stresses non-monetary causes of such variations.

Keynesians reject what they regard as the extreme Monetarist view that only money matters in explaining cyclical fluctuations. Many Keynesians believe that both monetary and non-monetary forces are important. Although they accept monetary mismanagement as one potential source of economic fluctuations, they do not believe that it is the only or even the major source of such fluctuations. Thus they deny the monetary interpretation of trade-cycle history. They believe that most fluctuations in the aggregate demand curve are due to variations in the desire to spend on the part of the private sector and are not induced by government policy. Such variations in private-sector desired expenditure functions are held by the Keynesians to be due to large shifts in expectations about the future – what Keynes himself called 'animal spirits' – which are uncontrollable by government policy. These fluctuations in desired expenditure in turn mean that fluctuations in aggregate demand will always occur, and the best thing that the government can do is to try to mitigate some of their most harmful consequences on employment and income through an active stabilization policy.

Keynesians also believe that the economy lacks strong natural corrective mechanisms that will always force it easily and quickly back to full employment. They believe that, although the price level rises fairly quickly to eliminate inflationary gaps, the price level does not fall quickly to eliminate recessionary gaps. Keynesians stress the asymmetries noted in earlier chapters which imply that although prices and wages rise quickly in response to inflationary gaps, they fall only slowly in response to recessionary gaps. As a result, Keynesians believe that recessionary gaps can persist for long periods of time unless eliminated by an active stabilization policy.

The second part of the Keynesian view of cyclical fluctuations is acceptance that, while there does exist a correlation between changes in the money supply and changes in national income, the causality often runs from changes in income to changes in the money supply. They offer several reasons for this, but only the most important need be mentioned.

Keynesians point out that from 1945 to the early 1970s many of the world's central banks often sought to stabilize interest rates in pursuit of their support function rather than seeking to vary rates in pursuit of their stabilization function. To do this, they had to increase the money supply during upswings in the trade cycle (so that a shortage of money would not cause interest rates to rise) and decrease the money supply during downswings (so that a surplus of money would not cause interest rates to fall). (This policy was analysed in Figure 37.2 on page 452).

Thus we see that, according to Keynesians, fluctu-

ations in national income are often caused by fluctuations in expenditure decisions, while fluctuations in national income cause fluctuations in the money supply. Nevertheless, most Keynesians also agree that policy-induced changes in the money supply, particularly when they are large and rapid, can cause major shifts in aggregate demand.

The Price Level

As we saw in Chapter 41, sustained inflation requires sustained expansion of the money supply. (A *sustained inflation* is one that has been going on for a long time, while an *entrenched inflation* is one that is expected to continue for a long time. Although one type of inflation often goes with the other, they are not the same thing.)

Governmental motives for excessive monetary expansions have varied from time to time and from place to place. Sometimes central banks have tried to hold interest rates well below their free-market levels. To do this, they buy bonds to hold bond prices up. We have seen that these open-market operations increase the money supply and so help to validate a demand inflation. At other times, central banks have tried to hold the exchange rate below its equilibrium level. The resulting purchase of foreign exchange is an open-market policy that expands the reserves of the commercial banking system. At still other times, central banks have helped governments finance large budget deficits by buying up the new public debt. These open-market operations provide what is popularly known as *printing press finance*. The steady increase in the money supply fuels a continuous inflation.

Monetarist Views: Many Monetarists hold that inflation is everywhere and always a monetary phenomenon. (See Chapter 41, page 498, for an assessment of this contention.) They thus focus on changes in the money supply as the key source of shifts in the aggregate demand curve. Many also believe that supply shocks, which cause *some* prices to rise, do not lead to inflation because, unless the money supply is also raised, some other prices will have to fall. This will cause changes in relative prices but no significant change in the price level. Thus, according to many Monetarists, all inflations are caused by excessive monetary expansions and would not occur without them.

Keynesian Views: Keynesians accept the view that a *sustained* rise in the price level cannot occur unless it is accompanied by continued increases in the money supply. To this extent, they agree with the Monetarists. Keynesians also emphasize, however, that temporary bursts of inflation can be caused by shifts in the aggregate demand curve brought about by increases in private- or public-sector expenditure functions (consumption, investment, exports and government expenditure). If such inflations are not validated by monetary expansion, they are brought to a halt by the monetary adjustment mechanism. Even when not validated, they can, however, persist long enough to worry policy-makers and governments concerned about the next election.

Keynesians also accept the importance of supply-shock inflations. They accept that such inflations cannot go on indefinitely unless accommodated by monetary expansion, but believe that they can go on long enough to be a matter of serious concern. Indeed, we have seen that such inflations can present the central bank with agonizing choices: whether to accommodate the shocks, thereby accepting a bout of inflation but avoiding unemployment, or not to accommodate the shocks, thereby accepting a period of unemployment but avoiding further inflation.

Many Keynesians also accept the existence of permanent wage-cost-push inflation that we studied in Chapter 42. This type of inflation, if it exists, makes full employment incompatible with a stable price level. Again the Bank is faced with the agonizing choice of whether or not to accommodate such a wage-cost-push inflation.

Growth

Laissez-Faire Views: Advocates of *laissez-faire*, and indeed most Monetarists, feel that in a stable environment free from government interference, growth will take care of itself. Large firms will spend much on research and development. Where they fail, or where they suppress inventions to protect monopoly positions, the genius of backyard inventors will come up with new ideas and will develop new companies to challenge the positions of the established giants. Left to itself, the economy will prosper as it has in the past, provided only that inquiring scientific spirit, and the profit motive, are not suppressed. Advocates of *laissez-faire* point out that much of the increase in employment in the 1980s has come from small businesses that embody the essence of the entrepreneurial spirit.

Interventionist Views: Interventionists, and indeed most Keynesians, are less certain about the ability of market forces to produce growth. While recognizing the importance of invention and innovation, they fear the stultifying hand of monopoly, and conservative business practices, that choose security over risk-taking. Therefore they believe that the government needs, at the very least, to give a nudge here and there to help the growth process along.

THE DIFFERENT PRESCRIPTIONS

The *laissez-faire* and the interventionist diagnoses of the economy's ills lead, not surprisingly, to very different prescriptions about the appropriate role of economic policy.

Laissez-Faire Prescriptions

It is not necessary to distinguish *laissez-faire* policies with respect to the three objectives of full employment, stable prices and economic growth. This is because advocates of *laissez-faire* believe all three goals will be achieved by the same basic policy: provision of a stable environment within which the free-market system can operate.

Providing a stable environment

We earlier mentioned *laissez-faire* policies for creating a stable microeconomic environment. Creating the stable macroeconomic environment may, however, be easier said than done. We focus on the prescriptions for establishing stable fiscal and monetary policies.

One major problem to keep in mind is that macro variables are interrelated. The stability of one may imply the instability of another. In such cases, a choice must be made. How much instability of one aggregate should be tolerated in order to secure stability in another related aggregate?

Assume, for example, that people are so worried about budget deficits that the government decides to stabilize the budget balance as part of the stable environment: the budget balance should be the same from year to year.

This 'stability' would require great *instability* in tax and/or expenditure policy. As we saw in Chapter 42, although governments can set tax *rates*, their tax revenues depend on the interaction between these tax rates and the level of national income. With given tax rates, tax revenues change with the ebb and flow of the business cycle. A stable budget balance would require that the government raise tax rates and cut expenditures in slumps, and lower tax rates and raise expenditures in booms.

Not only would this squander the budget's potential to act as a stabilizer, but great instability of the fiscal environment could be caused by continual changes in tax rates and expenditure levels. A stable fiscal environment requires reasonable stability in government expenditures and tax rates. Stability is needed so that the private sector can make plans for the future within a climate of known patterns of tax liabilities and government demand. This in turn requires that the budget balance should fluctuate cyclically, showing its largest deficits in slumps and its largest surpluses in booms.

Advocates of a stable macroeconomic environment are actually concerned to achieve a stable, and low, inflation rate – zero if possible. To accomplish this, the central bank is urged to set a target rate of increase in some measure of the money supply, usually M1, and hold to it. To establish the target, the central bank estimates the rate at which the demand for money (which depends on nominal income and the interest rate) would be growing if actual income equalled potential income and the price level were stable. As a first approximation, assuming no radical changes in the interest rate, this rate of growth in the demand for money can be taken to be the rate at which potential income itself is growing. This then becomes the target rate of growth of the money supply.

The key proposition is that the money supply should be changing gradually along a stable path that is independent of short-term variations in the demand for money caused by cyclical changes in national income. This is sometimes referred to as a k *per cent rule*, where k stands for the target rate of growth of the money supply.

Will the k per cent rule really provide monetary stability? The answer is 'not necessarily'. Assuring a stable rate of monetary growth does not assure a stable monetary environment because monetary shortages and surpluses depend on the relation between the supply of, *and the demand for*, money.

Problems for the k per cent rule arise when the demand for money shifts. For example, payment of interest on sight deposits – a development seen in several countries in recent years – increases the

demand for M1. In this event, if the central bank adheres to a *k* per cent rule, there will be an excess demand for money, interest rates will rise and contractionary pressure will be put on the economy.

Should the central bank commit itself to a specific *k* per cent rule or merely work toward unannounced, and possibly variable, targets? The pre-announced target makes it easier to evaluate how well the central bank is doing its job. It also helps to prevent the central bank from trying to fine tune the economy with repeated changes in its monetary policy.

One disadvantage of such a rule is that the central bank, in order to preserve its credibility, may fail to take discretionary action that would otherwise be appropriate. For example, after an entrenched inflation is broken, the economy may come to rest with substantial unemployment and a stable price level. There is then a case for a once-and-for-all discretionary expansion in the money supply to get the economy back to full employment. The *k* per cent rule precludes this, condemning the economy to a prolonged slump unless other means of stimulating the economy can be found.

Despite such problems, *laissez-faire* advocates believe the *k* per cent rule is superior to any known alternative. Some would agree that, in principle, the central bank could improve the economy's performance by occasional bouts of discretionary monetary policy to offset such things as major shifts in the demand for money. But they also believe that, once given any discretion, the central bank would abuse it in an attempt to fine tune the economy. The resulting instability would, they believe, be much more than any instability resulting from the application of a *k* per cent rule in an environment subject to some change.

Laissez-faire advocates also want to let growth take care of itself. They argue that governments cannot improve the workings of free markets and that their interventions can interfere with market efficiency. Thus they advocate reducing the current level of government intervention.

Given the complex web of government rules, regulations and tax laws that have grown up over many years, the *laissez-faire* agenda for reducing government intervention is usually a long one. Such an agenda was adopted in the United States by so-called *supply-siders* during the late 1970s and early 1980s. Some similar supply-side policies were also adopted by the Thatcher government from 1979 onwards in the UK.

Some of the most important aspects of supply-side economics were reviewed in Chapter 42 (see pages 522–3) and these should be reviewed at this point. Once again, support of supply-side measures can be associated with *laissez-faire*, and hostility with interventionists. However, supply-side policies cover a wide range and many economists in many philosophical camps support at least some of these.

Interventionist Prescriptions

Full employment

Interventionists call for discretionary fiscal and monetary policies to offset significant GNP gaps. Some of the major problems associated with discretionary stabilization policy have been discussed in earlier chapters. The issues in the debate that is sometimes known as 'rules versus discretion' were discussed in Chapter 42. Interventionists feel that in spite of lags and uncertainties of knowledge, the weakness of the forces leading to recovery from recessions will lead to the occasional occurrence of prolonged recession. These last long enough for expansionary fiscal and monetary policies to be employed without the instability issues that arise with fine-tuning in the face of continual shifts in the aggregate demand curve.

A stable price level

Some interventionists believe that the *k* per cent rule may not be enough to achieve full employment and stable prices simultaneously. This is because they accept the wage-cost-push theory of inflation also discussed in Chapter 42. These economists call for prices and incomes policies to restrain the wage-cost push and so make full employment compatible with stable prices. They believe that such policies should become permanent features of the economic landscape.

Incomes Policies: Permanent incomes policies might be of two types. The first type, commonly used in Europe in the past decades but now out of favour, is often called a *social contract*. Here labour, management and the government consult annually and agree on target wage changes. These are calculated to be non-inflationary, given the government's projections for the future and its planned economic

policies. Such a scheme is most easily initiated in an economy such as West Germany's, where a few giant firms and unions exert enormous power. It has sometimes been possible in Britain, especially under a Labour government whose strong links with unions have sometimes helped it to gain union co-operation in an incomes policy. But so far, such agreements have never been long-lived. They have tended to break down after some time when the feeling grew that wage restraint was acting to reduce real wages because it failed to produce as much restraint on prices and profits as on wages.

The other main type of incomes policy is the *tax-related incomes policy*, or as it is often called, TIPs. This policy, which we encountered in Chapter 42, provides tax incentives for management and labour to conform to government-established wage and price guidelines. Advocates of TIPs argue that their great advantage is in leaving decisions on wages and prices in the hands of labour and management while seeking only to influence behaviour by altering the incentive system. Critics argue that they would prove to be an administrative nightmare.

Growth

Policies for intervention to increase growth rates are of two sorts. Some policies seek to alter the general economic climate in a way favourable to growth. They typically include subsidization, or favourable tax treatment, for research and development, for purchase of plant and equipment, and for other profit-earning activities. Measures to lower interest rates are urged by some as favourable to investment and growth. We saw in Chapter 41 that monetary policy cannot be used to reduce the real rate of interest permanently in a fully employed economy – but subsidies on interest payments would do the job. Many interventionists support such general measures.

Some also support more specific intervention, usually in the form of what is called 'picking and backing winners'. Advocates of this view want governments to pick the industries, usually new ones, that have potential for future success and then to back them with subsidies, government contracts, research funds and all the other incentives at the government's command.

Opponents argue that picking winners requires foresight, and that governments do not have better foresight than private investors. Indeed, since politi-

cal considerations inevitably get in the way, the government may be less successful than the market in picking 'winners'. If so, channelling funds through the government rather than through the private sector may hurt rather than help growth rates. Many economists are sceptical of the government's ability to spot, and then back, potential winners. Sceptics point, for example, to the Concorde aircraft, which continued to absorb large amounts of investment expenditure, channelled to it for political reasons, long after any profit-maximizing firm would have dropped the project.

THE LONG-RUN PROSPECTS FOR GROWTH

We end this chapter, and this book, with a brief consideration of the long-run prospects for world growth. We have already observed several times that raising living standards depends critically on sustained economic growth (and also on controlling population). So many of the world's people live at extremely low living standards that little could be done to raise average living standards by redistributing existing income from the few 'have countries' to the many 'have not' countries. There are things that the rich countries can do by way of providing money and knowledge to encourage economic growth in poorer countries, but, in the long run, the prospect for raising living standards in those countries depends on the growth rates that they themselves can sustain. Similarly the prospects for raising living standards in the richer countries depends on their own growth rates.

It has been popular since the 1970s to argue that sustained growth is an impossible objective for the world. People who hold this view argue that the growth process will soon reach natural limits, and real incomes will then cease to grow throughout the world. Everything terrestrial has some ultimate limit. The ultimate of ultimate terrestrial limits will come when, as astronomers predict, the solar system itself dies with the burning out of the sun in another 6 billion or so years. To be of practical concern, therefore, a limit must be within some reasonable planning horizon. Best-selling books of the 1970s by Jay Forrester (*World Dynamics*, 1973) and D.H. Meadows *et al.* (*The Limits to Growth*, 1974) predicted the imminence of a 'growth-induced doomsday'.

These books both contributed to and reflected the fear, prevalent in the 1970s, that growth was coming to a permanent halt due to resource limitations.

But these disaster models were purely mechanical. They took technology as given – i.e. they did not allow for the very long run. The early models did not allow prices of materials to rise as scarcities grew, nor did they consider all the market reactions to such increases in relative prices. Some of the forms taken by market reactions turned out to be conservation of scarce materials, substitution of other materials within known technology, discovery of new sources of the materials, and, most important of all, the development of new technologies that substituted abundant materials for the scarce, high-priced materials. A parallel can be drawn with the famous pessimistic predictions of population growth outstripping food supplies, by the Revd Thomas Malthus, almost 200 years ago, who failed to foresee the massive improvements in nineteenth-century technology.

After a decade of the world's adjustment to high oil prices, from the mid-1970s to the mid-1980s, people now realize that such adjustments can, and do, occur on a massive scale. The sequence is growing shortage, rising prices, then the adaptations mentioned above – some of which will be spread over a decade or more. The biggest threat to such market-induced adjustments is, perhaps, that government will frustrate them by holding down the price of the increasingly scarce commodities through subsidies and price controls. Many governments tried to do this with oil prices after the first OPEC shock in 1974. (The motives were partially anti-inflationary and partly redistributive to protect lower income groups from rapidly rising prices of heating and transportation.) Only later, when governments allowed oil prices to rise to their market values, did a host of adjustments finally begin – adjustments that eventually relieved the world from its heavy dependence on OPEC oil.

The power of market signals, and market reactions, in inducing adaptations to major shortages is now much more clearly understood than it was two decades ago. Human ingenuity, directed by market incentives, is capable of making vast, almost undreamed of, adjustments within the short space of a decade or two. The market mechanism undoubtedly has inefficiencies, and it certainly causes inequities, but no one has yet succeeded in devising a command alternative with anything like the same power to induce, and co-ordinate, long-run adjustments. The

adaptation that has eroded within the short space of 15 years the near-monopoly of OPEC countries over the world's energy supplies – when in the mid-1970s contemporary observers could see no escape from the monopoly – is testimony to the power of the market to induce and co-ordinate millions of individual adaptations. This experience does not necessarily provide a case for pure *laissez-faire*, but for a mixed economy with significant reliance on markets for efficiency reasons even if there is substantial intervention for distributive reasons.

Oil, however, is not the world's only exhaustible resource and the years since the Second World War have seen a rapid acceleration in the consumption of many resources. We are all familiar with one reason for this accelerated consumption: world population growth. World population has increased from under 2.5 billion to nearly 5 billion in that period and this alone has greatly increased the demand for the world's resources.

A second major reason is growth in living standards for a *given* total of world population. Calculations have focused on the resources used by those people throughout the world who have living standards equal to the standards enjoyed by 90 per cent of the people in Western Europe and the United States. This so-called 'middle class', which today includes about one-sixth of the world's population, consumes 15 to 30 times as much oil per capita and, overall, at least 5 times as much of the earth's scarce resources per capita, as do the other 'poor' five-sixths of the world's population.

Economic growth has added nearly 4 per cent per year to the number of people throughout the world who achieve this 'middle class' standard over the post-war period. The number of persons realizing these living standards is estimated to have increased from 200 million to 800 million between 1950 and 1985.

Economic growth is a major cause of projected shortages of many natural resources: the increases in demand of the last three decades have outstripped discovery of new supplies and caused crises in energy, and in the supplies of many minerals, as well as food shortages. Yet the 4 per cent growth rate of the 'middle class', which is probably too fast for present resources to sustain, is too slow for the aspirations of the billions who live in underdeveloped countries and hope for economic growth to relieve their poverty. Thus the pressure on world resources of energy, minerals and food is likely to accelerate even if population growth is reduced.

Another way of looking at the problem of resource pressure is to note that present technology, and resources, could not possibly support the present population of the world at the standard of living of today's average Western European or North American family. For example, the demand for oil would increase nearly tenfold. Since these calculations (most unrealistically) assume no population growth anywhere in the world, and no growth in living standards for the richest sixth of the world's population, it is evident that resources are insufficient.

A Tentative Verdict

Most economists agree that conjuring up absolute limits to growth, based on the assumptions of constant technology and fixed supplies of known resources, is unwarranted. Yet there is surely cause for concern. Most agree that any single barrier to growth can be overcome by technological advances – *but not in an instant, and not automatically*. Clearly, there is a problem of timing: how soon can we discover, and put into practice, the knowledge required to solve the problems that are made ever more urgent by growth in population, growth in affluence, and by the aspirations of the billions who now live in poverty? There is no guarantee that a whole generation may not be caught by the transition, with social and political consequences that would certainly be enormous, and possibly cataclysmic.

The nightmares conjured up by the doomsday models may have served their purpose if they helped to focus attention both on the power of the market mechanism to induce and co-ordinate adjustments to change, and on the severe limitation that the existing supply of known resources puts on the possibilities of rapidly raising world living standards.

SUMMARY

1 In current policy debates, micro and macro issues are intertwined. The micro performance of the economy affects its macro performance, and vice versa.

2 On every policy issue, two extreme positions can be defined. The *laissez-faire* view would leave the issue to be settled by the free market, while the interventionist view would look to government intervention to produce a better result than would be produced by the unaided free market.

3 On the trade cycle, the *laissez-faire* view (which is roughly the Monetarist view) is that, in practice, stabilization policy worsens cyclical swings and it should not be used. The interventionist view, while wary of precise fine-tuning, holds that serious and prolonged slumps will occur from time to time and that these can be alleviated by conscious stabilization policy.

4 On the price level, the *laissez-faire* view calls for stable monetary targets consistent with a long-run, low inflation target and for no monetary fine-tuning. The interventionist view emphasizes non-monetary causes of changes in the price level and holds that non-monetary cures may be needed. Both sides accept, however, that the money supply and the price level are intimately associated.

5 On growth, the *laissez-faire* view is that governments should provide a stable background of law and order, and a steady price level, leaving private initiative, acting through free markets, to achieve a satisfactory growth rate. Supply-side economics includes measures designed to raise the growth rate by reducing the scope for government intervention and so increase the scope for private effort and initiative operating through free markets. The interventionist view emphasizes poor entrepreneurial performance and an alleged lack of risk-taking by large monopolistic firms and calls for government intervention to increase growth rates.

6 Sustained economic growth is required if the poorest of the world's population is to achieve anything like the living standards enjoyed by the richest. Achieving this result would put impossible strains on present resources under existing technology. The experience of the world's adjustment to high oil prices over not much more than ten years suggests, however, that market adjustments would occur and new technologies would be developed to avoid the severe restraints on long-term growth that would otherwise be exercised by growing scarcities of materials heavily used under present conditions.

Appendix to Chapter 1

Graphs in Economics

Economics is about quantities, and the relation between different quantities. In this appendix we deal with the method of showing these relations by using graphs. The ability to manipulate graphs is essential for every student of the subject. For some of you this appendix will be unnecessary; for others it will be a useful review; for yet others it will be a way of learning some of the topics covered in O-level maths that are needed to read this book.

A variable

At the outset we need to recall a term that was introduced in the text of the chapter and that you will constantly encounter. A *variable* is some quantity that can take on various values. For example, the price of wheat is a variable. It might be £90 per tonne at one time, and £110 per tonne at another time. The amount of wheat produced in a given year is also a variable. It might be 3 million tonnes in one year and 2.5 million tonnes in another.

Representation of the values of variables on a line

Part (i) of Figure 1A.1 shows a line. The arrowheads show that the line can be extended in either direction as far as we need. We now wish to represent on this line the value of some variable which we call X. To show that it is the value of X that we are measuring on the line, we write 'value of X' under the line. X might stand for the price of wheat, or the quantity of wheat produced, or any other variable quantity in which we are interested. We choose a point on the line and label it '0' to indicate the situation in which the value of the variable is zero. Next we mark off equal distances to the right to indicate positive values,

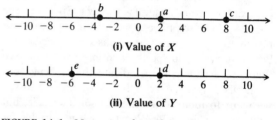

FIGURE 1A.1 Measuring the Values of a Variable on a Line

running on our line from 0 to 10 (we could extend the line further if we had values in excess of ten). We also mark off equal distances to the left of the zero point to indicate negative values of the variable, running up to −10 (again, we could go further if we needed to indicate values less than −10, say −15 or −2,453).

The SCALE of the line is the amount of distance corresponding to one unit of the variable's value. In this particular line the scale is 3mm = 1 unit.

Now let us show the value of the variable, X, on the line. If X is 2, we plot a point at the spot labelled 2 on the line. For ease of reference, we call this point *a*. If X is −3.5, we plot a point at −3.5, which is three-quarters of the way between the points labelled −2 and −4. We call this point *b*.

The exercise we have just gone through starts with values of the variable and then plots them on the line. We can also reverse the process. Say we are told that there is a point at *c* in the Figure. When we read the scale, we discover that this represents a value of 8 for the variable X.

In part (ii) of the Figure we draw another line and use it to represent values of a second variable that we call Y. Again, we indicate that it is the value of Y that

is measured on this line by writing 'value of Y' under the line. The procedure is the same as we used for the variable X in part (i) of the Figure. For example, the value of 2 is plotted as point d and, if we are told that there is a point at e, we know that this means a value for Y of -6.

Notation for specific but unspecified values of variables

So far we have given each variable specific, numerical values. Many times, however, we wish to indicate that a variable takes on some specific value, without saying what that value is. For example, let X be a person's age. This is our variable. A specific, numerical example would occur if we knew the person's age was 24. Then we have $X = 24$. But say we want merely to say that the person has some specific age, but do not want to specify its numerical value. We then use a subscript to indicate that specific, but unspecified, age. We write this as X_1. Now let us say we want to indicate another person's specific, but again unspecified, age. We let Y be the variable for that person's age and indicate the specific value as Y_1. Some years later, the two persons have different specific, but once again unspecified, ages and we write these as X_2 and Y_2. The subscript, therefore, tells us that we are referring to a specific value of the variable, and a second, different subscript that we are referring to another specific value. We shall soon make use of this technique.

A co-ordinate graph

Now let us say we want to know if there is any relation between the two variables X and Y. To do this, we can create what is called a co-ordinate graph. We place the two lines in Figure 1A.1 on one graph. We leave the line indicating variable X where it is and then place the line for Y at a right-angle to the line for X, so that the two points indicating zero for X and zero for Y coincide. This is done in Figure 1A.2.

The Figure now has two lines, one of which measures values of X and one of which measures values of Y. These two lines are called AXES. The horizontal line is called the HORIZONTAL AXIS or the X AXIS, and the vertical line is called the VERTICAL AXIS or the Y AXIS. The point where the two axes intersect, which corresponds to zero values of both X and Y, is called the ORIGIN.

We now have an extremely powerful analytical

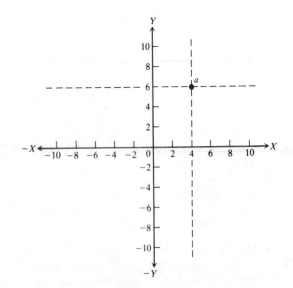

FIGURE 1A.2   A Co-ordinate Graph. Any point on the graph refers to a pair of values, one for X and one for Y

device – one which was invented some 300 years ago by the great French mathematician and philosopher René Descartes, and to this day the diagram shown in Figure 1A.2 is called a Cartesian diagram.

Now consider some point located in this diagram. The vertical distance to that point indicates its Y value. For example, every point on the broken line drawn through the value 6 on the Y axis indicates a value for Y of 6. Also, every point on the horizontal line drawn through 4 on the X axis indicates a value for X of 4. Now look at the point labelled a, where the vertical and the horizontal lines that we have just constructed intersect. This point indicates the combination of values $Y = 6$ and $X = 4$.

Every point on the co-ordinate graph corresponds to a *pair* of values. The vertical distance of the point from the X axis tells us its Y value while the horizontal distance of the point from the Y axis tells us its X value.

To facilitate plotting pairs of values as points, we erect vertical grid lines through equally spaced points on the X axis and horizontal grid lines through equally spaced points on the Y axis. These lines, which are drawn dashed in Figure 1A.3, form what is called a Cartesian grid. They make it easy to plot pairs of values. For example, the point a refers, as in the previous Figure, to a situation in which Y is 6 and X is 4. The point b refers to a case where X is 10 and Y is -4. Now, before reading on, try plotting the points

corresponding to the four pairs of values of $Y = 2$, $X = 5$; $Y = 10$, $X = 10$; $Y = -1$, $X = 9$; and $Y = -8$, $X = 0$. Note that the last point lies on the Y axis. Indeed, any point for which X is zero lies on the Y axis, while any point for which Y is zero lies on the X axis.

What you have learned so far is how to construct a graph and to plot points on it. You also need to be able to read a graph constructed by others. When you see such a graph, all you have to do is to reverse the procedure we have just gone through. To read the values indicated by any point on a graph, drop perpendiculars to the two axes and read the values of the two variables off the two axes. For example, what values for X and Y are indicated by the points c and d in Figure 1A.3? The perpendicular from c to the X axis tells us that the value of X at c is -6, while the perpendicular to the Y axis tells us that the value of Y at c is -8. A similar procedure for the point d tells us that d indicates values of $X = -2$ and $Y = 2$.

Notice that the two axes divide the graph into four segments. These are called QUADRANTS. This division is illustrated in Figure 1A.4. In the upper right-hand quadrant, both X and Y are positive; in the lower right-hand quadrant, X is positive while Y is negative; in the lower left-hand quadrant, both X and Y are negative; and, finally, in the upper left-hand quadrant, X is negative while Y is positive.

The upper right-hand quadrant, where both X and

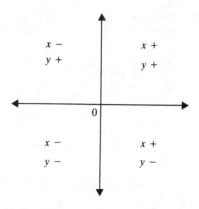

FIGURE 1A.4   The Four Quadrants of the Cartesian Graph. The two axes divide the graph into four quadrants

Y are zero or positive, is often called the POSITIVE QUADRANT. Many economic variables can only take on zero or positive values. For this reason many, although not all, economic diagrams only use the positive quadrant. Such a diagram is shown in part (i) of Figure 1A.5. The other quadrants are still there; we just do not bother to draw them in because we do not need to consider negative values of the variables being plotted.

Also in many economic diagrams we do not bother to draw in the full co-ordinate grid. To do so would clutter the Figure unnecessarily. The grid is still there; we just do not need all of it. When we wish to refer to a particular point, however, we often draw in the relevant parts of the grid. Thus, for example, point a in Figure 1A.5 refers to a situation in which Y is 6 and X is 4. This is shown in parts (i) and (ii) of Figure 1A.5. In part (i), the grid is there and a can be seen at the intersection of the horizontal line indicating $Y = 6$ and the vertical line indicating $X = 4$. In part (ii), the same point is shown but on a diagram where the full grid is not drawn in. But the two relevant parts of the grid are shown. The horizontal line drawn from a to the Y axis indicates that Y is 6, while the vertical line drawn to the X axis tells us that X is 4.

Notice that we read the Y value by moving up the Y axis till we reach the point horizontal to a. This value of 6 corresponds to the height of the Y axis at this point *and to the height of the line drawn from the X axis to a.* These two equivalent measures are indicated by the two braces marked $Y = 6$ in the Figure. Notice also that the value of $X = 4$ is indicated by the distance along the X axis to the point vertically below the point a and by the length of the grid line drawn

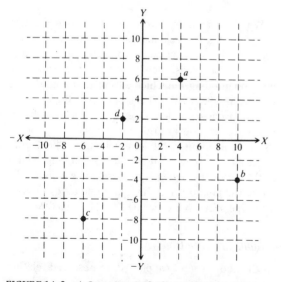

FIGURE 1A.3   A Cartesian Grid. The grid lines make it easy to plot and read the X and Y values corresponding to any point on the graph

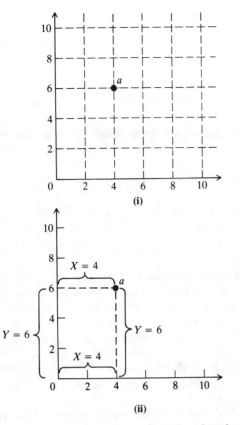

FIGURE 1A.5   The Cartesian Graph With and Without a Full Set of Grid Lines. Where the grid lines are suppressed, they can be drawn in where they are needed

Household	Annual income (£s)	Annual saving (£s)
1	7,000	1,500
2	3,000	1,000
3	10,000	3,000
4	6,000	2,000
5	8,000	3,000
6	1,000	0
7	2,000	500
8	5,000	1,500
9	4,000	500
10	9,000	2,500

TABLE 1A.1 Annual Income and Annual Saving for Eight Selected Households

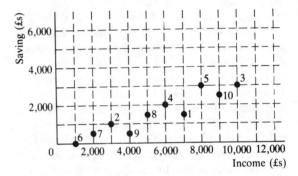

FIGURE 1A.6   A Scatter Diagram for Income and Saving. Each point on the diagram shows the income and the saving of a particular household

horizontally from the Y axis to a. These equivalent measures are shown by the two braces labelled $X = 4$ in the Figure. This point is worth emphasizing because it is natural, when first studying such graphs, to use lengths along the axes to measure values of the variables. It is common in such diagrams, however, to measure the values of X and Y as the distance of the grid lines from the X and Y axes to the point in question. The diagram makes it clear that the two measures are equivalent.

Graphs and schedules

A SCHEDULE is a list of values of particular variables. Let us say that we have a list of values of two economic variables. Assume, for example, that we have studied eight households and observed their annual income and the amount that each household saves. These values are listed in the schedule shown in Table 1A.1.

We wonder if these two variables are related and to 'see' any possible relation, we plot them on a co-ordinate diagram. We plot income on the X axis and saving on the Y axis. Each household then becomes a point on our diagram which tells us that household's income and its saving. This is shown in Figure 1A.6. Each household has been given a reference number in the above schedule and this number is written in over its corresponding point in the Figure. The Figure suggests a tendency that we shall use at length later in this book: the higher is a household's income, the larger the amount that the household tends to save. This type of graph is called a SCATTER DIAGRAM.

Graphs and equations

In the above graph we plotted an observed relation between two variables. We can also use co-ordinate graphs to plot relations between variables that are expressed in algebraic equations. This is very import-

TABLE 1A.2 Values of *Y* Corresponding to Selected Values of *X* on the Equation *Y* = 2*X*

Values of X	Values of Y
2	4
4	8
8	16
12	24

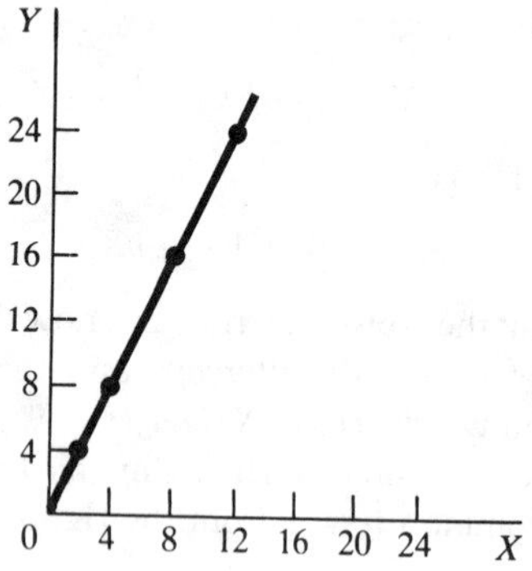

FIGURE 1A.7   The Graph of a Straight Line $Y = 2X$

ant because much of economics deals with assumed relations between variables that can be expressed in equations and graphs.

Let us say that some economic theory of the relation between two variables X and Y predicts that Y will always be twice as large as X. We can write this as the following equation:

$$Y = 2X.$$

The equation says just what we said in words above: the value of Y is always the value of X multiplied by 2.

We can investigate this relation by drawing up a schedule. To do so, we take selected values of X and calculate the corresponding values of Y. This is done for a few values in Table 1A.2.

These four points are plotted on a co-ordinate diagram in Figure 1A.7.

But what if we want a graph of the whole relation, at least for all positive values of X and Y? This we can do by plotting the line that corresponds to the equation $Y = 2X$. This line is shown by the solid line going through the four points that we have already plotted in Figure 1A.7.

Note that this line goes through the origin. This tells us that when X is zero, Y is also zero, which can be confirmed by setting X at zero in the above equation and noting that Y is also zero. Notice also that the line is upward-sloping. This indicates that as X increases, Y also increases. This is an example of what is called a positive association between the two variables; as one increases, so does the other. In such a case we say that the two variables are POSITIVELY RELATED to each other.

A linear relation

The equation $Y = 2X$ is an example of what is called a LINEAR RELATION between the two variables. The general equation of a linear relation is as follows:

$$Y = a + bX.$$

We must now look at this relation in some detail.

The *variables* in this equation are X and Y. As X takes on various values, Y takes on specific associated values.

The magnitudes a and b are called PARAMETERS. These are symbols that take on particular fixed values to define some specific example of the general relation. They are constants for that relation, but they take on other fixed values for other examples. Thus, when parameters are given specific values, the exact relation between X and Y is specified. For example, in the equation given earlier, a was zero and b was 2. This gave rise to the graph shown in Figure 1A.7. Two other examples are given by first letting a equal -4 and b equal 2, and then letting a equal 10 and b equal -1. These give rise to the two following equations:

$$Y = -4 + 2X$$
$$Y = 10 - X.$$

These two equations are graphed in Figure 1A.8.

Now we can show the key characteristics of the graph of the general linear relation, of which the above are two examples.

(1) The constant term a gives the value of the intercept of the graph on the Y axis. The Y INTERCEPT is the value of Y where the graph of the equation cuts the Y axis. It is found by letting X equal zero (as it is everywhere along the Y axis). Putting X at zero in the above two examples tells us that $Y = -4$ in the first example and $Y = 10$ in the second example.

(2) The sign of the parameter b tells us whether the slope of the line is positive or negative. In the first equation above, Y is positively related to X because the larger is Y, the larger is X. The graph of a positive relation between two variables slopes upward to the right. In the second equation above, Y is NEGATIVELY RELATED to X because the larger is X, the smaller is Y.

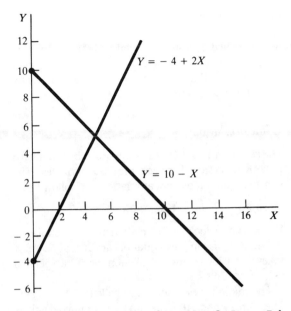

FIGURE 1A.8 The Graphs of Two Specific Linear Relations. The graph of a positive association between two variables slopes upward to the right; the graph of a negative association slopes downward to the right

The graph of a negative relation between two variables slopes downward to the right.

(3) The magnitude of the parameter b tells us how much Y changes every time X changes. The *larger* is the magnitude of b, the *more* does Y change every time X changes. The graphical expression of this is that the larger is the magnitude of b, the steeper is the line expressing the relation between the two variables. To be precise, b gives the slope of the line that graphs the equation. To show that this is so, we need to use a little algebra.

The slope of a linear relation

First, let us look at the example given above where $Y = -4 + 2X$. Let X take on the value of 2. Y is then $(2 \times 2) - 4$, which is 0. Now let X take on the value of 3. Y is now $(2 \times 3) - 4$, which is $+2$. This illustrates that the increase in Y for a unit change in X is 2, which is the value of the parameter b.

Now let us do this more generally. Let X take on any specific value, X_1, and calculate the corresponding value of Y, which we obtain by multiplying X_1 by b and adding a:

$$Y_1 = a + bX_1. \tag{1}$$

Now let X take on a second specific value, which we call X_2, and calculate the corresponding value of Y, called Y_2:

$$Y_2 = a + bX_2. \tag{2}$$

Next subtract the first equation from the second. To do this we subtract the LHS (which stands for the left-hand side) of (1) from the LHS of (2) and the RHS (which stands for the right-hand side) of (1) from the RHS of (2). This gives us:

$$Y_2 - Y_1 = (a + bX_2) - (a + bX_1). \tag{3}$$

This simplifies to:

$$Y_2 - Y_1 = bX_2 - bX_1. \tag{4}$$

Notice that the constant term a has now disappeared. It only determines the intercept, and has nothing to do with how Y *changes* as X *changes*.

Equation (4) can be further simplified by factoring out the common term b from the right-hand side to obtain:

$$Y_2 - Y_1 = b(X_2 - X_1). \tag{5}$$

This tells us that the change in Y is equal to b times the change in X. We now use a common device of symbolizing *the change in* any variable by the Greek letter delta, Δ. Thus we can rewrite the above as

$$\Delta Y = b\Delta X. \tag{6}$$

Equation (6) says exactly the same thing as equation (5), only it says it in our new notation where Δ means 'the change in' the variable to which it is attached.

Finally, if we divide through by ΔX, we obtain:

$$\Delta Y / \Delta X = b. \tag{7}$$

This tells us that the parameter b expresses the ratio of the change in Y to the change in X. In other words, it tells us the change in Y *per unit change in X*.

Finally, let us look at the graph of this equation, $Y = a + bX$. A specific case is shown in Figure 1A.9. The original point on the line is shown by the values X_1 and Y_1. The new point is shown by the values X_2 and Y_2. The change in Y, which is $Y_2 - Y_1$, is indicated in the Figure by ΔY, while the change in X, which is $X_2 - X_1$, is indicated by ΔX. In geometry, the slope of a line is given by the ratio of the change in Y divided by the change in X, which is $\Delta Y / \Delta X$ in the Figure. But we have already seen that this ratio is equal to b.

We conclude, therefore, that the parameter b in a linear equation gives the slope of the line that plots

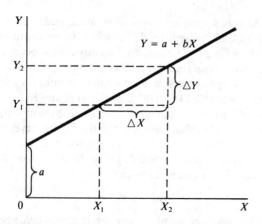

FIGURE 1A.9   **The Slope of a Straight-Line Graph.** The slope of a straight line measures the change in Y per unit change in X

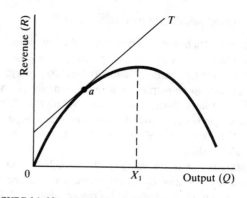

FIGURE 1A.10   **A Non-Linear Function**

that equation, and that this is the ratio of the change in Y to the change in X. This ratio tells us how much Y changes *per unit change in X*.

On a straight line, the slope is constant over its whole length. This is shown algebraically by the fact that the slope parameter b is a constant.

Non-linear relations

So far we have dealt only with linear relations – relations in which Y changes by the same amount every time X changes by one unit no matter where we are on the line. Many economic relations, however, are non-linear. An example is shown in Figure 1A.10. This relation relates the output of a large firm to the revenue that it can gain from selling that output. On the curve, the X axis refers to the firm's output and the Y axis refers to its sales revenue. We will study how this relation arises later in this book; in the meantime we merely accept it, and study its properties.[1]

Notice that when X increases from zero to X_1, Y also increases. Over this range, Y is positively related to X. But also notice that, as X increases beyond X_1, Y decreases. Over this range, Y is negatively related to X. Also note that, as X increases from zero, Y increases a great deal. This is shown by the steepness of the curve when X is close to zero. Note further that,

as X approaches the value of X_1, Y increases less and less as X increases, until, when X reaches X_1, Y is no longer increasing as X increases. This is shown by the flatness of the curve just to the left of X_1.

Evidently the slope of the curve relating Y to X tells us something about *how much* Y changes as X changes. To learn more about this relation, we need to study further what the slope of the curve tells us about the magnitude of the change in Y that accompanies given changes in X.

Tangents to curves

In the above discussion we judged the slope of a curve by looking at how steep or flat it appeared on the graph. This is rather impressionistic, and we need a precise measure of how steep or flat a curve is at some point. We do this in two steps.

We first construct what is called a tangent to the curve at the point where we want to measure the curve's steepness. A TANGENT to a curve at a particular point is a straight line that just touches the curve at a particular point. In Figure 1A.10 we have drawn a tangent to the curve at the point labelled a. The tangent is labelled T.

The second step is to measure the slope of the tangent. This is done in the manner discussed above. The tangent is a straight line, so its equation is $Y = a + bX$ and its slope is b. We saw above that this slope parameter b measures the ratio of the change in Y to the change in X (i.e. $\Delta Y/\Delta X$) along the line.

Thus the slope of any curve at a particular point is measured precisely by the slope of the tangent to the curve at that point, and it can be interpreted as showing how Y is tending to change *per unit change in X* at that point of the curve.

---

[1] The equation of this particular curve is $Y = a + bX + cX^2$, where a is zero, b is positive, and c is negative.

Marginal values and incremental ratios

Economic theory makes much use of what are called 'marginal' concepts. Marginal cost, marginal revenue, marginal rate of substitution and marginal propensity to consume are a few examples that we will meet later in this book. Marginal means on the margin or border, and the concept refers to what would happen if there were a small change from the present position.

Marginals refer to relations that can be expressed in curves. We draw the curve relating Y to X and we wish to know what would be the change in Y if X changed by a small amount from its present value. The answer is referred to as the marginal value of Y and is given various names depending on what economic variables X and Y stand for.

There are two ways of measuring the marginal value of Y. One is exact and the other is an approximation. Because the exact measure uses differential calculus, introductory texts in economics usually use the approximation, which depends only on simple algebra. Students are often justifiably confused because the language of economic theory refers to the exact measure while introductory examples use the approximation. For this reason it is worth explaining each at this time.

Consider the example shown in Figure 1A.11, in which a firm's output, Q, is measured on the X axis and the total revenue earned by selling this output, R, is measured on the Y axis.

The marginal concept that corresponds to this function is *marginal revenue*. It refers to the change in the firm's revenue when sales are altered slightly from their present level. But what do we mean by 'altered slightly'? There are two answers, depending on which marginal concept we use.

The approximation to marginal revenue is called the INCREMENTAL RATIO. Let sales in Figure 1A.11 be 6, with a corresponding revenue of £70. Now increase sales to 8, so that, according to the Figure, revenue rises to £100. The increase in sales is 2 and the increase in revenue is £30. Using the Δ notation for changes, we can write this as

$$\Delta R/\Delta Q = £30/2 = £15.$$

Thus the increment in revenue is £30 when sales change from 6 to 8. This means that sales are increasing at an average rate of £15 *per unit of commodity sold* over the range from 6 to 8 units. We may call this the marginal revenue at 6 units of output but, as we shall see, it is only an approximation to the true marginal revenue at that output.

Graphically, incremental revenue is the slope of the line joining the two points in question. In this case they are the two points on the revenue function corresponding to outputs of 6 and 8. This is shown in Figure 1A.12, which is an enlargement of the relevant section of the curve in Figure 1A.11. Now look at the triangle created by these points. Its base is 2 units long and its vertical side is 30 units in height. The slope of the hypotenuse of the triangle is $30/2 = 15$, which is the incremental revenue. Visually it is clear that this slope tells us the average gradient or steepness of the revenue function over the range from $Q = 6$ to $Q = 8$. It thus tells us how fast revenue is changing as output changes over that range of Q.

Incremental revenue will be different at different points on the function. For example, when output goes from 8 to 10, revenue goes from 100 to 115 and this gives us an incremental revenue of

$$\Delta R/\Delta Q = £15/2 = £7.50.$$

This calculation confirms what visual inspection of the Figure suggests: the larger is output (at least over the ranges graphed in the Figure), the less is the response of revenue to further increases in output.

The incremental ratio is an approximation to the true marginal concept, which is based on the derivative of differential calculus. The derivative is symbolized in general by dY/dx, and, in the case of the relation we are now considering between the two variables R and Q, it is symbolized by dR/dQ. It measures the tendency for R to change as Q changes

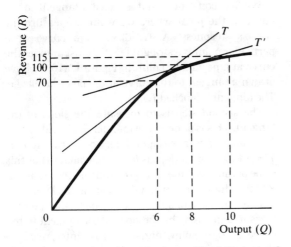

FIGURE 1A.11   **The Relation Between a Firm's Output and its Revenues**

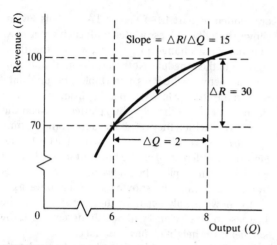

FIGURE 1A.12   Calculation of the Incremental Revenue on a Non-Linear Curve. The incremental revenue shows the average change in revenue per unit change in output over a range of the revenue curve

at a precise point on the curve (whereas the incremental ratio measures the average tendency over a range of the curve).

The value of the derivative is given by the slope of the tangent at the point on the function in which we are interested. Thus 'true' marginal revenue at 6 units of output is given by the slope of the tangent, T, to the curve at that point. This slope measures the tendency for R to change per unit change in Q at the precise value at which it is evaluated (i.e. the point on the function at which the tangent is drawn).

We saw in the example of Figure 1A.10 that the incremental ratio declined as we measured it at larger and larger values of Q. It should be visually obvious that this is also true for marginal revenue in that particular curve: the slope of the tangent to the curve will be smaller the larger is the value of Q at which the tangent is taken. Two examples are shown in Figure 1A.11; one, T, for $Q = 6$ and the other, T', for $Q = 8$.

Now try measuring the incremental ratio, starting at 6 units of output but for smaller and smaller changes in output. Instead of going from 6 to 8, go, for example, from 6 to 7. This brings the two points in question closer together and, in the present case, it steepens the slope of the line joining them. It is visually clear in the present example that as ΔQ is made smaller and smaller, the slope of the line corresponding to the incremental ratio starting from $Q = 6$ gets closer and closer to the slope of the tangent corresponding to the true marginal value evaluated at $Q = 6$.

Let us now state our conclusions in general for a curve relating the variables X and Y.

(1) The marginal value of Y at some initial value of X is the rate of change of Y per unit change in X, as X changes from its initial value.

(2) The marginal value is given by the slope of the tangent to the curve showing the relation to the two variables drawn at the value of X.

(3) The incremental ratio $\Delta Y/\Delta X$ measures the average change in Y per unit change in X over a range of the curve starting from the initial value of X.

(4) As the range of measurement of the incremental ratio is reduced (i.e. as ΔX gets smaller and smaller), the value of the incremental ratio eventually approaches the true marginal value of Y. Thus the incremental ratio may be regarded as an approximation to the true marginal value, the degree of approximation improving as ΔX gets very small.

Areas under curves: from marginal to total values

So far we have seen how to derive a marginal curve from a total curve. The marginal curve tells us how fast the total value of Y is changing as X changes at any point on the curve. Often in economics we are given the marginal curve and the problem is to determine the total value of Y at some point on the curve. This requires that we reverse the process of finding the marginal curve given the total curve, and,

TABLE 1A.3 Selected Values of X and Y for Some Given Relation Between the Two Variables

Value of X (1)	Value of Y (2)	Change in Y (3)	Value of Y (4)
1	10	+10	10
2	18	+8	18
3	25	+7	25
4	30	+5	30
5	34	+4	34
6	36	+2	36
7	37	+1	37
8	35	−2	35

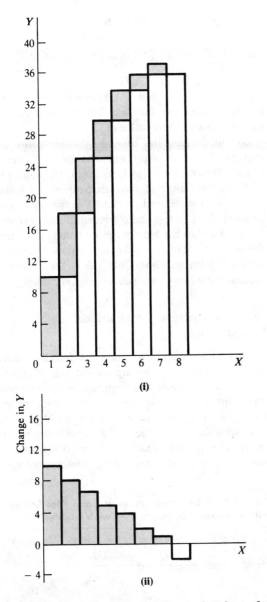

FIGURE 1A.13   The Total and Marginal Values of Y Associated with Each Value of X

are plotted in part (i) of Figure 1A.13. This Figure shows the value of Y associated with each value of X. The marginal change in Y is shown in the third column of the schedule. Note that the marginal data is placed between the rows of the table. Marginal data refer to the change in Y when going from one row to the next row, and they are thus plotted between the two rows to which they refer. The data from columns (1) and (3) of the schedule are plotted in part (ii) of the Figure. X is still plotted on the horizontal axis, but the vertical axis now plots the *change* in Y as X increases by one unit to the value shown on the horizontal axis.

It is now visually apparent that the smaller is the increase in Y associated with a unit increase in X, the smaller is the height of the marginal curve.

Now let us assume that all we know is the data in columns (1) and (3) of the above schedule, which data are plotted in part (ii) of the Figure. Our problem is to find columns (2) and (4) from which we can plot part (i) of the Figure. All we have to do is to add up the *changes* in Y up to any X value and we will have the *total value of Y* corresponding to that value of X. Thus the change in Y when X goes from 0 to 1 is +10, so the value of Y at X = 1 must be 10. The change in Y when X goes from 1 to 2 is 8, so the total value of Y must be equal to its value of 10 when X = 1 plus its change of 8 when X goes from 1 to 2, which makes a total of 18. The change in Y when X goes from 2 to 3 is 7, so the total value of Y must be its value of 18 when X = 2 plus its change of 7, which makes 25. In other words, *the total value of any variable is the sum of the marginal values.*

We can conclude that, if we know the changes in Y as X increases unit by unit, we can find the total value of Y for any value of X by adding up all the changes in Y that occur as X increases from zero to the value in question. This is done in column (4), and you will see that it reproduces column (2).

Now let us look at this process graphically. Figure 1A.13 (ii) gives the increase in Y for every unit increase in X. These increments are also shaded in part (i) of the Figure. The total value of Y for any value of X is the sum of these increases from zero up to the point in question. Thus the value of Y at, say, X = 5 is the sum of the marginal changes from zero to 5. This is the area of the second graph between 0 and 5 and it is equal to the height of the graph of Y in part (i) at X = 5.

Note that when Y decreases as X increases – which happens here when X goes from 7 to 8 – the marginal value is negative. All this means is that Y is decreas-

instead, find the total curve, given the marginal curve.

The problem is easiest understood if we deal with a case where X varies one unit at a time rather than continuously, as it does along a curve. Consider the schedule of X and Y values set out in Table 1A.3, where the columns have been numbered for easy reference.

The data from the first two columns of the schedule

ing. Negative values for Y are plotted, according to our graphical convention, below the X axis.

Inspection of Figure 1A.13 makes it clear that the height of the bar in part (i) for any value of X is equal to the total area of the bars in part (ii) between zero and the value in question.[1]

---

1 Students who have done calculus will recognize the marginal curve as the graph of the first derivative of Y with respect to X. They will also recognize the procedure of going from the marginal curve back to the total curve as the process of integrating the area under the marginal curve between zero and the X value in question. If we take a total curve, differentiate it with respect to X, and then integrate the result with respect to X, we get back to the original curve. This is what we have had to argue verbally, numerically and geometrically in the text for those of our readers who do not know elementary calculus.

Appendix to Chapter 7

The Derivation of Elasticity of Demand
at a Point on a Demand Curve

We are given a demand curve PQ and required to find the elasticity of demand at point t. The formula for elasticity of demand is

$$\eta = \frac{\Delta q}{\Delta p} \times \frac{P}{Q}$$

At price At, the value of η in the formula is

$$\eta = \frac{\Delta q}{\Delta p} \times \frac{At}{OA} \qquad (1)$$

The triangles trs and POQ are similar. Therefore the ratio of any two sides of those triangles are similar.

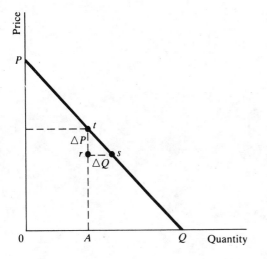

Thus

$$\frac{\Delta q}{\Delta p} = \frac{\Delta Q}{At} \qquad (2)$$

Substituting (2) in (1) to give

$$\eta = \frac{AQ}{At} \times \frac{At}{OA}$$

The At's cancel out, leaving

$$\eta = \frac{AQ}{OA}$$

Since At and OP are parallel,

$$\frac{AQ}{OA} = \frac{Qt}{tP}$$

Therefore

$$\eta = \frac{Qt}{tP}$$

At any point on a linear demand curve[1], the value of elasticity of demand is equal to the length from the point to the quantity axis divided by the length from the point to the price axis.

---

1 For curvilinear demand curves, draw a tangent to the point at which demand is to be measured. The statement above is now applicable to the tangent to the curve.

Appendix to Chapter 8

The Derivation of Market Equilibrium Price and Quantity Using Mathematical (Algebraic) Methods

Market equilibrium was derived in Chapter 8, using demand and supply schedules, and graphs. It is also possible to derive the equilibrium price and quantity using algebra.

As explained in the Appendix to Chapter 1, a line on a graph is an expression of a relationship between two variables, which can also be expressed in the form of an equation. Hence, we can find equations which are represented by the supply and demand curves for table wine, which are drawn on Figure 8.1 (see page 86). These are as follows:

The demand equation is
$$Q_d = 21 - 5p \qquad (1)$$

The supply equation is
$$Q_s = -6 + 10p \qquad (2)$$

(You might like to check these for yourself. Assume a value for p and, using equation (1), calculate the quantity demanded. For example, if $p = 3$, $q_d = 21 - (5 \times 3) = 6$. $p = 3$, $q = 6$, is one point on the demand curve. The supply equation can be similarly checked.)

To find the market equilibrium price and quantity, using the supply and demand equations, we need to bring in our definition of market equilibrium. This is that quantity demanded equals quantity supplied. In symbols this is:
$$Q_s = Q_d \qquad (3)$$

To find the value of p which will make the quantity demanded equal to the quantity supplied, we need, therefore, to solve equation (3), after substituting equations (1) and (2) for the simple $Q_s = Q_d$. In other words we must solve:
$$-6 + 10p = 21 - 5p \qquad (4)$$

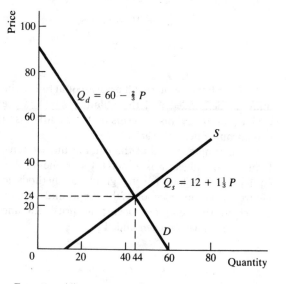

Equation (4) contains only a single unknown, p. So we solve it in the usual manner, by bringing all the terms with p to one side of the equation, leaving the terms without p on the other side (remembering to change the sign of any term which we transfer from one side of the equation to the other side).

Thus, equation (4) may be rewritten:
$$10p + 5p = 21 + 6$$

which simplifies to
$$15p = 27$$

and, therefore, also to
$$p = \frac{27}{15} = 1.8.$$

The solution to the equation for market equilibrium is that price is therefore 1.8.

The final step in the analysis is to find the quantity supplied and demanded at price 1.8. The quantity supplied at that price is found by substituting 1.8 for p in the supply equation (2):

$$Q_s = -6 + 10p$$
$$= -6 + (10 \times 1.8)$$
$$= -6 + 18$$
$$= 12.$$

The quantity demanded at the price 1.8 is found by substituting 1.8 for p in the demand equation (1):

$$Q_d = 21 - 5p$$
$$= 21 - (5 \times 1.8)$$
$$= 21 - 9$$
$$= 12.$$

Thus we have found that if price is equal to 1.8, the quantity demanded and the quantity supplied are each equal to 12. This confirms that the market is in equilibrium when price is 1.8.

We may note, too, that the equilibrium we have found using algebra is exactly the same as the equilibrium we found using graphical methods in Figure 8.1. The intersection of the supply and demand curves in that diagram occurs at price 1.8 and quantity supplied and demanded 12.

Index

Note – Where multiple page numbers occur after an index entry, the page numbers in **bold type** refer to a definition or main description of the term.